Associated Motion

Empirical Approaches to Language Typology

Editors
Georg Bossong
Bernard Comrie
Kristine Hildebrandt
Jean-Christophe Verstraete

Volume 64

Associated Motion

Edited by
Antoine Guillaume
Harold Koch

DE GRUYTER
MOUTON

ISBN 978-3-11-110408-9
e-ISBN (PDF) 978-3-11-069209-9
e-ISBN (EPUB) 978-3-11-069212-9

Library of Congress Control Number: 2021930508

Bibliographic information published by the Deutsche Nationalbibliothek
The Deutsche Nationalbibliothek lists this publication in the Deutsche Nationalbibliografie;
detailed bibliographic data are available on the Internet at http://dnb.dnb.de.

© 2022 Walter de Gruyter GmbH, Berlin/Boston
This volume is text- and page-identical with the hardback published in 2021.
Typesetting: Integra Software Services Pvt. Ltd.
Printing and binding: CPI books, GmbH, Leck

www.degruyter.com

Contents

Part I: Perspectives and general issues

Antoine Guillaume and Harold Koch
1 Introduction: associated motion as a grammatical category in linguistic typology —— 3

Daniel Ross
2 A cross-linguistic survey of Associated Motion and Directionals —— 31

Joseph Lovestrand and Daniel Ross
3 Serial verb constructions and motion semantics —— 87

Matthew S. Dryer
4 Associated motion and directionals: where they overlap —— 129

Aïcha Belkadi
5 Deictic directionality as associated motion: motion, complex events and event integration in African languages —— 163

Marine Vuillermet
6 A visual stimulus for eliciting associated motion —— 201

Part II: Australia and South Pacific

Harold Koch
7 Associated motion in the Pama-Nyungan languages of Australia —— 231

David Osgarby
8 Mudburra associated motion in an areal perspective —— 325

Lauren W. Reed and Kate L. Lindsey
9 "Now the story's turning around": Associated motion and directionality in Ende, a language of Papua New Guinea —— 357

Dineke Schokkin
10 Preverbal directionals as markers of associated motion in Paluai (Austronesian; Oceanic) —— 385

Part III: The Americas

Adam J.R. Tallman
11 Associated motion in Chácobo (Pano) in typological perspective —— 419

Alejandra Vidal and Doris L. Payne
12 Pilagá directionals and the typology of associated motion —— 451

Matthew S. Dryer
13 Associated motion in North America (including Mexico and Central America) —— 485

Néstor Hernández-Green and Enrique L. Palancar
14 Associated motion in the Otomi family —— 527

Part IV: Africa

Rozenn Guérois, Hannah Gibson and Bastian Persohn
15 Associated motion in Bantu languages —— 569

Sylvie Voisin
16 Associated motion and deictic directional in Atlantic languages —— 611

Denis Creissels and Alain Christian Bassène
17 Ventive, associated motion and aspect in Jóola Fóoñi (Atlantic) —— 665

Doris L. Payne
18 The extension of associated motion to direction, aspect and argument structure in Nilotic languages —— 695

Kazuhiro Kawachi
19 The 'along'–deictic-directional verb suffix complex in Kupsapiny —— 747

Manuel A. Otero
20 At the intersection of associated motion, direction and exchoative aspect in the Koman languages —— 779

Part V: **Asia**

Guillaume Jacques, Aimée Lahaussois and Shuya Zhang
21 Associated motion in Sino-Tibetan, with a focus on Gyalrongic and Kiranti —— 819

Brigitte Pakendorf and Natalia Stoynova
22 Associated motion in Tungusic languages: a case of mixed argument structure —— 855

Subject Index —— 899

Language Index —— 907

Name Index —— 917

Part I: **Perspectives and general issues**

Antoine Guillaume and Harold Koch

1 Introduction: associated motion as a grammatical category in linguistic typology

Abstract: This volume is the first book-length presentation of the relatively newly established grammatical category of Associated Motion (AM). It provides a framework for understanding a grammatical phenomenon which, though present in many languages, has gone unrecognised until recently. Previously known mainly from languages of Australia and South America, grammatical AM marking has now been identified in languages from most parts of the world (except Europe) and is becoming an important topic of linguistic typology. The 22 chapters provide a thorough introduction to the subject, discussion of the relation between AM and related grammatical concepts, detailed descriptions of AM in a wide range of the world's languages, and surveys of AM in particular language families and areas. All of the studies are richly illustrated by means of (approximately 2000) example sentences.

Keywords: associated motion, direction, aspect, location, typology, complexity, implicational hierarchies

1 Introduction

Associated Motion (AM) is a relatively newly established descriptive and comparative concept[1] that we define as *a verbal grammatical category, separate from tense, aspect, mood and direction, whose function is to associate, in different ways, different kinds of translational motion* (spatial displacement / change of location) *to a* (generally non-motion) *verb event*. As an illustration, example (1), from the Amazonian language Cavineña, shows seven suffixes (out of an inventory of 12) expressing different AM values, in combination with the verb 'see'.

---

[1] This introductory section is an updated summary of Guillaume (2016: 81–94, 2017a).

Antoine Guillaume, Laboratoire Dynamique du Langage (CNRS & Université Lumière Lyon 2), antoine.guillaume@cnrs.fr
Harold Koch, Australian National University, harold.koch@anu.edu.au

https://doi.org/10.1515/9783110692099-001

(1) Cavineña (Takanan; Guillaume 2006; 2008; 2009)
    ba-   'see O'
    ba-*ti*-   'go and see O'
    ba-*na*-   'come and see O'
    ba-*aje*-   'see O while going'
    ba-*be*-   'see O while coming'
    ba-*kena*- 'see O and go'
    ba-*dadi*- 'see O while O is moving away'
    ba-*tsa*-   'see O while O is approaching'
    etc.

AM can be expressed by *verbal affixes*, as in (1), but also by *clitics, particles or auxiliaries*, which, in different linguistic traditions, receive a wide range of descriptive labels such as "motion / motion-with-purpose / purposive / intentional", "(deictic) directional / directive", "ven(i)tive / andative / itive", "hither / thither", "centrifugal / centripetal", "cis- / trans- / dis- / (re-)locative", "displacement" or "(secondary / locative) aspect".

The category of AM is noteworthy from a theoretical point of view because it shows, among other things, that in some languages *the "fact-of-motion"* (Talmy 1985, 2007) *can be encoded grammatically*, by way of affixes or other grammaticalised elements, and not necessarily (or not only) lexically, contrary to what is generally assumed (Guillaume 2006: 433–435; Levinson & Wilkins 2006: 534). As pointed out by several authors, motion expression in AM falls outside of Talmy's motion event typology (verb frame / satellite frame distinction) because this typology only takes into consideration situations where the motion component is expressed by a lexical verb root (Slobin 2004: 243; Wilkins 2004: 147; Guillaume 2006: 433–435; Schultze-Berndt 2007: 223–224).

The phenomenon of AM was first recognised and labelled in the 1980s by linguists describing the verbal morphology of Aboriginal languages of *Central Australia* (starting with Koch 1984; Tunbridge 1988; Wilkins 1989: 270–298, 1991). In the 2000s, the term "associated motion" was borrowed from Australianist linguistics in studies of similar morphemes in languages from the Americas in *Western Amazonia* (starting with Guillaume 2000, 2006, 2008: 212–236, 2009; Sakel 2004), *Central America* (starting with Zavala Maldonado 2000; O'Connor 2004) and *North America* (Dryer 2002, 2007). In this period, one can also mention the first identification of AM in a language of *Papua New Guinea* by Levinson (2006: 197–199). Finally, a decade later, AM was also identified in languages from most of the rest of the world — with the notable exception of Europe — in *Africa* (starting with Voisin 2010, 2013; Kawachi 2011; Renaudier 2012: 97; Belkadi 2014, 2015, 2016; Kießling & Bruckhaus 2017; Persohn 2018), *Asia* (starting with Jacques 2013; Konnerth 2014:

232, 2015; Vittrant 2015: 588–589; Stoynova 2016; Boro 2017; Alonso de la Fuente & Jacques 2018),[2] the *Oceanic family in the South Pacific* (Meier 2020) and a few more cases in *Papua New Guinea* (Dryer 2013; Cleary-Kemp 2015).

The exploration of AM in languages from different parts of the world and different families has revealed the multifaceted nature of the phenomenon, in terms of the wide range of ways it is manifested cross-linguistically, from dedicated to non-dedicated systems, highly elaborated to very simple inventories, varied morphological exponence (affixes, clitics, particles, etc.) with different statuses (derivational, inflectional, neither), and possible etymologies and development paths.

In the remainder of this chapter, we first review several landmark contributions in the development of the field of AM studies (§2), before zooming in on a number of important issues that run throughout the papers of the volume: parameters of AM (§3), AM and other grammatical categories (§4) and further issues (§5). Finally, in §6, we summarise the contents of the specific chapters.

2 Landmark contributions in the development of the field of AM studies

In this section, we review three important findings which have paved the way for the study of AM in general and more specifically in the studies in this volume: the original recognition of the AM phenomenon in dedicated AM systems (§2.1), the subsequent identification of AM in non-dedicated systems (§2.2), and the first typological studies and proposals for implicational hierarchies (§2.3).

2.1 Dedicated AM

A first major development in the field of AM studies was the recognition and exploration of the phenomenon in a number of extensive studies of the Arandic languages of Central Australia (Koch 1984; Wilkins 1989, 1991) and Takanan languages of Western Amazonia (Guillaume 2006, 2008, 2009, 2013; Vuillermet 2012, 2013). These studies, which provided the main impetus for the recognition of AM as a phenomenon of cross-linguistic relevance, dealt with *highly elaborated and articulated*

---

[2] For more recent studies on AM in Asian languages, see Lamarre (2020), Zhang (2020), Lamarre et al. (to appear) and Genetti et al. (to appear). Of particular note is the recognition, in Lamarre (2020) and Lamarre et al. (to appear), of AM in Standard Mandarin and Japanese, two languages which have been extensively studied in the past.

systems, expressed by inventories of sometimes up to 15 grammaticalised markers in paradigmatic opposition (as in Mparntwe Arrernte), all dedicated to the expression of contrasting AM values. Crucially, the observation that these values were quite similar across the languages of the two languages families suggested a number of preliminary generalisations about the semantic parameters according to which AM systems are structured and can be compared cross-linguistically. It was found that, at the higher level of organisation, the recurrent semantic contrasts that distinguish AM forms are the *argument role of the moving figure* (subject versus non-subject, generally the object), the *temporal relation* between the motion and the verb event (prior versus concurrent versus subsequent), the *path* of motion (toward versus away from deictic centre, upward versus downward, straight versus return, etc.), and the *aspectual realisation* of the verb event (perfective / punctual versus imperfective / continuous / repeated); see (1) above for an illustration of several of these contrasts in the Takanan language Cavineña.

Subsequently, these parameters proved useful in identifying and describing other AM systems in languages from all over the world. These included systems somewhat similar to the Arandic and Takanan ones, in terms of semantic structure and degree of elaboration. This was the case, for instance, in a number of other Western Amazonian languages such as the isolate language Mosetén (Sakel 2004: 272–288), the Arawak language Trinitario (Rose 2015), and several languages of the Panoan family (Guillaume 2017b). But the newly recognised AM systems also included *much simpler ones, with inventories sometimes limited to just one or two markers*, as in, for instance, several African languages of the Atlantic branch of the Niger-Congo family (Voisin 2010, 2013), Japhug from the Rgyalongic branch of Sino-Tibetan (Jacques 2013); see also many such simple systems reported by Guillaume (2016) for South American languages. The simple system of AM in Wolof (Atlantic), which is restricted to a pair of subject prior motion markers in a single contrast (itive versus ventive path), is illustrated in (2).[3]

(2) Wolof (Atlantic, Senegal)
    a. *Dafa dox-**i** ci tefes gi.*
       EV.3SG walk-**GO&DO** LOC beach DEF
       'He <u>went to</u> walk on the beach.' (Voisin 2013: 142)

    b. *Waa-dëkk bépp a wall-**si** woon.*
       village_inhabitant all ES rescue-**COME&DO** PST
       'The whole village <u>came to</u> rescue.' (Voisin 2013: 142)

---

3 In the Wolof examples in (2), EV stands for 'emphatic verb' and ES for 'emphatic subject'.

2.2 Non-dedicated AM

A second significant development in the field of AM studies was the recognition in a number of African languages of *AM systems in languages which do not have dedicated AM markers, but markers which normally (or primarily) express other (non-AM) meanings, and only display AM meanings in specific contexts* (Belkadi 2014, 2015, 2016; building on observations in Bourdin 2006). Named D-AM (for "AM marked by deictic directionals") by Belkadi (2015: 50), this phenomenon is found to be characteristic of what is generally and indistinguishably called "deictic directionals" in the description of languages from the Afro-Asiatic (Berber, Chadic, Cushitic) and Nilo-Saharan (Nilotic) families. "Deictic directionals" in these languages consist of markers which primarily operate on motion verbs and (unless they have developed non-spatial meanings) specify the path (deictic orientation) of a motion already encoded by the verb. In (3a), for instance, the ventive enclitic =d of the Berber language Taqbaylit (Kabyle) specifies the path of a 'jumping' motion encoded by the verb root. In this context, the deictic directional does not express AM; it does not contribute a motion component distinct from that of the (motion) verb event. Yet there are contexts when the deictic directionals can give rise to AM readings similar to those expressed by dedicated AM markers, as when used with (at least certain) non-motion verbs. In (3b), for instance, the same ventive enclitic =d in Taqbaylit contributes a separate component of subsequent motion (specified for a ventive path) to the (non-motion) 'reading' event encoded by the verb root.

(3) Taqbaylit (Berber, Algeria)
    a. non-AM meaning (path only)
        t-jjlb   *=d*   *yr*   *tabla.*
        3SG.F-jump.PRF = VEN to table
        'She jumped on the table (<u>in the direction of the speaker</u>).' (Belkadi 2015: 64)

    b. AM meaning (subsequent motion and path)
        t-yra   *=d*   *taktaf*
        3SG.F-read.PRF =VEN book
        'She read the book somewhere else <u>and came back</u> (to the location of the speaker).' (Belkadi 2015: 64)

Interestingly, it was observed that when used with AM meanings, many of these non- (or less) dedicated AM systems do not behave as otherwise expected. Typically, as pointed out by Belkadi (2015), unlike what happens in dedicated AM systems, their exact AM values are not fixed but are dependent on context (inherent semantics of the verb, TAM settings, pragmatic situation, etc.). In the Cushitic language Somali, for instance, depending on the communicative situation, the subsequent motion that can be expressed by the 'itive' clitic *sii* can relate either to the subject argument of the verb (4i) or to a non-subject participant (4ii).

(4) Somali (Cushitic, Bourdin 2006: 18)
wuxu ***sii*** *joog-aa* *London*
FOC:3SG.M **ITIVE** stop/stand-PRS:3SG.M London
(i) 'He is in London right now and will continue on his way (towards a place where I am not).'
(ii) 'He is in London, where I or somebody else is going to join him.'

And in the same language, the ventive clitic *soo* can express all of the three main possible temporal relation values: prior motion (5i), concurrent motion (5ii), subsequent motion (5iii), as well as the more complex prior plus subsequent return motion (5iv).

(5) Somali (Cushitic, Bourdin 2006: 17–18)
soo *seexo*
VEN sleep:IMP.2SG
(i) 'Come sleep over here!' [face-to-face communication]
(ii) 'Get some rest (while you're traveling towards here)!' [phone conversation]
(iii) 'Get some rest (and then we'll get together)!' [phone conversation]
(iv) 'Go have a rest (and then come back here). / Go get some rest (and then we'll get together)!' [face-to-face communication]

In dedicated AM systems, each of these different values (subject versus non-subject motion, prior versus concurrent versus subsequent motion), if expressible, is normally encoded by way of a distinct marker.

2.3 Typology of AM

Finally, a third important development in the field of AM studies was a number of tentative typological proposals, in terms of implicational hierarchies, that make predictions in the way AM systems are structured cross-linguistically.

A first proposal, by Guillaume (2016), correlates the degree of complexity in the formation of AM systems (number of contrasting values) with the types of semantic values being manifested. On the basis of a survey in 44 South American languages from 36 distinct families or isolates, this typology included two implicational hierarchies.

The first hierarchy, based on the parameter of *temporal relation* and a suggestion by Levinson & Wilkins (2006: 534), predicts that, if a language has a marker for subsequent motion, it will also have a marker for prior and/or concurrent motion, and if it has a marker for concurrent motion, it will also have a marker for prior motion (*prior motion > concurrent motion > subsequent motion*).

The second hierarchy, based on the parameter of *moving argument*, states that if a language has an object AM marker, it normally has a subject AM marker as well, with a restriction that the subject AM inventory must be complex (in terms of number of AM morphemes) (*motion of the subject (complex inventory) > motion of the object*).

A second typological proposal, by Belkadi (2016), makes generalisations as to which readings, *directional versus AM*, particular semantic classes of verbs normally yield in non-dedicated polysemous (D-AM) systems. On the basis of a survey in 20 languages from the four main linguistic phyla in the African continent, Belkadi finds that on the following scale, the more the verbs are on the left-hand side, the more they tend to have directional readings, and the more they are on the right-hand side, the more they tend to have AM readings: *Path motion > Motion translational > Causative motion > Perception > (Natural phenomena and bodily secretions?) > Activities not involving translational motion > States*.

3 Parameters of AM

The typology of AM has been centred on three major semantic parameters: the temporal relation between the motion and the main event, the direction of the motion, and the grammatical role of the moving figure. Some further refinements are offered in the chapters of this book.

3.1 Direction

It should be noted at the outset that some authors refer to this dimension as "path" or "orientation" rather than "direction". Directions found in AM systems are frequently the deictic ventive (toward speaker) and itive (away from speaker) values. Note that in some languages, the deictic centre might be the addressee rather than the speaker (Otero ch. 20). But other directions also occur, including 'return' (Koch ch. 7), and, in the vertical dimension, 'up', 'down', and 'level'

(Schokkin ch. 10, Jacques et al. ch. 21). Included among AM markers are ones that indicate only the "fact-of-motion", with no specific direction (e.g. 'do while going along') and others that express indirect motion, such as random direction ('do here and there'). The latter, which may be called "distributive", is sometimes treated as AM but sometimes not, especially when its primary function appears to be to signal the spatial distribution of the event ('do in different places') rather than actual motion (see Koch ch. 7, Tallman ch. 11).

Efforts to establish a typology of AM are somewhat hampered by an overabundance of terminology, resulting partly from different descriptive traditions. As a guide to readers we provide in Table 1 a list of equivalents that are used by authors of these chapters (many further terms are used in the language descriptions on which these studies are based). Note that certain terms are used for different senses by different authors. The label based on the English gloss 'go' is ambiguous between a deictic sense 'away from speaker' and a neutral (unspecified) direction. "Andative" is used either for a deictic (away from speaker) sense or for motion in no particular direction ('go along'); some authors use "ambulative" for this second sense, while others use "ambulative" in a more distributive sense or for a specific 'around' meaning. "Returnative" has been used not for movement back to a prior location but for bidirectional movement (as noted by Dryer ch. 4). Our preferred terms are given first in each set.

Table 1: Equivalent directional terms.

Direction	Terms
toward deictic centre	ventive, venitive, centripetal, cislocative, HITHER, TOWARD, COM(ING)
away from deictic centre	itive, andative, centrifugal, translocative, THITHER, HENCE, AWAY, GO(ING)
no specific direction	andative, ambulative, mobilative, MOT(IVE) ALONG, NEUTRAL, GO(ING)
indirect, multiple locations	ambulative, distributive, AROUND, HERE AND THERE, HITHER AND THITHER, RANDOM, AIMLESS, circumlocative, circular
returning	reversive, returnative, BACK
bidirectional	roundtrip, counterdirectional, returnative, GO&DO&RETURN
reach endpoint	adlocative, arrive
depart	LEAVE

3.2 Temporal relation

Beside the temporal relation distinctions of prior (P), concurrent (C) and subsequent (S) motion, it is necessary to recognise polysemous markers that can flexibly indicate two or more relations (P/C, C/S, P/C/S): for examples see Dryer ch. 4, Belkadi ch. 5, Vidal & Payne ch. 12, Voisin ch.16, Creissels & Bassène ch. 17. A further complication is the encoding of two sequential motions (P+S), typically in opposite directions (i.e. a round trip 'go and do and return') – see Ross ch. 2, Dryer ch. 4, Koch ch. 7, Tallman ch. 11, Dryer ch. 13, Jacques et al. ch. 21, Pakendorf & Stoynova ch. 22. Perhaps related is interrupted motion in a consistent direction ('go and do then go again' or 'do while passing by') – see Ross ch. 2, Dryer ch. 4 – which however can be treated in some languages as an aspect-like punctual action within concurrent motion (= 'do once on the way') – see Koch ch. 7. Some scholars (e.g. Ross ch. 2), have indicated exceptions to Guillaume's (2016) temporal relation hierarchy P > C > S (cf. §2.3). Given that most of these exceptions (Reed & Lindsey ch. 9, Payne ch. 18, Kawachi ch. 19, Otero ch. 20) are in systems of the D-AM type, it is worth reconsidering to what extent the hierarchy is dependent on the type of AM system involved.

3.3 Argument role of the moving figure

A complication to the distinction of subject versus non-subject (usually object) as the moving figure is the situation where the subject and object together move after some action (e.g. 'do and bring') – see Jacques et al. ch. 21 and, earlier, Belkadi (2015: 61, 65). Contributors have pointed out some exceptions to Guillaume's (2016) generalisation that movement of a non-subject presupposes movement of the subject (cf. §2.3) – see Vidal & Payne ch. 12 for the D-AM system of Pilagá. Movement of the object of caused motion verbs (e.g. 'take and come/go') is characteristic of directional systems (Schokkin ch. 10, Otero ch. 20), so it is not surprising if this occurs in D-AM systems as well. Another exception to the generalisation concerns perception verbs in certain languages, also typically with D-AM systems, where expressions like 'see (object) coming/going' are frequently encountered (Ross ch. 2, Belkadi ch. 5, Creissels & Bassène ch. 17).

4 AM and other grammatical categories

AM has been characterised as a grammatical category separate from other typical verb categories such as tense, aspect, mood, and direction. Yet it bears some relations to many of these, and sometimes as well as to categories such as location, speed, and the roles and even persons of arguments.

4.1 AM versus motion with purpose

Prior AM can be hard to distinguish (in descriptions) from motion-with-purpose constructions (Lovestrand & Ross ch. 3), which express meanings such as 'go/come in order to do', with no implication that the doing is actually accomplished. These two constructions may overlap in irrealis (future, imperative) contexts (Jacques et al. ch. 21, Pakendorf & Stoynova ch. 22), and prior AM may develop historically from motion-with-purpose constructions (Koch ch. 7).

4.2 AM and direction

The motion co-event signaled by AM markers typically includes a direction specification (see §3.1). Directional markers are another kind of grammatical specification that in many languages mark the direction of verbs with inherent motion semantics. In some languages, directional markers which typically occur with motion verbs may be used in some circumstances to add a motion event to non-motion verbs, and therefore express AM. These have been called, following Belkadi (2015), D-AM systems (for "AM marked by deictic directionals") (§2.2); see Reed & Lindsey's (ch. 9) alternate proposal to rename D-AM as "inferential AM". About half of the specific languages described here (all the African chapters except Guérois et al. ch. 15 on Bantu and to some extent Voisin ch. 16 on Atlantic, Reed & Lindsey ch. 9, Schokkin ch.10, Vidal & Payne ch. 12) have such D-AM systems rather than what might be called "dedicated AM", "pure AM" or "canonical AM" systems. In other languages, the reverse type of extension can be found: the AM markers can be applied to motion verbs, in which case they add only a directional component, a phenomenon called "AM-D" by Voisin ch. 16 (for primary AM system with deictic directional extensions). A number of these studies (Ross ch. 2, Lovestrand & Ross ch. 3, Dryer ch. 4, Belkadi ch. 5, Otero ch. 20) explore overlaps between directionals and AM markers. For Koman languages, Otero ch. 20 further evaluates the predictions of Belkadi's (2016) hierarchy of semantic classes of verbs (cf. §2.3) and finds that her generalisations are generally confirmed but with some notable exceptions.

4.3 AM and aspect

Although AM has been characterised as a category separate from aspect, there are overlaps. Extension of AM markers to aspectual usages is especially prominent in the African systems described here. Phasal aspect may be marked by AM morphemes: inceptive has affinities with prior motion and "exchoative" (cessative) with subsequent motion (see Tallman ch. 11 for Chácobo and Otero ch. 20 for Koman languages). Tallman ch. 11 and Kawachi ch. 19 propose that AM is always aspectual. A further interaction is the fact that aspect-like contrasts are made within certain AM subcategories (cf. §2.1 on aspectual realisation of the verb event), especially concurrent motion (e.g. 'do once/repeatedly/continuously while going'; see Vuillermet ch. 6, Koch ch. 7). Possibly related to aspectual realisation are contrasts of speed that are found within AM systems (see Koch ch. 7)

4.4 AM and location

AM meanings are sometimes extended to indicate the location of the action, without reference to actual movement. Creissels & Bassène ch. 17 posit a semantic shift of the ventive marker of Jóola Fóoñi from 'do before coming' to 'do something while being away from here' – a usage for which the terms "altrilocal", "exlocative" or "distal" have been used (Ross ch. 2, Hernández-Green & Palancar ch. 14, Guérois et al. ch.15, Voisin ch. 16). The corresponding location near the deictic centre has been called "proximal" (Ross ch. 2).

4.5 AM and argument structure

While AM marking on verbs typically does not affect argument structure, in some languages adding a marker of motion permits the addition of spatial arguments (source, goal, trajectory) that are relevant to the motional component of the resulting verb (Pakendorf & Stoynova ch. 22). Furthermore, in some African languages, apparent extensions of AM markers include the manipulation of semantic roles, with and without valence change (Payne ch. 18). With respect to transitivity, in some languages AM markers display a kind of "transitivity harmony"; i.e. their form is conditioned by the transitivity of the verb stem (Koch ch. 7, Tallman ch.11).

5 Further issues

5.1 System complexity

Guillaume (2016) distinguishes AM systems by degree of complexity measured by the number of contrasting values in the system (cf. §2.1).[4] Ross (ch. 2) raises the question of how complexity should be measured, whether by the absolute number of contrasts, the number of parameters in the system, the interaction of AM with other grammatical values, or even by the formal complexity of its expression (Hernández-Green & Palancar ch. 14). Koch (ch. 7) questions whether a language with three AM markers within a system with two values in the relative timing parameter should count as more complex than a language with four markers within a single relative timing parameter.

5.2 Formal expression of AM

Most studies have focused on morphological marking by verb affixes, but AM values may be expressed by serial verb constructions (Lovestrand & Ross ch. 3), particles (Schokkin ch. 10, Dryer ch. 13), clitics (Dryer ch. 4, Belkadi ch. 5, Tallman ch. 11), or auxiliary constructions (Koch ch. 7, Guérois et al. ch. 15). AM (and directional) markers can be described in terms of their relative ordering within the verbal word or phrase (Ross ch. 2, Lovestrand & Ross ch. 3) – e.g. whether prefixes versus suffixes, or first versus final word in a serial verb construction. Another difference is whether AM markers are formally invariant or have variants (e.g. conditioned by the transitivity of the verb stem, see Koch ch.7, Tallman ch. 11) or whether they are expressed cumulatively with other grammatical features such as tense or subject-marking: the languages described by Reed & Lindsey ch. 9 and Hernández-Green & Palancar ch. 14 show great complexity in this sense.

---

4 Alternatively, this may be expressed in terms of the number of morphemes in the AM inventory.

5.3 Discourse function

The AM-marked verb may introduce both the main and the motion co-events (e.g. 'go and do'). Alternatively, it may redundantly "echo" (Guillaume 2006: 424, 432, 2016: 91, fn. 11) a motion event already introduced by a separate motion verb (e.g. 'go ... do (after going)'. In some languages it may *anticipate* a motion event to be separately introduced (e.g. 'do (before going) ... go'). These alternative uses have been described as "redundant" by Koch ch. 7, "pleonastic" by Pakendorf & Stoynova ch. 22, and "co-indexation" of motion by Tallman ch. 11. (There is no specific label for the anticipatory use, for which the term "echo" is not very suitable.) Many papers in the volume illustrate these discourse usages, and Pakendorf & Stoynova ch. 22 provide a detailed investigation of this topic. A related topic of interest is the overall frequency of use of AM markers in discourse, as well as the relative frequency of use of particular AM markers (Vuillermet ch. 6, Tallman ch. 11, Pakendorf & Stoynova ch. 22).

5.4 Diachrony of AM markers

Some genetically related languages display obviously cognate AM markers, but these are usually not sufficient to allow the reconstruction of complete AM systems (see Koch ch. 7 for Arandic and Pama-Nyungan, Hernández-Green & Palancar ch. 14 for Otomi, Guérois et al. ch. 15 for Bantu, Payne ch. 18 for Nilotic, Jacques et al. ch. 21 for Gyalrongic, and Pakendorf & Stoynova ch. 22 for Tungusic languages). These papers also offer many suggestions about the origins of the forms that mark AM. While verbal origins have been known for a long time (Koch 1984; Austin 1989; Wilkins 1991; Guillaume 2013), further evidence is provided here for verbal sources of several kinds. Verbs 'come' and 'go' are especially likely etymological sources (Jacques et al. ch. 21). Former auxiliary phrases are indicated for many Pama-Nyungan languages (Koch ch. 7) as well as for Bantu languages (Guérois et al. ch. 15). Serial verb constructions are argued as the source for Paluai AM markers (Schokkin ch. 10). In some situations where verbal origins are suggested for AM markers, details of their presumed earlier construction are not recoverable (or at least not explicitly discussed). It is apparent that attested AM markers reflect different degrees of grammaticalisation from their source constructions, a fact which sometimes makes it hard to be certain about their synchronic status. A non-verbal source of AM markers, not previously appreciated, is directional affixes, particles or clitics (Osgarby ch. 8,[5] Vidal & Payne ch. 12). Another diachronic development, apart from origins, is the further evolution of AM markers to non-AM values such as pure direction (Voisin ch. 16), aspect (Tallman ch. 11), and altrilocality (Creissels & Bassène ch. 17). These diachronic developments also present problems for their synchronic analysis.

5.5 AM and language contact

Previous studies have argued that, in Central Australia and Western Amazonia, AM is a highly diffusible category spread through language contact (Austin 1989; Wilkins 1991; Dixon 2002: 201–202; Koch 2007; Guillaume 2016). Further support for the influence of contact on the development of AM systems is provided in a number of papers in this volume (see especially Osgarby ch. 8, Voisin ch. 16).

5.6 Geographical distribution of AM

AM has been found to occur in languages of all inhabited continents except Europe. This volume adds considerably to the situation in Africa and North and Central America, but also includes Papuan and Oceanic languages. Not all parts of the world have been systematically studied, however.

6 Summary of the chapters

The introduction so far has set out the general framework within which studies of AM have been conducted and has highlighted some issues under discussion. In this section we summarise the contents of specific chapters. The contributions are ordered geographically.

First, however, we provide an indication of the overall scope of the papers, in terms of the coverage of the world's languages. Three of the chapters have worldwide scope: Ross ch. 2 on AM and directionals, Lovestrand & Ross ch. 3 on serial verb constructions and motion semantics, and Dryer ch. 4 on the overlap of AM and directionals. Two have continental scope: Belkadi ch. 5 on Africa and Dryer ch. 13 on North and Central America. Eight papers survey language families: Koch ch. 7 on

---

[5] Here it is suggested that the ventive AM marker in Mudburra derived from a former directional enclitic, which in turn reflected a non-subject enclitic first person pronoun.

Pama-Nyungan (Australia); Guérois et al. ch. 15 on Bantu, Voisin ch. 16 on Atlantic, Payne ch. 18 on Nilotic, and Otero ch. 20 on Koman – all in Africa; Jacques et al. ch. 21 on Gyalrongic and Kiranti within Sino-Tibetan, and Pakendorf & Stoynova ch. 22 on Tungusic – both in Asia; and Hernández-Green & Palancar ch. 14 on Otomi in Central America. Eight papers provide detailed studies of AM in particular languages: Osgarby ch. 8 on Mudburra (Pama-Nyungan, Australia); Tallman ch. 11 on Chácobo (Panoan) and Vidal & Payne ch. 12 on Pilagá (Guaycuruan) – both in South America; Creissels & Bassène ch. 17 on Jóola Fóoñi (Atlantic) and Kawachi ch. 19 on Kupsapiny (Nilotic) – both in Africa; Schokkin ch. 10 (Oceanic, Austronesian); and Reed & Lindsey ch. 9 (Pahoturi River family, Papua New Guinea).

6.1 Part I: General issues/perspectives

Part I is devoted to issues that transcend the description of particular languages. The four papers which immediately follow this introductory chapter study relations between AM and other verbal categories and/or constructions. The fifth paper is more methodological; it provides potential researchers with ideas on how data on AM may be collected.

Ross (ch. 2) presents a quantitative typological survey of the distribution of the morphological expression of AM and the distinct but overlapping grammatical category of directionals, based on a balanced sample of 325 languages. He finds AM attested in 26% and directionals in 35% of these languages, and both categories in 57 languages (i.e. about 17.5% of the 325 in the sample). Parameters investigated are: direction of motion (itive, ventive, etc.); temporal relationship with the lexical verb event (prior, concurrent and subsequent); moving argument (subject or object); and functional overlap of AM with directionals and other grammatical categories. Guillaume's (2016) hierarchies are tested and found to be generally supported. Ross also discusses some borderline cases which pose challenges for a precise description within the current framework of AM typology.

Lovestrand & Ross (ch. 3) explore the semantic relationship between markers of grammatical AM and motion verbs in serial verb constructions (SVCs). Their study is predicated on the fact that AM as a grammatical category, which has largely been studied as a morphological phenomenon, can also be expressed by means of multi-verb syntactic constructions. It thus complements the preceding chapter on the distribution of AM morphology. The authors find motion and/or directional semantics to be present in about 80.8% of their sample of 125 languages having SVCs. The most common motion SVCs are "directional SVCs", which combine a path-of-motion verb with another motion verb (typically manner of motion, e.g. 'run descend'), and "prior motion SVCs" (e.g. 'come and eat') or "purposive motion

SVCs" (e.g. 'come to eat'), which are difficult to distinguish from each other. SVCs expressing concurrent or subsequent motion and "caused accompanied motion SVCs" (e.g. 'take and come/go') are much rarer. The authors analyse the relative order of the two verbs in motion SVCs and find a clear tendency for the "restricted" motion verb to be in the first position in prior/purposive motion SVCs and in the second position in directional SVCs and subsequent motion SVCs. They propose explanations for these ordering patterns.

Dryer (ch. 4) explores the relationship between markers of AM and directional markers. He demonstrates that it is not uncommon for the same morphemes to be used for both functions; he finds this in 56 languages, from all continents in which AM occurs. When used with verbs having inherent motion semantics, these markers do not add a motion event, nor do they indicate temporal relation between motion and event, but they specify only the direction of motion. In contrast to "pure directionals", i.e. markers that do not indicate AM, Dryer proposes, these morphemes can be interpreted as a subtype of AM, akin to prior motion, concurrent motion, and so on. His on-line supplementary materials present examples from each of the languages mentioned in this chapter.

Belkadi (ch. 5) was the first to recognise the expression of AM by deictic directionals (D-AM) in many languages of Africa, showing that well-known itive and ventive markers are sometimes used to add a motion component to non-motion verbs (see §2.2). Here Belkadi addresses the problem of how AM, especially D-AM, relates to deictic directionality. Building on proposals from the literature on event semantics, the typology of event encoding and event integration, and her earlier work on an implicational hierarchy of semantic classes of verbs (cf. §2.3), she argues for an analysis in which AM and deictic directionality form a single grammatical category. A deictic directional expresses a complex event with the verb it modifies, just like an AM marker, but unlike AM it is fully integrated with (i.e. coextensive with) the motion event encoded by the host verb.

Vuillermet (ch. 6) describes a methodological tool for eliciting AM linguistic behaviour by means of visual stimuli, in the form of a picture storybook, *A Hunting Story*. The scenario incorporates the main parameters established in the AM literature, and it was specifically designed to elicit AM markers. The use of this tool with speakers of Ese Ejja, an Amazonian language of Bolivia and Peru (Takanan family), yielded not only examples of much of its complex AM system but also valuable data on sociolinguistics and discourse use. The author also provides some observations on strategies used to co-express motion and non-motion events in languages (which may or may not manifest grammatical AM) other than those for which this tool was designed.

1 Introduction: associated motion as a grammatical category in linguistic typology — 19

6.2 Part II: Australia and South Pacific

Part II begins with two studies on languages of Australia, the continent where AM was first recognised, then adds a study of D-AM in a Papuan language, Ende, plus a description of the system of directionals and AM of Paluai, an Oceanic (Austronesian) language of Papua New Guinea.

Koch (ch. 7) surveys AM in the Pama-Nyungan languages of Australia. He first updates the description of semantic contrasts within the very complex AM system of Kaytetye, the Arandic language for which the AM category was first described (Koch 1984). He then compares Kaytetye with other Arandic languages, which share similarly complex AM systems and have played an important role in early studies of AM (Wilkins 1989, 1991). The remainder of the paper is devoted to an exploration of the extent to which AM appears in other languages of the large Pama-Nyungan family, spoken across a large part of the Australian continent. It is organised according to the degree of complexity of the AM systems: very complex, with eight or more AM contrasts; moderately complex, with three to six; binary, with a two-way contrast; and languages with a single AM category. AM markers are found in 41 of the approximately 100 languages for which there is adequate data to make a judgement. The findings are summarised with respect to system complexity, semantic parameters involved, geographical distribution, and diachronic sources of the AM markers.

Osgarby (ch. 8) describes AM in Mudburra, a Pama-Nyungan language in north-central Australia in intimate contact with languages of the non-Pama-Nyungan Mirndi family, which includes Wambaya, where some AM forms have been previously reported (e.g. Nordlinger 2001). Mudburra has a two-way contrast of deictic direction: away from and toward the speaker. In addition to signaling (prior or concurrent) AM with non-motion verbs, these markers may be used with motion verbs to indicate either direction (e.g. 'fall toward speaker') or an added motion co-event (e.g. 'come and fall'). Unusual features, in the Australian context, are the fact that these markers do not combine with all tense-mood values and that they occur *after* rather than *before* TAM markers; both of these features reflect their origin as directional suffixes or enclitics. Osgarby shows that diachronically Mudburra has adapted its inherited directional markers (-*rni* 'hither' and -*rra* 'thither') to express the kind of information signaled in neighbouring Mirndi languages by forms derived from earlier verbs. He further shows that languages of north-central Australia, which belong to two different families (Mirndi and Pama-Nyungan) and three separate subgroups of Pama-Nyungan, form an areal group with respect to their AM systems.

Reed & Lindsey (ch. 9) describe the AM system of a Papuan language – a (non-genetic) group for which AM has been largely unknown (but cf. Levinson's

2006 account of Yélî Dnye). Ende, a member of the Pahoturi River language family in southern New Guinea, has a minimal AM system of the D-AM type: a ventive directional prefix can indicate concurrent, subsequent or prior motion of the subject and sometimes of other participants. The formal expression of ventive is not straightforward, but is embedded in a complex system of verbal morphological exponence. The authors also propose a new term *inferential associated motion* to distinguish the D-AM type from the canonical *dedicated associated motion* systems like that of Kaytetye.

Schokkin (ch. 10) offers one of the first explicit descriptions of AM in an Oceanic (Austronesian) language, Paluai, spoken on Baluan Island, a volcanic island in Manus Province, Papua New Guinea. Paluai has a directional system that combines three deictic values (ventive, itive and neutral) with four directions based on fixed bearings (up/inland, down/seawards, level/parallel to the shore, and unspecified). These are expressed by ten motion verbs in a serial verb construction, in which the directional verb specifies the direction of the intransitive subject or transitive object of a preceding main verb expressing motion, transfer or perception. At least seven of these directional forms can also occur as particles in a preverbal slot, between Core Aspect and Secondary Aspect slots. In this position they indicate direction with motion verbs and prior motion of subject with non-motion verbs; i.e. they function as markers of D-AM. This paper contrasts preverbal (AM or directional) and post-verbal (only directional) constructions, both of which originate from serial verb constructions.

6.3 Part III: The Americas

Part III presents four studies from the American continents (Vuillermet's chapter in Part I presents further data from South America).

Tallman (ch. 11) describes a complex system of at least seven dedicated AM morphemes in Chácobo, a southern Panoan language of the northern Bolivian Amazon. Most of the AM morphemes display allomorphy based on the transitivity of the verb stem. Ventive and andative directions are semantic components of several AM markers, but morphemes signaling "distributive" ('do in multiple places and multiple times') and "counterdirectional" (circular) meanings are also present. Relative timing of motion versus event may be prior, concurrent, subsequent, or prior plus subsequent ('go and do and return'). On the basis of natural text data, Tallman also studies the non-motional functions of AM markers (especially aspect and orientation), and explores from texts the extent to which each of the AM markers of prior, concurrent, and subsequent motion clearly expresses AM versus aspect or orientation/direction. He argues that the data support a fuzzy boundary between AM and other categories and suggests that this fuzziness can be measured for each AM category.

Vidal & **Payne** (ch. 12) offer a study of Pilagá, a Guaycuruan language from north-eastern Argentina, thus extending our knowledge of AM systems geographically into the periphery of the South American systems of Guillaume's (2016) survey. They describe the functions of a few (including ventive and itive) of the 14 members of a set of directional verbal suffixes. There are no dedicated affixes for AM distinct from those used for non-motion direction/location, as in other languages with D-AM systems; however, at least one non-deictic directional, 'straight ahead', glossed 'opposite', is used to add associated motion. The most likely target of AM is the object/patient of a transitive verb; the temporal relation between the motion and the main event is not fixed. Directional suffixes also function to indicate the location of the event and they sometimes have applicative functions.

Dryer (ch. 13) surveys AM in North and Central America, finding it to be widespread, attested in 94 languages (29 families and isolates), with only five families lacking any evidence of AM. About 70% of these languages have simple systems of just one or two AM subcategories. The highest number of contrasts is seven in Panamint (Uto-Aztecan) and six in Menomini (Algic). In terms of basic typological parameters, the author notes four temporal relations (here called "types" of AM): prior, concurrent, subsequent, and prior plus subsequent (with two subtypes, "round trip" and "passing by"); their relative frequency according to language is P > C > P+S > S. The most common directions coded by AM markers are the deictic ventive and itive (here called "andative"), but a non-deictic "random" ('ambulative', 'around') direction also occurs, typically with concurrent motion, as does "neutral" direction ('go/come and do'). Dryer presents numerous examples of the same markers being used to code AM with non-motion verbs and direction-only with motion verbs, as well as a few cases where a verb is modified by a combination of a pure directional and an AM marker (e.g. 'hither move&do'). A summary table presents the inventories of all the languages, and a set of online supplementary materials lists and describes the AM markers in each of the 94 languages.

Hernández-Green & **Palancar** (ch. 14) describe AM systems in three languages of the Otomi family in central Mexico. The languages differ in the degree of complexity of the AM system, from one (in the reduced Querétaro Otomi system) to four semantic contrasts. The moving argument is usually the subject. The directional and relative timing values of AM markers in these systems are ventive (prior, concurrent, or subsequent motion to the speaker's location), attested in all the languages; andative (concurrent motion in a direction other than toward the deictic centre); ambulative (concurrent motion in a random direction, 'here and there'), attested in one language; and adlocative (prior arrival at place of the action). Most AM categories can also be used to encode pure direction with motion verbs. Extended usages of AM marker include an "exlocative" (i.e. altrilocative) reading of the ventive and aspectual uses (progressive, customary) of the andative and the ambulative. A typologically interesting feature of these systems is the complexity of their formal realisation. There are no dedicated AM markers, but AM values are realised cumulatively with TAM and subject person in pre-verbal "inflectional formatives" and by stem alternations (involving consonant mutations and tone changes), both of which are morphologically conditioned by the conjugation class of the verb. The Otomi AM systems are also characterised by a substantial number of paradigmatic gaps. The authors point out that the complexity of exponence of AM is a different criterion for the complexity of AM systems than morphosemantic complexity (e.g. the number of AM subcategories).

6.4 Part IV: Africa

African languages, where ventive and itive directional marking has long been recognised, have been brought into the compass of AM typology by the pioneering studies of Voisin (2010, 2013) and Belkadi (2014, 2015). The six studies presented in this section describe AM systems in a representative sample of individual languages and groups of languages from the Niger-Congo and Nilo-Saharan phyla. Two chapters describe individual languages and four survey AM across a genetic group. (Examples from further African languages are presented in Belkadi's ch. 5 in Part I.) AM in African languages is generally of the D-AM type, but dedicated AM systems do occur in Bantu and some Atlantic languages. A considerable number of extended (especially aspectual and locational) functions are also described in these papers.

Guérois, Gibson & Persohn (ch. 15) study morphological and semantic aspects of AM across the whole Bantu family, where AM has not traditionally been recognised. They identify 54 languages with clear instantiations of AM. Most of these have systems consisting of only one or two forms, marking only prior motion; but one language, Fuliiru, marks eight subcategories involving five different directions and a contrast between prior and concurrent motion. AM markers are usually verbal prefixes originating from motion verbs constructed with a non-finite verb. Some AM forms have further evolved into markers of TAM, especially future or imperative, or location, such as altrilocality.

Voisin (ch. 16) surveys AM in the languages of the Atlantic branch of the Niger-Congo family. Some 20 languages (out of a total of 50) are considered, including representatives of all subgroups except Nalu. The AM systems generally contain few contrasting markers (one to three), which are always verbal

1 Introduction: associated motion as a grammatical category in linguistic typology — 23

affixes. Voisin classifies the languages according to whether they have: an "exclusive AM" system of dedicated AM affixes (with some non-motional extensions to markers of TAM or altrilocality); a D-AM system, where deictic directional (DD) markers attest AM readings with some specific verbs; or what she calls an "AM-D" system, which is explained as an AM system expanding toward deictic directional meanings; a few languages remain unclassified. Voisin then describes the distribution of these systems geographically and according to genetic subgroups, exploring what might have been their historical development within the family. She concludes tentatively that the dedicated AM system is the more ancient one in the family and that its markers were already "verbal extensions" rather than independent lexical motion verbs in proto-Atlantic.

Creissels & **Bassène** (ch. 17) provide a detailed description of the use of a single ventive marker in Jóola Fóoñi (aka Diola-Fogny), a language of the Atlantic family spoken in Senegal. Here, as in other D-AM systems, a verbal suffix (with two allomorphs) encodes deictic direction with movement verbs, but with non-movement verbs it adds a motion component. The motional semantics of this suffix is also extended to non-motional uses, expressing locational or aspectual information ('do something while being away from here') or 'development of a process in the direction of some outcome'.

Payne (ch. 18) explores the use of directional markers across the Nilotic family. Deictic directionals (ventive and itive) are found in the verbal morphology of all three branches, to express direction or orientation with motion verbs and also to add AM to non-motion verbs – in Southern Nilotic only in conjunction with ambulative (cf. Kawachi's 'along' morpheme in chapter 19). Payne explores further functions that presumably result from extensions of AM uses, including the manipulation of semantic roles (with or without valence change) and a large variety of aspectual senses. She further presents the results of a corpus study of Maasai texts, which shows that AM is not (any longer) the dominant function of the Maasai directionals.

Kawachi (ch. 19) describes the marking of direction and motion in Kupsapiny, a Southern Nilotic language of Uganda. Verbal suffixes marking deictic ventive and itive directions occur with motion verbs, but also with non-motion verbs in combination with an 'along' marker (called "ambulative" in Payne's chapter 18) to specify (usually concurrent) associated motion of the subject or even pure aspect without motion. The author emphasises that the "along-deictic-directional" marker always involves an aspectual component of continuation or iteration.

Otero (ch. 20) examines the highly polyfunctional deictic directional (DD) verbal morphology in the five living languages of the small Koman family (possibly belonging to the Nilo-Saharan phylum) spoken around the borderlands of Ethiopia and South Sudan. These suffixes mark two or three contrasting deictic directions – toward the speaker, toward the addressee or away from the deictic centre (according to language), or unspecified. Their function largely depends on the semantics of the host verb: direction (of intransitive subject or transitive object) with motion verbs, and subsequent motion of subject with dynamic non-motion verbs. At the more fine-grained level, Otero finds Belkadi's (2016) scale (see §2.3) to be generally confirmed by the Koman languages, while showing that in some of these languages one of the directional markers may indicate "exchoative" aspect rather than AM with verbs of state, and that several semantic subtypes of verbs allow alternative construals which do not conform to the predictions of Belkadi's hierarchy.

6.5 Part V: Asia

AM has only recently been discussed with respect to languages of Asia, and only in three families of languages: Sino-Tibetan, Tungusic and Japonic (see references in §1). In this volume, we provide two studies that further explore AM in Sino-Tibetan and Tungusic. Key issues addressed in these studies have been distinguishing AM from motion-with-purpose and directionals.

Jacques, Lahaussois & Zhang (ch. 21) survey the usage of AM in the languages of the Gyalrongic and Kiranti groups within the Sino-Tibetan family. They provide criteria for determining AM functions and for distinguishing AM from both motion-with-purpose constructions and from orientation/directional markers. Four Gyalrongic languages mark two contrasting deictic directions of prior motion of the subject ('come and verb', 'go and verb'), with prefixes grammaticalised from the motion verbs 'go' and 'come' in serial verb constructions. The Kiranti languages have more complex AM systems, with one to seven distinct markers, including: prior, concurrent, and subsequent temporal relations (plus one example of prior plus subsequent 'go and do and return'); "circumlocative" direction ('go around doing'); motion in the vertical dimension (up, down, level); and joint movement of subject and object (e.g. with 'bring', 'take'). AM markers originating from verbs in serial verb constructions have in some languages further grammaticalised into aspectual markers. The authors also mention a few other languages in the Sino-Tibetan family that manifest AM marking.

Pakendorf & Stoynova (ch. 22) survey AM in five Tungusic languages belonging to the Northern and Southern branches. All the Tungusic languages, including the now-extinct Classical Manchu, have a productive suffix, here labelled the "*ndA*-suffix", which marks prior motion of the subject in a deictically non-specific direction ('go and do'), and sometimes as well motion-with-purpose ('go to do'). Classical Manchu also had a distinct ventive suffix, and in some languages a further AM meaning 'go and do and return' is grammaticalising from a combination of *-ndA* with an imperfective marker. The AM suffixes occur in three constructions: in an AM-marked independent verb construction expressing both motion and main event ('go and/to VERB') and in two "pleonastic" constructions consisting of an independent motion verb plus either an AM-inflected verb ('go ... go and/to VERB') or a dependent AM-marked converb ('go ... go to VERB'). Unlike AM-marked verbs in many other languages, the Tungusic languages allow *ndA*-verbs to express spatial arguments (goal, source, trajectory) appropriate to the relevant motion, in addition to or instead of the arguments of the base verb. The authors compare discourse frequencies of AM-related variables (transitivity of base verb, construction type, argument expression) within and across the languages studied.

Acknowledgements: We are grateful to the people who worked with us to make the publication of this volume possible, including the authors of the articles, the reviewers (Aïcha Belkadi, Philippe Bourdin, Gerrit Dimmendaal, Matthew Dryer, Patti Epps, David Fleck, Carol Genetti, Rozenn Guérois, Guillaume Jacques, Kazuhiro Kawachi, Aimée Lahaussois, Joseph Lovestrand, Patrick McConvell, Lev Michael, Tatiana Nikitina, Doris Payne, Daniel Ross, Dineke Schokkin, Sylvie Voisin, Marine Vuillermet), Jean-Christophe Verstraete and the other editors of the EALT series, editorial staff at de Gruyter Mouton Julie Miess and Kirstin Boergen, and Suruthi Manogarane for supporting us during the production of the book. We thank the organisers of the 12th Conference of the Association for Linguistic Typology (ALT), held at the Australian National University, Canberra 10–15 December 2017, where earlier versions of some of the papers in this volume were presented at a workshop on "Associated Motion".[6] We also thank Kate Lindsey, Brigitte Pakendorf, Bastian Persohn, Lauren Reed and Dineke Schokkin for feedback on an earlier version of this introductory chapter. Finally, we are grateful to the ASLAN project (ANR-10-LABX-0081) of Université de Lyon, for its financial support within the program "Investissements d'Avenir" (ANR-11-IDEX-0007) of the French government operated by the National Research Agency (ANR).

---

6 http://www.ddl.cnrs.fr/fulltext/Guillaume/Workshop_programs/Associated%20motion_ALT2017_Epeire.pdf

References

Alonso de la Fuente, José Andrés & Guillaume Jacques. 2018. Associated motion in Manchu in typological perspective. *Language and Linguistics* 19(4). 501–524.

Austin, Peter. 1989. Verb compounding in central australian languages. *La Trobe University Working Papers in Linguistics* 2. 1–31.

Belkadi, Aïcha. 2014. Verb meaning and deictic paths in Taqbaylit Berber. In Aïcha Belkadi, Kakia Chatsiou & Kirsty Rowan (eds.), *Language Documentation and Linguistic Theory 4*. London: SOAS University of London.

Belkadi, Aïcha. 2015. Associated motion with deictic directionals: A comparative overview. *SOAS Working Papers in Linguistics* 17. 49–76.

Belkadi, Aïcha. 2016. Associated Motion Constructions in African Languages. *Africana Linguistica* 22. 43–70.

Belkadi, Aïcha. This volume, chapter 5. Deictic directionality as associated motion: Motion, complex events and event integration in African languages.

Boro, Krishna. 2017. *A Grammar of Hakhun Tangsa*. Eugene: University of Oregon doctoral dissertation.

Bourdin, Philippe. 2006. The marking of directional deixis in Somali: How typological idiosyncratic is it? In F. K. Erhard Voeltz (ed.), *Studies in African Linguistic Typology* (Typological Studies in Language 64), 13–41. Amsterdam: John Benjamins Publishing Company.

Cleary-Kemp, Jessica. 2015. *Serial verb constructions revisited: A case study from Koro*. Berkeley: University of California doctoral dissertation.

Creissels, Denis & Alain-Christian Bassène. This volume, chapter 17. Ventive, associated motion and aspect in Jóola Fóoñi (Atlantic).

Dixon, Robert M. W. 2002. *Australian languages. Their nature and development*. Cambridge: Cambridge University Press.

Dryer, Matthew. 2002. A comparison of preverbs in Kutenai and Algonquian. In David Pentland (ed.), *Proceedings of the 30th Algonquian Conference*, 63–94. Winnipeg: University of Manitoba.

Dryer, Matthew. 2007. Kutenai, Algonquian, and the Pacific Northwest from an areal perspective. In H. C. Wolfart (ed.), *Proceedings of the 38th Algonquian Conference*, 155–206. Winnipeg: University of Manitoba.

Dryer, Matthew S. 2013. *A grammatical description of Kara-Lemakot* (Studies in the Languages of Island Melanesia 2). Canberra: Asia-Pacific Linguistics Open Access Monographs.

Dryer, Matthew S. This volume, chapter 4. Associated motion and directionals: Where they overlap.

Dryer, Matthew S. This volume, chapter 13. Associated motion in North America (including Mexico and Central America).

Genetti, Carol, Kristine A. Hildebrandt, Alexia Fawcett & Nathaniel Sims. To appear. Direction and associated motion in Tibeto-Burman. *Linguistic Typology*.

Guérois, Rozenn, Hannah Gibson & Bastian Persohn. This volume, chapter 15. Associated motion in Bantu languages.

Guillaume, Antoine. 2000. Directionals versus associated motions in Cavineña. In Alan K. Melby & Arle L. Lommel (eds.), *LACUS Forum XXVI: The lexicon*, 395–401. Fullerton, CA: The Linguistic Association of Canada and the United States.

Guillaume, Antoine. 2006. La catégorie du "mouvement associé" en cavineña : apport à une typologie de l'encodage du mouvement et de la trajectoire. *Bulletin de la Société de Linguistique de Paris* 101(1). 415–436.
Guillaume, Antoine. 2008. *A grammar of Cavineña* (Mouton Grammar Library 44). Berlin & New York: Mouton de Gruyter.
Guillaume, Antoine. 2009. Les suffixes verbaux de mouvement associé en cavineña. *Faits de Langues : Les Cahiers* 1. 181–204.
Guillaume, Antoine. 2013. Reconstructing the category of "associated motion" in Tacanan languages (Amazonian Bolivia and Peru). In Ritsuko Kikusawa & Lawrence A. Reid (eds.), *Historical Linguistics 2011. Selected papers from the 20th International Conference on Historical Linguistics, Osaka, 25–30 July 2011*, 129–151. Amsterdam & Philadelphia: John Benjamins Publishing Company.
Guillaume, Antoine. 2016. Associated motion in South America: Typological and areal perspectives. *Linguistic Typology* 20(1). 81–177.
Guillaume, Antoine. 2017a. Associated motion: Australia, South America and beyond. Presented at the Workshop on "Associated Motion", held in conjunction with the 12th Conference of the Association for Linguistic Typology (ALT), 15 December, Canberra, Australia.
Guillaume, Antoine. 2017b. Sistemas complejos de movimiento asociado en las lenguas Takana y Pano: perspectivas descriptiva, tipológica e histórico-comparativa. In Antoine Guillaume & Pilar M. Valenzuela (eds.), *Estudios sincrónicos y diacrónicos sobre lenguas Pano y Takana*, vol. 39(1), 211–261. Paris: Amerindia – A.E.A.
Guillaume, Antoine & Harold Koch. This volume, chapter 1. Introduction: Associated motion as a grammatical category in linguistic typology.
Hernández-Green, Néstor & Enrique Palancar. This volume, chapter 14. Associated motion in the Otomi family.
Jacques, Guillaume. 2013. Harmonization and disharmonization of affix ordering and basic word order. *Linguistic Typology* 17(2). 187–215.
Jacques, Guillaume, Aimée Lahaussois & Shuya Zhang. This volume, chapter 21. Associated motion in Sino-Tibetan, with a focus on Gyalrongic and Kiranti.
Kawachi, Kazuhiro. 2011. Meanings of the spatial deictic verb suffixes in Kupsapiny, the southern Nilotic language of the Sebei region of Uganda. In Hieda Osamu (ed.), *Descriptive studies of Nilotic languages* (Studies in Nilotic Linguistics 3), 65–107. Tokyo: Research Institute for Languages and Cultures of Asia and Africa, Tokyo University of Foreign Studies.
Kawachi, Kazuhiro. This volume, chapter 19. The 'along'-deictic-directional verb suffix complex in Kupsapiny.
Kießling, Roland & Stefan Bruckhaus. 2017. Associated locomotion in Datooga (Southern Nilotic). In Kaji Shigeki (ed.), *Proceedings of the 8th World Congress of African Linguistics (WOCAL), Kyoto 2015*, 243–258. Tokyo: Tokyo University of Foreign Studies.
Koch, Harold. 1984. The category of "associated motion" in Kaytej. *Languages in Central Australia* 1. 23–34.
Koch, Harold. 2007. Language contact and the grammaticalisation of motion: a case study from central Australia. Presented at the 18th International Conference of Historical Linguistics, Montreal, August 6–11.
Koch, Harold. This volume, chapter 7. Associated motion in the Pama-Nyungan languages of Australia.

Konnerth, Linda. 2014. *A grammar of Karbi*. Eugene: University of Oregon doctoral dissertation.
Konnerth, Linda. 2015. A new type of convergence at the deictic center: second person and cislocative in Karbi (Tibeto-Burman). *Studies in Language* 39(1). 24–45.
Lamarre, Christine. 2020. An associated motion approach to northern Mandarin motion-cum-purpose patterns. In Janet Zhiqun Xing (ed.), *A typological approach to grammaticalization and lexicalization*, 131–163. Berlin/Boston: De Gruyter Mouton.
Lamarre, Christine, Alice Vittrant, Anetta Kopecka, Sylvie Voisin, Noëllie Bon, Benjamin Fagard, Colette Grinevald, Claire Moyse-Faurie, Annie Risler, Jinke Song, Adeline Tan & Clément Voirin. To appear. Deictic directionals revisited in the light of advances in typology. In Laure Sarda & Benjamin Fagard (eds.), *Neglected aspects of motion-event description*. (Human Cognitive Processing). Amsterdam: John Benjamins Publishing Company.
Levinson, Stephen C. 2006. The language of space in Yélî Dnye. In Stephen C. Levinson & David P. Wilkins (eds.), *Grammars of space. Explorations in cognitive diversity*, 157–205. Cambridge: Cambridge University Press.
Levinson, Stephen C. & David P. Wilkins. 2006. Patterns in the data: toward a semantic typology of spatial description. In Stephen C. Levinson & David P Wilkins (eds.), *Grammars of space. Explorations in cognitive diversity*, 512–552. Cambridge: Cambridge University Press.
Lovestrand, Joseph & Daniel Ross. This volume, chapter 3. Serial verb constructions and motion semantics.
Meier, Sabrina C. 2020. *Topics in the grammar of Mono-Alu (Oceanic)*. Newcastle, Australia: University of Newcastle doctoral dissertation.
Nordlinger, Rachel. 2001. Wambaya in motion. In Jane Simpson, David Nash, Mary Laughren, Peter Austin & Barry Alpher (eds.), Forty years on: Ken Hale and Australian languages, 401–413. (Pacific Linguistics 512) Canberra: Australian National University.
O'Connor, Loretta. 2004. Going getting tired: associated motion through space and time in Lowland Chontal. In Michel Achard & Suzanne Kemmer (eds.), *Language, culture and mind*, 181–199. Stanford: CSLI Publications.
Osgarby, David. This volume, chapter 8. Mudburra associated motion in an areal perspective.
Otero, Manuel A. This volume, chapter 20. At the intersection of associated motion, direction and exchoative aspect in the Koman languages.
Pakendorf, Brigitte & Natalia Stoynova. This volume, chapter 22. Associated motion in Tungusic languages: A case of mixed argument structure.
Payne, Doris L. This volume, chapter 18. The extension of 'Associated Motion' to aspect and argument structure in Nilotic languages.
Persohn, Bastian. 2018. Basic motion verbs in Nyakyusa: lexical semantics and associated motion. *Studies in African Linguistics* 47(1 & 2). 101–127.
Reed, Lauren W. & Kate L. Lindsey. This volume, chapter 9. "Now the story's turning around": Associated motion and directionality in Ende, a language of Papua New Guinea.
Renaudier, Marie. 2012. *Dérivation et valence en sereer. Variété de Mar Lodj (Sénégal)*. Lyon: Université Lumière Lyon 2 doctoral dissertation.
Rose, Françoise. 2015. Associated motion in Mojeño Trinitario: some typological considerations. *Folia Linguistica* 49(1). 117–158.
Ross, Daniel. This volume, chapter 2. A cross-linguistic survey of associated motion and directional.
Sakel, Jeanette. 2004. *A grammar of Mosetén* (Mouton Grammar Library 33). Berlin & New York: Mouton de Gruyter.

Schokkin, Dineke. This volume, chapter 10. Preverbal directionals as markers of associated motion in Paluai (Austronesian; Oceanic).
Schultze-Berndt, Eva. 2007. On manners and paths of refining Talmy's typology of motion expressions via language documentation. In Peter K. Austin, Oliver Bond & David Nathan (eds.), *Proceedings of Conference on Language Documentation and Linguistic Theory*. London: SOAS.
Slobin, Dan I. 2004. The many ways to search for a frog. In Sven Strömquist & Ludo Verhoven (eds.), *Relating events in narrative: typological and contextual perspectives*, vol. 2, 219–257. Mahwah, NJ: Lawrence Erlbaum Associates.
Stoynova, Natalia. 2016. Pokazateli "dviženija s cel'ju" i sobytijnaja struktura: suffiks -nda v nanajskom jazyke [Markers of "motion-cum-purpose" and event structure: -nda suffix in Nanai]. *Voprosy Jazykoznanija* (4). 86–111.
Tallman, Adam J. R. This volume, chapter 11. Associated motion in Chácobo (Pano) in typological perspective.
Talmy, Leonard. 1985. Lexicalization patterns: semantic structure in lexical form. In Timothy Shopen (ed.), *Language typology and syntactic description*, vol. 3, 57–148. Cambridge: Cambridge University Press.
Talmy, Leonard. 2007. Lexical typologies. In Timothy Shopen (ed.), *Language Typology and Syntactic Description*, vol. 3, 66–168. 2nd edn. Cambridge: Cambridge University Press.
Tunbridge, Dorothy. 1988. Affixes of motion and direction in Adnyamathanha. In Peter Austin (ed.), *Complex sentence constructions in Australian languages* (Typological Studies in Language 15), 267–283. Amsterdam: John Benjamins Publishing Company.
Vidal, Alejandra & Doris L. Payne. This volume, chapter 12. Pilagá directionals and the typology of associated motion.
Vittrant, Alice. 2015. Expressing motion. The contribution of Southeast Asian languages with reference to East Asian languages. In Nick J. Enfield & Bernard Comrie (eds.), *Languages of Mainland Southeast Asia: the state of the art* (Pacific Linguistics 649), 586–632. Berlin: De Gruyter Mouton.
Voisin, Sylvie. 2010. Les morphèmes -i et -si en wolof. *Sciences et Techniques du Langage, Revue du Centre de Linguistique Appliquée de Dakar* 10. 21–34.
Voisin, Sylvie. 2013. Expressions de trajectoire dans quelques langues atlantiques (groupe nord). *Faits de Langues. Sémantiques des relations spatiales* 42. 131–152.
Voisin, Sylvie. This volume, chapter 16. Associated motion and deictic directional in Atlantic languages.
Vuillermet, Marine. 2012. *A grammar of Ese Ejja, a Takanan language of the Bolivian Amazon*. Lyon: Université Lumière Lyon 2 doctoral dissertation.
Vuillermet, Marine. 2013. Dónde, cuándo, y con quién ocurren acciones: el movimiento asociado en ese ejja. In Ana María Ospina Bozzi (ed.), *Expresión de nociones espaciales en lenguas amazónicas*, 39–59. Bogota: Instituto Caro y Cuervo & Universidad Nacional de Colombia.
Vuillermet, Marine. This volume, chapter 6. A visual stimulus for eliciting associated motion.
Wilkins, David P. 1989. *Mparntwe Arrernte (Aranda). Studies in the structure and semantics of grammar*. Canberra: Australian National University doctoral dissertation.
Wilkins, David P. 1991. The semantics, pragmatics and diachronic development of "associated motion" in Mparntwe Arrernte. *Buffalo Papers in Linguistics* 1. 207–257.
Wilkins, David P. 2004. The verbalization of motion events in Arrernte. In Sven Strömquist & Ludo Verhoven (eds.), *Relating events in narrative: typological and contextual perspectives*, 143–157. Mahwah, NJ: Lawrence Erlbaum Associates.

Zavala Maldonado, Roberto. 2000. Olutec motion verbs: grammaticalization under Mayan contact. In Andrew K. Simpson (ed.), *Annual Meeting of the Berkeley Linguistics Society*, vol. 26, 139–151.

Zhang, Shuya. 2020. *Le rgyalrong situ de Brag-bar et sa contribution à la typologie de l'expression des relations spatiales : L'orientation et le mouvement associé*. Paris: Institut National des Langues et Civilisations Orientales doctoral dissertation.

Daniel Ross
2 A cross-linguistic survey of Associated Motion and Directionals

Abstract: This chapter investigates the morphological expression of Associated Motion (AM) and Directionals from a broad typological perspective based on a balanced sample of 325 languages worldwide. Directionals are found in about one-third of the languages surveyed, whereas AM is found in about one-fourth, in some cases beyond the traditional areas for research on these phenomena, and often based on very different descriptive traditions and terminology. It is determined that, although the distributions of AM and Directionals overlap, they represent distinct grammatical categories. Typically, Directionals combine with lexical motion verbs to specify path, whereas AM contributes motion to non-motion verbs. The main parameters of variation for AM are the moving argument (most often subject, alternatively object), and the temporal relationship of the motion to predicate (before, during or after). Prior AM is found to be the most common type, followed by Concurrent and Subsequent. Typological generalizations are presented based on the data, and challenging cases are discussed in detail, as well as implications for continued research.

Keywords: associated motion, directionals, typology, morphology, survey

1 Introduction

Associated Motion (AM) has only recently been recognized as a cross-linguistic category, and while volumes like this one and ongoing fieldwork around the world contribute to our understanding of the phenomenon, most research to date on AM has focused on individual languages or particular regions. The current paper addresses AM and the related concept of Directionals (DIR) from a broad typological perspective, centered around a balanced cross-linguistic survey of these features in 325 languages around the world. In addition to contributing directly to our typological understanding of these phenomena, such a survey is also beneficial for identifying challenging cases in particular languages that in turn may make us question and refine our understanding and potentially our working definitions as well. Just how widespread is AM? And what does

Daniel Ross, University of Illinois at Urbana-Champaign, djross3@illinois.edu cross-linguistic variation tell us about its nature? Which typological features are needed to explain the variation, and how does it relate to other phenomena?

The term *Associated Motion* was introduced by Koch (1984) for the description of languages in Australia, where it has caught on in descriptive and comparative work (Tunbridge 1988; Wilkins 1991; Dixon 2002; Koch, this volume; *inter alia*). More recently the term has also been applied to languages in South America (Guillaume 2013, 2016; Rose 2015; *inter alia*). Elsewhere, it has been used sporadically to describe individual languages in descriptive grammars and other publications (e.g. O'Connor 2004; Jacques 2013), but rarely for larger typological comparisons, with a few exceptions such as Belkadi (2016) and now a number of chapters in this volume. For more information about the history and scope of this research, see Guillaume (2016: 84–92), Guillaume & Koch (this volume), Ross (2021), and the references cited in each. The main typological parameters considered include direction of motion, temporal relationship (motion before, during or after the action of the verb), and the moving argument (typically subject, but sometimes another argument), as well as interaction with other grammatical features.

Descriptive studies have reported motion-related morphemes for a long time, albeit through the lenses of a wide array of often confusing and even contradictory terminology that may, in part, explain why a broad cross-linguistic typology has not yet been established. Browsing through descriptive grammars and other publications, the range of terminology used by different linguists to describe AM would be impressive if it were not for the inconsistency (see also Guillaume 2016: 101–102; Rose 2015: 120; *inter alia*). Trends mostly fall into regional traditions but may be inconsistent even there. In part this terminological variation has obscured commonalities in languages around the world, resulting in AM systems being reported as rarer or more regionally restricted than they actually are. Problematically, terminology for AM and DIR is rarely distinguished, with the same terms often used for both, or one term ambiguously used to describe a particular instance in a language that might be either. In some cases, AM morphemes have been thrown into the grab bag of *aspect* (e.g. Talmy 1985) or other existing categories, but frequently terms that might more appropriately be used for DIR, including *directionals*, have been used for AM. In Africa, the terms *itive/andative* ('going' from Latin roots) and *ventive/venitive* ('coming') have gained some traditional status (Bourdin 2006), alongside *centrifugal* ('outward') and *centripetal* ('inward') especially for Chadic languages (Frajzyngier 1987). In North America, the terms *translocative* ('away') and *cislocative* ('toward') are in relatively common usage (Mithun 1999). These pairs all have the same significance, just reflecting different descriptive traditions. Elsewhere the terms from one of those descriptive traditions may be adopted by individual researchers, as well as idiosyncratic labels. For this reason alone, a thorough cross-linguistic investigation of the relationship between the two categories of AM and DIR is warranted, not only to clarify terminology, but also because the confusion in traditional descriptions is not coincidental.

As suggested by the terms listed above, directionally-oriented verb markers often come in pairs contrasting 'away' or 'toward', labeled here Itive (ITV) and Ventive (VEN) for consistency. Terminologically, this contrast is often emphasized over their functions of marking AM and/or DIR. For this contrast in AM, consider examples (1)-(2) below:

(1) **Itive Prior AM:** Tzutujil, Mayan (Dayley 1985: 98)[1]
X-in-ee-war-i.
COMPL-1SG-**AM.PR.ITV**-sleep-FNL
'I went and slept.'

(2) **Ventive Prior AM:** Tzutujil (Dayley 1985: 98)
X-in-uj-war-i.
COMPL-1SG-**AM.PR.VEN**-sleep-FNL
'I came and slept.'

Whereas AM adds motion to a (typically non-motion) verb, DIR specifies the path for lexical motion verbs. That is, AM asserts fact-of-motion, while DIR describes an already asserted motion. Compare examples (1)-(2) to the similar directional semantics of DIR in (3) below. AM typically also encodes direction, while DIR often has more directional nuances such as in the case of Kiribati suffixes meaning 'up' and 'down' also functioning to mean 'eastward' or 'shoreward' and 'westward' or 'seaward' respectively.

(3) **DIR paradigm:** Kiribati, Oceanic (Groves, Groves & Jacobs 1985: 26–27)
biri	*biri-mai*	*biri-wati*
run	run-VEN	run-VEN2
'run'	'run toward speaker'	'run toward you'
biri-rake	*biri-rio*	*biri-rikaaki*[2]
run-UP	run-DOWN	run-REV
'run upwards'	'run downwards'	'run back'

---

1 Glossing adjusted for some examples for consistent notation and to highlight relevant morphosyntactic features.
2 This last form is attested in the *Gilbertese Bible* (Judges 20:45), from the Bible Society of the South Pacific.

The two categories of AM and DIR, though differing in important ways, share a number of properties and may even be expressed by the same morphemes in some languages. Distinguishing between the two, especially based on attested data in published grammatical descriptions, can be difficult. This paper takes up that challenge with a primary goal of presenting the results of a typological survey directly so that readers and future researchers may consider the data for themselves, for example to establish the place of an individual language in the context of regional trends within the worldwide typology. Questions of typological correlation and definition are also discussed. Section 2 will introduce the survey methodology and discuss the general distribution of AM and DIR in the sample. Section 3 compares AM and DIR, looking especially at cases of functional overlap, and establishes a general typology of AM. Section 4 highlights challenging cases and reconsiders the definition of AM.

2 Cross-linguistic survey

This is the first worldwide systematic survey of AM, expanding on earlier studies. This broad sample allows us to determine whether observations from previous, narrower studies are trends in particular regions or families, or whether they are widespread typological patterns. In particular, I consider specifically whether Guillaume's (2016) generalizations for South America, including implicational hierarchies, apply to other languages around the world (see also Guillaume & Koch, this volume).

2.1 Methodology

Following the methodology of the *World Atlas of Language Structures* (WALS: Haspelmath et al. 2005; Dryer & Haspelmath 2013), this paper surveys morphological marking of AM and DIR in a worldwide balanced sample of 325 languages based primarily on descriptive grammars, supplemented by published secondary sources and in some cases personal communication from fieldworkers or speakers. The selection of languages is an expanded version of the sample used in a WALS chapter by Haspelmath (2005/2013); for details see Ross (2021). It should be emphasized, however, that even a thorough review of the available literature does not necessarily fully represent the AM or DIR systems found in some languages, and in some cases such systems may be unknown for a particular language due to under-reporting. In particular, descriptions frequently provide a cursory overview of these phenomena and may, for example, lack clear discussion of secondary functions of the markers so that only the primary functions can be reported here. Accordingly, one of the goals of this paper is to provide the typological background from which fieldworkers can continue to explore these phenomena in greater detail (on methodology, see also Vuillermet, this volume).

This survey is limited in scope to only morphological realization of AM and DIR, primarily for practical reasons, but also following the trends in existing work on AM to establish the broader typological context for that line of research (e.g. Guillaume 2016). However, AM and DIR should not be mistaken as being only morphological phenomena: consider for example the English pseudocoordination constructions *go and get* or *come and see* expressing Prior AM (Ross 2016, 2021). Likewise, verb-particle constructions familiar from many European languages (e.g. English *take out, move on, bring up*) are a type of DIR (often with additional grammaticalized meanings), as are Polynesian postverbal directional particles (Hooper 2002) that function very similarly to the Kiribati suffixes in example (3) above. See Lovestrand & Ross (this volume) for a complementary study of AM and DIR as found in serial verb constructions, based on the same language sample as in this paper. See also Schokkin (this volume) and Otero (this volume) for other examples of AM beyond morphology.

The identification of AM follows the definition provided in the introduction to this volume: *a verbal grammatical category, separate from tense, aspect, mood and direction, whose function is to associate, in different ways, different kinds of translational motion to a verb event* (Guillaume & Koch, this volume). Only morphological marking is considered here, and only *productive* morphemes (found outside of lexicalized verb forms) were included. Additionally, only what were interpreted to be *systematic, grammatically established morphology* was included in the typology (see Lovestrand & Ross, this volume for a brief discussion of verb-verb compounds). In addition to identifying the languages with AM and the number of distinct morphemes in the system, several parameters were considered for each morpheme: (1) the direction of motion (Itive, Ventive, etc.); (2) the temporal relationship with the lexical verb (Prior, Concurrent and Subsequent); (3) overlap in function with DIR and other grammatical categories; (4) the moving argument (Subject or Object); and any other unique or interesting features.

DIR is defined as expressing the directional component of the path in a motion event, and limited here to morphological marking, as with AM. In contrast to AM, DIR markers do not attribute the fact-of-motion to the predicate, and therefore combine primarily with lexical motion verbs. The additional properties identified for DIR morphemes include: (1) the direction of motion; and (2) overlap in function with AM and other grammatical categories.

The results are summarized in the discussion that follows, as well as in the Appendix summarizing the distribution for all languages in the sample. See also Ross (2021) for an expanded appendix describing the AM and DIR systems (if any) for each language and including a morpheme-by-morpheme list for each language, as well as the sources consulted for the survey. It should be emphasized that for statistical purposes multi-functional morphemes were counted independently in each category to which they applied: languages in which AM and DIR overlap were considered to have both, even if represented by the same morphemes, and morphemes that could express multiple types of AM were counted independently for each of those categories, but only once when considering the total number of morphemes in the language.

Examples cited in this paper are adjusted to follow a consistent notation, based on paradigmatic contrasts, allowing for underspecification of morphemes for categories such as direction or temporal relationship.[3] I should emphasize that standardization of glosses like this highlights similarities, without intending to imply lack of diversity in nuance or other functions for these morphemes. Although in some cases changing the labels used to describe phenomena in a particular language could obscure the intent of the author in glossing certain forms in particular ways, from a comparative perspective it can often be difficult to interpret glossing found in descriptive grammars,[4] so I present these standardized forms for the benefit of the reader based on my close inspection of each of the languages discussed.

2.2 The distribution of AM and DIR

AM is found in 83 languages (26%) of the 325 in the sample, and the distribution clusters geographically, as shown in Figure 1. It is relatively common in South

---

[3] Specifically, I have used AM or DIR for morphemes of those categories (or MOT for a more general motion morpheme). These can be further specified for temporal relationship (PR, CONC, SUBS) or direction (ITV, VEN), as well as interaction with other morphosyntactic categories such as tense or aspect.

[4] As discussed above, terminology is often idiosyncratic, and even when presented clearly one must be familiarized with specific conventions for each language. Furthermore, while some authors, including those writing in this volume, do take special care in designing appropriate glosses for AM, the variety of often ambiguous or redundant terminology used by linguists not specializing in AM would suggest that much of the time terminology is not intended to be contrastive. Indeed, some grammars consulted did not even explicitly distinguish a category of AM, regardless of terminology.

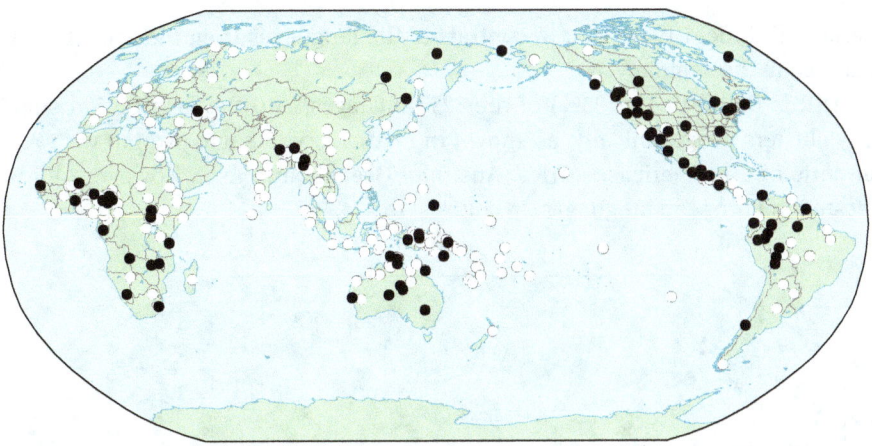

Figure 1: 83 (26%) of 325 languages with AM (black).

America[5] and Australia[6] (and Oceania) as would be suggested by earlier research, but also found extensively in North America,[7] as well as in Africa and Asia (see also the other chapters in this volume on these areas). It is conspicuously absent from Europe[8] (aside from the Caucasus), which may also have contributed to its relative neglect in comparative research.

This large-scale perspective is based on a balanced sample of languages, so it is generally representative of the distribution of these phenomena, but may obscure some diversity within regions. For example, although AM is not a widespread feature in India, Kui (Dravidian, not in sample) has developed AM

---

5 Although generally similar, the current results include outliers (e.g. Ika, Imbabura Quechua, Arawak, Hixkaryana, Mapudungun) in a larger geographic sample than Guillaume (2016: 107). AM in South America is not as narrow a regional phenomenon as suggested in that earlier study, which suggests possible independent development as well as contact effects. At the same time, these outliers are typologically distinct enough, both from each other and from the languages Guillaume surveyed, to lend some support to the possibility of contact effects within the more central group of languages. Finally, as suggested but not shown by Guillaume, AM is not found in the southeast.
6 Although complex AM systems are known for some Australian languages, their distribution here (as well as in Koch, this volume) shows that they are not especially widespread there geographically, but limited to a few languages/families.
7 See also Dryer (this volume, ch. 13), who presents a similar distribution and shows that AM is attested in most families of North (and Central) America. And for the prevalence of AM in Mesoamerica specifically, see also Nielsen & Messerschmidt (2020).
8 One exception appears to be developing in colloquial southern Italian dialects with *va-* 'go' as an invariant Prior Itive prefix (e.g. *va-ffazu* 'I go do'), in variation with its multi-verb source construction (Accattoli & Todaro 2017; Di Caro 2019).

marking (Winfield 1928: 112), in contrast to the languages from the same family included in the sample.

DIR is found in 114 (35%) of the 325 languages, and the distribution similarly clusters geographically, as shown in Figure 2, with some overlap with AM for parts of the Americas,[9] Africa, Australia/Oceania and Asia. However, DIR is attested in European languages, in contrast to AM.

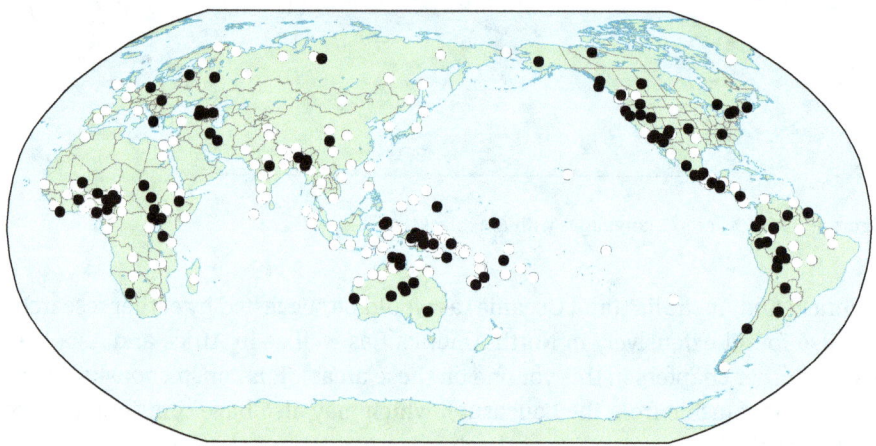

Figure 2: 114 (35%) of 325 languages with DIR (black).

3 Typology of AM and DIR

This section presents the results from the cross-linguistic survey of AM and DIR. First, the results for DIR are summarized, followed by a discussion of the relationship between AM and DIR. The remainder of this section surveys the main typological parameters of variation in AM, building on some of the generalizations found by Guillaume (2016) for South American languages, and extending and testing them for a worldwide sample. This is followed in Section 4 by discussion of challenges in classifying certain languages and some more difficult typological questions.

---

[9] See also Mithun (1999: 132–151) for discussion of DIR in North America, including some elaborate systems.

3.1 Typology of DIR

There is a lot of semantic variation with DIR, with as few as one DIR marker per language, but up to dozens in a single language. Fifteen languages in the sample have 10 or more DIR markers. Frequent are deictic contrasts like Itive and Ventive or general directions like 'up' and 'down', while languages with larger inventories may have highly specific semantics, including for example spatial relationships involving natural geography, for which see the examples in (4) below. The semantics of DIR in individual languages seems to vary rather freely, although certain types are widespread; for a comparison with AM, see Section 3.2. The six-marker DIR system of Kiribati, in (3) above, illustrated relatively basic contrasts. Compare this to several examples in (4) selected from dozens of DIR markers in Nisgha; semantically-specific DIR markers like these can be difficult to distinguish from Locationals, for which see Section 4.2.

(4) **Specific DIR markers:** Nisgha, Tsimshianic (Tarpent 1987: 518–548; Mithun 1999: 146–147)

spə 'horizontally off'   ḵisə 'downstream'   xlip 'at one end, at tip'
spə=qús (<'jump')   ḵisə=ʔúlkskʷ (<'drift')   xlip=qanqínks (<'chew')
'jump off (boat, car)'   'drift down the river'   'chew on the tip'

A structural component of variation is affix ordering in DIR morphology (for a comparison with AM, see Section 3.5). Compare the Kiribati DIR suffixes in (3) to the Nisgha markers that precede the verb in (4).[10] As discussed in Lovestrand & Ross (this volume), there is a strong tendency for Directionals in serial verb constructions to follow the lexical verb. Therefore, if this is a prominent path of grammaticalization for DIR morphology, we would expect to find mostly DIR suffixes.

Of the 114 languages with DIR morphology, 67 (59%) are suffixing, 41 (36%) are prefixing, and 6 (5%) have both prefixes and suffixes, as shown in Figure 3. Suffixing is the dominant strategy, although that is true of affixes cross-linguistically in general (Dryer 2005/2013; Jacques 2013). There are also regional trends: prefixing is relatively rare, except for two areas. Europe is almost exclusively prefixing, reflecting the phenomenon of DIR preverbs across several distinct families, which incidentally often are etymologically related to adpositions (Hewson & Bubenik 2006). Across the far north of North America, prefixation is also common, where polysynthetic

---

[10] In Nisgha, these are described as proclitics rather than prefixes, but for the purposes of the current study, only relative ordering of AM or DIR markers was considered, and both affixes and affix-like clitics were included in the survey, referred to here as "prefixes" and "suffixes" for convenience.

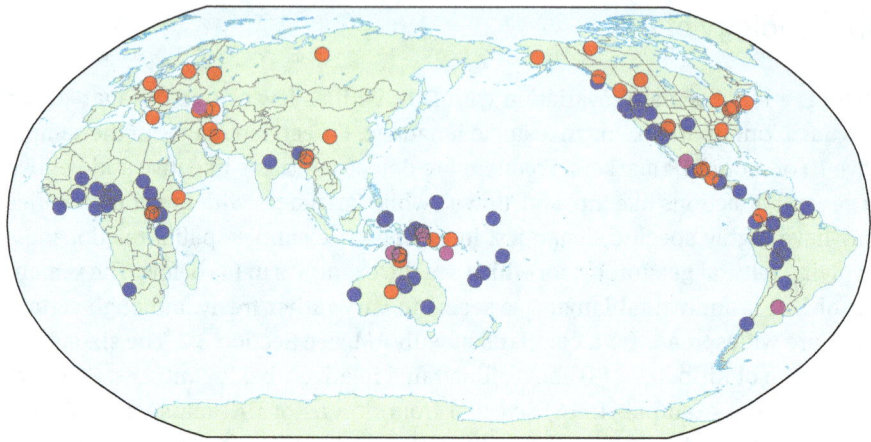

Figure 3: Affix ordering for DIR (red: prefixing; blue: suffixing; purple: mixed).

languages typically exhibit semantic modification of verb roots through preverbs (cf. Givón 2000; see the Nisgha examples in (4) above). These are also two regions in the world not known for having serial verb constructions. Therefore, the dominant suffixation found elsewhere is compatible with the possibility that serial verb constructions are a common source for the grammaticalization of DIR morphology.

In addition to those languages with both prefixes and suffixes, the morphology of several languages is not strictly limited to prefixes or suffixes: Ngalakan has distributive DIR marked with initial reduplication, classified here as prefixing, while Hausa (see example 28 below) and Lamang have a combination of tonal or templatic morphology and suffixation, classified here as suffixing. Outside the sample, an interesting case of non-concatenative morphology is Dinka (Nilotic) with tonal DIR marking that may also sometimes function as AM (Andersen 2012; see also Payne, this volume).

3.2 The relationship between AM and DIR

The somewhat similar distributions of AM and DIR add to the confusion caused by the inconsistent terminology often used in descriptive sources for languages in different regions. At the same time, a more fine-grained analysis of these two data sets reveals important differences. First, 57 languages have both AM and DIR; that is, 50% of the 114 DIR languages also have AM, or 69% of the 83 AM languages also have DIR. Of those 57 languages, 44 exhibit overlap in the function of individual markers for both AM and DIR, meaning that a significant minority of languages exhibit multi-functionality (53% of AM languages or 39% of DIR languages),¹¹ as shown in Figure 4. However, complete overlap of all AM/DIR markers in a language is very rare (found in only 14 languages). It seems at this point that AM and DIR are distinct grammatical categories.¹² We might still consider a functional relationship such as areal effects promoting the development of either AM or DIR due to contact, which could explain why many of the languages with multi-functional AM/DIR markers are found in what appear to be focal points of the distribution.

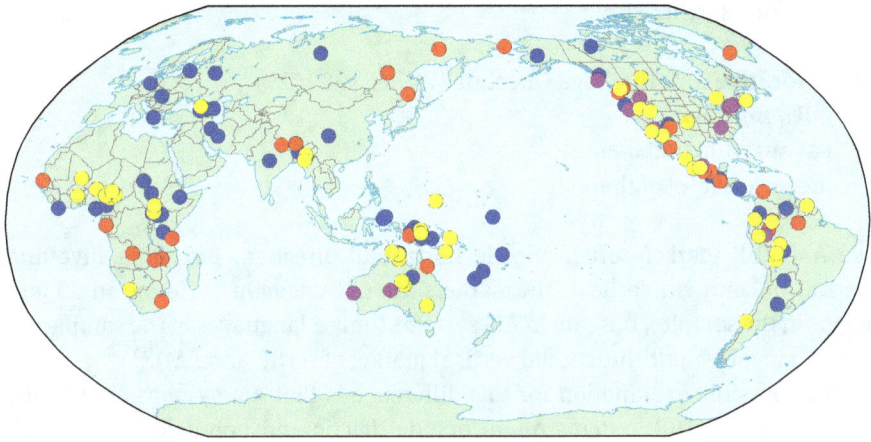

Figure 4: AM only (red); DIR only (blue); both (purple), with shared markers (yellow).

There is also variation in multi-functional markers. Some may contribute different motion semantics based on context and lexical semantics of the verb, such that individual examples may be vague or ambiguous.¹³ In other cases, multi-functional markers have varied but consistent functions. For example, in most varieties of Quechua, a single motion suffix -*mu* has distinct functions as AM and

---

11 Dryer (this volume, ch. 4) in a survey of 56 languages with individual overlapping markers for DIR and AM finds that 29 (52%) overlap for Prior, 24 (43%) for Concurrent, and 12 (21%) for Subsequent.
12 Dryer (this volume, ch. 4) introduces a potential counterargument, in that we classify different subtypes of AM (e.g. different temporal relationships) as a unitary phenomenon even if they overlap with each other even less often than AM and DIR in general.
13 See for example Vidal & Payne (this volume) on Pilagá. A particularly extreme example is Maasai (Nilotic, East Africa), as discussed in Ross (2021), where a simple two-way contrast between Itive and Ventive markers can have a wide range of interpretations as DIR or AM, and as AM do not specify a particular temporal relationship of the motion or even the moving actor (Tucker & Mpaayei 1955: 123–129; Payne 2013, this volume).

DIR, as shown in (5)-(6): for movement verbs, the marker acts as Ventive DIR, in contrast to the default interpretation of movement away, while as AM the marker is typically interpreted as Prior Itive (on this relatively systematic usage and additional details, see Bills 1972; van de Kerke & Muysken 1990; *inter alia*).

(5) **Ventive DIR:** Huallaga Quechua (Weber 1989: 28)
    Kay-man   aywa-mu-n.
    here-DAT   go-**MOT**-3
    'He comes to here.'

(6) **Prior Itive AM:** Huallaga Quechua (Weber 1989: 29)
    *mika-**mu**-shun*
    eat-**MOT**-1PL.INCL.IMP
    'Let's go eat (over there).'

Like AM, DIR markers often encode horizontal direction, including Itive and Ventive. In contrast, vertical DIR markers are not uncommon (found in 50 languages in the sample), but rare in AM systems (only 6 languages in the sample, all of which involve multi-functional vertical markers for DIR and AM).[14]

One possible explanation for this difference is that AM systems are usually deictic, whereas DIR systems often include deictic and non-deictic markers.[15] This makes sense when AM is a way of associating secondary motion to a grammatically-centered event (around the subject, speaker, etc.), whereas DIR can describe in wider semantic terms the path for motion in general. On the functional overlap of deictic DIR and AM, see also Belkadi (2015a, 2016, this volume), Dryer (this volume, ch. 4), Reed & Lindsey (this volume), Creissels & Bassène (this volume), Voisin (this volume), Vidal & Payne (this volume), Koch (this volume) and Lamarre et al. (to appear). The distribution of Itive and Ventive markers (corresponding to the deictic basic motion verbs 'go' and 'come') may at first appear to obscure this distinction: 58 (70%) of the languages with AM have one or both of these categories, compared to 94 (82%) of the languages for DIR. However, of the 25 languages with AM lacking both Itive and Ventive, most (19 languages) do

---

14 Generally (cf. Lamang, Matsés and Retuarã), this appears to be a secondary function of vertical DIR markers as AM, while in Alyawarra and Arrernte, related languages in central Australia, these may be AM markers with secondary functions as DIR. Lai has another variation on this usage, where AM and DIR markers contrast for horizontal direction (Itive and Ventive) as well as whether the motion is level, uphill or downhill.

15 Relevantly, Wilkins (1991:231–232) classifies the UP and DOWN Concurrent AM forms in Arrernte as non-deictic.

not distinguish direction at all, with AM markers expressing 'go/come and [verb]' or '[verb] while moving'.[16] Compare this to the remaining 20 languages with DIR lacking Itive and Ventive, which of course still express other kinds of non-deictic directional information.[17] Consider also that within individual languages there are often multiple DIR markers expressing contrasting directions, whereas even languages with a large number of AM markers tend instead to vary in the temporal relationship or paradigmatically with other inflectional features.

Another distinction between AM and DIR is the relative frequency of Itive and Ventive markers. 36 (43%) of the AM languages have both, while 13 (16%) have Itive only, and 9 (11%) have Ventive only. As mentioned above, directionally-unspecified AM markers (e.g. 'go/come and do') are also found in a number of languages, and these appear to be most often used in Itive contexts, away from the deictic center, likely because most motion events begin at the deictic center and go elsewhere; more generally, 'go' is more frequent and unmarked (compared to 'come') and may only function deictically in contrast to 'come' (Fleischman 1982; Wilkins & Hill 1995; Nordhoff 2020). Thus it would seem that in general motion 'away' is the most basic type, such that Itive AM markers, or those unspecified for direction but allowing for this interpretation, are especially common. But this is not the case for DIR, where the default interpretation of lexical motion verbs is often Itive (see example (3) for Kiribati above), so that Ventive DIR is more common: 70% (61%) of DIR languages have both, while 8 (7%) have Itive only, but 16 (14%) have Ventive only.[18]

More broadly, we can consider the typology of relationships between DIR and AM systems within a language. A crucial question is whether and how AM markers may combine with lexical motion verbs. We've already seen examples where the same markers are used for DIR (with motion verbs) and AM (with other verbs), but there are other languages where AM can freely combine with motion verbs, adding additional motion (e.g. Prior AM "go and walk [in the park]", as opposed to multi-functionality with DIR "walk away"). In these cases, another question is whether and how AM and DIR may combine: Can DIR be added to modify the semantics of AM? Or would AM add additional motion independently of the lexical verb already modified by DIR? Because these issues are typically

---

16 In a few languages, these directionally-unspecified AM markers may combine with DIR, while in other languages direction may remain unexpressed.

17 Like vertical direction described above, one other rare kind of AM overlapping with DIR is *distributive* ('around, about, in various places'), which is the type of direction found in 4 of those languages (see Section 4.1), while 2 others have reversive ('return, back') direction AM markers.

18 Consider the typically distinctive usage of the multi-functional motion suffix -*mu* in Quechua as Ventive DIR (versus default Itive interpretation) but Prior Itive AM, shown in (5)-(6) above.

not well-documented in language descriptions, I will set them aside for future research (but see Payne, this volume; Dryer, this volume, ch. 4).[19] For now, consider one example from the sample languages with systematic interaction between AM and DIR markers: in Barasano, a single motion suffix works together with other spatial suffixes to create what functions like a prototypical AM system with directional contrasts, as illustrated in (7):[20]

(7) **Compositional AM system**: Barasano, Tucanoan (Jones & Jones 1991: 104)
 adi-ʉ-re   ãbi-**a**-**di**-boa-bʉ   yʉ
 this-pole-OBJ   pick.up-**MOT**-**VEN**-MIR-N3.PST   1SG
 'I brought this pole (but it isn't needed).'

3.3 The typology of AM

The number of morphemes in a particular AM system varies considerably, but not quite to the extent of DIR as discussed above. Additionally, there are challenging definitional considerations when it comes to counting the number of markers in an AM system (see Section 4.4). Tentatively, taking a maximal approach to counting AM markers, based on the total number of distinct morphemes (e.g. in a paradigm listing all AM forms), we can look at the distribution.[21] Table 1 and Figure 5 show the distribution by number of AM markers:

Table 1: Number of AM markers in sample languages.

# AM markers	1	2	3	4	5	6	7	8	9	10	11	12	13	14	15
# Languages	30	27	5	5	2	4	2	3	–	–	–	1	–	2	2

---

19 See also Kawachi (this volume) and Payne (this volume) on Concurrent AM in Southern Nilotic languages obligatorily combining with DIR.
20 Barasano motion morphology is extremely complex, including multi-functionality and allomorphy. The suffix -*a* (*MOT*) acts as AM with non-motion verbs (with direction determined by other suffixes); it also combines with lexical motion verbs without any obvious effect, but it can be considered to generally express fact-of-motion (that is, indicating change-of-location for both motion and non-motion verbs).
21 This approach is useful for practical purposes, but is not ideal because it may conflate complexity of AM marking per se with fusion of other categories in the same morphemes such as tense/aspect or subject agreement; however, in general the distribution seems to reflect the number of contrastive features of AM, such as direction or temporal relationship, as well as intuitions about the most complex AM systems, setting aside the issue of multi-functionality. On the issue of counting how many AM markers are found in a language, see also Section 4.4.

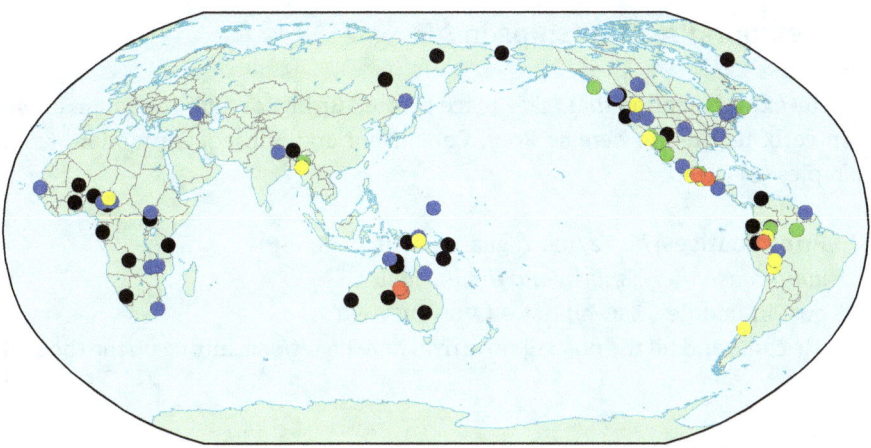

Figure 5: Number of AM markers (*black*: 1, *blue*: 2, *green*: 3–4, *yellow*: 5–8, *red*: 12–15).

In most of the world, simple systems of one to two markers per language are the most common configuration for AM morphology. Trends in previous research on AM suggest the most complex systems are found in Australia and South America, consistent with the results here, although most languages in Australia have simpler systems (see also Koch, this volume). Some complex systems in North America also stand out in this distribution, especially in Nahuatl languages (Uto-Aztecan) in southern Mexico. Given the relative extent and complexity of the AM systems found in South America, Guillaume (2016) is a reasonable starting point for the typology presented in this paper, and several points from that paper, including implicational hierarchies will be discussed in detail in the following sections. It should be kept in mind, however, that there do appear to be some different trends in other parts of the world, such as shown in Belkadi (this volume) for Africa where simpler systems and overlapping function of DIR and AM are more common.

In some languages, individual markers may be multi-functional. Remember that in these cases, for the purposes of the survey, these were considered independently when counting morphemes in each category. An extreme case is found in Bininj Gun-wok, where Ventive DIR *m-* "exhibits a number of semantic extensions. With some verbs the 'towards' motion may not be part of the verbal predicate itself, but of some contextually obvious subsequent, prior or concurrent action" (Evans 2003: 490), thus counted as DIR as well as AM (and independently as each of the three temporal relationships the morpheme may express).

3.4 Temporal relationships in AM

AM may express motion that takes place before, during, or after the action of the main verb, referred to here as Prior, Concurrent and Subsequent motion, as in examples (8)-(10):

(8) **Prior Ventive AM:** Yagua, Yaguan (Payne 1985: 256)
 juntú-tąąsá sa-jųvay-**nuvy̨i**-núúy-janu
 post-in.middle 3SG-hit-**AM.PR.VEN**-IPFV-PST3
 'He came and hit the post; upon arrival here he hit/was hitting on the (house) post.'

(9) **Concurrent AM:** Yagua (Payne 1985: 254)
 ray-maay-**títyiiy**-jancha
 1SG-sleep-**AM.CONC**-CONT
 'I sleep while going along (as in a car).'

(10) **Subsequent Itive AM:** Yagua (Payne 1985: 257)
 naada-suuta-**chiy**-núúy-jáy
 3DL[22]-wash-**AM.SUBS.ITV**-IPFV- PROX2
 'She washed and left; as the last thing before leaving, she washed yesterday.'

Guillaume (2016:83), following Levinson & Wilkins (2006: 534), proposed an implicational hierarchy based on the distribution of temporal relationships in South American AM systems: **Prior > Concurrent > Subsequent**. If this hierarchy applies worldwide, then we should find that Prior is the most common type, followed by Concurrent, then Subsequent. Taken in absolute terms, we should find no languages with Concurrent AM that do not also have Prior, and no languages with Subsequent that do not have Prior and Concurrent. Furthermore, there are implications for diachronic development, such that languages would develop first Prior, then Concurrent, and finally Subsequent AM morphology. See also Lovestrand & Ross (this volume) for discussion of these temporal relationships in AM serial verb constructions, which may have implications for diachronic development.

---

22 The dual is traditionally used for women who have borne children (Payne 1985: 42).

The results here show that Prior is by far the most common type cross-linguistically, found in 61 (73%) of the 83 languages with AM in the sample, as shown in Figure 6. This type is also consistently found across all regions with AM marking, except for parts of Africa. Markers of purposive motion are also counted in this category due to uncertainty of classification based on available descriptions of languages, although these may best be considered a distinct phenomenon (see Section 4.1).[23]

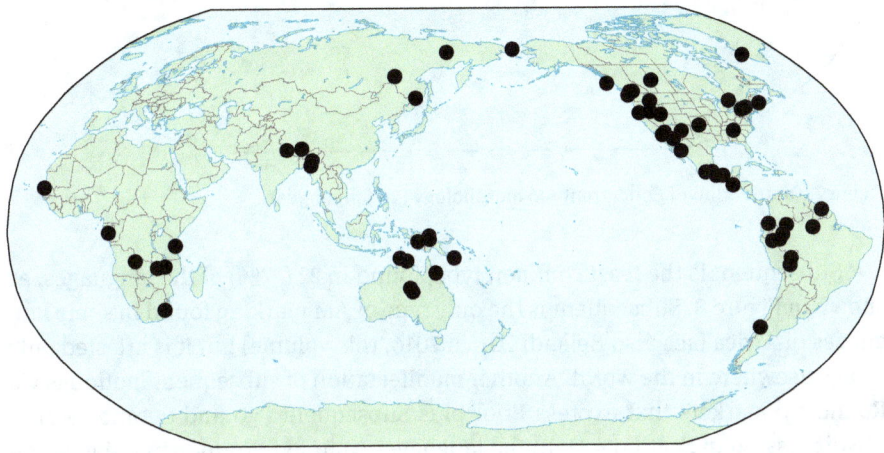

Figure 6: Distribution of Prior AM morphology (61 languages).

Concurrent is the next most common type, found in 36 (43%) of the languages, as shown in Figure 7. It is especially common in Australia and the Americas. In Australia there are several languages where this is the only type,[24] a distribution uncommon but attested sporadically in languages elsewhere. Classified as Concurrent were all morphemes expressing overlap between the motion and action of the lexical verb, regardless of specific temporal extent of the motion (for discussion see Section 4.1).

---

23 The reported frequency of Prior AM may therefore be somewhat inflated, but it is my impression that the majority of morphemes classified as 'Prior' in the results are in fact Prior rather than purposive, in part due to purposive semantics being introduced via glossing or translation rather than specified as a function of the morphemes. Regardless, a more nuanced analysis must be set aside for future research.
24 Koch (this volume) finds only Concurrent in 18 out of the 41 Pama-Nyungan languages in his sample.

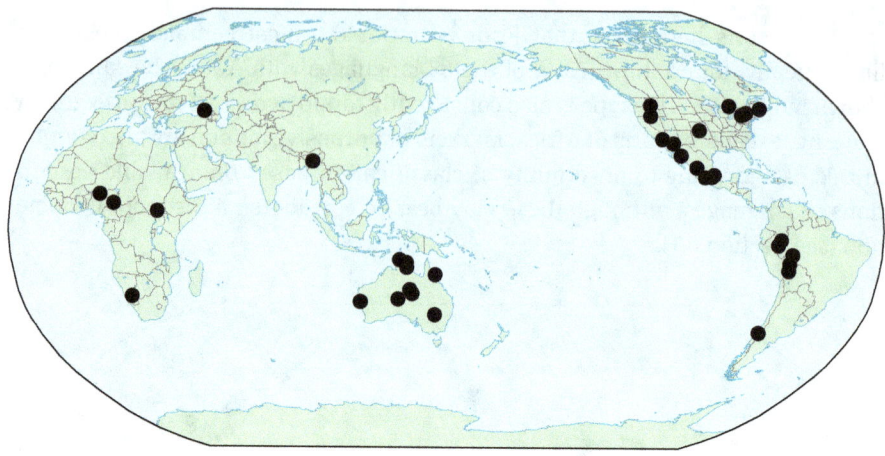

Figure 7: Distribution of Concurrent AM morphology (36 languages).

Subsequent is the least common type, found in 22 (27%) of the languages, as shown in Figure 8. Subsequent is the only type of AM marking found in some languages of Africa (see also Belkadi 2015a, 2016, this volume) but it is attested only rarely elsewhere in the world. Another manifestation of subsequent motion is via Roundtrip markers that express Prior plus Subsequent ('go and do and return': see discussion in Section 4.1). In the languages sampled, Roundtrip AM is found in 9 (11%) of the languages and exclusively in the Americas.[25] Interestingly it is only found in one language that also has Subsequent AM (Araona). Roundtrip is, however, found in some of the same languages that have Prior, and in fact these can sometimes be alternative interpretations for the same markers (e.g. 'go and do' with an implication of returning).

Quantitatively, Guillaume's generalization about the frequency of these temporal relationships is supported, although Subsequent is not much less frequent than Concurrent compared to the much larger gap between either and Prior. At the same time, these distributions show that the hierarchy has exceptions.[26]

---

[25] Outside the sample, Roundtrip AM is also found elsewhere in at least Kaytetye in Australia (Koch, this volume). Additionally, Roundtrip AM can be expressed by the combination of markers in at least 4 languages in the sample (Arawak, Haida, Nez Perce, Udihe), either by marking for both Prior and Subsequent or by Prior plus a special 'return' or 'reversive' marker.

[26] Guillaume (2016: 120) also reports 4 exceptional languages (of 43 total) with Concurrent but not Prior, and concludes that the implicational hierarchy is "a robust statistical tendency." For studies of exceptional languages, see Kawachi (this volume) on Kupsapiny, with only Concurrent and Subsequent AM, and Otero (this volume) on Koman, with only Subsequent AM.

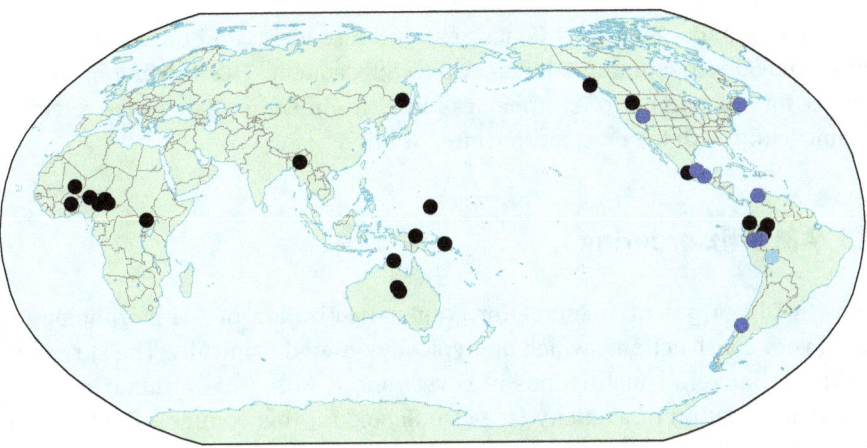

Figure 8: Distribution of Subsequent (black) and Roundtrip (blue) AM morphology (both: teal).

There are languages having only one type for each temporal relationship, as well as all possible combinations, as shown in Table 2.

Table 2: Distribution and co-occurrence of temporal relationships in AM systems.[27]

AM type(s)	PR (only)	CONC (only)	SUBS (only)	P+C	P+S	C+S	P+C+S
Languages	33	11	9	16	4	1	8

Eight languages have all three types, including some of the most complex systems in the sample: Alyawarra and Arrernte (in Australia), and Araona and Yagua (in South America); Purépecha (Mesoamerica) has a moderately sized inventory with complex marking of Concurrent AM along with less prominent Prior and Subsequent markers; Nez Perce (North America) has a relatively succinct set of 5 functionally diverse AM markers that are not multi-functional, while Meithei (Tibeto-Burman, India) has a mixed system with multi-functional morphemes, and Bininj Gun-wok, as mentioned above, has a particularly versatile Ventive DIR marker that may also express different temporal relationships for AM.

In summary, as a strong statistical trend, Prior is more common than the other two types, while the prominence of Concurrent over Subsequent is only marginally supported. The hierarchy is not supported in absolute terms due to

---

27 Combined categories indicate co-occurrence, not necessarily multi-functionality; multi-functional markers are counted individually for each category. Roundtrip markers are not included in the table, but have the following distribution: RT (only): 1; P+RT: 3; C+RT: 1; P+C+RT: 3; P+C+S+RT: 1.

the languages that have only Concurrent or Subsequent, and the combinations Prior plus Subsequent and Concurrent plus Subsequent. The distribution is also similar for the number of morphemes found in individual languages or cross-linguistically, with the most morphemes for Prior.

3.5 AM affix ordering

As with DIR, a potential source for grammaticalization of AM morphology is serial verb constructions, which are typically ordered iconically. The survey on motion serial verb constructions in Lovestrand & Ross (this volume) supports this generalization of iconicity (see also Schokkin, this volume): Prior motion markers should precede the main verb, while Subsequent motion markers should follow. If serial verb constructions are a primary source from which AM grammaticalizes, we might expect similar skews in prefixing vs. suffixing patterns in AM morphology. The results are mixed, however, and do not support this relationship: 21 (25%) of the languages with AM have prefixes, and 60 (72%) have suffixes, while 2 (2%) have mixed systems with both prefixes and suffixes, as shown in Figure 9.

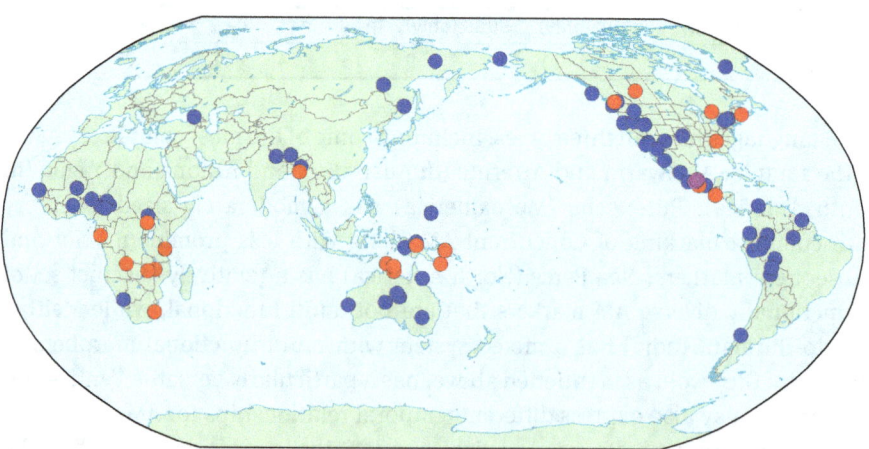

Figure 9: Affix ordering for AM (red: prefixing; blue: suffixing; purple: mixed).

There is a suffixing preference for AM, in fact stronger than for DIR. Given that Prior is the most common type and would be prefixing, the grammaticalization of iconic serial verb constructions is not supported as a general source for AM morphology, although it may be the source for some languages. Interestingly, the ordering is almost always consistent within each language, either prefixing or suffixing for both Prior and Subsequent (as well as Concurrent).[28] Perhaps iconicity is overridden by the formation of AM paradigms. There does not appear to be any effect of temporal relationship types on affix ordering, as shown in Table 3. In Prior-only two-morpheme systems contrasting Itive and Ventive (most likely to correspond directly to the basic motion verbs 'go' and 'come'), 7 are prefixing and compatible with development from iconic serial verbs, but 4 are suffixing and probably from another grammaticalization source. Among the most complex systems (12–15 AM markers), 4 are suffixing and 1 is mixed.

Table 3: Distribution of temporal relationships and affix ordering in AM systems.[29]

AM type(s)	PR (only)	CONC (only)	SUBS (only)	P+C	P+S	C+S	P+C+S
Prefixing	14	1	2	3	–	–	1
Suffixing	19	9	7	12	4	1	7
Mixed	–	1	–	1	–	–	–

Furthermore, prefixed AM appears to be correlated to some degree with prefixed DIR, which might indicate some kind of attraction to this position. Among the languages with AM but without DIR, 18 are suffixing, 8 are prefixing, and 1 is mixed. In the languages with both AM and DIR, most have the same configuration: 11 are prefixing for both, and 36 are suffixing for both. There are also 4 languages with suffixing AM and prefixing DIR, but no languages with prefixing AM and suffixing DIR.[30] In short, AM on its own appears to be heavily suffixing. As for DIR without AM, the distribution is similar to what was reported in Section 3.1 above but slightly more skewed toward suffixing: 24 languages with prefixing DIR, 31 suffixing, and 2 mixed. The attraction appears to primarily be an effect on AM of prefixing DIR, and possibly a slight effect on DIR from AM.

In summary, there is a strong preference for suffixing AM. This is exactly the opposite pattern we would expect from Prior AM serial verb constructions, in

---

[28] There are two exceptions (mixed type), both in southern Mexico: Nahuatl (Tetelcingo), which has a complex system of 12 AM suffixes in addition to 2 multi-functional DIR prefixes that can also express Concurrent AM, suggesting two distinct instances of grammaticalization; and Totonac, which has a mixed smaller system of 3 AM markers, with Roundtrip and Concurrent prefixes as well as another Concurrent suffix.

[29] Roundtrip AM languages are almost exclusively suffixing (including Ika with only Roundtrip AM); the two exceptions are Totonac, which has mixed ordering including prefixed Roundtrip, and Passamaquoddy-Maliseet which is consistently prefixing.

[30] Among the languages with mixed DIR, 2 have prefixing AM and 2 have suffixing AM. Additionally, both languages with mixed ordering for AM also have prefixed DIR.

which the motion verb is almost always first (Lovestrand & Ross, this volume). It is unlikely that serial verb constructions are the primary grammaticalization source for AM morphology. There is clearly no single iconic grammaticalization path for AM, although iconicity could still affect individual languages. There is also a possibility of interaction of word order and affix ordering; see also Jacques (2013). Detailed diachronic studies are crucial for our understanding of the phenomenon of AM (see also Koch 1986, this volume; Osgarby, this volume), but there are too few such analyses to make generalizations.[31] Similarly, the interaction between AM and DIR in the same language and their potential co-occurrence has not been sufficiently explored cross-linguistically. These are areas in immediate need of attention from researchers. Another relevant consideration is that the type of multi-verb construction may play a part in determining linear order: there is an overall correlation between VO word order and serial verb constructions (or pseudocoordination), and between OV word order and dependent-marked (e.g. converb), head-final verb combinations (Ross 2021). Aside from simple verb-verb compounds, there are also a small number of languages in the sample with a linking morpheme between the verbs (such as Djabugay: see Section 4.4), which can usually be reconstructed as a dependent-verb suffix. More research is required to fully understand the relationship between multi-verb constructions and AM affixes. There are also other possible sources of grammaticalization, such as Locationals, discussed in Section 4 along with other challenges.

4 Challenging cases and outlook

The sections above addressed some of the most prominent topics in research on AM and DIR and their typology and relationship. This section will explore some of the more challenging details, and discuss some open questions for future research. Applying a comparative concept to a large sample has a testing effect. Some languages are borderline cases, prompting us to revise our coding scheme and revisit the definition, thereby better understanding the limits of the phenomenon. Several

---

[31] Other diachronic studies also often result in quite complicated developments, including Guillaume (2013) on Takanan languages, who reconstructs several AM markers to the proto-language but posits that the rest developed through analogy rather than synchronic compounding, and Wilkins (1991: 238–251), who describes multiple sources for Arrernte AM forms including verb compounding, but also reanalysis of dependent-verb suffixes and areal diffusion in Australian languages.

challenging cases came up in the survey, and this section will address some of the more unusual properties of AM and DIR.[32]

4.1 Temporal relationships

Prior AM often has a sense of purpose, with the motion facilitating the action of the main verb. However, as discussed by Lovestrand & Ross (this volume) for serial verb constructions, there are also purposive constructions where completion of the lexical verb action is not entailed. That is, the two verb actions are not mutually contingent; the lexical verb action is subordinated as the goal of the motion, and that goal may or may not be accomplished. The same may apply to morphology. In several of the languages in the sample, apparent Prior AM morphology may in fact express a purposive relationship (sometimes called *motion-cum-purpose*), as in example (11): rather than associating a motion with the assertion of the lexical verb, the predicate may only assert that the motion occurred without specifying accomplishment of the lexical action.[33]

(11) **Purposive motion:** Cahuilla, Uto-Aztecan (Sauvel & Munro 1981: 160)
*Mamayaw-**llew**-qa'.*
help-**PURP.MOT**-PST.SG
'He went in order to help.'

Although this type appears relatively rare in the sample, it can be difficult to tease apart this relatively subtle semantic distinction, especially when it is rarely contrastive in context and when relying on available information in descriptive grammars. For discussion, see also Pakendorf & Stoynova (this volume) and Jacques, Lahaussois & Zhang (this volume). Glosses in English can also sometimes be misleading: 'go (in order) to [verb]' should be expected for purposives, whereas 'go and [verb]'[34] should be expected for Prior AM,[35] and rarely do grammars

---

[32] Due to space limitations, this section has been shortened, which I hope does not give an impression of homogeneity in AM systems in the world. See Ross (2021) for extended discussion.
[33] Compare also conative ('try to') or desiderative ('want to') affixes, such that the lexical verb is not entailed.
[34] That is, pseudocoordination (Ross 2016, 2021), which problematically is not itself widely recognized for its Prior AM semantics, resulting in potential confusion for both authors and readers of descriptive materials.
[35] Glosses in languages other than English are often similarly unhelpful, especially when these meanings are not typically distinguished (e.g. Spanish *ir* 'go' + INF, used to gloss either purposive 'go (in order) to' or Prior AM).

specifically describe the semantics of such constructions beyond the glosses. Given that it was not always possible to distinguish purposive from Prior, the category of Prior in the current survey includes both types, although in principle, given sufficient data to make this distinction consistently, I would prefer to exclude purposives by definition.[36]

Another challenging type is found as an extension of Prior or Subsequent, which sometimes may convey not just one-way movement, but a Roundtrip motion event with the action performed somewhere else, followed by returning to the original location. It is often unclear to what extent this meaning is expressed directly by the verb form or interpreted in context (see also Guillaume 2016: 118); note how easily the English glosses of such AM events could be understood to refer to roundtrip events, especially with certain lexical verbs (e.g. *I'll go get some help!*). Based on the limited number of examples in the survey, Roundtrip functions typically seem to develop as a contextual extension of Prior or Subsequent AM. Consider example (12), as a common contextual extension of Quechua -*mu* as Prior Itive illustrated in (6) above.

(12) **Distal Roundtrip AM:** Huallaga Quechua (Weber 1989: 137)
*Tanta-ta   ranti-ri-**mu**-y*
bread-ACC buy-PUNC-**MOT**-IMP
'Go buy bread (and return quickly).'

There is a contrast between two possible types of Roundtrip AM: whereas (12) from Quechua means 'go and do (there) and return (here)', another possibility is 'come and do (here) and return (there)'. We can refer to the former as Distal Roundtrip (e.g. Itive-Ventive), versus Proximal Roundtrip (e.g. Ventive-Itive), as

---

[36] Some definitions of AM (including the one used in this paper "to associate, in different ways, ... motion to a verb event") may leave room for interpretation to include purposives, but ideally we should exclude or at least distinguish purposives in the typology because they do not *add* motion to the verb but *subordinate* it semantically to the motion as a goal. Further motivation for this distinction comes from traditional definitions of AM emphasizing that the motion is *secondary*: Koch (1984: 26) discerns that "the indication of motion is subordinate to that of the main activity", and according to Wilkins (1991: 219, 251) the category function is "to foreground [the] event of [the] main verb against [the] background of [a] motion event" and "to locate events within the flow of space". Thus the main action (along with motion) is asserted, and the motion is not focused, whereas purposives entail only motion.

demonstrated in example (13) from Mecayapan Isthmus Nahuatl, which has two contrastive Roundtrip AM suffixes:

(13) **Proximal vs. Distal Roundtrip AM:** Nahuatl, Uto-Aztecan (Wolgemuth 2002: 88)

m<u>a</u>lti-**coya** m<u>a</u>lti-**toya**
bathe-PST.**AM.RT.PROX** bathe-PST.**AM.RT.DIST**
'He came and bathed and returned.' 'He went and bathed and returned.'

Roundtrip AM presents a methodological challenge, specifically in whether it should be considered a type of Prior or Subsequent (or both), or a distinct category (see also Rose 2015: 123–124; Guillaume 2016: 117–118; Dryer, this volume, ch. 4, this volume, ch. 13; Koch, this volume; Tallman, this volume). As discussed in Section 3.4, Roundtrip AM is found in 9 of the languages in the sample, a relatively rare feature and limited to the Americas. Although similar, there is also variation within these systems, such as whether, or which, parts of the path are emphasized or optional. Another possibility is the combination of affixes to express Roundtrip semantics. Consider example (14) from Udihe, where Itive AM can combine with a reversive suffix (see also Pakendorf & Stoynova, this volume).[37]

(14) **Complex AM marking:** Udihe, Tungusic (Nikolaeva & Tolskaya 2001: 321)

wakca- wakca-ne- wakca-ne-**se**-
hunt hunt-**AM** hunt-**AM**-**REV**
'hunt' 'go to hunt' 'come back after hunting'

Concurrent AM poses a different type of problem, namely that in some languages there are affixes expressing motion but not in any particular direction, which seem semantically unexpected in the cross-linguistic typology of AM but nevertheless associate motion with the verb. For example, several languages have Concurrent 'aimless' markers (see also Dryer, this volume, ch. 13), as in example (15). A more extreme type is distributives that indicate the action takes place in multiple locations, thus entailing motion for some lexical verbs, as in (16). Whereas including distributives might seem like stretching the definition too far, they are hard to rule out objectively. In this way, AM and DIR overlap with the typology of pluractionals (for which see Mattiola 2019 for a cross-linguistic survey and discussion).

---

[37] Similarly, Pech has an idiomatic verb compounding construction in which the roots 'go' and 'come' added together after a lexical root indicate "an entire process of going (or coming) somewhere, doing something, and returning" (Holt 1999: 68).

(15) **Aimless Concurrent AM:** Apuriña, Arawakan (Facundes 2000: 315)
hãkiti   akatsa-**ãpo**-ta-ru
jaguar   bite-**AM.CONC.AIMLESS**-VBLZ-3M.OBJ
'The jaguar ran around biting it/him aimlessly.'

(16) **Distributive:** Khoekhoe, Khoe (Hagman 1977: 74)
≠nṹu-**mãa**   !ũu-**mãa**   sã́i-**mãa**   !ùru-**mãa**
sit-**DISTR**   go-**DISTR**   cook-**DISTR**   thunder-**DISTR**
'sit around'   'go around'   'cook around'   'thunder around'

Concurrent AM may also be more flexible regarding the way in which the motion is distributed temporally. Whereas with Prior or Subsequent AM, the motion occurs immediately before or after the action of the lexical verb, there are multiple ways for the motion and action to co-occur temporally. As in example (15), Concurrent AM may partially or completely overlap with the main action, such as singing while going or coming, while in Distributives an action is iterated during motion to several locations. But another possibility, as in (17), is that the motion is interrupted by the action before continuing,[38] in contrast to (18) where the action occurs throughout the motion.

(17) **Interruptive Ventive AM:** Matsés, Panoan (Fleck 2003: 371)
onque-**cuëtsen**-o-sh
talk-**AM.INTERRUPT.VEN.INTR**-PST-3
'He stopped (once) to talk on his way here.'

(18) **Concurrent Ventive AM:** Matsés, Panoan (Fleck 2003: 371)
onque-**cho**-o-sh
talk-**AM.CONC.VEN.INTR**-PST-3
'He talked the whole way here.' or 'He kept stopping to talk on his way here.'

However, in a strict interpretation this would not be Concurrent at all, but both Prior and Subsequent, like Roundtrip, even though the direction of motion does

---

[38] Another possibility available for such markers that may be available in some languages is not *interruption* per se, but *punctuation* of the motion by an action like seeing a bird fly by (Guillaume 2016:117), although this seems to at least involve *diversion* of attention. Another interpretation of such contrasts would be by analogy with aspect, which only seems applicable within Concurrent AM (see Koch, this volume).

not change (cf. Dryer, this volume, ch. 4).³⁹ In Matsés, (continuous) Concurrent and Interruptive AM are contrastive. In other languages, though, the Concurrent marker may actually be ambiguous between these two meanings;⁴⁰ notice the similar ambiguity of English *during* and *on the way*. Although rare, these alternative types of Concurrent AM suggest we may need to revisit the typology of AM in terms of, for example, simple path versus complex path (see also Rose 2015: 123–124; Guillaume 2016: 116–117). Example (19) illustrates that in some languages these forms can combine, with a distributive meaning.⁴¹

(19) **Complex Concurrent/Interruptive Ventive AM:** Yagua, Yaguan (Payne 1985: 258)
sa-jimyiy-ri̧i̧-tityiiy
3SG-eat-**AM.INTERRUPT-AM.CONC**
'He (repeatedly) stops enroute while going along to eat.'

4.2 Locationals and other spatial functions

AM and DIR are not the only ways in which languages may grammaticalize spatial relationships via verbal morphology. Another common cross-linguistic type involves the marking of location where an action takes place but not necessarily any motion to or from that location (see also Guillaume 2016: 103; Guérois, Gibson & Persohn, this volume; Hernández-Green & Palancar, this volume; Voisin, this volume). For example, in addition to marking DIR and AM, the Quechua motion

---

39 Compare this to how Rose (2015: 123–124) describes what I call 'Roundtrip' as 'Interrupted', whereas Koch (pers. comm.) emphasizes that in Arandic languages even sleeping overnight while on a journey may be treated consistently as Concurrent. Cultural conceptualization determines what constitutes a single motion event, and one way to classify these forms would be based on subjective usage by speakers, rather than relying on an objective semantic typology. It should be emphasized, however, that even a Roundtrip journey may be conceptualized as a single event, which is another reason to consider a parallel between Interruptive and Roundtrip AM.
40 Mosetén provides another kind of evidence for this relationship, specifically that the Itive and Ventive Concurrent AM suffixes may be combined with a special Interruptive marker -*min* (Sakel 2004: 283–284) to specify that the motion was interrupted by the action of the verb, rather than occurring throughout.
41 Compare also Mapudungun, where two 'interruptive' suffixes (once vs. repeatedly) are used only in combination with other AM markers to indicate an action occurs as a break in the motion. Path-modifying morphemes like these, and other types such as 'reversive', or in Matsés a 'distributive' that combines with DIR/AM (Fleck 2003: 376), and so forth, are an important topic for further study.

suffix -*mu* can function as in (20) without indicating movement. We can refer to this usage as Locational (LCL).

(20) **Distal LCL:** Huallaga Quechua (Weber 1989: 137)
Tayta-: ospital-chaw keeda-ku-***mu***-sha
father-1 hospital-LOC remain-REFL-**MOT**-3PERF
'My father remained (over there) in the hospital.'

Weber (1989:134) glosses -*mu* as 'afar', while van de Kerke & Muysken (1990) describe it as *bilocational*, specifying a relationship between the location of the speaker and some other location, from which the various interpretations may be derived. Although there is still a directional component to the meaning in some cases (otherwise Itive or Ventive would be interchangeable), Quechua -*mu* is associated as much with location as with motion.

The focus of the cross-linguistic survey was limited to AM and DIR, although instances of LCL and other spatial morphology on the verb were observed in some languages, and impressionistically appear to be less common cross-linguistically.[42] Similar to the basic Itive-Ventive contrast found in some simple AM or DIR systems, there is often a contrast between Proximal and Distal LCL, as in (21)-(22).

(21) **Proximal LCL:** Meithei, Sino-Tibetan (Chelliah 1992: 165)
ləy-kon-tu khoy-mú-siŋ-tu pay-**lə**-e
flower-nest-DIST bee-black-PL-DIST fly-**LCL.PROX**-REAL.EMPH
'The garden is swarming with bees.'

(22) **Distal LCL:** Meithei (Chelliah 1997: 225)
má-nə apəl čá-**lək**-í
3-CONTRAST apple eat-**LCL.DIST**-REAL
'He ate an apple over there.'

There can be overlap between different spatial functions, as already seen for Quechua. Whereas -*lək* refers to Distal LCL in (22) above, it is interpreted as referring to Concurrent Ventive AM in (23), where the verb carries the progressive inflection.

(23) **Ventive AM:** Meithei (Chelliah 1997: 225)
má-nə apəl čá-**lək**-li
3-CONTRAST apple eat-**LCL.DIST**-PROG
'When he came here he was eating an apple.'

---

42 In the current sample, LCL morphology appears to be attested in about 15% of the languages.

Similarly, overlapping markers for DIR and LCL are also found, such as described by Abbott (1981) for Oneida, with a DIR interpretation for motion verbs, as in (24), but LCL interpretation for non-motion verbs, as in (25).

(24) **DIR:** Oneida, Iroquoian (Abbott 1981: 50; Michelson & Doxtator 2002: 64–65)
wa-h-ahkwé·nʌht-eʔ
AOR-3SG.M-descend-PFV
'he descended'

t-a-h-ahkwé·nʌht-eʔ   *y-a-h-ahkwé·nʌht-eʔ*
PROX-AOR-3SG.M-descend-PFV   **DIST**-AOR-3SG.M-descend-PFV
'he came down'   'he went down'

(25) **LCL:** Oneida (Abbott 1981:50; Michelson & Doxtator 2002: 550)
la-nákle-ʔ   *t-ha-nákle-ʔ*   *ye-ha-nákle-ʔ*
3SG.M-dwell-HAB   **PROX**-3SG.M-dwell-HAB   **DIST**-3SG.M-dwell-HAB
'he dwells'   'he lives there'   'he lives far away'

There are languages with extremely complex LCL systems. For example, Mithun (1999: 139–151) surveys several North American languages with dozens of affixes each. Often it can be difficult to distinguish between LCL and DIR among these semantically specific morphemes; see the examples from Nisgha in (4) above. Sometimes, LCL markers resemble incorporated objects but generally have somewhat bleached semantics and may co-occur with more specific, referential noun phrases.

Some languages offer even more ways to refer to the local environment through verbal morphology, such as with cross-linguistically rare elevationals (Forker 2019).[43] In Alamblak (Bruce 1984: 150–151), elevational prefixes are used for DIR, while elevational suffixes are used for LCL. These may co-occur, with distinct interpretations, as shown in example (26):

(26) **Elevational DIR and LCL:** Alamblak, Sepik (Bruce 1984: 151)
yua-muh-wë-r-we
DIR.VEN.UP-climb-IPFV-3SG.M-LCL.DOWN
'He is climbing up down there.'

Another related usage can be called orientational, which is not clearly a cross-linguistic category of its own but a recurring function of DIR in a number of languages. In an orientational function, DIR may be used beyond translational

---

43 The multi-functional AM and DIR markers in Lai also express relative elevation in addition to Itive vs. Ventive (VanBik & Tluangneh 2017).

motion verbs, such as for perception verbs like 'look', as in example (27). When used with a non-motion verb, sometimes another type of directional interpretation may be coerced, such as that of perspective,[44] as shown in example (28).

(27) **Orientational:** Jakaltek, Mayan (Craig 1993: 28)
xil-**ah-toj**   naj tet ix
saw-**UP-ITV**   he   to   her
'He looked at her (up-away from him).'

(28) **Orientational:** Hausa, Chadic (Newman 1983: 407)
sàyi   sayař
Buy   buy.**ITV**
'buy'   'sell'

We can also consider temporal parallels for these spatial morphemes. AM and DIR often grammaticalize as tense or aspect, such as the proximal future from 'come' and distal future from 'go' in Zulu (Botne 2006), following general cross-linguistic patterns of grammaticalization from spatial to temporal functions (Traugott 1974; Lakoff & Johnson 1980; *inter alia*). Another topic that has not been investigated in detail is the extent to which AM (or DIR) can express *fictive motion* (Talmy 1996; Matlock & Bergmann 2015; *inter alia*), or the description of spatial arrangements via metaphorical motion (cf. English *This road goes to the ocean*); this usage is attested in at least Arrernte (Wilkins 2006: 51–52; Ross 2016: 12).[45]

4.3 Non-subject AM

Non-subject AM is so sporadically attested and semantically distinct that we might want to consider it a separate phenomenon, if it were not for the attested multifunctionality of the same AM affixes for different moving arguments or shared paradigmatic roles of Subject and Object AM markers in some languages (cf. Guil-

---

[44] In some languages, this change of perspective has even grammaticalized as a part of person marking (Jacques & Antonov 2014: 312–313; *inter alia*).
[45] See also Belkadi (2015b: 25–26, 2018: 17–19, this volume) for related discussion about the functions of Berber clitics, as well as similar usage described by Vidal & Payne and in several other chapters in this volume.

laume 2016; Wilkins 1991).⁴⁶ On the other hand, although rare, this particular parameter of variation in AM systems is fundamental and independent of other factors such as temporal relationship and direction. Still, we have so few examples, and of several types, that only a preliminary typology can be proposed at this time. Only 17 languages in the sample (20% of the 83 with AM) have non-subject AM, and most of these are marginal extended functions of Directionals. These few languages are discussed below, along with additional examples from Guillaume (2016)⁴⁷ and other sources.⁴⁸ Cross-linguistically two types are most widespread for dedicated markers of Non-subject AM:

A. *Perception or interaction during object's motion.* Non-subject Concurrent AM is attested only in Nez Perce in the current sample, as in example (29), but it is also found in several other languages (Cavineña, Nomatsiguenga, Maasai). This often occurs with perception verbs, in addition to some other verbs of interaction such as speaking, insulting, cursing, hitting or capturing.

(29) **Non-subject Concurrent AM:** Nez Perce, Sahaptian (Aoki 1970: 95)
*hi-weh-**etk**-sik*
3-bark-**AM.OBJ.CONC.PASSING**-PRS.PL
'[The dogs] barked as we passed by.'

B. *Upon object's arrival, before object's departure.* Even if not in motion, the grammatical subject is still part of the action, so it is not surprising that Prior Ventive and Subsequent Itive are most common among non-concurrent motion types (while Prior Itive and Subsequent Ventive seem to be unattested as dedicated markers, though see discussion of Subsequent Ventive as an extension of DIR below). Consider examples (30)-(31):

(30) **Object Prior Ventive AM:** Tacana, Takanan (Guillaume 2016: 165)
*Miwa-**tsu**-ta-iti-a   mesa   kupari*
feed-**AM.OBJ.PR.VEN**-3.A-PFV-PST   3SG.GEN   compadre
'Heᵢ fed hisᵢ compadreⱼ after heⱼ arrived; he received his compadre with food.'

---

46 Nielsen & Messerschmidt (2020) also discuss the possibility of multi-functional AM markers allowing non-subject interpretations in some Mesoamerican languages, such as in for causee arguments in causative verbs in Filomena Mata Totonac (McFarland 2009: 143).
47 Guillaume found Non-subject AM in 6–7 (about 15%) of his sample of 44 South American languages with AM.
48 An especially unusual type is reported by Otero (this volume) for Koman languages where AM can actually be interpreted as Subsequent motion of the *speaker* following an event with a different subject (and for which the speaker is not necessarily a grammatical participant, possibly just an observer).

(31) **Object Subsequent Itive AM:** Tacana (Guillaume 2016: 165)
Miwa-***use***-ta-iti-a   mesa   kupari
feed-**AM.OBJ.SUBS.ITV**-3.A-PFV-PST   3SG.GEN   compadre
'He_i fed his_i compadre_j before he_j left; he sent his compadre off fed.'[49]

Regarding Non-subject Prior Ventive AM in Arrernte, Wilkins (1991:237) explains, "… the subject of the action is human and s/he has been consciously waiting for the object or dative-marked entity in order to do the verb action to them." The predicates that tend to occur in Non-subject Prior Ventive AM typically indicate *reactions* to the arrival of someone or something. This usage is found in Nez Perce as well as Alyawarra and Arrernte (and outside the sample the related language Kaytetye (Koch, this volume), as well as Ashéninca, Nomatsiguenga, Ese Ejja, and Tacana). Another variant is found with verbs meaning 'wait for someone to arrive' and is found in languages outside the sample, including Nivacle and Maasai. Specialized markers for Non-subject Subsequent Itive AM are attested in languages outside the sample (Ese Ejja and Tacana).

More often, Non-subject Subsequent AM is an extension of DIR markers, related also to orientational functions of DIR (Section 4.2); this is especially common with transitive verbs where the object, possibly accompanied by the subject, is set in motion. Consider the extension of DIR from caused-motion verbs like 'throw' to verbs applying a directional force on an object like 'push' and finally to non-motion verbs like 'hit' with a potentially similar meaning (see also Reed & Lindsey, this volume, for discussion of DIR expressing "inferential" AM with non-motion verbs, including for objects). Consider the functions of the Puluwat DIR suffixes in example (32). This extension of DIR to Non-subject Subsequent AM is relatively common and is found in at least 12 languages in the sample: Abkhaz, Banoni, Dagbani, Hausa, Kera, Koyraboro Senni, Lamang,[50] Ma'di, Matsés, Pero, Puluwat, and Retuarã. This usage seems especially common in Africa (see Belkadi, this volume; see also Wilkins 1991:208 on Hausa), but may represent a more widespread function of DIR markers in general even if not consistently reported in descriptive grammars.

(32) **Object Subsequent AM via DIR:** Puluwat, Oceanic (Elbert 1974: 51)
kkaru-**ló**   kkaru-**to**
cut-**ITV**   cut-**VEN**
'to cut and send away (e.g. a gift of bananas)' 'to cut and bring back'

---

[49] Alternative translation my own, illustrating tight semantic integration of motion and main action.
[50] Lamang has a large inventory of at least 6 DIR suffixes that can express Object Subsequent AM or Comitative AM, as discussed below, but not Subject AM.

Sometimes, the grammatical subject may actually be included in the motion, as may be the case in Puluwat. This creates a sort of collective or comitative AM. Regarding this phenomenon in African languages, Belkadi (2015a: 61) states "the [moving] figure is the object of the verb, while the subject of the verb is understood as the agent of the causative motion", as in example (33):

(33) **Comitative Subsequent Ventive AM:** Pero, Chadic (Frajzyngier 1989: 96; Belkadi 2015a: 61)
nī-ip-**nà**   tújè
1SG-catch-**VEN**   horse
'I caught a horse (and brought it).'

Another type of mutual motion between subject and object is attested outside the sample in Bora with an 'upon encountering' suffix (Thiesen & Weber 2012: 117–118; Guillaume 2016: 140–141). Motion is expressed, but it may be that of the subject, object or both meeting, upon which the lexical action occurs. In function, this is similar to Object Prior Ventive AM.

As with other parameters of variation for AM, there is a wide range of types of Non-subject AM, despite the relatively few known languages with this feature. The remainder of this section will discuss two generalizations about Non-subject AM proposed by Guillaume (2016). Neither is without exception, although they are valid statistical generalizations, as was the case for the implicational hierarchy for temporal relationships discussed in Section 3.4.[51]

First, Guillaume (2016: 83) proposed an implicational hierarchy based on the distribution of moving arguments in South American AM systems: **Motion of the Subject > Motion of the Object**. That generalization certainly holds statistically,[52] but an exception (Nivacle) was already observed by Guillaume (2016: 113). Another possibility is Puluwat, discussed above, as well as several others, with only

---

51 Interestingly, the distribution of temporal relationships within Non-Subject AM appears to possibly be the opposite, with Subsequent AM most common, followed by Concurrent and Prior, presumably because DIR most easily extends to Subsequent AM. In the current sample, though too limited for reliable generalizations, 12 languages had only Subsequent, 2 had only Prior, and 1 had Prior and Concurrent; Concurrent would also be more common if including continuous caused motion (e.g. 'push') when not extended to Subsequent. Roundtrip Non-subject AM is unattested, while a partially analogous Separative type was found in 2 languages, for which see below.
52 This is reinforced by the fact that even in languages with both types, typically in complex AM paradigms, there are usually fewer morphemes encoding Non-subject AM. See also Koch (this volume) for discussion of the Arandic languages, in which the only Non-subject AM category involves Prior motion to the location of the subject.

Subsequent Itive AM as an extension of DIR, except that an interpretation of the subject moving with the object is often possible.

Second, Guillaume (2016: 91) specifically observes that AM systems seem to operate on a nominative-accusative basis: most AM markers indicate movement of intransitive subjects (S) or transitive agents (A), while others (for Non-subject AM) apply to transitive patients (P). He was not aware of any AM systems functioning on an ergative-absolutive basis. This generalization also applies statistically, but ergative-absolutive systems are in fact attested, albeit extremely rarely.

One apparent counterexample in the sample is a marginal type of AM found in Arapesh, which we might consider to be a type of Separative AM, in a way the counterpart to the Collective Prior Ventive type described for Bora above. Called a "permanent aspect" directional by Conrad & Wogiga (1991: 19–20), the suffix *-úk* indicates *non-motion*, as well as motion. As seen in examples (34)-(35), it operates on an ergative-absolutive basis, with transitive patients (P) behaving like intransitive subjects (S), remaining in place (or more generally a lasting resulting state), while transitive agents (A) are understood to leave.[53] Consider also the different semantics of English *leave* in transitive and intransitive usage.[54] Even if we only consider the motion of A to count as true AM (and not the non-motion of the other arguments), this determination of Subsequent is still ergative, whereas Prior motion is absolute in both cases.

(34) **"Permanent" intransitive:** Arapesh, Torricelli (Conrad & Wogiga 1991: 20)
 *Énan   n-a-nak-**úk**.*
 3SG.M   3SG-REAL-GO-**PERM**
 'He went (and did not return).'

(35) **"Permanent" transitive:** Arapesh (Conrad & Wogiga 1991: 20)
 *Y-a-húlú-búk-úm-ag-**úk***   *wah.*
 1SG-REAL-3PL.OBJ-put-BEN-here-**PERM** sun
 'I put them [sago leaves] in the sun and they will remain there, and I went.'

Vidal & Payne (this volume) discuss what appears to be a true case of absolutive AM in Pilagá, where DIR markers can also function to mark AM for intransitive

---

[53] Conrad & Wogiga (1991: 19–20) describe these functions clearly and explicitly but only provide a limited number of examples, so it is unclear exactly how this suffix functions when combining with a full range of lexical verbs.
[54] At least for the transitive usage, a parallel is found in Lai, which Peterson (2007: 20–21) calls "relinquitive" and considers a type of applicative.

subjects (S) or transitive patients (P), but not transitive agents (A). (There does not appear to be an alternative ergative AM equivalent for A.)

Similar to the cases above for AM functioning on an ergative-absolutive basis, an apparent parallel for absolutive DIR may exist in Matsés (Fleck 2003: 373–375), where vertical DIR markers are only used for movement of intransitive subjects (S) and transitive patients (P), not transitive agents (A).[55] In fact, this usage also appears to extend to Subsequent (Patient) AM from the available examples (e.g. 'pull *down* fruits'), thus also one of very few examples of vertical AM (cf. Section 3.1).

In summary, Non-subject AM is rare and its typology not yet fully understood – a clear area for continued research especially in languages with more extensive usage. On the difficulty and uncertainty of identifying what should be considered Non-subject AM, see Lovestrand & Ross (this volume).

4.4 What is associated motion?

This paper has expanded on previous studies of AM in individual languages or regions and provided the first worldwide account of AM, building on the foundation for a comprehensive typology of the phenomenon. However, it is still in some ways unclear how to define or describe AM. What are the required features for AM, and how do they relate to other categories? Instead of a conclusion this sub-section will attempt to understand the nature of AM as a grammatical category and guide further research.

The ranking of AM systems by number of markers in Section 3.3 is a reasonable starting point for comparing languages, but by considering only paradigm size, other aspects of the complexity of AM systems may be overlooked, and there are also more fundamental questions of definition. All AM systems express motion, so there is no reason to think of some languages as having *more motion* than others: fact-of-motion is associated with verbs whether there is one form in a paradigm or more than a dozen. Should we consider temporal relationship and moving argument, given that this is *how* the motion is associated with the verb? These may be the core components of AM, and languages with all three temporal relationship types and variation in the moving argument do generally correspond to the languages with the largest paradigms (see also Guillaume 2016: 106–123; Koch, this volume). However, it is important to consider not only by the

---

[55] See also Foley (1991: 349–350) on similar usage in Yimas, and Guillaume (2000, 2008: 307) for Cavineña.

number of forms, but also by the range of meanings for multi-functional forms (see Tallman, this volume); see also Hernández-Green & Palancar (this volume) about morphological complexity.

Many of the most complex paradigms seem to come not from more complex AM per se, but from more overlap with other categories. In some languages, AM morphemes have fused with inflectional categories. Popoloca Itive prefixes vary by tense and person, as the diachronic result of the irregular verb 'go' compounding with another verb root to create a new tense-like paradigm shown in in Table 4, as illustrated in example (36). (Similar interaction of tense and AM is found in Nahuatl. Or consider Matsés, which has pairs of AM suffixes that vary by transitivity of the verb.)

Table 4: Metzontla Popoloca Itive paradigm (Veerman-Leichsenring 1991: 267).[56]

	Past	Present	Future
1st Person	xuì-	thì-	chì/sì-
2nd/3rd Person	xuí-	thī-	chī/sī-

(36) **AM fused with inflection:** Popoloca, Oto-Manguean
(Veerman-Leichsenring 1991: 267)
xuí-xíngʔāxìą̀   kuāyē čìʔ
AM.PR.ITV.PST.1-lower.1 many pot
'I went to get down many pots.'

There are also AM affixes in several languages that are only used with imperatives (e.g. Hixkaryana, Makah, Matsés, Tibetan and Tiwi; also, Kalkatungu and Iraqw for DIR). Would these be more complex AM systems (or perhaps less)?

Regarding AM paradigms, consider also compositionality, specifically the possibility for multiple AM affixes to combine with one another (or with DIR). We have already seen examples in Section 4.1 above: complex Roundtrip in (14) and iterated interruptive Concurrent in (19). In fact, many of the most complex AM systems appear to have some internally morphologically complex forms. For example, Wilkins (1991) acknowledges that some forms in Arrernte are morphologically complex, but presents them in a large paradigm, while others (Henderson 2002, 2013; Dras et al. 2012) have described these forms as compounds rather than

---

[56] These forms could be analyzed as compositional, but note that these Itive prefixes function paradigmatically like tense inflection, while *agreeing* with person inflection on the root. There is also a Ventive counterpart but not enough information to determine the paradigm from the brief description (Veerman-Leichsenring 1991: 271).

morphology in the narrow sense. On the one hand, this means that to varying degrees the most complex systems may not be the best candidates to measure from a paradigmatic perspective. On the other hand, this is actually evidence that AM is an active category in the grammar, not only synchronically but also diachronically as more forms (and functions) are added within an increasingly complex system. This would also suggest that different markers in AM systems may grammaticalize independently, for example following the statistical distribution described by the implicational hierarchies discussed above, which likewise suggest that some markers tend to grammaticalize after others are already established (e.g. Concurrent or Subsequent after Prior).

For several reasons, then, paradigm size does not seem to be the best way to compare AM systems. This becomes even more apparent when we consider multi-verb constructions with AM functions (cf. Lovestrand & Ross, this volume; Ross 2021). There are also a few cases of specialized syntactic AM systems such as Trumai motion auxiliaries (Guirardello-Damian 2012), as in example (37).

(37) **AM auxiliary:** Trumai, isolate (Guirardello-Damian 2012: 186)
 *hai-ts   ha   mut   xoxan **katsu**.*
 1SG-ERG 1SG clothing wash   **AUX.AM.PR.RIVER**
 'I went to the river to wash my clothing.'

Consider also the difficulty in distinguishing between morphological AM and compound verbs in the current survey. Indeed, if we were to include compound verbs and measure them from the perspective of paradigmatic complexity, we would find that a language like Asmat, with extensive verb-verb compounding, would have 40 or more AM markers (Drabbe 1959: 20–21).

There are other cases where AM may not be fully morphologized, as discussed above for the disputable paradigm for Arrernte. Another example is Djabugay, which appears to have a typical AM system as found in other Australian languages (Patz 1991: 285), as shown in (38). However, two transparently verbal stems are linked together with a dependent verb suffix (in fact indicating incorporation of the lexical verb into the motion verb). As discussed by Wilkins (1991: 238), this linker would eventually be lost in a fully morphologized AM system (see also Koch 1986, this volume; Austin 1989).

(38) **Compound AM with linker:** Djabugay, Pama–Nyungan (Patz 1991: 285)
 gudji   nyinya-y-garra-ny   buimba-:
 3SG.SBJ sit-**LNK**-come-PST   camp-LOC
 'He came to sit in the camp.'

This paper has also demonstrated the widespread distribution of Directionals in languages of the world, often semantically more varied than the spatial meanings in AM. These categories interact, but there is also cross-linguistic variation in terms of how they divide up different functions in expressing spatial meaning in languages. The results of the survey supported the need to distinguish these phenomena, but we should also recognize their similarities. In particular, AM markers often also express directional contrasts. At the same time, as also observed by Dryer (this volume, ch. 4), the *only* property that AM and DIR necessarily share is that they are related to motion: DIR does not predicate fact-of-motion, while AM is not inherently directional. We might then consider whether typical directional AM is in fact a hybrid category of AM plus DIR, or another more general grammatical category of Direction which can be expressed by either.[57] This may also be the connection that explains the development of multi-functional markers of AM and DIR in some languages. On the other hand, Belkadi (this volume) asks whether DIR itself might be a subtype of AM, which is not an unreasonable position if we take it to predicate the *translational* fact-of-motion: compare for example manner-of-motion verbs that lexically express a motion event but do not, strictly speaking, predicate change of location (compare 'run around' to 'run away'). Conversely, "echo" phenomena (Wilkins 1991: 251; Jacques, Lahaussois & Zhang, this volume; Pakendorf & Stoynova, this volume; *inter alia*), where AM combines with multi-verb constructions expressing motion or other contextually-established motion events, suggest that AM might function more like agreement or reinforcement, instead of independently predicating fact-of-motion itself. There is, therefore, some conceptual overlap as well, in addition to attested multi-functionality.[58]

Instead of a definitive conclusion, I will end with a question: in what sense is AM a *grammatical category* (as in the definition used in this paper and in this volume)? We might ask whether AM could be considered inflectional or deriva-

---

[57] Indeed, despite the combinatorial differences in AM and DIR systems, the resulting predicates in either case express directional motion events and can behave similarly: for example, grammaticalization of Itives and Ventives (AM or DIR) in tense/aspect-marking is well known, and similarly grammaticalization of Itive-marked predicates with a 'surprise' reading is attested in a number of languages around the world (Ross 2016, 2021).

[58] These connections between AM and DIR might also alleviate the need to differentiate between instances of DIR functioning as AM versus AM functioning as DIR, as proposed by various researchers, but without any clear metric for making this distinction, except perhaps etymology. One intriguing possibility is that if indeed DIR were a type of AM, then it would be underspecified for temporal relationship and moving argument, such that Reed & Lindsey's proposal (this volume) of "inferential" AM from DIR would apply for how to interpret the motion with non-motion verbs and explain why that reading is not readily available for all predicates.

tional morphology. Although it likely varies by language, this distinction is difficult to make. In terms of affix ordering, with derivational morphology typically immediately adjacent to the verb root and inflectional morphology at the outside of the word, AM affixes seem to often appear in the middle. Overlap (whether agreeing or as fused forms) with other inflectional categories such as tense, aspect, or person would suggest AM properly belongs to inflectional morphology. Similarly, AM is known to further grammaticalize into tense or aspect marking. These factors, in addition to the paradigmatic nature (or at least our habits as analysts in writing AM in paradigms), support an analysis as inflection. On the other hand, overlap with DIR in some languages would suggest AM is derivational; it is also possible to consider AM to create new lexemes because certain combinations are known to lexicalize in some languages as well. Furthermore, despite the temptation to think of AM like TAM marking, we may first also want to consider other possible similar categories such as Associated Posture (Enfield 2002, and indeed several of the languages in the survey have affixes for posture similar to those for motion). Obligatoriness is not a good criterion in this case because AM markers are used to add semantic information, although they are not really optional in that case, much like English plurals for example. Consider also the possible "echo" function of AM, reinforcing rather than introducing information about an established motion event. The frequency of use of these forms also varies greatly cross-linguistically. In the end, perhaps AM is instead good evidence for not making a sharp distinction between inflectional and derivational morphology, nor between morphology and syntax. Even if not often described using the same terminology, expression of AM via multi-verb and other syntactic constructions is also common cross-linguistically (Ross 2016, 2021; Lovestrand & Ross, this volume).

All that can be concluded with confidence is that continued research on Associated Motion is welcome, and the contributions to this volume are an important step in the right direction. More cross-linguistic research, especially comparative and taking into account syntactic forms, is still needed. The current survey has shown that Guillaume's (2016) parameters of variation for South America can be productively applied to languages elsewhere. At its core, Associated Motion expresses the translational movement of a syntactic argument before, during or after the lexical action of a verb. Information about the direction of motion is also often encoded, although for describing the path of lexical motion verbs a distinct category of Directionals expresses that information, which may sometimes interact or overlap with Associated Motion. The cross-linguistic distributions also highlight languages beyond the traditional areas for research on these phenomena to further our understanding, as well as areas without morphological marking that would suggest further research on syntactic expression to determine just how widespread Associated Motion is as a grammatical – not just morphological – category.

Abbreviations

Abbreviations follow Leipzig Glossing Rules, with the following additions:

1/2/3	person or remoteness	MIR	mirative
AM	associated motion	MOT	motion
AOR	aorist	PERM	permanent
CONC	concurrent	PR	prior
CONT	continuous	PUNC	punctual
DIR	directional	REAL	realis
EMPH	emphatic	REV	reversive
FNL	phrase-final suffix	RT	roundtrip
HAB	habitual	SUBS	subsequent
ITV	itive	VBLZ	verbalizer
LCL	locational	VEN	ventive
LNK	linker	VEN2	toward 2nd person

Acknowledgments: I would like to thank Antoine Guillaume, Harold Koch and Matthew Dryer for comments on earlier drafts of this paper, as well as the participants of the ALT 2017 Workshop on Associated Motion and contributors to this volume for their feedback, including especially Joseph Lovestrand and Bastian Persohn.

The maps in this paper were generated using the WALS Interactive Tool by Hans-Jörg Bibiko.

The initial stages of this survey project were completed with the help of research assistants Ryan Grunow, Kelsey Wise, George Jabbour and Jack Dempsey. I would like to thank Joseph Lovestrand for a number of rewarding discussions about methodology and classification. And I am grateful to Matthew Dryer for providing me with his personal notes on AM and DIR systems in a long list of languages worldwide which allowed for verification and in some cases revision of the classification assigned to a number of languages in the sample. My survey has also greatly benefitted from all of the chapters in this volume, including especially those with overlapping languages.

Appendix: Quantitative summary of associated motion and directionals survey

This appendix includes a quantitative summary of the data points for each language as represented in the maps and statistical comparisons in this paper. See Ross (2021) for an expanded version including sources and information about the forms and functions of AM and DIR in individual languages, as well as more general background information about the survey.

The table below summarizes the following information: the language name (following WALS); the WALS code identifying the language; and information about AM and DIR affixes, including the number of morphemes and affix ordering (⇆ ⟵ for prefixes, ⟶ for suffixes, and ⇆ for mixed prefixes and suffixes), and whether Itive and Ventive affixes are attested. AM is also classified for temporal relationship to the motion event, including Prior, Concurrent, Subsequent and Roundtrip, and DIR is also classified for whether Vertical markers are attested. The last column indicates the number of individual affixes that overlap (∩), functioning as both AM and DIR.

Language	WALS	AM	⇆	ITV	VEN	PR	CONC	SUBS	RT	DIR	⇆	ITV	VEN	VERT	∩
Abkhaz	ABK	2	⟶	+	+	–	+	–	–	106+	⇆	+	+	+	2
Abun	ABU	0	–	–	–	–	–	–	–	0	–	–	–	–	–
Acehnese	ACE	0	–	–	–	–	–	–	–	0	–	–	–	–	–
Acoma	ACO	1	⟶	–	–	+	–	–	–	0	–	–	–	–	0
Agarabi	AGA	0	–	–	–	–	–	–	–	0	–	–	–	–	–
Ainu	AIN	0	–	–	–	–	–	–	–	0	–	–	–	–	–
Alamblak	ALA	8	⟵	+	+	+	–	–	–	8	⟵	+	+	+	8
Alyawarra	ALY	15	⟶	+	+	+	+	+	–	5	⟶	–	+	+	5
Ambae (Lolovoli Northeast)	AML	0	–	–	–	–	–	–	–	0	–	–	–	–	–
Amele	AME	0	–	–	–	–	–	–	–	0	–	–	–	–	–
Apurinã	APU	2	⟶	–	–	–	+	–	–	2	⟶	–	–	–	2
Arabic (Egyptian)	AEG	0	–	–	–	–	–	–	–	0	–	–	–	–	–
Araona	ANA	7+	⟶	+	+	+	+	+	+	5+	⟶	+	+	–	5
Arapesh (Mountain)	ARP	2	⟶	–	+	+	–	+	–	3	⟶	+	+	–	2
Arawak	ARA	2	⟶	+	+	+	–	–	–	2	⟶	+	+	–	2
Arop-Lokep	ALK	0	–	–	–	–	–	–	–	0	–	–	–	–	–
Arrernte (Mparntwe)	AMP	15	⟶	+	+	+	+	–	–	5+	⟶	–	+	+	4

(continued)

Language	WALS	AM	⇆	ITV	VEN	PR	CONC	SUBS	RT	DIR	⇆	ITV	VEN	VERT	⌒
Asmat	ASM	1	→	+	−	+	−	−	−	0	−	−	−	−	0
Babungo	BAB	0	−	−	−	−	−	−	−	0	−	−	−	−	−
Badimaya	BDM	0	−	−	−	−	−	−	−	0	−	−	−	−	−
Bagirmi	BAG	0	−	−	−	−	−	−	−	0	−	−	−	−	−
Baka (in Cameroon)	BAK	0	−	−	−	−	−	−	−	0	−	−	−	−	−
Bali-Vitu	BVI	0	−	−	−	−	−	−	−	0	−	−	−	−	−
Banoni	BNN	1	←	−	−	−	−	+	−	1	←	−	−	−	1
Barasano	BRS	1	→	−	−	+	−	−	−	3+	→	+	+	−	0
Basque	BSQ	0	−	−	−	−	−	−	−	0	−	−	−	−	−
Batak (Karo)	BKR	0	−	−	−	−	−	−	−	0	−	−	−	−	−
Bawm	BAW	0	−	−	−	−	−	−	−	0	−	−	−	−	−
Berber (Middle Atlas)	BMA	0	−	−	−	−	−	−	−	0	−	−	−	−	−
Bininj Gun-Wok	BBW	1	←	−	+	+	+	+	−	2	←	+	+	−	1
Bozo (Tigemaxo)	BOZ	0	−	−	−	−	−	−	−	0	−	−	−	−	−
Brahui	BRH	0	−	−	−	−	−	−	−	0	−	−	−	−	−
Brokskat	BKT	0	−	−	−	−	−	−	−	0	−	−	−	−	−
Buduma	BUD	0	−	−	−	−	−	−	−	0	−	−	−	−	−
Buma	BUM	0	−	−	−	−	−	−	−	0	−	−	−	−	−
Burmese	BRM	0	−	−	−	−	−	−	−	0	−	−	−	−	−
Burushaski	BUR	0	−	−	−	−	−	−	−	0	−	−	−	−	−
Busa	BUS	0	−	−	−	−	−	−	−	0	−	−	−	−	−
Cahuilla	CAH	6	→	+	+	+	+	−	−	4	→	+	+	−	4
Canela-Krahô	CKR	0	−	−	−	−	−	−	−	0	−	−	−	−	−
Cantonese	CNT	0	−	−	−	−	−	−	−	0	−	−	−	−	−
Cayuga	CYG	2	→	−	−	+	+	−	−	2	←	+	+	−	0
Chamorro	CHA	0	−	−	−	−	−	−	−	0	−	−	−	−	−
Chechen	CHC	0	−	−	−	−	−	−	−	0	−	−	−	−	−
Chemehuevi	CMH	4	→	+	+	+	−	−	−	3+	→	+	−	−	0
Chichewa	CIC	2	←	+	+	+	−	−	−	0	−	−	−	−	0
Chocho	CCH	0	−	−	−	−	−	−	−	0	−	−	−	−	−
Chukchi	CHK	1	→	−	−	+	−	−	−	0	−	−	−	−	0
Coahuilteco	COA	0	−	−	−	−	−	−	−	0	−	−	−	−	−
Coos (Hanis)	COO	0	−	−	−	−	−	−	−	1	→	−	−	−	0
Coptic	COP	0	−	−	−	−	−	−	−	0	−	−	−	−	−
Cree (Plains)	CRE	2	←	+	+	+	−	−	−	1	←	−	+	−	1

2 A cross-linguistic survey of Associated Motion and Directionals — 73

(continued)

Language	WALS	AM	↹	ITV	VEN	PR	CONC	SUBS	RT	DIR	↹	ITV	VEN	VERT	∩
Daga	DAG	0	–	–	–	–	–	–	–	0	–	–	–	–	–
Dagbani	DGB	1	→ı	–	+	–	–	+	–	1	→ı	–	+	–	1
Dani (Lower Grand Valley)	DNI	0	–	–	–	–	–	–	–	1	→ı	–	+	–	0
Dargwa	DRG	0	–	–	–	–	–	–	–	8	←ı	+	+	+	0
Degema	DEG	0	–	–	–	–	–	–	–	0	–	–	–	–	–
Dhaasanac	DHA	0	–	–	–	–	–	–	–	0	–	–	–	–	–
Dhivehi	DHI	0	–	–	–	–	–	–	–	0	–	–	–	–	–
Djabugay	DJA	0	–	–	–	–	–	–	–	0	–	–	–	–	–
Doyayo	DOY	1	→ı	–	–	–	+	–	–	2	→ı	–	+	–	1
Drehu	DRE	0	–	–	–	–	–	–	–	0	–	–	–	–	–
Dullay (Gollango)	DUG	0	–	–	–	–	–	–	–	0	–	–	–	–	–
English	ENG	0	–	–	–	–	–	–	–	0	–	–	–	–	–
Erromangan	ERR	0	–	–	–	–	–	–	–	5	→ı	–	–	+	0
Evenki	EVE	1	→ı	–	–	+	–	–	–	0	–	–	–	–	0
Ewondo	EWO	0	–	–	–	–	–	–	–	0	–	–	–	–	–
Fijian	FIJ	0	–	–	–	–	–	–	–	0	–	–	–	–	–
Finnish	FIN	0	–	–	–	–	–	–	–	0	–	–	–	–	–
Fongbe	FON	0	–	–	–	–	–	–	–	0	–	–	–	–	–
French	FRE	0	–	–	–	–	–	–	–	0	–	–	–	–	–
Gapapaiwa	GAP	0	–	–	–	–	–	–	–	0	–	–	–	–	–
Garo	GAR	0	–	–	–	–	–	–	–	6+	→ı	+	+	+	0
Georgian	GEO	0	–	–	–	–	–	–	–	10+	←ı	+	+	+	0
German	GER	0	–	–	–	–	–	–	–	25+	←ı	+	+	+	0
Gola	GOL	0	–	–	–	–	–	–	–	0	–	–	–	–	–
Gooniyandi	GOO	0	–	–	–	–	–	–	–	0	–	–	–	–	–
Grebo	GRB	0	–	–	–	–	–	–	–	4	→ı	+	+	–	0
Greek (Modern)	GRK	0	–	–	–	–	–	–	–	17+	←ı	–	–	+	0
Greenlandic (West)	GRW	1	→ı	–	–	+	–	–	–	0	–	–	–	–	0
Guaraní	GUA	0	–	–	–	–	–	–	–	0	–	–	–	–	–
Gujarati	GUJ	0	–	–	–	–	–	–	–	0	–	–	–	–	–
Gunbalang	GNB	0	–	–	–	–	–	–	–	3	←ı	+	+	+	0
Gurr-goni	GRG	0	–	–	–	–	–	–	–	0	–	–	–	–	–
Haida	HAI	3	→ı	+	–	+	–	+	–	12	→ı	+	–	+	0
Hamtai	HAM	0	–	–	–	–	–	–	–	0	–	–	–	–	–
Hatam	HAT	0	–	–	–	–	–	–	–	0	–	–	–	–	–

(continued)

Language	WALS	AM	⇌	ITV	VEN	PR	CONC	SUBS	RT	DIR	⇌	ITV	VEN	VERT	∩
Hausa	HAU	1	→ı	−	+	−	+	+	−	5	→ı	+	+	+	1
Hawaiian	HAW	0	−	−	−	−	−	−	−	0	−	−	−	−	−
Hebrew (Modern)	HEB	0	−	−	−	−	−	−	−	0	−	−	−	−	−
Hindi	HIN	0	−	−	−	−	−	−	−	0	−	−	−	−	−
Hixkaryana	HIX	4	→ı	+	−	+	−	−	−	0	−	−	−	−	0
Hmong Njua	HMO	0	−	−	−	−	−	−	−	0	−	−	−	−	−
Hoava	HOA	0	−	−	−	−	−	−	−	0	−	−	−	−	−
Hungarian	HUN	0	−	−	−	−	−	−	−	8+	⊢	+	+	+	0
Hunzib	HZB	0	−	−	−	−	−	−	−	0	−	−	−	−	−
Ika	IKA	1	→ı	−	−	−	−	+	−	0	−	−	−	−	0
Imonda	IMO	0	−	−	−	−	−	−	−	0	−	−	−	−	−
Indonesian	IND	0	−	−	−	−	−	−	−	0	−	−	−	−	−
Iraqw	IRQ	0	−	−	−	−	−	−	−	4	→ı	−	+	−	0
Irish	IRI	0	−	−	−	−	−	−	−	0	−	−	−	−	−
Italian	ITA	0	−	−	−	−	−	−	−	0	−	−	−	−	−
Itzaj	ITZ	0	−	−	−	−	−	−	−	0	−	−	−	−	−
Jabêm	JAB	0	−	−	−	−	−	−	−	3	⊢	+	+	−	0
Jakaltek	JAK	0	−	−	−	−	−	−	−	10	→ı	+	+	+	0
Jaminjung	JAM	0	−	−	−	−	−	−	−	0	−	−	−	−	−
Japanese	JPN	0	−	−	−	−	−	−	−	0	−	−	−	−	−
Ju|'hoan	JUH	0	−	−	−	−	−	−	−	0	−	−	−	−	−
Kairiru	KRR	0	−	−	−	−	−	−	−	0	−	−	−	−	−
Kalkatungu	KGU	0	−	−	−	−	−	−	−	2	→ı	+	+	−	0
Kamaiurá	KMA	0	−	−	−	−	−	−	−	0	−	−	−	−	−
Kambera	KAM	0	−	−	−	−	−	−	−	0	−	−	−	−	−
Kana	KAN	0	−	−	−	−	−	−	−	1	→ı	+	−	−	0
Kannada	KND	0	−	−	−	−	−	−	−	0	−	−	−	−	−
Kanuri	KNR	0	−	−	−	−	−	−	−	0	−	−	−	−	−
Karen (Pwo)	KPW	0	−	−	−	−	−	−	−	0	−	−	−	−	−
Karok	KRK	1	→ı	−	−	+	−	−	−	45+	→ı	+	+	+	0
Kashmiri	KAS	0	−	−	−	−	−	−	−	0	−	−	−	−	−
Kâte	KAT	0	−	−	−	−	−	−	−	0	−	−	−	−	−
Kayardild	KAY	0	−	−	−	−	−	−	−	0	−	−	−	−	−
Kera	KER	2	→ı	+	+	−	−	+	−	2	→ı	+	+	−	2
Ket	KET	0	−	−	−	−	−	−	−	3+	⊢	+	+	+	0
Kewa	KEW	0	−	−	−	−	−	−	−	2	→ı	−	−	+	0
Khalkha	KHA	0	−	−	−	−	−	−	−	0	−	−	−	−	−

Language	WALS	AM	⇆	ITV	VEN	PR	CONC	SUBS	RT	DIR	⇆	ITV	VEN	VERT	∩
Kham	KMH	2	→	+	+	+	−	−	−	0	−	−	−	−	0
Khanty	KTY	0	−	−	−	−	−	−	−	0	−	−	−	−	−
Khasi	KHS	0	−	−	−	−	−	−	−	0	−	−	−	−	−
Khmu'	KMU	0	−	−	−	−	−	−	−	0	−	−	−	−	−
Khoekhoe	KHO	1	→	−	−	−	+	−	−	3	→	−	+	−	1
Kiowa	KIO	2	→	+	−	+	+	−	−	3	→	+	+	−	1
Kiribati	KRB	0	−	−	−	−	−	−	−	6	→	+	+	+	0
Koasati	KOA	2	←	+	+	+	−	−	−	4	←	−	−	+	0
Kobon	KOB	0	−	−	−	−	−	−	−	0	−	−	−	−	−
Kolami	KOL	0	−	−	−	−	−	−	−	0	−	−	−	−	−
Kombai	KMB	0	−	−	−	−	−	−	−	0	−	−	−	−	−
Korean	KOR	0	−	−	−	−	−	−	−	0	−	−	−	−	−
Korku	KKU	0	−	−	−	−	−	−	−	2	→	+	+	−	0
Koromfe	KFE	0	−	−	−	−	−	−	−	0	−	−	−	−	−
Korowai	KRW	0	−	−	−	−	−	−	−	0	−	−	−	−	−
Koyraboro Senni	KSE	1	→	−	+	−	+	−	−	1	→	−	+	−	1
Krongo	KRO	0	−	−	−	−	−	−	−	2	→	+	+	−	0
Kugu Nganhcara	KNC	0	−	−	−	−	−	−	−	0	−	−	−	−	−
Kukú	KUK	2	→	+	+	−	+	−	−	2	→	+	+	−	2
Kuot	KUO	0	−	−	−	−	−	−	−	0	−	−	−	−	−
Kutenai	KUT	0	−	−	−	−	−	−	−	0	−	−	−	−	−
Kwaio	KWA	0	−	−	−	−	−	−	−	0	−	−	−	−	−
Lai	LAI	5	←	+	+	+	−	−	−	5	←	+	+	+	5
Lak	LAK	0	−	−	−	−	−	−	−	0	−	−	−	−	−
Lakhota	LKT	0	−	−	−	−	−	−	−	0	−	−	−	−	−
Lamang	LMG	6+	→	+	+	−	+	−	−	10	→	+	+	+	6
Lango	LAN	0	−	−	−	−	−	−	−	1	→	−	+	−	0
Latvian	LAT	0	−	−	−	−	−	−	−	11	←	+	+	+	0
Lavukaleve	LAV	0	−	−	−	−	−	−	−	0	−	−	−	−	−
Laz	LAZ	0	−	−	−	−	−	−	−	24+	←	+	+	+	0
Lele	LEL	0	−	−	−	−	−	−	−	0	−	−	−	−	−
Lepcha	LEP	0	−	−	−	−	−	−	−	0	−	−	−	−	0
Lezgian	LEZ	0	−	−	−	−	−	−	−	0	−	−	−	−	−
Lillooet	LIL	0	−	−	−	−	−	−	−	0	−	−	−	−	−
Longgu	LGU	0	−	−	−	−	−	−	−	0	−	−	−	−	−
Lugbara	LUG	0	−	−	−	−	−	−	−	1	←	−	+	−	0
Luvale	LUV	1	←	+	−	+	−	−	−	0	−	−	−	−	0

(continued)

Language	WALS	AM		ITV	VEN	PR	CONC	SUBS	RT	DIR		ITV	VEN	VERT	∩
Ma'di	MAD	1	←	−	+	−	−	+	−	1	←	−	−	−	1
Maale	MLE	0	−	−	−	−	−	−	−	0	−	−	−	−	−
Madurese	MDR	0	−	−	−	−	−	−	−	0	−	−	−	−	−
Maithili	MAI	0	−	−	−	−	−	−	−	0	−	−	−	−	−
Makah	MAK	1	→	+	−	+	−	−	−	0	−	−	−	−	0
Malagasy	MAL	0	−	−	−	−	−	−	−	0	−	−	−	−	−
Malayalam	MYM	0	−	−	−	−	−	−	−	0	−	−	−	−	−
Mam	MAM	0	−	−	−	−	−	−	−	2	→	+	+	−	0
Mandarin	MND	0	−	−	−	−	−	−	−	0	−	−	−	−	−
Mangarrayi	MYI	0	−	−	−	−	−	−	−	0	−	−	−	−	−
Mangghuer	MGG	0	−	−	−	−	−	−	−	0	−	−	−	−	−
Maori	MAO	0	−	−	−	−	−	−	−	0	−	−	−	−	−
Mapudungun	MAP	6	→	+	+	+	+	−	+	4	→	+	+	−	4
Marathi	MHI	0	−	−	−	−	−	−	−	0	−	−	−	−	−
Maricopa	MAR	0	−	−	−	−	−	−	−	2	→	+	+	−	0
Marquesan	MRQ	0	−	−	−	−	−	−	−	0	−	−	−	−	−
Martuthunira	MRT	0	−	−	−	−	−	−	−	0	−	−	−	−	−
Matsés	MYR	14	→	+	+	+	+	−	+	2	→	−	−	+	0
Maung	MAU	0	−	−	−	−	−	−	−	2	→	+	+	−	0
Maybrat	MAY	0	−	−	−	−	−	−	−	0	−	−	−	−	−
Mbay	MBY	0	−	−	−	−	−	−	−	0	−	−	−	−	−
Mbili	MBI	0	−	−	−	−	−	−	−	0	−	−	−	−	−
Meithei	MEI	4	→	+	+	+	+	+	−	6	→	+	+	+	2
Midob	MID	0	−	−	−	−	−	−	−	2	→	+	+	−	0
Mixtec (Chalcatongo)	MXC	0	−	−	−	−	−	−	−	0	−	−	−	−	−
Miya	MIY	0	−	−	−	−	−	−	−	0	−	−	−	−	−
Mocoví	MCV	0	−	−	−	−	−	−	−	15	↔	+	+	+	0
Mohawk	MOH	2	→	−	−	+	+	−	−	2	←	+	+	−	0
Monumbo	MBO	0	−	−	−	−	−	−	−	0	−	−	−	−	−
Mosetén	MOS	6	→	+	+	+	+	−	−	2	→	+	+	−	2
Mundari	MUN	0	−	−	−	−	−	−	−	0	−	−	−	−	−
Mupun	MUP	0	−	−	−	−	−	−	−	0	−	−	−	−	−
Musgu	MGU	0	−	−	−	−	−	−	−	0	−	−	−	−	−
Mussau	MUS	0	−	−	−	−	−	−	−	0	−	−	−	−	−
Nabak	NAB	0	−	−	−	−	−	−	−	0	−	−	−	−	−
Nagatman	NAG	0	−	−	−	−	−	−	−	5+	→	+	+	−	0

2 A cross-linguistic survey of Associated Motion and Directionals — 77

(continued)

Language	WALS	AM	⇆	ITV	VEN	PR	CONC	SUBS	RT	DIR	⇆	ITV	VEN	VERT	∩
Nahuatl (Mecayapan Isthmus)	NMI	12	→	+	+	+	−	−	+	0	−	−	−	−	0
Nahuatl (Tetelcingo)	NHT	14	⇆	+	+	+	+	−	−	2	←	+	+	−	2
Nambikuára (Southern)	NMB	0	−	−	−	−	−	−	−	0	−	−	−	−	−
Navajo	NAV	0	−	−	−	−	−	−	−	100+	←	+	+	+	0
Ndebele (in South Africa)	NDB	0	−	−	−	−	−	−	−	0	−	−	−	−	−
Ndjébbana	NDJ	0	−	−	−	−	−	−	−	1	←	−	+	−	0
Nelemwa	NEL	0	−	−	−	−	−	−	−	0	−	−	−	−	−
Nepali	NEP	0	−	−	−	−	−	−	−	0	−	−	−	−	−
Newar (Dolakha)	NWD	0	−	−	−	−	−	−	−	0	−	−	−	−	−
Nez Perce	NEZ	5	→	+	+	+	+	+	−	4	→	+	+	−	0
Ngalakan	NGL	1	←	−	−	−	+	−	−	1	←	−	−	−	1
Ngbandi	SAN	0	−	−	−	−	−	−	−	0	−	−	−	−	−
Ngiyambaa	NGI	1	→	−	−	−	+	−	−	2	→	−	−	−	1
Nhanda	NHA	1	→	−	−	−	+	−	−	2	→	−	+	−	0
Nias	NIA	0	−	−	−	−	−	−	−	0	−	−	−	−	−
Nisgha	NSG	0	−	−	−	−	−	−	−	62	←	−	−	+	0
Niuafo'ou	NIF	0	−	−	−	−	−	−	−	0	−	−	−	−	−
Niuean	NIU	0	−	−	−	−	−	−	−	0	−	−	−	−	−
Nivkh	NIV	0	−	−	−	−	−	−	−	0	−	−	−	−	−
Nkore-Kiga	NKO	0	−	−	−	−	−	−	−	0	−	−	−	−	−
Nsenga	NSE	2	←	+	+	+	−	−	−	0	−	−	−	−	0
Nuaulu	NUA	0	−	−	−	−	−	−	−	0	−	−	−	−	−
O'odham	OOD	3	→	−	−	+	+	−	−	1	→	−	−	−	1
Obolo	OBO	0	−	−	−	−	−	−	−	0	−	−	−	−	−
Ojibwa (Eastern)	OJI	4	←	+	+	+	+	−	−	4	←	+	+	−	3
Oneida	OND	2	→	−	−	+	+	−	−	2	←	+	+	−	0
Oromo (Harar)	ORH	0	−	−	−	−	−	−	−	2	←	+	+	+	0
Otomí (Mezquital)	OTM	0	−	−	−	−	−	−	−	0	−	−	−	−	−
Paamese	PMS	0	−	−	−	−	−	−	−	0	−	−	−	−	−
Páez	PAE	0	−	−	−	−	−	−	−	7	←	−	−	+	0
Paiute (Northern)	PNO	2	→	+	−	+	+	−	−	3	→	+	+	−	2
Paiwan	PAI	0	−	−	−	−	−	−	−	0	−	−	−	−	−

(continued)

Language	WALS	AM	↔	ITV	VEN	PR	CONC	SUBS	RT	DIR	↔	ITV	VEN	VERT	∩
Palauan	PAL	0	–	–	–	–	–	–	–	0	–	–	–	–	–
Passamaquoddy-Maliseet	PSM	3	←	+	+	+	+	–	+	9	←	+	+	–	1
Pech	PEC	0	–	–	–	–	–	–	–	0	–	–	–	–	–
Pero	PER	2	→	–	+	–	–	+	–	2	→	–	+	–	2
Persian	PRS	0	–	–	–	–	–	–	–	7+	←	–	–	+	0
Pirahã	PRH	0	–	–	–	–	–	–	–	0	–	–	–	–	–
Pitjantjatjara	PIT	1	→	–	–	–	+	–	–	5	←	+	+	–	0
Popoloca (Metzontla)	POP	8+	←	+	+	+	–	–	–	0	–	–	–	–	0
Puluwat	PUL	2	→	+	+	–	–	+	–	7	→	+	+	+	2
Purépecha	PUR	7	→	+	+	+	+	+	–	4	→	+	+	–	2
Qafar	QAF	0	–	–	–	–	–	–	–	0	–	–	–	–	–
Qiang	QIA	0	–	–	–	–	–	–	–	8	←	+	+	+	0
Quechua (Huallaga)	QHU	1	→	+	–	+	–	–	+	5	→	–	+	+	1
Quechua (Imbabura)	QIM	1	→	–	+	+	–	+	–	1	→	–	+	–	1
Rama	RAM	0	–	–	–	–	–	–	–	2	→	+	+	–	0
Rapanui	RAP	0	–	–	–	–	–	–	–	0	–	–	–	–	–
Retuarã	RET	3	→	+	+	–	–	+	–	3	→	+	+	+	3
Rotuman	ROT	0	–	–	–	–	–	–	–	3	→	+	+	–	0
Russian	RUS	0	–	–	–	–	–	–	–	8	←	–	–	+	0
Saami (Kildin)	SKI	0	–	–	–	–	–	–	–	0	–	–	–	–	–
Saami (Northern)	SNO	0	–	–	–	–	–	–	–	0	–	–	–	–	–
Salt-Yui	SYU	0	–	–	–	–	–	–	–	0	–	–	–	–	–
Sangu	SGU	1	←	+	–	+	–	–	–	0	–	–	–	–	0
Sanuma	SNM	0	–	–	–	–	–	–	–	3	→	+	+	–	0
Selknam	SEL	0	–	–	–	–	–	–	–	0	–	–	–	–	–
Selkup	SKP	0	–	–	–	–	–	–	–	0	–	–	–	–	–
Sentani	SNT	0	–	–	–	–	–	–	–	6	→	+	+	+	0
Shoshone	SHO	2	→	+	–	+	–	–	+	6	→	+	+	–	2
Siar	SIR	0	–	–	–	–	–	–	–	0	–	–	–	–	–
Siuslaw	SIU	0	–	–	–	–	–	–	–	0	–	–	–	–	–
Slave	SLA	0	–	–	–	–	–	–	–	50+	←	+	–	+	0
So	SO	0	–	–	–	–	–	–	–	2	→	+	+	–	0
Somali	SOM	0	–	–	–	–	–	–	–	0	–	–	–	–	–

2 A cross-linguistic survey of Associated Motion and Directionals —— 79

(continued)

Language	WALS	AM	⇄	ITV	VEN	PR	CONC	SUBS	RT	DIR	⇄	ITV	VEN	VERT	∩
Southeast Ambrym	SEA	0	–	–	–	–	–	–	–	0	–	–	–	–	–
Spanish	SPA	0	–	–	–	–	–	–	–	0	–	–	–	–	–
Squamish	SQU	2	←	+	+	+	–	–	–	2	←	+	+	–	2
Sudest	SUD	1	←	–	–	+	–	–	–	7	⇄	+	+	+	1
Suena	SUE	0	–	–	–	–	–	–	–	0	–	–	–	–	–
Sundanese	SUN	0	–	–	–	–	–	–	–	0	–	–	–	–	–
Supyire	SUP	0	–	–	–	–	–	–	–	0	–	–	–	–	–
Swahili	SWA	1	←	+	–	+	–	–	–	0	–	–	–	–	0
Taba	TAB	0	–	–	–	–	–	–	–	0	–	–	–	–	–
Tagalog	TAG	0	–	–	–	–	–	–	–	0	–	–	–	–	–
Taiof	TAF	0	–	–	–	–	–	–	–	0	–	–	–	–	–
Tamabo	TMM	0	–	–	–	–	–	–	–	0	–	–	–	–	–
Tamil	TML	0	–	–	–	–	–	–	–	0	–	–	–	–	–
Tarao	TAO	0	–	–	–	–	–	–	–	2	←	–	–	+	0
Tauya	TAU	0	–	–	–	–	–	–	–	0	–	–	–	–	–
Tepehuan (Southeastern)	TPS	2	→	–	–	–	+	–	–	3	⇄	+	+	+	1
Teribe	TRB	0	–	–	–	–	–	–	–	0	–	–	–	–	–
Tetun	TTN	0	–	–	–	–	–	–	–	0	–	–	–	–	–
Thai	THA	0	–	–	–	–	–	–	–	0	–	–	–	–	–
Thompson	THO	1	→	+	–	+	–	–	–	0	–	–	–	–	0
Tibetan (Shigatse)	TIS	1	→	–	+	+	–	–	–	0	–	–	–	–	0
Tidore	TID	0	–	–	–	–	–	–	–	7	→	+	+	+	0
Tigrinya	TIG	0	–	–	–	–	–	–	–	0	–	–	–	–	–
Tikar	TIK	0	–	–	–	–	–	–	–	2	→	+	+	–	0
Tinrin	TIN	0	–	–	–	–	–	–	–	6	→	+	+	+	0
Tiwi	TIW	2	←	+	–	+	+	–	–	2	⇌	+	–	–	1
Tobelo	TLO	0	–	–	–	–	–	–	–	6	→	+	+	+	0
Tommo So	TMS	0	–	–	–	–	–	–	–	0	–	–	–	–	–
Totonac (Xicotepec de Juárez)	TXJ	3	⇄	–	–	–	+	–	+	1	←	–	–	–	0
Trumai	TRU	0	–	–	–	–	–	–	–	0	–	–	–	–	–
Tsat	TST	0	–	–	–	–	–	–	–	0	–	–	–	–	–
Tugun	TGN	0	–	–	–	–	–	–	–	0	–	–	–	–	–
Tukang Besi	TUK	0	–	–	–	–	–	–	–	0	–	–	–	–	–

(continued)

Language	WALS	AM	⇆	ITV	VEN	PR	CONC	SUBS	RT	DIR	⇆	ITV	VEN	VERT	∩
Turkish	TUR	0	–	–	–	–	–	–	–	0	–	–	–	–	–
Tuvaluan	TVL	0	–	–	–	–	–	–	–	0	–	–	–	–	–
Tzutujil	TZU	2	←	+	+	+	–	–	–	0	–	–	–	–	0
Udihe	UDH	2	→	–	–	+	–	+	–	0	–	–	–	–	0
Udmurt	UDM	0	–	–	–	–	–	–	–	0	–	–	–	–	–
Ulithian	ULI	0	–	–	–	–	–	–	–	0	–	–	–	–	–
Upper Kuskokwim	UKU	0	–	–	–	–	–	–	–	16+	←	+	–	+	0
Urubú-Kaapor	URK	0	–	–	–	–	–	–	–	0	–	–	–	–	–
Usan	USA	0	–	–	–	–	–	–	–	0	–	–	–	–	–
Vafsi	VAF	0	–	–	–	–	–	–	–	3	←	–	–	+	0
Vietnamese	VIE	0	–	–	–	–	–	–	–	0	–	–	–	–	–
Walman	WAL	0	–	–	–	–	–	–	–	0	–	–	–	–	–
Warao	WRA	0	–	–	–	–	–	–	–	0	–	–	–	–	–
Wardaman	WRD	0	–	–	–	–	–	–	–	0	–	–	–	–	–
Wari'	WAR	0	–	–	–	–	–	–	–	2	→	+	+	–	0
Wichí	WCH	0	–	–	–	–	–	–	–	3	→	+	–	+	0
Wichita	WIC	0	–	–	–	–	–	–	–	0	–	–	–	–	–
Wolof	WLF	2	→	+	+	+	–	–	–	0	–	–	–	–	0
Yagua	YAG	8	→	+	+	+	+	+	–	0	–	–	–	–	0
Yaqui	YAQ	4	→	–	–	+	+	–	–	0	–	–	–	–	0
Yawelmani	YWL	0	–	–	–	–	–	–	–	0	–	–	–	–	–
Yawuru	YWR	0	–	–	–	–	–	–	–	0	–	–	–	–	–
Yidiny	YID	2	→	+	+	+	+	–	–	0	–	–	–	–	0
Yimas	YIM	0	–	–	–	–	–	–	–	9	⇆	+	+	+	0
Yoruba	YOR	0	–	–	–	–	–	–	–	0	–	–	–	–	–
Yukaghir (Kolyma)	YKO	1	→	–	–	+	–	–	–	0	–	–	–	–	0
Zapotec (Quiegolani)	ZAQ	0	–	–	–	–	–	–	–	0	–	–	–	–	–
Zoque (Chimalapa)	ZCH	0	–	–	–	–	–	–	–	5+	←	+	–	+	0
Zulu	ZUL	2	←	+	+	+	–	–	–	0	–	–	–	–	0
Zuni	ZUN	0	–	–	–	–	–	–	–	1	→	–	–	–	0

References

Abbott, Clifford. 1981. Here and there in Oneida. *International Journal of American Linguistics* 47(1). 50–57. https://doi.org/10.1086/465673
Accattoli, Matilde & Giuseppina Todaro. 2017. Verbes de mouvement et grammaticalisation : le cas du sicilien *vaffazzu*. In Malinka Velinova (ed.), *Normes et grammaticalisation : le cas des langues romanes*, 187–210. Sofia: CU Romanistika.
Andersen, Torben. 2012. Verbal directionality and argument alternation in Dinka. In Angelika Mietzner & Ulrike Claudi (eds.), *Directionality in grammar and discourse: Case studies from Africa*, 35–53. Köln: Rüdiger Köppe.
Aoki, Haruo. 1970. *Nez Perce grammar*. Berkeley: University of California Press.
Austin, Peter. 1989. Verb compounding in Central Australian languages. *La Trobe Working Papers in Linguistics* 2(4). 43–71.
Belkadi, Aicha. 2015a. Associated motion with deictic directionals: A comparative overview. *SOAS Working Papers in Linguistics* 17. 49–76. https://www.soas.ac.uk/linguistics/research/workingpapers/volume-17/
Belkadi, Aicha. 2015b. Deictic directionality and space in Berber: A typological survey of the semantics of =d and =nn. *Corpus* 14. https://journals.openedition.org/corpus/3574
Belkadi, Aicha. 2016. Associated motion constructions in African languages. *Africana Linguistica* 22. 43–70. https://doi.org/10.2143/AL.22.0.3197351
Belkadi, Aicha. 2018. Aspects of the semantics of the Berber directionals and microvariations. In Dymitr Ibriszimow, Kerstin Winkelmann, Rainer Vossen & Harry Stroomer (eds.), *Ètudes berbères VIII: Essais sur la linguistique berbère et autres articles*, 11–26. Köln: Rüdiger Köppe.
Belkadi, Aicha. This volume, chapter 5. Deictic directionality as associated motion: Motion, complex events and event integration in African languages.
Bills, Garland D. 1972. The Quechua directional verbal suffix. *Papers in Andean Linguistics* 1(1). 1–15.
Botne, Robert. 2006. Motion, time, and tense: On the grammaticalization of *come* and *go* to future markers in Bantu. *Studies in African Linguistics* 35(2). 127–188.
Bourdin, Philippe. 2006. The marking of directional deixis in Somali: How typologically idiosyncratic is it? In F. K. Erhard Voeltz (ed.), *Studies in African linguistic typology*, 13–41. Amsterdam: John Benjamins. https://doi.org/10.1075/tsl.64.03bou
Bruce, Les. 1984. *The Alamblak language of Papua New Guinea (East Sepik)* (Pacific Linguistics C-81). Canberra: Australian National University.
Chelliah, Shobhana L. 1992. A study of Manipuri grammar. Austin: University of Texas at Austin Ph.D. dissertation.
Chelliah, Shobhana L. 1997. *A grammar of Meithei*. Berlin: Mouton de Gruyter. https://doi.org/10.1515/9783110801118
Conrad, Robert J. & Kepas Wogiga. 1991. *An outline of Bukiyip grammar* (Pacific Linguistics C-113). Canberra: Australian National University.
Craig, Colette G. 1993. Jacaltec directionals: Their meaning and their function. *Languages of the World* 7(2). 23–36.
Creissels, Denis & Alain Christian Bassène. This volume, chapter 17. Ventive, associated motion and aspect in Jóola Fóoñi (Atlantic).
Dayley, Jon P. 1985. *Tzutujil grammar*. Berkeley: University of California Press.

Di Caro, Vincenzo. 2019. Multiple Agreement Constructions in southern Italo-Romance: The syntax of Sicilian Pseudo-Coordination. Venice: Università Ca'Foscari di Venezia Ph.D. dissertation.

Dixon, Robert M. W. 2002. *Australian languages: Their nature and development*. Cambridge: Cambridge University Press. https://doi.org/10.1017/cbo9780511486869

Drabbe, Peter. 1959. *Grammar of the Asmat language*. (Trans.) Joseph Fichtner. Syracuse, Indiana: Our Lady of the Lake Press.

Dras, Mark, Benjamin Börschinger, Yasaman Motazedi, Myfany Turpin, François Lareau, Robert Dale, Owen Rambow & Morgan Ulinski. 2012. Complex predicates in Arrernte. In Miriam Butt & Tracy Holloway King (eds.), *Proceedings of the LFG12 Conference*. Stanford: CSLI Publications.

Dryer, Matthew S. 2005/2013. Prefixing vs. suffixing in inflectional morphology. In Martin Haspelmath, Matthew S. Dryer, David Gil & Bernard Comrie (eds.), *World atlas of language structures*, 110–113. Oxford: Oxford University Press. https://wals.info/feature/26A

Dryer, Matthew S. This volume, chapter 4. Associated motion and directionals: Where they overlap.

Dryer, Matthew S. This volume, chapter 13. Associated motion in North America (including Mexico and Central America).

Dryer, Matthew S. & Martin Haspelmath (eds.). 2013. *The world atlas of language structures online*. Leipzig: Max Planck Institute for Evolutionary Anthropology. http://wals.info

Elbert, Samuel H. 1974. *Puluwat grammar* (Pacific Linguistics B-29). Canberra: Australian National University.

Enfield, N. J. 2002. Cultural logic and syntactic productivity: Associated posture constructions in Lao. In N. J. Enfield (ed.), *Ethnosyntax: Explorations in culture and grammar*, 231–258. Oxford: Oxford University Press. https://doi.org/10.1093/acprof:oso/9780199266500.003.0010

Evans, Nicholas. 2003. *Bininj Gun-wok: A pan-dialectal grammar of Mayali, Kunwinjku and Kune*. 2 vols. (Pacific Linguistics 541). Canberra: Australian National University.

Facundes, Sidney da Silva. 2000. The language of the Apurinã people of Brazil (Maipure/Arawak). Buffalo: State University of New York at Buffalo Ph.D. dissertation.

Fleck, David W. 2003. A grammar of Matses. Houston: Rice University Ph.D. dissertation. http://hdl.handle.net/1911/18526

Fleischman, Suzanne. 1982. The past and the future: Are they *coming* or *going*? Berkeley Linguistics Society 8. 322–334.

Foley, William A. 1991. *The Yimas language of Papua New Guinea*. Stanford: Stanford University Press.

Forker, Diana. 2019. Elevation as a category of grammar: Sanzhi Dargwa and beyond. *Linguistic Typology* 23(1). 59–106. https://doi.org/10.1515/lingty-2019-0001

Frajzyngier, Zygmunt. 1987. Ventive and centrifugal in Chadic. *Afrika und Übersee* 70(1). 31–47.

Frajzyngier, Zygmunt. 1989. *A grammar of Pero*. Berlin: Dietrich Reimer Verlag.

Givón, Talmy. 2000. Internal reconstruction: As method, as theory. In Spike Gildea (ed.), *Reconstructing grammar: Comparative linguistics and grammaticalization*, 107–159. Amsterdam: John Benjamins. https://doi.org/10.1075/tsl.43.05giv

Groves, Terab'ata R., Gordon W. Groves & Roderick Jacobs. 1985. *Kiribatese: An outline description* (Pacific Linguistics D-64). Canberra: Australian National University.

Guérois, Rozenn, Hannah Gibson & Bastian Persohn. This volume, chapter 15. Associated motion in Bantu languages.
Guillaume, Antoine. 2000. Directionals versus associated motions in Cavineña. In Alan K. Melby & Arle Lommel (eds.), *LACUS Forum 26: The lexicon*, 395–401. Fullerton, CA: Linguistic Association of Canada and the United States.
Guillaume, Antoine. 2008. *A grammar of Cavineña*. Berlin: Mouton de Gruyter. https://doi.org/10.1515/9783110211771
Guillaume, Antoine. 2013. Reconstructing the category of "associated motion" in Tacanan languages (Amazonian Bolivia and Peru). In Ritsuko Kikusawa & Lawrence A. Reid (eds.), *Historical linguistics 2011: Selected papers from the 20th International Conference on Historical Linguistics, Osaka, 25–30 July 2011*, 129–151. Amsterdam: John Benjamins. https://doi.org/10.1075/cilt.326.11gui
Guillaume, Antoine. 2016. Associated motion in South America: Typological and areal perspectives. *Linguistic Typology* 20(1). 81–177. https://doi.org/10.1515/lingty-2016-0003
Guillaume, Antoine & Harold Koch. This volume, chapter 1. Introduction: Associated motion as a grammatical category in linguistic typology.
Guirardello-Damian, Raquel. 2012. Um estudo sobre o léxico trumai: Verbos e auxiliares de movimento. In Cristina Martins Fargetti (ed.), *Abordagens sobre o léxico em línguas indígenas*, 171–195. Campinas: Editora Curt Nimuendajú.
Hagman, Roy Stephen. 1977. *Nama Hottentot grammar*. Bloomington: Indiana University Press.
Haspelmath, Martin. 2005/2013. Nominal and verbal conjunction. In Martin Haspelmath, Matthew S. Dryer, David Gil & Bernard Comrie (eds.), *World atlas of language structures*, 262–265. Oxford: Oxford University Press. https://wals.info/feature/64A
Haspelmath, Martin, Matthew S. Dryer, David Gil & Bernard Comrie (eds.). 2005. *World atlas of language structures*. Oxford: Oxford University Press.
Henderson, John. 2002. The word in Eastern/ Central Arrernte. In Robert M. W. Dixon & Alexandra Y. Aikhenvald (eds.), *Word: A cross-linguistic typology*, 100–124. Cambridge: Cambridge University Press. https://doi.org/10.1017/cbo9780511486241.005
Henderson, John. 2013. *Topics in Eastern and Central Arrernte grammar*. Munich: LINCOM Europa.
Hernández-Green, Néstor & Enrique L. Palancar. This volume, chapter 14. Associated motion in the Otomi family.
Hewson, John & Vit Bubenik. 2006. *From case to adposition: The development of configurational syntax in Indo-European languages*. Amsterdam: John Benjamins. https://doi.org/10.1075/cilt.280
Holt, Dennis. 1999. *Pech (Paya)*. Munich: LINCOM Europa.
Hooper, Robin. 2002. Deixis and aspect: The Tokelauan directional particles mai and atu. *Studies in Language* 26(2). 283–313. https://doi.org/10.1075/sl.26.2.04hoo
Jacques, Guillaume. 2013. Harmonization and disharmonization of affix ordering and basic word order. *Linguistic Typology* 17(2). 187–215. https://doi.org/10.1515/lingty-2013-0009
Jacques, Guillaume & Anton Antonov. 2014. Direct/inverse systems. *Language and Linguistics Compass* 8(7). 301–318. https://doi.org/10.1111/lnc3.12079
Jacques, Guillaume, Aimée Lahaussois & Shuya Zhang. This volume, chapter 21. Associated motion in Sino-Tibetan, with a focus on Gyalrongic and Kiranti.
Jones, Wendell & Paula Jones. 1991. *Barasano syntax*. Dallas: Summer Institute of Linguistics & University of Texas at Arlington.

Kawachi, Kazuhiro. This volume, chapter 19. The 'along'-deictic-directional verb suffix complex in Kupsapiny.

Koch, Harold. 1984. The category of "associated motion" in Kaytej. *Language in Central Australia* 1. 23–34.

Koch, Harold. 1986. "Associated motion" in Australian languages. Paper presented at the Australian Linguistic Society, Brisbane, August 7, 1986.

Koch, Harold. This volume, chapter 7. Associated Motion in the Pama-Nyungan languages of Australia.

Lakoff, George & Mark Johnson. 1980. *Metaphors we live by*. Chicago: University of Chicago Press.

Lamarre, Christine, Alice Vittrant, Anetta Kopecka, Sylvie Voisin, Noëllie Bon, Benjamin Fagard, Colette Grinevald, Claire Moyse-Faurie, Annie Risler, Jinke Song, Adeline Tan & Clément Voirin. To appear. Deictic directionals revisited in the light of advances in typology. In Laure Sarda & Benjamin Fagard (eds.), *Neglected aspects of motion-event description*. (Human Cognitive Processing). Amsterdam: John Benjamins.

Levinson, Stephen C. & David P. Wilkins. 2006. Patterns in the data: Toward a semantic typology of spatial description. In Stephen C. Levinson & David P. Wilkins (eds.), *Grammars of space: Explorations in cognitive diversity*, 512–552. Cambridge: Cambridge University Press. https://doi.org/10.1017/cbo9780511486753.015

Lovestrand, Joseph & Daniel Ross. This volume, chapter 3. Serial verb constructions and motion semantics.

Matlock, Teenie & Till Bergmann. 2015. Fictive motion. In Ewa Dabrowska & Dagmar Divjak (eds.), *Handbook of cognitive linguistics*, 546–562. Berlin: De Gruyter. https://doi.org/10.1515/9783110292022-027

Mattiola, Simone. 2019. *Typology of pluractional constructions in the languages of the world*. Amsterdam: John Benjamins.

Michelson, Karin & Mercy Doxtator. 2002. *Oneida-English/English Oneida dictionary*. Toronto: University of Toronto Press.

Mithun, Marianne. 1999. *The languages of native North America*. Cambridge: Cambridge University Press.

Newman, Paul. 1983. The efferential (alias 'causative') in Hausa. In Ekkehard Wolff & Hilke Meyer-Bahlburg (eds.), *Studies in Chadic and Afroasiatic linguistics: Papers from the International Colloquium on the Chadic Language Family and the Symposium on Chadic within Afroasiatic, at the University of Hamburg, September 14–18, 1981*, 397–418. Hamburg: H. Buske.

Nielsen, Mads & Maria Messerschmidt. 2020. Backgrounded motion events: A crosslinguistic study of associated motion in Mesoamerica. Presented at the *53rd Annual Meeting of the Societas Linguistica Europaea (SLE 2020)*, Online, August 26, 2020. https://osf.io/tqwg3/

Nikolaeva, Irina & Maria Tolskaya. 2001. *A grammar of Udihe*. Berlin: Mouton de Gruyter. https://doi.org/10.1515/9783110849035

Nordhoff, Sebastian. 2020. Frequencies in language archives. Email. *Lingtyp: Discussion list for the Association for Linguistic Typology*. http://listserv.linguistlist.org/pipermail/lingtyp/2020-April/007777.html

O'Connor, Loretta. 2004. Going getting tired: "Associated motion" through space and time in Lowland Chontal. In Michel Achard & Suzanne Kemmer (eds.), *Language, culture and mind*, 181–199. Stanford: CSLI Publications.

Osgarby, David, chapter 8. This volume. Mudburra associated motion in an areal perspective.
Otero, Manuel A. This volume, chapter 20. At the intersection of associated motion, direction and exchoative aspect in the Koman languages.
Pakendorf, Brigitte & Natalia Stoynova. This volume, chapter 22. Associated motion in Tungusic languages: A case of mixed argument structure.
Patz, Elizabeth. 1991. Djabugay. In Robert M. W. Dixon & Barry J. Blake (eds.), *The handbook of Australian languages*, vol. 4, 244–347. Melbourne: Oxford University Press Australia.
Payne, Doris L. 1985. Aspects of the grammar of Yagua. Los Angeles: University of California, Los Angeles Ph.D. dissertation.
Payne, Doris L. 2013. The challenge of Maa "away." In Tim Thornes, Erik Andvik, Gwendolyn Hyslop & Joana Jansen (eds.), *Functional-historical approaches to explanation: In honor of Scott Delancey*, 259–282. Amsterdam: John Benjamins. https://doi.org/10.1075/tsl.103.13pay
Payne, Doris L. This volume, chapter 18. The extension of associated motion to direction, aspect and argument structure in Nilotic languages.
Peterson, David A. 2007. *Applicative constructions*. Oxford: Oxford University Press.
Reed, Lauren W. & Kate L. Lindsey. This volume, chapter 9. "Now the story's turning around": Associated motion and directionality in Ende, a language of Papua New Guinea.
Rose, Françoise. 2015. Associated motion in Mojeño Trinitario: Some typological considerations. *Folia Linguistica* 49(1). 117–158. https://doi.org/10.1515/flin-2015-0004
Ross, Daniel. 2016. Going to surprise: The grammaticalization of itive as mirative. In Jacek Woźny (ed.), *Online proceedings of Cognitive Linguistics in Wrocław Web Conference 2016*. Wrocław: Polish Cognitive Linguistics Association & University of Wrocław. http://hdl.handle.net/2142/108897
Ross, Daniel. 2021 Pseudocoordination, serial verb constructions and multi-verb predicates: The relationship between form and structure. Urbana: University of Illinois at Urbana-Champaign Ph.D. dissertation.
Sakel, Jeanette. 2004. *A grammar of Mosetén*. Berlin: Mouton de Gruyter. https://doi.org/10.1515/9783110915280
Sauvel, Katherine Siva & Pamela Munro. 1981. *Chem'ivillu' (let's speak Cahuilla)*. Los Angeles & Morongo Indian Reservation, Banning, CA: American Indian Studies Center, UCLA & Malki Museum.
Schokkin, Dineke. This volume, chapter 10. Preverbal directionals as markers of associated motion in Paluai (Austronesian; Oceanic).
Tallman, Adam J. R. This volume, chapter 11. Associated motion in Chácobo (Pano) in typological perspective.
Talmy, Leonard. 1985. Lexicalization patterns: Semantic structure in lexical forms. In Timothy Shopen (ed.), *Language typology and syntactic description III: Grammatical categories and the lexicon*, 57–149. Cambridge: Cambridge University Press.
Talmy, Leonard. 1996. Fictive motion in language and "ception." In Paul Bloom, Mary A. Peterson, Lynn Nadel & Merrill F. Garrett (eds.), *Language and space*, 211–276. Cambridge: MIT Press.
Tarpent, Marie-Lucie. 1987. A grammar of the Nisgha language. Victoria: University of Victoria Ph.D. dissertation. http://hdl.handle.net/1828/9496
Thiesen, Wesley & David Weber. 2012. *A grammar of Bora with special attention to tone*. Dallas: SIL International.

Traugott, Elizabeth Closs. 1974. Explorations in linguistic elaboration: Language change, language acquisition, and the genesis of spatio-temporal terms. In John M. Anderson & Charles Jones (eds.), *Historical linguistics I: Syntax, morphology, internal and comparative reconstruction. Proceedings of the First International Conference on Historical Linguistics, Edinburgh, 2nd-7th September 1973*, 263–314. New York: Elsevier.

Tucker, A. N. & J. Tompo Ole Mpaayei. 1955. *A Maasai grammar with vocabulary*. London: Longmans, Green & Co.

Tunbridge, Dorothy. 1988. Affixes of motion and direction in Adnyamathanha. In Peter Austin (ed.), *Complex sentence constructions in Australian languages*, 267–283. Amsterdam: John Benjamins. https://doi.org/10.1075/tsl.15.12tun

van de Kerke, Simon & Pieter Muysken. 1990. Quechua *mu* and the perspective of the speaker. In Harm Pinkster & Inge Genee (eds.), *Unity in diversity*, 151–163. Berlin: De Gruyter. https://doi.org/10.1515/9783110847420.151

VanBik, Kenneth & Thlasui Tluangneh. 2017. Directional pre-verbal particles in Hakha Lai. *Himalayan Linguistics* 16(1). 141–150. https://doi.org/10.5070/H916130390

Veerman-Leichsenring, Annette. 1991. *Gramática del popoloca de Metzontla: con vocabulario y textos*. Amsterdam: Radopi.

Vidal, Alejandara & Doris L. Payne, chapter 12. This volume. Pilagá directionals and the typology of associated motion.

Voisin, Sylvie. This volume, chapter 16. Associated motion and deictic directionals in Atlantic languages.

Vuillermet, Marine. This volume, chapter 6. A visual stimulus for eliciting associated motion.

Weber, David. 1989. *A grammar of Huallaga (Huánuco) Quechua*. Berkeley: University of California Press.

Wilkins, David P. 1991. The semantics, pragmatics and diachronic development of "associated motion" in Mparntwe Arrernte. *Buffalo Papers in Linguistics* 1. 207–257.

Wilkins, David P. 2006. Towards an Arrernte grammar of space. In Stephen C. Levinson & David P. Wilkins (eds.), *Grammars of space: Explorations in cognitive diversity*, 24–62. Cambridge: Cambridge University Press. https://doi.org/10.1017/cbo9780511486753.003

Wilkins, David P. & Deborah Hill. 1995. When "go" means "come": Questioning the basicness of basic motion verbs. *Cognitive Linguistics* 6(2–3). 209–260. https://doi.org/10.1515/cogl.1995.6.2-3.209

Winfield, W. W. 1928. *A grammar of the Kui language*. Calcutta: Baptist Mission Press.

Wolgemuth, Carl. 2002. Gramática náhuatl (mela'tájtol) de los municipios de Mecayapan y Tatahuicapan de Juárez, Veracruz. 2nd edn. México, D.F.: Instituto Lingüístico de Verano.

Joseph Lovestrand and Daniel Ross
3 Serial verb constructions and motion semantics

Abstract: This chapter investigates the expression of associated motion and directional motion in the form of serial verb constructions (SVCs). In a sample of 125 languages with SVCs, 101 have motion SVCs. The most common types are directional SVCs, in which a path-of-motion verb combines with another motion verb, and prior associated motion SVCs expressing motion prior to the activity or state predicated by the other verb in the construction. Concurrent motion and subsequent motion are much less common. In a prior motion SVC, the motion verb nearly always precedes the other verb, and the figure on the path of motion is the subject. In a directional SVC, the path-of-motion verb nearly always follows the other verb, and the grammatical function of the figure on the path of motion can vary according to the semantics of the main verb in the construction.

Keywords: serial verb constructions, associated motion, directional, typology

1 Introduction

Associated motion has almost exclusively been treated as a morphological phenomenon in previous literature (e.g. Koch 1984; Wilkins 1991; Guillaume 2016), but as a grammatical category it can be expressed in other forms. Compared to most contributions to this volume, this chapter takes a broader perspective and turns to the syntactic expression of associated motion through serial verb constructions (SVCs).[1] For many of the languages that do not have a morphological expression of associated motion, multi-verb constructions take on this role (Ross 2021).

Consider the following examples, each of which expresses prior associated motion in a different form. Example (1) is an SVC of the type that is discussed in detail in

---

[1] Other authors have made an explicit connection between associated motion and SVCs including Koch (1986), Nordlinger (2010) and Cleary-Kemp (2015). The connection was independently suggested by Patrick Caudal (personal communication).

Joseph Lovestrand, School of Oriental and African Studies, University of London, jl119@soas.ac.uk
Daniel Ross, University of Illinois at Urbana-Champaign, djross3@illinois.edu

https://doi.org/10.1515/9783110692099-003

this chapter. Example (2) is a verb-verb compound, where the verb stems form a single grammatical word.[2] Similar meanings can be expressed through pseudocoordination (e.g. English *go and get*: Ross 2016) or other constructions with an overt linking morpheme, as in example (3). Example (4) is a converb construction, in which one of the verbs is marked in a dependent, non-finite form. It also expresses prior motion.

(1) Serial verb construction: Nuaulu, Austronesian (Bolton 1990: 159)
Au **u-eu keta** sanue isa.
I **1SG-go shoot** bird a
'I'm going to go and shoot a bird.'

(2) Verb-verb compound: Rama, Chibchan (Craig 1991: 484)
naas ngulkang **alais-traal-i**
I wild.pig **hunt-walk-TNS**
'I go hunt the wild pig.'

(3) Pseudocoordination: Mayrinax Atayal, Formosan (Shibatani 2009: 256)
wah-an ʔiʔ **m-itaal** niʔ yumin ʔiʔ yaya=niaʔ
come-FOC LINKER **FOC-see** GEN Yumin NOM mother=3SG.GEN
'Yumin came to see his mother.'

(4) Converb complex predicate: Nara, Nilo-Saharan (Tucker & Bryan 1966: 330)
o go **mes-ing** ot-o
me to **speak-CVB** come.AOR-3SG
'He came to speak to me.'

Although a thorough survey encompassing all types of multi-verb constructions would be desirable, this chapter only explores the distribution of motion semantics in SVCs. In addition to expanding our understanding of associated motion beyond morphology, this study of multi-verb constructions also gives us some initial insight into the ways in which morphological associated motion is more or less likely to develop historically.

SVC is a traditional descriptive category normally reserved for constructions in which at least two verbs occur in the same clause with no morphological marker linking the verbs or indicating that one is subordinate to the other (e.g. Foley & Olson 1985; Sebba 1987; Joseph & Zwicky 1990; Lefebvre 1991b; Durie 1997; Aikhenvald 2006; 2018; Lovestrand 2021). This excludes, for example, any

---

[2] Some linguists consider verb-verb compounds to be a subtype of SVCs. We treat them as a separate type of construction. This is discussed in Section 2.

construction which requires a verb to appear in a non-finite or participial form. One way that SVCs can differ from asyndetic (unmarked) coordination of verbs is that SVCs may restrict which verbs can appear in the construction. It has long been reported that the most common type of SVC restricts one of its verbs to a class of motion verbs (Durie 1997: 310; Aikhenvald 2006: 47; 2018: 56, 156). Foley & Olson (1985: 47) call motion verbs "the serializing verb type *par excellence*."

There are actually several types of motion SVCs with different semantic properties, but this diversity is frequently glossed over, conflating distinct types of motion into one general category. In this chapter we follow the volume as a whole in making a distinction between directional semantics and several types of associated motion semantics. A directional morpheme is one that combines with a predicate that already has a motion component in its meaning, as in the SVC in example (5), which shows the combination of the path verb 'go' with the manner-of-motion verb 'run'. Typically, directionals contribute information about the orientation of the path of motion, such as deixis or relative direction.

(5) Directional SVC: Pero, Chadic (Frajzyngier 1989: 251)
 tà-yí-ù **tánà wáatò** mínà nín-cákkà
 FUT-make-FORM.B **run go** home SBJ-3M
 'He will run home.'

In contrast, associated motion is "a verbal grammatical category, separate from tense, aspect, mood and direction, whose function is to associate, in different ways, different kinds of translational motion (spatial displacement / change of location) to a (generally non-motion) verb event" (Guillaume & Koch, this volume). A prototypical parameter of an associated motion system is that it will "distinguish the time of motion relative to the main activity – whether the motion is prior to, subsequent to, or concurrent with the time of the main activity" (Koch 1984: 26). All three of these types of associated motion (prior, subsequent, concurrent) can be expressed by a restricted verb in an SVC, as shown in examples (6) through (8).

(6) Prior motion SVC: Arapesh, Papuan (Conrad & Wogiga 1991: 56)
 U-nak *w-i-chúlokuh*
 3PL.F.SBJ.IRR-go 3PL.F.SBJ.IRR-wash
 'They will go and wash.'

(7) Concurrent motion SVC: Kayardild (Evans 1995: 309–310)
 niwan-burri-yarrba **yathuyii-ja warra-ja,** jungarra-ya dulk-i
 3SG-emerge-PRECON **laugh-ACT go-ACT** big-LOC place-LOC
 'Having come out of [the sea], [Kajurkju] went along laughing...'

(8) Subsequent motion SVC: Taba, Austronesian (Bowden 2001: 354)
 n=*tua* yan n=*mul*
 3SG=buy fish **3SG=return**
 'He's returned from buying fish.'

We searched for examples of these three types of associated motion SVCs, as well as directional SVCs, in a sample of 325 languages, 125 of which have some type of SVC. An overview of the results is shown in Table 1. More detailed quantitative results are given in Section 3. We find that 101 of these languages have motion SVCs. Directional SVCs are slightly more common than SVCs that express associated motion, while 43 languages have both types. Among associated motion SVCs, prior motion is by far the most common in our results, although, as discussed in Section 3.2, it is often difficult to distinguish prior motion from purposive motion. Concurrent motion and subsequent motion SVCs are rare. There is also a type of SVC that combines a motion verb with the verb 'take' with possible subsequent motion interpretations. This construction is discussed separately in Section 3.5.

Table 1: Distributional results for types of motion SVCs in sample.

Type of motion SVC	# of languages out of 101
Directional SVC	70
Prior/purposive motion SVC	68
Concurrent motion SVC	5
Subsequent motion SVC	6

We also find that in a prior motion SVC the restricted motion verb nearly always precedes the other verb, regardless of the general word order properties of the language, and that the figure on the path of motion is always the subject.[3] In a directional SVC, the restricted motion verb nearly always follows the other verb, and the identity of the figure on the path of motion is determined by the semantics of the event.

The rest of this chapter is organized as follows. In Section 2, we further elaborate on our definition of motion SVCs, and explain how the criteria were interpreted in the process of identifying SVCs in our sources. In Section 3, we give

---

[3] As found by Ross (2021), there is a trend towards SVCs being more likely in languages with head-initial (S)VO basic word order than in languages with a verb-final, (S)OV, basic word order. However, there is no indication of a correlation between basic word order and the verb order in motion SVCs.

more background on our distributional study and present the quantitative results with subsections focusing on the distribution of each type of motion semantics. In Section 4, we show that there is a strong correlation between verb order and motion semantics, and discuss possible explanations for some exceptional cases. In Section 5, we discuss how the figure on the path of motion is identified in different types of motion SVCs. Section 6 is a brief conclusion emphasizing the importance of including multi-verb constructions in associated motion research.

2 Defining motion SVCs

In this section, we explain what criteria we used to determine whether a language in our sample is considered to have a motion SVC. We discuss some borderline cases that we have not included in our study of motion SVCs, and explain the distinction we make between SVCs and verb-verb compounds.

2.1 Defining SVCs

The definition used in this study is based on Ross et al. (2015) and Ross (2021). For a particular construction to be considered an example of an SVC, it must at least have the following characteristics: (1) two or more verbs, (2) with no marker of dependency or linking element, (3) with shared tense-aspect-modality and negation, and (4) shared arguments. While the criteria used in this definition are not all uncontroversial, they are well-grounded in the literature on SVCs (see further discussion in Ross 2021; Lovestrand 2021).

Like many traditional categories in descriptive linguistics, there is no consensus on a set of necessary and sufficient criteria by which to identify an SVC in any given language. Our definition represents a middle ground covering most of the major themes in previous descriptive and typological work on SVCs. There are both narrower and broader views of SVCs found in the literature, but we have not found them to be practical for our purposes. The number of languages in our sample makes it impractical to assume a more narrow definition of SVCs because, as others have also found, "SVCs are rarely described in sufficient detail in descriptive grammars" (Haspelmath 2016: 291). There are simply some criteria for which it is not possible to find enough information in the available source material, for example, intonation (cf. Givón 1991). On the other hand, our definition of SVCs proves to be sufficiently narrow to find strong correlations between the semantic and formal characteristics we are investigating in this analysis.

A broader definition would result in a less homogenous set of constructions with more variables to control in order to find correlations in the data.

We view verbhood as a lexical category defined on a language-specific basis using criteria such as morphology and syntactic distribution. There is a tendency for verb roots in SVCs to grammaticalize and change their lexical category which, in some cases, creates uncertainty concerning the lexical status of a particular morpheme in a putative SVC (e.g. Westermann 1930: 129–130; Ansre 1966; Crowley 1990; Hamel 1993; Lord 1993). While recognizing this potential complication, in practice, we have followed the judgement of the linguist presenting the data.

2.2 Some constructions not included in our study

Most constructions discussed under the term SVC involve multiple verb roots that are each separate grammatical words.[4] Similar constructions that have all the same characteristics as SVCs, but in which two verb roots form a single grammatical word have been called (verb-verb) compounds as a way to distinguish them from multi-word SVCs (e.g. Lord 1973; Déchaine 1993; Crowley 2002). Following these authors, we do not include single-word constructions as SVCs. Nonetheless, we recognize that some linguists do treat them as a type of SVC (e.g. Foley & Olson 1985; Durie 1997; Nishiyama 1998; Aikhenvald 2006, 2018).

The absence of any marker or linking element in SVCs has been a point of interest since the very first publication on SVCs in Akan by Riis (1854: 103), who described a "connection of sentences without any conjunction." However, as early as Hyman (1971), linguists have pointed out that there are constructions that appear to be identical to prototypical cases of serialization except for the presence of some type of linking morpheme (cf. Lord 1993: 2; Carlson 1994: 283–283; Foley 1997: 382; Shibatani 2009). While these constructions certainly merit more cross-linguistic study than they have received, for practical reasons the current study excludes constructions such as those shown in examples (3) and (4) in Section 1.

Finally, the definition of SVCs used for selecting the sample also excludes a relatively rare type of construction that uses repeated subject pronominals or tense-aspect markers that appear to be syntactically and phonologically separate from the verb, such as in example (9) where the repeated subject pronouns form a clitic cluster with a number marker.

---

4 This is assuming that it is possible to distinguish between grammatical and phonological words (Tallman 2020). In practice, we have generally followed the wordhood assumptions of the linguist presenting the data.

(9) Ambae (Lolovoli Northeast), Oceanic (Hyslop 2001: 276)
*maraga   ra=ru   mo   **singi**   ra=ru   mo   **hivo***
get.up   3NSG.SBJ=DU   REAL **sing**   3NSG.SBJ=DU REAL **go.down**
'Then the two of them sang as they went down.'

In our examination of the expression of motion, we have only included two-verb SVCs, although longer sequences of verbs can also form SVCs. For example, the Thai directional SVC in example (10) has two directional verbs following a manner-of-motion verb.[5]

(10) Thai, Tai-Kadai (Muansuwan 2001: 237)
*Piti   **dən**   **khûn**   **paj***
Piti   **walk**   **ascend** **go**
'Piti walked up, away from the speaker.'

Our definition of SVCs in no way precludes the possibility of further studies into the semantics of motion in the types of multi-verb constructions that are not included in this particular study. Further studies could show whether motion semantics are as frequently reported in other types of multi-verb constructions as they are in SVCs, and whether other constructions show the same correspondences between semantic types of motion and the order of the verbs in the construction.

2.3 Defining motion SVCs

Our focus in this study is further limited to what Aikhenvald (2006; 2018) calls "asymmetric" SVCs. Asymmetric SVCs restrict one of the verb slots in the construction to a particular class of verbs. We call this the "restricted" verb.[6] We have

---

[5] One implication of this limitation is that it prevents our study from systematically capturing the frequency of another type of associated motion in SVCs, those with explicit "roundtrip" or "interrupted motion" semantics (cf. Rose 2015; Ross, this volume). Impressionistically, this type of SVC is not as common as prior motion SVCs or directional SVCs, but it is not uncommon to find constructions that express a round trip with three verbs, e.g. 'go', 'do', 'come'. This may be most frequently used to express "fetch" events (Schalley 2003), and in some languages the construction might be restricted to this particular event. One analytical question this raises is whether these roundtrip SVCs should be considered a separate type, or an instance of a prior motion SVC embedded in a subsequent motion SVC or vice versa. Note, however, that at least some two-verb SVCs can imply a round trip. See footnote 22.
[6] Sebba (1987: 40) calls the restricted verb "fixed", and Aikhenvald (2006; 2018) calls it "minor".

made an effort to exclude cases of symmetric SVCs, such as those with resultative or sequential meaning, as well as cases of asyndetic coordination. Asyndetic coordination and symmetric SVCs allow, in principle, any verbs to occur in the construction. In contrast, the restriction on what verbs can occur in an asymmetric SVC indicates that the construction is grammaticalized in the sense that it has a specialized role in the language for expressing a grammatical function.

Out of the set of all constructions that meet our definition of an SVC, this particular study is interested in two-verb SVCs which restrict one of their verbs to a verb of motion, such as verbs glossed 'go', 'come', 'go up' or 'go in'. The verb form in question must be able to express what Guillaume (2016) calls "translational" motion (a literal change of location), but does not necessarily need to express a path of motion. While we did not specifically search for transitive motion verbs, we noted only one case where the restricted motion verb is a transitive motion verb (example (35), Section 5).[7] In every other case, the restricted motion verb is intransitive.

We exclude SVCs where the restricted motion verb has lost its translational meaning. It is relatively common for motion verbs in multi-verb constructions to take on aspectual meaning such as the verb *yà* 'come' in Khwe in example (11) which has a prospective meaning.

(11) Khwe, Khoisan (Kilian-Hatz 2006: 117)
ǹǁí̵̌ ǁgὲɛ-khòὲ-hὲ *yà* ǁʼó-à-tè
DEM female-person-3SG.F **come** die-FORM.I-PRS
'This woman is about to die.'

3 Distribution of types of motion SVCs

There have been at least three previous quantitative studies of the distribution of semantics of motion in SVCs, but with a smaller scope than our study. Maurer & Michaelis (2013) find directional SVCs in 30 of 75 creole languages examined. In a study of 16 languages of eastern Indonesia, van Staden & Reesink (2008) find prior or purposive motion SVCs in eight languages, and directional SVCs

---

[7] Example (35) shows a construction in Kayardild that uses the transitive verb 'send' to convey concurrent motion of the object in an SVC. Kayardild also has concurrent SVCs with a restricted intransitive motion verb.

in ten languages.[8] Unterladstetter (2020) expands on van Staden & Reesink's work, examining "multi-verb constructions" (MVCs) from 32 languages of eastern Indonesia.[9] Every language has an MVC that expresses prior/purposive motion, and all but one language has an MVC with directional meaning (Unterladstetter 2020: 249, 347). Verb order patterns and argument structures of motion MVCs in eastern Indonesia are shown to follow the same patterns we observe in our data (Sections 4 and 5).

Our distributional study is an extended analysis of the sample used in Ross (2021; this volume) using the same, balanced sample of 325 languages which includes the 200-language sample of the *World Atlas of Language Structures* (Dryer & Haspelmath 2013). Ross identifies 125 languages (38.5%) that have at least one type of SVC. The geographic distribution of the languages in the sample with at least one type of SVC is shown in Figure 1.[10] As can be seen in the breakdown in Table 2, the relevant subset of the balanced sample results in a relatively representative set of languages that are spread across many language families and geographic areas.[11] For more details on the language sample and the survey methodology, see Ross (2021; this volume).

We reviewed the available data on SVCs for these 125 languages and found motion SVCs in 101 of them (80.8%).[12] This confirms that motion is the most common semantic type of SVC, and provides a more precise quantification of this tendency.[13] The full record of types of motion SVCs found, language by language, is given in Appendix A. The summary is given in Table 1 in Section 1. Note that many languages have more than one type of motion SVC. Also, in some languages,

---

8 Van Staden & Reesink (2008) include verb-verb compounds in their definition. Excluding these would result in one less language with prior/purposive motion SVCs and two less languages with directional SVCs.
9 Most MVCs in Unterladstetter's data can be considered SVCs. Prior or purposive motions SVCs are considered a type of "stage-relating" construction, specifically called "motion-to-action". Directional SVCs are considered a type of "component-relating" construction divided into three types: "motion complex" (intransitive), "direction complex" (transitive) and "transport complex" (caused accompanied motion, Section 3.5).
10 This map and the similar maps below were generated using the WALS Interactive Reference Tool by Hans-Jörg Bibiko.
11 However, there is a relatively large number of Austronesian languages in the sample (52 languages of 325), and this family also has a relatively high rate of languages with SVCs (34 languages, 65.4%). For this reason, we checked our results by splitting the data between Austronesian and non-Austronesian languages, and found no significant differences in the distribution.
12 Among the 34 Austronesian languages that have an SVC, 27 of them (79.4%) have a motion SVC.
13 See Ross & Lovestrand (2018) for a comparison to the frequency of other common semantic types of SVCs.

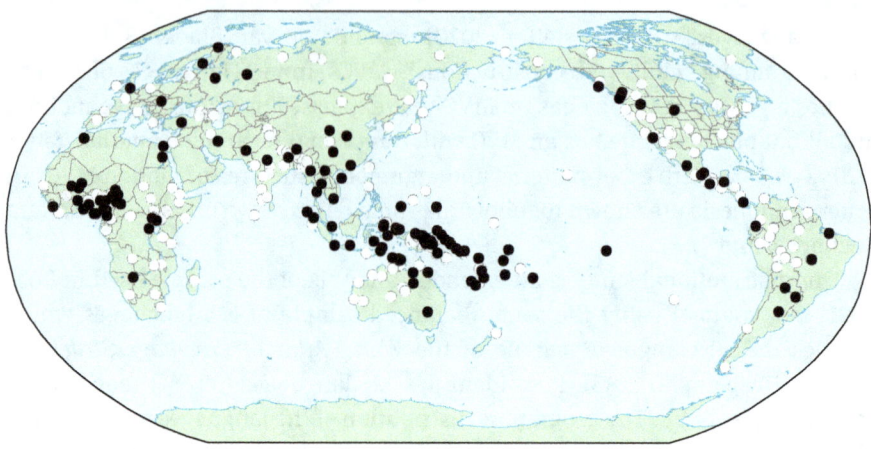

Figure 1: Distribution of languages with SVCs (Ross 2021); black = has SVC, white = no SVC.

Table 2: Languages in the sample with SVCs by geographic area and language family.

– Africa: **26**	– Pacific, PNG & Indonesia: **49**
– Afro-Asiatic, Chadic: 5	– Austronesian, Oceanic: 23
– Afro-Asiatic (other): 3	– Austronesian (other): 11
– Niger-Congo, Bantoid: 4	– Trans-New Guinea: 5
– Niger-Congo (other): 8	– West Papuan: 3
– Nilo-Saharan: 5	– Torricelli: 2
– Khoisan: 1	– other Papuan: 5
– Eurasia: **21**	– North & Central America: **13**
– Indo-European: 5	– Salishan: 3
– Uralic: 4	– Uto-Aztecan: 3
– Sino-Tibetan: 5	– Other: 7
– Other: 7	– South America: **6**
– Australia: **10**	– Tupian: 3
– Pama-Nyungan: 3	– Other: 3
– Other: 7	

one form of SVC can express more than one of the types of motion. In these cases, the language is counted as having all the types of motion SVC that the single form can express.

In addition, we find verb-verb compounds in 72 languages in the sample, including some languages that have both SVCs and verb-verb compounds. Verb-verb compounds are less common than SVCs, and the expression of motion in verb-verb compounds is also less frequent than in SVCs. We have identified 37 languages (51%) with a verb-verb compound that includes a motion verb.[14] Detailed results are given in Appendix B. However, these results may be underreported in cases where there is some ambiguity about whether a specific morpheme has grammaticalized into an associated motion marker. For example, Ross (this volume) classifies as morphology a number of forms which could potentially be called compounds (derived from motion verbs) that appear to function paradigmatically (consider, for example, Kham, Watters 2002: 107–108).[15] Further research in this area is still needed.

In the following subsections, we further explore the distribution of the four semantic types of motion SVCs introduced in Section 1, as well as caused accompanied motion SVCs involving the verb 'take'. The latter are difficult to classify, and so have been set aside as a separate category.

3.1 Directional SVCs

A directional SVC combines a path-of-motion verb with another motion verb, often one that expresses a manner of motion. The interpretation is that the two verbs describe a unitary motion event, as seen in example (12), as well as example (5) above.

(12) Egyptian Arabic, Afro-Asiatic (Woidich 2002: 181; cited in Versteegh 2009: 197)
 miši *rāḥ* *fēn*
 3SG.M.walked 3SG.M.went.away where
 'Where did he go?'

Directional SVCs are the most common type of motion SVC, found in 70 languages.[16] The geographic distribution of languages with a directional SVC is shown

---

14 Unterladstetter (2020:292, 346) finds a similar pattern in 32 eastern Indonesian languages. Motion semantics appear to be less frequent in verb-verb compounds compared to other types of multi-verb constructions.
15 The results of these two studies are complementary, with morphological markers in Ross (this volume) not considered compounds here. As with the other classifications in this sample, classifications were based on our best judgment from the evidence available to us.
16 Among the 27 Austronesian languages that have a motion SVC, 22 of them (81.5%) have a directional SVC.

in Figure 2 (black dots), contrasted with languages with motion SVCs, but no directional SVCs (white dots).

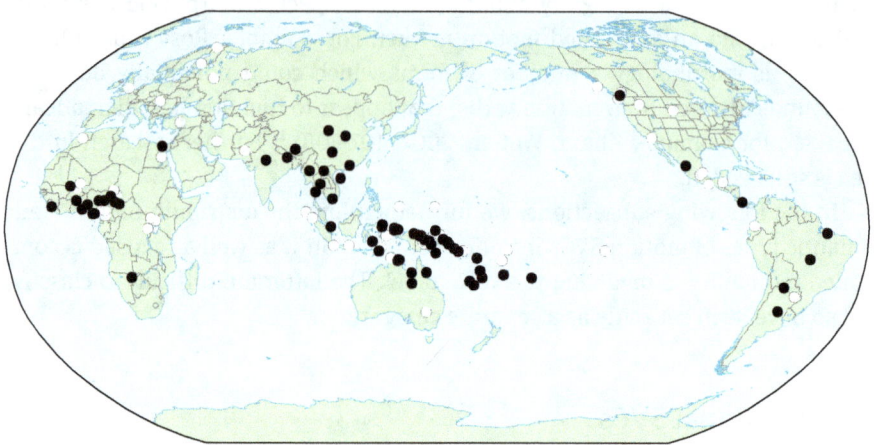

Figure 2: Distribution of languages with a directional SVC; black circle = has directional SVC, white circle = no directional SVC.

3.2 Prior motion SVCs and purposive SVCs

For practical reasons, our study conflates two types of motion semantics that are so similar that it is often difficult to distinguish them based on the information available in our sources. These types are prior motion and purposive motion.[17] In a prior motion SVC, a motion verb, typically one glossed 'go' or 'come', combines with another verb. The other verb is generally not restricted to a particular lexical or semantic class, but is typically a non-motion verb.[18] The interpretation is sequential, not simultaneous. The restricted motion verb indicates that the subject changes location before the event or activity predicated by the other verb takes place, as seen in example (13), and example (6) above.

---

[17] For similar issues in the description of morphological AM, see Ross (this volume), Pakendorf & Stoynova (this volume) and Jacques, Lahaussois & Zhang (this volume).
[18] Although prior/purposive motion SVCs typically involve a motion verb and a non-motion verb, it is possible, at least in some languages, for both verbs to be motion verbs (e.g. Lovestrand 2018: 116). Despite this, in the following discussion we use "non-motion" verb to refer to the not-necessarily-motion verb that occurs in the open or unrestricted slot of the SVC.

(13) Ewe, Niger-Congo (Essegbey 2004: 483)
 Kofi **va** **ɖe** *nyɔnu-a* (*gake wo-gbe)
 Kofi **come** **marry** woman-DEF but 3SG-refuse
 'Kofi came and married the woman (*but she refused).'

A purposive motion SVC is very similar to a prior motion SVC in that a motion verb combines with another verb and indicates a change of location of the subject (immediately) before the activity or event of the other verb takes place.[19] The difference is that, in the case of a purposive motion SVC, the activity or event predicated by the unrestricted (non-motion) verb is only intended and not asserted. Thus the two actions are not mutually contingent. Whereas a prior motion SVC might be translated into English as "go and (then) V", a purposive motion SVC could be translated as "go (in order) to V," as in example (14).[20]

(14) Sranan, Surinamese creole (Sebba 1987: 104)
 mi ben **go trow** *nanga a uma ma a no ben*
 1SG PST **go marry** with DEF woman but 3SG NEG PST
 wani mi
 want 1SG
 'I went to marry the woman, but she didn't want me.'

The difficulty in distinguishing these two semantic types stems from the fact that purposive motion can result in an implicature that the intended activity or event predicated by the non-motion verb did in fact occur following the motion. On the other hand, prior motion SVCs suggest (or may even entail) that the motion takes place for the purpose of bringing about the activity or event predicated by the non-motion verb. Presumably for this reason, free translations of these constructions are often ambiguous or inconsistent in regards to the distinction between prior motion and purposive motion.

---

19 Note that Ross (2021) excludes purposive motion from the category of SVCs because the verbs are not "mutually contingent". Since Ross' sample is the basis of this study, there is a slight possibility that a few languages which have only purposive motion constructions may have been excluded from the list of languages with SVCs.
20 A very loose reading of the definition of associated motion might allow that motion can be associated with a non-asserted purpose verb phrase. However, we do not consider purposive motion to be a subtype of associated motion. Whereas prior motion clearly associates motion with a verb event, it is debatable whether the same can be said of purposive motion.

A simple test can clarify whether the activity or event of the non-motion verb is implied or entailed. In the prior motion SVC in example (13) above, it is a direct contradiction for a conjoined clause to state that the event predicated by the second verb, *ɖe* 'marry', did not take place. The occurrence of this event is entailed by the prior motion SVC. In contrast, in the purposive motion SVC in example (14) it is possible to conjoin another clause stating that the event predicated by the second verb, *trow* 'marry', did not take place. This is because in a purposive motion SVC, the occurrence of the event is only implied, not entailed. Since this distinction is often unclear in our sources, these two types of motion are counted together as a single type of SVC in our study.

Of the 101 languages in our sample that have motion SVCs, we found a prior or purposive motion SVC in 68 of them. Only a relatively small number of sources make an explicit claim about the distinction between prior and purposive motion. We estimate that around half of these are prior motion, and half are purposive motion. This suggests that prior motion is still by far the most commonly expressed type of associated motion in SVCs, but there are too many unclear cases to make a more reliable count of each type. The geographic distribution of languages with a prior/purposive motion SVC is shown in Figure 3 (black dots), in contrast with languages that have motion SVCs, but no prior/purposive motion SVC (white dots). Note that 38 languages have both a directional SVC and a prior/purposive motion SVC, appearing in both Figures 2 and 3.

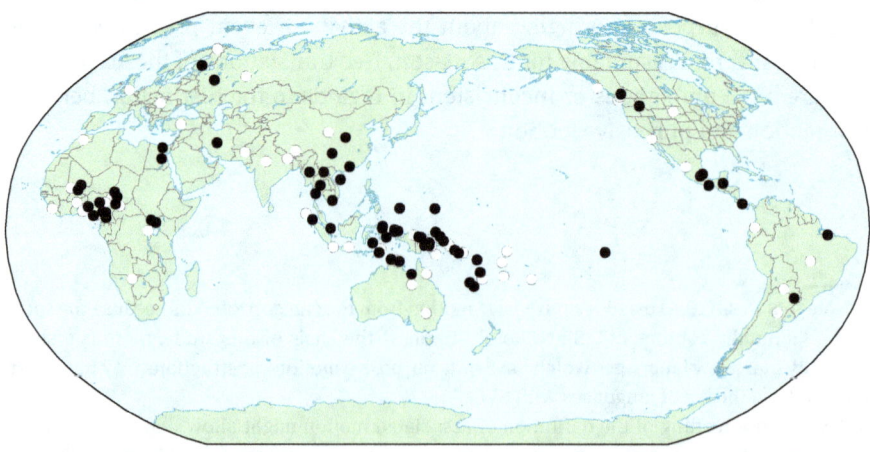

Figure 3: Distribution of languages with a prior/purposive motion SVC; black circle = has prior/purposive motion SVC, white circle = no prior/purposive motion SVC.

3.3 Concurrent motion SVCs

Among the 101 languages with motion SVCs, there are only 5 languages with evidence of concurrent motion SVCs.[21] The geographic distribution of languages with a concurrent motion SVC is shown in Figure 4 (black dots), contrasted with languages that have motion SVCs, but no concurrent motion SVC (white dots). Notably, 3 of the 5 languages that have concurrent motion SVCs are Australian languages.

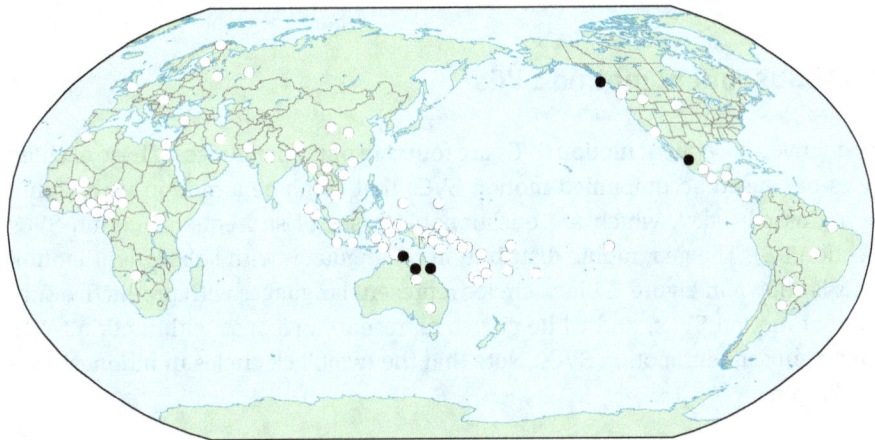

Figure 4: Distribution of languages with a concurrent motion SVC; black circle = has concurrent motion SVC, white circle = no concurrent motion SVC.

Concurrent motion SVCs are similar to directional SVCs in that the activity of the motion verb and the activity of the other verb in the SVC are understood to take place simultaneously. The distinction between concurrent motion and directional SVCs is whether the main verb can express a motion event. In a directional SVC, the restricted directional verb modifies a motion event expressed by another verb by contributing path of motion. In a concurrent motion SVC, the motion verb combines with a non-motion verb contributing a meaning like 'V while going' as in examples (15) and (16).

---

[21] Note that example (9) in Section 2.2 is semantically a concurrent motion construction, but it was ruled out as an example of an SVC since it has two independent subject pronouns.

(15) Kayardild, Non-Pama-Nyungan (Evans 1995: 309)
 jiki-ja   warra-ja   karn-ki
 light.fire-ACT go-ACT   grass-LOC
 '[They] went along setting fire to the grass.'

(16) Southeastern Tepehuan, Uto-Aztecan (García Salido 2007: 10)
 gu   chioñ su-suaki-t   jii
 ART man   REDUP-cry-PST.3SG   move.PST
 'The man went crying.'

3.4 Subsequent motion SVCs

Productive subsequent motion SVCs are found in only 6 languages. These exclude cases of caused accompanied motion SVCs that combine a motion verb with a verb glossed 'take', which are questionable cases of subsequent motion SVCs (Section 3.5). The geographic distribution of languages with subsequent motion SVCs is shown in Figure 5. Black circles represent languages with productive subsequent motion SVCs, and white circles represent languages with motion SVCs, but no subsequent motion SVCs. Note that the two black circles in Indonesia are overlapping.

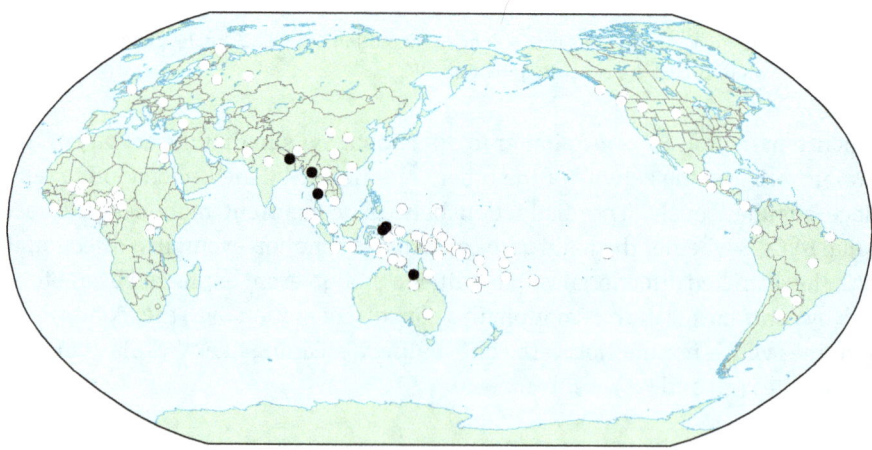

Figure 5: Distribution of languages with a subsequent motion SVC; black circle = has subsequent motion SVC, white circle = no subsequent motion SVC.

Semantically, subsequent motion SVCs are the inverse of prior motion SVCs. The motion verb in a subsequent motion SVC indicates a change of location by at least one of the arguments (immediately) following the activity or event, as in example (17).

(17) Maithili, Indo-Aryan (Yadav 1996: 203)
 pəiṛh ae-l-ah
 read come-PST-3.HONORIFIC
 'He read and came.'

Two languages spoken in the Halmahera region (Maluku Islands, Indonesia), Tidore and Taba, have a subsequent motion SVC that appears to exclusively use a motion verb glossed 'return' as shown in example (8) above.²² The restriction to one particular verb to express subsequent motion is strong evidence that this is not a case of standard meaning composition in asyndetic coordination, but a specialized syntactic construction for expressing associated motion. A similar construction in Kayardild allows the verb *danathu* 'leave' to express subsequent motion, as in example (18). In other contexts, the same construction can also express concurrent motion.

(18) Kayardild, Non-Pama-Nyungan (Evans 1995: 310)
dand-da	*jardi*	*kurulu-tha*	*mutha-ya*	*yakuri-y,*
this-NOM	mob	kill-ACT	many-LOC	fish-LOC
diya-a-nangku,	*dathin-a*	**narrkiri-ju**	**dana-thu**	
eat-M-NEG.POT	that-NOM	**bury-POT**	**leave-POT**	

 'These people killed lots of fish, more than could be eaten, they'll bury them there before leaving.'

The SVC with a subsequent motion interpretation in Pwo Karen is remarkable for being ambiguous with a purposive motion interpretation, as seen in example (19). The same structure is also used for directional SVCs, as shown in example (27) below.

---

22 Evans (1995: 308–309) discusses an SVC in Kayardild with the verb 'return' in the second position explaining that the construction expresses an intended subsequent motion, but the 'return' motion is not necessarily entailed. The construction also implies (or perhaps entails) a prior motion before the event or activity of the first verb, and is "used in describing short round trips" (Evans 1995:309). Similar interpretations of subsequent motion are discussed by Bourdin (2006) and Belkadi (2015).

(19) Pwo Karen, Sino-Tibetan (Kato 2003: 644)
  jə-yɛ.   ʔaN: mI̠
  1SG-come   eat   rice
  'I came after having lunch.' *or* 'I came to eat lunch.'

3.5 Directed caused accompanied motion SVCs with 'take'

There is a relatively common subtype of SVC occurring in at least 16 languages in our sample that combines a verb glossed 'take' and a motion verb expressing "caused accompanied motion" towards a goal (Margetts et al. 2019).[23] The geographic distribution of these 16 languages is shown in Figure 6.

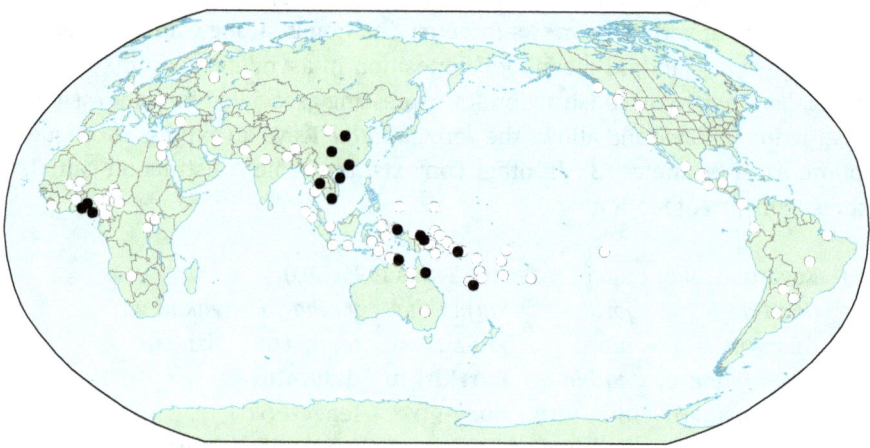

Figure 6: Distribution of languages with a 'take' caused accompanied motion SVC; black circle = has CAM SVC, white circle = no CAM SVC.

Whereas directed caused accompanied motion can be expressed by a single verb *bring* in English, the same meaning is frequently expressed by a combination of morphemes in other languages, such as the use of an SVC which combines a verb glossed 'take' with a motion verb, as in example (20).[24]

---

23 We also observe that all 16 languages with CAM SVCs also have directional SVCs, suggesting a functional or at least historical relationship between these types. See also "Comitative Subsequent Itive AM" in Ross (this volume).
24 Directed caused accompanied motion can also be expressed by an SVC with a verb glossed 'carry' combined with a directional verb. Assuming that a gloss of 'carry' indicates an unambig-

(20) Cantonese, Sino-Tibetan (Matthews 2006: 76)
 lei₅ **lo₂** di₁ saam₁ **lai₄**
 you **take** PL clothing **come**
 'Bring some clothes.'

It is unclear if these 'take' SVCs expressing caused accompanied motion can be considered a type of subsequent motion SVC, a type of directional SVC or (at least in some cases) idiomatic or lexicalized SVCs. Taking the viewpoint of a literal, word-for-word translation, these can be thought of as a type of subsequent motion SVC. First an object is acquired, and then the acquirer of that object moves in some direction together with the object acquired. However, van Staden and Reesink (2008) view these constructions as a type of directional SVC.[25] Note that for van Staden and Reesink, the main verb of a directional SVC does not necessarily have to express a motion event. In the context of our study of associated motion, their definition would blur the distinction between directional and associated motion meaning.

These caused accompanied motion SVCs might still be considered directional SVCs if verbs glossed 'take' can express a motion event. In an analysis of the semantics of taking events, Narasimhan et al. (2012: 5) offer the following definition: "Removal (or 'taking') events are events in which an agent causes an object to move away from a location." However, it is doubtful that all verbs glossed 'take' necessarily convey motion semantics, particularly in the context of SVCs. For example, in the well-known case of instrumental SVCs, as in example (21), the object of the verb 'take' has the semantic role of instrument. There is no immediate indication that this SVC should be construed as expressing translational motion.

(21) Fon, Niger-Congo (Lefebvre 1991a: 39)
 Kɔ́kú **sɔ́** àtî̃ **hò** Àsíbá
 Koku **take** stick **hit** Asiba
 'Koku hit Asiba with a stick.'

Narasimhan et al. (2012: 10) note that "some placement events involving transfer ... may additionally involve a notion of possession that causes such scenes to be excluded from the category of 'placement'." In other words, at least in some

---

uous motion verb, we consider SVCs like example (30) to be a type of directional SVC. In this section, we are only interested in the analysis of SVCs that use a verb glossed 'take'.
25 Unterladstetter (2019:303–305) also groups caused accompanied motion constructions with constructions we consider directional, but concedes that the evidence for this analysis is less than clear. See also Dryer's discussion of Huasteca Nahuatl in Chapter 4 of this volume.

contexts, a verb glossed 'take' might be conceived of as expressing possession instead of a removal event. Making a distinction between 'take' as a motion or a non-motion verb would require a precise analysis of the lexical semantics of the verb 'take' in SVCs in different languages. This is beyond what can be accomplished in this analysis, and so these examples are set aside as interesting data for future study.

A further issue with caused accompanied motion SVCs is that of restriction and productivity. Our focus is on asymmetric SVCs which restrict one verb to a class of motion verbs. However, in at least some languages, there is a type of SVC where the verb 'take' is the restricted verb that can be combined with an unrestricted number of main verbs, including motion verbs (Shluinsky 2017; Lee 2019). This is the case in Fon, as shown in examples (21) and (22).[26] Strictly speaking, the SVC in example (22a) does not meet our definition of a motion SVC, since it is not the motion verb that is in the restricted position in the construction.

(22) Fon, Niger-Congo (Lefebvre 1991a: 39)
    a. *Kɔ́kú* **sɔ́** *àsɔ̃́* **yì** *àxì*
       Koku **take** crab **go** market
       'Koku brought the crab to the market.'

    b. *Kɔ́kú* **sɔ́** *àsɔ̃́* **ɖó** *távò-jĭ*
       Koku **take** crab **put** table-on
       'Koku put the crab on the table.'

    c. *Kɔ́kú* **sɔ́** *àsɔ̃́* **nà** *Àsíbá*
       Koku **take** crab **give** Asiba
       'Koku gave the crab to Asiba.'

3.6 Discussion

The distribution of associated motion semantics in SVCs is roughly similar to the distribution of motion semantics in verbal affixes (Guillaume 2016; Ross, this volume). Among associated motion affixes, prior motion is the most common, while concurrent and subsequent motion are relatively rare. However, the most common type of motion SVCs are not associated motion SVCs, but directional SVCs. The high frequency of directional SVCs can be partially accounted for by assuming that the semantics of direction (the goal of motion) is intrinsically

---

[26] Lefebvre (1991b) argues that all of the main verbs in these 'take' SVCs, including the verb hò 'hit', are verbs of motion expressing a "change of location".

related to result semantics (Talmy 2000; Beavers, Levin & Tham 2010). Observing that there is an apparent restriction against (or very strong tendency to avoid) co-lexicalization of manner and result semantics in a single verb root (Rappaport Hovav & Levin 2010), the conclusion is that direction semantics, just like result semantics, cannot combine with manner-of-motion semantics in a single verb root. Directional SVCs are a strategy for circumventing this restriction by placing two verb roots into a single construction.

A further issue to consider is the co-occurrence of different types of motion SVCs in a single language. When a language has only one type of motion SVC, that type is normally either prior motion (30 languages) or directional (27 languages), with the exception of Haida where concurrent motion is the only type identified. On the other extreme, only one language (Kayardild) has all four types of motion SVC, and this is also the only instance of a language with both concurrent motion and subsequent motion SVCs. While the instances of concurrent and subsequent motion SVCs may be too small to draw statistical generalizations, it is worth noting that that these two rarer types of associated motion are mostly found in languages with a directional SVC (again with the exception of Haida). In contrast, only 2 of the 5 languages with a concurrent motion SVC also have a prior motion SVC. 5 of the 6 languages with a subsequent motion SVC also have a prior motion SVC.

4 Semantic types and verb order

Having established the relatively high frequency of directional motion SVCs and prior/purposive motion SVCs, we now turn to a syntactic pattern that correlates with these two semantic categories. In purposive motion and prior motion SVCs, it is nearly always the case that the motion verb is in the first position in the construction. In directional SVCs, it is normally the case that the directional motion verb is in the second position in the construction. The precise quantification of this tendency in our sample is shown in Table 3.

Table 3: Motion SVC type and verb order.

Type of motion SVC	Total in sample	Restricted verb first	Restricted verb second	Variable ordering
Directional SVC	70	6	63	1
Prior/purposive motion SVC	68	64	1	3
Concurrent motion SVC	5	1	3	1
Subsequent motion SVC	6	1	5	0

4.1 Verb order in prior/purposive motion SVCs

As shown in Table 3, of the 68 languages that have a purposive/prior motion SVC, in 64 of them (94.1%) the restricted motion verb is always reported to be in the first position, as seen in examples (6), (13) and (14) above. One of the other four languages, Kayardild, always has the restricted motion verb in the second position, as shown in example (23). Note that the same verb order is used for a concurrent motion SVC in this language, as seen above in example (15). Evans (1995: 309–210) writes: "*Warra-ja* ... as an associated motion verb it usually means 'go/come along while Ving' ... Less frequently a purposive/sequential meaning is conveyed: 'go/come to V'."

(23) Kayardild, Non-Pama-Nyungan (Round 2013: 110)
*Bardakantha   ngijuwa   **wuyiijuuntha   warrajuunth.***
belly.SEJ   1sg.SEJ   **put.POT.SEJ   go.POT.SEJ**
'I'll go and feed myself.'

The three other exceptional languages have a flexible pattern. These are Arop-Lokep, Russian and Urubú-Kaapor. Most of the examples given of prior/purposive motion SVCs in Urubú-Kaapor have the motion verb in the second position, but there is at least one example of an apparent prior/purposive motion SVC with the more iconic verb order, namely the motion verb in the first position (Kakumasu 1986: 332, 347). In Russian prior motion SVCs (often called "double-verb" constructions), either verb order is possible without any apparent change in meaning, as in example (24).

(24) Russian, Indo-European (Weiss 2012 and personal communication)
priš-li   *poznakomi-li-s'*   / *poznakomi-li-s'*
come-PAST.PL   introduce-PAST.PL-REFL   introduce-PAST.PL-REFL
priš-li
come-PAST.PL
'They came and introduced themselves.'

Arop-Lokep has two different prior/purposive motion SVCs. In one type of prior/purposive motion SVC, the restricted motion verb is in the first position, as expected, and any directional motion verb can be found in the first position of this construction. The other prior/purposive motion SVC in Arop-Lokep places an uninflected verb *pa*, glossed 'walk', after the main verb, as in example (25).[27]

(25) Arop-Lokep, Oceanic (D'Jernes 2002: 262–263)
    A-riu   ***pa***
    1SG-bathe   **walk**
    'I am going to bathe.'

In summary, the motion verb of a prior/purposive motion SVC precedes the other verb in the SVC in nearly every case, with just a few exceptions. There are other exceptions to this pattern in languages that are not included in our sample. Wambaya, an Australian (Mirndi, Non-Pama-Nyungan) language, has a prior motion SVC in which the motion verb can either precede or follow the other verb (Nordlinger 2014). There are also at least two Sino-Tibetan languages that have a prior/purposive motion SVC with the motion verb in the second position, Boro (Boro 2012) and Hakhun Tangsa (Boro 2017).

4.2 Verb order in directional SVCs

Turning to directional SVCs, we see a tendency for the verbs to occur in the opposite order. In 63 of 70 languages (90%) that have a directional SVC, the directional verb is in the second position, as in examples (5) and (12) above. In six languages, the directional verb is in the first position, and in one language the order is variable. In three of the languages that have a directional SVC in which the directional verb is in the first position, Pwo Karen (Sino-Tibetan), Lavukaleve (Papuan) and Tukang Besi (Austronesian), the construction is ambiguous between a directional interpretation and a prior/purposive motion interpretation. This can be seen in example (26) from Tukang Besi, where two possible interpretations of the construction are given in the free translation.

---

27 Although it is most frequently used as a manner-of-motion verb, in some contexts, the verb *pa* can be interpreted as a more general verb of motion (D'Jernes, personal communication). As an uninflected stem, it is difficult to establish conclusively that *pa* is a verb in this context. It may turn out to be the case that the word is better analyzed as an adverbial or other modifier in this context.

(26) Tukang Besi, Austronesian (Donohue 1999: 184)
Te   anabou iso **no-wila**   **no-kee-ngkee**   kua wunua.
core   child   yon **3.REAL-go** **3.REAL-REDUP-hop**   ALL house
'The child went hopping to the house.'
or 'The child went to the house in order to hop.'

A similar pattern is found in Pwo Karen, except that the construction does not only overlap with prior/purposive meaning, but also with subsequent motion. This can be seen by comparing the structure of the directional SVC in example (27) with the ambiguous prior/purposive or subsequent motion SVC from Pwo Karen in example (19) above.

(27) Pwo Karen, Sino-Tibetan (Kato 2003: 644)
ʔəwe.   yɛ.   **kli:**
3SG   **come**   **run**
'He came running.'

Southeastern Tepehuan has a directional SVC with a directional verb in the first position – the same verb order as a concurrent motion SVC. In directional SVCs in Mbay (Nilo-Saharan), only the verb, *tèḕ* 'go out', can occur in the first position (Keegan 1997: 86–87). Other motion verbs cannot be used.

In only one language, Kayardild, is there a productive and unambiguous directional SVC in which the directional verb always occurs in the first position. In this language, all other motion SVCs have the restricted motion verb in the second position, as in example (23), and directional SVCs have the restricted motion verb in the first position, as in example (28). In terms of verb order in motion SVCs, Kayardild exhibits the inverse of a nearly universal pattern.

(28) Kayardild, Non-Pama-Nyungan (Evans 1995: 580)
ra-yin-da   **thula-thi**   jawi-ji
south-from-NOM **go.down-IMMED** **run-IMMED**
'From the south (they) run down now.'

4.3 Verb order in concurrent and subsequent motion SVCs

Less can be said about verb order in the few examples of concurrent and subsequent motion SVCs. In three of five cases of concurrent motion SVCs, the motion verb is in the second position, and in one language it occurs in the first position. Variable verb order is reported in Southeastern Tepehuan (García Salido 2007:

8–10). In Gurr-goni, Yidiny and Southeastern Tepehuan, the verb order for concurrent motion SVCs is the same as for directional SVCs, in second position. In Kayardild, the verb order for concurrent motion SVCs (motion verb in the second position) is the same as that for prior motion SVCs, but not the same as directional SVCs (first position). In five of six languages with unrestricted subsequent motion SVCs, the motion verb is in the second position. The exceptional order is found in Pwo Karen, where the subsequent motion SVC is ambiguous with a prior/purposive motion SVC, as shown in example (19) above.

4.4 Discussion

In summary, there is a clear tendency for the motion verb to be in the first position in a prior/purposive motion SVC and in the second position in a directional SVC. The motion verb in the few examples of concurrent and subsequent motion SVCs is also usually in the second position. Verb order in prior and subsequent motion SVCs can be seen as reflex of the principle of temporal iconicity which requires the linear order of verbs in the construction to follow the chronological order of the events they represent (e.g. Tai 1985; Li 1993: 480, 500; Durie 1997: 330; Good 2003: 437, 444). However, this explanation does not account for the four languages with exceptional verb order in prior motion SVCs (Kayardild, Russian, Pwo Karen, Arop-Lokep). It is also worth noting that the verb order in prior motion SVCs does not correspond to the strong tendency for prior motion morphology to be suffixing, rather than prefixing (Ross, this volume). This suggests that it is unlikely that SVCs are a common diachronic source for prior motion morphology. Austin (1989: 68–69) notes a similar pattern in Central and Eastern Australian languages where verb order in compound verbs makes them an unlikely source for associated motion morphology.

The strong tendency for the directional verb to be in the second position of a directional SVC cannot be directly explained by an appeal to temporal iconicity because the actions associated with each verb in the construction are simultaneous. A better explanation for verb order tendency in directional SVCs can be derived by treating them as a type of resultative construction (Levin & Rappaport Hovav 1992: 265). The tendency in resultative constructions is that if the result is expressed by a single verb, the result predicate follows the cause predicate (Williams 2008).

A few of the seven cases of exceptional verb order in directional SVCs have a straightforward explanation. In three languages, the directional SVC shares its structure with a prior motion SVC. The directional interpretation is limited to when the main verb can express a motion event. The directional meaning can be seen as a type of extension of the more basic prior motion meaning.[28] Another case of exceptional word order in a directional SVC, Southeastern Tepehuan, is possibly due to directional meaning being derived from a concurrent motion SVC. Two other exceptional cases, Mbay and Arop-Lokep, are marginal examples of directional SVCs which only allow one specific verb to occur in the restricted position. We have no explanation for the exceptional verb order in Kayardild directional SVCs.

5 Identifying the figure on the path of motion

In a small number of languages with an extensive associated motion morphology system, there can be particular forms to indicate that a non-subject argument of the verb is the figure on the path of associated motion (Wilkins 1989: 293–294; Guillaume 2016: 5–6; Ross, this volume). Only in one case (example (35) below) have we found an example of an associated motion SVC that specifies that a non-subject argument is the figure on the path of motion. In the case of prior/purposive motion SVCs, the figure is always the subject, as in examples (6), (13), (14), (23), (24) and (25) above. In the case of directional SVCs, the identity of the figure on the path of motion is determined by the semantics of the event, and it is not always the subject. It is often the case that the main verb is a manner-of-motion verb with only one argument. In these cases, that single argument, the subject, is necessarily also the figure on the path of motion, as in examples (5), (12), (27) and (28) above. The main verb in a directional SVC can also be a transitive motion verb, such as 'throw' or 'send', in which the second argument is propelled along a path of motion by the first. In these cases, the second argument, typically an object, is the figure on the path of motion, as in example (29).

(29) Maybrat, Papuan (Dol 2007: 217)
t-ai bola *m-amo*
1SG-throw ball **3-go**
'I throw the ball away.'

---

28 See also Belkadi (this volume), Dryer (Chapter 4 of this volume) and Voisin (this volume). Schokkin (this volume) discusses preverbal "directionals" in Paluai that can express both prior motion and directional motion, arguing that it is a case of associated motion meaning extended from a directional marker (D-AM in the terminology of Belkadi 2015). However, the word order patterns and argument structure of the construction suggest that the construction can be equally or better described as a case of a prior motion SVC that can extend to a directional meaning (AM-D in the terminology of Voisin, this volume).

There are at least two other possibilities for the identity of the figure on the path of motion in directional SVCs. One possibility is for the figure to be both the subject and the object. This cumulative interpretation is commonly the case when the main verb is 'carry', as in example (30).

(30) Abun, Papuan (Berry & Berry 1999: 67)
An **gwat** buku **ma** mo nu
3SG **carry** book **come** LOC house
'He brought the book to the house.'

In some cases, there may be ambiguity. With main verbs like 'pull' or 'push', as in example (31), it could be understood that the subject is moving together with the object, or that the subject is propelling the object along a path of motion, but not moving itself.

(31) Fon, Niger-Congo (Lefebvre & Brousseau 2002: 423)
Kɔ̀kú **dɔ̀n** àzìnkpò ɔ́ **wá** fí
Koku **pull** chair DEF **come** here
'Koku pulled the chair over here.'

Finally, there are also cases of directional SVCs where the figure is not any of the arguments of the main verb, but the orientation of the event itself.[29] In the directional SVC in example (32), neither the subject of the verb *onoono* 'look' nor the thing being looked at is moving. The directional verb refers to the gaze itself which is abstractly conceived of as moving from the eyes of the perceiver up and away towards the thing perceived.[30]

---

29 See also Ross, this volume, on orientational uses of morphological associated motion, and Dryer, Chapter 4, this volume discussing the use of directional marker with a non-motion verb in Yakima, as well as the discussion of "emanation" in Matsumoto (2020).
30 On a strict reading of the criteria for SVCs given in Section 2.1, the construction in example (32) does not meet the "shared argument" criterion. This type of construction, and others known as "ambient" serialization (Crowley 1987: 40), are just one example of how treating the criteria for SVCs as a cross-linguistic set of necessary and sufficient conditions ends up arbitrarily dividing what is clearly a natural set of constructions in a language like Niuean. Niuean also has the more prototypical type of argument-sharing directional SVC, so in any case it counts as a language with directional SVCs. We are not aware of any language which has metaphorical/ orientational directional SVCs, but does not also have the more prototypical type.

(32) Niuean, Oceanic (Seiter 1980: 19)
Ne **onoono hake** a ia ke he mahina
PST **look go.up** ABS he to moon
'He was looking up at the moon.'

With so few examples of concurrent and subsequent motion SVCs, less can be said about how the figure on the path of motion is identified in these constructions. Generally, these constructions are more like directional SVCs than prior/purposive motion SVCs in that the identity of the figure on the path of motion is not necessarily fixed to a particular argument in the construction. In a subsequent motion SVC with a monovalent main verb, it is necessarily the subject that is the figure on the path of motion, as in examples (17), (18) and (19) above. It would be possible to have a cumulative interpretation in which both the subject and object are moving together on the path of motion, and such would be the case if the caused accompanied motion SVCs discussed in Section 3.5 are considered subsequent motion SVCs. In concurrent motion SVCs, it is commonly the case that the subject is the figure on the path of motion, as in examples (7) and (15) above. However, if the main verb in a concurrent motion SVC is transitive, it may be understood that a non-subject argument moves along with the subject, as in example (33).

(33) Kayardild, Non-Pama-Nyungan (Evans 1995: 309)
walmathi bath-in-d **burldi-burldi-ja warra-j,** burldi-ja
high west-from-NOM **roll-REDUP-ACT go-ACT** roll-ACT
birrk-i
string-LOC
'High up, moving from the west she came along, rolling string as she went.'

Example (34) is a concurrent motion SVC in which it is possibly only the object of the main verb *njirrrrerrmirri* 'pound' that is the figure on the path of motion. The subject, the rain, is large enough that it can continue to pound a moving object without moving along the same path of motion itself.

(34) Gurr-goni, Non-Pama-Nyungan (Green 1995: 261)
njirr-rre+rrmi-rri **njiwurr-ma-bay**
3SG.ERG>1PL.ABS-pound+ REDUP-REAL **1PL.ABS-go.along-REAL**
gut-djardi wana
3IV-rain big
'We went along being pelted by heavy rain.'

There is a particularly interesting type of concurrent motion SVC in Kayardild in which the figure on the path of motion must be the object of the main verb. Evans (1995: 310) describes a concurrent (or subsequent) motion SVC with the motion verb *dana-tha* 'leave' which expresses motion by the subject overlapping with (or subsequent to) the action or event of the main verb. Evans contrasts this with another concurrent motion SVC, shown in example (35), using the verb *wara-tha* 'send' which means, "V OBJ as OBJ moves away, or ... 'you look and he's going'" (Evans 1995: 310).[31]

(35) Kayardild, Non-Pama-Nyungan (Evans 1995: 310)
yan-d, ngakuluwan-ju **kurri-ju wara-thu** balung-ku
now-NOM 1PL.INCL-FUT **look-POT send-POT** westward-FUT
'Now (the short people) are looking out at us (from their hiding places beneath the cliffs) as we go westwards.'

To summarize, each of the two most common types of motion SVCs has its own way of determining the identity of the figure on the path of motion. In prior/purposive motion SVCs, it is always the subject that is the figure on the path of motion. In directional SVCs, the figure on the path of motion depends on the semantics of the event, and can be the subject, the object, cumulative or metaphorical. We did not identify any examples of directional SVCs in which the figure on the path of motion is a non-core argument. In most cases, the identity of the figure in a subsequent or concurrent motion SVC depends on the semantics of the event; however, in Kayardild there is an example of a concurrent motion SVC in which the selection of a particular verb in an SVC can determine whether the figure on the path of motion is the subject or object.

6 Conclusion

Motion semantics are very common in asymmetric SVCs, particularly in the form of directional SVCs. Prior associated motion is also relatively common, but in descriptions it is not always clearly distinguished from purposive motion. Concurrent motion and subsequent motion are rare. More frequent are directed caused accompanied motion SVCs using the verb 'take' that arguably express a type of subsequent motion. Prior/purposive motion SVCs nearly always have the

---

31 This is the one exception we noted to the rule that the restricted verb in a motion SVC will always be an intransitive verb.

motion verb in first position, and the subject of the construction is the figure on the path of motion. Directional SVCs nearly always have the directional motion verb in the second position, and the identity of the figure on the path of motion is determined by the semantics of the event. The few examples of concurrent and subsequent motion SVCs available indicate that they are more like directional SVCs than like prior motion SVCs: they more frequently occur in languages with directional SVCs, they usually occur following the main verb, and they do not always restrict the moving argument to the subject.

Having laid out a picture of the major patterns found in the expression of motion in SVCs, it is still possible that additional relevant patterns were not included in our sample. We hope that by presenting what is already commonly described, researchers working with languages that exhibit ways of expressing motion in SVCs that we have not considered here will be motivated to bring those additional data to the forefront of the discussion of the grammar of motion. Our typological study suggests some guidelines for major features to consider, such as the distinction between directional SVCs and (at least) three types of associated motion SVCs, the distinction between prior and purposive motion, verb order patterns, and the identity of the figure on the path of motion. In particular, rarer cases of SVCs in which the figure of motion is a non-subject deserve some additional attention, as well as motion SVCs with more than one restricted motion verb.

In this chapter and Ross (this volume), we have established that there is substantial similarity in the distribution of associated motion as expressed in verbal morphology and in SVCs. The same range of temporal ordering – prior, concurrent and subsequent – is found in both forms, and the prior type is most common. Non-subject associated motion also appears to be cross-linguistically rare in SVCs, as it is in morphological systems. We also note that there are very few languages that express associated motion in both verbal morphology and SVCs.[32] The evidence clearly shows that these forms are functionally equivalent, expressing the same grammatical category. A motion verb in an associated motion SVC, therefore, has the properties of a grammaticalized verb in terms of its function, even though it retains its verbal morphology and the core of its lexical meaning (cf. Cardinaletti & Giusti 2001).

Earlier work on associated motion is often explicitly limited to morphological paradigms (e.g. Guillaume 2016). This volume is more open as to the form of expression of associated motion, although the introductory chapter (Guillaume

---

[32] For discussion of languages that use both syntactic and morphological means of expressing associated motion and directional meaning, see Jacques, Lahaussois & Zhang (this volume), Otero (this volume) and Pakendorf & Stoynova (this volume).

& Koch, this volume) does not explicitly address the issue of multi-verb constructions. Some chapters refer to the expression of associated motion in multi-verb constructions (e.g. Otero, this volume), while others ignore this possibility or explicitly restrict their scope to morphological expressions. There may be practical reasons to restrict the scope of a particular study, but conceptually it makes no more sense to exclude SVCs (and other multi-verb constructions) from the analysis of associated motion than it would to exclude SVCs from the analysis of tense and aspect, or any other grammatical category frequently expressed in multi-verb constructions. Restricting associated motion to morphology significantly reduces our understanding of the phenomenon. For example, the claim by Guillaume & Koch (this volume) that associated motion has not been found in Europe should be clarified to state that the *morphological expression* of associated motion has not been found, since associated motion is expressed in multi-verb constructions in Russian, English and other European languages. This is not merely a terminological issue, but a substantive one, because the different forms express the same grammatical category. A holistic understanding of associated motion will not be achieved if its expression in multi-verb constructions is systematically overlooked.

Abbreviations

The following abbreviations are used in the interlinearized examples according to how they are glossed in the cited source:

1	first person	FOC	focus	PL	plural
3	third person	FUT	future	POT	potential
ABS	absolutive	GEN	genitive	PRECON	precondition
ACT	actual	IMMED	immediate	PST	past
ALL	allative	IMP	imperative	REAL	realis
AOR	aorist	INCL	inclusive	REDUP	reduplication
ART	article	IRR	irrealis	REFL	reflexive
COMPL	completive	LOC	locative	SBJ	subject
CVB	converb	M	masculine	SEJ	sejunct
DEF	definite	NEG	negation	SEQ	sequential
DU	dual	NOM	nominative	SG	singular
ERG	ergative	NSG	non-singular	TNS	tense marker
F	feminine	PFV	perfective		

Acknowledgements: Thanks to the participants of the ALT 2017 Workshop on Associated Motion for their insightful feedback, and in particular to Antoine Guillaume and Marine Vuillermet for their detailed constructive criticism of an earlier draft of this chapter, as well as Harold Koch and Jean-Christophe Verstraete for their helpful input on the content and structure. Naturally, the views expressed and any remaining shortcomings are our own.

Appendix A: detailed list of languages with serial verb constructions

The following table shows the distribution of types of SVCs for 125 languages in the sample. The names and three-letter codes are based on the conventions in WALS. For more information about this survey including the languages and sources, see Ross (2021; this volume). For each language, the columns indicate whether specific motion subtypes are attested (Y) or not (N). In the Subsequent column, the abbreviation "CAM" indicates that only a caused accompanied motion SVC with the verb 'take' was found, as described in Section 3.5, but no other type of subsequent motion SVC.

Language	WALS code	Prior/ Purposive	Concurrent	Subsequent	Directional
Abun	abu	Y	N	N	Y
Acehnese	ace	N	N	N	N
Arabic (Egyptian)	aeg	Y	N	N	Y
Arapesh (Mountain)	arp	Y	N	N	Y
Arop-Lokep	alk	Y	N	N	Y
Babungo	bab	Y	N	N	N
Bagirmi	bag	Y	N	N	N
Banoni	bnn	N	N	N	Y
Batak (Karo)	bkr	Y	N	N	N
Berber (Middle Atlas)	bma	N	N	N	N
Bininj Gun-Wok	bbw	N	N	N	Y
Bozo (Tigemaxo)	boz	N	N	N	Y
Brahui	brh	N	N	N	N
Buduma	bud	Y	N	N	N
Buma	bum	Y	N	N	Y
Burmese	brm	Y	N	Y	Y
Cahuilla	cah	N	N	N	N
Cantonese	cnt	Y	N	CAM	Y
Coptic	cop	Y	N	N	N
Dagbani	dgb	N	N	N	Y
Degema	deg	Y	N	CAM	Y
English	eng	N	N	N	N

(continued)

Language	WALS code	Prior/ Purposive	Concurrent	Subsequent	Directional
Erromangan	err	N	N	N	Y
Ewondo	ewo	Y	N	N	N
Fijian	fij	N	N	N	Y
Finnish	fin	Y	N	N	N
Fongbe	fon	N	N	CAM	Y
Gapapaiwa	gap	N	N	N	Y
Gola	gol	N	N	N	Y
Guaraní	gua	Y	N	N	N
Gunbalang	gnb	N	N	N	N
Gurr-goni	grg	Y	Y	CAM	Y
Haida	hai	N	Y	N	N
Hatam	hat	Y	N	CAM	Y
Hindi	hin	N	N	N	Y
Hmong Njua	hmo	Y	N	CAM	Y
Hoava	hoa	Y	N	N	Y
Hungarian	hun	N	N	N	N
Indonesian	ind	Y	N	N	Y
Itzaj	itz	Y	N	N	N
Jabêm	jab	N	N	N	Y
Juǀ'hoan	juh	N	N	N	Y
Kairiru	krr	Y	N	CAM	Y
Kalkatungu	kgu	N	N	N	Y
Kamaiurá	kma	N	N	N	Y
Kana	kan	N	N	N	Y
Karen (Pwo)	kpw	Y	N	Y	Y
Kayardild	kay	Y	Y	Y	Y
Khmu'	kmu	Y	N	N	Y
Kobon	kob	N	N	N	N
Koromfe	kfe	Y	N	N	N
Koyraboro Senni	kse	Y	N	N	N
Kuot	kuo	Y	N	N	N
Kwaio	kwa	N	N	N	N
Lakhota	lkt	N	N	N	N
Lamang	lmg	N	N	N	Y
Lango	lan	Y	N	N	N
Lavukaleve	lav	Y	N	CAM	Y
Lele	lel	Y	N	N	Y
Lillooet	lil	Y	N	N	N
Lugbara	lug	Y	N	N	N
Madurese	mdr	N	N	N	N

(continued)

Language	WALS code	Prior/ Purposive	Concurrent	Subsequent	Directional
Maithili	mai	N	N	Y	Y
Makah	mak	N	N	N	N
Mandarin	mnd	Y	N	CAM	Y
Mangghuer	mgg	N	N	N	Y
Marquesan	mrq	Y	N	N	N
Maung	mau	N	N	N	N
Maybrat	may	Y	N	N	Y
Mbay	mby	N	N	N	Y
Mocoví	mcv	N	N	N	Y
Monumbo	mbo	N	N	N	N
Mupun	mup	Y	N	N	Y
Mussau	mus	Y	N	N	Y
Nabak	nab	Y	N	N	N
Nahuatl (Tetelcingo)	nht	Y	N	N	N
Ndjébbana	ndj	N	N	N	Y
Nelemwa	nel	Y	N	N	Y
Nez Perce	nez	Y	N	N	N
Ngiyambaa	ngi	N	N	N	N
Niuean	niu	N	N	N	Y
Nkore-Kiga	nko	N	N	N	N
Nuaulu	nua	Y	N	N	N
Paamese	pms	N	N	N	Y
Palauan	pal	Y	N	N	N
Pero	per	N	N	N	Y
Persian	prs	Y	N	N	N
Puluwat	pul	Y	N	N	N
Quechua (Imbabura)	qim	N	N	N	N
Rotuman	rot	N	N	N	N
Russian	rus	Y	N	N	N
Saami (Northern)	sno	N	N	N	N
Salt-Yui	syu	Y	N	N	N
Sentani	snt	N	N	N	Y
Siar	sir	Y	N	N	Y
Southeast Ambrym	sea	Y	N	N	Y
Squamish	squ	N	N	N	Y
Sundanese	sun	N	N	N	N
Taba	tab	Y	N	Y	Y
Taiof	taf	N	N	N	Y
Tauya	tau	Y	N	N	N
Tepehuan (Southeastern)	tps	N	Y	N	Y

(continued)

Language	WALS code	Prior/ Purposive	Concurrent	Subsequent	Directional
Teribe	trb	Y	N	N	Y
Tetun	ttn	Y	N	N	Y
Thai	tha	Y	N	CAM	Y
Tibetan (Shigatse)	tis	N	N	N	Y
Tidore	tid	Y	N	Y	Y
Tikar	tik	Y	N	N	N
Tinrin	tin	Y	N	CAM	Y
Tiwi	tiw	Y	N	N	N
Totonac (Xicotepec de Juárez)	txj	Y	N	N	N
Tsat	tst	Y	N	CAM	Y
Tugun	tgn	N	N	N	N
Tukang Besi	tuk	Y	N	N	Y
Turkish	tur	N	N	N	N
Tuvaluan	tvl	N	N	N	N
Udmurt	udm	N	N	N	N
Urubú-Kaapor	urk	Y	N	N	Y
Usan	usa	N	N	CAM	Y
Vietnamese	vie	Y	N	CAM	Y
Walman	wal	Y	N	N	Y
Wichí	wch	N	N	N	Y
Yidiny	yid	N	Y	CAM	Y
Yoruba	yor	Y	N	CAM	Y
Zapotec (Quiegolani)	zaq	Y	N	N	N

Appendix B: detailed list of languages with verb-verb compounds

The following table shows the distribution of types of verb-verb compounds for 72 languages in the sample. The names and three-letter codes are based on the conventions in WALS. The format is the same as for SVCs in Appendix A.[33]

---

[33] Specifically in the case of Southeast Asian languages without verbal inflection (including Burmese, Cantonese, Hmong Njua, Karen (Pwo), Mandarin and Vietnamese), the distinction between SVCs and verb-verb compounds is not clear, such that for the current typology we have included both but elected to classify productive, compositional motion forms as SVCs.

Language	WALS code	Prior/ Purposive	Concurrent	Subsequent	Directional
Acehnese	ace	Y	N	CAM	N
Ainu	ain	N	N	N	N
Alamblak	ala	N	N	CAM	N
Apurinã	apu	N	N	N	N
Araona	ana	N	N	N	Y
Arop-Lokep	alk	N	N	N	N
Asmat	asm	Y	N	N	Y
Banoni	bnn	N	N	N	N
Barasano	brs	N	N	N	N
Brokskat	bkt	N	N	N	N
Burmese	brm	N	N	N	N
Cahuilla	cah	N	N	CAM	N
Cantonese	cnt	N	N	N	N
Chemehuevi	cmh	N	Y	Y	N
Chukchi	chk	Y	N	N	Y
Dani (Lower Grand Valley)	dni	N	N	N	N
Drehu	dre	N	N	N	N
Gapapaiwa	gap	N	N	N	N
Garo	gar	Y	N	N	N
Haida	hai	N	N	N	N
Hmong Njua	hmo	N	N	N	N
Imonda	imo	N	Y	Y	Y
Kairiru	krr	N	N	N	Y
Kamaiurá	kma	N	N	N	N
Kambera	kam	N	N	CAM	Y
Karen (Pwo)	kpw	N	N	N	N
Kâte	kat	N	N	N	N
Ket	ket	N	N	N	N
Khasi	khs	Y	N	N	Y
Khoekhoe	kho	N	N	CAM	N
Kiowa	kio	Y	N	N	N
Kombai	kmb	N	N	N	Y
Korean	kor	N	N	N	N
Korku	kku	N	N	N	N
Korowai	krw	N	N	N	Y
Lakhota	lkt	Y	N	Y	N
Lepcha	lep	Y	N	N	Y
Longgu	lgu	N	N	N	N
Mandarin	mnd	N	N	N	N
Mapudungun	map	N	N	N	Y
Matsés	myr	N	N	N	N

(continued)

Language	WALS code	Prior/ Purposive	Concurrent	Subsequent	Directional
Midob	mid	N	N	N	N
Monumbo	mbo	N	N	N	N
Mundari	mun	N	N	N	Y
Nabak	nab	Y	N	N	N
Nambikuára (Southern)	nmb	N	N	N	N
Nez Perce	nez	N	N	N	N
Ngalakan	ngl	N	N	N	N
Ngiyambaa	ngi	N	N	N	N
Nivkh	niv	N	N	N	N
Paiute (Northern)	pno	N	Y	N	Y
Pech	pec	Y	N	CAM	Y
Pirahã	prh	Y	N	N	Y
Qiang	qia	Y	N	N	N
Rama	ram	Y	N	N	N
Retuarã	ret	Y	Y	N	N
Sanuma	snm	N	N	N	N
Shoshone	sho	Y	Y	N	Y
Sudest	sud	N	N	N	Y
Tamabo	tmm	N	N	N	Y
Tauya	tau	N	N	N	N
Tugun	tgn	Y	N	N	N
Tukang Besi	tuk	N	N	N	Y
Vietnamese	vie	N	N	N	N
Wari'	war	N	N	N	Y
Wichita	wic	N	N	N	N
Yagua	yag	N	N	N	Y
Yaqui	yaq	N	Y	CAM	N
Yimas	yim	N	N	N	N
Zapotec (Quiegolani)	zaq	N	N	N	N
Zoque (Chimalapa)	zch	Y	N	CAM	Y
Zuni	zun	N	N	N	Y

References

Aikhenvald, Alexandra Y. 2006. Serial verb constructions in typological perspective. In Alexandra Y. Aikhenvald & Robert M. W. Dixon (eds.), *Serial verb constructions: A cross-linguistic typology*, 1–68. Oxford: Oxford University Press.

Aikhenvald, Alexandra Y. 2018. *Serial verbs*. Oxford: Oxford University Press.
Ansre, Gilbert. 1966. The verbid – A caveat to "serial verbs." *Journal of West African Languages* 3(1). 29–32.
Austin, Peter. 1989. Verb compounding in Central Australian languages. *La Trobe University Working Papers in Linguistics* 2(4). 43–71.
Beavers, John, Beth Levin & Shiao Wei Tham. 2010. The typology of motion expressions revisited. *Journal of Linguistics* 46(02). 331–377.
Belkadi, Aïcha. 2015. Associated motion with deictic directionals: A comparative overview. *SOAS Working Papers in Linguistics* 17. 49–76.
Belkadi, Aïcha. This volume, chapter 5. Deictic directionality as associated motion: Motion, complex events and event integration in African languages.
Berry, Keith & Christine Berry. 1999. *A description of Abun: A West Papuan language of Irian Jaya*. Canberra: Pacific Linguistics.
Bolton, Rosemary Ann. 1990. *A preliminary description of Nuaulu phonology and grammar*. The University of Texas at Arlington MA thesis.
Boro, Krishna. 2012. Serialized verbs in Boro. In Gwendolyn Hyslop, Stephen Morey & Mark W. Post (eds.), *North East Indian Linguistics*, vol. 4, 83–103. New Delhi: Cambridge University Press India.
Boro, Krishna. 2017. *A grammar of Hakhun Tangsa*. Eugene OR: University of Oregon PhD dissertation.
Bourdin, Philippe. 2006. The marking of directional deixis in Somali: How typologically idiosyncratic is it? In F. K. Erhard Voeltz (ed.), *Studies in African Linguistic Typology*, 13–42. Amsterdam: John Benjamins.
Bowden, John. 2001. *Taba: Description of a South Halmahera language*. Canberra: Pacific Linguistics.
Cardinaletti, Anna & Giuliana Giusti. 2001. "Semi-lexical" motion verbs in Romance and Germanic. In Norbert Corver & Henk van Riemsdijk (eds.), *Semi-lexical categories: The function of content words and the content of function words*, 371–414. Berlin: Mouton de Gruyter.
Carlson, Robert. 1994. *A grammar of Supyire*. Berlin: Mouton de Gruyter.
Cleary-Kemp, Jessica. 2015. *Serial Verb Constructions revisited: A case study from Koro*. University of California, Berkeley PhD.
Conrad, Robert J & Kepas Wogiga. 1991. *An outline of Bukiyip grammar*. Canberra: Pacific Linguistics.
Craig, Colette. 1991. Ways to go in Rama: A case study in polygrammaticalization. In Elizabeth Closs Traugott & Bernd Heine (eds.), *Approaches to grammaticalization*, vol. 2, 454–492. Amsterdam: John Benjamins.
Crowley, Terry. 1987. Serial verbs in Paamese. *Studies in Language* 11(1). 35–84.
Crowley, Terry. 1990. Serial verbs and prepositions in Bislama. In John W.M. Verhaar (ed.), *Melanesian Pidgin and Tok Pisin: Proceedings of the First International Conference on Pidgins and Creoles in Melanesia*, 57–90 Amsterdam: John Benjamins.
Crowley, Terry. 2002. *Serial verbs in Oceanic: A descriptive typology*. Oxford: Oxford University Press.
Déchaine, Rose-Marie. 1993. Serial verb constructions. In Joachim Jacobs, Arnim von Stechow & Theo Vennemann (eds.), *Syntax: Ein internationales Handbuch zeitgenössischer Forschung = An international handbook of contemporary research*, vol. 1, 799–825. Berlin: Walter de Gruyter.

D'Jernes, Lucille. 2002. Arop-Lokep. In John Lynch, Malcolm Ross & Terry Crowley (eds.), *The Oceanic languages*, 249–269. London: Routledge.

Dol, Philomena Hedwig. 2007. *A grammar of Maybrat: A language of the Bird's Head Peninsula, Papua Province, Indonesia*. Canberra: Pacific Linguistics.

Donohue, Mark. 1999. *A grammar of Tukang Besi*. Berlin: Mouton de Gruyter.

Dryer, Matthew. This volume, chapter 4. Associated motion and directionals: Where they overlap. Guillaume & Koch ch 1,

Dryer, Matthew S & Martin Haspelmath. 2013. *The World Atlas of Language Structures online*. Leipzig: Max Planck Institute for Evolutionary Anthropology. http://wals.info. (1 July 2018).

Durie, Mark. 1997. Grammatical structures in verb serialization. In Alex Alsina, Joan Bresnan & Peter Sells (eds.), *Complex predicates*, 289–354. Stanford: CSLI Publications.

Essegbey, James. 2004. Auxiliaries in serialising languages: On COME and GO verbs in Sranan and Ewe. *Lingua* 114(4). 473–494.

Evans, Nicholas D. 1995. *A grammar of Kayardild: With historical-comparative notes on Tangkic*. Berlin: Mouton de Gruyter.

Foley, William A. 1997. Polysynthesis and complex verb formation: The case of applicatives in Yimas. In Alex Alsina, Joan Bresnan & Peter Sells (eds.), *Complex predicates*, 355–395. Stanford, CA: CSLI Publications.

Foley, William A & Mike Olson. 1985. Clausehood and verb serialization. In Johanna Nichols & Anthony C. Woodbury (eds.), *Grammar inside and outside the clause*, 17–60. Cambridge: Cambridge University Press.

Frajzyngier, Zygmunt. 1989. *A grammar of Pero*. Berlin: Reimer.

García Salido, Gabriela. 2007. Serial Verb Constructions in Southeastern Tepehuan: A Uto-Aztecan language. In *Proceedings of the Conference on Indigenous Languages of Latin America-III*. University of Texas at Austin, October 25–27, 2007. https://ailla.utexas.org/sites/default/files/documents/Garcia_CILLA_III.pdf. (23 April 2020).

Givón, Talmy. 1991. Some substantive issues concerning verb serialization: Grammatical vs. cognitive packaging. In Claire Lefebvre (ed.), *Serial verbs: Grammatical, comparative and cognitive approaches*, 137–184. Amsterdam: John Benjamins.

Good, Jeffrey. 2003. *Strong linearity: Three case studies towards a theory of morphosyntactic templatic constructions*. University of California, Berkeley PhD dissertation.

Green, Rebecca. 1995. *A grammar of Gurr-goni*. Canberra: Australian National University PhD dissertation.

Guillaume, Antoine. 2016. Associated motion in South America: Typological and areal perspectives. *Linguistic Typology* 20(1). 81–177.

Guillaume, Antoine & Harold Koch. This volume, chapter 1. Introduction: Associated motion as a grammatical category in linguistic typology.

Hamel, Patricia J. 1993. Serial verbs in Loniu and an evolving preposition. *Oceanic Linguistics* 32(1). 111–132.

Haspelmath, Martin. 2016. The Serial Verb Construction: Comparative concept and cross-linguistic generalizations. *Language and Linguistics* 17(3). 291–319.

Hyman, Larry M. 1971. Consecutivization in Feʔfeʔ. *Journal of African Languages* 10(2). 29–43.

Hyslop, Catriona. 2001. *The Lolovoli dialect of the North-East Ambae language, Vanuatu*. (Pacific Linguistics 515) Canberra: Research School of Pacific and Asian Studies.

Jacques, Guillaume & Aimée Lahaussois & Shuya Zhang. This volume, chapter 21. Associated motion in Sino-Tibetan, with a focus on Gyalrongic and Kiranti.

Joseph, Brian D & Arnold M Zwicky (eds.). 1990. *When verbs collide: Papers from the 1990 Ohio State mini-conference on serial verbs*. Ohio State University, Dept. of Linguistics.

Kakumasu, James. 1986. Urubu-Kaapor. In Desmond C. Derbyshire & Geoffrey K. Pullum (eds.), *Handbook of Amazonian languages*, vol. 1, 326–403. Berlin: Mouton de Gruyter.

Kato, Atsuhiko. 2003. Pwo Karen. In Graham Thurgood & Randy J LaPolla (eds.), *The Sino-Tibetan languages*, 632–648. London: Routledge.

Keegan, John M. 1997. *A reference grammar of Mbay*. München: Lincom Europa.

Kilian-Hatz, Christa. 2006. Serial Verb Constructions in Khwe (Central-Khoisan). In Alexandra Y. Aikhenvald & Robert M. W. Dixon (eds.), *Serial verb constructions: A cross-linguistic typology*, 108–123. Oxford: Oxford University Press.

Koch, Harold. 1984. The category of 'associated motion' in Kaytej. *Languages in Central Australia* 1. 23–34.

Koch, Harold. 1986. "Associated motion" in Australian languages. Presented at the Australian Linguistic Society, Brisbane, 7 August 1986.

Lee, Taegyeong. 2019. *A cross-linguistic typology of 'take' Serial Verb Constructions*. University of New Mexico MA thesis.

Lefebvre, Claire. 1991a. Take serial verb constructions in Fon. In Claire Lefebvre (ed.), *Serial Verbs: Grammatical, comparative and cognitive approaches*, 37–78. Amsterdam: John Benjamins.

Lefebvre, Claire (ed.). 1991b. *Serial verbs: Grammatical, comparative and cognitive approaches*. Amsterdam: John Benjamins.

Lefebvre, Claire & Anne-Marie Brousseau. 2002. *A grammar of Fongbe*. Berlin: Mouton de Gruyter.

Levin, Beth & Malka Rappaport Hovav. 1992. The lexical semantics of verbs of motion: the perspective from unaccusativity. In I.M. Roca (ed.), *Thematic structure: Its role in grammar*, vol. 16, 247–269. Berlin: Foris.

Li, Yafei. 1993. Structural head and aspectuality. *Language* 69(3). 480–504.

Lord, Carol. 1973. Serial verbs in transition. *Studies in African Linguistics* 4(3). 269–296.

Lord, Carol. 1993. *Historical change in serial verb constructions*. Amsterdam: John Benjamins.

Lovestrand, Joseph. 2018. *Serial verb constructions in Barayin: Typology, description and Lexical-Functional Grammar*. University of Oxford PhD dissertation.

Lovestrand, Joseph. 2021. Serial verb constructions. Annual Review of Linguistics (7), In press.

Margetts, Anna, Nikolaus Himmelmann, Sonja Riesberg, Harriet Sheppard, Stefan Schnell & Nicholas Thieberger. 2019. BRING and TAKE: Caused accompanied motion events in Austronesian languages. Presented at the 11th International Austronesian and Papuan Languages and Linguistics Conference (APLL11), Leiden University, 13–15 June, 2019.

Matsumoto, Yo. 2020. Neutral and specialized path coding: Toward a new typology of path-coding devices and languages. In Yo Matsumoto & Kazuhiro Kawachi (eds.), *Broader perspectives on motion event descriptions*, 281–316. Amsterdam: John Benjamins.

Matthews, Stephen. 2006. On serial verb constructions in Cantonese. In Alexandra Y. Aikhenvald & Robert M. W. Dixon (eds.), *Serial verb constructions: A cross-linguistic typology*, 69–87. Oxford: Oxford University Press.

Maurer, Philippe, Susanne Maria Michaelis & the APiCS Consortium. 2013. Directional serial verb constructions with "come" and "go." In Susanne Maria Michaelis, Philippe Maurer, Martin Haspelmath & Magnus Huber (eds.), *Atlas of Pidgin and Creole Language Structures online*. Leipzig: Max Planck Institute for Evolutionary Anthropology. http://apics-online.info/parameters/84. (27 April 2020).

Muansuwan, Nuttanart. 2001. Directional serial verb constructions in Thai. In Dan Flickinger & Andreas Kathol (eds.), *Proceedings of the 7th International HPSG Conference, UC Berkeley (22-23 July, 2000)*, 229–246. Stanford: CSLI.

Narasimhan, Bhuvana, Anetta Kopecka, Melissa Bowerman, Marianne Gullberg & Asifa Majid. 2012. Putting and taking events: A crosslinguistic perspective. In Anetta Kopecka & Bhuvana Narasimhan (eds.), *Events of putting and taking: A crosslinguistic perspective*, 1–20. Amsterdam: John Benjamins.

Nishiyama, Kunio. 1998. V-V Compounds as serialization. *Journal of East Asian Linguistics* 7(3), 175–217.

Nordlinger, Rachel. 2010. Complex predicates in Wambaya: Detaching predicate composition from syntactic structure. In Mengistu Amberber, Brett Baker & Mark Harvey (eds.), *Complex predicates: Cross-linguistic perspectives on event structure*, 237–258. Cambridge: Cambridge University Press.

Nordlinger, Rachel. 2014. Serial verbs in Wambaya. In Rob Pensalfini, Myfany Turpin & Diana Guillemin (eds.), *Language description informed by theory*, 263–282. Amsterdam: John Benjamins.

Otero, Manuel. This volume, chapter 20. At the intersection of associated motion, direction and exchoative aspect in the Koman languages.

Pakendorf, Brigitte & Natalia Stoynova. This volume, chapter 22. Associated motion in Tungusic languages: A case of mixed argument structure.

Rappaport Hovav, Malka & Beth Levin. 2010. Reflections on manner/result complementarity. In Malka Rappaport Hovav, Edit Doron & Ivy Sichel (eds.), *Syntax, lexical semantics, and event structure*, 21–38. Oxford: Oxford University Press.

Riis, Hans Nicolaus. 1854. *Grammatical outline and vocabulary of the Oji-language, with especial reference to the Akwapim-dialect, together with a collection of proverbs of the natives*. Basel: Bahnmaier.

Rose, Françoise. 2015. Associated motion in Mojeño Trinitario: Some typological considerations. *Folia Linguistica* 49(1), 117–158.

Ross, Daniel. 2016. Going to surprise: The grammaticalization of itive as mirative. In Jacek Woźny (ed.), *Online proceedings of Cognitive Linguistics in Wrocław Web Conference 2016*. Wrocław, Poland: Polish Cognitive Linguistics Association & University of Wrocław. http://hdl.handle.net/2142/108897.

Ross, Daniel. 2021. *Pseudocoordination, Serial Verb Constructions and multi-verb predicates: The relationship between form and structure*. University of Illinois at Urbana-Champaign Ph.D. dissertation.

Ross, Daniel. This volume, chapter 2. A cross-linguistic survey of associated motion and directionals.

Ross, Daniel, Ryan Grunow, Kelsey Lac, George Jabbour & Jack Dempsey. 2015. Serial Verb Constructions: A distributional and typological perspective. Presented at Illinois Language and Linguistics Society (ILLS) 7, University of Illinois at Urbana-Champaign, April 17, 2015. http://hdl.handle.net/2142/88844.

Ross, Daniel & Joseph Lovestrand. 2018. What do serial verbs mean? A worldwide survey. Presented at Syntax of the World's Languages 8. INALCO, Paris, 3–5 September 2018. https://swl8.sciencesconf.org/data/pages/Ross_Lovestrand_SWL8.pdf. (23 April 2020).

Round, Erich R. 2013. *Kayardild morphology and syntax*. Oxford: Oxford University Press.

Schalley, Andrea C. 2003. A cross-linguistic comparison of the event-structure of FETCH: Possible coding alternatives and their realizations. *Views & Voices–Inquiries into the English Language and Literature* 1(2). 69–92.
Schokkin, Dineke. This volume, chapter 10. Preverbal directionals as markers of associated motion in Paluai (Austronesian; Oceanic).
Sebba, Mark. 1987. *The syntax of serial verbs: An investigation into serialisation in Sranan and other languages*. Amsterdam: John Benjamins.
Seiter, William J. 1980. *Studies in Niuean syntax*. New York: Garland.
Shibatani, Masayoshi. 2009. On the form of complex predicates: Toward demystifying serial verbs. In Johannes Helmbrecht (ed.), *Form and function in language research*, 309–336. Berlin: Mouton de Gruyter.
Shluinsky, Andrey. 2017. An intragenetic typology of Kwa serial verb constructions. *Linguistic Typology* 21(2). 333–385.
Staden, Miriam van & G Reesink. 2008. Serial verb constructions in a linguistic area. In Gunter Senft (ed.), *Serial verb constructions in Austronesian and Papuan languages*, 17–54. Canberra: Pacific Linguistics.
Tai, James H.-Y. 1985. Temporal sequence and Chinese word order. In John Haiman (ed.), *Iconicity in syntax: Proceedings of a Symposium on Iconicity in Syntax, Stanford, June 24–6, 1983*, 49–72. Amsterdam: John Benjamins.
Tallman, Adam J. R. 2020. Beyond grammatical and phonological words. *Language and Linguistics Compass* 14(2).
Talmy, Leonard. 2000. *Toward a cognitive semantics*. Cambridge, MA: MIT Press.
Tucker, Archibald N & Margaret A Bryan. 1966. *Linguistic analyses: The non-Bantu languages of north-eastern Africa*. London: Oxford University Press.
Unterladstetter, Volker. 2020. *Multi-verb constructions in Eastern Indonesia*. Berlin: Language Science Press.
Versteegh, Kees. 2009. Serial verbs. In Kees Versteegh (ed.), *Encyclopedia of Arabic language and linguistics*, vol. 4, 195–199. Leiden: Brill.
Voisin, Sylvie. This volume, chapter 16. Associated motion and deictic directionals in Atlantic languages.
Watters, David E. 2002. *A grammar of Kham*. Cambridge: Cambridge University Press.
Weiss, Daniel. 2012. Verb serialization in northeast Europe: The case of Russian and its Finno-Ugric neighbours. In Björn Wiemer, Bernhard Wälchli & Björn Hansen (eds.), *Grammatical replication and borrowability in language contact*, 611–646. Berlin: De Gruyter.
Westermann, Dietrich. 1930. *A study of the Ewe language*. Translated by A.L. Bickford-Smith. London: Oxford University Press.
Wilkins, David P. 1989. *Mparntwe Arrernte (Aranda): Studies in the structure and semantics of grammar*. Canberra: Australian National University PhD dissertation.
Wilkins, David P. 1991. The semantics, pragmatics and diachronic development of 'associated motion' in Mparntwe Arrernte. *Buffalo Papers in Linguistics* 1. 207–257.
Williams, Alexander. 2008. Word order in resultatives. In Charles B Chang & Hannah J Haynie (eds.), *Proceedings of the 26th West Coast Conference on Formal Linguistics, Somervillie, MA*, 507–515. Somerville, MA: Cascadilla Press.
Woidich, Manfred. 2002. Verbalphrasen mit asyndetischem perfekt im Ägyptisch-Arabischen. *Estudios de dialectología norteafricana y andalusí* 6. 121–192.
Yadav, Ramawatar. 1996. *A reference grammar of Maithili*. Berlin: Mouton de Gruyter.

Matthew S. Dryer
4 Associated motion and directionals: where they overlap

Abstract: The literature frequently distinguishes associated motion morphemes from directional morphemes. The goal of this chapter is to provide evidence that it is not uncommon for languages to use the same morphemes to cover both of these functions, coding associated motion with non-motion verbs and direction with motion verbs. In fact, it seems to be more common for a language to use a morpheme either for associated motion or as a directional than it is for a language to use a morpheme that covers more than one type of associated motion. While this could be interpreted as an argument that directionals ought to be treated as a type of associated motion, this chapter argues that the frequency of morphemes that function either as markers of associated motion simply reflects the naturalness of extending markers of associated motion to use as directionals.

Keywords: associated motion, directional, ventive, andative

1 Introduction

The general notion of associated motion morphemes (hereafter AM) is that they are morphemes that add a motion event to the event denoted by the verb, typically though not necessarily combining with non-motion verbs. Guillaume (2013, 2016), like Koch (1984) among others, distinguishes them from directional morphemes, morphemes that combine only with verbs of motion to denote the direction of motion.[1] Conceptually, this makes sense since AM morphemes add a meaning of motion to the verb they combine with while directional morphemes

---

[1] The distinction between directional morphemes and associated motion is only implicit in Guillaume (2016). His definition of associated motion morphemes as morphemes which "express motion, in the specific sense of translational motion", which implicitly excludes directionals, and his discussion of associated motion in languages in South America excludes instances of directional morphemes.

Note: Supplementary material for chapters 4 and 13 can be accessed on the publisher's website https://www.degruyter.com/view/title/569942?language=en&result=1&rskey=k0pRD4

Matthew S. Dryer, University at Buffalo, dryer@buffalo.edu

https://doi.org/10.1515/9783110692099-004

do not. The primary goal of this chapter, however, is to demonstrate that it is not uncommon for languages to have morphemes that can be used to indicate either AM when used with non-motion verbs or direction when used with motion verbs. Guillaume (2016) acknowledges the existence of this phenomenon, citing Belkadi (2015), primarily in a number of languages in Africa. The goal of this chapter is to demonstrate the fact that this phenomenon is more widespread than the existing literature might suggest. See also Belkadi (this volume, ch. 5).

This chapter discusses 56 languages in which there are morphemes that function either as markers of AM or as directionals. Among these languages, 14 are in Africa, 14 are in South America, 22 are in North America (including Mexico and Central America), 4 are in Australia, one is in Asia, and one is in New Guinea.[2]

An initial example of a language with a morpheme that functions both as a marker of AM and as a directional is Karbi, illustrated in (1) and (2). Karbi has a proclitic *nang=* that Konnerth (2014) calls cislocative, that functions as an indicator of prior AM, as in (1),[3] where it combines with a non-motion verb *làng* 'see' to yield the complex meaning 'come to see'.[4]

---

[2] The sample of languages discussed in this paper is rather ad hoc. It originally grew out of a search for languages with either associated motion or directional morphemes, based on sources for which I had a searchable PDF in which I found, in searching, various words associated with associated motion like 'motion', 'direction', 'directional', 'andative', 'ventive', 'venitive', 'centripetal', 'centrifugal' and 'cislocative' (and their equivalents in French and Spanish). The fact that the highest number of languages is in North America is probably an artifact of the fact that I have examined associated motion much more extensively in this area (see Dryer this volume, ch. 13). This study does not provide a good basis for estimating just how frequently languages have morphemes that are used either as directionals or as markers of associated motion. However, the study of associated motion in North America (Dryer this volume, ch. 13), which found such morphemes in 22 out of 94 languages, provides an estimate of the frequency in North America. Ross (this volume, ch. 2) reports that in his sample 53% of the languages with markers of associated motion employ at least one of these as a directional.

[3] The interlinear glosses used in this chapter are in general the original glosses in the source, except for (1) standardizing abbreviations for the same thing; (2) improving a few glosses, where the gloss in the source was not user-friendly; and (3) translating glosses in non-English sources to English.

[4] Some contributors to this volume (e.g. Lovestrand and Ross, this volume, ch. 3) do not consider motion with purpose to be instances of associated motion. I do not distinguish motion with purpose from motion without an implication of purpose, largely because it is in general difficult to determine from sources whether purpose is part of the morphemes in question. The fact that examples may receive English translations implying purpose may reflect nothing more than an implicature in context, rather than purpose being part of the meaning of the morpheme in question. Although the translation for (1) suggests purpose, it is clear from other examples cited by Konnerth that employ the morpheme *nang* that this morpheme does not code purpose. I suspect that morphemes that also function as directionals are less likely to code motion with purpose when functioning as markers of associated motion.

4 Associated motion and directionals: where they overlap — 131

(1) Karbi (Kuki-Chin-Naga, Sino-Tibetan; India)
   ... lasō **nang**=k-làng-dūn=ta.
       this **CISLOC**=NMLZ-see-along=ADDIT
   '... they came to watch this.' (Konnerth 2014: 232)

The same morpheme occurs in (2) as a directional, where it combines with a motion verb *sūn* 'descend' to indicate the direction of the descending as reflected by the gloss 'came down'.

(2) Karbi (Kuki-Chin-Naga, Sino-Tibetan; India)
   ... a-pō   abàng=tā   **nang**=sūn-tùk-lò.
       POSS-father NPDL=ADDIT **CISLOC**=descend-sound.of.stepping-REAL
   '... the father came down ...' (Konnerth 2014: 230)

In both (1) and (2), this morpheme has ventive meaning, i.e. motion towards the deictic centre, as reflected by the use of the English verb *come* in the sentence glosses for both (1) and (2). The English verb *come* differs from the verb *go* in that *come* denotes motion towards the deictic centre, while the verb *go* denotes motion away from the deictic centre (and sometimes just motion when the issue of motion relative to the deictic centre does not arise). Although this ventive morpheme denotes motion towards the deictic centre in both (1) and (2), in (1) it denotes such motion prior to the event denoted by the verb, while in (2) it simply denotes the direction of the motion expressed by the verb.

A second example is provided by Cora. The prefix *a'-* 'away' functions as a marker of prior AM in (3).

(3) Cora (Corachol, Uto-Aztecan; Mexico)
   áuuh víit^{y}e **a'**-u-ta-hée-va   ta-váuhsi-m^{w}a'a.
   LOC   rains   **AWAY**-COMPL-PFV-call-HAB 1PL-elder-PL
   'Go off and call back here your elders, The Rains.' (Casad 1984: 203)

This prefix is similar to the ventive clitic in Karbi illustrated in (1) in adding motion that is prior to the event denoted by the verb root (*hée* 'call'), but differs in that the motion is andative, i.e. motion away from the deictic centre.[5] This prefix is also

---

[5] Some scholars use "itive" to refer to motion away from the deictic centre and use "andative" to refer to motion without specification of whether the motion is away from the deictic centre or towards it. In my experience, it is generally difficult to determine from sources whether a morpheme is itive or andative in this broader sense, unless the language has a contrast between such a morpheme and a ventive morpheme (in which case it probably, though not necessarily, codes

used as a directional, as in (4), where it also has andative meaning, combining with the verb for 'go' to denote going away from the deictic centre.

(4) Cora (Corachol, Uto-Aztecan; Mexico)
 á'-u-ye'i-mɨ   *m^wéeci ham^wan.*
 AWAY-COMPL-go-DESID   you   with
 'He wants to go with you.' (Casad 1984: 240)

The markers in (1) from Karbi and (3) from Cora both denote prior AM, i.e. motion prior to the event denoted by the verb. In contrast, the suffix *-pia* in (5) from Imonda[6] codes motion that is concurrent with the event denoted by the verb root *ōb* 'hear'. Like the AM clitic illustrated in (1) from Karbi, it denotes ventive motion.

(5) Imonda (Border family; Papua New Guinea)
 ne-m   *ka*   *heual-ōb-i-**pia**-fna.*
 2-GOAL   1   hear-NON.SG-LINK-**COME**-PROG
 'I came here hearing you.' (Seiler 1985: 125)

The suffix *-pia* also functions as a directional, as in (6), where it denotes the direction of the flying.

(6) Imonda (Border family; Papua New Guinea)
 tetoad   *paiha-i-**pia**-n.*
 bird   fly-LINK-**COME**-PAST
 'The bird came flying.' (Seiler 1985: 108)

Note that although this suffix is like the AM clitic in Karbi illustrated in (1) in denoting ventive motion when it is used for AM, it denotes concurrent AM, while the ventive clitic in Karbi denotes prior AM. However, when these two morphemes are used as directionals, as in (2) and (6), they share the same meaning since both simply denote ventive direction of the motion denoted by the verb they attach to.

---

motion away from the deictic centre). For this reason, I use "andative" in this chapter as a label for morphemes that specifically code motion away from the deictic centre and for morphemes for which it is unclear whether they specifically code motion away from the deictic centre as opposed to coding only motion, without reference to the direction relative to the deictic centre.
6 The Imonda constructions generally involve directional-motion morphemes that also function as verb stems on their own. But in the directional-motion constructions the form consists of verb root + motion verb root forming a single verb stem and this construction is apparently restricted to compounds where the second verb is a motion verb, so I take this to be grammaticalized.

There are also languages in which a morpheme that is used for subsequent AM is also used as a directional. For example, Bole has a ventive suffix *-àakóo* that is used either for subsequent AM, as in (7), or as a directional, as in (8).

(7) Bole (West Chadic, Chadic, Afro-Asiatic; Nigeria)
    màté   à   lòoɗ-*àakóo*-yí.
    3PL   3SUBJ   ask-**VENT**-OBJ
    'They will ask and come with the answer.' (Gimba 2000: 135)

(8) íshí   à   pàt-*àakóo*
    3SG   3SUBJ   go.out-**VENT**
    'He will come out.' (Gimba 2000: 135)

Again, the use as a ventive directional has the same meaning as the directional use of the ventive morphemes in Karbi and Imonda, even though it has a different meaning when used as a marker of AM.

The remainder of this chapter is organized as follows. In §2, I discuss a refinement of the definition of the distinction between AM and directionals. In §3, I present various types of morphemes that serve both as markers of AM and as directionals. In §4, I discuss the question of how to interpret the phenomenon which such markers represent. In the Appendix, I provide a summary table of the morphemes that are used both for AM and as directionals in the 56 languages in the sample. In the Supplementary Materials,[7] I present more detailed data for the 56 languages, with relevant examples.

2 Refining the definition of the distinction between AM and directionals

A preliminary characterization of the distinction between AM and directionals is that markers of AM only occur on verbs that do not denote motion while directionals only occur on verbs that do denote motion. A better characterization, however, is that markers of AM add a motion event to the event denoted by the verb, while directionals do not, only adding direction. There are a couple of ways in which these two characterizations differ. First, there are instances of

---

[7] Supplementary Material for chapter 4 can be accessed on the publisher's website https://www.degruyter.com/view/title/569942?language=en&result=1&rskey=k0pRD4

directionals on verbs that might not be thought of as motion verbs, but where there is some motion, possibly metaphorical, denoted by the verb and the directional specifies the direction of that motion. For example, the andative suffix -*(n)kik* in Yakima (glossed 'TSL' for 'translocative' by Jansen) occurs in (9) on a verb for 'fall into water' that is clearly a motion verb.

(9) Yakima (Sahaptian, Plateau Penutian; Oregon, U.S.)
*i-xdtamalii-**kik**-a.*
3SG-fall.into.water-**TSL**-PAST
'He fell into the water.' (Jansen 2010: 109)

In (10), however, it occurs on a verb meaning 'cough', which one would not usually think of as a motion verb. It is functioning as a directional in (10) in that it does not add a motion event, but simply denotes the direction that the subject is facing when they cough.

(10) Yakima (Sahaptian, Plateau Penutian; Oregon, U.S.)
*i-kukuwi-**nkik**-a.*
3SG-cough-**TSL**-PAST
'S/he coughed (away).' (Jansen 2010: 109)

Similarly the distinction between 'buy' and 'sell' in Tamashek, illustrated in (11), involves a contrast of centripetal (ventive) versus centrifugal (andative) directionals, in terms of whether the metaphorical motion of what is bought or sold involves motion towards the buyer/seller or away from them.

(11) Tamashek (Berber, Afro-Asiatic; Mali)
a. *əžž-ənš-æɣ=ə́dd*
CAUS-be.sold.PFV-1SG=**CENTRIP**
'I bought' (Heath 2005: 602)

b. *əžž-ənš-æɣ=ín*
CAUS-be.sold.PFV-1SG=**CENTRIF**
'I sold' (Heath 2005: 602)

And the centripetal (ventive) directional form of the verb meaning 'tell' in (12) from Datooga indicates that the metaphorical motion of the thing said is going towards the speaker.

(12) Datooga (Nilotic; Tanzania)
 ándá   qáyi   g-í-rùknêaní   bìi.
 why   PAST   AFF-2SG.SUBJ-tell.CP.1SG.OBJ   Q
 'Why did you say it to me before?' (Mitchell 2015 : 261)

In all these cases, a morpheme combines with a verb that might not seem to be a motion verb. It nevertheless functions as a directional since it specifies the direction of some motion implicit in the verb rather than adding a motion event to the meaning.

There are also cases of the opposite situation, where a morpheme must be considered to be a marker of AM rather than a directional, even though it combines with a motion verb. This is the case when the motion denoted by the AM marker is a distinct motion event from the motion denoted by the motion verb. For example in (13) from Yine, the elative (andative) suffix attaches to a verb meaning 'enter', but the andative does not code the direction of the entering, but rather represents a motion event prior to the event of entering.

(13) Yine (Southern Maipuran, Arawakan; Peru)
 kosina   hima   t-çihloka-**pa**   t-nikanri-yehi.
 kitchen   QUOT   3SG.F-enter-**ELV** 3SG.F-food-LOC
 'She went and entered the kitchen where her food was.' (Hanson 2010: 161)

Hence, although the andative is attached to a motion verb, it is a marker of AM, not a directional. Similarly, in (14) from Koasati, the ventive prefix combines with a motion verb meaning 'pass through', but the ventive denotes a separate motion event that is prior to the passing through, not the direction of the passing through.

(14) Koasati (Muskogean; southeastern United States)
 ... **it-ł**opótli-t   ałí:ya-k
      COME.AND-pass.through-SS   go.SG-DISTANT.PAST
 '... and he came and passed through and went off.' (Kimball 1991: 149)

Finally, in (15) from Sochiapan Chinantec, the ventive prefix attaches to a verb meaning 'push'. If this were a directional, it would mean something like 'push this rock towards me', with the ventive representing the direction of the pushing. But in this case, the ventive motion is a separate motion event that is prior to the event of pushing.

(15) Sochiapan Chinantec (Chinantecan, Otomanguean; Mexico)
 ɲiá^M-ʔliá^H   tiá^l kḯ^H lá^M ɲiú^H.
 VENT.IMPER-push.INAN.IMPRT.2SUBJ SUPPL rock this friend
 'Please come and push this rock, friend.' (Foris 2000: 109)

The general point is that what distinguishes AM from directionals is that AM adds a motion event while directionals do not, only adding the direction of the motion denoted by the verb.

It is not always clear, however, whether a morpheme is adding a separate motion event. One situation where there can be uncertainty is cases where a verb is glossed with something like 'carry, take, bring'. Consider (16) from Huasteca Nahuatl.

(16) Huasteca Nahuatl (Aztecan, Uto-Aztecan; Mexico)
 ni-h-walika-ti-**walah**-ki.
 1SG-3SG-bring-CONN-**COME**-PAST
 'I brought it as I came.' (Beller and Beller 1979: 285)

In (16), a ventive suffix (glossed 'come') combines with a verb glossed as 'bring'. One possibility is that the ventive suffix here is simply a directional, coding the direction of the bringing. The English verb *bring* is inherently ventive, but there are other Huasteca Nahuatl examples cited by Beller and Beller (1979) with the same verb *walika* that occurs in (16) but which Beller and Beller gloss as 'take', so it could be that it is really the ventive suffix that yields the meaning 'bring' rather than 'take'.

If the verb *walika* really does represent a motion event, then the ventive suffix in (16) is probably best viewed as a directional. However, a second possibility is that the event of bringing and the event of coming should be considered two separate motion events, in which case the ventive suffix in (16) is a marker of AM, not a directional. We must be careful, however, not to read too much into the way a verb is glossed. The English verbs *carry*, *take*, and *bring* all inherently code motion, but there may be cases where a verb that is glossed as 'carry', 'take' or 'bring' can be used to include instances of holding, where there is no motion. If a ventive or andative morpheme combines with a verb of this sort, then it probably should be treated as a marker of AM rather than as a directional. In this chapter, I treat morphemes that combine with verbs glossed as 'carry' or 'take' as directionals rather than as markers of AM. However, some of these cases may turn out to be cases where the verb can mean something like 'hold', in which case the morpheme should be treated as a marker of AM.

This issue of whether there is one motion event or two arises in general with transitive motion verbs where it is the object of the verb that moves. It is not obvious, for example, whether (17) from Kaytetye should be viewed as a single event of pushing in this direction or as two concurrent events, an event of pushing and an event of coming.

(17) Kaytetye (Arandic, Pama-Nyungan; Australia)
 Mwernart-atheke erntwe-***yernalpe***-rranytye.
 this.way-toward push-**WHILE.COMING**-PROG
 '(They) are pushing (the car) this way.' (Koch 1984: 30)

Note that both the car and the ones pushing are in motion in (17) and although these two motions are causally linked, they could be viewed as separate motion events. Again, although I cite examples in this chapter of transitive verbs of motion illustrating what I claim to be directional uses, if it turns out that a particular morpheme cannot be used with intransitive verbs of motion (as a directional), I would take that as evidence that the use with transitive verbs might be better viewed as an instance of concurrent AM. Hence some of the morphemes cited in this chapter that I treat as instances of morphemes that function either as markers of AM or as directionals might be better analysed only as markers of AM. However if the type of AM coded by a morpheme is something other than concurrent AM, I take the use with such transitive verbs as sufficient evidence that the morpheme functions as a directional.

3 Different types of markers of AM that also function as directionals

In this section, I illustrate various types of AM morphemes that also function as directionals. Each of the subsections here is defined on the basis of the use as a marker of AM, the section title specifying the direction (ventive, andative, random, upward or returnative) followed by the type of AM associated with uses of that morpheme when it is used for AM (prior AM, concurrent AM, subsequent AM, or prior plus subsequent AM). For each morpheme in each language, I in general cite two examples, the first illustrating the AM use, the second the directional use. §3.1 to §3.3 discuss cases where the AM use involves prior AM, §3.4 to §3.8 discuss uses involving concurrent AM, §3.9 to §3.10 discuss uses involving subsequent AM, and §3.11 and §3.12 discuss uses involving prior plus subsequent AM, while §3.13 to §3.18 discuss uses involving more than one type of AM (like prior and concurrent).

3.1 Ventive prior motion

Examples (1) and (2) above from Karbi illustrate an instance of a ventive morpheme that can be used either as a marker of prior AM or as a directional. A second example of this is given in (18) and (19) from Tafi, where (18) illustrates the AM use of a ventive prefix *bo- ~ be-*, while (19) illustrates the directional use.

(18) Tafi (Kwa, Niger-Congo; Ghana)
 *kídēso pɪ ó-**bo**-yú ki-vu nɪ be-kusi*
 why CONN 2SG.DEP-**VENT**-dance NC-dance COMIT NC.PL-chief
 e-dzini nɪ́.
 NC-wife DEF
 'Why did you come and dance with the queens?' (Bobuafor 2013: 253)

(19) *é-dzyúī ko yɪ é-**bé**-kóéyī nɪ́ o-zi nɪ́ kɪmɪ ...*
 NC-rat just 3SG.INDEP NC-**VENT**-exit LOC NC-hole DEF inside
 'A mouse just came out of the hole ...' (Bobuafor 2013: 172)

Other examples of ventive morphemes functioning either as markers of prior AM or as directionals are provided in the Supplementary Materials, including (S85) to (S86) from Rikbaktsa,[8] (S91) and (S92) from Yanomami, (S98) and (S99) from Guatusa, (S100) and (S101) from Kekchi, (S156) to (S158) from Ineseño Chumash, (S159) and (S160) from Creek, and (S169) and (S170) from Cree.

3.2 Andative prior motion

Examples (3) and (4) above from Cora illustrate an instance of an andative morpheme that is used for both prior AM and as a directional. A second example is given in (20) and (21) from Buwal where the andative particle *āzà* (glossed 'IT' for 'itive') is used either for prior AM, as in (20), or as a directional, as in (21).

(20) Buwal (Biu-Mandara, Chadic, Afro-Asiatic; Cameroon)
 *ndā ŋ́ bān **āzà** ménégē?*
 go INF wash **IT** TAG.IMP
 'Go and wash there, won't you?' (Viljoen 2013 : 518)

---

[8] Example numbers of the form (S...), like (S85), refer to examples in the Supplementary Materials.

(21) ā-xēj āntā **āzà** skʷá?
3SG-run 3SG.POSS **IT** Q.FAM
'Did he run away?' (Viljoen 2013: 280)

Other examples illustrating morphemes of this sort in the Supplementary Materials include (S72) to (S74) from Yine, (S133) and (S134) from Shoshone, and (S149) to (S151) from Northern Paiute.

There are languages where there are pairs of ventive and andative morphemes that are used either for prior AM morphemes or as directionals. The examples in (22) and (23) illustrate this for the ventive in Nomatsigenga, (24) and (25) for the andative. (Lawrence refers to the ventive as 'allative' and the andative as 'ablative').

(22) Nomatsigenga (Southern Maipuran, Arawakan; Peru)
p-oga-og-**ap**-ima-ri-ni p-ikongiri ...
2SG-CAUS-drink-**ALL**-IRREAL-3M-IPFV.ANIM 2SG.POSS-uncle
'Come and drink with your uncle, ...' (Lawrence 2013: 88)

(23) na-N-ar-**ap**-e-ni.
1SG-IRREAL-fly-**ALL**-IRREAL-IPFV.ANIM
'I will come flying.' (Lawrence 2013: 87)

(24) na-N-áge-**an**-e-ne-ri-ni oká.
1SG-IRREAL-grab-**ABL**-IRREAL-BEN-3M-IPFV.ANIM DEM.PROX
'I'm going to grab all of what's here for him.' (Lawrence 2013: 135)

(25) i-isig-**an**-k-a.
3M-run-**ABL**-PFV-REAL
'He ran away.' (Lawrence 2013: 88)

Other examples of languages with paired ventive and andative morphemes that occur both as markers of prior AM and as directionals are illustrated in the Supplementary Materials, namely (S62) to (S65) from Moseten, (S79) to (S82) from Baure, (S83) and (S84) from Kanamari, and (S104) to (S107) from Sochiapan Chinantec.

3.3 Returnative prior motion

Chimariko has a suffix -*(yu)wu* which Jany calls 'returnative' and which involves prior motion, but with the additional semantic element that the one moving is returning somewhere to do something, i.e. with the presupposition that the one moving has previously been at the location they are moving to.[9] Example (26) illustrates this suffix as a marker of AM, while (27) and (28) illustrate its use as a directional with motion verbs.

(26) Chimariko (Isolate; California, U.S.)
*n-ixoda-**yuwu***
IMPER.SG-watch-RETURN
'go back and look at him!' (Jany 2009: 108)

(27) *h-iwo-**wu**-k-ta.*
3-fall.over-RETURN-DIR-ASP
'He fell over backwards.' (Jany 2009: 41)

(28) *h-atqa-**wu**-k-ta*   *šəvəl-op.*
3-take.away-RETURN-PAST-3PL.NONSPEC   shovel-DEF
'They took the shovel away from him.' (Jany 2009: 211)

The meaning of this suffix as a directional is not entirely clear from the examples in (27) and (28). It seems unlikely that the motion in (27) is returnative in the sense that the one falling is falling to a location that they were previously located; rather it seems to convey motion that is the opposite of typical motion, which is motion forward. And it is not clear whether the use in (28) involves taking back the shovel, as opposed to simply taking it. See §3.6 and §3.15 below for two languages with similar returnative morphemes.

3.4 Ventive concurrent motion

Examples (5) and (6) above from Imonda illustrate a ventive suffix used either for concurrent AM or as a directional. Examples (29) and (30) illustrate a second

---

[9] Note that Michael (2008) uses the term returnative in a distinct sense, as a label for a prior plus subsequent associated motion in Nanti, discussed in §3.12 below.

instance of this, from Mparntwe Arrernte, where (29) illustrates the concurrent AM use, (30) the directional use.

(29) Mparntwe Arrernte (Arandic, Pama-Nyungan; Australia)
 Kenhe kwele artwe just arlenge-nge-anteye ar-**intye**-ke.
 but QUOT man just far-ABL-as.well see-**DO.COMING**-PAST.COMPL
 'But supposedly the man had just seen (everything) from afar as he came.'
 (Wilkins 1989: 319)

(30) ... artnerr-**intye**-p-**intye**-rlenge.
 crawl-**DO.COMING**-FREQ-**DO.COMING**-DS
 '[... started rapidly taking out the burrs, prickles, and thorns that had stuck into the baby] as it had come crawling along. (Wilkins 1989: 531)

Other examples illustrating this pattern are (S89) and (S90) in the Supplementary Materials from Yanomami and (S183) and (S184) from Kaytetye.

3.5 Andative concurrent motion

The examples in (31) and (32) from Lowland Tarahumara illustrate an andative suffix -*si* that is used either for concurrent AM, as in (31), or as a directional, as in (32).

(31) Lowland Tarahumara (Tarahumaran, Uto-Aztecan; Mexico)
 maha-ga basí-**si**-le=turu.
 scare-CONT throw.stones.at-**ASSOC.MOT**-PAST=FOCUS
 'Scared, they went throwing stones at him.' (Valdez Jara 2013: 177)

(32) lége ma-**si**-é-ko warú rosobócu-go-me
 downwards run-**ASSOC.MOT**-PAST-IRREAL big grey-CONT-PTCPL
 gasá-tiri.
 grass-LOC
 'It ran away, the big grey one, by the grass.' (Valdez Jara 2013: 177)

Other examples illustrating morphemes of this sort include (S96) and (S97) from Garifuna, (S161) to (S164) from Kwak'wala, and (S187) and (S188) from Wirangu.

Just as some languages have pairs of ventive and andative morphemes that serve both as markers of prior AM and as directionals, there are also languages with pairs of ventive and andative morphemes which code concurrent motion when they are used for AM. For example, Tonkawa (Hoijer 1949 ; Isolate;

south-central U.S.) has a pair of suffixes *-ta* and *-na* which are ventive and andative and appear to be concurrent AM suffixes, as in *naw-ta* 'to come along setting fires', *naw-na* 'to go off setting fires', *na·xsok-ta* 'to come raiding', and *na·xsok-na* 'to go off raiding'. These also function as directionals, as in *yancicxil-ta* 'to come running' and *yancicxil-na* 'to run off'.

Two other languages with similar pairs of ventive and andative markers of concurrent AM that also function as directionals are Kashibo-Kakataibo and Yaminahua (both Panoan languages), illustrated in (S44) to (S48) and (S49) to (S53) respectively.

3.6 Returnative concurrent motion

Mparntwe Arrernte has a returnative suffix *-irtne*, denoting motion that involves returning to a location, similar to the returnative suffix in Chimariko discussed in §3.3 above, but differing in that the Chimariko suffix involves prior AM, while the returnative suffix in Mparntwe Arrernte involves concurrent AM. The example in (33) illustrates the use of this suffix as a marker of concurrent AM, while (34) illustrates its use as a directional.[10]

(33) Mparntwe Arrernte (Arandic, Pama-Nyungan; Australia)
 *Nthenhe   arrantherre   arlkw-**irtne**-tyenhe   Thursday-nge?*
 where   2PL(A)   eat-**REVERS**-NONPAST.COMPL   Thursday-ABL
 'Where will you eat on your way back on Thursday?' (Wilkins 1989: 277)

---

10 As Antoine Guillaume has pointed out to me, according to the classification of types of associated motion that I assume in this chapter and in Chap. 13 of this volume, (33) does not really illustrate concurrent motion since the natural reading of (33) is that the subject is not eating while going back, but is stopping to eat while going back. This would involve what I call prior plus subsequent motion of the passing-by type in Chap. 13 of this volume, except that it has the additional sense of returning. However, it is clear from the discussion and examples in Wilkins (1989) that it is a general property of markers of concurrent associated motion in Mparntwe Arrernte that they cover both instances in which the activity denoted by the verb is concurrent with motion and instances in which the activity denoted by the verb temporarily interrupts the motion, implying that the verb form in (33) could also be used to denote instances where the eating and motion occur simultaneously. In other words, the implication that (33) involves interrupting the motion to eat arises, not due to the associated motion morpheme on the verb, but due to the word *nthenhe* 'where'. In other words, if the question had been 'Why will you eat on your way back on Thursday?' or 'What will you eat on your way back on Thursday?', the sentence would have been vague as to whether the eating was truly concurrent with the motion or only occurred during an interruption to the motion.

(34) Kele   arrpenhe-le   tyarre-kng-**irtne**-ke.
     OK   other-ERG   pull.out-carry/take-**REVERS**-PAST.COMPL
     'So the other one dragged him back (towards the water).' (Wilkins 1989: 277)

3.7 Random concurrent motion

With markers of concurrent AM, there is a distinct type of direction, which I call random, where the motion involves moving around without a particular direction. The example in (35) from Apurinã illustrates a suffix -*ãpo* of this sort.

(35) Apurinã (Southern Maipuran, Arawakan; Brazil)
     nhi-nhika-**ãpo**-ta-ru.
     1SG-eat-**RANDOM**-VBLZ-3SG.M.OBJ
     'I went around aimlessly eating it.' (Facundes 2000: 284)

Example (36) illustrates the same suffix being used as a directional, with a verb of motion meaning 'run', where the running involves running around, rather than from a particular place or towards a particular goal.

(36) Apurinã (Southern Maipuran, Arawakan; Brazil)
     nota   mutekã-**ãpo**-ta.
     1SG   run-**RANDOM**-VBLZ
     'I ran around.' (Facundes 2000: 249)

A second instance of a morpheme like this is illustrated by the Ojibwa morpheme *biba:(m)-* in (37) and (38).

(37) Ojibwa (Algonquian, Algic; eastern Canada and eastern U.S.)
     biba:-mo:nah-maškikiw-e:-w.
     AROUND-dig-medicine-INCORP-3
     'He is gathering medicinal herbs.' (Rhodes 1976: 265)

(38) **biba:m**-bato:-w.
     AROUND-run-3
     'He is running around.' (Rhodes 1976: 244)

Examples in the Supplementary Materials illustrating other languages with random motion morphemes that are used either for concurrent AM or as directionals include (S60) and (S61) from Kashinawa, (S108) and (S109) from

Sochiapan Chinantec, (S112) and (S113) from Huehuetla Tepehua, (S126) and (S127) from Cupeño, (S143) to (S148) from Panamint, and (S152) to (S155) from Northern Paiute.

3.8 Upward and downward concurrent motion

Shipibo-Konibo has a morpheme that codes upward motion that is used either as a directional or as a marker of upward concurrent motion when used as a marker of AM. Example (39) illustrates the concurrent AM use, (40) the directional use.

(39) Shipibo-Konibo (Panoan; Peru)
 *Sani-ra bewa-**inat**-ai.*
 Sani.ABS-EVID sing-**GOING.UP**-INCOMPL
 'Sani is going up the river singing.' (Valenzuela 2003: 269)

(40) *Jainoa-xa no-a jo jó-**ina**-ke,* ...
 there.LOC-ABL-INTR.S:EVID 1PL-ABS come come-**GOING.UP**-COMPL
 'From there, we came up the river ...' (Valenzuela 2003: 269)

Similarly, Shipibo-Konibo has an AM morpheme *-pake(t)* for downward motion, as in (41), that is also used as a directional, as in (42).

(41) Shipibo-Konibo (Panoan; Peru)
 ... *jato yoi yoi-**paket**-i*
 3PL.ABS tell tell-**GOING.DOWN**-SIMUL.SS:INTR.S
 '... they went down the river inviting the people (to the Ani Xeati ceremony).' (Valenzuela 2003: 593)

(42) ... *wetsa ka-a iki toxbá-**paket**-i*
 other.ABS go-COMPL.PTCPL AUX float-**GOING.DOWN**-SIMUL.SS:INTR.S
 '... while the second one floated down the river.' (Valenzuela 2003: 270)

3.9 Ventive subsequent motion

The preceding sections describe morphemes involving either prior AM or concurrent AM. The third basic type of AM involves subsequent motion, i.e. motion following the event denoted by the verb. The examples in (43) and (44) illustrate a ventive suffix -ŋ ~ -iŋ for this for Tima, the second example illustrating the directional use.

(43) Tima (Kordofanian; Sudan)
mɔ́ɔ́k-**iŋ**
drink-**VENT**
'drink and come towards me' (Bashir 2010: 187)

(44) dîîk-**iŋ**
go-**VENT**
'come' (Bashir 2010: 187)

Morphemes like this that function as markers of ventive subsequent AM or as ventive directionals are found in 12 of the 14 languages of Africa in the sample discussed in this paper but in none of the languages outside Africa. Examples illustrating ventives like this are (S5) and (S6) from Koyra Chiini, (S7) and (S8) from Koyraboro Senni, (S9) and (S10) from Kwarandzyey, (S17) and (S18) from Päri, (S19) to (S21) from Ma'di, (S22) and (S24) from Tamashek, (S28) and (S29) from Bole, (S30) and (S31) from Ngizim, (S32) and (S33) from Lele, (S34) and (S35) from Buwal, and examples cited in §S1.14 in the Supplementary Materials from Gude. §3.10 below describes Camus, where there are both ventive and andative morphemes of this sort.

3.10 Andative subsequent motion

Kaytetye has an andative suffix *-layte ~ rrayte* 'AND.GO' which marks subsequent AM in (45) but functions as a directional in (46).[11]

(45) Kaytetye (Arandic, Pama-Nyungan; Australia)
Alarre-**layte**-nke   nhartepe   kwerarte-pe   atnwenthe-pe.
kill-**AND.GO**-PRES that.ACC   it.ACC-TOP   animal.ACC-TOP
'(The hawk) kills that animal and goes off.' (Koch 1984: 29)

---

[11] Harold Koch (p.c.) now analyses the verb form in (46) and similar forms with verbs of motion as involving a derivational process distinct from forms like that in (45) that involve associated motion. For the purposes of this paper, however, these examples show the same phonological form being used either as a marker of associated motion or as a directional with motion verbs.

(46) *alhwenge-theye artnpe-**rrayte**-nye.*
hole-ABL run-**AND.GO**-PAST
'[The goanna] ran away from its hole.' (Koch 1984: 29)

Camus has both ventive and andative morphemes that can code subsequent AM, as in (47) and (48), or as directionals, as in (49) and (50).

(47) Camus (Nilotic; Kenya)
*k-á-idóŋ-**u** n-kérá-í.*
ASP-1SG-beat-**VENT** F-CHILD.OBJ-SG
'I beat the child until he comes back.' (Heine 1980: 124)

(48) *k-á-ídóŋ-**oo** n-kérá-í.*
ASP-1SG-beat-**ANDAT** F-child.OBJ-SG
'I beat the child until he runs away.' (Heine 1980: 124)

(49) *a-rum-**ú***
INF-push-**VENT**
'to push this way' (Heine 1980: 124)

(50) *a-rum-**oó***
INF-push-**ANDAT**
'to push away' (Heine 1980: 124)

Note that the AM examples in (47) and (48) involve motion by the object rather than the subject. It is unclear whether the ventive and andative suffixes can be used for AM by the subject.

3.11 Prior plus subsequent AM or ventive directional

The fourth basic type of AM involves a combination of prior plus subsequent AM, going or coming somewhere, doing something, and then returning. The Huallaga Quechua suffix *-mu*, which Weber (1989) glosses 'afar' is used either for prior AM, as in (51), or for prior plus subsequent AM, as in (52). There is apparently usually (though not always) an implication that, after going somewhere, the subject returns.[12]

---

[12] This morpheme differs from the returnative morphemes discussed in §3.3 and §3.6 above in that the returnative morphemes code returning to do something while the suffix *-mu* 'afar' in

(51) Huallaga Quechua (Quechuan; Peru)
mikU-**mu**-shun
eat-**AFAR**-12.IMPER
'let's go eat (over there)' (Weber 1989: 29)

(52) Wasi-:-ta   watqa-ykU-**mu**-nki.
house-1POSS-OBJ   spy-impact-**AFAR**-2
'Please spy on my house (and then come back).' (Weber 1989: 101)

When used as a directional, this morpheme has ventive meaning, as in (53).

(53) Huallaga Quechua (Quechuan; Peru)
... pukutay   ura-ka-rpU-**mu**-ra-n.
     cloud   descend-pass-DOWN-**AFAR**-PAST-3
'... the clouds came down about them.' (Weber 1989: 123)

The fact that the directional use has ventive meaning supports the idea that when used as a marker of AM, the return is usually part of the meaning.

3.12 Prior plus subsequent for both AM and as a directional

Nanti also has a suffix -*ut* which Michael (2008) calls 'returnative' and which codes prior plus subsequent AM with non-motion verbs, as in (54).

(54) Nanti (Southern Maipuran, Arawakan; Peru)
i=p-**ut**-i=ri.
3SG.M=give-**RETURN**-REAL=3SG.M.OBJ
'He gave it to him (going to him, giving it to him, then returning).' (Michael 2008: 258)

It is also used as a directional, in which case it still involves a combination of prior and subsequent motion, as in (55).

Huallaga Quechua codes going to do something and then returning. Note that in Dryer (this volume ch. 13), I distinguish two types of prior plus subsequent associated motion, a round trip type in which the subsequent motion involves a reverse of the direction of the prior motion and a passing-by type, in which the subsequent motion involves continuing in the same direction as the prior motion. The prior plus subsequent associated motion in Huallaga Quechua and that in Nanti, discussed below in §3.12, are both of the round trip type.

(55) Nanti (Southern Maipuran, Arawakan; Peru)
 i=shig-**ut**-i.
 3SG.M=run-**RETURN**-REAL
 'He ran there and back.' (Michael 2008: 258)

This suffix has a meaning similar to the suffix in Huallaga Quechua discussed in §3.11, but when used as a directional, the Huallaga Quechua suffix codes ventive direction, while the direction coded by the Nanti suffix involves motion in one direction followed by motion in the reverse direction. It is not clear whether this combination in Nanti involves a combination of andative direction followed by ventive direction, or whether the direction of the prior motion could be ventive (i.e. motion towards the deictic centre) and the direction of the subsequent motion andative (i.e. motion away from the deictic centre), or whether the motion is simply neutral with respect to direction.

3.13 Ventive prior or concurrent motion

The remaining types, discussed in §3.13 to §3.18, involve morphemes that are used for two types of AM, but also as a directional. The morpheme discussed in this section is a ventive prefix -wal from Tetelcingo Nahuatl which Tuggy (1979) glosses as 'hither' and which is homophonous with the verb stem for 'come'. This morpheme codes either ventive prior AM, as in (56), or ventive concurrent AM, as in (57).

(56) Tetelcingo Nahuatl (Aztecan, Uto-Aztecan; Mexico)
 šı-k-cahcı-lı ıhkı-u kiemı nı-k-**wal**-ıhto.
 IMPER-3SG.OBJ-shout-APPLIC be-DIST like 1SG-3SG.OBJ-**HITHER**-say
 'Shout to him like I came and said to.'[13] (Tuggy 1979: 129)

(57) k-**wal**-teh-tiekı-lı in-u pah-tlı koš
 3SG.OBJ-**HITHER**-REPET-pour-APPLIC DEM-DIST medicine-ABS whether
 ɔ-cin-tlı.
 water-DIM.HON-ABS
 'He comes sprinkling that medicine on him if it is liquid.' (Tuggy 1979: 132)

This prefix also functions as a ventive directional, as in (58).

---

13 The sentence gloss I give for (56) is the one given by Tuggy. What it seems to mean is something like 'Shout to him, saying the same thing that I came and said to him'.

(58) Tetelcingo Nahuatl (Aztecan, Uto-Aztecan; Mexico)
 por taha tɪ-wala ye nɪ-**wal**-temu-k.
 for 2SG 2SG-come already 1SG-**HITHER**-descend-PFV
 'Because you came, I've managed to get down here.' (Tuggy 1979: 134)

Examples of morphemes of this sort that are cited in the Supplementary Materials are (S22) to (S24) from Tamashek and (S171) to (S174) from Malecite-Passamaquoddy.

3.14 Ventive and/or andative prior or concurrent motion

Tamashek has an andative clitic =(h)ín that is used for prior AM, as in (59), for concurrent AM, as in (60), or as a ventive directional, as in (61).

(59) Tamashek (Berber, Afro-Asiatic; Mali)
 i-kfa=**hín** ázrəf è mæssi-s.
 3SG.M.SUBJ-give.PFV=**CENTRIF** money DAT master-3SG.POSS
 'He went and gave the money to his master.' (Heath 2005: 600)

(60) i-kša=**hín**
 3SG.M.SUBJ-eat.PFV=**CENTRIF**
 'It (=brush fire) ate up (the vegetation) going away that way.' (Heath 2005: 599)

(61) a=**hín** ăs-æy.
 FUT=**CENTRIF** arrive.IPFV-1SG.SUBJ
 'I will come (there).' (Heath 2005: 600)

Panamint[14] has a ventive suffix -(k)kin and an andative suffix -(k)kwan that are both used for prior AM, concurrent AM, or as directionals. These three uses of the ventive are illustrated in (62) to (64), and similarly in (65) to (67) for the andative.[15]

---

14 Panamint is also known as Tümpisa Shoshone, though this name is potentially confusing since it might imply that Panamint is a dialect of Shoshone, which it is not.
15 Dayley does not gloss individual morphemes consistently. For example, he glosses the suffix -(k)kin in (62) as 'come and', where it is used for prior associated motion, but as 'hither' when it is used for concurrent associated motion, as in (63), or as a directional, as in (64). I use his glosses throughout.

(62) Panamint (Numic, Uto-Aztecan; California, United States)
Sümü-ttü-sü   ma   tükka-**kin**-tu'ih.
one-NUM-ABS   3SG.OBJ   eat-**COME.AND**-FUT
'One will come and eat it.' (Dayley 1989: 65)

(63) hipi-**kkin**
drink-**HITHER**
'coming drinking' (Dayley 1989: 421)

(64) Satü   süngkia-**kin**-na.
that   stagger-**HITHER**-NONFUT
'He is coming staggering.' (Dayley 1989: 66)

(65) Nü   hipi-**kwan**-tu'ih.
1sg   drink-**GO.AND**-FUT
'I will go and drink.' (Dayley 1989: 66)

(66) Nüü   ma   kwüü-**kkwan**-tu'ih.
1SG   3SG.OBJ   catch-**AWAY**-FUT
'I'm going away catching it.' (Dayley 1989: 66)

(67) Mungku   mimi'a-**kwan**-tu'ih.
2DU   go.DUAL-**AWAY**-FUT
'You two are going away.' (Dayley 1989: 130)

3.15 Returnative prior or concurrent motion

Arabana has a suffix *-thika* that is similar to the suffixes in Chimariko and Mparntwe Arrernte described above in §3.3 and §3.4 respectively in denoting motion returning somewhere. It differs from the suffixes in these other languages in that, when used for AM, it can be used for either prior AM or concurrent AM. Its use for prior AM is illustrated in (68), its use for concurrent AM in (69), and its use as a directional in (70).

(68) Arabana (Karnic, Pama-Nyungan; Australia)
Pitha-palti-nha   kanhangarda   kaRu   thawi-**thika**-rna.
Pitha-palti-PROP   there   thither   throw-**RETURN**-IPFV
'(The place called) Pitha-palti-nha, that is where we went back to throw it away.' (Hercus 1994: 89)

(69) KaRu uka-ru tharki-tharki-l-**thika**-rna pirra-maka.
there he-ERG show-show-BEN-**RETURN**-IMPV message-stick
'He went back, showing people the message stick (on his way).' (Hercus 1994: 208)

(70) Antha wadna-**thika**-rnda.
I run-**RETURN**-PRES
'I'm running back (to last night's camping place).' (Hercus 1994: 207)

3.16 Ventive prior or subsequent motion

Päri has centripetal (ventive) morphology which can be used for prior AM, subsequent AM, and directional meaning. The different categories are realized by stem changes, including tone. Compare the form in (71), without the relevant marking, with the ventive form in (72), where it codes prior AM.

(71) Päri (Nilotic; South Sudan)
ùbúr á-kwʌ̀d-ò.
Ubur COMPL-steal.ANTIPASS.HAB-SUFF
'Ubur used to steal.' (Andersen 1988: 301)

(72) ùbúr á-kwʌ̀nn-ò.
Ubur COMPL-steal.ANTIPASS.**CENTRIP**-SUFF
'Ubur came to steal.' (Andersen 1988: 301)

Example (73) illustrates the use of a ventive form to denote subsequent AM (differing from the form in (72) in that it is not antipassive).

(73) dhòk á-kwʌ́l` ùbúrr-ì.
cows COMPL-steal.**CENTRIP** Ubur-ERG
'Ubur stole the cows (and brought them here).' (Andersen 1988: 301)

Example (74) illustrates the use of a ventive form as a directional.

(74) Päri (Nilotic; South Sudan)
á-múll`-ò
COMPL-crawl.**CENTRIP**-SUFF
'He crawled (hither).' (Andersen 1988: 302)

3.17 Ventive concurrent or subsequent motion

Tamashek has ventive and andative clitics that code various types of AM. The andative clitic, which can express prior AM, concurrent AM and direction, is discussed in §3.14 above. The use of the ventive clitic =ə́dd for concurrent AM is illustrated in (75), for subsequent AM in (76), and as a directional in (77).

(75) Tamashek (Berber, Afro-Asiatic; Mali)
*i-ššəyæl=**ə́dd**.*
3SG.M.SUBJ-work=**CENTRIP**
'He came working.' (= 'He was working as he came.') (Heath 2005: 599)

(76) *Muss,   əɣtəs=**ə́dd**   i-sǽyer-æn.*
go.IMPRT cut.IMPRT=**CENTRIP** PL-wood-M.PL
'Go, cut (and bring) the pieces of wood!' (Heath 2005: 598)

(77) *ərjǽš-æɣ=**ə́dd**   ɣor   ʔǽ-wet   hàr   a-m-ǽzzaɣ.*
walk.PFV-1SG-**CENTRIP** chez SG-market until SG-??-camp
'I walked from the market all the way to the camp.' (Heath 2005: 291)

It is possible that both the ventive and the andative clitics can be used for prior or concurrent or subsequent AM, but I was unable to find examples in Heath (2005) illustrating the ventive clitic being used for prior AM or the andative clitic used for subsequent AM.

3.18 Andative concurrent or subsequent motion

Yanomami has an andative clitic =*huru*, which can serve as a marker of concurrent AM, as in (78), or subsequent AM, as in (79), or as a directional, as in (80). (Perri Ferreira glosses it as 'DIR.AND' for 'andative directional').

(78) Yanomami (Yanomamic; Brazil)
*thuë   thë=pë=heri=**huru**=ma.*
woman CLSFR=3PL=chant=**DIR.AND**=PAST
'The women were singing (moving away).' (Perri Ferreira 2017: 352)

(79) *kama   xaraka   e=kɨ=huhe=ku=**huru**=ma.*
3   arrow   DS=PL=release=PFV=**DIR.AND**=PAST
'He put down his arrows and went away.' (Perri Ferreira 2017: 357)

(80) pora a=kãyo=rërë=rayu=**huru**=ma.
     ball 3SG=APPLIC=run=PFV=**DIR.AND**=PAST
     'He ran away with the ball.' (Perri Ferreira 2017: 202)

Kashibo-Kakataibo and Shipibo-Konibo have similar morphemes, illustrated in the Supplementary Materials in (S41) to (S43) (for Kashibo-Kakataibo) and (S54) and (S55) (for Shipibo-Konibo).

4 Interpretation

The number of languages with morphemes that function both as markers of AM and as directionals all over the world raises questions about treating the two as different categories or crosslinguistic comparative concepts. In this section, I discuss a number of ways of viewing the situation.

One interpretation is that treating the two as distinct is a mistake, that directionals should simply be viewed as a type of AM. One might argue against this on the grounds that morphemes for AM can be used as directionals in only 53% of the languages discussed by Ross (this volume, ch. 2). In the sample of languages from North America discussed by Dryer (this volume, ch. 13), the percentage is even lower: in only 22 out of 94 language were there morphemes that are used both for AM and as directionals. But one can counter this argument by pointing out that other combinations of different types of AM are even less common: the most common other combination of different types among the 94 languages in North America is morphemes that are used for either prior AM or concurrent AM but there are only four such languages. Hence, the fact that only a minority of languages have morphemes that are used either as markers of AM or as directionals can hardly be used as an argument that directionals are not a type of AM.

However, there is another way to explain the relatively high frequency of languages with morphemes that either code AM or function as directionals, without treating directionals as a type of AM. If a language has AM morphemes that are not used as directionals, this means that these morphemes either cannot be used with motion verbs or, if they can, must be restricted to instances where the AM involves a distinct motion event, as in (13) to (15) above. Situations where there is a separate motion event probably arise much less often than situations where a particular motion event has a particular direction. For example, situations where someone came here and then walked are probably much less common than situations where someone walked here. What this means is that if a language has an AM marker for ventive prior AM, then either the language will simply disallow using this marker with motion verbs, or it will require that it be interpreted as a distinct prior motion when used with a motion verb, or it will interpret it as simply coding the direction of the motion denoted when used with a motion verb. The fact that I found evidence of AM markers being used as directionals in only about one quarter of languages in North America suggests that the first two of these options are common, but in the minority of languages where I did find AM markers being used as directionals, it appears that in these languages the third option was chosen. Furthermore, it seems that a language is more likely to choose this third option if the language has an andative-ventive contrast in its markers of AM or at least a marker of AM that codes ventive or random direction, these being the "non-default" directions (in contrast to andative). Among the 94 languages in North America with markers of AM, 42 exhibit a directional contrast or use only a ventive or random AM as a directional and 17 of them (or 40%) use at least one of the morphemes that are used for AM as a directional. In contrast, of the remaining 50 languages, only 5 (or 10%) have only an andative directional. In other words, if a language has a directional contrast or at least a ventive or random AM marker, it is more likely to extend the use of that directional coding to motion verbs.

One of the striking things about the results of this chapter is the extent to which markers of AM are used as directionals in ways that seem somewhat surprising in the sense that the type of AM (i.e. prior, concurrent, or subsequent) is lost when it is used as a directional.[16] One might have expected that the most common type of marker of AM to be used as a directional would be a marker of concurrent AM since with directions, the direction is in a sense necessarily concurrent with the motion. But in only 24 of the 56 languages discussed in this chapter did I find markers of concurrent AM being used as directionals.[17] Contrast this with the fact that 38 of the 56 languages either have markers of prior AM that are also used as directionals or have markers of subsequent AM that are also used as directionals.[18] What this suggests is that the explanation for the relatively

---

16 A partial exception to this is the suffix -*ut* in Nanti discussed in §3.12, which codes prior plus subsequent motion either as a marker of associated motion or as a directional. Although as a directional, it involves motion in one direction followed by motion in the reverse direction, it is not clear from Michael (2008) whether this is necessarily a sequence of andative direction followed by ventive direction or whether it could be a sequence of ventive direction followed by andative direction.

17 Seven of these 24 languages have markers of associated motion that cover both concurrent motion and either prior or subsequent motion.

18 The sum of 24 and 38 is 62, six more than 56. This is because there are six languages that have both markers of concurrent motion that also function as directionals as well as markers of prior motion or subsequent motion that also function as directionals. Among the 38 languages with

high frequency with which markers of AM are used as directionals (relatively high compared to the frequency with which markers of AM are used for two different types of AM) is the apparent naturalness of extending a marker of AM to use as a directional.

The use of a marker of AM as a directional contrasts with the situation of using a marker of AM for more than one type of AM. For example, if a marker of AM is used for both prior AM and concurrent AM, then sentences employing such a marker will be more ambiguous or vague than if the AM marker were used for a single type of AM. This contrasts with the situation with morphemes that serve either as markers of AM or as directionals, where the use with non-motion verbs will be unambiguously one of AM and the use with motion verbs will (in at least some languages) be unambiguously directional. We thus have an explanation for why markers of AM that are used as directionals are more common than markers of AM that are used for more than one type of AM, without interpreting this as reason for treating directionals as a type of AM.

One might still argue that even if one wants to treat directionals as distinct from markers of AM, then that implies that there is some higher category or comparative concept that subsumes the two. They do share the property that they involve motion (though in a different way). Note, however, that they do not all share direction, since there are languages with AM markers that do not code direction at all. For example, Cree has a prior AM morpheme *nitawi-* illustrated in (81) that is neutral with respect to direction.

(81) Cree (Algonquian, Algic; Canada)
   piko   ka-**nitawi**-atoskê-yân   anohc.
   necessary   IRREAL-**GO**-work-1   today
   'I have to go to work.' (Cook 2014 : 299)

This morpheme combines with a ventive directional *pê-* in (82) to code ventive prior AM.

(82) Cree (Algonquian, Algic; Canada)
   ... pâmwayês   **pê-nitaw**-âyamihâ-yêk!
       before   **COME-GO**-pray-2PL
   '... before you come here to pray.' (Cook 2014: 279)

---

markers of prior motion or subsequent motion used as directionals, 29 have markers of prior motion used as directionals and 12 have markers of subsequent motion used as directionals.

That *nitaw(i)-* is itself neutral with respect to direction is implied by the fact that one combines a ventive morpheme *pê-* with *nitaw(i)-* to code ventive direction. In the absence of *pê-*, the direction will be assumed to be andative, although in that situation the direction is coded by the absence of *pê-* rather than by *nitaw(i)-*. There are many other languages where it is unclear from the description whether a morpheme is andative or neutral with respect to direction. For example, Yakima has a prefix *wyá-* illustrated in (83) that Jansen (2010: 218) glosses as 'while going along' suggesting that it codes concurrent AM without direction.

(83) Yakima (Sahaptian, Plateau Penutian; Oregon, U.S.)
míimi   pa-**wyá**-pshata-na   áyat-ma.
long.ago 3PL-**WHILE.GOING**-gather-PAST woman-PL
'Long ago, women went along gathering.' (Jansen 2010: 77)

The only property that such markers of AM that do not code direction share with directionals is that they involve motion.

The conceptual difference between markers of AM and directionals is that markers of AM add motion to the meaning of a verb while directionals do not. Directionals do not add motion since motion is already coded in the verb. Another way of putting this is to say that motion is part of the meaning of markers of AM while motion is only a presupposition of directionals. What, however, do we want to say about morphemes that both code AM and function as directionals? Since they are used as markers of AM, this implies that motion is part of their meaning. It would be odd to say that they presuppose motion when they are used as directionals since in their AM use motion is not a presupposition but part of the meaning. I think that the most natural way to describe the use of such morphemes as directionals is to say that they have motion as part of their meaning but when used as directionals, this motion is redundant.[19]

What this implies is that the use of markers of AM as directionals is different from pure directionals, morphemes that can only be used with verbs of motion, in that motion is part of the meaning of the former while it is only a presupposition with the latter. What this further implies is that when markers of AM are used as directionals, directionals are a subtype of AM, akin to prior AM, concurrent AM, and so on. In other words, we need to distinguish pure directionals, which are not instances of AM, from the use of AM marker as directionals, which is an instance of AM.

---

19 Belkadi (this volume, ch. 5) makes a similar proposal for morphemes that are used either as markers of associated motion or as directionals.

5 Conclusion

In this chapter, I have documented the fact that it is common for languages to have morphemes that are used either as markers of AM or as directionals. The fact that it is common might suggest that we should treat directionals as a type of AM. However, while we might say that directionals and AM constitute two subtypes of a higher-level crosslinguistic category or comparative concept, there is an alternative explanation for the frequency of languages with morphemes that serve both functions. There appear to be three options a language with markers of AM has as far as the occurrence of these markers on verbs of motion is concerned. One option is that these markers of AM are never used on motion verbs. A second option is that these markers (or some of them) can occur on motion verbs, but when they do, they always represent a distinct motion event from the motion event denoted by the motion verb itself. The third option is that they (or some of them) can be used on motion verbs but, when they do, they function as directionals. This third option is more common among languages that have a directional contrast in markers of AM or at least have an AM that codes ventive or random direction, suggesting that these AM markers coding direction are naturally extended to motion verbs as directionals. We thus have a natural explanation for why many languages employ markers of AM as directionals without treating directionals as a type of AM.

Abbreviations

1	first person	ABS	absolutive
12	first person plural inclusive	ACC	accusative
1PL	first person plural	ADDIT	additive
1POSS	first person possessor	AFF	affirmative
1SG	first person singular	ALL	allative
2	second person	ANDAT	andative
2DU	second person dual	ANIM	animate
2PL	second person plural	ANTIPASS	antipassive
2SG	second person singular	APPLIC	applicative
2SUBJ	second person subject	ASP	aspect
3	third person	ASSOC.MOT	associated motion
3M	third person masculine	AUX	auxiliary
3PL	third person plural	BEN	benefactive
3SG	third person singular	CAUS	causative
3SUBJ	third person subject	CENTRIF	centrifugal
ABL	ablative	CENTRIP	centripetal

CISLOC	cislocative	M	masculine
CLFSR	classifier	NC	noun class marker
COMIT	comitative	NMLZ	nominalizer
COMPL	completive	NON.SG	nonsingular
CONN	connective/connector	NONFUT	nonfuture
CONT	continuative	NONSPEC	nonspecific
DAT	dative	NPDL	noun phrase delimiter
DEF	definite	OBJ	object
DEP	dependent	PFV	perfective
DESID	desiderative	PL	plural
DIR	directional	POSS	possessive
DIST	distal	PRES	present
DS	different subject	PROG	progressive
ELV	elative	PROP	proper noun marker
ERG	ergative	PROX	proximal
EVID	evidential	PTCPL	participle
F	feminine	Q	question
FREQ	frequentative	QUOT	quotative
FUT	future	REAL	realis
GEN	genitive	REPET	repetitive
HAB	habitual	RETURN	returnative
HON	honorific	REVERS	reversative
IMPRT	imperative	SG	singular
INAN	inanimate	SIMUL	simultaneous
INCOMPL	incompletive	SS	same subject
INCORP	incorporation	SUBJ	subject
INDEP	independent	SUFF	suffix
INF	infinitive	SUPPL	supplication
INTR.S	intransitive subject	TOP	topic
IPFV	imperfective	TSL	translocative
IRREAL	irrealis	VBLZ	verbalizer
LOC	locative	VENT	ventive

Acknowledgements: I acknowledge helpful comments from Lea Brown, Harold Koch, Antoine Guillaume, Philippe Bourdin, and Jean-Christophe Verstraete on earlier drafts of this chapter. I also acknowledge assistance from Harald Hammarström in obtaining copies of some of my sources.

Appendix

Table 1 summarizes the data for the 56 languages discussed in this chapter. Details are found in the Supplementary Materials.

Table 1: Summary of languages with AM markers that are also used as directionals.

§S1.1	Tafi	Niger-Congo	Pv
§S1.2	Tima	Kordofanian	Sv
§S1.3	Koyra Chiini	Songhai	Sv
§S1.4	Koyraboro (Koroboro) Senni	Songhai	Sv
§S1.5	Kwarandzyey	Songhai	Pa
§S1.6	Camus	Nilotic	Sv, Sa
§S1.7	Päri	Nilotic	P/Sv
§S1.8	Ma'di	Central Sudanic	Sv
§S1.9	Tamashek	Berber, Afro-Asiatic	C/Sv, P/Ca
§S1.10	Bole	Chadic, Afro-Asiatic	Sv
§S1.11	Ngizim	Chadic, Afro-Asiatic	Sv
§S1.12	Lele	Chadic, Afro-Asiatic	Sv
§S1.13	Buwal	Chadic, Afro-Asiatic	Sv, Pa
§S1.14	Gude	Chadic, Afro-Asiatic	Sv
§S2.1	Huallaga Quechua	Quechuan	P/PSv
§S2.2	Kashibo-Kakataibo	Panoan	Cv, Ca, C/Sa
§S2.3	Yaminahua	Panoan	Cv, Ca
§S2.4	Shipibo-Konibo	Panoan	C/Sa, Cup, Cdown
§S2.5	Kashinawa	Panoan	Cr
§S2.6	Moseten	Moseten-Chimane	Pv, Pa
§S2.7	Apurinã	Arawakan	Cr
§S2.8	Nomatsigenga	Arawakan	Pv, Pa
§S2.9	Yine	Arawakan	Pa
§S2.10	Nanti	Arawakan	Pv, PSps
§S2.11	Baure	Arawakan	Pv, Pa
§S2.12	Kanamari	Katukinan	Pv, Pa
§S2.13	Rikbaktsa	Macro-Ge	Pv
§S2.14	Yanomami	Yanomamic	Pv, Cv, C/Sa
§S3.1	Garifuna	Arawakan	Ca
§S3.2	Guatusa	Chibchan	Pv
§S3.3	Kekchi	Mayan	Pv
§S3.4	Lowland Chontal	Tequistlatecan	Pv
§S3.5	Sochiapan Chinantec	Otomanguean	Pv, Pa, Cr
§S3.6	Huehuetla Tepehua	Totonacan	Cr
§S3.7	Tetelcingo Nahuatl	Uto-Aztecan	P/Cv

Table 1 (continued)

§S3.8	Cora	Uto-Aztecan	Pa
§S3.9	Lowland Tarahumara	Uto-Aztecan	Ca
§S3.10	Cupeño	Uto-Aztecan	Pv, Cv, Cr
§S3.11	Shoshone	Uto-Aztecan	Pa
§S3.12	Panamint	Uto-Aztecan	P/Cv, P/Ca, Cr
§S3.13	Northern Paiute	Uto-Aztecan	Pa, Cr
§S3.14	Ineseño Chumash	Chumash	Pv
§S3.15	Creek	Muskogean	Pv
§S3.16	Kwak'wala	Wakashan	Ca
§S3.17	Menomini	Algonquian, Algic	Pv
§S3.18	Ojibwa	Algonquian, Algic	Pv, Cr
§S3.19	Cree	Algonquian, Algic	Pv
§S3.20	Malecite-Passamaquoddy	Algonquian, Algic	P/Cv
§S3.21	Chimariko	Isolate	Pret
§S3.22	Tonkawa	Isolate	Cv, Ca
§S4.1	Mparntwe Arrernte	Pama-Nyungan	Cv, Cret
§S4.2	Kaytetye	Pama-Nyungan	Cv, Sa
§S4.3	Wirangu	Pama-Nyungan	Ca
§S4.4	Arabana	Pama-Nyungan	P/Cret
§S5	Imonda	Border	Cv
§S6	Karbi	Sino-Tibetan	Pv

Key to Table 1

Pv	prior AM, ventive direction
Pa	prior AM, andative direction
Pret	prior AM, returning
Cv	concurrent AM, ventive direction
Ca	concurrent AM, andative direction
Cret	concurrent AM, returning
Cr	concurrent AM, random direction
Cup	concurrent AM, upward direction
Cdown	concurrent AM, downward direction
Sv	subsequent AM, ventive direction
Sa	subsequent AM, andative direction
PSps	prior plus subsequent AM, prior plus subsequent directional
P/Cv	prior or concurrent AM, ventive direction
P/Ca	prior or concurrent AM, andative direction

P/Cret	prior or concurrent AM, returning
P/Sv	prior or subsequent AM, ventive direction
C/Sv	concurrent or subsequent AM, ventive direction
C/Sa	concurrent or subsequent AM, andative direction
P/PSv	prior or prior plus subsequent AM, ventive direction

References

Not including references cited only in the Supplementary Materials; a separate list of references for those items cited in the Supplementary Materials is at the end of the Supplementary Materials.

Andersen, Torben. 1988. Ergativity in Päri, a Nilotic OVS language. *Lingua* 75. 289–324.
Bashir, Abeer Mohamed Ali. 2010. *Phonetic and phonological study of the Tima language*. University of Khartoum doctoral dissertation.
Belkadi, Aicha. 2015. Associated motion with deictic directionals: A comparative overview. *SOAS Working Papers in Linguistics* 17: 49–76.
Belkadi, Aicha. This volume, chapter 5. Deictic directionality as associated motion: Motion, complex events and event integration in African languages.
Beller, Richard & Patricia Beller. 1979. Huasteca Nahuatl. In Ronald W. Langacker (ed.), *Studies in Uto-Aztecan grammar 2: Modern Aztec grammatical sketches*, 199–306. Dallas: Summer Institute of Linguistics and the University of Texas at Arlington.
Bobuafor, Mercy. 2013. *A grammar of Tafi*. Rijksuniversiteit te Leiden doctoral dissertation.
Casad, Eugene H. 1984. Cora. In Ronald W. Langacker (ed.), *Studies in Uto- Aztecan grammar 4: Southern Uto-Aztecan grammatical sketches*, 153–459. Dallas: Summer Institute of Linguistics and the University of Texas at Arlington.
Cook, Clare. 2014. *The clause-typing system of Plains Cree: Indexicality, anaphoricity, and contrast*. Oxford: Oxford University Press.
Dayley, Jon P. 1989. *Tümpisa (Panamint) Shoshone grammar*. Berkeley and Los Angeles: University of California Press.
Dryer, Matthew S. This volume, chapter 13. Associated motion in North America.
Facundes, Sidney da Silva. 2000. *The language of the Apurinã people of Brazil (Maipure/Arawak)*. State University of New York at Buffalo doctoral dissertation.
Foris, David P. 2000. *A grammar of Sochiapan Chinantec*. Dallas: Summer Institute of Linguistics and the University of Texas at Arlington.
Gimba, Alhaji Maina. 2000. *Bole verb morphology*. University of California at Los Angeles doctoral dissertation.
Guillaume, Antoine. 2013. Reconstructing the category of "associated motion" in Tacanan languages (Amazonian Bolivia and Peru). In Ritsuko Kikusawa & Lawrence A. Reid (eds.), *Historical Linguistics 2011: Selected papers from the 20th International Conference on Historical Linguistics, Osaka, 25–30 July 2011*, 129–151. Amsterdam: Benjamins.
Guillaume, Antoine. 2016. Associated motion in South America: Typological and areal perspectives. *Linguistic Typology* 20: 81–177.

Hanson, Rebecca. 2010. *A grammar of Yine (Piro)*. LaTrobe University doctoral dissertation.
Heath, Jeffrey. 2005. *A grammar of Tamashek (Tuareg of Mali)*. Berlin: Mouton de Gruyter.
Heine, Bernd. 1980. *The Non-Bantu languages of Kenya*. Berlin: Dietrich Reimer.
Hercus, Luise A. 1994. *A grammar of the Arabana-Wangkangurru language Lake Eyre Basin, South Australia*. (Pacific Linguistics C-128) Canberra: Australian National University.
Hoijer, Harry. 1949. *An analytical dictionary of the Tonkawa language*. (University of California publications in linguistics 5.1). Berkeley: University of California Press.
Jansen, Joana Worth. 2010. *A grammar of Yakima Ichishkíin/Sahaptin*. University of Oregon doctoral dissertation.
Jany, Carmen. 2009. *Chimariko grammar: Areal and typological perspective*. Berkeley and Los Angeles: University of California Press.
Kimball, Geoffrey D. 1991. *Koasati grammar*. Lincoln: University of Nebraska Press.
Koch, Harold J. 1984. The category of 'associated motion' in Kaytej. *Language in Central Australia* 1. 23–34.
Konnerth, Linda. 2014. *A grammar of Karbi*. University of Oregon doctoral dissertation.
Lawrence, Aimee Lynn. 2013. *Inflectional verbal morphology in Nomatsigenga*. University of Texas at Austin MA thesis.
Lovestrand, Joseph, and Daniel Ross. This volume, Chapter 3. Serial verb constructions and motion semantics.
Michael, Lev David. 2008. *Nanti evidential practice: Language, knowledge, and social action in an Amazonian society*. University of Texas at Austin doctoral dissertation.
Mitchell, Alice. 2015. *Linguistic avoidance and social relations in Datooga*. University at Buffalo doctoral dissertation.
Perri Ferreira, Helder. 2017. *Yanomama clause structure*. Radboud Universiteit Nijmegen doctoral dissertation.
Rhodes, Richard Alan. 1976. *The morphosyntax of the Central Ojibwa verb*. University of Michigan doctoral dissertation.
Ross, Daniel. This volume, Chapter 2. A cross-linguistic survey of associated motion and directionals.
Seiler, Walter. 1985. *Imonda, a Papuan language*. (Pacific Linguistics B-93) Canberra: Australian National University.
Souag, Lameen. 2010. The Western Berber stratum in Kwarandzyey. In D. Ibriszimow, M. Kossmann, H. Stroomer & R. Vossen (eds.), *Études berbères V – Essais sur des variations dialectales et autres*, 177–189. Cologne: Rüdiger Köppe.
Tuggy, David H. 1979. Tetelcingo Náhuatl. In Ronald W. Langacker (ed.), *Studies in Uto-Aztecan grammar 2: Modern Aztec grammatical sketches*, 1–140. Dallas: Summer Institute of Linguistics and the University of Texas at Arlington.
Valdez Jara, Yolanda. 2013. *Predication in Rarómuri (Urique Tarahumara)*. University of Oregon doctoral dissertation.
Valenzuela, Pilar M. 2003. *Transitivity in Shipibo-Konibo grammar*. University of Oregon doctoral dissertation.
Viljoen, Melanie Helen. 2013. *A grammatical description of the Buwal language*. LaTrobe University doctoral dissertation.
Weber, David John. 1989. *A grammar Huallaga (Huánuco) Quechua*. Berkeley and Los Angeles: University of California Press.
Wilkins, David P. 1989. *Mparntwe Arrernte (Aranda): Studies in the structure and semantics of grammar*. Australian National University doctoral dissertation.

Aïcha Belkadi
5 Deictic directionality as associated motion: motion, complex events and event integration in African languages

Abstract: The ambivalent cross-linguistic relationship between the categories of associated motion and deictic directionality has been noted in recent studies: they express different meanings but have complementary distributions and are frequently realised by the same exponents depending on their linguistic environment. My main aim in this paper is to address this yet unexplained theoretical and typological puzzle. Based on the properties and distributions of polysemous exponents across various languages indigenous to Africa, I develop a unifying semantic account of associated motion and deictic directionality. Following the views that paths can refer to events, that events are not necessarily atomic and can be decomposed into multiple temporally related sub-events, I argue that deictic directionality constitutes a subtype of associated motion. Like the latter, it is used to express complex events, differing only in how the motion it expresses temporally integrates with the event encoded by the host verb.

Keywords: associated motion, path/directionality, complex event, macro-event, event integration, African languages

1 Introduction

Since its recognition as a valid morphosyntactic concept (Koch 1984; Wilkins 1991; Guillaume 2016), associated motion (henceforth AM) has been compared to other motion-related categories, such as path and directionality. At first sight, AM could be considered to be an instance of path or directionality. In the following examples from Cherang'any, a Kalenjin language from the Great Rift Valley in Kenya, the deictic directional suffix -tá and the AM suffix -λλtí appear to have very similar functions. Both forms occur in constructions which refer to motion in one way or another, both anchor this motion with respect to the speaker and both are expressed by 'grammatical' forms bound to a verb (Guillaume 2016).

Aïcha Belkadi, SOAS, University of London, ab105@soas.ac.uk

https://doi.org/10.1515/9783110692099-005

(1) Cherang' any (Nilotic, Kenya; Mietzner 2015: 201)
   a. *wìr̀-tá*
   throw-ITV
   'S/he throws away' (from deictic anchor)

   b. *til-λλtí*
   cut-MOB.ITV
   'S/he cuts while going' (from deictic anchor)

Most generally, AM is distinguished from path and particularly deictic directionality on the grounds that it expresses motion while the latter does not. As discussed in more detail in the introductory chapter of this volume (Guillaume & Koch this volume and references therein), an AM form encodes an additional motion event which is temporally linked to another event lexicalised by its host verb. By contrast, a deictic directional is considered to simply orient the motion event expressed by its host verb with respect to a deictic centre (Guillaume 2006, 2016; Voisin 2013; Vuillermet 2013; Belkadi 2015b). In other words, an AM construction can be described as a mono-verbal strategy expressing a complex event constituted of at least two subevents: one encoded by a lexical verb and a second encoded by an AM exponent. This difference in surface semantics between the two categories is clearly visible in (1). In (1a), the verb describes a motion whose direction is deictically anchored by the directional *-tá*. In (1b), a complex event is described: the main verb describes a cutting event, while the suffix *-λλtí* describes a motion event occurring simultaneously.

Although seemingly trivial, this established dichotomy has important typological and theoretical ramifications. On the one hand, it justifies treating AM as a cross-linguistically valid grammatical category, separate from other motion-related concepts such as direction. On the other, it makes AM typologically exceptional since languages most generally lexicalise motion in lexical items, such as verbs, rather than grammatical forms (Levinson & Wilkins 2006; Guillaume 2016; Guillaume & Koch this volume). Yet, recent research on so-called 'deictic-associated motion' (henceforth D-AM) casts critical doubt on the validity of this distinction. The term D-AM, introduced by Belkadi (2015a),[1] refers to

---

[1] As will be discussed in more detail in this paper, contrary to what is assumed in Belkadi (2015a), there seems to be no ontological differences between canonical AM and D-AM. Nevertheless, the term D-AM is adopted here for convenience to refer without ambiguity to associated motion encoded by forms which also express pure deictic directionality and by extension, to forms which are polysemous between AM encoding and pure deictic directionality encoding. Forms like the Berber ventive clitic in (2) can thus be considered to be D-AM forms. Note that

the cross-linguistic phenomenon whereby a single form may encode both AM and deictic directionality depending on the context. D-AM is found in a range of unrelated languages spoken in various regions of the globe (see Dryer this volume chapter 4 and Ross this volume for detailed cross-linguistic overviews of where deictic directionality and AM overlap), including, for instance, African languages (e.g. Dimmendaal 2015; Belkadi 2016; and several chapters in this volume: Creissels & Bassene; Kawachi; Otero; Payne; Voisin), South American languages (Weber 1989; Payne & Vidal this volume), Tibeto-Burman languages (Genetti et al. 2017) and some languages of Papua New Guinea (Reed & Lindsey this volume). The interpretation of D-AM, as either marking deictic directionality or AM, is contingent on the meaning of the main verb of the clause inside which it occurs and the type of event the latter expresses (Bourdin 2006; Alamin et al. 2012; Claudi 2012; Belkadi 2015a, 2016; Dimmendaal 2015). For example, the ventive directional clitic =d of Taqbaylit, a Berber language spoken in northern Algeria, is used most canonically to orientate the motion event encoded by a verb towards the location of the speaker or prominent deictic centre, as in (2a). There are a number of verbs, such as the counterpart of 'swim' in (2b), with which =d expresses instead a separate motion event, occurring after the event encoded by the verb.

(2) Taqbaylit Berber (Afro-Asiatic, Algeria: own data)
 a. *i- ruḥ* =*d*
    3SGM- go.PFV =VEN
    'He came.'

 b. *i-ʕum* =*d*.
    3SGM-swim.PFV =VEN
    'He (went somewhere) swam and came back (to the location of the speaker or to his house).'

The intrinsic properties, semantic ambiguity and distribution of D-AM across languages are being increasingly described and are now starting to be better understood. But such forms also point to strong similarities between AM and deictic directionality, which have been considerably neglected. Addressing the issue is yet crucial for a complete understanding of AM and the development of a valid definition for this new concept. Such a discussion can, furthermore, also greatly contribute to a better understanding of deictic directionality, a

---

canonical AM can also be, and is very often, deictically-oriented. The term D-AM is not meant to refer to this type of motion or to contrast with non-deictically oriented AM.

concept still very much understudied, and its status in the network of categories composing motion events. My main goal in this chapter is precisely to address these questions. Based on data and findings presented in my previous research focussing on D-AM across African languages (Belkadi 2015a, 2016a, 2016b), I argue that the properties, distribution and idiosyncrasies of D-AM support an analysis of AM and deictic directionality as forming a single grammatical category. Specifically, building on proposals from the literature on event semantics, the typology of event encoding and event integration (Tenny & Pustejovsky 1997; Krifka 1999; Levin & Rappaport Hovav 1999; Talmy 2000b; Rappaport Hovav 2008; Gehrke 2006; Ramchand 2008; Bohnemeyer et al. 2007; Bohnemeyer et al. 2009), I advance the claim that deictic directionality, at least in some languages, constitutes a form of AM.

The chapter is organised as follows. Section 2 clarifies the terminology as well as the theoretical and empirical assumptions followed in this paper. It defines the concepts of motion, AM and deictic directionality in detail and explains how the latter two categories interact with other components of the motional network. Section 3 introduces the phenomenon of D-AM and its main morphosyntactic, semantic and discourse properties across African languages. Section 4 presents a unifying analysis of AM and deictic directionality based on the properties of D-AM. Finally, Section 5 concludes the chapter and summarises my main arguments.

2 Deictic directionality and associated motion in the motional network

Deictic directionality and associated motion (AM) are used across languages to locate, in one way or another, events in space (Koch 1984; Wilkins 1991). Since they both occur in the descriptions of motion events, a clear definition of these two concepts first necessitates an understanding of what motion is and how it is encoded across languages.

A motion situation, or event, is one involving the continuous change in the position of a figure relative to a ground[2] (Langacker 1991; Talmy 2000b ; Zlatev 2007; Blomberg and Zlatev 2009; Zlatev, Blomberg, and David 2010; Fagard et al. 2013). This change in position of a figure generally involves a path, which

---

[2] Figure and Ground can be referred to respectively as Trajector and Landmark (Langacker 1987 amongst others).

minimally consists of a vector encompassing the concepts of source, traversal and goal, and a conformation, defined as a region relating the figure to the ground (Talmy 2000b; Zlatev 2007). For example, in (3) below, the figure in the noun phrase 'the man' moves with respect to a ground, encoded by the expression 'the room'. The path of motion, encoded by the verb 'enter', is composed of the vector 'to' – expressing the concept of goal – and the conformation 'in'.

(3) *The man entered the room.*

The semantic functions of both deictic directionality and AM often interact with the particular way in which a motion event is experienced and thus, of course, how it is expressed (see section 4).

According to Blomberg and Zlatev (2009), motion events can be experienced in the following ways. Motion can be perceived as translocative, as in (3) above, where the motion described involves a change in the figure's location, or as non-translocative, in which case the figure moves while staying in the same location. This is the case in example (4) below, in which the verb 'run' describes a motion occurring in the same location. Many non-translocative situations involve a figure moving in a certain manner; these events are thus often referred to as manner of motion events.

(4) *John ran on the treadmill for forty-five minutes.*

In addition, motion can be bounded or unbounded.[3] Bounded motion involves the crossing of a boundary, such as the departure from a source, the passing through a route or the arrival at a goal location (Blomberg and Zlatev 2009: 50). Example (3) involves bounded motion since the event of 'entering' involves a boundary crossing (exterior to interior) and ends when the figure reaches the interior of the room. An unbounded motion, such as 'running' in example (4), has, on the other hand, neither a set beginning nor a delimited end.

---

3 Many researchers (e.g. Pourcel & Kopecka 2006, Zlatev, Blomberg & David 2009) make a distinction between motion events and motion processes based on boundedness: motion events are bounded while motion processes are unbounded. This contrast mirrors the general distinctions between telic and atelic verbs or verb phrases based on their aktionsart properties. In this paper, the term 'event' is not used in contrast to the term 'process'. As discussed in the following section, 'event' is used here as a neutral term to refer to actions or 'action sequences' individuated in time and space (Bohnemeyer et al. 2009). So, a 'motion event' is, according to the terminology adopted here, an action involving motion, bounded or unbounded.

Finally, motion can be conceived of as either self-contained[4] – the figure moves on their own as in (3) and (4) above – or as caused by an external agent. Example (5) below, in which the agent 'John' causes the change of location of the figure 'the book', illustrates causative motion.

(5) *John put the book on the table.*

These various components and properties of motion events are encoded differently across languages, but there are some strong tendencies. Motion, path, manner and cause of motion are quite frequently lexicalised by verbs (Talmy 2000b; Levinson and Wilkins 2006; Beavers, Levin and Tham 2010). Furthermore, path and manner of motion are never encoded together in a single verb root (Talmy 2000b; Beavers, Levin and Tham 2010). After Talmy (1985, 2000b), languages are often categorised depending on which of path or manner the main verb of a clause encodes. In so-called 'verb-framed' languages, the main verb of a clause canonically lexicalises path while manner is encoded in a satellite construction, such as a converb (e.g. Japanese) or a subordinate clause (e.g. French). In 'satellite-framed' languages, the main verb lexicalises manner and path is expressed by adpositions, particles (e.g. English) or affixes (e.g. Russian). In 'equipollently-framed' languages, path and manner of motion are often encoded in serial verb constructions (Talmy 2000b; Slobin 2004; Zlatev &. Yangklang 2004; Ameka & Essegbey 2006).

In the motion literature, deictic directionality is considered to be either a subtype of path, on a par with vector and conformation (Talmy 2000b; Nakazawa 2006), or a distinct component of motion (Blomberg and Zlatev 2009; Zlatev, Blomberg and David 2010; Fagard et al. 2013). Its canonical function is to specify the trajectory of the figure of a motion event with respect to a deictic 'ground' (Talmy 2000b; Nakazawa 2006). This deictic ground may be the speaker, the addressee, a logophoric topic or a prominent location. The two most common types of deictic direction are the ventive and the itive, in which the deictic ground is respectively the goal (or intended goal) and the source. The verbs 'go' and 'come' in English are typical examples of verbs denoting deictic direction. 'Go' expresses itive[5] direction; it describes a motion which does not have a deictic anchor as its goal. 'Come', by contrast, expresses ventive[6] semantics. Its goal is

---

[4] The terminology used here to describe the various ways in which motion can be experienced is adopted from Blomberg & Zlatev (2009). The term 'self-contained motion', which, in this instance, refers to non-causative motion, is also often used by other authors, particularly Talmy (2000b), to refer to non-translocative motion.

[5] Also referred to as distal (cf. Levinson 1983) or andative.

[6] Also referred to as proximal (cf. Levinson 1983) or venitive.

the deictic anchor's location. Cross-linguistically, deictic directionality can be expressed in various ways; by verb roots, as in English, by satellites – such as particles or affixes –, as in (6), and in serial verb constructions, as in (7).

(6) Ghadamsi (Berber, Libya; Kossmann 2013: 55)
    a. *i-kri*   =*yasăn*   =**dd**
        3SGM-return.PFV =3PLM:DAT =VEN
        'He came back to them (over here/towards the speaker).'

    b. *t-əkre*   =**yin**   *iy* *əššu*   =*ye*
        3SGF-return.PFV =ITV to food =ANP
        'She went back (over there/ not towards the speaker) to the food.'

(7) Khwe (Central-Khoisan, Namibia; Kilian-Hatz 2010:116)
     Céɛ-ɛ   **xùú**
     take   **leave**
     'Take away.'

Some languages lexicalise deictic directionality in the same way as they do path (i.e. vector and conformation), but it is very often the case that path and deictic directionality are encoded using different morphosyntactic strategies[7] (Talmy 2000b; Lamarre 2008; Morita 2011; Fleisch 2007, 2012; Belkadi 2015b). Thus, in English, which is a satellite-framed language, deictic direction is encoded in verbs while other path notions are most canonically encoded by satellites. In Berber languages, which are most canonically verb-framed, deictic directionality is encoded by clitics and path is lexicalised in the main verb (Fleisch 2007, 2012; Belkadi 2015b).

AM is a recently recognised morphosyntactic concept expressing the translocative motion of one of a verb's arguments (Koch 1984, 2019; Wilkins 1991, 2006; Levinson & Wilkins 2006; Vuillermet 2013; Guillaume 2016; Guillaume & Koch this volume). A typical construction involving AM is mono-verbal but expresses two events, one of which involves motion. The motion event in the construction is encoded by a 'grammatical morpheme' (Guillaume 2016) and always occurs in addition to another event, encoded by a verb. According to Koch (1984, 2019) and Wilkins (1991, 2006), it is an inflectional category. Wilkins (1991), in particular, draws a parallel between AM and the category of tense: in an AM construction, a motion event locates the main verb's event in space in the same way that tense locates an event

---

[7] There are also many languages in which deictic directionality cannot co-occur with other path components (cf. Choi-Jonin & Sarda 2007; Morita 2011).

in time. Some other sources, for instance Bond & Reid (in preparation), analyse AM as a derivational category. Most canonically, AM is marked on a verb by affixes, but its exponents can also consist of particles, serial verbs or converbs (Koch 1984, 2019; Austin 1988; Wilkins 1991, 2006; Levinson & Wilkins 2006; Guillaume 2016; Lovestrand 2018; Ross this volume amongst others). AM paradigms can be quite complex and contrast features pertaining to the time of the additional motion event relative to the time of the verb's event, its path shape and the identity of its figure (Wilkins 1991, 2006; O'Connor 2007; Guillaume 2009, 2016; Rose 2015; Vuillermet 2013 amongst others). The examples in (8) and (9) from the Tacanan languages Ese Ejja and Cavineña, illustrate AM patterns quite clearly. In (8a), the affix -*nana* encodes a subsequent motion event with a path that is bounded at the beginning. The affix -*ñaki*, in (8b), encodes a motion with a path bounded at the end, occurring prior the verb's event. In (9), the affix -*tsa* encodes a simultaneous motion event, with a ventive deictic path and a figure of motion which is the object of the verb.[8]

(8) Ese Ejja (Tacanan, Bolivia & Peru; Vuillermet 2013: 8)
  a. *Ewanase =pa jama a-ka-**nana**-ani-naje* (...)
   Wife =REP so say-3A-**DO&LEAVE**-IPFV-PAS
   'Before leaving, he used to say to his wife (...)'

  b. *kya-kiyo =se ani-**ñaki**-ani.*
   APF-hot =1INCL.ABS sit-**ARRIVE&DO**-PRS
   'It is hot and we sit when we arrive.

(9) Cavineña (Tacanan, Bolivia; Guillaume 2009: 197)
   *tume =pa =taa =tuja =tu ba-**tsa**-ya ekwita...*
   then =REP =EMPH =3SG.DAT =3SG see-**COME(O)**-IPFV Person
   'He saw a person coming in his direction.'

As explained in section 1, AM and deictic directionality are now generally considered to form distinct categories (Levinson and Wilkins 2006; Guillaume 2006, 2016; Voisin 2013; Vuillermet 2013; Belkadi 2015a, b). The distinction is based on the fact that the categories each have their own set of paradigms and positions in the verbal or clausal template of some languages (Guillaume 2006; Vuillermet 2013), and, most crucially, on the fact that they relate differently to motion. Deictic directionals modify motion events while AM encodes motion. Deictic directionals occur with verbs of motion while AM markers occur with verbs which do not express

---

[8] For more information on the geographical distribution and typological properties of the AM category, the reader is referred to Guillaume and Koch's introduction to this volume.

motion. In many languages, however, AM and deictic directionality categories can be expressed by the same forms (Bourdin 2006; Alamin et al. 2012; Claudi 2012; Voisin 2013; Belkadi 2014, 2015b, 2016; Dimmendaal 2015; Guillaume 2016; see also Ross this volume and Dryer this volume chapter 4 for typological overviews). In the next section, I discuss in more detail the semantics of these forms as they occur in African languages and the contexts in which their different interpretations are found. The discussion there is strongly based on my previous work on the issue in Belkadi (2015a; 2016a).

3 D-AM across African languages

Consider the examples in (10) below:

(10) Taqbaylit (Berber, Algeria; Belkadi 2016a: 197)
    a. *i-ʕum*
        3SGM-swim.PFV
        'He swam.'

    b. *i-ʕum*   *=d.*
        3SGM-swim.PFV =VEN
        'He (went somewhere) swam and came back (to the location of the speaker or to his house).'
        '*He swam (towards or to the location of the speaker)'.

The Berber clitic *=d*, already discussed in sections 1 and 2, normally expresses the ventive deictic goal of a motion event (see example 2a). In (10b), however, it seems to encode AM. Its presence obligatorily implies the realisation of a motion event occurring in addition and subsequently to the 'swimming' event encoded by the verb. Notice that this separate motion event is not implied in (10a), where the clitic is absent.

As mentioned in section 1, this phenomenon, referred to as deictic-associated motion (D-AM) after Belkadi (2105a), is cross-linguistically frequent and is particularly common in African languages. It is found in the four major linguistic phyla indigenous to Africa. In Afro-Asiatic, the phenomenon is displayed by many languages from the Berber, Chadic and Cushitic branches (Frajzyngier 1989, 2001; Newman 2000; Jaggar 2001; Heath 2005; Bourdin 2006; Claudi 2012; Kossmann 2013; Belkadi 2014, 2015b). In Nilo-Saharan, the category figures prominently in the Songhay, Nilotic and Koman groups (Heath 1998, 1999; Otero 2017; Mietzner 2012; Dimmendaal 2015). In Niger-Congo, languages from the Atlantic, Bantu,

Kordofanian and Mande groups have been reported to have such forms (Voisin 2013, this volume; Creissels 2014, this volume; Belkadi 2016a; Persohn 2018). In Khoisan,[9] the category is also found, mainly marked by directional serial verb constructions (Kilian-Hatz 2010; Kießling 2014; Güldemann pc).

African D-AM is formally encoded in a variety of ways. In most languages from the Niger-Congo and Nilo-Saharan phyla, D-AM is expressed morphologically on the verb, by both concatenative and non-concatenative processes. In Atlantic and some Nilo-Saharan languages (including some Nilotic languages), D-AM is encoded by affixes (11, 12). In most Nilotic languages, AM is expressed by vowel or consonantal changes to the stem (13, 14). In some languages, D-AM is associated with a particular verb class. This is the case in Otoro (15) where ventive direction is encoded by the so-called 3rd stem and in Hausa (Chadic) where it is expressed by the well-known grade 6.

(11) Jóola Banjal (Atlantic, Niger-Congo; Bassène, 2007: 177)
 ti-cig-me   nu-vven-**úl**   ikki   u-ɲak   si-mbal-i
 13-arrive-SUBOR 2SG-row-**VEN** until 2SG-pull 4-net-PSS2S
 'When it arrives, you row and come to pull your net.'

(12) Kenga (West Sudanic, Nilo-Saharan, Chad: Neukom, 2010: 135)
 ɔ́k   tâs   sé   ə̄-túg-íň-**ó**!
 2:take cup ART 2-wash-**3SGO**-VEN
 'Take the cup, wash it and bring it back.'

(13) Dinka (Southern Nilotic, South Sudan: Andersen, 2012: 39)[10]
 a. ḓɔ̀ɔk   à̰=t̪ḛ̀l   wḛ́ŋ   t̪ɔ̰́ooc.
    boy   D=pull   cow:ABS   swamp:LOC
    'The boy is pulling a cow in/ from the swamp.'

---

9 Originally coined by Greenberg (1963), the term Khoisan is used to refer to non-Bantu and non-Cushitic click languages spoken in Southern Africa, which do not form a genetic group.
10 In Dinka, Anywa and several other Nilotic languages (Reh 1996; Andersen 2012; Bond & Reid in preparation), AM exponents are categorised within larger systems of verb 'extensions' or 'derivations' which mark, amongst other things, valence changing processes. This is the case in example (13) from Dinka and (14) from Anywa, where ventive and itive paths are marked by the directional derivation. Directional derivations and AM in Nilotic languages may often also have functions that are very similar to those of the applicative morphology found in many other languages from across the globe (Andersen 2012; Reh 1996; Payne this volume, chapter 18).

b. d̪ɔ̀ɔk ą̀=t̪è̥el wę́ŋ t̪ô̥ooc
   boy D=pull:**VEN** COW:ABS swamp:LOC
   'The boy is pulling a cow to / from the swamp (towards the deictic anchor).'

(14) Anywa (Nilotic, Nilo-Saharan; Sudan-Ethiopia: Reh, 1996: 257)
   a. *téeD*
      do.cooking
      'cook'

   b. *téennó*
      cook.INF.**VEN**
      'to come and cook for somebody'

(15) Otoro (Kordofanian, Sudan; Stevenson 2009: 264)
   a. *dhir-ɔ*   b. *dhir-a*
      sleep-2ND STEM   sleep-3RD STEM
      'Sleep!'   'Sleep and return!'

In Afro-Asiatic, Khoisan and very few Niger-Congo languages, D-AM most commonly surfaces verb externally as preverbal or post-verbal particles, clitics or minor verbs in serial verb constructions. In example (16) below, from Lele, the ventive particle *jè* is separated from the verb by the subject pronoun *dí*. Similarly, in (17), from Mandinka, a number of functional heads intervene between the ventive *naŋ* and the main verb *kúmándí* 'call'.

(16) Lele (Chadic, Nigeria; Frajzyngier 2001: 115)
   Se   dí   **jè**   dà   dèbréŋ   lìŋdà   nè
   Leave   3M   **VEN** PREP debreng   yesterday COP
   kínè   cà-y
   return.FUT   head-3M
   'He came from Debreng yesterday, and he is going to return here.'

(17) Mandinka (Mande, West Africa; Creissels, 2014: 97)
   díndíŋ-o   kúmándí   ń   yé   **naŋ**!
   child-DET   call   1SG   BEN   **VEN**
   'Call the child on my behalf in order for him to come here.'

In terms of its semantic properties, D-AM involves the same kind of features as those described in section 2 for canonical AM. The motion event can thus be simultaneous (concurrent) with or sequential to the event encoded by the verb, in which case it may precede (prior) or follow it (subsequent). In example (18), from Tamasheq, the motion event encoded by the ventive clitic =ə́dd is concurrent to the event of 'working' lexicalised by the verb. In (19), from Päri, the motion event is prior to the event of 'cutting' expressed by the verb. Finally, in (20), from Pero, the motion event encoded by *ínà* is subsequent to the event of 'falling' encoded by the verb.

(18) Tamasheq (Berber, Mali; Heath 2006: 599)
i-ššəyæ =*ə́dd*
3SGM-work.PFV =VEN
'He came working (he was working as he came).'

(19) Päri (Nilotic, South Sudan; Andersen 1988: 88)
ùbúr *á-ŋùtò*
Ubur C-cut+ITV+AP+INTR
'Ubur went to cut.'

(20) Pero (Chadic, Nigeria; Frajzyngier 1989: 94)
cúg-ínà tù púccù
fall-COMPL.VEN PREP there
'He fell there and came.'

The path of a motion event encoded by D-AM forms may be bounded or unbounded and simple or complex, for instance expressing a return-shaped motion, but it always includes deictic direction. The motion events presented in the previous examples all involve simple deictic paths. (18) and (20), for instance, involve ventive paths while (19) encodes an itive path. In (10b), repeated in (21) below for convenience, the path of the motion event encoded by the clitic =d is a complex return-shaped one: the figure is understood to have moved to a certain location, away from that of the deictic anchor, where they performed the event described by the verb, and then to have come back to the location of the deictic anchor.

(21) Taqbaylit (Berber, Algeria: own data)
i-ʕum =***d***.
3SGM-SWIM.PFV =VEN
'He (went somewhere) swam and came back (to the location of the speaker or to his house).'

The figure of the motion is most canonically the subject argument of the main verb as in the examples presented thus far. However, the figure can also be the

O argument of the main verb, as in (22). Motion of O alone, as in (22a), is less frequent and most often involves movement of A too, as in (22b).

(22) Mandinka (Mande, West Africa; Creissels 2014: 98–99)
    a. súŋkút-óo   ye   Tumáanî jé   **Naŋ** a   níŋ   nins-óo-lu
       girl-DET   PFV Toumani see **VEN** 3SG with COW-DET-PL
      'The girl saw Toumani come towards her with the cows.'

    b. í   Faamâa   táa-tá   deem-óo   la,
       2SG   father.DET go-ACPP hunting-DET OBL
       wŏ   Le   yé   Ñíŋ   sub-óo   făa   **naŋ**
       DEM   FOC   ACPP DEM   game-DET kill **VEN**
      'Your father went hunting, it is he who killed the game and brought it here.'

D-AM is strongly context-dependent: its occurrence and properties, such as the time of the motion event expressed or the identity of its figure, depend on the meaning of the main verb of the clause, the type of event it describes and often, the direct extra-linguistic context. Time of motion variations in a single language are well illustrated by the ventive particle *soo* of Somali in (23).

(23) Somali (Cushitic, Afro-Asiatic; Bourdin, 2006)
    a. waan   **soo**   seex-day
       FOCUS:1SG **VEN**   sleep-PST:1SG
      (i) 'I took a nap before coming here.'
      (ii) 'I took a nap on my way here (on the bus).'

    b. **soo**   seexo
       VEN   sleep:IMPER.2SG
      'Come sleep over here!' [face to face conversation]
      '*Sleep and come over here.'

Bourdin (2006) shows that motion events encoded by *soo* are interpreted as concomitant with the main verb's events, instead of or in addition to sequential, if the pragmatic context allows or forces it. In (23a), the event expressed by the verb *seex* 'to sleep' can be understood as occurring before the motion event marked by the ventive *soo* (as in interpretation i). Alternatively, if the subject of the verb is known by the speech participants to have travelled prior to the time of utterance – for instance by bus – the verb's event can be presupposed to have occurred during this particular motion situation (interpretation ii). In some contexts, however, the motion event expressed by *soo* can only be interpreted as occurring prior to the verb's event. In (23b), the ventive is used with the same verb as in (23a) in a face to face conversation. In this context, a prior motion of the subject must be derived. The reason for this is that a sleeping event usually implies the impossibility of motion of its subject while it unfolds. What's more, the result state it triggers usually lasts for some time. Thus, a motion following this event, in the short time interval presupposed by a face to face conversation is rather unlikely. Given this, the most relevant type of motion is one which is prior to the verb's event.

Similarly, many languages have the same form marking different types of path. Path ambiguity may be triggered by the nature of the event encoded by the verb modified. It appears to be the case in Taqbaylit, for instance, where the ventive D-AM usually expresses a motion with a return-shaped path (24i), but with some verbs, it also express a simple bounded path ('to arrive') (24ii).

(24) Taqbaylit (Berber, Afro-Asiatic, own data)
 t-bazg =**d** iman =is yakʷ.
 3SGF-be.wet.PFV =**VEN** self =GEN.3SG all
 (i) 'She went somewhere, soaked herself and came back' or
 (ii) 'She arrived soaking wet (to the location of the speaker)'.

Most languages also display variations in the grammatical role of the figure of D-AM events. These variations frequently depend on the argument structure of the verb and the nature of the event it describes. Therefore, motion of O with A, instead of motion of A alone, is found with transitive verbs (25a). Motion of O alone is also possible, particularly with transitive verbs involving so-called 'fictive' motion; that is, motion occurring across a metaphorical path, extending from a perceiver to a perceived entity or vice versa (Talmy 2000a: 115; Slobin 2008: 198). Seeing verbs (25b), verbs of calling (25c) and other goal-oriented verbs of emission for instance (26), thus very often involve motion of the O argument.

(25) Mandinka (Mande, West Africa; Creissels 2014: 98–99)
 a. í faamâa táa-tá deem-óo la,
  2SG father.DET go-ACPP hunting-DET OBL
  wŏ le yé ñĭŋ sub-óo fǎa **naŋ**
  DEM FOC ACPP DEM game-DET kill **VEN**
  'Your father went hunting, it is he who killed the game and brought it here.'

 b. súŋkút-óo ye Tumáanî jé **naŋ** a níŋ nins-óo-lu
  girl-DET PFV toumani see **VEN** 3SG with cow-DET-PL
  'The girl saw Toumani come towards her with the cows.'

c. *Musu-kéebáa   ye   wul-oo   kílí **naŋ**.*
woman-old.DET ACPP dog-DET call **VEN**
'The old woman called the dog in order for it to come.'

(26) Maasai (Nilotic, Kenya; Tucker & Tompo Ole Mpaayei 1955: 124)
ɛ-tɛ-dɛk-u-a   iyíóók
3-PF-CURSE-VEN-PF   1PL[11]
'He came cursing us'
'He cursed us as we came'

With some verbs, the figure of motion may even be an entity which is not an argument of the verb. The figure can, for example, be a speech participant or some other prominent discourse entity. Thus, in Somali, D-AM may force a subject-figure 'disjointness' or 'switch-reference' (Bourdin 2005; Claudi 2012), whereby the figure is a discourse participant rather than the main verb's subject. In Somali, disjointness obligatorily applies with the itive form ***sii***. As shown in examples (27a, b & c), the figures of the motion events encoded by the form are respectively the addressee and the speaker, rather than the subjects of the verbs.

(27) Somali (Cushitic, Somalia; Claudi 2012: 83–85)
 a. *Aad   baan   u   **sii**   cun-i*
    much   FOCUS:1SG to/for ITV   eat-infn
    'I'm going to stuff my face, while you are out.'

 b. ***Sii**   joog*
    ITV   stop/stay
    'Stay here until I come back.'

 c. *muus   wuu   **sii**   cun-eyaa*
    banana FOCUS ITV   eat-PRSPRG:3SGM
    'He is eating a banana while I'm absent.'

Comparable examples of this phenomenon are also found in other languages of the Afro-Asiatic phylum, such as Hausa (Jaggar pc) and Berber. In (28) and (29), respectively from Taqbaylit and Tamasheq, the ventive D-AM form *=dd/=ə́dd* is used with the verb 'to sit'. In (28), the deictic expression 'there' is not overtly expressed but implicitly understood and provided in the translation. This deictic expression, which locates the unfolding of the state as distinct from the deictic

---

[11] Tucker & Tompo Ole Mpaayei do not provide glosses for this example.

anchor, clashes with the ventive semantics of the D-AM used. This unexpected inference is easily explained by assuming that there is motion expressed there. However, the figure of this motion is not the subject of the verb — who is described as remaining in a distinct location — but the speaker or another participant. A similar explanation can be provided for the interpretation in (29).

(28) Taqbaylit (Berber, Algeria; Mettouchi 2011: 6)
 tə-qqim =**dd** faṭima tuhṛiʃt-nni
 3SGF-sit.PFV =VEN Fatima clever-DEM
 '(There) remained Fatima.'

(29) Tamasheq (Berber, Mali; Heath 2006: 599)
 æqqìm-əɣ-**ə́dd**
 sit.PFV-1SG-VEN
 'I stayed here (i.e. I didn't go).'

Whether a D-AM form encodes deictic directionality or AM depends on the semantics of the host verb, particularly on the degree of prototypicality of the motion event encoded by the verb (Belkadi 2015a, 2016a, 2016b). Forms are more likely to be interpreted as marking deictic directionality with verbs expressing translocative motion of S or A. Thus, in a study of D-AM in 20 African languages (Belkadi 2016a), no AM was found with verbs expressing bounded motion and canonical translocational motion of S or A arguments, such as those expressing entering and running events.[12] On the other hand, such interpretations were observed to be rarer with manner of motion verbs not perceived as involving translocationality, such as the verbs expressing dancing events.[13] Verbs whose motion can be experienced as translocative or not derive either AM or deictic directionality interpretations. For example, the sentences in (30) and (31), respectively from Pero and Sereer, describe the same event of falling. In Pero, it seems not to be perceived as translocative (at least not in 30a). The ventive form -*ínà* is interpreted with AM semantics and in fact occurs after the event of falling expressed by the verb. In Sereer, by contrast, the motion expressed by the D-AM affix -*iid* deictically anchors the event of falling.

---

[12] A verb like 'run' encodes unbounded translocational self-contained motion. Such motion has been shown to be very similar to bounded translocational self-contained motion (i.e. path motion) (Gehrke 2008; Levin et al. 2009; Nikitina 2008; Kopecka 2009; Croft et al. 2007).
[13] See Croft et al. (2007) for a typological discussion of prototypical translocative motion.

(30) Pero (Chadic, Nigeria; Frajzyngier 1989 : 94)
 cúg-ìnà   *tù*   *púccù*
 fall-COMPL.VEN   PREP   there
 'He fell there and came.'

(31) Sereer (Atlantic, Niger-Congo; Voisin 2013:148)
 Ten   *yen-**iid**-u*   *ga-kall*   *al-e*   (...)
 3SG   fall-VEN-foc   CL-inlet   CL-PROX
 'She fell in the inlet (in the direction of the island where the speaker is).'

There may also be variations with the same (polysemous) verbs in individual languages, depending precisely on how the event encoded by the former is interpreted. The following examples in (32) from Taqbaylit illustrate this phenomenon. Thus, in (32a), the verb glossed as 'turn' describes a bounded translocative motion; the motion of the car involves the crossing of a boundary (Blomberg and Zlatev 2009: 50). The ventive motion expressed by the clitic =d is interpreted as deictic direction. However, in (32b), the event described by the same verb root involves motion that is unbounded and not as prototypically translocative. Wandering around the world involves discontinuous motion – one can presume that the figure in (32b) travelled to different areas of the world and stayed for some periods of time in these countries, thus making the motion interrupted – that has neither a set beginning nor a delimited end. The ventive clitic is thus interpreted with AM semantics.

(32) Taqbaylit (Berber; Afro-Asiatic, own data)
 a. *t-dəwwər*   =***d***   *tumubil.*
     3SGF-turn.PFV   =VEN   car
     'The car turned (in the direction of the speaker).'

 b. *t-dəwwər*   =***d***   *dunit*   *kaml̥.*
     3SGF-turn.PFV   =VEN   world   whole
     'She wandered around the world and came back (to the speaker).'

Similarly, causative translocational motion, that is motion of arguments other than S/A, such as O arguments, may yield either interpretation of D-AM forms. In Hausa, the ventive on the verb is given a directional semantics with most verbs describing events involving translocative motion of the A and O arguments (33a, b) or the O arguments alone (34, 35).

(33) Hausa (Chadic, Afro-Asiatic; Jaggar 2001: 257–260)
    a. *kai*   b. *kāwō*
       take   bring

(34) a. *tūrà̄*   b. *tūrō*
       send   send (in the direction of the speaker)

(35) a. *sâkà̄*   b. *sāwō*
       put/ place   put/place here

However, some events that could be thought of as involving motion or transfer of an O argument also derive AM. Thus, the verb 'buying' in (36), which could be thought of as involving a transfer of the O argument and hence motion, triggers AM.[14]

(36) a. *sàyā*   b. *Sayō*
       buy   buy and bring

The last factor which seems to play a role in the interpretation of D-AM forms is whether the event encoded by the verb can be perceived as involving metaphorical or fictive motion. Fictive motion is a type of motion occurring across a metaphorical path, extending from a perceiver to a perceived entity or vice versa (Talmy, 2000a: 115; Slobin, 2008: 198). It is often argued that seeing events (e.g. see, look) and those involving verbal emission (e.g. tell, call) and appearance (appear, find) are cognitively conceived of in terms of motion (Talmy 2000a; Johnson, Fillmore et al. 2001; Slobin 2008). Cross-linguistically, it is undoubtedly very common for such events to be grammatically realised in constructions more canonically associated with motion. Path expressions, for instance, are used in many languages to specify verbs describing these events. In English, one can 'look out', 'look over', 'look into' or 'look towards' (Slobin 2008: 216). In Russian, the directional prefix *vy-*, more commonly used to specify the path of a motion event (37a) is also often used with verbs of seeing as in (37b).[15]

---

[14] One of the reviewers doubts that a verb like 'buy' could derive directional interpretations of a D-AM form, but in Taqbaylit Berber, the verb 'buy' very frequently co-occurs with the ventive marker =*d*. In such contexts, speakers do not translate the ventive as marking a separate motion event. Rather, it appears that in such contexts, the clitic encodes a goal (I bought myself something) or deictically anchors the goal argument.

[15] In the same vein, events describing change of states (e.g. become, clean) are also very often lexicalised in the same way as motion events (Lakoff & Johnson 1980; Aske 1989; Levin & Rappaport Hovav 1992; Talmy 2000b amongst others).

(37) Russian (Indo-European; Slobin 2008: 199)
   a. *Ptica* **vy**-*letela Iz Okna*
      Bird **out**-flew From Window
      'The bird flew out from the window.'

   b. *starik* **vy**-*gljanul iz okna*
      Old.man **out**-looked from window
      'The old man looked out from the window.'

The semantics of D-AM markers with events involving fictive motion varies across and within languages. In the examples in (38) from Maasai, the ventive affix -*u*- acquires AM semantics with the verbs meaning 'look' in (38a) and (38b). The examples in (39) from Bijogo show that telic verbs of emission, those that encode a path or a scale (Beavers 2008; Rappaport-Hovav 2010; Belkadi 2014, 2015a) like 'tell' are more likely to be interpreted as involving fictive motion, and thus derive directional readings, than atelic activities such as 'interrogate', which derive AM readings.

(38) Maasai (Eastern Nilotic, Kenya; Tucker & Mpaayei 1955: 124)
   a. ɪŋɔr-**u**-a=kɪ[16]
      2.SG.IMP:look.FOR-VEN-SUBJ=1SG.OBJ
      'Come and look for me.'

   b. *edol*-**u**-*ni*
      3.see-**VEN**-PASS
      'He is seen coming this way.'

(39) Bijogo (Atlantic, Niger-Congo; Voisin 2013: 147)
   a. *dit-a*   b. *dit-am*
      tell-**VEN**   tell-**ITV**
      'tell (to the speaker)/ 'tell (not to the speaker)/
      *come and tell.'   *go and tell.'

   c. *tɛmm-a*   d. *tɛmm-am*
      interrogate-**VEN**   interrogate-**ITV**
      'come to interrogate.' 'go to interrogate.'

The phenomenon of D-AM described above, and its properties, highlights the equivocal nature of the relation between AM and deictic directionality. While these two concepts have, on the surface, clearly different meanings, they are,

---

[16] Tucker & Mpaayei (1955) provide no glossing for this example.

as evidenced by African languages, very often realised by the same exponents. In previous research on the topic, including my own (Belkadi 2015a, 2016a), deictic directionality and AM have consistently been treated as separate concepts or categories based on their meaning divergences. In the next section, I take a different stance and develop a unifying semantic account of associated motion and deictic directionality.

4 Deictic directionality as associated motion: a temporal integration approach

In my previous work on the topic (see for instance Belkadi 2015a: 64–72), I contrast the strong contextual nature of D-AM described in the previous to the fixed distribution and meaning of canonical AM markers. The latter, I claim there, conventionally encode a contrastive bundle of information about the motion component, occur with all kinds of verbs – including motion verbs lexicalising an orientation or direction (except deictic ones) – and also often involve more refined semantic oppositions between markers, including aspect and manner specifications, or information about the outcome of the AM motion event (see section 2). Based on these differences, I analyse D-AM and canonical AM as two distinct categories, developed from divergent sources. I take the two categories to be at different stages of the grammaticalisation cline and thus at different points of semantic reanalysis. Canonical AM forms often, but do not exclusively, develop directly from motion verbs (Austin 1987; Wilkins 2006; Guillaume 2009, 2013, 2017) and are at the end of the grammaticalisation cline. D-AM, on the other hand, develops exclusively from deictic directional forms and constitutes an earlier stage of the grammaticalisation process. The variable semantics and distribution of D-AM are due to the fact that they are not yet fully reanalysed as functional markers of AM and not yet paired with fixed meanings. However, there are a number of important problems with this analysis of AM and D-AM as separate entities.

The first of these issues concerns the definition of deictic directionality assumed there and the grammaticalisation approach developed. If one assumes that deictic directionality does not express a motion event, but simply encodes a set of locations traversed by a figure, whose motion is specified by the verb, the hypothesised deictic directionality to AM pathway does not present the characteristic properties of grammaticalisation. Grammaticalisation is a process in which a lexical item gradually comes to acquire functional meanings and in doing so loses parts or all of its lexical meaning and semantics (Hopper & Traugott 2003; Heine & Kuteva 2002; Lehmann 2015). D-AM – and canonical AM in general –

does not express a more functional or less lexical meaning than deictic directionality. In fact, since it expresses a complete motion event, separate from the event of the verb, D-AM could be considered to have more lexical content than deictic directionality.

The second problem is that the meaning of canonical AM is not as fixed as presupposed above and, in fact, can vary as well (Belkadi 2016b). Canonical AM forms may indeed also be interpreted with different paths or directions depending on the context in which they are used. In the following example from Noon, the AM affix -*nee* 'move & do' is associated with a ventive path in (40a) but has an itive path interpretation in (40b).

(40) Noon (Atlantic, Senegal; Soukka 2000: 172 cited in Voisin 2013: 143)
    a. *Ya   jom   ki-heel-**nee**   Sookoon*
       s/he   should INF-get-**MOVE&DO** Firewood
       'She should go to get firewood.'

    b. *Hay-aa   dii,   futaas-**nee**   paam-fu*
       come-IMP DEM.LOC answer-**MOVE&DO** father-POSS
       'Come here and answer your father.'

Furthermore, AM markers may encode meanings more similar to those encoded by deictic directionals, particularly when hosted by verbs of motion. Example (41a) below, from Kaytetye, encodes two events: the event encoded by the verb *alarre-* 'kill' is understood to be followed by a motion event encoded by the affix -*lalpe*/-*rralpe* 'do & return'. By contrast, example (41b) appears to refer to one event encoded by the verb *artnpe-* 'run'. The affix -*lalpe*/-*rralpe* 'do & return' contributes there a return-shaped path.

(41) Kaytetye (Arandic; Central Australia: Koch, 1984: 29)
    a. *alarre-**lalpe**-nhe?*
       kill-**DO&RETURN**-PST
       'Did you kill it before you came back?'

    b. *artnpe-**rralpe**-ne   apmere-warle*
       run-**DO&RETURN**-IMP camp-ALL
       'Run back to the camp!'

Strikingly, the two possible interpretations of ambiguous AM forms, such as -*lalpe*/-*rralpe*, occur in the same types of contexts as those of D-AM markers (Belkadi 2016b, 2016c). Thus, additional motion event interpretations for both AM and D-AM are most often found with verbs not encoding motion. By contrast, directional or path interpretations are most often found with verbs which encode motion (Voisin 2013; Vuillermet 2013; Rose 2015), particularly those encoding self-contained, bounded, translocative motion (Belkadi 2015a, 2016a). Furthermore, motion and directional or path interpretations appear to be in complementary distributions across single languages (Belkadi 2016a). It is thus extremely rare for a form to be ambiguous between a directional interpretation and an additional motion event interpretation with a single verb (unless this verb is polysemous, in which case each interpretation is only possible with a particular meaning of the verb).[17]

The fuzzy boundaries between deictic directionality and AM are reinforced by the fact that in some languages the two categories appear to form single paradigms. In Cherang'any, for instance, deictic directionals and AM (referred to as mobilitive) markers occur in the same position in the verb template and are in complementary distribution (Mietzner 2015). This is illustrated in the examples in (42) below.

(42) Cherang'any (Nilotic, Kenya; Mietzner 2015: 201)
    a. *wìr-tá*
       throw-**ITV**
       'S/he throws away' (from deictic anchor)

    b. *wìr-u*
       throw-**VEN**
       'S/he throws towards.' (deictic anchor)

    c. *til-λλtí*
       cut-**MOB.ITV**
       'S/he cuts while going.' (from deictic anchor)

    d. *til-λλnu*
       cut-**MOB.VEN**
       'S/he cuts while coming.' (towards deictic anchor)

---

17 The only example of a D-AM exponent being interpreted with either deictic directionality or associated motion with the same verb in the exact same type of context I have come across is from Nuer (West Nilotic, South Sudan and Ethiopia) discussed in Bond & Reid in preparation):

ųą̈n   jèeṭ-ą́   nāaaṭ   ɲjāl
1SG.SUBJ spear.AM-1SG people up

(i) 'I am spearing people whilst (I am) moving (towards) upstairs.'
(ii) 'I am spearing people in the direction of upstairs.'

It is quite evident that D-AM cannot necessarily and categorically be distinguished from AM. And if a clear-cut dichotomy between AM and D-AM is not possible, it does not seem pertinent to continue to treat deictic directionality and AM as distinct morphosyntactic categories. Take the Berber clitic =*d* and the Kaytetye affix -*rralpe*/-*lalpe* discussed in examples (10) and (41) respectively. The suffix -*rralpe*/-*lalpe* is categorised by Koch (1984) as a member of the category AM while =*d* is classified by Berber linguists as a deictic directional. However, since the former can encode directionality and the latter can encode AM, it is quite difficult to categorically contrast them. Why should one belong to the category of AM and not the other? A plausible alternative analysis is that deictic directionality also expresses a motion event. In the remainder of this paper, I argue that these similarities stem from the fact that deictic directionality constitutes a form of associated motion.

The analysis of deictic directionality as expressing motion is neither new nor unchallenged. Dryer (this volume, chapter 4), while conceding that D-AM forms do encode motion – which, he assumes, becomes redundant with verbs expressing motion –, discounts a generalised analysis of directionality as associated motion. For him, only associated motion encodes motion; directionality presupposes it. Evidence for keeping a dichotomy comes from a number of American languages in which associated motion markers are never interpreted with deictic directional semantics.[18] Bourdin (2005), on the other hand, proposes a motion analysis for deictic directionals, focussing on the Somali itive and ventive markers (i.e. *sii* and *soo*). The following quote summarises his proposal:

> [The ventive and itive satellites] refer to motion events (M) which take place in physical space. Syntactically they modify a verb which itself refers to a process (P). The relation between P and M may be one of identity, coincidence or contiguity. There is identity if the process designated by the verb is M itself, there is coincidence if P and M are concomitant, and there is contiguity if M frames P. (Bourdin 2006: 18)

Although akin in essence, the account under development here contrasts with Bourdin's in subtle ways and it is important to clarify this divergence from the onset. My analysis principally seeks to unify the concepts of deictic directionality and AM, and to this aim relies exclusively on time relations between the motion event argued to be encoded by deictic directionality and the event lexicalised by the host verb. Indeed, as discussed in section 2, one of the most characteristic and canonical functions of AM is to temporally link a motion event to some other event

---

18 One reviewer also notes that in some languages deictic directionals do not also mark associated motion.

expressed by a verb. Particularly, and this will be explained in more detail below, I take constructions which involve deictic directionality to express complex events, just like constructions involving AM. The differences between the two constructions lie in the particular way in which the events they involve temporally relate to each other; specifically, in their degree of temporal integration (after Levin & Rappaport 1999; Rappaport Hovav 2008). Bourdin (2006) does not attempt to link deictic directionality to AM. Furthermore, while the concept of 'coincidence' he adopts in the previous quote implies such a temporal relation between his M (motion) and P (process) events, the other concepts of 'identity' and 'contiguity' do not.

My proposal is first and foremost based on the assumption that events, defined as actions or sequences of actions individuated in time and space, are not necessarily 'atomic units' (Tenny & Pustejovsky 1997: 7; see also Reichenbach 1947; Davidson 1966; Parsons 1990; Link 1998; Bohnemeyer et al. 2009 amongst others). Events may have internal structure and be composed of multiple subevents (Davidson, 1967; Miller and Johnson-Laird 1976; Jackendoff 1990; Hale & Keyser 1993; Levin & Rappaport Hovav 2005; Ramchand 2008; Bohnemeyer et al. 2009 amongst others). For example, as discussed in Tenny & Pustejovsky (1997: 8), the event expressed in (43) can be analysed as complex. Specifically, it can be thought of as being composed of one subevent which refers to John acting agentively to slice the bread and a second subevent referring to the change of state undergone by the bread.

(43) *John sliced the bread.*

In the fields of cognitive semantics and lexical-conceptual semantics, events which include a path expression are considered to form such complex events. That is, the path components of motion events are taken to express events (Tenny & Pustejovsky 1997; Krifka 1999; Levin & Rappaport Hovav 1999; Talmy 2000; Rappaport Hovav 2008; Bohnemeyer et al. 2007; Bohnemeyer et al. 2009; Beavers 2008). There are a number of arguments supporting this view. One of these is detailed in Rappaport Hovav (2008: 16), who discusses the English examples below:

(44) a. *John ran to the store.*
 b. *John rolled the barrel to the store.*
 c. *The cup fell to the floor.*

(45) a. *I threw the ball to Mary (but aimed badly and she didn't catch it).*
 b. *I sent the package to France (but the ship sank and the package never arrived).*
 c. *We launched the rocket to the moon (but it blew up before it got there).*

Both sets of sentences in (44) and (45) include path expressions involving the preposition *to*. However, the relations between the motions of the figures and the '*to*-paths' are different. In the set of examples presented in (44), the figures are interpreted as traversing the paths in their entirety. Thus, in (44a), for John to have run to the store, he must have reached it. By contrast, in the set of sentences given in (45), the figures do not have to traverse the path. In (45a), for instance, the ball may be thrown without Mary catching it. For Rappaport Hovav (2008; see also Krifka 1999), these distinct interpretations show that the path components in (44) and (45) encode motion events. In (44), the path motion events necessarily co-occur with the event encoded by the verb. This is not necessarily the case in (45): the throwing of the ball event may happen while the motion of this ball to Mary does not.

In particular, manner of motion, causative motion events and motion events consisting of a complex path are often argued to form macro-events in English (Levin & Rappaport Hovav 1999; Talmy 2000; Bohnemeyer et al. 2007; Bohnemeyer et al. 2009); that is, a complex event conceptualised and lexicalised as a unitary event (Talmy 2000). The degree of semantic integration between subevents can be measured on the basis of morphosyntactic criteria, in which case any sequence of events encoded in a single clause forms a macro-event (Pawley 1987; Givón 1991; Talmy 2000; Dixon 2006; Dooley 2010 amongst others). Event integration can alternatively be measured on the basis of temporal criteria (Bohnemeyer et al. 2007). In this case, a series of events form a macro-event only if they all fall under the scope of some temporal operator. The complex motion from Japanese given below, for example, can be described as having the macro-event property as the two subevents respectively expressed by 'go from the tree' and 'go to the house' are both necessarily under the scope of the time adverbial *kinoo* 'yesterday'.

(46)   Japanese (Bohnemeyer et al. 2007: 511)
(Kinoo)   ki-no   tokoro-kara   ie-made   it-ta.
yesterday   tree-GEN   place-ABL   house-until   go-PAST
'[One] went from the tree to the house (yesterday).'

Whichever definition one adopts for macro-events, there seems to be a clear agreement that the subevents they are composed of can temporally relate to each other in various ways. Recall, for instance, the English sentences discussed in (44) and (45) above which all involve macro-events with one path of motion subevent. Despite being formally very similar, these constructions yield different interpretations. According to Rappaport Hovav (2008), these come from the different temporal relations between subevents. In (44), the subevents are 'coextensive': the temporal progress of one is dependent on the temporal progress of the other, and so they necessarily unfold at the same time and have the same starting and end points (Rappaport Hovav 2008: 17; Levin & Rappaport Hovav 1999: 207). The subevents in (45), by contrast, are not. The interpretations of subevents as either coextensive or not depend primarily on the verbs used in the constructions. Thus, the verbs in (44) are classified by Rappaport Hovav (2008) as having a coextensive property, those in (45) are classified as lacking this property.

The close link between deictic directionality and path (cf. section 2) justifies an analysis of motion events involving deictic directionals as forming macro-events too.[19] Similarly, Dimmendaal (2015) proposes an analysis of complex events involving AM as macro-events.[20] Given that deictic directionality and AM encode motion events which form (complex) macro-events with the events encoded by the verb they morphosyntactically combine with, they can both be considered to form one single category. Following the work cited above, I propose that the difference in interpretations between AM and deictic directionality lies, in fact, in the temporal integration between the motion subevent they encode and the subevent described by the verb they occur with. In directional interpretations

---

[19] A macro-event usually consists of a framing event which determines "the overall temporal and aspectual frame of the sentence and its argument structure" and a subordinate event which "fill in, elaborate, add to, or motivate the framing event" (Talmy 2000: 219–220). In macro-events involving path and manner or cause, the path is the framing event while either manner or cause constitutes the subordinate co-event. It is not possible at this stage to establish which of the events in a macro-event involving deictic directionality constitutes the framing event. At least in some languages, the deictic motion is the subordinate event rather than the main/framing event. In Taqbaylit, for instance, the ventive =d does not generally affect the aspectual structure of a predicate. However, it is possible that deictic directionality has properties of framing events in other languages. More research is needed to determine this.

[20] If one follows the second definition of macro-events (i.e. the definition proposed by Bohnemeyer et al. 2007), it is not clear that complex events involving AM interpretations form such macro-events. Indeed, particularly in constructions in which the associated motion event occurs prior or subsequently to the event of the verb, subevents are not necessarily under the scope of all temporal operators. Thus, in the following example from Taqbaylit Berber, the temporal adverbial phrase *f tnac* 'at noon' modifies the main verb's event but cannot modify the motion event encoded by the ventive clitic.

Taqbaylit (Berber, Algeria, own data)
ičča   =*d*   f   tnac.
3SGM-eat.PFV   =VEN   at   twelve
'He ate at noon and then came back.'
*'He ate and came back at noon.'

I leave these issues for further research and, for the purpose of the present discussion, follow Dimmendaal (2015) in treating complex events involving AM interpretations as macro-events.

the relation between the deictic motion event and the motion event encoded by the verb can be described as coextensive: the subevents are the same and have the same starting and end points (Levin & Rappaport Hovav 1999: 207; Rappaport Hovav 2008: 17). Example (47) from Tima clearly illustrates this relation. The ventive deictic motion event expressed by the suffix *-íŋ* can be defined as coextensive with the motion event encoded by the verb 'walk'. Indeed, the temporal progress of the figure's motion towards the school is dependent on the event of walking: every part of the sub-event of walking corresponds in effect to a part of the sub-event of moving towards the school.

(47) Tima (Niger-Congo, Nuba Mountains; Alamin et al. 2012: 21, 27)
 kì-címbʌ́rí én-díík-**íŋ** áỳm̩t̩ś mádə̀ràsà
 NC.SG-child TAM-walk-**VEN** DIR:SPEAKER.there school
 'The child is walking towards the school (where I am).'

In AM interpretations, by contrast, subevents are less integrated. Associated motion subevents can take place before, after or at the same time as those subevents lexicalised by the main verb. However, the former and latter do not temporally depend on each other and do necessarily have the same starting point or endpoint. Take the following two AM examples from the Tacanan languages Ese Ejja and Cavineña, previously discussed in section 2.

(48) Ese Ejja (Tacanan, Bolivia & Peru; Vuillermet 2013: 8)
 Ewanase =pa jama a-ka-***nana***-ani-naje (...)
 Wife =REP so say-3A-**DO&LEAVE**-IPFV-PAS
 'Before leaving, he used to say to his wife (...)'

(49) Cavineña (Tacanan, Bolivia; Guillaume 2009: 197)
 tume =pa =taa =tuja =tu ba-***tsa***-ya ekwita...
 Then =REP =EMPH =3SG.DAT =3SG see-**COME(O)**-IPFV person
 'He saw a person coming in his direction.'

In (48), the two events involved do not unfold at the same time. The event described by the verb 'to say' is presented as finished when the associated motion subevent starts; i.e. the saying subevent occurs before the leaving one. In (49), the two events involved occur simultaneously – the figure of motion (*the person*) is coming while the experiencer (*he*) is seeing. While there is temporal concordance between them, these two subevents are undoubtedly not temporally integrated or coextensive. First, it is not the case that the temporal progress of one depends on the other. Indeed, the referent of 'person' can stop moving while still being seen by the referent of 'him' or, alternatively, can continue to move even if not seen by 'him' anymore. Second, the 'subjects' of the subevents in the macro-event are divergent: the most agentive argument of the seeing event is thus not the figure of the motion subevent.

As already stated a number of times already, the analysis of deictic directionality as AM is strongly supported by the very occurrence of D-AM. The fact that a same form can yield deictic directional and AM interpretations in complementary types of contexts is indeed a compelling sign that this form encodes both concepts. Incidentally, the distribution of these interpretations, particularly the fact that they are determined by the semantics of the main verb, further corroborates the account developed here. It was shown in section 3 that the degree of prototypicality of the motion event encoded by the hosting verbs triggers variations in the interpretations of polysemous. The ventive suffix -íŋ in Tima illustrates this phenomenon quite nicely. In (47) above, it occurs on the verb 'walk' and the motion event it encodes is interpreted as coextensive with the event of the verb. In (50) below, the same suffix is used on the non-motion verbs 'build' and 'drink'. The motion event it encodes is interpreted as not coextensive with the verb's event.

(50) Tima (Niger-Congo, Nuba Mountains; Alamin et al. 2012: 21, 27)
  a. *kɔ́yɔ̀-ɔÃŋ*   k-ùrtú
     build.IMP:SG-VEN   NC.SG-house
     'Build the house and come.'

  b. *mɔ́ɔ̀k-íŋ*
     drink.IMP:SG-VEN
     'Drink and come.'

If the different interpretations of D-AM are taken to derive from variations in the degree of temporal integration between the motion event they encode and the event expressed by their host verb – i.e. how coextensive they are –, the role of the motion semantics of the main verbs is easily explained. Indeed, the more motional a subevent encoded by a verb is, the more likely the motion subevent expressed by a D-AM form is to be temporally integrated with it, and vice-versa. The more similarities in their semantics, the more two subevents are likely to be interpreted as coextensive.

In Belkadi (2016a, b), I proposed the ranking of verbs in (51)[21] and argued that D-AM forms that do not have coextensive relations with verbs on the left-hand

---

[21] Some of the terms used to differentiate aspects of motion events in Belkadi (2016a, b) differ from those adopted in this paper and described in section 2. Thus: Path Motion in Belkadi (2016a)

side of the scale are more likely to be 'real' markers of motion and belong to the category of AM, while those with coextensive relations to verbs from the right-hand side of the scale are more likely to be directional expressions. Following the unified analysis argued for here and the evidence provided in the range of data above, the implications of this verb ranking should be modified. Thus, the types of events lexicalised by verbs on the left-hand side of the scale are more likely to fully temporally integrate with the motion encoded by an AM/D-AM form. Those on the right-hand side are more likely not to temporally integrate with the latter.

(51) Path Motion > Motion translational > Causative motion > Perception > (Natural phenomena and bodily secretions?) > Activities not involving translational motion > States (Belkadi 2016a: 64)

5 Conclusion

In the typological and theoretical literature focussing on motion events and path encoding, deictic directionality is often either left out or only briefly discussed. In descriptive work, where it is more often considered, the focus is generally on the range of deictic contrasts grammaticalised by some languages (e.g. Gurzdeva 2007). As a result, there are a number of contrastive analyses of the role and place of deictic directionality in the network of components forming motion event expressions. I hope to have shown in this paper that deictic directionality plays an essential linguistic role in a number of languages from across Africa. It is not only used to specify the deictic anchor of a motion event encoded by a verb but also to locate a range of non-motion events across space in certain languages.

This second function of deictic directionality makes it very similar to another (also not as widely studied but increasingly popular) morphosyntactic category: associated motion (Wilkins 2006; Koch 2019). In the previous sections, I have developed an analysis which accounts for the similarities between deictic directionality and associated motion while also explaining the role of the former in the network of components forming motion events. Based on the distribution and semantic meanings of so-called D-AM forms – forms which express both deictic directional and associated motion meanings depending on their linguistic environment – in a number of languages from the four linguistic phyla indigenous to Africa, I proposed that deictic directionality is a type of associated motion: it

---

corresponds here to self-contained, translocative and bounded motion, and Motion Translational in Belkadi (2016a) corresponds here to self-contained, translocative unbounded motion.

encodes motion events and as such constitutes a mono-verbal strategy to encode multiple (complex) events. The seemingly different semantics between the two concepts is due to the different ways in which the events they encode temporally integrate with the events encoded by the verb they modify. With deictic directional interpretations, temporal integration between events is coextensive; with associated motion interpretations, the events are not fully or not at all temporally integrated.

The analysis argued for in this paper has a number of advantages. Besides accounting for the strong similarities between AM and deictic directionality as well as the phenomenon of D-AM itself, it straightforwardly explains and, in fact predicts, variations in the range of contexts in which AM vs. deictic directionality can be found cross-linguistically. Yet at this stage, it leaves some questions unanswered. One of these is whether deictic directionals should always be considered to encode motion, even in languages where they never have AM interpretations. For example, as discussed briefly in section 4, Dryer (this volume, chapter 4) does not believe that all directionals encode motion; only those that actually express associated motion do. For my part, I believe that it is difficult to gauge, and not possible to predict, how different parts of an event are linguistically broken down and encoded in different languages (see Levinson & Wilkins 2006 or Bohnemeyer et al. 2007 for discussions of this issue) and there might be a number of independent reasons why a deictic directional does not encode associated motion in a particular language. In some, an exponent interpreted as realising deictic directionality in some particular contexts or in combination with some other entity encoding direction or path may in fact primarily function as a locative marker. Such forms would, of course, not be expected to encode motion. The locative prepositions of many Romance and Germanic languages, for instance, have directional meanings with verbs that encode directed or canonically translocative motion (Gehrke 2006; Nikitina 2008; Ramchand 2008 amongst others). In French, the preposition *à* is interpreted as locative with the non-motion verb 'eat' (*J'ai mangé à la maison* 'I ate at home') but it is interpreted with directional semantics with the verb of translocative motion 'run' (*J'ai couru à la maison* 'I ran to the house'). In others, it could be that deictic directionals do not encode motion at all. Future typological and theoretical research on deictic directionality and D-AM in languages from various areas of the globe and linguistic families might help settle the question. For now, despite the high frequency of D-AM forms cross-linguistically pointing to a fundamental link between motion and deictic directionality, my analysis cannot be categorically generalised to deictic directionals outside of Africa.

Abbreviations

1	first person	F	feminine	PASS	passive
2	second person	FOC	focus	PC	past completive
3	third person	FUT	future	PFV	perfective
ABS	absolutive	GEN	genitive	PL	plural
ACC	accusative	HORT	hortative	POSS	possessive
ALL	allative	IMP	imperative	PROX	proximal
ANP	anaphoric deictic pronoun	INF	infinitive	PST	past
		INS	instrumental	PURP	purposive
AOR	aorist	IPFV	imperfective	REP	reported
CAUS	causative	IS	inflectional suffix	RES	resultative
COM	comitative	ITN	itinerant	SBJ	subject
D	declarative	ITV	itive	SG	singular
DAT	dative	LOC	locative	SUB	subordination marker
DEM	demonstrative	M	masculine		
DET	determiner	MOB	mobilitive	TAM	tense/aspect/mood
DIR	directional	NC	noun class		
EMPH	emphatic	NOM	nominative	TR	transitive
ES	subject emphatic	OBJ	object	VEN	ventive.
EV	verb emphatic	OBL	oblique		

Acknowledgements: I have had the opportunity to present the materials and ideas in this paper at several conferences and I am grateful to the audiences for their comments and questions. I thank all those who have discussed the ideas in this paper with me or shared examples and information about D-AM in the languages they work on: the editors of this volume Antoine Guillaume and Harold Koch who provided extensive and valuable comments on different versions, Gerrit Dimmendaal who reviewed an earlier draft of this paper, Samir Ben Si Said, Denis Creissels, Tom Güldemann, Phil Jaggar and Serge Sagna, Doris payne.

References

Alamin, Suzan, Gertrud Schneider-Blum & Gerrit J. Dimmendaal. 2012. Finding your way in Tima. In Angelika Mietzner & Ulrike Claudi (eds), *Directionality in grammar and discourse: Case studies from Africa*, 9–34. Köln: Rüdiger Köppe Verlag.

Ameka, Felix K. and James Essegbey. 2006. Elements of the grammar of space in Ewe. In Steven C. Levinson & David Wilkins (eds), *Grammars of space*, 359–398. Cambridge: Cambridge University Press.

Andersen, Torben. 1988. Consonant alternation in the verbal morphology of Päri. *Afrika und Ubersee* 71. 63–113.

Andersen, Torben. 2012. Verbal directionality and argument alternation in Dinka. In Angelika Mietzner & Ulrike Claudi (eds.), *Directionality in grammar and discourse: Case studies from Africa*, 35–54. Köln: Rüdiger Köppe Verlag.

Aske, Jon. 1989. Path predicates in English and Spanish: A closer look. *Annual meeting of the Berkeley linguistics society*. 1–14. Berkeley CA: University of California Press.

Austin, Peter K. 1988. *Complex sentence constructions in Australian languages*. (Typological Studies in Language 15) Amsterdam & Philadelphia: John Benjamins.

Bassène, Alain C. 2007. *Morphosyntaxe du jóola banjal: Langue atlantique du Sénégal*. (Grammatische Analysen Afrikanischer Sprachen 32) Köln: Köppe.

Beavers, John. 2008. Scalar complexity and the structure of events. In Johannes Dölling, Tatjana Heyde-Zybatow and Martin Schäfer (eds.), *Event structures in linguistic form and interpretation*, 245–265. Berlin: Mouton de Gruyter.

Beavers, John, Beth Levin & Shiao Wei Tham. 2010. The typology of motion expressions revisited. In *Journal of Linguistics* 46 (2). 331–377.

Belkadi, Aicha. 2014. Verb meaning and deictic paths in Taqbaylit Berber. In Aicha Belkadi, Kakia Chatsiou & Kirsty Rowan (eds.), *Language Documentation and Linguistic Theory 4*. London: SOAS University of London.

Belkadi, Aicha. 2015a. Associated motion with deictic directional A comparative overview. In Charlotte, Hemmings & Vivian Lee (eds), *SOAS Working Papers in Linguistics 16*, 49–76. London: SOAS.

Belkadi, Aicha. 2015b. Deictic directionality and space in Berber: A typological survey of the semantics of =d and =nn. In Sabrina Bendjaballah & Samir Ben Si Said (eds.), Corpus 14. Base, Corpus, Langage, UMR 6039. https://journals.openedition.org/corpus/2672 (last accessed on 20th April 2020).

Belkadi, Aicha. 2016a. Associated motion constructions in African languages. *Africana Linguistica*, 22. 43–70.

Belkadi, Aicha. 2016b. Verb semantics and the category of associated motion. Paper presented at the 6th UK Cognitive Linguistics Conference, Bangor University, Bangor (UK), 19–22 July 2016.

Belkadi, Aicha. 2016c. Towards a definition of the category associated motion. Paper presented at the 49th Annual Meeting of the Societas Linguistica Europaea, University of Naples Federico II, Naples (Italy), 31 August-03 September 2016.

Bentolila, Fernand. 1969. Les modalités d'orientation du procès en berbère (1). *La Linguistique* 5 (1). 85–96

Bentolila, Fernand. 1969. Les modalités d'orientation du procès en berbère (2). *La Linguistique* 5 (2). 91–111.

Blomberg, Johan and Jordan Zlatev. 2009. Linguistic relativity, mediation and the categorization of motion. In Jordan Zlatev, Mats Andrén, Marlene Johansson Falck and Carita Lundmark (eds.), *Studies in language and cognition*, 46–61. Newcastle upon Tyne: Cambridge Scholars Publishing.

Bohnemeyer, Jürgen, Nicholas J. Enfield, James Essegbey, Iraide Ibarretxe, Sotaro Kita, Friederike Lüpke and Felix K. Ameka. 2007. Principles of event encoding: The case of motion events. *Language 83 (3)*. 495–532.

Bohnemeyer, Jürgen, Nicholas J. Enfield, James Essegbey & Sotaro Kita. 2009. The macro-event property: The segmentation of causal chains. Ms.

Bond, Oliver and Tatiana Reid. In preparation. Associated motion in Nuer.

Bourdin, Philippe. 2006. The marking of directional deixis in Somali How typologically idiosyncratic is it? In Voeltz, F.K. Erhard (ed.), *Studies in African linguistic typology*, 13–41. Amsterdam & Philadelphia: John Benjamins.
Choi-Jonin, Injoo & Laure Sarda. 2007. The expression of semantic components and the nature of ground entity in orientation motion verbs: a cross-linguistic account based on French and Korean. In Michel Aurnague, Maya Hickmann and Laure Vieu (eds.), *The categorization of spatial entities in language and cognition* (Human Cognitive Processing 20), 123–149. John Benjamins.
Claudi, Ulrike. 2012. Who moves, and why? Somali deictic particles. In Angelika Mietzner, & Ulrike Claudi (eds.), *Directionality in grammar and discourse: Case studies from Africa*, 77–88. Köln: Rüdiger Köppe Verlag.
Creissels, Denis. 2014. Le développement d'un marqueur de déplacement centripète en Mandinka: Une influence possible du contact avec les langues atlantiques. In Carole De Féral, Maarten Kossmann and Mauro Tosco (eds.), *In and out of Africa: Languages in question, in honour of Robert Nicolai vol 2* (Language contact and language change in Africa), 95–102. Louvain-La-Neuve: Peeters.
Creissels, Denis & Alain C. Bassene. This volume, chapter 17. Ventive, associated motion and aspect in Jóola Fóoñi (Atlantic).
Croft, William, Jóhanna Barðdal, Willem Hollmann, Violeta Sotirova, and Chiaki Taoka. 2007. Revising Talmy's typological classification of complex event. In Hans C. Boas (ed)., *Contrastive Construction Grammar*, 201–237. Amsterdam: John Benjamins Publishing.
Davidson, Donald. 1966. The logical form of action sentences. In Donald Davidson (ed.) *Essays on actions and events*, 105–121. Oxford: Clarendon Press.
Dimmendaal, Gerrit J. 2012. The grammar of knowledge in Tima. In Alexandra Aikhenvald & Robert M. W. Dixon (ed.), *The grammar of knowledge: A cross-linguistic typology*. (Explorations in Linguistic Typology 7), 245–259. Oxford: Oxford University Press.
Dimmendaal, Gerrit J. 2015. Alloying as an economy principle in morphology. Ms.
Dixon, Robert M. W. 2006. Serial verb constructions: Conspectus and coda. In Alexandra Y. Aikhenvald & Robert M. W. Dixon (ed) *Serial verb constructions: A cross-linguistic typology*, 338–350. Oxford: Oxford University Press.
Dooley, Robert A. 2010. Exploring Clause Chaining. SIL Electronic Working Papers 2010–001.
Dryer, Matthew. This volume, chapter 4. Associated motion and directionals: Where they overlap.
El Mountassir, Abadallah. 2000. Langage et espace. Les particules d'orientation -d/-nn en berbère (tachelhit). In Salem Chaker & Andrzej Zaborky (eds.), *Études berbères et chamito-sémitiques: Mélanges offerts à Karl-G. Prasse*, 129–154. Leuven: Peeters.
Fagard, Benjamin, Jordan Zlatev, Anetta Kopecka, Massimo Cerruti & Johan Blomberg. 2013. The expression of motion events: A quantitative study of six typologically varied languages. *Berkeley Linguistics Society* 39. 364–379.
Fleisch, Axel. 2007. Orientational clitics and the expression of path in Tashelhit Berber (Shilha). *Annual Publication in African Linguistics* 5. 55–72.
Fleisch, Axel. 2012. Directionality in Berber: Orientational clitics in Tashelhit and related varieties. In Angelika Mietzner & Ulrike Claudi (eds.) *Directionality in grammar and discourse: Case studies from Africa*, 127–146. Köln: Rüdiger Köppe Verlag.
Frajzyngier, Zygmund. 1989. *A grammar of Pero*. Berlin: D. Reimer.
Frajzyngier, Zygmund. 2001. *A grammar of Lele*. (Stanford Monographs in African Languages). Chicago: University of Chicago Press.

Gehrke, Berit. 2006. Putting path in place. In Estela Puig-Waldmüller (ed.), *Sinn und Bedeutung* 11, 244–260.
Genetti, Carol, Kristin Hildebrandt, Alexia Fawcett, Patrick Hall & Nathaniel Sims. 2017. Argument structure functions of spatial-encoding sub-systems in Tibeto-Burman languages. Paper presented at the 12th Conference of the Association for Linguistic Typology (ALT), Australian National University, Canberra, Australia, 12–14 December 2017.
Givón, Talmy. 1991. Serial verbs and the mental reality of 'event.' In Elizabeth C. Traugott and Bernd Heine (eds.). *Approaches to grammaticalization* vol. 1, 81–127. Amsterdam: John Benjamins.
Guillaume, Antoine. 2006. La catégorie du 'mouvement associé' en cavineña: Apport à une typologie de l'encodage du mouvement et de la trajectoire. *Bulletin de la Société Linguistique de Paris* 101 (2). 415–436.
Guillaume, Antoine. 2009. Les suffixes verbaux de 'mouvement associé' en cavineña, *Faits de Langues, Les Cahiers 1.* 181–204. Gap, Paris : Ophrys.
Guillaume, Antoine. 2013. Reconstructing the category of "associated motion" in Tacanan languages (Amazonian Bolivia and Peru). In Ritsuko Kikusawa & Lawrence A. Reid (eds.), *Historical Linguistics 2011. 20th International Conference on Historical Linguistics, Osaka, 25–30 July 2011*, 129–151. Amsterdam & Philadelphia: John Benjamins Publishing Company.
Guillaume, Antoine. 2016. Associated motion in South America: Typological and areal perspectives. *Linguistic Typology* 20 (1). 2–95.
Guillaume, Antoine. 2017. Sistemas complejos de movimiento asociado en las lenguas Takana y Pano: perspectivas descriptiva, tipológica e histórico-comparativa. In Antoine Guillaume & Pilar M. Valenzuela (eds.), *Estudios sincrónicos y diacrónicos sobre lenguas Pano y Takana,* 39(1). 211–261. Paris: Amerindia – A.E.A.
Guillaume, Antoine & Harold Koch. This volume, chapter 1. Introduction: Associated Motion as a grammatical category in linguistic typology.
Gurzdeva, Ekaterina. 2007. Challenging theory: Spatial deixis in Nivkh. In Peter K. Austin, Oliver Bond & David Nathan (eds.), *Language Documentation and Linguistic Theory 1,* 103–113. London: SOAS University of London.
Hale, Kenneth & Samuel J. Keyser. 1993. On argument structure and the lexical expression of syntactic relations. In Kenneth Hale & Samuel J. Keyser (eds.), *View from Building 20: Essays in Linguistics in Honour of Sylvain Bromberger,* 53–109. (Current Studies in Linguistics 24 Cambridge, Ma.: MIT Press.
Heath, Jeffrey. 1998. *A grammar of Koyra Chiini.* Berlin: Mouton de Gruyter.
Heath, Jeffrey. 1999. *A grammar of Koyraboro (Koroboro) Senni.* Köln: Rüdiger Köppe Verlag.
Heath, Jeffrey. 2005. *Grammar of Tamashek (Tuareg of Mali).* Berlin: Mouton de Gruyter.
Heine, Berndt, Ulrike Claudi & Friederike Hünnemeyer. 1991. *Grammaticalization: A conceptual framework.* Chicago: University of Chicago Press.
Heine, Berndt & Tania Kuteva. 2002. *World lexicon of grammaticalisation.* Cambridge: Cambridge University Press.
Hopper Paul J. & Elisabeth Traugott. 2003. *Grammaticalization.* (Cambridge Textbooks in Linguistics) Cambridge: Cambridge University Press.
Jackendoff, Ray. 1990. *Semantic structures.* Cambridge, Mass.: MIT Press.
Jaggar, Phil. 2001. *Hausa.* Amsterdam & Philadelphia: John Benjamins.
Johnson, Christopher, Charles J. Fillmore, Esther Wood, Josef Ruppenhofer, Miriam Petruck, and Collin Baker. 2001. The FrameNet Project: Tools for Lexicon Building. Berkeley: ICSI-University of California at Berkeley.

Kawachi, Kazuhiro. This volume, chapter 19. The 'along'–deictic-directional verb suffix complex in Kupsapiny.
Kießling, Roland. 2014. Verb serialisation in Taa (Southern Khoisan). In Alena Witzlack-Makarevitch and Martina Ernszt (eds.), *Khoisan languages and linguistics: Proceedings of the Second International Symposium, July 6–10, 2008*. 33–60. Cologne: Köppe.
Kilian-Hatz, Christen. 2010. Serial verb constructions vs. converbs in Khwe. In Matthias Brenzinger & Christa König (eds.), *Proceedings of the 1st International Symposium, January 4–8, 2003, Riezlern/Kleinwalsertal*, 115–143. Köln: Köppe.
Koch, Harold. 1984. The category of 'associated motion' in Kaytej. *Language in Central Australia* 1. 23–34.
Koch, Harold. 2019. Morphosyntactic reanalysis in Australian languages: Three studies. In Lars Heltoft, Iván Igartua, Brian D. Joseph, Kirsten Jeppesen Kragh and Lene Schøsler (eds.), *Perspectives on language structure and language change: Studies in honor of Henning Andersen*. (Current Issues in Linguistics theory 345). Amsterdam & Philadelphia: John Benjamins.
Kossmann, Maarten. 2011. *A grammar of Ayer Tuareg (Niger)*. Köln: Rüdiger Köppe Verlag.
Kossmann, Maarten. 2013. *A grammatical sketch of Ghadames Berber (Libya)*. Köln: Rüdiger Köppe Verlag.
Krifka, Manfred. 1999. Manner in dative alternation. *Proceedings of WCCFL* 18, 260–271. Somerville: Cascadilla Press.
Lakoff, George & Mark Johnson. 1980. *Metaphors we live by*. Chicago: University of Chicago Press.
Lamarre, Christine. 2008. The linguistic categorization of deictic direction in Chinese – With reference to Japanese. In Dan Xu (ed.), *Space in languages of China*, 69–97. Dordrecht: Springer.
Langacker, Ronald. 1991. Cognitive Grammar. in Flip G. Droste and John E. Joseph (eds.), *Linguistic theory and grammatical description: Nine current approaches*. (Current Issues in Linguistic Theory 75), 275–306. Philadelphia: John Benjamins.
Lehmann, Christian. 2015. *Thoughts on grammaticalization*. 3rd edn. Berlin: Language Science Press.
Levin, Beth and Malka Rappaport Hovav. 1999. Two structures for compositionally derived events. *Semantics and linguistic theory (SALT)* 9. 199–223.
Levin, Beth & Malka Rappaport Hovav. 2005. *Argument realization*. (Research Surveys in Linguistics) Cambridge: Cambridge University Press.
Levinson, Stephen C. 1983. *Pragmatics*. Cambridge: Cambridge University Press.
Levinson, Stephen & David Wilkins. 2006. *Grammars of space: Explorations in cognitive diversity*. (Language Culture and Cognition 6) Cambridge: Cambridge University Press.
Link, Godehard. 1998. Algebraic Semantics in Language and Philosophy. Center for the Study of Language and Information Publication Notes, Vol. 74.
Lord, Carol. 1993. Historical change in Serial Verb Constructions. (Typological Studies in Language 26) Amsterdam: John Benjamins.
Lovestrand, Joseph. 2018. Serial verb constructions in Barayin: Typology, description and lexical-functional grammar. Unpublished Doctoral Dissertation. Oxford University.
Mettouchi, Amina. 2011. The grammaticalization of directional clitics in Berber. Paper presented at the workshop "Come and Go off the grammaticalization path", convened by J. van der Wal and M. Devos at the 44th Annual meeting of the Societas Linguistica Europaea. University de la rioja (Spain). 8–11 September 2011.

Mietzner, Angelika. 2012. Spatial orientation in Nilotic languages and the forces of innovation. In Angelika Mietzner & Ulrike Claudi (eds.), *Directionality in grammar and discourse: Case studies from Africa*, 165–176. Köln: Rüdiger Köppe Verlag.

Mietzner, Angelika. 2015. The philosophy of walking – motion and the verbs of walking in Cherang'any (Kalenjin). In Angelika Mietzner and Anne Storch (eds.), *Nilo-Saharan – Models and descriptions*. (Nilo-Saharan 28), 199–210. Köln: Rüdiger Köppe Verlag.

Miller, George A. and Philip N. Johnson-Laird. 1976. *Language and perception*. Cambridge, MA: Harvard University Press.

Morita, Takahiro. 2011. Intratypological variations in motion events in Japanese and French: Manner and deixis as parameters for cross-linguistic comparison. *Revue de l'Association Française de Linguistique Cognitive 6*. https://journals.openedition.org/cognitextes/498 (Last accessed online on 29th April 2020).

Nakazawa, Tsuneko. 2006. Motion event and deictic motion verbs as path-conflating verbs. In Stephen Müller (ed.), *Proceedings of the 13th International Conference on Head-Driven Phrase Structure Grammar* held at the Bulgarian Academy of Sciences, Sofia 24–27 July 2006, 284–304. Stanford : CSLI Publications.

Neukom, Lukas. 2010. *Description grammaticale du kenga (langue nilo-saharienne du Tchad)*. (Nilo-Saharan 25) Köln: Köppe.

Newman, Paul. 2000. *The Hausa language An encyclopaedic reference grammar*. (Yale Language Series) Princeton: Yale University Press.

Nikitina, Tatiana. 2008. Pragmatic factors and variation in the expression of spatial goals: The case of *into* vs. *in*. In Anna Asbury, Jakub Dotlăcil, Berit Gehrke, and Rick Nouwen (eds.), *Syntax and semantics of spatial P*, 175–209. Amsterdam: John Benjamins.

O'Connor, Loretta. 2007. *Motion, transfer and transformation: The grammar of change in Lowland Chontal*. (Studies in Language Companion Series 95) Amsterdam: John Benjamins.

Otero, Manuel. 2017. (Deictic) direction/ associated motion in Ethiopian Komo: A typological perspective. Paper presented at the 12th Conference of the Association for Linguistic Typology (ALT), Canberra, Australia.

Otero, Manuel. This volume, chapter 20. At the intersection of associated motion, direction and exchoative aspect in the Koman languages.

Parsons, Frederick W. 1960. The verbal system in Hausa. *Afrika und Übersee* 44. 1–36.

Parsons, Terence. 1990. *Events in the semantics of English: A study in sub-atomic semantics*. Cambridge, Mass.: MIT Press.

Pawley, Andrew. 1987. Encoding events in Kalam and English: Different logics for reporting experience. In Russell S. Tomlin (ed.), *Coherence and grounding in discourse*, 329–60. Amsterdam: John Benjamins.

Payne, Doris. This volume, chapter 18. The extension of Associated Motion to Direction, Aspect and argument structure in Nilotic Languages.

Persohn, Bastian. 2018. Basic motion verbs in Nyakyusa: Lexical semantics and associated motion. *Studies in African Linguistics 47*. 101–127.

Pourcel, Stephanie & Anetta Kopecka. 2006. Motion events in French: *Typological intricacies*. Ms., University of Sussex, Brighton, and Max Plank Institute for Psycholinguistics, Nijmegen.

Ramchand, Gillian. 2008. *Verb meaning and the lexicon: A first phase syntax*. Cambridge: Cambridge University Press.

Rappaport Hovav, Malka. 2008. Lexicalized meaning and the internal temporal structure of events. In Susan D. Rothstein (ed.), *Theoretical and crosslinguistic approaches to the*

semantics of aspect (Linguistik Aktuell/Linguistics Today 110), 13–42. John Benjamins Publishing.
Rappaport Hovav, Malka and Beth Levin. 2010. Reflections on manner/result complementarity. In Edith Doron, Malka Rappaport Hovav, and Ivy Sichel (eds.), *Syntax, lexical semantics, and event structure*, 21–38. Oxford: Oxford University Press.
Reed, Lauren W. & Kate L. Lindsey. This volume, chapter 9. 'Now the story's turning around': Associated motion and directionality in Ende, a language of Papua New Guinea.
Reh, Mechthild. 1996. *Anywa language: Description and internal reconstructions.* (Nilo-Saharan, linguistic analyses and documentation 11) Köln: Rüdiger Köppe.
Reichenbach, Hans. 1947. *Elements of symbolic logic*. New York & London: The Free Press Collier.
Rose, Françoise. 2015. 'Associated Motion in Mojeño Trinitario: Some typological considerations. In *Folia Linguistica* 49 (1). 117–158.
Slobin, Dan I. 2004. The many ways to search for a frog: Linguistic typology and the expression of motion events. In Sven Strömqvist & Ludo Verhoeven (eds), *Relating events in narrative* Vol. 2. 219–257. Mahwah, NJ: Lawrence Erlbaum Associates.
Slobin, Dan I. 2008. Relations between paths of motion and paths of vision: A Crosslinguistic and developmental exploration. In Virginia M. Gathercole (ed.), *Routes to language: Studies in Honor of Melissa Bowerman*, 197–221. Mahwah, NJ: Lawrence Erlbaum Associates.
Soukka, Maria. 2000. *A descriptive grammar of Noon: A Cangin language of Senegal.* Munich: Lincom Europa.
Stevenson, Roland C. 2009. *Tira and Otoro. Two Kordofanian grammars.* Köln: Rüdiger Köppe Verlag.
Talmy, Leonard. 1985. Lexicalization patterns: Semantic structure in lexical forms. In Timothy Shopen (ed.), *Language typology and syntactic description*, Vol. 3: *Grammatical categories and the lexicon*, 57–149. Cambridge: Cambridge University Press.
Talmy, Leonard. 2000a. *Towards a cognitive semantics* Vol. 1. Cambridge, Mass.: MIT Press.
Talmy, Leonard. 2000b. *Towards a cognitive semantics* Vol. 2. Cambridge, Mass.: MIT Press.
Tenny, Carol & James Pustejovsky. 1997. A history of events in linguistic theory. In Carol Tenny and James Pustejovsky (eds.), *Events as grammatical objects: The converging perspectives of lexical semantics and syntax.* (CSLI lecture notes 100) Stanford: CSLI Publications.
Tucker, Archibald N. & John Tompo Ole Mppaayei. 1955. *A Maasai grammar.* (Publications of the African Institute) Leyden: Longmans, Green and Co.
Vidal, Alejandra & Doris Payne. This volume, chapter 12. Pilagá Directionals and the typology of Associated Motion.
Voisin, Sylvie. 2013. Expressions de trajectoire dans quelques langues atlantiques (groupe Nord). *Faits de Langues* 42(1). 131–152.
Voisin, Sylvie. This volume, chapter 16. Associated Motion and Deictic Directionals in Atlantic languages.
Vuillermet, Marine. 2013. Spatial obsession in the Ese Ejja verbal domain: A look at its associated motion system. Paper presented at Fieldwork Forum, University of California Berkeley. http://linguistics.berkeley.edu/~fforum/handouts/vuillermet_AM_fforum_handoutFINAL.pdf (last accessed 20 June 2016).
Weber, David J. 1989. *A grammar of Huallaga (Huánuco) Quechua.* Berkeley: University of California Press.

Wilkins, David P. 1991. The semantics, pragmatics, and diachronic development of 'associated motion' in Mparntwe Arrernte. Buffalo Papers in Linguistics 91. 207–257.

Wilkins, David P. 2006. Towards an Arrernte grammar of space. In Steven C. Levinson and David P. Wilkins (eds.), *Grammars of space: Explorations in cognitive diversity*. Cambridge: Cambridge University Press.

Zlatev, Jordan. 2007. Spatial semantics. In Dirk Geeraerts & Hubert Cuyckens (eds.), *The Oxford handbook of cognitive linguistics*, 318–350. Oxford: Oxford University Press.

Zlatev, Jordan & Peerapat Yangklang. 2004. A third way to travel: The place of Thai in motion-event typology. In Sven Strömqvist & Ludo Verhoeven (eds.), *Relating events in narrative Vol. 2* 159–190. Mahwa, NJ: Lawrence Erlbaum.

Zlatev, Jordan, Johan Blomberg, and Caroline David. 2010. Translocation: Language and the categorization of experience. In Vyvyan Evans (ed.), *Language, cognition, and space: The state of the art and new directions*, 389–418. London: Equinox.

Marine Vuillermet
6 A visual stimulus for eliciting associated motion

Abstract: Pictures and video stimuli help investigate specific semantic domains and/or grammatical categories. Such stimuli not only help to collect more occurrences of a given (possibly rare) morpheme in a semi-spontaneous setting, but also allow the study of variation across speakers and diversity across languages. The paper describes a stimulus in the form of a storybook, *A Hunting Story*, specifically conceived to elicit associated motion (AM) morphemes in Ese Ejja, an Amazonian language with a complex system of 14 such morphemes. The pictures of the storybook therefore represent an Amazonian setting, and the scenario incorporates the main parameters established in the AM literature (such as path/directionality, temporal relation, moving argument), as well as less frequent ones (such as aspectual realization). The paper describes the data collected from 14 speakers of Ese Ejja as well as data collected with the same stimulus in other languages, including languages with no morphological AM system.

Keywords: experimental stimulus, visual stimulus, elicitation, associated motion, Amazonian languages

1 Introduction: a visual stimulus for eliciting associated motion

Pictures and video stimuli have long proven to be useful in investigating specific semantic domains and/or grammatical categories (e.g. Hellwig 2006), especially for comparative work (e.g. Levinson et al. 2003; or Kopecka & Narasimhan 2012). *A Hunting Story* (Vuillermet & Desnoyers 2013) is the first storybook conceived to elicit Associated Motion (henceforth AM), i.e. morphemes or constructions which mark the association of a backgrounded motion to a main action (Koch 1984; Wilkins 1991; Guillaume 2006, 2016; Guillaume & Koch this volume). This storybook was specifically designed to collect AM morphemes in Ese Ejja, an Amazonian language from the Pano-Takanan family of Bolivia and Peru that displays a

---

Marine Vuillermet, Department of Comparative Language Science & Center for the Interdisciplinary Study of Language Evolution, University of Zürich & Laboratoire Dynamique du Langage (CNRS & Université Lumière Lyon 2), marine.vuillermet@uzh.ch

https://doi.org/10.1515/9783110692099-006

very complex system of 14 AM verbal affixes. For instance, example (1), collected with the Hunting Story stimulus, illustrates the Ese Ejja AM morpheme -*ña* DO.ARRIVING which indicates that the (non-motion) event of eating will happen upon the arrival of the speaker.[1]

(1) *'Bo'bi-kwakwa,   iya-'io-kwe   ekweya e-ijjia-**ña**-'io-jji,*
    food-cooked   sit.TR-TEL-IMP   1GEN   PURP-eat-**DO_ARRIVING**-TEL-PURP
    kia-shoe-nei-nei=ya   kwe-je-'io   eya.
    APF-hungry-very-very=FOC   come-FUT-TEL   1SG.ABS
    'Put cooked food aside for me to eat (when I arrive), I will arrive home very hungry.' {JulHS01}

All the pictures in this storybook illustrate main actions that occur in the context of a journey – e.g. eating *while arriving*, as in (1), checking the rifle *before leaving*, waving to one's family *while going away*, greeting friends *passing by*, etc. This particular stimulus aims to:
1. facilitate the collection of AM morphemes and yield a greater number of tokens, produced in a variety of contexts;
2. better understand the semantic features of each AM morpheme and of the system as a whole (inventory);
3. allow the comparison of intraspeaker and interspeaker variation and examine the possible influence of various parameters such as age, gender and level of fluency;
4. permit the investigation of the discourse use of the morphemes;
5. enable cross-linguistic comparisons, in terms of inventories and discourse use;
6. study AM with an onomasiological approach, i.e. as a functional domain, by examining any strategy used to co-express a non-motion and a (backgrounded) motion event (instead of AM morphology alone).

The storybook is accompanied by a protocol for its use.[2] They are the result of a one-year postdoctoral fellowship at the University of California, Berkeley; the

---

[1] All examples in this paper are responses to the stimulus 'A Hunting Story'. In the translation line, HS## in brackets indicates the page number of the picture described, preceded by the recording ID used by the researcher.

[2] Both are available online at the TulQuest archive for linguistic questionnaires (http://tulquest.huma-num.fr/fr/node/46). TulQuest is an online interactive archive developed by a research team led by A. Lahaussois (HTL, CNRS) and supported by the CNRS Fédération de Typologie et Universaux Linguistiques (TUL, FR2559) between 2014 and 2018. The archive allows users to both retrieve and deposit Questionnaires, defined by our project as any methodological tool de-

Fyssen Foundation provided the financial support, and Antoine Desnoyers, a painter and graphic-designer, effected the drawings.[3]

The present paper is organized as follows: Section 2 details the parameters selected to design the stimulus, and discusses the various domains one might want to explore. Section 3 presents the entire kit: the AM storybook and its 22 scenes, the precautions to be taken to ensure that the pictures are accessible to people unfamiliar with Western modes of representation, and the optional steps in the protocol. Section 4 examines the AM morphemes collected in the Ese Ejja *Hunting Stories*. Section 5 offers a glance at data collected by other researchers using the stimulus in languages with or without AM morphology, not only spoken in Amazonia but also Nepal and Papua New Guinea.

2 The etic grid and the domains to be explored

2.1 Parameters identified and selected for the AM storybook *A Hunting Story*

According to the descriptions of complex[4] AM systems currently available, three main parameters play a role:
- PATH / DIRECTIONALITY – motion away or towards a point of reference, distributed over space, and, much less frequently, upward /downward, as e.g. in Arrernte (Pama-Nyungan) in Wilkins (1991), or reversive, as in Mojeño Trinitario (Arawak; Rose 2015: 144);
- TEMPORAL RELATION TO THE MAIN ACTION – motion event is prior, concurrent or subsequent, as e.g. in Kaytetye (Pama-Nyungan) in Koch (1984: 26) or in Cavineña (Pano-Takanan) in Guillaume (2009);
- MOVING ARGUMENT – the subject, the object (e.g. Guillaume 2016) or, exceptionally, a non-core argument, as in Arrernte (Wilkins 1991: 236–238).

---

signed to collect linguistic data. The archived Questionnaires are categorized according to a taxonomy of features and written with a capital letter to highlight this special use of the term, and are accompanied by additional materials beyond basic metadata, ranging from a summary of usage protocol, development context, reviews and user tips, as well as the possibility of linking together questionnaires that have been adapted from an original version, reflecting the dynamic nature of questionnaire use. See Lahaussois (2019) for more details.
3 www.antoinedesnoyers.com
4 "Complex" here is used in the sense of Guillaume (2016: 109), who distinguishes between three levels of complexity in the system of Amazonian languages: simple systems (1 or 2 AM morphemes), complex systems (3 to 5 AM morphemes) and very complex ones (6 or more AM morphemes).

Other attested parameters are:
- ASPECTUAL REALIZATION (ongoing vs. punctual main action, e.g. 'do all along or repeatedly' vs. 'do only once during a translational motion');
- FEATURES OF THE GROUND (new or topic, as distinguished in Yagua (isolate; Payne 1984), permanent, unstable or transitional);[5]
- the TYPE OF RELATION between the action and the motion (purpose vs. plain temporal relation, e.g. in Ese Ejja (Vuillermet 2013: 47), -*ki* 'go to do' vs. -*ña* 'do arriving');
- the MANNER (hurried or unspecified, as in Arrernte (Wilkins 1991: 235)).

This list of parameters constitutes the etic grid (Majid 2012: 62–65) for this stimulus. The storybook takes into account all these parameters (but the manner) and contrasts most values. (See Table 1 in §3 for the list of the concepts targeted with each scene.)

2.2 Goals and domains explored

The main goals of the stimulus are to collect more AM morphemes, and to investigate which semantic features a given system is sensitive to. Is "subsequent motion" part of the system or is the AM system restricted to prior (and concurrent) motion (cf. Guillaume's (2016: 90) implicational scale)? Is the reference point the speaker, or any salient place or entity from the previous discourse? Additional goals are as follows:

Discourse use
The stimulus helps examine the AM system of a language in terms of discourse use. How systematic is the use of AM morphemes? In a language with AM morphemes encoding different temporal relations to the main action, are the prior, concurrent and subsequent motion used (a) symmetrically; i.e. are prior motion AM forms for instance more frequent? Does the language manifest the "echo phenomenon" (Wilkins 1991: 251; Guillaume 2006: 424, 432) and if it does, how systematic is it? Which main path verbs (e.g. 'go', 'come', 'move towards', 'leave', etc.) are echoed by which AM morphemes?

---

[5] An action realized at a transitional Ground ('go and do at a *transitional* place and leave again') can alternatively be interpreted as being concurrent motion with a punctual main action ('do once while going', see Koch, this volume), or as an action preceded and followed by a motion event (see Dryer, this volume ch.13). See also Guillaume & Koch, this volume (§3.2).

Intra- and interspeaker variation
Speakers may vary in terms of their AM inventories and in their use of their AM morphology (frequency and discourse use). In Mparntwe Arrernte, for instance, Wilkins (1991: 226, 229) observes ongoing semantic shifts in the systems of younger speakers (under 18) and mentions that not using AM morphemes is seen as "resorting to children's speech" or as being "uncooperative" if the path is known. Collecting data with a large variety of consultants may thus provide interesting clues in the domains of language acquisition or language decay.

In addition, the protocol in §3.3 suggests different tasks to examine the use of AM morphology by the same speaker in different stories – using *A Hunting Story* vs. personal narrations.

Cross-linguistic variation
The data collected with the same stimulus in distinct languages should, in the longer term, facilitate cross-linguistic comparison between AM systems, again in terms of inventories, frequency and discourse use. It also helps the systematic study of AM as a functional domain rather than of AM morphology only. This onomasiological approach allows for the inclusion of any type of AM expression, instead of only those which consists of morphological markers.

3 The stimulus kit

3.1 The AM storybook

The AM storybook consists of 22 drawings. They feature an Ese Ejja person who goes hunting and experiences a series of subevents. Each scene was conceived as being potentially described with at least one type of AM morpheme of the kind that has been reported so far in at least one language. Each of the 22 scenes thus represents a main action that can be perceived in the framework of a journey. Picture 1 (#14 in the picture book) illustrates the hunter rinsing his machete on his way back home, and one of the corresponding descriptions in Ese Ejja is found in (2a). Picture 2 (#21 in the picture book) illustrates the mother monkey coming to steal her baby monkey back, and (2b) is a corresponding description.

(2) a. *Ani-ñaki-o'oya-naje,*   *'baa*   *shakwa-ka-ani.*
sit-**ARRIVE&DO&LEAVE**-AGAIN-PST   machete   rinse-3A-PRS
'He stopped again (lit. he arrived, sat and then left) and rinses the machete.' {JulHS14}

Picture 1: 'arrive & sit & leave' – ex. (2a)/#14.

Picture 2: 'go to steal X' – ex. (2b)/#21.

 b. *Sii-**ki**-ka-'io-naje*   *enaese=a* *o=kawi=jo=ya.*
   steal-**GO.TO.DO**-3A-TEL-PST mother=ERG 3=sleep=TMP.DS=FOC
   'She (the mother monkey) came (lit. went) to steal (her baby) back,
   the mother, when they were asleep.' {JulHS21}

Familiarity with the distinct main and backgrounded events is important, to guide the consultant during the familiarization phase through the many events depicted (Task 1, see § 3.3 for a summary of the protocol), or to conduct more specific elicitation with a selection of pictures to test a given context. The first column of Table 1 summarizes the story picture by picture. The second column mentions the various

Table 1: Detailed event account and AM morphemes expected.

Pict.	Description of the picture	Targeted verb event and AM meanings
#1	A man is getting ready to go hunting, checking his rifle.	check rifle BEFORE LEAVING (HOME)
#2	He leaves his home with his rifle; he waves at his wife & baby who stand at the door, the boy is holding back the dog who wants to follow his master.	– wave & GO AWAY (FROM HOME) – (the boy) holds the dog back AT Z's DEPARTURE – (the dog) wants to go AT Z's DEPARTURE (Z stands for a non-core argument)
#3	He walks past a field in which a couple is working and they wave at each other.	wave / say hi PAST (A NEW PLACE)
#4	He finds some fruits and collects them.	collect (punctual) WHEN GOING
#5	He loses fruits on his way because his bag has a hole.	lose (atelic) WHEN GOING
#6	He is walking, is hot and tired (or: he chases flies/mosquitoes).	'be hot/tired' WHEN GOING
#7	He goes down to a river and drinks / refreshes himself / fills his water sack.	– GO DOWNWARD & drink – drink WHILE STOPPING TRANSITORY (NEW PLACE)
#8	He walks again and feels much better.	be happy WHEN RESTARTING A JOURNEY AFTER A SHORT STOP (AT A TRANSITORY PLACE)
#9	He hears capybaras.	– (the man) hear O (the capybaras) COMING TOWARD A – (the capybaras) hear O (the man) COMING TOWARD A
#10	He shoots one capybara out of three. The other two run away in the opposite direction.	– shoot O (the capybara) COMING TOWARD A – see / miss O (the capybaras) GOING away from A
#11	He puts the capybara into his bag (but it is too big) and goes back home.	load AND RETURN HOME
#12	Vultures try to get some pieces of meat / attack him on his way.	– be attacked WHILE RETURNING HOME – attack WHILE O's MOVING
#13	He disembowels the capybara and throws the guts to the vultures so that they eat them & leave him in peace.	disembowel/throw/ WHILE RETURNING / WHILE STOPPING (AT A NEW PLACE)
#14	He goes back (down) to the river to refresh / drink; he sees a baby monkey.	drink WHILE RETURNING HOME / WHILE STOPPING SHORTLY (AT A KNOWN PLACE)

Table 1 (continued)

Pict.	Description of the picture	Targeted verb event and AM meanings
#15	He captures the baby monkey; the monkey's mother witnesses the scene.	capture O WHILE RETURNING HOME / WHILE STOPPING SHORTLY (AT A KNOWN PLACE) / BEFORE RETURNING HOME
#16	He passes by the field of the same couple, who are interested in exchanging some meat for bananas.	wave / say hi PAST BACK (KNOWN PLACE)
#17	His child runs towards him as he is arriving; the monkey's mother (crying/hiding) has followed him.	− (Mother Monkey) hide/cry WHILE FOLLOWING Z − run towards Z AT Z'S ARRIVAL
#18	He ties the monkey with his rifle still on the shoulder (= WHEN ARRIVING); the neighbor / woman working in the field brings banana to exchange them for meat.	− tie WHEN ARRIVING − bring banana AT Z'S ARRIVAL − COME MOMENTARILY TO A PLACE TO bring/exchange banana − give X AT ARRIVING somewhere AND RETURN
#19	The neighbor / woman working in the field leaves the house / goes back home with the meat that was exchanged for bananas.	− COME TO exchange X − exchange X and LEAVE/RETURN
#20	The wife cooks the animal; the children play around with their father & the monkey; the monkey's mother is looking through the window.	− cook X BROUGHT
#21	The family sleeps at night, and the monkey's mother sets him free.	− COME TO free X
#22	They both run back into the forest while smiling / eating banana.	− run / steal banana + GO FOR GOOD

AM concepts targeted. (The main, non-motion event is written in lower case while the AM event is in small caps.) This table is actually the storyboard on which the illustrator Antoine Desnoyers based his work. He was asked to focus on the main action(s) of each scene, and to incorporate it/them in an environment familiar to the Ese Ejja, an environment to which he had had previous exposure.

3.2 Ecology of the stimulus: an Amazonian setting

Most linguists acknowledge that stimuli are useful in the process of data collection and documentation (see e.g. Lüpke 2009; Majid 2012) and even necessary for the careful investigation of specific semantic categories sometimes poorly represented in corpora (see e.g. Ponsonnet 2014; or San Roque et al. 2012). This subsection addresses the precautions taken for the *Hunting Story* stimulus to be as accessible as possible to people from non-WEIRD societies (for 'Western, Educated, Industrialized, Rich and Democratic', see Henrich, Heine & Norenzayan 2010).

Miller (1973) had already pointed to two main ingredients for a pictorial stimulus to be easily recognizable: familiarity with the represented entity and familiarity with the pictorial cues. Therefore, the *Hunting Story* drawings represent actions occurring in an Amazonian setting which the Ese Ejja are familiar with. This resulted in that the Ese Ejja speakers and, more generally, most speakers from the Amazonian region who participated in the experiment, easily identified the pictorial representation, despite, or maybe because of the graphic density of the drawings. It was also found that even beyond Amazonia, consultants had no specific trouble understanding the pictures, as with Papitalai speakers from Papua New Guinea or Khaling speakers from Nepal, although the assumed identity of non-endemic entities was heavily discussed among the speakers – e.g. the *capybara* (a type of rodent) (A. Lahaussois, p.c. October 2018). The familiarity of the main storyline – people in a community living in wooden huts, cooking over the fire, collecting fruits and hunting in the forest, and fetching young animals to domesticate them – seems to have been transparent enough for speakers from very different environments.

People unfamiliar with Western modes of representation sometimes encounter difficulties understanding pictorial cues. Wilkins (1991: 217) mentions for instance the confusion of the Arrernte speakers with Western pictorial conventions depicting people lying rather than standing upright, because of the aerial view of events in Arrernte drawings. In drawing the pictures of the *Hunting Story*, Antoine Desnoyers avoided such techniques as 'shot-countershot' (where the viewpoint changes from one participant to another), which may not have been spontaneously understood by "non-Western" consultants.

To help gain familiarity with pictorial cues, Miller (1973) has emphasized the importance of the training phase: "the more experience an individual has with cues other than familiarity cues (e.g. depth cues, orientation cues), the greater the probability that he will be able to match a picture of an unfamiliar object with the actual object represented". (See also Cáceres (2017) on her experience with the Fish film in an Amazonian context.) This is the reason why the first task for this storybook is to leaf through the story with the consultant, discuss it, and make sure that he understands the succession of isolated pictures as a coherent story.

Note that elderly people seemed less at ease with the storybook, probably reflecting their limited exposure to Western modes of representation. As with any stimulus, the researcher should make sure that the consultant does not feel uncomfortable while completing any of the tasks. If such situations should arise (all the more likely in the context of linguistic insecurity), researchers are encouraged to limit stimulus use to other speakers more familiar with storybook narratives. The next section details the various steps of the protocol.

3.3 The full protocol

The full protocol consists of five tasks, detailed in a separate document available online (http://tulquest.huma-num.fr/fr/node/46). The list below is a summary.

Task 1. Becoming familiar with the story and describing each picture (in the target language). The goal of this task is threefold: (a) to make sure that the different drawings are easily interpreted and understood as a single story (cf. §2.2); (b) to highlight the presence of backgrounded elements that could be missed, like the hidden mother monkey who follows her captured baby; (c) to compare this first narrative to the second one (cf. re-telling the story in Task 2). If performed with several consultants, this first task is likely to give rise to interesting very natural discussions about the different perspectives of each speaker (see San Roque et al. 2012 for a similar primary task).

Task 2. Re-telling the story to a native speaker who does not know the story already so as to collect the most natural data in this artificial setting (see Himmelmann's (1998) "staged communicative events"). These first two steps should make it possible to test whether the consultant uses more AM morphemes once more familiar with the journey.

Task 3. Giving feedback to the researcher. Positive feedback included that the speakers were at ease and enjoyed themselves when performing the tasks – the Ese Ejja really enjoyed finding elements from their everyday life in a storybook. Negative feedback included for instance issues with elderly people, due to sight problems or to their unfamiliarity with this kind of material. This third task is of importance for future users of the *Hunting Story* stimulus, and more generally for the design of future stimuli.

Task 4. Telling a complementary similar story. Besides obtaining more spontaneous data, the interest of collecting such complementary data is to compare the relative frequency of use of AM morphemes when the itinerary is maybe clearer in the consultant's mind, as in personal (or reported) experiences in a well-known environment, rather than a made-up story. Possible prompting questions could be the following: Did the story remind you of a personal experience, or of that of a friend? Could you tell me about your last / best hunting / fishing trip, or describe a typical day of hunting / fishing, or your last trip?

Task 5. Looking for support from direct elicitation. As already mentioned above, yet another useful task is to test the felicity of known AM morphemes with the relevant pictures, even if they did not come up in Task 1 or 2. The visual support will facilitate working with a shared existing context and determining whether the use of a given AM morpheme is felicitous or not.

Task 6. Running The Pear Film experiment. At this point, the researcher could elicit another narrative using the well-known "Pear Film". (www.linguistics.ucsb.edu/faculty/chafe/pearfilm.htm). One of the main advantages of this video stimulus is the absence of a "real" home as a reference point, which can help investigate whether an AM morpheme is exclusively associated with homes or with more general reference points established in any journey.

Most Ese Ejja consultants performed the first three tasks in about half an hour. The three additional tasks lengthen the procedure considerably, which may be problematic in some fieldwork situations. These tasks are however fairly independent of one another and the researcher can plan to use them in subsequent sessions.

3.4 Bonuses

The stimulus did more than just collect comparable stories with AM morphemes. This subsection lists several extra goals accomplished with the stimulus, such as comparing dialectal variants (lexical and phonological differences), yielding several infrequent constructions (e.g. *lest*-clauses and mistaken belief constructions, cf. Spronk 2017), providing pedagogical material to teachers of the community, and establishing more confident relationships with speakers.

The storybook seems to enhance linguistic confidence in consultants. A Tacana consultant put great effort into a written version of the story, which ended up looking like a traditional story with reported speech markers (A. Guillaume, p.c. November 2013); such a written task can actually reassure insecure consultants and help them plan their story. K. Neely (p.c. October 2013) also noticed that the stimulus was not only a good springboard to get personal narratives for people unfamiliar and ill-at-ease with recording devices, but also a good introduction to more complex stimuli like *Man and Tree* (Levinson et al. 1992). She also reported that the *Hunting Story* stimulus had served as a basis for discussions between consultants, yielding interesting very spontaneous interactions involving questions, answers, explanations and disagreements about what certain images represented (as did A. Lahaussois, p.c. October 2018).

4 A pilot study: the Ese Ejja and the *Hunting Story*

After a brief presentation of the Ese Ejja speakers and their language (§4.1), the present section discusses a pilot study run in 2013 with 14 Ese Ejja consultants who performed the first two tasks of the protocol. The data collected make use of half of the morphemes present in the Ese Ejja AM system (§4.2). Surprisingly, the data suggest that younger consultants do not necessarily produce fewer AM morphemes than older consultants, and that the consultants from the community with the best degree of vitality were not the ones who produced the most AM morphemes (§4.3).

4.1 The Ese Ejja speakers and their language (and its AM system)

Approximately 1,700 Ese Ejja live in southwestern Amazonia, in 9 villages in Bolivia and Peru. Ese Ejja (ISO 639–3: ese) is classified as a Pano-Takanan language, with approximately 1,500 Ese Ejja speakers and three variants: Madidi, Sonene and Baawaja. The Baawaja variant is the most distinct and is moribund; the Madidi and Sonene variants are very close and still used on a daily basis in most villages, but are not always transmitted to the younger generations (Vuillermet 2012b: 58, 69ff.). The data examined here include all three varieties and come from original fieldwork with consultants from five different communities located in Bolivia and Peru.

The language displays ergative alignment (ergative marker =*a* and limited, third person Agent indexation -*ka*, see (2b)). Table 2 shows the morphological template for inflecting verbal predicates. A verb may appear with more than one

Table 2: Morphological template for verbal predicates.

-3	-2	-1	0	+1	+2	+3	+4	+5	+6	+7	+8	+9	+10	+11
Tense/Mood	Valency	Nominal Root	Verbal Root 1	Verbal Root 2	Manner Adj. Root	Adverbials	Valency	Associated Motion / Adverbials	Indexation	Associated Motion	Tense/Mood	Adverbials	Aspect	Tense/Mood

root, as is for instance the case with noun incorporation or verb compounding. A full verb takes inflectional morphology (in bold), i.e. indexation (limited to third person) and tense or mood. AM morphology (in bold and small caps), together with adverbials and valency-changing morphology, belongs to the non-inflectional morphology. Like most other non-inflectional categories, AM morphology appears in two different slots.

Table 3 classifies the 14 AM suffixes in Ese Ejja according to the three main parameters: 1) path/direction, 2) temporal relation to the non-motion main event, 3) moving argument.

Table 3: Ese Ejja AM system[6] & the morphemes used in the stimulus.

	IN THE HUNTING STORIES			PATH / DIRECTIONALITY*	TEMPORAL RELATION TO THE EVENT	MOVING ARGUMENT
1	✓	-ña	'do after arriving'	toward	prior motion	S / A
2	✓	-ñaki	'arrive&do&leave'	toward&away	prior & subsequent***	
3	✓	-ki	'go to do'	away from	prior + purpose	
4	✓**	-wa	'come to do'	toward		
5	✓	-poki	'do while going'	away from	concurrent motion	
6	✓	-je'be	'do while coming'	toward		
7	✓	-nana	'do&leave'	away from	subsequent motion	
8	✓	-na	'do&return'	toward		
9		-'aeki	'do here&there'	away from	concurrent motion	
10	✓**	-jjeki	'come (O)'	toward A	prior motion	O
11		-no'bi	'do while going in'	boundary crossing		S / A
12		-kwaya	'do while going out'			
13		-sowa	'do while going upstream'	absolute frame of reference	concurrent motion	S / O
14		-'oke	'do while going downstream'			

* See Vuillermet (2012a; 2012b: Chap. 15; 2013) for a thorough discussion of the semantics of the system.
** These two morphemes were only used after I suggested them (NB: not all suggestions were accepted).
*** Alternatively analyzed a punctual aspectual realization away from the point of reference (do *once* while *going away*); see e.g. Guillaume (2009).

---

[6] See Vuillermet (2012a, 2013) for a discussion of the semantics of the AM system.

4.2 AM morphemes collected in Ese Ejja

Fourteen Ese Ejja consultants used the stimulus, eight males and six females, aged 7 to 73. One consultant spoke the Baawaja variant (from the Baawaja community), five the Sonene (4 from the community of Palmareal and 1 from Portachuelo Alto), and eight the Madidi (from Portachuelo Bajo).

Exactly half of the 14 AM morphemes present in the system were collected spontaneously, as shown in the second column of Table 3. Two additional morphemes (double-starred) were suggested by the researcher during Task 1, and repeated either during Task 1 or 2; see (4a) below for an illustration of one of these. The remaining five AM morphemes appear to be cross-linguistically less frequent in AM systems and were actually not targeted in any of the 22 pictures of the storybook: they encode distributed action & motion (#9), boundary crossing motion (#11–12) and motion within an absolute frame of reference (#13–14).

The following examples are Ese Ejja narratives of a *A Hunting Story*, and are presented with the corresponding pictures preceding the examples. The path/directionality parameter is illustrated in (3a-b), and the temporal relation parameter in (4a-d). An additional parameter relevant to the Ese Ejja AM system, namely purpose of the main action is illustrated in (5).

Picture 3: 'scatter X while going' – ex. (3a)/#5.

Picture 4: 'run while coming' – ex. (3b)/#13.

(3) PATH / DIRECTIONALITY: do going (a), do coming (b)

a. *Aekwá... e'a'bojji=pajja=me wejja-jji*
   what.is.it.again backpack=DISC=DISC hole-PROPR
   *jja-wojjajia-ki-**poki**-ani oya.*
   MID-scatter-MID-**DO.GOING**-PRS 3ABS
   'And then what is it again... (his) backpack has a hole, he scatters it (<u>while going</u>).' {BawHS05}

b. *E-'bakwa kwaji~kwaji-**je'be**-ani akwe.*[7]
   NPF-child run~RDP-**DO.COMING**-PRS CONFIRM
   'The child <u>comes</u> running, doesn't he?' {BawHS17}

---

7 The AM morpheme *-je'be* 'DO.COMING' occurs here with a motion verb, and it could thus be analyzed as being used as a directional, i.e. not expressing motion at all (see e.g. Dryer, this volume ch. 4 or Voisin, this volume). Such an analysis however implies that the motion component of *-je'be* is present only when used with a non-motion verb, and absent when used with a motion verb. I prefer analyzing the form *kwajikwaji-je'be-* as being redundant for motion, avoiding thus to resort to two semantic analyses depending on the verb type it collocates with.

Picture 5: 'come to give' – ex. (4a)/#18.
'lay X on the table at arrival' – ex. (4b).

Picture 6: 'run after while coming' – ex. (4c)/#16.

(4) TEMPORAL RELATION to the main event: prior (a–b), concurrent (c), prior & subsequent (d)
    a. *Ejjawi*   *kia-ka-**wa**-ani*   *no?*   *noe=sosejje.*
        banana   give-3A-**COME.TO.DO**-PRS   no(Sp)   meat=IN.EXCHANGE.FOR
        'She <u>comes to</u> give banana, right? In exchange for meat.' {BawHS18}

b. *Majoya kane owaya (...) mesa='biajje wana-ka-naje,*
then meat(Sp) 3ERG table=ON lay-3A-PST
wana-ka-ña-'io-naje e-jaja-te'a-jji.
lay-3A-**DO.ARRIVING**-TEL-PST PURP-cut-tear.apart-PURP
'Then he laid the meat, he laid it onto the table <u>when he arrived home</u>, to cut it up.' {JulHS18}

c. *Okwekwaji-ka-**je'be**-ani, (e-naese) e-'bakwa*
run.after-3A-**DO.COMING**-PRS NPF-mother NPF-child
ichaji-'oshe=ya e-naese=ya,
howling.monkey-white=ERG NPF-mother=ERG
*okwekwaji-ka-**je'be**-ani.*[8]
run.after-3A-**DO.COMING**-PRS
'She runs after him, her child, the mother monkey, she runs after him.' {JulHS16}

d. *'Ba-ka-**ñaki**-naje kweyo.*
see-3A-**ARRIVE&DO&LEAVE**-PST fruit_sp
'He saw *kweyo* fruit <u>on his way</u>.' {JulHS04}

Picture 7: 'arrive & see & leave' — ex. (4d)/#4.

---

8 See footnote 7.

Picture 8: 'go to steal' — ex. (5)/#21.

(5) ADDITIONAL PARAMETERS: PRIOR MOTION AWAY + **PURPOSE**
 O-kawi-jo=ya   meka=jje   pojja'a sii-**ki**-ka-'io-naje.
 3-sleep-TMP.DS=FOC night=PERL maybe   steal-**GO.TO.DO**-3A-TEL-PST
 'When they were sleeping, at night maybe, she goes to steal him (back)'.
 {IzrHS16}

4.3 Preliminary results

The storybook proved successful, yielding as many as 22 AM morphemes in a single narrative. As expected, there was also a lot of variation across consultants and across communities, and one consultant (from the Baawaja community, where the few Ese Ejja speakers no longer use their language daily) did not produce any AM morphemes.

In the context of a minority language mostly spoken by bilinguals, I was interested in examining whether the AM system, very typical of Ese Ejja, was losing ground. My two main research questions were thus primarily aimed at comparing the AM use across speakers of different ages and communities.
1.   Do elderly speakers use more AM morphemes than younger ones?
2.   Do speakers from communities where the language is best preserved use more AM morphemes than speakers from other communities?

The results were not straightforward. The two youngest consultants (7 and 10 years old) from Portachuelo Bajo actually produced up to 4 more AM morphemes than adults in the same community (whose members speak their native language daily at all ages). These results are even more surprising as the two young consultants are also very fluent in Spanish, unlike other Ese Ejja children of the same age. Children in this community still acquire (at least part of) the AM system, despite the heavy influence of Spanish in their everyday life, e.g. at school. Conversely, a 26-year-old woman in this same community produced only a single AM morpheme. Unfortunately, my sample did not include young consultants of the same age from other communities.

However, the young speakers mostly used lexicalized forms (other older speakers did too). A sheer count of the tokens misses important cues if it does not differentiate combination with a random action verb from more lexicalized forms like *ani-ñaki-* 'stop, lit. arrive and sit and leave or sit once on one's way', as using only the latter certainly points to a loss in productivity of the AM system.

Unsurprisingly, and as already mentioned above, the only consultant from the Baawaja community did not produce a single AM morpheme. However, consultants from the community of Palmareal, where language transmission is broken (but where people in their 30's still speak it daily), produced many more AM morphemes than consultants from Portachuelo Bajo, where the whole population speaks the language daily. In addition, the Palmareal consultants used the AM morphemes more productively, with a wider range of verbs.

One possible factor that could have triggered a higher production is the degree of comfort with the task. The Palmareal consultants seemed to have enjoyed themselves the most in telling the story, producing very flowing stories (e.g. with dialogues between the characters as in ex.(1)), while the production of the Portachuelo Bajo consultants was more halting. However, enjoyment was not the only factor at play. At least one of the Portachuelo Bajo consultants told a very fluid and lively story (with lots of discourse particles and interaction with his audience) and produced only two AM morphemes. This consultant is a politician and is therefore more exposed to Spanish than most other Ese Ejja, something which could have influenced his production. These results suggest, on the one hand, the need for limiting the number of variants (age vs. gender vs. community vs. education level, etc.), i.e. targeting a less heterogenous sample. On the other hand, having access to a detailed picture of the individual language use allows researchers to take into account finer-grained sociolinguistic parameters that are key in interpreting the results from such an experiment.

5 Hunting stories in other languages: preliminary results

This section shows the kind of utterances elicited with the *Hunting Story* in several other languages, mostly spoken in the Amazonian region, but also much further beyond, in Asia and Oceania. Table 4 shows that eight researchers used the stimulus, yielding interesting AM constructions in most cases.[9]

Table 4: List of the languages for which *Hunting Stories* have been recorded, and the researchers.

Choapan Zapotec	Oto-Manguean	North America	Erin Donnelly
Purepecha	Tarascan	South America	Alejandra Capistran
Máíhɨ̃ki	Tukanoan	Peru	Lev Michael
Yaminahua	Pano-Takanan	Peru	Kelsey Neely
Tacana	Pano-Takanan	Bolivia	Antoine Guillaume
Dâw	Nadahup	Brazil	Karolin Obert
Thulung	Sino-Tibetan, Kiranti	India; Nepal	Aimée Lahaussois
Papitalai (Koro dialect)	Austronesian, Oceanic	Papua New Guinea	Jessica Cleary-Kemp

Some languages tested have morphological AM systems. The first two examples are from Tacana (A. Guillaume, p.c. November 2018), a language with a very complex system of 13 morphemes (Guillaume 2017: 224), and display two AM morphemes that respectively encode prior and concurrent motion.

(6) a. *Y-asease-**ti***   =da   ema   e-wane.
FUT-hunt-**GO.TO.DO** =PTC 1SG NPF-wife
'"I'm going to go to hunt (in the jungle), my wife" (the man said to his wife)' {ye008HS01}

b. *Senda=je*   *e-uru-**u***   *tumi*   =*mu*.
path=PERL **IPFV**-fall-**IPFV.GOING** motacú_palm =CONTR
'The motacú nuts were falling along the path (from the hunter's bag.)' {ye008HS5}

---

[9] Two researchers reported that their consultants did not produce the expected AM morphology, but I did not see their data and do not know if and how the consultants possibly co-expressed the motion and non-motion events instead. Note that the following examples are courtesy of various researchers. They are only illustrating the kind of AM expression collected with the stimulus, and in depth analyses fall out of the scope of this paper.

Yaminahua (K. Neely, p.c. November 2018) also has a very complex AM system of 11 morphemes. In addition to this, the language has a multi-verb construction associating a non-finite verb with the auxiliary *ka-* 'go'. The three examples below illustrate (a) an AM morpheme used alone, (b) the multi-verb construction with *ka-* 'go', and (c) an AM morpheme on a non-finite verb, within the multi-verb construction with *ka-* 'go'. (Note the intransitive/transitive allomorphy of *-kai~-waid* 'do.going' in (7a) and (7c).)

(7) a. wibi=Ø   pake-**kai**-i
    fruit=ABS   fall-**DO.GOING.INTR.SG**-IPFV
    'The fruit is going falling.' {0159HS05} (The fruit is falling from the backpack of the hunter.)

  b. afimefi=Ø   ichu-i   **ka**-i
    capybara=ABS   escape-NF   **go.SG**-IPFV
    'The capybara(s) are going to escape / going running.' {0159HS10}

  c. shidu=Ø   wi-afi-**waid**-i   **ka**-i
    monkey=ABS   take-MAL-**GO.DOING.TR**-NF   **go.SG**-IPFV
    '(He's) taking the monkey (to its mother's detriment) as he goes.' {0165HS15-16}

By contrast, the *Hunting Story* in Thulung (A. Lahaussois, p.c. October 2018), did not contain the single AM morpheme the language has.[10] Instead, plain motion verbs where used and coordinated with a general conjunction *-ma* that can also combine non-motion events to a concurrent motion event as (8a) or a prior motion event to a non-motion event (8b). (Note how the capybara, absent from Nepal, was interpreted as a deer.)

(8) a. me   səkhli   bɯ:-rɯ-**ma**   dər
    DEM   hunt   do-3SG>3SG.PST-**CONJ**   deer
    kur-rɯ-**ma**   bik-ta-lo
    carry-3SG>3SG.PST-**CONJ**   come-3SG.PST-TEMP
    'when he hunted and carried the deer and came'

---

10 This AM morpheme encodes distributed motion (called "ambulative" by A. Lahaussois) and might correspond to the morpheme *-'aeki* 'do here & there' in Ese Ejja. Distributed motion is not specifically represented in the pictures of *A Hunting Story* and is also absent from the Ese Ejja narratives collected with this storybook.

b. *memma lʌs-ta-**ma*** *meram sokse-ku tse-lai*
then go-3SG.PST-**CONJ** DEM monkey-GEN child-DAT
tsum-ru (...)
catch-3SG>3SG.PST
'He went and caught the baby monkey.'

Other languages tested do not have morphological AM systems. For instance, the Dâw consultants used a serial verb construction as illustrated in (9) (K. Obert, p.c. October 2018). The construction seems to express concurrent events only.

(9) a. *dâw xut soob **ween rãm** ka'*
person M hand **wave go** PROG
'The man was waving (while) going' {HS2}

b. *dâw xut **yêd yâa** tir nŭr-ŭuy*
person M **hide return** 3SG.POSS head-DOM
'The man goes back (home) (while) hiding his head (from the vultures)' {HS12}

Unlike Dâw, Papitalai (J. Cleary-Kemp, p.c. November 2018) used a sequential AM serial verb construction, with *le* or *la* 'go to' as V1 and a main action verb as V2. It indifferently expresses 'go and V2' or 'go to V2', as in (10a). Cleary-Kemp reports that this construction is extremely common in Koro narratives and appeared a lot in *A Hunting Story*. In addition, two bi-clausal constructions were also frequent: one with two main clauses, conjoined with *mwa* 'and' or simply juxtaposed with no coordinator; and a (semantically) subordinate clause[11] with *taim* 'when/while' and a "main" clause. These were usually connected with coordinator *mwa*. In (10b), the first clause is a (semantically) subordinate clause, indicated by *taim* 'when'. (Note in this last example how the vulture was interpreted as a sea eagle.)

(10) a. *ayou k-u **le kah** nderi tih pu ne, tih*
1SG.SBJ IRR-1SG **go.to look.for** small one pig or one
lawat ne, tih cha
cuscus or one what
'I am going to go to look for a small pig, or a cuscus, or whatever.'
{HS1-2, Mary Clara Hinduwan v2013-07-30-AV-01 00:00:30}

---

11 There is no morphological indication on either of the verbs that this is a subordinate clause construction.

b. ***Taim***   *i*   *ri*   *la,*   ***mwa***   *menuwai*   *i*
   when/while   3SG   stay   walk   **COORD**   sea.eagle   3SG
   hung-eya Ø
   smell-TR3SG.INAN.OBJ
   "He was walking and a sea eagle smelled it (the pig)"
   (p.12 of the story, Mary Clara Hinduwan v2013-07-30-AV-01 00:03:50)

Finally, Máíhɨ̃ki (Lev Michael, p.c. November 2018) used clause chaining. Interestingly, it is the verb of motion (mostly 'go') that is finite and appears in the main clause, while the activity verbs are not finite and appear in multiple non-finite (nominalized) chained subordinate clauses, with either simultaneous or sequential markers on them. The two examples in (11) show two types of "simple" subordinate clauses (simultaneous vs. sequential), and (12) shows two types of multiple chained subordinate clauses.

(11) a. [*Hásu*   *deba-**re***]   *máká*   ***sái̯-hɨ̃***.
       shotgun   put.in.order-**SUB.SEQ.SS**   forest   **go**-3M.SG.PRS
       'Having put his shotgun in order, he goes to the forest.'

   b. *ĩ̯i*   ***sái̯-hɨ̃***   [*hásu*   *kwá̯ɨ-**ki***]
      3SG.PRO   **go**-3M.SG.PRS   shotgun   carry.on.shoulder-**SUB.SIM.SS**
      'He goes carrying his shotgun on his shoulder.'

(12) a. [*neá-**re***]   ***sái̯-hɨ̃***,   *yuara-re*
       grab-**SUB.SEQ.SS**   **go**-3MASC.SG.PRES   paca-ACC
       [*bee-**ki***]
       carry.on.back-**SUB.SIM.SS**
       'Having grabbed (it), he goes, carrying the paca on his back.'

   b. [*hɨ̃ti*   *dóá-**re***]   [*na*   *ókó*   *ǔku-**re***]
      hand   wash-**SUB.SEQ.SS**   again   water   drink-**SUB.SEQ.SS**
      [*háso*   *íní-kwá̯ɨ-**ki***]   ***sái̯-hɨ̃***
      shotgun   get-carry.on.shoulder-**SUB.SIM.SS**   **go**-3M.SG.PRS
      'Having washed his hands, having drunken water again, getting and carrying his shotgun on his shoulder, he goes.'

This section has shown that *A Hunting Story* proves to be an efficient tool to not only collect AM *morphology* but also a variety of non-morphological constructions co-expressing motion and non-motion events. The many patterns attested show constructions ranging from mono-clausal to multi-clausal ones, including grammatical (AM), semi-grammatical (auxiliaries), semi-lexical (SVCs[12]) and lexical means (full lexeme & subordinated/coordinated clauses).

6 Conclusion

The storybook *A Hunting Story* is the first visual stimulus designed to elicit motion events in the background of main, (prototypically) non-motion events. It can serve various goals, from descriptive (collection of AM morphology and constructions) or sociolinguistic (comparison across speakers and communities), to typological ones (comparison across languages). Designed for linguistic fieldwork in non-urban communities, special attention was given to the ecology of the story itself (an everyday hunting activity) and its setting (an ordinary-looking wooden house with a thatched roof, dense vegetation, etc.). It is noticeable that consultants from very distinct origins have welcomed and enjoyed the storybook, with some even using it as pedagogical material. Nevertheless, as with any methodological tool, success always depends on the consultant's preparation to the task.

The first results presented in this paper show that the collection of morphological AM was successful in most cases and yielded AM morphemes, as long as the pictures represented the targeted AM concepts. In the future, it may be worth adding some pictures that represent less frequent AM morphemes, such as absolute-frame-of-reference motion co-events ('do while going up/downriver') or boundary-crossing ones ('do while going in/out'). If used for descriptive and sociolinguistic goals, the researcher needs to be well aware of the sociolinguistic profile and language use of each consultant.

Although initially designed for morphological AM, the storybook opens the possibility of comparing the variety of strategies used to co-express motion and non-motion events in an onomasiological approach. Is the Máíhɨ̃ki strategy of clause chaining governed by the motion verb typical across languages? Do languages with AM morphology use bi-clausal strategies in addition to AM morphology? *A Hunting Story* will hopefully become an essential part of the toolkit for fieldworkers and will help to build a comparative corpus that will enrich our understanding of the co-expression of motion events.

---

12 In the sense that SVCs have a conventionalized order, and are thus not "pure lexical constructions".

Abbreviations

The abbreviations used follow the Leipzig Glossing Rules, except for the following ones:

APF	adjective prefix	FUT	future	RDP	reduplication
CONJ	conjunction	MAL	malefactive	SEQ	sequential
CONTR	contrastive	MID	middle	SIM	simultaneous,
DISC	discourse particle	NF	non-finite	_sp	species
DOM	differential object marker	NPF	noun prefix	SS	same subject
		PERL	perlative	SUB	subordinate
DS	different subject	PRO	pronoun	TEL	telic
INAN	inanimate	PROPR	proprietive	TMP	temporal
INCL	inclusive	PTC	particle		(subordinator).

Acknowledgements: This research has been supported by a one-year grant from the Fyssen Fundation in 2012–2013 at UCB and the paper was finalized during a postdoctoral fellowship from LABEX ASLAN (ANR-10-LABX-0081) of the Université de Lyon within the program "Investissements d'Avenir" (ANR-11-IDEX-0007). I want to thank Antoine Desnoyers for the beautiful work he achieved and his patient collaboration. My thanks go to the Ese Ejja people, who taught me their language with much patience and friendship over the years. I am grateful to Lev Michael who has been a great sponsor during my postdoctoral stay at the University of California at Berkeley. I am very indebted in Jessica Cleary-Kemp, Antoine Guillaume, Aimée Lahaussois, Lev Michael, Kelsey Neely, and Karolin Obert for having enthusiastically used the stimulus and shared their data for the present paper. I am very grateful to Antoine Guillaume and Harold Koch for having accepted this original contribution to their volume, and for their constructive comments and those of Aimée Lahaussois, which helped me to greatly improve the paper. All remaining mistakes are, of course, my own.

References

Cáceres, Natalia. 2017. Adapting experimental visual stimuli protocols for wider use. Presented at the Workshop on questionnaires for linguistic description and typology, University of Paris Diderot, Paris, France, November 9.

Dryer, Matthew S. This volume, chapter 4. Associated motion and directionals: Where they overlap.

Dryer, Matthew S. This volume, chapter 13. Associated Motion in North America (including Mexico and Central America).

Guillaume, Antoine. 2006. La catégorie du mouvement associé en cavineña: Apport à une typologie de l'encodage du mouvement et de la trajectoire. *Bulletin de la Société Linguistique de Paris* 415–436.

Guillaume, Antoine. 2009. Les suffixes verbaux de "mouvement associé" en cavineña. *Les Cahiers de Faits de Langues* 1. 181–204.

Guillaume, Antoine. 2016. Associated motion in South America: Typological and areal perspectives. *Linguistic Typology* 20(1). 81–177.

Guillaume, Antoine. 2017. Sistemas complejos de movimiento asociado en las lenguas de las familias Tacana y Pano: perspectivas descriptiva, comparativa y tipológica. In Antoine Guillaume & Pilar Valenzuela (eds.), *Amerindia (Numéro thématique: Estudios sincrónicos y diacrónicos sobre lenguas Pano y Takana: fonología, morfología y sintaxis)* 39(1). 211–261.

Guillaume, Antoine & Harold Koch. This volume, chapter 1. Introduction: Associated motion as a grammatical category in linguistic typology.

Hellwig, Birgit. 2006. Field semantics and grammar-writing: Stimuli-based techniques and the study of locative verbs. In Felix K Ameka, Alan Charles Dench & Nicholas Evans (eds.), *Catching language: The standing challenge of grammar writing*, 321–358. Berlin & New York: M. de Gruyter.

Henrich, Joseph, Steven J. Heine & Ara Norenzayan. 2010. The weirdest people in the world? *Behavioral and Brain Sciences* 33(2–3). 61–83. doi:10.1017/S0140525X0999152X.

Himmelmann, Nikolaus P. 1998. Documentary and Descriptive Linguistics. *Linguistics* 36. 161–195.

Koch, Harold. 1984. The category of "associated motion" in Kaytej. *Language in Central Australia* 1. 23–34.

Koch, Harold. This volume, chapter 7. Associated Motion in the Pama-Nyungan languages of Australia.

Kopecka, Anetta & Bhuvana Narasimhan (eds.). 2012. *Events of putting and taking: A crosslinguistic perspective* (Typological Studies in Language 100). Amsterdam & Philadelphia: John Benjamins.

Lahaussois, Aimée. 2019. The TULQuest linguistic questionnaire archive. *Language Documentation & Conservation* 16 [Special issue *Methodological tools for linguistic description and typology* edited by Aimée Lahaussois & Marine Vuillermet]. 97–123.

Levinson, Stephen C., Penelope Brown, Eve Danziger, Lourdes De León, John B. Haviland, Eric Pederson & Gunter Senft. 1992. Man and Tree & Space games. doi:10.17617/2.2458804. http://pubman.mpdl.mpg.de/pubman/item/escidoc:2458804 (8 November, 2018).

Levinson, Stephen C., Sergio Meira & Language and Cognition group, Max Planck Institut für Psycholinguistics Netherlands. 2003. "Natural concepts" in the spatial topological domain–Adpositional meanings in crosslinguistic perspective: An exercise in semantic typology. *Language* 79(3). 485–516. doi:10.1353/lan.2003.0174.

Lüpke, Friederike. 2009. Data collection methods for field-based language documentation. *Language Documentation and Description* 6. 53–100.

Majid, Asifa. 2012. A guide to stimulus-based elicitation for semantic categories. In Nicholas Thieberger (ed.), *The Oxford handbook of linguistic fieldwork*, 54–71. New York: Oxford University Press.

Miller, Robert J. 1973. Cross-cultural research in the perception of pictorial materials. *Psychological Bulletin* 80(2). 135–150.

Payne, Thomas. 1984. Locational relations in Yagua narrative. *Work Papers of the Summer Institute of Linguistics* 28. 157–192.

Ponsonnet, Maïa. 2014. Documenting the language of emotions in Dalabon (Northern Australia): Caveats, solutions and benefits. In Aicha Belkadi, Kakia Chatsiou & Kirsty Rowan (eds.), *Proceedings of the Conference on Language Documentation and Linguistic Theory 4*, 1–13. School of Oriental and African Studies, University of London.

Rose, Françoise. 2015. Associated motion in Mojeño Trinitario: Some typological considerations. *Folia Linguistica* 49(1). 117–158. doi:10.1515/flin-2015-0004.

San Roque, Lila, Lauren Gawne, Darja Hoenigman, Julia Colleen Miller, Alan Rumsey, Stef Spronk, Alice Carroll & Nicholas Evans. 2012. Getting the story straight: Language fieldwork using a narrative problem-solving task. *Language Documentation and Conservation* 6. 135–174.

Spronk, Stef. 2017. Reckoning wrong: Mistaken belief in Australian Aboriginal languages as a window onto the syntax of perspective. Presented at the 12th Conference of the Association for Linguistic Typology (ALT), Canberra, Australia, December 12.

Voisin, Sylvie. This volume, chapter 16. Associated Motion and Deictic Directional in Atlantic languages.

Vuillermet, Marine. 2012a. Une typologie en cheminement : Contribution de l'ese ejja à l'étude du mouvement associé. In Caroline Imbert & Nathalie Vallée (eds.), *LIDIL*, 79–100.

Vuillermet, Marine. 2012b. *A grammar of Ese Ejja, a Takanan language of the Bolivian Amazon*. Université Lumière Lyon 2 Doctoral dissertation.

Vuillermet, Marine. 2013. Dónde, cuándo, y con quién ocurren acciones: El movimiento asociado en ese ejja. In Ana María Ospina (ed.), *Expresión de nociones espaciales en lenguas amazónicas*, 33–53. Bogota: Universidad Nacional de Colombia e Instituto Caro y Cuervo.

Vuillermet, Marine & Antoine Desnoyers. 2013. A hunting story – Yendo a cazar: A visual stimulus for eliciting constructions that associate motion with other events. Linguistic Department, UC Berkeley, ms. http://tulquest.huma-num.fr/fr/node/46.

Wilkins, David P. 1991. The Semantics, pragmatics and diachronic development of "Associated Motion" in Mparntwe Arrernte. *Buffalo Papers in Linguistics* 207–257.

Part II: **Australia and South Pacific**

Harold Koch
7 Associated motion in the Pama-Nyungan languages of Australia

Abstract: This paper describes the systems of Associated Motion that are found in the Pama-Nyungan family of Australian languages, based on a survey of about 100 language descriptions, in terms of the typology which has been developed in recent years. The very complex systems (with up to 17 subcategories) of languages of Central Australia, which have been known since the 1980s, are presented in terms of their semantic parameters, and illustrated most fully by means of an updated analysis of Kaytetye, the Arandic language for which AM was first reported (Koch 1984). Other languages are discussed according to the complexity of their system: moderately complex, binary (two AM values) and unitary. Comparison of all the systems found in 41 languages distributed widely over the continent shows an apparently independent recurrent development of AM from similar precursor constructions as well as increasing complexity of systems around a core area in the centre of the continent.

Keywords: associated motion, typology, complexity, direction, temporal relation, aspect, speed

1 Introduction

1.1 Aims and scope of the study

This study aims to present a survey of Associated Motion (AM) in the languages of the large Pama-Nyungan family of Australia, analysed according to the international typological framework that has developed over recent decades. This applies both to the complex systems that have been previously studied (Koch 1984 for Kaytetye, Wilkins 1991 for Mparntwe Arrernte, and Tunbridge 1988 for Adnyamathanha) but also to simpler systems, which have been either described in ad hoc ways or totally overlooked (see Osgarby this volume, for an Australian example of a simpler AM system). With respect to the former, I aim to present an updated description of the very complex AM system of Kaytetye and to compare the AM systems across the whole Arandic subgroup. A further aim is to determine

Harold Koch, Australian National University, harold.koch@anu.edu.au

https://doi.org/10.1515/9783110692099-007

as far as possible to what extent AM is present in the whole Pama-Nyungan family. Finally, I explore the historical sources of AM markers, with a view to contributing to the diachronic typology of AM.

1.2 The typological framework of AM

AM has been defined by Guillaume (2016: 12) thus: "An AM marker is a grammatical morpheme that is associated with the verb and that has among its possible functions the coding of translational motion." Motion must involve spatial displacement; movement of parts of the body while remaining in one location (e.g. shaking one's head) thus does not count as translational. In AM systems the motion is presented as a co-event with the main action or state denoted by the verb. The AM-marked verb may introduce both the main and the motion co-events (e.g. 'go and do') or may redundantly "echo" a motion event already introduced by a separate motion verb (e.g. 'go ... do (after going))' or anticipate a motion event to be introduced separately (e.g. 'do (before going) ... go').[1] AM is defined as grammatical marking; lexically expressed motion (e.g. *go and eat, go around gossiping* in English) does not count as AM. Grammatical markers may be affixes, clitics, particles, or auxiliaries – but note that Guillaume's study is restricted to verbal affixes (Guillaume 2016: 19). Although Guillaume defines AM in terms of "morphemes", the recognition of AM grammatical markers does not depend on the use of a classic morphemic approach, in my opinion.[2]

The main focus of typological study of AM has been on the semantic parameters of AM systems. All AM markers contribute to the verb an indication of some motion, which typically includes a specification of direction: Itive, Ventive, up, down, etc.;[3] they may also distinguish the time of the motion co-event relative to that of the main event: prior, concurrent, or subsequent. Also relevant may be the grammatical role of the moving entity, whether subject or non-subject (usually object). Two implicational hierarchies have been proposed, which are typically but not obligatorily satisfied: (1) the moving entity is more likely to be the subject than a non-subject; (2) Prior (P) Motion is more likely to be expressed than Concurrent (C) Motion, which is more likely than Subsequent (S) Motion (Guillaume

---

[1] These usages are called "pleonastic constructions" in Pakendorf & Stoynova (this volume).
[2] This is especially relevant where AM is expressed by an auxiliary phrase; see examples in this chapter.
[3] Forms meaning 'do while moving along or around' could be argued to involve no specific direction of motion.

2016: 3).⁴ In some languages the Relative Time may be variable: an AM form may express polysemously either Prior or Concurrent Motion (P/C), or even any of the three relative times (P/C/S). A fourth Relative Time relation has been mentioned in the literature, but analysed in different ways: the combination of Prior and Subsequent (P+S) Motion (typically in the reverse direction); i.e. a round trip 'go/come and do and then return'. Further minor parameters have been observed; these include distinctions of Speed of the motion (e.g. 'go quickly and do') and distinctions of an aspectual nature (e.g. 'do once, repeatedly, or continuously while going').⁵ AM systems can be distinguished by their degree of complexity, i.e. the number of AM subcategories, and by the semantic parameters the systems distinguish. For western Amazonian languages Guillaume (2016: 29) distinguishes simple, complex, and very complex systems according to whether the system includes one or two forms, three to five, or six of more forms respectively.

AM as a category of grammatical specification is distinct from other (typically verb-related) categories including Tense⁶ and Aspect.⁷ AM has also been distinguished from Motion with Purpose ('go to do'), where the event is only intended but not realised.⁸ AM is also distinct from Direction markers, which typically occur only with verbs denoting motion (e.g. 'move/take (something) toward/away from speaker'), or, with non-motion verbs, to specify orientation; e.g. 'look toward/away from speaker'.⁹

A further development within AM studies, however, relates (deictic) directionals more specifically to studies of AM. Belkadi (2015) has shown that in many languages of Africa "deictic directionals", especially Ventive and Itive, whose primary function is to specify direction on motion verbs, can be used in specific contexts with non-motion verbs to add a distinct motion co-event; e.g. 'look and come' rather than just 'look toward speaker'. She has given the label D-AM to

---

4 The second hierarchy was tentatively proposed by Levinson & Wilkins (2006: 534), who nevertheless included with Prior Motion ('go and VERB') Motion with Purpose ('go to VERB'), which is typically treated in AM studies as a separate phenomenon.
5 See Rose (2015) on the treatment of these extra parameters. Guillaume (2013) and Vuillermet (this volume) describe the latter as "aspectual realisation" of the verb event/action.
6 Nevertheless AM subcategories may be distinguished by the Relative Timing of the motion and main co-events.
7 Nevertheless aspect-like distinctions may be made within an AM subcategory, such as Concurrent Motion; e.g. how the main event is temporally linked to the motion co-event, e.g. occurring once or for a short while, repeatedly, or continuously.
8 Nevertheless Prior Motion markers may evolve historically from earlier Motion with Purpose constructions, and some scholars include Motion with Purpose in studies of AM.
9 Nevertheless the Associated Motions subcategories typically do involve a directional component; e.g. 'come and do', 'do and go away'.

AM marked by deictic directionals. This extension of AM brings many more languages into considerations of AM. Typically languages with D-AM have "simple" AM systems, marking only one or two deictic directions of AM.

Relations between expressions of AM values, whose motion components typically involve directions, and pure directional markers has received recent attention (see Dryer this volume chapter 4, and Ross this volume). When, as sometimes occurs, a dedicated marker that signals an AM value with non-motion verbs (e.g. 'come and see') can also occur with a verb of pure (necessarily concurrent) motion (e.g. 'move') to specify direction only (e.g. 'move toward speaker', i.e. 'come'), how should this be described? The position adopted in this paper is this: If a marker productively indicates an additional motion co-event in non-motion verbs but also occurs with a few motion verbs, it is treated as AM;[10] on the other hand, where a marker's primary function is to signal direction on verbs of motion, and in addition is sometimes used to add motion to non-motion verbs, it is treated as D-AM.[11]

1.3 Pama-Nyungan languages and subgroups

Pama-Nyungan (PN) is generally recognised as the largest family of Australian languages (see Koch 2014; Miceli 2015). The languages of this family were spoken over about 90% of the mainland. The family included upwards of 200 languages.[12] The majority of languages are no longer spoken, although revitalisation programs are in place for some languages for which there is historical documentation. The PN languages have been classified into thirty or more subgroups (including isolates) – see Bowern & Atkinson (2012: 820) for a map of "major current subgroups". The results of their computational phylogenetic study suggest four tentative highest-level subgroups (Bowern & Atkinson 2012: 837–838).[13] The main subgroups to be mentioned here and their locations are shown in Table 1 (see the map, Figure 2, in the Appendix).

---

10 See the discussion of Kaytetye in §2.4, where the issue of glossing for the motion verbs is canvassed.
11 An Australian example is Yalarnnga (see §7.2).
12 Dixon's (2002: xxx-xxxix) catalogue, which conservatively joins varieties that others would separate, includes 183 PN languages (although he does not recognise Pama-Nyungan as a genetic entity). Bowern & Atkinson's (2012) phylogenetic study compares lexical data from 194 PN languages; a later study (Bouckaert et al. 2017) uses data from 299 PN separate languages, some of which could be considered co-dialects.
13 Their Bayesian phylogenetic methods, based on cognate sets for 189 English glosses from 194 PN languages, supported 25 previously identified PN lowest-level subgroups (Bowern & Atkinson 2012: 830), but further considerations suggest there are several more.

Table 1: Pama-Nyungan subgroups discussed in this paper.

Subgroup	Region
Arandic	Southern part of Northern Territory (N.T)
Thura-Yura	South Australia (S.A)
Karnic	northeastern S.A and western Queensland
Warumungu (isolate)	mid-N.T. (north of Arandic)
Ngumpin-Yapa	SW N.T. and northern Western Australia (W.A.)
Wati (Western Desert)	Central W.A., northwestern S.A., southwestern N.T.
Marrngu	northwestern W.A.
Ngarna (Warluwarric)	northwestern Queensland and eastern N.T.
Kalkatungic	northwestern-central Queensland
Maric	east-central Queensland
Paman	northeastern Queensland
Central New South Wales	central New South Wales
Yuin	southeastern New South Wales

Typologically the PN languages have agglutinative, mainly suffixing, morphology, with rich case systems including Ergative, and verb inflection (in many languages varying according to inflectional class or "conjugation") for various tenses, moods, aspects, and sometimes directionals and "associated motion" values, but rarely for marking of subject or object person-number.[14]

1.4 Scope and structure of the paper

For this survey of Pama-Nyungan AM I have investigated approximately 100 languages, which includes practically all the PN languages for which grammatical descriptions are available. I discuss all the languages which are judged to manifest AM. The order of presentation is according to decreasing degrees of complexity of their AM systems. I begin with the most complex systems, those with eight or more AM subcategories. The current interpretation of the system of Kaytetye, where AM was first recognised, is presented in considerable detail in §2 as an example of a very complex system. Then in §3 the other Arandic languages are compared with one another and with Kaytetye. In §4 the Adnyamathanha system, reported by Tunbridge (1988), is briefly described, along with the incomplete evidence for its co-dialect Kuyani. §5 presents four systems with moderate complexity (3 to 6

---

[14] Mudburra, as described by Osgarby (this volume), has a typical PN morphological structure.

AM values): Arabana-Wangkangurru, Warumungu, and Warlmanpa from central Australia – adjacent to the languages with very complex systems – and Yir Yoront from northeastern Australia. §6 describes binary systems with two markers, and §7 those with a single AM category. For each language I present the forms considered to be AM markers, indicate how they have been described in the relevant grammar, give examples of the forms, and offer my analysis in terms of AM parameters. I also mention any non-AM uses of the formatives, and comment on their likely diachronic sources. In §8 I discuss some "precursor constructions" found in languages without grammaticalised AM, indicating the latent potential in Pama-Nyungan languages from which AM grammatical forms are likely to have developed. In §9 I summarise the findings according to system complexity (Tables 16–19), geographical distribution (see the map, Figure 2 in the Appendix), and diachronic sources.

2 The very complex AM system of Kaytetye

2.1 Sources of the data

This analysis of Kaytetye AM is based primarily on examples from Koch (n.d.), which consists of texts I collected in the field in Central Australia (mainly the Tara Community) during the late 1970s and 1980s as part of my documentation of the language.[15] The texts describe the traditional way of life of Kaytetye people: many are narratives, but they include procedural texts and explanatory descriptions of flora and fauna. The collection includes 128 stories with a total of 2870 sentences. Some 240 AM forms occur in these texts. Supplementary data for the present discussion comes from Turpin & Ross' (2012) dictionary, which includes further text data compiled by Myfany Turpin from the late 1990s to about 2010 and example sentences written by the late Alison Ross, a native speaker.

2.2 Principal AM functions

This section summarises the current analysis of the 12 major AM subcategories of Kaytetye, which supersedes my earlier analyses (Koch 1984). Fuller justification and illustration is given in Koch & Turpin (in preparation). Table 2 shows

---

[15] In the examples cited from this collection the source of each is abbreviated thus: KKT 9.8 refers to *Koch Kaytetye Texts*, Text 9, Sentence 8.

Table 2: Semantic dimensions of Kaytetye AM.[16]

Arg	RelTime	Speed/Aspectual	Direction		
nSbj	Prior		NSBJ.ARRIVE -yayte		
Sbj	Prior		GO&DO -yene	RETURN&DO -yalpe	COME&DO -yetnye
Sbj	Prior	Quick	GO.QUICK&DO -nyeyene		
Sbj	Subsequent		DO&GO -layte / -rratye	DO&RETURN -lalpe / -rralpe	
Sbj	Concurrent	Neutral	DO.ALONG -rrapereyne / -rrape		
Sbj	Concurrent	Once	DO.ONCE.ALONG -lpVCe		DO.COMING -yernalpe
Sbj	Concurrent	Continuous	DO.ALL.ALONG- lVCelarre / -rrVCerrenye		
Sbj	Prior+Subs		GO&DO&RETURN -nyeyaytne		

the system of semantic contrasts, and their exponents, according to the major parameters of Moving Argument, Relative Time of MOTION and EVENT (as I shall describe the meanings of the verb stem and the motional modification), the Direction of MOTION, and minor parameters of Speed, applicable only within Prior Motion, and other Aspectual[17] values, which combine only with Concurrent Motion. All but one of the AM subcategories refer to motion of the subject. Prior motion of the non-subject (NSBJ.ARRIVE) is discussed last, in §2.2.5.

Before proceeding further, it is worth showing the morphological structure of Kaytetye verbs. The basic template is given in (1), where brackets indicate optional categories and slashes different categories which occupy the same slot: there are three inflectional slots that follow the verb stem: The AM and Aspect slots are optional; only the final slot (which includes marking for Tense or Mood, or more rarely Negation or Subordination) is obligatory. An example of a verb with three slots filled is (2).

---

16 Where two forms are given in the same cell, the first occurs after transitive verb stems and the second after intransitive stems.
17 I use "aspectual" in the sense of Comrie (1985: 343–244). Note, however, that these are separate from the Kaytetye inflectional category of Aspect.

(1) Verb Stem (Associated Motion) (Aspect) Tense/Mood/Negative/Subordinator

(2) Aynanthe=pe   are-**rapereynte-rantye-wethe** nhakerre   weye-we
    1PL.INCL.ERG=TOP[18] see-**ALONG-IPFV-PURP**   around.here   meat-DAT
    'We'll go looking for meat around here.' (Turpin & Ross 2012: 156)

A slight complication to the formula in (1) is the fact that a directional enclitic =*rne* HITHER[19] may follow some Tense markers in verbs of motion, in particular *ape-nke* 'go (in an unspecified direction)', *alpe-nke* 'return', and *artnpe-nke* 'run, go quickly' – citing them in the PRS inflection -*nke* – to specify toward speaker deixis: *ape-nke=rne* 'come', *alpe-nke=rne* 'come back', and *artnpe-nke=rne* 'run in this direction'.[20]

2.2.1 Prior Motion of subject

This subsection describes and illustrates the four markers of Prior Motion of the subject (the marker for non-subject motion is discussed in §2.2.5). GO&DO, marked by the suffix -*yene*, indicates that the subject moves (in an unspecified direction) and then performs the EVENT, or equivalently, the subject does the EVENT after changing location. The verb may express both MOTION and EVENT, as in (3), where a euro (hill kangaroo) moves forward to inspect a pebble thrown by the hunter. Alternatively, it may redundantly allude to MOTION which has already been specified by an independent motion verb (as an "echo"; see §1.2), as in (4), where the euro, after being speared, runs off and then dies.

(3) *Are-nke=lke*   *re,*   *wethapenye* *are-**yene**-nke*   *weye-le=pe*
    look-PRS=THEN   3SG.ERG   thus   look-**GO&DO**-PRS animal-ERG=TOP
    'It (euro) looks then, the animal goes and has a look.' (KKT 9.8)

(4) *Nharte=pe* **artnpe**-*nke* *ampwarre*-**yene**-*nke*
    then=TOP   **run**-PRS   die-**GO&DO**-PRS
    'Then it runs and then dies (after going some distance).' (KKT 9.11)

---

18 Non-singular pronouns include specification for relative social categories of moiety and alternative generation, which in this paper is omitted from the gloss.
19 A variant =*ngerne* occurs after PST, e.g. *ape-nhe=ngerne* 'go-PST=HITH'.
20 Some Tense-Mood inflections are rather based on a suppletive stem which includes deixis, e.g. *aperrernenye-ye* 'come-FUT'.

RETURN&DO, marked by -*yalpe*, indicates that the subject does EVENT after returning to the subject's base or former location. In (5) the sense of returning motion, of both the independent verb *alpe*- and the AM formative -*yalpe*, is reinforced by the presence of 'camp' in both clauses. The second clause, (5b), a purposive subordinate clause, indicates a subsequent event of eating. Here the -*yalpe* inflection is redundant, merely echoing the motion specified in (5a). The meaning of (5b) is not *'in order to return and eat it in camp' but 'in order to eat it in camp (after returning)'.[21]

(5) a. **Alpe**-*nke*=*lke*   *apmere-warle*
       return-PRS=THEN   camp-ALL

   b. *apmere-warle*=*lke*   *ayne*-**yalpe**-*wethe*
       camp-ALL=THEN   eat-**RETURN&DO**-PURP
       'Then [he] goes back to camp, to eat [it] in the camp (after getting back).'
       (Koch 1984: 27, translation revised)

COME&DO, signaled by -*ye(t)nye*-,[22] indicates that EVENT occurs after the subject has moved to the location where the speaker is. (6) describes a situation where I had taken a dead bird to show my consultants for identification. The toward speaker deixis is guaranteed by the verb 'bring' and the directional modifier *mwernarte*.

(6) a. *Kwerepenharte*=*pe*   *re*   *aperneyne-nye*   *mwernarte*
       then=TOP   3SG.ERG   bring-PST   hither

   b. *Re*   *wethapenye*   *erlwewarre-wethe*   *kwerarte*=*pe*
       3SG.ERG   thus   show-PURP   3SG.ACC=TOP

   c. *Thangkerne*=*pe*   *erlwewarre*-**yenye**-*nye*
       bird(ACC)=TOP   show-**COME&DO**-PST
       'After that he brought it along this way.
       So he could show it [to us].
       He showed [us] the bird after he came.' (KKT 72.4–6)

The suffix -*nyeyene* GO.QUICK&DO marks both Speed and Prior Motion. Example (7) shows that it is MOTION and not the EVENT which is speedy. The stockmen Alec (the speaker) and his colleague Sam had been waiting (expressed by

---

21 For the use of Allative rather than Locative in (5b), see §2.6.
22 The prestopping of the nasal is often not expressed.

'stand') on their horses, but when the mustering helicopter came close, they moved quickly away and took up a stance where they could hold the approaching cattle.

(7) a. *Old.Sam=pe*   ***artnpe**-nhe*   *akngerrake*
Old.Sam(NOM)=TOP   **run**-PST   east

b. *Aylanthe*   *atne-**nyeyene**-nhe*   *akngerrake.*
1DU.INCL.NOM   stand-**GO.QUICK&DO**-PST   east
'Old Sam rode to the east.
The two of us went quickly and stood to the east.' (KKT 81.94–95)

Speed of motion (or possibly hurried action) has been identified as a subcomponent of AM in other Australian languages: with Prior Motion in Adnyamathanha (§4.1) and marginally in Kuuk Thaayorre (§6.1.3), and with Subsequent Motion in other Arandic languages (see §3.3). Rose (2015: 127), for South American languages, chooses to "regard this parameter as a sub-component of the timing parameter ... where the boundary between lexical action and motion is particularly tight: 'do and go immediately after'". This is a possible interpretation; but note that in the Kaytetye system of AM contrasts it could alternately be regarded as part of an "aspectual" dimension, along with the distinctions made within the (non-ventive) Concurrent Motion subcategory. I treat Speed as a separate parameter, while noting – as can be seen in Table 2 – that markers of Speed and Aspectual never co-occur within the same Relative Timing subcategory.

Regarding the forms of the Prior Motion markers, we note that they all include the consonant *y*, preceded in the speedy form *-nyeyene* by *nye*, which distinguishes it from *-yene* GO&DO, and that only *-yalpe* RETURN&DO includes a recognisable verb root, *alpe-* 'return'. Comparison with other Arandic languages (see §3.3) indicates that *y* derives (by lenition) from earlier *ty*; *-yalpe* thus reflects a phonological reduction (including vowel elision) from a phrasal construction *VERB-*tye alpe-*. It can be surmised that *-yene* GO&DO and *-yetnye* COME&DO likewise reflect *VERB-*tye* plus former verbs of motion, which however have not survived into the modern language.

2.2.2 Subsequent Motion

Markers of Subsequent Motion include alternate forms conditioned by the transitivity of the verb stem. The only semantic contrast made within this subcategory is a twofold distinction of Direction: unspecified vs. return to base. DO&GO,

marked by *-layte* or *-rrayte*,[23] after transitive vs. intransitive stems respectively, signals that the subject moves away, in an unspecified direction, from the location of the action they performed – seeing in (8), getting out of a car in (9), and covering in (10). The fact that DO&GO is unspecified for the direction of MOTION is clearly demonstrated by (10), where the direction is actually indicated by the verb *alpe-* as a return to one's base in the (b) sentence. The corresponding DO&RETURN form *-lalpe* (transitive) or *-rralpe* (intransitive) is very infrequent, and there are no clear examples in my texts;[24] (11) is from my fieldnotes. Formally, the Subsequent Motion markers include the recognisable verbs *ayte-* and *alpe-* after an element *l* or *rr* in transitive and intransitive verbs respectively. While *-lalpe* DO&RETURN reflects the meaning of the free verb *alpe-* 'return', *ayte-* as a free verb means 'grow, rise'. Turpin & Ross (2012: 301), however, note another sense 'set off' of *ayte-*, used only by older speakers, which matches better the sense of departure of the DO&GO form. Note that, in the contrasting pair *-yalpe* RETURN&DO and *-lalpe* DO&RETURN, it is only the initial consonant (*y* vs. *l*) that distinguishes the relative time of MOTION and EVENT.

(8) Well   re   atyenge   atere-le   are-**layte**-nhe
    well   3SG.ERG   1SG.ACC   frightened-ERG   see-**DO&GO**-PST
    'Well, it (bird) saw me and flew off frightened.' (KKT 18.4)

(9) a. *Ertwe-nhe   aynanthe   ertwe-**rayte**-nyerre*
       descend-PST   1PL.INCL.NOM   descend-**DO&GO**-PST

    b. *Ape-nhe   aynanthe   alperre=lke   aynanthe*
       go-PST   1PL.INCL.NOM   foliage(ACC)=THEN   1PL.INCL.ERG
       erntwe-nherre
       pick-PST
       'We got out (of the car) and walked away.
       We went and then broke off some leaves.' (KKT 32.8–9)

---

[23] *rr* (a tap or trill) is replaced by *r* (an approximant) after a preceding apical consonant, by a general rule.
[24] The intransitive form *-rralpe* does not occur in my data. The Dictionary (Turpin & Ross 2012: 572) entry suggests that (at least for some speakers) it can also denote concurrent motion, 'do while returning', as in *ante-ralpe-* 'return by car or bus'; i.e. 'sit while returning'.

(10) a. *Alperre-le=lke*   *enpe-**layte**-nke*
 foliage-LOC=THEN   cover-**DO&GO**-PRS

 b. *Nharte=pe*   ***alpe**-nke*   *apmer-arle=lke*
 then=TOP   **return**-PRS   camp-ALL=THEN
 'He covers him (a dead companion) with leaves before he goes off. Then he goes back to camp.' (KKT 82.18–19)

(11) a. *arntwe*   *kwathe-**lalpe**-nhe*;
 water(ACC)   drink-**DO&RETURN**-PST

 b. *apmere*   *kwereyenge-warle*   ***alpe**-nhe.*
 camp   3SG.POSS-ALL   **return**-PST
 '(He) drank some water (before going back) and went back to his camp.' (Koch 1984: 29)

2.2.3 Concurrent Motion

There are four contrasting Concurrent Motion values in Kaytetye. The markers of three of these are alternative formatives conditioned by the transitivity of the verb stem. Two of the exponents of Concurrent Motion involve reduplication. Semantically, the Concurrent Motion forms distinguish two directions of MOTION, one deictic, DO.COMING, toward where the speaker is located, and the other unspecific, here rendered as DO.ALONG.[25] Within Concurrent Motion a further parameter applies, which has been called the "aspectual realisation of the verb action" by Guillaume (2013: 134; cf. Guillaume & Koch, this volume). Whereas the Tacanan languages described by Guillaume make a two-way distinction of repetitive/continuous (imperfective) vs. punctual (perfective), Kaytetye makes a three-way contrast, but only within the unspecified (i.e. non-ventive) direction, while the DO.COMING form is indifferent to this contrast. This three-fold distinction is made according to the degree to which the EVENT overlaps with the extent of time and space of the associated MOTION event. This aspectual subcategory is not the same as the inflectional category of Aspect, however. Kaytetye verbs manifest a contrast between Imperfective and unmarked Aspect. The marking of Imperfective Aspect occurs in a verbal slot between AM and Tense, or fused in its exponence with Tense, as in (12 and 13), where both AM and Aspect:Tense co-occur.

---

25 To save space I omit DO from the glosses in example sentences.

The DO.ALL.ALONG form, -lVCelarre (tr.) /-rrVCerrenye (intr.), indicates that the EVENT takes place during the whole of the MOTION path; EVENT and MOTION are coextensive. The forms involve the addition of an element *l(e)* after a transitive stem and *rr(e)*[26] after an intransitive stem, reduplication of the last *VCe*[27] of the verb stem together with the added *l* or *rr*, plus the addition of *-arre* with transitive and *-enye* with intransitive verbs. It is presumably the reduplication that conveys the sense of total overlap between the EVENT and the MOTION. Diachronically it seems that the construction consisted of a non-finite (participial) form ending in *-le* or *-rre*, conditioned by transitivity, (partially) reduplicated and followed by a (no longer extant) verb of motion (i.e. *are-le-are-l(e) arre-), yielding a Kaytetye form something like a pseudo-English 'look-ing-ook-ing go'. (12) shows a continuous transitive EVENT, as well as illustrating the DO.COMING form. In (13) the jumping EVENT, while not continuous as with 'see', consists of jumps that are repeated over the whole MOTION path, since this is the way a marsupial runs. Note the symmetrical relationship between 'run' and 'jump' in (13b); the *-ngele* subordinating suffix indicates simultaneous action by the same subject as that of the main clause.

(12) Nharte=pe   are-**larelarre**-yayne   atye=pe,
     then=TOP   look-**ALL.ALONG**-IPFV.PST   1SG.ERG=TOP
     are-**yernalpe**-yayne   atye
     look-**COMING**-IPFV.PST   1SG.ERG
     'Then I kept watching all the way along,
     I watched as we came this way.' (KKT 26.2)

(13) a. Antye-**rrantyerrenye**-rrane;
        jump-**ALL.ALONG**-IPFV.PRS

     b. antye-nke...   artnpe-ngele=pe;   artnpe-nke=pe
        jump-PRS...   run-SSBJ=TOP   run-PRS=TOP
        re,   antye-ngele.
        3SG.NOM,   run-SSBJ
        'It (marsupial mouse) jumps along;
        it jumps while running; it runs while jumping.' (KKT 87.2)

---

26 *e* is elided before a following vowel by a general rule, and *rr* changes to *r* by another rule.
27 Here C may be a consonant cluster (as in (13)). Where the verb stem includes only a short, VCe, root, reduplication includes the whole verb stem. VCe, which is common in Arandic reduplication, corresponds to a minimal prosodic word.

The DO.ONCE.ALONG form, *-lpVCe*, consists of *lp* plus the reduplication of the last *VCe* of the verb stem (which, like all morphemes in the language, ends in *e*), whether this is transitive or intransitive. It indicates that the EVENT occupies only a small part of the MOTION path, typically occurring just once or for a short duration. Thus (14), like (12), involves the speaker seeing a plant while travelling in a car. Whereas in (12) the seeing involved constant watching, in (14) it is the momentary act of catching sight of the plant. In (15) the eating EVENT was of short duration in comparison to the whole MOTION of droving the cattle (and occurred at a single point along the motion path); it also shows that the EVENT need not take place while the subject is in motion but it is enough that it takes place along a motion path. Formally, this reduplicated structure resembles a non-AM, quasi-aspectual Attenuative formation in other Arandic languages, which I suggest is its etymological source (Koch 2020).

(14) *Kwerepenharte=pe,   are-**lpare**-nherre   kwerarte=pe   kwenpaye...*
then=TOP   see-**ONCE.ALONG**-PST   3SG.ACC = TOP   fan.flower(ACC)
'After that (I) saw the fan-flower plant as we went along.' (KKT 57.12)

(15) *Nharte=pe   atewanthe   apereyne-nke=lke,   dinner   elkwerre*
then=TOP   3PL.ACC   take-PRS=THEN   dinner   middle
*ayne-**lpayne**-ngele.*
eat-**ONCE.ALONG**-SSBJ
'Then we drove them (cattle) along, stopping to eat lunch on the way.' (KKT 80.5)

A third Concurrent Motion form, *-rrape* (intr.) / *-rrapereyne* (tr.) DO.ALONG, indicates that the main event occurs in the course of a concurrent motion, but does not specify to what extent the EVENT overlaps with the MOTION. Typically the action is repeated. This is implied in (16) but is more obvious in (17) and (18). The form is *-rrape* after intransitive verb stems and *-rrap(er)eyne* after transitive stems.[28] Here *rr* appears to be the same linking consonant as in the Subsequent Motion form *-rrayte* DO&GO, *ape-* is identical to the free verb 'go' (in no specific direction), and *eyne* is a transitivising suffix occurring in factitive verbs. By itself *ap(er)eyne-* is a verb meaning 'take, carry', but that sense is not reflected in the AM form.

---

28 *rr* is altered to *r* after a preceding apical consonant and *n* is changed to *nt* before certain following suffixes, by rules which apply elsewhere in the morphology. The dictionary (Turpin & Ross 2012: 573) gives the longer form of the transitive marker as its main entry and attributes the shorter form to older speakers. My (older) sources used only the shorter form.

(16) *Are-**rapeynte**-rantye   re,   arlelke=pe,   ape-rrane-ngele=pe.*
look-**ALONG**-IPFV.PRS 3SG.ERG hunting=TOP go-IPFV-SSBJ=TOP
'He looks about while going along hunting.' (KKT 43.19)

(17) *Marnte-le   eyterrty-eynenge   eyle-**rapereynte**-rantye.*
bus-ERG   person-COLL(ACC) get-**ALONG**-IPFV.PRS
'The bus travels along, picking up people on its way.' (Turpin & Ross 2012: 383)

(18) *Marnte   antethente-**rape**-rrane   eyterrty-eynenge-we*
bus(NOM) stop-**ALONG**-IPFV.PRS person-COLL-DAT
'The bus stops for people as it goes along.' (Turpin & Ross 2012: 130)

The DO.COMING form, *-yernalpe*, in contrast to the three ALONG (i.e. non-ventive) forms, is indifferent to the aspectual distinctions of the latter. In (12) above it refers to the same event of continuous watching as is described by means of the DO.ALL.ALONG form. In (19) it refers to the single act of killing the prey while in flight. In (20) it refers the intermittent chopping of honey from hollow trees while on a journey to the place where the speaker was at the time of telling. The suffix *-yernalpe* consists of three recognisable elements: *y(e)*, which otherwise occurs in Prior Motion suffixes; *rne*, which is identical to the HITHER directional enclitic; and *alpe-*, which is identical to the free verb 'return'. This suggests an origin as a phrasal construction *VERB-*tye=rne alpe-*, which should mean 'return hither and do', i.e. 'come back and do'. If this was the earlier meaning, there has been a semantic shift from Prior to Concurrent Temporal Relation plus a loss of the 'return' direction.

(19) *Pekapeyne-**yernalpe**-ngele wenhe   alarre-nke.*
paralyse-**COMING**-SSBJ   same(ACC) kill-PRS
'Coming down it (eaglehawk) paralyses (the prey) and kills it. (KKT 93.10)

(20) *Eylpweralke   atye   arte-**yernalpe**-yayne,*
sugarbag(ACC) 1SG.ERG chop-**COMING**-IPFV.PST
'I've been chopping sugarbag (wild honey) while coming along.' (KKT 126.14)

2.2.4 Prior plus Subsequent Motion

A form that earlier was poorly understood is now treated as indicating motion both before and after the main event: *-ny(ey)ay(t)ne-*[29] GO&DO&RETURN. The

---

[29] The *ey* may be elided and the prestopping of the nasal may be omitted.

dictionary definition is "1. Go and do something lots or times or for some time and then return; 2. Back and forth; to and fro" (Turpin & Ross 2012: 524). (21) and (22) illustrate the return phase, the former implicitly since it refers to sleeping away from one's camp, and the latter by means of the verb 'take back', describing termites fetching and cutting off grass for their new home. Most of the available examples involve habitual (hence repeated) events, which in my opinion has given rise to the (unnecessary) interpretation that the verb form includes iterative or durative components. For example, (23) refers to a man gathering a lot of firewood to build a large fire in a pit in which he will cook a euro (hill kangaroo). The duration of the wood-collecting activity, which involves many small trips, is signalled by the Extensive enclitic =ee. The etymology of this AM suffix is not at all clear, but is possibly cognate with Adnyamathanha *wadnii-* 'return' and an AM suffix in other Arandic languages (e.g. EC Arrernte *-irtne* DO.GOING. BACK).[30]

(21) *Erlkwe   aynewantheyenge   ane   mamey-eynenge*
     old.man   1PL.INCL.POSS(NOM)   and   mother-COLL
     *aynewantheyenge   enwe-**nyeyaytne**-nke.*
     1PL.INCL.POSS(NOM)   lie-GO&DO&RET-PRS
     'The old men and our mothers used to go and camp out and return.'
     (Turpin & Ross 2012: 334)

(22) *Kngwere-l-amerne   re   athe=rtame   rntwe-**nyayne**-ngele*
     other-ERG-PL   3SG.ERG   grass(ACC)=CNTR   cut-GO&DO&RET-SSBJ
     alpereynte-ranytye   nthe-warl-arte   athe
     take.back-IPFV.PRS   that-ALL-DEF   grass(ACC)
     'Some of them going and cutting grass take it back to that (termite mound).'
     (KKT 106.9)

(23) a. *Ware=lke   re   nharte=pe   arre-**nyayne**-yerr=ee;*
        fire(ACC)=THEN   3SG.ERG   then=TOP   put-GO&DO&RET-FUT=EXT
     b. *ware=pe   elenhe-ye   errwele*
        fire(ACC)=TOP   throw-FUT   high(ACC)
        'Then he will go back and forth for a long time putting firewood (into the hole); he will throw the firewood in until it is (piled) high.' (KKT 9.44)

---

30 There are free verbs *aytne-* 'spear' and *ayne-* 'eat' in Kaytetye, but neither would provide a suitable source.

A similar AM subcategory has been noted in other languages. Alternative interpretations have been proposed to avoid positing a fourth relative time value. Rose (2015: 123, 140) suggests that the Mojeño Trinitario form -*pono* (and allomorphs) REV.MOT marks "interrupted motion" on a reversive path. The "interrupted" label, however would be misleading for Kaytetye, since Concurrent Motion forms meaning DO.ONCE.ALONG may involve interruption of the motion, e.g. Kaytetye (15) above, stopping to eat on the way.³¹ Guillaume (2016: 38) mentions a number of apparently similar forms in South American languages and comments:

> From a typological point of view, such forms could arguably be interpreted in a range of different ways. They could represent a new subcategory of temporal relation (prior-and-subsequent-return motion). Or they could be categorized under one of the already established subcategories, such as concurrent motion (prior and subsequent return motion construed as a single "circular" motion) or prior motion (subsequent return motion merely implied). For the sake of the present study, I opted for the latter analysis, classifying all these forms under the subcategory of prior motion, which seems to be their primary meaning.

For Kaytetye, the alternative analysis as Prior Motion with implied return would introduce a new subcategory within the GO&DO subcategory. Treating it as doing (once) while going on a round trip would introduce another directional distinction to Concurrent Motion. The most straightforward solution, in my opinion, is to posit a fourth value within the relative time parameter.

2.2.5 Prior Motion of non-subject

The form -*yayte* NSBJ.ARRIVE represents a new parameter – grammatical role of the moving entity (subject vs. non-subject) – which is now recognised for Kaytetye and for an equivalent subcategory of other Arandic languages, since Wilkins' (1989) analysis of Mparntwe Arrernte DO.ON.Z'S.ARRIVAL. The -*yayte* form, previously analysed in Koch (1984) as (subject) APPROACH&DO means rather 'do on the arrival (prior motion) of a non-subject'. Thus *arntarrtye-yayte-nke* means 'grabs (a ball thrown to you) when it arrives'. The translation of (24) corrects the version cited as (9a) in Koch (1984: 18) and interpreted there as 'others would go up [i.e. approach] and ask (him) for tobacco'. The point is rather that those who had stayed in camp would ask the hunter returning with freshly picked native tobacco for a share, after he had come to where they were.

---

31 A similar example is found in the Panoan language Matses (Fleck 2003: 371, cited in Guillaume 2016: 117), glossed 'He stopped (once) to talk on his way here.'

(24) *Kngwerangkwerre-le=pe... ngkwarle-we... lwengelwengaye-**yayte**-yayne.*
others-ERG=TOP   delicacy-DAT   ask-**NSBJ.ARRIVE**-IPFV.PST
'Others would ask him for tobacco once he arrived.' (Koch 1984: 18)

In (24) the moving non-subject is a direct object. But it may also be the dative complement of a verb like 'speak', or even a non-argument of the verb, as shown in (25). Here the subordinate clause 'when a person moves' explicitly marks (by means of *-ngewarle*) that the subject of *ape-* is different from that of the main clause.

(25) *atyewe=rteye   apmwe   entwe-yane...*
awake(NOM)=COND   snake(NOM)   lie-IPFV.PRS
*antye-**yayte**-nke   eyterrtye   ape-ngewarle=pe.*
jump-**NSBJ.ARRIVE**-PRS person(NOM)   go-DSBJ=TOP
'If the snake is awake (it) jumps when a person comes along.' (Turpin & Ross 2012: 579)

2.3 Other possible AM forms

Beyond the 12 forms discussed above there are a few more apparent AM form. It is not certain whether these are productive or rather nonce creations made according to the wider patterns or perhaps adaptations of forms in other Arandic languages. There is an example (26) of a formation *-yalpereyne*, which includes the verb *alpereyne-* 'take back', the transitive version of *alpe-* 'return', i.e. 'take back'. The meaning in the context is 'return it and do', or equivalently 'do after returning it', or perhaps just 'do after returning' with the verbal element of the AM marker unusually adding the transitivising suffix on the analogy of the DO.ALONG form of transitive verbs, *-rrapereyne-* (see §2.2.3).

(26) *Alperneyne-yayne   pwe-**yalpereyne**-yayne.*
bring.back-IPFV.PST   cook-**RETURN(TR)&DO**-IPFV.PST
'We would bring it [kangaroo] back and cook it (after getting it back).' (KKT 128.38)

Another rare form involves a suffix *-yernayte*, which seems to consist of the element *y* found in Prior Motion forms, the HITHER enclitic *rne* and the verb *ayte-* 'rise' (cf. *-yernalpe* DO.COMING). It means 'rise and do', or equivalently, 'do after rising' (27). (The verb for rising or getting up is *atneyayte-*, which is derived from the root *atne-* 'stand'.) Since getting up (from a lying or sitting position) does not involve motion across space, this cannot be an example of prototypical AM.

(27) Ngwetyanpe-ngwetyanpe   wethapenye   perrtye-**yernayte**-yayne   rewenhe
     morning-morning   in.same.way   tie-RISE&DO-IPFV.PST   3SG.REFL
     'Every morning after getting up (lit. rising) he would tie himself [i.e. his hair] in the same way.' (KKT 66.45)

The dictionary (Turpin & Ross 2012: 524) gives a form -*nyeyalpe* with a meaning 'return and do and then go'. The form suggests that it should rather mean 'return quickly and do' (cf. -*nyeyene* GO.QUICK&DO). This is compatible with an example of bees bringing back pollen and putting it into their nest (formed from *akwe-* insert'), since the flight of bees could be considered quick motion. Another form found in the dictionary (Turpin & Ross 2012: 521) is -*nyangkeletne*, said to mean 'come and do quickly or for a short time and then go back'; this appears to include the Kaytetye verb *eletnhe-* 'throw', except that the nasal in the suffix is apical vs. the laminodental of the free verb. This form could possibly have been influenced by a neighbouring Arandic language, Alyawarr or Anmatyerr (which many Kaytetye people speak), where the verb 'throw' is involved in the formation of derived verbs of quick action.

2.4 Non-AM uses of AM forms

Not all uses of AM forms indicate literal motion; there are metaphorical uses.[32] Concurrent Motion forms of verbs of state may signal spatial distribution only. Thus *enwe-yernalpe-rrane* 'lie-COMING-IPFV.PRS' was used of a range of hills extending in the direction of the speaker (KKT 126.65). And the DO.ALL.ALONG form of *ane-* 'sit', *ante-ranterenye-*, is glossed in Turpin & Ross (2012: 129) as 'be, stay, sit, live (of things spread out)'. AM forms can also be used with change of state verbs in a metaphorical sense (28). This is especially true of weather phenomena (29).

(28) arwele=pe   re=pe   alperre=pe   errpwerlarre-**nyeyene**-ye
     tree=TOP   3SG.NOM=TOP   foliage(NOM)=TOP   get.black-**GO.QUICK&DO**-FUT
     'The leaves of the tree will quickly become black (in the boiling water).' (KKT 68.9)

(29) Kweretheyarte=pe,   ahepertewarre-**yernalpe**-yaynenke
     then=TOP   become.summer-**COMING**-IPFV.PST
     'Afterwards it would come to be hot weather time.' (KKT 93.22)

---

[32] Metaphorical or fictive motion is also discussed in this volume's chapters by Ross, Dryer (ch. 4), and Belkadi.

AM forms are used in the Respect Language (RL) register employed between a mother and her daughter in talking about the latter's husband – the relation between mother-in-law and son-in-law being one of strict avoidance (Turpin & Ross 2012: 14). The RL register involves special vocabulary, such as *weyapele* or *weyalyerre* in place of *weye* 'meat' and *ntayle-*, here rendered 'transfer', in place of 'give' or 'get'. Verbs in RL typically occur with AM inflections (Myfany Turpin, pers. comm.). Four AM forms are given in Turpin & Ross (2012: 508) as sub-entries of *ntayle-* 'transfer'. Two of these are illustrated here: ONCE.ALONG in (30) and GO.QUICK&DO in (31). The use of AM forms, especially in commands, suggests that the politeness strategy consists in the fiction that the subject is already on the move ('give while you're on your way') or that the activity will not take much time ('pop over and give'). The verb *arre-* 'put', when suffixed with an otherwise unattested AM form *-nyeyernalpe-*, is used in RL in the sense 'take or bring' (Turpin & Ross 2012: 194, 196), as in (32). This seems to be a modification of *-yernalpe* DO.COMING by the addition of the *nye* seen in *-nyeyene* GO.QUICK&DO, which would give a literal sense 'put while coming quickly', using both motion and speed to convey politeness.

(30) *Weyapele   nte   katye   ntayle-**lpayle**-ne.*
   meat(ACC) 2SG.ERG for s.o.   transfer-**ONCE.ALONG**-IMP
   'Take this meat and give it to him (my son-in-law).' (Turpin & Ross 2012: 508)

(31) *Ntayle-**nyeyene**-wen=awe,   rtwaltye*
   transfer-**GO.QUICK&DO**-OBLG=EXCLAM   daughter's husband(ACC)
   'Go and give this meat (to my son-in-law).' (Turpin & Ross 2012: 508)

(32) *Weyalyerre   arre-**nyeyernalpe**-rrantye=pele.*
   meat(ACC)   put-**COME.BACK.QUICK&DO?**-IPFV:PRS=THUS
   '(My son-in-law) is bringing some meat back.' ["running me some meat"]
   (Turpin & Ross 2012: 640)

AM forms also occur with (intransitive only) verbs that inherently denote motion, especially *ape-* 'go, move', *alpe-* 'return', and *artnpe-* 'run, move quickly'. But in this use the semantic features added are not identical to those of regular AM forms with non-motion verbs. No distinct motion co-event is added, since motion is already specified by the verb root. It follows that there is no indication of the time of EVENT relative to time of MOTION. The moving argument is always the subject, even with *-yayte*, which as a regular AM suffix marks Prior Arrival of a non-subject. As illustrated in (33) to (35), the directions indicated by the forms are largely congruent with those of the corresponding regular AM forms that are used with non-motion verbs, but with some different nuances. *-yayte* indicates approach, often but not necessarily toward the speaker's location; see (33). *-rrayte*, which occurs only with *artnpe-*, contributes the sense 'away', as it does as the AM marker DO&GO (34). *-yene* with *ape-* and *alpe-* seems to add an extended spatial sense of moving 'around' or 'along' (35).³³ In (36) *-yernalpe* adds 'hither' direction to *ape-*; but since 'come' could have been expressed by *ape-nhe=ngerne* 'go-PST=HITHER', the longer suffix perhaps accentuates the spatial extent of the motion. As a result of these considerations I treat these verbs not as AM-inflected motion verbs but rather as separate derived lexemes, which happen to use the same morphology as the AM inflections.³⁴

(33) Nharte   re   ape**yayte**-rane   arrere
     then   3SG.NOM   approach-IPFV.PRS   close
     'Then it (emu) is coming close (to where the hunter is hiding).' (KKT 7.6)

(34) Alarre-nke   kwere   elperarte   artnpe**rrayte**-meketye
     kill-PRS   3SG.ACC   quickly   run.away-APPREH
     'He kills it quickly before it can run away.' (KKT 15.10)

(35) Artweye   apmere-theye   alethele   alpe**yente**-yane
     man(NOM)   camp-ABL   travelling   go.along-IPFV.PRS
     'A man is going along travelling away from the camp.' (KKT 100.1)

(36) Re=pe   aylekanth-angkwerr-apenye=pe   kwenenge=pe   ape**yernalpe**-nhe
     3SG.NOM   1DU.EXCL-PERL-LIKE=TOP   low=TOP   come-PST
     'He (helicopter pilot) came down low around where the two of us were.'
     (KKT 81.97)

2.5 Issues of formal analysis

I have treated the markers of AM as members of a paradigm of contrasting values within an inflectional category of AM. This analysis is reflected in my segmentation of words and the glossing of AM exponents as unitary segments. It may be objected that these markers include phonological elements that can be cor-

---

33 *alpe-* here does not indicate return direction; it is sometimes used in this direction-neutral sense. The insertion of *t* in *-yene* is regular before the IPFV.PRS suffix.
34 There are other derived verbs that use the same suffixes; e.g. *atneyayte-*, 'stand up, get up', derived from *atne-* 'stand', uses the suffix whose AM value is NSBJ.ARRIVE.

related with semantic components of the AM value. The clearest instance of this analysability is the contrast between -*yalpe* RETURN&DO and -*lalpe* DO&RETURN, where *alpe* indicates the semantic component 'return' and the choice between *y* and *l* appears to mark priority vs. subsequence of the motion event. Wilkins (1989, 1991) for Mparntwe Arrernte indicates this sub-analysis by using a dot to separate these formal elements; the corresponding forms in Kaytetye could thus be marked as -*y.alpe* and -*l.alpe*. Apart from the undesirability of recognising meaningful subparts of morphemes, which were defined by Bloomfield (1933: 161) as minimal units of form and meaning, in Kaytetye the formal elements lack enough semantic consistency to make this a plausible synchronic analysis, in my opinion.[35]

These forms, however, clearly derive historically from complex structures consisting of a non-finite suffix followed by an erstwhile auxiliary verb (cf. §3.4). There are, moreover, synchronic traces of this phrasal structure – in the form of (rare) instances of enclitics occurring in the middle, immediately before the more verbal part, of a complex AM marker. Thus the sequencing enclitic =*lke* THEN interrupts -*yalpe* in (37)[36] and the reduplicated -*lpeRDP* in (38).

(37) *Errke-ye<lk>alpe-nke* *errke-yalpe-nke=lke* re
 carve-RETURN<THEN >&DO-PRS carve-RETURN&DO-PRS=THEN 3SG.ERG
 'He goes back then and carves it (boomerang), he goes back and carves it then.' (Koch 1984: 28)

(38) *Ape-nhe atanthe eyle-lpe<lk>eyle-nye*
 go-PST 3PL.NOM get-ONCE<THEN>ALONG-PST
 'Then they went out and then gathered (bush onions) on the way.' (KKT 125.34)

2.6 Argument structure of AM forms

Previous studies (e.g. Koch 1984: 26) have emphasised that, even if an etymological verb of motion can be discerned in a verb form marking AM, which may

---

[35] See however Panther & Harvey (2020) for arguments in favour of a synchronic syntactic phrasal analysis of Kaytetye AM forms, where separate meanings are attributed to each of these elements.
[36] Note that in the second instance of the verb, the enclitic =*lke* rather follows the whole inflected verb, which is its normal position.

descend from a participle plus auxiliary verb construction, it is the verb denoting the main event that determines the transitivity of the whole, and not the AM marker. While this is true for subject marking, the case-marking of locationals is more variable. Simpson (2001: 180) observes that Warlpiri verb compounds that signal AM may in fact alter the argument structure of the verb by adding a directional argument by virtue of the meaning of the motion verb included in the compound. Kaytetye in fact shows some variability in the marking of location with AM forms. (39) has the expected Locative case for the place where eating-after-return takes place. In (40b) and (5b) above, however, the Allative case appears to be motivated by the motion part of the complex event. Similarly, the Ablative case in (41) seems to be licensed by the motion sense within the complex verb.[37]

(39) a. *Alpe-werne=lke   aynanthe   apmer-arl=ane.*
         return-OBLG=THEN 1PL.INCL.NOM   camp-ALL=EMPH

   b. *Apmere-**le**   ayne-**yalpe**-wethe.*
      camp-**LOC**   eat-**RETURN&DO**-PURP
      'We should go back to camp now.
      To eat it in camp (after getting back).' (KKT 7.34–35)

(40) a. *Nharte   kwer-akak-arte=pe   alpe-nke=lke   apmer-arle.*
         then   3SG-PROP-DEF=TOP   return-PRS=THEN   camp-ALL

   b. *Apmer-**arle**=lke   re   ayne-**yalpe**-wethe.*
      camp-**ALL**=THEN   3SG.NOM   eat-**RETURN&DO**-PURP
      'Then he goes back to camp with [carrying] it.
      To eat it (after getting back) in camp.' (KKT 43.28–29)

(41) *Anteyerre-**theye**=lke   eyle-**yernalpe**-nherre   kwer-arte=pe*
      south-**ABL**=THEN   get-**COMING**-PST   3SG.ACC-DEF=TOP
      pweleke=pe;   nharte   alpalpangenhe   artne-we=pe.
      cattle(ACC)=TOP   that   huge.mob(ACC)   scrub-DAT=TOP
      'He (the helicopter) came along from the south now getting the cattle, that huge mob, out from the scrub.' (KKT 81.90)

---

[37] 'From the south' cannot be an argument of 'get', since verbs of extraction/separation require the Dative to mark the object/location from which the object is separated.

3 AM in other Arandic languages

3.1 The Arandic subgroup

The Arandic subgroup of the Pama-Nyungan language family is justified in Koch (2004). Their internal genetic relations, known since Hale (1962), consist of two primary branches, Kaytetye vs. the rest, which can be labelled with the older name "Aranda". This Aranda branch subdivides into Lower Arrernte vs. the rest, which Hale labelled "Upper Aranda". The varieties of Upper Aranda were treated by Hale (whose classification was based on lexicostatistics) as a dialect continuum, but they are now usually treated as separate languages: Eastern Arrernte, Central Arrernte, Western Arrernte (with a Southern subvariety), Anmatyerr, and Alyawarr. Their relations are shown schematically in Figure 1. Their geographical positions can be seen on the map (Figure 2 in the Appendix).

Arandic
    Kaytetye
    Aranda
        Upper Aranda
            Alyawarr
            Anmatyerr
            Western Arrernte
            Central Arrernte
            Eastern Arrernte
        Lower Arrernte

Figure 1: Genetic relations among the Arandic languages.

3.2 Eastern and Central (EC) Arrernte

The fullest descriptions of AM in other Arandic languages are those for Mparntwe (Central) Arrernte by Wilkins (1989: 270–298, 1991, 2006). Central and Eastern Arrernte are similar enough to have been treated together as Eastern and Central (EC) Arrernte (cf. Henderson & Dobson 1994, Henderson 2013[1997]). Wilkins treats the markers of AM as "quasi-inflections" for the following reasons: the forms all occur in the same slot[38] in the verb structure; they form a coherent paradigmatic set of meanings; they can be productively applied to any verb (except the four basic motion verbs); and, although some forms are partially analysable as including verb roots, these cannot be analysed as synchronic verb compounding since the verbal elements do not retain the full semantics of their independent counterparts. For example, *alhe-*'go' and *alpe-* 'go back' lose their 'away from speaker' deictic value in AM forms and, in *-inty.alhe* DO.COMING.THRU, *alhe-* occurs with the opposite 'toward speaker' deixis. Note that Wilkins uses a dot to separate identifiable components of the complex suffixes[39] – a practice that has been followed in other descriptions of Arandic languages and which will be used in the following presentation of comparative Arandic AM forms.

Table 3: EC Arrernte AM forms.[40]

Path & Speed	Concurrent Hither	+ Deixis Neutral	Subsequent	Prior
Back	*-inty.alpe* COMING.BACK	*-irtne* GOING.BACK	*-rl.alpe* &GO.BACK	*-ty.alpe* GO.BACK& &GO.BACK
Back Quick			*-artn.alpe* QUICK&GO.BACK	
Unsp	*-intye* DO.COMING	*-rl.ape* DO.ALONG	*-rl.alhe* DO&GO	*-ty.alhe* GO&DO
Unsp Quick			*-artn.alhe* QUICK&GO	
Past/Thru	*-inty.alhe* COMING.THRU	*-nhe* IN.PASSING[41]		
Down	*-inty.akerle* COMING.DOWN	*-ty.akerle* DOWN		

---

38 The AM slot comes between the verb stem and three other quasi-inflectional slots marking (two marking Aspect and one for Subject Number Agreement) which precede the final obligatory Tense/Mood slot (Wilkins 2006: 28).
39 The boundary between the two components of the complex suffixes is also the location for the insertion of the Plural Subject Agreement marker and potentially some clitics (see further §3.4).
40 To save space in glosses I have omitted the component DO from all but the shortest glosses, and the suffixes -WARDS from DOWNWARDS and UPWARDS, and -LY from QUICKLY. 'Unsp' refers to 'unspecified'.
41 I use IN.PASSING in place of Wilkins' DO.PAST to prevent confusion with Past Tense where necessary.

Path & Speed	Concurrent Hither	+ Deixis Neutral	Subsequent	Prior
Down Quick		-artn.akerle QUICK.DOWN		
Up		-ty.antye[42] UP		
(nSbj) Arrive				-ty.intye ON.Z'S.ARRIVAL[43]

Table 3 presents 17 AM forms, arranged here according to the parameters of: Path, Deixis, Speed, and Relative Timing of motion. The role of the moving figure is always the subject except for the last form DO.ON.Z'S.ARRIVAL, where Z is a non-subject, usually an object or dative complement. The forms include the 15 presented in Wilkins' (2006: 49) Table 2.5. I have added an additional form, *-inty. akerle* '(do something) while coming downwards towards the person speaking', cited from the south-eastern subdialect (Henderson & Dobson 1994: 390). I also include a somewhat ambiguous form *-rl.ape* (variant *-rle.pe*), which is analysed by Wilkins as a marker of Aspect, 'do continuously while going along', contrasting with *-rl.ane* (variant *-rle.ne*) 'do continuously' and *-rliwe* 'do quickly' (Wilkins 1989: 252–254), but which often has a sense of 'do while going in an unspecified direction' (Wilkins 2006: 50).[44] An example of both the aspectual and concurrent motion senses is shown by (42).

(42) *Thomas   ulyenty-le   ne-**rle.pe**-me*
Thomas   shade-LOC   sit-**DO.ALONG**-NPST.PROG
'Thomas is continually sitting in the shade as he goes along.' (i.e. either 'Thomas is going along from shade to shade' or 'Thomas is sitting while going along in the shade; e.g. in a car'.) (Wilkins 1989: 253)

The EC Arrernte AM system, while sharing its overall complexity with Kaytetye, shows many differences in detail. In terms of semantic values: it lacks a Prior plus

---

[42] *-ty.intye* in the south-eastern subdialect (Henderson & Dobson 1994: 563).
[43] *-ty.antye* in the north-eastern subdialect (Henderson & Dobson 1994: 565).
[44] According to Wilkins (1989: 275), the *-rl.ape* form can occur in the (Aspect) slot after AM forms and, unlike AM forms generally, can be added to motion verbs. The cognate forms in Alyawarr and Lower Arrernte have been analysed as markers of AM (see §3.3).

Subsequent motion form; it combines Speed with Subsequent and Concurrent Motion but not with Prior Motion; it includes directions in the vertical dimension (upwards and downwards); it makes greater use of 'toward speaker (coming)' deixis; it involves extra 'past' and 'through' Paths, which I here treat as the same; and it lacks an aspectual distinction within Concurrent Motion. There is a hint, however, of an aspectual contrast. Whereas Concurrent Motion forms in general may involve single, repeated, or continuous action along the motion path, the -*rl.ape* form "does **not** permit the interpretation that the verb action happens only once in the midst of motion" (Wilkins 1989: 275 [emphasis in original]). This suggests that -*rl.ape* was at least formerly a Concurrent AM form contrasting in an aspectual dimension with -*nhe*. The difference between Unsp(ecified) and Past/Thru paths in Table 3 (as I have arranged the forms) may, I suggest, reflect an aspect-like contrast between punctual and continuous (or iterative) distribution within Concurrent Motion.

In terms of the forms of EC Arrernte AM markers, we can observe the following. The elements -*intye* and -*artne* consistently mark hither deixis and Speed respectively. Verb roots recognisable as elements of AM forms are *alpe*- 'go back', *alhe*- 'go', *antye*-/*intye*- 'climb, ascend', *akerle*- 'move down' – the last occurring in EC Arrernte (Henderson & Dobson 1994: 63) although not in Wilkins' Mparntwe. The element -*ape* in -*rl.ape*, complementary in function to -*alhe*, etymologically reflects a proto-Arandic *ape- 'go', which is still attested in Kaytetye (Wilkins 1989: 253). The element -*irtne* DO.GOING.BACK, complementary to -*alpe*, may reflect an earlier verb cognate with Adnyamathanha *wadnii*- 'return' (Wilkins 1989: 278). The similarity of the elements *antye* and *intye* of DO.UPWARDS and DO.ON.Z'S.ARRIVAL is intriguing, given that the verb 'ascend' occurs in variant forms *antye*- and *intye*- within EC Arrernte (Henderson & Dobson 1994: 163).

3.3 Arandic AM forms compared

I now present and compare the forms known from the various Arandic languages.[45] Further discussion of the etymology of forms is in §3.4. Note that, apart from ECArrernte, AM has been explicitly described only for Alyawarr by Moore (2012)[46] and Lower Arrernte by Humphris' (2017) analysis of the (relatively sparse) data compiled by Breen (2002). The Anmatyerr forms are taken from

---

45 Abbreviations used in the tables are: Aly Alyawarr, Anm Anmatyerr, ECAr Eastern and Central Arrernte, LAr Lower Arrernte, Kay Kaytetye, and WAr Western Arrernte.
46 There are some indications in Yallop's (1977) earlier description as well.

Green's (2010) dictionary; there has not been a systematic grammatical study. Western Arrernte forms are supplied from T. Strehlow (1944: 172–175), using the updated orthography of Breen (2000), following the interpretations of Wilkins, which are based on parallels to EC Arrernte forms and work with a Western Arrernte speaker.[47] This has been supplemented by forms found in the newly available dictionary by Carl Strehlow (2018[1909]). An even earlier source of Western Arrernte AM forms, although admittedly not fully understood by the author, is Kempe (1891), who must now be acknowledged as the first grammarian to present AM verbal forms for an Australian language (Stockigt 2016: 389–391). These historic sources allow us to conclude that practically all the subcategories recognised for EC Arrernte are represented in Western Arrernte, although some of the examples are not clear (cf. Henderson 2018: 93).[48] The forms cited from Carl Strehlow (2018[1909]) and Kempe (1891) have been put into the modern orthography in the following tables. Here Eastern and Central Arrernte includes both Wilkins' Mparntwe Arrernte and data from other lects represented in Henderson & Dobson's (1994) dictionary and Henderson's (2013 [1997]) dissertation. The inventory of forms cited here may not be complete, and further study could be done to refine the semantic distinctions.

Tables 4 and 5 present the Prior and Subsequent forms respectively. (Table 5 also includes the Prior plus Subsequent form which is found only in Kaytetye.) Note that the complex suffixes of both subtypes include the verb roots *(a)lhe-* 'go' and *alpe-* 'return' preceded by linking suffixes (ligatives) *-tye-* (lenited to *-ye-* in Alyawarr and Kaytetye) in Prior formations and *-rle-* (*-rre-* and *-le-* in Kaytetye) in Subsequent formations. The NSBJ.ARRIVE forms, which refer to the movement of a non-subject to the place where the event occurs, involve a verb 'rise' – Kaytetye *ayte-*, **aynte-*, with divergent phonological developments, in the other lects – preceded by *-tye-* (except in Western Arrernte). The marker of Speed, *-artne-* QUICK, of unknown etymology, co-occurs with *-(a)lhe* and *-alpe* but without a preceding ligative in EC Arrernte and Western Arrernte. Alyawarr has a distinctive marker of Speed, *-elpe*, which is not recognisable as an independent verb.

---

[47] "For Western Arrernte Strehlow (1944: 171–174) presents as series of forms which he calls 'Derived ("Periphrastic") Verbs'. In the long list of forms, all based on the simple verb *tuma* 'hit', one can discern certain associated motion forms which are cognate to the Mparntwe Arrernte forms" (Wilkins 1989: 275).

[48] The only form I have not been able to identify is *-artn.akerle* QUICKLY.DO.DOWNWARD. On the other hand, there appear to be numerous forms consisting of combinations, not attested elsewhere, of AM elements.

Table 4: Prior Motion in Arandic languages.

	NSBJ.ARRIVE	GO&DO	RETURN&DO	COME&DO	GO.QUICK&DO
LAr	-ty.irnte	-tye.lhe	-ty.alpe		
WAr	-intye, -antye[49]	-tye.lhe	-ty.alpe		
ECAr	-ty.intye, -ty.antye[50]	-ty.alhe	-ty.alpe		
Anm		-ty.alhe	-ty.alpe		
Aly	-y.aynte	-y.alhe	-y.alpe		-y.elpe
Kay	-y.ayte	-yene	-y.alpe	-yetnye	-nyeyene

Table 5: Subsequent Motion in Arandic languages.

	&GO	&RETURN	&GO.QUICK	&RETURN.QUICK	GO&DO&RETURN
LAr	-rle.lhe	-rl.alpe			
WAr	-rle.lhe	-rl.alpe	-artne.lhe	-artn.alpe	
ECAr	-rl.alhe	-rl.alpe	-artn.alhe	-artn.alpe	
Anm	-rl.alhe	-rl.alpe			
Aly	-rl.alhe	-rl.alpe	-rl.elpe		
Kay intr.	-rr.ayte	-rr.alpe			-nyeyaytne-
Kay tr.	-l.ayte	-l.alpe			

Table 6: Concurrent Motion in Arandic languages: Unspecified direction.

	ALONG	ONCE.ALONG/ IN.PASSING	ALL.ALONG
LAr	-rl.ape	-arlp(unt)e	
WAr	-rl.ape	-nhe	
ECAr	-rl.ape	-nhe	
Anm	-rl.ape	-nhe	
Aly	-rl.ape	-nhe	
Kay intr.	-rr.ape	-lpe.RDP	-rre.RDP.rre.nye
Kay tr.	-rr.apereyne		-le.RDP.l.arre

---

49 According to T. Strehlow (1944: 178) -*antye* is the form in the Southern Arrernte subdialect. Movement of a non-subject figure seems to be guaranteed by the gloss for *kamirr-antye-*: 'to rise towards someone else (e.g. to rise towards a guest who has just arrived)'. His glosses 'see upon approach' for *ar-antye* is ambiguous, but C. Strehlow's gloss '(herankommen) sehen', 'see (approaching)' for *r-intye-* clearly indicates movement of the object.

50 According to Henderson & Dobson (1994: 565), -*ty.antye* occurs in the north-eastern dialect.

Concurrent Motion forms are presented in Tables 6–8. Table 6 shows those that do not mark deictic or oriented direction (according to Wilkins' directionality terminology). All the non-Kaytetye languages include a form *-rl.ape* or *-rle.pe*, consisting of a ligative *-rle* and a reflex *ape-* or *pe-* of a Proto-Arandic verb *ape- reflected in Kaytetye *ape-* 'go (in a non-specific direction)' and in the other Arandic languages in *(a)petye-* 'come'. Lower Arrernte *-rl.ape* is glossed as DO.GO-ING (Humphris 2017: 111), a marker of AM. Alyawarr *-rlape* CONV is likewise treated as a marker of AM, although described in terms of 'doing while being conveyed or conveying along a path' (Moore 2012: 111–112) – a situation which applies to some situations but not very plausibly to telling stories when travelling around. For Anmatyerr the form is said to show "that the verb action happens continuouly or over a period of time while in motion, or while going along" (Green 2010: 294). This interpretation echoes the interpretation as Aspect of Mparntwe Arrernte mentioned in §3.2. T. Strehlow's (1944: 172) description of Western Arrernte *twe-rl.ape-me* involves two glosses 'keep on hitting' and 'hit while going along', which mirrors Wilkins' analysis of Mparntwe Arrernte.

The *-nhe* form in EC Arrernte is described in terms of "oriented" Concurrent Motion, 'do on the way past some reference point' (Wilkins 1989: 284); the identical suffix in Alyawarr (Green 1992: 134) and Anmatyerr (Green 2010: 291) has been defined in similar terms. Moore (2012: 91), however, defines Alyawarr *-nhe* as doing 'at a point along a motion path'. This meaning is very similar, except in omitting a reference point on the path which is "passed". The meaning of the Alyawarr form is also close to that of the Kaytetye *-lpe.*RDP inflection – thus allowing for the marking of momentary vs. continuous action on a concurrent motion path. Lower Arrernte has a few instances of *-nhe*, but it is interpreted by Humphris (2017: 118) as THITHER, a marker of direction away from the speaker,[51] which can occur after *-arlp(unt)e* DO.ALONG. The etymology of *-nhe* is unknown.

Humphris (2017: 111) gives two Concurrent Motion forms which seem to overlap in function, *-rlape* DO.GOING and *-arlp(unt)e* DO.ALONG. The element *-arlpe* is otherwise unknown, but *unte-* is identical to the independent verb 'run'. Most of Humphris' examples of *-arlp(unt)e* include the following Continuative Aspect suffix *-ane*, but she notes that "when occurring without the Continuative *-an*, the suffix *-arlpunt* may imply sudden and non-continuing motion" (Humphris 2017: 117). The *-rlape* form, on the other hand, "has an interpretation of (a) 'going from place to place and doing sth' or (b) 'going along doing sth (on the

---

[51] 'Thither' is a typical gloss for this deixis, but, as observed by Blake & Breen (1971: 178) with regard to a Pitta-Pitta form, it "is probably not the best translation of this suffix, which is the converse of 'hither'. 'Thither' implies motion to a specific place, whereas this suffix probably just means 'away from here' (= 'hence')."

way)'" (Humphris 2017: 111), quoting Breen (2002: 68)), illustrated by (43).⁵² This recurrent occurrence is compared to the aspect-like contrast made by Kaytetye within Concurrent Motion (Humphris 2017: 116). This is the only explicit mention of a possible aspectual contrast within the AM system of an Arandic language other than Kaytetye.

(43) Ila   unthe-**lape**-me   tne-**rlape**-mele
     3SG.NOM   walk.about-**DO.GOING**-NPST stand-**DO. GOING**-SS
     irle-**rlape**-me
     sing-**DO.GOING**-NPST
     'He moves around everywhere, and then he stops from time to time and sings.' (Breen 2002: 68)

Only Kaytetye has a separate AM form that indicates total coextension of the motion and the main action. Doubtless it is the reduplication that provides the main signal for this semantic component. The complex suffix probably includes etymologically a reduplicated participle followed by a (no longer recoverable) verb root *(e)nye or *arre. Note that the ligatives included in Concurrent forms are the same as those in the Subsequent forms. Presumably the phrasal precursors of these forms were expressions such as 'doing move', which could be understood as indicating either simultaneous or prior action, i.e. 'doing move' or 'having done move'.

The forms in Table 7 (Concurrent Motion with specified deictic direction) involve elements -intye and -irtne that mark respectively motion toward the speaker and back to a former location. Lower Arrernte -antye is analysed as a HITHER directional suffix rather than an AM marker; it is not certain whether it is cognate with -intye of the other languages. Note that when -(a)lhe or -alpe is added after -intye, there is no ligative. The Kaytetye form -yernalpe, unrelated to -intye, was explained in §2.2.3 above.

Table 8 shows that only Kaytetye lacks AM markers of vertical motion. The UPWARDS forms include the verb root 'rise'; the DOWNWARDS forms include a verb root 'descend'; in Alyawarr and Eastern Anmatyerr, however, the DOWNWARDS value is expressed in combination with the transitive verb root arrerne- 'put (down)' (Moore 2012: 118). The ligative occurring before -(a)kerle is variably -tye or -rle. The presence of a ligative before -artne in -ty.artne.kerle – perhaps a nonce form from C. Strehlow (1909) – is unparalleled. An interesting issue concerns

---

52 I have normalised the orthography. The l of -lape results from regular conditioning of rl after a laminodental consonant. Note that the AM marker is added to a motion verb unthe- and that the main verbs are 'moves about' and 'sings [his verse] (while going about)', the middle verb being a subordinate form 'stopping [literally standing] (while going about)'.

the relation between the UPWARDS forms and those that mark Prior Arrival of a non-subject participant (see Table 4). Moore (2012: 115–117) for Alyawarr and Humphris (2017: 114–115) for Lower Arrernte treat the forms as the same morpheme with two distinct uses.[53]

Table 7: Concurrent Motion in Arandic languages: Specified directed deictic.

	COMING	COMING.THROUGH	COMING.BACK	GOING.BACK
LAr	-antye ?	–	–	–
WAr	-intye	-intye.lhe	-inty.alpe	-irtne
ECAr	-intye	-inty.alhe	-inty.alpe	-irtne
Anm	-intye	-inty.alhe	-inty.alpe	-rne
Aly				-eyne
Kay	-yernalpe			

Table 8: Concurrent Motion in Arandic languages: Oriented.

	UPWARDS	DOWNWARDS	DOWNWARDS.QUICK
LAr	-ty.irnte	-rl.akerle	
WAr	-ty.intye -ty.antye	-rle.kerle, -tye.kerle	-ty.artne.kerle
ECAr	-ty.antye -ty.intye[54]	-ty.akerle	-artn.akerle
Anm	-ty.aynte ?	-rl.arrerne (E) -ty.akerle (W)	
Aly	-y.aynte	-rl.arrerne	
Kay	–	–	–

The number of semantic distinctions within the AM category in Arandic languages varies from nine[55] in Lower Arrernte to 16, arguably 17 if *-rl.ape* is included, in EC Arrernte. Non-subject as the moving figure is not documented for Anmatyerr and only weakly for Western Arrernte. With respect to the Relative Timing parameter, all languages contrast Prior, Subsequent and Concurrent motion; only Kaytetye has a clear Prior plus Subsequent subcategory. The main directional

---

53 The only Lower Arrernte examples cited are *tne-ty.irnte-*, whose gloss 'stand up', rather than 'stand while going up' suggests a derivational rather than an AM usage; cf. Kaytetye *atneyayte-* 'stand up', etymologically 'stand-LIG-rise', which however is not analysed as AM.
54 According to Henderson & Dobson (1994: 563) *-ty.intye* occurs in the south-eastern dialect.
55 Assuming that the COMING form is a mere directional rather than an AM marker.

contrast is between 'go' (neutral direction) and 'return', but motion toward the speaker ('come') is also well represented. Motion in the vertical dimension, 'up' and 'down' is relatively rare in attestation, even in its use in languages where it has been found (cf. Wilkins 2006: 51). The dimension of Speed is sporadically attested. Aspectual distinctions within Concurrent Motion (continuous vs. punctual, coextensive vs. unspecified) are restricted to Kaytetye; but the distinction in the other languages between the Continuous Aspect, derived from 'do while going', and Punctual Aspect 'do at a point or in passing' appears to reflect a similar difference in the temporal (and spatial) contour of an action in relation to its framing path. The Lower Arrernte difference between *-rl.ape* DO.GOING and *-arlp(unt)e* DO.ALONG may also reflect such a contrast.

3.4 Sources of Arandic AM forms

This section explores the diachronic sources of Arandic AM forms and how this is reflected in their synchronic structure.[56] Several facts about Arandic AM markers are obvious: (a) many forms include recognisable verb roots; (b) the elements that connect these "verbs" to the stem – i.e. the "ligatives" – have recurrent functions; and (c) many of these formal elements and their functions are shared across many of the languages. Table 9 summarises these shared elements. Here "Aranda" indicates all the Arandic languages other than Kaytetye, and P, C, and S refer to Prior, Concurrent and Subsequent Motion respectively. The full forms have been presented in Tables 4–8 of §3.3.

Table 9: Shared elements of Arandic AM forms.

Verb	*-tye	-(r)le	-rre
alpe- 'return'	all: P Kaytetye: C	all: S	Kaytetye: S
(a)lhe- 'go'	all Aranda: P	all Aranda: S	
ayte- 'rise'	Kaytetye: P(NSBJ)	Kaytetye: S	Kaytetye: S
*aynte- 'rise'	all Aranda: P, C		
*ape- 'move'		all Aranda: C	Kaytetye: C
akerle- 'descend'	ECAr, WAr, WAnm: C	WAr, LAr: C	
arrerne- 'put down'		Aly, EAnm: C	

---

56 For earlier comments on diachrony see Koch (1984, 2019, 2020) and Wilkins (1989: 296, 1991: 238–250).

Some of the recognisable verbs, when used as part of an AM formation, have meanings somewhat different from those of the corresponding independent verbs. All languages use *alpe-* 'return' and all the Aranda languages likewise employ *(a)lhe-* 'go' as an element of both Prior and Subsequent AM forms. Wilkins (1989: 291) notes, however, that in Mparntwe Arrernte these motion verbs lose their deictic component 'away from speaker' when forming part of an AM marker. The Kaytetye verb *ayte-* 'rise', which has a cognate in Warumungu (cf. §5.2), is used in the AM system to mark both Subsequent Motion away from the location of the main event (DO&GO) and Prior Arrival of a non-subject to the location of the main event (NSBJ.ARRIVE). The Aranda languages use their verb 'rise, ascend', which are reflexes of *aynte-, to mark both UPWARDS Concurrent Motion and Prior Arrival of a non-subject.[57] It is not clear why these two separate AM values would use the same verb. Note that Wilkins' (2006: 49) analysis assigns *-ty.antye* DO.UPWARDS and *-ty.intye* DO.ON.Z'S.ARRIVAL to separate AM subcategories. Moore (2012: 114–117) and Humphris (2017: 114–115) attribute both uses to the same form for Alyawarr and Lower Arrernte respectively. A Proto-Arandic verb *ape-, preserved in Kaytetye as *ape-* 'go (with no specific direction)' and in Aranda in an extended form *(a)petye-* 'come', is used as an element *-(a)pe-* of a Concurrent Motion form *-rl.ape/ -rle.pe* DO.ALONG in all languages, with possible extensions to Continuous Aspect marking in some varieties of Arrernte.

There are a number of other elements of AM forms which appear in a similar construction, following a ligative, but which are not identifiable as contemporary independent verb roots. In Alyawarr an apparent verb *-elpe* occurs in *-y.elpe* GO.QUICK&DO and *-rl.elpe* DO&GO.QUICK. Kaytetye has the most of such apparently former verbs: *-ene* in *-y.ene* GO&DO and in *-nye.y.ene* GO.QUICK&DO, *-etnye* in *-y.etnye* COME&DO and perhaps *-rre.RDP.rr.enye* ALL.ALONG, *-arre* in *-le.RDP.l.arre* ALL.ALONG, and *-aytne* in *-nye.y.aytne* GO&DO&RETURN.[58]

The semantic contribution of the ligatives is not consistent, although some generalisations can be made. The reflexes of Proto-Arandic *-tye (> -ye in Kaytetye and Alyawarr) most often occur in Prior Motion formations, but are also found in Concurrent UPWARDS and DOWNWARDS forms, as well as in Kaytetye *-yernalpe* DO.COMING, which has apparently shifted semantically from an earlier Prior Motion sense 'come back and do'. Aranda *-rle* and (the probably cognate) Kaytetye *-le* occurs in Subsequent formations but also in Concurrent forms: Aranda *-rl.ape*,

---

[57] I assume sound changes involving loss of initial *a* and change of *y* plus apical consonant(s) to palatal consonant(s). The presence of these forms in Anmatyerr is uncertain. Note the absence of a ligative in the Western Arrernte NSBJ.ARRIVE form.
[58] *-aytne* is possibly cognate with ECAr and WAr *-irtne* GOING.BACK, which could have a distant cognate in Adnyamathanha *wadnii-* 'return'.

some DOWNWARDS forms, and the Kaytetye reduplicated transitive allomorph -*le.RDP.l.arre* DO.ALL.ALONG. Kaytetye -*rre* occurs in Subsequent forms after intransitive stems, but also in the Concurrent reduplicated intransitive allomorph -*rre.RDP.rr.enye* DO.ALL.ALONG and in the -*rr.ape(reyne)-* DO.ALONG form.

It is assumed that that ligatives continue earlier non-finite verb suffixes. The value of the *-tye forms was presumably future-oriented in constructions with a motion verb; i.e. a possible Motion with Purpose construction 'go to do' was reinterpreted as 'go and do'. The use of -*ye* in the Kaytetye Concurrent form -*ye.rn.alpe-* results from a language-internal semantic shift from a Prior form (§2.2.3). The use of -*tye* with Aranda vertical (UPWARDS and DOWNWARDS) Concurrent markers is apparently arbitrary, since -*rle* is also found in these constructions. The -*(r)le* and (uniquely Kaytetye) -*rre* elements were hypothetically non-finite forms marking contemporaneous time; with motion verbs the construction was thus 'while doing go'. This is reflected in Aranda -*rl.ape* and Kaytetye -*rr.ape*. These forms are structurally parallel to (Aranda) Continuous or (Kaytetye) Imperfective Aspect markers, where the ligative combines with *ane-* 'sit' to form Aranda -*rl.ane* and Kaytetye -*rr.ane*.[59] A simultaneous action semantics of the ligatives is also presupposed by the Kaytetye reduplicated DO.ALL.ALONG forms -*le.RDP.l.arre* and -*rre.RDP.rr.enye* – occurring after transitive vs. intransitive stems respectively – which would have literally meant 'doing doing go'.[60]

I hypothesise that the use of Aranda -*rle* and Kaytetye -*rre* in Subsequent Motion constructions results from extending the simultaneity of the dependent verb to immediately preceding action; thus 'doing go' can be used for 'having done go'. A similar usage of a non-finite verb in contemporary Kaytetye can be seen in (44), where the Same Subject subordinate form of 'kill' actually refers to a completed event (not the literal 'while killing' but 'after killing'), yielding an instance of subsequent (transitive) motion.

(44) nharte=pe   re   alarre-**ngele**,   alpereyne-yayne.
     then=TOP   3SG.ERG   kill-**SSBJ**   take.back-IPFV.PST
     'Then when he had killed it he would take it back.' (KKT 11.17)

Some of the elements of AM formatives cannot obviously be analysed as either verb roots or non-finite verbal suffixes. These include Aranda -*irtne* GOING.BACK,[61] -*intye* COMING, -*nhe* DO.IN.PASSING, -*artne* QUICK, plus Lower Arrernte -*arlpe*

---

59 In spite of their etymology, these forms do not have an associated posture interpretation.
60 With the second instance of the verb truncated; e.g. * ... VCe-le VCe-le arre-.
61 But perhaps cognate with the Adnyamathanha verb *wadnii-* 'return', which may have another reflex in the *aytne* of Kaytetye -*nye.y.aytne* GO&DO&RETURN.

DO.ALONG, Kaytetye -*nye* in -*nye.y.ene* GO.QUICK&DO and possibly -*nye.y.aytne* GO&DO&RETURN. In Koch (2020) I have proposed that Kaytetye -*lpe* in the reduplicated -*lpe*.RDP ONCE.ALONG form was in origin probably a clitic occurring as an element of the reduplicating Attenuative formation found in other Arandic languages. Apart from -*lpe* the etymology of these elements is unknown.

Any attempt to synchronically analyse the AM markers into component morphemes encounters problems with the verbal elements, the ligatives, and the semantic compositionality of the formations. Some of the verbal elements have a different meaning in AM forms from that of the homophonous free verb; e.g. Kaytetye *ayte* in -*y.ayte* NSBJ.ARRIVE and -*rr.ayte*/-*l.ayte* in DO&GO versus *ayte*- 'rise'. And for Kaytetye especially, some of the verbal elements have no corresponding free verb. If the ligatives were treated as separate synchronic morphemes, they would have different interpretations in different constructions; e.g. Aranda -*rle* would mean 'before' in Prior Motion constructions but 'during' in Concurrent Motion constructions. Furthermore, what signals relative timing of MOTION and EVENT in AM forms that lack a ligative, e.g. EC Arrernte -*artn.alhe* QUICKLY.DO&GO (prior) vs. -*artn.akerle* QUICKLY.DO.DOWNWARDS (concurrent)? Finally, the meaning of the whole construction would not always be predictable from the meaning of the components: e.g. how can the NSBJ.ARRIVE forms consisting of 'PRIOR-rise' be treated as compositional? For an analysis of Kaytetye AM in terms of analytical components, however, see Panther & Harvey (2020).

It seems clear that those AM forms that consist etymologically of a nonfinite suffix and a motion verb result from auxiliary phrases which were already grammaticalised as markers of AM. Their monoclausal phrase structure is clear from the fact that the valency of the whole complex is determined by the main verb stem rather than by the motion auxiliary. The fact that contrasting constructions are formed with the same auxiliary but differentiated only by the nonfinite suffix should not be surprising; it is well-known, for instance, that in the Romance languages both Future and Perfect markers derive from Latin phrases combining 'have' with an infinitive or passive participle respectively. Further diachronic changes can be presumed to have followed the genesis of grammatical AM phrases. Univerbation took place; i.e. the combination of both verbs into a single prosodic word, albeit with possible retention of secondary stress on the second verbal element. And increasing opacity of some constructions resulted from the loss of the corresponding free verb as well as from semantic shifts such as affected Kaytetye -*ye.rn.alpe* DO.COMING < *COME.BACK&DO.

A trace of the earlier phrasal status of AM markers can nevertheless be seen in the fact that (some) complex AM forms can be interrupted by clitics, which are placed before the erstwhile auxiliary motion verb; for Kaytetye examples of the sequencing enclitic =*lke* THEN see (37) and (38). Insertable elements include Plural Subject markers; e.g. Anmatyerr *arlkwe-**rl<atherr>ape**-tyarte* eat-**DO<PL.SBJ>ALONG**-PST.CONT '(they) used to come along eating' (Green 2010: 259) and Mparntwe Arrernte *are-**tye<te>lhe**-me* 'see-**GO<PL.SBJ>&DO**-NPST.PROG '(plural subjects) go and see' (Wilkins 1989: 295). In EC Arrernte the PL.SBJ *-te* fuses with the ligative *-rle* to produce *-rlte.pe* as the PL.SBJ form of DO.ALONG (Wilkins 1989: 253).[62]

There appears to be some flexibility within the AM systems with respect to possible semantic values, which makes it hard to view Arandic AM as a stable and tightly constructed system. Hints of incipient new meanings and forms in Kaytetye have been mentioned in §2.3 above. Particular languages may combine two AM markers, creating possible new senses (which could be further explored); e.g. Alyawarr has examples of *-nhe-y.alhe* and *-nhe-y.alpe* (Moore 2012: *passim*); for Western Arrernte forms such as *-ty.alpe.irtne*, *-ty.alpe-nhe*, *-irtne.nhe*, *-irtn-alpe-nhe* can be found in the older materials by Kempe (1891) and C. Strehlow (1909). For EC Arrernte Henderson (2013 [1997]: 242–245) describes a reduplicated form, without an unreduplicated counterpart, that adds *-rl.alpe*, which otherwise marks DO&RETURN, to signal repeated or continuous action while going along.[63] Further flexibility within the Arandic AM system is indicated by the loss of AM subcategories (especially UPWARDS and DOWNWARDS) or shift in their sense. Thus Wilkins (2006: 51) reports that younger speakers of Mparntwe Arrernte use only eight[64] of the AM forms, having lost all the forms marking quickness and UPWARDS or DOWNWARDS motion, as well as DO.COMING.THROUGH and DO.ON.Z'S. ARRIVAL, and having shifted the meaning of *-intye* from Concurrent DO.COMING to Prior COME&DO. According to Henderson & Dobson (1994: 389) the form *-inty.alhe-* DO.COMING.THROUGH is used by some speakers as equivalent to *-intye* DO.COMING, which suggests a neutralisation without loss of the form.

The forms and subcategories of Kaytetye are the most distinctive among the Arandic languages, which reflects the fact that Kaytetye constitutes a separate branch within the Arandic subgroup (Koch 2004: 130). How many of the forms compared in Tables 4–8 can be reconstructed to a Proto-Arandic stage, ancestral to Kaytetye and all the other languages? Probably at most three forms: *-tye alpe- RETURN&DO, *-(r)le/-rre alpe- DO&RETURN, *-(r)le/-rre ape

---

62 Henderson (2013 [1997]: 222–227) treats the insertions within AM and other verb forms in EC Arrernte as a manifestation of a synchronic process of splitting a prosodic word into two separate words. Panther & Harvey (2020) for Kaytetye treats them as evidence for synchronic phrasal syntactic structure.
63 Note that *rle* here marks concurrent rather than subsequent motion and that *alpe* lacks any sense of 'return'.
64 Nine if we include DO.ALONG. See Table 3 for the conservative system.

DO.ALONG. These were probably grammaticalised motion phrases rather than single words.[65] The second and third of these presuppose that *alpe- and *ape- occurred with participial forms, one of which had allomorphs *-le and *-rle, and that Kaytetye continued a further (possibly conjugation-dependent) allomorph *-rre, and that the two branches of Arandic made different choices about which participial form was continued. For many of the other subcategories the diverging branches of Arandic may have had parallel grammatical constructions realised with different auxiliary verbs – like the Karnic subgroup situation described by Austin (1989); cf. §8 below.

4 AM in the Thura-Yura subgroup

This section summarises the complex system of two closely related varieties of the Thura-Yura subgroup (Simpson & Hercus 2004) located to the south-east of the Arandic languages. The Adnyamathanha system was described by Tunbridge (1988); the apparently similar system of Kuyani is inferred from the relatively sparse documentation by Hercus (n.d.).

4.1 Adnyamathanha

The 10 AM distinctions made by Tunbridge (1988: 273–274) are shown in Table 10.[66] The moving argument is always the subject. The system distinguishes Prior, Concurrent, and Subsequent motion. There is a sub-parameter of Speed within Prior Motion. The speed is said to apply either to the motion or to the action: 'come/go quickly and do' or 'come/go and do quickly'; see (45) (Tunbridge 1988: 270–271). Quick action presumably also includes action of short duration: in a text example from Schebeck (1974: 144) the consultant provided for *ika-nha-wara-nytyu*, a (Future) form of *ika-* 'sit', a translation "he goes, sits for a little while".[67] The most consistent Directions of motion are deictic, where *-mana* and *-vara* occur in the Prior Motion forms. The direction of *-enhi* 'ceaseless motion' is not specific and that of Subsequent Motion is "in a direction away from the event location"

---

[65] This is an example of where reconstruction from morphology yields earlier syntactic constructions; this was illustrated with examples from Arandic (including these forms) in Koch (2015: 296–297).
[66] Tunbridge also describes a further, purely directional, suffix *-na* 'hither'.
[67] Here the forms are given as *-nha* vs. Tunbridge's *-na* and *-wara* vs. Tunbridge's *-vara*.

Table 10: Adnyamathanha AM system.

	toward speaker	away from speaker	unspecified
Prior	-*mana* come &	-*vara* go &	
Prior: Speedy	-*namana* come quickly &	-*navara* go quickly &	
Subsequent			-*wandha* & leave
Concurrent: once	-*ndhena* once coming	-*ndheli* once going	
Concurrent: continuous [iterated]	-*nali* cont coming	-*nangga* go along	
Concurrent: ceaseless motion			-*enhi* keep moving

(Tunbridge 1988: 273); -*wandha* is identifiable as the transitive verb 'leave' (Tunbridge 1988: 274). A three-way aspect-like contrast within Concurrent Motion resembles that of Kaytetye (§2.2.3). The 'once' and 'continuous' values may involve a temporary pause along the motion path (46, 47), but the 'ceaseless motion' (48) may not and furthermore implies that the motion continues after the main event.

(45) Urdlu   ngarlku-***namana***-angg=adna.
     kangaroo   eat-**COME.QUICKLY&**-PRF=3PL.ERG
     'They came and ate the kangaroo then went.' or
     'They came and ate the kangaroo in a hurry.' (Tunbridge 1988: 270)

(46) Mai   ngarlku-***ndhena***-k=alpurla.
     food   eat-**ONCE.COMING**-NARR=1PL.ERG
     'We stopped and ate (once) on the way home.' (Tunbridge 1988: 271)

(47) Mapi-***nangga***-angga=ai.
     rest-**GO.ALONG**-PRF=1SG.NOM
     'I had a spell here and there as I went.' (Tunbridge 1988: 272)

(48) Ardla   irrarlda-***enhi***-k=athu
     fire   light-**KEEP.MOVING**-NARR=1 SG.ERG
     'I lit fires – I didn't stop – I kept going, lighting fires as I went.'
     (Tunbridge 1988: 272)

The AM formatives are only partially analysable and provide little clarity about their etymological origins. Speed is apparently marked by the element *na*. A separate *na*, marking motion toward the speaker (cf. Tunbridge 1988: 270), may be involved in the Concurrent 'toward speaker' forms. *-mana* and *-vara* of the Prior Motion formatives may be from verb roots: the initial *v* of *-vara* is best explained as a reflex of a word initial *p* (Tunbridge 1988: 275); the functional equivalent and possibly cognate suffix in the closely related Kuyani is *-pira-* (Hercus n.d.). The *ndhe* part of the concurrent once suffixes is plausibly related to the participial suffix *-ndha* (with *e* conditioned by the preceding laminodental consonant) and may have been followed by a verb of uncertain origin (Tunbridge 1988: 276).

4.2 Kuyani

Four of the Adnyamathanha formatives have apparent cognates in Kuyani. These are illustrated in (49–52), with glosses supplied as for Tunbridge's Adnyamathanha. Note that the three-way aspectual contrast within Concurrent Motion is attested. Not represented are any forms marking toward speaker deixis, speed terms, or subsequent motion. It is not known whether a fuller documentation of this language would have yielded a system as rich as that of Adnyamathanha. No AM forms have been noted in other languages of the Thura-Yura subgroup[68] (which are not well documented and are no longer actively spoken), except for the single marker in Wirangu, which has been explained as the result of borrowing from the Western Desert language (see §7.8).

(49) *kuty'-alypila wangka-**piRa**-nta*
 other-two talk-**GO&**-PRS
 'The other two are going away to talk.' (Hercus n.d.)

(50) *papiwirri parlu kati-**thali**-nta*
 father.and.son meat carry-**ONCE.GOING**-PRS
 'Father and son are carrying meat over there.' (Hercus n.d.)

(51) *yapaapa-**nangka**-ta*
 poke.with.stick-**GO.ALONG**-PRS
 'He went poking (with a stick under the house).' (Hercus n.d.)

---

[68] For the subgroup in general see Simpson and Hercus (2004).

(52) kakaak-**anyi**-nya
come.as.group-**KEEP.MOVING**-PRS.CONT
'They keep coming.' (Hercus n.d.)

5 Moderately complex AM systems

This section describes moderately complex AM systems, defined here as those with three to six AM values. The closely related West Karnic varieties of §5.1 are adjacent to both the Arandic and Thura-Yura languages described in previous sections. Warumungu (§5.2) and Warlmanpa (§5.3) – of the Ngumpin-Yapa subgroup – are north and northwest respectively of Arandic. Yir Yoront (§5.4) is a long way to the northeast but closer to other Paman languages that have binary AM systems.

5.1 Karnic subgroup: Arabana-Wangkangurru

Arabana-Wangkangurru appears to have at least six AM sub-categories. The AM suffixes occur before markers of Aspect, Tense and Mood. Most of the markers of AM are transparently derived from verb roots combined in a single phonological word with a verb stem and often a linking element -*rnda*/-*rda*[69]/ -*rna*, which is an apparent reflex of a Karnic non-finite suffix; here I gloss it as participle (PTCP), following the practice of Austin (1989). This PTCP link is absent from Prior Motion forms, obligatory in Subsequent Motion forms, and optional but usual in Concurrent Motion forms unless the stem is reduplicated. The one AM marker that is not related to a free verb is what Hercus labels the "transitory" (TRN) suffix and treats as a marker of Aspect: Arabana -*ka*, Wangkangurru -*yiwa* (with allomorphs). Hercus (1994: 199–200) explains its use thus: "the transitory form conveys the nuance that the action is being performed during the course of travelling, in transit … The transitory form is very common indeed in the speech of the oldest and most fluent people, in all accounts of travels and everyday mobility." The subject need not be in motion at the time of the main event, as (53) shows.

---

[69] -*rnda* is orthographic for a homorganic retroflex nasal plus stop cluster. The allomorph -*rda* occurs after a preceding nasal plus stop cluster as the result of a rule of nasal cluster dissimilation.

(53) Arni thangka-**rda-ya**-rna thiti puntha-lhuku
   we   sit-**PTCP-TRN**-IPFV   tea   drink-PURP
   'We were stopping on our way for a little while to have a drink of tea.'
   (Wangkangurru: Hercus 1994: 200)

Of the AM forms most transparently related to a free verb, those including *thika* 'return' are the most frequently used (Hercus 1994: 206). There are contrasting constructions distinguishing Prior Motion, without the linking participial form (54), and Subsequent Motion, where the participle is always present (55). The redundant or echo usage of prior motion marking (56) is noted (Hercus 1994: 207): "It is a particularly common turn of phrase to use the verb *thika-* (or its causative form *thiki-*) as an independent verb, and then explain the situation further by using *-thika* as part of a compound verb."

(54) athu   mani-**thika**-rnda
   I.ERG   get-**RETURN**-PRS
   'I go back to get something.' (Arabana: Hercus 1994: 209)

(55) athu   mani-**rnda-thika**-rnda
   I.ERG   get-**PTCP-RETURN**-PRS
   'I get something and come back.' (Arabana: Hercus 1994: 209)

(56) kari-ri   **thiki**-lhiku   ukunha
   they-ERG   **take.back**-HIST   him
   ngura-nga   kari-kunha   thadna-**thika**-lhuku
   camp-LOC   they-POSS   leave-**RETURN**-HIST
   'They took him back with them, they went back and (then) left him in their own camp.'[70] (Arabana: Hercus 1994: 206)

The same *thika-* can be used to mark Concurrent Motion. The participial connective may be omitted, which occurs most frequently after reduplicated stems, which are used "when the action is repeated over the length of the trip" (Hercus 1994: 208), as in (57): here the actor kept resting by laying down the heavy grindstone he was carrying on his head. An apparent example of concurrent return without reduplication is (58), describing the actions of the mythological Firemaker.[71]

---

[70] I suggest that, in place of Hercus' overly literal translation, a more appropriate rendering is: 'they took him back and left him in their camp (after their return)'.
[71] Here I have based my translation on two different versions, as well as the context, of the story.

(57) uka   kudni-kudni-**thika**-lhuku
     he   RDP-put.down-**RETURN**-HIST
     'he put it down again and again on his way back' (Arabana: Hercus 1994: 208)

(58) maka   mapa-**rna-thika**-rnda   nguyu-nga-ma-rna
     fire   collect-**PTCP-RETURN**-PRS   one-LOC-MAKE-IMP
     nguyu-nga-ma-rna-ki
     one-LOC-MAKE-IMP-EMPH
     'On his way home he gathered the fires, combining them (at each place).'
     (Wangkangurru: Hercus et al. 2013: 144)

Other Concurrent Motion formations involve the (non-deictic) motion verbs *yuka* 'go' (rare and only in Arabana) and *marka* 'crawl'. The first adds unspecified motion (59), while the second (60) "implies slow and steady movement" (Hercus 1994: 210). The second also illustrates: reduplication of the verb stem, Aspect-marking following the AM marker, and the non-literal meaning of *marka* when used in this construction.

(59) Kutha   madli   puntha-**rda-yuka**-rnda
     water   cool   drink-**PTCP-GO**-PRS
     'He is going along drinking a (can of) soft drink.' (Arabana: Hercus 1994: 212)

(60) Thupu   puntha-puntha-**marka**-nangka-rda
     smoke   RDP-drink-**CRAWL**-CONT-PRS
     '(He) is walking along slowly, smoking as he goes.' (Arabana: Hercus 1994: 211)

Hercus' (1994: 204–209) explicit discussion of Associated Motion is centred on the forms based on *thika* 'return'. The TRANSITORY forms are described in terms of Aspect. Other "compound verb" constructions, including -*marka* and the rare and Arabana-only -*yuka* (Wangkangurru has a similar construction with -*wapa*) are said to generally follow the pattern of -*thika* (Hercus 1994: 209–212). My analysis results in an AM system that can be summarised as in Table 11. It involves two distinctions of motion Path/Direction (return vs. unspecified), three Relative Time relations, and distinctions of duration and speed within Concurrent Motion – the transitory form here interpreted as brief action vs. the slow and the unmarked actions.[72]

---

[72] Although the marker of slowness contains the verb 'crawl', it is possible (although not demonstrable from the few examples) that within the AM system the form rather marks an aspectual value, the total overlap of EVENT and MOTION.

Table 11: Semantic distinctions in the Arabana-Wangkangurru AM system.

	Unspecified direction	Return direction
Prior		RETURN&DO
Subsequent		DO&RETURN
Concurrent (unspecified)	DO.WHILE.GOING	DO.WHILE.RETURNING
Concurrent: momentary	DO.BRIEFLY.WHILE.GOING	
Concurrent: slow	DO.WHILE.GOING.SLOWLY	

5.2 Warumungu

In Warumungu there are three AM markers, described by Simpson (1998: 720–723; 2001: 174–179; 2002: 135–137). These markers "can attach to most verbs" (Simpson 2002: 135). There are three Directional values, labelled HITHER, AWAY/THITHER, SETTING OUT/INCEPTIVE.[73] The first two involve direction toward or away from the deictic centre, and the third away from the action. The markers of the first two values consist of complex verb suffixes which express TAM values as well as Direction and vary formally according to the conjugation of the preceding verb stem. Table 12, quoted from Simpson (2001: 176, 178), shows the Neutral and AM inflectional forms of *pari-* 'get', a member of the Y conjugation (omitting the modal forms Imperative, Admonitive and Irrealis). Dots are used (by Simpson) to separate elements that are partially recognisable etymologically. The element -*nji* is elsewhere a nominalising suffix; an element *rr* of unknown provenance is omitted by some speakers, and the rest of the form is not fully analysable. The SETTING OUT/INCEPTIVE forms are more transparent, since they consist of the nominaliser (plus *rr*) followed by TAM-inflected forms of *parti-*, whose free form means 'get up, arise, set off'.[74] These forms suggest an origin of the suffixes as having been grammaticalised from constructions consisting of a participle followed by a finite verb (Simpson 2001: 177).

---

[73] Where two different glosses are given, the first is from Simpson (1998) and the second from Simpson (2001).
[74] This is cognate with the Kaytetye verb *ayte-* 'rise, grow' and the element *-ayte*, which occurs in the subsequent motion markers *-rr.ayte* and *-l.ayte* 'DO&GO'.

Table 12: Partial paradigm of Warumungu *pari-* 'get'.

TAM	NEUTRAL	HITHER	THITHER	INCEPTIVE
Future	*pari*	*pari-nji.rra*	*pari-nji.(rr).karl*	*pari-nji.(rr).parti*
Past Punctual	*parinyi*	*pari-nji.(rr)ka.rni*	*pari-nji.rr.a.rni*	*pari-nji.(rr).parti-nyi*
Past Cont	*parinjina*	*pari-nji.rr.ajina*	[unattested]	*pari-nji.(rr).parti-na*
Present	*paranjan*	*pari-nji.rr.apan*	*pari-nji.rr.arnta*	*pari-nji.(rr).parta-n*

The SETTING OUT/INCEPTIVE forms express prior motion. Although no sentence example is given in the sources, *para-nji.(rr).parti* is glossed 'will go off and get' (Simpson 2001: 178). The other AM forms are said to express Prior, Concurrent or Subsequent Motion.[75] No example is given in the sources quoted of Subsequent Motion. (61) illustrates Concurrent Motion. (62) is an example of Prior Motion. This sentence also illustrates the typical redundant or echo use of AM, the literal meaning being 'I'll go, I'll see him (after going)'.

(61) *Wangarri   =ajju   wanppi-**rrajina***
    money(ABS) 1SG.NONSUBJECT fall-**PST.CONT.AWAY**
    'The money fell out of my pockets as I was walking along.'
    (Simpson 1998: 721)[76]

(62) *Api-**rr.karl**   arni,   nya-**nji.rr.karl**   arni*
    go-**AWAY.FUT** I   see-**AWAY.FUT** I
    'I'll go and see him.' (Simpson 2002: 136)

(62) also illustrates another usage of the deictic AM forms: they can be used on verbs of inherent motion, in which case they mark direction only. They turn the non-deictic *api-* 'move' into 'go' vs. 'come' and *juku-* 'carry' into 'take' vs. 'bring'. The deictic forms are found as well on 'run', 'enter', 'set off', and may occur to specify orientation without motion: there is an example of a road lying away toward the north (Simpson 1998: 721).

---

75 "The time of this movement or direction relative to that of the main event may ... be concurrent with, or overlapping, the main event ('do on the way, do while going along'), or may precede it ('do after movement, go and do'), or follow it ('do before going, do and go')." (Simpson 2001: 174)
76 In spite of the translation, I assume that the meaning is that the money fell out (from me) on the way, while it was moving (i.e. being carried) along.

5.3 Warlmanpa (Ngumpin-Yapa)

Warlmanpa[77] is the western neighbour or Warumungu but belongs with Warlpiri (§6.4.1) to the Yapa branch of the Ngumpin-Yapa subgroup. There are three suffixes that mark Concurrent AM; these occur between the verb root plus an "infinitive augment" and a following TAM inflection: *-nja* MOT 'go around VERBing', *-nji* MOT.TWD 'come VERBing', and *-nya* MOT.AWAY 'go away VERBing'. The first of these marks motion that is not specified as either toward or away from the speaker and is translated as 'around'. The other two mark deictic directions. All three AM markers can occur on motion verbs, where they specify direction only. The language also has a contrasting set of deictic direction markers, *-rni/-rti* Centripetal/TWD and *-rra/-pa* Centrifugal/AWAY – which occur after the TAM inflections.[78] These do not have AM uses, but TWD can be used in a verb marked with the MOT AM suffix, as in *ka-**nja**-nu-**rnu***[79] take-**MOT**-PST-**TWD** 'used to bring'. Etymologically, two of the AM suffixes appear to have been built on the nominalising (infinitive) suffix – *nja* – as have AM forms in Warumungu (§5.2) and the Inceptive in Warlpiri (§6.4.1)[80] – followed by the inflected verb **ya-* 'go'.

5.4 Yir Yoront (SW Paman)

Yir Yoront is a language of north Queensland, an immediate neighbour of Kuuk Thaayorre (discussed in §6.1.3); both have been classified in the Southwest Paman subgroup (Black 2004: 252). Verbs can be productively compounded. Alpher (1991: 51–52; more detail in Alpher 1973: 383–390) describes four productive verbal compounds, where the second member is a truncated form of a verb of motion and is preceded by a connective suffix whose form is determined by the conjugation of the preceding verb stem. Both verb stems receive equal stress (Alpher 1991: 8); the second member receives the TAM inflections of the corresponding free verb (determined by its conjugation class), but the transitivity of the whole is determined by the first element. Within the verb structure the Motion markers occur after the markers of Voice and before the markers of Continuative Aspect and the final Tense-Mood inflection (Alpher 1991: 41). Table 13 shows the four compounding forms with their conjugation class, their meaning in compounds, and the free verbs from which they are derived. The fourth form does not correspond to any

---

77 Warlmanpa data is from Mitch Browne (pers. comm. 19.11.2019 and 21.11.2019).
78 The second allomorph of each set, i.e. *-rti* and *-pa*, are used after Imperative.
79 The vowel of *-rnu* (instead of *-rni*) is conditioned by harmony with the preceding vowel.
80 Warlmanpa has an Inceptive 'start VERBing', which is homophonous with *-nji* MOT.TWD.

Table 13: Yir Yoront AM verbal formatives.

Compounding form	Grammatical meaning	Free verb
-wa- L	'go and' (unspecified direction)'	wa- 'go' (unspecified direction)
-aw- RR	'go and'	yaw- 'go' (directed)
-al- L2	'return and'	ṯal- 'return'
-an- NH	'come and'	(none synchronically)

synchronic free verb in Yir Yoront but a cognate verb *yan* 'go' occurs in the closely related Kuuk-Thaayorre language.

These forms suggest an AM system consisting of four markers of Prior Motion in four distinct directions. The two 'go and' forms partially overlap in their uses, as do the corresponding free verbs, although the verb "YAW carries a necessary implication of 'with definite direction', which WA+ lacks" (Alpher 1991: 573). Examples of each are given in (63–66). Note the echo effect of the RETURN& form in (65), as well as the use of a 'hither' directional to provide deixis. The +*wa* form has a further (non-motional) aspectual usage as an inceptive 'begin to'.

(63) Ngoyo   pan   wun-**n**+**wa**-*l*
     I   sleep   lie-**GO&**-NPST
     'I'll go lie down and sleep.' (Alpher 1991: 574)

(64) kawn-thilhl   i   nga   karr-*l*+**aw**
     water-running.down.bank   that   ?   see-**GO&**.IMP
     'Go and look at that water running over the bank.' (Alpher 1991: 132)

(65) Ngul   olowr,   pal   **thal**-*l*   ngeyn
     then   last-mentioned   hither   **return**-PST   1PL.EXCL
     nhoq   nhin-**n.al**-   ngeyn
     here   stay-**RETURN&**-PST   1PL.EXCL
     'Then at that time we came back this way; we came back here and stayed at this place.' (Alpher 1991: 127)

(66) Kana   nin-**n**+**an**-*l*   pul
     just   sit-**COME&**-PST   3DU
     'They came and sat down.' (Alpher 1991: 129)

The source of these constructions seems to be the univerbation of a motion verb with a non-finite form of the other verb: the connective suffix that precedes the (truncated) motion root has the same (conjugation-determined) consonant (C) as the future-oriented Purposive and Desiderative suffixes -*Ce* and -*Cə* respectively. This suggests an origin as a Motion with Purpose construction.

6 Binary AM systems

This section describes AM systems that make a two-way distinction. All the languages in §6.1 belong to the Paman subgroup of northeast Queensland: the first two are adjacent to each other, while the third is a direct neighbour of Yir Yoront (§5.4). The two languages of §6.2 belong to the Ngarna or Warluwarric subgroup (Breen 2004a).[81] §6.3 discusses five languages of the large Karnic subgroup: Wangka-Yutyuru, which belongs to the northern branch, along with Pitta-Pitta (Blake 1979b: 184; see §7.3); Wangkumara, an East Karnic language; and three varieties from the Central Karnic banch: Yandruwandha, Ngamini, and its co-dialect Diyari. §6.4 gives data from the Warlpiri and Mudburra, members respectively of the Yapa and Ngumpin branches of Ngumpin-Yapa.

6.1 Paman subgroup

6.1.1 Jabugay

The fullest description of a two-way AM contrast is given for Jabugay and Yidiny. The relevant motions are the deictic 'go' and 'come'. In fact the verbs *kali-* 'to go' and *karra-* 'to come' are transparently included within the complex verb word. Both Hale (1976b: 239) and Patz (1991: 285) describe the forms as consisting of the productive "compounding" of a verb stem with the motion verb into a single word. The resulting verb forms signal that the motion involves the subject of the main verb and that this motion is prior to the main event. Although both authors normally gloss the construction as 'go/come to VERB', as in (67) and (68),[82] which suggests a Motion with Purpose meaning, it is clear from an example given in Hale (1976a: 326), presented in modernised orthography in (69) – as well as from

---

[81] A third Ngarna language, Wakaya has a single AM marker (see §7.1). Another Ngarna language, Yanyuwa, spoken further to the north, separated by intervening non-Ngarna languages, does not appear to have any AM markers.
[82] Here I have supplied the morpheme-by-morpheme glosses, including LIGative, which both authors leave unglossed.

text examples in Patz (1991) – that the verbal activity is not merely intended but actually accomplished. (69) further illustrates the characteristic "echo" phenomenon found in AM systems; i.e. the sense here is not 'he came and came to see me' but 'he came and saw me (after coming)', with the AM marker in the second verb merely providing the fact of motion as background information.

(67) ŋawuŋku ma: puka-**y-karra**-n^y
 1SG.ERG food eat-**LIG-come**-PST
 'I came to eat food.' (Hale 1976b: 239)

(68) ŋawuŋku min^ya paka-**la-kali**-na
 1SG.ERG meat spear-**LIG-go**-FUT
 'I will go to spear meat.' (Hale 1976b: 239)

(69) kutyi **karra**-ny nganya nguntala-**karra**-ny
 that **come**-PST me see-**come**-PST
 wangal-nta kipa-yi-ya
 boomerang-LOC scrape-ANTIP-REL
 'He came along and saw me while I was scraping the boomerang.'
 (Hale 1976a: 326)

In terms of grammatical category, Hale (1976b: 239) makes no comment apart from describing the complex forms as the result of "productive compounding of verb stems with the motion verbs *kali-* 'to go' and *kara-* 'to come'". Patz (1991: 285) describes the resulting function as marking "the aspects 'to go to (verb)' and 'to come to (verb)'". In terms of form, Hale (1976b: 239) describes the element -y- ~ -la- that intervenes between the verb stem and the motion root as an "incremental suffix".[83] Patz (1991: 285) makes it clear that the choice between these elements depends on whether the verb stem belongs to the *y* or the *l* conjugation, where these consonants appear as segments before various TAM or subordinating suffixes.

6.1.2 Yidiny

The corresponding formations in Yidiny are described by Dixon (1977: 219–227) as GOING and COMING "aspects". These markers of "aspect" are included among the "derivational" affixes that occur between a verb root and the final inflection

---

83 Note that in (69) Hale has not separated the *la* of *nguntala* as a separate morpheme.

which marks Tense, Mood and Subordination. Derivational aspects are divided into those which affect valency – the COMITATIVE (with applicative and causative uses) and an ANTIPASSIVE (which also marks Reflexive) – and these markers of deictic motion, which "do not alter the transitivity of the verb" (Dixon 1977: 219). In Dixon (2002: 201) they are described as "derivational suffixes marking what is called 'associated motion'". The GOING and COMING suffixes occupy a verbal slot between the valence-changing suffixes (either or both of which may occur, ordered by their semantic scope) and the final Tense/Mood/Subordination suffixes.[84]

The temporal relation between the motion (of the subject) and the main event differs from that of Jabugay; in Yidiny the motion may be either prior to or concurrent with that of the main event, e.g. 'go and look' or 'look while going'. Dixon (1977: 221) also mentions that speakers favour the redundant use of an AM marker after an explicit verb of motion – a phenomenon he calls "aspect agreement" – as in (70) and (71). This is the "echo" phenomenon noted in other studies of AM. The use of the Yidiny AM forms is amply exemplified in the large collection of stories in Dixon (1991).[85]

(70) ngayu **gali**-ng minyaa-gu, minya duga-**ali**-na
 I **go**-PRS fish-PURP fish catch-**GOING**-PURP
 'I'm going for fish, going to catch fish.' (Dixon 1977: 221)

(71) minjam nganjdji **gada**-ng njina-**ngada**-ng
 animal-ABL we-S/A **come**-PRS sit-**COMING**-PRS
 'We come home after [hunting] animals, come to stay at home.'
 (Dixon 1977: 232–233)

The AM forms vary according to which of the three verb conjugations the preceding verb stem belongs to (see Table 14).[86] These suffixes are apparently derived etymologically from combinations of a suffixed form of the verb[87] and motion verbs

---

[84] Dixon (1977: 225) posits a possible ordering of a general aspect-marking suffix -Vrri- before the comitative -nga, but this is more plausibly analysed as a unitary comitative suffix -Vrringa.
[85] Here, and as is the case in (70) and (71), Dixon's translations are often overly literal, reflecting directly the redundant use of AM forms.
[86] V in Table indicates the lengthening of the preceding vowel.
[87] It is not clear what was the source form – I could suggest a Purposive ('go/come to Verb') or possibly a serial construction (these do occur in Yidiny) – nor exactly how the phonological reductions took place (cf. discussion in Dixon 1977: 223–224).

Table 14: Yidiny AM suffixes.

	COMING	GOING
N-conjugation	-ng(g)ada-	-ng(g)ali-
L-conjugation	-Vlda-	-Vli-
R-conjugation	-Vda-	-Vri-
free verb	gada-	gali-

gali- 'go' and *gada-* 'come', which are cognate with Jabugay *kali-* and *karra-* respectively, but with considerably more phonological reduction than the corresponding Jabugay forms (Dixon 1977:223–224). Support for this diachronic source comes from: the fact that the resultant form inflects according to the N-conjugation as do the free motion verbs, the occasionally heard fuller forms in the N-conjugation which include the initial *g* of the free motion verbs, and the fact that the Tablelands dialect includes further forms that add *-nggada* or *-nggali* to the normal AM suffixes; here the complex suffix probably reflects a reduplicated motion verb (e.g. *-galing-gali) which preserves its initial consonant. The meaning of these extra AM forms is uncertain but possibly 'going/coming right up and doing' or 'going/coming right away and doing' (Dixon 1977: 227). A text example of a reduplicated 'going' form is (72).

(72) ngadjin wagal wawa-**alinggaali**-ng
 my wife see- **GOING.RDP**-PRS
 'I'll go right up and have a look at my wife.' (Dixon 1977:536)

It should be noted that the AM suffixes may be added to verbs which inherently denote motion, such as 'run', in which case they contribute an extra sense of direction only; e.g. *dyungga-ngali-ng* 'is running away' vs. *dyungga-ngada-ng* 'is running here'.

6.1.3 Kuuk Thaayorre

Kuuk Thaayorre has two formatives that have been described as markers of Associated Motion (Gaby 2017: 300–305). These are verb suffixes *-nha-*, glossed GO&, and *-(nh)ic*, glossed 'RUN&'. The forms consist of the Subjunctive suffix *-nh* followed by truncated versions of the verbs *ya-* 'go' and *riic* 'run' respectively. The derived AM verbs share the same TAM inflections as the independent motion verbs, including the portmanteau expression of TAM with 'go' (see Table 15, from Gaby 2017: 301).

Table 15: GO& formative vs. TAM inflections of *ya-* 'go'.

	'GO&'	*ya-* 'go'
Nonpast	-nhan	yan
Past perfective	-nhat	yat
Imperative	-nharr	yarr
Subjunctive	-nhancnh	yancnh

The forms mark Prior Motion of the subject. The motion does not indicate a deictic direction. In spite of the obvious derivation of RUN& from 'run', a contrast in speed is not obvious (Gaby 2017: 305). The redundant or echo usage of the AM forms is attested, as seen in (73) and (74).

(73) a. *ii-rr-kuw* **therk**-*r* *yuuwir-n*
there-to-west **return**-P.PFV ocean-DAT

b. *wuurr nhangn-man nhaat-**nhat***
fishtrap 3SGGEN.DAT look-**GO&.PST.PFV**
'he went back west to the ocean
and looked at his fishtrap.' (Gaby 2017: 492)

(74) a. *minh kanharr **riica**-rr ii-rr-kuw*
meat fresh.croc(NOM) **run**-PST.PFV there-to-west

b. *mun-**ica**-rr ii-rr-kaw*
summon-**RUN&**-PST.PFV there-to-east
'The freshwater crocodile sped to the west to summon [the saltwater croc] to the east.' (Gaby 2017: 492)

The source construction of the AM forms is obvious, especially since a GO& expression such as *kath-nha-n* 'trim-GO&-NONPST' may also be expressed by means of two separate words *kath-nh ya-n* for the sense 'go and make (a spear)'. The Subjunctive category expressed by *nh* is used to encode a range of future-oriented senses, including desire, purpose, intention, and potential (Gaby 2017: 284). So it seems clear that here the AM forms developed from "a subjunctive verb (encoding an intended event) combined with a motion verb" (Gaby 2017: 301). Although the AM form probably originated as a Motion with Purpose construction, the contemporary form indicates that the non-motion event is realised, as indicted by the consultant's translation of (75), where *bin* is the Aboriginal English Past Tense marker.

(75) ngul   raak   yiirr   waath-**nhat**
     then   place   other(ACC)   search-**GO&.PST.PFV**
     "they walk all the way, till they bin find another place" (Gaby 2017: 303)

Another (non-motional) function of the GO& construction is the aspectual-inceptive usage, indicating the beginning of a process, sometimes expressing surprise or the suddenness of the event (Gaby 2017: 303–305).

6.2 Ngarna subgroup

6.2.1 Warluwarra

Warluwarra has a "motive marker",[88] with various conjugation-dependent allomorphs, including -*tha*, -*tya*, and -*rra*. Its function is to indicate that an action is "performed by an agent who is walking, or moving along, or who is travelling but not necessarily in motion at time of the action, or who was travelling immediately before the action or will be travelling immediately afterwards" (Breen 1971: 116). The relative time of the motion with respect to the main action may thus be concurrent (76), prior (77) or subsequent (78). The most typical usage, however, is concurrent. The motive marker does not indicate any specific direction, but 'hither' deixis can be specified by the addition of the directional enclitic =*mi* (see (76)).[89]

(76) Yarra-ka   ngarna   nguna-**tha**-rna=mi
     creek-LOC   I:NOM   sleep-**MOT**-PST=HITH
     'I camped at the creek yesterday (while on my way here).' (Breen 1971: 118)

(77) yanu   nguna-rna   ngarna   karri-**tya**-rna   nhunda
     they:NOM   sleep-PST   I:NOM   stand-**MOT**-PST   then
     'When they went to sleep,[90] I went away.' (i.e. 'I went and stood somewhere else.') (Breen 1971: 119)

---

[88] In later work this was glossed 'along' or 'while going' (Breen 1976b: 334).
[89] An alternative means of expressing concurrent motion is by a relatively transparent combination of the tense-inflected verb *nhanda-* 'go' with a (first conjugation) verb stem followed by -*rri*, which seems to be nominalising suffix; e.g. *paka-rri-nhanda-rna* 'hopped along' vs. *paka-rna* 'hopped' (Breen 1971: 117).
[90] *Nguna-* means just 'sleep': as in the previous example, no motion is involved.

(78) *Wata ngarna   yina   nguta-**rra**-thiyi*
     money I:ERG   you:ACC give-**MOT**-PURP
     'I'll give you money before I go.' (Breen 1971: 119)

Another marker which appears to mark only Prior AM, without specification of direction, and typically after a previous mention of motion, is the so-called "conjunctive affix", described by Breen (1971: 121). This marker has allomorphs *-thiwarra, -tyiwarra,* and *-iwarra,* depending on the conjugation of the preceding verb stem, with the syllable *rra* dropped before the past inflection *-rna*.[91] (79) shows that the subject's case marking is determined by the transitive stem 'see', and shows directional marking, signalled by the enclitic *=mi*, co-occurring with an AM marker. (80) illustrates the redundant use of an AM form after an explicit verb of motion; literally 'went and killed (after going)'. (81), in contrast to (79) and (80), is an example of a Motion with Purpose construction, indicated by the PURP marking on the final verb – even though it, like (80), redundantly marks motion: literally 'I have come in order to see you (after coming)'.[92] In (82) we see the ordering of markers within the verb: AM-Aspect-Tense.

(79) *yiwa thawa-ku yina   yanga-**thiwarra**-a=mi*
     that man-ERG   you(ACC) see-**CONJ**-POT=HITH
     'That man might be coming to see you.' (Breen 1971: 123)

(80) *ngarna **nhanda**-rna math-**iwa**-rna ngarna yinya   thuwana*
     I   **go**-PST   kill-**CONJ**-PST I   it(ACC) snake
     'I went and killed the snake.' (Breen 1971: 122)

(81) *ngarna **nhanda**-rna=mi   yinda   yanga-**thiwarri**-yi*
     I   **go**-PST=HITH   you(PURP) see-**CONJ**-PURP
     'I have come to see you.' (Breen 1971: 124)

(82) *karla yanu nguna-**thiwarra**-ka-tya*
     meat   they sleep-**CONJ**-HAB-PRS
     'The cattle always go and sleep [there].' (Breen 1971: 125)

---

91 Breen describes the marker as consisting of *-wa(rra)* added to the (nominalising) "gerund" suffix, which has the form *-thi/-tyi/-i*, but his sentence glosses label it as a unitary morpheme CONJ.
92 It was possibly the use of CONJ in discourse cohesion seen in examples like (81) which led Breen to label the affix "conjunctive".

I analyse Warluwarra as manifesting a two-way contrast of AM values, distinguished by the relative timing of the motion and the main event – Prior CONJ vs. Concurrent MOT, with the latter potentially extended to immediately prior or subsequent – and with the specific direction of motion indicated (if at all) not by the AM formative but by a directional enclitic. Both AM formatives appear to include a nominalising suffix of the verb, but the remainder is unclear. The nominalising suffix is thought to ultimately reflect an earlier form *-ntha, which is cognate with the -nji element occurring in the Warumungu AM formatives.

6.2.2 Bularnu

For Bularnu Breen (1980: 64–65) says: "The verb *baga* 'to go' is used ... in a ... type of compounding in which it is added to a verb in the present or imperfect tense to convey the meaning 'do while going along' or 'go and do' ... the form based on the present tense means 'do while going' and the form based of the imperfect means 'to go and do'". I interpret this as an AM system of two values indicating Prior (83) vs. Concurrent (84) motion in an unspecified direction: direction toward the speaker may however be specified by a 'hither' enclitic. I suspect that the formatives preceding *-baga* are (at least etymologically) different non-finite verbal suffixes. The presumed origin would then have been a construction consisting of a non-finite verb followed by a motion verb, as in the corresponding AM forms of the Arandic languages.

(83) warama-**ḍi-baga**-ṇa   ŋaṇa
      look.for-**IMPERF-GO**-PST   I
      "I went and had a look there." (Breen 1980: 64)

(84) ŋulaḍa yaŋa-**ḍara-baga**-ra=ḍi
      back   look-**PRS-GO**-PRS=HITHER
      'He's going along looking back all the time.' (Breen 1980: 64)

6.3 Karnic subgroup

6.3.1 Wangka-Yutyuru

For Wangka-Yutyuru Blake and Breen (1971: 178–179) describe two verbal suffixes, *-rna* (with allomorphs *-rnu* and *-rni*) and *-rta* (with allomorph *-rtanyi*), both of which precede the tense inflection or non-finite *-lhi*. They "refer to an action which is taking place at the same time as another action ... normally ... that of walking ... *rta* is used when the action occupies only a short time ... *-rna* is used when the action and the walking continue together for an appreciable time". The contrast is illustrated by (85) vs. (86). The direction of motion is unspecific, but deictic directional suffixes (or enclitics) may be added to the verb to indicate direction toward or away from the speaker. I analyse Wangka-Yutyuru as have an AM system marking Concurrent Association Motion, of unspecific direction, with an aspectual distinction analysable as Punctual vs. Continuous. This is reflected in the glosses I have supplied (the authors do not provide a gloss). A complication is that the Punctual form is said to allow a sense of immediately following (i.e. subsequent) motion, with a possible translation of (86) being 'I looked at him and walked away'. (87) is an example of this subsequent motion usage.

(85) ngathu   nhanaparra   thalha-**rna**-nya
     I:ERG   him   see-**ALONG.CONT**-PST
     'I was watching him as I went along.' (Blake & Breen 1971: 179)

(86) ngathu   nhanaparra   thalha-**rta**-nya
     I:ERG   him   see-**ALONG.PUNC**-PST
     'I looked at him as I walked past.' (Blake & Breen 1971: 179)

(87) nganhu   thalha-**rtanyi**-lhinga
     I:FUT   see-**ALONG.PUNC**-PURP[93]
     'I'm going to have a look and go away.' (Blake & Breen 1971: 179)

6.3.2 Wangkumara

In Wangkumara a suffix *-ka* signals Prior Motion, "that an action is preceded by a period of movement which is necessary to take the agent to the place where the action must be carried out" (Breen 1981b: 35); see (88). Another formative *-manja* is used for Concurrent Motion, "to denote that the action is being carried out while the agent is going along" (Breen 1981b: 35), as in (89). The same formative can be used with verbs of motion to emphasise the idea of progression. While *-manja* is identical to the free verb meaning 'crawl', *-ka* is not related to any known verb in the language (Austin 1989: 52).

---

93 Here I have changed the authors' gloss of *-lhinga* from "ing-for", i.e. nominalisation plus dative, to Purposive, since that is the function of the form as a whole (Blake & Breen 1971: 143).

(88) *Mandha-**ka**-nga*   *ngathu* *wii-nhanha*
carry-**PRIOR**-IMM.PST I.ERG firewood-ACC
'I went and got some firewood.'
(Wangkumara: Austin 1989: 54, from Breen 1981b ex. 151)

(89) *Yantha-garla* *nhia-guru* *thaltha-**manja**-garla*
go-PRS   he-there   eat-**ALONG**-PRS
'He is walking along eating.'
(Wangkumara: Austin 1989: 52, from Breen 1981b ex. 149)

6.3.3 Yandruwandha

Yandruwandha makes a two-way aspectual contrast within Concurrent Motion. "The formative *-rduda* denotes a continued or frequently repeated action carried out while the actor is travelling" (Breen 2004b: 150), as in (90). Two other synonymous morphemes, *-thawa* and *-mini*, both "denote that an action is performed in an interval between stages in a journey" (Breen 2004b: 150), as in (91) and (92). Breen (1976c: 752) describes the function as denoting "momentary action carried out while the agent is in motion". *-thawa-* and *-mini* are identical to the verbs 'go' and 'run' respectively, but *-rduda* does not correspond to a lexical verb in the contemporary language.

(90) *Maka* *nhu-tjadu* *mangga-**rduda**-rla*
fire   3SG-THERE burn-**ALONG**-PRS
'The bushfire's burning along.' (Breen 2004b: 150)

(91) *Karirr-yi* *nganyi* *thuda-**thawa**-na*
creek-LOC 1SG-NOM lie-**GO**-IMM.PST
'I camped at the creek while I was on the way here.' (Breen 2004b: 151)

(92) *Kurra-paṉḍi* *ṉiŋguru* *ṯanuṯanu*
put-down   there   in.the.middle
*mandri-**tawa**-la* *ŋaṯu* *yita*
get-**GO**-PRS   1SG.ERG there
'Put it down in the middle. I'll pick it up as I'm going home.'
(Breen 1976c: 752)[94]

---

[94] Breen (1976c) uses a different orthography from Breen (2004b).

6.3.4 Ngamini

In Ngamini the markers of AM occur in tightly bound phrases following a main verb in a non-finite, participial form. The (grammaticalised) markers of AM are recognisable verbs *parka-* 'run' and *marka-* 'crawl', but in this construction they are used "for momentary action whilst moving" and "for continuing action whilst moving" respectively (Austin 1989: 55); see (93) and (94). This is an aspectual distinction within Concurrent Motion.

(93) ṉula-ya   ŋaṉa   ṉirrka-**ṉa**   **parka**-yi
     he(ERG)-HERE   me   look-**PTCP**   **PASSING**-PRS
     'He looked at me as he went past.' (Ngamini: Breen 1976a: 748)

(94) ṯana-ya   yara   wapa-yi   kiḍari-**ṉa**   **marka**-ṉa
     they(PL)-HERE hither   go-PRS   call.out-**PTCP** **ALONG**-REL$_{ss}$
     'They are coming here, singing out as they come.' (Ngamini: Breen 1976a: 748)[95]

6.3.5 Diyari

In Diyari the cognate of Ngamini *parka-* is *paḷka-* and means 'travel'; in the verb phrase construction it indicates "action performed whilst in motion, typically whilst on a journey" (Austin 1981: 99); see (95). There is also a "prolative" verb suffix *-iŋa*, not related to any recognisable verb, which functions "to indicate that the subject of the verb ... is in motion"; no particular direction of motion is specified; see (96–98). Both of these markers seem to indicate Concurrent Motion, but it is not clear what the difference is: perhaps the former involves a longer time span of the associated motion. I tentatively classify the distinction as an aspect-like one of Continuous vs. Unmarked: the continuous marker can apparently not be characterised as indicating momentary action.

(95) ḍiṯi   palpa   ṯuraṟa-**ṉa**   **paḷka**-yi
     day   some   sleep-**PTCP** **GO.ON**-PRS
     'They slept on their journey for some days.' (Austin 1981: 244)

---

95 I have altered the glosses in accordance with the interpretation in Austin (1989).

(96) kapidi   ṉuṟa   ṯarka-**iṉa**-yi
     goanna   tail(ABS) stand-**PROL**-PRS
     'Goannas' tails stand up as they move.' (Austin 1981:207)[96]

(97) ṯukudu   wakaṟa-yi kupadu   piḷi-ṉi   ŋama-**iṉa**-ṉaṉi
     kangaroo(ABS) come-PRS   young(ABS) pouch-LOC sit-**PROL**-RELDS
     'A kangaroo is coming with a joey sitting in its pouch (as it goes along).' (Austin 1981:79)

(98) ŋadimaṯa-li   ṉiṉa   kupa   mani-**iṉa**-ṉḍa   pudi-yi
     flood-ERG   3SG.NFOBJ   child(ABS) get-**PROL**-PTCP   AUX-PRS
     'The flood took the child as it went past.' (Austin 1981:79)

6.4 Ngumpin-Yapa subgroup

6.4.1 Warlpiri

Warlpiri has two AM forms that are marked by verb morphology. One, labelled Inceptive, illustrated in (99), "expresses the idea that the event denoted by the verb is initiated, probably by some movement" (Simpson 2001: 184). The formal expression consists of a suffix *-nji/-rninji/-ninji*, with allomorphs determined by the conjugation class of the verb. This is identical to the nominalised form of the verb, *-nja/-rninja/-ninja*, except with a final vowel *i* in place of *a*. This vowels of the suffix are subject to regressive vowel assimilation to *u* in the following suffix. The formation is considered to result from the grammaticalisation of the nominalised verb compounded with the verb *ya-* 'go', with phonological reduction of the *aya* sequence to *i* (Simpson 2001: 184). The meaning of (99) suggests prior motion in an unspecified direction (*ya-* 'go' does not have a deictic sense).[97] The other formation consists transparently of the *-nja* (and allomorphs) nominaliser, which Simpson calls a participle, plus *-yalpi*, which does not exist as a free verb, but is considered to have been borrowed from Arandic languages (Simpson 2001: 182).[98] The meaning is 'return and do' (100), but the free Warlpiri verb 'return' is *kulpa-* (Nash

---

[96] This example is from the Dhirari dialect of Diyari.
[97] Another example given by Simpson is more ambiguous, and may imply concurrent motion.
[98] More specifically, the source must have been Kaytetye, where RETURN&DO is *-y.alpe*, rather than one of the other Arandic languages in contact with Warlpiri, i.e. Anmatyerr or Western Arrernte, where the form is rather *-ty.alpe*. Note that *-yalpi* is added to Warlpiri *-nja*, although the *y* of *-yalpi* is probably, like Warlpiri, a reflex of the same Pama-Nyungan nominalisation suffix *-ntha.

1982: 192). I treat Warlpiri as having two morphological AM markers, both signalling Prior Motion, with the directions 'return' and 'unspecified motion'. (See further §8 below for Warlpiri AM meanings expressed by more transparent formations.)

(99)   *Kuyu=lpa*   *luwa-**rnunju**-nu*   *ka-ngu=rnu=lpa*
       game=IPFV   shoot-**INCEP**-PST   carry-PST=HITH=IPFV
       'He went and killed some animal and brought it back.' (Simpson 2001: 184)

(100)   *Nguna-**nja-yalpi**-ja=lu*
        lie-**PPL-?return**-PST=3PL.SBJ
        'They went back and lay down.' (Simpson 2001: 182)

6.4.2 Mudburra

Osgarby (this volume) describes the AM system of Mudburra in terms of markers 'toward' and 'away from' the deictic centre. The relative time of the motion may be Prior or Concurrent, depending largely on whether the verb as a whole is Perfective or Imperfective respectively. Unlike most other Pama-Nyungan languages, the markers occur verb-finally, after or fused with Tense-Mood markers. This probably reflects the origin of at least some allomorphs of the AM markers as directionals (as in Yalarnnga, cf. §7.2) – =*rni* 'hither' and -*rra* 'thither' having these functions in other Ngumpin-Yapa languages. Mudburra has been influenced by neighbouring languages of the (non-Pama-Nyungan) Mirndi family, where Ventive and Itive directions are expressed by markers which, unlike Mudburra, reflect former verbs.[99]

7 Unitary AM systems

This section presents data from a large number of languages, belonging to nine subgroups and distributed over widely scattered parts of the continent. A few of these languages belong to subgroups already mentioned: Wakaya (§7.1) to Ngarna, Pitta-Pitta (§7.3) to (North) Karnic, and Wirangu (§7.8) to Thura-Yura. The other languages belong to subgroups not previously discussed with respect to AM (but see Table 1 above): Kalkatungic (§7.2), Maric (§7.4), Central New South Wales (§7.5), Yuin (§7.6), Wati or Western Desert (§7.7), and Marrngu (§7.9).

---

99 For the D-AM system of Wambaya, see Nordlinger (2001).

7.1 Ngarna subgroup: Wakaya

Wakaya has a form labelled "Andative Present", marked by a suffix with variants *-arr*, *-al*, *-tarr*, *-thal*, *-nthal*, *-tyal* (consisting of the gerund suffix plus *rr* or *l* of uncertain origin), which "denotes action being carried out in the present time (?) while the agent is in motion or travelling, and seems to be best translated 'along'" (Breen 1974: 113). Elicited examples of AM usage with transitive and intransitive non-motion verbs are (101) and (102) respectively. (Breen had trouble getting spontaneous examples.) Note that the suffix does not specify the direction of motion, but that deictic direction toward and away from the speaker may be indicated by adverbs and/or enclitics.

(101) *theperr mernt-**arre**=kanye=pulu*
grass eat-**ALONG.PRS**=AWAY=this
'It (kangaroo) is eating grass as he goes along.' (Breen 1974: 137)

(102) *pakepaki-k yuwerr-**arre**=kanye=pulu*
buggy-LOC sit-**AND.PRS**=AWAY=that
'He's going along in a buggy.' (Breen 1974: 113)

This suffix occurs most readily with verbs of motion. Example (103) illustrates the use of ALONG with both the transitive non-motion verb 'eat' and the intransitive manner-of-motion verb 'crawl', with 'hither' direction marked by means of a directional adverb and enclitic.

(103) *kuritye=kertiy=pulu mernt-**arre** irrke-**tyal***
to.here=TO.HERE=that eat-**ALONG.PRS** crawl-**ALONG.PRS**
'It (kangaroo) is coming this way and having a feed as he comes along.' (Breen 1974: 136)

7.2 Kalkatungic subgroup: Yalarnnga

Yalarnnga is a language of western Queensland that has been classified with its northern neighbour Kalkatungu in a Kalkatungic subgroup.[100] Its other neigh-

---

100 Dixon (2002: xxxvi) puts both languages in a non-genetic "areal group", and Breen & Blake (2007: 83–84) refrain from attributing their shared features to a distinctive genetic relationship. Evans (2005: 260–261) argues for the plausibility of their forming a genetic subgroup – a view which I accept.

bours are Warluwarra to the west and Pitta-Pitta to the south. Dixon (2002: 202) includes Kalkatungu and Yalarnnga (his "W group") among the languages that mark just two AM values. Both languages have suffixes (or perhaps rather enclitics) occurring on motion verbs – in Kalkatungu attested only on Imperatives (Blake 1979a: 92) – that mark direction toward or away from the speaker. Yalarnnga examples are (104) and (105). This, however, does not constitute Associated Motion, since no separate motion event is indicated by these deictic suffixes. In Yalarnnga, however, there are a few examples where the HITHER suffix does contribute an extra motion event. Examples (106–108) involve transitive verbs, where the directional marker contributes Subsequent Motion involving the subject and object together; i.e. 'do and bring'. There are two markers of motion toward the speaker: *-ati*, which follows the imperative suffix and *-nyanharrirta*, which combines Future with 'hither' (Breen & Blake 2007: 47). It is not known how general this usage is: whether *-anthu* HENCE can be used in this way, and whether the deictic markers can similarly add a motion event to intransitive verbs. At any rate, Yalarnnga presents an example of Belkadi's (2015) D-AM, i.e. AM marked by deictic directionals, where markers whose primary function is to specify the direction of a verb of motion (perhaps also orientation in non-motion verbs such as 'look in the direction of speaker') can be extended to add a motion co-event to a verb that is not inherently motional in its semantics. This has not been explicitly described for Australian languages before now.

(104) *Piyaka-mala-mpa   ngap(a)-**anthu**-wa*
son.in.law-your-ALL go.IMP-**HENCE**-?[101]
'Go over to your son-in-law.' (Breen & Blake 2007: 31)

(105) *Kaya tjala kanyi-l-**ati**   ngatji-wampa*
child this bring-IMP-**HITH** 1SG-ALL
'Bring the kid over to me.'[102] (Breen & Blake 2007: 46)

(106) *watjani   thingka-l-**ati***
firewood chop-IMP-**HITH**
'Chop some firewood and bring it here.' (Breen & Blake 2007: 46)

---

101 ? marks a "prosodic suffix", of unclear meaning.
102 The verb glossed 'bring' really means 'carry', 'take', or 'bring'; i.e. its sense does not include inherent direction.

(107) miya-l-***ati***   tjala warrramparta
       get-IMP-**HITH** this   axe
       'Pick up that axe and bring it here.' (Breen & Blake 2007: 46)

(108) Thangani-ma   kunhu-ta   miya-li-***nyanharrirta***
       run.away-PRS   water-PURP   get-ANTIP-**FUT.HITH**
       'He's going to fetch water.' (Breen & Blake 2007: 47)

7.3 N Karnic subgroup: Pitta-Pitta

For Pitta-Pitta Blake (1979b: 204) describes a verbal suffix -*yarnta* ALONG, which means 'do something while walking along'. The only non-motion verb cited is 'eat', which is illustrated in (109), where the direction of motion is indicated by the deictic enclitic. Blake and Breen (1971: 71), however, mention another verb, *rtarri-**yarnta**-* 'hop along', compared to *rtarri-* 'jump'. The same suffix can be added to a motion verb, in which case it seems to add a notion of extended time and/or space, as in (110), where ergative agreement on the motion verb indicates the subordinate status of its clause.[103]

(109) thatyi-***yarnta***=yangu
       eat-**ALONG**=HITHER
       'He's coming this way eating as he comes.' (Blake 1979b:204)

(110) tyirra-nha   nhu-lu-ka   thawi-ka   karnta-***yarnta***-ka-lu
       boomerang-ACC   he-ERG-HERE   throw-PST   go-**ALONG**-PST-ERG
       'While walking along he hurled the boomerang.' (Blake 1979b:204)

7.4 Maric subgroup

7.4.1 Bidyara

Three closely related Maric varieties have been described by Breen in terms which suggest a single AM grammatical form. For Bidyara Breen (1973: 100) describes a verbal suffix, which he glosses ALONG, as follows: "The affixing of -*ndyarra* to

---

[103] See §6.3.1 for a similar situation in the closely related Wangka Yutyuru, where there is furthermore a contrast between two markers of Concurrent AM.

a verb stem indicates that the action is taking place while the actor is moving along." Examples include 'burn along (of a bush fire)', 'eat while travelling', 'talk while walking along'. (111) and (112) illustrate the effect of this suffix on the verb 'jump', which does not otherwise indicate change of location. I interpret this as a marker of Concurrent AM. No specific direction of motion is indicated.

(111) gandu   dhumba-la
       boy   jump-PST
      'The boy jumped.' (Breen 1973: 101)

(112) ngarrgu   dhumba-**ndyarra**-la
       kangaroo jump-**ALONG**-PST
      'The kangaroo hopped along.' (Breen 1973: 101)

The ALONG suffix has further uses which do not involve adding motion: it is used "superfluously" on motion verbs 'walk' and 'run', yielding 'walk/run along' – apparently indicating spatial extent – and with intransitive process verbs (apparently indicating gradualness): examples are 'getting better (from being sick)' and 'growing' (Breen 1973: 101).

7.4.2 Margany

For Margany Breen (1981a: 322) describes two verb suffixes that mark "extended actions", -*ta.ba* glossed ALONG and -:*la.ba* glossed ABOUT (where ":" marks lengthening of the preceding vowel). Both appear to include an element *ba*, which may have been derived from *waba*- 'go, walk' (without specific direction). The *ta* in -*taba* is "probably to be identified with the conjunctive" (Breen 1981a: 322), a non-finite suffix used in various subordinate clauses (Breen 1981a: 318). The source of -:*la* is unknown. The suffixes signify either "(a) that an action is performed while the actor is going along or immediately after he goes somewhere or (b) that the action is spread out over an area"[104] (Breen 1981a: 322). In spite of the different glosses, both suffixes occur in sentences where the meaning is 'going along'. (113) is an example with -*taba*; a form *dhumba-**alaba**-nhi* 'hop-**ABOUT**-PST' (from *dhumba*- 'jump') was used of a kangaroo hopping along.[105] Breen's

---

104 The only clear example of spatial distribution without motion is with -:*laba* suffixed to the stative verb *nguna*- 'lie', to describe 'dogs lying around everywhere' (Breen 1981a: 323).
105 Cf. the similar Bidyara example in §7.4.1.

consultant furthermore glossed *binda-**taba**-nhi* (from *binda-* 'sit') as "I went over there and I sat down over there". This suggests that the construction may mark prior as well as concurrent motion. I therefore consider the Margany system to include a single AM category of either Concurrent or Prior motion in an unspecified direction, expressed by two synonymous suffixes. The hypothesised origin of the *-taba* forms is the univerbation of a verb marked with a non-finite suffix plus (a truncated form of) the motion verb *waba-* 'move'.

(113) bula   ngandhi-***taba***-nhi
       3DU   talk-**ALONG**-PRS
       'Those two are walking along talking.' (Breen 1981a: 322)

These suffixes can be added to verbs of inherent motion; there are examples of both suffixes occurring with *waba-* 'go' and of *-taba-* with *wara-* 'run'. Example (114) illustrates both the addition of *-:laba* to a verb of motion and the use of the "conjunctive" suffix in a (simultaneous) subordinate clause. (115) shows the (Imperative form of the) general motion verb used with a deictic adverb to give the sense 'come', plus the use of the "conjunctive" suffix in a subordinate clause of purpose.[106]

(114) waba-***alaba***-nhi   nhula   bulu   dhala-ta
       go-**ALONG**-PRS   3SG   tucker   eat-CONJ
       'He's eating along (i.e. eating as he goes)'. (Breen 1981a: 318)[107]

(115) ugu   waba   binda-ta
       hither   come   sit-CONJ
       "Come inside and sit down." (Breen 1981a: 318)

7.4.3 Gunya

Another possible instance of a language with a single AM marker is neighbouring Gunya, for which Breen (1981a: 330) describes a verbal suffix *-yi/-ya*, glossed CONT, which "seems to denote a continuing action, or perhaps an action carried out while the agent is going along". While some examples suggest a purely aspectual function (e.g. grass growing, meat cooking, and CONT added to *wadya-* 'go'),

---

[106] A comparison of (115) with the form *binda-**taba**-nhi* cited above helps us see how the latter could have evolved from a construction *binda-ta waba-nhi*.
[107] The same sentence is repeated on page 322 with the substitution of the gloss ABOUT.

example (116) parallels (112) from Bidyara. CONT followed by Future Tense seems to signal "an intended continuing action", according to Breen (1981: 331). Nevertheless, examples provided, such as (117), "all have a reasonable interpretation with prior motion", as noted by Austin (1989: 68). Like Margany, then, the formative may mark Concurrent or Prior Motion, with a possible implication of continuous aspect. The source of this suffix is not certain: Breen (1981a: 330) suggests a possible origin as a truncated form of the verb *wadya-* 'go' (without specific direction), which presupposes lenition of *dy* to *y*, and notes that this would parallel the suggested source of the *ba* of Margany *-taba*. Against this proposal is the fact that this would require direct combining of the motion root with the preceding verb stem, with no intervening material such as the *ta* of the Margany suffix (and possibly the *ntya* of the Bidyara suffix).

(116)   *gula*   *dhumba-yi-nhi=la*
        kangaroo   jump-CONT-PRS=3SG
        'The kangaroo is hopping along.' (Breen 1981a: 334)

(117)   *gamu*   *dhala-ya-nggi=ya*
        water   eat-CONT-FUT=1SG
        'I'm going to have a drink of water.' (Breen 1981a: 331)

7.5 Central New South Wales subgroup

7.5.1 Ngiyambaa

For Ngiyambaa Donaldson (1980: 190–191) describes a verb suffix *-wa*, glossed MOVING, which "attached to a non-stative verb indicates that the event takes place while the subject or agent is in motion". Examples are 'sit while traveling along' (118) and 'eat while going along' (119). This formative is described as one of a set of "aspectual suffixes", which do not affect the transitivity of the preceding verb stem and which occur after valency-changing suffixes and before the final Tense-Mood suffix (Donaldson 1980: 183). Most verbal suffixes have variant shapes conditioned by the conjugation class of the preceding element, and themselves belong to one of the conjugation classes. The elements *-l-* and *-y-* of (119) are glossed by Donaldson as "conjugation markers" (CM); I have included them within the segmented AM or Mood formative.[108] The presence of these CMs

---

[108] Some conjugations involve a zero CM, which is not indicated here.

indicates that the suffixes were formerly themselves verbs that have come to be compounded phonologically with their hosts.

(118)   winar   wi:-**wa**-nha   wilba:ra
        woman(NOM)   sit-**MOVING**-PRS   cart.LOC
        'A woman is sitting in a sulky, (driving) along.' (Donaldson 1980: 190)

(119)   dha-**l.wa**-y.ŋabi-guwa-y.aga=lu=na
        eat-**MOVING**-NIGHT-PITY-IRR=3ERG=3ABS
        'Poor thing! She will eat as she goes along during the night.' (Donaldson 1980: 184)

The MOVING suffix also occurs with verbs of motion, such as 'go (in a non-specific direction)', 'run', 'fly', where it is glossed 'along', as in (120).

(120)   yarur   yana-**wa**-y.ga:-nha   dhi:nbay-buwan
        slow(ABS)   go-**MOVING**-A.BIT-PRS   walking.stick-COM(ABS)
        '(He) walks along a little, slowly, with a walking stick.' (Donaldson 1980: 109)

The same suffix attached to a stative verb like 'be sick' marks Inchoative, and is then glossed GETTING. Donaldson (1980: 191) treats this developing state as a metaphorical use of motion.

7.5.2 Yuwaalaraay-Yuwaaliyaay-Gamilaraay

Giacon (2017: 252–257) analyses the verbal suffix -waa (with allomorphs, including -laa, conditioned by the class of the preceding verb stem), glossed MOVING, as one of two contrasting "Continuous Aspect" markers, this one being used when the subject is in motion. The matching Continuous Aspect suffix which does not involve motion is glossed Continuous (CTS) and has -lda as one of its allomorphs. The contrast between the moving and non-moving Continuous Aspect markers is illustrated in (121) vs. (122). For the inherently motion verb 'run' the addition of the suffix is said to add linearity (Giacon 2017: 253) – not deictic direction since this is specified by dhaay – whereas for 'bark' it marks a concurrent motional action.

(121)   maadhaay dhaay   banaga-**waa**-nha,   gula-**laa**-nha
        dog   to.here   run-**MOV**-PRS   bark-**MOV**-PRS
        'The dog is running here and barking.' (Giacon 2017: 253)

(122) *ngaarma   nguu   guld-**lda**-nha*
      there   3SG.ERG   bark-CTS-PRS
      'He is barking there now (at the base of the tree).' (Giacon 2017: 253)

Verbal forms with AM meanings were noted already in R. H. Mathews' grammatical sketch of "Yualeai" (Yuwaaliyaay), in his comment on forms of the verb 'beat': "There are forms of the verb to express beating going along the road ..." (Mathews 1902: 142). Williams (1980: 74) quotes from his notebook a sentence *illa ngulli bumullawai* 'we'll fight going along', where the last word can now be analysed as *bumali-waa-y* 'fight-MOV-FUT'.

7.5.3 Wiradjuri

Wiradjuri is the southernmost language of the Central NSW subgroup. Although we lack a modern grammar of the language, the dictionary compiled from old sources includes, among the plenteous verbal suffixes, forms that suggest Concurrent Associated Motion; e.g. *buma-**l.balaa**-nha* 'hits while going along' and *ngu-**m.balaa**-nha* 'gives while going along' – analysable as 'hit/give-ALONG-PRS', where the movement marker includes a conjugation-dependent consonant (Grant and Rudder 2010: 349–353).

7.6 Yuin subgroup

7.6.1 Ngunawal

Languages of the Yuin subgroup were spoken in south-eastern New South Wales, both along the coast south of Sydney and further inland. The closely related Ngunawal and Gundungurra – probably co-dialects of the same language – were southern neighbours of Wiradjuri. Both appear to have a similar marking for Concurrent Associated Motion, according to the glosses provided in the sketch grammar by R. H. Mathews. For Ngunawal he cites (123) as an example of "different shades of meaning" imparted by verbal affixes – for which I offer a segmentation and morphemic glossing in the second and third lines.[109] (Mathews 1904: 298).

---

109 I thank Louise Baird for bringing this form to my attention.

(123) *dhaimballinyirrimuingga*
       *dhayimbali-**nyiri**-muyi-ngga*
       eat-**ALONG**-PST.CONT-1SG
       'I was eating going along.' (Mathews 1904: 298)

7.6.2 Gundungurra

For Gundungurra, Besold (2004: 54) cites from Mathews' notebook the form in (124), and suggests that it may contain a motion suffix. My interpretation, which differs somewhat from Besold's, is provided in the segmentation and morphemic glosses of the second and third lines. Nothing is known about the origin of this formation: note that the AM marker is added directly after the verb stem. Nothing similar appears in the (rather meagre) descriptions of the other Yuin languages, which are summarised in Besold (2013).

(124) *yerrinyirrimuingga*
       *yiri-**nyiri**-muyi-ngga*
       throw-**ALONG**-PST.CONT-1SG
       'I threw going along.' (Besold 2004: 54)

7.7 Western Desert language

7.7.1 Yankunytjatjara

The huge Western Desert language has many named dialects. The term Wati has been used as the name of the subgroup which includes this single language plus Warnman. An AM formation is found in several of the more easterly dialects. For Yankunytjatjara Goddard (1985: 118–119) describes a form one of whose functions is to express 'to do so-and-so going along', which he compares to Dixon's (1977: 219) Yidiny "going aspect". The formation consists of suffixing *-kati*, which as an independent verb stem means 'carry', to the so-called "neutral stem" of a verb. The suffix serves to add a concurrent motion co-event, in an unspecified direction, to the verb, and the valence of the modified verb is not changed by the addition of *-kati*, as can be seen in (125–126). The same formation can have another usage, that of assuming a posture, when added to stance verb; thus *ngari-kati-* is ambiguous between the AM sense 'lie while going along' and the "assume stance" sense 'lie down'. Goddard uses the same gloss PROCESS for both uses.

(125) *paluru   ngari-**kati**-ngi   Uluru-la*
      DEF(NOM)   lie-**PROCESS**-PST.IPFV   Uluru-LOC.NAME
      'He slept on the way past Uluru.' (Goddard 1985: 119)

(126) *Ngayulu   mayi   nyanga-tja   ngalku-**kati**-nyi*
      1SG(ERG)   food(ACC)   this-EVIDENT   eat-**PROCESS**-PRS
      'I'll eat this food while going along.' (Goddard 1985: 119)

7.7.2 Pitjantjatjara

Essentially the same situation is found in the Pitjantjatjara dialect. Eckert & Hudson (1988: 251) state that -*kati*- is "added to many types of verbs to mean 'while going along'". (127) illustrates this usage.

(127) *Paluru mungartji-kutju   ngalya-alti-**kati**-pai.*
      he   yesterday-only   toward-call-**WHILE.GOING**-CHAR
      'Only late in the afternoon would he call for her (on his way home).'
      (Eckert & Hudson 1988: 252)

7.7.3 Pintupi

In Pintupi the equivalent marker has variants (according to sub-dialect) -*kati* and -*ti* and is interpreted by Hansen & Hansen (1975: 161) as 'unit action (UNIT)', which "emphasises an action which is accomplished once. One definite action is in focus and is usually carried out speedily". In (128) the suffix appears to add concurrent motion ('look while going') and allows the directional particle (or proclitic) *ma* to be added to the verb, specifying the movement 'away'.

(128) *kingkaru-ku=latju   kanintjarra-lu   ma   nyaku-**ti**-malpa*
      kangaroo-DAT=1PL.EXCL.ERG   inside-ERG   away   see-**UNIT**-FUT.CONT
      'From inside (the car) we will continue to look for kangaroos.'
      (Hansen and Hansen 1975: 161)

I analyse all three of these dialects as manifesting a single Concurrent Associated Motion category.

7.8 Thura-Yura subgroup: Wirangu

The southwesternmost Thura-Yura language, Wirangu, which has been heavily influenced by the adjacent (and now co-located) Kukata variety of the Western Desert language, has a formation that closely resembles the *kati*-form of Western Desert. Hercus (1999: 129) explicitly describes it as an Associated Motion marker, which produces verbal forms that mean 'while travelling along' or 'on the way', "exactly parallel to the use of the same verb -*kati*- in Western Desert languages (Goddard 1985: 118)". The form is spelled -*gadi* in Hercus' orthography. Speakers do not associate it with the independent verb *gadi*- 'carry'. As an AM marker it usually drops the *i* vowel and is preceded by what may be a non-finite form of the main verb stem (though labelled PRESENT), and the vowel preceding PRESENT is sometimes changed to *i*, which is said to mark Continuous-Repetitive (Hercus 1999: 130). Examples (129) and (130) show two of Hercus' examples, with her glosses. Although Wirangu belongs to the same subgroup as Adnyamathanha and Kuyani, which have complex AM systems, the single Wirangu AM marker appears to have been borrowed from its Western Desert neighbours.

(129) *Bala-ngu   rabbiti   gurndi-**rn-gad(i)**-na*
      he/she-ERG   rabbit   kill.CONT-**PRS-GO**-PST
      'She went round killing rabbits.' (Hercus 1999: 132)

(130) *bala-ngu   maa   ngalgu-**rn-gad**-n*
      he/she-ERG   food   eat-**PRS-GO**-PRS
      'He is eating as he is walking along.' (Hercus 1999: 131)

7.9 Marrngu subgroup: Nyangumarta

In the Nyangumarta language of Western Australia,[110] a verb phrase construction consisting of a nominalised verb followed by *kawa*- 'repeat' indicates "that the event of the main verb happens over time, often in different places. It can also

---

110 This is the only language of Western Australia in which AM has been found. The only other possible candidate is a poorly understood verbal inflection (or possibly enclitic) -*nggula* of the southwestern language Nhanda, which has been glossed 'Ambulative' and whose meaning includes 'while going along, while walking along' (Blevins 2001: 105). [Late addition: a cognate construction, based on a nominalised verb compounded with *ka*- 'carry', with (subsequent or concurrent) AM semantics, can now be recognised in Nyangumarta's neighbouring Marrngu language, Mangarla (Agnew 2020: 273, 285–287.]

include the idea of travelling", as in (131) (Sharp 2004: 231–232). This phrasal construction, with *kawa-* as an auxiliary verb, qualifies as a grammatical AM marker. The so-called verb *kawa-*, glossed 'repeat', which occurs only in this construction, may derive from a reanalysis of the monosyllabic verb **ka-* 'carry, take', whose prehistoric Imperative form was **kawa*. If so, this construction bears some resemblance to the use of *kati-* 'carry' to mark Concurrent Motion in the closely related Western Desert language (see §7.7).

(131) *Pala-nga   nga-**ninya** **kawa**-nikinyi pulu   kuyi*
      that-LOC   eat-**NMLZ**   **repeat**-IPFV   3DU.SBJ   meat
      'And there those two went along eating meat.' (Sharp 2004: 232)

8 Precursor constructions

A number of languages display somewhat grammaticalised constructions which link a motion verb in a modifying role with another verb, typically in a non-finite form, yielding meanings related to and perhaps sometimes including associated motion, yet not being restricted to having an AM sense. It is likely that constructions of this kind are a potential source of grammaticalised AM markers. I call such antecedent structures "precursor constructions".

Dhanggati, a language of northeastern New South Wales, employs an expression that has been described as "associated motion aspect". Here a phrasal construction consisting of a verb in a nominalised form followed by the motion verb *manha-* 'go', indicates a sense "going about doing the action of the first verb" (Lissarrague 2007: 46). In spite of the occurrence of the inflected verb of motion, the sense of spatial distribution ('about') seems to be a more consistent semantic feature of the construction than that of motion ('going'), as can be seen from its use with stative verbs, where the derived sense is 'sit or stand about'. The construction is thus better described as "distributive" (Lissarrague, pers. comm.).

Warlpiri, in addition to the two morphological markers of Prior Motion discussed in §6.4.1, has a less grammaticalised construction consisting of a main verb in its non-finite "infinitive" form *-nja* (with allomorphs)[111] followed by a motion verb: *ya-* 'go', *parnka-* 'run', or *pardi-* 'arise', meaning 'go/run/arise VERBing' (Nash 1986: 44), with concurrent motion. That this construction is somewhat grammaticalised is evident from: the syntactic fact that it is the main verb that determines the argument structure of the clause, including ergative marking of

---

111 Nash's "infinitive" is the same form as Simpson's (2001) "participle" mentioned in §6.4.1.

the subject of a transitive verb;[112] the phonological facts that the motion verb has reduced stress and the initial consonant of *ya-* may be omitted;[113] and the semantic fact that the meaning may be spatial extension rather than literal motion (133).[114] On the other hand, directional enclitics may occur after the infinitive and before the inflected motion verb, as shown in both (132) and (133).

(132) ...*jurlarda=lku   paka-**rninja**-rni-**ya**-ntarla   kujarni-rli=ji*
sugarbag=THEN   strike-INF-HITH-**go**-IRR   other.side-ERG=TOP
'(...so we) would come chopping sugarbag on the other side.' (Nash 1986: 45)

(133) *Nungu   ka   nguna-nguna-**nja**=rni   **ya**-ni*
sugar   PRS   RDP-lie-INF-HITH   **go**-NPST
'The (best) sugar lies from one end to another (of the beehive).' (Nash 1986: 146)

Somewhat similar to the Warlpiri form is a formation in the Pintupi dialect of Western Desert, which consists of the conjugation-dependent participial suffix *-la/-ra/-rra* followed (with deletion of *a*) by an element *i* (*a* in some sub-dialects), which inflects according to the *n*-class just like *ya-* 'go'. The earlier form of (134) would thus have been *pungku-la yanku-payi, where *yanku* is a form of the verb *ya-* 'go'. This Pintupi inflection, labelled Intermittent (Continuous) Action, "implies that the actor is carrying out the action while moving around or that the action is repeated many times over a long period of time" (Hansen & Hansen 1975: 159). Since many of the sentences illustrating this form include motion verbs (135), and the form can be added to stative verbs (136), it seems that the contribution of the formation is primarily to mark spatial distribution rather than AM.

(134) *Palunya-lu   ngaya   pinyi   pungku-**linku**-payi*
that-ERG   cat   many   hit-INTM-CHAR
'That one always kills many cats (when it goes hunting).'
(Hansen & Hansen 1975: 160)

---

112 The Ergative in (132) results from co-reference with the transitive subject.
113 The construction is written as a single word in (132) but as two words in (133).
114 Here both 'go' and the reduplication of the main verb contribute to the sense of spatial extent.

(135) *Kayili=nyurra yanku-**linku**-mara*
 north=2PLS   go-**INTM**-SUBJ
 'You all should have walked around the north side.'
 (Hansen & Hansen 1975: 160)

(136) *Wamaku=nyurra ngaangka nyina-**ri**-ninpa*
 beer=2PLS   here   sit-**INTM**-PRS
 'Are you all sitting here for beer?' (Hansen & Hansen 1975: 159)

A similar formation is found in other Western Desert dialects. For example, Eckert & Hudson (1988: 252–253), for the Pitjantjatjara dialect, describe the function of the suffix *-ri* (after most verb stems), glossed 'recurrently' (RECUR), in aspectual terms ("means that the action referred to by the basic verb is carried on over a reasonably lengthy period of time either recurrently or sometimes continuously"), yet claim that the resultant verb has "a very similar meaning to the *-kati-* verbs which is 'doing (something) while going along'". The examples provided all seem to include an element of spatial distribution – even the stative verb 'sit' yields 'live in various places' (137). In (138) the *-ri* form adds a sense of 'about' to both the motion verb *kati-* and the action verb *ninti-* 'show' (here motion is obviously implied: 'show while going around'). In (139) the suffix more clearly adds motion to *tili-* 'light fire' and allows the resulting verb to take a directional prefix *ma-* 'away'.

(137) *nganana iriti   kakarara nyina-**ri**-nanyi.*
 we   long.ago east   sit-**RECUR**-PST
 'Long ago we lived around about (in various places) in the east.'
 (Eckert and Hudson 1988: 253)

(138) *Ngayu-lu ngayu-ku malpa   kati-**ri**-nangi   ngura tjuta-wanu*
 1SG-ERG   1SG-DAT   friend take-**RECUR**-PST   place many-PERL
 *munu=na   ninti-**ri**-nangi.*
 and=1SG.SBJ show-**RECUR**-PST
 'I was taking my friend around various communities and showing him about.' (Eckert and Hudson 1988: 253)

(139) *Nyaratja   paluru   waru ma-tili-**ri**-nanyi.*
 that.over.there 3SG.ERG fire away-light-**RECUR**-PRS
 'That's him making off over there, lighting fires as he goes.'
 (Eckert and Hudson 1988: 253)

Languages of the Karnic subgroup (except those of the northern sub-branch, which consists of Pitta-Pitta and Wangka Yutyuru) manifest a large set of motion verbs that modify other verbs in senses that include direction, manner, associated motion, associated stance, time of day, aspectual notions such as continuous action or action done to completion, or action done for oneself. These have been discussed in Austin (1989). The formal aspect of these constructions differs according to languages: in the dialect continuum Diyari-Ngamini-Yarluyandi they are phrases consisting of a nominalised verb (i.e. a participial form) plus an inflected verb (VERB$_1$-PTCP VERB$_2$-INFL); in Arabana-Wangkangurru they involve complex verbs uniting both of these elements in a single phonological word (VERB$_1$-PTCP-VERB$_2$-INFL), plus some formations which lack the linking participial suffix; in Yandruwandha and Wangkumara they consist of two verbal roots in combination without an intervening nominalising suffix (VERB$_1$-VERB$_2$-INFL). Austin (1989) argues that the latter did not necessarily result from a gradual grammaticalisation from a biclausal structure but that contact within a well-recognised linguistic and cultural area led to the copying of constructions between languages.

I have claimed in §6.3 that only two of these modifying verbs are genuine AM markers in each of these languages except the westernmost Arabana-Wangkangurru, for which I posit at least six AM forms (§5.1). This language is located between languages with very complex AM systems, Adnyamathanha and Kuyani to the south and Arandic languages to the north. I suggest that under the influence of these languages Arabana-Wangkangurru has adapted several of these Karnic constructions to AM usage. One verb that occurs in all these languages is *thika-* 'return'. As a marker of direction it means 'action directed back to origin' (Austin 1989: 56). If the main verb is transitive, it is the object that moves, as illustrated in (140). When used as a marker of AM in Arabana-Wangkangurru, however, it is always the subject that moves (see §5.1). This is a clear indication of the difference between pure directional and AM markers, even though the latter include direction as a semantic component.

(140) *Yindi*   *kurrha-rnda*   **thika**
      you.ERG   put-PTCP   **return**(IMP)
      'You put (it) back!' (Yarluyandi: Austin 1989: 55)

The use of certain verbs in a modifying role occurs in various Pama-Nyungan languages. In the languages of the Yolngu subgroup, located in an enclave in the northeastern corner of north-central Australia, surrounded by non-Pama-Nyungan languages, these modifying verbs typically include the stance verbs 'sit', 'stand', and 'lie', but also the general motion verb 'move'.[115] "Yolngu languages use a closed set of motion and stance verbs as auxiliary verbs in order to express durative aspect, with varying nuances according to the actual auxiliary verb used" (Waters 1989: 131). Here the construction is formally verb serialisation. The greatest number of such auxiliary verbs is reported from Djinang (Waters 1989: 131–136). An example of *kiri-* 'go' being used for Progressive Aspect is (141). Other modifying motion verbs are: *giri-* 'go' (i.e. *kiri-* with initial voicing), Habitual Aspect; *nunydjirri* 'go quickly, run', Hastitive aspect 'do hastily'; *wali-* 'crawl about', Ramblitive Aspect 'do from place to place arbitrarily' (see (142)); and *gukirr-* 'walk about', aspectually 'do while walking about' (only one attested example). Although the stance verbs when used as auxiliaries can bear an associated posture meaning, the motion verbs are not used for associated motion.[116] The Yolngu languages, like the Karnic languages, provide evidence for the kind of constructions involving motion verbs which in certain languages have given rise to grammaticalised Associated Motion constructions; i.e. they demonstrate the latent potential for AM that exists among the Pama-Nyungan languages.

(141) *bambuli*   *nyani*   *ngami-n*   **kiri-m**
bark.painting   3SG.ERG   paint-PRS   **PROG-PRS**
'He is busy painting the bark.' (Waters 1989: 133)

(142) *giliwilim*   *bil*   *ngurri-ny*   ***wali-ny***
together   3DU.NOM   sleep-REMOTE.PST.CONT   **RAMBL-REMOTE.PST.CONT**
'They slept together in various places.' (Waters 1989: 136)

9 Summary and conclusions

9.1 Summary tables

Tables 16–19 summarise our findings, sorted according to the level of complexity of the AM systems. The four categories of complexity are indicated in these tables and on the map (Figure 2 in the Appendix) by means of letters: D = very complex (eight or more values), Table 16; C = moderately complex (three to six values),

---

[115] Languages for which this has been reported include Djapu, Djambarrpuyngu, Ritharrngu, Djinang, and Djinpa.
[116] The unique example *dirradji-m gukirr* 'eat-PRS walk.about(PRS)' '(pigs) are walking about eating' (Waters 1989: 132), however, does apparently show AM semantics.

Table 16: Very complex AM systems in Pama-Nyungan languages.

Subgroup	Language	MOV ARG	REL TIME	DIRECTION	SPEED / ASPECTUAL	§	Map ref
Arandic	Kaytetye	NSBJ	1P	AR		2	D1
		SBJ	4P	IT, VEN, RET	QUICK		
		SBJ	2S	AND, RET			
		SBJ	4C	UN, VEN	PUNC, UN, CONT		
		SBJ	1P+C	AND+RET			
	Alyawarr	NSBJ	1P	AR		3.3	D2
		SBJ	3P	AND, RET	QUICK		
		SBJ	3S	AND, RET	QUICK		
		SBJ	5C	AND, RET, UP, DN	±PUNC		
	EC Arrernte	NSBJ	1P	AR		3.2	D5
		SBJ	2P	AND, RET			
		SBJ	4S	AND, RET	±QUICK		
		SBJ	10C	UN, VEN,[117] RET, UP, DN	QUICK,[118] ±PUNC[119]		
	L Arrernte	NSBJ	1P	AR		3.3	D6
		SBJ	2P	AND, RET			
		SBJ	2S	AND, RET			
		SBJ	4C	AND, UP, DN	±PUNC[120]		
Thura-Yura	Adnyamathanha	SBJ	4P	IT, VEN	±QUICK	4.1	D8
		SBJ	5C	IT, VEN, AND	PUNC, UN, CONT		
		SBJ	1S	AND			
	Kuyani[121]	SBJ	1P	IT		4.2	D7
		SBJ	3C	AND	PUNC, UN, CONT		

Table 17; B = binary (two values), Table 18; and A = unitary (one value), Table 19. The tables provide the following information: languages, their subgroup, the section of the chapter where each is discussed, their map reference, and the AM parameters and contrasting values within the system of each language. The MOV(ING) ARG(UMENT) is non-subject (NSBJ) vs. subject (SBJ). REL(ATIVE) TIME values are

---

117 Occurs alone or combined with UN, RET
118 Combines only with DN.
119 Interpretation of Past/Thru, combined with UN, VEN (see Table 3).
120 Possible aspectual distinction, only with AND.
121 Kuyani is classified as a very complex system rather than a moderately complex one, in spite of its mere four AM values, on the grounds that, given its limited documentation and its close dialect relationship with Adnyamathanha, it is likely to have had a system similar to that of Adnyamathanha.

Table 17: Moderately complex AM systems in Pama-Nyungan languages.

Subgroup	Language	MOV ARG	REL TIME	DIRECTION	SPEED / ASPECTUAL	§	Map ref
WKarnic	Arabana & Wangkangurru	SBJ	1P	RET		5.1	C2,3
		SBJ	1S	RET			
		SBJ	4C	AND, RET	PUNC, UN, CONT		
(isolate)	Warumungu	SBJ	2P/C/S	IT, VEN		5.2	C4
		SBJ	1P	AND			
Ngumpin-Yapa	Warlmanpa	SBJ	3C	AND, VEN, IT		5.3	C5
Paman	Yir Yoront	SBJ	4P	AND, IT, VEN, RET		5.4	C1

Table 18: Binary AM systems in Pama-Nyungan languages.

Subgroup	Language	MOV ARG	REL TIME	DIR	SPEED / ASP	§	Map
Paman	Jabugay	SBJ	2P	IT, VEN		6.1.1	B1
	Yidiny	SBJ	2P/C	IT, VEN		6.1.2	B2
	Kuuk Thaayorre	SBJ	2P	AND	±QUICK?	6.1.3	B3
Ngarna	Warluwarra	SBJ	1P,1C	AND		6.2.1	B9
	Bularnu	SBJ	1P,1C	AND		6.2.2	B10
NKarnic	Wangka-Yutyuru	SBJ	2C	AND	±CONT	6.3.1	B8
EKarnic	Wangkumara	SBJ	1P,1C	AND		6.3.2	B4
CKarnic	Yandruwandha	SBJ	2C	AND	±CONT	6.3.3	B5
	Ngamini	SBJ	2C	AND	±CONT	6.3.4	B7
	Diyari	SBJ	2C	AND	±CONT	6.3.5	B6
Ngumpin-Yapa	Warlpiri	SBJ	2P	AND, RET		6.4.1	B12
	Mudburra	SBJ	2P/C	VEN, IT		6.4.2	B11

P(RIOR), C(ONCURRENT), S(UBSEQUENT), P+C (PRIOR plus CONCURRENT in the reverse direction), P/C (PRIOR or CONCURRENT), and P/C/S (PRIOR, CONCURRENT, or SUBSEQUENT). Directions are specified with a consistent set of abbreviated terms, which may differ from the glosses used in the discussion of individual languages above: IT(IVE): deictic 'go (away from speaker)'; VEN(TIVE): deictic toward speaker, 'come'; AND(ATIVE): non-deictic 'go (along)', 'move', 'depart' (with sub-

Table 19: Unitary AM systems in Pama-Nyungan languages.

Subgroup	Language	MOV ARG	REL TIME	DIR	SPEED / ASP	§	Map
Kalkatungic	Yalarnnga	SBJ	1S	VEN		7.2	A10
Ngarna	Wakaya	SBJ	1C	AND		7.1	A11
NKarnic	Pitta-Pitta	SBJ	1C	AND		7.3	A9
Maric	Bidyara	SBJ	1C	AND		7.4.1	A8
	Margany	SBJ	1P/C[124]	AND		7.4.2	A6
	Gunya	SBJ	1P/C	AND		7.4.3	A7
CNSW	Ngiyambaa	SBJ	1C	AND		7.5.1	A4
	Yuwaalaraay	SBJ	1C	AND		7.5.2	A5
	Wiradjuri	SBJ	1C	AND		7.5.3	A3
Yuin	Ngunawal	SBJ	1C	AND		7.6.1	A2
	Gundungurra	SBJ	1C	AND		7.6.2	A1
Wati	Yankunytjatjara	SBJ	1C	AND		7.7.1	A14
	Pitjantjatjara	SBJ	1C	AND		7.7.2	A13
	Pintupi	SBJ	1C	AND		7.7.3	A12
Thura-Yura	Wirangu	SBJ	1C	AND		7.8	A15
Marrngu	Nyangumarta	SBJ	1C	AND		7.9	A16

sequent motion)'; RET(URN); AR(RIVE);[122] UP(WARDS); D(OW)N(WARDS), UN(SPEC-IFIED). SPEED combines with PRIOR, where it may refer to the short duration of either MOTION or EVENT, or with SUBSEQUENT, where it refers to the duration of EVENT, but rarely with CONCURRENT. In the tables SPEED is indicated by means of (±)QUICK, i.e. 'quick' or 'not quick'.[123] ASPECTUAL refers to the relative degree of overlap (in time and space) of the EVENT with the MOTION path: terms used are CONT(INUOUS), PUNC(TUAL), and UN(SPECIFIED).

9.2 Generalisations on complexity and parameters

AM has been found in 41 distinct language varieties of the approximately 100 that were investigated;[124] the number could be reduced to 35 *languages* if some of the

---
[122] AR(RIVE) occurs only in Prior NSBJ forms, where there is no contrasting direction.
[123] The DO.WHILE.GOING.SLOWLY value of Arabana-Wangkangurru is here categorised as the aspectual value CONT(INUOUS) (see §5.1).
[124] It is unknown whether the same proportion would have applied in the remaining 100 or so Pama-Nyungan languages for which insufficient data could be found.

dialects are grouped together (the three Wati or Western Desert, the three Maric, and the two Yuin varieties, Arabana and Wangkangurru).[125] It is found in 13 subgroups, which is about 40% of some 30–35 Pama-Nyungan lower-level subgroups.[126]

Of the 41 languages with AM, eight languages (20%) have very complex systems: six belonging to the Arandic and two to the Thura-Yura[127] subgroups respectively; five languages (12%), including the co-dialects Arabana and Wangkangurru, manifest complex systems making three to six distinctions; binary systems are found in 12 languages (29%) and unitary systems in 16 (39%) – see Table 20. The complexity measured here is based on the number of AM subcategories expressed. Another possible measure would be the number of (e.g. relative timing) parameters distinguished; thus the moderately complex language Warumungu (four subcategories) with two contrasting relative timing values would be classified as more complex than Yir Yoront, with four AM subcategories all expressing Prior Motion, and Warluwarra (two subcategories), with a contrast of Prior and Concurrent, would be more complex than Wangka-Yutyuru (also two subcategories), with two Concurrent markers.[128]

Table 20: Number of languages with Moving Argument and Relative Time parameters.

	Very complex D	Complex C	Binary B	Unitary A	Total
% of lgs	19.5%	12.2%	29.3%	39%	100%
No. of lgs	8	5	12	16	41
P(NSBJ)	6	0	0	0	6
P	8	4	6	0	18
C	8	3	6	13	30
S	7	2	0	1	10
P+S	1[130]	0	0	0	1
P/C	0	0	2	2	4
P/C/S	0	1	0	0	1

---

125 The figures cited in this section include Arabana and Wangkangurru as two languages and include data from Anmatyerr and Western Arrernte, which are not given in Table 16 (see tables in §3.3).
126 Cf. §1.3 for figures on the number of languages and subgroups.
127 I include Kuyani, for which only four are attested, on the grounds that it is so incompletely documented; but it is very close genetically to Adnyamathanha and geographically adjacent to Arabana and Lower Arrernte.
128 Cf. Ross (this volume: §4.4) on possible alternative ways of measuring complexity of AM systems.
129 It is possible that close study, with an awareness of this potential subcategory, could reveal further instances of P+S.

Generalisations can be made concerning parameters that are signalled (Tables 16–19). It is useful to count the semantic distinctions according to the complexity of the systems. Table 20 indicates the number of languages manifesting the Moving Argument and Relative Timing parameters. Only very complex systems indicate a moving argument other than the subject – in fact, only (and all) the Arandic languages, but not Adnyamathanha.[130] And the only motion involving a non-subject is the prior motion of arrival at the location of the main event. With respect to Relative Timing, Prior plus Subsequent is clearly attested only in Kaytetye; it is possible, however, that closer study might find it to be present in other Arandic languages or elsewhere. The other three temporal relations (of subjects) are almost equally frequent (in terms of languages) in very complex and moderately complex systems, as are Prior and Concurrent in binary systems. Concurrent is vastly most favoured in unitary systems, and Subsequent is totally absent from all simple systems except Yalarnnga, where VEN derives from a directional marker (see §7.2). The relative number and percentage of languages (of the 41) manifesting each Relative Timing (of subject) value is: C 30 (73.2%), P 18 (43.9%), S 10 (24.4%). The Prior figure is increased to 23 (56%) if we include the five languages that have polysemous markers of P/C and P/C/S. Our findings with respect to the frequency of P and C thus do not match the hierarchy P > C > S found by Guillaume (2016: 40) as a "robust statistical tendency" for western Amazonian languages. The Concurrent Motion figure in the Pama-Nyungan languages, however, is primarily due to the predominance of C in languages with a single AM marker. If we omit these (the A languages in Table 19), the figures for P and C in the remaining 25 languages have P 18 (72%) slightly exceeding C 17 (68%).[131]

Generalisations can also be made concerning the parameter of Path/Direction: see Table 21. In unitary systems the sole path is almost always AND, i.e. movement without a specific direction. The only exception is Yalarnnga, where VEN derives from a directional marker (fuller documentation might have revealed the presence of a contrasting IT marker). AND is also the most prevalent path in binary systems, but three of the 11 B languages manifest a deictic VEN vs. IT contrast. One language, Warlpiri, contrasts AND with RET, but the RET marker has been borrowed from neighbouring Arandic languages (see §6.4.1). All five of the moderately complex languages have a marker of AND, while VEN, IT, and RET paths are each signalled in three languages. In the very complex systems of the Arandic and Thura-Yura

---
130 This accords with Guillaume's (2016: 34) implicational scale that movement of a non-subject (typically object) implies movement of a subject and the existence of a complex AM system. Cf. Ross (this volume: §4.3) for further findings on non-subjects as moving arguments.
131 Cf. Ross (this volume: §3.4) for qualifications to the temporal relation hierarchy based on his worldwide sample.

languages: AND occurs in all the languages, RET in all six Arandic languages, and ARRIVE (of non-subject) in five Arandic languages (not securely documented in Anmatyerr), UP and DOWN in all five Aranda (i.e. non-Kaytetye) languages, VEN in five languages (not documented as AM in Kuyani, Lower Arrernte,[132] or Alyawarr), and an IT marker contrasting with VEN only in Adnyamathanha and Kaytetye.

Table 21: Path/Direction in Pama-Nyungan languages.

	Very complex D/8	Complex C/5	Binary B /12	Unitary A/16	Total/41
AND	8	5	9	15	35
VEN	5	3	3	1	11
IT	2	3	3	0	7
RET	6	3	1	0	9
ARRIVE	5	0	0	0	5
UP	5	0	0	0	5
DOWN	5	0	0	0	5

Contrasts of Speed are largely limited to complex systems; Kuuk Thaayorre, in a binary system, however, has Prior forms based on both the verbs 'go' and 'run', although without a clear semantic contrast in the AM forms (§6.1.3). In the very complex systems, QUICK combines with Prior in Kaytetye and Alyawarr (GO.QUICK&DO) and Adnyamathanha (GO.QUICK&DO, COME.QUICK&DO), with Subsequent in Alyawarr (DO&GO.QUICK), EC and W Arrernte (DO&GO.QUICK, DO&RETURN.QUICK), and with Concurrent in EC and W Arrernte (DO.DOWNWARDS.QUICK). Arabana-Wangkangurru has a marker of slow Concurrent motion (§5.1).

Aspectual contrasts occur only within Concurrent Motion. I suggest that most of these can be interpreted in terms of a contrast between a punctual (or momentary or semelfactive) and a continuous relation of the EVENT to the MOTION, and that where there is a three-way contrast, the continuous value marks coextension of EVENT with MOTION and the middle value is unmarked with respect to both marked values. According to my analysis, a three-way contrast is attested in Adnyamathanha, Kuyani, Kaytetye, and possibly Arabana and Wangkangurru (if the "slow" value is treated as Aspectual rather than Speed). A two-way contrast occurs in all the Aranda (non-Kaytetye Arandic) languages, but also in some Karnic languages with binary AM systems: Wangka-Yutyuru, Yandruwandha, Ngamini, Diyari. This amounts to a total of 14 (34%) of the 41 languages. Genetically, however, these are in only three subgroups: Arandic, Thura-Yura, and Karnic, all of which are located in central Aus-

---

132 But -antye occurs as a Ventive directional marker.

tralia. A generalisation that results is that an aspectual contrast occurs most readily in complex, especially very complex AM systems, but is possible also in a simple (necessarily binary) system, and may result from regional influences.

9.3 Generalisations regarding geographical and genetic distribution

It is clear that the most complex systems are to be found in a relatively small area in the centre of the continent, comprising all languages of the Arandic subgroup plus Adnyamathanha and Kuyani of the Thura-Yura subgroup (see the map, Figure 2, in the Appendix). Systems of moderate complexity are found in two languages adjacent to these most complex systems, Arabana-Wangkangurru between Arandic and Thura-Yura and Warumungu to the north of Arandic, as well as Warlmanpa adjacent to Warumungu. This concentration of AM systems in central Australia has been commented on before (Tunbridge 1988; Austin 1989; Wilkins 1991; Dixon 2002). Dixon (2002: 202) mentioned that AM occurs in a number of further subgroups surrounding this core area, without specifying particular languages,[133] and claimed that, apart from these, AM occurs only in the distant northeastern Jabugay and Yidiny. Our study has found, however, that AM occurs in a wide scattering of languages that are not contiguous to the core: we have added Nyangumarta (Marrngu) in the west, Wirangu in the southwest,[134] further Paman languages in the northeast (Yir-Yoront and Kuuk Thaayorre), and languages from the Maric,[135] Central New South Wales and Yuin subgroups in eastern Australia. It is thus clear that contact cannot have been the sole factor responsible for the distribution of AM.

9.4 Generalisations regarding diachronic sources

The most recurrent source construction of AM markers is a non-finite subordinate verb followed by a verb of motion. In a number of languages the ultimate source of the non-finite verb marker is the Proto Pama-Nyungan nominalisation suffix *-ntha (for which see Evans 1988: 94), which is reflected as -ntya in languages without a laminal contrast between th and ty and which may be simpli-

---

[133] His inclusion of group W (Kalkatungic) on the basis of two (purely) directional suffixes in Kalkatungu needs to be amended; however, its neighbour Yalarnnga does show AM use of its directional, as noted in §7.2.
[134] This language was not included by Dixon in the Thura-Yura subgroup.
[135] Austin (1989: 68) included (Maric) Margany and Gunya among the languages expressing AM.

fied by the loss of the nasal or the stop or by lenition of the stop to *y*. Instances in our data are the *tye* or *ye* element of Arandic *-(t)y.alpe*, *-nji* in Warumungu and Warlpiri, *-nh* in Kuuk Thaayorre – all of which mark prior motion – and in Warluwarra, Bidyara, Nyangumarta, and possibly Adnyamathanha concurrent motion forms *-ndhena* and *-ndhela*. An alternative non-finite verbal form is used especially in concurrent motion forms (e.g. Arrernte *-rl.ape*, Kaytetye *-rr.ape*), with possible extension to subsequent motion (e.g. Arrernte *-rl.alpe*, Kaytetye *-rr.alpe*). The Western Desert participial *-la/-rra/-ra* used with *ya- 'go' in the distributive construction mentioned in §8 is another example. Some of the Karnic languages also use a nominalised verb form in constructions with motion verbs (§5.1, 6.3.4–5, 8).

In these formations the mechanism of change would appear to involve grammaticalisation: a biclausal structure with the motion verb in the main clause, with a favouring of the non-finite clause being positioned directly before the motion verb, is reanalysed as a single clause, with the motion verb downgraded to an auxiliary verb and the erstwhile subordinate verb now determining the argument structure of the unified clause, the motion auxiliary reduced phonologically (sometimes in a truncated form) to a member of a compound phonological verbal word, and possibly reanalysed as a mere suffix; for this diachronic scenario see Austin (1989: 65); Wilkins (1991: 240); Simpson (2001: 186–188); Koch (2019: 302–306). AM forms with this history may display different degrees of grammaticalisation, which partly accounts for the ambiguities in their synchronic analysis.

Another source of AM markers is the direct compounding of a motion verb stem with another verb stem. This is seen in the Western Desert *-kati* forms, where *kati-* is the (transitive) motion verb 'carry' (§7.7). Direct compounding of verb stems is also present among the Karnic languages, although here some of the motion verbs have not (yet) developed into grammatical AM markers. In some cases, however, these Verb-Verb compounds may result from the deletion of an intervening non-finite suffix (Austin 1989, see also §8).

A different kind of source is found where AM markers derive from directional clitics; examples in our data are Yalarnnga (§7.2) and Mudburra (§6.4.2 and Osgarby this volume).

Another consideration that should not be overlooked is that, once an (especially complex) AM system has been established, it is liable to be elaborated by the creation of further forms for potential cells in the paradigm – based on analogies within the system. The new forms may come from the combination of existing AM forms in the system, or from the "ad hoc copying" of motion verb roots (Guillaume 2013: 146–147), for example. Wilkins (1991: 245–250) suggests a number of possible sources for AM markers other than grammaticalisation from syntactic structures.

Semantic shift may affect some forms. For example, Kaytetye -*yernalpe* has apparently shifted from *'return hither and do' to 'do while coming', and a reduplicated aspectual "attenuative" marker ('do a bit of') has in Kaytetye entered the AM system and provided an aspect-like 'do once while going' value within Concurrent Motion (§2.2.3 and Koch 2020). On the other hand, a Concurrent Motion form can be extended to also encode Aspect, in addition to its AM meanings (Arrernte -*rlape* 'do while going' > 'continuous while in motion' (§3.2–3).[136]

Finally, contact may be the source of AM markers. Thus Warlpiri has borrowed -*yalpi* from Kaytetye -*yalpe* RETURN&DO and added it to its infinitive to create its own AM form -*njiyalpi* of the same meaning (§6.4.1). The Wirangu AM form -*rn.gad(i)* is also presumed to be the result of direct borrowing of the Western Desert -*kati* construction (§7.8). Not only direct borrowing but imitation of a neighbouring language's subcategory, and perhaps even calquing its formation, have long been suspected to be responsible for the origin of some AM subcategories (Tunbridge 1988: 281; Austin 1989: 68; Wilkins 1991: 241; Dixon 2002: 202), although specific forms or subcategories have rarely been mentioned. Osgarby (this volume, cf. §6.4.2) shows how Mudburra has adapted its inherited directional suffixes (or enclitics) to the marking of AM, under the influence of neighbouring languages of north-central Australia.

9.5 Conclusions

AM as a grammatical category may include a number of internal semantic parameters, which resemble notions expressed elsewhere in the grammar. The grammatical role of subject is involved as the moving entity (with the exception of one subcategory), even though in all these languages the case system marks transitive subject (A) with a different marking from that of intransitive subject (S), by Ergative vs. Nominative respectively. Relative Time is indicated, but this differs from Tense in that it relates the component subevents to one another, while Tense relates a verb to the speech situation, and the whole EVENT+MOTION complex may be further inflected for Tense. Direction of motion is inherent in some subcategories, even though the language may have separate markers of (especially deictic) direction as well, and these may co-occur with some AM subcategories, especially those marking movement in a nonspecific direction. Aspect-like distinctions may occur within AM, even though the whole EVENT+MOTION complex

---

[136] Rose (2015: 137–139) discusses the extension of AM markers to aspect values.

may be further inflected for Aspect.[137] The Aspectual distinctions within AM, like clausal Aspect, refer to the temporal contour, but not that of the verbal event but of the relationship (degree of overlap) between the contour of the EVENT relative to the MOTION. Unlike pure Aspect, moreover, Aspectual Realisation within AM involves contours of space as much as of time, specifying the extent to which the EVENT overlaps with the MOTION path both temporally and spatially. Finally, the Speed dimension reflects an area of semantics that is otherwise generally expressed lexically.

Geographically, complex systems cluster in the centre of the continent but simple AM systems are widely distributed across other parts of the continent where Pama-Nyungan languages were spoken.

Diachronically, many AM markers derive from grammaticalised auxiliary verb constructions involving a non-finite verb and an inflected motion verb. Two such sources appear to be 'go to VERB', that is a Motion with Purpose construction, which gets to be reanalysed as a Prior Motion construction, and a 'VERB while going along' construction, which can turn into a Concurrent Motion construction. Most complex systems include forms with both kinds of source constructions. One might hypothesise that complex systems arise when both kinds of AM (Prior and Concurrent) coexist. It also seems possible that once complex systems arise they are liable to expand by the creation of further terms, taken from various sources, to fill out potential cells implied by the parameters in the system, augmented by semantic change and possibly the imitation of forms in neighbouring languages (cf. Wilkins 1991: 249–250; Guillaume (2013: 146–147).

Finally, it is worth remembering the cultural context in which Pama-Nyungan languages developed AM systems. Wilkins (1991: 212–218) noted the cultural preoccupation, reflected in discourse patterns of Aboriginal people, especially in the arid interior of Australia, with locating events in space. This is not surprising, given that both daily hunting and seasonal migration for food and other resources were constant facts of life. I might add that the daily rhythm of outward movement from and return to camp may partly be responsible for the frequency of 'return' as one of the directional subcategories of AM in Australian languages.

---

[137] Thus it should be possible to express as a repeated or habitual event a situation that involves a single sub-event correlated with a motion co-event such as: 'During the period of time when he used to eat his breakfast (at some point) on his way to work, he would always arrive late in the office.'

Abbreviations

(Standard Leipzig glosses are used, plus the following):

ALL.ALONG	do all the way along	LIG	ligative
ALONG	do while going along	MOT	motive
AND	andative	MOV	moving
APPREH	apprehensive	NARR	narrative
AR	arrive	NSBJ.ARRIVE	do when non-subject arrives
CHAR	characteristic	OBLG	obligative
COLL	collective	ONCE.ALONG	do once on the way
COMING	do while coming	PERL	perlative
CONJ	conjunctive	POT	potential
CONT/CTS	continuous	PROL	prolative
CONV	do while being conveyed	PROP	proprietive
DN	downwards	PUNC	punctual
DS/DSBJ	different subject	RAMBL	ramblitive
EMPH	emphatic	RDP	reduplicant
EXCLAM	exclamation	RECUR	recurrently
HAB	habitual	RET	return
HIST	historic	SS/SSBJ	same subject
HITH	hither	TRN	transitory
IMM	immediate	TWD	toward
IMPERF	imperfect	UN	unmarked or unspecified
INCEP	inceptive	UNIT	unit action
INTM	intermittent	VEN	ventive.
IT	itive		

Acknowledgements: I gratefully acknowledge the many useful comments on earlier versions of this paper by Antoine Guillaume, Pattie Epps, and Jean-Christophe Verstraete, I thank fellow Arandicists David Wilkins, Myfany Turpin and David Moore for insights into Arandic AM. I thank Billy McConvell for producing the map.

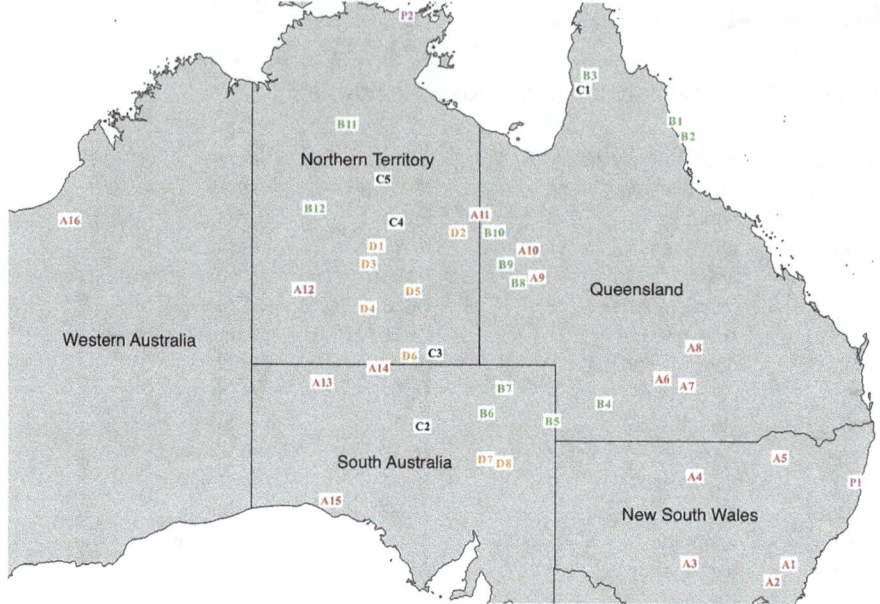

Figure 2: Distribution of Pama-Nyungan AM systems.

Appendix

The map (Figure 2) shows the location of Pama-Nyungan languages with AM markers, categorised by complexity (see §9.1 and Tables 16–19), with the addition of Dhanggati (P1) and Djinang (P2) as representative of precursor constructions. The languages are designated by alphanumeric codes, which are explained in Table 22.

Table 22: Key to Figure 2 map.

Adnyamathanha	D8	Ngunawal	A2
Alyawarr	D2	Nyangumarta	A16
Anmatyerr	D3	Pintupi	A12
Arabana	C2	Pitjantjatjara	A13
Bidyara	A8	Pitta-Pitta	A9
Arrernte, EC	D5	Wakaya	A11
Arrernte, Lower	D6	Wangkangurru	C3
Arrernte, Western	D4	Wangka-Yutyuru	B8

Table 22 (continued)

Bularnu	B10	Wangkumara	B4
Dhanggati	P1	Warlmanpa	C5
Diyari	B6	Warlpiri	B12
Djinang	P2	Warluwarra	B9
Gundungurra	A1	Warumungu	C4
Gunya	A7	Wiradjuri	A3
Jabugay	B1	Wirangu	A15
Kaytetye	D1	Yalarnnga	A10
Kuuk Thaayorre	B3	Yandruwandha	B5
Kuyani	D7	Yankunytjatjara	A14
Margany	A6	Yidiny	B2
Mudburra	B11	Yir Yoront	C1
Ngamini	B7	Yuwaalaraay	A5
Ngiyambaa	A4		

References

Agnew, Brigitte. 2020. *The core of Mangarla grammar*. Melbourne: University of Melbourne PhD dissertation. http://hdl.handle.net/11343/241927
Alpher, Barry. 1973. *Son of ergative: The Yir Yoront language of northeast Australia*. Ithaca, N.Y.: Cornell University dissertation.
Alpher, Barry. 1991. *Yir-Yoront lexicon: Sketch and dictionary of an Australian language* (Trends in Linguistics, Documentation 6) Berlin: Mouton de Gruyter.
Austin, Peter. 1981. *A grammar of Diyari, South Australia*. Cambridge: Cambridge University Press.
Austin, Peter. 1989. Verb compounding in Central Australian languages. *La Trobe Working Papers in Linguistics* no. 2. 43–71.
Belkadi, Aïcha. 2015. Associated motion with deictic directionals: A comparative overview. *SOAS Working Papers in Linguistics* 17. 49–76.
Belkadi, Aïcha. This volume, chapter 5. Deictic directionality as associated motion: Motion, complex events and event integration in African languages.
Besold, Jutta. 2004. *Sketch grammar of Gandangara (Gundungurra): A 'sleeping' language of South Eastern New South Wales*. Bundoora, Victoria: La Trobe University BA(Hons) thesis.
Besold, Jutta. 2013. *Language recovery of the New South Wales South Coast Aboriginal languages*. Canberra: Australian National University dissertation.
Black, Paul. 2004. The failure of the evidence of shared innovations in Cape York Peninsula. In Claire Bowern & Harold Koch (eds.), *Australian languages: Classification and the comparative method*, 241–267. Amsterdam & Philadelphia: John Benjamins.

Blake, Barry J. 1979a. *A Kalkatungu grammar*. (Pacific Linguistics B-57) Canberra: Australian National University.
Blake, Barry J. 1979b. Pitta-Pitta. In R. M. W. Dixon & Barry J. Blake (eds.), *Handbook of Australian languages* Vol. 1, 182–242. Canberra: Australian National University Press.
Blake, Barry J., & J. G. Breen. 1971. *The Pitta-Pitta dialects*. (Linguistic Communications 4) Melbourne: Monash University.
Blevins, Juliette. 2001. *Nhanda: An Aboriginal language of Western Australia*. (Oceanic Linguistics Special Publication 30) Honolulu: University of Hawai'i Press.
Bloomfield, Leonard. 1933. *Language*. London: George, Allen & Unwin.
Bouckaert, Remco R., Claire Bowern & Quentin D. Atkinson. 2018. The origin and expansion of Pama-Nyungan languages across Australia. *Nature Ecology and Evolution*. https://www.nature.com/articles/s41559-018-0489-3
Bowern, Claire, & Quentin D. Atkinson, 2012. Computational phylogenetics and the internal structure of Pama-Nyungan. *Language* 88. 817–845.
Breen, J. G. 1971. *A desciption of the Warluwara language*. Clayton, Victoria: Monash University MA thesis.
Breen, J. G. 1973. *Bidyara and Gungabula grammar and vocabulary*. (Linguistic Communications 8) Melbourne: Monash University.
Breen, John Gavan. 1974. *Wagaya grammar*. Unpublished manuscript (MS122), Australian Institute of Aboriginal and Torres Strait Islander Studies, Canberra.
Breen, J. G. 1976a. Ngamini, and a note of Midhaga. In R. M. W. Dixon (ed.), *Grammatical categories in Australian languages*, 745–750. Canberra: Australian Institute of Aboriginal Studies.
Breen, J. G. 1976b. Warluwara and Bularnu. In R. M. W. Dixon (ed.), *Grammatical categories in Australian languages*, 250–257, 331–335, 586–590. Canberra: Australian Institute of Aboriginal Studies.
Breen, J. G. 1976c. Yandruwandha. In R. M. W. Dixon (ed.), *Grammatical categories in Australian languages*, 750–756. Canberra: Australian Institute of Aboriginal Studies.
Breen, Gavan. 1980. *Bularnu phonology and grammar: Preliminary [draft] with semantic vocabulary*. Unpublished manuscript (MS 1457), Australian Institute of Aboriginal and Torres Strait Islander Studies, Canberra.
Breen, J. G. 1981a. Margany and Gunya. In R. M. W. Dixon & Barry J. Blake (eds), *Handbook of Australian languages* Vol. 2, 274–393. Canberra: Australian National University Press.
Breen, J. G. 1981b. Wangkumara. Unpublished manuscipt. Canberra: Australian Institute of Aboriginal and Torres Strait Islander Studies.
Breen, Gavan. 2000. *Introductory dictionary of Western Arrernte*. Alice Springs: IAD Press.
Breen, Gavan. 2002. *[Lower Arrernte dictionary]*. Unpublished manuscript.
Breen, Gavan. 2004a. Evolution of the verb conjugations in the Ngarna languages. In Claire Bowern & Harold Koch (eds.), *Australian languages: Classification and the comparative method*, 223–240. Amsterdam & Philadelphia: John Benjamins.
Breen, Gavan. 2004b. *Innamincka talk: A grmmar of the Innamincka dialect of Yandruwandha with notes on other dialects*. (Pacific Linguistics 558) Canberra: Australian National University.
Breen, Gavan & Barry J. Blake. 2007. *The grammar of Yalarnnga: A language of western Queensland*. (Pacific Linguistics 584) Canberra: Australian National University.
Comrie, Bernard. 1976. *Aspect*. Cambridge: Cambridge University Press.
Dixon, R. M. W. 1977. *A grammar of Yidiny*. Cambridge: Cambridge University Press.

Dixon, R. M. W. 1991. *Words of our country. Stories, place names and vocabulary in Yidiny, the Aboriginal language of the Cairns-Yarrabah region*. St. Lucia, Qld: University of Queensland Press.

Dixon, R. M. W. 2002. *The Australian languages: Their nature and development*. Cambridge: Cambridge University Press.

Donaldson, Tamsin. 1980. *Ngiyambaa, the language of the Wangaabuwan*. Cambridge: Cambridge University Press.

Dryer, Matthew S. This volume, chapter 4. Associated motion and directionals: Where they overlap.

Eckert, Paul & Joyce Hudson. 1988. *Wangka Wiru: A handbook for the Pitjantjatjara learner*. Underdale, S.A.: University of South Australia.

Evans, Nicholas. 1988. Arguments for Pama-Nyungan as a genetic subgroup, with particular reference to initial laminalization. In Nicholas Evans & Steve Johnson (eds.), *Aboriginal Linguistics 1*. 91–110. Armidale, NSW: Department of Linguistics, University of New England.

Evans, Nicholas. 2005. Australian languages reconsidered: A review of Dixon (2002). *Oceanic Linguistics* 44. 242–286.

Fleck, David W. 2003. *A grammar of Matses*. Houston, Texas: Rice University dissertation. https://scholarship.rice.edu/handle/1911/18526

Gaby, Alice R. 2017. *A grammar of Kuuk Thaayorre*. (Mouton Grammar Library 74) Berlin & New York: de Gruyter Mouton.

Giacon, John. 2017. *Yaluu: A recovery grammar of Yuwaalaraay and Gamilaraay: A description of two New South Wales languages based on 160 years of records*. (A-PL 36). Canberra: Asia-Pacific Linguistics, Australian National University. http://hdl.handle.net/1885/132639.

Goddard, Cliff. 1985. *A grammar of Yankunytjatjara*. Alice Springs, N.T.: Institute for Aboriginal Development.

Grant, Stan & John Rudder. 2010. *A new Wiradjuri dictionary: English to Wiradjuri, Wiradjuri to English, categories of things, and reference tables*. [Canberra]: Restoration House.

Green, Jenny. 2010. *Central & Eastern Anmatyerr to English dictionary*. Alice Springs: IAD Press.

Guillaume, Antoine. 2013. Reconstructing the category of "Associated Motion" in Tacanan languages (Amazonian Bolivia and Peru). In Ritsuko Kikusawa & Lawrence A. Reid (eds.), *Historical Linguistics 2011: Selected papers from the 20th International Conference on Historical Linguistics, Osaka, 25–30 July 2011*, 129–151. Amsterdam: John Benjamins.

Guillaume, Antoine. 2016. Associated motion in South America: Typological and areal perspectives. *Linguistic Typology* 20 (1). 81–177.

Hale, Kenneth. 1962. Internal relationships in Arandic of Central Australia. In A. Capell, *Some linguistic types in Australia (Handbook of Australian Languages, Part 2)*, 171–183. Sydney: University of Sydney.

Hale, Kenneth. 1976a. Dja:bugay. In R. M. W. Dixon (ed.), *Grammatical categories in Australian languages*, 321–326. Canberra: Australian Institute of Aboriginal Studies.

Hale, Kenneth. 1976b. Tya:pukay (Djaabugay). In Peter Sutton (ed.), *Languages of Cape York*, 236–242. Canberra: Australian Institute of Aboriginal Studies.

Hansen, K. C., & L. E. Hansen. 1975. *The core of Pintupi grammar*. Alice Springs, N.T.: Institute for Aborginal Development.

Henderson, John. 2013 [1997]. *Topics in Eastern and Central Arrernte*. (Outstanding Grammars from Australia 12) Muenchen: Lincom Europa.

Henderson, John. 2018. Assessing Carl Strehlow's dictionary as linguistic description: Present value and future potential. In Carl Strehlow, *Carl Strehlow's 1909 comparative heritage dictionary: An Aranda, German, Loritja and Dieri to English dictionary with introductory essays*, Translated and edited by Anna Kenny, 63–99. Canberra: ANU Press.

Henderson, John & Veronica Dobson (eds.). 1994. *Eastern and Central Arrernte to English dictionary*. Alice Springs N.T.: Institute for Aboriginal Development.

Hercus, Luise A. 1994. *A grammar of the Arabana-Wangkangurru language of the Lake Eyre Basin, South Australia*. (Pacific Linguistics C-128) Canberra: Australian National University.

Hercus, Luise A. 1999. *A grammar of the Wirangu language from the west coast of South Australia*. (Pacific Linguistiics C-150) Canberra: Australian National University.

Hercus, Luise A. n.d. *Kuyani list*. Electronic file. Australian National University, Canberra.

Hercus, Luise A., Mick McLean Irinyili, Colin Macdonald & Grace Koch. 2013. *The Fire history*. Canberra: Luise Hercus.

Humphris, Kathryn Celeste. 2017. *A morphosyntactic sketch of Lower Arrernte, Central Australia*. Brisbane: University of Queensland BA(Hons) thesis.

Kempe, H. 1891. A grammar and vocabulary of the language spoken by the Aborigines of the Macdonnell Ranges, South Australia. *Transactions of the Royal Society of South Australia* 14 (1). 1–54.

Koch, Harold. 1984. The category of 'associated motion' in Kaytej. *Language in Central Australia* no. 1. 23–34.

Koch, Harold. 2004. The Arandic subgroup of Australian languages. In Claire Bowern & Harold Koch (eds.), *Australian languages: Classification and the comparative method*. 127–150. Amsterdam & Philadelphia: John Benjamins.

Koch, Harold. 2014. Historical relations among the Australian languages: Genetic classification and contact-based diffusion. In Harold Koch & Rachel Nordlinger (eds.), *The languages and linguistics of Australia: A comprehensive guide*, 23–89. Berlin: de Gruyter Mouton.

Koch, Harold. 2015. Morphological reconstruction. In Claire Bowern & Bethwyn Evans (eds.), *The Routledge handbook of historical linguistics*, 286–307. (Routledge Handbooks in Linguistics) London: Routledge.

Koch, Harold. 2019. Morphosyntactic reanalysis in Australian languages: Three studies. In Lars Heltoft, Iván Igartua, Brian D. Joseph, Kirsten Jeppesen Kragh & Lene Schøsler (eds.), *Perspectives on language structure and language change: Studies in honour of Henning Andersen*, 295–309. Amsterdam & Philadelphia: John Benjamins.

Koch, Harold. 2020. Development of aspect markers in Arandic languages, with notes on Associated Motion. *Journal of Historical Linguistics* 10 (2): 209–250.

Koch, Harold. n.d. *Koch Kaytetye texts*. Electronic ms. Canberra, Australian National University.

Koch, Harold & Myfany Turpin. In preparation. *Kaytetye Grammar*.

Levinson, Stephen C. & David P. Wilkins, 2006. Patterns in the data: Towards a semantic typology of spatial description. In Stephen C. Levinson & David P. Wilkins (eds.), *Grammars of space: Explorations in cognitive diversity*, 512–552. Cambridge: Cambridge University Press.

Lissarrague, Amanda. 2007. *Dhanggati grammar and dictionary with Dhanggati stories*. Nambucca Heads, NSW: Muurrbay Aboriginal Language and Culture Cooperative.

Mathews, R. H. 1902. Languages of some native tribes of Queensland, New South Wales and Victoria. *Journal and Proceedings of the Royal Society of New South Wales* 36. 135–190.

Mathews, R. H. 1904. The Wiradyuri and other languages of New South Wales. *The Journal of the Anthropological Institute of Great Britain and Ireland* 34. 284–305.

Miceli, Luisa. 2015. Pama-Nyungan. In Claire Bowern & Bethwyn Evans (eds.), *The Routledge handbook of historical linguistics*, 704–725. London: Routledge.
Moore, David. 2012. *Alyawarr verb morphology*. Perth: University of Western Australia MA thesis.
Nash, David. 1982. Warlpiri verb roots and preverbs. In S. Swartz (ed.), *Papers in Warlpiri grammar: In memory of Lothar Jagst*, 165–216. Darwin: Summer Institute of Linguistics Australian Aborigines Branch.
Nash, David. 1986. *Topics in Warlpiri grammar*. (Outstanding Dissertations in Linguistics) New York & London: Garland.
Nordlinger, Rachel. 2001. Wambaya in motion. In Jane Simpson, David Nash, Mary Laughren, Peter Austin & Barry Alpher (eds.), *Forty years on: Ken Hale and Australian languages*, 401–413. (Pacific Linguistics 512) Canberra: Australian National University.
Osgarby, David. This volume, chapter 8. Mudburra associated motion in an areal perspective.
Pakendorf, Brigitte & Natalia Stoynova. This volume, chapter 22. Associated motion in Tungusic languages: A case of mixed argument structure.
Panther, Forrest & Mark Harvey. 2020. Associated Path in Kaytetye. *Australian Journal of Linguistics* 40 (1). 74–105. https://www.tandfonline.com/doi/full/10.1080/07268602.2019.1703644
Patz, Elisabeth. 1991. Djabugay. In R. M. W. Dixon & Barry J. Blake (eds.), *Handbook of Australian languages* Vol. 4: *The Aboriginal language of Melbourne and other grammatical sketches*, 245–347. Melbourne: Oxford University Press.
Rose, Françoise. 2015. Associated motion in Mojeño Trinitario: Some typological considerations. *Folia Linguistica* 49 (1). 117–158.
Ross, Daniel. This volume, chapter 2. A cross-linguistic survey of Associated Motion and directionals.
Schebeck, Bernhard. 1974. *Texts on the social system of the Atynyamaṯaṉa people with grammatical notes*. (Pacific Linguistics D-21) Canberra: Australian National University.
Sharp, Janet Catherine. 2004. *Nyangumarta: A language of the Pilbara region of Western Australia*. (Pacific Linguistics 556) Canberra: Australian National University.
Simpson, Jane. 1998. Warumungu (Australian – Pama-Nyungan). In Andrew Spencer & Arnold M. Zwicky (eds.), *The handbook of morphology*, 707–736. Oxford: Blackwell.
Simpson, Jane. 2001. Preferred word order and the grammaticalization of Associated Path. In Miriam Butt & Tracy Holloway King (eds.), *Time over matter: Diachronic perspectives on morphosyntax*, 173–208. Stanford: Centre for the Study of Language and Information.
Simpson, Jane. 2002. *A learner's guide to Warumungu*. Alice Springs: IAD Press.
Simpson, Jane & Luise Hercus. 2004. Thura-Yura as a subgroup. In Claire Bowern & Harold Koch (eds.), *Australian languages: Classification and the comparative method*, 179–206. Amsterdam & Philadelphia: John Benjamins.
Stockigt, Clara. 2016. *Pama-Nyungan morphosyntax: Lineages of early description*. Adelaide, South Australia: University of Adelaide dissertation.
Strehlow, Carl. 2018 [1909]. *Carl Strehlow's 1909 comparative heritage dictionary: An Aranda, German, Loritja and Dieri to English dictionary with introductory essays*. Translated and edited by Anna Kenny. (Monographs in Anthropology Series) Canberra: ANU Press.
Strehlow, T. G. H. 1944. *Aranda phonetics and grammar*. (Oceania Monographs 7) Sydney: Australian National Research Council.
Tunbridge, Dorothy. 1988. Affixes of motion and direction in Adnyamathanha. In Peter Austin (eds.), *Complex sentence constructions in Australian languages*, 267–283. Amsterdam & Philadelphia: John Benjamins.

Turpin, Myfany & Alison Ross. 2012. *Kaytetye to English dictionary*. Alice Springs: IAD Press.
Vuillermet, Marine. This volume, chapter 6. A visual stimulus for eliciting associated motion.
Waters, Bruce E. 1989. *Djinang and Djinpa: A grammatical and historical perspective*. (Pacific Linguistics C-114) Canberra: Australian National University.
Wilkins, David P. 1989. *Mparntwe Arrernte: Studies in the structure and semantics of grammar*. Canberra: Australian National University dissertation.
Wilkins, David P. 1991. The semantics, pragmatics and diachronic development of 'associated motion' in Mparntwe Arrernte. *Buffalo Papers in Linguistics* 91 (1). 207–257.
Wilkins, David P. 2006. Towards an Arrernte grammar of space. In Stephen C. Levinson & David P. Wilkins (eds.), *Grammars of space: Explorations in cognitive diversity*, 24–62. Cambridge: Cambridge University Press.
Williams, Corinne. 1980. *A grammar of Yuwaalaraay*. (Pacific Linguistics B-74) Canberra: Australian National University.
Yallop, Colin. 1977. *Alyawarra: An Aboriginal language of central Australia*. Canberra: Australian Institute of Aboriginal Studies.

David Osgarby
8 Mudburra associated motion in an areal perspective

Abstract: Associated motion (AM) in Mudburra, an Australian language from the Pama-Nyungan family, is expressed by means of verbal suffixes distinguishing two paths of motion: away from versus towards the deictic centre. As such Mudburra AM is simple in terms of "degree of elaboration", especially in comparison to the highly complex systems of Arandic AM found to its south. This chapter describes the forms, functions and distribution of AM markers in Mudburra. The Mudburra AM system makes similar contrasts to that of the neighbouring non-Pama-Nyungan language Wambaya (Ngurlun, Mirndi), despite the fact that they possess entirely distinct grammatical structures. Morphology cognate to Mudburra AM suffixes functions as deictic directionals in related languages, and morphemes cognate with Wambaya AM morphemes function as verbs in related languages. Mudburra and Wambaya have thus independently converged in their repurposing of these morphemes as markers of AM: a situation that makes the Northern Central Australia region of particular interest to the study of the diachronic development of AM systems.

Keywords: Mudburra; Ngumpin-Yapa languages; Pama-Nyungan languages; Australian languages; associated motion; language description; morphosyntax; historical linguistics.

1 Introduction

Mudburra is a language spoken by the Mudburra people of the Barkly Tableland and Victoria River District of the Northern Territory of Australia. Mudburra exhibits verbal inflections that function to encode a motion event additional to the event depicted by the lexical verb. These 'associated motion' (AM) inflections make a two-way distinction between motion away from the deictic centre, as in (1), and motion towards the deictic centre, as in (2).[1]

---

[1] The terms 'away' and 'towards' used here (following Nordlinger 1998: 151) are equivalent to the terms 'itive' and 'ventive' respectively, found in other descriptive traditions.

David Osgarby, Australian National University, david.osgarby@anu.edu.au

https://doi.org/10.1515/9783110692099-008

(1) *Ba=rnayinangulu nyang-ku-**rru** yali-ngkurra=rni*[2] *Kulumindini-ngkurra=rni,*
    DECL=1PL.EXCL>3PL see-POT-**AWY** DIST-ALL=RSTR Elliott-ALL=RSTR
    ngayu-walija-li=ma.
    1-PL-ERG=TOP
    'We will go back there to Elliott and see you, all of us.'
    (SD: DOS1-2017_ 029-01: 3641288_3645502)

(2) *Marndaja ba=rnangku nyanga-**nnginyi**.*
    later DECL=1SG>2SG see-**POT.TWD**
    'I will come and see you later.'
    (TN: KHA1-701_29_10_11-01: 856715_858585)

This chapter will first describe the phenomenon of AM in Mudburra, and detail its interactions with other verbal features (§2.1), its exponents (§2.2), the functions that AM morphemes exhibit (§2.3), and the temporal relation of the motion event and the event depicted by the verb (§2.4). It will then compare this to other documented cases of AM in North Central Australian languages, such as the Mirndi language Wambaya (§3.1), and four Pama-Nyungan languages(Warumungu, Warlpiri, Warlmanpa and Wakaya) (§3.2) and consider the development of AM as an areal phenomenon (§3.3). The remainder of this section will introduce the Mudburra language (§1.1) and some key aspects of Mudburra grammar (§1.2).

1.1 Mudburra and its geographical neighbours

Mudburra is a Pama-Nyungan language of the Ngumpin-Yapa subgroup spoken in the Northern Territory of Australia (Osgarby 2018a). There are two main dialects of the language: Eastern Mudburra and Western Mudburra (see Figure 1). Mudburra is critically endangered, with fewer than ten fluent speakers as of 2019; however, many more people have some knowledge of the language.

To the west, south and south-east of Mudburra are other Pama-Nyungan languages (shown in black bold font in Figure 1) such as: the Ngumpin-Yapa languages Bilinarra (Meakins and Nordlinger 2014), Gurindji (McConvell 1996; Meakins et al. 2013), Warlpiri (Nash 1986; Simpson 1991) and Warlmanpa (Nash 1979), the family-level isolate Warumungu (Simpson and Heath 1982; Simpson 1998), and Wakaya (Breen 1974) – to the southeast of Warumungu, not shown

---

[2] While the restrictive clitic *=rni* is homophonous with the towards suffix *-rni*, its distributional and semantic properties are distinct.

8 Mudburra associated motion in an areal perspective — 327

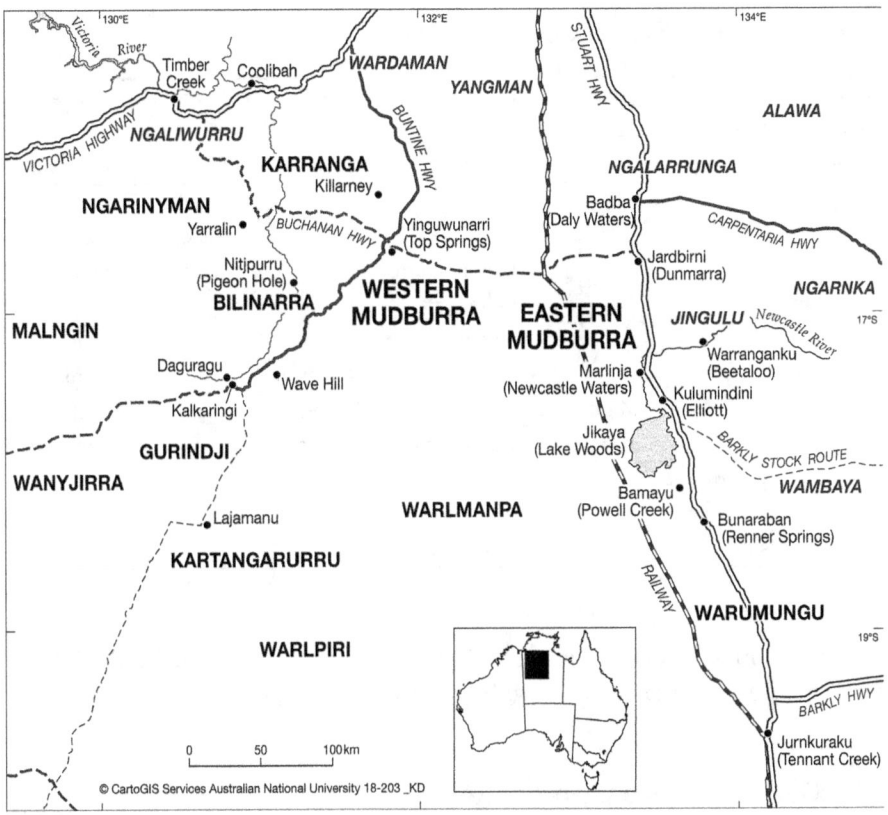

Figure 1: Map showing location of dialects of Mudburra and nearby languages (Non-Pama-Nyungan languages in grey italic font; Pama-Nyungan in black bold font).

in Figure 1. To the east of Mudburra are non-Pama-Nyungan languages (shown in grey italic font in Figure 1) of the Mirndi family, such as Jingulu (Pensalfini 2003), Ngarnka (McQuay 2005; Osgarby 2014) and Wambaya (Nordlinger 1998). In a non-contiguous region to the north-west are more Mirndi languages such as Jaminjung and Ngaliwurru (Schultze-Berndt 2000). Directly north of Mudburra is the non-Pama-Nyungan language Wardaman (Merlan 1994) and the closely related varieties Yangman and Dagoman. The genetic classification of these languages is shown in Table 1.

Mudburra therefore lies on an important typological and genetic boundary between largely dependent-marking suffixing Pama-Nyungan languages, and largely head-marking prefixing non-Pama-Nyungan languages. Borrowing between Mirndi and Ngumpin languages is well documented in the lexical domain (Black 2007; McConvell 2009; Meakins and Pensalfini to appear; Pensalfini and

Table 1: Genetic classification of languages mentioned.

Pama-Nyungan family	Ngumpin-Yapa subgroup	Ngumpin subgroup	Ngarinyman	**Mirndi family**	Yirram subgroup	Nungali
			Bilinarra			Jaminjung
			Malngin			Ngaliwurru
			Gurindji		isolate	Jingulu
			Wanyjirra		Barkly subgroup	Ngarnka
			Kartangarurru			Binbinka
			Karranga			Gudanji
			Mudburra			Wambaya
			inter alia	**Non-Pama-Nyungan isolate**		Wardaman
		Yapa subgroup	Warlpiri			Yangman
			Warlmanpa			Dagoman
	Warluwarric subgroup		Wakaya			
	isolate		*inter alia*			
			Warumungu			

Meakins to appear), and AM may constitute a grammatical domain in which Mudburra has been influenced by neighbouring Mirndi languages.

1.2 Mudburra verbal predicates

Mudburra verbal predicates comprise a verb with finite verbal inflection as well as an optional coverb.[3] The predicate arguments are expressed by bound pronouns and optional nominals. The verbal predicate in (3) is a typical verbal predicate that exhibits AM (in bold).

(3) *Jardbirni-ngkurra ba=rna ngaluny~nga-lu-**rru** walanja,*
   Dunmarra-ALL   DECL=1SG.S   IPFV~eat-POT-**AWY**   goanna[ACC]
   nyinawurda, yunba-yaru.
   echidna[ACC]   foot-COM
   'I will go along on foot eating goannas and echidnas on the way to Dunmarra.' (SD: DOS-2017_029-01: 1515370_1519991)

---

[3] The term 'coverb' is used in the Australianist literature to refer to an open part of speech whose members usually occur as the lexical component of a light verb construction. An example of a coverb is *durlmak* 'pick up' in (7). The light verb, such as *warnd-* in (7), is known as the '(inflecting) verb', and often occurs with no coverb in a simple verb construction, as in *nga-* 'eat' in (3).

The verb *ngalunyngalurru* 'will go along eating' exhibits a finite tense/mood suffix *-lu* indicating potential mood, leftward verbal reduplication *ngaluny~* as a marker of imperfective aspect, and an AM suffix *-rru* that indicates translational movement away from the deictic centre. The sentence has an auxiliary (that usually appears in second position) that registers sentient event participants such as the first singular subject, and that can make a limited range of modal distinctions by means of the auxiliary base. While predicate arguments are frequently not expressed, they can be overt as is the case for the direct objects *walanja* 'goanna' and *nyinawurda* 'echidna', in (3), that are in the unmarked accusative case. Predicate adjuncts are obligatorily marked with case suffixes to indicate their function within the clause. Example (3) exhibits a goal *Jardbirni-ngkurra* 'to Dunmarra' inflected for the allative case indicating the goal of motion, and an instrument adjunct *yunba-yaru* 'on foot' inflected for the comitative case indicating the means of motion.

2 Mudburra associated motion

Associated motion is the encoding of translational motion by means of a grammatical rather than lexical morpheme (Guillaume 2016: 92). For example, the inherent semantics of the verb *nyang(a)-* 'see' in (4) does not entail any translational motion, whereas the same verb bearing AM morphemes in (1) and (2) entail translational motion. These morphemes therefore fall within the scope of the category of AM.

(4) Ba=njurrangulu **nyang-ku** nyundu-ya=ma mayilawik.
    DECL=3PL>2PL **see-POT** 2-PL=TOP <week_identifier>[4]
    'They will see you next week.'
    (SD: DOS1-2017_029-01: 3538911_3540884)

However, Mudburra AM differs significantly from such phenomena described in the related Arandic language languages to the south – such as Kaytetye (Koch 1984, this volume) – in that it only grammatically encodes two paths of motion: away from the deictic centre, as in (1); and towards the deictic centre, as in (2). As such, it is "simple" according to Guillaume's (2016) metric of "degree of

---

[4] This word is used to refer to every second week. The *mayila* component is of unknown origin, and the *wik* is a borrowing of the English word 'week'. Every other week is identified as *binjinawik* (< English 'pensioner week'), referring to the week the Age Pension is paid.

elaboration", and resembles more closely the AM system described for the nearby unrelated language Wambaya (Nordlinger 2001).

This section will outline the form and function of AM markers in Mudburra, with a focus on the interaction of AM with other verbal morphosyntactic features (§2.1), the formal encoding of AM (§2.2), the functions that AM markers can have in Mudburra (§2.3), and the relative tense interpretation of the motion event and the event depicted by the verb (§2.4).

2.1 Mudburra verbal features

There are three verbal morphosyntactic features: tense/mood, aspect and associated motion. The tense/mood feature is realised by verbal suffixes corresponding to the 13 feature values shown in Table 2. The aspect feature is realised by means of prefixal or infixal partial verbal reduplication. Unreduplicated verbs are perfective, and reduplicated verbs are imperfective. The AM feature has three values; neutral (no AM), away and towards, exemplified in (2)–(4). In order for each inflected verb to be specified for each verbal feature, the feature value 'neutral' is used (following Chadwick 1975 : 24; Nordlinger 1998: 155; Pensalfini 2003: 228) for

Table 2: Verbal morphosyntactic features.

Feature		Tense/Mood	Aspect	Associated Motion
Feature values	(Realis values)	Past	Perfective	Neutral (no AM)
		Habitual	Imperfective	Away
		Narrative*		Towards
		Customary		
		Actual*		
		Present		
	(Irrealis values)	Speculative*		
		Potential*		
		Purposive		
		Imperative*		
		Deontic		
		Subjunctive*		
		Counterfactual		

* These tense/mood values combine with away and towards.

the case in which no AM is encoded.[5] Values of AM are realised by means of verbal suffixes following the tense/mood suffixes, or by means of portmanteau morphs that encode both tense/mood and AM. A simplified verbal structure showing the locus of exponence of each verbal morphosyntactic feature is provided in (5).

(5) ASPECT~ verb root −TENSE/MOOD −ASSOCIATED MOTION

The fact that AM morphology follows the finite tense/mood inflection distinguishes Mudburra AM morphology from that described for most other Pama-Nyungan languages (Koch this volume). AM in other Pama-Nyungan languages is best described as formally compounding or derivational in nature, in which AM morphology derives a verb stem (that can belong to a different conjugation class), that subsequently bears TAM inflection. In Mudburra, by contrast, AM morphology follows TAM inflection and does not affect the conjugation class of the verb; as such, it is formally inflectional rather than derivational. This is significant in the context of the historical development of AM in Mudburra (§3.3).

The features tense/mood, aspect and AM do not combine freely, in that not all combinations of feature values for each feature are possible. For every tense / mood value, both perfective and imperfective values of the aspect feature are possible. However the AM feature values 'away' and 'towards' only combine with some tense/mood values, as shown in Table 2 by means of asterisks. The full verbal paradigm for the verb *ba-* 'hit' is provided in Table 3.

The first six values of tense/mood listed in Table 2 are the realis values, and the remaining seven values are irrealis. While the narrative tense combines with away and towards, the away versus towards distinction is neutralised throughout all other realis tense values (past, habitual, customary, present and actual), and in contexts calling for these feature values, the actual mood is used. The speculative, potential, imperative and subjunctive moods combine with away and towards; but the purposive, deontic and counterfactual values do not. These moods employ the potential, imperative and subjunctive moods respectively when occurring with away and towards.[6]

---

5 Note that this feature value of the AM feature does not encode any motion. However it may be used in predicates that encode motion, therefore the term 'neutral' is used rather than a possible alternative 'absent' or 'no motion'.
6 The purposive, deontic and counterfactual inflections are formally related to the potential, imperative and subjunctive inflections, by means of the addition of the *+arn* 'imperfective' formative. However, synchronically, unlike in other Ngumpin-Yapa languages the *+arn* formative does not constitute an exponent of aspect.

Table 3: Verbal paradigm of Mudburra verb *ba-* 'hit' (Exponents of AM in bold).

Tense/Mood	Aspect	Associated Motion		
		Neutral (no AM)	Away	Towards
Past	Perfective	*ba-rni*	–	–
	Imperfective	*barniny~ba-rni*	–	–
Habitual	Perfective	*ba-rniwu*	–	–
	Imperfective	*barniny~ba-rniwu*	–	–
Narrative	Perfective	*ba-rnirra*	*ba-rnirra-**ra***	*ba-rnirra-**rni***
	Imperfective	*barniny~ba-rnirra*	*barniny~ba-rnirra-**ra***	*barniny~ba-rnirra-**rni***
Customary	Perfective	*ba-la*	–	–
	Imperfective	*ba-rnanybala*	–	–
Present	Perfective	*ba-rnini*	–	–
	Imperfective	*barniny~ba-rnini*	–	–
Actual	Perfective	*ba-rna(na)*	*ba-rna-**rra***	*ba-rna-**ni***
	Imperfective	*barnany~ba-rna(na)*	*barnany~ba-rna-**rra***	*barnany~ba-rna-**ni***
Speculative	Perfective	*ba-rnarra*	*ba-rnarra-**ra***	*ba-rnarra-**rni***
	Imperfective	*barnany~ba-rnarra*	*barnany~ba-rnarra-**ra***	*barnany~ba-rnarra-**rni***
Potential	Perfective	*ba-rru*	*ba-rru-**ru***	*ba-**rrarnnginyi***
	Imperfective	*barruny~ba-rru*	*barruny~ba-rru-**ru***	*barnarn~ba-**rrarnnginyi***
Purposive	Perfective	*ba-rrarnku*	–	–
	Imperfective	*barrarn~ba-rrarnku*	–	–
Imperative	Perfective	*ba-rra*	*ba-rra-**ra***	*ba-**rrarn***
	Imperfective	*barrany~ba-rra*	*barrany~ba-rra-**ra***	*barrarn~ba-**rrarn***
Deontic	Perfective	*ba-rrarnda*	–	–
	Imperfective	*barrarn~ba-rrarnda*	–	–
Subjunctive	Perfective	*ba-rrala*	*ba-rrala-**rra***	*ba-rrala-**rni***
	Imperfective	*barrany~ba-rrala*	*barrany~ba-rrala-**rra***	*barrany~ba-rrala-**rni***
Counterfactual	Perfective	*ba-rrarndala*	–	–
	Imperfective	*barrarn~ba-rrarndala*	–	–

2.2 Form of Mudburra AM suffixes

The non-orthogonality of feature values is one way in which the morphosyntactic feature of AM creates a non-canonical inflectional paradigm (Stump 2016). In addition, the morphemes themselves involved in expressing AM exhibit significant departures from canonical inflection (Corbett 2009). Both away and towards feature values can in some morphological contexts be realised by means of portmanteau suffixes encoding both tense/mood and AM.

The morph that realises the 'away' value usually follows the tense/mood morpheme and is usually of the form -*rra*, as in (6).

(6) *Kadi-li=ma   ba=nyanu   ja<manji>~ma-rna-**rra**   mayingka=ma*
    DIST-ERG=TOP DECL=REFL <IPFV>~grind-ACT-**AWY** axe=TOP
    kuya-barda=wanya.
    thus-THITH=SEQ
    'That one is going that way now sharpening his axe.'
    (SD: DOS1-2017_021-01: 3648795_3655134)

However the vowel of the suffix shows some variability. In (7) and (8), this AM suffix follows the imperative and the potential suffixes with characteristic *a* and *u* vowels respectively. In these examples the vowel of the 'away' suffix seems to assimilate in quality to that of the preceding tense/mood suffix.

(7) *Kadi=ma   durlmak   warnd-a-**rra**!*
    DIST=TOP pick_up get-IMP-**AWY**
    'Go and pick up that person!'
    (SD: DOS1-2017_003-03: 1617078_1618378)

(8) *Ngurra-ngkurra   yanan~ja-na-rra.   Marruny~ma-rru-**ru**[7]   nyangarlu.*
    home-ALL IPFV~go-ACT-AWY IPFV~say-POT-**AWY** one
    'He is going home. He'll talk to himself all the way.'
    (SD: DOS1-2017_023-01: 199318_201710)

However the difference in vowel quality in the two tense/mood environments is preserved even when there is no concomitant difference in preceding vowel. For

---

[7] 'Rhotic dissimilation' (Laughren 1978: 15; Nash 1986: 76–77) is a phonological process applying here to transform an underlying alveolar tap *rr* into a retroflex central approximant *r*, as in (8) and below in (28).

example, verbs of conjugation II, such as *ku(ya)-* 'throw', have null imperative and potential suffixes. In these cases, the only exponent of the tense/mood distinction is the 'away' morpheme. Like the potential and imperative 'towards' portmanteaux, they are analysed in these contexts as portmanteau morphs expressing the features tense/mood and AM, as in (9) and (10).

(9) Lun   *kuya-**rra**=yina!*
    drop_off throw-IMP.**AWY**=3PL.NS
    'Go and drop it off with them!'
    (SD: DOS1-2017_006-02: 592893_594077)

(10) *Ba=rna   manyan kuya-**rru**   kanju.*
     DECL=1SG.S lie   throw-**POT.AWY** inside
     'I will go and lay it (the child) down inside (to sleep).'
     (SD: DOS1-2017_007-01: 1821254_1822504)

The form of the 'towards' value is conditioned by the morphological environment. Usually the tense/mood feature and the AM feature are realised by two adjacent morphs, as in (11). The form of the 'towards' morph is *-ni* when followed by a syllable with a retroflex onset, and *-rni* elsewhere.

(11) *Ja<manji>~ma-**rna-ni**.*[8]
     <IPFV>~grind-**ACT-TWD**
     'He was coming sharpening it (his axe).'
     (SD: DOS1-2017_21-01: 3372557_ 3373913)

However when in the potential or imperative moods, the 'towards' value is encoded by means of a portmanteau morph realising both the tense/mood feature and the AM feature, as in (12) and (13) respectively.

(12) *Jawardi-la   ba=ngku   ba-**rrarnnginyi**, ba=yi   ma-rnana.*
     tomorrow-LOC DECL=2SG.NS hit-**POT.TWD**   DECL=1SG.NS do/say-ACT
     'He told me that tomorrow he would come and hit you.'
     (SD: DOS1-2017_021-01: 2401026_2403146)

---

8 Mudburra verbal reduplication is variable and complex, involving a prefixed or infixed reduplicant. It is represented with a tilde, and in the case of an infixed reduplicant, also pointy brackets. The internal structure of the reduplicant is omitted here, but a full description of the forms of verbal reduplication is provided by Osgarby (2018a).

(13) Yali=ma   karu=ma   dak⁹ kanga-**rn**   lurrbu=rni=ma!
      DIST=TOP child=TOP sit   take-**IMP.TWD** return=RSTR=TOP
      'Bring that child back here (while he is) sitting up!'
      (SD: DOS1-2018_003-01: 1054090_1057608)

The forms of these two portmanteau morphs are likely derived historically from encliticized forms of the verb *ya-* 'go', as shown in (14) and (15). While in Pre-Mudburra, the encliticized verb *ya-* 'go' could likely refer to motion either away or towards the deictic centre, the paradigmatic co-existence of these forms with the motion 'away' form *ba-rru-ru* 'will go and hit' and *ba-rra-ra* 'go and hit' likely caused a semantic narrowing of the forms in question to the 'towards' feature in opposition to the 'away' forms. The motivation for the adoption of these suppletive inflections at the expense of regular forms such as **ba-rru-rni* and **ba-rra-rni* remains unclear.¹⁰

(14) Pre-Mudburra ba-rru=ya-ni-nginyi   → Mudburra ba-rrarnnginyi
                   hit-POT=go-INF-GEN   hit-POT.TWD
                   'will hit after going/coming'   'will come and hit'

(15) Pre-Mudburra *ba-rra=ya-ni   → Mudburra ba-rrarn
                   hit-IMP=go-INF   hit-IMP.TWD
                   ?   'come and hit'

2.3 Functions of Mudburra AM suffixes

Mudburra AM markers can encode either direction of a motion event inherent in the lexical verb, or they can depict an independent motion subevent with a specified deictic path. The motion encoded by the AM marker is always of the subject (S or A argument) and can only be interpreted as motion of the object (O)

---

9 When the AM markers attach to a verb participating in a light verb construction, it modifies the event depicted by the entire complex predicate. However, the topic of conceptually merging three types of elements that can all contribute predicate sub-events (i.e. coverb, verb and AM inflection) remains to be further investigated.

10 In Warlpiri, the cognate directional enclitic *=rni* 'towards', undergoes progressive vowel harmony when encliticized to hosts with a final *u*, motivating the allomorph *=rnu* (Laughren 1978: 15). This suggests that the form *=rni* following *u* is dispreferred, and is avoided in Warlpiri, by harmonizing the vowel of the enclitic with that of the final syllable of the host. It is possible that in Mudburra, a similar dispreference for forms such as **ba-rru-rni* was resolved by the adoption (and semantic narrowing) of the extant and phonologically preferred form illustrated in (13).

when the object accompanies the moving subject, as in (13), for instance, with the verb *kang(a)-* 'take'. When occurring on verbs with no inherent translational motion, the AM suffixes always contributes a motion subevent. In (16) the motion event encoded by the AM suffix has an overt source, 'far in the west', and in (17) the motion event encoded by the AM suffix has an overt goal, 'towards us'. In neither utterance can the AM suffix be interpreted as a 'direction/orientation of wetting' or 'direction/orientation of hitting'.

(16) *Karla-yin-ngurlu   ba=ngalawarna   kunja-rna-**ni**,*
 west-DABL-ABL   DECL=1PL.INCL.NS   wet-ACT-**TWD**
 karlayin~karla-yin-ngurlu.
 FAR~west-DABL-ABL
 'It (the storm) came from far off in the west and wet us.'
 (AC: PMC1-M8-01: 2829371_2834515)

(17) *Kuya-njala=wanya   barnany~ba-rna-**ni**   ngayu-walija-ngkurra=wanya*
 thus-HITH=SEQ   IPFV~hit-ACT-**TWD**   1-PL-ALL=SEQ
 ba=ngalawa.
 DECL=1PL.INCL.NS
 'He's coming this way while hitting him, towards us now.'
 (SD: DOS1-2017_021-01: 670669_674291)

While these functions are identical to those described for the nearby unrelated language Wambaya (Nordlinger 2010), they contrast with the function of a cognate suffix in a closely related neighbouring language Bilinarra, that attaches to non-motion verbs with a directional function. In (18), the suffix *-rni* contributes a direction/orientation for the calling out event with no implication of any motion towards the deictic centre.[11] The distinction between the function of *-rni* in Mudburra, as shown in (16) and (17), and Bilinarra, as shown in (18), is key in distinguishing an AM system from a Directional system.

---

11 The Bilinarra example provided in (18) is one of the few examples provided by Meakins and Nordlinger (2014) of the towards suffix *-rni* affixed to a non-motion verb. However, given that *ma-* 'do/say' cannot take an allative complement to express destination of motion, it does not qualify as a motion verb. While verbs of sound emission may be said to express "fictive" or "abstract" motion (which indeed may have contributed to the acceptability of the marker with this particular verb), the 'towards' suffix is not interpreted as a marker of translational motion, and hence illustrates the above point.

(18) *Wayarrib-ba=rla   ma-la-**rni**   nyila.*
call_out-EP=3OBL say-PRS-**TWD** that
'He's calling out to him (this way). (lit. He's calling this way for him.)'
(Bilinarra: Meakins and Nordlinger 2014: 309)

When occurring with verbs encoding inherent translational motion,[12] the Mudburra AM feature can specify the direction of the motion with respect to the deictic centre. The verb *karlama-* 'approach' has inherent translational motion and an inherent goal registered in this example in the auxiliary. The AM suffix stipulates that the motion inherent in *karlama-* 'approach' is towards the deictic centre.

(19) *Nyamba-wu   ba=yin   nyundu-lu=ma   nanga~nangaj*
what-DAT   DECL=2SG>1SG   2-ERG=TOP   PLUR~sneak
*karla<manji>~ma-rna-**ni**?*
<IPFV>~approach-ACT-**TWD**
'Why are you sneaking up on me this way?'
(SD: DOS1-2017_021-03: 22059_24683)

Motion verbs with inherent vertical directionality can occur with AM suffixes. In these cases, the AM suffixes perform one of two operations to the event: they *modify* the path horizontally, or they *add* an additional horizontal motion event. In (20), the path of motion inherent in the verb *wandi(ya)-* 'fall' is modified horizontally, such that the path implied by the inflected verb is downwards and towards the deictic centre (the speaker in this instance). Similarly, the path of motion inherent in the verb *duma-* 'rise' is modified in (21), such that the path implied by the inflected verb is upwards and away from the deictic centre.

(20) *Karu, jurd   **wandiya-rn**   kuya-njala!*
child go_down   **fall-IMP.TWD** thus-HITH
'Kid, come down this way.'
(SD: DOS1-2017_036-03: 2346442_2347998)

---

12 The Mudburra verbs encoding inherent translational motion are *ya-* 'go', *kang(a)-* 'take', *karlama-* 'approach', *duma-* 'rise' and *wandi(ya)-* 'fall'. The first two verbs, *ya-* 'go' and *kang(a)-* 'take', have no inherent direction with respect to the deictic centre, so could be translated into English as 'go'/'come' and 'take'/'bring' respectively. To specifiy other manners or paths of motion, for the most part these verbs are used in concert with coverbs in light verb constructions. It should be noted however there are light verb constructions that encode translational motion by means of a non-motion light verb, such as *kayang ba-* [sprint hit] 'sprint'. As mentioned in footnote 11, the topic of combining complex predication and AM remains to be investigated.

(21) *Mardba-ngurlu* **du**<*manyi*>~**ma**-*rna*-**rra** *Yingawurnarri.*
Montejinni-ABL <IPFV>~**rise**-ACT-**AWY** Top_Springs
'From Montejinni it went up to Top Springs.'
(AC: PMC1 M16, PM Notes pp. 34–40 l. 9)

Alternatively, with the same verb, the AM suffix can add an additional motion event to the event depicted by the lexical verb. In (22) the motion event inherent in the lexical verb *wandi(ya)-* 'fall' has a downwards path. Unlike in (20), the addition of the 'towards' affix to *wandi(ya)-* 'fall', in (22), does not angle the path of motion such that the rain falls downwards and towards the deictic centre. Instead, it adds an additional motion component with a horizontal path of motion for the entire falling event. As such, both the lexical verb and the AM affix encode independent motion events.

(22) *Minya*   *madayi*   *diyija*   *yanan~ja-na-rni.*
     PROX   cloud   big   IPFV~go-ACT-TWD
     Nguku=barra *ba=ngalawa* **wandiya-rnnginyi.**
     water=DUB   DECL=1PL.INCL.NS **fall-POT.TWD**
'These big clouds are coming. Maybe the rain will come and fall on us.'
(SD: DOS1-2017_036-03: 2934719_2939921)

Although the depiction of translational motion by means of a grammatical path morpheme on a non-motion verb is sufficient to establish an AM function, it seems the presence of a grammatical path morpheme on a motion verb is not sufficient to establish that the path morpheme has a directional function. It may, as in (22), be functioning to encode an additional motion event, and as such be considered a true AM marker. For the reasons, the Mudburra AM system is not considered an illustration of the phenomenon of 'Deictic Associated Motion' (D-AM, Belkadi this volume).

2.4 Relative temporal interpretation

The relative temporal interpretation of the event depicted by the lexical verb and the motion event depicted by the AM marker is underspecified in Mudburra, unlike in other Australian languages with complex AM systems (Koch this volume). While there is no evidence that a *subsequent* motion interpretation is available, contextual features coerce either a *prior* or a *concurrent* temporal interpretation of the motion event.

One factor that seems crucial in the interpreted relative temporality of subevents is the aspect feature (recall §2.1). If a verb realises the perfective aspect (e.g. it is unreduplicated), it most frequently has a prior motion interpretation, as in (23)–(26).

(23) Marndaj dulyurr ba-rnana buliki=ma, ba=rlawa=wanya
okay shoot hit-ACT bullock=TOP DECL=1PL.INCL.S=SEQ
biyang-ku-**rru**.
[**PFV**]cut-POT-**AWY**
'He has now shot the bullock. Now we'll go and cut it up.'
(SD: DOS1-2017_012-02: 1342980_1346718)

(24) Kadi jawaranya darndarn warnd-a-**rra**=yi marru-ngkurra
DIST billycan inside [**PFV**]get-IMP-**AWY**=1SG.NS house-ALL
karu! Ba=rna lalija kamb-u.
child DECL=1SG.S tea cook-POT
'Go inside the house and get me that billycan, kid! I am going to heat up some tea.' (SD: DOS1-2018_004-01: 1127371_1131318)

(25) Nyundu=wanya ba=yinan kamb-u-**rru** ngarina=ma
2=SEQ DECL=2SG>3PL [**PFV**]cook-POT-**AWY** meat=TOP
wawirri=ma kadi-ya-wu jabaka-wu=wanya.
plains_kangaroo=TOP DIST-PL-DAT old_woman-DAT=SEQ
'You should go and cook kangaroo meat for those old women now.'
(SD: DOS1-2017_029-03: 2509602_2516383)

(26) Nyanu-nya karlaj-nyana ba=rla wuj
3-GEN younger_sibling-3.POSS DECL=3SG.OBL search
bung-**annginyi** ngaba-wu nyanu-nya-wu.
[**PFV**]poke-**POT.TWD** elder_sibling-DAT 3-GEN-DAT
'His younger brother will come and look for (lit. search poke) his elder brother.'
(SD: DOS1-2017_002-04: 909986_914212)

There are exceptions, however, as there are also infrequent examples of a concurrent motion interpretation for such unreduplicated verbs, such as that illustrated in (27).

(27) Ba=li jurduk ma-**rnirra-rni**.
DECL=3PL.S search_for do-**NAR-TWD**
'They came searching.'
(PD: PMC1-PM1-01: 2210667_2213140)

If the verb realises the imperfective aspect value (e.g. it is reduplicated), it has a concurrent motion interpretation, as in (28)–(31).

(28) *Karu!   Langa-jija   ba=n.*
child   ear-ABE   DECL=2SG.S
*Ngayi-li=ma   ba=rnangku   **barruny~ba-rru-ru.***
1-ERG=TOP   DECL=1SG>2SG   **IPFV~hit-POT-AWY**
'Hey kid! You're deaf (you never listen)! I'll go along hitting you!'
(SD: DOS1-2017_021-01: 1426339_1430286)

(29) *Yali-li   ba=yina   durlk-karra   **barnany~ba-rna-rra**,   winymi-yaru.*
DIST-ERG   DECL=3PL.NS   shoot-DLOC   **IPFV~hit-ACT-AWY**   walk-COM
'He is going away shooting them, on foot.'
(SD: DOS1-2017_012-02: 987993_991174)

(30) *Wangku-lu   **janki~**janki-yina-**rni**=wanya.   Wakurni   minya=ma*
sun-ERG   **IPFV~**burn-act-**TWD**=SEQ   nothing   PROX=TOP
kamuru=rni.
dark=RSTR
'The sun is coming (up) and heating up now. It isn't dark anymore.'
(SD: DOS1-2017_008-03: 2049480_2056400)

(31) *Ngada<**yin**>~ja-yina-**rni**   kadi=ma?   Bu<**nganji**>~nga-na-**rni**.*
<**IPFV**>~do_what-ACT-**TWD**   DIST=TOP   <**IPFV**>~poke-ACT-**TWD**
'What is that one doing coming this way? She's dancing (lit. poking) her way here.'
(SD: DOS1-2017_029-01: 1016471_1020116)

The relative time of the motion event results from the interaction of the event depicted by the AM marker, and the viewpoint aspect of the inflected verb. While the translational motion event depicted by the AM marker necessarily has durative Aktionsart, the Aktionsart of the event depicted by the verb stem varies; and so, for the viewpoint aspect of the combined event to hold, there are only certain temporal configurations possible. If the viewpoint aspect of the event depicted by the inflected verb is imperfective, the durative motion event can be temporally superimposed without issue as a concurrent motion event. However, if the viewpoint aspect of the event depicted by the inflected verb is perfective, the only way to maintain a perfective interpretation of the combined event is to interpret the durative motion event as prior to the culmination of the event depicted by the verb stem.

3 Associated motion in North Central Australian languages

AM in Mudburra is not an isolated phenomenon in North Central Australia. Similar phenomena have been observed in the Mirndi language Wambaya (§3.1), and four neighbouring Pama-Nyungan languages: Warumungu, Warlpiri, Warlmanpa and Wakaya (§3.2). Three types of system are found, as summarised in Table 4: "Directionality", where markers of direction specify direction (only) on both motion and non-motion verbs; "Associated Motion", where markers serve to add a motion event to non-motion verbs but when used with motion verbs specify its direction; and "Directional Associated Motion", where markers specify direction for motion verbs but may add a separate motion event to non-motion verbs. The latter corresponds to Belkadi's (this volume, note 1) "deictic-associated motion" (D-AM), which is used to refer to "associated motion encoded by forms which also express pure deictic directionality and by extension, to forms which are polysemous between AM encoding and pure deictic directionality encoding." AM in these languages will first be described, before a discussion of the diachronic development of AM in Mudburra and Wambaya (§3.3).

Table 4: Contribution of Directional/Associated Motion markers.

	Directionality	Directional Associated Motion	Associated Motion
With motion verbs	Direction	Direction	Direction (/Associated Motion)
With non-motion verbs	Direction	Direction/Associated Motion	Associated Motion

3.1 AM in Wambaya (Mirndi)

Nordlinger (1998, 2001) describes AM in Wambaya in some detail. She observes that, only two paths of motion are distinguished: away and towards. As in Mudburra, the AM feature is not orthogonal to the features encoding tense, aspect and modality, as shown in Table 5.

Table 5: Tense/Aspect/Mood/Associated Motion[13] morphemes in Wambaya (Nordlinger 1998: 144–156).

Tense	Aspect/Mood	Associated Motion		
		Neutral (no AM)	Away	Towards
Past	Simple	-a	-(g)any	-amany
Past	Habitual	-aji	?	?
Past	Progressive	-a-n	?	?
Past	Non-actual	-uda ~ -uja	?	?
Present/Non-past	Simple	-a ~ Ø	-(g)uba	-ulama
Non-past	Habitual	-ala	?	?
Present	Progressive	-a-n ~ -n	?	?
Present	Non-actual	-udi ~ -uji	?	?
Future	Simple	-u ~ Ø	?	?
—	Hypothetical	-agba	?	?
—	Imperative	Ø (SG) ~ gurl (DU) ~ girr (PL)	gama (SG) ~ gurl+i (DU) ~ girr+i (PL)	ga (SG) ~ gurl+ama (DU) ~ girr+ama (PL)

Despite the fact that there are eleven permissible combinations of the tense and aspect/mood features when the AM feature is neutral, when it is either 'away' or 'towards', there are only three documented combinations in the Wambaya corpus: past simple, non-past simple and imperative. The highly defective paradigm in Wambaya results from the historical auxiliation of an erstwhile verbal part of speech with an ostensibly more canonical inflectional paradigm (Green 1995; Harvey 2008; Osgarby 2018b).

The Wambaya AM morphemes are not affixed to the verb, but rather form part of a second position auxiliary that also encodes tense/aspect/mood and person/number of predicate arguments. The motion event depicted by the Wambaya AM morphemes is almost always interpreted as prior to the event depicted by the lexical verb, as in (32) and (33).

(32) **Mirra ny-uba** jajiliga-yi nganginga-ni
 sit 2SG.S-NPST.AWY daughter.F-LOC 2SG.POSS.F-LOC
 'You'll go and sit with your daughter.'
 (Wambaya: Nordlinger 1998: 86)

---

[13] Nordlinger (1998; 2001) refers to these morphemes as "directional", but they are described as having the functions attributed here to markers of "associated motion".

(33) **Ngajbi wurlu-ng-amany** ngurra ngarl-warda.
see **3DU.A-1.O-PST.TWD** 1PL.INCL.ACC talk-INF
'They came to watch us talking.'
(Wambaya: Nordlinger 1998: 152; 2001: 407)

The only example of a concurrent motion interpretation is when AM morphology appears with the lexical verb *yabu* 'have' and renders the interpretations 'take' and 'bring', as in (34) and (35) respectively.

(34) Baraj-bali **gun-uba** irra **yabu**.
old_man-PL.M **3SG.M.A-NPSTAWY** 3PL.ACC have
'He takes all the old men.'
(Wambaya: Nordlinger 1998: 140)

(35) Juguna-yi **gin-amany** *yabu*.
uncle.M-ERG **3SG.M.A.PST.TWD** have
'Uncle brought him.'
(Wambaya: Nordlinger 1998: 84)

3.2 AM in Warumungu, Warlpiri, Warlmanpa and Wakaya (Pama-Nyungan)

AM is also observed in several Pama-Nyungan languages in the North Central Australian region. Warumungu (isolate), Warlpiri (Ngumpin-Yapa subgroup), Warlmanpa (Ngumpin-Yapa subgroup) and Wakaya (Warluwarric subgroup) all exhibit systems of AM, and belong to country roughly between Mudburra and the Arandic languages to the south (see map in Figure 1 and Koch this volume).

Verbal path morphemes in Warumungu can have both a directional function with motion verbs, as in (36), and an AM function with non-motion verbs, as in (37).

(36) Karnanti aki-nyi, kampaju aki-nyi=angkuljarnikki
mother 3SG.DAT-GEN father 3SG.DAT-GEN=3PL>1PL
kili=karn api-**karni** karlampi-kkina.
angry=now go-**TWD.PSTPUNC** creek-ALL/LOC
'His mother and father angrily came to us to the creek.'
(Warumungu: Simpson 1998: 732)

(37) Nya-**njirrkarl**=arni   nyangirr-ji-nta=ama   ajji-nyi   kartungunyu.
     see-**AWY.FUT**=1SG.S   how-INCH-PRS=3SG.S   1SG.NS-GEN   wife
     'I will go and see what my wife is doing.'
     (Warumungu: Simpson 2002a, 151)

However, with non-motion verbs, they can exhibit a directional function, such as in (38). This suggests that underlyingly they are directionals, but that they can have an AM function in some contexts.[14] Warumungu therefore serves as an illustration of 'Deictic Associated Motion' (D-AM) (Belkadi this volume).

(38) Ngalanya   yuwaji   ngu-**njirranta**   kajunu.
     this   road   lie-**AWY.PRS**   north
     'This road goes north.'
     (Warumungu: Simpson 1998: 721)

Unlike in Mudburra, the Warumungu verbal path morphemes *precede* the tense inflection. A full paradigm of the verb *paka-* 'poke, spear' is given in Table 6.

Simpson (2001: 177) observes that the conjugation class of the marked AM values can be different from that of the neutral value, as shown by the differing present tense suffixes in (39), where only one of the AM forms inflects with the -*nta* Present of the verb root. Furthermore, she identifies traces of a historical structure within the directional affixes. For example she suggests that the present tense 'towards' suffix in (39) is likely historically composed of a nominaliser and an inflected form of the verb *apa* meaning 'go'.

(39) *paka-nta*   'is spearing'
     *paki-ntirr+**apa**-n*   'is spearing this way, is coming spearing' (cf. *apa-n* 'is going')
     *paki-ntirr+**a**-nta*   'is spearing that way, is going spearing'
     *paki-nti(rr)+**parta**-n* 'is setting off spearing' (cf. *parta-n* (verb) 'is setting off')

While the Warumungu AM feature is almost entirely orthogonal to the tense feature, as shown in Table 6, the marked AM feature values ('away', 'towards' and 'setting out'), do not have a nominal stem inflection (an infinitive nominalised

---

14 However it should be noted that in the Arandic AM systems, AM markers typically have some metaphorical usages parallel to that of (38).

Table 6: Warumungu verbal inflections for paka- 'poke, spear' showing directional affixes.

TAM	Directionality			
	Neutral (L class)	Away (≈L class)	Towards (≈Ø class)	Setting Out (Ø class)
Future	pakki-*l*	paki-nti(rr)+**ka**-*rl*	paki-njirr+**a**	paki-nti(rr)+**parti** ~ paki-nji(rr)+**parti**[2]
Imperative	pakki-*l*=a	paki-nti(rr)+**ka**-*rl*=a	paki-njirr=a	paki-nti(rr)+**part**=a ~ paki-nji(rr)+**part**=a[2]
Present	paka-*nta*	paki-ntirr+**a**-*nta*	paki-ntirr+**apa**-*n*	paki-nti(rr)+**parta**-*n* ~ paki-nji(rr)+**parta**-*n*[2]
Past Punctual	paki-*nni* ~ paki-*(n)nyi*	paki-ntirr+**a**-*rni*	paki-nti(rr)+**ka**-*mi* ~ paki-nji(rr)+**ka**-*mi*	paki-nti(rr)+**parti**-*nyi* ~ paki-nji(rr)+**parti**-*nyi*[2]
Past Continuous	paki-*njina*	–	paki-ntirr+**a**-*jina*	paki-nti(rr)+**parti**-*na* ~ paki-nji(rr)+**parti**-*na*[2]
Admonitive	paka-*nkurn*	paki-ntirr+**a**-*rnkkurn*	paki-nti(rr)+**pu**-*nkkurn*	paki-nti(rr)+**parta**-*kurn* ~ paki-nji(rr)+**parta**-*kurn*[2]
Optative/ Irrealis	paka-*nnga(ri)*	paki-ntirr+**a**-*rnnga(ri)*[1]	paki-nti(rr)+**pu**-*nnga(ri)*[1]	paki-nti(rr)+**parta**-*nga(ra)* ~ paki-nji(rr)+**parta**-*nga(ri)*[1,2]

Underline: TAM suffix. Bold: Possible directional morph. Paradigm and segmentation is based on that of Simpson (1998: 722) with updates taken from Simpson (Simpson 2002a: 163) as footnoted. [1]Simpson (2002a: 163) records the final vowel as the high front vowel *i*. [2]Simpson (2002a: 163) states that variants with the palatal are also attested.

verb form), and there is a single gap in the paradigm combining past continuous with 'away', maked with an em rule in Table 6 (Simpson and Heath 1982: 34).

A single AM marker is observed in Warlpiri, and it is discussed by Simpson (2001; 2002b). It is referred to as the 'inceptive' and expresses translational motion with no inherent path, as in (40) and (41).

(40) Jinta-ngku   ka=jana   yangka yapa-ngku   wirrpiyi-rli
     one-ERG   PRS=3PL.O the   person-ERG   enlisting-ERG
     yaja-**rninji**-ni.
     recruit-**INCEP**-NPST
     'One person goes enlisting support asking them to join in with him.'
     (Warlpiri: Simpson 2001: 184)

(41) *Kuyu=lpa   luwa-**rnunju**-nu,   ka-ngu=rnu¹⁵=lpa.*
     game=IPFV   shoot-INCEP-PST   carry-PST=TWD=IPFV
     'He went and killed some animal, and brought it back.'
     (Warlpiri: Simpson 2001: 184)

Warlmanpa, a southern neighbour of Mudburra, seems to also exhibit at least one AM morpheme, as in (42), although the distribution and function of the morpheme is presently unclear (Mitch Browne, in preparation).

(42) *Jinjirla=n   paka-**nyanya**.*
     sneeze=2SG.S   hit-PRS.AWY
     'You're sneezing, going away from me.'
     (Warlmanpa: DK, wrl-20180614-02, 5:34min)

Wakaya, a language located to the southeast of Warumungu, has a verbal paradigm of 11 finite verbal inflections and a nominalizing gerund suffix (Breen 1974: 104–118). One of these finite verbal inflections is identified as an "Andative present". While it largely appears on verbs of motion with a directional function, it is also observed on non-motion verbs contributing a motion subevent (Breen 1974: 113–114), as in (43) and (44) which show two distinct allomorphs of the andative present.

(43) *pakepaki-k yuwerr-**arre**=kanye=pulu*
     buggy-LOC   sit-AND.PRS=AWY=that
     'He's going along in a buggy.'
     (Wakaya: Breen 1974: 113)

(44) *mare-**jale**=kany   pule-wiy*
     talk-AND.PRS=AWY   that-DU
     'Those two fellows were (?) walking along talking.'
     (Wakaya: Breen 1974: 113)

In addition, Wakaya has directional morphemes that do not inherently encode motion, but that distinguish direction towards and away from the deictic centre. As in Mudburra and Wambaya, the 'towards' inflection has only been observed in conjunction with some TAM feature values (see Table 7) (Breen 1974: 122).

---

15 The Warlpiri enclitic *=rni ~ =rnu* in this word is cognate with the Mudburra 'towards' AM marker; however it is a pure directional in Warlpiri.

Table 7: Wakaya verbal inflections for *penk* 'go' showing directional suffixes.

TAM	Directionality	
	Neutral	**Towards**
Imperative	*penk*	*penk-art*
Negative imperative	*penk-anhi*[†]	?
Optative	*penk-arl*	?
Potential	*penk-ii*[†]	?
Past	*penke-rniy*	*penke-rn-**ant** (penke-rn-**art**)*
Imperfect	*penke-thiy*[†]	?
Gerund	*penk-a*	?
Present	*penke-tiy*	?
Andative present	*penk-arr*	?
Future	*penke-rl*	*penke-**nyint*** (E, W), *penke-rl-**art*** (E)
Irrealis	*penk-arliy*[†] (W), *penke-murliy*[†] (E)	*penk-arli-**nt*** (W), *penke-murli-**rt*** (E)
Purposive	*penk-ariy*	*penk-ari-**rt*** (W), *penk-ariy-**art*** (E)

W: West, E: East. Breen (1974) does not provide a verbal paradigm. He discusses the following verbal inflections: Imperative (p. 104), Negative imperative (p. 105), Optative (pp. 105–106), Potential (pp. 106–107), Past (p. 107), Imperfect (p. 108), Gerund (pp. 110–111), Present (p. 112), Andative present (pp. 113–114), Future (p. 114), Irrealis (pp. 115–117) and Purposive (pp. 117–118). Unmarked forms are attested by Breen (1974), whereas daggered forms are predicted based on the relevant description.

The 'away' enclitic is illustrated in (43) and (44), while the 'towards' suffix, which usually follows TAM suffixation, is illustrated in (45); when co-ocurring with the future TAM value, directionality is encoded as part of a portmanteau morph, as in (46).

(45) *penke-**rn-ant**=arn,   wera-rl=anh   ma-rniy   ngethemerlt*
     go-**PST-TWD**=1SG.NOM, dog-ERG=1SG.ACC hit-PST   calf
     'As soon as I came here the dog bit my leg.'
     (Wakaya: Breen 1974: 123)

(46) *murrpunga penke-**nyint**=imp,   inge-rl=imp   urinhathi*
     tomorrow   go-**FUT.TWD**=2SG.NOM, see-FUT=2SG.NOM younger_sister
     'If you come here tomorrow, you'll see my sister.'
     (Wakaya: Breen 1974: 123)

Therefore, Wakaya seems also to conform to the demonstrated areal tendency to (1) make a two-way directional distinction, (2) show restrictions on the combination of path markers and the tense/mood feature, and (3) for some such combinations, exhibit portmanteau morphemes expressing path and tense/mood.

3.3 Development and loss of AM in Mudburra and Wambaya

3.3.1 Etymology of Mudburra AM suffixes

It is likely that Proto-Ngumpin-Yapa had the suffixes (or clitics) *-rra* and *-rni*, and that they had a directional function, given that this is the function of reflexes in other Ngumpin-Yapa languages, for example Warlpiri (Laughren 1978). While the etymology of the 'away' suffix is unclear, the Proto-Ngumpin-Yapa towards affix *-rni* likely has a pronominal origin (Harold Koch, pers. comm.). It probably developed from the borrowing of a first person singular non-subject enclitic pronoun from Wati languages. In these languages there is a clear bridging context for the use of the bound pronoun as a directional morpheme, as shown in Pintupi and Wangkajunga in (47) and (48).

(47) *Ngalya   kati-ngu=**ni**[16]=ra*
     toward   bring-PST=1SG.ACC=3SG.DAT
     'He brought (it) to me for her.'
     (Pintupi: Hansen & Hansen 1978: 124)

(48) *Wati-wirrja-rnu=**rni**   jii-janu.*
     across-run-PST=1SG.O   DEM-ABL
     'It ran across to me from there.'
     (Wangkajunga: Jones 2011: 179)

The same process of grammaticalisation of the first person singular non-subject enclitic pronoun to a directional suffix is clear in Yingkarta (Kartu, Pama-Nyungan). Dench (1998: 48) states, "to the extent that the goal of motion is the speaker, the *-rni* suffix is very like a first person object pronoun. However [...] the goal of motion need not be the speaker specifically", as shown by (49).

(49) *Thinha   pipi-jura-wu   mayu   pirlipilya-nma-**rni**.*
     this   mother-POSS-DAT   child   run-IPFV-TWD
     'This mother's child is running to her.'
     (Yingkarta: Dench 1998: 48)

---

[16] The grapheme ⟨n⟩ in Pintupi represents a retroflex nasal phoneme, written ⟨rn⟩ in the other orthographies used by languages in this paper.

3.3.2 Development of AM in Wambaya

In the non-Pama-Nyungan Mirndi family, Green (1995) proposes that Proto-Mirndi verbs underwent auxiliation in the Barkly languages (Jingulu, Ngarnka, Binbinka, Gudanji and Wambaya), such that the only remaining reflexes of the verbs are the "light verbs" of Jingulu and Ngarnka, and the "auxiliaries" of Binbinka, Gudanji and Wambaya. The maintenance of reflexes of motion verbs, that distinguish different paths of motion in the modern languages, can be seen as convergence to the areal tendency – shown by Arandic languages and Warumungu – to grammatically encode path of motion subevents.

In Jingulu and Ngarnka reflexes of Proto-Mirndi verbs remain the head of verbal predicates (Pensalfini 2004). This leads to the unusual situation in which there are only three verbal predicate heads encoding the concepts: 'go' ('event involving motion away from the deictic centre'), 'come' ('event involving motion towards the deictic centre'), and 'do' ('event unspecified for motion').[17] The majority of verbal predicates are therefore light verb constructions consisting of a coverb and one of these three verbs acting as the "light verb".

However in Binbinka, Gudanji and Wamabya, the reflex of the Proto-Mirndi verb has further grammaticalised to an inflectional auxiliary rather than a predicate head. In Wambaya, the deictic motion meaning is maintained. However as these morphemes have developed into purely grammatical morphemes, Wambaya is considered to be a language that encodes motion by means of grammatical morphemes, yielding an AM construction (Nordlinger 2001). In Gudanji and Binbinka, the morphemes cognate to the Wambaya AM morphemes have further grammaticalized to markers of tense. Reflexes of 'go' have grammaticalized as an index of future temporality, and those of 'come' have grammaticalized as an index of past temporality (Osgarby 2018b: 237–238).

3.3.3 Development of AM throughout the region

Of the six languages in North Central Australia that exhibit AM, three languages – Warlpiri, Warlmanpa and Wakaya – seem to exhibit a single AM marker unspecified for path. The three others – Mudburra, Wambaya and Warumungu – form a geographic bloc directly north of the Arandic languages, and distinguish

---

[17] Pensalfini (2014) observes the development of a spatial deictic function for the light verbs, beyond their function as motion verbs.

'towards' and 'away' from the deictic centre, and in the case of Warumungu, a third category of 'set out'.

Directional AM markers in Warumungu are similar to those of other Pama-Nyungan languages in being formally derivational; i.e. they precede finite TAM inflection, and occur with the full range of TAM feature values. However, in both Mudburra and Wambaya, AM morphemes are restricted in their coocurrence with values of the Tense-Mood/Tense-Aspect feature, and they are inflectional in nature – following the finite TAM inflection in Mudburra, and occurring in a second position auxiliary in Wambaya.

Beyond these languages exhibiting AM morphemes, Jingulu and Ngarnka (Mirndi) similarly afford an important grammatical role to motion away and towards the deictic centre, expressed by way of one of three light verbs: 'do', 'go' and 'come'; the vast majority of verbal predicates in these two languages being light verb constructions. This information is summarised in Table 8.

Table 8: Summary of Associated Motion categories in some North Central Australian languages.

Family	Subgroup	Language	Function	Formal type	Number and types of values
Pama-Nyungan	Warluwarric	Wakaya	AM	Suffix	1: PRS.AND
	Ngumpin-Yapa	Warlpiri	AM	Derivational suffix	1: INCEPTIVE
		Warlmanpa	AM	Suffix	1: PRS.AWY?
		Mudburra	AM	Inflectional suffix	2: AWY, TWD
	isolate	Warumungu	D-AM	Derivational suffix	3: AWY, TWD, SETOFF
Mirndi	Ngurlun	Wambaya	AM	Auxiliary	2: AWY, TWD
		Ngarnka	**Light verb**	Verb	2: GO, COME
	isolate	Jingulu	**Light verb**	Verb	2: GO, COME

The development of AM in these languages is likely relatable to two distinct areal phenomena. The development of D-AM morphemes in Warumungu is the result of the grammaticalisation of motion verbs as markers of AM in a complex predicate construction. The Warumungu D-AM morphemes derive from a fixed inflected form of the main verb, combined into a single word with a finite motion verb. The development of AM affixes is due to the grammaticalisation of this structure. The same process has been suggested for the development of Adnyamathanha AM morphemes (Tunbridge 1988: 274–280). The verb in (50) is inflected for the features present and towards, as shown in the gloss of (50b); however this derives from a complex predicate involving some non-finite form of the lexical verb, and the finite motion verb 'go', as shown in (50a).

(50) a. *[VERB STEM   −NON-FINITE INFLECTION]   [MOTION VERB
       *paki-   -ntirr   =apa
       *poke   -NFIN   =go
       −FINITE INFLECTION]
       -n
       -PRS

   b. VERB STEM   −ASSOCIATED MOTION
      paki   -ntirr+apa-n
      poke   -TWD-PRS

The grammaticalisation of verbs as markers of D-AM in Warumungu is likely an influence of the Arandic languages directly to the south, which have complex systems of AM that exhibit path morphemes also preceding finite tense morphemes (see Koch, this volume). By contrast, the development in Mudburra of a dedicated AM function for what are directional affixes in other Ngumpin-Yapa languages seems to be a more complex process, given that the paradigm is sourced from both directional morphology, in the case of -*rra* and -*rni*, as well as encliticised verbs, in the case of -*Carnnginyi* [POT.TWD] and -*Carn* [IMP.TWD].

3.3.4 Development of AM in Mudburra

Returning to the unresolved issue of the development of Mudburra AM morphemes, the repurposing of the directional morphology as AM morphology likely occurred due to contact with Jingulu. Mudburra is the only Ngumpin-Yapa language to have dedicated inflectional AM morphology and given its close proximity and contact history with Jingulu – a language which makes precisely the same deictic motion contrasts in its verbal inventory – it is likely that this is a semantic schema that is borrowed from Jingulu. The "light verbs" of Jingulu 'do', 'go' and 'come' have been calqued to the Mudburra verbal path morphemes realising the features 'neutral', 'away' and 'towards' respectively. The fact that the Jingulu verbs encode inherent motion is evident in Mudburra in the repurposing of the directional morphology as that of AM. This repurposing of the inherited directional morphemes accounts for most of the Mudburra AM suffixes, the rest deriving from phonological vowel assimilation and motion verb encliticisation as described in (§2.2).

Mudburra, Warumungu, Wambaya, Ngarnka, and Jingulu therefore constitute a genetically diverse area that accords privileged grammatical status to motion subevents. In Jingulu and Ngarnka, 'do', 'go' and 'come' are the only concepts lexicalised in the verbal part of speech, and in Wambaya, Mudburra and Warumungu they constitute a small set of grammatical path morphemes (in addition to the 'set out' category in Warumungu). This convergence area notably excludes neighbouring and related languages with no evidence of AM, such as Bilinarra (closely related to Mudburra), and Gudanji and Binbinka (closely related to Wambaya).

4 Conclusion

This chapter has described the form and function of AM morphemes in Mudburra; it has compared them to AM morphemes in the nearby unrelated language Wambaya; and it has contrasted them to AM morphemes in the related languages Warumungu, Warlpiri, Warlmanpa and Wakaya. AM in Mudburra, as in Wambaya, does not co-occur with all TAM feature values, and when it does, it is in some cases realised as portmanteau TAM–AM morphs.

Mudburra, in contact with the unrelated language Jingulu, has developed an AM function out of the erstwhile directional morphemes, and has innovated new forms to supplement these morphemes when occurring in combination with certain tense/mood values by means of encliticisation of the generic verb of motion *ya-* 'go'.

The development of AM morphemes in both Mudburra and Wambaya is likely an areal convergence, given the areal tendency to make only a few distinctions in grammatical path of motion morphemes. The North Central Australian region therefore constitutes a convergence zone of "simple" systems of AM, in contrast to languages directly south of this region that express a greater number of path distinctions in AM morphemes (Koch this volume).

Abbreviations

1	first person	ABE	abessive suffix
2	second person	ABL	ablative case
3	third person	ACC	accusative case
-	morpheme boundary	ACT	actual mood
=	clitic boundary	ALL	allative case
~	reduplication boundary	AND	andative
>	agent–patient relation	AWY	away
A	transitive subject	COM	comitative case

D	directionality	LOC	locative case
DABL	derivational ablative suffix	M	masculine gender
D-AM	directional associated motion	NFIN	non-finite inflection
DAT	dative case	NPST	non-past tense
DECL	declarative mood	NS	non-subject
DEM	demonstrative	O	object,
DEO	deontic mood	OBL	oblique
DIST	distal demonstrative	PFV	perfective
DLOC	derivational locative suffix	PL	plural number
DU	dual number	PLUR	pluractional
DUB	dubitative	POSS	possessive suffix
EP	epenethesis	POT	potential
ERG	ergative case	PRS	present tense
EXCL	exclusive	PST	past tense
F	feminine gender	PURP	purposive mood
FUT	future tense	REFL	reflexive
GEN	genitive case	RSTR	restrictive
HITH	hither	S	(intransitive) subject
HYP	hypothetical (auxiliary)	SEQ	sequential
IMP	imperative mood	SG	singular number
INCH	inchoative	THITH	thither
INCL	inclusive	TOP	topic
INF	infinitive	TWD	towards
IPFV	imperfective		

Acknowledgements: I would like to thank all of my Mudburra colleagues, in particular Shannon Dixon, Wendy Hughes, Raymond Dixon, Janey Dixon, Maureen Bill, Raylene Bill and Sarah Bill. It is only in learning Mudburra from these wonderful teachers that I have gained insights into this phenomenon. Language examples included are taken from both archival materials and my own recordings across several genres (for the most part narrative and elicitation), and were gathered as part of research towards an MPhil dissertation (Osgarby 2018a), for which fieldwork funding was provided by Australian Research Council Discovery Project grant (DP150101201, 'Trilingual language contact in an Indigenous community', 2015–2018, CI Meakins and Pensalfini). The map in Figure 1 was created with funds provided by the UQ School of Languages and Cultures Postgraduate Research Support Scheme. I would also like to thank Rob Pensalfini, Felicity Meakins, Rachel Nordlinger, Jane Simpson, Mitch Browne, Harold Koch, Antoine Guillaume, Jean-Christophe Verstraete, an anonymous reviewer and audiences at the University of Queensland, Laboratoire Dynamique Du Langage (CNRS and Université Lyon 2) and Universität Zürich for useful discussion and suggestions. Any errors or omissions are my own.

References

Belkadi, Aïcha. This volume, chapter 5. Deictic directionality as associated motion: Motion, complex events and event integration in African languages.
Black, Paul. 2007. Lexicostatistics with massive borrowing: The case of Jingulu and Mudburra. *Australian Journal of Linguistics* 27 (1): 63–71. https://doi.org/10.1080/07268600601172959.
Breen, Gavan. 1974. Wakaya grammar. Unpublished MS, Australian Institute of Aboriginal and Torres Strait Islander Studies, Canberra.
Browne, Mitchell. in preparation. *A grammatical description of Warlmanpa: A Ngumpin-Yapa language spoken around Tennant Creek (Northern Territory)*. St Lucia: University of Queensland PhD Thesis.
Chadwick, Neil. 1975. *A descriptive study of the Djingili language*. Canberra: Australian Institute of Aboriginal Studies.
Corbett, Greville G. 2009. Canonical inflectional classes. In Fabio Montermini, Gilles Boyé & Jesse Tseng (eds.), *Selected proceedings of the 6th Décembrettes*, 1–11. Somerville: Cascadilla Proceedings Project.
Dench, Alan. 1998. *Yingkarta*. (Languages of the World/Materials 137) Munich: Lincom Europa.
Green, Ian. 1995. The death of 'prefixing': Contact induced typological change in Northern Australia. In *Proceedings of the twenty-first annual meeting of the Berkeley Linguistics Society: General session and parasession on Historical Issues in Sociolinguistics/Social Issues in Historical Linguistics*, 414–425. Berkeley: Berkeley Linguistics Society.
Guillaume, Antoine. 2016. Associated Motion in South America: Typological and areal perspectives. *Linguistic Typology* 20 (1). 81–177. https://doi.org/10.1515/lingty-2016-0003.
Hansen, Kenneth Carl & Lesly Ellen Hansen. 1975. *The core of Pintupi grammar*. Alice Springs: Institute for Aboriginal Development.
Harvey, Mark. 2008. *Proto Mirndi: A discontinuous language family in northern Australia*. (Pacific Linguistics 593) Canberra: Australian National University. https://doi.org/10.15144/PL-593.
Jones, Barbara. 2011. A grammar of Wangkajunga: A language of the Great Sandy Desert of north western Australia. (Pacific Linguistics 636) Canberra: Australian National University. https://doi.org/10.15144/PL-636.
Koch, Harold. 1984. The category of 'associated motion' in Kaytej. *Language in Central Australia* no. 1. 23–34.
Koch, Harold. This volume, chapter 7. Associated motion in the Pama-Nyungan languages of Australia.
Laughren, Mary. 1978. Directional terminology in Warlpiri (a Central Australian language). In Thao Lê & Mike McCausland (eds), *Working Papers in Language and Linguistics* 8. 1–16. Launceston: Tasmanian College of Advanced Education.
McConvell, Patrick. 1996. Gurindji grammar. Unpublished manuscript. Canberra.
McConvell, Patrick. 2009. Loanwords in Gurindji, a Pama-Nyungan language of Australia. In Martin Haspelmath & Uri Tadmor (eds.), *Loanwords in the world's languages: A comparative handbook*, 790–822. Berlin: Walter de Gruyter. https://doi.org/10.1515/9783110218442.790.
McQuay, Colleen Ruth. 2005. *The structure and inflections of verbs in Ngarnka, an Aboriginal language of the Northern Territory*. St Lucia: University of Queensland BA Honours Thesis.

Meakins, Felicity, Patrick McConvell, Erika Charola, Norm McNair, Helen McNair, & Lauren Campbell. 2013. *Gurindji to English dictionary*. Batchelor: Batchelor Press.

Meakins, Felicity & Rachel Nordlinger. 2014. *A grammar of Bilinarra: An Australian Aboriginal language of the Northern Territory*. (Pacific Linguistics 640) Berlin: De Gruyter Mouton. https://doi.org/10.1515/9781614512745.

Meakins, Felicity & Rob Pensalfini. to appear. Holding the mirror up to converted languages: Two grammars, one lexicon. *International Journal of Bilingualism*.

Merlan, Francesca C. 1994. *A grammar of Wardaman: A language of the Northern Territory of Australia*. (Mouton Grammar Library 11) Berlin: Mouton de Gruyter.

Nash, David. 1979. *Grammatical preface to Vocabulary of the Warlmanpa language*. http://www.anu.edu.au/linguistics/nash/aust/wpa/wpa-vocab.intro.html.

Nash, David. 1986. *Topics in Warlpiri grammar*. New York: Garland.

Nordlinger, Rachel. 1998. *A grammar of Wambaya, Northern Territory (Australia)*. (Pacific Linguistics C–140) Canberra: Australian National University. https://doi.org/10.15144/PL-C140.

Nordlinger, Rachel. 2001. Wambaya in motion. In Jane Simpson, David Nash, Mary Laughren, Peter Austin & Barry Alpher (eds.), *Forty years on: Ken Hale and Australian languages*, 401–414. (Pacific Linguistics 512) Canberra: Australian National University. https://doi.org/10.15144/PL-512.401.

Nordlinger, Rachel. 2010. Complex predicates in Wambaya: Detaching predicate composition from syntactic structure. In Mengistu Amberber, Brett Baker & Mark Harvey (eds.), *Complex predicates: Cross-linguistic perspectives on event structure*, 237–58. Cambridge: Cambridge University Press. https://doi.org/10.1017/CBO9780511712234.009.

Osgarby, David. 2014. *Nominal morphology of Ngarnka, Northern Territory (Australia)*. St Lucia: University of Queensland BA Honours Thesis.

Osgarby, David. 2018a. *Verbal morphology and syntax of Mudburra: An Australian Aboriginal language of the Northern Territory*. St Lucia: University of Queensland MPhil Thesis.

Osgarby, David. 2018b. Reconstructing Proto-Mirndi verbal morphology: From particles and clitics to prefixes. *Australian Journal of Linguistics* 38 (2). 223–92. https://doi.org/10.1080/07268602.2018.1400504.

Pensalfini, Rob. 2003. *A grammar of Jingulu: An Aboriginal language of the Northern Territory*. (Pacific Linguistics 536) Canberra: Australian National University. https://doi.org/10.15144/PL-536.

Pensalfini, Rob. 2004. Towards a typology of configurationality. *Natural Language & Linguistic Theory* 22 (2). 359–408. https://doi.org/10.1023/B:NALA.0000015794.02583.00.

Pensalfini, Rob. 2014. Verbs as spatial deixis markers in Jingulu. In Rob Pensalfini, Myfany Turpin & Diana Guillemin (eds), *Language description informed by theory*, 123–52. (Studies in Language Companion Series 147) Amsterdam: John Benjamins Publishing Company. https://doi.org/10.1075/slcs.147.07pen.

Pensalfini, Rob & Felicity Meakins. to appear. Gender lender: Noun borrowings between Jingulu and Mudburra in Northern Australia. *Journal of Language Contact*.

Schultze-Berndt, Eva. 2000. *Simple and complex verbs in Jaminjung: A study of event categorisation in an Australian language*. (MPI Series in Psycholinguistics 14) Wageningen: Ponsen & Looijen.

Simpson, Jane. 1991. *Warlpiri morpho-syntax: A lexicalist approach*. (Studies in Natural Language & Linguistic Theory 23) Dordrecht: Kluwer Academic Publishers.

Simpson, Jane. 1998. Warumungu (Australian – Pama-Nyungan). In Andrew Spender & Arnold M Zwicky (eds.), *The handbook of morphology*, 707–36. Oxford: Basil Blackwell. https://doi.org/10.1002/9781405166348.ch32.

Simpson, Jane. 2001. Preferred word order and the grammaticalization of Associated Path. In Miriam Butt & Tracy Holloway King (eds.), *Time over matter: Diachronic perspectives on morphosyntax*, 173–208. (Studies in Constraint-Based Lexicalism) Stanford: Centre for the Study of Language and Information.

Simpson, Jane. 2002a. *A learner's guide to Warumungu: Mirlamirlajinjjiki Warumunguku apparrka*. Alice Springs: Institute for Aboriginal Development.

Simpson, Jane. 2002b. From common ground to syntactic construction: Associated Path in Warlpiri. In Nick Enfield (ed.), *Ethnosyntax: Explorations in grammar & culture*, 287–307. (Oxford Linguistics) Oxford: Oxford University Press.

Simpson, Jane & Jeffrey Heath. 1982. Warumungu sketch grammar. Unpublished manuscript.

Stump, Gregory. 2016. *Inflectional paradigms: Content and form at the syntax-morphology interface*. (Cambridge Studies in Linguistics 149) Cambridge: Cambridge University Press.

Tunbridge, Dorothy. 1988. Affixes of motion and direction in Adnyamathanha. In Peter Austin (ed.), *Complex sentence constructions in Australian languages*, 267–284. (Typological Studies in Language 15) Amsterdam: John Benjamins. https://doi.org/10.1075/tsl.15.12tun.

Lauren W. Reed and Kate L. Lindsey

9 "Now the story's turning around": Associated motion and directionality in Ende, a language of Papua New Guinea

Abstract: In this paper, we provide one of the first descriptions of associated motion in a Papuan language. Ende, a language of southern Papua New Guinea, has one directional affix that codes path towards the deictic centre when combined with verbs of motion or transfer. When this affix is combined with other verbs, it gives rise to interpretations of an associated, secondary motion event. This type of "deictic associated motion" was first explicitly described by Belkadi (2015) in several languages of Africa. Ende's deictic associated motion system is unlike prototypical associated motion systems, such as that in Kaytetye (Pama-Nyungan, Australia), in that Ende does not have dedicated affixes that code associated motion. Instead, Ende's associated motion expression relies on inference on the part of speakers and hearers to give rise to the motion readings. Accordingly, we propose the terms *dedicated associated motion* and *inferential associated motion* to distinguish these two very different associated motion systems, one of which relies on dedicated affixes or other structures, and the other, which relies on speakers' and hearers' inferences.

Keywords: associated motion, directionality, deictic associated motion, Ende, Papua New Guinea, Papuan languages

1 Introduction

Associated motion was first described by Koch (1984) in Kaytetye (Pama-Nyungan, Australia). In Kaytetye, associated motion is a grammatical category expressed by a set of dedicated affixes, which associate the main verb with a secondary event of motion. This motion event is specified temporally in relation to the main verb. In the first example below, the motion follows the action of the main verb, while in the second, the motion precedes the action of the main verb.

Lauren W. Reed, Australian National University, lauren.reed@anu.edu.au
Kate L. Lindsey, Boston University, klindsey@bu.edu

https://doi.org/10.1515/9783110692099-009

(1) *Alperre-le=lke   enpe-**layte**-nke.*
    foliage-LOC=then cover-**DO&GO**-PRS
    'He covers him (a dead companion) with leaves before he goes off.'
    (Kaytetye; Koch, this volume, ex [10a])

(2) *Are-nke=lke   re   wethapenye are-**yene**-nke   weye-le=pe.*
    look-PRS=then 3SG.ERG thus   look-**GO&DO**-PRS animal-ERG=TOP
    'It (euro) looks then, the animal then goes and has a look.'
    (Kaytetye; Koch, this volume, ex [3])

Associated motion has since been explicitly described in other Australian languages, including Adnyamathanha (Tunbridge 1988) and Arrernte (Wilkins 1989, 1991), and in several languages of South America (Guillaume 2016) including Cavineña (Guillaume 2008) and Mojeño Trinitario (Rose 2015). Prototypical associated motion systems such as these have dedicated affixes whose only function is to code motion associated with a verb event.

Languages may also have directional systems, where they have one or more morphemes that code direction. The direction may be oriented in absolute space or oriented deictically. For example, Matukar Panau (Austronesian, Papua New Guinea) has directional morphemes that code a seaward or inland distinction, as well as morphemes which code path to or away from the deictic centre (Barth & Anderson 2015). Directionals prototypically code path and do not code motion.

However, Belkadi (2015) describes a phenomenon in the South American language Quechua and several African languages where deictic directional morphemes can give rise to associated motion readings. That is, depending on the inherent semantics of the host verb and the pragmatic context, a deictic directional morpheme can express a separate, secondary motion event that is oriented temporally in relation to the main verb, as exemplified in (3):

(3) *t-cdh   =**d**   di tamyra*
    3SGF-dance.PRF =**VEN** in wedding
    'She danced at the party and came back.' (Taqbaylit Berber; Belkadi 2015: 59)

While this function of directionals has been identified in the past (Payne 1982; Haviland 1993: 42–43; Lichtenberk 2003: 160–166; Bourdin 2006), Belkadi (2015) was the first to explicitly link it to associated motion as a grammatical category, terming it *D-AM or deictic associated motion* (Belkadi 2015: 50, 2016: 49, this volume).

This paper presents the way in which associated motion is expressed in Ende, a Papuan language of Papua New Guinea. Ende is one of six varieties in the Pahoturi River language family in southern New Guinea and is spoken by around 600 people living in three villages in remote rural Western Province. Ende people are primarily subsistence farmers who supplement their palm sago production and slash-and-burn agriculture with hunting and fishing. Ende is still being acquired by children. Papua New Guinea is a known hotspot of linguistic diversity, and southern New Guinea even more so (Evans & Klamer 2012; Evans 2012).

Ende has one directional affix which codes motion towards the deictic centre. When the marker is used with a verb of motion or transfer, as in (4), it codes directionality. However, when it is used with a verb that is not of motion or transfer, as in (5), it gives rise to a secondary, associated motion meaning.

(4) *Ine   ulle da   bogo   ade   gongällbänän   a   tater ingoll*
    ine   uɽe=da   bogo   ade   go-ŋaɽbən-ən   a   tater=iŋoɽ
    water   big=NOM   3SG.NOM   then   REM-rise-3SGS   and   mat=SIM
    ngädnanngädnan   deyarnän.
    ŋəd-nan~ŋəd-nan   d-**ej**-a-r-n-ən
    ADV~roll-PLS   REM-**VEN**-SGS-go.SGS-DUR-3SGS
    'The water rose up and came rolling in like a mat.' (J. Sowati 2016: 8)

(5) *Ngämlle   sokpa de   yazgi.*
    ŋəmɽe   sokpa=de   **j**-a-zgi
    1SG.DAT   tobacco=ACC   FUT.**VEN**.2SG>3SG-RT.EXT-wrap
    'Wrap and bring that tobacco to me.' (S. Jerry 2016: 3)

This pattern is similar to that expressed by the Taqbaylit Berber deictic directional morpheme in (3), which indexes two separate events: (i) the dancing and (ii) the return. Similarly, in (5), the Ende directional affix gives rise to an interpretation where there is (i) a main event (wrapping) and (ii) a secondary associated motion event (bringing). Like Taqbaylit Berber, Ende uses its deictic directional marker to index associated motion; hence, like Taqbaylit Berber, Ende exhibits what Belkadi (2016) terms "deictic associated motion".

Associated motion has only been briefly described in one Papuan language, the isolate Yélî Dnye of Rossel Island (Levinson 2006: 197–199) (see also Dryer's [this volume, ch. 4] analysis of Imonda [Border, Papua New Guinea]). Belkadi (2015: 69) mainly surveyed languages in Africa and was concerned that deictic associated motion might be "quite geographically concentrated". In this paper, we present the first extended description of associated motion in a Papuan language. In doing so, we explicitly identify deictic associated motion in a geographically and genetically unrelated language to those surveyed by Belkadi (2015). (See also Schokkin, Vidal & Payne, and Dryer [this volume, ch. 13], for descriptions of deictic associated motion in other non-African languages.)

We also propose alternative terms to those posited by Belkadi (2015, 2016). Belkadi (2015: 45) termed dedicated associated motion systems such as that in Kaytetye as "AM expressed by inflectional affixes" or *I-AM*. Belkadi (2015, 2016: 49) termed systems like Taqbaylit Berber and Ende, which repurpose directional morphemes, as D-AM or deictic associated motion. We hold that these terms are confusing. So-called deictic associated motion systems regularly make use of inflectional affixes, as Ende does. In addition, dedicated associated motion markers in some languages are not inflectional affixes but are instead derivational affixes (see Osgarby, this volume), particles, clitics, or auxiliaries. Guillaume (2016: 99–100) proffers an example of the same from Baure (Arawak, Bolivia), where an "intentional particle" expresses prior motion:

(6) ač   ri=im=ro   yiti   ač   **kač**   ri=nik
    and   3SG.F=put=3SG.M chili   and   **go**   3SG.F=eat
    'And she put chili in it [the food] and she [another woman] went to eat.'
    (Baure; Danielson 2007: 277, as cited in Guillaume 2016: 100)

Furthermore, some languages express associated motion using serial verb constructions (see Lovestrand & Ross, this volume). Hence, in light of this variability of means for expressing AM cross-linguistically, we propose the term *dedicated associated motion* rather than I-AM for systems such as those in Kaytetye, Cavineña, and Baure, where markers exist with no other function than to express associated motion.

The term "deictic associated motion" is also imprecise because many dedicated associated motion markers also have a deictic component. Consider the following pair of examples from Cavineña (Tacanan, Bolivia), which feature two dedicated associated motion markers coding prior motion:

(7) *Tudya*   *=ekwana*   *ba-**ti**-kware*   *takure*
    then   =1PL   see-**go**.TEMP-REM   chicken
    'So we went to see the chicken (in the back of the bus).'
    (Cavineña; Guillaume 2008: 212)

(8) *Jadya=tibu=dya*   *=mikwana*   *ba-**na**-wa*
    thus=reason=FOC   =2PL   see-**come**.TEMP-PERF
    'This is why I have come to see you (plural) (here in your village).'
    (Cavineña; Guillaume 2008: 212)

The affixes -*ti* and -*na* are respectively dedicated associated motion markers, but they are also deictically oriented: -*ti* away from the deictic centre and -*na* towards it. Hence, the term "deictic associated motion" for non-dedicated systems (such as Taqbaylit Berber and Ende) is confusing, as the associated motion suffixes in (7) and (8) are both dedicated *and* deictic.

Belkadi (this volume) clarifies that the terms "D-AM" and "deictic associated motion" are meant to refer to associated motion systems where a single form encodes either associated motion or deictic directionality depending on the context. At the same time, she notes that "canonical AM" (or I-AM) is often deictically oriented. Given the fact that deictic orientation can figure in *both* D-AM and I-AM systems, we suggest that rather than incorporating the term "deictic" in the name for only *one* of these systems, it would be less analytically opaque to select a different term altogether. As such, inspired by Haviland (1993: 43), we propose *inferential associated motion* as a designation for systems such as that in Ende, which, in order to express associated motion, repurpose morphemes that have other primary functions. The term "inferential" highlights how pragmatics and context drive the way in which deictic directionals give rise to associated motion meanings.

The paper is structured as follows. In section 2, we present the form of the Ende ventive. In section 3, we illustrate cases where the Ende ventive morpheme has a canonical directional function. In contrast, in section 4, we present those cases in which the ventive morpheme has an inferential associated motion function. Those cases that do not fit neatly into either category are described in section 5, and in section 6, we discuss our findings and revisit our proposed new terminology. This study is grounded in a corpus of naturalistic speech, primarily narratives, collected over 11 months from 2015 to 2018 in Limol, Western Province, Papua New Guinea (Lindsey 2015). All examples in the paper are naturally occurring utterances arising from the corpus except for (38), which was elicited.

2 Form of the ventive prefix

The form of the ventive prefix has three allomorphs. The underlying form *i-* is realised as *y-* /j/ when word-initial and immediately preceding a vowel (9), as *ey-* /ej-/ when word-medial but still before a vowel (10), and as *i-* elsewhere, that is when immediately preceding a consonant (11).[1] When the prefix is realised as

---

[1] The Ende orthography is used for in-text language examples. IPA equivalents of non-transparent orthographs include: <ä> = /ə/, <dd> = /d͡z/, <ll> = /ɽ/, <ng> = /ŋ/, <ny> = /ɲ/, <tt> = /t͡s/, <y> = /j/, <z> = /z/~/d͡ʒ/.

a high /i/ vowel, it triggers height-sensitive vowel harmony throughout the verb (see Lindsey [2019: 190]; and cf. a similar system in Idi in Gast [2017]).

(9) *Ag me   yuwenyan.*
    ag=me   ju-weɲ-an
    morning=LOC   REC.**VEN**.3SGP-take-3SGA[2]
    'In the morning, he brought it back.' (B. Zakae 2016a: 12)

(10) *Gall   deyagllaenalla   gänyo.*
     gaɽ   d-**ej**-a-gɽaj-n-aɽa   gəɲo
     canoe   REM-**VEN**.3SGP-RT.EXT-paddle-DUR-1NSGA   here
     'We paddled the canoe here.' (W. Warama 2016: 27)

(11) *Skul a   sens de   biwenyän.*
     skul=a   sens=de   b-**i**-weɲ-ən
     school=NOM   change=ACC   FUT-**VEN**.3SGP-take-3SGA
     'Education will bring change here.' (E. Sali 2018: 95)

The ventive prefix is limited in its distribution in two ways. Semantically, the ventive prefix does not occur in transitive verbs with first- or second-person patients. This constraint is evidenced by contrasting the (a) and (b) examples in (12) and (13), which have a first-person and third-person patient, respectively. Note how the andative (a) and ventive (b) forms are identical in (12) but differ in (13). Of note, here we use "andative" to refer to motion with a non-specific or deictically unmarked path (see Guillaume & Koch, this volume).

(12) a. *Ngänäm   gänyo   **datramän**.*
        ŋənəm   gəɲo   d-a-tram-ən
        1SG.ACC here   REM-RT.EXT-lead-3SGA
        'He brought me here.' (C. Soma 2018: 25)

---

[2] Ende verbal morphology contains multiple types of distributed exponence, complicating a one-to-one gloss of form to meaning. Since the verbal morphology is not the topic of this paper, the glosses have been simplified. Only the intended meaning is glossed, not all the meanings possible with the shown form.

b. *Ngänäm   danglläbänän   abo   **datramän***
   ŋənəm   d-a-ŋɾəbən-ən   abo   d-a-tram-ən
   1SG.ACC REM-RT.EXT-get-3SGA then   REM-RT.EXT-lead-3SGA
   do   sel   ma we.
   do   sel   ma=we
   there   cell   place=ALL
   'He got me and then took me to jail.' (Y. Sowati 2018: 22)

(13) a. *Gänyaolle   dindugän   bogo.   Ngämo   mang bom*
        gənaoɾe   d-indug-ən   bogo   ŋəmo   maŋ=bom
        towards.here REM-run-3SGS 3SG.NOM 1.SG.POSS brother=3SG.ACC
        *ngattong   **ditramän.***
        ŋaʈʂoŋ   d-i-tram-ən
        first   REM-VEN.3SGP-lead-3SGA
        'He ran this way. He brought my brother first.' (P. Wäziag 2018: 59)

   b. *Ine da   däbe   llig   kälsre de   **dätramän**   duli.*
      ine=da   dəbe   ɾɪg   kəlsre=de   d-ə-tram-ən   duli
      water=NOM   that   child   small=ACC   REM-3SGP-lead-3SGA there
      'The water took that small child there.' (T. Warama 2016: 21)

Structurally, the ventive prefix is constrained in two ways: (i) it must replace a patient agreement prefix and (ii) it may precede a transitive root extension, but not an intransitive one. The exact mechanics of this are not at issue for this paper. In summary, the Ende ventive marker has three phonologically-conditioned allomorphs, *i-*, *ey-*, and *y-*, which occur only in transitive prefix templates indexing third-person or dummy patients, either by replacing the patient agreement prefixes or by preceding a transitive root extension.

3 Directionality

Ende has one directional, which codes orientation towards the deictic centre. Terms by which this is known in the literature include *ventive*, *venitive*, *cislocative*, *centripetal*, and *hither*. The ventive can be contrasted with motion away from the deictic centre, referred to as *andative*, *itive*, *translocative*, *centrifugal*, and *thither* (see Guillaume & Koch, this volume). In this paper, we understand motion as fundamentally involving the displacement of an entity (Frawley 1992: 171). In their canonical form, directionals do not code motion, but only path (Guillaume 2016:

13–14). Jackendoff (1983: 163) describes how path may consist of a "path-function" and a "reference-object" or "reference place". In the following English example, *from* is the path function and *under the table* is the reference place:

(14) *The mouse ran from under the table.*
      (Jackendoff 1983: 163)

Critically, here, the preposition *from* does not encode motion. Instead, motion is encoded by the semantics of the verb. Similarly, Talmy (1975: 181) defines path as "the respect in which one object is considered as moving or located to another object".

In Ende, the deictic centre may be the speaker (15). It may be the location where the speaker is, was, or will be in, or the typical place where the speaker is, usually the village of Limol, where much of the corpus was recorded (16). In narratives, a third-party protagonist may be the deictic centre (17). Figure 1 shows the context in which example (17) was uttered.

(15) *Ngämo   nag   deyarän   ada,   "Wiya."*
      ŋəmo   nag   d-**ej**-a-r-ən   ada   wiya
      1SG.POSS   friend REM-**VEN**-RT.EXT-go-3SGS   like.this come.IMP
      'My friend came to me and said, "Come!"' (Dareda 2016: 18.1)

(16) *Ngämi   baebol   skul i   yaralla*
      ŋəmi   bajbol   skul=i   j-a-r-aɽa
      1NSG.EXCL.NOM bible   school=ALL   REC.**VEN**-RT.EXT-go.SGS-1NSGS
      ngäna   abo   gänyaolle   Llimoll e   dedam
      ŋəna   abo   gənaoɽe   ɽimoɽ=e   dedam
      1SG.NOM   then   towards.here   Limol=ALL   here
      yaran,   naentin   eiti   wan.
      j-a-r-an   najntin   ejti   wan
      REC.**VEN**-RT.EXT-go-1SGS   nineteen   eighty   one
      'We went to bible school, and then I came back here to Limol, in 1981.'
      (D. Sobam 2018b: 122)

(17) *Ge   lla da   abo   yaran   abo,   mälla da*
      ge   ɽa=da   abo   j-a-r-an   abo   məɽa=da
      this   man=NOM   then   REC.**VEN**-RT.EXT-go-3SGS then   woman=ACC
      wa   llig a   nabllenegan   abo.
      wa   ɽɪg=a   n-a-bɽe-neg-an   abo
      and   child=ACC   REC-RT.EXT-greet-SG>PL-1|3SGA   then
      'Then this man came and greeted his wife and child.' (D. Sobam 2018a: 77–78)

9 "Now the story's turning around": Associated motion and directionality in Ende — 365

Figure 1: #15 Real Return (San Roque et al. 2012).

As shown in examples (4) and (15–17), the Ende ventive is often found with motion verbs and adds a path specification to the motion already expressed by the verb. However, it may occur with stative verbs with no motion component, denoting the orientation of the event, as in (18).

(18)   *Ubi*   *didämawän*   *gänyaolle.*
       ubi   d-*i*-dəma-wən   gəɲaoɾe
       3NSG.NOM   REM-**VEN**-sit.pl-3PLS   this.way
       'They were sitting down facing this way.' (T. Warama 2018: 99)

In Ende, verbs of transfer such as 'haul' and 'carry' entail motion. When the Ende ventive is used in these contexts, it adds a path specification to the motion entailed by the verb, as in the following examples.

(19) Käsre   mälla da   gobällän   wayati
    kəsre   məɾa=da   go-bəɾ-ən   wajati
    then   woman=NOM   REM-go.PLS-3PLS watermelon
    deyangmereyo.
    d-**ej**-a-ŋmer-ejo
    REM-**VEN**-RT.EXT-haul-3NSGA
    'Then the women went and hauled the watermelons back here.' (J. Dareda 2016: 93)

(20) Däbem   matta   digegiyu   gänyowe   de
    dəbem   ma͡tsa   d-**i**-geg-iyu   gəɲo=we   de
    that.ACC shoulder REM-**VEN**.3SGP-AUX-3NSGA here=ALL FOC
    Kurupel pate.
    kurupel pat=e
    Kurupel body=ALL
    'They carried him on their shoulders here to Kurupel.' (W. Kurupel 2017a: 76)

Many narratives in the Ende corpus involve a departure and a return to a place, usually the village of Limol. The title of this paper quotes Ende speaker Wendy Bewag, who remarked that the ventive morpheme means that "now the story's turning around". That is, the switch from unmarked verbs to ventively marked verbs signal to the hearer that the path of the action has now switched towards the deictic centre. In the following examples, drawn from a single narrative, the verb is first used in a neutral sense (21) and then oriented to the deictic centre to indicate that the protagonists are now returning (22).

(21) Gall   dagllaenalla   do   gongkaemam   Parade.
    gaɾ   d-a-gɾaj-n-aɾa   do   go-ŋkajm-mam   Parade
    canoe   REM-RT.EXT-paddle-DUR-1NSGA there REM-start-1PLS   Parade
    'We paddled the canoe (away from the village) until we got to Parade.' (W. Warama 2016: 9)

(22) Gall   deyagllaenalla   gänyo-o, Eramang   gall
    gaɾ   d-**ej**-a-gɾaj-n-aɾa   gəɲo-o   eramaŋ   gaɾ
    canoe   REM-**VEN**-RT.EXT-paddle-DUR-1NSGA here-VOC Eramang canoe
    tap   ma.
    tap   ma
    moor   place
    'We paddled back all the way here to Eramang canoe mooring place.' (W. Warama 2016: 27)

9 "Now the story's turning around": Associated motion and directionality in Ende

Example (23) is drawn from a story in part about a cure for an illness, where a crocodile tooth is shot at a man's back, and a cassowary chick is then removed from the man's chest, curing the illness.

(23) a. *Käsre   bägäl de   diwenyän   käza   ngoe*
       kəsre   bəgəl=de   d-i-weɲ-ən   kəza   ŋoj
       then   bow=ACC   REM-**VEN**.3SGP-carry-3SGA   crocodile   tooth

   ereya   tär peyang   itrel att.
   er=eja   tər=pejaŋ   itrel=a͡tʂ
   where=COP.PST.SGS   string=COM   sickness=ABL

   'Then [the healer] brought a bow and a healing crocodile tooth tied with string.'

   b. *Ttatta   pallall e   dedme   deyazuwän.*
      t͡ʂat͡ʂa   paɽaɽ=e   dedme   d-**ej**-a-zu-wən
      lower.back   direction=ALL   there.LOC   REM-**VEN**-RT.EXT-shoot-3SGA

   '[The healer] shot it into [Sali's] back.'

   c. *Sali bo   guwo watt   dirom   llig de*
      sali=bo   guwo=a͡tʂ   dirom   ɽɪg=de
      Sali=3SG.POSS   inside=ABL   cassowary   child=ACC

   ekaekong   digezänän.
   eka~eka=aŋ   d-**i**-gezən-ən
   ADV~sound=ATT   REM-**VEN**.3SGP-take.out.NPL-3SGA

   '[The healer] took the chirping cassowary chick out of Sali's body.'

   d. *Sali   abo   ai   gogän.*
      sali   abo   aj   go-g-ən
      Sali   then   good   REM-AUX-3SGS

   'Then, Sali became well.' (W. Kurupel 2017a: 82–84, 87, 98)

In both (23a) and (23b), Sali, the sick man, is the deictic centre. Accordingly, the use of the ventive indexes motion towards Sali. The use of the ventive in (23c) also indexes directionality, but it is less clear who the deictic centre is. Example (23c) could be read as a shift in the deictic centre to the healer, who brings the chick out towards himself. Alternatively, this could be seen as a continuation of Sali as the deictic centre, as the cassowary chick emerges into his field of vision. Cross-linguistically, deictic directionals have been found to mark a contrast of visibility (Fortis & Fagard 2010: 10).

Similarly, the event in (24) involves a hook, which is extracted towards the deictic centre. However, it is unclear whether the deictic centre is Karama Popo, the cutter who removed the hook, or both Karama Popo and the speaker, as the hook emerges into both of their fields of view and hence towards them.

(24) Karama Popo eraya   bogo   aya
     karama popo er=aja   bogo   aj=ja
     Karama Popo where=COP.PST.SGS 3SG.NOM who=COP.PST.SGS
     dapellaemnän,   dägageyo,   dägageyo,
     d-a-peɾajm-n-ən   d-ə-gag-ejo   d-ə-gag-ejo
     REM-RT.EXT-cut-DUR-3SGA   REM-3SGP-AUX-3NSGA REM-3SGP-AUX-3NSGA
     tudi   käp de   däbe   digezäneyo.
     tudi   kəp=de   dəbe   d-i-gezən-ejo
     fishing   hook=ACC   that   REM-VEN.3SGP-take.out.NPL-3NSGA
     'Karama Popo was the one who cut me open. They cut and cut and took the fish hook out.' (W. Bewag 2017: 63)

All the previous examples in this section index actual motion, where an entity moves in real space and time. In Ende, motion and corresponding path can also be metaphorical, as in (25).

(25) Oke, ge   ttoen a   oba   taem e   deyarän,
     oke   ge   t͡sojn=a   oba   tajm=e   d-ej-a-r-ən
     okay this story=NOM   3NSG.POSS time=ALL REM-VEN-RT.EXT-go.SG-3SGS
     deyarän,   deyarän.
     d-ej-a-r-ən   d-ej-a-r-ən
     REM-VEN-RT.EXT-go.SGS-3SGS REM-VEN-RT.EXT-go.SG-3SGS
     'Okay, this story has been coming all the way to their time.' (R. Kurupel 2017: 16)

In this section, we have described how the Ende ventive is used in a classic directional sense; that is, where it codes path only. Any motion or non-motion is expressed not by the directional morpheme, but by the semantics of the host verb. We now turn to examples where the Ende ventive codes not only path but also associates a motion event with the main verb.

4 Inferential associated motion

When the Ende ventive is combined with a verb that has no motion semantics, it adds a secondary motion event to the clause, in addition to a path specification (see Guillaume & Koch, this volume; Dryer, this volume, ch. 4; Belkadi, this volume). We

9 "Now the story's turning around": Associated motion and directionality in Ende — 369

call this an *inferential associated motion* system because it is based on inference and implicature. Ende's inferential associated motion system can give rise to the association of a motion event occurring prior to, subsequent to, or simultaneous with the action of the host verb. The moving entity or "figure of the event" (Talmy 1975: 181) may be an intransitive subject, transitive object, or transitive subject and object together. In this next section, we systematically explore each of these possibilities in Ende and contextualise them in terms of associated motion typological tendencies.

In the following example, the speaker is running from a bright light that is pursuing him through the forest.

(26) *Däbe   ngäna   ddone   deyangttäneg*
     dəb=e   ŋəna   ɖʐone   d-**ej**-a-ŋʈʂə-nəg
     that=COP.PST.SGS 1SG.NOM   not   REM-**VEN**-RT.EXT-count-SG>PL
     ada llo   tubu   deya   o
     ada ɾo   tubu   da=jja   o
     like tree stump INT.DEM=COP.PST.SGS OR
     kupkup   deya.
     kup~kup   da=jja
     DIM~hole   INT.DEM=COP.PST.SGS
     'I didn't count how many small logs or potholes there were as I was coming back.' (Sowati Kurupel 2017: 48)

In (26), when the ventive directional is added to the verb 'count', the resulting reading is that there is concurrent motion associated with the counting. In other words, the speaker is in motion while he is counting. Here, the ventive codes two properties: motion and orientation of that motion towards the deictic centre. Similarly, in (27), the ventive on the verb 'hide' results in a prior motion reading associated with the hiding.

(27) a. *Mänmän a   komlla ten   ada   gotbanegän,*
        mənmən=a   komɾa   ten   ada   go-tba-negən
        girl.PL=NOM   two   ten   like.this REM-plan-3PLS
        "Ibi   tatuma   ibi wi   dag."
        ibi   tatuma   ibi=wi   da=g
        1NSG.INCL.NOM   washing.place   GO=ALL   INT.DEM=COP.PRS.PLS
        'Twenty girls were planning, "Let's go bathe."'

b. *Käsre   ada   gognegän,   tatuma   gobällän.*
   kəsre   ada   go-g-negən   tatuma   go-bəɽ-ən
   then   like.this REM-AUX-3PLS   washing.place   REM-go.PL-3PLS
   'Then they went like this, they went to the bathing spot.'

c. *Lla da   ditgewän   ada   mänmän,   "Gidre! Gidre!"*
   ɽa=da   d-**i**-tge-wən   ada   mənmən   gidre   gidre
   man=NOM   REM-**VEN**-hide-3PLS like.this girl.PL   enemy   enemy
   'Men had come and hid, and the girls went, "Enemy! Enemy!"' (P. Wäziag 2016: 1)

In terms of the moving entity, associated motion of intransitive subjects or transitive subjects *without* their object (as in [26] and [27]) are rare in the Ende corpus. However, associated motion of either transitive objects alone, or transitive subjects and objects together, are more common. It is perhaps significant, then, that the slot that the directional morpheme usurps in the Ende verbal complex is one customarily dedicated to object marking (see section 2).

As discussed in section 3, in Ende, verbs of transfer such as *kongkom* 'carry' and *matta dägag* 'shoulder' entail movement. In these verbs, the subject and the object move together (as in [19] and [20]). Given that Ende verbs of transfer already entail movement, by our definition, the ventive in these sentences is coding path only and not motion (see Dryer [this volume, ch. 4], for a related discussion). Conversely, in the following examples, the host verbs are 'search' (28), 'dig' (29), and 'pick' (30). These are actions, but they do not necessarily entail motion like actions such as 'go' (15–17), 'haul' (19) or 'paddle' (21, 22). When the directional morpheme is combined with the former set of verbs, a secondary motion event is entailed. In other words, the motion event associated with the main verb is expressed by the directional morpheme alone.

(28) *Mani di   niyagnegnan.*
     mani=di   n-**i**-jag-neg-n-an
     money=ACC   REC-**VEN**.3PLP-search-SG>PL-DUR-3SGA
     'She searched for and brought back money.' (Sarbi Kurupel 2018: 315)

(29) *Gaguma we   abo   bidaebneyo.*
     gaguma=we   abo   b-**i**-d-ajb-n-ejo
     yamhouse=ALL then   IRR-**VEN**.3PLP-dig.out.NPL-NSG>PL-DUR-3NSGA
     'They would dig the yams and bring them to the yamhouse.' (J. Dareda 2017: 74)

9 "Now the story's turning around": Associated motion and directionality in Ende — 371

(30) Ngämo   lla da   nge   yaddänan   a
     ŋəmo   ɾa=da   ŋe   j-a-ʤən-an   a
     1SG.POSS man=NOM   coconut REC.**VEN**-RT.EXT-pick-3SGA and
     imneimne   ngäna   wätät yu.
     imne~imne   ŋəna   wətət ju
     ADV~after   1SG.NOM food   fire
     'My husband picked and brought a coconut, and afterwards, I cooked.'
     (M. Bewag 2018: 227)

In examples (27–30), with perception and utterance verbs, the transitive subject and the transitive object move in conjunction. However, in the following examples, the transitive subject is stationary, and the transitive object is the moving entity. The context in which example (31) was uttered can be seen in Figure 1 (also used to show the context for [17]).

(31) O   lligda   bogo   ikop **dey**addägnän.
     o   ɾɪg-da   bogo   ikop d-**ej**-a-ʤəg-n-ən
     oh   child-3.POSS 3SG.NOM see   REM-**VEN**-RT.EXT-bite[3]-DUR-3SGA
     'Oh, his boy was watching him come up.' (D. Sobam 2018a: 15)

(32) To   indrang de   ngäna   ikop dige.
     to   indraŋ=de   ŋəna   ikop d-**i**-ge
     light bright=ACC   1SG.NOM see   REM-**VEN**.3SGP-AUX
     'I saw the bright light coming towards me.' (Sowati Kurupel 2017: 30)

(33) Daolle   dallän   abo   tatraem de
     daoɾe   da-ɾ-ən   abo   tatrajm=de
     towards.there   REM-go-3SGS   then noise=ACC
     yaya   **dey**andärän.
     jaja   d-**ej**-a-ndər-ən
     father   REM-**VEN**-RT.EXT-hear-3SGA
     'He walked until his father heard him coming.' (W. Kurupel 2017b: 37)

---

3 The collocation of the uninflecting verb 'see' and the inflecting verb 'bite' is an idiomatic expression in Ende, which translates as 'to watch'.

(34) *Lla da   deyamballigallo   ngänaeka alle*
     ɽa=da   d-**ej**-a-mbaɽɪg-aɽo   ŋənajka=aɽe
     person=NOM   REM-**VEN**-RT.EXT-welcome-HAB.PLA tears=INS
     tärämpmenyang de.
     tərəmpmeɲ=aŋ=de
     funeral.act=AGT=ACC
     'The people will welcome with tears the returning person who slept with the deceased's bag.' (B. Zakae 2016b: 29)

Again, the host verbs in examples (31–34) have no motion semantics.[4] Instead, the directional morpheme expresses both the motion and path of the moving entity, which in these examples is the object argument. This associated motion of the object may be typologically unusual, given Ross's (this volume) finding that "non-subject" associated motion is rare. Belkadi (this volume), surveying D-AM systems in several African languages, notes that motion of the object is "quite rare", and where it occurs, is associated with verbs of perception, utterance, or "goal-oriented verbal emission", such as cursing or welcoming. Belkadi's analysis of the semantics of verbs that can drive an object-only motion reading, therefore, accords with this phenomenon in Ende (31–34).

A core component of associated motion is that the secondary motion event is ordered temporally in relation to the main verb. In dedicated associated motion systems such as Adnyamathanha (Pama-Nyungan, Australia), prior (35), concurrent (36) and subsequent (37) temporal orderings are possible:

(35) *Mai   ngarlku-**mana**-angg-athu.*
     food eat-**come.and**-PERF-1SG.ERG
     'I came and ate the food.' (Adnyamathanha; Tunbridge 1988: 270)

(36) *Awi   yarra-**nali**-ku.*
     rain-NOM fall-**CONT.coming**-NARR
     'It's raining, and it's heading this way (from a long way off).'
     (Adnyamathanha; Tunbridge 1988: 272)

---

4 Antoine Guillaume makes a good observation here that "in some languages, such verbs behave like motion verbs, and the authors talk about 'fictive' motion. But in these languages, the directional specifies the direction of this fictive motion (of the 'gaze', for instance, with verbs like 'look at'), and not about the motion of the O, which [exists] in Ende" (p.c. 28 April 2020).

(37) *Artu-nga   veldha   marli-**wandha**-anggu.*
   woman-ERG clothes   wash-**and.leave**-PERF
   'The woman washed the clothes and cleared off.' (Adnyamathanha; Tunbridge 1988: 273)

Despite the fact that Ende has a single associated motion morpheme, the Ende ventive prefix can still give rise to a prior (27), concurrent (26, 31–34), or subsequent (5, 28–30) sense of motion. In dedicated associated motion systems such as Adnyamathanha (35–37), there are dedicated affixes for each temporal ordering. This is not the case in Ende, where context and pragmatics determine which temporal reading is generated. Ende speaker Warama Kurupel Suwede reported in elicitation that the events in (38) can be interpreted with either a subsequent or a concurrent motion reading.

(38) *Ngäna   nge   ine de   inewan.*
   ŋəna   ŋe   ine=de   *i*-ne-wan
   1SG.NOM coconut water=ACC REC.**VEN**.3SGP-drink-3SGA
   'I drank coconut water and came.'
   'I drank coconut water while I was coming.' (W. Kurupel p.c. 2017)

When we consider our naturalistic corpus, some generalisations emerge in terms of which inferred reading is more likely. Using the ventive with an intransitive verb seems to yields prior associated motion (27), while the motion of the transitive object only seems to yield concurrent associated motion (31–34).[5] However, the motion of transitive subject and transitive object together can generate a concurrent (26) or subsequent associated motion reading (28–30).

This variability in possible temporal interpretations is in contrast with the inferential associated motion system in five languages of the Koman family (Ethiopia/South Sudan), which can only express subsequent motion (Otero, this volume). Temporal ordering in Ende appears freer than that in Paluai (Oceanic, Papua New Guinea), where preverbal and postverbal directionals give, respectively, strict prior and subsequent associated motion readings (Schokkin, this volume). In Ende, the prevalence of concurrent and subsequent motion and the relative scarcity of prior motion goes against crosslinguistic proposals and findings from Levinson and Wilkins (2006: 534), Guillaume (2016: 120, 127), and Ross (this volume).

---

5 We thank an anonymous reviewer for this insight.

5 Other functions of the directional morpheme

There are several examples in Ende where the ventive may denote the assumption or intention of motion, rather than necessarily actualised motion. The following is an excerpt of a conversation:

(39) Ao,   nga   be**y**antämonaemeya
 ao   ŋa   b-**ej**-a-ntəmon-ajm-eja
 yes now FUT-**VEN**-RT.EXT-wait-NSG>PL-1NSGA
 'Yes, now we will wait for them to come.' (P. Madura 2016: 21)

Here, motion is associated with the host verb 'wait'. The figure of the secondary motion event is the object, namely, the girls who are washing. However, the motion has not yet occurred, and indeed, may not; for example, the girls may not come back to the waiting speaker. Similarly, in the following example, the subject calls towards the object to come (i.e., move), but there is no entailment that the object will necessarily carry out the motion coded by the directional. That is, the children will not necessarily come following their being called.

(40) Llig   kläkle   olle   **ig**nigan.
 ʈɩg   kləkle   oɽe   **i-g**-nig-an
 child small.PL call REC.**VEN**.3PLP-AUX-SG>PL-1SGA
 'I called the children over.' (K. Baewa 2018: 331)

There is a parallel here with the "anticipated ventive" marker in Nivacle (Mataguayan, Paraguay), exemplified in (41):

(41) j-ovalh-**c'oya**
 1(>3)-watch-**AM.ANT.VEN**
 'I watched, waiting for him/her/them to come.' (Nivacle; Fabre 2013: 11, cited in Guillaume 2016: 144)

The "anticipated ventive" marker in Nivacle marks motion that is "temporarily postponed or expected ... towards the [subject/actor]" and where the "associated actor [is] invisible at the time of the event" (Fabre 2013: 11, cited in Guillaume 2016: 144). This accords with (39) and (40) in Ende; however, in Ende, there is no entailment that the associated actor is nonvisible.

It is an open question whether examples such as (39) and (40) should be considered associated motion or not, given that it is not certain whether the motion will take place or not.[6] Antoine Guillaume (p.c., 28 April 2020) highlights a more interesting pattern in this data, in that it may reflect the "mirror image" of what is commonly referred to as "motion with purpose". As Guillaume points out, motion with purpose is overwhelmingly discussed in the context of *prior* motion in the literature (see, for example, Lovestrand & Ross, this volume). However, Ende appears to permit the expression of *subsequent* motion with purpose, which may be cross-linguistically quite unusual.

By way of further example, other uses of the Ende ventive are better translated as 'so as to come …' rather than encoding an actual secondary motion event. This could be seen as a sort of path-oriented intentionality. In (42), Donae Kurupel describes the aftermath of capturing a crocodile in her net while fishing in the swamp. Having placed the crocodile in the canoe, she arrives back at the mooring place, throws the crocodile on the ground, kills it with the help of her sister, and then they carry it back to the village.

(42) a. *Gall e   tap   dägag.   Za de   ngäna*
       gaɽ=e   tap   d-ə-gag   za=de   ŋəna
       canoe=ALL   dock   REM-3SGP-AUX   thing=ACC   1SG.NOM
       dägaz.
       d-ə-gaz
       REM-3PLP-take.out.PLP
       'The canoe docked. I took out our things.'

   b. *Käza de   däbe   bogo   gall*
      kəza=de   dəbe   bogo   gaɽ
      crocodile=ACC   that   3SG.NOM   canoe
      ik mi   ada   any   gogän.
      ik=mi   ada   aɲ   go-g-ən
      inside=LOC   like.this   something   REM-AUX-3SGS
      'That crocodile was inside the canoe and was going like this.'

   c. *Ngäna   däbe   käza de   eraeya*
      ŋəna   dəbe   kəza=de   era=jja
      1SG.NOM   that.ACC   crocodile=ACC   where=COP.PST.SGS
      net alle   daeya   any   dägag.
      net=aɽe   da=jja   aɲ   d-ə-gag
      net=INST   INT.DEM=COP.PST.SGS   thing   REM-3SGP-AUX
      'I got the crocodile with the net, and went like this.'

---

[6] We thank Antoine Guillaume for this point, and for drawing our attention to the Nivacle data.

d. *Gänyeri   tutu wi   deyaspun.*
   gəɲeri   tutu=wi   d-**ej**-a-spun
   here.ALL   land=ALL   REM-**VEN**-RT.EXT-throw
   'I threw [the crocodile] onto the shore [so as to return home].'
   'I threw [the crocodile] onto the shore [towards home].'
   #'I threw [the crocodile] onto the shore [and brought it home].'

e. *Gall   ik att de   dägazen   ume ttäp a*
   gaɾ   ik=atş=de   d-ə-gazen   ume tşəp=a
   canoe   inside=ABL=ACC   REM-3SGP-take.out   mouth=NOM
   eraeya   ttatt a   gottalamän.
   era=jja   tşatş=a   go-tşalam-ən
   where=COP.PST.SGS   jaw=NOM   REM-break-3SGS
   'When I took it out from the canoe, the jaw cracked open.'

f. *Ngäna   däbe   giri   tupi da   ngämi*
   ŋəna   dəbe   giri   tupi=da   ŋəmi
   1SG.NOM   that.ACC   knife   long=NOM   1NPL.EXCL.NOM
   eraeya   ada   ume ttäp e   dätrəkne.
   era=jja   ada   ume tşəp=e   d-ə-trək-ne
   where=COP.PST.SGS   like.this   mouth=ALL   REM-3SGP-push-DUR
   'I took my big knife and started pushing it into the crocodile's mouth.'
   (D. Kurupel 2017:51–56)

Example (42d) could be translated as 'I threw it on the shore and carried it home', just as in (28–30), where the translation indexes two events. However, the next part of the story recounts how the protagonist struggles with and kills the crocodile on the shore. It is only after that that she and her sister shoulder the crocodile and carry it back to the village. Hence, (42d) translates best as 'I threw it on the ground (so as to return home)', or 'I threw it on the ground (towards home)'. It is not well-translatable as 'I threw it on the ground and brought it home' as there are multiple events following this sequence where the crocodile is killed before it is then carried home. This interpretation is in contrast to uses of the directional in examples (28–30), which involve two distinct events per clause.

Coding for directionality or associated motion is optional in Ende. Example (42) is revelatory in that although the ventive could appear in (42a), (42c) and (42e), it does not. The switch back and forth from ventively marked to neutral verbal forms appears more stylistic than strictly grammatical. Indeed, the directional morpheme is often co-combined with a directional adverb or deictic postposition, as with (43) and (44) in the following examples:

(43) Gänye   gänyerimae   **de**yangkämänggeya
      gəɲe   gəɲerimaj   d-**ej**-a-ŋkəmə-ŋg-eja
      here   this.way.closer REM-**VEN**-RT.EXT-take-APPL-1NSGA
      ako-o   aumawang e ae.
      ako=o   au=ma=waŋ=e=aj
      then=VOC   grave=place=ATT=ALL=VOC
      'Then we took a shortcut this way towards the graves.' (J. Karea 2016:11)

(44) Minong   gänyaollemae
      minoŋ   gəɲaoɾemaj
      Minong   towards.here.closer
      ditäräpmällnän   ngämo pate.
      d-**i**-tərəp-məɾ-n-ən   ŋəmo=pate
      REM-**VEN**.3SGP-cut.across-DUR-DUR-3SGA   1SG.POSS=ALL.ANIM
      'Minong cut across towards me.' (J. Karea 2016:43)

Remarking on the use of the ventive in its directional sense, speaker Warama Kurupel Suwede called it "a shortcut". His comment hints at speakers' intuition of the use of the ventive as an efficient way to package a lot of information in a single clause. This shortcut is optional in Ende, but it is nevertheless used quite often.

6 Discussion

In Taqbaylit Berber, Belkadi (2015: 59) finds that when a directional is used with a verb which does not encode an event expressing motion, an associated motion reading arises. The exclusion of inferential associated motion with verbs with motion semantics in Taqbaylit Berber "suggests that the phenomenon is primarily derived pragmatically, as a kind of 'last-resort' interpretation" (Belkadi 2015: 60; also see Belkadi, this volume). Faced with a deictically orientated non-motion verb (such as 'sleep', 'eat' or 'work'), speakers "seek among the implicatures" of the directional and construct the most pragmatically likely meaning (Hooper 2002: 297). Motion coded by directionals appears a matter of "inferential ingenuity", not syntax (Haviland 1993: 43).

Ende's associated motion system is similar to those in geographically widely-dispersed languages, such as those discussed in this volume by Dryer (this volume, ch. 4) and Belkadi (this volume). Prior to Belkadi's (2015, 2016: 49) proposal of the term "deictic associated motion" or "D-AM", this function of directionals was variously termed "displaced directionality" (Lichtenberk 2003: 160–166), "time referentials" (Payne 1982), or given no specific term at all (Haviland 1993: 43). The lack of convergence on a standard term meant that studies were scattered orphan-like throughout the literature. The term "deictic associated motion" has created an explicit link to the existing associated motion literature, and indeed has been taken up by several scholars in this volume.

However, as outlined in section 1, we have concerns that the term "deictic associated motion" is somewhat imprecise and potentially confusing, as prototypical associated motion markers very often also have a deictic orientation. As such, we restate our new terminological proposals here, which we argue are both clearer and capture a greater range of form possibilities. For "I-AM" systems such as in Adnyamathanha, Cavineña, and Kaytetye, we propose the term *dedicated associated motion*. For "D-AM" systems such as in Ende, we propose the term *inferential associated motion*. The expression of associated motion is common to both types of systems, but what differs is whether the sense of the marker is dedicated and hence unambiguous, or whether it rests on inference. By focusing on this dimension of *dedication* vs *inference*, we avoid questions of form; that is, we allow for the possibility that either type of associated motion may be expressed by any morphological form, be it verbal inflections, derivations, particles, or some other construction.

To see the power of this terminological distinction in action, we consider Kayardild (Tangkic, Australia). Here, when a verb is followed directly by a motion verb, this gives rise to a concurrent or subsequent motion reading (Evans 1995: 308). For instance, when the verb *warra-ja* is used as a main verb, it translates as 'go (to)' or 'come (to)'. However, when it appears in a "motion complex", that is, directly following a "main verb", it gives rise to a concurrent motion reading, as in (45).

(45) *Jiki-ja   warra-ja   karn-ki.*
    light.fire-ACT go-ACT   grass-MLOC
    '(They) went along setting fire to the grass.' (Evans 1995: 309)

Evans (1995: 309–310) notes that this concurrent motion reading is "usually" generated from this serial verb construction; less frequently, a motion with purpose reading is generated. Depending on how predictable and "usual" the concurrent motion reading indeed is, we would have grounds to classify these Kayardild serial verb constructions as either dedicated associated motion (if they are heavily predictable) or inferential associated motion (if not).[7]

---

[7] See also Lovestrand & Ross (this volume) for a treatment of Kayardild and associated motion serial verb constructions more generally.

7 Conclusion

Ende has one directional morpheme, which codes motion towards the deictic centre. When the directional morpheme is inserted into a verb of motion or transfer, it codes path only. When it is inserted into a verb that is not of motion or transfer, it associates a secondary motion event with the host verb. This motion event can be prior to, concurrent with, or subsequent to the main verb. The directional can also code the assumption or intention of motion. Despite a lean directional system with only one morpheme, Ende speakers use context and pragmatics to give rise to a feast of possible meanings.

We agree with Belkadi (2015, this volume) that this phenomenon warrants analysis as a special type of associated motion. However, we identify some issues with Belkadi's (2015, 2016) terms "I-AM", "D-AM", and "deictic associated motion". We instead propose that associated motion systems with dedicated markers or structures, such as those in Kaytetye and Cavineña, be termed *dedicated associated motion*. Meanwhile, systems such as those in Ende, which rely on other markers such as directionals to express associated motion, should be termed *inferential associated motion*. Importantly, by following Belkadi's lead and arguing for a link between these Ende phenomena and associated motion, we contribute to "turning the story around" for this function of directionals, which has hitherto been only peripherally acknowledged.

Abbreviations

Glossing abbreviations follow Leipzig's Glossing Rules (Comrie, Haspelmath, & Bickel 2008). Less-standard abbreviations are as follows:

|	or	HAB	habitual	RT.EXT	root extension
>	acting on	MLOC	modal locative	SIM	similative
ACT	actual	NSG	nonsingular	TEMP	temporarily
AM	associated motion	PERF	perfective	VEN	ventive
ANIM	animate	REC	recent past		
ANT	anticipated	REM	remote past		

Acknowledgements: We wish to thank and acknowledge the Ende tribe, in particular Warama Kurupel Suwede, Wagiba Geser, Wendy Bewag, Takeya (Mecklyn) Dieb, and Wareya (Wesley) Giniya for their assistance in data collection and analysis and for sharing their lives and language with us. We also gratefully acknowledge funding from the Firebird Foundation for Anthropological Research to conduct this research and for equipment loans from the Centre of Excellence for the Dynamics of Language. For comments and feedback on this paper, thanks go to Antoine Guillaume, Harold Koch, Nicholas Evans, Jean-Christophe Verstraete, an anonymous reviewer, and the attendees of the workshop "Directionality or associated motion? Evidence from diverse languages" held at the Australian National University on 22 June 2018.

References

Baewa, Kols. 2018. Sociolinguistic Questionnaire – Kols Baewa. *LSNG08*.[8]
   http://www.paradisec.org.au/collections/LSNG08/items/SE_PI113.
Barth, Danielle, & Gregory D. S. Anderson. 2015. Directional constructions in Matukar Panau. *Oceanic Linguistics* 54(1). 206–239.
Belkadi, Aicha. 2015. Associated motion with deictic directionals. *SOAS Working Papers in Linguistics* 17. 44–71.
Belkadi, Aicha. 2016. Associated motion constructions in African languages. *Africana Linguistica* 16. 44–70.
Belkadi, Aïcha. This volume, chapter 5. Deictic directionality as associated motion: Motion, complex events and event integration in African languages.
Bewag, Maki (Lynette). 2018. Sociolinguistic Questionnaire – Maki (Lynette) Bewag. LSNG08. http://www.paradisec.org.au/collections/LSNG08/items/SE_PI095.
Bewag, Wendy. 2017. Wendy's Fishing Story. *LSNG08*. http://www.paradisec.org.au/collections/LSNG08/items/SE_SN039.
Bourdin, Philippe. 2006. The marking of directional deixis in Somali. In F. K. Erhard Voeltz (ed.), *Studies in African linguistic typology*, 13–41. Amsterdam & Philadelphia: John Benjamins.
Comrie, Bernard, Martin Haspelmath, and Balthasar Bickel. 2008. The Leipzig Glossing Rules: Conventions for interlinear morpheme-by-morpheme glosses (modified 05/31/2015). *Department of Linguistics of the Max Planck Institute for Evolutionary Anthropology & the Departemtn of Linguistics of the University of Leipzig*. https://www.eva.mpg.de/lingua/resources/glossing-rules.php.
Danielsen, Swintha. 2007. *Baure: An Arawak language of Bolivia*. Leiden: Research School of Asian, African, and Amerindian Studies (CNWS), Universiteit Leiden.
Dareda, Jerry. 2016. Watermelon Story (retelling). *LSNG08*. http://www.paradisec.org.au/collections/LSNG08/items/SE_PN010.
Dareda, Jerry. 2017. Sisor otät ttängäm ngasnges ttoen (Yam Gardens: Planting and Harvest). *LSNG08*. http://www.paradisec.org.au/collections/LSNG08/items/SE_SN045.
Dobola, Kaoga. 2018. Sociolinguistic Questionnaire – Kaoga Dobola. *LSNG08*. http://www.paradisec.org.au/collections/LSNG08/items/SE_PI110.

---

[8] References to collection *LSNG08* refer to the PARADISEC archival collection by Lindsey (2015). Years refer to the date of recording.

Dryer, Matthew S. This volume, chapter 4. Associated motion and directionals: where they overlap.
Dryer, Matthew S. This volume, chapter 13. Associated motion in North America (including Mexico and Central America).
Evans, Nicholas. 1995. *A grammar of Kayardild: With historical-comparative notes on Tangkic*. Berlin & New York: Mouton de Gruyter.
Evans, Nicholas. 2012. Even more diverse than we had thought: The multiplicity of Trans-Fly languages. In Nicholas Evans & Marian Klamer (eds.), *Melanesian Languages on the Edge of Asia: Challenges for the 21st Century. Language Documentation & Conservation*. Special publication (5). 109–49.
Evans, Nicholas, & Marian Klamer. 2012. Introduction: Linguistic challenges of the Papuan region. In Nicholas Evans & Marian Klamer (eds.), *Melanesian Languages on the Edge of Asia: Challenges for the 21st Century. Language Documentation & Conservation*. Special publication (5). 1–12.
Fabre, Alain. 2013. Applicatives and associated motion suffixes in the expression of spatial relations: A view from Nivacle (Mataguayo family, Paraguayan Chaco). Unpublished manuscript. https://www.academia.edu/12443688/ (accessed 17 May 2020).
Fortis, Jean-Michel & Benjamin Fagard. 2010. Space and language, Part V – Deixis. Leipzig summer school in typology. https://www.eva.mpg.de/lingua/conference/2010_summerschool/pdf/course_materials/Fortis_5.DEIXIS.pdf (accessed 7 March 2018).
Frank, Wendy. 2018. Sociolinguistic Questionnaire – Wendy Frank. *LSNG08*. http://www.paradisec.org.au/collections/LSNG08/items/SE_PI058.
Frawley, William. 1992. *Linguistic semantics*. Hillsdale, New Jersey: Lawrence Erlbaum Associates.
Gast, Volker. 2017. Directional inflection in Sidibiri Idi (Southern PNG). Paper presented to Workshop on the Languages of Papua 4, Manokwari, Indonesia. 23 January. https://www.researchgate.net/publication/313242611_Directional_inflection_in_Sibidiri_Idi_Southern_PNG (accessed 6 March 2018).
Geser, Wagiba. 2017. Llimollang aba giddoll ttoen. *LSNG08*. http://www.paradisec.org.au/collections/LSNG08/items/SE_SN066.
Guillaume, Antoine. 2008. *A grammar of Cavineña*. Berlin: De Gruyter Mouton.
Guillaume, Antoine. 2016. Associated motion in South America: Typological and areal perspectives. *Linguistic Typology* 20(2). 81–177.
Guillaume, Antoine & Koch, Harold. This volume, chapter 1. Introduction: Associated motion as a grammatical category in linguistic typology.
Haviland, John B. 1993. The syntax of Tzotzil auxiliaries and directionals: The grammaticalization of "motion". In *Proceedings of the Nineteenth Annual Meeting of the Berkeley Linguistics Society: Special Session on Syntactic Issues in Native American Languages*. 35–49. https://www.researchgate.net/publication/268384840_The_Syntax_of_Tzotzil_Auxiliaries_and_Directionals_The_Grammaticalization_of_Motion_Authors (accessed 16 October, 2018).
Hooper, Robin. 2002. Deixis and aspect: The Tokelauan directional particles *mai* and *atu*. *Studies in Language* 26(2). 283–313.
Jackendoff, Ray. 1983. *Semantics and cognition*. Boston: MIT Press.
Jerry, Samuel. 2016. Ause Ur (Children's song). *LSNG08*. http://www.paradisec.org.au/collections/LSNG08/items/SE_SS024.
Karea, Jugu (Mado). 2016. Mado's Pig Story. *LSNG08*. http://www.paradisec.org.au/collections/LSNG08/items/SE_SN030.

Koch, Harold. 1984. The category of "associated motion" in Kaytej. *Language in Central Australia* 1. 23–34.
Koch, Harold. This volume, chapter 7. Associated motion in the Pama-Nyungan languages of Australia.
Kurupel, Donae, author. 2016. Kurupel bo pepeb (reading). *LSNG08*. http://www.paradisec.org.au/collections/LSNG08/items/RE_EN015.
Kurupel, Donae. 2017. Donae's Crocodile Story. *LSNG08*. http://www.paradisec.org.au/collections/LSNG08/items/SE_SN033.
Kurupel, Donae. 2018. Sociolinguistic Questionnaire – Donae Kurupel. *LSNG08*. http://www.paradisec.org.au/collections/LSNG08/items/SE_PI051.
Kurupel, Rex. 2017. Story of the Limol/Malam coconut tree. *LSNG08*. http://www.paradisec.org.au/collections/LSNG08/items/SE_SN049.
Kurupel, Sarbi. 2018. Sociolinguistic Questionnaire – Sarbi Kurupel. *LSNG08*. http://www.paradisec.org.au/collections/LSNG08/items/SE_PI114
Kurupel, Sowati. 2017. Iddob Kabama Ibiatt. *LSNG08*. http://www.paradisec.org.au/collections/LSNG08/items/SE_PN024.
Kurupel (Suwede), Warama. 2017a. Sali's Pig Story. *LSNG08*. http://www.paradisec.org.au/collections/LSNG08/SE_SN041.
Kurupel (Suwede), Warama. 2017b. Auma we ibiatt ttoen (retelling)." *LSNG08*. http://www.paradisec.org.au/collections/LSNG08/items/SE_PN026.
Levinson, Stephen C. 2006. The language of space in Yélî Dnye. In Stephen C. Levinson & David P. Wilkins (eds.), *Grammars of space: Explorations in cognitive diversity* (Language Culture & Cognition), 157–205. Cambridge: Cambridge University Press.
Levinson, Stephen C. & Wilkins, David P. 2006. Patterns in the data: Towards a semantic typology of spatial description. In Stephen C. Levinson & David P. Wilkins (eds.), *Grammars of space: Explorations in cognitive diversity* (Language Culture & Cognition), 512–552. Cambridge: Cambridge University Press.
Lichtenberk, Frantisek. 2003. Directionality and displaced directionality in Toqabaqita. In Erin Shay & Uwe Seibert (eds.), *Motion, direction and location in languages: In honour of Zygmunt Frajzyngier*. 151–75. Amsterdam & Philadephia: John Benjamins.
Lindsey, Kate L. 2015. *Language corpus of Ende and other Pahoturi River languages* (LSNG08). Digital collection managed by PARADISEC. [Open Access]. DOI: 10.26278/5c1a5cfcaacde. http://catalog.paradisec.org.au/collections/LSNG08.
Lindsey, Kate L. 2019. *Ghost elements in Ende phonology*. Stanford, CA: Stanford University doctoral dissertation. https://purl.stanford.edu/ys194fp6634.
Lovestrand, Joseph & Ross, Daniel. This volume, chapter 3. Serial verb constructions and motion semantics.
Madura, Pitepo. 2016. Conversation. *LSNG08*. http://www.paradisec.org.au/collections/LSNG08/items/SE_SI001.
Osgarby, David. This volume, chapter 8. Mudburra associated motion in an areal perspective.
Otero, Manuel. This volume, chapter 20. At the intersection of associated motion, direction and exchoative aspect in the Koman languages.
Payne, Judith. 1982. Directionals as time referentials in Ashéninca. *Anthropological Linguistics* 24(3). 325–337.
Rose, Françoise. 2015. Associated motion in Mojeño Trinitario: Some typological considerations. *Folia Linguistica* 49(1). 117–158.

Ross, Daniel. This volume, chapter 2. A cross-linguistic survey of associated motion and directionals.
Sali, Erabal. 2018. Sociolinguistic Questionnaire – Erabal Sali. *LSNG08*. http://www.paradisec.org.au/collections/LSNG08/items/SE_PI064.
San Roque, Lila, Lauren Gawne, Darja Hoenigman, Julia C. Miller, Alan Rumsey, Stef Spronck, Alice Carroll & Nicholas Evans. 2012. Getting the story straight: Language fieldwork using a narrative problem-solving task. *Language Documentation and Conservation* 6. 135–174.
Schokkin, Dineke. This volume, chapter 10. Preverbal directionals as markers of associated motion in Paluai (Austronesian; Oceanic).
Sobam, Duiya. 2018a. Family Problems Picture Task 4.4. *LSNG08*. http://www.paradisec.org.au/collections/LSNG08/items/SE_PI041.
Sobam, Duiya. 2018b. Sociolinguistic Questionnaire – Duiya Sobam. *LSNG08*. http://www.paradisec.org.au/collections/LSNG08/items/SE_PI072.
Soma, Christina. 2018. Sociolinguistic Questionnaire – Christina Soma. *LSNG08*. http://www.paradisec.org.au/collections/LSNG08/items/SE_PI046.
Sowati, Jubli (Joe), author. 2016. Ause da llig kälsre peyang (The old woman and the small boy). *LSNG08*. http://www.paradisec.org.au/collections/LSNG08/items/RE_EN003.
Sowati (Kurupel), Maryanne. 2016. Emi bo mänddmänddatt eka (Emi's drowning story). *LSNG08*. http://www.paradisec.org.au/collections/LSNG08/items/SE_PN004.
Sowati, Yuga. 2018. Family Problems Picture Task 2.4. *LSNG08*. http://www.paradisec.org.au/collections/LSNG08/items/SE_PN036.
Talmy, Leonard. 1975. Semantics and syntax of motion. In John P. Kimball (ed.), *Syntax and semantics*, vol 3, 181–238. New York: Academic Press.
Tunbridge, Dorothy. 1988. Affixes of motion and direction in Adnyamathanha. In Peter Austin (ed.), *Complex sentence constructions in Australian languages*, 267–283. Amsterdam & Philadephia: John Benjamins.
Vidal, Alejandra & Payne, Doris L. This volume, chapter 12. Pilagá directionals and the typology of associated motion.
Warama, Tonny (Tonzah). 2016. Ause da llig kälsre peyang (The old woman and the small boy). *LSNG08*. http://www.paradisec.org.au/collections/LSNG08/items/SE_PN003.
Warama, Tonny (Tonzah). 2018. Kate's Notebook 2018b. *LSNG08*. http://www.paradisec.org.au/collections/LSNG08/OE_SI005.
Warama, Winson. 2016. How we went to dive. *LSNG08*. http://www.paradisec.org.au/collections/LSNG08/items/SE_PN021.
Wäziag, Pingam. 2016. Tatuma ibiatt pepeb. *LSNG08*. http://www.paradisec.org.au/collections/LSNG08/items/WE_PN009.
Wäziag, Pingam. 2018. Sociolinguistic Questionnaire – Pingam Wäziag. *LSNG08*. http://www.paradisec.org.au/collections/LSNG08/items/SE_PI062.
Wilkins, David P. 1989. *Mparntwe Arrernte (Aranda): Studies in the structure and semantics of grammar*. Canberra, Australia: Australian National University PhD thesis.
Wilkins, David P. 1991. The semantics, pragmatics and diachronic development of "associated motion" in Mparntwe Arrernte. *Buffalo Papers in Linguistics* 1. 205–257.
Zakae, Bibiae. 2016a. Funeral traditions. *LSNG08*. http://www.paradisec.org.au/collections/LSNG08/items/SE_SN013.
Zakae, Bibiae, author. 2016b. Funeral traditions (reading). *LSNG08*. http://www.paradisec.org.au/collections/LSNG08/items/RE_EN022.

Dineke Schokkin
10 Preverbal directionals as markers of associated motion in Paluai (Austronesian; Oceanic)

Abstract: This chapter discusses the directional paradigm of Paluai, an Oceanic language spoken on Baluan Island in Manus Province, Papua New Guinea. It shows that these forms are used as preverbal particles not only to indicate direction with motion verbs, but also associated motion (AM) with non-motion verbs. This paper is the first to claim that an AM system based on deictic directionals can clearly be recognized as a category in an Oceanic language, thus setting a precedent for further study of this phenomenon in this particular subgroup, and perhaps also in the Austronesian language family more generally. Secondly, a systematic comparison is made between directionals used either preceding or following the main verb, and it is argued that only the former are attested as markers of AM. It turns out that iconicity is a strong guiding principle in the usage of directionals in Paluai.

Keywords: associated motion, directionals, serial verb constructions, Oceanic languages

1 Introduction

A phenomenon commonly encountered in Oceanic languages consists of verb-like forms that indicate the direction of motion verbs, which go by different names depending on the analysis (Pawley 1973; Durie 1988), but will henceforth be referred to with the term "directional". This paper discusses the directional paradigm of Paluai (South East Admiralty subgroup), spoken on Baluan Island in Manus Province, Papua New Guinea; see Figure 1 for the location of Manus Province, and Figure 2 for the location of Baluan within the province. The analysis is based on a corpus of naturalistic speech about 69,000 words in size, which was collected on Baluan Island by the author between 2010 and 2012. The main text genres represented in the corpus are narratives, task-based elicitation (picture-matching tasks), and public speeches.

Dineke Schokkin, University of Canterbury/The Australian National University, dineke.schokkin@canterbury.ac.nz

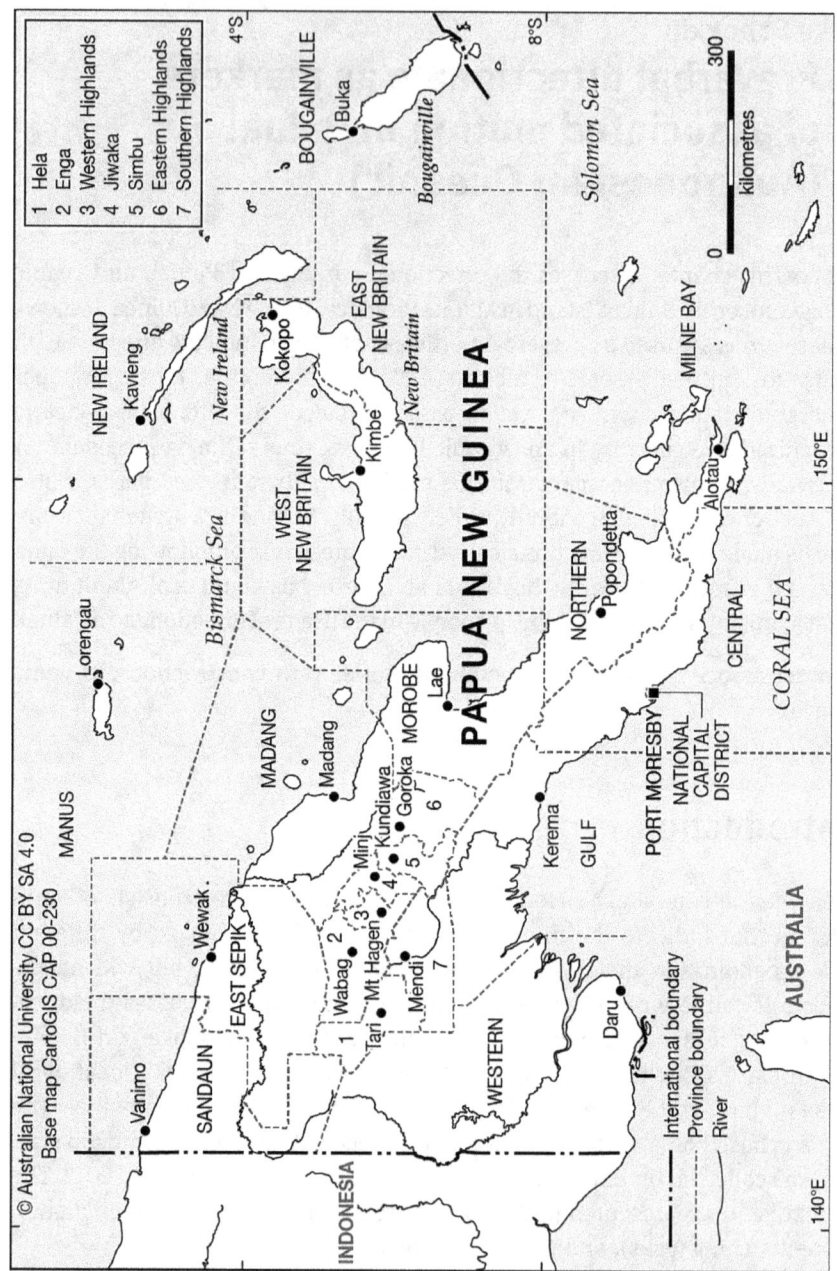

Figure 1: Provinces of Papua New Guinea.

10 Preverbal directionals as markers of associated motion in Paluai — 387

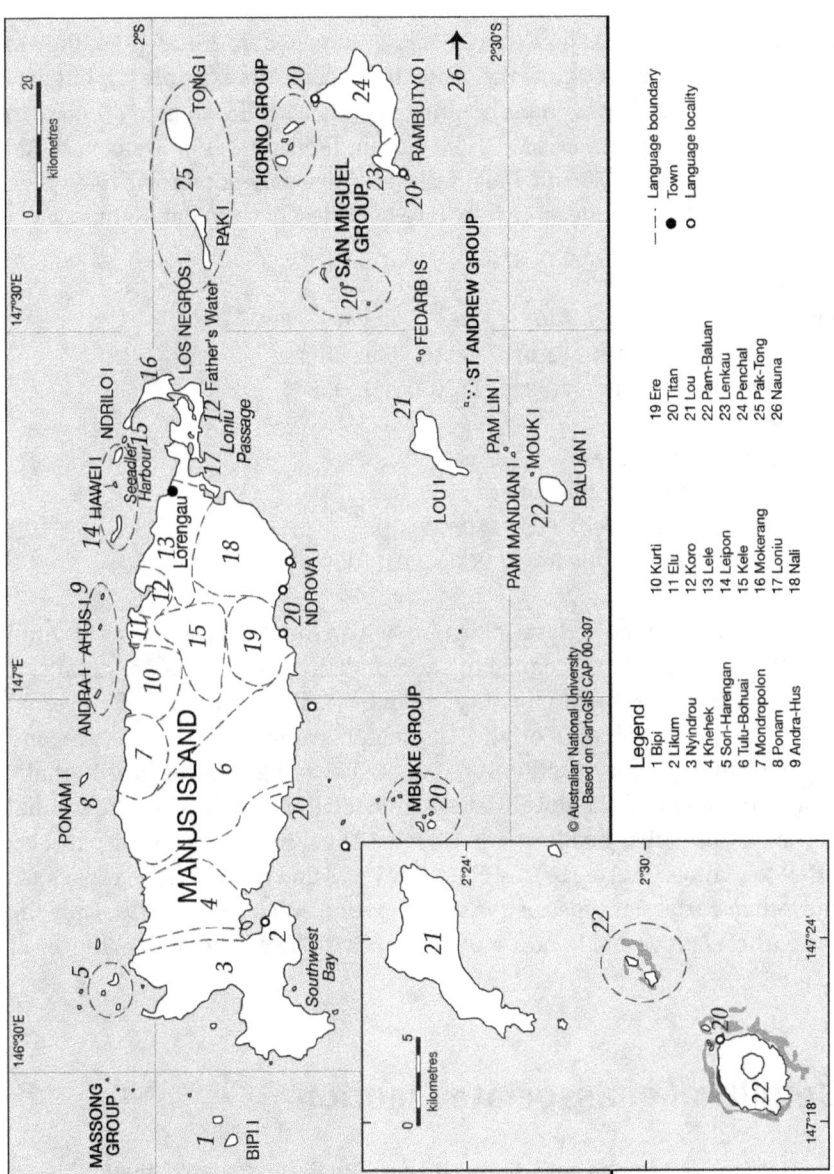

Figure 2: Location of Baluan Island within Manus Province.

The current paper will show that in Paluai, directionals are used not only to indicate direction with motion verbs, as with *me* 'come' in example (1), but also associated motion (AM) with non-motion verbs, as with the same *me* 'come' in (2). It is therefore an example of a D-AM system (Belkadi 2015). Systems of AM may be present in other Oceanic languages, but they may not always have been recognized as such and none appear to have been described in detail thus far.

(1) *epme ret liliu la Lipan*
    ep$_S$=**me**   **tet**   **liliu**   la   Lipan
    1pl.EXC=**come** **walk** **return** go.to place.name
    'We came back to Lipan village.' (KM060111_0084)

(2) *ipme lêp nganngan teyo*
    ip=**me**   **lêp**   nganngan   te-yo
    3pl=**come** **take** food   EMP-DEM.INT
    'They came and took the food.' (KM060111_0092)

Paluai shows widespread verb serialisation, with a number of subtypes of serial verb constructions (SVCs) recognised; see Schokkin (2020) for more details. It has no tense, but aspect and modality are indicated by a number of preverbal particles that may be verbal in origin. Alignment is nominative-accusative, and constituent order is fairly rigidly SVO. It has a paradigm of ten directionals, introduced in more detail below, that are attested in three different functional slots: 1) as main verbs, heading a predicate; 2) as grammaticalised particles preverbal to main lexical verbs, both motion verbs and non-motion verbs; 3) as second verb in particular types of SVCs with motion and transfer verbs. Only the uses as particles preverbal to non-motion verbs will be considered instances of D-AM.

2 Definition of associated motion

As discussed in Guillaume and Koch (this volume), "associated motion" as a category was first recognised for indigenous languages of Australia, but is now gaining more currency among people working with a variety of other language families across the world. Belkadi (2015) proposes a distinction between I-AM and D-AM systems, the former involving inflectional elements dedicated to marking AM whereas the latter contain forms that stem from, and can be simultaneously used as, markers of deictic orientation. She also puts forward the hypothesis that the former system can develop out of the latter. In Belkadi (2015: 53), D-AM is defined as follows:"[I]n D-AM contexts, deictic directionals presuppose a motion event which occurs *in addition to* the event encoded by the verb stem they modify." (emphasis mine).

Guillaume (2016: 13) puts forward the following definition: "An AM marker is a grammatical morpheme that is associated with the verb and that has among its possible functions the coding of translational motion." While this definition is often interpreted as referring to bound verbal morphology, it can be extended to include other grammatical elements such as particles, even if these are also attested as free forms. This is the approach taken in the current chapter. Even though all Paluai directionals currently occur as main verbs, as preverbal particles they function as grammatical elements that are closely associated with the main verb, as the analysis in the subsequent sections will show.

3 AM in Oceanic languages

Grammatical elements that indicate direction on motion verbs are a characteristic feature of Oceanic languages, and much attention has been devoted to them, over several decades (see e.g. Pawley 1973; Durie 1988; Hamel 1993; Wilkins & Hill 1995; Senft 2000; Ross 2004; Næss 2011; Schokkin 2013; Barth & Anderson 2015). They can indicate deictic direction (itive 'go' vs. ventive 'come'), direction with regard to a cardinal orientation system ('seawards', 'inland', 'parallel to the shore'), or a combination of both.

Given recurrent findings in the typological literature with respect to the link between directionals and AM in other language families, it would be expected to also find this link in Oceanic languages where directionals are frequently employed. This isn't often made explicit for Oceanic languages, however, which may just simply be due to unfamiliarity with the term "associated motion" in the Oceanic research tradition. There are a few exceptions. Cleary-Kemp (2015), in her dissertation on SVCs in Koro, an Admiralties language spoken on Manus mainland, analyses one type of SVC as denoting associated motion. This construction looks very similar to the one in Paluai that uses preverbal directionals to indicate AM. Dryer (2013) also explicitly analyses the suffix *-maan* 'come' and the preverbal particles *maa* 'come.and' and *fe* 'go.and' as AM markers in his description of the Lemakot dialect of Kara. Meier (2020) is another recent dissertation that discusses AM, for the Northwest Solomonic language Mono-Alu.

4 The Paluai directional paradigm

Each motion event includes "a Figure in Motion along a Path oriented with respect to one or more Grounds" (Wilkins & Hill 1995: 217). The source (the location where the motion starts) and the goal (where the motion terminates) are sometimes, but not always, explicitly stated. When referring to motion in Paluai, two dimensions are important: whether or not the motion is oriented or grounded with regard to a deictic centre (DC), and whether or not the motion is oriented or grounded with regard to an absolute Frame of Reference (FoR) based on fixed bearings (Levinson 2003; Levinson & Wilkins 2006).

Paluai directionals form a closed subclass of active intransitive verbs, which have become grammaticalised to function as direction markers for or related to the action expressed by a main verb. They do, however, also appear as head of a predicate. A feature that distinguishes them from regular active intransitive verbs is that they cannot be nominalised. Table 1 shows the directional paradigm. It is likely that some of the directionals were in fact morphologically complex forms, and the presumable Proto-Oceanic (POc) roots are indicated for each of them.

Table 1: Directional paradigm.

Form	Paraphrase	POc root(s)
1) [+deixis −FoR]		
me	come, motion towards DC	**mai* 'come, hither'
la, lak	go to, motion away from DC	**lako* 'go, thither'
2) [+deixis +FoR]		
si	come seawards (down), towards DC	**sipo* 'go down'
sa, sak	come inland (up), towards DC	**sake* 'go up'
wot	go parallel to the shore (horizontally), away from DC	**ua[tu]* 'go to addressee'
suwot	go seawards (down), away from DC	**sipo* + **ua[tu]*
sot	go inland (up), away from DC	**sake* + **ua[tu]*
3) [−deixis +FoR]		
wen	move parallel to the shore (horizontally)	**pano* 'go, walk (away)'
suwen	move seawards (down)	**sipo* + **pano*
sen	move inland (up)	**sake* + **pano*

Paluai has eight directionals that are specified with regard to an absolute FoR. For these, a three-way distinction is made between 1) movement seawards, 2) movement inland, and 3) movement parallel to the shore. As for other Austronesian languages, the land–sea axis is an important concept within spatial reference. Baluan is a cone-shaped volcanic island; its highest point is the crater of the now dormant volcano located more or less in the middle. Therefore, going inland always means going up, and going towards the shore always means going down. In addition, since motion parallel to the shore (i.e. intersecting the land–sea axis) usually means moving on more or less the same level, this has obtained the secondary meaning of 'moving on a horizontal level'. At sea, the system is extrapolated: thus, for moving towards the shore the same directionals are used as for moving inland, and for moving out to sea the same directionals are used as for moving towards the shore (i.e. seawards) when on land.

Seven of the ten directionals are specified for deixis, indicating motion either towards or away from a deictic centre. Most often, the speaker of the utterance can be understood as the DC, but this can be varied for pragmatic reasons. Five of the directionals specified for deixis are additionally specified for the absolute FoR. The other three of the ten directionals are specified with regard to the absolute FoR, but are not deictically anchored. This means that, in most cases, both the source and the (intended) goal of the motion are located at points removed from the DC, and thus the motion is directed neither towards nor away from the DC. Thus, these terms are often used for motion transverse to the DC. For instance, when speaker and addressee from their DC slightly uphill are commenting on a third person walking along the shore, the form *wen* could be used. No distinction is made between motion from left to right or the reverse. Two directionals, *la* and *me*, are deictically anchored, but not specified for the absolute FoR.

This interrelation is illustrated in Table 2. The first three columns in the first and third row of the table show forms all ending in *-ot* and *-en* respectively, and it is possible that the forms in the first column start with the same formative *si-* ~ *su-*. Note that there are two omissions in the paradigm: first, there is no antonym of *wot*, a directional indicating motion towards the DC, parallel to the shore. This slot is filled by *me*, as discussed below. In addition, there is no term that is neither specified with regard to the absolute FoR, nor deictically anchored. This is not surprising, as such a term would not add meaningful information to a lexical motion verb.

Table 2: Organisation of the directional paradigm along two dimensions: absolute FoR and deixis.

Absolute FoR Deixis	down, seawards (on land); out to sea (on water)	up, inland (on land); towards the shore (on water)	parallel to the shore, level, horizontally	not specified
away from deictic centre	*suwot*	*sot*	*wot*	*la, lak*
towards deictic centre	*si*	*sa, sak*	–	*me*
not deictically anchored	*suwen*	*sen*	*wen*	–

The directional paradigm provides a precise reference structure with ample use in discourse. For virtually all actions that in some sense involve motion (including perception-based actions such as seeing/looking, speaking or listening), the direction of the action will be specified with a directional, something that is very common in Oceanic languages. In Paluai, this is done either by a directional as preverbal particle, or by a SVC in which the directional follows the main verb.

There are semantic differences between the directionals that are not specified above. For instance, *la* is telic, with an endpoint to the motion inherent in its meaning; it is therefore systematically translated with 'go to'. *wot*, on the other hand, seems to lack an inherent endpoint. Forms indicating motion towards the DC are a bit different again: these motion events are telic in nature, since it is implied that the Figure's arrival at the DC will terminate the motion. This may be part of the reason that *me* is used as an antonym to *wot* in many instances. Firstly, the semantics of *me* do not clash with this reading, and secondly, with 'come' forms, the arrival at DC may be the meaning facet that speakers focus on most, rather than the exact direction the Figure of Motion came from.

As in other Oceanic languages, the deictic centre does not necessarily have to be the current position of the speaker, but it can be varied in order to put a certain constituent or discourse participant in focus (cf. Hamel [1993, 1994] for the related language Loniu). In addition, directionals are used to keep track of who did what to whom, because they specify the locations of speech act participants relative to each other.

Below, examples are given of the directional *la(k)* in each of the functional slots: as preverbal particle in (3), as main verb in (4), and as V2 in a SVC in (5). Two directionals have two different forms attested: *la~lak* and *sa~sak*. The long form is used when the directional appears by itself (either as main verb or in a SVC) and does not introduce a constituent (a following adverb or noun phrase), as in (4a); the short form is used in all other contexts (preverbal particle, main verb or secondary verb in an SVC when introducing a constituent), as in with (4b)

(3) *wuikala au nayek ansê alilêt*
    wui=ka-**la**   wau   nayek an-sê   alilêt
    1du.EXC=IRR.NS-**go.to** move about PART-DIM forest
    'We would go and walk around a bit in the bush.' (KM050995_0003)

(4) a. *ngalak*   b. *ngala um*
       nga=**lak**   nga=**la**   wumwa
       1sg=**go.to**   1sg=**go.to** house
       'I went.'   'I went home.'

(5) *ino ro lêp la um*
 i=no to lêp=Ø la wumwa
 3sg=IPFV CONT take=3sg.ZERO **go.to** house
 'He was taking [it] home.' (NP210511_1_0050)

5 Structure of the Paluai verb complex

Directionals, in particular the most common forms *la* 'go (away from DC)', 'thither', and *me* 'come (towards DC)', 'hither' are frequently found in a preverbal particle slot. The Paluai verb complex[1] exhibits three preverbal slots for particles expressing Tense-Aspect-Mood (TAM) and direction, obligatorily preceded by either a bound pronoun proclitic or irrealis prefix cross-referencing the subject argument, or both of these. In Figure 3, the preverbal part of the verb complex of a declarative clause is schematically represented. Some material can occur after the main verb, but should not concern us here; please refer to Schokkin (2020) for a fuller discussion of the verb complex and the TAM system more generally.

(ProSubj=)	IRR°	(CoreAsp)	(DIR)	(SecAsp)		VERB**
	kV-	PFV *pe*		CONT/HAB	*to*	
		PRF *an**		PROG	*yen*	
		MOD *sa*		STAT CONT	*tu*	
		IPFV *no*				

° The subject bound pronoun is obligatory for realis clauses and 2sg irrealis clauses, but not for other persons in irrealis. Irrealis is obligatory when the reference demands so, but is formally unexpressed for 2sg.
* When *an* is present, no other preverbal matter except a subject bound pronoun is allowed.
** The main verb (head of the verb complex) can consist of a SVC.

Figure 3: Schematic representation of the Paluai verb complex.

The subject argument is cross-referenced strictly only once per verb complex, on the first element, also when it contains more than one verb. The first particle slot

---

[1] The term "verb complex" is used following Pawley (2003) who defines it as a phonological phrase which has word-like properties (rigid order of elements, single intonation contour with no pauses and stressed only once), but is unwordlike in the sense that it can be made up of a sequence of free forms.

can be filled by forms analysed as Core Aspect particles, specifying perfective, imperfective or perfect aspect, or by a marker of modality; none of these can be clearly traced back to a full verbal source they grammaticalised from. The second particle slot is reserved for one of the ten directionals. The third slot can be occupied by forms indicating Secondary Aspect, which are formally identical to the posture/existential verbs *to(k)* 'be, stay; sit', *tu* 'stay (for a longer period)'[2] and *yen* 'lie', and thus clearly have grammaticalised from full verbs.[3] They indicate continuative/habitual, stative continuative, or progressive aspect. None of the particle slots is obligatorily filled. An example with a form occupying each slot is given in (6).

(6) *ipkape la ro wau nayek ayi pulek*
 ip$_S$=ka-pe la to wau nayek a-i pulek
 3pl=IRR.NS-PFV go.to CONT walk around OBL-3sg also
 'They will go and wander around there [at the hot springs] too.'
 (MS250311_0007)

Preverbal directionals appear to have a very similar status to the Secondary Aspect particles, where there are identical forms synchronically functioning both as a full lexical verb and as a grammatical element modifying other verbs. These sequences may have developed from nuclear-layer SVCs (Foley & Olson 1985; Crowley 2002) indicating associated motion/direction for directionals and associated posture (Enfield 2002; Newman 2002) for posture verbs, then further grammaticalising towards aspectual markers (for posture verbs) and indicating distance from the deictic centre (for the directional *la* 'go to').[4]

The Secondary Aspect particles seem to have grammaticalised further than most directionals, however. Most uses of directionals (either pre- or postverbal) still denote a sense of genuine translational motion, whereas the particles stemming from posture/existential verbs are purely aspectual, and not postural, in meaning. This raises the issue of whether directionals could be considered full

---

[2] *tu* is a reflex of POc *tuqur 'stand', but is not attested with this meaning in the present-day language.
[3] *to~tok* is similar to *la~lak* and *sa~sak* discussed above, in that it exhibits a long form when used on its own as a main verb and not followed by a constituent.
[4] The term "nuclear layer" is part of the Role and Reference Grammar framework (Foley & Van Valin 1984), in which clauses are analysed as having a layered structure. The nuclear layer consists of the inflected verb(s), while the core layer contains the inflected verbs (the nucleus) plus arguments (and a third layer, the periphery, includes non-core arguments). Paluai SVCs with a directional as V2 (discussed in Sections 7 and 8) are considered to be core-layer SVCs.

verbs instead of particles in all instances, including in their preverbal use. This would mean that instances of preverbal directionals would also count as SVCs. There are two main arguments for analysing preverbal directionals as particles, and not full verbs. The first is a phonological one: in contrast to postverbal directionals (in SVCs), preverbal directionals are never independently stressed. The second one is based on distributional criteria: directionals are found in a slot occurring between two slots that can exclusively be filled by grammatical items. Thus, while preverbal directional particles and Secondary Aspect particles may very well have developed out of full verbs in SVCs (as discussed in the previous paragraph), the sequences they occur in are not analysed as SVCs in the present-day language.

6 Preverbal directionals as markers of AM

Directional particles often occur preverbal to intransitive motion verbs, specifying direction for the translational motion indicated by the main verb. The seven deictic directionals also frequently occur preposed to non-motion verbs, and then indicate deictically anchored, i.e. itive or ventive, motion prior to the event described by the main verb ('go/come and do X').[5] In this function, directionals can be considered markers of AM (Belkadi 2015).

The following sections discuss and give examples of the occurrence of the various directionals in the preverbal slot, both as markers of direction with motion verbs, and as markers of AM with non-motion verbs. The relevant sequences of directional and lexical verb (with the lexical verb represented by a SVC in some cases) are shown in bold.

6.1 *La* 'go to'

La(k) 'go to' is the most frequently used directional, with 2,193 tokens of *la* and 220 tokens of *lak* in a corpus of about 69,000 words. This directional underwent the most semantic bleaching and grammaticalisation; still, it is very often used to refer to genuine translational motion. The sentences below demonstrate its use. Example (7) shows the long form *lak* as a main motion verb in the first clause,

---

[5] Due to my previous unfamiliarity with the term "associated motion", in Schokkin (2013) these constructions were called "sequential/purposive", but essentially their analysis has not changed.

followed by a coordinated clause in which the short form *la* is used as a preverbal directional to *lêp* 'take', indicating prior associated motion; this is also called "echo construction" (Guillaume & Koch this volume). It frequently occurs in Paluai, as it does in other languages with AM markers.

(7) *wuipe lak a wuipe la lêp China*
    wui$_S$=pe   **lak**   *a*   *wui$_A$=pe*   **la**   **lêp**   [China]$_O$
    1du.EXC=PFV   **go.to**   and   1du.EXC=PFV   **go.to** take   proper.name
    'We went and (after going) we took China [a dog].' (MK060211_0043)

In example (8), the first clause shows the short form *la* as a main verb followed by the locative constituent *alilêt* 'bush'.[6] Subsequently, *la* is used three times as a marker of prior motion AM. The entire sentence has irrealis reference, which is not formally marked for a 2sg subject. The speaker relates how, after a ceremony was done for her, the taboos of a specific place were lifted and she was told she could move around freely and do things. Each action, except for *tapot nik* 'smoke fish' which was presumably done at or very near the deictic centre, is accompanied by *la* as a marker of a separate associated motion event.

(8) *wono la alilêt, wono la lêp yaum le wono la tun pau le wono la yim lêp mwei le wono rabot nik, le ...*
    wo=no   **la**   *alilêt*   *wo=no*   **la**   **lêp**   *yaum*   *le*
    2sg=IPFV   **go.to**   bush   2sg=IPFV   **go.to**   take   mudcrab   or
    wo=no   **la**   *tun*   *pau*   *le*   *wo=no*   **la**   **yim.lêp**
    2sg=IPFV   **go.to**   boil   coconut.oil or   2sg=IPFV   **go.to**   dive. take
    mwei   *le*   *wo=no*   *tapot*   *nik*   *le*
    clam.meat   or   2sg=IPFV smoke   fish   or
    '[They told me,] "You can go to the bush, you can go catch mudcrabs, or you can go boil coconut oil, or you can go dive for clamshells, or you can smoke fish, or ..."' (LL030611_0059)

Note that in both (7) and (8), the subject of each coordinated clause is obligatorily cross-referenced by a bound pronoun. This excludes a possible analysis of the juxtaposition of *la* and another verb, e.g. *lêp*, as an instance of coordi-

---

6 *alilêt* is not marked by a preposition *a-* even though it functions as an adverbial (locative goal) constituent. This is due to a well-described feature of many Oceanic languages, namely a distinction between local, common and personal nouns (Lynch, Ross, & Crowley 2002). In Paluai, this means that local nouns are not marked by a preposition, in contrast to common nouns, for which this is obligatory in locative uses. See also Schokkin (2020).

nation of two clauses without overt marking, as there is no cross-referencing of the subject on the second verb. Since a bound subject pronoun occurs only once per verb complex, we conclude that the two forms must belong to a single verb complex and thus a single clause. The fact that the semantic contribution of the directional in subsequent clauses in both (7) and (8) is superfluous (after all, this motion event was already expressed by the main verb in the first clause) is further evidence that preverbal directionals are indeed grammaticalised elements.

As mentioned, cases of preverbal *la* in combination with the Secondary Aspect particle *to* have acquired another meaning: that the action referred to by the main verb is taking place at a distance removed from the DC (usually the speaker); this corresponds to what is called "atrilocal", "exlocative" or "distal" function in §4.4 of the Introduction (Guillaume and Koch this volume).[7] Cognates of *la* with this function are found in other Oceanic languages (Lichtenberk 1991); a Paluai example is given in (9). There is no sense of motion in this statement, in contrast to AM uses of *la* such as in (8).

(9)   *urêro pe yong yamat te ila ro pe kolon wat*
     wurê=pe   yong   yamat   te   i=**la**   to   pe   kolo-n
     1pc.EXC=PFV   hear   person   REL   3sg=**go.to**   CONT   do   mouth-3sg.POSS
     wat
     up.high
     'We heard someone shouting [lit. 'doing mouth'] up high.' (NP210511_2_0024)

6.2 Me 'come'

Example (10) below, repeated from (1), shows the use of *me* as a directional marker for the motion verb *tet* 'move, walk'.

(10)   *epme ret liliu la Lipan*
      ep$_S$=**me**   tet   liliu   la   Lipan
      1pl.EXC=**come**   walk   return   go.to   place.name
      'We came back to Lipan village.' (KM060111_0084)

---

[7] There are a few constructions with other directionals found in the corpus that exhibit the same semantics. Since these are so rare, it is concluded that grammaticalisation into a 'distance from DC' marker may be only incipient for these forms, whereas it is firmly established for *la*.

Example (11), from the same story, shows a use of *me* as a marker of AM, indicating prior motion towards the DC. The action represented by the main verb is giving back food. The inanimate O argument is elided, and not cross-referenced on the verb, which is a regular feature of Paluai discourse. The Goal argument bears the alimentary classifier *ka-*, which indicates both its Animate Goal status, and that the Theme transferred is a food item. Note that, while the main verb is a transfer verb, preverbal *me* is not related in any way to the motion of the O inherent in the transfer, which is expressed by *la* following the main verb. *me*, in this case, only entails the motion associated with the A argument of the main verb, prior to the action entailed in that verb.

(11) *ippe me rou liliu la kep*
     ip$_A$=pe   **me**   *tou*   *liliu=Ø*   *la*   *ka-ep*
     3pl=PFV   **come**   **give**   **return=3sg.ZERO**   go.to   CLF.food-1pl.EXC.POSS
     'They came and gave (it) [=food] back to us.' (KM060111_0087)

6.3 *Wot* 'go (on the same level)'

Example (12) shows the use of *wot* in a deictic directional sense, with a motion verb.

(12) *mui reo ibe ngui rou ngoyai, onga ngoyai reo ibe wot terepelek*
     mui   *te-yo*   *i=pe*   *ngui.tou*   *ngoyai*   *ong.a*   *ngoyai*
     dog   EMP-DEM.INT   3sg=PFV   snarl.give   cuscus   and.so   cuscus
     te-yo   *i=pe*   **wot**   **terepelek**
     EMP-DEM.INT   3sg=PFV   **go.level**   **run**
     'The dog 'snarled after' the cuscus, and so the cuscus ran away (from him).' (LL010711_0069)

In example (13), preverbal *wot* with a non-motion verb means 'go ahead (and)', indicating a sequence of events. When *wot* follows a non-motion main verb in a SVC, the predicate obtains a different, aspectual meaning: 'do for an extended period of time'; see example (14).

(13) *eppe wot lêpi ran mwanen Parugui*[8]
    ep=pe   **wot**   **lêp**=i   ta-n   mwane-n
    1pl.EXC=PFV **go.level** **take**=3sg CLF.AL-3SG.POSS brother-3sg.POSS
    Parugui
    person.name
    'We went ahead and took her of/from her brother Parugui.' (KM060111_0035)

(14) *uno rok wot*
    u=no   **tok**   **wot**
    3du=IPFV **stay** **go.level**
    'They were staying/living (together) for some time.' (LL10711_0011)

6.4 *Sot* 'go up'

Example (15) shows a deictic directional use, with a motion verb.

(15) *irê not teo no sot tet panu rang*
    irê   not   te-yo   no   **sot**   tet   panu   ta-ng
    3pc   child EMP-DEM.INT IPFV **go.up** walk front CLF.AL-1sg.POSS
    '[I stopped walking and] the boys were going past, in front of me.'
    (NP210511_2_0040)

Sentence (16) below shows an AM use of *sot*, and could have two interpretations: either a sequence of motion and action, or an instance where there is simultaneous motion and action, i.e. 'going up' and 'hunting' happening at the same time. This is because the verb *yik* is ambiguous as to whether there is motion happening while the action is carried out, or not, and thus semantically both interpretations are allowed. It is possible that the proper reading is pragmatically determined, as is the case in various other languages discussed in this volume (e.g. Vidal & Payne this volume). Examples of temporal vagueness of this kind are rare in the Paluai corpus, however.

---

8 *lêp* 'take' is one of the few trivalent verbs in Paluai, which do not need to be serialised with a directional to form a ditransitive predicate (see Section 7 below, and Schokkin (2020) for full discussion). The Source semantics of the third argument is not explicitly expressed by any grammatical element but needs to be inferred from the lexical semantics of *lêp*.

(16) *eppwa kasot yik ngoyai*
 ep=pwa ka-sot yik ngoyai
 1pl.EXC=want.to IRR.NS-**go.up** search.for cuscus
 'We were about to go uphill and hunt for / hunting for cuscus.' (NP210511_2_0011)

6.5 *Sa* 'come up'

In sentences (17) and (18), we see again a directional used first in a deictic directional sense, and as a marker of sequential AM.

(17) *kumun teo kipe sa wau la wat*
 kumun te-yo ki-pe sa wau la wat
 sprout EMP-DEM.INT IRR.3sg-PFV **come.up** move go.to up.high
 'The sprout will come up high.' (NK290311_1_0028)

(18) *wuipe sa lêpi*
 wui=pe sa lêp=i
 1du.EXC=PFV **come.up** take=3sg
 'We came up and got her.' (MK060211_0044)

6.6 *Suwot* 'go down'

In (19), the directional *suwot* is used in combination with a motion verb.

(19) *irou parayon suwot net a isuwot tet la net*
 i=tou parayo-n suwot net a i=suwot tet
 3sg=put front-3sg.POSS go.down sea and 3sg=**go.down** walk
 la net
 go.to sea
 'He turned his face toward the sea and went down into the water.' (WL020711_0096)

Sentence (20) illustrates a sequence of events with *suwot*.

(20) osuwot ilili la pulen kone areo
 wo=**suwot** *ilili* la *pulen.kone* a-te-yo
 2sg=**go.down** stand.up go.to beach OBL-EMP-DEM.INT
 'You go down and stand up on the beach there.' (LL030611_0051)

6.7 *Si* 'come down'

Example (21) shows a deictic directional use of *si* 'come down', whereas (22) shows a purposive sequential AM use.

(21) kanun kuyen deo ino si ret si pulikalon paye
 kanun kuyen te-yo i=no **si** tet
 drops dye EMP-DEM.INT 3sg=IPFV **come.down** spread
 si *puli.kalo-n* *paye*
 come.down elbow-3sg.POSS down.below
 'Drops of dye are trickling down his elbow.' (Game4_280812_0067)

(22) kisi wut kem a ...
 ki-**si** *wut* *kem* *ya*
 IRR.3sg-**come.down** fetch salt.water then
 'When she will come down to the shore to fetch sea water, then ...' (LK100411_0090)

6.8 Non-deictic directionals *wen*, *sen* and *suwen*

The three directionals indicating motion that is not deictically anchored (*sen* 'move upwards', *wen* 'move horizontally' and *suwen* 'move downwards') are rarely used in the corpus, and therefore very few instances were found of their use as preverbal particles (in the case of *sen* 'move upwards' none at all). They are sometimes used in combination with a motion verb, with a directional meaning, as in (23). When we find them with non-motion verbs, their interpretation can usually be metaphorical, and there are therefore no instances of these directionals where they unambiguously indicate AM.[9] It is unclear whether this is because

---

9 Metaphorical usage of verbs of motion (i.e. not expressing spatial relations or translational motion in a literal sense, but for instance with reference to the passage of time) is very common

they cannot be used to express AM, or these cases are just not present in the corpus because of the relatively low frequency of the forms. In sentence (23), there is a simultaneous action of moving and getting closer together. This reading is possible because Paluai stative verbs, such as *pit*, are ambiguous between a stative and inchoative semantic reading, and *pit* can thus mean either 'be close' or 'become closer'. The second instance of *wen* in this example, as a main verb, refers to a location rather than a movement.

(23) *apkawen pir ai pulen kone re iwen telo*
*ap=ka-**wen*** ***pit*** *a-i* *pulen.kone* *te*
2pl=IRR.NS-**move.level** **become.closer** OBL-3sg beach REL
i=wen *te-lo*
3sg=move.level EMP-DEM.DIST
'You will gather together on the sand beach that is over there.'
(NP210511_2_0009)

6.9 Summary

The above sections have shown that only a prior motion sense is attested when preverbal directionals are used with non-motion verbs (with the possible exception of (16), with the verb 'hunt'). What these cases also have in common is that the motion semantics are associated with the S/A argument of the clause. These properties are in line with Guillaume's (2016) two implicational hierarchies based on cross-linguistic observations for AM as a comparative concept in South American languages (prior motion > concurrent motion > subsequent motion and motion of the subject > motion of the object). While there are many examples of preverbal directionals in the corpus that have purposive meanings (motion with the intention of doing an action: 'go/come TO do X'), in all these instances the clause is marked for irrealis, which can be assumed to contribute the purposive semantics. When preverbal directionals occur with past reference, the action following the motion is always realised, and never just purposed. See also Section 4.1 of the introduction (Guillaume & Koch this volume) for examples of motion-with-purpose constructions; note that not all authors (e.g. Lovestrand & Ross this volume) consider these instances of AM.

---

cross-linguistically and is also often found for the other Paluai directionals discussed in this paper. While a very interesting topic in its own right, discussing this in detail was deemed to lie outside the scope of the current paper.

The AM sense of preverbal directionals is based on a complementary distribution: when they precede a motion verb, they indicate direction of that motion, and when they precede a non-motion verb, they indicate AM. Their AM sense is based on inference, and therefore the system can be considered an example of "inferential AM", as opposed to "dedicated AM" systems where a given morpheme always has an AM interpretation (Reed & Lindsey this volume). There appears to be some leakage in the system when a main motion verb is used in an ambulative sense, as is the case in (24) below (repeated from (3)). Because in this case, *wau* 'move, walk' is modified by *nayek* 'about, around', there are two separate motion events: first an itive motion event from the DC to the bush, specified by *la*, followed by an ambulative motion event inside the bush, indicated by *wau nayek*. Thus, *la* indicates prior AM, and not direction for the main motion verb. This example underlines the inferential nature of the system, as it is highly dependent on verb semantics and the pragmatic context.

(24) *wuikala au nayek ansê alilêt*
 *wui=ka-**la*** *wau* *nayek* *an-sê* *alilêt*
 1du.EXC=IRR.NS-**go.to** move about PART-DIM forest
 'We would go and walk around a bit in the bush.' (KM050995_0003)

Since there are (at least) seven different terms that can express AM in the Paluai inventory of directionals, the Paluai AM system can be considered "very complex" according to the classification put forward by Guillaume (2016: 109). Guillaume does not distinguish between systems that make distinctions based on a vertical cline (motion 'up' vs. 'down') and those that don't. However, systems that do, like Paluai, have been attested elsewhere, such as in Sino-Tibetan languages (Jacques et al. this volume).

The most frequently encountered form, *la*, appears to have grammaticalised to a larger extent than other directionals. In many of its preverbal occurrences in combination with the secondary aspect particle *to*, it can be interpreted as marking an event that takes place at a distance removed from the DC.

7 Directionals in SVCs

This section will briefly discuss what SVCs containing a directional look like, in order to set the stage for a comparison of the use of directionals either preceding or following the lexical verb, as will be done below in Section 8. For a more in-depth discussion of serialisation in Paluai, see Schokkin (2020). For the purposes of this paper it suffices to use the narrow definition of a SVC as given by Haspelmath (2016: 296): "A serial verb construction is a monoclausal construction consisting of multiple independent verbs with no element linking them and with no predicate–argument relation between the verbs." As a reminder, directionals can occur in three different slots: preverbally, as main verb, and following the main verb in SVCs. There are many instances in which two different directionals are encountered in the same clause: one preverbally, the other following the main verb (but a directional as main verb is never combined with another directional in either slot). This is an indication that the preverbal and postverbal slots can function independently from each other.

Directionals used as V2 in SVCs, like preverbal directionals, indicate deictic (or occasionally, non-deictic) direction of a path with main verbs, most typically but not limited to verbs of motion. Almost any verb describing an action which has motion or transfer inherent in it can be (and preferably is) accompanied by a directional; this type of serialisation is very common for Oceanic languages (Durie 1988; Crowley 2002). But while it is highly preferential to indicate direction for any motion and transfer event by serialising the main verb with a directional, this doesn't seem to be obligatory. While not numerous, examples such as (25) are found in which a lexical motion verb, in this case *liliu* 'return', is not followed by a directional. These cases, showing the optionality of directional serialisation, are also evidence against a full reanalysis of postverbal directionals as argument markers and/or prepositions.

(25) *aukala liliu um tao*
 au=ka-la   liliu   wumwa   ta-o
 2du=IRR.NS-go.to return   house   CLF.AL-2sg.POSS
 'You two must return to your (sg) house.' (KM060111_0027)

Directionals can be serialised with either transitive or intransitive verbs. Each will be discussed in turn; again, relevant verb forms will be shown in bold. Typically, directionals serialise with motion verbs, but they are also very frequently encountered with other intransitive verbs, e.g. referring to perception or bodily functions. When the directional does not introduce a constituent, it merely modifies the main verb for direction; the destination or goal of the movement is left unspecified, but it will be retrievable from the discourse context. A directional can also introduce an Oblique constituent of an intransitive clause, preceding a noun phrase headed either by a local or a common noun, or a spatial adverbial or demonstrative. This SVC is of the same-subject type. It does not have to be contiguous: an adverb can be inserted between the main verb and the serialised directional.

The following sentences are examples of the directional *me* modifying the main verb, in (26) without introducing a Locative constituent, and in (27) with a Locative.[10] In (26), the inherent endpoint can be understood to be the current location of the speaker (the DC).

(26) ong kope liliu me
 wong ko-pe **liliu me**
 1sg.FREE IRR.1sg-PFV **return come**
 'I will come back (here).' (KW290311_0007)

(27) uro aluk liliu me panu
 u$_S$=to **aluk liliu me** panu
 3du=CONT **paddle return come** village
 'They were paddling back to the village.' (NP210511_1_0021)

Below, two examples are given of directional serialisation with verbs of perception: (28) shows intransitive *ningning* 'look' (formed by reduplication of transitive *ning* 'see'), and (29) shows transitive *tiy* 'observe, watch'. Sometimes a locative constituent is introduced by the directional, such as in (29). In other cases, just the direction of the event of perception is indicated, as in (28). When V1 has an overt O argument, this intervenes between the two verbs, as in (29). Note that with perception verbs, there is no translational motion in a literal sense, only a metaphorical motion of e.g. a gaze.

(28) ipwa kiningning suwot …
 i=pwa ki-**ning~ning suwot**
 3sg=want.to IRR.3sg-RED~**see go.down**
 'He was about to look down …' (LL010711_0052)

(29) iriy maloan suwor ai laliyon
 i=**tiy** maloa-n **suwot** a-i laliyon
 3sg=**observe** reflection-3sg.poss **go.down** OBL-3sg pool
 'He looked down at his reflection in the pool.' (LL010711_0052)

---

10 The exact syntactic status of NPs introduced by directionals (whether they are arguments or not) is often unclear due to several complicating factors. This argument will not be pursued further here, and the reader is referred to Schokkin (2020) for more elaborate discussion.

With transitive verbs, directionals have the function of adding a Goal argument. They thus introduce another participant to the clause, one that the main verb is not subcategorised for, in order to express a three-participant event (Margetts & Austin 2007). This SVC is of the switch-subject type, with the O of V1 functioning as the S of V2, and is always discontiguous: V2 follows the shared argument if this is overtly expressed.[11] The types of argument specified by this SVC are Locative Goal, often expressed by a local noun, and Animate Goal (which includes Recipient and Beneficiary). Paluai only has a handful of genuine three-place verbs that do not necessitate introduction of a third participant by a SVC (for an example of such a verb, see (13) above), making this a very common strategy to express three-participant events, by means of a ditransitive complex predicate consisting of one transitive and one intransitive verb.

Some examples of directionals introducing a Locative Goal argument are given in (30) and (31).

(30) *urê yokari si suk*
 wurê **yokat**=i **si** suk
 1pc.EXC **carry**=3sg **come.down** shore
 'We carried him down to the shore.' (NP210511_2_0063)

(31) *irou liliuip la panu*
 i$_A$=**tou** **liliu**=ip **la** panu
 3sg=**send** **return**=3pl go.to place
 'He sent them back to their village.' (LL300511_1_0022)

An Animate Goal argument is obligatorily preceded by the general alienable possessive classifier *ta-* (which takes a pronominal suffix specifying number and person of the referent), or, alternatively, by the alimentary possessive classifier *ka-* (also taking a suffix) when the Theme is a food item. This kind of argument is typically encountered with verbs of transfer that involve motion of a Theme to a human Recipient, such as *tou* 'give' (32) and *pul* 'tell' (33), but is encountered with other transitive verbs as well, as (34) shows.

---

11 When the O argument is not overtly expressed, as is usually the case when it refers to an inanimate object, it is still assumed that there is a zero trace of the O argument between V1 and V2.

(32) ikipe si rou kokon la rararê
 i=ki-pe   si   tou   kokoni la   ta-tarê
 3sg=IRR.3sg-PFV come.down **give** money **go.to** CFL.AL-1pc.INC.POSS
 'He should come here and give money to us.' (OBK040311_0193)

(33) ngapwa kopul sot tao la remenin telo
 nga$_A$=pwa   ko-**pul**=∅   **sot** ta-o   la
 1sg=want.to IRR.1sg-**tell**=3SG.ZERO **go.up** CFL.AL-2sg.POSS go.to
 temenin   te-lo
 thus   EMP-DEM.DIST
 'I am going to tell you as follows ...' (PK290411_3_0076)

(34) ipe sui yapi reo la kau rinan
 i=pe   **sui** yapi te-yo   la   ka-u   tina-n
 3sg=PFV **fry** sago EMP-DEM.INT **go.to** CLF.food-3du.POSS mother-3sg.POSS
 'She fried the sago for him and his mother (to eat).' (KW290611_0036)

The directional *la* is attested most frequently, but occasionally another directional is found expressing an Animate Goal argument; see (33). Most cases of directionals other than *la* are attested with the verb *pul* 'tell'. The speaker of sentence (33), which was uttered during a public ceremony, stands on a lower level than his addressee, and thus it is more appropriate to use the directional *sot*, specified for the absolute Frame of Reference, instead of the unspecified *la*. It appears that when the cardinal direction (i.e. landwards or seawards) of the motion indicated by the main verb is known, an appropriate directional has to be used. However, when the cardinal direction of the action relative to the deictic centre is unknown or backgrounded, *me* or *la* can be used, since these are only deictic and not specified for the absolute FoR.

8 Comparison of directionals preceding and following the main verb

To summarise: the preceding sections have shown how the same set of forms, the paradigm of ten directionals in Paluai, can be used both as preverbal particle and serialised with a main verb (and additionally, as main verbs). As preverbal particles, they are used in order to indicate direction (with motion verbs) or AM (with non-motion verbs, and perhaps excepting non-deictic forms). Serialised with a main verb, they serve to specify the direction or goal of a translational motion event, and, in the case of three-participant events, introduce a third argument. This section will discuss the main differences between the two uses, and argue why it is that only directionals in preverbal position are attested as markers of AM.

Firstly and most notably, the two construction types including a directional (preceding a main verb on the one hand, and following a main verb on the other) consist of, or have developed from, two different types of SVC. Preverbal directional particles, as mentioned, have probably developed from nuclear-layer SVCs, which necessarily shared their arguments. Directionals following the main verb, in contrast, form core-layer SVCs, in which there can be a switch in arguments: the O argument of V1, if transitive, will be the S argument of V2. In ditransitive constructions, V2 introduces a third argument, while the main verb it is serialised with is only subcategorised for two. Thus the transitivity of the construction as a whole is determined by V1 and V2 both, whereas in nuclear-layer SVCs the valency of the main lexical verb always determines the transitivity of the construction. In addition, core-layer SVCs do not have to be contiguous, in contrast to nuclear-layer SVCs.

Secondly, a directional preceding the main verb is always related to motion by the S/A argument, whereas the same directional following the main verb is describing the completion of motion by a Figure specified by the verb semantics towards a goal. For intransitive verbs, this Figure is the S argument; for transitive verbs it is the O, as we will see below.[12] As an illustration of the former, consider the following pair, made up of the intransitive main verb *terepelek* 'run' plus the directional *wot* 'go (on the same level)':

(35) *mui reo ibe ngui rou ngoyai, onga ngoyai reo ibe wot terepelek*
 mui te-yo i=pe ngui.tou ngoyai ong.a ngoyai
 dog EMP-DEM.INT 3sg=PFV snarl.give cuscus and.so cuscus
 te-yo i=pe **wot terepelek**
 EMP-DEM.INT 3sg=PFV **go.level run**
 'The dog "snarled after" the cuscus, and so the cuscus ran away (from him).' (LL010711_0069)

---

12 Transitive verbs of perception form an exception to this, as there is no literal translational motion in these instances and thus neither the A nor the O argument could be seen as a Figure of motion. Rather, it is the act of perceiving that functions as the Figure, and the directional indicates the Path of perception.

(36) som iterepelek wot a ipung nupun som
som   i_S=**terepelek** **wot**   a   i=pung   nupu-n
one.ANIM   3sg=**run**   **go.level** and 3sg=smell bottom-3sg.POSS
som
one.ANIM
'One (dog) ran over (to the other dogs) and sniffed the bottom of another.' (LL300511_1_0075)

In (35), *wot* occurs preverbally, and its function is to indicate that the cuscus started running away from a certain location, the DC, and away from the dog. In contrast, in (36) *wot* follows the main verb *terepelek*. This highlights the motion by the S argument away from a DC, arriving at a goal location where the main action of the coordinated clause, 'sniffing', takes place.

A further set of sentences, only a few utterances apart in a narrative, shows that this "minimal pair" of DIR-V and V-DIR is not coincidental. Compare (37) and (38):

(37) *Sakumai ipe moto a urêpe me terepelek la Baon*
Sakumai   i=pe   moto   a   wurê=pe   **me**   **terepelek**
person.name 3sg=do   engine and 3p=PFV   **come** **run**
la   Baon
go.to   place.name
'Sakumai operated the engine and we sped off towards Baon.' (NP210511_2_0066)

(38) *ip not pari Lou, ipterepelek me a ippwa "tenepa?"*
ip   not   pari   Lou   ip=**terepelek** **me**   a
3pl   child belonging.to   place.name 3pl=**run**   **come** and
ip=pwa   tenepa
3pl=say how
'The children from Lou Island, they came running over [to us] and asked, "What's the matter?" (NP210511_2_0069)

Example (37) describes how a dinghy is departing; interestingly, ventive preverbal *me* is used. By contrast, (38) describes how, after the dinghy arrived at Baon, children came running towards it and its passengers and started asking questions. Here the emphasis is on the completion and goal location of the 'running' event (by the children, not the dinghy) and the event that followed after, and thus postverbal *me* is used.

We can summarise the differences in semantics and pragmatics of the two constructions as in Table 3:

Table 3: Comparison of two constructions involving directional + main verb.

1. DIR – Main V	2. Main V – DIR
1. When expressing **direction**: specifies direction of motion by Figure S entailed in the semantics of V 2. When expressing **AM**: specifies motion by S/A **prior** to action entailed in the semantics of V	Specifies direction of motion by Figure entailed in the semantics of V (S of intransitive V, O of transitive V)
Highlights source location	Highlights goal location / participant
Emphasizes inception of the event	Emphasizes completion of the event

Evidence that the two grammatical slots are functioning independently of each other comes from the fact that there are many instances in the corpus where the same or a different directional is chosen to occupy either. There were already several examples of this throughout the paper (see e.g. (19), (21), (32) and (37)); one of them is repeated below (from (11)).

(39) *ippe me rou liliu la kep*
 ip_A=pe **me** tou liliu=Ø **la** ka-ep
 3pl=PFV **come** give return=3sg.ZERO **go.to** CLF.FOOD-1PL.EXC.POSS
 'They came and gave (it) [=food] back to us.' (KM060111_0087)

This sentence describes how a party involved in a bride price ceremony came to the speaker's house and gave the family an amount of food. The preverbal directional *me* reflects this: the A argument *ip* moved to the current location of the speaker, the DC. However, *me* 'come' does not encompass the direction of the transfer that the food subsequently makes when it is given, but instead *la* 'go to' is serialised with the main verb to indicate this motion to the Goal argument. This example shows that both directional positions operate independently of each other, referring to distinct (associated) motion and transfer sub-events. The most frequent directional *la* is often used also when strictly speaking a more specific directional would be more appropriate. *La* thus seems to be highly grammaticalized, and functions here primarily as an argument marker. It is very much bleached of its original 'motion from DC' semantics. After all, since the transfer of the food would also have been towards the speaker (and thus the DC), one would expect the use of ventive *me* to mark the Goal argument.

It appears that the usage of ventive directionals to mark motion to a Goal that is the current DC only happens when a speaker adds particular (e.g. contrastive) focus to the fact that motion is directed towards him or her, and not somewhere else; this is shown below in (40). The example is from the beginning of a recording of the *Man and Tree* game (Levinson et al. 1992). The two players are discussing how the game should be played. In this utterance, the speaker wants to confirm whether he should pass the photo to his interlocutor (using *wot*) or whether the interlocutor should pass it to him (using *me*). It appears that only in this kind of contrastive situation, use of *me* for a ventive 'towards me' meaning is required.

(40) korou wot le worou me?
 ko-**tou**=Ø **wot** le wo$_A$=**tou**=Ø **me**
 IRR.1sg-**give**=3sg.ZERO **go.level** or 2sg=**give**=3sg.ZERO **come**
 'Should I give (it) to you or should you give (it) to me?'
 (Game1_021012_0020)

Example (41) shows 'round-trip motion' (i.e. 'go and come back', cf. Belkadi 2015: 59) semantics, which involve prior motion, an action and subsequent motion back to the same location. We see that the prior motion, going away from the deictic centre by the A argument, is expressed by preverbal *la*. The subsequent motion, bringing the coconut (back) to the DC and arriving there, is expressed by a directional *me* which follows the main verb plus the very long constituent that makes up the O argument.[13] Alternatively, it is possible that *lêp* 'take' has additional motion semantics, in which case there would be no subsequent AM meaning, but *me* would merely specify the 'hither' direction of the motion, as in other cases of directional serialisation.

While, of course, in this case the A argument moves back to the DC as well, it is the motion/direction of the O argument back to the DC that this construction specifies. In order to specifically express motion back to the DC of the A argument, a SVC expressing round-trip motion would be infelicitous. Instead, a biclausal construction is used, as shown in (42) and (43), in which the S/A argument is cross-referenced again on the first verb or particle in the coordinated clause. Note that nevertheless, a preverbal particle is expressing the prior AM in the first clause, while in the second clause, a directional serialised with the main motion verb is used to express the direction for the subsequent motion of the S argument back to the original location.

---

13 One reviewer enquired whether this type of subsequent motion AM only occurs with the 'take' verb, as this is a cross-linguistically fairly common pattern. This appears to be the case, but due to the paucity of constructions with clear round-trip semantics in the corpus it is hard to say with certainty.

(41) *ola lêp kong payanpôl sip te ila ro arelo me*
 wo=**la**   **lêp** ka-ng   payan.pôl   sip   te
 2sg=**go.to** **take** CLF.food-1sg.POSS dry.coconut one.INANIM   REL
 i=la   to   a-te-lo   **me**
 3sg=go.to   be   OBL-EMP-DEM.DIST   **come**
 'You go and get my coconut (to eat) that is over there, (and bring it) here (to me).' (LK100411_0063)

(42) *kola ning Maluan a koliliu me*
 ko-**la**   ning   Maluan   a   ko-**liliu**   **me**
 IRR.1sg-**go.to** see   person.name   and   IRR.1sg-**return** **come**
 'I will go and see Maluan and come back (here).' (KM050995_0006)

(43) *kala yik yapi a kape liliu sa Paluai pwo*
 ka-**la**   yik   yapi   a   ka-pe   **liliu**   **sa**
 IRR.NSG-**go.to** find   sago   and IRR.NS-PFV   **return** **come.up**
 Paluai   pwo
 place.name   DEM.PROX
 'We would go find sago and come back to Paluai.' (OL201210_0053)

This is more evidence that postverbal, serialised directionals are associated with completion of the event. In the case of transfer verbs, where the Figure in Motion is the item transferred, this entails specifying the location where the Figure ends up. Consequently, in a three-participant transfer situation, this type of directional SVC came to be used to introduce (animate) Goal arguments. It also explains why postverbal uses of directionals are excluded from being considered AM markers. The only non-motion verbs they occur with are transfer verbs, which by definition are not analysed as verbs triggering AM contexts since they already have translational motion inherent in their semantics. If subsequent motion of the S/A argument is expressed, a biclausal construction with a main motion verb serialised with a directional, or with a directional as main verb, has to be used. Thus, in Paluai we do not find postverbal directionals to indicate subsequent AM of S/A arguments.

It appears that motion serialisation in Paluai, including AM meanings, works under strong iconic principles. This is shown by the fact that preverbal directionals, coming before the main verb and when expressing AM, can only express prior motion, and, being closer to the bound subject pronoun, are most strongly associated with motion of the S/A argument. Contrastively, postverbal directionals, when used with non-motion verbs, can only express direction for subsequent motion of the O arguments of transfer verbs. One question that remains for preverbal directionals is whether their AM meaning grammaticalised from an earlier directional use with motion verbs, or whether the directional sense developed out of an earlier prior motion SVC with an AM sense. The latter is the more likely explanation for two reasons.[14] Firstly, across languages a prior motion sense is commonly expressed by a motion verb preceding another verb, while directional meaning expressed by a verb in this position appears to be quite rare; see Lovestrand and Ross (this volume) for a cross-linguistic overview. Directional verbs tend to follow the main verb, as they do in the other Paluai construction, analysed as a SVC. It seems therefore reasonable to conclude that Paluai preverbal directionals primarily had prior motion meaning, and acquired an additional directional meaning at a later stage. A second fact suggesting that prior motion is the primary function of the preverbal directionals is the restriction on only expressing motion of the S/A argument. Again, this is a cross-linguistically common feature of prior motion SVCs. Thus, in addition to AM meanings being a possible grammaticalisation path for deictic directionals as suggested by Belkadi (2015), it appears that the opposite route is also a possibility, with a more general directional sense developing out of an associated motion sense. Further evidence for this possibility is provided by Voisin (this volume), who proposes the term "AM-D" for systems that have AM as their primary meanings and developed an additional directional sense.

9 Conclusions

The aim of this chapter has been twofold. Firstly, it has claimed that D-AM can clearly be recognized as a category in an Oceanic language, thus setting a precedent for further study of this phenomenon in this particular subgroup, and perhaps also in the Austronesian language family more generally. Secondly, a systematic comparison has been made between directionals used either preceding or following the main verb, and it has been argued that only the former can be analysed as markers of AM. It turned out that iconicity is a strong guiding principle in the usage of directionals in Paluai. Moreover, the chapter has shown that deictic directionality and associated motion meanings are closely intertwined, as put forward elsewhere (Dryer this volume [ch. 4]; Belkadi this volume). Either one of them appears to be able to develop out of the other (Voisin this volume) and it is even possible that they may develop in parallel (Creissels & Bassène this volume). These outcomes show that the development of directionals and AM markers may

---

[14] I thank Joey Lovestrand for first suggesting this as a possible analysis.

be another instance of *polygrammaticalisation* (Craig 1991), a process whereby one specific element can evolve into multiple different grammatical markers.

Abbreviations

AL	alienable	HAB	habitual	pl	plural
ANIM	animate	INANIM	inanimate	POSS	possessive
CLF	classifier	INC	inclusive	PRF	perfect
CONT	continuative	INT	intermediate	PROG	progressive
DEM	demonstrative	IPFV	imperfective	PROX	proximate
DIM	diminutive	IRR	irrealis	RED	reduplicant
DIR	directional	MOD	modal	REL	relative clause marker
DIST	distal	NS	non-singular		
du	dual	OBL	oblique	sg	singular
EMP	emphatic	PART	partitive	STAT	stative
EXC	exclusive	pc	paucal		
FREE	free pronoun	PFV	perfective		

Acknowledgements: First and foremost, thanks are due to the Paluai speech community on Baluan Island and elsewhere, for their support, hospitality and friendship over the years. I also wish to thank the volume editors, Antoine Guillaume and Harold Koch, for inviting me to contribute a paper and giving me a chance to revisit and deepen my understanding of a phenomenon that captured my fascination many years ago. I am grateful to a reviewer and the editors for helpful comments on the chapter, which much improved the analysis. Any remaining errors are of course my own.

References

Barth, Danielle, & Gregory D. S. Anderson. 2015. Directional constructions in Matukar Panau. *Oceanic Linguistics* 54(1). 206–239. doi:10.1353/ol.2015.0009
Belkadi, Aicha. 2015. Associated motion with deictic directionals: A comparative overview. *SOAS Working Papers in Linguistics 17*. 49–76.
Belkadi, Aicha. This volume, chapter 5. Deictic directionality as associated motion: Motion, complex events and event integration in African languages.
Cleary-Kemp, Jessica. 2015. *Serial verb constructions revisited: A case study from Koro*. Berkeley: University of California dissertation.
Craig, Colette. 1991. Ways to go in Rama: A case study in polygrammaticalization. In Elizabeth C. Traugott & Bernd Heine (eds.), *Approaches to grammaticalization*, 455–492. Amsterdam/Philadelphia: John Benjamins.

Creissels, Denis & Alain Christian Bassène. This volume, chapter 17. Ventive, associated motion and aspect in Jóola Fóoñi (Atlantic).
Crowley, Terry. 2002. *Serial verbs in Oceanic: a descriptive typology*. Oxford: Oxford University Press.
Dryer, Matthew. 2013. *A grammatical description of Kara-Lemakot*. Canberra: Pacific Linguistics.
Dryer, Matthew. This volume, chapter 4. Associated motion and directionals: where they overlap.
Durie, Mark. 1988. Verb serialization and "verbal-prepositions" in Oceanic languages. *Oceanic Linguistics 27*. 1–23.
Enfield, Nick J. 2002. Cultural logic and syntactic productivity: associated posture constructions in Lao. In Nick J. Enfield (ed.), *Ethnosyntax: Explorations in culture and grammar*, 231–258. Oxford: Oxford University Press.
Foley, William A., & Mike Olson. 1985. Clausehood and verb serialization. In Johanna Nichols & Anthony C. Woodbury (eds.), *Grammar inside and outside the clause: Some approaches to theory from the field*, 17–60. Cambridge: Cambridge University Press.
Foley, William A. & Robert D. Van Valin. 1984. *Functional syntax and universal grammar*. Cambridge: Cambridge University Press.
Guillaume, Antoine. 2016. Associated motion in South America: Typological and areal perspectives. *Linguistic Typology 20*(1). 81–177.
Guillaume, Antoine and Harold Koch. This volume, chapter 1. Introduction: Associated motion as a grammatical category in linguistic typology.
Hamel, Patricia J. 1993. Serial verbs in Loniu and an evolving preposition. *Oceanic Linguistics 32*(1). 111–132.
Hamel, Patricia J. 1994. *A grammar and lexicon of Loniu, Papua New Guinea*. Canberra: Pacific Linguistics.
Haspelmath, Martin. 2016. The serial verb construction: Comparative concept and cross-linguistic generalizations. *Language and Linguistics 17*(3). 291–319. doi:10.1177/2397002215626895
Jacques, Guillaume, Aimée Lahaussois, & Shuya Zhang. This volume, chapter 21. Associated motion in Sino-Tibetan, with a focus on Gyalrongic and Kiranti.
Levinson, Stephen C. 2003. *Space in language and cognition: Explorations in cognitive diversity* (Vol. 5). New York: Cambridge University Press.
Levinson, Stephen C., P. Brown, E. Danziger, L. De León, J.B. Haviland, E. Pederson, & Gunter Senft. 1992. Man and tree & space games. In Stephen C. Levinson (ed.), *Space stimuli kit 1.2: November 1992*. Nijmegen: Max Planck Institute for Psycholinguistics.
Levinson, Stephen C., & David Wilkins. 2006. *Grammars of space: Explorations in cognitive diversity*. Cambridge: Cambridge University Press.
Lichtenberk, Frantisek. 1991. Semantic change and heterosemy in grammaticalization. *Language 67*(3). 475–509.
Lovestrand, Joseph, & Daniel Ross. This volume, chapter 3. Serial verb constructions and motion semantics.
Lynch, John, Malcolm Ross, & Terry Crowley. 2002. *The Oceanic languages*. Richmond, Surrey: Curzon.
Margetts, Anna, & Peter Austin. 2007. Three-participant events in the languages of the world: Towards a crosslinguistic typology. *Linguistics 45*(3). 393–451.

Meier, Sabrina C. 2020. *Topics in the grammar of Mono-Alu (Oceanic)*. Newcastle, Australia: University of Newcastle dissertation.

Næss, Åshild. 2011. Directional verbs in Vaeakau-Taumako. *Oceanic Linguistics 50*(1). 120–139.

Newman, John (ed.). 2002. *The linguistics of sitting, standing, and lying*. Amsterdam/Philadelphia: John Benjamins.

Pawley, Andrew. 1973. Some problems in Proto-Oceanic grammar. *Oceanic Linguistics 12*. 102–188.

Pawley, Andrew. 2003. Grammatical categories and grammaticisation in the Oceanic verb complex. In Anastasia Riehl & Thess Savella (eds.), *Cornell Working Papers in Linguistics*, 149–172. Ithaca, NY: Cornell University.

Reed, Lauren W. & Kate L. Lindsey. This volume, chapter 9. "Now the story's turning around": Associated motion and directionality in Ende, a language of Papua New Guinea.

Ross, Malcolm. 2004. Demonstratives, local nouns and directionals in Oceanic languages: a diachronic perspective. In Gunter Senft (ed.), *Deixis and demonstratives in Oceanic languages*, 175–204. Canberra: Pacific Linguistics.

Schokkin, Dineke. 2013. Directionals in Paluai: semantics, use, and grammaticalization paths. *Oceanic Linguistics 52*(1). 169–191.

Schokkin, Dineke. 2020. *A grammar of Paluai: The language of Baluan Island, Papua New Guinea*. Berlin: De Gruyter Mouton.

Senft, Gunter. 2000. COME and GO in Kilivila. In Bill Palmer (ed.), *Proceedings of the second international conference on Oceanic linguistics: Volume 2, Historical and descriptive studies*, 105–136. Canberra: Pacific Linguistics.

Vidal, Alejandra & Doris L. Payne. This volume, chapter 12. Pilagá directionals and the typology of associated motion.

Voisin, Sylvie. This volume, chapter 16. Associated motion and deictic directionals in Atlantic languages.

Wilkins, David, & Deborah Hill. 1995. When "go" means "come": questioning the basicness of basic motion verbs. *Cognitive Linguistics 6*. 209–259.

Part III: **The Americas**

Adam J.R. Tallman

11 Associated motion in Chácobo (Pano) in typological perspective

Abstract: This paper has two related goals. The first goal is to provide a revised description of associated motion (AM) in Chácobo, a southern Pano language of the northern Bolivian Amazon. Previous studies reported only 3 AM markers, but I argue that there are at least 7, which express the three timing relations or prior motion, concurrent motion and subsequent motion. The second goal is to take up the non-motional readings of these markers and their importance for the definition and the typology of AM, in particular that concerned with the ranking of timing relations in terms of an implicational hierarchy. I argue that AM markers in Chácobo can be understood as varying according to how dedicated they are to their motion function as opposed to other non-motional functions (path, aspect, etc.). Data from naturalistic speech suggest that the prior motion morpheme is less dedicated than the concurrent and subsequent morphemes. The relative ranking of concurrent and subsequent motion morphemes vis-à-vis prior motion morphemes depends on how the diagnostics for identifying AM markers are understood. I assess the implications of this study for the general typology of AM markers.

Keywords: Pano, Amazonian, AM, aspect, discourse

1 Introduction

As in all documented Pano languages (Guillaume 2017), Chácobo has a complex set of Association Motion (AM) morphemes. AM morphemes combine with a lexical verb root with which they associate a motion event as illustrated in (1) which shows the lexical verb root *ara* 'cry' in combination with various AM morphemes.

(1) a. *ara=kaná* 'cry while going'
    b. *ara=kayá* 'cry and then go'
    c. *ara=koná* 'go away, cry and return'
    d. *ara=honá* 'cry while coming'
    ...

Adam J.R. Tallman, Laboratoire Dynamique du Langage (CNRS & Université Lumière Lyon 2), adam.tallman@cnrs.fr; Friedrich Schilller, Universität – Jena (Germany), adam.james.ross.tallman@uni-jena.de

https://doi.org/10.1515/9783110692099-011

The motion event expressed by AM morphemes has a specific timing relation with the event denoted by the lexical verb (prior, concurrent, subsequent, among others). AM morphemes are also a closed class and occupy a position in the syntactic structure distinct from the verb root. In this paper I revise the description of associated morphemes in Chácobo, based on original data gathered over approximately two years of field work. More examples of AM morphemes in Chácobo can be found in Tallman (2018). Previous literature identified only 3 AM morphemes (Guillaume [2016, 2017] citing data in Prost [1967] and Zingg [1998]). I argue that there are at least 7 and possibly 8 depending on what is considered to be a dedicated AM morpheme. The second goal of this paper is concerned with the importance of Chácobo's AM system for the typology of AM generally. Based on a survey of 66 languages of South America, Guillaume (2016) argues that there is an implicational scale in the timing relations encoded by AM morphemes: prior > concurrent > subsequent. To illustrate the predictions of Guillaume's scale above, (1a) and (1d) are a examples of a concurrent AM marking: the motion event is concurrent with the event denoted by the lexical root or main verb. (1b) is an example of subsequent AM marking. According to Guillaume's scale, if a language has subsequent AM marking it is likely to have concurrent AM marking, and if it has concurrent AM marking it is likely to have prior AM marking. Thus, we should predict that Chácobo to have prior AM marking.

The revised description of AM in Chácobo suggests that the language has a highly developed system of concurrent and subsequent motion without a concomitantly complex system for marking prior motion. This paper explores the extent to which this revised description presents a counterexample to Guillaume's implicational scale of timing relations in AM morphemes. I argue that this depends on how broadly or narrowly the notion of a "dedicated" AM morpheme is understood. The problem in definition arises because of the numerous circumstances in naturalistic speech where AM morphemes do not express or do not uniquely express motion events. For instance, the AM morpheme =kaná~=boná typically expresses concurrent translation motion, but occasionally only expresses continuative semantics.

I show that there are strong asymmetries across prior, concurrent, and subsequent morphemes in this regard that suggest that prior motion is on its way out in Chácobo's AM system. I suggest that these asymmetries arise from the aspectual semantics that emerge from AM timing relations in combination with the other syntactic resources of Chácobo for expressing motion events. Evidence for this thesis is primarily based on the distribution of meanings of AM markers found in naturalistic speech. In Section 2 I provide some background on the Chácobo language and the data for this study, before moving into a revision of the description of AM in the language in Section 3. Section 4 provides a critical discussion of definitions of AM. I argue that while AM is a distinct domain from aspect, it is not orthogonal to it. Section 5 is concerned with non-motion meanings that emerge from AM morphemes and provides some quantitative data with respect to the frequency of motion vs. non-motion events across the different AM markers in Chácobo. Section 5 summarizes the results and discusses future research.

2 Chácobo language: an overview

Chácobo is a southern Pano language of the northern Bolivian Amazon, spoken by approximately 1200 people in 20 communities along the Geneshuaya, Ivon, Benicito and Yata rivers. The language is still being learnt as a first language. Education in some of the Chácobo communities is partially in Chácobo. However, many Chácobo move to the Bolivian town of Riberalta for a better education, where the language is not spoken in day-to-day life (Córdoba, Villar, Valenzuela 2012).

The language has a fairly simple phonological inventory with four vowels (/i, o, a, ɨ/) and 16 consonants (/p, t, k, β, ts, tʃ, ɾ, h, ʔ, n, m, w, j, s, ʃ, ʂ/). Syllable structure is (C)V(C) and only sibilants can occur in coda position. Chácobo has a tonal system that distinguishes high tone marked syllables from toneless syllables. The tonal system is lexically contrastive (e.g. *haná* 'vomit' vs. *hana* 'leave'; *kaṣá* 'play' vs. *káṣa* 'be angry'). Tone sandhi in Chácobo is complex and highly dependent on the type of juncture.

An important distinction in Chácobo syntax is between verbal and non-verbal predicate constructions. Verbal predicate constructions are defined by containing at least one verb root and a morpheme that encodes clause-type (Declarative, Interrogative, Imperative, Hortative). Non-verbal predicate constructions contain a special class of clause-type morphemes and involve juxtaposition of two constituents. Since non-verbal predicate constructions are not relevant to the category of AM they will not be discussed further (for more details see Tallman 2018). An example of a verbal predicate construction is provided in (2) below.

(2) honi kiá ***ara**=kana=tiki(n)=ní=kɨ*
　　man REP **CRY**=GOING:ITR:SG=AGAIN=REMP=**DEC:P**
　　'It is said that the man went along crying again (a long time ago).' ELIC

Chácobo has a rich inventory of closed class bound morphemes that modify the verb, including tense, aspect, temporal distance, AM, modality, evidentiality, and adverbial concepts, some of which are seen in (2), including the AM morpheme

=*kana* 'while going'. Only the verb root and the clause-type rank morpheme are obligatory for the verbal predicate construction, as in *ara* 'cry' and =*ki* 'declarative, past/anterior' (in bold above). All other elements, including overt expressions of arguments (such as *honi* 'man') can be dropped. Non-overt arguments are always interpreted as third person.

Another notable property of Chácobo is that it displays an ergative case marking system on full NPs. Pronouns display an accusative alignment. There are a number of circumstances where the alignment system in case marking is neutralized. With some minor caveats, Chácobo is a dependent marking system. Arguments are not indexed on the verb.

Chácobo displays transitivity harmony across its grammar. Transitivity harmony refers to a system where a given verbal modifier displays suppletive allomorphy conditioned by the transitivity of the verb (see Valenzuela 2017 for transitivity harmony in Pano generally). Transitivity harmony will be illustrated in the context of the description of AM in Chácobo since it is a property of most AM morphemes.

The data for this paper are based on 26 hours of naturalistic speech and thousands of elicited sentences gathered by the author during approximately 22 months of original fieldwork. More details on the Chácobo language can be found in Tallman (2018) and much of the data gathered is archived at the Endangered Language Archive (ELAR).[1] The documentation project involved recording approximately 120 Chácobo speakers and running workshops in the Chácobo communities on documentation techniques.

Examples in this paper that are not from elicitation are presented with an English and Spanish free translation, where available. The Spanish translations correspond as much as possible to translations given by Chácobo in their own Spanish. Sometimes, the motion event expressed by AM morphemes is not expressed in these Spanish translations, which is to be expected given that the motion events expressed by AM markers are often backgrounded. In order to give the reader access to the raw data the Spanish translation is provided. For clarity, readability and in order to present the reader with my understanding of the sentence, I have provided literal English translations. Phonemic transcriptions of Chácobo follow the practice in Tallman (2018: Chapter 1 for details).

---

[1] https://elar.soas.ac.uk/Collection/MPI485795

3 AM categories

This section provides a description of AM categories in Chácobo and a discussion of the distinction between AM morphemes and lexical motion verbs. The full inventory of AM morphemes is provided in Table 1.[2]

Table 1: AM morphemes in Chácobo.

AM morpheme[3]		Temporal relation with verb event	Orientation to point of reference	Further semantic contribution on main verb
=kaná~=boná	GOING	concurrent	NA	durative
=honá~=biná	COMING		towards	
=kayá~=bayá	DO&GO	subsequent	away from	completive
=kiriá~=biriá	DO&COME		towards	
=koná~=boʔoná	CNTRDIR	counterdirectional	away from + towards	
=kó~=boʔó	DISTR	distributive	NA?	pluractional
=tá(n)	GO&DO	prior	away from	incipient
=tiarí	COME_INTO_VIEW	concurrent/ subsequent	towards	

Previous descriptions identified only the concurrent motion morphemes =kaná~=boná and =honá~=biná and the prior motion morpheme =tá(n) as distinct markers of AM (see Guillaume 2016, 2017). A revised description also includes the subsequent morphemes =kayá~=bayá and kiriá~biriá, the counterdirectional =koná~boʔoná, the distributive =kó~=boʔó and the coming-into-view morpheme =tiarí.

As stated above, most AM morphemes in Chácobo display transitivity based allomorphy. Six of the AM categories in Chácobo display this type of allomorphy.

---

[2] In related Pano languages AM morphemes are classified as suffixes (Fleck 2003; Valenzuela 2003; Zariquiey 2018; Valle 2017). I classify AM morphemes in Chácobo as clitics because they can be interrupted by free forms (see Tallman 2018: Section 3.2 and Section 5.2.2 for details on the constituency of the verb complex). In other Pano languages, free forms do not interrupt the verb complex to my knowledge; however, future research on the internal constituency of "words" in other Pano languages might reveal that the distinction between suffixes and enclitics in this case is terminological rather than empirical.

[3] The left-hand variant refers to the intransitive allomorph and the right-hand variant to the transitive allomorph.

I illustrate it with the concurrent andative (away from point of reference) below. The form =*kaná* surfaces when the verb it combines with is intransitive (3a) and the form =*boná* when it is transitive (3b).

(3) a. *tsaʔo=**kaná**=ki*
 sit=**GOING:ITR**=DEC:NONP
 'He sits down (repeatedly) while going.' ELIC

 b. *tsáya=**boná**=ki*
 see=**GOING:TR**=DEC:NONP
 'S/he sees him/her/them while going.' ELIC

Transitivity harmony in AM morphemes interacts with the number and person of the subject. When the subject (A or S argument) is expressed by a plural third person pronoun *(ha) ... =kán*, the transitive allomorph surfaces even when the main verb is intransitive as in (4a). Otherwise, when the subject argument is expressed by a plural NP or a 1st or 2nd person pronoun (singular or plural), the intransitive allomorph surfaces on intransitive verbs as in (4b) and (4c).

(4) a. *tsaʔo=**bona**=ká(n)=ki*
 sit=**GOING:TR**=PL=DEC:NONP
 'They sit down (repeatedly) while going.' ELIC

 b. *hóni=bo*   *tsáʔo=**kaná**=ki*
 man=PL   sit= **GOING:ITR**=DEC:P
 'The men sat down.' ELIC

 c. *ma/no*   *tsaʔo=**kaná**=kɨ*
 2PL/1PL   sit=**GOING:ITR**=DEC:P
 'You (pl)/we sit down (repeatedly) while going.' ELIC

Only the prior motion =*tá(n)* and the concurrent/subsequent =*tiarí* do not participate in the system of transitivity harmony.

As indicated in Table 1, AM morphemes are distinguished according to three other variables: (i) timing, (ii) orientation and (iii) aspectual semantics. AM morphemes in Chácobo always relate to the movement of the subject (A/S) and never other arguments. The display of paradigmatic relations provided in Table 1 somewhat oversimplifies the orientation parameter since it does not distinguish between orientations which are entailed and those which are pragmatic defaults. The distinction is teased out in the discussion below.

3.1 Timing

The most frequent AM morphemes express the simple relations of prior motion, concurrent motion and subsequent motion. The three timing relations are illustrated in (5)-(7) below: subsequent motion with =*bayá* in (5); concurrent motion with =*boná* in (6); prior motion with =*tá(n)* in (7).

(5) hátsi kiá hawɨ şani ha bi=**baya**=ní=kɨ
    then REP 3SG:GEN pubic_hair 3 grab=**DO&GO:TR** =REMP=DEC:P
    'Entonces él recogió el pendejo y después él se fue.'
    'Then he (the man) grabbed her (his grandmother's) pubic hair and left (went away from his grandmother).' TXT 083: 104

(6) ʃino no şɨrɨ-ʔa=şo pi=**bona**=ʔái=na
    monkey 1PL boil-TR=PRIOR:A eat=**GOING:TR** =NMLZ =EPEN
    'Después de sancuchar el mono, comíamos de ida.'
    'After boiling the monkey, we left and ate it (the monkey) while going.'
    TXT 045: 153

(7) tʃama=yá tʃani-na=**tá(n)**=ki
    leader=com converse-intrc2=**GO&DO**=dec:nonp
    'Ella/él se va y habla con el capitán.'
    'S/he goes and speaks with the leader.' ELIC

In many Panoan languages, AM morphemes are polysemous with respect to concurrence and subsequence, rather than strictly encoding subsequence (Guillaume 2017). Based on data in Valenzuela (2003: 159), Guillaume (2016: 153, 2017: 237) categorizes two morphemes in Shipibo, the andative *-kain/-bain* and the ventive *-kiran/ -beiran*, which are partly cognate to the subsequent =*kayá*~=*bayá* and =*kiriá*~=*biriá* of Chácobo, as concurrent-subsequent. However, the polysemy displayed by the corresponding subsequent morpheme in Chácobo, summarized in (8), is different from the polysemy of Shipibo. Importantly, the completely overlapping concurrent reading in (8iv) is not compatible with the semantics of the morpheme (it apparently is in Shipibo). This example shows that subsequent AMs in Chácobo are subsequent morphemes (for more details see Tallman 2018: Section 12.2) in the sense of requiring that the motion continue after the termination of the main event.[4]

---

4 For many authors the 'on the way' reading in (9iii) is a concurrent reading because motion occurs prior and subsequent to the main event (Koch 1984; Guillaume 2016). In my view, the fact

(8) tsaya=**bayá**=ki
　　see=**DO&GO:TR/PL**=DEC:P
　　(i) 'S/he visited him/her/them for a while and left.'
　　(ii) 'S/he looked/glanced at him/her/them and then went.'
　　(iii) 'S/he saw him/her/them on the way.'
　　(iv) *'S/he was looking at him/her/them the whole-time s/he was going.' ELIC

The counterdirectional and distributive AM markers are not strict with respect to the timing relation they have with the main verb. They are discussed below in the context of orientation.

3.2 Orientation

Another basic parameter of variation within Chácobo's AM system is orientation to a point of reference. The path encoded by an AM morpheme can refer to a source and a goal. The source or goal are not necessarily the speaker or addressee but can refer to a salient place (see Vuillermet 2012: 660); "away from" from refers to a trajectory with an explicit source; "towards" refers to a path with an explicit goal. A typical distinction in this regard is between the andative/itive and the ventive, the former encoding an "away from" orientation and the latter a "towards" orientation with respect to a point of reference. In this paper, I use the term "andative" markers as those without a ventive "towards" orientation, rather than as a marker that necessarily has an "away from" orientation. The term "itive" is used for those AM markers that *always* seem to code an away from orientation. The only AM markers that might fit this description are subsequent AM markers.

In Chácobo the distinction between AM morphemes according to orientation crosscuts the concurrent and subsequent morphemes. The distinction between itive and ventive AM can be discerned by comparing (5) with (9). In (5), the subsequent motion is away from the point of reference (the subject's grandmother). In (9) the subsequent motion is towards the point of reference (the subject's home) (see Tallman 2018: 951–961; 977–983).

---

that a concurrent reading is possible with a subsequent morpheme does not provide sufficient evidence to consider this morpheme to be concurrent. The translation evidence in (9i) and (9ii) suggests that subsequent motion is entailed, while concurrent motion emerges contextually. In other words, the translation in (9iii) does not imply that =*kayá*/=*bayá* 'do and go (transitive)' *encodes* concurrent motion, just that motion could be occurring concurrently.

(9) şɨbi   ho=kí   nó   bi=**biria**=itá=kɨ
     motacu   come=CONCUR:A   1pl   grab=**DO&COME:TR**=RECP=DEC:P
     'De regreso hemos cogido motacu'
     'We grabbed the motacusillo (type of palm tree) and came (towards our home, here).' TXT 094:058

The distinction between itive and ventive seems to relevant for subsequent AM markers. However, there is an asymmetry in concurrent motion such that the ventive requires an orientation, whereas the andative has a particular orientation as a pragmatic default. Evidence for this comes from the fact that "andative" AM morphemes can co-index (or "echo": Guillaume 2016: 91, fn11) a motion event that is expressed by a ventive lexical motion verb in the same clause. By co-index I mean that the motion event that seems to be expressed by an AM marker is also expressed by a lexical motion verb. The reverse does not appear to be true, however: when ventive AM morphemes co-index a lexical motion verb, it must be a ventive motion verb; see §3.3 for more discussion on this co-indexing/echo phenomenon. The asymmetry is partially illustrated in (10) where the andative =*boná* appears to co-index a motion event with the lexical motion verb *ho* 'come'.

(10) hó=ki   hó=ki   habi   yóşa=bo
     come=DEC:NONP   come=DEC:NONP   surely   woman=PL
     ka=ʔá=kato=́   tsi   şɨtɨ=**boná**=kiá
     go=NMLZ:P=REL=SPAT LNK   smell=**GOING:TR**=REP
     'Viene, viene, viene, atrás de las dos mujeres, se fue oliendo en camino.'
     'He (the jaguar) is coming ... he (the jaguar) keeps coming, surely he is smelling while going/coming where the women have gone.' TXT 050: 204–206

More evidence of the weak orientation for the "andatives" in Chácobo comes from the fact that they do not have to encode a direct path. Speakers associate situations where a participant "wanders-about" in no particular direction with the "andative" AMs.[5] For instance, a participant that follows a path like the one

---

[5] Guillaume (2017: 236–239) shows that "wandering-about" (Spanish deambulando) or "indirect motion" is a distinct category from the andative in certain Panoan languages such as Kashibo-Kakataibo and Kashinawa. Perhaps the "andative" morphemes in Chácobo should not be classified as andative because they do not imply a straight path. Alternatively, the meaning of the "andative" morphemes in Chácobo suggests that Guillaume's (2016, 2017) clas-

depicted in Figure 1 while performing some action will be described with an andative AM as in (11).

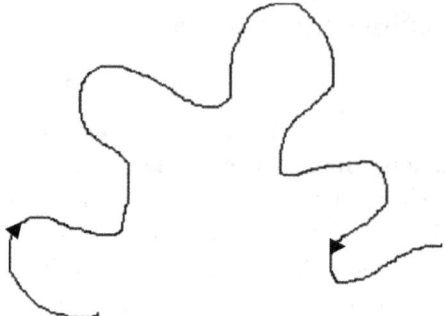

Figure 1: Indirect motion of the Chácobo andative, as drawn by a Chácobo speaker.

(11)   *mɨra=**bona**=ʔái=na*
       look_for=**GOING:TR/PL**=NMLZ:IPV=EPEN
       'He was looking while going.' ELIC

Chácobo also contains morphemes that express more complex path semantics. The AM morpheme *=koná~=boʔoná* associates one or more motion events with the main verb that move in opposing directions. The timing relation with respect to the main event is unspecified, being timed concurrently or non-concurrently depending on context.[6] For concurrent motion events the counterdirectional denotes a circular path such as (12).

(12)   *ho=ṣó   ha-to   hói-wa=**boʔoná**   hini*
       come=PRIOR:A   3-ACC:PL   speak-V:TR=**CNTRDIR:TR**   chicha
       ama=kán=ikiá
       send=PL=REP
       'Llega y saluda después se anda invitandoles chicha.'
       'When he arrived, he greeted them and offered them chicha (fermented yuca beverage) (going around in a circle where they were seated passing it around).' TXT 001:006

---

sification of path semantics could be made more fine grained to account for the distinction between entailed meanings and those that arise via implicature (see Wilkins and Hill 1995).
6 Here context could refer to the aspectual class of the main verb or the discourse context. How different timing relations emerge out of discourse requires future research.

For non-concurrent timing, the counterdirectional expresses motion events prior to and subsequent to the main event that have orientations in opposite directions as in (13).

(13) toka=ʔá   tsi   káko   aʃi=**kona**=ʔá
     do_so=NMLZ:P   LNK   Caco   bathe=**CNTRDIR:ITR**= NMLZ:P
     tsi   aʃi=kí=a   iwĩ
     LNK   bathe=DEC:NONP=1SG   EXCLAM
     i   kia   ha   =ní=kɨ
     say   REP   3   =REMP=DEC:P

'Cuando Caco hizo así, vino "voy a bañarme, ¡¿pero que es eso?!" dice él (Caco) a su otro hermano.'
'And after he (Caco) did this, Caco went to bathe himself and then came back.' (before he went to bathe himself, he said) "I'm going to go bathe myself. But what's this?!" he said (and then he turned back). TXT 026: 328

Chácobo also displays a distributed AM that encodes that the event took place in multiple places and multiple times. In all text examples I have, it implies motion. The distributive *ko~boʔó* requires the verb to reduplicate. An example is provided in (14) below.

(14) ha-ʔ-ɨwa   ara=**ko**   ara=**ko**=ʔái=ka
     3-EPEN-mother   cry=**DISTR:ITR**   cry=**DISTR:ITR**=NMLZ:IPV=REL
     obiyá
     over_there

'Su madre empezaba a llorar en toto lugar, y allí está.'
'(After losing her daughter in the woods), her mother was crying in multiple places everywhere she went (stopping and starting to cry again) "And look now she's over there!" (her mother said).' TXT 110:009

Finally, Chácobo has a morpheme =*tiarí* which encodes that one of the participants of the event denoted by the main verb is coming or will come into view. The morpheme =*tiari* does not display suppletive allomorphy according to the transitivity of the verbal predicate. Also, it does not always encode motion as it can just refer to the fact that an event is being performed away from the speaker. However, ventive motion meanings often emerge from its use and some examples of this are provided in (15), (16) and (17).

(15) hísikɨ=**tiarí**　　　　　hóno　i=kiá
　　 appear=COME_INTO_VIEW　taitetu　say=REP
　　 '"De repente va a aparecer más allá taitetu." le dice a su mujer.'
　　 '"Perhaps a taitetu will appear (coming) within our vision" (he) said (to his wife).' Txt 807:061

(16) hawɨ　　　　hoi=nomarí　　　　　　　　　　　　　　pa　　　i-kí
　　 3SG:GEN　　speech=IMAGIN　　　　　　　　　　　　MIR　　1SG-DAT
　　 pístia=ka　　nia=**tiarí**=ki　　　　　　　　　　　　　ható　　tʃaʔíta
　　 small=REL　throw_away=COME_INTO_VIEW=DEC:NONP　3PL:GEN　uncle
　　 bóka
　　 Boca
　　 'A ver si es cierto su palabra de su abuelo Boca de repente me va a dar algo con eso puedo comprar Lima yo digo también.'
　　 'Perhaps his (Boca's uncle's) word (can be trusted) and Boca's uncle will come (to Alto Ivon) to give (throw away) me a little something (i.e. money).' Txt 2153: 435

(17) mató　　　　　mi-ʔ-ípa　　　　　ʂo
　　 2PL:GEN　　　2-EPEN-father　　DEC
　　 hawɨ　　　　píʃa　　　　　　　a=**tiari**=ʔái=na
　　 something　　small　　　　　　kill=COME_INTO_VIEW=NMLZ:IPV =EPEN
　　 tiʃiná=ki　　　mi-ʔ-ípa
　　 thirsty=DEC:NONP　2-EPEN-father
　　 'Por allí tu padre mata algo bicho viene con sed.'
　　 'From there your father kills a little something and comes (towards us) and your father is thirsty.' Txt 582: 241

The counterdirectional, distributional and coming-into-view morphemes are not very common in naturalistic speech compared to the other AM markers. More details can be found in Tallman (2018: Chapter 12).

3.3 Lexical motion verb roots versus AM clitics

There are three lexical motion verbs that are similar in form and function to AM morphemes with which they are probably diachronically related (see Guillaume 2017 for such correspondences across the Pano family). The verb root *ka~bo* 'go' is related in form and orientation to the andative and itive AMs (=**kaná~**=**boná** 'do while going', =**kayá~**=**bayá** 'do and go'), except that the subsequent itive begins with *ba* rather than *bo*. The verb root *ho~bi* 'come' is related in form and orientation to the ventive AMs (=**honá**~=**biná** 'do while coming', =**kiriá**~=**biriá** 'do and come'), with the exception of the intransitive allomorph of the subsequent, which appears to not be related. The verb root *kó~boʔó* 'hunt, go and return' is related in form and orientation to the counterdirectional and the distributive AMs (*koná~boʔoná* and *kó~boʔó* respectively). Across the board these three lexical motion verbs display the same transitivity harmony that is displayed in the AMs. There are corresponding lexical motion verbs for the prior AM =*tá(n)* and the coming-into-view AM =*tiari*.[7]

The discussion above has focused on the semantic properties that distinguish AM morphemes from each other. Since Chácobo also contains formally related lexical motion verbs, it is important to discuss how these are distinct from AM morphemes. Three properties distinguish them, listed below.

- **Selection:** Lexical motion verb roots do not require another lexical verb root to combine with in order to surface. AM morphemes cannot surface without a lexical verb root.
- **Class size:** Lexical motion verb roots pattern syntactically and phonologically with lexical verb roots in general, which are open class. AM morphemes are, in contrast, closed class morphemes.
- **Pragmatic backgrounding:** Compared to lexical motion verbs, AM morphemes are more likely to express backgrounded motion events rather than introduce new motion events into discourse (Wilkins 1991: 251).

Selection and class size are fairly straightforward. They are important criteria for identifying AM morphemes because they are what distinguish AM constructions from serial verb constructions with a motion verb (I assume that serial verb constructions involve the combination of open class lexical verb roots).

Pragmatic backgrounding is less obvious because it refers to a tendency. That an AM encodes pragmatically backgrounded motion can be seen from redundant repetition of the same AM marker or redundant use of an AM marker following or preceding a lexical motion verb that expresses the same semantics (cf. the coindexing/echoing function described in §5.2). Examples of such redundant repetition are provided in (18) for the concurrent and (19) for the subsequent (more examples are found in Tallman 2018: Chapter 12). The AM morphemes repeated in these examples are encoding the same motion event.

---

[7] One exception might be the lexical verb *nata(n)* 'pass by'. However, the relationship in form is less clear.

(18) bona   mira=**boná**=ʔikiá   pi=**boná**=ʔikiá   noʔó
     ant   look=GOING:TR=REP   eat=**GOING:TR**=REP   1SG:GEN
     yotʃi   yoi   mira=**bona**=kí=a
     peppers SYMP   look_for=**GOING:TR**=DEC:NONP=1SG

'Buscando tuandero, comiendo en camino, "estoy buscando mi querido aji." (dijo el oso bandera).'

'(The anteater was climbing up the tree) looking for ants <u>while going</u>, eating them on the way (<u>lit. while going</u>) (the ant eater said) "I'm looking for my precious peppers <u>on the way (lit. while going)</u>" he said.' TXT 061: 743–744

(19) a(k)=**biriá**   ha-to   ipáisa   hawɨ
     do=DO&COME:TR   3-GEN:PL   uncle   3SG:GEN
     kuenta   kopi=biriá   toa
     account   pay= DO&COME:TR   DEM2
     wai   a(k)=**biriá**   tsi   haʔarí
     farm_plot   do=DO&COME:TR   LNK   again
     ho=tiki(n)=ki   no-a   nia=́no
     come=AGAIN=DEC:NONP 1PL-EPEN   here=SPAT

'Después de hacer pagar la cuenta de su tio después de hacer chaco otra vez vamos a regresar aquí.'

'We do it (harvesting the farm plot in Alegre) and come here, paying the debt (account) of their uncle, and harvesting that farm plot (the one in Siete Almendros).'

(lit. we will do it (harvest the farm plot in Alegre) and then we <u>will come</u>, and we will pay their uncle's account and we <u>will come,</u> and we do that farm plot (the one in Siete Almendros) we <u>will come</u>, and we will come here again.).' TXT 101: 108–110

Unmarked use of lexical motion verbs does not involve redundant repetition in this fashion.

3.4 Other meanings of AM morphemes

AM morphemes cannot combine with deictic motion verb roots such as those discussed above. However, AM morphemes do combine with motion-manner and motion-path verbs. When an AM morpheme combines with a certain motion verbs, the motion event expressed by the AM morpheme is redundant; other aspects of the semantics of AM morphemes are not.

For instance, in (20) the function of the concurrent ventive AM =honá~=biná is to add an orientation.

(20) no-ki=rí   ʃiʃo=**honá**=ki   no-a
1PL-EPEN=AUG stroll_by=**COMING:ITR**=DEC:NONP 1PL-EPEN
'Estamos llegando a pasear.'
'We are arriving (onto you) as we go along / stroll.' (lit. we are strolling while coming).' TXT 004:018

In certain contexts the function of AM morphemes appears to be purely aspectual, even when they do not combine with a motion verb. For instance, the concurrent andative in (21) expresses durative semantics rather than incipience per se and no motion.

(21) hakirikɨ̂   oʃo=**kaná**=ʔi   tsi
after_that become_thin=**GOING:ITR**=CONCUR:S LNK
riso=ki   ínaka
die=DEC:NONP dog
'Cuando el perro come, después, él está flaqueciendo poco a poco/de ida y el perro muere.'
'(After the dog eats the contaminated meat), the dog becomes progressively thinner and dies. TXT 114:018–019

The prior motion AM =ta(n) very frequently expresses quick succession between events. This is illustrated in (22) below. It is rare that this morpheme expresses motion semantics.

(22) matoṣ=yo=ta(n)=ṣó   tsi a(k)=aí   i   kópa
dice=CMPL=**GO&DO**=PRIOR:A LNK do=INTER:NONP:2SG say Copa
=kɨ   a(k)=kí=a
=DEC:P   do=DEC:NONP=1SG
'Después de picar, hemos jalado agua.'
'After finishing dicing all of it (the yuca) Copa said "are you going to do it?". (I replied) "Yes, I will."' Txt 093:026

In fact, most of the AM morphemes have occasional aspectual functions (see Table 1 for an overview). The rest of this paper is concerned with the non-motional interpretations of AM markers and what they mean for the typology of AM.

4 The boundaries of AM

The function of AM morphemes not only bleeds into other functional domains, but the non-motion semantics of AM morphemes seems to be the more important function in certain contexts. In this section we engage with the definition and/or the diagnostic criteria that distinguish AM morphemes from other functional categories. I take up the distinction between AM and aspect and then the distinction between AM and directionals.

Wilkins (1991: 211–212) put forth important arguments for treating AM as a category distinct from aspect. Wilkins (1991: 211) states that "AM forms contain none of the information that would typically be considered aspectual." This is not obviously true (in Chácobo and generally) as it depends on how aspectual content is defined and which aspectual categories are considered (see Guillaume 2013: 134, 2017: 244, 228; Rose 2015: 125–126 for additional comments). Specifically, the timing relations encoded by AM markers impose temporal boundaries on the main event in a fashion similar to some aspectual markers. Prior motion will tend to implicitly impose a clear initiation on the main event. Subsequent motion will do the same for the termination of the main event. In other words, subsequent motion AMs impose completive semantics on the main event and concurrent motion imposes atelic-durative meaning. This is illustrated in (23) and (24). The verb roots *oṣa* 'sleep' and *raka* 'lie down, live' are stative predicates. But in combination with subsequent AM markers, they are obligatorily construed as achievements (events with inherent end points).

(23) *nia=rá*   *wistí*   *oṣa=**kaya***   *há*
 here=AUTH   one   sleep=**DO&GO:ITR:SG**   3
 bo=tikɨ(n)=ká(n)=ʔ=itá=ki
 go=AGAIN=PL=EPEN=RECP=DEC:P
 'Por cierto, uno durmió y se fue otra vez.'
 'Here (for certain) one (of the traveling men) slept and then went again.'
 TXT 117:061

(24) *raka=**kiriá***   *tsi*   *pɨ̂*   *tóa*   *há*
 lie_down=**DO&COME:ITR:SG**   LNK   ANX   DEM2   3
 ho=tikɨ̂(n)=ki
 come=AGAIN=DEC:P
 'Él vivía allí y otra vez él llegó.'
 'He lived there (in Nucleo, where the rubber center was), and then came (home).' TXT 043:024

There is a class of aspectual markers in Chácobo that are durative and atelic (see Smith 1997: 19; Givón 2001: 287 for definitions of these concepts); =*paó* 'durative, habitual'; =*baʔiná* 'during the day'; =*ʃiná* 'during the night' (see Tallman 2018: Chapter 11 for a description of aspectual morphemes in Chácobo). Atelic-durative aspectual morphemes and subsequent AM morphemes cannot co-occur in the same verb complex. I have no examples showing such combinations in naturalistic speech and speakers reject the co-occurrence of these morphemes in elicitation, as illustrated in (25) and (26).

(25) a. **tsaʔo=kayá=baʔiná=kɨ*
     sit=DO&GO:ITR=ALL/EACH_DAY=DEC:P

   b. **tsaʔo=baʔiná=kayá=kɨ*
     sit=ALL_DAY=DO&GO:ITR=DEC:P
     'S/he sat down during the day and then went.' ELIC

(26) a. **tsaya=baʔiná=bayá=kɨ*
     see=ALL_DAY=DO&GO:TR=DEC:P

   b. **tsaya=bayá=baʔiná=kɨ*
     see=ALL_DAY=DO&GO:TR=DEC:P
     'S/he saw him/her/them during the day and then went.' Elic

In contrast, speakers accept the combination of the atelic-durative aspectual morphemes with concurrent AM markers, which express durative meanings, as in (27) below from elicitation. (Note that examples that combine aspectual markers with AM markers are rare in naturalistic speech.)

(27) *tsaʔó   tsaʔó   =**kana=baʔiná**=kɨ*
     sit   sit   =**GOING:ITR=ALL_DAY**=DEC:P
     'S/he was sitting while going all day.'

(28) | naa | niama | ma | wisiwisi |
| --- | --- | --- | --- |
| DEM1 | far_away | 2PL | each |
| ma | ko=ʔiní | tʃaʔita | tiani=yá |
| 2PL | wander=INTER:NONP | grandfa | Tëani=COM |
| mi-ʔ-ípa | yamábo=yá | ma | raká |
| 2-EPEN-father | deceased=COM | 2PL | lie_down/live |
| raká | =**hona=pao**=ní=na | | |
| lie_down/live | =**COMING:ITR=DUR**=REMP=EPEN | | |

'¿Este que ustedes andaban lejos con Taita Rabi y con tu papa finado que andaban ustedes que ustedes venían viviendo viviendo?'
'This one (how about the story) each one of you wandering with your deceased grandfather Tëani, you used to come living (resting and/or setting up settlements)?' TXT 1867: 343

The incompatibility of the atelic-durative markers with the subsequent AM markers, and the compatibility of the atelic-durative markers with concurrent AM markers suggest that the Chácobo AM morphemes encode aspectual semantics (even if most aspectual markers are non-motional). Rather than defining AM as *not* involving aspect, one could define it positively as necessarily expressing motion.[8] Other linguists (Guillaume (2006, 2016); Rose (2015)) take this approach in distinguishing AM markers from directionals. Directionals only encode orientation, whereas AM markers encode motion and optionally orientation (Guillaume 2016: 92). This definition has the advantage of dealing with AM markers that have occasional non-motional functions such as those in (20), (21) and (22). A potential problem with this definition is that it may cast too wide a net, potentially obscuring typological variation and/or typological generalizations. For some morphemes, motion semantics might be nearly obligatorily, whereas for others motion semantics only emerges in specific contexts (see Belkadi 2015, this volume, and Dryer this volume chapter 4) for data that support this observation). Given that AM markers can encode non-motional semantics without encoding motion in certain contexts (see Belkadi this volume; Hernández-Green & Palancar this volume; Otero this volume; Voisin this volume), the motional semantics of a given morpheme could be conceptualized as a matter of degree.

Previous literature on AM made an important contribution by arguing that AM should be regarded as a functional domain in its own right, alongside aspect,

---

[8] Prior to Koch (1984) and Wilkins (1991), associated motion in Australian languages was described as a type of aspect. Note also that in defense of the idea that AM markers are not aspectual markers, Wilkins (1991: 221) states that in Mparntwe Arrernte "the motion event referred to by an associated motion form is never constrained (by meaning or form) to being specifically continuous, punctual or iterative". I do not understand why this fact is relevant to the issue of the status of AM markers as distinct from aspect. Aspectual markers modify the temporal constituency of main event, and if AM markers do the same thing, they could be categorized as a type of aspect marker that also encodes motion, as is done by Talmy (2000: 122–123) under the label of "secondary aspect". Understanding AM markers as a subtype of aspect marker would not make them less interesting any more than considering relative tense relations or perfect markers as subtypes of aspect does (e.g. Klein 1992, 1994). Whether the AM markers in Mparntwe Arrernte are aspectual markers will depend on how aspect is understood and defined as much as it relates to the facts in Mparntwe Arrernte.

tense, mood and direction (Koch 1984; Wilkins 1991; Guillaume 2006, 2016; Rose 2015), in the same way that some authors (e.g. Aikhenvald 2004; Michael 2008) have claimed that evidentiality should be regarded as its own domain, contrary to earlier views that considered it as a type of modality. However, that AM is a distinct functional domain does not need to imply complete orthogonality with respect to other domains. We might posit that morphemes display different degrees of fuzzy category membership in the domain of AM. I suggest that corpus data from Chácobo support this idea.

5 Non-motional functions of AM morphemes

Guillaume's (2016: 92) definition of AM as a "comparative concept" is stated below.

> An AM marker is a grammatical morpheme that is associated with the verb that has among its possible functions the coding of translational motion.

One potential problem with this definition is that it does not distinguish between cases where the expression of motion is saliently present in many or most contexts and those where the expression of motion is marginal. Other definitions in the literature are also problematic in this regard. For instance, Rose states: "AM markers express motion on all kinds of verb stems except, on the whole, on motion verbs themselves, and 'motion' constitutes the core of their semantics" (2015: 210; see Guillaume and Koch this volume for a similar statement). In this section I will provide a summary of the statistical distribution of non-motional readings across prior, concurrent and subsequent AM markers. I suggest that the statistical distributions reveal that Rose's definition of AM markers is too vague. Specifically, it is not clear what "on the whole" means and how to determine precisely when motion is in the "core semantics" or not. The problem with Guillaume's (2016) comparative concept is that the strength of the implicational scales he proposes could vary depending on how membership in the AM category is assessed.

I counted AM markers in texts. Coding for their timing properties and the frequency of morphemes in the resulting database are displayed in Table 2. I went through the texts in consecutive order as they are listed in Tallman (2018: 48–53). In this study I did not code counterdirectional and distributive AM markers since they are too infrequent in my corpus to provide reliable results.

Table 2: Counts of prior, concurrent and subsequent AM markers.

Timing	Orientation	Allomorphy		# of morhs in text	Total
Prior			=tán	149	149
Concurrent	Andative	Intransitive	=kaná	27	226
		Transitive	=boná	96	
	Ventive	Intransitive	=honá	57	
		Transitive	=bɨná	46	
Subsequent	Itive	Intransitive	=kayá	38	227
		Transitive	=bayá	79	
	Ventive	Intransitive	=kiriá	45	
		Transitive	=bɨriá	65	

The most straightforward way to code how often a given AM marker expresses motion is to count cases throughout texts where a motion event is expressed in a clause that contains an AM. The variable of motion expression can actually be divided into three values which are described below.

- **Yes:** The AM marker is clearly expressing translational motion as can be seen from the context and/or the translation provided by a linguistic consultant.
- **No:** The AM marker is not expressing translational motion. It could be expressing orientation, aspect, or some other category, but no translational motion is involved in the sentence that the AM marker occurs in.
- **Unclear:** It is not clear whether the AM marker expresses translational motion because translational motion is simultaneously expressed somewhere else, either when the AM marker combines with a motion verb or elsewhere in the same clause in cases of co-indexation/echo (see above). The motion semantics of the AM marker appears be redundant and, thus, it is unclear what semantic contribution it is making.

Cases where an AM marker is coded "Yes" with respect to the expression of motion are provided in (5), (6) and (7) above (Section 3). In each of these cases the context and the consultant's translations made clear that translational motion is involved and there are no other elements in the sentence that could also be expressing translational motion.

An example where an AM is coded as "No" for expressing translational motion is provided in (29). The AM marker =kaná~=boná is expressing the enlarging of a perforation in a person's ear lobe, not the translational motion of the ear or the person (see (21) above for another example of an AM marker that is coded "No" with respect to the expression of motion).

(29) hiwi   bara   raa=kan=(ʔ)á=ka   habi
     stick   clean send=PL=NMLZ:P=REL   surely
     raa=**bona**=kí   tsi   ani=**kana**=kí   tsi
     send=**GOING:TR**=CONCUR:A LNK   grow=**GOING:ITR**=CONCUR:A LNK
     tóka   tsi   ha
     do_so   LNK   3
     i=ka(n)=pao=ní=kɨ
     be=PL=HAB=REMP=DEC:P
     'Cuando le ponen una barita de palo debe meter despacio y mientras que ancheaba despacio así eran ellos antes.'
     'When they put the little stick (in their ear), as they continued to put it in, it continued to widen, that's how they did it before.' Txt 115: 154

Cases where an AM marker would be coded as "Unclear" with respect to the expression of motion are provided in (11) above for the concurrent and (30) below for the subsequent (see also 21 and 22). In the example in (30) below the subsequent AM marker occurs with/on a verb that stands in an asyndetic coordinate relation with the lexical motion verb *ka* 'go'.

(30) pi=**bayá**   tsi   no   ka=tɨkɨ(n)=ní=kɨ   bakiʃmarí
     eat=**DO&GO:TR**   LNK   1PL   **go**=AGAIN=REMP=DEC:P   morning
     'Después de comer fuimos otra vez temprano.'
     'We ate and then went in the morning.' Txt 011:020

In this case one can either say that =*bayá* does not express motion or that it co-expresses it with the motion verb. Assuming that the lexical motion verb expresses motion in such cases, the semantic contribution of the AM marker is unclear. Similarly, in (18) one can either say that =*honá* does not express translational motion or that it expresses it redundantly, marking only orientation. I coded such cases as "Unclear" because, while one cannot rule out the idea that the AM marker expresses motion, it is difficult to tell from context because of the presence of another element encoding motion.

Table 3 and Figure 2 summarize the variable of motion expression across the AM markers grouped according to their timing relations.

Table 3: Motion expression across prior, concurrent and subsequent AM markers (counts and percentages).

	Prior	Concurrent	Subsequent	Total
No	86 (57%)	14 (6%)	0	100 (16%)
Unclear	24 (16%)	53 (24%)	139 (61%)	216 (35%)
Yes	39 (27%)	161 (70%)	88 (39%)	288 (48%)

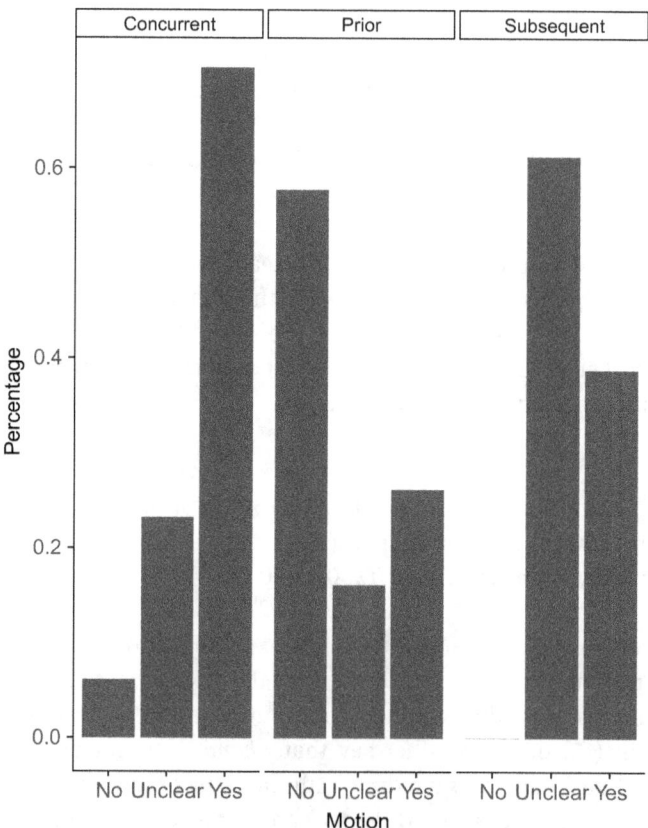

Figure 2: Motion expression across prior, concurrent and subsequent AM markers (percentages).

The data reveal stark asymmetries between AM markers in terms of how often they express and/or clearly express translational motion. Below I provide a discussion of each of the AM categories with reference to the non-motional functions of each morpheme. A final discussion provides an overview.

5.1 Concurrent

70% of the cases of concurrent AM markers clearly express motion; 70% of the time concurrent markers combine with non-motional lexical verbs and motion is expressed. 24% of the time it is unclear whether the AM expresses a motion event, because it combines with a lexical motion-manner or motion-path verbs such as *haba* 'run', *waʃa* 'row'; *tia* 'go in circle, surround'; *nini* 'trot'; *ʃobiri* 'spin around'; *paki* 'fall', *bibo* 'overcome (with movement), interrupt', *ʃiʃo* 'stroll'. When the AM marker combines with a motion verb it can be seen as contributing either towards/ventive-orientation or continuative aspect.

(Ventive) Orientation: When AM markers combine with motion+manner verbs, orientation can be seen as their primary contribution to the semantics of the resulting verb complex. An example is provided in (18) above, where the ventive concurrent AM marker combines with the manner+motion verb *ʃiʃo* 'pass by'. Overall ventives combine with manner+motion verbs more frequently than andatives/itives do. 17% (21/123) of concurrent andatives combine with manner+motion verbs, compared to 31% (33/103) of concurrent ventives. This makes sense if one of the primary functions of AM markers in combination with motion verbs is orientation. Recall from Section 3 that andatives do not seem to encode orientation explicitly, whereas ventives do. Thus, it is less likely that combination with an andative AM marker contributes path semantics to a manner+motion verb, whereas combination with the ventive does.

Continuative aspect: 6% of concurrent AM markers contribute no motional semantics at all. In such cases the semantic contribution appears to be continuative. Examples are provided in (19) *oʃo=kaná* 'continue thinning out' and (23) *ani=kaná* 'continue widening' and *raa=boná* 'continue to put/send'. All examples of concurrent AM markers contributing only aspectual semantics come from andatives. Concurrent ventives contribute either motion and orientation or just orientation, but never continuative aspect. Thus, there seems to be some complementarity in the non-motional functions of concurrent AMs. To a large extent, andatives contribute continuative aspect and ventives contribute orientation.

5.2 Subsequent

Most subsequent AMs (61%) occur in constructions where it is unclear whether it can be said that they contribute motional semantics. Typically this involves asyndetic coordinate structures where the subsequent AM modifies the first verb and the second verb is a lexical verb as in the schema in (25).

(31) [(NP$_O$) VERB$_1$-AM] [(NP$_O$) NP$_{A/S}$ VERB$_2$] CLAUSE-TYPE

When VERB$_2$ is a lexical motion verb, the construction is coded as unclear. An example of such a construction with the itive morpheme is provided in (30) above and an example with the ventive is provided in (32).

(32) mai= no ho=ʔá=ka [oṣa=kiriá]
ground=SPAT 1PL come=NMLZ:P=REL [sleep=**DO&COME:ITR:SG**]
tsi [nobá ṣobo=kí no
LNK [1PL:GEN house=DAT 1PL
kaʔɨ]=ní=kɨ
arrive_here]=REMP=DEC:P
'Cuando venimos a pie, en el medio dormimos y de allí llegamos a casa a pie.'
'When we had been coming on the ground, we slept (before leaving) and then came at our house.' Txt 102:035–036

57% of instances of AM markers of all types occur in such constructions. In the examples in (23) and (24) the second verb is a deictic motion verb. The second verb can also be a motion+manner verb as in (33).

(33) [rooṣ a(k)=**bayá**] tsi kiá [hawî
[IDEO_shove_inside do=**DO&GO:TR/PL**] LNK REP [3S:GEN
raís **haba**]=ní=kɨ]
in_law **run**]=REMP=DEC:P]
'Cuando lo mitió (en su ano), su suegro se escapó.'
'After he (the in-law) shoved it (up the other in-law's anus) (before going), he (the in-law) went running away (lit. he went and ran away).' Txt 084:079

11% (25 examples) of asyndetic coordinate constructions with AM markers contain non-motion verbs as the second verb root as in (34). In the rest of asyndetic coordinate constructions the second verb is a motion verb (89%).

(34) [bi=**bayá**] tsi kiá [yoṣa=yá
[receive=**DO&GO:TR**] LNK REP [woman=COM
rakɨpi-na]=ní=kɨ
lie_with-INTRC2]=REMP=DEC:P
'Después de recibirla y llevarla, se acostó con la mujer.'
'After he (Isha) met her (lit. received her), he went (with her) and lay with the woman.' Txt 008:016

There are no cases where subsequent AM markers clearly do not express motion. That is, AM subsequent markers either express motion or co-index a motion event with a lexical motion verb in the same clause. In the latter case the subsequent AM marker contributes completive semantics to the main verb it is attached to.

Completive aspect: As noted in Section 3, an important function of subsequent AM markers is that they encode completion of the event of the verb root with which they combine. Furthermore, subsequent AM markers display aspectual constraints such that they cannot co-occur with certain imperfective modifications. The importance of the aspectual function compared to translational motion can be seen from the fact that subsequent AM markers clearly express motion only 39% of the time.

Orientation: In cases where the subsequent AM marker co-occurs with a motion+manner verb root as in (31) that does not encode orientation such as in (32), orientation is a plausible semantic contribution. The cases where it clearly has this function are relatively few, however. For subsequent andative AM markers in asyndetic coordinate constructions where the second verb is a motion verb, only 25% (11 of 44) of the motion verbs are manner+motion rather than deictic. For subsequent ventive AM markers the proportion is 35% (39 out of 60). Thus, while orientation could be an important function of subsequent AM markers, the prevalence of cases where an AM marker redundantly occurs with a deictic motion verb that expresses the same orientation as in (30) and (32) suggests that this is not its most important non-motional function. The primary non-motional function of subsequent AM markers, therefore, appears to be the expression of completive semantics on the first verb.

5.3 Prior

As can be seen from Table 3 and Figure 2 above, the prior AM marker =tá(n) only clearly expresses motion 27% of the time. While this would classify it as an AM marker according to Guillaume's (2016) typology, it is clearly *less* dedicated to the expression of translational motion than the other AM markers of this study. Below I provide a brief overview of some of its other functions. I also point out that motional versus non-motional readings are not distributed evenly across all constructions where =tá(n) occurs.

Non-motional interpretations of =tá(n) are 'quick succession' or 'for a short period'. The quick succession interpretation typically arises when =tá(n) occurs in same and different subject clauses as in (35) and (36); see another example in (20).

(35) hatsi kiá   ha miʂ-a-**ta(n)**=ʂó   tsi kia
     then REP   3   grab-TR-**GO&DO**=PRIOR:A LNK REP
     há   a(k)=ní=ki
     3   do=REMP=DEC:P
     'Entonces el momento que él lo arrancó, lo hizo.'
     'Then as soon as he grabbed it (the branch) he hit (did) him (the caiman)'
     Txt 061: 287

(36) ma-pɨk-a   ha-ʔ-á   tsi   kiá
     head-open-TR   3-EPEN-SPAT   LNK   REP
     yoʂa   háʔi=bo   atʃ-a-**ta(n)**=kɨ̂
     woman   girl=PL   grab-TR=**GO&DO**=PRIOR:D{A,S}
     ɾi-tóo   há   wa=ʔái=na
     nose-hit   3   TR=NMLZ:IPV=EPEN
     'Abrieron y allí están las muchachas, y el momento que la cogió lo golpeó en la nariz.'
     'They opened it (the door), and there were the young (Maina) women, the moment that he (one of the Chácobo men) grabbed her (one of the Maina women he wanted to take home), she (the Maina woman) pegged him (the Chácobo man) on the nose. Txt 007: 275–276

The other reading expresses that the event of the main verb took a short period to complete. For the sentence in (37) speakers provide two translations. One is a motion reading and the other is a short period of time reading. The former reading is fairly rare and/or hard to discern from texts and is better attested in elicitation than in naturalistic speech (as in (7)).

(37) habi   tóa   ʂaba   hiko=**tá(n)**=ki
     surely   DEM2   savannah   enter=**SHORTLY/GO&DO**=DEC:NONP
     pɨ̂   hóno
     ANX   collared_peccary
     'De allí en la entrada de la pampa el taitetu entró después de un rato / entró después de viajar.'
     'And for sure, in that savannah, a collared peccary entered shortly / a collared peccary travelled and entered the savannah.' Txt 092: 194–195

The short period to completion reading seems to always be present in Chácobo even where prior motion is expressed. The short period reading could have naturally extended into quick succession as in (36) and (32). The most common case for prior motion to be expressed is in imperative and intentional constructions. An example is provided in (38) below.

(38) niá=ʂo   i-a   mana=wɨ̂   i   boi   a(k)=**tá(n)**=no
     here =A 1SG-ACC wait=IMPER 1SG yatorana do=**GO&DO**=INTENT
     '(Después de acostarse con su mujer se levantó) "Esperama aquí, voy a matar una yatorana (dijo el hombre adentro de la casa en el pueblo)"'
     '(After sleeping with his wife and getting up from bed) "Wait for me here. I intend to go (to the river) and catch (lit. do) yatorana (type of fish)." (the man said from in the house inside the village).' Txt 008:024

An overview of the distribution of motion expression across the five constructions where the prior motion AM is found is provided in Table 4.

Table 4: Expression of motion by the prior motion AM across five constructions.[9]

	No	Unclear	Yes
Same/different subject =ʔi, =kɨ́,=ʔáʂ, =ʂó, =pama	75	15	8
Declarative =kɨ, =ki	1	2	4
Nominalization =ʔai, =ʔá	3	0	1
Intention =no	2	6	17
Imperative =wɨ̂	0	1	5

The domain of prior motion is less developed and least integrated into the system of AM markers in Chácobo for a few reasons. First, there is no distinction between andative and ventive prior motion; the morpheme =tá(n) always seems to express

---

[9] A reviewer suggests that there are multiple different morphemes with the form =tá(n) even if they occur (or seem to occur?) in the same position in the verb complex. To the extent that this suggestion is about speaker knowledge (do Chácobo speakers store different versions of =tá(n) in their mind?), I simply do not have the data to answer it. If it concerns synchronic analysis, the problem here has more to do with the definition of a morpheme than with the marker =tá(n). It simply remains the case that there is no method for determining the correct morphemic analysis in ambiguous cases such as these (see Blevins 2016). I thus remain agnostic concerning whether there is one or more =tá(n) morphemes. If there are two morphemes, then the variation in meaning is reduced to a certain extent.

andative motion, but this issue requires future research. Second, the prior motion AM marker =*t(á)n* does not display transitivity harmony as the other AM markers do. Finally, the summary above suggests that the motion semantics of the prior AM marker are eroding, although the erosion has not spread evenly across constructions.[10]

5.4 Discussion

If the diagnostic for whether a morpheme is an AM marker is the simultaneous combination with a non-motion lexical verb and expression of motion (Rose 2015: 210), then the data from naturalistic speech in Chácobo reveal a language specific ranking of AM markers with respect to this diagnostic. The AM markers can be ranked from more to less dedicated as in (39).

(39) Ranking of AM timing categories according to the frequency of clear expression of motion (Percentage coded "Yes" from Table 3):
Concurrent (70%) > Subsequent (39%) > Prior (27%)

Assuming a discrete division between AM, aspect and directionals, the ranking reveals that it is not clear when a morpheme stops becoming an AM marker. Is 39% expression of motion enough to classify the subsequent AM in Chácobo as a dedicated AM marker? Is 27% expression of motion enough to classify the prior AM in Chácobo as a dedicated AM marker?

There are different ways of measuring the strength of motional semantics from natural speech. If expression of motion at the clause level regardless of whether there is a co-indexed lexical verb is understood as the diagnostic, the subsequent AM could be considered the most dedicated AM marker and a different ranking emerges.

(40) Ranking of AM timing categories according to the frequency with which they clearly express or possibly express motion. (Percentage coded "Yes" or "Unclear" from Table 3):
Subsequent (100%) > Concurrent (94%) > Prior (44%)

---

[10] It is probably the case that the erosion has not spread across all speakers. Whether there is dialectal variation with respect to the motion vs. non-motional expression of =tá(n) requires future research.

These data suggest that the current diagnostics for classifying morphemes as AM either result in ambiguous or fuzzy classification or obscure potentially important variation. It is unclear how to reconcile the gradient data in Chácobo with the statement that AM markers are those that express motion as their "core semantics" and combine with non-motional verbs "on the whole" (Rose 2015: 210). On the other hand, assuming that any morpheme that expresses motion in any context is a bona fide AM marker (Guillaume 2016), while practical, obscures the fact that some morphemes might be *more* dedicated to expressing motion than others, which may be important for constructing robust typological scales, and for understanding the diachronic trajectory of AM and its relationship to other functional categories.

6 Conclusions and future research

This paper has argued that Chácobo has a more complex system of grammaticalized AM than previously described. As has been described for many systems of AM, the AM markers in Chácobo encode more than just motion, but also express notions related to orientation and aspect. The importance of these non-motional functions can be understood as varying according to context, when the diagnostics for identifying AM markers are applied to natural speech. The corpus data of Chácobo reveal asymmetries with respect to the prevalence of motional vs. non-motional semantics across different AM markers in a way that would seem to undermine any attempt to keep AM distinct from other categories in a discrete fashion. Prior motion morphemes seem to be *less* dedicated to the expression of motion than concurrent and subsequent morphemes. Whether concurrent or subsequent AM markers are considered more or less dedicated depends on how the strength of motion is measured from the natural speech.

Future research might reveal that some statistically meaningful and testable concept of "core motion semantics" can be established based on data from naturalistic speech. Combining corpus data with a set of clear semantic tests that can be applied in elicitation (e.g. Waldie et al. 2009) to diagnose whether a morpheme encodes "core motion semantics" might also help. Furthermore, in this paper I have not systematically investigated the relationship between the lexical class of the main verb and the semantic contribution of the AM morpheme. Raw frequencies might obscure the possibility that non-motional meanings are distributed differently according to the semantic class of the main verb (see Otero this volume). Whatever new methodologies come to the fore, moving forward with the typology of AM will need to involve dealing with the gradience of motional semantics that emerges from naturalistic speech in individual languages and relating it to the proposed typological scales such as that in Guillaume (2016).

Abbreviations

I use the following glossing conventions:

A	subject of transitive clause	HAB	habitual
ACC	accusative	IDEO	ideophone
AGAIN	again	IMAGIN	imaginative
ALL_DAY	all day	INTRC	interactional
ANT	anterior	INTER	interrogative
ANX	anxietive	INTENT	intentional
AUG	augmentative	IPV	imperfective
AUTH	authoritative	ITR	intransitive
CMPL	completive	NMLZ	nominalizer
CNTRDIR	counterdirectional	NONP	non-past
COM	comitative	P	past
CONCUR	concurrent dependent clause	P5	position 5 morpheme
DAT	dative	PL	plural
DEC	declarative	PRIOR	prior dependent clause
DEM1	proximal (speaker oriented) demonstrative	SG	singular
		SHORTLY	shortly
DEM2	distal (addressee oriented) demonstrative	SPAT	spatial
		SYMP	sypathetic
DISTR	distributive	TXT	data from naturalistic speech
ELIC	data from elicitation	RECP	recent past
EPEN	epenthetic formative	REL	relativizer
EXCLAM	exclamative	REMP	remote past
GEN	genitive	REP	reportative
GOING	going	TR	transitive

Acknowledgements: I would like to thank my Chácobo collegues and language teachers, especially Caco Moreno Ortiz, Boca (Miguel) Chácobo Ortiz and Paë Yaquë Roca. Data for this paper were gathered in the context of a documentation project funded by the National Science Foundation (Grant BCS-1360783) and the Endangered Language Documentation Project (Grant IGS0230). I am grateful to the editors Antoine Guillaume and Harold Koch for insightful comments as well as David Fleck. All mistakes are my own.

References

Aikhenvald, Alexandra Y. 2004. *Evidentiality*. Cambridge: Oxford University Press.
Belkadi, Aicha. 2015. Associated motion with deictic directionals: A comparative overview. *SOAS Working Papers in Linguistics* 17: 49–76.
Belkadi, Aicha. This volume, chapter 5. Deictic directionality as associated motion.
Blevins, James P. 2016. *Word and Paradigm Morphology*. Oxford: Oxford University Press.
Córdoba, Lorena, Pilar M Valenzuela, and Diego Villar. 2012. Pano meridional. In Mily Crevels and Pieter Muysken (eds.), *Lenguas de Bolivia, Vol. 2, Amazonía*, 27–69. La Paz: Plurales Editores.
Dryer, Matthew. This volume, chapter 4. Associated motion and directionals: where they overlap.
Fleck, David. 2003. *A Grammar of Matses*. Houston: Rice University PhD Thesis.
Givón, Talmy. 2001. *Syntax: An Introduction (Volume II)*. Amsterdam: John Benjmains.
Guillaume, Antoine. 2006. La catégorie du mouvement associe en cavineña: Apport à une typologie de l'encodage du mouvement et de la trajectoire. *Bulletin de la Société Linguistique de Paris* 101 (1): 417–438.
Guillaume, Antoine. 2013. Reconstructing the category 'associated motion' in Tacanan languages (Amazonian Bolivia and Peru). In Ritsuko Kikusawa and Lawrence Reid (eds.) In *Historical Linguistics 2011. Selected papers from the 20th International Conference on Historical Linguistics, Osaka, 25–30 July 2011*, 129–151. Amsterdam: John Benjamins.
Guillaume, Antoine. 2016. Associated motion in South America: Typological and areal perspectives. *Linguistic Typology* 20 (1): 81–177.
Guillaume, Antoine. 2017. Sistemas complejos de movimiento asociado en las lenguas Tacana y Pano *Amerindia* 39 (1): 211–261.
Guillaume, Antoine, and Harold Koch. This volume, chapter 1. Associated Motion as a grammatical category in linguistic typology.
Hernández-Green, Néstor, and Palancar Enrique. This volume, chapter 14. Associated motion in the Otomi family.
Klein, Wolfgang. 1992. The Present Perfect Puzzle. *Language* 68 (3): 525–552.
Klein, Wolfgang. 1994. *Time in Language*. London: Routledge.
Koch, Harold. 1984. The Category 'Associated Motion' in Kaytej. *Language in Central Australia* 1: 23–24.
Michael, Lev David. 2008. *Nanti evidential practice: Language, knowledge, and social action in an Amazonian society*. PhD Thesis, University of Texas at Austin.
Otero, Manuel A. This volume, chapter 20. At the intersection of associated motion, direction and exchoative aspect in the Koman languages.
Prost, Gilbert. 1967. Chacobo. In Esther Mattseon (ed.), *Bolivian Indian Grammars 1* (Summer Institute of Linguistics International Publications in Linguistics 16). Norman: Summer Institute of Linguistics of the University of Oklahoma.
Rose, Francoise. 2015. Associated motion in Mojeño Trinitario: Some typological considerations. *Folia Linguistica* 49 (1): 117–158.
Smith, Carlota. 1997. *The Parameter of Aspect* (2nd edn). Dordrecht: Kluwer.
Tallman, Adam J.R. 2018. *A Grammar of Chácobo, a southern Pano language of the northern Bolivian Amazon*. Austin: University of Texas at Austin PhD thesis.
Talmy, Leonard. 2000. *Toward a Cognitive Semantics (Volume II, Typology and Process in Concept Structuring)*. Cambridge: The MIT Press.

Valenzuela, Pilar M. 2003. *Transitivity in Shipibo-Konibo Grammar*. Oregon: University of Oregon PhD thesis.
Valenzuela, Pilar M. 2017. Armonía transitiva en las lenguas Pano y Takana. *Amerindia* 39 (2): 407–453.
Valenzuela, Pilar M. & Antoine Guillaume (eds.). 2017. Estudios sincrónicos y diacrónicos sobre lenguas Pano y Takana [Special issue]. *Amerindia* 39.
Valle, Daniel. 2017. *Grammar and Information Structure of Kakataibo*. Austin: University of Texas at Austin PhD thesis.
Voisin, Sylvie. This volume, chapter 16. Associated Motion and Deictic Directional in Atlantic languages.
Vuillermet, Marine. 2012. *A Grammar of Ese Ejja, A Takanan language of the Bolivian Amazon*. Lyon: l'Université Lumière Lyon 2 PhD thesis.
Waldie, Ryan, Tyler Peterson, Hotze Rullmann, and Scott Mackie. 2009. Evidentials as Epistemic Modals or Speech Act Operators: Testing the Tests. Handout for presentation given at the Workshop on Structure and Constituency in the Languages of Americas. Purdue University, 3 April 2009.
Wilkins, David P. 1991. The Semantics, Pragmatics and Diachronic Development of 'Associated Motion' in Mparntwe Arrente. *Buffalo Working Papers in Linguistics* 91: 207–257.
Wilkins, David P., and Deborah Hill. 1995. When 'go' means 'come': Questioning the basicness of basic motion verbs. *Cognitive Linguistics* 6 (2/3): 209–259.
Zariquiey, Roberto. 2018. *A Grammar of Kakataibo* (Mouton Grammar Library 75). Berlin: Mouton de Gruyter.
Zingg, Philippe. 1998. *Diccionario chácobo-castellano, castellano-chácobo con bosquejo de la gramática chacobo y con apuntes culturales*. La Paz: Ministerio de Desarrollo Sostenible y Planificación Viceministro de Asuntos Indígenas y Pueblos Originarios.

Alejandra Vidal and Doris L. Payne

12 Pilagá directionals and the typology of associated motion

Abstract: Pilagá (Guaycuruan) has fourteen directional verb suffixes that code location, spatial configuration, and deictic and non-deictic path. The directionals also sometimes have applicative and some associated motion (AM) functions. This study focuses on the AM function of the deictic directionals *-ge(')* 'itive' and *-get* 'ventive' and on the non-deictic directional *-ege* 'opposite'. The extent to which an AM meaning is evident with these directionals depends on a combination of communicative pragmatics and the lexical root semantics. The system is technically vague as to whether an AM is interpreted as prior to, or simultaneous with the action of the lexical verb. AM targets an intransitive S or a transitive O argument, thus displaying absolutive alignment. This is counter to Guillaume's (2016) prediction that if an O can be interpreted as undergoing AM, then subjects (both A and S) can also be so interpreted. Part of the explanation for the Pilagá absolutive pattern may be the conflation of AM with an applicative function.

Keywords: deixis, deictic motion, Guaycuruan family, applicative, absolutive

1 Introduction

Guaycuruan languages have complex paradigms of verbal suffixes that, in previous literature, are commonly called directionals (see Klein 1973, 1981, and Messineo 2003 on Toba; Gualdieri 1998: 279 and Carrió 2011 on Mocoví; Vidal 2001 for previous work on Pilagá; Sandalo 1997 on Kadiwéu; among others). Guaycuruan directionals encode location, deictic and non-deictic path, and spatial configuration relevant to a lexical event or situation. They sometimes also have applicative and associated motion functions. Here we use the term "directional" as a name for the paradigm of morphemes, regardless of the function or meaning in any occasion of use.

Alejandra Vidal, University of Formosa & Consejo Nacional de Investigaciones Cientificas y Técnicas, vidal.alejandra@conicet.gov.ar
Doris L. Payne, University of Oregon & SIL International, dlpayne@uoregon.edu

https://doi.org/10.1515/9783110692099-012

This paper is a preliminary investigation of the conceptual category of associated motion (AM) in the grammar of Pilagá verbal directionality.[1] Pilagá is spoken by about 5,000 people in the province of Formosa, northeastern Argentina (INDEC 2004). Formosa is part of the Gran Chaco in the lowlands of South America, which spans four countries (Argentina, Brazil, Paraguay and Bolivia), across an area of approximately one million square kilometers.

Figure 1 shows the internal relationships of the Guaycuruan family (Viegas Barros 2013: 29), which consists of five languages: 1) Kadiwéu, the only extant member of the northern branch, is spoken in Mato Grosso, Brazil; 2) Pilagá, 3) Mocoví, 4) Toba (who prefer the ethnonym Qom), and 5) the extinct language Abipón belong to the Southern branch. Pilagá and Mocoví are spoken in Argentina and Toba (Qom) is spoken in Argentina, Paraguay, and Bolivia. Both Toba and Pilagá have several dialects. In Figure 1, language names are in bold.

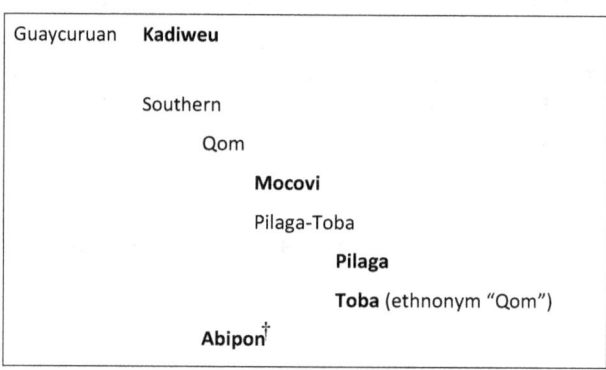

Figure 1: Guaycuruan linguistic family.

In Guillaume's (2016) survey of AM in South American languages, Pilagá is classified as not having AM. However, as this paper shows, some directionals can have either a deictic direction function that doesn't imply a separate motion event from the one communicated by the lexical root, like the 'ventive' in (1), or sometimes they can indeed have an AM function, like the same 'ventive' in (2). In the latter situation, they communicate that a translational motion event accompanies the event expressed by the main lexical predicate.[2]

---

[1] To our knowledge, AM has not been noticed in other Guaycuruan languages. However, we expect that further study of Guaycuruan directionals will likely reveal that AM is not exclusive to Pilagá.
[2] Throughout this paper we use the practical orthography for Pilagá, in accord with orthographic systems in use in Northern Argentina. This orthography is Spanish-based but phonemic: <ʕ> = a pharyngeal stop or flap, <q> = a uvular stop, <č> = /tʃ/, <λ> = palatal /lj/, <ƀ> = a labiovelar glide

(1) nač'e   ha-so'   yawo   yataqta   ø-ka'a-**get**
    then   F-CLF:FAR   woman   very   A3-go-**VEN**
    so'   taʕade-na'
    CLF:FAR   father-ancestor
    'Then, the woman came closer to the father' (pil050MujerMonte, 1.6)

(2) č'e yemta   de-mače-**get**-'a   noqo'   so'   t'ae-'m
    then   A3-listen-**VEN**-OBJ.SG   when   CLF:FAR   be.little-DEM
    l-owa-'   wotakie-'
    POS.3-spouse-PL   kiskadee-PL
    'Then, the women heard their little kiskadee (bird sp.) spouses coming (towards them).' (pil011Kitilipi, 1.8)

Two of the directionals are specifically deictic: -ge(') 'itive' (IT) and -get 'ventive' (VEN), and both can function as AM markers. The non-deictic members of the directional system signal that the lexical event progresses through a certain path or takes place at a location with a particular spatial configuration, but they do not signal that the event is deictically anchored. This paper addresses the AM features of the system, focusing only on the deictic directionals -ge(') 'itive' (IT) and -get 'ventive' (VEN) and on the non-deictic directional morpheme -ege 'opposite' (OPP). The semantics of the other directional morphemes are more cursorily mentioned by way of background (more information can be found in Vidal 2001, 2006).

The paper demonstrates several features of AM in Pilagá relative to AM systems more generally. First, it shows that AM exists in Pilagá as part of a larger grammatical system that pays detailed attention to spatial configuration and path (including deictic direction), but where not all 14 members of the system have AM functions. A semantic, and at least sometimes historical association between directionality and AM has been pointed out for a number of languages, including from Africa (Payne 2013 and this volume, Belkadi 2015 and this volume, Payne & Otero 2016, Otero 2018 and this volume), South America (Guillaume 2000, 2016; Vuillermet 2012; Fabre 2013; Rose 2015; Otero, Vidal & Payne 2017), and elsewhere (Dryer, this volume; Ross, this volume). This study thus complements other work on directional systems that do and do not have AM as part of their meaning features.

Second, the paper argues that the likelihood of a Pilagá directional being construed as having AM meaning can depend on the pragmatics of the communicative

---

/w/, and <'> = a glottal stop /ʔ/ or glottalization on a consonant. Examples from text have a text reference at the end of the free translation; otherwise, examples are elicited.

situation and on whether the lexical root is a motion, non-motion active, or stative root. For instance, *-ge(')* 'itive', *-get* 'ventive', and *-ege* 'opposite' can communicate literal (physical) AM with non-motion active roots, but with translational motion roots they signal the path through which an event progresses.

Third, the Pilagá directional suffixes which participate in AM are technically vague as to whether their motion component is interpreted as prior to, simultaneous with, or subsequent to the action of the lexical verb. Simultaneous action is, by far, the dominant interpretation, but 'prior' can (rarely) be inferred depending on pragmatics of the communication context, shared assumptions between speaker and hearer, and particular verb roots.

Fourth, in its AM functions, the Pilagá system always codes motion of an intransitive S or of a transitive O participant of the lexical verb root, although in some instances pragmatic factors may allow an inference that the A of a transitive event may also have moved in addition to the O. Thus, the system operates on an absolute alignment basis, which is somewhat counter to one of the typological claims in Guillaume's (2016) study of other South American AM systems. We suggest that the applicative function of Pilagá directionals may intersect with why the AM function strongly targets the O role.

The paper is organized as follows. Section 2 introduces relevant aspects of the Pilagá verbal directional paradigm and participant indexation, situating the three morphemes under focus in this paper as part of a larger system of directionals. In the process, a few refinements are made to the earlier analysis of directionality in Pilagá found in Vidal (2001, 2006). Section 3 discusses directional and AM functions of *-ge(')*, *-get*, and *-ege* with different verb classes. Section 4 addresses the features of AM in Pilagá from a typological perspective. Section 5 concludes the paper.

2 The grammar of verbal directionality in Pilagá

Before specifically exploring the AM functions of *-ge(')*, *-get* and *-ege*, we introduce the complete verbal directional system so as to set the directionals that are primarily under discussion within their larger context. To help the reader understand examples, we also comment briefly on verbal participant indexation and on nominal classifiers, both of which are part of the grammar of directionality.

Table 1 presents the full paradigm of Pilagá directionals, classified into deictic (labeled as such in Table 1) and non-deictic from the perspective of either the speaker or some other participant. The non-deictic members of the set signal that the event progresses along a certain path (Jackendoff 1983, Talmy 2000), or takes place at a static location with a particular spatial configuration (what Talmy 2000 calls "conformation"; see also Grinevald 2006), but is not deictically anchored in the speech situation.

Table 1: Pilagá Directional Suffixes.

-ge(')	'itive' (deictic)	-get	'ventive' (deictic)
-segem	'upward'	-ñi	'downward to ground'
		-som	'downward to water source'
-lege	'on, over'	-ot	'up', 'under'
-owe	'inward'	-wo	'outward'
-yi	'to/at the inside'	-ta	'to/at the side'
-iyi	'in straight line, aligned'	-sop	'in circles with'
-ege	'opposite of, straight ahead/ forward, horizontal'		

As will be seen throughout our discussion, Pilagá directional suffixes occur on all sorts of verb roots including motion, non-motion active, and stative roots.[3] However, not all directionals can occur with all lexical verb roots.

A simplified verb template for Pilagá is in (3). This shows that the directional suffixes occur in the penultimate position, between aspect and object number suffixes. Like the other affixes in parentheses, the directionals are optional with most roots.[4] To our knowledge, a given verb token cannot synchronically carry more than one directional at a time.

(3) Simplified template of Pilagá verb structure:
(NEG)-(OBJ)-(INDEF.SUBJECT)-SUBJ–STEM–(SUBJ.NUMBER)-(ASP)-(**DIR**)-(OBJ. NUMBER)

We now briefly introduce how the directionals function. Example (4) has a stative verb root *eta* 'be'. This root must always carry a directional suffix. In (4), -*lege* 'on, over' shows the relationship between the figure (in this case a semantic THEME) 'he' and the ground (here a semantic LOCATION) 'donkey' where the figure is located.

---

[3] The directionals may also occur in non-verbal predications with the copular verb 'be' to predicate spatial location of a participant (Payne, Vidal & Otero 2018).
[4] Certain verb roots cannot be used without a particular directional suffix. A full treatment of co-occurrence restrictions is a topic for further research.

(4) n-eta-**lege**   so'   la-lo-asena   wayodaʕa-ik
B3-be-**OVER** CLF:FAR.VIS POSS.3-domestic.animal-donkey be.crippled-M
'He was on his crippled donkey.' (pil021Asien, 1.4)

In (5), the root *k'ataʕa* 'go' lexically expresses motion. Here, the directional meaning of the suffix *-som* 'downward to water' is salient. In (5), *-som* also has a locative applicative function.

(5) ni-yamaq-a't   da'   yi-k'ataʕa-**som**-'a   ga'   lačika'age
B3-meet-RECP SUB A3-go-**DOWNWARD.WATER**-OBJ.SG CLF:DIST lagoon
'They meet together to go down to the lagoon.' (pil017Pesca1, 1.1)

With non-motion verb roots, the suffixes *-ge(')*, *-get* and *-ege* can entail AM meanings. This is seen in (6) through (9) and (2) above. We defer fuller treatment of AM to Section 3, but briefly introduce these morphemes here. The morpheme *-ge(')* was previously glossed as 'away from the reference point' by Vidal (2001: 231) and as 'away' by Otero, Vidal & Payne (2017); here we gloss it as 'itive' (IT), in keeping with the terminology used in this volume. In (6), it indicates that the participant is moving away from the reference point while performing another activity; but as we will see later, it does not always imply motion.

(6) ya-saʕa-ta-**ge'**
A3-laugh-PRG-**IT**
'He/she is laughing while going away.'

The morpheme *-get*, previously glossed 'hither' in Vidal (2001: 235–236), is here glossed 'ventive' (VEN). Its meaning is to 'move or be oriented toward the point of reference', as can be seen in (2).

The morpheme *-ege* 'opposite' indicates that the participant is passing by horizontally or opposite someone, as illustrated in (7). Though *-ege* can sometimes have an AM function, it is not deictic (despite some English translations). (We will comment shortly on the phonetic transcription.)

(7) se-sowe-tape-**(e)ge**   [sesoweta'peɣe]
A1-criticize-PRG-**OPP**
'I am (repeatedly) criticizing someone who is (now) passing by.' (e.g. across my line of sight, but not particularly toward or away from me)

One might ask if *-ege* is not just an allomorph of *-ge(')* 'itive', or even of *-get* 'ventive', judging by their close formal and perhaps semantic similarities. However, the evidence shows that, at least synchronically, they are separate morphemes that cannot be confused. This can be seen by comparing the prosody in the minimal pair (7) and (8), where *-ege* and *-ge(')* are used with the same verb *sowe* 'criticize'. In both examples, the directional suffix adds a motion co-event, related to the O argument, to an otherwise non-motion event. With *-ege* in (7), the prosodic stress falls on the penultimate syllable, perhaps due to the two vowels that would come together underlyingly in {*-tape-ege*}, and the final syllable is pronounced with a lenis [ɣ]. In contrast, in (8) with *-ge('),* the stress falls on the last syllable which has a plosive (it is possibly slightly glottalized). The two different forms indicate different paths of the motion co-event traversed by the O of *sowe* 'criticize'. Both the phonological and the semantic facts show that *-ge(')* and *-ege* are not the same morpheme.

(8) *se-sowe-tape-**ge'***   [sesowetape'ge?]
A1-criticize-PRG-**IT**
'I am (repeatedly) criticizing someone who is departing/went away (=who is now far from the deictic center).'

Example (9) shows that *-get* 'ventive' also contrasts with *-ege*.

(9) *se-sowe-ta-**get***
A1-criticize-PRG-**VEN**
'I am criticizing someone who is coming towards here.'

Not all directionals in Table 1 can have AM meanings. Examples (10) through (13) illustrate the conformation or trajectory (path) function of the formally similar but semantically distinct directionals *-yi* '(to, at) the inside' and *-iyi* 'in a straight line'. Example (10) concerns how a bird's eyes became colored (red), and uses the verb root 'paint' together with *-yi* in reference to the inner part of the eye. In (11), Fox speaks to Monkey and complains about Monkey (already) being inside Fox's own home. In these examples, *-yi* indicates that the figure is inside something conceptualized as a closed container; it does not express AM.

(10) *n-'ami-n-**yi***
B3-paint-NPRG-**INSIDE**
'He (Fox) painted them inside.' (pil003ZorroPaloma, 5.1)

(11) Ten   maeč'e   yi-wabik   ena   o-neta-**yi**
     INTJ   own   POSS.1-creeper   CLF:PROX   B2-be-**INSIDE**
'Hey, it is inside my own creeper that you are.' (pil009ZorroMono, 1.6)

In (12) with the verb 'go', Fox hurts himself with the arrow he threw when he tried to imitate Pitoqchen, a mythical bird. The arrow is stuck in his head, extending from side to side. Here the directional suffix *-iyi* clearly specifies the path followed by the arrow as well as the resulting static conformation of the arrow with respect to the head. In (13), *-iyi* is added to the root *lo* 'see/look', yielding the meaning 'stare', that is, to watch in a straight line without taking one's eyes from the referent.

(12) nač'e   le-wo-taeyi   t-a-t-**iyi**   na'   l-qaik.
     And   A3-walk-COMPl   A3-go-PRG-**STRAIGHT.LINE**   CLF:PROX   POS.3-head
     'and (the arrow) hit and pierced his head.' (pil012Pitoqchen, 1.23)

(13) se-lo-t-**iyi**   ha-da'   María
     A1-see/look-PRG-**STRAIGHT.LINE**   F-CLF:VERT   Mary
     'I am watching Mary.'

Most directionals can have applicative functions, allowing an O participant to occur with an otherwise intransitive or sometimes labile root.[5] That is, they create derived argument frames. (Pilagá has no adpositional oblique phrases or nominal case marking for core arguments.) In (14) and (15), for instance, the labile verb *wose* 'cook' occurs without a directional and it means just 'cook/cook it'. In (16), *wose* occurs with *-lege* 'on, over'; here, *-lege* functions syntactically as an applicative marker with a benefactive meaning.[6]

(14) *de-wose-tak*
     A3-cook-PRG
     'She is cooking.'

(15) *se-wose*   *na'*   *lapat*
     A1-cook   CLF:PROX   meat
     'I cook the meat'

(16) *de-wose-**lege***   *na'*   *tesoqo*
     A3-cook-**OVER**   CLF:PROX   uncle
     'She/he cooks for her/his uncle.'

---

[5] Pilagá tries to avoid ditransitive (i.e., two object) constructions. If a speaker wants to add a third core participant, the preferred strategy is to add an extra verb to bring in the third participant. Adding a directional to a transitive root may change the semantic role or interpretation of trajectory of the O, but it does not usually allow a third NP argument in the clause.

[6] Full discussion of the applicative function of the directionals is beyond the scope of this article.

Somewhat similarly, in (17) the directional *-ta* indicates that the location of the O is 'on/at the other side' from where the person indexed by the grammatical prefix is. In (18) with the translational motion verb 'go', *-ta* indicates that the only participant moves to the other side.

(17) *ya-saqa-**ta***
A3-throw-SIDE
'He/she throws something out.' (The thrower is inside the water; the item thrown ends up outside of the water.)

(18) *di'   yi-y'odo   kal'i   qamase'   t-a-**ta***
CLF:HORIZ POS.1-father.in.law before CONJ A3-go-SIDE
keda nč'e onolek di'   neta-ñ-'a
far and one/only CLF:HORIZ be-DOWNWARDS-specific.place
'However, my father-in-law never went outside (or far from the community); he was in a specific place (his community) only.' (pil052RelatoAnciana, 9.1)

It is important to point out that Pilagá has other grammatical means for signaling deictic directionality besides the 'ventive' and 'itive' directional suffixes. One system involves what we call nominal "classifiers", which also participate in nominal tense/evidentiality (Vidal 2001; Payne and Vidal, 2020). Three classifiers relate to shape of stationary objects: *di'* 'horizontally extended', *da'* 'vertically extended', *ñi'* 'bunched up. Three others in the same paradigm concern deictic direction and/or visibility, but also have temporal and evidential senses in certain contexts: *na'* 'near, coming to the reference point', *so'* 'far, departing from the reference point, past', and *ga'* 'unseen, absent, irrealis/future'. Some of these will be mentioned in passing because of how they interact with the directionals in particular examples.

Another salient means of signalling deictic directionality resides in the system of person-indexation. Pilagá has a Split-S system, employing what Vidal (2001, 2008) calls Set A and Set B for transitive and intransitive subjects. Some roots may alternate participant markers from Sets A and B to indicate either different degrees of affectedness of a participant or, interestingly, opposite paths like 'thither' versus 'hither'. This is illustrated in (19) through (21) with the motion verb *enot* 'jump in place, jump straight up and down'. Line (19a) shows that without any directional, the sense of the verb is really to jump in a stationary place. The directional suffix *-ege* in (20) and (21) indicates translational motion but without a deictic meaning; here one could argue that the directional creates an AM stem but we find that it is difficult to distinguish this from a pure semantic directional function since the lexical meaning of 'jump' involves displacement, regardless of how it is oriented. The third person prefix *n-* 'B3' in (20) indicates 'hither' while the third person prefix *w-* 'A3' in (21) allows the interpretation of 'thither'.

(19) a. nač'e   qataʕa   *w-**enot***
        then   also   A3-**jump**
        'then he (Fox) jumped (straight up)'

   b. nač'e   w-a-ñ-'a
       then   A3-go-BELOW-OBJ.SG
       'then he (ended up) below (on the ground)' [because he hurt himself]
       (pil009ZorroMono.015)

(20) ***n**-enot-ege*
     B3-jump-OPP
     'he/she jumps towards here'

(21) ***w**-enot-ege*
     A3-jump-OPP
     'he/she jumps towards there'

The option of alternating participant indexation sets is not available for all motion verbs, but probably just for the oldest, basic, or most frequently used ones. Nevertheless, where it does occur, it shows that deictic directionality does not always depend on the presence of a directional suffix. (For more details on this pattern and the system of indexation, see Vidal 2001, 2008.)

Finally, we comment briefly on a formative */pe/* (not included in Table 1). The form */pe/* can precede certain directionals such as *-ge(')* and *-ege*. For the closely related language Toba, Klein (1973, 1981: 232) analyzed the cognate *-pe* as meaning 'circular position'. For Pilagá, Vidal (2001, 2006) included *-pe* in the list of directional suffixes and provisionally glossed it as 'along with', and by semantic extension as 'concurrent motion'. However, recent elicitation confirms that Pilagá *-pe* never occurs without *-ta* (allomorphs *-tak/-t*) 'progressive', yielding the progressive form *-tape*.[7] In fast speech there is considerable phonological reduction of complex aspect+directional forms, especially if both the aspect and directional morphemes are bi-syllabic. Thus {*tape*+ *ege*} often results in /*pege*/. In sum, while *-pe* may well mean 'circular position' in Toba, in Pilagá it may be developing into a type of imperfective aspect. It never occurs on its own, but sur-

---

7 Some data suggest that adding *-pe* to *-ta* indicates iterative or repeated action.

faces with another imperfective aspect morpheme. For this reason we do not consider it here as a directional morpheme, but as part of an aspect complex.

3 Directionals and associated motion in Pilagá

3.1 Overview of issues

As indicated earlier, we use the term "deictic directional" for morphemes that express how a path extends, or how a participant moves along a path towards ('ventive') or away ('itive') from a deictic center. Belkadi (2015, this volume) was perhaps the first to explicitly discuss a kind of deictic associated motion (D-AM) in some languages of Africa. In that region of the world, directional 'itive' and 'ventive' constructions have long been recognized, and such morphemes can sometimes, but do not always add a motion co-event to the event expressed by the lexical root. The motion co-event can be added to non-motion verb roots, or sometimes an additional motion event can be added to a verb which itself lexically expresses motion (cf. Dryer, this volume).

Prior to, and in some contrast with Belkadi's recognition of D-AM systems, the concept of AM was introduced to account for dedicated morphological paradigms or structures in several languages of Australia (Koch 1984, Wilkins 1989, 1991) and South America (Guillaume 2000, 2016) that add translational co-motions to lexical events, separate from paradigms or structures which code just directionality.

Though Pilagá is found in South America, it corresponds to the D-AM language type, rather than to the type with a dedicated AM paradigm distinct from directionals. In this section we discuss how the two deictic directionals -ge(') 'itive' and -get 'ventive' and the non-deictic directional -ege 'opposite', introduced in Section 2, can function both as pure directionals with a broad variety of verb types and as AM markers with a more restricted distribution, especially with intransitive active non-motion verbs and transitive speech, cognition and perception verbs. AM is particularly possibile with the two deictic directionals, but there are instances in which -ege also has AM functions. For the most part, these three directionals can be used with the same verb roots, though there are some idiosyncracies involving particular combinations, and directionals with AM meaning are never obligatory.[8] For instance, -ge' or -get can yield an AM reading

---

[8] As we will see, some roots, such as 'pour', always require one or another directional. But to our knowledge no root always requires a directional that conveys AM meaning. For instance, 'pour'

with a particular root, but *-ege* with that root might express just path information and not also AM. We will see that the interpretation of a directional depends on a combination of the context and the host root to which the directional attaches. Furthermore, the directionals play a role in some lexical derivations, to the point that they are fully lexicalized with some roots; and they sometimes function as applicatives. Altogether, this section shows that the directionals are multifunctional and that neither just directionality nor just AM sufficiently characterizes their functions.

Because it is not possible to cleanly separate one function from another in many instances, we organize this section by the type of verb root that the directionals combine with, rather than by function. Section 3.2 looks at their combination with translational and non-translational motion roots, Section 3.3 concerns active but non-motion roots, Section 3.4 concerns speech, cognition, and perception roots, and Section 3.5 very briefly considers stative roots.

3.2 Use with translational and non-translational motion verbs

This section illustrates the 'itive', 'ventive', and 'opposite' directionals with translational and non-translational motion roots.

In (22a), the 'itive' directional combins with an intransitive translational motion root 'move', and in (22b) it combines with a stative root 'be' (which we will discuss further in Section 3.5.). With *qaya'a* 'move', the 'itive' only marks path, and with *weta* 'be' it only marks location; neither is an instance of AM.

(22) a. *da'*   *siyaʕawa*   *Ø-wenta*   *ga'*   *la-qaya*   *m'e*
CLF:VERT   man   A3-think   CLF:DIST   POSS.3-brother   REL
*Ø-qaya'a-**ge'***
A3-move-IT

b. *da'*   *weta-**ge***
SUB   3.be-**IT**
'The man thinks about his brother who went away, (the brother) is (now) away.'

---

can combine with directionals that allow AM, but also with directionals that do not, such as *-lege* 'on, over, benefactive' or a directional that shows shape of a container.

Similarly, *-ege* 'opposite' can occur with translational movement roots, where it adds horizontal path information but not AM. The dynamic root *aq(a)* 'move' is a one that always requires a directional. In (23), *aq(a)* occurs with the 'downward' directional *-ñi*, yielding the sense of 'fall'. Logically, the primary if not only path for naturally moving fruits is 'downwards'. But at least for some speakers, *aq(a)* 'move' can also occur with *-ege*, as in (24), yielding the sense of 'horizontal' orientation, for instance in a scenario where fruits fall from a truck moving along a road, or from a basket on a moving bicycle.

(23) *n-aq-tapi-**ñi***
 B3-move-PRG-**DOWNWARD**
 'It is falling down.'

(24) *n-aq-tap-**ege**   ha-'n   hala-pi*
 B3-move-PRG-**OPP**   F-CLF:PROX   fruit-PL
 'The fruits fall.' (possibly along a path)

As we saw in (19a), the intransitive root *enot* means 'jump in place'.[9] The 'ventive' *-get* in (25) allows addition of 'the man' towards which the subject (e.g., an animal) jumps. Here, *-get* indicates that the man is approaching, taking the perspective of the participant that jumps as the deictic center. Note that the postverbal 'man' is an applied O. In contrast, the speaker clarifies that in (26), postverbal *so' siyaq* 'animal' has to be the one doing the action, but again *-get* functions as an applicative with *hayim* '1SG' as the applied O. (Note that subjects occur both before and after the verb, though it tends to operate on an absolutive basis; Vidal 2001: 164). Altogether, it is evident that deictic directionals can code path or location of a referent, as well as deictic motion of a participant.

(25) *w-enot-te-**get**   so'   siyaʕawa*
 A3-jump-PRG-**VEN**   CLF:FAR.VIS   man
 'Something (e.g., an animal) jumped/s on/towards the man that is/was coming.'

---

9 *Enot* 'jump' may be labile. Without a suffix it can indicate 'jump (in place)', with no implication of an object. However, an explicit plural-object suffix *-lo* can be added for the sense of 'to jump over several people'. If the directional *-get* occurs, as in (25), the verb is specifically transitive. Since *enot* can carry a plural object suffix even in the absence of a directional, it is not clear that *-get* acts like a classic applicative in (25) to add an object; though its presence ensures that the clause is transitive.

(26) hayim   w-enot-te-**get**   so'   siyaq
     1SG   A3-jump-PRG-**VEN** CLF:FAR.VIS animal
     'The animal jumped on me when I was coming towards it.'

As noted earlier, -*ege* marks a roughly horizontal or straight path, whether 'forward' or 'backward', and it is not deictically anchored. In (27) it explicitly adds such a path to the event of 'jump', denoting the trajectory covered by the monkey (possibly moving forward while also from tree to the ground; see also (20) and (21) above). Here, -*ege* does not create a transitive clause.

(27) nač'e e-so'   woyem   w-enot-**ege**
     and   M-CLF:FAR.VIS monkey A3-jump-**OPP**
     'And the monkey came down (lit. 'jumped forward').'

As a verb, *sot* 'dance' communicates an intransitive activity (the root also has the nominal sense of 'torso'). Without a directional, it indicates 'dancing in place', without translational motion (e.g., as during a religious service), as in (28).

(28) sa-sot-(t)ak
     A1-dance-PRG
     'I am dancing.'

The 'itive' directional with 'dance' can yield the meaning of either 'dance far away' (static location), or a future intention of 'dance far away'. According to our consultant, (29) does not communicate that the participants have moved anywhere, though the 'itive' can imply a future 'far away' location in the right context, as in (30), and hence one might infer possible future translational motion. However, we understand that potential future motion is a pragmatic inference, rather than something linguistically expressed in the sentence. In sum, the directionals in (29) and (30) are not really instances of AM.

(29) da-sot-(e)da-**ge'**
     A3-dance-PL-**IT**
     'They (will) dance far away.'

(30) setake da-sot-(e)da-**ge'**
     want   A3-dance-PL-**IT**
     'They want to go dancing in a distant place.'

The 'ventive' with *sot* also does not yield AM, but interestingly, the idiosyncratic and static location sense of 'be in front of somebody (as in a row)', shown in (31).

(31) awa-sot-'a(t)-**get**   ñi'   Sedaʕakie'n
     A2-dance/torso-RECP-**VEN**   CLF:NO.EXT   proper.name
     'You are standing in front of *Sedaʕaki'en*' / 'Stand in front of *Sedaʕaki'en*'
     (lit. 'You be torso-to-torso.')

We now illustrate the directionals with transitive motion roots. We start with the verb 'throw'.[10] We first discuss it without directionals to clarify its basic argument structure and the interpretation of what moves. In its simple root form, *saqa* can take either the THEME which moves (32), or the LOCATION to which something is thrown (33, 34) as the O. The past time interpretations in (32) and (33) arise from the classifier *so'*, which can specify something far distant, going out of view, or past time. In (33), *ñi* specifies that the truck is in a 'sitting' or bunched up in a stationary position.

(32) sa-saqa-n   so'   qa'
     A1-throw-NPRG   CLF:FAR   stone
     'I threw a stone (distant/going out of view/past).'

(33) sa-saqa-tak   so'   mayo   pata'g
     A1-throw-PRG   CLF:FAR   bird   nest
     'I was throwing (something) to the bird nest (distant/going out of view/past).'

(34) sa-saqa-tak   ñi'   camión
     A1-throw-PRG   CLF:NON.EXT   truck
     'I am throwing (something) at the (bunched-up and stationary) truck.'

Contrasting with (34), in (35) the classifier *so'* gives rise to the interpretation that the truck is moving (past or present interpretation). Importantly, this is not a case of AM as the motion does not arise from a verb affix.

(35) sa-saqa-tak   so'   camión
     A1-throw-PRG   CLF:FAR   truck
     'I am/was throwing (something) at the truck (moving away).'

---

10 This verb has variant pronunciations *saqa* and *saʕa* depending on what affixes are added. We consistently write it here in the form saqa.

We now examine *saqa* 'throw' with the deictic directionals. In (36), the 'itive' indicates that the stone is thrown 'far away'. Comparison of (36) with (32) suggests that in (36) the 'itive' is just functioning as a directional to show 'far away', as there is no movement beyond that found in (32).[11] The consultant is insistent that the A participant is stationary.

(36) *sa-saqa-**ge'** he-n qa'*
 A1-throw-**IT** M-CLF:PROX stone
 'I throw this stone far away.' (I do not move.)

The 'itive' does not increase valence in (36), but other examples suggest that a deictic directional can function as an applicative with 'throw', and arguably also as an AM marker. Example (37) is a rare optionally ditransitive clause in which *-get* 'ventive' correlates with adding *so' mayopi* 'birds' to the sentence. *So'* suggests the birds are far away, and the consultant clearly indicates that the birds are moving.

(37) *sa-saqa-ta-**get** (he-n qa') so' mayo-pi*
 A1-throw-PRG-**VEN** M-CLF:PROX stone CLF:FAR bird-PL
 'I (stationary) am throwing (a stone) at the (moving) birds.'

The argument that *-get* communicates AM in (37) is developed by comparing (38) with the 'ventive', (39) with the 'itive', and (40). Recall that the classifier *ñi* implies a stationary participant in (34) above. This same classifier occurs in (38) and (39), again with 'truck'; but unlike (34), the results in (38) and (39) are ungrammatical. Here, the ungrammaticality can only come from *-get* or *-ge'* co-occurring with *ñi*. We thus conclude that the deictic directionals on 'throw' communicate motion of the O 'truck', which clashes with the classifier *ñi* which specifies a stationary O.

(38) **sa-saqa-tape-**get** ñi' camion*
 A1-throw-PRG-**VEN** CLF:NON.EXT truck
 ('I am/was repeatedly throwing (something) at the sitting/stationary truck while it comes.')

---

11 Or, one might argue, the lexical movement component in *saqa* 'throw' effectively masks the AM meaning that the 'itive' might (also) impart.

(39) *sa-saqa-**ge'** ñi' camión
A1-throw-**IT** CLF:NON.EXT truck
('I throw throwing (something) at the sitting/stationary truck while it moves away.')

Example (40) resolves the conflict between the O-related AM function of the deictic directionals with transitive 'throw' and the classifier of the O.[12] This is analogous to the morphosyntactic arrangement in (37).

(40) sa-saqa-tape-**get** so' camión
A1-throw-PRG-**VEN** CLF:FAR truck
'I am/was repeatedly throwing (something) at the truck that is passing/moving along/no longer in view.'

We now examine the directionals with kod(e) 'pour, spill'. Unlike 'throw', in which the A and O are typically conceptualized as (ultimately) distant from each other, 'pour, spill' is an action which normally involves close proximity between A and O. Like saqa 'throw', 'pour, spill' lexically implies movement of the THEME. Somewhat differently from saqa, the verb kod(e) nearly always carries a directional. -Ege is the most common, as in (41); this is an elicited example but it is a very typical expression for depicting dumping out the entire contents of a yerba mate container (i.e. wet leaves and liquid together.) Any translational movement in (41) applies only to the contents of what is 'poured'. It is not clear that -ege expresses AM here, but just a horizontal orientation of the movement inherent in the lexical semantics of 'pour'. The suffix -tape indicates that this is done several times. As with 'throw', the A is not moving.

(41) yi-kode-tape-**(e)ge**
A3-pour-PRG-**OPP**
'He/she is pouring away (i.e. discarding) (the contents) several times.'

With -ge(') in (42) and -get in (43), 'pour' allows an AM interpretation where both the A doing the pouring and the (liquid) O move during the pouring. Given that AM strongly targets the absolutive (S/O) category in Pilagá, we surmise that the interpretation of A also moving in (42) and (43) results from the pragmatics of a

---

12 The function of so' in (40) is ambiguous outside of a larger discourse context: either the truck is passing and so' reinforces an idea of motion also provided by -get; or so' is functioning as a nominal tense form, providing past time information (Payne and Vidal, 2020).

pouring action: it is difficult if not impossible to pour something without being in close proximity to the item poured. Hence, if a liquid is undergoing translational motion toward or (far) away from the deictic center, the A participant must accompany it. Note that the meaning in (42) with -*ge(')* entails the participants are moving far away from the deictic center, and the A is pouring a liquid (on the ground) while moving 'far away'; throwing 'far away' cannot be done without moving, whereas 'throwing horizontally opposite' in (41) is not necessarily remote from the deictic center.

(42) *yi-kod(e)-tape-**ge***'
    A3-pour-PRG-IT
    'He/she is (repeatedly) pouring (a liquid) while going away from the deictic center.' (AM is interpreted as applying to both the agent and the liquid.)

Example (43) shows that -*get* 'ventive' is also possible with *kod(e)* 'pour, spill'. The liquid is undergoing translational motion toward the deictic center. Again, the A is pragmatically implicated to also be moving, since in normal circumstances pouring cannot be done without the agent and theme in close proximity.

(43) *yi-kod(e)-ta-**get***
    A3-pour-PRG-VEN
    'He/she is pouring (a liquid) coming towards the deictic center.' (AM is interpreted as applying to both the agent and the liquid.)

Example (43) cannot be interpreted as spilling or pouring some liquid towards the agentive self while being in a static position. A reflexive suffix would be required to express this, rather than the 'ventive' directional.[13]

Another active concept is that of 'mix', expressed in Pilagá by the intransitive lexeme *elte* and transitive *lekte*. The transitive form illustrates lexicalization of the root with deictic directional -*get*.[14] The concept of 'mix' inherently involves movement, though one might treat the intransitive form *elte* together with kinetic non-motion roots due to its salient basic meaning: *elte* designates an old custom of creating a specific rich dish involving combining meat and the fat of an animal, eaten in ancient times. We gloss *elte* as 'mix.meat+fat', as in (44). Note that it does

---

13 The consultant also explained that if there were an extra participant on whom the liquid was poured, the correct expression would require -*lege* 'on, over', yielding *yi-kod(e)-lege* 'he/she poured liquid on someone'. In this case, there is no AM involving any participant (other than movement of a THEME inherent in the concept of 'pour').

14 The two forms may be historically related, with metathesis of consonants.

not refer to just any instance of mixing meat and fat, but to the creation of this specific dish. An O NP cannot be added with this root form.

(44) qo-n-elte-n
 INDF-B3-mix.meat+fat-NPGR
 'Somebody does the mixing (of meat+fat for the rich dish).' (pil045Tapir 1.9)

A more general scenario of mixing any ingredients is possible with *lekte*. In this case the verb must carry a Set A prefix (with or without an indefinite subject marker) and also *-get* 'ventive', as in (45) and (46). We consider this to be a case of co-lexicalization as *lekte* is ungrammatical if the ventive is omitted. In this combination we gloss *lekte* just as 'mix'. Here the directional may have a (historical) applicative function, as the whole is transitive. The person who mixes the ingredients is not moving (indeed, (45) and (46) are parts of cooking scenarios), but the consultant indicates that the ingredients 'move' during the preparation. Motion is implied on the part of the O, but not of the A. Thus, in addition to functioning as an applicative, one might argue that *-get* functions to show AM of the O, as ingredients are brought together into the food.

(45) *qanač'e qo-ya-lekte-n-**get**   ga=m'e   nosek*
 then   INDF-A3-mix-NPRG-VEN   CLF:FAR=DEM   cooked.food
 'Then it (its ashes) are mixed with the food' (pil109Ethno28Planta 03)

(46) *ya-lekte-n-**get**   ñi-m'e   četa qataʕa di'   lapat*
 A3-mix-NPGR-VEN   CLF-DEM1:NEUT   fat   and   CLF:EXT   meat
 'He mixed the fat and the meat.' (Does not refer to the special old dish)

Table 2 summarizes the patterns illustrated with movement verbs. With intransitive translational motion verbs, the three directionals add (deictic) path, but not AM. With 'jump in place', they add (deictic) path, but one might argue that this is ambiguous with AM according to Dryer's (this volume) conception of AM. With non-translational motion 'dance', the directionals communicate static location. Where a directional increases valence of an otherwise intransitive root, AM can only apply to the O. With transitive verbs involving motion, the (deictic) directionals can indicate simultaneous AM that targets the (potentially derived) O. Only in the case 'pour', where the lexical nature of the action requires close contact between the A and O, is there an implication of the A moving along with the O (i.e. A+O). But with transitive 'throw' and 'mix', only the O moves.

Table 2: Attested functions of *-get* 'ventive' (VEN), *-ge(')* 'itive' (IT), *-ege* 'opposite, horizontal' (OPP) with motion verbs.

Root Type	Specific roots	DIR: functions	Grammatical role targeted when AM	Temporal interpretation when AM
INTR transl motion	*k'ate* 'go', *qaya'a* 'move', *aq* 'move'	VEN, IT, OPP: (deictic) path		
INTR non-transl motion	*enot* 'jump in place'	OPP: path, AM. VEN: APPL+AM	S, applied O	SIMUL
	(a)sot 'dance'	IT, VEN: static location		
TR transl motion	*kode* 'pour'	OPP: path. IT, VEN: AM	A+O	SIMUL
	saq 'throw', *lekte* 'mix'	IT, VEN: APPL+AM, deictic path	O/applied O	SIMUL

3.3 Use with active non-motion verbs

The three directionals easily combine with active intransitive non-motion roots, but their use is more constrained with active transitive non-motion roots, and is not at all possible with some. We first look at intransitive, then labile, and then transitive roots.

With intransitive active non-motion roots, the deictic directionals can add AM. Example (6) above shows this with 'laugh'; the AM event targets the base S participant. This is also true in (47) with intransitive 'knit fiber', and in (48) and (49) with 'cry'.

(47) *d-'onaʃa-tape-**ge'**   so'   Adela*
 A3-knit.fiber-PRG-**IT**   CLF:FAR   Adela
 'Adela is moving away while she knits the carandillo (a type of palm) fiber.'

(48) *n-oye-tape-**ge'***
 B3-cry-PRG-**IT**
 'He/she goes away crying (repeatedly).'

(49) *n-oye-ta-**get***
 B3-cry-PRG-**VEN**
 'He/she came/comes crying.'

With non-motion roots, the directionals can again function as applicatives. When they do so, they can simultaneously communicate AM of the new applied O, rather than of the base S. This may be especially true with the deictic directionals. In (50) 'her mother' is both licenced by the 'itive' directional *-ge(')* and is interpreted as moving away. (The AM here cannot be interpreted as applying to the A of a derived transitive.) The consultant's comment is that it is customary for people to cry "after" someone has left or died (which could be implicated in (50), especially if the classifer on the noun were *di'* 'horizontal'). That is, the reading in (50) is of prior motion, but we understand this is due to what is a pragmatically normal or customary cause-and-effect situation.

(50) *n-oye-ta-**ge**   so'   la-t'e*
       B3-cry-PRG-IT CLF:FAR POSS3-mother
       'He/she was crying (because) her mother (had) departed.'

Example (51) shows *-ege* with 'cry'. Here the function of *-ege* is not AM. It helps signal the static location where the applied argument (the mother) is.

(51) *n-oye-tape-(e)**ge** ha-so'   la-t'e*
       B3-cry-PRG-OPp   F-CLF:FAr POSS3-mother
       'He/she was (repeatedly) crying for her mother (out of view, distant).'

In its intransitive use, the labile verb *wose* 'cook' can take the 'itive' directional to yield a reading of static 'far away' location, as in (52). Our consultant rejects an AM interpretation for the intransitive S. This is pragmatically sensible, given that one normally cooks with fire and this is impossible while moving. The transitive use of *wose*, as in (15) above, need not carry a directional, and our consultant finds a combination with the 'itive' unnatural; compare (53) with (15). The unnaturalness is due to a combination of factors. One does not normally (simultaneously) cook something that is 'far away' (a static location interpretation), and 'meat' or 'food' cannot move on its own (an O AM interpretation). The consultant allows that (53) could imply that one has an intention to cook (currently proximate) meat far away, but that there is no idea of motion (instead, only of future static location). In sum, 'cook' also fails to show that AM can target an A.

(52) *se-wose-**ge'***
       A1-cook-IT
       'I cooked far away.' (static location)

(53) ?se-wose-**ge'** na' lapat
A1-cook-IT CLF:PROX meat
'I cook meat [that is] far away'

Certain other active transitive non-motion verbs do not accept the three directionals in focus here at all. For example, *yoy* 'wash' can be used with O NPs like 'face hands, dishes, cloth', etc., without any directional, as in (54). Some directionals are possible (e.g. if one wants to indicate the shape of a container in which washing is done), but the 'ventive', 'itive', and 'opposite' directionals are rejected. They also are rejected with *'ame* 'paint'.

(54) si-yoy-' na' yi-wa-'
A1-wash-PL CLF:PROX POS1-hand-PL
'I wash my hands.'

Table 3: Attested functions of *-get* 'ventive' (VEN), *-ge(')* 'itive' (IT), *-ege* 'opposite, horizontal' (OPP) with active non-motion verbs.

Root Type	Specific roots	DIR: attested functions	Grammatical role targeted when AM	Temporal interpretation when AM
INTR active non-motion	saʕa 'laugh', oye 'cry', yom 'drink', ke'e 'eat', enaʕa 'shoot gun', 'onaʕa 'knit fiber'	IT, VEN: AM IT: APPL+AM OPP: static location	S, applied O	SIMUL, PRIOR
TR active non-motion	'ame 'paint', yoy 'wash'	No DIR (pragmatically not sensible with AM)		
	wose 'cook' (labile)	IT: static location (pragmatically not sensible with AM)		

Table 3 summarizes what happens with active non-motion roots.[15] The deictic directionals easily combine with intransitive roots to communicate AM of the S. This is nearly always simultaneous AM, but prior AM is sometimes understood. The deictic directionals can sometimes function as applicatives, in which case the derived O can be interpreted as undergoing simultaneous or sometimes prior AM.

---

15 For conciseness, Table 3 includes some intransitive active non-motion verbs illustrated in Section 4.2.

The three directionals appear to be dispreferred with non-motion active (derived or basic) transitives. The combination is basically unattested in our text corpus. In elicitation, we find that with labile 'cook', the directionals are fine with the intransitive sense, implying static location; but are interpreted as odd or not possible with the transitive sense. They do not combine at all with transitive 'wash' and 'paint'.

3.4 Use with speech, cognition, and perception verbs

In contrast to transitive active non-motion verbs, the directionals easily combine with transitive speech, cognition, and perception verbs. Examples (7) through (9) above show them with the speech verb 'criticize'. Example (55) shows the 'ventive' with the perception root 'observe'. In (7) through (9), the first-person speech-act referent (A) is at the deictic center and is not moving, while the participant criticized (O) moves away from, towards, or across the speaker's line of sight. In (55), the O participant, the one observed, is not overtly marked since it is third person; nevertheless, it is understood as moving toward 'you' as the deictic reference point.

(55) awa-wa't(e)ta-**get**
A2-observe-**VEN**
'You are watching him/her coming.'

In (56) and (57) with 'see/look', the O of the base predicate is similarly the one interpreted as moving in the motion co-event.

(56) se-la-**ge'**
A1-see/look-**IT**
'I see him going away.' (Vidal 2001:238)

(57) nač'e yi-la'a-**get** so' yawo
Then A3-see/look-**VEN** CLF:FAR woman
da' i-ɓide-wo di' taʕade-na'
SUB A3-go-OUTWARD CLF:HORIZ father-relative
'And he saw the coming woman who left to see (lit. go outward to) my (e.g. deceased) father.'

It is not the case that -ge('), -get, and -ege are always interpreted as expressing AM with speech, cognition, and perception roots. They can just communicate that an action or situation holds in a static location. Consider (58) and (59) with *mače* 'listen'. In (58), *-get* 'ventive' indicates that a sound is (fictively or literally) moving toward the deictic center (i.e. this is AM). But in (59), *-ge(')* 'itive' indicates that a sound is simply distant, and thus not very audible.

(58) *se-mače-tape-**get***
A1-listen-PRG-VEN
'I am (repeatedly) listening to a sound that is coming towards me.'

(59) *se-mače-tape-**ge'***
A1-listen-PRG-IT
'I am (repeatedly) listening to a distant sound.'

Interestingly, there is a lexical co-occurrence restriction such that *mače* 'listen' cannot be combined with *-ege*, shown by (60).

(60) **se-mače-tap-**ege***   *[sematʃetaˈpege]
A1-listen-PRG-OPP

Table 4 summarizes what we have seen with speech, cognition, and perception verbs. The directionals can add an associated literal or fictive movement that concerns the O argument. However, AM is not always entailed.

Table 4: Attested functions of -get 'ventive' (VEN), -ge(') 'itive' (IT), -ege 'opposite horizontal' (OPP) with cognition, perception and utterance verbs.

Root Type	Specific roots	DIR: attested functions	Grammatical role targeted when AM	Temporal interpretation when AM
TR cognition, perception, utterance	*sowe* 'criticize', *wa'te* 'observe', *mače* 'listen', *la/lo* 'see/look'	IT, VEN, OPP: AM IT: static location OPP: path	O	SIMUL

3.5 Use with stative verbs

We briefly comment here on use of the directionals with stative verbs. In (61), *-ege* codes path semantics, describing a technically static situation. We could, however, view (61) as depicting fictive motion involving a change between a narrower and a wider portion of the road. This fictive AM targets the S participant.

(61) Ø-leka'a-**ege** di' na'a-ik
 A3-be.big-**OPP** CLF:HORIZ road-M
 'The route is wide/widens.'

Example (22b) above shows that with stative 'be', the deictic directionals can also code static location relative to a reference point (see Payne, Vidal, and Otero 2018 for further elaboration). Attested functions of the three directionals in focus are summarized in Table 5.

Table 5: Attested functions of *-get* 'ventive' (VEN), *-ge(')* 'itive' (IT), *-ege* 'opposite horizontal' (OPP) with stative intransitive verbs.

Root Type	Specific roots	DIR: attested functions	Grammatical role targeted when AM	Temporal interpretation when AM
INTR stative	*weta* 'be', *leka'a* 'be.big'	IT: static location OPP: (fictive) AM	S	SIMUL

Altogether, the data throughout Section 3 show that the three directionals in focus here are multi-functional. Though they can express AM, they are not dedicated AM morphemes. In the next section, we turn to explicitly discuss the Pilagá AM patterns relative to the typology of AM systems.

4 Pilagá directionals and the typology of AM

Guillaume (2000, 2016) and Guillaume & Koch (this volume) discuss various parameters relevant to the cross-linguistic comparison of AM systems. Here we examine how Pilagá AM patterns fit with the typology of AM proposed by Guillaume (2016), who suggests implicational hierarchies based on the behavior of AM constructions in South American languages. These include the grammatical role of the moving argument as transitive subject (A), transitive object (O), or intransitive subject (S), and the temporal relationship between the main event and the motion co-event.

4.1 The grammatical role targeted by AM

Guillaume's implicational hierarchy about the grammatical role of the moving argument concerns roles of the base predicate (Guillaume 2016: 113–116). For instance, in the following Cavineña (Takanan) example, the 'man' is the moving argument, and he is also the O of 'see'. (The fact that the man could be interpreted as the intransitive S argument of the motion co-event is not at issue; presumably all motion co-events are understood as intransitive.)

(62) Cavineña (Guillaume 2008: 234)
peadya ekwita=tuke=Ø ba-dadi-wa ...
one person=3SG=1SG see-go(O)-PRF
'I saw a man going away from me.'

The implicational hierarchy states that if object (O) referents of transitive base predicates can be understood as undergoing motion due to the addition of an AM morpheme in some language, then in that language subject referents (both transitive A and intransitive S subjects) of base predicates can also undergo AM (Guillaume 2016: 83).

In Pilagá, AM always targets the intransitive S or the transitive O (whether base or derived). That is, AM in Pilagá operates on a S/O (absolutive) rather than on a S/A (nominative, or subject) basis. Rarely the transitive A (as discussed for 'pour' in Section 3.2) is interpreted as moving along with the O (i.e. A+O). We have seen multiple examples of the absolutive patterning, especially with intransitive non-movement verbs and with transitive cognition, perception and speech verbs. However, even with these, AM is not always evident. Here we give a more extended text excerpt to illustrate the variable interpretation of directionals even with a single verb root, and to underscore how with transitives, AM targets the O – even with a verb where one could theoretically easily move while carrying out an action such as 'see/look'. Example (63) shows several instances of the perception verb *la/lo* 'see/look' carrying directionals, but only in (63c) with *-ge(')* 'itive' is there a clear sense of motion. (Notice the spatial contrast that arises from the same root in combination with the directional markers *-segem* in (63a) versus *-ege* in (63d).) In (63c), the motion co-event targets the O of the perception verb. Consultants agree that here *yila'age* communicates a motion co-event in which the bee moves. This movement goes on while the beekeeper looks for the hive, but the beekeeper is not moving; it is well-known among this historically hunter-gatherer group that one must remain stationary and quiet while looking for bees (or other prey) so as not to make them leave.

(63) a. *nač'e e-so   siyaʕawa l-qaya   yi-**lo**-tapi-**segem***
    then M-CLF:FAR person POSS.3-another A3-see/look-PRG-**UPWARD**
    'Another person **looks up** (for bees)' [no motion]

  b. *yi-**lo**-t-ake   qatek-lapaʕat*
    A3-see/look-PRG-DES bee-insect
    'he **looks** (with intention) for the bees' [no motion]

  c. *eda yi-**la'a-ge***
    SUB   A3-see/look-IT
    'when he **sees** it (the bee) moving away' [the bee is moving, not the person]

  d. *nač'e yi-**lo**-t-**ege***
    then   A3-see/look-PRG-OPP
    'then he **looks ahead** [no motion] (for the bee)

  e *m'e Ø-ta-yi-'a*
    REL   A3-go-INSIDE-O.SG
    'that goes into a specific place (the hive).' [the bee moves inside]
    (pil013Pesca2, 1.4)

The root *la/lo* 'see/look' appears to be a basic transitive root, as seen in (63b) with the overt O argument following the verb with no directional.[16] In this excerpt, then, the directionals on *la/lo* 'see/look' do not function as classic valence-increasing applicatives, but rather specify features of the direction of looking in (63a) and (63d), and AM in (63c). Note that the movement in (63e) is due to the lexical root *ta* 'go', and not to a directional suffix.

If it were the case that when functioning as AM morphemes, all directionals also had an applicative valence-related function, then the link between a derived O and the argument targeted by the motion co-event would be completely motivated. One might, in fact, argue that the particular semantic role of the O in (63c) is a result of the directional -*ge(')* and that it is not so much that the AM "targets" a base O, as it manipulates and/or adds an O with a specific participant role like "mover" (ie. THEME), just as other directionals add specific paths or conformations. Thus, given the relationship between applicative function and O, and the typological strength of a THEME-S/O grammatical link, the absolutive patterning of the Pilagá AM system is sensible.

---

[16] The form *yi-lo-tapi-segem*, in (63a), is clearly transitive in other text examples where it can be followed directly by a noun for monkey, bird, etc., as in 'he looks up for/at the monkey.'

To conclude this section, the strong S/O AM pattern in Pilagá is apparently counter to Guillaume's (2016) proposed implicational hierarchy based on other South American AM systems. Though AM targeting S/O is clearly the dominant pattern in Pilagá, we have noted a (very) few instances in the data where the pragmatics of the situation lead to an interpretation also involving a moving A participant. This is the case with *kode* 'pour' in Section 3.2. But even where AM can be interpreted as applying to an A, it includes this as part of a whole event also involving movement of the O, since 'pour' typically involves an A in close proximity to the poured O.

4.2 Temporal interpretation of the motion co-event

Guillaume's second implicational hierarchy predicts that if a motion co-event can occur temporally subsequent to the lexical verb event (i.e., 'do.VERB then move'), then the system will also allow motion co-events to occur simultaneously with ('do.VERB while moving') or prior to (i.e., 'move then do.VERB') the primary lexical verb event. For the Pilagá consultants, the motion co-event in AM constructions is most commonly simultaneous with the lexical event, and in some situations this is the only possible interpretation. According to consultants' interpretation, in (64) the AM co-event is simultaneous with 'drink', targetting the intransitive S. Similarly, in (65) and (66), the motion co-events are interpreted as simultaneous with 'eat' and 'shoot'. That is, the temporal reading in the following three examples is not ambiguous between prior and simultaneous (or subsequent) motion.

(64) *ni-yom-tape-**ge***'
 B3-drink-PRG-IT
 'He goes away while drinking (repeatedly).'

(65) *de-ke'e-tape-**ge***'
 A3-eat-PRG-IT
 'He eats (repeatedly) while he leaves (on his journey, on his way.')

(66) *da-enaʕa-tape-ge*
 A3-shoot.gun-PRG-IT
 'He/she moves away shooting (repeatedly)/He shoots (repeatedly) while moving away.'

Aside from the elicited sentences in (29) and (30) above, where there might be an implication of a future movement, the only other – very arguable – example we have found of potential 'subsequent' movement is (67), involving the verb *kop'a* 'elapse'. In fact, the consultant states that it is very difficult to assess whether the participant will come later, so we do not believe this really asserts AM.

(67) Ø-*kop'a-te-get*   *na' siyaʕawa*
      A3-elapse-PRG-**VEN**   CLF   Man
      'The man is belated/delayed.' (It is difficult to assess whether he will come later).

Kop'a 'elapse' is a defective verb, inflecting only for third person and typically taking a time expression as the argument. In (68), the 'itive' -*ge(')* with 'elapse' suggests either fictive motion with an imaginary trajectory of 'time'; or physical motion of someone who has just left or gone away from the perspective of the speaker, which would be 'prior' motion – not subsequent.

(68) Ø-*kop'a-te-**ge(')***
      A3-elapse-PRG-**IT**
      i. 'It (=time) elapses/passes/goes by.'
      ii. 'He/she has just left.'

In sum, we conclude that subsequent movement is hardly attested in the Pilagá AM system, if at all. Whether Pilagá AM events are interpreted as occurring prior to (as in (50) above), instead of simultaneously with the lexical verb event depends highly on speaker-hearer shared knowledge and other pragmatic conditions. However, considering that the motion co-event is sometimes (though rarely) interpreted as occurring prior to the lexical co-event, Pilagá conforms to Guillaume's (2016) predictions.

It should be noted that the interpretation of temporal concurrence of events in (64) through (66) is not due to the progressive aspect suffix -*tape* which happens to sometimes co-occur with the directional suffixes. To see this, examine (69) through (71), as well as (49) through (50) above, where morphological aspect has no effect on interpretation of temporal co-occurrence versus sequentiality of the motion and lexical events. Both (69) and (50) have the progressive aspect form -*ta*, but (69) is interpreted as indicating simultaneous motion while (50) is interpreted as having prior motion of an applied O argument. Again, (50) is the only example where our consultant accepted there could be prior motion of the object 'her mother'.

(69) *n-oye-ta-**ge(')***   (*hen la*dik)
      B3-cry-PRG-**IT**   DEM   road
      'He/she is crying (on the road) while going away.'

Example (70) has the progressive variant -*tape*, and also conveys simultaneous AM. Example (71) has non-progressive aspect and the event of 'cry' is interpreted as punctuating the motion event. (In (71), note that the 'itive' directional functions as an applicative to allow an overt LOCATIVE O, but the base S is the moving participant.)

(70) *n-oye-tape-**ge'***
 B3-cry-PRG-IT
 'He/she goes away crying (repeatedly).'

(71) *n-oye-n-**ge(')*** (*hen la*dik)
 B3-cry-PRG-IT DEM road
 'He/she cried (on the road) (sometime during the event of) going away.'

In sum, temporal concurrence is not tied to progressive or to non-progressive marking, nor to absence of any overt aspect.

5 Concluding remarks

With this study, we have aimed to amplify documentation of AM and D-AM systems by looking at three Pilagá directionals, two deictic and one that is not deictically anchored. With lexical motion roots, -*ge(')* 'itive' and -*get* 'ventive' encode deictic path semantics and -*ege* 'opposite' codes a non-deictic path. When combined with non-motion predicates, these three directionals can, but need not always, express AM. We have seen that the directionals can sometimes add a THEME, LOCATIVE or other O argument, as would an applicative derivation.

We have seen that in Pilagá, it is not the case that a discrete AM morphological paradigm exists, separately from a directional category (i.e. unlike in Australian and certain other South American languages). That is, this is a D-AM system in which there are no dedicated affixes for AM distinct from those used for non-motion direction/location (Belkadi 2015). In fact, the use of (deictic) directional morphemes for AM in South America is not restricted to Pilagá, as it is also found in the Mataguayan language Nivaĉle (Fabre 2013, 2017; Otero, Vidal & Payne 2017) spoken in the Chaco region, similarly to the systems found in D-AM systems in other regions of the world such as Nilotic (Payne 2013, and this volume; Payne & Otero 2016), Koman (Otero, this volume), and some other families (Belkadi, this volume; Dryer, this volume). The existence of such systems in multiple languages from various parts of the world suggests that AM may be a common semantic extension of deictic directionals, or vice-versa; or that both may develop directly and independently from a single source (possibly a directed motion verb root).

A second significant difference found in the Pilagá system compared to previously described AM and D-AM systems is that Pilagá AM targets an absolutive (S/O) category and not a nominative (S/A) category. That is, the grammatical role of the moving figure in associated motion situations is the S/O (absolutive) argument of the lexical root verb, or a derived O. The absolutive figure (which may be simultaneously agentive, or not) performs or undergoes the motion. Whether the figure is an intransitive S or an O depends on the lexical verb root, on whether the directional also functions as an applicative, and on pragmatics. Indeed, it is noteworthy that at least sometimes the Pilagá directionals (including the three markers under scrutiny here) behave like applicatives, creating derived stems that allow an additional new core participant. The A may sometimes (though very rarely) be interpreted as also undergoing movement when the pragmatic situation allows, but we analyze this as a pragmatic inference rather than being part of what the system grammatically codes. Given the findings of this paper, we suggest that the typology of associated motion proposed in Guillaume (2016) needs refinement with respect to grammatical roles.

The Pilagá directionals that allow AM are underspecified for the temporal relation they express between the lexical and associated motion events: prior or simultaneous meanings are possible in AM situations, though simultaneous meaning is by far most common in our data, and often is the only reading.

In sum, this preliminary study of AM in Pilagá extends our understanding of the geographical distribution of AM systems into the periphery of the area surveyed in Guillaume's (2016) South American study. It also extends our typological knowledge beyond dedicated AM systems to better understand D-AM grammatical systems which allow associated motion as just one of multiple functions.

Abbreviations

1	first person	COMPL	completive
2	second person	DEM	demonstrative
3	third person	DES	desiderative
A	actor argument of a transitive predicate	DIST	distal
		F	feminine
A	Set-A pronominal prefix	HORIZ	horizontal
ADV	temporal adverb	INDF	indefinite subject/agent
B	Set-B pronominal prefix	INTJ	interjection
CLF	classifier	INTR	intransitive

IT	itive	PROX	proximate
M	masculine	RECP	reciprocal
NON.EXT	non-extended	REL	relative
NPRG	non-progressive	S	single argument of an intransitive predicate
O	non-actor (or "other") argument of a transitive predicate	SG	singular
OBJ	object	SUB	subordinate
OPP	opposite	TR	transitive
PL	plural	VEN	ventive
POSS	possessive	VERT	vertical
PRF	perfect	VIS	visible
PRG	progressive		

Acknowledgments: We are grateful to Pilagá speakers Ignacio Silva and José Miranda, who have given their time and dedication to this project. We would like to acknowledge Antoine Guillaume, Harold Koch, Lev Michael, Daniel Ross and Jean-Christophe Verstraete for their comments and suggestions on this paper. Research has been supported in part by NSF grant 1263817 to the University of Oregon, and by the Argentinean CONICET.

References

Belkadi, Aicha. 2015. Associated motion with deictic directionals: A comparative overview. *SOAS Working Papers in Linguistics* 17. 49–76.

Belkadi, Aicha. This volume, chapter 5. Deictic directionality as associated motion: Motion, complex events and event integration in African languages.

Carrió, Cintia. 2011. Conflation in verbs of motion: Construction of location and direction in the Mocovi language. *Suvremena lingvistika* [*Contemporary Linguistics*] 37(1). 1–25.

Doris L. Payne & Alejandra Vidal. 2020. Pilagá determiners and demonstratives: Discourse use and grammaticalisation. In Åshild Næss, Anna Margetts & Yvonne Treis (eds.), *Demonstratives in discourse*, 149–183. Berlin: Language Science Press. DOI: 10. 5281/zenodo.4055824.

Dryer, Matthew. This volume, chapter 4. Associated motion and directionals: Where they overlap.

Fabre, Alain. 2013. Applicatives and associated motion suffixes in the expression of spatial relations: A view from Nivaĉle (Mataguayo family, Paraguayan Chaco). Unpublished manuscript. https://zenodo.org/record/344498#.Xp8tipl7k2w (accessed 21 April, 2020).

Fabre, Alain. 2017. Morphosyntax of the Nivacle verb and some comparisons with the other languages of the Gran Chaco region and elsewhere. Unpublished manuscript. https://independent.academia.edu/AlainFabre (accessed 17 October, 2017).

Grinevald, Colette. 2006. The expression of static location in a typological perspective. In Maya Hickmann & Stephane Robert (eds.), *Space in languages: Linguistic systems and cognitive categories*, 29–58. Amsterdam: John Benjamins.

Gualdieri, Beatriz. 1998. *Mocovi (Guaycurú) Fonologia e morfossintaxe.* Campinas: Universidade Estadual de Campinas PhD Thesis.
Guillaume, Antoine. 2000. Directionals versus associated motions in Cavineña. In Alan Melby & Arle Lommel (eds.), *LACUS Forum XXVI: The lexicon*, 395–401. Fullerton, CA: Linguistic Association of Canada and the United States.
Guillaume, Antoine. 2008. *A grammar of Cavineña.* Berlin: Mouton de Gruyter.
Guillaume, Antoine. 2016. Associated motion in South America: Typological and areal perspectives. *Linguistic Typology* 20(1). 81–177.
Guillaume, Antoine and Harold Koch, this volume, Chapter 1. Introduction: Associated Motion as a grammatical category in linguistic typology.
Instituto de Estadísticas y Censos (INDEC). 2004. Encuesta complementaria de pueblos indígenas. Dirección Nacional de Estadísticas. Argentina.
Jackendoff, Ray. 1983. *Semantics and cognition.* Cambridge, MA: MIT Press.
Klein, Harriet M. 1973. *A grammar of Argentine Toba.* New York: Columbia University PhD dissertation.
Klein, Harriet M. 1981. Location and direction in Toba: Verbal morphology. *International Journal of American Linguistics* 47(3). 227–235.
Koch, Harold. 1984. The category of 'associated motion' in Kaytej. *The Languages of Central Australia* 1. 23–34.
Messineo, Cristina. 2003. *Lengua toba (guaycurú). Aspectos gramaticales y discursivos.* (Lincom Studies in Native American Linguistics, 48) München: Lincom Europa.
Otero, Manuel A. 2018. Directional verb morphology in Ethiopian Komo. In Helga Schröeder, & Prisca Jerono (eds.), *Nilo-Saharan issues and perspectives*, 165–177. Köln: Rüdiger Köppe Verlag.
Otero, Manuel A. This volume, chapter 20. At the intersection of associated motion, direction and exchoative aspect in the Koman languages.
Otero, Manuel A., Alejandra Vidal, & Doris L. Payne. 2017. Associated motion and AWAY in the Chaco: Nivaĉle and Pilagá. Paper presented at the 2017 meeting of the Society for the Study of Indigenous Languages of the Americas (SSILA), Austin, TX.
Payne, Doris L. 2013. The challenge of Maa 'Away'. In Tim Thornes, Gwendolyn Hyslop, & Joana Jansen (eds.), *Functional-historical approaches to explanation: In honor of Scott DeLancey*, 259–282. Amsterdam: John Benjamins.
Payne, Doris L. This volume, chapter 19. The extension of associated motion to direction, aspect and argument structure in Nilotic languages.
Payne, Doris L., & Manuel A. Otero. 2016. Deictic (Associated) Motion and the tense-aspect domain: Evidence from Nilotic & Koman. Paper presented at the Syntax of the World's Languages VII, Workshop on Associated Motion, Mexico City, Mexico.
Payne, Doris L., Alejandra Vidal & Manuel A. Otero. 2018. Locative, existential and possessive predication in the Chaco: Nivaĉle (Mataguayan) and Pilagá (Guaykuruan). In Spike Gildea, Rosa Vallejos & Simon Overall (eds.), *Non-verbal predication in Amazonian languages*, 263–294. Amsterdam: John Benjamins.
Rose, Francoise. 2015. Associated motion in Mojeño Trinitario: Some typological considerations. *Folia Linguistica* 49(1). 117–158.
Ross, Daniel. This volume, chapter 2. A cross-linguistic survey of associated motion and directionals.
Sandalo, Filomena. 1997. *A grammar of Kadiwéu with special reference to the Polysynthesis Parameter.* (Occasional Papers in Linguistics 11) Cambridge, MA: MIT.

Talmy, Leonard. 2000. *Toward a cognitive semantics, Vol 2*. Cambridge, MA: MIT Press.
Vidal, Alejandra. 2001. *Pilagá Grammar (Guaycuruan)*. Eugene: University of Oregon PhD dissertation.
Vidal, Alejandra. 2006. De la direccionalidad al aspecto verbal en pilagá. *Revista de Lenguas Indígenas y Universos Culturales* 3. 89–107. Universidad de Valencia.
Vidal, Alejandra. 2008. Affectedness and viewpoint in Pilagá (Guaykuruan). In Mark Donohue & Søren Wichmann (eds.), *The typology of semantic alignment*, 412–430. Oxford: Oxford University Press.
Viegas Barros, J. Pedro. 2013. *Proto-Guaicurú: Una reconstrucción fonológica, léxica y morfológica*. (LINCOM Studies in Native American Linguistics) München: LINCOM.
Vuillermet, Marine. 2012. *A grammar of Ese Ejja, a Takanan language of the Bolivian Amazon*. Lyon: Université Lumière Lyon 2 doctoral dissertation.
Wilkins, David P. 1989. *Mparntwe Arrernte: Studies in the structure and semantics of grammar*. PhD dissertation. Australian National University, Canberra.
Wilkins, David P. 1991. The semantics, pragmatics and diachronic development of 'associated motion' in Mparntwe Arrernte. *Buffalo Papers in Linguistics* 91(1). 207–257.

Matthew S. Dryer
13 Associated motion in North America (including Mexico and Central America)

Abstract: This chapter is a survey of associated motion in North America (including Mexico and Central America), showing that it is widespread, being found in 94 languages in twenty-nine families and isolates. The majority of sources do not distinguish markers of associated motion from directionals and in general seem unaware of associated motion as something found in other languages. The majority of languages lack the degree of complexity found in some languages in Australia and South America and almost half of them have only a single marker of associated motion. The languages with the most markers of associated motion are among Algonquian, Sahaptian, and Uto-Aztecan languages.

Keywords: associated motion, directional, andative, ventive

1 Introduction

This chapter is a survey of associated motion (hereafter AM) in North America (including Mexico and Central America). It will show that AM is widespread in North America. In fact, apart from a number of isolates and very small families, there were only five families in which I was unable to find evidence of AM: Misumalpan, Yuman, Siouan, Salishan, and Nadene. I describe AM in 94 languages, in 29 families and isolates in North America.[1] For the majority of languages, especially in Canada and the United States, the sources show little awareness of AM as a phenomenon found in other languages.[2]

---

1 The sample of languages is rather ad hoc. It includes all sources for which I had a searchable PDF in which I found, in searching, various words associated with AM like 'motion', 'direction', 'directional', 'andative', 'ventive', 'venitive', 'centripetal', 'centrifugal' and 'cislocative' (and their equivalents in French and Spanish).
2 Many of the morphemes characterized in this chapter as AM morphemes have other uses, but for the sake of brevity and in order to focus on the topic of this chapter, I have ignored those

---

Note: Supplementary material for chapters 4 and 13 can be accessed on the publisher's website https://www.degruyter.com/view/title/569942?language=en&result=1&rskey=k0pRD4

Matthew S. Dryer, University at Buffalo, dryer@buffalo.edu

https://doi.org/10.1515/9783110692099-013

In the main body of this chapter I describe the overall patterns and in the Supplementary Materials[3] describe the markers of AM in each of the languages in question. The main body of this chapter is organized in terms of a typology of AM, illustrating how different types are found among the languages of North America. I assume a basic typology of four types of AM, namely prior AM, concurrent AM, subsequent AM, and a combination of prior plus subsequent AM, exemplified in (1) to (4).[4] I treat a construction as involving AM if there is some evidence of grammaticalization. In most cases, this involves affixes, but it also includes instances of nonverbal noninflecting words and instances of compounding when the compounding construction is limited to motion verbs or to motion verbs and stance verbs.[5]

Prior AM:
(1) Panamint (Numic, Uto-Aztecan; California, United States)
    Nü   hipi-**kwan**-tu'ih.
    1sg drink-**GO.AND**-FUT
    'I will go and drink.' (Dayley 1989: 66)

Concurrent AM:
(2) Sochiapan Chinantec (Chinantecan, Otomanguean; Mexico)
    hã́u^M huṍu^{LM} cá^{M}mi̵^{L} hmi̵$^{\tilde{H}}$ ʔi̵^{H}-ʔó̵ʔ^{LM} ʔi̵^{L} ʔi̵^{H}-ʔo^M ...
    so   many.ANIM   woman   TERMIN   **MOT**-shout.3   and   **MOT**-cry.3
    'So many women were walking along shouting and crying ...' (Foris 2000: 111)

Subsequent AM:
(3) Nez Perce (Sahaptian, Plateau Penutian; western United States)
    ʔimí-**we**-se
    camp.for.digging.roots-**RETURN.FROM**-IPFV.PRES.SG
    'I am returning from digging roots.' (Cash 2004: 74)

---

other uses as well as questions about the relationship between these other uses and their uses as markers of AM. It is possible that in some cases, careful examination of these other uses might lead us to analyse the morphemes as coding something other than AM.

3 Supplementary Material for chapter 13 can be accessed on the publisher's website https://www.degruyter.com/view/title/569942?language=en&result=1&rskey=k0pRD4

4 Guillaume (2016) treats prior plus subsequent AM as a type of prior AM. I discuss my reasons for treating it as a separate type below.

5 The interlinear glosses used in this chapter are in general the original glosses in the source, except for (1) standardizing abbreviations for the same thing; (2) improving a few glosses, where the gloss in the source was not user-friendly; and (3) translating glosses in non-English sources to English.

Prior plus subsequent AM:[6]
(4) Malecite-Passamaquoddy (Algonquian, Algic; northeastern U.S. and eastern Canada)
ht-áp-təmím-a-l
3-GO-hire-DIRECT-3OBV
'He goes somewhere and hires the other (and returns).' (LeSourd 1993: 173)

I need to emphasize at the outset that this survey is based on what is in many languages rather brief descriptions of morphemes and more detailed study would probably lead to a revision of how I classify some of the morphemes. In particular, it is likely that some of the languages have more AM morphemes than I was able to find in sources and that some of the morphemes I discuss have uses that go beyond what I describe. In some families I found more associated morphemes in some languages than in others and I suspect that in many cases the languages where I found fewer AM morphemes actually have more.

Although AM is widespread in North America, very few languages have systems of AM that are nearly as complex as some of those that Guillaume (2016) describes for South America or Koch (1984) for the Pama-Nyungan language Kaytej spoken in Australia. For 41 (or almost half) of the 94 languages I found evidence of only a single marker of AM and in only 29 of these 94 languages did I find more than two.[7]

The remainder of this chapter is organized as follows. In §2, I discuss the coding of direction with AM morphemes. In §3, I discuss the four types of AM. In §4, I discuss possible combinations of the types of direction discussed in §2 with the four basic types of AM discussed §3. In §5, I discuss morphemes that code AM with non-motion verbs but also function as directionals with motion verbs. In §6, I discuss cases where directional morphemes and AM morphemes co-occur. In §7, I discuss different types of inventories of AM morphemes, different types of associated morphemes that occur in the same language. In §8, I discuss AM morphemes that only occur with imperative meaning. In §9, I discuss a number of AM oddities found in languages of North America. The Appendix provides a summary table for each of the 94 languages. The Supplementary Materials illustrates the

---

[6] Although LeSourd glosses the prefix *áp-* in (4) simply as 'go', his description of the prefix makes it clear that it denotes both going somewhere and then returning.

[7] In describing the number of AM markers in particular languages in this chapter, I only intend to mean the number that I was able to find. I should also add that in these counts, I intend the number of markers that contrast in different types of AM. I do not count multiple markers that code a single type of AM that vary along some other dimension like tense or aspect (though I mention these in the Supplementary Materials).

AM morphemes found in all of the 94 languages, plus one additional borderline case, where I decide that the morphemes in question are not sufficiently grammaticalized to count as markers of AM. Figure 1 gives a map showing the location of the 94 languages.

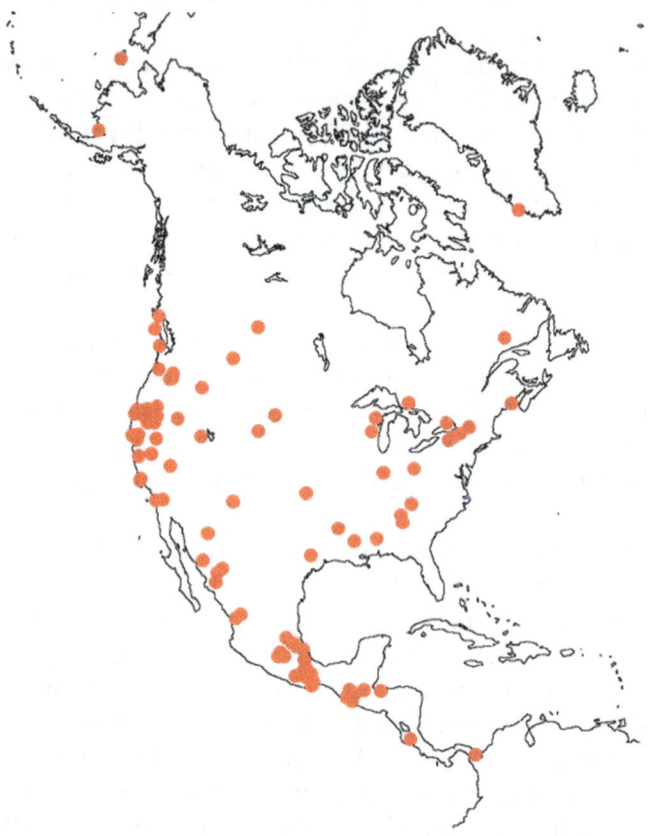

Figure 1: Map showing the 94 languages discussed in this chapter.

2 Coding of direction with AM morphemes

The typology of four types of AM (prior AM, concurrent AM, subsequent AM, and a combination of prior plus subsequent AM) further interacts with a dimension of direction. I assume, following Guillaume (2016), that pure directional morphemes, morphemes that only occur with motion verbs to code the direction of motion, need to be distinguished from AM morphemes, which primarily combine with non-motion verbs to add motion to the meaning of the verb.[8] Although this study did not directly examine directional morphemes, my search for morphemes coding AM suggests that directional morphemes are even more common in North America than morphemes coding AM. The examples in (5) and (6) illustrate directional affixes in two languages that are in families where I was unable to find evidence of AM.

(5) Nxa'amxcin (Columbia Moses) (Salishan; northwestern U.S.)[9]
 c-nəqínm.
 DIR-go.in
 'He came in.' (Willett 2003: 263)

(6) Tolowa (Athapaskan, Nadene; Oregon, U.S.)
 see-na-ł-da.
 UP-MOT-CLSFR-run
 'S/he runs up.' (Bommelyn 1997: 23)

I need to explain briefly how I use the terms "directional" and "direction". I use the term "directional" to refer to morphemes that combine with motion verbs to indicate the direction of the motion. The term "direction", however, applies not only to the direction coded by directional morphemes, but also to the direction coded by AM morphemes that combine with non-motion verbs that add not only an idea of motion but at the same time add an idea of the direction of that motion. I also distinguish two uses of the term directional. The first of these is what we might call "pure directional" morphemes, which only combine with motion verbs. The examples in (5) and (6) above are instances of pure directional morphemes; I will not discuss these further in this chapter. The second use of the term directional

---

8 As noted by Guillaume (2016), AM morphemes also occasionally combine with motion verbs. When they do, they can either express AM, denoting a separate motion that is distinct from that is denoted by the verb, as in (i), or they can express pure direction. In (i), for example, the motion denoted by the AM suffix *-pa* denotes motion that occurs prior to the motion of entering denoted by the verb. (Hanson glosses the suffix *-pa* as 'ELV' for 'elative', which she explains as meaning 'movement away from the deictic centre').

(i) Yine (Southern Maipuran, Arawakan; Peru)
    kosina   hima   t-çihloka-pa   t-nikanri-yehi.
    kitchen   QUOT   3sg.f-enter-**ELV**   3SG.F-food-LOC
    'She went and entered the kitchen where her food was.' (Hanson 2010: 161)

9 Willett (2003) glosses the Nxa'amxcin prefix *c-* in (5) as 'DIR' for 'directional' but describes it a cislocative, coding motion 'this way', i.e. towards the deictic centre.

is one that will play a role in this chapter. Namely, there are AM morphemes that combine both with non-motion verbs and with motion verbs, where they code AM when they combine with non-motion verbs and direction when they combine with motion verbs. I will refer to morphemes of this sort as "AM morphemes that also function as directionals". These are the topic of §5 below, as well as Dryer (this volume, ch. 4). It is also discussed by Belkadi (this volume).

The topic of this section is the way in which AM morphemes code direction in addition to one of the four basic types of AM. For example, the ventive suffix -*way* in the Lowland Chontal (§S5.1)[10] example in (7) codes prior AM, but also codes motion towards the speaker or deictic centre.

(7) Lowland Chontal (O'Connor 2007; Tequistlatecan; Mexico)
*sago-**way**-jle´.*
eat-**VENT**-IPFV.PL
'Come and eat!' (O'Connor 2007: 131)

I distinguish here four directions that occur with AM morphemes, namely "andative", "ventive", "random" and "neutral". The most common directions coded by AM morphemes are andative (motion away from the deictic centre) and ventive (motion towards the deictic centre). Example (1) above from Panamint (§S7.13) illustrates an andative morpheme, while (7) from Lowland Chontal illustrates a ventive morpheme, in both cases involving prior AM.

A third directional value is random direction, illustrated in (8) from Northern Paiute (§S7.14).

(8) Northern Paiute (Numic, Uto-Aztecan; western United States)
*tɨhoawai-**nimi**   nɨ.*
hunt-**RANDOM.SG**   1SG
'I've been hunting around.' (Thornes 2003: 417)

I gloss the suffix -*nimi* in (8) as RANDOM, indicating that the path of motion is an irregular one, not specifically away from or towards the deictic centre, and will refer to this direction type as random direction (although it more generally simply lacks a specific direction). English glosses for such random motion often use the word 'around' as in (8) and the example from Sochiapan Chinantec (§S4.6) in (9).

---

10 Section numbers starting with '§S' refer to sections in the Supplementary Materials. Similarly, example numbers that are cited which begin with '(S' refer to examples in the Supplementary Materials.

(9) Sochiapan Chinantec (Chinantecan, Otomanguean; Mexico)
 ŋii^L**-hui**^{MH} cú^M ha^H ʔŋiú^L ʔi^L té ʔ^{ML} rãi ʔ^{MH}.
 AMB-whistle.3 3PRO among house COMP call.PRES.3 companion.3POSS
 'He walks around in the streets calling his companions.' (Foris 2000: 104)

Note that these random direction AM morphemes are sometimes called ambulative (as in the gloss of *ŋii*^{L}- in (9)); while these may most often be used for instances of walking around randomly, this may reflect nothing more than the fact that walking is traditionally the most common manner of motion. After all, most instances of andative and ventive AM also involve walking. Random motion is apparently only found with AM morphemes coding concurrent motion[11].

The fourth direction type is essentially the absence of a specification of direction. I refer to this as neutral direction. The prefix glossed 'go' in (10) from Malecite-Passamaquoddy (§S29.13) codes prior AM, like the ventive suffix in (7), but is neutral as to whether the motion is away from the deictic centre or towards it.

(10) Malecite-Passamaquoddy (Algonquian, Algic; northeastern U.S., and eastern Canada)
 nát-*ewət-ów-an.*
 GO-arrange-TRANS.ANIM-DIRECT
 'He comes (or goes) and gets it for the other.' (LeSourd 1993: 378)

Yurok (§S29.1), Cree (§S29.11), and West Greenlandic (§S30.1) also have prior AM morphemes that are neutral as to direction. I will refer to this type of direction as neutral. Note that random direction is not the same as neutral direction. Random direction represents motion that is neither andative nor ventive while neutral direction is simply vague as to whether the motion is andative, ventive, or random. In other words, a marker of random direction specifically conveys the

---

[11] Random motion is sometimes found with AM morphemes that also function as directionals. For example, the suffix *-ãpo* in the Apurinã example is used in (i) for random concurrent AM, but in (ii) it is used as a directional, with a motion verb, where it does not add a separate motion event but simply denotes the random direction of the motion (Southern Maipuran, Arawakan; Brazil).

(i) nhi-nhika-ãpo-ta-ru.
  1SG-eat-RANDOM-VBLZ-3SG.M:OBJ
  'I went around aimlessly eating it.' (Facundes 2000 : 284)

(ii) nota   mutekã-ãpo-ta.
  1SG   run-RANDOM-VBLZ
  'I ran around.' (Facundes 2000: 249)

fact that the motion is neither andative nor ventive, while a marker of neutral direction does not and includes motion that is andative or ventive. We thus have four direction types, andative, ventive, random, and neutral.

It is not always clear whether a particular morpheme coding AM is neutral with respect to direction. For example, England (1983) describes a suffix *-7kj* in Mam (§S3.4) which she glosses as 'PROC' for 'processive' but translates as 'go and', illustrated in (11).

(11) Mam (Mayan; Guatemala)
*ma ø-txi7 t-la-**7kj** axi7n t-uj plaas.*
REC.PAST 3SG.ABS-DIR 3SG.ERG-see-**PROC** corn 3SG-in market
'He went and saw the corn in the market.' (England 1983: 109)

But it is not clear whether this suffix is specifically andative or whether it is neutral with respect to direction, since a gloss involving 'go and' is a natural way to gloss either an andative morpheme or a morpheme that is neutral with respect to direction.

While it is generally possible to classify AM morphemes as one of these four directions (except in cases when it is not clear whether a morpheme is neutral with respect to direction), there is one instance in my data of an AM morpheme that seems to be both andative and random. The Cupeño (§S7.10) example in (12) involves a concurrent AM suffix *-ngiy* which Hill (2005) glosses as 'MOTG' for 'motion going' and translates as 'go off doing, go around doing' but seems to involve random direction in most of her examples. In (12), the sentence gloss suggests both motion away from the deictic centre as well as random motion.

(12) Cupeño (Cupan, Uto-Aztecan; California, USA)
*Ta'a-la'a-la'a-la'a-pe-yi-**ngiy**.*
stagger-REPET-REPET-REPET-3SG-THEME-**MOTG**
'He went off staggering.' (Hill 2005: 270)

3 More on the four types of AM

In (1) to (4) above, I illustrate the four types of AM that I assume in this chapter: prior AM; concurrent AM; subsequent AM; and prior plus subsequent AM. The most common type of AM is prior AM: all but thirteen of the 94 languages (that is, 81 languages) have at least one morpheme coding prior AM. Among the thirteen languages lacking prior AM, seven have only concurrent AM, one has only subsequent AM, four have only concurrent AM and prior plus subsequent AM, and one has only prior plus subsequent AM. One of the seven languages with only concurrent AM is Garifuna (§S2), which has an andative concurrent AM suffix *-yna*, as in (13).

(13) Garifuna (Haurholm-Larsen 2016; Arawakan; Belize to Nicaragua)
    bueno aban wé-ydi-n   aríya-hè-**yna**   wa-gíya
    well   CONN 1PL-go.1SUBJ-USPEC look.for-DISTR-**ANDAT** 1PL-DEM
    pádnà.
    companion
    'Well, then we left, looking for company on our way.' (Haurholm-Larsen 2016: 225)

The only language in which I found only markers of subsequent AM is Sipakapense (§S3.2), which actually has three AM particles, all three of which denote subsequent AM. The first one, *b'ik*, illustrated in (14), denotes andative subsequent AM.

(14) Sipakapense (Mayan; Guatemala)
    Mariy x-tz'ul-ij   **b'ik**   Wan.
    Mariy COMPL-hug-MODAL **DIR.GO** Wan
    'Mariy hugged Wan and left.' (Barrett 1999: 131)

The second one, *ul*, is ventive, denoting motion towards the deictic centre ending in arrival after the event denoted by the verb.

(15) X-ø-tz'ub-j   **ul**.
    COMPL-3SG.ERG:3SG.ABS-kiss- **DIR.ARRIVE.HERE**
    MODAL
    'S/he kissed him/her before coming here.' (Barrett 1999: 133)

The third one, *pon*, is the reverse of *ul*, denoting arrival after motion away from the deictic centre.

(16) X-oq'   **pon**.
    COMPL.3SG-buy **DIR.ARRIVE.THERE**
    'S/he bought it before they (he/she) arrived.' (Barrett 1999: 132)

This particle *pon* is andative, like the particle in (14), but differs in that the one in (14) focuses on the departure after the act denoted by the verb, while the one in

(16) focuses on the arrival at some other place after the act denoted by the verb. For none of the languages in the sample was I able to find only markers of prior plus subsequent AM.

The types of AM other than prior AM are considerably less common among the languages in North America (and probably in general, as noted by Levinson and Wilkins 2006 and Guillaume 2016). Compared to the 81 languages with prior AM morphemes, there are only 28 languages with concurrent AM morphemes, 11 languages with prior plus subsequent AM morphemes and 6 languages with subsequent AM morphemes.

Some further discussion of prior plus subsequent AM morphemes is warranted, because Guillaume (2016) treats them as prior AM in his survey of AM in South American languages (while recognizing the possibility of treating them as a distinct type of AM). In addition to (4) above from Malecite-Passamaquoddy, examples of this type of AM from North America are given in (17) to (19). This is illustrated in (17) for Tepetotutla Chinantec (§S4.7), in (18) for Upper Necaxa Totonac (§S6.1), and in (19) for Washo (§S19).[12]

(17) Tepetotutla Chinantec (Chinantecan, Otomanguean; Mexico)
 ka^M-i^H-$lio\textglotstop^{LH}$ $hnia\textglotstop^{LH}$.
 PAST-**RETURN.COMPL.1PL**-bathe.1PL   1PL.EXCL
 'We went and bathed and returned.' (Westley 1991: 22)

(18) Upper Necaxa Totonac (Totonacan; Mexico)
 *ka-**kiː**-tayḁ*   *laːsu*
 OPT-**RETURN**-take.2SUBJ.PFV   rope
 'Go get a rope (and bring it back)!' (Beck 2004: 77)

(19) Washo (Isolate; western United States)
 *beguíweʔ-**il***
 buy-**GO.AND.RETURN**
 'to go and buy something and bring it back' (Jacobsen 1964: 567)

As noted above, in his survey of AM in South American languages, Guillaume (2016) treats all the morphemes which possibly code prior plus subsequent AM as instances of prior AM. To some extent, this makes sense: normally if one goes to do something, one returns after doing it, so it is often unclear whether the return

---

12 Westley (1991) and Beck (2004) gloss the prior plus subsequent AM morphemes as 'RT' for 'round trip'. I use this label below for one subtype of prior plus subsequent AM.

is part of the meaning of the morpheme or simply an implication in context. Guillaume opted for treating all possible instances of prior plus subsequent AM as prior AM rather than distinguishing a separate prior plus subsequent type of AM for two apparent reasons. First, in many of the instances in his study, it was unclear whether they would be classified as prior AM or prior plus subsequent AM, because in these cases, it was unclear whether the return is part of the meaning. And second, in all the translations of possible instances of prior plus subsequent AM in his study, the subsequent return was placed in parentheses.

There are a couple of reasons why I am treating prior plus subsequent AM as a distinct type of AM. First, the descriptions of some of these morphemes strongly imply that the return motion is definitely part of the meaning. In fact, they suggest that if anything, the return is the more fundamental part of the meaning than the prior motion. Second, and perhaps more importantly, in a number of the languages in North America with prior plus subsequent AM, these morphemes are in paradigmatic opposition to morphemes coding just prior AM. Since the sources distinguish the two morphemes on the basis of the fact that one involves returning while the other does not, the implication again is that the return is part of the meaning of those characterized as going and returning. For example the prior plus subsequent AM prefix in Tepetotutla Chinantec (§S4.7) illustrated in (17) above is in paradigmatic contrast with a prior AM prefix illustrated in (20).

(20) Tepetotutla Chinantec (Chinantecan, Otomanguean; Mexico)
   zi^L-*lioʔ*^{M} za^M.
   GO.INCOMPL.2-bathe   3PRO
   'S/he will go and bathe.' (Westley 1991: 21)

Similarly, the prior plus subsequent AM preverb in Malecite-Passamaquoddy (§S19.13) illustrated in (4) above is in paradigmatic contrast with a prior AM preverb illustrated in (21).[13]

(21) Malecite-Passamaquoddy (Algonquian, Algic; northeastern U.S., and eastern Canada)
   náci-ksə́m-əw-an
   GO-saw-TRANS.ANIM-3.PASSV
   'he goes somewhere to have it sawn for him' (LeSourd 1993: 390)

---

13 See the discussion of preverbs in Ktunaxa and Algic languages in §S28 and §S29 in the Supplementary Materials.

For these reasons, I continue to treat prior plus subsequent AM as a fourth type of AM, with the understanding that further research might show that some languages that I have classified as having morphemes of this sort might be shown to be better classified as having prior AM (or subsequent AM) instead.

A second difference between my typology and that of Guillaume (2016) is that some of the morphemes that I classify as prior plus subsequent AM are of a type that Guillaume classifies as concurrent. These are morphemes whose meaning is something like 'to do something while passing by', in which case the temporal interval for the verb event is a brief subinterval of the temporal interval for the motion event. Examples are given from Kekchi (§S3.3) in (22), from Upper Necaxa Totonac (§S6.1) in (23), and from Nez Perce (§S9.2) in (24).[14]

(22) Kekchi (Mayan; Guatemala)
x-in-x-**nume7**-b'oq.
COMPL-1SG.ABS-3SG.ERG-**WHILE.PASSING**-call
'He called me as he was passing.' (Stewart 1980: 73)

(23) Upper Necaxa Totonac (Totonacan; Mexico)
ʈuːn   maːn=tsa   ʈuːn=tsa   kin-**te:**-wan-níɬ   wayaya   an-ɬ.
PTCL   only=now   thus=now   1OBJ-**PATH**-say-BEN-PFV   IDPH   go-PFV
'He just came by to say mean things to me and took off.' (Beck 2004: 76)

(24) Nez Perce (Sahaptian, Plateau Penutian; western United States)
hi-wehin-**á·t**-six.
3NOM-bark-**AS.OBJECT.PASSES.BY**-IPFV.PRES-PL
'They were barking at us as we went by.' (Cash 2004: 73)

Guillaume (2016) describes affixes like these in a number of languages in South America, but classifies them as a subtype of (temporally non-coextensive) concurrent AM, as does Koch (this volume, ch. 7). However, I think that these morphemes are better viewed as a subtype of prior plus subsequent AM, since the act denoted by the verb may interrupt the motion, as in (23), where the individual passing by may have stopped moving temporarily while speaking. And even if the motion continues through the act denoted by the verb, as might be the case in (22), what seems crucial to the meaning of such morphemes is that there is

---

14 Note however that the sentence gloss for both (22) and (24) shows that at least in these examples, the one performing the act denoted by the verb is different from those in motion. Guillaume (2016) treats these as a distinct type of AM. I found few instances of this type of AM in North America.

prior motion and subsequent motion, while this is not otherwise the case with morphemes denoting concurrent AM. I suspect that in general these morphemes are vague as to whether the motion continued through the act denoted by the verb or whether the motion is interrupted. For example while the motion might continue through the act denoted by the verb in (22), it is not clear that it matters whether the motion stopped temporarily or not. For example the same Kekchí prefix -*nume7* in (22) occurs in (25), where the motion presumably stopped temporarily while the speaker bathed.

(25) Kekchí (Mayan; Guatemala)
 *x-in-**nume7**-atin-q.*
 COMPL-1SG-**WHILE.PASSING**-bathe-DIR
 'I stopped to bathe while passing by.' (Stewart 1980: 74)

A second reason for treating AM morphemes of this sort as a subtype of prior plus subsequent AM rather than as concurrent is that there are languages which have both morphemes of this sort and morphemes that are more unambiguously morphemes coding concurrent AM. For example, in addition to the passing-by prefix illustrated above in Upper Necaxa Totonac illustrated above in (23) is the concurrent AM ambulative suffix illustrated in (26).

(26) Upper Necaxa Totonac (Totonacan; Mexico)
 ... *le·n-ɬ   dulces   wi:li:-**te:ɬa**-ɬ   xa: ka:-lé:n-ɬ   ix-ta:ta.*
    take-PFV sweets   put-**AMB**-PFV   NEG   PL.OBJ-take-PFV   3POSS-father
 '[One of his sisters,] she brought sweets and went along dropping them where their father was taking them.' (Beck 2004: 75)

The difference in meaning between the passing-by AM prefix in (23) and the concurrent AM suffix in (26) appears to be that the former denotes an event preceded and followed by motion while the latter simply denotes concurrent motion. Filomena Mata (§S6.2) and Menomini (§S29.8) also distinguish concurrent AM morphemes from passing-by morphemes.

For these reasons, I classify these passing-by morphemes as a subtype of prior plus subsequent AM, differing from the ones illustrated in (4) and (17) to (19) above in that the subsequent motion is not the reverse of the prior motion. It is nevertheless useful to distinguish the two subtypes, which I will call the "round trip" type (following terminology used by Beck (2004) among others in discussing such morphemes in Totonacan languages) and the "passing-by" type.

Although I have given reasons why I treat these "passing-by" morphemes as a type of prior plus subsequent AM rather than concurrent AM, I am not claiming that it is wrong to treat them as a type of concurrent AM. In fact, it may actually be the case that languages differ in how they should be classified, depending on how they fit into the AM system of the language. Koch (this volume, ch. 7) describes a DO.ONCE.ALONG suffix in Kaytetye that has a meaning similar to the prior plus subsequent AM morphemes of the "passing-by" type discussed in this chapter, but this suffix is in paradigmatic opposition to a do.all.along concurrent suffix, where the latter is clearly concurrent by all criteria. In Upper Necaxa Totonac, in contrast, while the language does have a concurrent AM morpheme, the "passing-by" morpheme is not in paradigmatic opposition to this concurrent AM morpheme since the former is a prefix while the latter is a suffix. However, the "passing-by" morpheme is in paradigmatic contrast to a prior plus subsequent AM morpheme of the round trip type, illustrated in (18) above, since that morpheme is a prefix, like the passing-by morpheme. The situation in Filomena Mata Totonac is similar, as discussed in §S6.2. Hence it may be correct to analyse the DO.ONCE.ALONG suffix in Kaytetye as coding a type of concurrent AM while at the same time analysing the "passing-by" prefixes in Upper Necaxa Totonac and Filomena Mata Totonac as instances of a type of prior plus subsequent AM. For the other five languages in North America with "passing-by" morphemes, the situation is less clear. In Menomini, discussed in §S19.8, the "passing-by" morpheme *is* in paradigmatic opposition to both morphemes coding prior plus subsequent AM of the round trip type and concurrent AM morphemes. In none of other four languages with passing-by morphemes, namely Kekchí (§S3.3), Ixil (§S3.5), Chuj (§S3.7), and Nez Perce (§S9.2), did I find either concurrent AM morphemes or morphemes coding prior plus subsequent AM of the round trip type. For these five languages, either analysis seems possible.

Among the 11 languages with prior plus subsequent AM morphemes, 7 have morphemes of the round trip type and 7 have morphemes of the passing-by type. As noted in the preceding paragraph, three languages, Upper Necaxa Totonac (§S6.1), Filomena Mata Totonac (§S6.2), and Menomini (§S29.8), have morphemes of both types.

4 Combinations of direction and AM

In §2, I discussed four directional values found with AM morphemes. In this section I look at the different combinations of these four directional values, with the four basic types of AM discussed in the preceding section. Since there are four basic types of AM and four possible directional values, we might think that there would be sixteen possible ways to combine them. This is not quite the case for a number of reasons. First, random direction seems restricted to concurrent AM. Second, although one can imagine two subtypes of prior plus subsequent AM of the passing-by type, one where one passes somewhere while going somewhere and one where one passes somewhere while coming somewhere, no such distinction is found among the languages of North America that I examined.[15] Similarly, although one can imagine a distinction between two subtypes of prior plus subsequent AM of the round trip type, one where one comes somewhere and then goes back and one where one goes somewhere and then comes back, in the data I have for North America there is not such distinction.[16] In fact, it is clear from McFarland (2009) that the round-trip morpheme in Filomena Mata (§S6.2) can be used for either one, given the sentence glosses for (27) and (28).

(27) Filomena Mata Totonac (Totonacan; Mexico)
 kii-kaa-štlawan-áw.
 RETURN-LOC-adorn-1PL
 'We went to adorn the place and returned.' (McFarland 2009: 143)

(28) hkiiwaayánči.
 k-**kii**-waa-nan-či-li
 1SUBJ-**RETURN**-eat-HABIT-here-PFV
 'I came here to eat and returned.' (McFarland 2009: 143)

This leaves three possible directional subtypes of prior AM and of subsequent AM (andative, ventive, and neutral) and four possible subtypes of concurrent AM. All of these possibilities are attested in the languages I examined, except for subsequent AM that is neutral with respect to direction.[17]

Examples of the three types of direction associated with prior AM morphemes include the andative prefix in Tepetotutla Chinantec given in (20) above, the ventive suffix in Lowland Chontal given in (7) above, and the prior AM preverb

---

15 However, as illustrated in (67) below, it is possible in Kekchi to combine the passing-by associated morpheme with an andative or ventive morpheme to code the direction of the motion of passing by.
16 Outside North America, this possibility is attested in Matses, a Panoan language spoken in Peru and Brazil, where there is a contrast between two prior plus subsequent AM suffixes, one meaning go and do something and come back, the other meaning come and do something and then go back (Fleck 2003: 367–368).
17 I have interpreted (14) above from Sipakapense as an instance of andative subsequent AM, but it is conceivable that it is really neutral with respect to direction.

in Malecite-Passmaquoddy that is neutral with respect to direction illustrated in (10) above.

Examples of each of the four types of direction found with concurrent AM morphemes include the andative suffix in Garifuna illustrated in (13) above, the random AM suffix in Northern Paiute illustrated in (8) above and the ambulative prefix in Sochiapan Chinantec illustrated in (9) above, the ventive concurrent suffix in (29) from Cupeño (§S7.10), and the neutral concurrent suffixes in (30) from Kashaya (§S14), in (31) from Central Tarahumara (§S7.4), and in (2) above from Sochiapan Chinantec.

(29) Cupeño (Cupan, Uto-Aztecan; California, USA)[18]
 Qwa'i-**veneq**.
 eat-**MOTCA**
 'He came eating something on the way,' (Hill 2005: 271)

(30) Kashaya (Pomoan; California, United States)
 pihmoy-**á·dad**-u
 smile-**MOT**-VERB
 'to smile while walking along' (Oswalt 1961: 208)

(31) Central Tarahumara (Tarahumaran, Uto-Aztecan; Mexico)
 we ko'á-**simi**.
 INTENS eat-**MOT**
 'They are going along eating.' (Caballero 2008: 418)

It is actually not usually clear whether concurrent morphemes that are neither ventive nor random are andative or neutral. The sentence gloss for (31), for example, employs the English verb 'go' in the sentence gloss, but this might be that they are andative or that they are neutral and the glosses use 'go' because it is the default verb of motion in English.

Among subsequent AM morphemes, (14) above from Sipakapense illustrates andative subsequent AM and (15) above also from Sipakapense illustrates ventive subsequent AM, as does (3) above from Nez Perce. I have no clear instance of subsequent AM that is neutral with respect to direction.

Single morphemes that code prior plus subsequent AM should not be confused with single morphemes that code one type of AM or another. In the former

---

[18] Hill glosses the ventive concurrent AM suffix -veneq as 'MOTCA' for 'motion coming along VERBing'.

case, the morpheme specifically codes that there was both prior motion *and* subsequent motion. In the latter case, the morpheme codes one type *or* the other. For example, the suffix *-ya* in (32) from Huasteca Nahuatl (§S7.1) codes either prior AM or concurrent AM.[19]

(32) Huasteca Nahuatl (Beller and Beller 1979; Aztecan, Uto-Aztecan; Mexico)
*ni-tlakowa-ti-**ya**-s.*
1SG-buy-CONN-**go**-FUT
'I go and buy.' or 'I buy as I go.' (Beller and Beller 1979: 232)

Most of the AM morphemes that I have found in North America that cover either of two types of AM are like Huasteca Nahuatl in covering prior AM or concurrent AM. But the prefix *we·ˊ-* in Northern Sahaptin (§S9.3) seems to cover prior AM, as in (33), or concurrent AM, as in (34), or subsequent AM, as in (35).

(33) Northern Sahaptin (Sahaptian, Plateau Penutian; western U.S.)
*i-**we·ˊ**-wi-cabni-ya.*
3SG-**MOT**-many-ask-PAST
'He went and asked many people.' (Jacobs 1931: 149)

(34) *i-**we·ˊ**-t'łqwəd-na.*
3SG-**MOT**-catch-PAST
'He caught it as it went.' (Jacobs 1931: 149)

(35) *i-**we·ˊ**-wina'-utp-a.*
3SG-**MOT**-hurriedly-dress-PAST
'He dressed hurriedly and went.' (Jacobs 1931: 149)

Note, however, that the concurrent AM in (34) is motion by the object, not the subject.

Table 1 provides a summary of the different types of markers of AM found in my survey in the languages in North America. The rows represent the four types of markers of AM, with a further distinction of the two subtypes of prior plus subsequent AM, the round trip subtype and the passing-by subtype. Apart from the column showing the number of languages in the sample with each of the types

---

[19] In saying that the suffix *-ya* in (32) codes either prior AM or concurrent AM, I do not intend to imply that the suffix is ambiguous. It may just be vague, covering the space of both prior AM and concurrent AM.

of AM, the columns represent the four directions found with AM. The numbers in the cells are the numbers of examples in this paper illustrating the combination of the type of AM and the direction, with asterisks representing logically possible combinations not attested in the sample. As noted above, random direction is normally only found with concurrent AM.

Table 1 assumes that every AM marker can be assigned to one of the four directions. However, as discussed above, (12) above from Cupeño illustrates a morpheme that simultaneously codes andative and random direction. In fact, in principle, random direction is really a third dimension, since it is logically possible for random direction to combine with the other three directions. For example, it is logically possible to have a morpheme coding random ventive concurrent AM, coding doing something while moving randomly towards the deictic center. However, because I am aware of only one instance of a morpheme combining random direction with andative or ventive, I treat random direction as one of four types of directions. For the purposes of the table, I code the direction of instances of prior plus subsequent AM of the round trip type in terms of the direction of the prior motion, which seems to always be andative, though there are other logical possibilities, such as ventive motion followed by andative motion. The two subtypes of prior plus subsequent AM are distinguished by the direction of the subsequent motion relative to that of the prior motion, the subsequent motion being necessarily the reverse of the prior motion in the case of round trip AM but not the reverse in the case of passing-by AM.

Table 1: Types of AM with Example Numbers Illustrating That Type.

	Number Lgs in sample	andative	ventive	random	neutral
prior	81	(1)	(7)	*	(10)
concurrent	28	(13)	(29)	(8)	(2)
subsequent	7	(14)	(3)	*	*
prior plus subsequent	11				
round trip	7	(4)	*	*	(27)
passing-by	7	*	*	*	(22)

5 AM morphemes that also function as directionals

In addition to cases where a morpheme codes either of two (or three) subtypes of AM are cases where a morpheme codes AM with non-motion verbs but direction with motion verbs (see also Dryer this volume, ch. 4). For example, the ventive prefix *tonh-* in Guatusa (§S1.2) codes prior AM in (36), but serves as a directional in (37), since it is combining with a motion verb.[20]

(36) Guatusa (Chibchan; Costa Rica)
 mi-***tonh***-usírra.
 1-**COME**-talk
 'I came to talk.' (Constenla 1998: 124)

(37) lacá=lha   i-***tonh***-min.
 ground=3.on 3-**COME**-fall
 'He fell to the ground in this direction.' (Constenla 1998: 124)

Twenty-two of the languages of North America discussed in this chapter have morphemes of this sort, functioning as markers of AM with non-motion verbs, but as directionals with motion verbs. Seventeen of these languages have morphemes that code prior AM with non-motion verbs but serve as directionals with motion verbs, like Guatusa in (36) and (37) and Ineseño Chumash (§S11.2), where the ventive prefix *akti-* is used either for prior AM, as in (38), or as a directional, as in (39). In fact, the use as a directional in (39) illustrates what appears to be the normal way to express the meaning 'come' in Ineseño Chumash, combining the ventive prefix with the verb for 'go'.[21]

---

[20] A reviewer raises the interesting question whether these morphemes can also function as markers of AM with motion verbs, denoting a separate motion event, whether some uses are ambiguous between an AM reading and a directional meaning, whether in combination with a motion verb meaning 'enter' the meaning could mean either 'he came in' or 'he came and then entered'. I don't recall seeing any data that would bear on this question. Note that the issue of ambiguity would apparently not arise if the particular type of AM was concurrent, since it is difficult to imagine a case of a concurrent AM morpheme denoting a separate motion event from the motion event denoted by the verb.

[21] The gloss to (38) suggests prior motion with purpose. Some contributors to this volume (e.g. Lovestrand and Ross, this volume, ch. 3) do not consider motion with purpose to be instances of associated motion. I do not distinguish motion with purpose from motion without an implication of purpose, largely because it is in general difficult to determine from sources whether purpose is part of the morphemes in question. The fact that examples may receive English translations implying purpose may reflect nothing more than an implicature in context, rather than purpose being part of the meaning of the morpheme in question.

(38) Ineseño Chumash (Chumashan; California, United States)
s-**akti**-kep'.
3SG-**COME**-bathe
'He comes to bathe.' (Applegate 1972: 339)

(39) kay-wun' siš-**akti**-naʔ.
3-PL 3DU-**COME**-go
'The two of them are coming.' (Applegate 1972: 554)

There are twelve languages among the languages described here that have concurrent AM morphemes that are also used as directionals, though three of these languages are ones where there are morphemes that code prior AM or concurrent AM, or function as directionals, namely Tetelcingo Nahuatl (§S7.2), Panamint (§S7.13), and Malecite-Passamaquoddy (§S29.13).[22] This is illustrated for Malecite-Passamaquoddy in (40) to (43). The ventive preverb pét- ~ péc- in Malecite-Passamaquoddy codes prior AM in (40), concurrent AM in (41) and serves as a directional in (42) and (43).

(40) Malecite-Passamaquoddy (Algonquian, Algic; northeastern U.S. and eastern Canada)
h-**pét**-təmím-a-l
3-**ARRIVE**-hire-DIRECT-3OBV
'he comes and hires the other' (LeSourd 1993: 282)

(41) **pét**-témo
ARRIVE-cry.3
'he comes crying' (LeSourd 1993: 283)

(42) **péc**-óhse
ARRIVE-walk.3
'he comes walking' (LeSourd 1993: 378)

(43) **pécí**-ph-â
ARRIVE-carry-passv.3
'he arrives being carried' (LeSourd 1993: 68)

---

22 In addition to these three languages where there are morphemes that serve as markers of prior or concurrent AM as well as functioning as directionals are four other languages where there are both prior AM morphemes that also function as directionals and distinct concurrent AM morphemes that also function as directionals, namely Sochiapan Chinantec (§S4.6), Cupeño (§S7.10), Northern Paiute (§S7.14), and Ojibwa (§S29.10).

There are additional examples in the Supplementary Materials illustrating morphemes coding either prior AM or concurrent AM but also functioning as a directional. Tetelcingo Nahuatl (§S7.2) has a ventive morpheme similar to that in Malecite-Passamaquoddy performing these three functions, illustrated in (S85) to (S89), while Panamint has both ventive and andative morphemes performing these three functions, illustrated in (S121) to (S124) for the ventive and (S125) to (S128) for the andative.

An example of a language with a morpheme that codes concurrent AM but not prior AM, but which also functions as a directional is Garifuna. The andative concurrent suffix in Garifuna illustrated above in (13) also functions as a directional in (44).

(44) Garifuna (Haurholm-Larsen 2016; Arawakan; Belize to Nicaragua)
 éybuge-**yna** l-ínya Aléru aban l-achúgera-gu-n yára.
 walk-**ANDAT** 3M-COP Alero then 3M-stumble-REFL-UNSPEC.TENSE there
 'Alero is walking down the road and then stumbles there.' (Haurholm-Larsen 2016: 236)

Similarly, the suffix -*si* in Lowland Tarahumara (§S7.5) codes andative concurrent AM in (45), but functions as an andative directional in (46).

(45) Lowland Tarahumara (Valdez Jara 2013; Tarahumaran, Uto-Aztecan; Mexico)
 maha-ga basí-**si**-le=turu.
 scare-CONT throw.stones.at-**ASSOC.MOT**-PAST=FOCUS
 'Scared, they went throwing stones at him.' (Valdez Jara 2013: 177)

(46) lége ma-**si**-é-ko warú rosobócu-go-me gasá-tiri.
 downwards run-**ASSOC.MOT**-PAST-IRREAL big grey-CONT-PTCPL grass-LOC
 'It ran away, the big grey one, by the grass.' (Valdez Jara 2013: 177)

There is one language in the sample with a ventive concurrent AM morpheme that also functions as a directional but that cannot be used for prior AM. The ventive concurrent suffix in Cupeño illustrated above in (29), also functions as a directional, as in (47).

(47) Cupeño (Cupan, Uto-Aztecan; California, USA)
 Mu=ku'ut pe' kawisi-sh pe-cha$hwin-**veneq** pe-yik.
 and=REPORT DET fox-NONPOSS 3SG-crawl-**MOTCA** 3SG-to
 'And it is said Fox came crawling toward him.' (Hill 2005: 271)

There are six languages in the set of languages examined where a random concurrent AM morpheme also serves as a random motion directional. The ambulative suffix *-t'ajun* in Huehuetla Tepehua (§S6.4) functions as a random concurrent AM suffix in (48) and as a directional in (49).

(48) Huehuetla Tepehua (Totonacan; Mexico)
*tiix laqxtu=ch   juu   lhii-t'aqap'a-**t'ajun**?*
why   alone=ALREADY REL   APPL-get.drunk-**AMB.IPFV**
'Why do you go around getting drunk?' (Kung 2007: 291)

(49) *maa   x-7alhtanan-**t'ajun**   juu laka-x-taanqaa   juu*
RPT   PAST-walk-**AMB.IPFV**   ART   CASE-3POSS-bottom   ART
laka-kin-lakakapen-an.
CASE-1POSS-coffee.field-PL
'He went around walking below my coffee fields.' (Kung 2007: 291)

Other examples in the Supplementary Materials illustrating this phenomena are (S42) and (S43) from Sochiapan Chinantec, (S110) and (S111) from Cupeño, (S129) and (S130) from Panamint, (S147) though (S150) from Northern Paiute, and (S267) and (S268) from Ojibwa.

All of the AM morphemes that also function as directionals code either prior AM or concurrent AM (or both). In other words, I did not find any instances among the languages examined of morphemes coding subsequent AM or prior plus subsequent AM that function as directionals.[23]

The fact that there are fewer instances of concurrent AM morphemes that also function as directionals compared to the number of prior AM morphemes that also function as directionals might seem surprising, given that directionals are in a sense inherently concurrent. I assume that this simply reflects the fact that prior AM morphemes are in general more common than concurrent AM morphemes (Guillaume 2016, Ross this volume).

There is an interesting pattern in the differences in frequency of the different types of direction among morphemes that serve both as markers of AM and as directionals. Namely, there are fourteen languages with ventive morphemes of this sort, but only ten languages with andative morphemes of this sort. It is possible that I overlooked andative morphemes of this sort in some languages, but in some

---

[23] While I found no languages in North America with subsequent AM morphemes that also function as directionals, I report in Dryer (this volume, ch. 4) on a number of languages of this sort spoken in Africa. See also Belkadi (2015).

of these languages, the sources contained numerous examples with ventive morphemes of this sort, suggesting that even if andative associated morphemes can be used as directionals, this happens less often. I suspect that this is because the default motion is andative, so that coding the less expected ventive motion is more common. Note that we do not find the same phenomenon when we compare all andative and all ventive morphemes, not just those used as directionals. Namely, 49 languages have at least one andative morpheme while only 44 have at least one ventive morpheme. I suspect that we find a different pattern here (more andative than ventive markers) since AM morphemes add motion and the most common type of added motion will be andative. But when used as directionals, there is no added motion, so it will often be implicit that the motion that is already denoted by the verb is andative and direction is only specified when the motion is ventive.

It is also not surprising that AM morphemes that do not code direction of movement would not also serve as directionals. However, one language where this does happen is Sochiapan Chinantec (§S4.6). This language has a prefix $ʔi^H$- illustrated in (2) above that codes concurrent AM, apparently without coding a direction (in contrast to a ventive prefix used for either prior AM or concurrent AM which does), which Foris (2000: 111) says "does not imply a direction". In (50), however, it does occur with a motion verb, but Foris implies that this use is restricted to motion by things that are inanimate.

(50) Sochiapan Chinantec (Chinantecan, Otomanguean; Mexico)
      hláʔ^H ré^M ʔi^H-cau^{LM} ʔmá^{M}li̠ʔ^{LM} lá^M.
      really well **MOT**-go.3SG wagon this
      'This wagon really moves along well.' (Foris 2000: 111)

Thus, while the coding of motion is apparently redundant in these cases, it is motivated by the less expected phenomenon of something inanimate moving. Although this prefix is combining with a motion verb, it is not clear that we should be analysing it as directional, since it is not clear that it codes direction, nor is it apparently functioning as a marker of AM, since it does not add a distinct motion event.

6 Co-occurrence of directionals with AM morphemes

The simple characterization of directional morphemes is that they are morphemes that combine with motion verbs to specify the direction of the motion. There are some languages in which directional morphemes occur with non-motion verbs that bear AM affixes. For example, (51) illustrates a prior AM suffix -*mira* in Southeastern Tepehuan (§S7.8).[24]

(51) Southeastern Tepehuan (Tepiman, Uto-Aztecan; Mexico)
... *day gu jajannuhl na-ñ-ich*
only ART clothes SUBORD-1SG-PAST.PFV
*tu-vopcoñ-**mira**-c.*
EXTENT-wash-**PRIOR.SG**-PAST.PUNC
'... I just went to wash clothes.' (Willett 1991: 115)

The same suffix occurs in (52), but in this case the verb is preceded by a ventive particle *bai*.

(52) *Mo=ñ* **bai'** *va-m-tañ-**mira**-'* *gu vacax* ...
uncertain=1SG **VENT** COMPL-2SG-order-**PRIOR.SG**-FUT ART meat
'I may come and buy some meat ...' (Willett 1991: 170)

This particle is apparently a pure directional morpheme since it only occurs with motion verbs. However, although the verb stem *tañ* 'order' is not a motion verb, the addition of an AM suffix in effect converts it into a motion verb.

Similarly, Karok (§S17) has a prior AM suffix -*ar̃*, illustrated in (53).

(53) Karok (Isolate; California, U.S.)
ʔíh-ar̃
dance-**GO.IN.ORDER.TO**
'to go in order to dance' (Bright 1957: 106)

In (54), a pure directional ventive suffix -*uk* is added to the form in (53), giving the direction of the prior motion.[25]

(54) *ʔíh-ar̃-uk*
dance-**GO.IN.ORDER.TO-VENT**
'to come in order to dance' (Bright 1957: 106)

---

24 Willett glosses the AM suffix -*mira* as 'OBJ' for 'objective', the idea that someone goes somewhere with the objective of performing the act denoted by the verb stem.
25 Note that although *ʔíh* 'dance' is in one sense a motion verb, -*ar̃* in (53) and (54) still counts as AM, since the motion it denotes is separate from the motion of the dancing.

13 Associated motion in North America (including Mexico and Central America) — 509

Similar phenomena are illustrated in (S139) in Panamint and in (S174) in Lower Chinook.

7 Inventories of AM morphemes

I turn finally to an examination of the relationship between the number of AM morphemes in a language and which of the four basic types of AM are coded.[26]

7.1 Languages with just one AM morpheme

As noted early in this chapter, in 41 of the languages examined there is a single AM morpheme. In 35 of these languages, the sole morpheme codes prior AM, while in six languages, it codes concurrent AM and in one language it codes either prior AM or concurrent AM. In the majority of languages (four out of the seven) where the sole morpheme codes concurrent AM (including the one language where it also codes prior AM), the morpheme also serves as a directional. But curiously, in only four of the 35 languages where the morpheme only codes prior AM does the morpheme also function as a directional.

For most of the languages with one AM morpheme, where that morpheme codes prior AM, it is unclear from sources whether the morpheme is andative or neutral with respect to direction, since the glosses using the English verb 'go' could be interpreted either way. However, in a few languages, it is clear that the morpheme does not code direction. For example, in Southeastern Tepehuan (§S7.8), there are two prior AM suffixes, one for singular subjects and one for plural subjects (but I treat this as one AM suffix since only one type of AM is coded and the difference between the two does not involve direction or AM). The singular form is illustrated in (52) above, the plural in (55). But note that the direction is coded separately by a ventive directional particle in (52) above that is absent in (55). This ventive particle is a pure directional particle, not an AM particle, since

---

[26] In counting the number of AM morphemes in a language, I count the number of distinct types of AM, including both the four basic types (prior, concurrent, etc.) and the different types of direction, as well in a few cases other aspects of the motion itself (like arriving, leaving, returning, going out, etc.). Where a language has AM morphemes that also code other grammatical features not directly related to motion, like tense-aspect or features of the subject, I do not count these as separate AM morphemes. For example, the Sochiapan Chinantec examples in (57) and (59) below illustrate distinct past andative and future andative prefixes, but I count them as one "morpheme" for the purpose of counting AM morphemes since only one AM value is coded.

it only occurs with verbs of motion. As noted above, however, in this case, it is the AM suffix on the verb that makes the verb count as a motion verb.[27]

(55) Southeastern Tepehuan (Tepiman, Uto-Aztecan; Mexico)
Tová-tam=ach tu-sava'n-**po**-' ji'cchi gu cosas.
turkey-place=1PL DUR-buy-**OBJ.PL**-FUT a.few ART things
'We're going to Turkey Town to buy a few things.' (Willett 1991: 130)

However, the fact that the ventive direction is coded by a ventive directional particle implies that the AM suffix on the verb is neutral as to direction. Mayo also has a prior AM morpheme that is neutral to direction, as described in §S7.6.

7.2 Languages with two AM morphemes

There are 24 languages in which I found exactly two AM morphemes and in 16 of these, the two express andative prior AM and ventive prior AM. In one other language with two AM morphemes (Wappo, discussed in §9.7 below and §S12), both code andative prior AM, with one specifying going out to do something, the other ordinary andative prior AM. One language, Tonkawa (§S23), has two AM morphemes, both of which code concurrent AM, one andative and one ventive. The remaining six languages with two AM morphemes combine two of the four basic types of AM. Four of them combine prior plus subsequent AM of the round trip type with another type of AM, three with concurrent AM (Huehuetla Tepehua (§S6.4), Tlachichilco Tepehua (§S6.5), Washo (§S19)) and one with subsequent AM (Misantla Totonac (§S6.3)). What is perhaps surprising is that there are only two languages with exactly two AM morphemes that combine prior AM with another of the other basic types, both with concurrent AM (Southeastern Tepehuan (§S7.8), Northern Paiute (§S7.14)). However, most of the languages with more than two AM morphemes combine prior AM with one of the other three basic types.

7.3 Languages with three or more AM morphemes

There are 20 languages in the sample with exactly three AM morphemes. In this section, however, I focus on languages with more than three AM morphemes since these are the languages with an unusually large number of AM morphemes (at

---

[27] Willett glosses the AM suffix -*mira* as 'OBJ' for 'objective'.

least unusual for North America). There are nine such languages in the sample. I will not discuss these in detail here since they are described in detail in the Supplementary Materials. Six of these have four AM morphemes, Sochiapan Chinantec (§S4.6), Comaltepec Chinantec (§S4.8), Cupeño (§S7.10), Nez Perce (§S9.2), Northern Sahaptin (§S9.3), and Meskwaki (§S29.9). One has five AM morphemes, Huasteca Nahuatl (§S7.1), one has six, Menomini (§S29.8), and one has seven, Panamint (§S7.13).[28] Two of these nine languages (Nez Perce, Northern Sahaptin) lack an andative-ventive contrast, though one of them, Nez Perce, has an andative prior AM morpheme and a ventive subsequent AM morpheme. Two of these nine languages (Nez Perce, Northern Sahaptin, both Plateau Penutian languages) have morphemes coding subsequent AM, two have morphemes coding return trip prior plus subsequent AM (Menomini, Meskwaki, both Algonquian languages) and two have morphemes coding passing-by prior plus subsequent AM (Nez Perce, Menomini). Five of the nine languages only have morphemes for prior AM and concurrent AM (Comaltepec Chinantec, Sochiapan Chinantec, Cupeño, Huasteca Nahuatl, and Panamint).

8 Imperative AM morphemes

A number of languages have AM morphemes that are exclusively imperative, as in the Luiseño (§S7.11) example in (56).

(56) Luiseño (Cupan, Uto-Aztecan; California, USA)
 yáx-ŋi   póy.
 say-GO.IMPRT   3SG.ACC
 'Go and tell him.' (Davis 1973: 151)

In Luiseño this appears to be the only AM morpheme. The Wakashan languages Makah (§S27.1) and Nuuchahnulth (§S27.2) are similar. In other languages, the imperative associated morpheme co-exists with other AM morphemes, as in Mam (§S3.4), Sochiapan Chinantec (§S4.6), Mutsun (§S8.3) and Barbareño Chumash (§S11.1).

---

28 These nine languages fall in four language families: Otomanguean (Sochiapan Chinantec and Comaltepec Chinantec), Uto-Aztecan (Huasteca Nahuatl, Cupeño, Panamint), Plateau Penutian (Nez Perce, Northern Sahaptin) and Algic (Meskwaki, Menomini).

9 Some AM oddities

In this section, I describe a few oddities found among the languages examined.

9.1 Co-occurring AM affixes in Sochiapan Chinantec

First, Sochiapan Chinantec (§S4.6) allows both ventive and andative morphemes to occur in the same word, as in (57) and (58) (though always with the ventive morpheme first).

(57) Sochiapan Chinantec (Chinantecan, Otomanguean; Mexico)
Má^M **kuá^M-ŋii^H-ʔnia**ʔ^M cú^M ca^{L}kuá^H hoʔ^H
PFV VENT.PAST-ANDAT.PAST-search.3 3PRO horse have.3
la^{L}kã̂u ...
in.vicinity.of
'S/he has returned from searching for her/his horse in the vicinity of [Quetzalapa].' (Foris 2000: 232)

(58) **kuá^M-ŋii^H-kiãu^M** cá^{M}huú^M θáï^M ʔi^L
VENT.PAST-ANDAT.PAST-bring.3 townspeople sand COMP
tioʔ^{HL} ...
be.PRES.PL
'The townspeople went and brought back sand [from along the river.]' (Foris 2000: 233)

Both of these morphemes, when used alone, code prior AM. But both (57) and (58) resemble cases of prior plus subsequent AM of the roundtrip type. This is explicit in the sentence gloss for (58) and implicit in (57), where the use of 'return' in the sentence gloss implies that the individual who moved went somewhere and then returned. However, the two examples differ in that the verb in (58) is a motion verb meaning 'take, bring', while the verb in (57) is not, meaning 'search'. It is possible, in fact, for the verb for 'take, bring' in (58) to occur with just an andative prefix, without the ventive prefix but apparently without a difference in meaning, as in (59), where there is an implication in context that there was subsequent motion.[29]

---

29 Note that the AM prefixes in Sochiapan Chinantec vary for tense. For example, (58) contains a past tense andative prefix -ŋii^h, while (59) has a future tense andative prefix -ca^l.

(59) ... ca^L-kiãu^M ʔi^L cĩ^H cii͂^{LM} hná^{HL}.
      ANDAT.FUT-bring.3   thing   place.3   head.1SG   1SG
      '[No one is able to] go and bring the thing which my head rests on.' (Foris 2000: 109)

Furthermore, since the ventive prefix is used not only for prior AM but also as as a directional, the ventive prefix in (58) could be interpreted as a directional, indicating the direction of the bringing, since this verb can mean either 'take' or 'bring'. Such an interpretation of the ventive prefix does not seem possible in (57). Although the combination of the andative prefix and the verb 'search' creates a motion verb meaning 'to go and search for', the ventive prefix cannot here be representing the direction of the motion, since the direction of the motion is andative. Rather the ventive here is apparently denoting the separate motion of returning. This is unexpected given the fact that when this prefix is a marker of AM (and does not co-occur with the andative prefix), it codes prior AM not subsequent AM.

It is also possible in Sochiapan Chinantec to combine a concurrent AM prefix that is neutral with respect to direction with a ventive prefix to express ventive concurrent AM, as in (60).

(60) ó^{LM} bíʔ^H má^M **ʔi͂^{H}-há^M**-héiʔ^{LM} cú^M hui^{LM}.
     yonder   AFFIRM   PFV   **MOT-VENT.PRES**-slash.3   3PRO   trail
     'From over there they are coming along slashing (the overgrowth beside) the trail.' (Foris 2000:111)

9.2 Co-occurring AM suffixes in Cupeño

Cupeño (§S7.10) has both an andative prior AM suffix -*lu(')* (glossed 'MOTP' for 'purposive motion') and a ventive prior AM suffix -*mi'aw* (glossed 'arrive'), illustrated in (61) and (62) respectively.

(61) Cupeño (Cupan, Uto-Aztecan; California, USA)
     Ne'=ne   *tewa̲-**lu**'-vichu-qa.*
     1SG.SUBJ=1SG.ERG   see-**MOTP**-DESID-PRES.SG
     'I want to go and see.' (Hill 2005: 269)

(62) *Hanaka   pe̲m-enew   tan-pe'-men-**mi'aw**.*
     again   3PL-with   dance-3PL-PL-**ARRIVE**
     'Again they came and danced with them.' (Hill 2005: 273)

The ventive suffix also functions as a directional, as in (63).

(63) *Yaw-**mi'aw**-wene   pem-ne̱mxa-y.*
 carry-**ARRIVE**-HABIT   3PL-treasure-OBJ
 'They would bring their treasures.' (Hill 2005: 274)

It is possible for both the ventive suffix *-mi'aw* used as a directional and the prior andative suffix to co-occur in the same verb, as in (64).

(64) *Mu=ku'ut   axwa̱-nga   aya   pi-yaw-**mi'aw-lu***
 and=REPORT   DEM.NONVIS-in   then   3SG.OBJ-carry-**ARRIVE-MOTP**
 ne-t   pe̱-ve.
 chief-NONPOSS   3SG-on
 'He went to bring it there to the chief.' (Hill 2005: 272)

The ventive suffix *-mi'aw* is being used as a directional in (64), similar to its use in (63). Although the combination of *yaw* 'carry' and the ventive suffix *-mi'aw* in (64) denotes a motion event of bringing, the motion denoted by the andative AM suffix *-lu* is a separate motion event, preceding the event of bringing.

9.3 Co-occurring AM prefixes in Kekchi

Kekchi (§S3.3) has three AM prefixes, two denoting prior AM (ventive *ol-* illustrated in (65) and andative *ox-*, illustrated in (66)) and one, *nume7-*, illustrated above in (22) and (25) that denotes prior plus subsequent AM of the passing-by type.

(65) Kekchi (Mayan; Guatemala)
 *x-**ol**-in-x-b'oq.*
 COMPL-**COME**-1SG.ABS-3SG.ERG-call
 'He came to call me.' (Stewart 1980: 73)

(66) *x-**ox**-in-x-b'oq.*
 COMPL-**GO**-1SG.ABS-3SG.ERG-call
 'He went to call me.' (Stewart 1980: 73)

The ventive and andative prior AM prefixes can co-occur with the passing-by prefix to indicate the direction of the motion while passing by, illustrated in (67) for the ventive prefix.

(67) Kekchi (Mayan; Guatemala)
*X-ol'-laj-ex-in'-**nume**'-sak'.*
COMPL-**COME**-REPET-2PL-1SG-**WHILE.PASSING**-hit
'As I was coming, I hit each one of you.' (Hún Macz 2005: 58)

It is not clear whether the andative and ventive prefixes can function as directionals with verbs where the motion is denoted by the verb itself rather than by the passing-by prefix.

9.4 Arriving AM in Comaltepec Chinantec

Comaltepec Chinantec (§S4.8) has two AM prefixes gi^L- and gui^L- based on arriving, the first of which means 'to arrive there and do something', the second 'to arrive here and do something'. These are illustrated in (68) and (69).

(68) Comaltepec Chinantec (Chinantecan, Otomanguean; Mexico)
$ko:^L$ $hmî:^{LH}$ ka^L-**gi^L**-$guä^L$ $tiú^H$ hui^{LM} $dó^M$.
one   day   PAST-**ARRIVE.THERE**-sit   Peter   road   there
'One day Peter arrived to sit there.' (Anderson 1989: 16)

(69) ka^L-**gui^L**-$hé:n^L$ $ʔį^L$ $zä^L$ $dó^M$ la^L-$ŋîn^M$ $ʔinʔ^{LH}$ $hóʔ^L$.
PAST-**ARRIVE.HERE**-bring   REL   person   that   various   kind   animal
'That man arrived here bringing all kinds of animals.' (Anderson 1989: 16)

At first sight, the prefix in (68) might just seem to be an ordinary prior AM andative prefix, but the language also has a distinct prior AM andative prefix, illustrated in (70).[30]

(70) ka^L-$ŋo^L$-$lä̂^L$=a.
COMPL-GO.COMPL.1SUBJ-bathe=1sg
'I went and bathed' (Anderson 1989: 15)

While the prefix in (68) seems to represent prior AM, the prefix in (69), appears to be functioning as a kind of concurrent AM morpheme, but in some respects like a subsequent AM morpheme in that the period of time of the act denoted by the

---

[30] See the distinction in Sipakapense between arriving here and arriving there illustrated in (15) and (16) above.

verb ends with the arrival and mostly precedes the arrival. Note that while a verb meaning 'bring', as in (69), is a kind of motion verb, the event of arriving and the event of bringing are clearly distinct since the latter mostly took place prior to the arrival.

9.5 Leaving AM in Huasteca Nahuatl

Huasteca Nahuatl (§S7.1) has a type of AM, illustrated in (71), that could be considered the opposite of the type illustrated in (62) above from Cupeño, in that the AM in Cupeño involves arriving while that here involves leaving.

(71) Huasteca Nahuatl (Beller and Beller 1979; Aztecan, Uto-Aztecan; Mexico)
*ni-h-wika-ti-**kisa**-s*
1SG-3SG-take-CONN-**LEAVE**-FUT
'I will take it on leaving.' (Beller and Beller 1979: 284)

Like the arriving AM prefix in Comaltepec Chinantec in the preceding section (§9.4), the meaning is a kind of concurrent AM, but the period of time for the act denoted by the verb extends longer than the motion of leaving.

See also the discussion of (14) above from Sipakapense, where the leaving is subsequent to the act denoted by the verb.

9.6 Go back and do in Chimariko

Chimariko (§S16) also has an AM morpheme that involves a more specialized directional motion, namely that of returning to do something. The suffix *-yuwu* denotes a type of andative prior AM, but apparently with the added presupposition that the motion is returning to a location that the subject has traveled from, as in (72).

(72) Chimariko (Isolate; California, U.S.)
*n-ixoda-**yuwu**.*
IMPRT.SG-watch-**RETURN**
'Go back and look at him!' (Jany 2009: 108)

Note that this resembles prior plus subsequent AM of the round trip type in that there is implicit motion in one direction followed by motion in the reverse direction, but is not an instance of this, since both the original motion and the return motion in the opposite direction precede the event denoted by the verb.

9.7 Go out to do something in Wappo

Wappo (§S12) has two andative prior AM suffixes. The first is an ordinary andative prior AM morpheme, while the second, illustrated in (73), has the meaning to 'go out of a building to do something', in other words with the additional presupposition that the one going was inside at the beginning of the motion.

(73) Wappo (Thompson et al 2006; Yuki-Wappo; California, U.S.)
 heyh-**imeʔ**
 saw-**GO.OUT.TO**
 'to go out to saw' (Thompson et al 2006: 65)

9.8 Doing while carrying in Achumawi

Achumawi (§S15.2) has a suffix which de Angulo and Freeland (1930) describe as meaning 'to do something while carrying something', but do not exemplify it.

9.9 Andative prefixes varying for distance traveled in Creek

Creek (§S25.3) has two andative prior AM prefixes, illustrated in (74) and (75), which have the unusual property of differing in whether the subject traveled a short distance or a longer distance.

(74) Creek (Muskogean; southeastern United States)
 ma   óywa   atĭː^{n}k-os-aːn   ił-hôył-in   ...
 that water   up.to-DIM-REF   **DIR.FAR**-stand.SG:RES.PFV-DS
 'He went to the water's edge and stood ...' (Martin 2011: 342)

(75) ła:-hopoy-itá
 DIR.SHORT-look.for-inf
 'to go a short distance and look for' (Martin 2011: 325)

Abbreviations

1OBJ	first person object	F	feminine
1PL	first person plural	FUT	future
1POSS	first person possessor	HABIT	habitual
1SG	first person singular	IDPH	ideophone
1SUBJ	first person subject	IMPRT	imperative
2PL	second person plural	INCOMPL	incompletive
2SG	second person singular	INF	infinitive
2SUBJ	second person subject	INTENS	intensifier
3	third person	IPFV	imperfective
3.ON	third person 'on'	IRREAL	irrealis
3DU	third person dual	LOC	locative
3M	third person masculine	M	masculine
3NOM	third person nominative	MOT	motion
3OBV	third person obviative	MOTCA	motion coming along VERBing
3PL	third person plural	MOTG	motion going
3POSS	third person possessive	MOTP	purposive motion
3PRO	third person pronoun	NEG	negative
3SG	third person singular	NOM	nominative
ABS	absolutive	NONPOSS	not possessed
ACC	accusative	NONVIS	nonvisible
AFFIRM	affirmative	OBJ	object
AMB	ambulative	PASSV	passive
ANDAT	andative	PFV	perfective
ANIM	animate	PL	plural
ART	article	PRES	present
BEN	benefactive	PROC	processive
CLSFR	classifier	PTCL	particle
COMP	complementizer	PTCPL	participle
COMPL	completive	PUNC	past punctiliar
CONN	connector/connective	QUOT	quotative
CONT	continuative	REC.PAST	recent past
COP	copula	REF	referential
DEM	demonstrative	REFL	reflexive
DESID	desiderative	REPET	repetitive
DET	determiner	REPORT	reportative
DIM	diminutive	RES.PFV	resultative perfective
DIR	directional	RETURN	returnative
DIR.FAR	directional far away	SG	singular
DIR.SHORT	directional short distance away	SUBORD	subordinate
DIRECT	direct (as opposed to inverse)	TERMIN	terminative
DISTR	distributive	TRANS	transitive
DS	different subject	UNSPEC	unspecified
DUR	durative	USPEC	underspecified verb
ELV	ellative	VBLZ	verbalizer
ERG	ergative	VENT	ventive
EXCL	exclusive		

Acknowledgements: I acknowledge helpful comments from Lea Brown, Harold Koch, Antoine Guillaume, Daniel Ross, and Jean-Christophe Verstraete on earlier drafts of this chapter. I also acknowledge assistance from Harald Hammarström in obtaining copies of some of my sources.

Appendix

Table 2 summarizes the data given in the Supplementary Materials for each language.

Table 2: Details summarizing data in the Supplementary Materials.

	Language	Family	Prior	Conc	Sbsq	P&S	#
§S1.1	Kuna	Chibchan	1				1
§S1.2	Guatusa	Chibchan	A, Vd				2
§S2	Garifuna	Arawakan		Ad			1
§S3.1	Tzutujil	Mayan	A, V		A		3
§S3.2	Sipakapense	Mayan			A,[31] V		3
§S3.3	Kekchí	Mayan	Ad, Vd[32]			Pas	3
§S3.4	Mam	Mayan	1				1
§S3.5	Ixil	Mayan	A, V			Pas	3
§S3.6	Quiché	Mayan	A, V				2
§S3.7	Chuj	Mayan	A, V			Pas	3
§S4.1	Ocuilteco	Otomanguean	1				1
§S4.2	Tilapa Otomí	Otomanguean	A,[33] V				3
§S4.3	Yosondúa Mixtec	Otomanguean	A, V				2
§S4.4	San Juan Guelavía Zapotec	Otomanguean	A, V				2
§S4.5	San Bartolome Zoogocho Zapotec	Otomanguean	A, V				2
§S4.6	Sochiapan Chinantec	Otomanguean	Ad, Vd	N, Rd			4
§S4.7	Tepetotutla Chinantec	Otomanguean	A, V			RT	3

---

31 Sipakapense has two andative subsequent particles, one of which has the added entailment of arriving somewhere.
32 The prior AM prefixes in Kekchi can co-occur with the passing-by prefix to denote the direction of the motion denoted by the passing by. It is unclear whether the prior AM prefixes can otherwise occur as directionals.
33 There are two andative prior AM markers in Tilapa Otomí. See §S4.2 for further information. See also Hernández-Green and Palancar (this volume, Ch 14) for a detailed description of associated motion in Otomian languages, including Tilapa Otomí.

Table 2 (continued)

	Language	Family	Prior	Conc	Sbsq	P&S	#
§S4.8	Comaltepec Chinantec	Otomanguean	A, V[34]				4
§S4.9	Lealao Chinantec	Otomanguean	A, V[35]				3
§S4.10	Palantla Chinantec	Otomanguean	A, V				2
§S5.1	Lowland Chontal	Tequistlatecan	A,[36] Vd				3
§S5.2	Tequixistlan Chontal	Tequistlatecan	1				1
§S6.1	Upper Necaxa Totonac	Totonacan		N		RT, Pas	3
§S6.2	Filomena Mata Totonac	Totonacan		N		RT, Pas	3
§S6.3	Misantla Totonac	Totonacan			A	RT	2
§S6.4	Huehuetla Tepehua	Totonacan		Rd		RT	2
§S6.5	Tlachichilco Tepehua	Totonacan		N		RT	2
§S7.1	Huasteca Nahuatl	Uto-Aztecan	A, V, Ac, Vc[37]	Ap, Vp			5
§S7.2	Tetelcingo Nahuatl	Uto-Aztecan	Vcd[38]	Vpd			1
§S7.3	Cora	Uto-Aztecan	Ad				1
§S7.4	Central Tarahumara	Uto-Aztecan		N			1
§S7.5	Lowland Tarahumara	Uto-Aztecan		Ad			1
§S7.6	Mayo	Uto-Aztecan	1				1
§S7.7	Yaqui	Uto-Aztecan	1				1
§S7.8	Southeastern Tepehuan	Uto-Aztecan	1	N			2
§S7.9	Eudeve	Uto-Aztecan	1				1
§S7.10	Cupeño	Uto-Aztecan	A, Vd	Vd, Rd			4
§S7.11	Luiseño	Uto-Aztecan	1				1
§S7.12	Shoshone	Uto-Aztecan	Ad				1
§S7.13	Panamint	Uto-Aztecan	Acd,	Apd, Vpd,[39]			7

---

34 Comaltepec Chinantec has two andative prior AM markers and two ventive prior AM markers. The difference for both pairs of markers is that one member of the pair code arriving and doing something, while the other seems to be an ordinary prior AM marker.

35 Lealao Chinantec has three prior AM marker, an andative, a ventive, and one involving arriving.

36 Lowland Chontal has two andative prior AM markers; it is not clear what the difference is.

37 Huasteca Nahuatl has five AM markers. Two are andative and ventive prior AM suffixes. Two of the others andative and ventive, with either prior or concurrent AM. The last is like the previous two, but with the motion of leaving.

38 Tetelcingo Nahuatl has a ventive prefix that covers both prior AM and concurrent AM.

39 Panamint has seven concurrent AM suffixes. Two of them are andative and ventive suffixes respectively which also code prior AM and function as directionals. Three of them code random

Table 2 (continued)

	Language	Family	Prior	Conc	Sbsq	P&S	#
			Vcd	Nd, R, Rd			
§S7.14	Northern Paiute	Uto-Aztecan	Ad	Rd			2
§S8.1	Sierra Miwok	Utian	A, V		V		3
§S8.2	Lake Miwok	Utian	1				1
§S8.3	Mutsun	Utian	A, V				2
§S9.1	Klamath	Plateau Penutian	A, V				2
§S9.2	Nez Perce	Plateau Penutian	A1		V	Pas	4
§S9.3	Northern Sahaptin	Plateau Penutian	A	N, As	Ac		4
§S9.4	Yakima	Plateau Penutian		N			1
§S10.1	Lower Chinook	Chinookan	1				1
§S10.2	Kathlamet	Chinookan	1				1
§S11.1	Barbareño Chumash	Chumashan	1				1
§S11.2	Ineseño Chumash	Chumashan	A, Vd				2
§S12	Wappo	Yuki-Wappo	1[40]				2
§S13	Yana	Isolate	A, V	N			3
§S14	Kashaya	Pomoan		N			1
§S15.1	Atsugewi	Palaihnihan	1				1
§S15.2	Achumawi	Palaihnihan	1	N[41]			3
§S16	Chimariko	Isolate	Ad[42]				1
§S17	Karok	Isolate	1				1
§S18	Shasta	Isolate	1				1
§S19	Washo	Isolate	1c	Np		RT	2
§S20	Acoma	Keresan	1				1
§S21	Kiowa	Kiowa-Tanoan	1				1
§S22	Caddo	Caddoan	1				1
§S23	Tonkawa	Isolate		Ad, Vd			2
§S24	Natchez	Isolate	1				1
§S25.1	Koasati	Muskogean	A, V				2
§S25.2	Choctaw	Muskogean	A, V				2
§S25.3	Creek	Muskogean	A,[43] Vd				3

AM, one of which can also be used as a directional. The description of the remaining two suggests that they are neutral with respect to direction, but both can also be used as directionals where they code random direction.

40 Wappo has two prior AM suffixes, one of which specifically means 'go out and do something'.
41 Achumawi has two concurrent AM suffixes, where the difference in meaning is not clear.
42 The andative prior AM suffix in Chimariko has the added semantic component of returning to do something.
43 Creek has two andative prior AM prefixes, differing in that one denotes a shorter distance of the motion, the other a longer distance.

Table 2 (continued)

	Language	Family	Prior	Conc	Sbsq	P&S	#
§S26.1	Seneca	Iroquoian	A, V	R			3
§S26.2	Oneida	Iroquoian	1				1
§S26.3	Cayuga	Iroquoian	1				1
§S26.4	Mohawk	Iroquoian	1				1
§S26.5	Wyandot	Iroquoian	1				1
§S26.6	Cherokee	Iroquoian	A, V	R			3
§S27.1	Makah	Wakashan	1				1
§S27.2	Nuuchahnulth	Wakashan	A,[44] V				3
§S27.3	Kwak'wala	Wakashan			Ad		1
§S29.1	Yurok	Algic	1				1
§S29.2	Wiyot	Algic	A, V				2
§S29.3	Blackfoot	Algic	1				1
§S29.4	Arapaho	Algic	A, V				2
§S29.5	Cheyenne	Algic	A, V				2
§S29.6	Shawnee	Algic	1				1
§S29.7	Kickapoo	Algic	A, V				2
§S29.8	Menomini	Algic	A, Vd	N, R		RT, Pas	6
§S29.9	Meskwaki	Algic	A, V	R		RT	4
§S29.10	Ojibwa	Algic	A, Vd	Rd			3
§S29.11	Cree	Algic	A, Vd				2
§S29.12	Montagnais	Algic	1				1
§S29.13	Malecite-Passamaquoddy	Algic	1, Vcd	Vpd		RT	3
§S30.1	West Greenlandic	Eskimo-Aleut	1				1
§S30.2	Central Alaskan Yupik Eskimo	Eskimo-Aleut	1				1
§S30.3	Siberian Yupik Eskimo	Eskimo-Aleut	1				1

Key to Table 2:
Abbreviations for column headings:

Conc   Concurrent
Sbsq   Subsequent
P&S   Prior plus subsequent

---

[44] Nuuchahnulth has two andative prior AM prefixes; it is not clear what the difference in meaning is.

Abbreviations for annotations in the prior AM column:

1	there is only one prior AM marker and it is either neutral with respect to direction or it is not clear whether it is neutral or andative
A	andative prior AM
V	ventive prior AM
A, 1	two prior AM markers, one andative, one neutral with respect to direction
Ac	andative marker for both prior AM and concurrent AM
Vc	ventive marker for both prior AM and concurrent AM
1c	marker that is used for both prior AM and concurrent AM that is apparently neutral with respect to direction
Ad	andative marker for both prior AM and as a directional
Vd	ventive marker for both prior AM and as a directional
Acd	andative marker that is used for prior AM, concurrent AM or as a directional
Vcd	ventive marker that is used for prior AM, concurrent AM or as a directional

Abbreviations for annotations in the concurrent AM column (Conc):

N	concurrent AM that may be neutral, though it might be andative or random
R	random concurrent AM
A	andative concurrent AM
V	ventive concurrent AM
Ap	andative marker for both prior AM and concurrent AM
Vp	ventive marker for both prior AM and concurrent AM
Np	marker of prior or concurrent AM that appears to be neutral with respect to direction
Ad	andative marker for concurrent AM that also functions as a directional
Nd	marker for concurrent AM that is neutral with respect to direction, but also functions as a directional
Rd	random marker for concurrent AM that also functions as a directional
Apd	andative marker that functions as a marker of prior AM, concurrent AM, or as a directional
Vpd	ventive marker that functions as a marker of prior AM, concurrent AM, or as a directional
Ns	marker of concurrent AM that appears to be neutral with direction but that also functions as a directional

Abbreviations for annotations in the subsequent AM column (Sbsq):

A	andative subsequent AM
V	ventive subsequent AM
Ac	andative marker for both concurrent AM and subsequent AM

Abbreviations for annotations in the prior plus subsequent AM column (P&S):

RT round trip prior plus subsequent AM
Pas passing by prior plus subsequent AM

References

Not including references cited only in the Supplementary Materials; a separate list of references for those items cited in the Supplementary Materials occurs in the Supplementary Materials.

Anderson, Judi L. 1989. *Comaltepec Chinantec syntax*. Dallas: Summer Institute of Linguistics and the University of Texas at Arlington.
Angulo, Jaime de & Lucy S. Freeland. 1930. The Achumawi language. *International Journal of American Linguistics* 6. 77–120.
Applegate, Richard Brian. 1972. *Ineseño Chumash grammar*. University of California at Berkeley doctoral dissertation.
Barrett, Edward R. 1999. *A grammar of Sipakapense Maya*. Austin: University of Texas at Austin doctoral dissertation.
Beck, David. 2004. *A grammatical sketch of Upper Necaxa Totonac*. München: Lincom.
Belkadi, Aicha. 2015. AM with deictic directionals: a comparative overview. *SOAS Working Papers in Linguistics* 17: 49–76.
Belkadi, Aicha. This volume, chapter 5. Deictic directionality as associated motion: Motion, complex events and event integration in African languages.
Beller, Richard & Patricia Beller. 1979. Huasteca Nahuatl. In Ronald W. Langacker (ed.), *Studies in Uto-Aztecan grammar 2: Modern Aztec grammatical sketches*, 199–306. Dallas: Summer Institute of Linguistics and the University of Texas at Arlington.
Bommelyn, Loren Me'lashne. 1997. *The prolegomena to the Tolowa Athabaskan grammar*. University of Oregon MA thesis.
Bright, William. 1957. *The Karok language*. Berkeley and Los Angeles: University of California Press.
Caballero, Gabriela. 2008. *Choguita Raramuri (Tarahumara) phonology and morphology*. University of California at Berkeley doctoral dissertation.
Cash, Phillip. 2004. Nez Perce verb morphology. Ms.
Constenla Umaña, Adolfo. 1998. *Gramática de lengua Guatusa*. Heredia, Costa Rica: EUNA.
Davis, John F. 1973. *A partial grammar of simplex and complex sentences in Luiseño*. University of California at Los Angeles doctoral dissertation.
Dayley, Jon P. 1989. *Tümpisa (Panamint) Shoshone grammar*. Berkeley and Los Angeles: University of California Press.
Dryer, Matthew S. This volume, chapter 4. Associated motion and directionals: Where they overlap.
England, Nora C. 1983. *A grammar of Mam, a Mayan language*. Austin: University of Texas Press.
Fleck, David W. 2003. *A grammar of Matses*. Rice University doctoral dissertation.
Foris, David P. 2000. *A grammar of Sochiapan Chinantec*. Dallas: Summer Institute of Linguistics and the University of Texas at Arlington.

Guillaume, Antoine. 2016. Associated motion in South America: Typological and areal perspectives. *Linguistic Typology* 20: 81–177.
Hanson, Rebecca. 2010. *A grammar of Yine (Piro)*. LaTrobe University doctoral dissertation.
Haurholm-Larsen, Steffen. 2016. *A grammar of Garifuna*. Universität Zürich doctoral dissertation.
Hernández-Green, Néstor & Enrique L. Palancar. This volume, chapter 14. Associated motion in the Otomi family.
Hill, Jane A. 2005. *A grammar of Cupeño*. Berkeley and Los Angeles: University of California Press.
Hún Macz, Carlos Federico. 2005. *Historia de la lengua Kekchí*. Universidad de San Carlos de Guatemala MA thesis.
Jacobs, Melville. 1931. A sketch of Northern Sahaptin grammar. *University of Washington Publications in Anthropology* 4. 85–292.
Jacobsen, William H. Jr. 1964. *A grammar of the Washo language*. University of California at Berkeley doctoral dissertation.
Jany, Carmen. 2009. *Chimariko grammar: areal and typological perspective*. Berkeley and Los Angeles: University of California Press.
Koch, Harold. 1984. The category of 'associated motion' in Kaytej. *Language in Central Australia* 1: 23–34.
Koch, Harold. This volume, chapter 7. Associated motion in the Pama-Nyungan languages of Australia.
Kung, Susan Smythe. 2007. *A descriptive grammar of Huehuetla Tepehua*. Austin: University of Texas at Austin doctoral dissertation.
LeSourd, Philip S. 1993. *Accent and syllable structure in Passamaquoddy*. New York: Garland.
Levinson, Stephen C. and David P. Wilkins. 2006. Patterns in the data: Toward a semantic typology of spatial description. In Levinson & Wilkins (eds.), *Grammars of space: Explorations in cognitive diversity*, 512–552. Cambridge: Cambridge University Press.
Lovestrand, This volume, chapter 3. Serial verb constructions and motion semantics.
Martin, Jack B. 2011. *A grammar of Creek (Muskogee)*. Lincoln: University of Nebraska Press.
McFarland, Teresa Ann. 2009. *The phonology and morphology of Filomeno Mata Totonac*. University of California at Berkeley doctoral dissertation.
O'Connor, Loretta. 2007. Motion, transfer, and transformation: *The grammar of change in Lowland Chontal*. Amsterdam: John Benjamins.
Oswalt, Robert L. 1961. *A Kashaya grammar (Southwestern Pomo)*. University of California at Berkeley doctoral dissertation.
Ross, Daniel. This volume, chapter 2. A cross-linguistic survey of associated motion and directionals.
Stewart, Stephen. 1980. *Gramática Kekchí*. Guatemala: Editorial Academica Centro Americana.
Thompson, Sandra A., Joseph Sung-Yul Park & Charles N. Li. 2006. *A reference grammar of Wappo*. Berkeley and Los Angeles: University of California Press.
Thornes, Timothy Jon. 2003. *A Northern Paiute grammar and texts*. University of Oregon doctoral dissertation.
Valdez Jara, Yolanda. 2013. *Predication in Rarómuri (Urique Tarahumara)*. University of Oregon doctoral dissertation.
Westley, David O. 1991. *Tepetotutla Chinantec syntax*. Studies in Chinantec languages 5. Dallas: Summer Institute of Linguistics and the University of Texas at Arlington.
Willett, Marie Louise. 2003. *A grammatical sketch of Nxa'amxcin (Moses-Columbia Salish)*. University of Victoria doctoral dissertation.

Néstor Hernández-Green and Enrique L. Palancar
14 Associated motion in the Otomi family

Abstract: In this paper, we introduce the associated motion systems that we find in the Otomi family of languages (Oto-Manguean; Oto-Pamean; Mexico). We focus on three different languages: Acazulco Otomi, Tilapa Otomi and Querétaro Otomi. The three languages vary in degree of morphological conservatism: while in Acazulco Otomi and Tilapa Otomi the expression of associated motion makes for a robust system, having categories such as ventive, andative, adlocative and even ambulative, in Querétaro Otomi only the ventive has persisted and only restricted to the third person. Most AM categories in Otomi languages can also be used as directionals, i.e. to encode direction with motion verbs. From a typological point of view, what is most interesting about the associated motion system in Otomi is the formal encoding of the different distinctions. This is because there is no dedicated marking to realize them. The encoding is achieved through morphologically conditioned allomorphy and stem alternants. Besides, the system also has a substantial number of paradigmatic gaps. Towards the end of the paper and to provide an areal context for the Otomi system, we also briefly introduce the systems found in two other Mesoamerican language families: Nahuatl and Chinantec, which are also known to have systems involving associated motion.

Keywords: Otomi, associated motion, inflectional morphology, spatial semantics

1 Introduction

Otomi (Oto-Manguean; Oto-Pamean) is a family of indigenous languages or 'language variants' from Central Mexico spoken in total by c. 300,000 people, although the number of speakers per variant ranges dramatically from less than half a dozen speakers for Tilapa Otomi to about 80,000 for Mezquital Otomi. From a phonological point of view, Otomi languages are tonal and have a rich inventory of vowels and consonants. Morphosyntactically, they are head-marking. Syntactically, their basic word order is VO and they tend to have very few prepositions.

Néstor Hernández-Green, Centro de Investigaciones y Estudios Superiores en Antropología Social, Unidad Ciudad de México, nestorhgreen@gmail.com
Enrique L. Palancar, Laboratoire Structure et Dynamique des Langues (CNRS, INALCO & IRD), Enrique.PALANCAR@cnrs.fr

https://doi.org/10.1515/9783110692099-014

Verbs constitute the most morphologically complex word class and they fall into several classes: they can inflect for person, number, tense, aspect, mood, as well as for associated motion categories. In this chapter, we describe the morphology and use of these associated motion categories in three Otomi language variants, namely: Tilapa Otomi (less than a dozen speakers, critically endangered), Acazulco Otomi (~300 speakers, severely endangered), and Querétaro Otomi (~33,000 speakers, definitely endangered; see degrees of endangerment in UNESCO 2003). Tilapa Otomi and Acazulco Otomi are morphologically conservative in that they have retained much of the rich inflectional distinctions present in the old form of the common language spoken in the 16th century and described in Cárceres (1580/1907). In contrast, Querétaro Otomi pertains to a chain of very innovative dialects, which in Palancar (2013) have been treated under the umbrella of one language called 'Northern Otomi'. As we will show, the innovative character (in the sense of getting rid of old distinctions) of Querétaro Otomi can be seen in the fact that the AM system in this language is much simpler than the one we find in the other two languages.

The phenomenon labeled as 'associated motion' (henceforth AM) was first described for Kaytej (Pama-Nyungan; Australia) by Koch (1984). More recently, based on data from a set of South American languages, Guillaume (2009; 2016) proposes an elaborate typology of AM that (among others) includes the following parameters: (a) orientation of motion with respect to a reference point; (b) temporal relation between the verb action and the motion event; and (c) the moving argument, whether its function is of S, A, or P. For the purpose of this volume, a fourth parameter concerning the aspectual realization (perfective vs. imperfective) of the verb event is added (see Guillaume & Koch, this volume), and AM is defined as a verbal grammatical category, separate from tense, aspect, mood and direction, whose function is to associate, in different ways, semantic notions of translational motion to a (generally non-motion) verb event.

Four different AM categories can be found in the grammar of Otomi languages: **ventive** (i.e. toward the deictic center); **andative** (i.e. any direction, except toward the deictic center);[1] **ambulative** (i.e. random direction); and **adlocative**. The adlocative is an AM category that profiles the arrival of the subject at a location after a motion event, without encoding a specific orientation with respect to the speaker. The ventive and the andative categories can have either directional (with motion verbs) or associated motion functions (with non-motion verbs; see Dryer,

---

[1] We use the term 'andative' to refer to motion in an unspecified direction, although other authors use it to refer to motion specified as "away from the deictic center" (see Guillaume & Koch, this volume).

this volume, ch 4). AM morphology in Otomi languages has various degrees of inflectional complexity according to which language variant and which aspects of inflection are considered. Some dimensions of morphological complexity include (a) number of (morphological) elements (in the system and in a word); (b) principles of morphological combination; and (c) complexity of exponence (Guillaume 2016: 109–113). In §5.4, we introduce dimensions that are relevant to Otomi morphology in more detail, namely, cumulative, zero and empty exponence, allomorphic exponence, and paradigmatic stem alternations.

This chapter is organized as follows. In the next section, we introduce the basics of Otomi verbal inflectional morphology. In §3, we elaborate and illustrate the semantics and uses of the different AM categories found in this family. The extensions of AM categories to domains other than space are presented in §4. In §5, we concentrate on the formal aspects of AM morphology. §6 concludes.

2 Basics of the inflectional morphology of Otomi verbs

The basic inflectional categories of Otomi verbs are tense, aspect, mood, person, and number. Other inflectional categories include AM (discussed in the following sections), location, and adverbial inflection (Palancar 2012b; Hernández-Green 2016). Adverbial inflection involves the cross-referencing of focused adjuncts in the verbal complex and, as we show in §4, it interacts paradigmatically with AM in Tilapa Otomi. Verbal lexemes in Otomi are organized in conjugation classes (or inflectional classes, in the sense of Aronoff 1994). Such classes further involve some of the diathesis alternations in these languages. Verb stems may display (often lexicalized) noun incorporation.

TAM values are realized in the verb via pre-verbal markers that we call 'inflectional formatives'. Inflectional formatives further encode person of subject in a cumulative fashion, although the indexation for 3rd person subject is achieved indirectly for active verbs (i.e. the formatives used when the subject is 3rd person encode other information than person).[2] The formatives have some degree of

---

[2] The fact that inflectional formatives used with a 3rd person subject do not inherently encode information about 3rd person can be seen in the inflection of patientive and stative verbs. Such verbs encode person of subject by means of suffixes (with the same set that encodes object for transitive verbs). However, those verbs still select the same inflectional formatives used with active verbs when the subject is 3rd person, e.g. QRO active *xi=ma* {[3s]PRF=SS\go} 'she/he's/they're gone' vs. patientive *xi=no-'-a='i* {PRF=become.fat-2s$_o$-B=2s$_o$} 'you're fat'.

internal structure, and some authors (Andrews 1993; Hernández-Green 2015) have attempted an internal segmentation, but for the most part the exponence of TAM and person of subject remains non-dissociable. Table 1 shows three basic (discourse frequent) TAM subparadigms in the three focal languages. In the table, the subparadigm for the irrealis corresponds to the perfective irrealis in Acazulco and Tilapa Otomi; in Querétaro Otomi there is no aspect distinction in this mood.

Table 1: Basic TAM/person combinations in Otomi (Palancar 2009a, 2012a; Hernández-Green 2015).

mood	tense~aspect	person	Acazulco Otomi	Tilapa Otomi	Querétaro Otomi
REALIS	IPFV~PRS	1st	drá[3]	tŕá	dí
		2nd	grá	grá	gí
		[3rd]	ra	ra	[Ø]
	PFV~PST	1st	dí	tú̱	dá
		2nd	gí	gú̱	gá
		[3rd]	bi	bi	bi
IRR	(PFV)	1st	gu̱	gu̱	ga
		2nd	gi	gi	gi
		[3rd]	da	ta	da

Monosyllabic inflectional formatives (like the ones in Table 1) procliticize to the stem when the verbal complex occurs at the beginning of an intonational phrase (indicated by #), as in (1a), but they also often encliticize to the previous word in other circumstances, as shown in (1b). In Acazulco and Tilapa Otomi, there are also disyllabic formatives. These behave more like independent words, as shown in (1c). The label "{txt}" indicates that the example comes from a natural text.

(1) a. **#bi**=mbenti
ACA   [3S]PFV=NAS\send
         'He sent him.' {txt}

---

[3] Practical orthography of Otomi (when deviant from IPA; slightly modified from INALI 2014): <ä> [ã], <ch> [tʃ], <ę> [ɛ], <f> [pʰ, ɸ], <h> [h, ʰ], <'> [ʔ, ˀ], <j> [kʰ, x], <ñ> [ɲ], <o̱> [ɘ], <r> [ɾ], <ř> [ɻ], <u> [u, w, ʷ], <u̱> [ɨ], <x> [ʃ], <y> [j], <ý> [dʒ], <ž> [ʒ].

b. #óra=**bi** mbenti
   now=[3S]PFV NAS\send
   'Then he sent him.'

c. **radi** xah=a
   [3S]IPFV pray=ENCL
   'They're praying.' {txt}

The encoding of AM is also achieved by inflectional formatives, but by a special set that also encodes TAM and person/number of subject, as is shown in (2). We treat the formal encoding of AM in §5.

(2) a. **dú**=tû=ga='mbe=yu   ză
ACA 1S.PFV.VEN=have.on.back=1=PL.EXCL=DET.DIST.PL wood
   'We brought firewood.' {txt}

b. **tár**=ʰtsi='a
TIL 1S.AND=eat=3SG_PRO
   'I'm eating it as I go.' {txt}

In §5, we will further show that inflectional formatives have allomorphs conditioned by conjugation class. For example, the two different markers of the ventive imperfective in (3) are allomorphs, i.e. their selection responds to the fact that the two verbs belong to different classes.

(3) a. **ba**=hyon=nu   jö'i
ACA [3S]IPFV.VEN=PAL\look.for=DET.DIST.SG person
   'That man is coming looking for him.' {txt}
   (Hernández-Green 2015: 376)

b. ta=**badi** njungi=a='u
   INT=[3S]IPFV.VEN be.in.a.line=ENCL=3PL_PRO
   'They were even coming in a line.' {txt}
   (Hernández-Green 2015: 376)

In this section, we have introduced the basics of Otomi inflection that are necessary to understand the encoding of AM. We get back to details about the formal aspects of encoding such categories in §5. In the following sections, we focus on the semantics of AM categories.

3 The semantics of AM in Otomi

AM categories such as ventive and andative are reckoned with respect to the deictic center, others are not. In Otomi languages, the deictic center is firmly grounded on the location of the speaker, and it is not transferrable to other locations as it can be, for instance, in English (e.g. *are you coming to my party?* said from a location other than the place where the party takes place). The deictic center is often extendable to the speaker's home or village (as long as the speaker is located in those places at the moment of speaking). In narratives, it can occasionally be transferred to a location where the speaker happened to be at in the past. As it is common in languages with AM inflection (see Dryer, this volume, ch 4), some AM markers in Otomi can further have directional functions.

In the following sections, §3.1 to §3.4, we describe each of the AM categories that are found in the focal languages of this study. In §3.5 and §3.6, respectively, we focus on aspects about the moving argument in AM constructions, and on the temporal relation between the motion event and the situation described by the verb (i.e. prior, concurrent or subsequent motion; see Guillaume 2016).

3.1 Ventive

AM inflection in the three focal languages includes a ventive. The ventive in Otomi can have interpretations where the motion occurs prior, concurrent, or subsequent to the situation described by the verb (see §3.6 about the circumstances and categories where each of such cases occurs). The examples in (4) illustrate the function of the ventive in concurrent motion scenes. In examples (4a) and (4b) the ventive inflection indicates that the event described by the non-motion verb occurs as the agent moves toward the deictic center: in (4a), the flaring of an evil spirit's flames as he came flying towards the village; and in (4b), the action of looking for the addressee. The ventive is used as a directional in (4c), which refers to the action of walking by a man and his wife while they were coming back home.

(4)   a.   *ta=**badi***   *uãngi=k'ụ*   *tsibi*
ACA   INT=[3S]IPFV.**VEN**   flutter=DET.NV.PL   fire
             'Those flames come flaring intensely.' {txt}
             (Hernández-Green 2017: 298)

TIL   b.   ***tátụ***   *hon-k'i*
         1S.IPFV.**VEN**   look.for-2O
         'I'm looking for you (as I'm coming here).' {txt}

QRO	c.	ya	**ba**=ñ-'o=wi		ma	n'agi
		PRTCL	[3S]PST.**VEN**=MID-walk=DU		another	once

'He walked hither with her once more.' {txt}
(Palancar 2009b: 52)

The inflectional formatives of the ventive can also be used in prior motion scenes, where the situation described by the verb occurs after (and not simultaneous to) the motion event. This is illustrated in (5). In (5a), the speaker is referring to the people who came to her place and gave her the news that her brother had passed away; in (5b) the people in question have to come to a given place to exhibit their textiles; and in (5c), the act of arriving precedes the act of giving.[4]

(5) a. ACA   tŏk'o=**ba**   xih-ki=ga='mbe=a
            who=[3S]IPFV.**VEN**   tell-1O=1=PL.EXCL=ENCL
   'Those who were coming to tell us (the bad news).' {txt}
   (Hernández-Green 2015: 377)

TIL b. ñü=k'u̱   to=ra ^{h}petsu̱=yí   sku̱   kostura,
        PRTCL=DEM.PL.NV$_{PRO}$ who=[3S]IPFV   keep.AS=PL.3POSS   DIM   sewing
        bati   presenta=k'u̱
        [3S]IPFV.**VEN**   present=DEM.PL.NV$_{PRO}$
   'Those who have sewn goods of their making,
   bring them and present them!' {txt}

QRO c. **ba**='ra^h-k=he=n'a   'bada   t'ëi
        [3S]PST.**VEN**=give.to.1/2-1DAT=1PL.EXCL=one   recipient   atole
   'She came and gave us a recipient full of *atole*.' {txt}
   (Palancar 2009a: 446)

Finally, example (6) shows a case where the ventive is used to indicate motion that is subsequent to the event described by the verb, as for example the verb *tu̱ki* 'pick (fruit)' in Querétaro Otomi. This kind of interpretation has been observed only in the imperative; similar uses of the ventive are also possible in both Acazulco and Tilapa Otomi.[5]

---

[4] In these examples, the AM categories only indicate that the motion is prior to the situation described by the verb; the purposive semantics observed in the examples is a result of pragmatic implicature.
[5] Subsequent temporal relations in imperative constructions with ventive markers are also observed in Opo (Otero, this volume).

(6) **ba**=tu̱-g-a=gi='na
QRO IMP.**VEN**=pick-1O-B=1=QUOT
'Pick it (and bring it to me).' {txt}
(Palancar 2009: 197)

Direction with respect to the deictic center is not specified in the semantics of the verbs inflected in the ventive in the examples above. In Otomi languages, the ventive inflection is obligatory (when paradigmatically available) for verbs that describe movement toward a deictic center. This is illustrated in (7) with two instances of the verb *ëhë* 'come' where the AM markers are used with directional function. As shown in (8) with the verb *pá* 'go', verbs describing movement away from the deictic center do not accept the ventive.[6]

(7) a. ***ra/ba**=ëhë*
ACA [3S]IPFV/[3S]IPFV.**VEN**=come
'S/he comes.' {txt}
(Hernández-Green 2015: 385)

TIL b. 'a   ke   ***grá/gwá**='ëh=a?*
         how COP 2.IPFV/2.IPFV.**VEN**=come.AS=ENCL
'How is it that I was going to come?' {txt}

(8) ***ba**=pá*
ACA [3S]IPFV.**VEN**=go
Intended reading: 'S/he's going toward here.'

The inflectional formatives of the ventive in the perfective aspect are often also used to convey an exlocative reading in all three focal languages. The **'exlocative'** is used to indicate that the scene described by the verb occurs at a location other than the location where the speaker is located at the time of speaking.[7] Although this semantic extension of the ventive is not an AM category itself, it is discussed here because it seems to be formally and/or diachronically related to the ventive in Otomi, as well as in other languages such as Oneida (Ross, this volume) and Jóola Fóoñi (Creissels & Bassène, this volume).

---

[6] Verb forms where the motion given by the AM inflection contradicts the motion specified in the semantics of the verb are not acceptable, regardless of how pragmatically acceptable they may appear given the appropriate context.
[7] The exlocative would be equivalent to the category that Ross (this volume) refers to as the 'distal locational'.

Exlocative usages of the ventive are illustrated in (10) in Acazulco Otomi when compared to (9). While in (9), the ventive describes motion toward the deictic center (i.e. its more basic reading), in (10) the same ventive formatives are used to describe a situation that took place in a location other than the deictic center.

(9) a. *ja=**bú***   'mbent=k'ų   súndaro='na
ACA   and=[3S]PFV.**VEN**   IMPRS\send=DET.NV.PL   soldier=QUOT
     'And they say they sent the army (to this town).' {txt}

     b. *kéra=**du***   tą́h=nų
       if.only=[3S]IRR.PFV.**VEN**   fall=3SG.DIST
       'If only that (apple) would fall (my way).' {txt}

(10) a. *xo=**bú***   'mbá̱'t'i=a
ACA   so=[3S]PFV.**VEN**_{EXLOC}   IMPERS\shoot=ENCL
     'So they shot him (there on the plains).' {txt}

     b. ***du**=fa̱'=k'ų=chí*   tȩ́hti =a
       [3S]IRR.PFV.**VEN**_{EXLOC}=watch=DET.NV.PL=DIM   sheep=ENCL
       'They used to herd the sheep (there on the fields).' {txt}

Exlocative readings can even imply prior motion to a location other than the deictic center. This is shown in (11). This extension appears to be similar to the extensions of the usages of the suffix -*mu* 'AFAR' in Quechua, which functions as a ventive directional, but can also be used to express prior motion to a location other than the deictic center (see Dryer, this volume, ch 4).[8]

(11) a. *máx*   *néhe=k'ų*   *'yó=**du***   hnų́=a
ACA   perhaps   as.well=DET.NV.PL   cane=[3S]IRR.**VEN**_{EXLOC}   IMPERS\see=ENCL
     'They might go and check out also the sugar cane.' {txt}

TIL   b. *kha*   ***gwų**=ʰtsi-hme=hų=k'u='na*
       FOC.LOC   1S.IRR.PFV.**VEN**_{EXLOC}=ingest-tortilla=PL.INCL=LOC.NV=QUOT
       '(And) apparently it's there where we're going and have lunch.' {txt}
       (Or: '... we're going to have lunch.')

---

[8] The suffix can even be used to describe subsequent motion in Quechua, just like the imperative ventive in Querétaro Otomi in (6).

QRO c. *go   ge   bi=zix='ä,*
     FOC COP [3S]PST=SS\take.away.[3O]AS=3SG
     *no   **ba**=tsoh='pu̱='ä*
     REL[SG] [3S]PST.VEN_EXLOC=leave.AS=there=3SG
     'He's the one (who) took him away, the one who (went and) left him there.' {txt}
     (Palancar 2009: 180)

For the imperfective aspect, to express exlocative semantics all three focal languages have a dedicated subparadigm of inflectional formatives. Examples are given in (12). In all these examples, the speaker refers to a location different from where they are located while speaking, regardless of whether that location is far away or not.

(12) a. *pá=**bí**   'mbon=k'u='a   huä̌hi=a*
ACA   indeed=[3S]IPFV.EXLOC lie=LOC.NV=P.LOC   cornfield=ENCL
        'They're indeed lying there at the cornfield.' {txt}
        (Hernández-Green 2015: 444)

TIL b. *kha=**gí**   'oh=wi   mixa*
        LOC.FOC=2S.IPFV.EXLOC hear=PL   mass
        'You (PL) hear the mass (over there).' {txt}

QRO c. *ha ya   **bí**='bu̱h='pu̱=tho*
        if already [3S]PRS.EXLOC=be.located/live.AS=there=DEL
        'If they're still there.' {txt}
        (Palancar 2009a: 178)

Unlike the ventive, the exlocative in examples like (12) is not an AM category, because it does not entail a motion event as the background of the scene being described. However, the question remains as to how it is possible that ventive inflection is also used to express exlocative readings at least in perfective subparadigms, where there is not a dedicated exlocative morphology (see §3.6 for semantic interactions between aspect and AM categories). The phenomenon is found in all Otomi languages: it is observed in Mezquital Otomi (Bartholomew 2010: 504); in Ixtenco Otomi (Lastra 1997: 44–45); and most probably in Eastern Highlands Otomi as well (Voigtlander & Echegoyen 1985: 123–128). Furthermore, judging from the data in Stewart (1966: 63–65), one can argue that it is also found in Mazahua, the sister language of Otomi, strongly suggesting that the phenomenon is not a recent development, but goes back to the proto-language of this subbranch of

Oto-Pamean.[9] In this connection, Hernández-Green (2015: 392) has proposed that exlocative uses of ventive inflection may have arisen through a string of subsequent semantic extensions of ventive uses; namely, from expressions like "get X (from somewhere else)" to "get somewhere else and do X (and come back)", then to "do X somewhere else (and come back)", and finally ending up in just "do X somewhere else" doing away with the ventive component. A similar semantic shift involving a ventive marker is proposed for Jóola Fóoñi (Creissels & Bassène, this volume). Another alternative could be to appeal to a possible way of talking about events that happened away from the speech act location that involved a shift in conceptual perspective, treating this other location as the deictic center to where the actants of the events to be described were portrayed as having arrived there. In any event, regardless of how the exlocative extension of the ventive may have developed, we believe that they resulted from a historical process that is no longer at work when speakers of Otomi-Mazahua report of states of affairs happening away from the deictic center. Once the exlocative uses of the ventive are well established, uses of prior motion to a location other than the deictic center (as in (11) above) can be explained as arising by pragmatic implicature, as doing something somewhere else often implies having gone there in the first place.

Further evidence that the exlocative extensions of ventive inflection represent independent usages from the ventive comes from the fact that ventive inflection is possible with verbs like *pá* 'go', which describe movement away from the deictic center. This is shown in (13), which can only have the interpretation in (13a), and never the ventive reading in (13b).

(13) mehor **gwu̱**=mba=ga   gwu̱=tha̱-'ki
TIL better 1S.IRR.PFV.**VEN**_{EXLOC}=SS\go=1 1S.IRR.PFV.VEN_{EXLOC}=find-2o
  a. 'It's better that I'll go over there to find you there.' {txt}
  b. *'... I'll come over there to find you there while coming there.'

3.2 Andative

The andative is only found in Acazulco and Tilapa Otomi as a separate inflectional category, but not in Querétaro Otomi. The andative in Otomi only pairs with the imperfective aspect, and it always indicates that the situation described

---

9 Isomorphism between ventive and exlocative expressions has also been observed outside Oto-Pamean, as it is attested in Mohawk (cf. Deering & Harries-Delisle 1976: 105), in the directional and locational uses of the proximal (~ventive) in Oneida (see Ross, this volume), and in Jóola Fóoñi (Creissels & Bassène, this volume).

by the verb is concurrent with the motion in a direction other than toward the deictic center. In (14a), the motion event is concurrent with the holding by the evil spirit; in (14b), the motion event is concurrent with the event of peeling fruit and eating it.

(14) a. *ta='ënä ngú=m=**ár** the̱x=a='na*
ACA INT=seems like=PST=[3S]IPFV.**AND** hold.in.arms=ENCL=QUOT
'It was just as if it were carrying him away in its arms.' {txt}

TIL b. ***ar**=xönt'i 'ne=**ar** tsa*
[3S]**AND**=peel and=[3S]**AND** bite
'They were peeling them and eating them as they went.' {txt}

Apart from the AM uses observed in (14), the andative can also be used as a directional, as is shown in (15) with the motion verbs *'yó* 'walk' and *chíts'i* 'take (person) away' (Acazulco Otomi), and in (16) with the motion verbs *te̱ni* 'follow' and *pa* 'go' (Tilapa Otomi).

(15) a. *nu̱=chí bădu=**ar** 'yo=**ar** 'yo*
ACA DET.DIST.SG= DIM duck= [3S]IPFV.**AND** LT.walk= [3S]IPFV.**AND** LT.walk
'The little duck goes walking, goes walking.' {PMC 06-01}

 b. *xo=**ar** chíx=a*
so=[3S]IPFV.**AND** take.away=ENCL
'She takes them away.' {txt}

(16) a. *'ne=k'u̱ to=**ar** te̱ni*
TIL and=DEM.NV.PL who=[3S]**AND** follow
'And those who went following him.' {txt}

 b. *'ne=**ar** pa=k'u*
and=[3S]**AND** go=LOC.NV
'And they were going there.' {txt}

3.3 Ambulative

The ambulative is only found in Tilapa Otomi, and it is used to describe situations concurrent with motion in a random direction. One example of this AM category is shown in (17): in (17a), the setting for the movement is a street market and the mover is said to go shopping from one stall to the next; in (17b) the mover is a street vendor of clothes. The ambulative can also have directional uses, like in

(18). Acazulco Otomi used to have an ambulative category like Tilapa Otomi, but as will be seen in §4 it was reanalyzed as the inflection for the habitual aspect. This reanalysis happened through an extension that is still attested in the usages of the ambulative in Tilapa Otomi.

(17) a. **gádí**   ʰts<u>a</u>   di   ʰt<u>a</u>
TIL   2S.IPFV.**AMB** be.busy NMLZ buy
       'You're busy shopping here and there.' {txt}

   b. **adi**   mb<u>a</u>   i   tŕeʰxtyü
      [3S]IPFV.**AMB** ss\sell   PL   clothes
      'He's selling clothes here and there.' {txt}

(18)   hin=kho'=**tádí**   n-tx'o='mbe
TIL   NEG=not.exist.AS=1S.IPFV.**AMB**   MED-AS\walk=PL.EXCL
       'There's no one with whom I may walk here and there.' {txt}
       (Lit. 'There isn't (who) we can be walking here and there.')

3.4 Adlocative

The adlocative foregrounds the moment the mover arrives at a reference point after a motion event. The morphology exists in Acazulco Otomi and in Tilapa Otomi, but it is not found in Querétaro Otomi. However, we have but a few examples of the adlocative in our textual corpora, which made it difficult to understand its semantics, let alone reconstruct its paradigm. It was only after the careful implementation of a set of animated stimuli designed by Benedicto (2017) with speakers of Acazulco Otomi that this AM category became clearer to us. The stimuli in question show different movers moving in different directions. Examples in (19) illustrate it: (19a) describes a bird flying away from the speaker and landing on a far-away wooden fence; (19b) describes a similar scene, but this time with the bird flying toward the speaker and landing on a nearby fence. In both cases, the landing event is encoded using adlocative inflection. As the gloss indicates, the adlocative only occurs in the perfective aspect.[10]

---

10 In Benedicto & Salomón's (2014) typology of grammatical categories in movement predicate constructions, telicity is one of the relevant parameters in such constructions. Under their approach, the adlocative of Acazulco Otomi is a telic AM category (as an anonymous reviewer also suggests).

(19) a. bi=ntsháhki=bi   mbá   ta=**ín**
ACA   [3S]PFV=jump=[3S]PFV   NAS\go   until=[3S]PFV.**ADLOC**
       tǫ́h=nu̱
       stand.on.top=LOC.DIST
       'It flew away until it landed there.' {PMC 01-04}

    b. bú=ntsháhki   óra=**ín**   ýox=nu̱
       [3S]PFV.VEN=jump   now=[3S]PFV.**ADLOC**   be.on.top=LOC.DIST
       'It flew this way and then it landed there.' {PMC 01-05}

In (20) we give three more examples where the trajectory of an inanimate mover is from right to left (from the speaker's point of view) (20a), away from the speaker (20b), and toward the speaker (20c). The inclusion of inanimate movers is to control for the possibility that the speaker may be taking the mover's perspective (and thus making it possible that the adlocative is a deictic AM category).[11] However, as the examples in (20) show, this is not the case.

(20) a. ja=**ín**   tsó=nu̱='a
ACA   and=[3S]PFV.**ADLOC**   fall=LOC.DIST=LOC
       méro=ra   já=nu̱   cubeta
       right=[3S]IPFV   be.located=DET.DIST.SG   bucket
       'It (i.e. the paper plane) ended up right there on the bucket.' {PMC 02-02}

    b. **ín**=tsó=nu̱=ra   já=nu̱   red
       [3S]PFV.**ADLOC**=fall=LOC.DIST=[3S]IPFV   be.located=DET.DIST.SG   net
       'It (i.e. the ball) ended up in the net.' {PMC 10-02}

    c. ja=**ín**   tsó=nu̱=ra
       and=[3S]PFV.**ADLOC**   fall=LOC.DIST=[3S]IPFV
       já=nu̱=́r   gánu̱sta
       be.located=DET.DIST.SG=SG.3POSS   basket
       'It (i.e. the ball) ended up in the basket.' {PMC 10-02}

Speakers of Tilapa Otomi often translate instances of the adlocative into Spanish using the periphrasis *pasar a V* 'pass to V', which suggests that this is their best way to render the nuance of reaching a goal that is conveyed by this inflection. An example is given in (21).

---

[11] As an anonymous reviewer suggests.

(21) **grí**=tsohki-bi=ga   nt'a sku sentabo a   mu
TIL 1S.IRR.IPFV.**ADLOC**= SS\leave-3DAT=1 one DIM cent   DEF.SG 1POSS♂
mbe^y ...
mother
'I'm going to get there and leave a small cent for my mother ...' {txt}

Furthermore, the adlocative is the only AM category where no directional functions have been attested. In the corpus and in elicitation, the adlocative in Acazulco Otomi occurs with stative verbs such as *tǫ́ye* 'stand on top' and *'ǫ́ts'i* 'be on top' in (19), verbs of change of state such as *tsó* 'fall' in (20), and also with the activity verb *zoni* 'weep' and the transitive verb *'ét'i* 'put in', shown in (22) below.

(22) a. té=**gír**   zongi=a
ACA   why=2S.PFV.**ADLOC**   weep=ENCL
         'Why did you go there and weep?' {txt}

     b. óra=**ín**   'yět'=ru=ra
         now=[3S]PFV.**ADLOC**   PAL\put.in= LOC.DIST=[3S]IPFV
         já=nu   kăha
         be.located= DET.DIST.SG box
         'Then he went and put it in the box (when he arrived there).' {PMC 06-15}

3.5 Moving argument

For the clear majority of the cases, in all three focal Otomi languages discussed here the moving argument (Guillaume 2016: 113–116) in expressions using AM inflection is an S/A.[12] This is shown in the examples in (23) and (24) with the ventive. Here the mover functions as an S in the (a) examples, while in the (b) examples the ventive describes the motion of an A. In (24c), we have an instance of a demoted A. Although the examples shown are only inflected in the ventive, the use of AM inflection to describe the motion of S/A applies to all AM categories in Otomi (Palancar 2012a; Hernández-Green 2018b: 12).

---

12 S equals the only participant of an intransitive predicate, and A the most agent-like participant of a transitive predicate.

(23) a. *axta* **ba**=*peng-a=ma*   *n'agi=r*   *jö'i*   mover: S
QRO   until   [3S]PST.**VEN**=return-B= another   once=SG   person
        'Until the man came back once more.' {txt}
        (Palancar 2009a: 201)

     b. *ntonse ya*   **ba**=*hö=pya='na*   mover: A
         then   PRTCL   [3S]PST.**VEN**=have=now=QUOT
         'Then he brought it.' {txt}
         (Palancar 2009a: 179)[13]

(24) a. *nų=chí=bădu=***ba**   *'yó*   mover: S
ACA   DET.DIST.SG=DIM=duck=[3S]IPFV.**VEN**   walk
         'The little duck is walking this way.' {PMC 06-04}

     b. **ba**=*xih-ki=ga='mbe*   mover: A
         [3S]IPFV.**VEN**=tell-1O=1=PL.EXCL
         'They come to tell us.' {txt}

     c. **ba**=*t-'a̱'-k'i*   mover: (A)
         [3S]IPFV.**VEN**=IMPRS-ask.for-2O
         'They're coming to ask for your hand in marriage.' {txt}
         (Hernández-Green 2018b: 12–13)

The AM inflection describes the motion of P only with transitive verbs where the object is set in motion (see Ross, this volume), as illustrated in (25). This switch involving the moving argument may be due to the semantics of the verbs in question (i.e. where A causes P to move without A moving along) rather than being an idiosyncrasy of the grammar of AM in Otomi. In contrast to what is observed with the motion of S/A, which is possible with all AM categories, the description of the motion of P only occurs with the ventive. The ventive with verbs of sending is so strongly associated with the motion of P that interpretations where the A is the mover instead (i.e. 's/he came and sent it') do not obtain. In (25a), the deictic center where Death is sent to is the narrative's; in (25b) the deictic center is the speaker's village.[14]

---

13 The verb *hö* profiles a situation where A has P on himself/herself, and it does not imply motion. The motion component is provided by the ventive. The composite meaning that results is "A moves toward here while having P". Although both A and P are moving toward the deictic center, it is the motion of A that is profiled.

14 The interpretation of the temporal frame is different with verbs of sending with ventive than with verbs of other types. With verbs of sending, the motion event of P always follows the event of sending.

(25) a. ba=pehn-a=ma   n'agi **no=r**   **Ndöte**   mover: P
QRO   [3S]PST.VEN= send-B=another once **DEF.SG=SG** **Death**
       'He (i.e. God) sent Death once more (to the deictic centre).' {txt}
       (Palancar 2009a: 385)

ACA b. ja=bú   'mbent=**k'u**   **súndaro**='na   mover: P
       and=[3S]PFV.VEN   IMPRS\send= **DET.NV.PL** **soldier**=QUOT
       'And they say they sent the army (to this village).' {txt}

3.6 Temporal relation

As shown in §3.1 to §3.4, AM categories can have interpretations where the motion occurs either prior, concurrent, or subsequent to the situation described by the verb. Table 2 summarizes the different readings each AM category of the three focal Otomi languages can have in terms of temporal relation. As shown in §3.5 and §3.1, subsequent interpretations of the ventive are observed with verbs of sending and the imperative mood.

Table 2: Temporal relation of Otomí AM categories.

		prior	concurrent	subsequent
ventive	ACA	✓	✓	(✓)
	TIL	✓	✓	(✓)
	QRO	✓	✓	(✓)
andative	ACA		✓	
	TIL		✓	
ambulative	TIL		✓	
adlocative	ACA	✓		
	TIL	✓		

Temporal relation seems to be determined by the grammatical aspect in the AM categories of Acazulco and Tilapa Otomi, especially in the andative and adlocative: the former, which only pairs with the imperfective, has concurrent motion interpretations, whereas the latter, pairing only with the perfective, has prior motion interpretations. Similar correlations between aspect and temporal relation is found in Mudburra (Osgarby, this volume) and in Chácobo (Tallman, this volume).[15] Two examples of each AM category, with data from Acazulco Otomi, are given in (26) and (27).

(26) a. ***ardi***   x*a̱*h=a='*u̱*
    ACA   [3s]IPFV.**AND**   pray=ENCL=3PL
            'They are praying as they go.' {txt}

      b. *há'yu̱=**ar***   hu̱hki='na
         nothing=[3s]IPFV.**AND**   hold.up=QUOT
         'Nothing seemed to hold him back as he went.' {txt}

(27) a. óra=ta   y*ă*=***in***   mp'*ę̆*ngi=a
    ACA   now=INT   far=[3s]PFV.**ADLOC**   NAS\be.lying=ENCL
            'It (i.e. the bucket) ended up lying a little further.' {txt}

      b. xo=***ír***   f*ų̆*nts'=r*u̱*='a   'y*ų̂*
         xo=[3s]PFV.**ADLOC**   fall=LOC.DIST=LOC   way
         'So he went and tripped on the road.' {txt}

In the ventive, the temporal relation between the motion event and the situation described by the predicate correlates with the pragmatic implications of the meaning of the inflected verb (cf. Hernández-Green 2015: 394–396).[16] This mainly involves whether the motion is compatible with a situation that is possible, adequate or culturally expected, in such a way that situations that are possible/adequate/expected tend to have concurrent motion interpretations, while situations that are not, tend to have prior motion interpretations. Concurrent motion is observed with verbs of (caused) motion, as in the examples in (28) (the examples are from Acazulco and Querétaro Otomi, but the same situation can be found in Tilapa Otomi). The same goes for the situations in (29), which involve being arranged in a line (29a), lighting fireworks (29b), sitting on a horse (29c), and running (29d).[17] Further note that in these examples both motion and non-motion verbs can be inflected in the imperfective or the perfective.

---

15 This correlation is, of course, not necessarily always the case, as is shown for Pilagá in Vidal & Payne (this volume).
16 Hernández-Green (2015) also proposes that lexical aspect also plays a role in these interpretations, but the semantics of the verb seems to be a more consistent criterion here.
17 The AM inflection has directional functions in example (29d), as it also does in (28b) and (28c).

(28) a. gá'tho=**bú**   'ndṹ=a
ACA   all=[3S]PFV.**VEN**   IMPRS\have.on.back=ENCL
       'They brought them all here.' {txt}

b. **ba**=zí=a
   [3S]IPFV.**VEN**=LEN\bring.person=ENCL
   'He was bringing them (i.e. the gypsies) here.' {txt}

c. ja=**bú**   kṍ=nt'a='a   myö='na
   and=[3S]PFV.**VEN** descend=one=LOC above=QUOT
   'And one from above descended.' {txt}

QRO d. kwando mí=ma   ma   n'agi   **ba**=hö=r   dehe
       when   [3S]IMPF=SS\go another once   [3S]PST.**VEN**= have=SG water
       'When she went back there to bring water.' {txt}
       (Palancar 2009: 468)

(29) a. ta=**badi**   njųngi=a='ų
ACA   INT=[3S]IPFV.**VEN** be.in.line=ENCL=3PL
       'They were coming one after the other.' {txt}

b. ja=**ba**   fóh=yų   nzafi=a
   and=[3S]IPFV.**VEN** blow.up=DET.DIST.PL   fireworks=ENCL
   'And they were lighting fireworks as they came.' {txt}

c. **badi**   tó'=k'ų=í=chí   fáni=a=k'ų
   [3S]IPFV.**VEN**   stand.on.top=DET.NV.PL= PL.3POSS=DIM horse=ENCL=3PL.NV
   'They were coming on horseback.' {txt}

QRO d. xa=**ba**=nïxt'ï   **ba**='ëhë='na
       INT=[3S]PST.**VEN**=run   [3S]PST.VEN=come=QUOT
       'They say that he ran very fast as he came.' {txt}
       (Palancar 2009: 363)

Conversely, the situation types in (30) involve asking for someone in marriage (30a), paying a visit to a shrine (30b), telling lies (30c), and leaving someone somewhere (30d). All such situations are not expected to be performed while in motion and thus have a prior motion interpretation when the ventive inflection is used.

(30) a. **ba**=t-'a̱'-k'i
ACA   [3S]IPFV.**VEN**=IMPRS-ask.for-2O
       'They're coming to ask for your hand in marriage.' {txt}
       (Hernández-Green 2018b: 12–13)

b. ***badi***   *zéngua=yu̱*   *péregrino*
   [3S]IPFV.VEN   greet=DET.DIST.PL   pilgrim
   'The pilgrims come to visit.' {txt}

QRO   c. ***xpa**=möng-a=r*   *ñhëhmyo,*   *nu='mu̱*   *pödi*
   [3S]PRF.VEN=talk-B=SG   lie   PRTCL=if   [3S]know.F
   'That he who came to tell lies knows.' {txt}
   (Palancar 2009: §322)

d. *go*   *ge*   *bi=zix='ä,*   *no*
   FOC   COP   [3S]PST=SS\take.away.AS[3O]=3SG   REL(.SG)
   ***ba**=tsoh='pu̱='ä*
   [3S]PST.VEN=leave.AS=there=3SG
   'He's the one who took him away, the one who came and left him there.' {txt}
   (Palancar 2009: 180)

In this section we have shown that some AM categories in Otomi specify a temporal relation between the motion event and the situation described by the predicate (the adlocative and the andative), while others (the ventive) do not have such specification. In the latter case, the interpretation of the temporal relation depends on pragmatics, in terms of whether the situation described by the predicate is possible, or culturally expected, while in motion.

4 Extensions of AM categories

In the previous section, we have elaborated on the semantics of the AM categories in the three focal Otomi languages when used to describe AM scenes. In this section, we focus on the extension of AM inflection for uses other than encoding aspects of the spatial domain.

The andative has extended to the aspectual domain as it is used to convey progressive and continuative readings, such as for example in (31) and (32), as well as pluractionality involving a plurality of individuals, like in (33).

(31) a. ***ardi***   *'mbe̱h=na*   *édioma*
ACA   [3S]IPFV.AND   be.lost=DET.PROX.SG   language
'This language is being lost (gradually).' {txt}

      b. ***ar**=tsó-gi=ga='mbe*
         [3S]IPFV.**AND**=leave-1O=1=PL.EXCL
         'They (gradually) let us (weave by ourselves).' {txt}

TIL c. *'ne   pöhto   **ar**=te   'ne **ar**=te=a   sku̱ 'yo*
       and suddenly [3S]**AND**=grow and [3S]**AND**=grow=DEF DIM dog
       'And next thing you know, the little dog is (gradually) growing and growing.' {txt}

(32) a. *jak'u **ardi**   yőngi=a*
ACA   thus [3S]IPFV.**AND** help[RECP]=ENCL
       'That's how they help each other (as time goes by).' {txt}

      b. ***gar**=ẽ̱n-k'i   ja=gi   thöh=a?*
         1S.IRR.**AND**=say-2O and=2S.IRR answer=ENCL
         'Do I go on telling you (as the camera rolls) and you answer?' {txt}

(33) a. ***ar**='mbu̱h=yu̱   m-'nda*
ACA   [3S]IPFV.**AND**=live=DET.DIST.PL other-some
       'The others were born (one by one).' {txt}

      b. *ja=**gardi**   pu̱nts'i=a*
         and=2S.IRR.**AND** flip.over=ENCL
         'And then you flip them (i.e. the agave branches) over (one by one).' {txt}

Extensions of AM inflection may involve diachronic change too. For example, the old ambulative of Colonial Otomi (16th century) in (34), still present as such in Tilapa Otomi, has been reanalyzed as habitual aspect in Acazulco Otomi. The ambulative is often used in Tilapa Otomi to refer to customary activities, as in (35). This extension was reinforced in Acazulco Otomi, to the extent that the old AM meaning has been almost fully replaced by habitual aspect readings.[18] This is why Hernández-Green (2018a: 315) proposes that, for the synchronic grammar of Acazulco Otomi, the old ambulative is better analyzed nowadays as a habitual, which is a morphology that "describes imperfective situations of the gnomic type, by picturing the situation referred to by the verb as characteristic during an extended period of time, and not as a momentary, incidental property of it". Two examples of the habitual in Acazulco Otomi are given in (36).

---

[18] Ambulative readings of verbs inflected in the habitual can still be obtained, but only in elicitation (Hernández-Green 2015: 135).

(34) Colonial Otomi TIL ACA
       (AMB>HAB?) (AMB>HAB) (*AMB>HAB)
1st täni tá/tádi/táti dán/dádi
2nd käni gá/gádi/gáti gán/gádi
3rd ani a/adi/ati an/adi

(35) **gáti** ʰkhüh-kụ='mbe
TIL 2S.IPFV.**AMB** bring.AS-1O=PL.EXCL
'You're bringing us all the time.'
(Lit. 'You're bringing us here and there.') {txt}

(36) a. xo=**an** 'yó-xụ='ä
ACA so=[3S]**HAB** walk-night=3SG
'So she walks by night (as a habit).' {txt}

b. nt'a=jye nt'a=jye=**dán** pọ́n=ga='mbe
one=year one=year=1S.**HAB** go.out=1=PL.EXCL
'We go out on a trip every year.' {txt}
(Hernández-Green 2018a)

While the extension to the aspectual domain of AM constructions is typologically common, one not-so-common extension is observed in Tilapa Otomi. In most languages of the Otomi-Mazahua group, there is a special inflection to signal the discourse salience of an adjunct/adverbial element in the clause which has been placed in focus (Palancar 2012; Hernández-Green 2016). In Tilapa Otomi, there are dedicated formatives for this function in the irrealis as shown in (37): in (37a) the goal location is in focus; in (37b) the focus is on the manner adverb *k'u* 'that way' (originally a locative adverb 'there'). Discourse salience is represented with small caps.

(37) a. mehor **gátá** mba=ga 'A ESTADOS UNIDOS
TIL better 1S.IRR.PFV.**ADV** SS\go=1 P.LOC US
'I'd better go to the US.' {txt}

b. **gátátí** khah-pụ='mbe=k'u=a
1S.IRR.PFV.**ADV** do.AS-3DAT.AS=PL.EXCL=LOC.NV>that.way=ENCL
'We'll do it THAT WAY.' (Lit. 'We'll do it like THERE.') {txt}

But for the realis, the ambulative is used to cover this function. This is illustrated in (38). Example (38a) is an instance of a cleft. Here we have a headless relative clause where the instrument in the relative clause has been promoted to subject in focus. Example (38b) is a focus construction that places a location in focus. Example (38c) is like (37b), but this time the adverb *k'u* has a locative reading.

(38) a.   'ne   keh=a   [***tátu***   ^h*pem=p'e=a*   ___INSTR
TIL   and   COP=ENCL   1S.IPFV.**AMB**   wash[3O].AS=PL.EXCL
    range=i   txuxu]
    with=PL   blanket
    'THAT's (what) we used to wash it with along with the blankets.' {txt}

b.   *kha=**tátu***   ^h*tsotu='mbe=k'u=a*
    LOC.FOC=1S.IPFV.**AMB**   arrive.up.there.AS=PL.EXCL=LOC.NV=ENCL
    'We came up to THERE.' {txt}

c.   *bweno*   MADIKHA   ***támátu***   ^h*kum=p'e*
    well   long.ago   1S.IMPF.**AMB**   grind.AS=PL.EXCL
    'We used to grind chili LONG AGO.' {txt}

A final extension we have observed involves the ventive. This AM category is used for the TAM inflection of inchoative verbs in Tilapa Otomi, which are a subclass of patientive predicates. An example is given in (39).

(39)   *pero*   *porke*   ***b^wu**=tu*   *'un-gi*
TIL   but   because   PFV.**VEN**=INCHO   get.ill-1S$_O$
    'But because I got ill.' {txt}

In this section we have presented three extensions of the AM categories in Tilapa and Acazulco Otomi that fall outside of the spatial domain: two typologically common aspectual extensions in Acazulco Otomi (andative → pluractionality; ambulative → habitual), another typologically common aspectual extension in Tilapa Otomi (change of place → change of state, as in (39)),[19] and one rather rare extension related to the syntactic and discourse prominence of adverbials in Tilapa Otomi (ambulative → adjunct focus). One of the extensions in Acazulco Otomi (andative → pluractionality) coexists with genuine AM uses, whereas the other extension (ambulative → habitual) is a more complete shift of meaning, as the corresponding verb forms are no longer used as AM categories.

---

19 See Creissels & Bassène (this volume) for a semantically related aspectual extension of the ventive in Jóola Fóoñi, which the authors describe as "development of a process in the direction of some outcome"; see also Guérois et al. (this volume) and Payne (this volume).

5 The morphology of AM in Otomi

Having discussed the semantics of AM categories and their extensions, in this section we now concentrate on the formal aspects of the encoding of such categories in morphological terms. To understand this encoding, it is important to note that verbs in Acazulco and Tilapa Otomi fall into several conjugation classes. The conjugations are based on two morphological criteria: (a) the set and distribution of inflectional formatives a verb selects, and (b) the type and distribution of stem alternations that occur across the verbal paradigm. Such conjugations are inflectional classes in the sense in Aronoff (1994). In other words, membership to the classes is not motivated by the phonological properties of the stem, by the syntactic profile of the verb or by its semantics. This is illustrated in Acazulco Otomi with the verbs *pè̱nti* 'send' and *pè̱nt'i* 'grab' in Table 3. In the imperfective aspect (IPFV), a verb of Conjugation I like *pè̱nti* 'send' selects a set of formatives (*drá, grá, ra*), which are different from the set selected by a verb of Conjugation III like *pè̱nt'i* 'grab' (*drádi, grádi, radi*); (in the examples, the person enclitic for 1st person =*ka*, or =*k'a* due to phonological adjustment after /t'/, is obligatory in Acazulco Otomi).

Table 3: Some morphological contrasts between conjugations I and III in Acazulco Otomi.

			Conjugation I			Conjugation III	
			pè̱nti (tr) 'send'			*pè̱nt'i* (tr) 'grab'	
IPFV	1st	**drá**	*pè̱nt=ka*	'I send it'	**drádi**	*pè̱nt=k'a*	'I grab it'
	2nd	**grá**	*pè̱nti*	'you send it'	**grádi**	*pè̱nt'i*	'you grab it'
	3rd	**ra**	*pè̱nti*	'he sends it'	**radi**	*pè̱nt'i*	'he grabs it'
PFV	1st	*dí*	*pè̱nt=ka*	'I sent it'	*dí*	*pè̱nt=k'a*	'I grabbed it'
	2nd	*gí*	*pé̱nti*	'you sent it'	*gí*	*pè̱nt'i*	'you grabbed it'
	3rd	*bi*	*mbè̱nti*	'he sent it'	*bi*	*pè̱nt'i*	'he grabbed it'

Table 3 also shows how stem alternations are characteristic of conjugational classes. Verbs from Conjugation I may undergo stem alternations in the perfective aspect (PFV), consisting of consonant mutations (e.g. compare the form *ra pè̱nti* 'he sends it' with *bi mbè̱nti* 'he sent it') or tonal stem changes (e.g. compare *grá pè̱nti* 'you send it' with *gí pé̱nti* 'you sent it'). Such alternations do not occur in verbs from Conjugation III.

In the previous sections, we have shown that AM categories are encoded in Otomi by special sets of inflectional formatives that also encode TAM and person.

Portmanteau morphemes combining AM categories with TAM values are also observed (in certain morphological contexts) in Mudburra (Osgarby, this volume) or in Warumungu (Koch, this volume). In the next section, we show that for the encoding of AM there may be different morphologically conditioned allomorphs, selected by the different conjugations. Some cells in AM subparadigms further require stem alternations of the type we have seen in Table 3. We first discuss the AM inflectional formatives of Acazulco Otomi, then we introduce those in Tilapa Otomi, and we finish with Querétaro Otomi, which is the simpler system.

5.1 The encoding of AM by means of inflectional formatives

The AM paradigm in Acazulco Otomi is presented in Table 4 (adapted from Hernández-Green 2015).[20] In all the tables that follow, the rows correspond to TAM/person categories, and the columns to AM categories and conjugation classes. The labels "I.tr" and "I.intr" refer to transitive and intransitive verbs of Conjugation I, respectively. The exlocative (not an AM category) is only included in Table 4 because of the exlocative readings it shares with the ventive category in the perfective (see §3.1).

Table 4: The AM paradigm in Acazulco Otomi.

mood	aspect	person	AND		ADLOC			VEN		EXLOC
			I/II	III	I/II/III	I.tr		I.intr/II	III	I/II/III
REALIS	PFV	1st			dín		dú		dí	
		2nd			gín		gú		guí	→ [VEN]
		3rd			ín		bú		bí	
	IPFV	1st	dár	dárdi		dádi	dá		dádi	dí
		2nd	gár	gárdi		guádi	guá		guádi	gí
		3rd	ar	ardi			ba		badi	bí/rá
IRR	PFV	1st			gín		gu		guí	
		2nd			gín		gu		guí	→ [VEN]
		3rd			dín		du		dí	
	IPFV	1st	gar	gardi		guadi	gua		guadi	
		2nd	gar	gardi		guadi	gua		guadi	
		3rd	dar	dardi			da		dadi	

---

[20] In Hernández-Green (2015), the andative and adlocative TAM markers are analyzed as the imperfective and perfective markers of the 'translocative' category (here treated as 'andative').

Table 4 shows that for the realization of some of the AM categories there is allomorphy involving the formatives. In the cells of the imperfective aspect (also called incompletive), contrasting allomorphy is based on the presence/absence of the inflectional class marker *di* (Hernández-Green 2015).[21] Note that the ventive pairs with both the imperfective and the perfective in both the realis and the irrealis. In contrast, the andative only pairs with the imperfective, while the adlocative only pairs with the perfective. Table 4 points to the existence of paradigmatic gaps, which appear in shading. Such gaps are further discussed in §5.3.

The AM paradigm of Tilapa Otomi is shown in Table 5. This paradigm is very similar to the one we find in Acazulco Otomi, except for the ambulative. The inflectional class marker *ti* (cognate of Acazulco Otomi *di*) is now typically associated with Conjugation III. As for category pairings, the andative also pairs with the imperfective, as does the ambulative, while the adlocative pairs with the perfective, although at present we have not been able to find clear examples of it in the perfective realis. The ventive is again the AM category pairing with more TAM values.

---

[21] The marker *di* has no morphosyntactic function; it points to a class distinction that is purely morphological.

Table 5: The AM paradigm in Tilapa Otomi.

mood	tense	person	AND I/II	AND III	ADLOC I/II	ADLOC III	AMB I	AMB II	AMB III	VEN I.tr	VEN I.intr	VEN II	VEN III	EXLOC I	EXLOC II	EXLOC III
REALIS	PFV	1st			?	?					tṹ		tí			
		2nd			?	?					gwṹ	gwí		[VEN] →		
		3rd			?	?					bwṹ	bí				
	IPFV	1st	tár	tárti			táti/tátu̱	tádi	táti	tátu̱	tá		táti	tí		títi?
		2nd	gár	gárti			gáti/(gátu̱)	gádi	gáti	gwátu̱	gwá		gwáti	gí		gíti?
		3rd	ar	arti			a	adi	ati		ba		bati	brṹ		brṹti?
	IMPF	1st					támátu̱	támádi	támáti							
		2nd					gámáti	gámádi	gámáti							
		3rd						mádi	máti							
IRR	PRF	1st								xkwṹ	xtṹ		xtí?			
		2nd			grí	gríti				xpa	xkwṹ	xkwí		[VEN] →		
		3rd			grí	gríti						xpwu̱	xpí/(xpwu̱)			
						tí										
	PFV	1st								gwatu̱	gwṹ		gwí			
		2nd								gwatu̱	gwṹ		gwí	[VEN] →		
		3rd									t(w)u̱		tí			
											ta					
	IPFV	1st	gar?	garti?							gwa	gwa	gwati			
		2nd	gar?	garti?							gwa	gwa	gwati	[VEN] →		
		3rd	tar	tarti?							ta		tati			
	PST	1st									gwu̱gwu̱					
		2nd									gwu̱gwu̱			[VEN]		
		3rd									tugwu̱					

Finally, the AM inflection in Querétaro Otomi is given in Table 6 from Palancar (2009a), which shows that the paradigm is small as it only involves a ventive category. The ventive and the exlocative (not an AM category) are further restricted to pairings with the 3rd person. The ventive only pairs with the dependent imperfect (used in sequential clauses), the past and the perfect tenses, while the exlocative only pairs with the present tense. All category pairings in Table 6 occur in the realis, and none in the irrealis. Note that Querétaro Otomi inflectional formatives do not have allomorphs.

Table 6: The AM paradigm in Querétaro Otomi.

mood	tense	person	VEN		EXLOC
REALIS	PRS	1st			
		2nd			
		3rd			bí
	IMPF(DEP)	1st			
		2nd			
		3rd	mba		
	PST	1st			
		2nd			
		3rd	bá	→	[VEN]
	PRF	1st			
		2nd			
		3rd	(x)pá	→	[VEN]
IRR					

5.2 Stem alternation patterns in the cells involved in AM

Apart from inflectional formatives, the morphological realization of AM categories may also involve stem alternations by means of consonant mutations and tone changes. This only happens in morphologically conservative languages like Acazulco Otomi and Tilapa Otomi; the system has been morphologically levelled in Querétaro Otomi. Here, we only briefly introduce the stem alternations in Acazulco Otomi (at the current stage of the research, we know less of the alternations of Tilapa Otomi).

Stem alternations by consonant mutations involve lenition, nasalization, or palatalization of the onset consonant of the stem. This is illustrated in the examples in (40), which show contrasts between forms for the 3rd person imperfective realis with no AM and with AM (ventive).

(40)   Imperfective (no AM)   Imperfective ventive
ACA a.   *ra tṹ*   's/he has it'   *ba dṹ*   's/he brings it'
        ra pë   's/he steals it'   *ba bë*   's/he steals it as s/he comes'

    b.   *ra fe̱*   's/he gathers them'   *ba mbe̱*   's/he gathers them as s/he comes'
        ra pé̱i   's/he plays it'   *ba mbé̱i*   's/he plays it as s/he comes'

    c.   *ra honi*   's/he looks for it'   *ba hyoni*   's/he looks for it as s/he comes'
        ra 'a̱di   's/he asks for it'   *ba 'ya̱di*   's/he asks for it as s/he comes'

The type of mutated stem that obtains is predictable from the phonology of the lexical (basic) stem, although not for all cases. As a general rule, only the verbs whose stems begin with the segments (or segment clusters) listed in Table 7 have stem alternations; the rest do not. Stem mutation type is sensitive to conjugation class. The outcome for the mutated stem (lenition or nasalization) for verbs of Conjugation I whose stems begin with /p, f/ is lexically conditioned.[22]

Table 7: Consonant mutations in Acazulco Otomi (Hernández-Green 2015).

Conjugation I			Conjugation II	
lenition	nasalization	palatalization	nasal prefix	
p, f → b	p, f → mb	'V → 'yV	j → n-j	
		hV → hyV	f → m-f	
t, th → d			th → n-th	
			z → n-z	
ts → z			'mb → m-p'	
ch → ž			'nd → n-t'	
k, j → g			'y → n-ch'	
			t → n-d	
kw, jw → gw			ts → n-z	

In certain cells in the AM paradigm, stems also undergo tonal changes. When it happens, stems take either a high tone or a low tone under specific morphotactic circumstances (no matter what their lexical tone might be). This is illustrated in

---

22 A few intransitive verbs do not present stem alternants, although they meet the phonological criteria. For example, *thóyi* 'pass by', *thót'i* 'go downhill', *thëye* 'be completed/consumed', and *fṵnts'i* 'tumble' of Conjugation I, and *té* 'grow up', *té* 'scrub agave fiber', *tínt'e̱* 'thresh barley', *tó̱ye* 'be on top', *tsàhte* 'bite people', *tsíhme* 'eat', *tsṹ* 'be frightened', *tsu̱hte* 'scold people', *tṹhü* 'sing', and *tṵhü* 'sow' of Conjugation II.

(41) where the tone of the verb in the imperfective (with no AM) is the lexical tone. Note that the stem in (41a) shifts to high tone in the andative. This happens because the verb stem has the stem formative +*hi*. When the verb is monosyllabic, as in (41b), the form for the andative has low tone.[23]

(41)   IPFV of REALIS (no AM)   IPFV of REALIS + AND (AM)
ACA a. *ra tǐ+hi* 's/he runs'   *ar tí+hi* 's/he runs as s/he goes'
     b. *ra 'yǒ* 's/he walks'   *ar 'yò* 's/he walks as s/he goes'

The stem alternations occur in a fixed set of cells in the AM paradigm.[24] Table 8 shows the case for Acazulco Otomi, where the cells in question are indicated by 'CM' for 'consonant mutation' and by 'T' standing for 'tonal alternation'. With a very few exceptions (not discussed here), the patterns represented in Table 8 are the same for both the realis and the irrealis. In the table, the underscore ___ indicates cells where there are no changes in the stem.

Table 8: Stem alternations in Acazulco Otomi (Hernández-Green 2015).

aspect	person	AND			ADLOC			VEN			EXLOC		
		I.tr	I.intr/II	III	I.tr	I.intr	II/III	I.tr	I.intr/II/III		I.tr	I.intr/II	III
PFV	1st		___	___	___	___	___	___	___	___			
	2nd				CM/T	T		___	___	___			
	3rd				CM			___	___	___			
IPFV	1st	___	T	___				___	___		___	T	___
	2nd	___	T	___				CM/T	___		___	T	___
	3rd	___	T	___				CM	___		___	T*	___

Note: * The tonal alternation only occurs with the formative *bí*=, not with *rá*= (LOW).

---

[23] Apart from stem formatives, other circumstances that trigger high tone include noun incorporation; when the stem exhibits the antipassive suffix -*te* or when the stem co-occurs with enclitics, such as the plural exclusive enclitics, the counterfactual enclitic =*mö(hö)*, or the enclitic = *tshẹ* 'self'. In all other circumstances, low tone applies (for more details see Hernández-Green 2015: 287).

[24] There is one exception to this generalization. The nasal stem alternant of the verb *pá* 'go' extends to 2nd and 1st person; it is also the only verb that has stem suppletion conditioned by number and clusivity: *pẹ* with enclitics =*ui* 'DU' and =*'mbe* 'PL.EXCL' (historically a dual); and *pạ* with the enclitics =*hụ* 'PL' and =*he* 'PL.EXCL' (the historical plural, nowadays almost extinct in natural use).

5.3 Paradigmatic gaps involving AM

In the previous section, we have seen that the verb paradigm can have gaps where a certain AM category (or categories) does not pair with certain TAM/person categories (or person values). We have extensively investigated these paradigmatic gaps in both natural language samples and in elicitation. As far as our knowledge goes, we are certain that such gaps exist in the places where we have identified them. Similar paradigmatic gaps can also be found in other languages, such as Mudburra (Osgarby, this volume).

Whenever the event being described may involve motion, but the adequate AM category is not available in the grammar, one of two strategies are used. The first one is not to encode it all. However, this is not an option which is often taken by speakers, who normally resort to the second strategy. This other strategy involves encoding notions of AM by making use of syntactic means. This happens very frequently when the situation involves a ventive scene, as in (42) from Acazulco Otomi. Here the event in question is portrayed as a customary activity with the habitual aspect, but as there is no ventive inflection for the habitual aspect, the only way to convey ventive notions is by means of a purpose construction that has the verb *ëhë* 'come' as a matrix verb. In the construction, the embedded purpose clause that follows is asyndetic (i.e. it is not introduced by a subordinator). Needless to say, the motion event precedes the visiting.

(42) *mí=an='ëh=a*   *mí=adi*   *zéngua-gi=ga='mbe*
ACA   PST=HAB=LT.**come**=ENCL   PST=HAB   visit-1O=1=PL.EXCL
     'They used to come and visit us.' {txt}

A similar case is seen in Querétaro Otomi, where we have seen that AM inflection is only available for the 3rd person. Example (43) involves a ventive scene involving the speaker. As there is no ventive for 1st person, the construction in (43) is used instead. The adverbial construction in (43) depicts two simulatenous events (see Palancar 2009: 514*ff*). Here the first predicate belongs to the matrix clause, where the motion verb appears in an asyndetic embedded clause that follows.

(43) [*dá=nïxt'ï*]   [*dá='ë=he*]]
QRO   **1.PST**=run   **1.PST**=come.AS=PL.EXCL
     'We ran back.' {txt} (Lit. 'We ran, we came.')

Employing syntactic means like in (42) and (43) to encode typical notions of AM is not only restricted to cases where there are paradigmatic gaps, but forms part of a common discourse strategy in Otomi which is used to express aspects of AM in a given event. In this connection, it is relatively common to find examples like (44) in natural discourse: (44a) is an instance of the andative; (44b) and (44c) of the ventive. Note that both predicates involved in these constructions share the same AM inflection (when this is possible).

(44) a. 'ne   [**ar**=pa   [**arti**   heh=a=k'i   dulse]]
TIL   and   [3S]IPFV.**AND** [3S]IPFV.**AND** give.out.AS=ENCL= DEM.PL.NV candy
       'And they go and give out candy as they go.' {txt}

   b. 'ne   [ha̲n=**gwá**   'ëh=a   [**gwá**='yo=tho]]
      and   again=1S.IPFV.**VEN** come.AS=ENCL   1S.IPFV.**VEN**=walk=DEL
      'And I come back just walking back.' {txt}

QRO c. ah   [xa=**bá**=nïxt'ï   [**bá**='ëhë]]='na
       and   INT=[3S]PST.**VEN**=run   [3S]PST.**VEN**=come=QUOT
       'Ah, he quickly ran back.' {txt} (Lit. 'He ran a lot, he came.')

5.4 A note about the morphological complexity of AM inflection in Otomi

We have presented the formal encoding of AM categories in Otomi, which is achieved by means of markers that are cumulative with TAM values and with person of subject. Here we discuss some formal aspects of the system in the light of the dimension of morphological complexity, as introduced in Guillaume (2016). Guillaume (2016) uses a measure of morphological complexity for AM systems that is based on the total number of AM morphemes that the language has. He applies such a measure to a survey of 44 South American languages with AM. In this respect, one of the most complex AM systems in his survey is Cavineña (Takanan; northern Bolivia), where we find up to a dozen AM suffixes that may encode direction of motion, temporal relation, type of goal, aspect, and/or role of moving argument. Guillaume's approach to morphological complexity is morphosemantically oriented in that it involves richness of semantic distinctions encoded by richness in morphological items. Under such a perspective, Cavineña is rightly considered one of the most complex systems surveyed. Under the same perspective, Otomi languages look simpler because they only encode path distinctions in a clear way, leaving other notions morphologically underspecified.

Guillaume's approach to measuring morphological complexity is one among other possibilities. We know that levels of complexity of inflectional systems vary much depending on the type of complexity measure that we use (see Sagot & Walther 2011; Stump & Finkel 2015a, 2015b, among others). To defend a strictly morphological approach to morphological complexity of AM systems, we follow the take on morphological complexity in Baerman et al. (2009, 2015), where it is seen as the amount of morphological information speakers need to contend with in order to inflect a given lexeme for a given inflectional category. Under such an approach, the Otomi AM system, which is rather simple in Guillaume's approach, becomes rather complex.

In §5, we have shown that the Otomi AM system does not involve specific dedicated markers that are used in the verbal template when the semantics of a certain AM category is called upon. In our view of complexity, such a system would be morphologically very simple, because it would reveal a one-to-one mapping between semantics (i.e. a given AM meaning) and form (i.e. an affix). The Otomi system distances itself significantly from this agglutinative model because, for the encoding of AM, Otomi speakers need to contend with a great deal of morphological information which involves the following dimensions:

a. *Portmanteau morphemes*: AM is always expressed by means of inflectional formatives that also realize TAM values and person. This means that there is not a single morpheme in the inflection of all Otomi languages which can be isolated in the segmentation as an exponent of an AM category.
b. *Stem alternations*: In the realization of certain AM cells, a special alternant form of the stem is required, which may further involve consonant mutation, tone mutation or both under complex circumstances. The distribution of the stem alternants does not follow a natural class; in other words, it is purely morphological (i.e. 'morphomic' in the sense of Aronoff 1994).
c. *Syncretism*: most inflectional formatives encoding AM for the irrealis subparadigms have a syncretism of 1st and 2nd person. There is also extended syncretism across some cells of different conjugational classes, but such syncretism patterns are not systematic.
d. *Paradigm gaps involving TAM*: AM is not found across all TAM subparadigms. Speakers need to know when the possibility for the morphological encoding of an AM category is viable and when it is not.
e. *Paradigm gaps involving person*: There is defective AM inflection for some person values: the ventive is only found for the 3rd person in Querétaro Otomi. These structural gaps make of the Otomi AM system a typological rarity.
f. *Inflectional class distribution*: In the conservative Otomi languages, there is allomorphy of AM inflectional formatives determined by inflectional class, and membership of such classes is dictated by the lexicon.

Paradigm size is yet another dimension that calls for attention in measuring the morphological complexity of an AM system. In this regard, the size of the AM paradigm of conservative Otomi languages like Acazulco Otomi and Tilapa Otomi is substantially larger than that of Querétaro Otomi, because it involves 24 and 34 cells in each one, respectively, against only 3! Such paradigms considerably increase the information load that speakers need to contend with when they face the task of realizing AM categories.

We contend that an AM system like that of Otomi becomes rather complex from a formal point of view, even though the number of AM categories to be realized by the morphology is not substantially high. Likewise, in the materials on the Cavineña system from Guillaume (2009, 2016), one can but infer a few traces that point to morphological complexity of exponence. Firstly, most (if not all) AM markers in Cavineña are also portmanteau morphemes, as they can encode up to five grammatical categories in a cumulative fashion; other South American languages with portmanteau AM markers include Tacana and Yagua (Guillaume 2016: 163–165, 167).[25] Secondly, three of the Cavineña AM suffixes display syncretism in the sense that they can encode either prior or concurrent motion. And finally, the AM paradigm presented by Guillaume (2016: 88) also has gaps, so there is some degree of paradigmatic defectiveness: (a) the area corresponding to the moving argument does not have deictic or temporal relation markers; (b) the area corresponding to subsequent motion only has one marker available; and (c) markers that encode aspect are only found in the area corresponding to concurrent motion. An explicit account of these and other criteria in the dimension of complexity of exponence that we are postulating would be worth exploring in a typological account of AM systems in languages of the world.

6 Final remarks: Otomi in the light of Mesoamerica

In this paper, we have described the AM system found in the Otomi family of languages, by concentrating on three focal languages: Tilapa Otomi, Acazulco Otomi and Querétaro Otomi. Regarding types of AM categories, although all three languages have a ventive, that is the only category that is found in Querétaro Otomi; the other two languages, which are morphologically more conservative, have an andative and an adlocative. Tilapa Otomi has also ambulative morphology, which was preserved in Acazulco Otomi, but reanalyzed as habitual. We have proposed that the marking of the AM system in Otomi is morphologically complex from the morphological perspective, because its realization in inflection is intri-

---

25 Tacana also has three circumfixes in its AM system (Guillaume 2016: 163–165), which could be considered more complex than simple affixation (see Anderson 2015: 16–24).

cate, involving a large number of cells, portmanteau markers and stem alternation, allomorphy of exponence, and paradigmatic gaps.

While the Otomi AM system is remarkable, AM systems are known to exist in other languages of the Oto-Pamean branch of Oto-Manguean (i.e. in Mazahua, in Matlatzinca and in Chichimec). This means that the Otomi system is not a recent development, but one inherited from proto-Oto-Pamean. What the proto-system was like would necessarily remain as an open question for further research; a question that could be addressed as the descriptions of related languages generates more and better knowledge of their respective AM systems.

Outside of Oto-Pamean, our knowledge of the existence and distribution of AM systems in Mesoamerica is still poor, although Dryer (this volume, ch 13) is a good starting point. From the available descriptions, we know of the existence of AM systems in at least two other Mesoamerican language families. For example, Nahuatl (Uto-Aztecan) is known to have a simple system involving an andative and a ventive, which nonetheless pair with three TAM different values: two of them involving 'motion-cum-purpose' and a third one (i.e. the so-called 'transitory perfective') involving a round trip. This is shown in (45) and (46) from Mecayapan Nahuatl, a Gulf dialect (data adapted from Wolgemuth 1981: 88).

(45) AND:
NAH a. ma:lti:-ti [3s]bathe.AS-IPFV.AND 'S/he is going to take a bath'
b. ma:lti:-to [3s]bathe.AS-PFV.AND 'S/he went off to take a bath'
c. ma:lti:-to:ya[26] [3s]bathe.AS-TRANS.PFV.AND 'S/he went and took a bath and came back'

(46) VEN:
NAH a. ma:lti:-qui [3s]bathe.AS-IPFV.VEN 'S/he comes to take a bath'
b. ma:lti:-co [3s]bathe.AS-PFV.VEN 'S/he came to take a bath'
c. ma:lti:-co:ya [3s]bathe.AS-TRANS.PFV.VEN 'S/he came and took a bath and got back'

Within the Oto-Manguean stock to which Otomi belongs, the Chinantecan branch of languages is also known to have an AM system. The best described system is found in Foris (2000) and it involves a system of three AM categories: an ambulative,[27] an andative and a ventive. However, while the encoding of the

---

[26] One anonymous reviewer has pointed out to us that the round trip marker appears to be complex. In such an analysis, the portion /ya/ of both markers –to:ya and –co:ya could be analyzed precisely as an exponent of 'round trip'.
[27] The ambulative appears to have a sense of 'undirected' motion (see Foris 2000: 110).

ambulative is rather simple (achieved by means of the prefix *ŋii̯ᴸ-*, with low tone), the exponence for the andative and the ventive includes the prefix paradigms in Table 9 in Sochiapan Chinantec. The prefixes in question also encode TAM values and person (except in the completive, where the prefixes are invariant for person).

Table 9: The AM prefixes in Sochiapan Chinantec (Foris 2000: 106, 108).

	AND				VEN			
	1sg	2nd	3rd	1pl	1sg	2nd	3rd	1pl
HAB	*ŋiĩᴹ-*	*kuaᴸ-*	*cáᴹ-*	*cáᴹ-*	*hã́ᴹ-*	*ŋiaᴸ-*	*hã́ᴹ-*	*hã́ᴹ-*
INCPL	*ŋiĩᴹ-*	*kuaᴸ-*	*hã́ᴹ-*	*cáᴹ-*	*haᴸ-*	*ŋiaᴸ-*	*haᴸ-*	*haᴸ-*
IRR	*ŋiĩᴴ-*	*kuáᴴ-*	*caᴸ-*	*cáᴴ-*	*hã́ᴴ-*	*ŋiã́ᴴ-*	*haᴸ-*	*hã́ᴴ-*
IMP	—-	*kuáᴹ-*	—-	—-	—-	*ŋiã́ᴹ-*	—-	—-
CPL	*ŋiĩᴴ-*	*ŋiĩᴴ-*	*ŋiĩᴴ-*	*ŋiĩᴴ-*	*kuaᴸ-*	*kuaᴸ-*	*kuaᴸ-*	*kuaᴸ-*

In the making of the inflectional forms involving AM, as indicated in Foris (2000: 60), there is a special set of rules for the stem selection of the verb. Although the ambulative has only one invariant prefix, the verb requires two special stems (each with its own inflectional tone) for the 2nd and the 3rd person, respectively. Such stems are provided by the lexicon (i.e. they need to be learned; they cannot be generated by rule). For the 1st person (singular and plural), the irrealis stem is used. For the andative and the ventive, another special stem (but the same one) is required for the 3rd person. For the 1SG and 2nd person, the andative and ventive use the completive stem, while the irrealis stem is used for the 1PL.

We know little about the semantics of such categories. As for their origin, Foris (2000) proposes that prefixes are likely to have evolved from old verbal roots via verbal composition. In this respect, the ambulative prefix reminds one of the verb *ŋi*ᴸᴹ 'walk', as do some forms of the andative prefix, while other forms derived from historical inflected forms of the verb *cau*ᴸᴹ 'go home' or the verb *cã'*ᴸᴹ 'go other place but home'. Similarly, some forms of the ventive are related to forms of either the verb *hã̂u*'ᴹᴸ 'come back home'[28] or the verb *ha*ᴸᴹ 'come back to other place than home'. While synchronically there is little connection with these verbs and there is much suppletion in the prefix paradigms, the fact that we can still observe formal similarities with existing verbs is informative not only about the sources, but also that the system as such may be of relatively recent development. For Otomi, however, given the morphological nature of the exponence, a reconstruction in terms of a possible grammaticalization path is not easy to

---

28 The acute accent indicates ballistic stress in the Chinantec data in Foris (2000).

propose, although there are hints that seem to suggest that some bits in the AM inflectional formatives could be the remnants of old adverbials.

All in all, the existence of AM systems in these languages reveal that AM systems as proposed in Guillaume (2016) for South-American languages also exist in the Mesoamerican languages, where andative and ventive appear to be common values. At the current stage of the research, the typological study in Dryer (this volume, ch 13), which covers a sample of different language families in Mesoamerica, represents a promising start. However, it is based on sources (most of them written in English) that offer but glimpses of information about AM systems. We are in need of dedicated studies using similar methodology or at least the same conceptual language. Such studies would be bound to reveal important data not only to enrich our general understanding of AM systems in general, but about how that area may have contributed to the making of Mesoamerica as the linguistic area advocated in Campbell et al. (1986).

Abbreviations

ACA	Acazulco Otomi	F	free shape of a verb	O	object
ADLOC	adlocative			PRTCL	particle
ADV	adverbial inflection	H	high tone	PAL	palatal stem
		HAB	habitual	PFV	perfective
AM	associated motion	IMP	imperative	PL	plural
AMB	ambulative	IMPF	imperfect	POSS	possessor
AND	andative	IMPRS	impersonal	PRF	perfect
AS	adjusted stem	INCHO	inchoative	PROX	proximal
B	bound shape of a verb	INFL	inflectional	PRS	present
		INT	intensive	PST	past
COP	copula	IPFV	imperfective	QRO	Querétaro Otomi
DAT	dative	IRR	irrealis	QUOT	quotative
DEF	definite	L	low tone	RECP	reciprocal
DEL	delimitative	LEN	lenis stem	REL	relative
DET	determiner	LOC	locative	S	subject
DIM	diminutive	LOW	lower level	SG	singular
DIST	distal	LT	low-tone stem	SS	secondary stem
DU	dual	M	mid tone	TIL	Tilapa Otomi
ENCL	enclitic	MID	middle	TRANS	translocative
EXCL	exclusive	NAS	nasal stem	VEN	ventive
EXLOC	exlocative	NMLZ	nominalizer		
FOC	focus	NV	non-visible		

Acknowledgements: We would like to thank the editors, Antoine Guillaume and Harold Koch, for all the work and time they have invested in putting together this book, as well as Jean-Christophe Verstraete for his comments and recommendations. We are also very grateful to the people of San Ildefonso Tultepec, Santiago Tilapa, and San Jerónimo Acazulco, and especially to Mrs Anastacia Cruz Vázquez (RIP), Mrs Petra de la Cruz Gutiérrez Mora, Mr Benito Mendoza (RIP), Mrs Trinidad Beltrán, and Mr Felipe Sánchez (RIP) for their patience and willingness to teach us their respective languages. Our thanks go also to ELDP (SOAS, University of London; Small Grant 0036) for funding the documentation of Acazulco Otomi. Finally, we would like to thank the anonymous reviewers. All shortcomings in this paper remain our own.

References

Anderson, Stephen. R. 2015. Dimensions of morphological complexity. In Matthew Baerman, Dunstan Brown, & Greville G. Corbett (eds.), *Understanding and Measuring Morphological Complexity*, 11–26. Oxford: Oxford University Press.

Andrews, Henrietta. 1993. *The Function of Verb Prefixes in Southwestern Otomi*. Arlington: Summer Institute of Linguistics, University of Texas at Arlington.

Aronoff, Mark. 1994. *Morphology by Itself: Stems and Inflectional Classes*. Cambridge, Massachusetts: The MIT Press.

Baerman, Matthew, Dunstan Brown, & Greville G. Corbett. 2009. Morphological Complexity: A typological perspective. Paper read at "How do we cite words in action: Interdisciplinary approaches to understanding word processing and storage". Pisa, 11–14 October.

Baerman, Matthew, Dunstan Brown, & Greville G. Corbett. 2015. Understanding and measuring morphological complexity: An introduction. In Matthew Baerman, Dunstan Brown, & Greville G. Corbett (eds.), *Understanding and measuring morphological complexity*, 3–10. Oxford: Oxford University Press.

Bartholomew, Doris A. 2010. Notas sobre la gramática del Hñähñu otomí. In Luis Hernández, Moisés Victoria, & Donald Sinclair (eds.), *Diccionario del hñähñu otomí del Valle del Mezquital, estado de Hidalgo*. Mexico City: Instituto Lingüístico de Verano.

Benedicto, Elena. 2017. Motion predicates: Moving along. Purdue University Research Repository PURR. Doi:10.4231/R7PN93M4

Benedicto, Elena, & Elizabeth Salomón. 2014. Trayectoria y manera en los predicados de movimiento en mayangna: propiedades morfo-sintácticas y estructurales en construcciones seriales. In Lilián Guerrero (ed.), *Movimiento y espacio en lenguas de América*, 53–92. Mexico City: Instituto de Investigaciones Filológicas, Universidad Nacional Autónoma de México.

Campbell, Lyle, Terrence Kaufman, & Thomas C. Smith-Stark. 1986. Meso-America as a linguistic area. *Language* 62 (3). 530–570.

Cárceres, Fray Pedro de, 1580/1907. Arte de la Lengua Othomi. Edited by Nicolás León. *Boletín del Instituto Bibliográfico Mexicano* 6. 38–155.

Creissels, Denis, & Alain Christian Bassène. This volume, chapter 17. Ventive, associated motion and aspect in Jóola Fóoñi (Atlantic).
Deering, Nora, & Helga Harries-Delisle. 1976. *Mohawk Teaching Grammar Preliminary version.* Quebec: The Thunderbird Press.
Dryer, Matthew. This volume, chapter 4. Associated motion and directionals: Where they overlap.
Dryer, Matthew. This volume, chapter 13. Associated motion in North America (including Mexico and Central America).
Foris, David P. 2000. *A grammar of Sochiapan Chinantec* [Studies in Chinantec Languages, 6]. Summer Institute of Linguistics International and The University of Texas at Arlington.
Guérois Rozenn, Hannah Gibson, & Bastian Persohn. This volume, chapter 15. Associated motion in Bantu languages.
Guillaume, Antoine. 2009. Les suffixes verbaux de mouvement associé en Cavineña. *Faits de Langues: Les Cahiers* 1. 181–204.
Guillaume, Antoine. 2016. Associated motion in South America: Typological and areal perspectives. *Linguistic Typology* 201. 81–177.
Guillaume, Antoine, & Harold Koch. This volume, chapter 1. Introduction: Associated Motion as a grammatical category in linguistic typology.
Hernández-Green, Néstor. 2015. Morfosintaxis verbal del otomí de Acazulco. PhD Thesis, Centro de Investigaciones y Estudios Superiores en Antropología Social, Mexico City.
Hernández-Green, Néstor. 2016. Registration versus applicative constructions in Acazulco Otomi. *International Journal of American Linguistics* 82. 353–383.
Hernández-Green, Néstor. 2017. Relatos de tradición oral en otomí de San Jerónimo Acazulco. *Revista de Literaturas Populares* XVII (2). 281–305.
Hernández-Green, Néstor. 2018a. El sistema aspectual del otomí de Acazulco. *Cuadernos de Lingüística de El Colegio de México* 52. 279–333.
Hernández-Green, Néstor. 2018b. Tres fuentes de las construcciones impersonales en otomí. *LIAMES* 18 (1). 7–29.
Koch, Harold. 1984. The category of "associated motion" in Kaytej. *Language in Central Australia* 1. 23–34.
Koch, Harold. This volume, chapter 7. Associated Motion in the Pama-Nyungan languages of Australia.
Lastra, Yolanda. 1997. *El otomí de Ixtenco.* Mexico City: Instituto de Investigaciones Antropológicas, Universidad Nacional Autónoma de México.
Osgarby, David. This volume, chapter 8. Mudburra associated motion in an areal perspective.
Otero, Manuel A. This volume, chapter 20. At the intersection of associated motion, direction and exchoative aspect in the Koman languages.
Palancar, Enrique L. 2008. The emergence of active/stative alignment in Otomi. In Mark Donohue, & Søren Wichmann (eds.), *The Typology of Semantic Alignment,* 357–379. Oxford: Oxford University Press.
Palancar, Enrique L. 2009a. *Gramática y textos del Hñöñhö: Otomí de San Ildefonso Tultepec, Querétaro* Vol. 1: Gramática. Mexico City: Plaza y Valdés.
Palancar, Enrique L. 2009b. *Gramática y textos del Hñöñhö: Otomí de San Ildefonso Tultepec, Querétaro* Vol. 2: Textos. Mexico City: Plaza y Valdés.
Palancar, Enrique L. 2011. The conjugations of Colonial Otomi. *Transactions of the Philological Society* 109 (3). 246–264.

Palancar, Enrique L. 2012a. The conjugation classes of Tilapa Otomi: An approach from canonical typology. *Linguistics* 50 (4). 783–832.
Palancar, Enrique L. 2012b. Verbal inflection with applicative-like function? The adverbial tenses in Otomi-Mazahua. Paper read at the Syntax of the World's Languages V. Dubrovnik.
Palancar, Enrique L. 2013. The evolution of number in Otomi: The many faces of the dual. *Studies in Language* 37 (1). 94–143.
Payne, Doris L. This volume, chapter 18. The extension of associated motion to direction, aspect and argument structure in Nilotic languages.
Ross, Daniel. This volume, chapter 2. A cross-linguistic survey of Associated Motion and directionals.
Sagot, Benoît, & Géraldine Walther. 2011. Non-canonical inflection: data, formalisation and complexity measures. *Proceedings of 2011 Systems and Frameworks in Computational Morphology. Communications in Computer and Information Science series*, 23–45. Berlin/Heidelberg: Springer.
Stewart, Donald. 1966. Gramática de mazahua. MS. Summer Institute of Linguistics.
Stump, Gregory, & Raphael Finkel. 2015a. Contrasting modes of representation for inflectional systems: Some implications for computing morphological complexity. In Matthew Baerman, Dunstan Brown, & Greville G. Corbett (eds.), *Understanding and Measuring Morphological Complexity*, 119–140. Oxford: Oxford University Press.
Stump, Gregory, & Raphael Finkel. 2015b. The complexity of inflectional systems. *Linguistics Vanguard* 11. 101–117.
Tallman, Adam J.R. This volume, chapter 11. Associated motion in Chácobo (Pano) in typological perspective.
UNESCO. 2003. Language Vitality and Endangerment. International Expert Meeting on UNESCO. Programme Safeguarding of Endangered Languages. Paris. http://www.unesco.org/new/fileadmin/MULTIMEDIA/HQ/CLT/pdf/Language_vitality_and_endangerment_EN.pdf
Vidal, Alejandra, & Doris L. Payne. This volume, chapter 12. Pilagá directionals and the typology of associated motion.
Voigtlander, Katherine, & Artemisa Echegoyen. 1985. *Luces contemporáneas del otomí. Gramática del otomí de La Sierra*. Mexico City: Instituto Lingüístico de Verano.
Wolgemuth, Carl. 1981. *Gramática náhuatl de Mecayapan*. México, D. F.: Instituto Lingüístico de Verano.

Part IV: **Africa**

Rozenn Guérois, Hannah Gibson and Bastian Persohn
15 Associated motion in Bantu languages

Abstract: Associated motion (AM) is not a widely used term in literature on Bantu languages. However, on the basis of a set of 55 Bantu languages, all of which have markers for associated motion, this chapter makes a case that the grammatical category of AM is indeed robustly attested throughout this language family. The chapter offers a comparative-typological survey of the encoding of associated motion in Bantu, and constitutes the first systematic examination of the category in this language family. It considers the morphological and semantic features of AM, their geographic distribution and how many AM distinctions are encoded in the languages. Further variation is also considered in relation to: i) the grammatical function of the moving figure, ii) the order of the main event and the motion co-event, iii) the restriction of markers to specific Tense-Aspect-Mood constructions, and iv) additional semantic developments associated with AM markers. By developing a small-scale typology of AM across the Bantu language family, this chapter contributes to the emerging typology of the AM category in the world's languages, as well as to our understanding of this category in Bantu.

Keywords: associated motion, morphology, semantics, complexity, grammaticalization, distribution, variation, Bantu languages

1 Introduction

The term 'associated motion' (AM) has been considered as both a conceptual notion and a corresponding grammatical category since Koch's (1984) pivotal paper and follow-up work such as that by Wilkins (1991) and Guillaume (2009, 2016). As outlined by Guillaume and Koch (this volume), AM can be defined as "a verbal grammatical category, separate from tense, aspect, mood and direction, whose function is to associate, in different ways, different kinds of translational motion (spatial displacement / change of location) to a (generally non-motion) verb event" (vis-à-vis e.g. Guillaume's [2016] survey of South American languages, which is restricted to affixal markers). An illustrative example of a typical

---
Rozenn Guérois, LLACAN-CNRS & University of KwaZulu-Natal, rozenn.guerois@cnrs.fr
Hannah Gibson, University of Essex, h.gibson@essex.ac.uk
Bastian Persohn, University of Hamburg, persohn.linguistics@gmail.com

https://doi.org/10.1515/9783110692099-015

Bantu AM marker is provided in (1) from Mpoto where the AM prefix *ka-* adds the notion of 'go and' (itive) to the 'take' event.[1]

(1) Mpoto (N14 Tanzania)[2] (Botne 2019: 717)
 *Ti-**ka**-tol-ayi*   *ku-va-pel-a*   *v-ana*   *v-itu*
 SP1PL-**IT**-take-SBJV   15.INF-OP2-give-FV   2-child   2-POSS1PL
 'We should go and take [it (food)] to give to our children.'

This chapter examines the encoding of AM in the Bantu language family – a group of some 500 languages spoken across much of central, eastern and southern Africa (Van de Velde and Bostoen 2019). The morphemes used in Bantu languages to encode deictic relations and to associate translational motion to non-motion verb events have not traditionally been analyzed under the label of Associated Motion. A number of other terms have been employed such as 'ka-movendi' (Watkins 1937), 'movement grams' (Nicolle 2002, 2013; Persohn 2017), 'distal aspects' (Nicolle 2003), 'directional markers' (Mkochi 2017), 'deictic markers' (Sitoe 2001), 'itive/ventive' markers (Nurse 2008; Guérois 2015; Botne 2019), 'distal imperative' (Botne 2003: 397) and 'subsecutive imperative' (Devos 2008).

This chapter seeks to examine morphological and semantic aspects of the encoding of AM, and to develop a small-scale typology of the AM category across the language family. The chapter represents the first systematic study of AM in the Bantu languages. It makes an innovative contribution and integrates observations from the Bantu language family into the broader typological discussion of AM. It complements and expands on existing comparative studies of AM in African languages (which typically looked at non-Bantu languages) such as Belkadi (2016, this volume).

The study is based on a survey of 55 Bantu languages (listed in the Appendix) all of which have at least one strategy to express AM. In most cases, the data are taken from published descriptive work, although in some instances, this has been supplemented with material from unpublished sources. A representative sample from across the Bantu-speaking area has been attempted. However, there is an over-representation of Eastern languages. This is explained by two

---

[1] In keeping with the approach adopted throughout this volume, AM markers are glossed as in the original sources. However, for coherence and ease of reading, the other grammatical functions are presented in a uniform manner.
[2] The Bantu languages are conventionally divided into 16 geographic zones (each assigned a letter) following the work of Guthrie (1967–1971), with an update by Maho (2009). This purely geographic system was introduced before the ISO 639-3 coding and has become the standard way of identifying Bantu languages.

factors: Firstly, more descriptive work is available for a greater number of Eastern Bantu languages. Secondly, the accounts available for Western (and specifically North-Western) Bantu languages, seem to indicate that AM is less commonly attested in these regions. The reader should also bear in mind that while the final number of languages analyzed in this chapter is 55, a bigger sample has been considered. In the final set we retain only those languages with clear instantiations of AM. However, it is possible that AM is attested – but simply not described – in many of the languages that we ultimately excluded.

The study is structured around two primary domains of investigation. Firstly, it explores the way in which AM is encoded in Bantu – with three main strategies identified, i.e. prefixation of an AM marker, circumfixation of an AM marker, and use of auxiliary constructions. Secondly, it examines the degree of 'complexity' covered by these AM systems – i.e. how many AM distinctions are encoded. Four additional domains of variation are also considered: i) the grammatical function of the moving figure, ii) the relative order of the main event and the motion co-event, iii) the restriction of AM markers to specific Tense-Aspect-Mood (TAM) constructions, and iv) additional semantic developments the AM markers have undergone.

The chapter is structured as follows. Section 2 illustrates the strategies used to express AM in the surveyed languages. Section 3 identifies the levels of complexity in the encoding of AM in Bantu. Section 4 focuses on other parameters of variation, particularly the moving argument, temporal relations and TAM restrictions. Section 5 highlights a number of challenges in relation to AM in contrast to locational verbal morphology and deixis, while Section 6 constitutes a conclusion.

2 The encoding of associated motion in Bantu

2.1 Bantu verbal structure

Bantu languages are known for their dominant SVO word order, predominantly head-marking morphology and in many cases are characterized by noun classes with extensive systems of agreement. Bantu languages also tend to have a rich (agglutinative) verbal morphology.[3] The verbal complex commonly consists of a

---

[3] This is with the exception of many north-western Bantu languages which have more analytical morphology.

string of elements that appear in a strict order organized around a stem nucleus, which is built upon a verbal root optionally hosting one or several derivational suffixes. The elements that appear in these verbal slots convey a range of grammatical information, as can be seen on examination of Table 1 below. As will be seen throughout this chapter, AM markers regularly appear in the post-initial slot.

Table 1: Template of the finite Bantu verb (based on Güldemann 1999: 546).

Slot	pre-initial	initial	post-initial	pre-radical	radical	pre-final	final	post-final
Function	TAM/ polarity	subject	TAM/ polarity/ AM	object	verb root	derivation/ TAM	TAM	clause type/ object/ polarity

The example from Nyakyusa in (2) illustrates the ordering and type of information that may appear in the verb, with temporal and aspectual information, subject agreement, negative polarity and object agreement all appearing as prefixes (or proclitics), while the verb root also hosts the applicative suffix and a class 17 locative marker in the post-final position.

(2) Nyakyusa (M31 Tanzania) (Persohn 2017: 53)
 aa=tʊ-ti-kʊ-ba-jaat-ɪl-a=ko
 FUT=SP1PL-NEG-NON.PST.IPFV-OP2-walk-APPL-FV=17.LOC
 'We will not visit them there.'

Several studies have examined the form and relatedness of tense-aspect markers across the language family (see Nurse 2003; Nurse and Philippson 2006; Nurse 2008, amongst others). However, the morphological encoding of spatial relationships within the Bantu verb has received considerably less attention.

2.2 Encoding AM in Bantu: an overview

Across Bantu, motion co-events can be encoded through: i) the prefixation of an AM marker; ii) the addition of a circumfix (which is found in just one surveyed language), or iii) a grammaticalized auxiliary construction. These are discussed in turn below.

The first (and most widespread) strategy consists of prefixing an AM marker to the verbal form. The most common AM marker is *ka-* (or a variant thereof). This marker is attested in 36 out of 55 sampled languages (65%) and is considered historically to derive from the verb of motion *ka 'go' reconstructed by Meinhof (1910) (see also Meeussen [1967] and Botne [1999] for a study of ka- in a wider sample of languages). The marker ka- usually appears in the post-initial slot, following polarity and TAM markers (where present) and preceding the verbal (macro)stem. This is illustrated in Nyamwezi (3), where the AM prefix ka- is preceded by the future marker ku-.

(3) Nyamwezi (F22 Tanzania)
(Maganga and Schadeberg 1992: 108; glosses added)
*a-ku-**ka**-mal-a*
SP1-FUT-**IT**-finish-FV
'He will go and finish.'

The prefix ka- is widespread across Bantu. As can be seen in Map 1, its distribution goes from south-western to eastern Bantu, covering 8 out of 16 Guthrie's geographic zones: R, K, L, M, F, N, G and P. (See also Botne [1999: 475] who notes a similar distribution).

The form ka- is not the only prefix used to encode AM across Bantu languages. Prefixes that can still transparently be traced back to verbs of motion are also attested, especially 'come' and 'go' verbs. These verbs were originally part of auxiliary constructions of the shape SP-go/come (possibly further inflected with TAM(P) morphology) + INF-Stem and have undergone subsequent grammaticalization, whereby i) the infinitive prefix was either deleted or merged with the preceding motion auxiliary; ii) the former motion auxiliary subsequently became a prefix attached to the verb stem. This is exemplified in (4) with Changana where the AM markers ya- 'IT[IVE]' (< verb stem ya 'go') and ta- 'VENT[IVE]' (< ta 'come') occupy the post-initial slot in the verb.

(4) Changana (S53 South Africa, Mozambique) (Sitoe 2001: 104)
*Hi-yanakany-a ku-**ya/ta**-haq-a doropa*
SP1PL-think-FV 15.INF-**IT/VENT**-besiege-FV town
'We are thinking of going/coming and besieging the town.'

The AM prefixes in Digo and Shona are also transparently grammaticalized from constructions involving 'come' and 'go' verbs as illustrated in (5). The mid vowel /o/ in Shona is the result of fusion of the default final vowel -a and the high vowel /u/ of the infinitive prefix (Fortune 1984: 96).

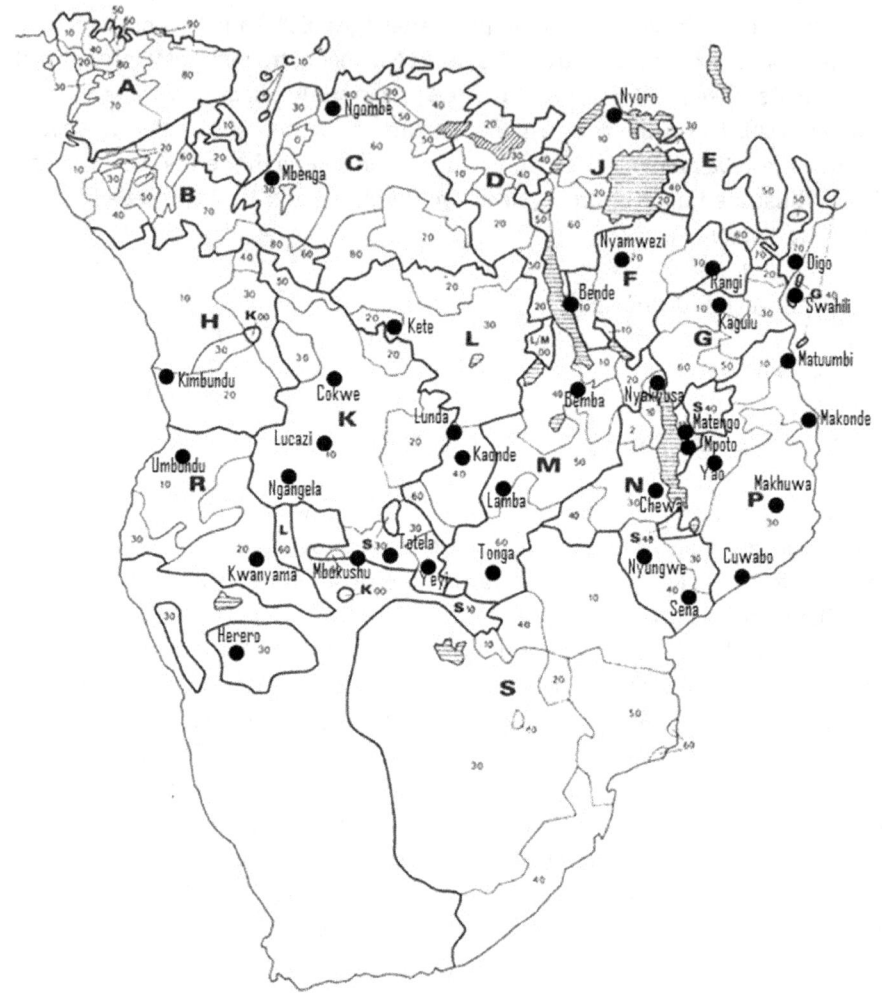

Map 1: Distribution of *ka-* as itive marker. (Background map from Blench [2014: 247])

(5) | Language | AM prefix | Source verb stem | Proto-Bantu (Bastin et al. 2002)
    | Changana | *ta-* VENT | *ta* 'come' | ?
    | | *ya-* IT | *ya* 'go' | **gì*
    | Digo | *edza-* VENT | *edza* 'come' | **jìj*
    | | *enda-* IT | *enda* 'go' | **gènd*
    | | *ya-* IT | *phiya* 'go' | **pít*
    | Shona | *zo-* VENT | *za* 'come' | **jìj*
    | | *ndo-* IT | *enda* 'go' | **gènd*
    | | *sviko-* ADLOC | *svika* 'arrive' | **pìk*

It should be noted that in some present-day languages the source verbs are obsolete. This is the case in Digo, where the source verb *enda* 'go', which developed into the AM affix *enda-*, is no longer available as a lexical verb (Nicolle 2013: 172). Only the verb stem *phiya*, which in turn grammaticalized into the AM prefix *ya-*, is synchronically observed with the meaning 'go' in Digo. Similarly, in Shona, the lexical verb *za* 'come' has become obsolete in general use and is only found in formulaic expressions and proverbs (Fortune 1955: 334; Mberi 2002: 115).

A second strategy for encoding AM in Bantu consists of circumfixing an AM marker to the verb. In our study, this strategy is only attested in Mongo (Democratic Republic of the Congo) where an AM circumfix seemingly of the shape *yu-* ... *-e* (~ *yo-* ... *-e*) can be added to imperative verb forms, as illustrated in (6).[4]

(6) Mongo (C61 DRC) (Hulstaert 1965: 444, glosses added)
 a. **yŭ**-tel-**e**   i-faká
    AM-take-**AM**   19-knife
    'go back (sg.) to take the knife'
 c. **yŏ**-kol-**e**   ló-ngo
    AM-pick_up-**AM** 11-hoe
    'go/come (sg.) and pick the hoe up'

 b. *loó-sang-e*
    SP2PL.**AM**-say-**AM**
    'come and say (pl.)!'
 d. *lɔ́-l-ɛ*
    SP2PL.**AM**-eat-**AM**
    'go and eat (pl.)!'

(7) Mongo (DRC)   (Ruskin 1934: 106–107)
 a. tanga   'name (sg.)!'
    lo-tanga   'name (pl.)!'
 b. boma   'kill (sg.)!'
    lo-oma   'kill (pl.)!'
 c. ena   'see (sg.)!'
    l-ena   'see (pl.)!'

On the basis of these examples, the nature of AM marking in Mongo is, however, difficult to determine precisely, and the following should be seen as a tentative hypothesis based on Hulstaert's (1965) descriptive account. Hulstaert (1965: 444) reports the existence of two AM-linked forms in Mongo: *yŏ-* ... *-e* used in the 2nd person singular imperative (6a), and *lŏ-* ... *-e* used in the 2nd person plural

---

4 Note that 1) both vocalic and tonal differences between *yŭ* and *yŏ* are unexplained by Hulstaert; 2) the directionality of the AM marker *yu-* ... *-e* (as both 'go' and 'come' in Hulstaert's translations) is briefly discussed in Section 3.2.1 below.

imperative (6b).[5] In terms of formal properties, the final vowel -*e* (or -*ɛ* when the vowel of the verb root is /ɛ/ or /ɔ/, see Hulstaert [1961: 35–40] on vowel harmony in Mongo), common to both singular and plural forms, does not appear in basic imperative constructions, i.e. those unmarked for AM, as shown in (7). The suffix -*e* thus seems to be an element marking AM in Mongo. The fact that the 2nd person singular imperative is formally identical to the verb stem, while its plural equivalent is expressed by the addition of a second person plural subject marker (with some morpho-phonological effects on the surface), as can be seen in (7), suggests that the 'raw' AM prefix is obtained in the 2nd person singular imperatives with the form *yǜ*- or *yŏ*- shown in (6a). Therefore, 2nd person plural imperatives seem to merge the 2nd person plural subject prefix *lo*- with the *yŏ*- AM variant, resulting in a CVV syllable with a back mid-vowel quality (6b). If this analysis is correct, it would mean that AM in Mongo is achieved through both prefixation and suffixation, i.e. circumfixation, something which has otherwise not been observed for the expression of AM in Bantu languages.

The third strategy for encoding AM across Bantu is the use of a grammaticalized auxiliary construction involving a verb of motion. Among the surveyed languages, only Nyakyusa (8) and Fuliiru exhibit this strategy.

(8) Nyakyusa (M31 Tanzania) (Persohn 2018: 118)
 ʊ-**j**-ile kʊ-bomb-a?
 SP2SG-**go**-PFV 15.INF-work-FV
 'Did you go (and) work?'

In the case of Nyakyusa, the AM auxiliary *(j)a* 'go' can be traced back to a former verb of motion which is no longer synchronically available as a lexical item (Persohn 2017, 2018). Evidence of the process of grammaticalization, however, comes from the observation that the complement of *(j)a* may host morphemes which are not generally available in infinitives, e.g. the imperfective suffix -*aga*, and that *(j)a* has developed further meanings, combining motion with prospective aspect (Persohn 2017: 317–322, 2018).

This contrasts with the situation in Zulu, where a widespread construction is one employed in directive speech acts in which an imperative is followed by a subjunctive verb form (9). Although the form *yana* 'go!' (derived from *ya* 'go') is interpreted as conveying a motion meaning, an alternative lexical verb could equally be used instead. This construction in Zulu therefore does not fit within

---

5 In other TAM categories, motion events are expressed by means of complex constructions based on the auxiliaries *yá* 'come' and *tswá* 'go' followed by an infinitive verb (see Hulstaert 1966: 318).

the definition of AM employed in the current volume in which AM markers must constitute a distinct grammatical category.

(9) Zulu (S42 South Africa) (Doke 1947: 331; glosses added)
 Y-a-na u-leth-e
 go-FV-IMP.SG SP2SG-bring-SBJV
 'Go and bring'

On the basis of the available descriptions, grammatical markers expressing AM appear to be much less common in the northwestern languages, as can be seen on examination of Map 2 in Section 3.4 below.

2.3 'Iterative' or 'echo' use of AM across Bantu

In Bantu languages, as in other language families of the world, AM markers are typically attached to non-motion verbs in order to add a semantic component of movement. However, it has been reported for several geographically and genetically unrelated languages (see Wilkins [1991, 2006] and Guillaume [2009, 2016: fn 11] among others) that a verb carrying an AM marker may be preceded by a lexical motion verb that expresses the same motion semantics. In this usage, the AM appears to 'reiterate' or 'echo' the motion event introduced by the lexical motion verb. Analogous uses have been reported across the Bantu language family (e.g. Fleisch 2000 for Lucazi; Nicolle 2007, 2013 for Digo; Persohn 2017, 2018 for Nyakyusa). An example from Cuwabo is provided in (10). In (10a), the itive prefix á- 'go and' is the sole marker of motion in the clause, whereas in (10b), á- appears in addition to the motion verb *dhowa* 'go'.[6]

(10) Cuwabo (P34 Mozambique) (Guérois 2015: 389–390)
 a. ddi-ḿ-fun-á ni-á-cey-e m-búga
 SP1SG-IPFV.CJ-want-FV SP1PL-IT-sow-SBJV 3-rice
 'I want us to go and sow rice.'

 b. ń-**dhow**-e ni-á-aredh-e
 SP1PL-**go**-SBJV SP1PL-IT-have.fun-SBJV
 'Let's go and have fun.'

---

6 The AM prefix á- in Cuwabo is a cognate of the widespread *ka-* marker, which has been reduced due to consonant loss in the intervocalic position. When used word-initially though, i.e. in imperative forms, the full CV shape is obtained (see example (28) below).

3 Complexity in AM systems in Bantu

3.1 Levels of complexity

In a survey of AM in South American languages, Guillaume (2016) introduces three different categories of complexity for AM systems: simple systems (1–2 markers), complex systems (3–5 markers) and very complex systems (≥ 6 markers). In this section, we discuss the different levels of complexity found in Bantu AM systems. For the purposes of the current discussion, we follow the approach adopted by Guillaume (2016) and consider 'complexity' only in terms of the number of AM markers found; see Ross (this volume) and Koch (this volume) for a problematization of the concept of complexity.

We begin with general observations about complexity in AM systems and the numerical and geographic distribution of the levels of complexity across Bantu languages (Section 3.1).[7] We then take a closer look at the distinctions encoded in simple systems (Section 3.2) and complex systems (Section 3.3). None of the languages in our sample exhibit the very complex systems of Guillaume's (2016) study – those with more than 6 markers –, so this category is not discussed. Finally, we present correlations in terms of the complexity of AM systems, their associated semantics and geographic distribution (Section 3.4).

In terms of numerical distribution, simple systems make up 93% (51 out of 55 languages) of our set of languages. The remaining 7% (4 out of 55) languages have complex systems. As discussed more in detail in Section 4.3, AM markers in Bantu, particularly those of the shape *ka-* (or similar), appear to be highly restricted in terms of the TAM forms with which they can co-occur.

Lastly, in contrast to what is found in some languages of South America (Guillaume 2016) and Australia (e.g. Koch 1984; Wilkins 1991), no AM system in the Bantu languages surveyed includes a strategy for encoding complex motion paths such as return paths. Rather, only simplex motion events (mostly itive and ventive) are attested.

---

[7] In some cases, AM markers may have lost their core meaning of translational motion and developed into locational markers (see also Section 5.1). Similarly, in some instances the available descriptive literature does not provide a clear analysis of lexical verbs, AM markers and locational markers. In case of doubt, we have counted markers as AM. In general, we believe the phenomenon has been under-reported in Bantu and as such our approach may have led to a slight over-representation in our language sample.

3.2 Simple systems

In this section we look at those AM systems that are classified as 'simple' in the terms of Guillaume (2016), i.e. those systems with one or two markers.

3.2.1 Simple systems with one marker

From the surveyed languages with only one AM marker, 27 out of 34 (almost 80%) use the prefix *ka-* (or similar). Kaonde (11) is a language where *ka-* is the only AM marker reported (see also Nyamwezi (3) and Cuwabo (10) above).

(11) Kaonde (L41 Zambia) (Wright 2007: 32; glosses added)
 a. *w-a-ká-leet-a* *buta*
    SP1-PST-IT-bring-FV 9.gun
    'he went and brought the gun'

 b. *u-saku-ká-leet-a* *mu-pando*
    SP1-NEAR.FUT-IT-bring-FV 3-chair
    'he will go and bring the chair'

As shown in Map 1, simple AM systems with *ka-* cover most of the south-western, central and eastern areas of the Bantu zone, i.e. from Angola and the Democratic Republic of the Congo to Tanzania and northern Mozambique.

The Mongo AM system, with the circumfix *yù- ... -e ~ yŏ- ... -e* (see Section 2.2), is also simple in terms of complexity. When translating the examples given in (6), Hulstaert (1965) proposes two possible interpretations in terms of directionality, i.e. both 'go' and 'come'. However, no additional information is provided in terms of whether – or indeed, when – one interpretation is preferred over the other one. It is very likely that context is crucial in disambiguating the meanings, but this hypothesis cannot easily be substantiated without further research. As such, we consider Mongo to have a simple AM system with only one marker, but with two possible interpretations (which might, in turn, relate to some sort of semantic underspecification).

From the 34 languages with only one AM marker, 28 (82%) of these encode an itive function. In addition to the Mongo AM circumfix discussed above, in Iyaa (12) and Mbuun (DRC) and in Mbugwe (Tanzania), only 'come' is expressed through AM.

(12) Iyaa (B73c DRC) (Mouandza 2001: 391; glosses added)
 bó *bá-yí-yòlò*
 PRO2 SP2-VENT-take
 'they came and took'

3.2.2 Simple systems with two markers

Simple AM systems comprising two markers are widespread across Bantu (see also Map 2 in Section 3.4 below). In most cases, the reported pair of AM markers represents cognates of verb forms expressing 'go' and 'come'. In (13), two examples are provided from Southern Sotho which has itive *ĕa-* 'go and' and ventive *tla-* 'come and'. Note that these two markers have also developed into an immediate future and an ordinary future marker respectively (see Section 4.4). However, according to Doke and Mofokeng (1957: 205), "[t]he idea of motion in the use of *ĕa* is still felt", as shown in (13a). The marker *tla-*, in turn, encodes the idea of motion only when it is associated with a remnant of the perfect suffix *-ile* which is present in the original periphrastic construction. In this case, the AM prefix and the perfect marker are merged and appear as the prefix *tlil'-* (13b). When used on its own – i.e. when directly followed by the verb stem without being associated with the (former) perfect marker – no motion is conveyed on the event, and *tla-* merely expresses an ordinary future (such use is illustrated in (30b) below).

(13) Southern Sotho (S33 South Africa)
(Doke and Mofokeng 1957: 206–207; glosses added)
a. *Kē-ĕa-ba-bòn-a,   ha   kē-fihl-a   Maseru*
   SP1SG-**IT**-OP2-see-FV when SP1SG-arrive-FV Maseru
   'I shall see them / I am going to see them when I reach Maseru.'

b. *Johanne   ō-tlil'-o-rē-bòn-a*
   Johanne SP1-**VENT**.PRF-15.INF-OP1PL-see-FV
   'John has come to see us.'

Nyakyusa is another language with two AM markers. However, unlike Southern Sotho and other languages in this category, both Nyakyusa AM markers are itive. One is expressed by means of the auxiliary *(j)a* 'go', ((8) above) while the second marker is the common Bantu prefix *ka-*, illustrated in (14). Unlike *(j)a*, *ka-* is restricted to the subjunctive mood. Furthermore, this marker has also developed locational, i.e. non-motion uses (see Section 5.1).[8]

---

[8] The voicing of the initial segment (*ka > ga*) is an effect of the preceding first person singular subject prefix *n-*.

(14) Nyakyusa   Persohn (2017: 283)
    po   ʊ-sota   bo jɪ-fum-ile   n-kʊ-jaat-a
    then   AUG-9.python   as SP9-come_from-PFV 18.LOC-15.INF-walk-FV
    *jɪ-lɪnkʊ-tɪ   "n-**ga**-keet-e   ii-fumbɪ ly-angʊ"*
    SP9-NARR-say   SP1SG-IT-watch-FV 5-egg   5-POSS1SG
    'Python, when it had come from taking a walk, said "I'll go look after my egg."'

3.3 Complex systems

In this section we look at complex AM systems – i.e. those which feature between three and five markers of AM. Of the surveyed languages, 7% (4 out of 55) exhibit a complex system.

3.3.1 Complex systems with three markers

Shona is an example of a language which has three AM markers: the itive *ndo-* (15a), ventive *zo-* (15b), and adlocative ('on arrival') *sviko-* (15c). These three prefixes are all grammaticalized from the collocation of a motion verb stem (*enda* 'go', *za* 'come', and *svika* 'arrive') and the infinitival class 15 prefix *ku-*, i.e. they all originate from periphrastic constructions involving finite motion verbs and infinitival complements. The merging of these two morphemes results in the deletion of the prefix consonant /k/ and is followed by vowel coalescence between the verb stem final vowel *-a* and the vowel /u/ of the infinitive prefix.

(15) Shona (S10 Zimbabwe)
    a. *nd-aká-**ndo**-chér-á   m-vúrá*
       SP1SG-REM.PST-IT-draw-FV   3-water
       'I went to draw water.' (Fortune 1984: 97; glosses added)

    b. *ci-**zo**-rar-a*
       now-VENT-sleep-FV
       'Come now and sleep!' (Fortune 1955: 334; glosses added)

c. *mu-kadzi   uyu   aka-**sviko**-mbundir-an-a*
   1-woman   1.DEM.PROX   SP1.REM.PST-**ADLOC**-embrace-RECP-FV
   no-mw-eni   w-ake
   COM-1-visitor   1-POSS3SG
   'This woman, on arrival, embraced each other with her visitor [sic].'
   (Mberi 2002: 139)

Shona *zo-* 'come' seems to serve as a ventive AM marker only in imperatives (15b). In other TAM constructions, it has developed a metaphorical meaning of 'coming to VERB' (see Sections 3.4 and 4.4). The translation 'go to VERB' in (15a) suggests that the notion of purpose may play a role in the semantics of certain AM markers in Bantu (see Section 4.4).

3.3.2 Complex systems with four or five markers

Two languages in our survey have more than three markers of AM: Digo and Fuliiru. Among the five Digo markers *ka-*, *enda-*, *ya-*, *edza-*, and *cha-*, the first three are itive. More specifically, *ka-* and *enda-* are complementarily distributed, depending on TAM categories. While *ka-* is restricted to the subjunctive mood (16a), *enda-* is used with all other TAM markers (16b). The third itive marker *ya-* (16c) additionally conveys a future-oriented meaning, whereby "the action described by the verb is subsequent to some temporal reference point" (Nicolle 2003: 6). The fourth marker *edza-* (16d) is a ventive.

(16)   Digo (E73 Kenya, Tanzania)   (Nicolle 2013: 169–173)
   a. ***Ka**-som-e*
      IT-study-SBJV
      'go and study'

   b. *a-pig-a   m-biru   a-ch-**enda**-mu-endz-a*
      SP2-hit-FV   9-horn   SP2-SEQ-**IT**-OP1-search-FV
      'they blew the horn and went and looked for him'

   c. *U-**ya**-hend-a-dze   Kwale?*
      SP2SG-FUT.**IT**-do-FV-Q   Kwale
      What are you going to do in Kwale?'

   d. *Li-gundzu   a-chetu   a-k-**edza**-hek-a   ma-dzi.*
      11-morning   2-woman   SP2-SEQ-**VENT**-draw-FV   6-water
      'In the morning the women came and drew water.'

The status of the fifth Digo marker *cha-* (17) is more problematic.

(17) Digo (Kenya, Tanzania) (Nicolle 2013: 168)
 u-**cha**-mu-amb-ir-a
 SP2SG-**DIST**-OP1-tell-APPL-FV
 'You tell her (over there).'

According to Nicolle (2013: 167), *cha-* denotes an "action at a distance from the deictic centre", which does not necessarily involve a motion co-event. As we discuss in more detail in Section 5.1, when in doubt we have opted to include such borderline cases in our survey.

Fuliiru is another case of a complex system with five markers. The AM markers in this language form part of a larger set of what van Otterloo (2011) terms "adverbial auxiliaries". At first glance, it appears that Fuliiru has not only five, but eight AM markers. However, a closer look reveals that Fuliiru has a combination of five verbs that participated in the grammaticalization process, namely *génd* 'go', *yíj* 'come', *lèng* 'pass (a location)', *híkir* 'arrive + APPL' and *taah* 'go home' and two different morphosyntactic frames, which in a slightly simplified form can be schematized as in (18). Example (19) illustrates the use of *génd* 'go' in these two frames.[9,10] Example (20) illustrates *lèng* 'pass' in the *ga*-frame.

(18) *i*-frame: ... -*i* macrostem
 ga-frame: ... -FV SP-*ga(a)*-macrostem

(19) Fuliiru (JD63 DRC) (van Otterloo 2011: 278–286)
 a. à-ná-**gênd-ì**   tèg-á   i-ny-àmîishwá   í-rú-bàkò
  SP1-SEQ-**going-i** trap-PFV AUG-10-wild_animal 23.LOC-11-forest
  'He went and trapped wild animals at the forest'

 b. à-ná-**génd**-àg-à   á-**gá**-lóòz-á   á-bá-kàzì
  SP1-SEQ-**going**-EMPH-FV SP1-**ga**-seek-FV AUG-2-woman
  'And he went looking for women'

---

9 The *i* suffix relates to what was originally an infinitive prefix (of class 5) on the following verb. Coalescence between the final vowel of the motion verb and the infinitive prefix paved the way to reinterpreting /i/ as a suffix of the motion verb (van Otterloo 2011: 264).
10 The prefix *ga(a)-* is described as a "future/intentional" prefix by van Otterloo (2011).

(20) Fuliiru (DRC) (van Otterloo 2011: 280)
*lyê-ry-ó   í-fárásì   z-àná-**lèng**-à   zì-gwétì*
EMPH-5-right_then 5-horse SP10-SEQ-**passing**-FV SP10-PROG
*zí-**gá**-tîmb-à   í-bí-sìndò*
SP10-**ga**-beat-FV AUG-8-sound
'Right then the horses passed making a pounding sound.'

Of the five (former) motion verb bases, three (*génd* 'go', *yíj* 'come', and *lèng* 'pass') are found in both morphosyntactic frames, while *híkìr* 'arrive' is only found in the *ga*-frame and *taah* 'go home' only in the *i*-frame.

As for the semantic contribution of the two frames, van Otterloo (2011: 278) mentions that the *i*-frame with *génd* 'go' and *yíj* 'come' yields a reading of prior motion, while the same roots in the *ga*-frame denote concurrent motion. With the other three verbal bases (*lèng* 'pass', *híkìr* 'arrive + APPL' and *taah* 'go home'), the absence of counterexamples to this generalization suggests that the link between temporal relation and morphosyntactic frame generally holds for Fuliiru. This means that Fuliiru is the only Bantu language that we are aware of that systematically distinguishes two temporal relations in the domain of AM (see also Section 4.2). The different distribution of the grammaticalized motion verb bases with the two morphosyntactic frames yields a four-way distinction for each temporal relation, as illustrated in (21).

(21) prior motion (*i*-frame):   itive vs. ventive vs. 'pass' vs 'go home'
     concurrent motion (*ga*-frame): itive vs. ventive vs. 'pass' vs. adlocative

3.4 Generalizations and geographic distribution

An examination of the AM systems in the languages surveyed gives rise to a number of generalizations: Firstly, when a language has only one AM marker, in most cases (82%), it expresses an itive sense (see exceptions in Section 3.2.1). Secondly, two-way AM systems predominantly display a distinction between itive and ventive. Thirdly, more complex systems, which include additional semantic distinctions such as 'arrive and VERB', 'pass and VERB' and 'go home and VERB' in the case of Fuliiru (see Section 3.3.3), reveal that itive and ventive are by far the categories most frequently used in discourse. Percentages calculated on the basis of 1,320 attestations of AM constructions in van Otterloo's (2011) corpus of Fuliiru are provided in Table 2.

The frequency of occurrence of AM markers in complex systems is likely to be linked to the meaning encoded by each marker: the more semantically specialized a marker is ('go home', 'pass' or adlocative 'arrive'), the more limited its usage ($\leq 5\%$). Furthermore, if the Fuliiru results mirror the lexical frequency of the

Table 2: Percentage distribution of the occurrences of AM markers in Fuliiru (based on van Otterloo 2011: 277).

AM construction	Occurrences	Percentage
génd 'go'	764	57.88%
yíj 'come'	400	30.30%
taah 'go home'	73	5.53%
léng 'pass'	71	5.38%
híkir 'arrive'	12	0.91%
Total	1320	100%

source verbs (although this remains to be confirmed), it may explain why motions like 'go' and 'come' are more easily grammaticalized into AM markers (see Bybee et al. 1994: 5), and as a result, why more complex systems are generally rarer.

In terms of geographical distribution, Map 2 shows that simple AM systems are attested throughout the Bantu area (except the north-western). However,

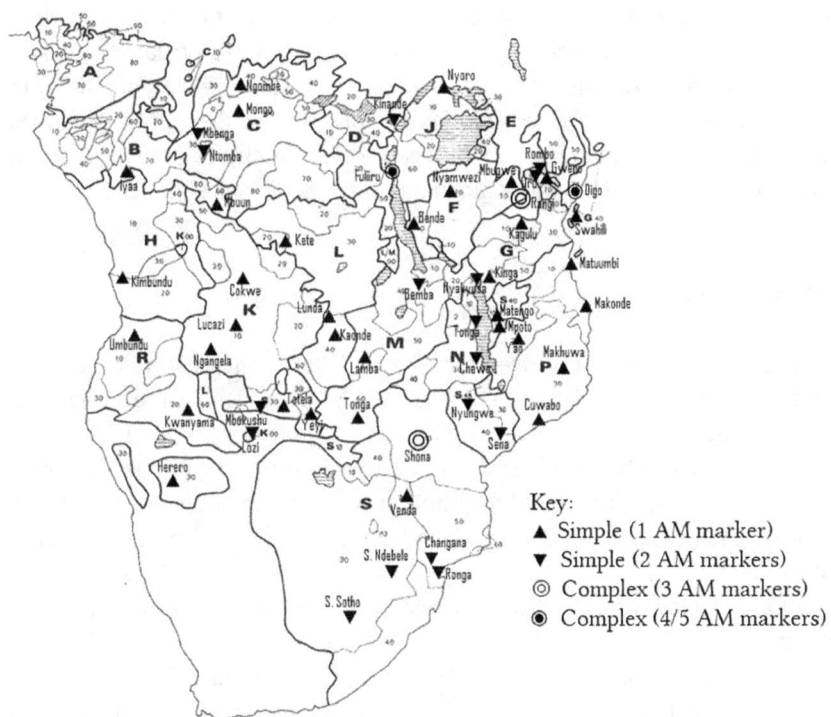

Map 2: Geographic distribution of simple and complex AM systems in Bantu (Background map from Blench [2014: 247]).

systems with one marker are predominantly found across the central and eastern areas, which corresponds to the zone associated with itive *ka-* (see Map 1). Systems with two AM markers are mostly present in the eastern and southern areas. More complex systems are much rarer and restricted to a couple of eastern languages. However, since most previous descriptive work dedicated to Bantu languages has not thoroughly investigated the expression of AM, it can be expected that the number and the associated distribution of AM systems is in fact higher.

Three generalizations can be made from this distribution. Firstly, simple systems are the norm in those Bantu languages exhibiting AM. Secondly, the few Bantu languages displaying a higher degree of variation and complexity in expressing AM are found in the eastern and southern regions. Thirdly, northwestern languages seem to be devoid of the AM category.

4 Other parameters of variation

In this section we discuss other parameters of variation in relation to the encoding of AM. In Section 4.1 we discuss the grammatical function (and associated semantic roles) of the moving figure. In Section 4.2 we discuss the relative temporal order of the main event described by the verb and the motion co-event. Section 4.3 examines the relation between AM marking and TAM categories. Finally, Section 4.4 looks at additional semantic developments which have occurred in some languages.

4.1 Moving figure

A parameter of variation introduced by Wilkins (1991) concerns the grammatical function of the moving figure, i.e. whether it is the subject or the object that undergoes translational motion. In all Bantu languages examined here, the moving entity is typically the subject (intransitive S or transitive A), not the object (see examples (11), (15a) and (16d) for illustration). This corroborates the strong preference for a moving subject observed by Guillaume (2016) for the languages of South America.

A few additional observations, however, merit discussion. Whereas Cuwabo causativized verbs typically entail the moving figure to be the subject-causer (22a), in some contexts, it may preferably be identified with the object-causee (22b). Although more examples combining AM markers with causativized verbs would be needed to draw further generalizations, the context is certainly a crucial factor in determining which argument is the moving figure.

(22) Cuwabo (Mozambique) (Guérois field notes)
   a. *ddi-**a**-mu-ttambilr-ih-e*   *mu-námalaba*
      SP1SG-**IT**-OP1-receive-CAUS-SBJV   1-worker
      Interpretation 1 (favoured): 'so that I go and pay [lit. make receive] the worker'
      Interpretation 2 (accepted): #'so that I make the worker go and receive'
   b. *ddi-**á**-rudd-ih-e*   *gulúwe*
      SP1SG-**IT**-urinate-CAUS-SBJV   9.pig
      Interpretation 1 (favoured): 'so that I make the pig go and urinate'
      Interpretation 2 (accepted): #'so that I go and make the pig urinate'

Further (apparent) counterexamples to our generalization come from Digo and Nyakyusa. First, Nicolle (2013: 173) notes for the Digo marker *edza-* that "[i]n most clauses containing *edza*, the subject of the clause is the participant [...] However, it is possible for *edza* to be used in cases where it is a participant other than the subject of the clause which moves". The passive in (23) Nicolle's (2013) translation implies a motion undergone by the oblique agent participant 'hyena'. A closer examination of Digo texts (Nicolle 2015) together with a discussion of (23) and similar examples (Steve Nicolle, p.c.), however, show that *edza-* has also developed a metaphorical meaning, indicating in this specific case the inevitability of the act of being taken (see also Section 4.4), rather than the motion of the oblique participant. This second interpretation, which seems to be the prevailing one, is in line with the generalization that the moving entity in Bantu languages is predominantly the subject.[11]

(23) Digo (Kenya, Tanzania)   (Nicolle 2013: 173)
   siku   *y-a*   *n-ne*   *y-a*   *tsano*   *yuya*   *mu-tu*
   9.day   9-CONN 9-four 9-CONN 9.five   1.DEM.DIST 1-person
   w-a-lum-w-a   *n'=chi-tswa*   *a-chi-fw-a*
   SP1-PST-pain-PASS-FV   COP=7-head   SP1-SEQ-die-FV
   na   *a-ch-**edza**-hal-w-a*   *ni*   *ma-fisi*
   and   SP1-SEQ-**VENT**-take-PASS-FV   by   6-hyena
   Original translation: 'On the fourth and fifth day that man had a headache, (then) he died and hyenas came and took him.' (lit. 'he came and was taken by hyenas')
   More likely: '... and he came to be taken (=was eventually or inevitably taken) by hyenas.'

---

[11] Persohn (2018) also discusses an apparent counterexample in Nyakyusa, which he links to the development of a prospective (future-oriented aspectual) reading of the construction in question.

4.2 Temporal relations

Variation in temporal relations relates to the relative order of the motion co-event and the main event. Three logical possibilities exist which tend to follow an implicational hierarchy: prior motion > concurrent motion > subsequent motion (Koch 1984; Guillaume 2016).

Our survey corroborates this observation, as prior motion predominates and is commonly the only available reading for Bantu AM markers. The only language that systematically distinguishes temporal relations in the domain of AM, specifically prior and concurrent motion, is Fuliiru (see Section 3.3.3). We are not aware of any Bantu language that has dedicated grammatical means to express subsequent motion.

Although prior motion is the prototypical reading of AM markers in all languages except Fuliiru, in some languages, when the relevant markers are used together with verbs of motion, they may denote a single motion event rather than adding a distinct motion co-event. Nicolle (2003: 7) states that the marker *enda*- 'go' in Digo "indicates that movement either precedes *or is an integral part of the action* described by the main verb" (emphasis added). Example (24) illustrates a case of concurrent motion: the grammatically construed notion of 'go' and the lexically encoded motion do not occur in sequence but rather simultaneously. An alternative (but less natural) translation could be something along the lines of 'That man left while (going and) following the track of the antelope to a cave.'

(24) Digo (Kenya, Tanzania) (Nicolle 2015: 45–46)
*yuya   m-lume   wa-uk-a   a-ch-**enda**-lungalung-a*
1.DEM.DIST 1-man   SP1.PST-leave-FV SP1-CONS-**IT**-follow-FV
hura   m-guruto   w-a   kulungu   hata   panga-ni
3.DEM.DIST 3-track   3-CONN   1a.antelope until   5.cave-LOC
'That man left and went and followed the track of the antelope to a cave.'

A similar case is discussed by Persohn (2018) for the marker *(j)a* in Nyakyusa. It is not entirely clear what the function of the AM marker is in these cases. A possible hypothesis is that it adds components of the motion event description (see Talmy 1985; Wilkins and Hill 1995) not included in the semantics of the lexical verb of motion.

4.3 Restrictions to specific TAM constructions

On the basis of our survey, it is quite common for at least one of the AM markers to be restricted to (or excluded from) specific TAM constructions and/or the infinitive. This is especially true with *ka*-. Botne (1999) notes that this itive marker is predominantly found in the imperative ('go and VERB'), the subjunctive mood ('so that I go and VERB'), the future tense and the infinitive. In a couple of languages though (e.g. Kaonde, illustrated in (11), and Umbundu), *ka*- is unrestricted in terms of TAM. By way of illustration, infinitive (25a), imperative (25b), present (25c), and past perfective (25d) TAM categories associated with AM *ka*- are shown below for Umbundu.

(25) Umbundu (R11 Angola)
 a. *óku-ka-up-á*
  15.INF-IT-take-FV
  'to go and take' (Schadeberg 1990: 52; glosses added)

 b. *on-gombe y-á-kop-a   ka-y-úp-é*
  9-cow   SP9-PST1-be.skinny-FV IT-OP9-take-FV
  'the cow is skinny, go and take/fetch it' (Valente 1964: 275; glosses added)

 c. *oci-mbungu ci-tund-a   v-oci-lala, ci-lil-a,   ci-ka-yev-a*
  7-wolf   SP7-go.out-FV 16-7-lair SP7-howl-FV SP7-IT-hunt-FV
  'the wolf goes out of the lair, howls and goes hunting.'
  (Valente 1964: 401; glosses added)

 d. *va-ka-tet-a   ovi-ti*
  SP2-IT-cut-FV   4-tree
  'they went and cut trees' (Valente 1964: 292; glosses added)

The AM marker *ka*- is attested in 65% (36 out of 55) of the surveyed languages. The percentage occurrence of *ka*- depending on TAM categories is given in Table 3. These results are in line with Botne (1999). The author further argues that this distribution might be a synchronic reflex of *ka*-, originating in imperative and/or subjunctive constructions, which gradually became more generalized to other TAM paradigms in some languages.

Table 3: Occurrences of AM *ka*- according to TAM.

TAM	Occurrences of AM *ka*-
Infinitive only	2 languages out of 36 (5.56 %)
Imperative only	1 language out of 36 (2.78 %)
Subjunctive only	17 languages out of 36 (47.22 %)
Subjunctive & Infinitive	2 languages out of 36 (5.56 %)
No TAM restriction	14 languages out of 36 (38.89 %)

Similar variation in terms of TAM restrictions occurs with other AM markers. For instance, in Changana, itive *ya-* and ventive *ta-* only occur in sequential constructions and with infinitives (see example (4) in Section 2.2). In Shona, while itive *ndo-* and adlocative *sviko-* may apply to any TAM category, ventive *zo-* seems to be available only with imperatives, as illustrated in (15b) in section 3.3.1.

4.4 Further semantic developments

As mentioned in Section 4.1, 'come'-markers may develop a metaphoric meaning, often with subsequent future-oriented development. This was shown in Digo with *edza-* (23). As also noted, the Shona prefix *zo-* 'come' displays AM semantics with imperatives only. Elsewhere it indicates "a sequel" (Fortune 1955: 353), or, as Carter and Kahari (1972: 30) put it, "the meaning [...] is roughly 'finally'". Similar metaphorical extensions have been described for the Tumbuka marker *zaka* (< 'come with') (Veil 1972: 465–466) and the Fuliiru marker *yíj* 'come' (van Oterloo 2011: 283–284).

It should be highlighted that this semantic development of 'come'-markers need not include an AM reading stage. Thus, the auxiliary *isa* 'come' in Ndali "contributes a sense of arriving at or reaching a particular state or condition, equivalent in English to come to, finally, ultimately" (Botne 2008: 123), but does not denote a co-event of physical motion. Likewise, in Nyakyusa, the verb stem *isa* 'come' may appear in the same syntactic frame as the AM marker *(j)a* 'go' but in this context, it only has an ingressive meaning of 'coming to/reaching a condition', and from there, has grammaticalized into a future marker, leaving no trace of an AM-related meaning (see Persohn 2017: 264–265, 320–322). See also Ebneter (1973), Traugott (1978) and Hilpert (2008) for similar developments outside Bantu.

In other Bantu languages, an AM marker may add a purposive meaning, where the verb event may not be the target. This is illustrated in (26) with the ventive *dza-* 'come' in Chewa. The translation 'come to VERB' leaves it open as to whether or not the subject of the verb actually achieved the aim of 'destroying'.

(26) Chewa (N31 Malawi, Mozambique) (Kiso 2012: 149)
 *Kodi mw-a-**dza**-ti-wonong-a ?*
 Q SP2PL-PRF-**VENT**-OP1PL-destroy-FV
 'Have you come to destroy us?'

The notion of purpose is relevant in AM systems with prior motion (also see Pakendorf and Stoynova [this volume] for the Tungusic languages). On the basis of the available descriptions, it is not clear how pervasive this parameter is in the semantics of Bantu AM markers, but the Chewa example in (26), as well as the Shona one in (15a), suggest that it may play a bigger role than expected. It is also not clear whether the purposive interpretation can be attributed solely to the AM markers or whether it is rather induced by the construction in which they appear. For instance, in Ronga, 'echo' constructions, whereby the AM marker found in the event verb stem reiterates the preceding motion verb, may easily indicate a purpose, as in (27a). Based on Bachetti's (2006) translation, such a purposive interpretation does not seem to obtain in 'non-echo' or simple constructions as in (27b).

(27) Ronga (S54 Mozambique)   (Bachetti 2006: 177–178; glosses added)
 a. *Tan-a   u-**ta**-tek-a   mali*
    come-FV SP2SG-**VENT**-fetch-FV 9.money
    'Come (in order to) fetch money.'

 b. *Ni-**ya**-tek-a   a-kaneta*
    SP1SG-**IT**-fetch-FV AUG-mug
    'I go and fetch the mug.'

More generally, AM markers in a number of Bantu languages have developed new meanings and functions in the realm of tense, aspect and modality. Such grammaticalization processes have productively created imperative and (more frequently) future markers.

In Cuwabo the AM marker *ka-* has been reanalyzed as a fully-fledged imperative marker, which always occupies the verb-initial position, as shown in (28).

(28) Cuwabo (Mozambique)   (Guérois 2015: 384)
 ***ka**-dhów-a   va-tákulu*
 IMP-go-FV   16-9.house
 'Go home!'

In Rangi, ventive *joo-* (29a) has grammaticalized into a future tense marker, with the possibility of appearing alongside the itive directional marker *koo-* (29b).

(29) Rangi (F33 Tanzania)
 a. *Sikʊ   ɪmwɪ   maa   a-kʊʊj-a   mʊ-tavana na*
    9.day   9.one then   SP1-come-FV   1-boy   CONN
    *mʊ-kaáya   kʊ-**joo**-mʊ-lool-a.*
    1-neighbour 15.INF-**VENT**-OP1-marry-FV
    'And then one day, our neighbour's boy came to marry her ...' (Stegen 2011: 418)

b. ***Joo**-koo-kan-y-a*   *v-íise*   *ʊ-hʊ*   *mʊ-ti.*
   FUT-DIR-fell-CAUS-FV   SP2-AUX   DEM-3   3-tree
   'They will [go to] fell this tree' (Gibson and Belkadi 2018: 22–23)

The development of future constructions involving both itive and ventive markers is also observed in Southern Sotho, where itive *ěa-* and ventive *tla-* (illustrated in (13) above) have respectively developed into an immediate future (30a) and an ordinary future marker (30b).

(30)   Southern Sotho (South Africa)
                                 (Doke and Mofokeng 1957: 206–207; glosses added)

     a.   *Rē-**ěa**-'mòn-a.*
         SP1PL-**PROX.FUT**-see-FV
         'We shall seem him; we are on the way to see him.'

     b.   *Mō-rèna*   *ō-**tla**-ah-a*   *ntlō*   *ea-haē*   *thabe-ng*
         1-chief   SP1-**FUT**-build-FV   9.house   9-POSS1   hill-LOC
         'The chief will build his house on the hill.'

In Zulu, another southern Bantu language, the prefix *zo-* (< *za ku-*'come INF-') is used to express a near future (31a). In contrast, the prefix *yo-* (< *ya ku-*'go INF-') indicates a more remote future (31b).

(31)   Zulu (South Africa)   (Doke 1947: 174)
     a.   *ngi-**zo**-thand-a*
         SP1SG-**PROX.FUT**-love-FV
         'I shall love (soon).'

     b.   *ngi-**yo**-thand-a*
         SP1SG-**REM.FUT**-love-FV
         'I shall love (later).'

In several southern languages, markers originating from motion verbs do not seem to operate as AM markers. The question remains whether these future prefixes once were AM markers (themselves originating from verbal sources) which further developed TAM functions, or whether the same verbal sources evolved distinct functions: as AM markers and TAM markers. From a synchronic point of view, it is difficult to find support for one path of grammaticalization over the other. However, Crane and Mabela (2019) make a case for Southern Ndebele and argue that in many cases directionality still plays a role in the selection of the future markers *yo-* and *zo-*. This suggests that motion was originally part of the meaning of these markers before future uses developed.

In a few western Bantu languages, such as Nzebi (32) and Lega (see Botne 2003: 440), *ka-* merely functions as a remote future marker. This is illustrated in Nzebi.

(32) Nzebi (B52 Gabon) (Marchal-Nasse 1989: 431)
 bi-vo:nda bí-**ká**-só:mb-á mɛ́:di
 8-old.person SP8-**REM.FUT**-buy-FV 6.oil
 'The old people will buy oil.'

More rarely, former AM markers may denote that the event expressed by the verb occurs at a different place, without indicating any movement (see Section 5.1).

5 Remaining issues

In this section we discuss two issues that provide challenges both for descriptive accounts of AM, as well as for comparative investigations. The first issue concerns the delimitation of AM markers from those markers that express the related notion of an event occurring at some location – also known as altrilocal markers (Section 5.1). The second issue concerns the question of the semantic relation between markers that translate as 'come' and those that translate as 'go', more specifically, whether a vector away from the deictic centre necessarily forms part of the meaning of 'go'-markers (Section 5.2).

5.1 Associated motion and locational marking

The definition of AM given in Section 1 crucially involves different kinds of translational motion. This means that to identify markers of AM, we need to determine whether spatial displacement of the figure forms part of the semantics of the paradigm in question and consequently exclude markers that do not satisfy this criterion. This proves to be a more challenging task than it might seem at first sight.

In several Bantu languages, we find markers which appear to have their origins in former AM markers, but which have lost or are in the process of losing their semantic connection to translational motion. Instead, they denote that the state-of-affairs encoded in the lexical verb takes place at some location, typically away from the deictic centre, but without indicating any movement. Seidel (2007) terms this function "altrilocal", whereas Ross (this volume) speaks of "distal" locational marking and Hernández-Green and Palancar (this volume) employ the term "exlocative" marking. It seems that a common pathway of change is from a lexical verb encoding motion to a marker of AM and in turn to a locational marker. Therefore, the task of identifying precisely where an element is along this pathway is not straightforward.

Cases like these seem to be recurrent in the languages of the world. Guillaume (2016: 103) observes similar instances in Tariana (Arawak, Brazil) and Andoke (isolate, Colombia). He stresses however, that the available material often does not allow for a clear-cut decision. In case of doubt, he opts to include those "static location" markers in his survey of AM in South America. In a similar vein, Ross (this volume) observes a functional overlap between AM markers and what he calls "locational" morphology, for instance in Huallaga Quechua (Quechuan). Hérnandez-Green and Palancar (this volume) describe how the 'come'-marker in the Otomi language family (a sub-branch of the Otomanguean phylum) can be employed to signal that the event took place at a location other than the speaker's. As for the African continent, Creissels and Bassène (this volume) observe a phenomenon reminiscent of the Otomi languages in Jóola Fóoñi (Atlantic). Following these authors, we have chosen to include the relevant markers in the present Bantu survey. Nevertheless, the issue warrants some additional discussion.

The first, and so far only, dedicated discussion of this phenomenon is the one by Seidel (2007). Seidel observes that the prefix *ka-* in Yeyi (R41) does not always entail a motion co-event, but rather denotes that an event takes place at a different location, as in (33).

(33) Yeyi (R41 Botswana, Namibia) (Seidel 2007: 185)
    a. *ku-dzw-a=po*   *nda-taa-yend-a*
       15.INF-come_out-FV=16.LOC   SP1SG-P.ANT-go-FV
       ku-ba-Masasa
       16.LOC-2a-Masasa
       *Nda-ri-**ka**-shak-a*   *i-namania=ku-wur-a.*
       SP1SG-REM.PST-**ka**-want-FV 9-calf.CONN9=15.INF-buy-FV
       *Nda-ri-**ka**-shangan-a*   *atikya*   *ba-mu-mbur-u.*
       SP1SG-REM.PST-**ka**-find-FV   that   SP2.ANT-OP1-kill-FV
       'Then I went to Masasa. I was looking for a calf to buy. I found that he/they had killed it (already).'

    b. *yuyu-mwe*   *ma-y-a*   *yuyu-mwe*   *ma-**ka**-kar-a*
       CONN1-other SP1.ANT-arrive-FV CONN1-other SP1.ANT-**ka**-remain-FV
       'The one came, the other one remained (over there).'

Referring to *ka-* in (33a), Seidel (2007: 185) states that "to include itive semantics into its basic meaning would run against its use in narratives to present a string of events that are subsecutively enacted at the same location". Given the widely observed 'iterative' or 'echo' use of AM markers (see Section 2.3), the use of *ka-* in this particular example might, however, still be understood as portraying the acts of wanting and finding against a backdrop of the preceding change of location. In the case of (33b), on the other hand, there is no motion event against which the act of remaining – the opposite of translational motion – could be understood.

Similarly, the prefix *ka-* in Nyakyusa "locates the state of affairs away from the deictic centre ... this often goes together with a sense of physical motion ... [but] ... this is not always the case" (Persohn 2017: 282–283). Crane (2019: 676) refers to the Totela prefix *ka-* as a "distal marker", meaning that the event denoted by the verb takes place elsewhere. Likewise, in Kaonde, Wright (2007: 31) states that "*ka-* has the meaning 'at a distance'", although his English translation 'go and V' in (11) does not make this element of the meaning explicit.

As mentioned in Section 3.3.2, Nicolle (2013) also describes the Digo prefix *cha-* as "a distal marker which expresses action at a distance from the deictic centre, implying prior movement on the part of the subject, although the movement itself is not part of the meaning of this morpheme" (Nicolle 2013: 167).

A more complex case is found in Chewa, which has two verbal prefixes that at first sight appear to be prime candidates for AM markers: *ka-*, which some authors trace back to *muka~mka* 'go', and *dza-* which is uncontroversially grammaticalized from *dza* 'come' (cf. anonymous 1969: 44; Hetherwick 1907: 156, 160; Thomson 1947: 38; Watkins 1937: 98). The proposed lexical sources as well as the descriptive accounts (anonymous 1969: 44; Bentley and Kulemeka 2001: 40–41; Harding 1966: 90; Lehmann 2002; Louw 1987: 111; Watkins 1937: 98) suggest that these two markers denote translational motion. For instance, according to Lehmann (2002: 37) "*ka-* implies 'going' and *dza-* 'coming'". However, a closer look at the Chewa data suggests that the two markers, at least in some uses and in some topolects, no longer necessarily connect the verb with translational motion. According to Peter Msaka (p.c.), the following examples based on Hetherwick's (1907) grammar do not evoke any sense of motion, but rather indicate that the act of building takes place away from (34a) or at/around the deictic centre (34b). As for the latter function, Ross (this volume) speaks of "proximal" location marking.

(34) Chewa (Malawi, Mozambique)   (Peter Msaka, p.c.; glosses added)
  a. *mu-mu-z-e   iye   a-**ka**-mang-e   nyumba y-ache*
     SP2PL-OP1-tell-SBJV PRON1   SP1-**ka**-build-SBJV 9.house 9-POSS1
     ku   bw-alo
     17.LOC   14-arena
     'Tell him to go and build his house at the *bwalo* [arena]' (Hetherwick 1907: 150)
     Comment: 'Tell him to build his house at the *bwalo* there (i.e. away from here).'

  b. *mu-mu-z-e   iye   a-**dza**-mang-e   nyumba y-ache*
     SP2PL-OP1-tell-SBJV PRO1   SP1-**dza**-build-SBJV 9.house 9-POSS1
     ku   bw-alo
     17.LOC   14-arena
     'Tell him to build his house at the *bwalo* here.'

This non-translational, locational interpretation is supported by the examples in (35), which feature an impersonal construction consisting of a locative subject prefix plus the passive voice and which cannot be interpreted as involving any translational movement (Peter Msaka p.c.).

(35) Chewa (Malawi, Mozambique)   (Peter Msaka, p.c.; glosses added)
  a. *Ku-**ka**-meny-edw-a   m-pira.*
     SP17.LOC-**ka**-beat-PASS-FV 3-ball
     'There (away) will be played football.'

  b. *Ku-**dza**-meny-edw-a   m-pira.*
     SP17.LOC-**dza**-beat-PASS-FV 3-ball
     'There (here about) will be played football.'

Based on these data, it appears that Chewa *ka-* and *dza-* have developed or are developing locational functions whereby the state-of-affairs encoded in the lexical verb takes place at (*dza-*) or away from (*ka-*) the deictic centre.

Future in-depth studies of the relevant morphemes and associated constructions, especially taking into account their use in discourse, might unveil more such cases across Bantu.

5.2 'go', 'come' and the question of deixis

Many descriptions of itive markers implicitly or explicitly assume inherent *deixis*, especially if they stand in opposition to a ventive. A closer inspection, however, shows that this is not always the case.

Before turning our attention to grammatical elements, it is worth examining lexical verbs of motion. In their seminal article, Wilkins and Hill (1995) show that go-verbs need not necessarily include reference to the deictic centre as part of their meaning: if there is a universal deictic opposition of 'come' versus 'go', then this opposition is found at the pragmatic rather than semantic level. Likewise, Levinson (2006: 118) states that the notions underlying 'go' "generally do not encode anything about alignment of vectors with the deictic centre [...] Rather, 'come' and 'go' verbs tend to be in privative opposition, with 'come' marked as having such an alignment and 'go' unmarked". According to Levinson, any deictic readings of 'go' are the result of scalar implicature. That is to say, the choice of the less informative 'go' suggests that the conditions for the use of the more informative 'come' are not met. In a similar vein, Langacker (1990: 155) describes English *go* as "a maximally generic motion verb".

For Bantu languages, Botne (2005) shows that the lexical semantics of the 'go' verbs in Ndali (M301, Tanzania and Malawi) does not include reference to the deictic centre. Persohn (2018) illustrates the same for Ndali's neighbouring language Nyakyusa. Sitoe (2001: 93) discusses the opposition between *ta* 'come' and *ya* 'go' in Changana and observes that "the primary deictic verb is *ku-ta* (where *ku-* is the infinitive marker) and *kuya* is not strictly the itive counterpart of *kuta*. The only deictic meaning of *kuya* is that the goal is not the deictic centre" – a pattern that fits well with Levinson's (2006) proposal of a privative opposition rather than a binary one.

Turning to grammaticalized markers of AM, we can make similar observations. For instance, van Otterloo (2011: 281) states that in narratives the Fuliiru itive marker *génd* "indicates that the deictic centre is changing. The subject of the verb is going towards the new deictic centre", which can then be referred to by the ventive *yíj*. On closer examination, however, we encounter examples such as (36).

(36) Fuliiru (DRC) (Roger van Otterloo, p.c.; glosses added)
 *i-ky-anya ky-o-ku-**gendi** yegerez-a a-ba-geni*
 AUG-7-time 7-CONN.AUG-15.INF-**going** greet-FV AUG-2-guest
 'at the time of [going and] welcoming guests'

In the first clause of the narrative, the setting is introduced ('One man had a feast at his place') and all events of the story take place there. This means that, the deictic centre – the setting of the story – is the space within which the feast takes place. After the man has instructed his helpers, the story begins with the subordinate clause in (36). The translational motion denoted by itive *génd* in (36) takes place within the space of the wedding feast and does not lead away from this deictic centre. There are also no textual indications of a switch in focal location from one spot at the feast to another one. If itive *génd* denotes motion away from the deictic centre, its use in (36) seems contradictory.

Van Otterloo also observes a strong tendency for the expression *kaaya* 'home' to co-occur with ventive *jíj* (2001: 285–287), which he explains by stipulating that "one does not 'go away' to home" (van Otterloo 2011: 287). In the light of the above cross-linguistic discussion and examples such as (36), this tendency, as well as the distribution of the itive and ventive in narrative discourse can be explained without resorting to a deictic component ('go away to') for itive *génd*. Instead, it can be assumed that the language-specific rules of "deictic projection" (Lyons 1977: 579) in Fuliiru allow both established focal locations in narratives, as well as home, to be treated as deictic centres. The use of the ventive and itive can then be understood as governed by the pragmatic considerations sketched out above.

A case similar to Fuliiru *génd* is found in Kinga with the prefix *tsi-*. This marker has been described as indicating "movement away from the deictic center" (SIL International n.d.) An examination of its use in the texts in Wolff (1905) shows that the translational motion denoted by *tsi-* typically, but not exclusively, leads away from the deictic centre. Consider (37) where the context is one in which the older of two sisters has sent the younger one to the river to fetch water. At this point in the narrative the perspective remains from their home.

(37) Kinga (G65 Tanzania) (Wolff 1905: 123; glosses added)
u̱-n-nūna a-ka-vu̱k-a ku̱ ma-ġasi; u̱-mw-e̱ne̱
AUG-1-younger.sibling SP1-NARR-go-FV 17.LOC 6-water AUG-1-PRO1
ku̱mbe̱le̱ a-ka-vuj-a a-k-ibat-a e-ṅuku̱
then SP1-NARR-return-FV SP1-NARR-grasp-FV AUG-9.chicken
e-ji-ṅge̱ a-ka-bud-a, u̱-n-twe a-ka-paġek-a
AUG-9-other SP1-NARR-kill-FV AUG-3-head SP1-NARR-put-FV
ku̱-ky-aṅya a-ka-ḻy-a. u̱-n-nūna
17.LOC-7-attic SP1-NARR-eat-FV AUG-1-younger.sibling
a-ka-**tsi**-vuj-a ku̱-ḻu-ġasi a-ka-sik-a
SP1-NARR-**IT**-return-FV 17.LOC-11-river SP1-NARR-arrive-FV
a-ka-t-a
SP1-NARR-say-FV
'The young one went to the water. She [older sibling], however, took and killed another chicken, put the head in the attic and ate. The young one [went and] returned from the water. She arrived [home] and said …'

The motion referred to by *tsi-* in Kinga (37) does not take place away from the deictic centre, but leads towards it. Moreover, the locative noun phrase *kuḷugasi* 'the river' denotes a source other than the deictic centre (the home). If the meaning of *tsi-* included a vector away from the deictic centre, (37) would represent a contradiction. It is conceivable that this use of *tsi-* with motion to(wards) the deictic centre is facilitated by the fact that the language does not have a grammaticalized ventive marker with which *tsi-* stands in opposition. Similarly, Persohn (2018) observes that the Nyakyusa itive marker *(j)a* is also attested with motion not directed away from the deictic centre.

In summary, it seems that not all itive markers in the Bantu languages necessarily include deixis as part of their meaning. In line with typological findings on lexical motion verbs, it rather seems that deictic readings arise at the level of pragmatic interpretation.

6 Conclusion

This chapter has presented an overview of the encoding of AM in Bantu, drawing on a set of 55 languages, all of which have at least one AM marker. It examined strategies employed for the encoding of AM and degrees of complexity found in these systems, as well as a number of other areas of variation. In terms of encoding, three strategies are commonly employed in Bantu. The first consists of prefixing an AM marker, most often grammaticalized from a motion verb. The most common AM prefix is *ka-* which has been reconstructed for Proto-Bantu as the verb of motion **ka* 'go' (Meinhof 1910; Bourquin 1923; Meeussen 1967; Botne 1999). This is found in 36 of the languages of our sample, i.e. 65%. The second strategy, only attested in Mongo imperatives, sees the use of a circumfix of the shape *yu-* ... *-e* (~ *yo-* ... *e*). The third strategy involves the use of a grammaticalized auxiliary construction in which movement is expressed through an auxiliary which has its origins in a motion verb.

In terms of variation with regard to the complexity of AM systems (i.e. how many distinct AM markers are encoded), the vast majority of simple systems made of one AM marker involve the use of the itive *ka-*. Simple systems with two AM markers typically distinguish between 'come' and 'go'. Complex AM systems are much rarer. A predominant tendency is that if a language has at least one AM marker, it tends to be itive.

As for the moving figure, Bantu languages strongly prefer moving subjects over moving objects. Concerning the temporal relation between the motion co-event and the main event, it has been shown that in the vast majority of languages only prior motion is available. Only one language (Fuliiru) systematically contrasts prior and concurrent motion. If AM prefixes in Bantu typically originate from lexical sources, and more specifically from verbs of motion, the function of the same prefixes has further evolved in a number of languages, distinguishing them from AM *sensu stricto*. At this stage, and on the basis of our survey, two different grammaticalization pathways have been observed (although some cases deserve further research): 1) AM prefixes developed into specific TAM categories, most often future or imperative; 2) AM prefixes developed into locational markers.

Lastly, it has been shown that itive markers in Bantu need not encode an element of deixis, which links the analysis of AM with both language-specific and typological findings on lexical verbs of motion.

Abbreviations

Glossing follows the Leipzig Glossing Rules, with the following additional abbreviations.

AUG	augment	NEAR.FUT	near future
AM	associated motion	NON.PST	non-past
CONN	connective	OP	object prefix
COM	comitative ('with', 'and')	P.ANT	past anterior
CONS	consecutive	POSS	possessive
CJ	conjoint	PRO	pronoun
DEM.DIST	distal demonstrative	PROX.FUT	proximal future
DIR	directional	REM.FUT	remote future
DIST	distal (verbal prefix)	REM.PST	remote past
EMPH	emphatic	SEQ	sequential
FV	final vowel	SP	subject prefix
INTERJ	interjection	VENT	ventive
IT	itive	1 ... 18	noun classes
NARR	narrative		

Acknowledgements: Parts of this research were supported by the Leverhulme Trust as part of the project 'Morphosyntactic variation in Bantu: Typology, contact and change' (Rozenn Guérois) and the British Academy 'Pathways of change at the northern Bantu borderlands' (Hannah Gibson), the authors gratefully acknowledge the generous support of these funders. The authors also would like to extend their gratitude towards Sylvie Voisin, Antoine Guillaume and Harold Koch as reviewers, Helen Eaton for making an unpublished Kinga grammar sketch available to us, to Rasmus Bernander for discussions pertaining to grammaticalization, to The Missionarios Colombianos for sending us a hardcopy of Martins (1991), to Roger van Otterloo for making Fuliiru texts available to us and discussing Fuliiru data with us, as well as to Joseph Koni Muluwa, Nancy Kula, Winfred Mkochi, Peter Msaka, Philip Mutaka, Steve Nicolle, Roger van Otterloo and Vera Wilhelmsen and Lizzie Poole for further insightful discussions of Mbuun, Bemba, Tonga, Chewa, Kinande, Digo, Fuliiru and Mbugwe data respectively. Any mistakes naturally remain our own.

Appendix: list of surveyed languages

The additional sources which we consulted in which no clear instances of Associated Motion could be identified are not included in the list below.

Guthrie Code + language / ISO 693–3	AM Markers	TAM categories	Source(s)
B73c Iyaa / iyx	*yi-* VENT	all	Mouandza (2001)
B87 Mbuun / zmp	*yí-* VENT	PST	Koni Muluwa & Bostoen (2008), Joseph Koni Muluwa (p.c.)
C31 Mbenga / –	*kó-* IT *yo-* IT	INF all	Motingea & Bonzoi (2008)
C35a Ntomba / nto	*to-* IT *yo-* VENT	IMP	Gilliard (1928), via Botne (1999: 484)
C41 Ngombe /ngc	*ka-* IT	SBJV	Ruskin & Ruskin (1937)
C61 Mongo / lol	*yŏ- ... -e* 'IT/VENT'	IMP	Ruskin & Ruskin (1934), Hulstaert (1965)
E622d Uru / –	*enda-* IT *tʃa-* VENT	FUT	Shinagawa (2012)
E623 Rombo / rof	*nde-* IT *ʃe-* VENT	FUT	Shinagawa (2012)
E65 Gweno / gwe	*ye-* IT	INF & SBJV	Philippson & Nurse (2000)
E73 Digo / dig	*ka-* IT *ya-* IT *enda-* IT *edza-* VENT *(cha-)*	SBJV ? all all all	Nicolle (2003, 2013, 2015), Steve Nicolle (p.c.)
F12 Bende / bdp	*ka-* IT	SBJV	Abe (2019: 207)
F22 Nyamwezi / nym	*ka-* IT	SBJV	Maganga & Schadeberg (1992), Nurse & Philippson (2006)
F33 Rangi / lag	*too-* IT *koo-* IT *joo-* VENT	all INF ALL	Stegen (2011), Gibson & Belkadi (2018)

(continued)

Guthrie Code + language / ISO 693-3	AM Markers	TAM categories	Source(s)
F34 Mbugwe /mgz	*ja-* VENT	PST, SEQ, HAB	Wilhelmsen (2018), Lizzie Poole (p.c.)
G12 Kagulu / kki	*ka-* IT	all	Petzell (2008)
G42 Swahili / swh	*ka-* IT	SBJV	Ashton (1947)
G65 Kinga / zga	*tsi-* IT	all	Wolff (1905), Schadeberg (1973), SIL (ms.)
H21a Kimbundu / kmb	*ka-* IT	SBJV	Chatelain (1888), Quintão (1934)
JD42 Kinande / nnb	*ya-* IT *syá-* VENT	all (?)	Bbemo Musubaho (1982), Mutaka (1994), Mutaka (n.d.), Kavutirwaki & Mutaka (2012), Ngessimo M. Mutaka (p.c.)
JD63 Fuliiru / flr	AUX *génd* IT AUX *yíj* VENT AUX *léng* 'pass' AUX *híkir* 'arrive' AUX *taah* 'go home'	all	Nicolle (2003), van Otterloo (2011), Roger van Otterloo (p.c.)
JE11 Nyoro / nyo	*ka-* IT	SBJV	Shigeki Kaji (p.c.)
K11 Cokwe / cjk	*ka-* IT	all	Van den Eynde (1960), dos Santos (1962), Guérois *field notes*
K12b Ngangela / nkn	*ka-* IT	SBJV	Maniacky (2003)
K13 Lucazi / lch	*ka-* IT	all	Fleisch (2000)
K21 Lozi / loz	*yo-* IT *to-* VENT	all	Gorman (1950), Gowlett (1967), Mwisiya (1977), Fortune (2001)
K333 Mbukushu / mhw	*ka-* IT *na-* VENT	all	Fisch (1998)
K41 Totela / ttl	*ka-*	all	Crane (2019)
L21 Kete / kcv	*ka-* IT	SBJV	Muzenga (1980)
L41 Kaonde / kqn	*ka-* IT	all	Wright (2007)
L52 Lunda / lun	*ka-* IT	all	Kawasha (2003)
M31 Nyakyusa / nyy	AUX *(j)a* IT *ka-* IT	all SBJV	Persohn (2017, 2018)
M42 Bemba / bem	*ka-* IT *so-* VENT	SBJV	Schoeffer (1907), Sharman (1963), Mann (1977), Nancy Kula (p.c.)
M54 Lamba / lam	*ka-* IT	IMP	Doke (1922: 83)
M64 Tonga (Zambia) / toi	*ka-* IT	SBJV	Hopgood (1992)
N13 Matengo / mgv	*ka-* IT	SBJV	Yoneda (2019: 429)

(continued)

Guthrie Code + language / ISO 693-3	AM Markers	TAM categories	Source(s)
N14 Mpoto / mpa	*ka-* IT	SBJV	Botne (2019)
N15 Tonga (Malawi) / tog	*ci-* 'go' *zi-* 'come'	all	Mkochi (2017), Winfred Mkochi (p.c.)
N31 Chewa / nya	*ka-* IT *dza-* VENT	all	Hetherwick (1907), Watkins (1937), Thomson (1947), Harding (1966), Anonymous (1969), Louw (1987), Lehmann (2002), Bentley & Kulemeka (2001), Kiso (2012), Peter Msaka (p.c.)
N43 Nyungwe / nyu	*ka-* IT *dza-* VENT	SBJV & INF	Courtois (1900), van der Mohl (1904), Martins (1991)
N44 Sena / seh	*ka-* IT *dza-* VENT	SBJV & INF	Moreira (1924)
P13 Matuumbi / mgw	*ka-* IT	SBJV	Odden (1996)
P21 Yao / yao	*ka-* IT	all	Whiteley (1966)
P23 Makonde / kde	*ka-* IT	SBJV	Leach (2010)
P31 Makhuwa / vmw	*a-* IT	SBJV	do Sacramento (1906), van der Wal (2009)
P34 Cuwabo / chw	*a-* IT	SBJV	Guérois (2015)
R11 Umbundu / umb	*ka-* IT	all	Valente (1964), Schadeberg (1990)
R21 Kwanyama / kua	*ka-* IT	all	Zimmermann & Hasheela (1998), Halme (2004)
R30 Herero / her	*ka-* IT	all	Möhlig & Kavari (2008)
R41 Yeyi / yey	*ka-*	all	Seidel (2007, 2008)
S10 Shona / sna	*ndo-* IT *zo-* VENT *sviko-* 'arrive'	all IMP all	Fortune (1955, 1984), Stevick et al. (1965), Brauner (1995), Mberi (2002), Mpofu-Hamadziripi et al. (2013)
S21 Venda / ven	*yo-* IT	all	Poulos (1990)
S33 Southern Sotho / sot	*ěa-* IT *tla-* VENT	INF & FUT PFCT	Doke & Mofokeng (1957)
S407 Southern Ndebele / nbl	*yo-* IT *zo-* VENT	FUT	Crane & Mabena (2019)
S53 Changana / tso	*ya-* IT *ta-* VENT	SEQ & INF	Ribeiro (1965), Sitoe (2001)
S54 Ronga / rng	*ya-* IT *ta-* VENT	all	Bachetti (2006)

References

Abe, Yuko. 2019. Bende (F12). In Daisuke Shinagawa & Yuko Abe (eds.), Descriptive materials of morphosyntactic microvariation in Bantu. 191–224. Tokyo University of Foreign Studies.

Anonymous. 1969. *Chichewa intensive course*. Lilongwe: Lilongwe Language Centre in association with the Malawian Catholic Church.

Ashton, Ethel O. 1947. *Swahili grammar (including intonation)*. London: Longmans, Green and Co.

Bachetti, Cláudio. 2006. *Gramática da língua Ronga*. Maputo: Paulinas Editorial.

Bastin, Yvonne, André Coupez, Evariste Mumba & Thilo C. Schadeberg (eds.). 2002. *Bantu lexical reconstructions 3*. Tervuren: Musée royal de l'Afrique centrale. Online database: linguistics.africamuseum.be/BLR3.html (accessed 15 November 2018).

Bbemo Musubaho, Tseme Mutatsapa. 1982. *Le Kinande, langue bantoue de l'est du Zaire (D.42): Phonologie et morphologie*. University of Ghent doctoral dissertation.

Belkadi, Aïcha. 2016. Associated motion constructions in African languages. *Africana Linguistica* 22. 43–70.

Belkadi, Aïcha. This volume, chapter 5. Deictic directionality as associated motion: Motion, complex events and event integration in African languages.

Bentley, Mayrene Elizabeth & Andrew T.C. Kulemeka. 2001. *Chichewa*. Munich: Lincom.

Blench, Roger. 2014. African agricultural tools: Implications of synchronic ethnography for agrarian history. In Chris J. Stevens, Sam Nixon, Mary Anne Murray & Dorian Fuller (eds.), *Archeology of African plant use*. 243–257. Walnut Creek, CA: Left Coast Press.

Botne, Robert. 1999. Future and distal -*ka*-'s: Proto-Bantu or nascent form(s)? In Jean-Marie Hombert & Larry M. Hyman (eds.), *Bantu Historical Linguistics*, 473–515. Stanford: Centre for the Study of Language and Information.

Botne, Robert. 2003. Lega (Beya dialect) (D25). In Derek Nurse & Gérard Philippson (eds), *The Bantu Languages*. 422–449. London: Routledge.

Botne, Robert. 2005. Cognitive schemas and motion verbs: coming and going in Chindali (eastern Bantu). *Cognitive Linguistics* 16 (1). 43–80.

Botne, Robert. 2008. *A grammatical sketch of Chindali (Malawian variety)*. Philadelphia: American Philosophical Society.

Botne, Robert. 2019. Chimpoto N14. In Mark Van de Velde & Koen Bostoen (eds), *The Bantu languages*. 2nd edn. 692–732. London: Routledge.

Bourquin, Walther. 1923. *Neue Ur-Bantu-Wortstämme, nebst einem Beitrag zur Erforschung der Bantu-Wurzeln*. Berlin & Hamburg: Verlag von Dietrich Reimer & C. Boysen.

Brauner, Siegmund. 1995. *A grammatical sketch of Shona*. Cologne: Rüdiger Köppe.

Bybee, Joan L., Revere Dale Perkins & William Pagliuca. 1994. *The evolution of grammar: Tense, aspect and modality in the languages of the world*. Chicago: University of Chicago Press.

Carter, Hazel & George P. Kahari. *Kuverenge Chishóna: An introductory Shona reader with grammatical sketch*. London: SOAS University of London.

Chatelain, Héli. 1888. *Grammatica elementar do Kimbundu ou Lingua Angola*. Geneve: The Gregg.

Courtois, Victor J. 1900. *Elementos de grammatica Tetense: lingua Chi-Nyungue* [Elements of Tete grammar: Chi-Nyungue language]. Coimbra: Imprensa da Universidade.

Crane, Thera. 2019. Totela K41. In Mark Van de Velde & Koen Bostoen (eds), *The Bantu languages*. 2nd edn. 645–691. London: Routledge.

Crane, Thera & Msuswa Petrus Mabena. 2019. Time, space, modality, and (inter)subjectivity: Futures in isiNdebele and other Nguni languages. *South African Journal of African Languages* 39 (3). 291–304.
Creissels, Denis & Alain Christian Bassène. This volume, chapter 17. Ventive, associated motion and aspect in Jóola Fóoñi (Atlantic).
Devos, Maud. 2008. *A grammar of Mawke (Palma, Mozambique)*. Munich: Lincom.
Doke, Clement Martyn. 1922. *The grammar of the Lamba language*. London: Kegan Paul, Trench, Trubner & Co.
Doke, Clement Martyn. 1947. *Text-book of Zulu grammar*. London: Longmans, Green and Co.
Doke, Clement Martyn & S. Machabe Mofokeng. 1957. *Textbook of Southern Sotho grammar*. London: Longmans, Green and Co.
Ebneter, Theodor. 1973. *Das bündnerromanische Futur. Syntax der mit vegnir und habere gebildeten Futurtypen in Gegenwart und Vergangenheit*. Bern: Franck.
Elmslie, Walter Angus. 1923. *Introductory grammar of the Tumbuka language*. Livingstonia: Mission Press.
Eynde, Karel van den. 1960. *Fonologie en morfologie van het Cokwe* (No. 2). Leuven: University of Leuven.
Fisch, Maria. 1998. *Thimbukushu grammar*. Windhoek: Out of Africa Publ.
Fleisch, Axel. 2000. *Lucazi grammar: A morphosemantic analysis*. Cologne: Rüdiger Köppe.
Fortune, George. 1955. *An analytical grammar of Shona*. London: Longmans, Green & Co.
Fortune, George. 1984. *Shona grammatical constructions II*. Harare: Mercury Press.
Fortune, George. 2001. *An outline of Silozi grammar*. Zambia: Bookworld Publishers.
Gibson, Hannah & Aicha Belkadi. 2018. The development of the encoding of deictic motion in Rangi: Grammaticalisation and change. Unpublished manuscript. University of Essex and SOAS University of London.
Gorman, W. A. R. 1950. *Simple Silozi: A guide for beginners*. London: Longmans, Green & Co.; Northern Rhodesia & Nyasaland Joint Publ. Bureau.
Gowlett, Derek F. 1967. *Morphology of the verb in Lozi*. Johannesburg: University of Witwatersrand M.A. dissertation.
Guérois, Rozenn. 2015. *A grammar of Cuwabo (Mozambique, Bantu P34)*. Lyon: Université Lumière Lyon 2 doctoral dissertation.
Guillaume, Antoine. 2009. Les suffixes verbaux de mouvement associé en cavineña. *Faits de Langues: Les Cahiers* 1. 181–204.
Guillaume, Antoine. 2016. Associated motion in South America: Typological and areal perspectives. *Linguistic Typology* 20 (1). 81–177.
Guillaume, Antoine & Harold Koch. This volume, chapter 1. Introduction: Associated motion as a grammatical category in linguistic typology.
Güldemann, Tom. 1999. The genesis of verbal negation in Bantu and its dependency on functional features of clause types. In Jean-Marie Hombert & Larry M. Hyman (eds.), *Bantu Historical Linguistics*, 545–587. Stanford: Centre for the Study of Language and Information.
Guthrie, Malcolm. 1967–1971. *Comparative Bantu: An introduction to the comparative linguistics and prehistory of the Bantu languages*, 4 vols. Letchworth: Gregg International.
Halme, Riikka. 2004. *A tonal grammar of Kwanyama*. Cologne: Rüdiger Köppe.
Harding, Deborah Ann 1966. *The phonology and morphology of Chinyanja*. Los Angeles: University of California doctoral dissertation.

Harjula, Lotta. 2004. *The Ha language of Tanzania: Grammar, texts and vocabulary*. Cologne: Rüdiger Köppe.
Hernández-Green, Néstor & Enrique L. Palancar. This volume, chapter 14. Associated motion in the Otomi family.
Hetherwick, Alexander. 1907. *A practical manual of the Nyanja language*. London: Society for Promoting Christian Knowledge.
Hilpert, Martin. 2008. Where did this future come from? The constructional grammaticalization of Swedish komma att V. In Alexander Bergs & Gabriele Diewald (eds.), *Constructions and Language Change*, 105–129. Berlin: Mouton de Gruyter.
Hopgood, Cecil Robert. 1992. *A practical introduction to Chitonga*. Lusaka: Zambia Educational Publishing House.
Hulstaert, Gustaaf. 1961. *Grammaire du lomongo. Première partie, phonologie*. Tervuren: Musée royal de l'Afrique centrale.
Hulstaert, Gustaaf. 1965. *Grammaire du lomongo. Deuxième partie, morphologie*. Tervuren: Musée royal de l'Afrique centrale.
Hulstaert, Gustaaf. 1966. *Grammaire du lomongo. Troisième partie, syntaxe*. Tervuren: Musée royal de l'Afrique centrale.
Kavutirwaki, Kambale & Ngessimo M. Mutaka. 2012. *Dictionnaire kinande-français. Avec index français-kinande*. Tevuren: Musée royal de l'Afrique centrale. http://www.africamuseum.be/sites/default/files/media/docs/research/publications/rmca/online/documents-social-sciences-humanities/dictionnaire-kinande-francais.pdf (last accessed 04 July 2018).
Kawasha, Boniface Kaumba. 2003. *Lunda grammar: a morphosyntactic and semantic analysis*.
Kiso, Andrea. 2012. *Tense and aspect in Chichewa, Citumbuka and Cisena*. Stockholm: Stockholm University doctoral dissertation.
Koch, Harold. 1984. The category of 'associated motion' in Kaytej. *Language in Central Australia* 1. 23–34.
Koch, Harold. This volume, chapter 7. Associated motion in the Pama-Nyungan languages of Australia.
Koni Muluwa, Joseph & Koen Bostoen. 2008. Un recueil de proverbes mbuun d'Imbongo (RD Congo, Bantu B87). *Annales Aequatoria* 29. 381–423.
Langacker, Ronald. 1990. *Concept, image, and symbol: The cognitive basis of grammar*. Berlin: Mouton de Gruyter.
Leach, Michael B. 2010. *Things hold together: Foundation for a systemic treatment of verbal and nominal tone in Plateau Shimakonde*. Utrecht: LOT.
Lehmann, Dorothea A. 2002. *An Outline of Cinyanja Grammar*. Lusaka: Bookworld Publishers.
Levinson, Stephen C. 2006. Deixis. In Laurence R. Horn & Gregory Ward (eds.), *The handbook of pragmatics*, 97–121. Malden: Blackwell.
Louw, Johan K. 1987. *Chichêwâ, a practical course*. Pretoria: University of South Africa.
Lyons, John. 1977. *Semantics*. vol. 2. Cambridge: Cambridge University Press.
Maganga, Clement & Thilo C. Schadeberg. 1992. *Kinyamwezi: Grammar, texts, vocabulary*. Cologne: Rüdiger Köppe.
Maho, Jouni Filip. 2007. The linear ordering of TAM/NEG markers in the Bantu languages. *SOAS Working Papers in Linguistics* 15. 213–225.
Maho, Jouni Filip. 2008. Comparative TAM morphology in Niger-Congo. *Interdependence of diachronic and synchronic analyses* 103. 283–298.

Maho, Jouni Filip. 2009. NUGL Online: The online version of the new updated Guthrie list, a referential classification of the Bantu languages. https://brill.com/fileasset/downloads_products/35125_Bantu-New-updated-Guthrie-List.pdf (accessed 5 July 2018).
Maniacky, Jacky. 2003. *Tonologie du ngangela: variété de Menongue (Angola)*. Munich : Lincom.
Mann, Michael. 1977. *An outline of Bemba Grammar*. In Mubanga E. Kashoki (ed.), *Language in Zambia: Grammatical sketches*, 6–61. Lusaka: Institute for African Studies, University of Zambia.
Marchal-Nasse, Colette. 1989. *De la phonologie à la morphologie du nzebi, langue bantoue (B52) du Gabon*. Brussels: Université libre de Bruxelles doctoral dissertation.
Martins, Manuel dos Anjos. 1991. *Elementos da língua nyungwe: gramática e dicionário (nyungwe-português-nyungwe)* [Elements of the Nyungwe language: Grammar and dictionary (Nyungwe-Portuguese-Nyungwe)]. Roma: Missionários Combonianos.
Mberi, Nhira Edgar. 2002. *The categorial status and functions of auxiliaries in Shona*. Harare: University of Zimbabwe doctoral dissertation.
Meinhof, Carl. 1910. *Grundriss einer Lautlehre der Bantusprachen, nebst Anleitung zur Aufnahme von Bantusprachen*. Berlin: Verlag von Dietrich Reimer.
Meussen, Achille Emile. 1967. Bantu grammatical reconstructions. *Africana Linguistica* 3. 79–121.
Mkochi, Winfred. 2017. Phonological variation of the present progressive aspect marker *-tu-* in Malawian Tonga: A prosodic analysis. *Southern African Linguistics and Applied Language Studies* 35 (4). 365–383
Mohl, Alexander van der. 1904. Praktische Grammatik der Bantu-Sprache von Tete, einem Dialekt des Unter-Sambesi mit Varianten der Sena-Sprache. *Mittheilungen des Seminars für Orientalische Sprachen* 7. 32–85.
Möhlig, Wilhelm J. G. & Jekura Uaurika Kavari. 2008. *Reference grammar of Herero (Otjiherero), Bantu language of Namibia*. Cologne: Rudiger Koppe.
Moreira, Alexandre. 1924. *Practical grammatical notes of the Sena language*. St Gabriel-Mödling: Anthropos.
Motingea, André Mangulu, and Mwamakasa Bonzoi. 2008. *Aux sources du Lingála: Cas du Mbenga de Mankaza-Nouvel Anvers*. Kyoto: Kyoto University Center for African Area Studies.
Mouandza, Jean-Daniel. 2001. *Éléments de description du iyaa (parler bantu du Congo-Brazzaville)*. Lille: ANRT
Mpofu-Hamadziripi, Nomalanga, Armindo Ngunga, Nhira Edgar Mberi & Francis Matambirofa. 2013 *A descriptive grammar of Shona*. Harare: CROBOL project.
Mundeke, Léon. 2011. *Etude morphosyntaxique de la langue mbuun (B87) (parler d'Elyob)*. Lubumbashi: Université de Lubumbashi doctoral dissertation.
Mutaka, Ngessimo M. n.d. *Kinande: a grammar sketch* (version 1.0). https://www.africananaphora.rutgers.edu/images/stories/downloads/casefiles/KinandeGS.pdf (last accessed 04 July 2018).
Mutaka, Ngessimo M. 1994. *The lexical tonology of Kinande*. Munich: Lincom.
Muzenga, J.G. Kamba. 1980. *Esquisse de grammaire kete*. Tervuren: Musée royal de l'Afrique centrale.
Mwisiya, M. W. 1977. *Introduction to Silozi grammar*. Lusaka: National Educational Company of Zambia.

Nash, Jay A. 1992. *Aspects of Ruwund grammar*. Urbana-Champaign: University of Illinois doctoral dissertation.
Nicolle, Steve. 2002. The grammaticalisation of movement verbs in Digo and English. *Revue de sémantique et pragmatique* 11. 47–67.
Nicolle, Steve. 2003. Distal aspects in Bantu languages. In Katarzyna M. Jaszczolt and Ken Turner (eds.), *Meaning Through Language Contrast*. vol. 2. 3–22. Amsterdam: Benjamins.
Nicolle, Steve. 2007. The grammaticalization of tense markers: A pragmatic reanalysis. *Cahiers Chronos* 17. 47–65.
Nicolle, Steve. 2013. *A grammar of Digo: a Bantu language of Kenya and Tanzania*. Dallas: SIL International.
Nicolle, Steve. 2015. Digo Narrative Discourse. https://www.sil.org/resources/publications/entry/61297 (accessed 4 July 2018).
Nurse, Derek. 2003. Aspect and tense in Bantu languages. In Derek Nurse & Gérard Philippson (eds). *The Bantu Languages*. 90–102. London: Routledge.
Nurse, Derek. 2007. Did the Proto-Bantu verb have a synthetic or an analytic structure? *SOAS Working Papers in Linguistics* 15: 239–256
Nurse, Derek. 2008. *Tense and aspect in Bantu*. Oxford: Oxford University Press.
Nurse, Derek & Gérard Philippson. 2006. Common tense-aspect markers in Bantu. *Journal of African Languages and Linguistics* 27. 155–196.
Odden, David. 1996. *The Phonology and morphology of Kimatuumbi*. Oxford: Clarendon Press.
Otterloo, Roger van. 2011. *The Kifuliiru language*. vol. 2: *A descriptive grammar*. Dallas: SIL International.
Pakendorf, Brigitte & Natalia Stoynova. This volume, chapter 22. Associated motion in Tungusic languages: A case of mixed argument structure.
Persohn, Bastian. 2017. *The verb in Nyakyusa: A focus on tense, aspect and modality*. Berlin: Language Science Press. http://langsci-press.org/catalog/book/141 (accessed 4 July 2018).
Persohn, Bastian. 2018. Basic motion verbs in Nyakyusa: Lexical semantics and associated motion. *Studies in African Linguistics* 47. 101–127.
Petzell, Malin. 2008. *The Kagulu language of Tanzania: Grammar, text and vocabulary*. Cologne: Rüdiger Köppe.
Philippson, Gérard & Derek Nurse. 2000. *Gweno, a little known language of northern Tanzania*. http://www1.ddl.ishlyon.cnrs.fr/fulltext/Philippson/Philippson_2000.pdf (last accessed 17 March 2020).
Poulos, George. 1990. *A linguistic analysis of Venda*. Pretoria: Via Afrika.
Quintão, José Luís. 1934. *Gramática de kimbundo*. Lisbon: Ed. Descobrimento.
Ribeiro, Armando. 1965. *Gramática changana (Tsonga)*. Caniçado: Editorial Evangelizar.
Ross, Daniel. This volume, chapter 2. A cross-linguistic survey of associated motion and directionals.
Ruskin, Edward Algernon & Lily Ruskin. 1934. *A grammar of the Lomongo language*. Belgian Congo: Congo Balolo Mission.
Ruskin, Edward Algernon & Lily Ruskin. 1937. *Notes on the Lingombe grammar*. Belgian Congo: Congo Balolo Mission.
Sacramento, José do. 1906. *Apontamentos soltos da lingua macúa*. Lisbon: Sociedade de Geographia de Lisboa.
Santos, Eduardo dos. 1962. *Elementos de gramática Quioca*. Lisbon: Agência Geral do Ultramar.

Schadeberg, Thilo C. 1973. Kinga: a restricted tone language. *Studies in African linguistics* 4. 23–48.
Schadeberg, Thilo. 1990. *A sketch of Umbundu*. Köln: Rüdiger Köppe Verlag.
Schoeffer, [Reverand]. 1907. G*rammar of the Bemba language as spoken in northeastern Rhodesia*. Oxford: Clarendon Press.
Seidel, Frank. 2007. The distal marker *-ka-* and motion verbs in Yeyi. *Annual publications in linguistics* 5. 183–195.
Seidel, Frank. 2008. *A grammar of Yeyi: A Bantu language of southern Africa*. Cologne: Rüdiger Köppe.
Sharman, John Campton. 1963. *Morphology, phonology and meaning in the single-verb forms in Bemba*. Pretoria: University of South Africa doctoral dissertation.
Shinagawa, Daisuke. 2012. Bidirectionality in the grammaticalization of 'come' and 'go' in Chaga. *Paper presented at World Congress on African Languages 7*, Buea 2012.
SIL International. n.d. *A grammar of Kinga*. Unpublished manuscript.
Sitoe, Bento. 2001. *Verbs of motion in Changana*. Leiden: Research School CNWS.
Stegen, Oliver. 2011. In quest of a vernacular writing style for the Rangi of Tanzania: Assumptions, processes, challenges. Vol 2: Appendices. University of Edinburgh doctoral dissertation.
Stevick, Earl W., M. Mataranyika & L. Mataranyika. 1965. *Shona basic course*. Washington DC: Foreign Service Inst., US Dept. of State.
Talmy. Leonard. 1985. Lexicalization patterns: Semantic structure in lexical forms. In Shopen, Timothy (ed.), *Language typology and syntactic description: Grammatical categories and the lexicon*. 57–149. New York: Cambridge University Press.
Thomson, Davidson. 1947. *A practical approach to Chinanja*. Salisbury: African Newspapers Ltd.
Traugott, Elizabeth Closs. 1978. On the expression of spatio-temporal relations in language. In Joseph H. Greenberg, Charles A. Ferguson & Edith A. Moravcsik (eds.), *Universals of human language*, vol. 3: *Word structure*. 367–400. Stanford: Stanford University Press.
Turner, William Y. 1996. *ChiTumbuka, chiTonga, English & English, chiTumbuka, chiTonga dictionary*. Blantyre: Central Africana.
Vail, Hazen Leroy. 1972. *Aspects of the Tumbuka verb*. Madison: University of Wisconsin doctoral dissertation.
Valente, José Fransisco. 1964. *Gramática Umbundu. A língua do centro de Angola*. Lisbon: Junta de Investigações Científicas do Ultramar.
Van de Velde, Mark & Koen Bostoen.. 2019. Introduction. In Mark Van de Velde & Koen Bostoen (eds.), *The Bantu languages*. 2nd edn. 1–13. London: Routledge.
Wal, Jenneke van der. 2009. *Word order and information structure in Makhuwa-Enahara*. Leiden: Leiden University doctoral dissertation.
Watkins, Mark H. 1937. *A grammar of Chichewa*. Philadelphia: Linguistic Society of America.
Whiteley, Wilfred Howell 1966. *A study of Yao sentences*. Oxford: Clarendon Press.
Wilhelmsen, Vera. 2018. *A linguistic description of Mbugwe with focus on tone and verbal morphology*. Uppsala: Uppsala Unviersity doctoral dissertation.
Wilkins, David P. 1991. The semantics, pragmatics and diachronic development of 'associated motion' in Mparntwe Arrernte. *Buffalo papers in linguistics* 1. 207–257.
Wilkins, David P. 2006. Towards an Arrernte grammar of space. In Stephen Levinson and David P. Wilkins (eds.), *Grammars of space: explorations in cognitive diversity*. 24–62. Cambridge: Cambridge University Press.
Wilkins, David P. & Deborah Hill. 1995. When "go" means "come": Questioning the basicness of basic motion verbs. *Cognitive linguistics* 6 (2–3). 209–260.

Wolff, R. 1905. *Grammatik der Kinga-Sprache (Deutsch-Ostafrika, Nyassagebiet) nebst Texten und Wörterverzeichnis*. Berlin: Kommissionsverlag von G. Reimer.
Wright, John Lisle. 2007. *An outline of Kikaonde grammar*. Lusaka: Bookworld Publishers & UNZA Press.
Yoneda, Nobuko. 2019. Matengo (N13). In Daisuke Shinagawa & Yuko Abe (eds.), Descriptive materials of morphosyntactic microvariation in Bantu. 418–439. Tokyo University of Foreign Studies.
Zimmermann, Wolfgang & Paavo Hasheela. 1998. *Oshikwanyama grammar*. Windhoek: Gamsberg Macmillan.

Sylvie Voisin
16 Associated motion and deictic directional in Atlantic languages

Abstract: This chapter provides an in-depth description of how the concept of Associated Motion (AM) is conveyed in Atlantic languages, which have been under-described in this matter in the existing literature. African languages have rarely been described as possessing a dedicated Associated Motion system (AM), i.e. verbal suffixes whose primary function is to add a motion co-event to the event expressed by the verb. Here I will show that, within some Atlantic languages, the dynamic deictic morphemes constitute a system of dedicated AM suffixes, whereas in others the dynamic deictic morphemes display both directional deictic and AM meanings. This so-called D-AM system is primarily a Directional Deictic system (DD) attesting AM readings with some specific verbs. The co-existence of these two distinct systems in the Atlantic languages leads us to consider their geographical and/or genetic distribution and to explore their possible origins.

Keywords: associated motion, Atlantic languages, directional deictic, motion events, motion verbs

1 Introduction

The concept of Associated Motion (AM) is defined as "a verbal grammatical category, separate from tense, aspect, mood and direction, whose function is to associate, in different ways, different kinds of translational motion (spatial displacement / change of location) to a (generally non-motion) verb event" (Guillaume & Koch, this volume). In the Niger-Congo languages, the category of AM has been poorly documented until recently, and the morphemes involved have long been designated as "directional" without further explanations.

In this study I show that in Atlantic languages AM is expressed by three types of systems. In the first type, which is common to African languages (Bourdin 2005, 2006; Belkadi 2015a; 2015b; Creissels & Bassène, this volume), AM is expressed as a peculiar function of a deictic directional morpheme. The primary function of these morphemes is to add a deictic orientation to motion events expressed

---
Sylvie Voisin, Aix Marseille Université & Laboratoire Dynamique du Langage (CNRS & Université Lumière Lyon 2), sylvie.voisin@cnrs.fr

by motion verbs in a discursive perspective. In this paper, this function will be referred to by the abbreviation DD (for Deictic Direction).[1] This directionality is oriented with respect to a deictic centre, usually the speaker. In example (1), the Jóola Fóoñi motion verb *riiŋ* 'arrive' is marked by the centripetal suffix *-ul(o)*, which indicates that the people arrived at a place where the speaker is situated, or where the speaker has located the deictic centre.

(1) ba~baj   buk-an   ká-riiŋ-**ulo**   fucen
    PERF~have   CL-someone   S.3PL-arrive-**CTP**   yesterday
    'There are people who arrived yesterday.'
    (Jóola fóoñi: Sambou 2014: 266)

However, as illustrated in example (2), the same suffix *-ul(o)* can also be used with a non-motion verb. In this example, the suffix is used with the dynamic verb *bʊj* 'kill'. As described by Creissels & Bassène (this volume), this derivation involves a movement "whose destination does not coincide with the point of departure". The specific meaning in this context is 'do while coming', more precisely 'you killed my husband while coming'.

(2) A-ta-ɔm,   jɩ-bʊj-**ul**-ɔɔ~bʊj   dɩ
    CLa-husband-I:1SG   SI:2PL-kill-**DO.COMING**-I:CLA~PERF   PREP
    bʊ-ɲar-a-b.
    CLb-road-D-CLb
    'My husband, you killed him on the way.'
    (Jóola fóoñi: Creissels & Bassène, this volume)

The 'do while coming' meaning coincides with one of the possible meanings of AM. In this study, following Belkadi (2015a, b, this volume), this type of system will be referred to by the abbreviation D-AM (primary DD system with AM extensions).

In the second type, which is rarely described in African languages (Voisin 2010, 2013), AM is the primary and exclusive function of the verbal suffixes, which are dedicated to the expression of AM meanings. In the Wolof example (3), for instance, the suffix *-i* adds a motion event realized before the action 'lie down'.

---

[1] Conversely to Belkadi or Ross (this volume), DD is not considered as a sub-type of path. Following Fagard et al. (2013), DD is seen as both a distinct component of motion and a distinct category of AM. For more details of these different points of view see Belkadi (this volume).

(3) Bala   nga=y   tër-**i**,   nanga   fat   basaŋ   b-i
     before S.2SG=IMPERF lie_down-**GO&DO** OBL.S.2SG   tidy mat   CL-PROX
     'Before you go to bed, you'll put the mat away.'
     (Wolof: Diouf 2003: 69)

Crucially, unlike the Jóola Fóoñi suffix *-ul(o)* in (1), the Wolof AM suffix *-i* cannot be used to add a deictic orientation to a motion verb – it never has DD extensions. The only known extension is TAM readings when *-i* is suffixed to non-dynamic verbs (§ 3.5). In this study, this type of system will be referred to by the abbreviation EAM (for Exclusive Associated Motion system).

Finally, in the third type of system, which is even much more rare than the preceding ones in African languages (and possibly elsewhere in the languages of the world), AM is the primary but non-exclusive meaning of the dynamic deictic morphemes, which can also have a DD function.[2] For instance, the following examples of Sereer display the same polyfunctionality as in the preceding examples of Jóola Fóoñi. In (4a), the suffix *-iid* has a pure centripetal function (DD), and in (4b) this same morpheme adds a motion event before the action 'eat' (AM). However, several differences between the system such as attested in Jóola Fóoñi vs. in Sereer allow us to consider that in Sereer the original system was an AM system, not a DD system as in Jóola Fóoñi.

(4) a. ten   yen-**iid**-u   ga-kall   al-e [...]
        3SG   fall-**CTP**-FOC   CL-arm_of_sea   CL-PROX
        'She fell into the inlet (towards the island where the speaker is located).'
        (Sereer: Renaudier 2012: 41)

    b. tiit   k-e   a-ñaam-**iid**-aa   kaaf   k-e
        bird   CL-PROX   s.3-eat-**COME&DO**-IMPERF millet   CL-PROX
        'Birds come to eat millet.'
        (Sereer: Renaudier 2012: 97)

In my earlier publications (Voisin 2010, 2013), this third type of system was referred to as "Mixed system". Here, it will be referred to by the abbreviation AM-D (for primary AM system with DD extensions). In Atlantic languages, the DD system always displays extensions towards AM meanings (D-AM),

---

[2] The description of AM systems, such as in Amerindian or Australian languages (Guillaume 2016), does not imply an extension towards DD interpretations.

and these AM extensions encode subsequent and/or concurrent motion.³ The paper is organized around the following main question: to which of these three types of systems do the affixes that express AM meanings belong in the Atlantic languages: D-AM, EAM or AM-D)? The chapter is structured with five further sections. In section 2, I present the language sample and introduce the genetic relationships and typological features of Atlantic languages. Section 3 is devoted to the description of dedicated AM systems (EAM) and some of their semantic extensions related to space, such as distal (or altrilocative), or TAM. Section 4 handles non-dedicated AM systems in which AM meanings are carried by polyfunctional affixes which can fulfill other kinds of (non-AM) functions. On the one hand, as in many other African languages, the AM meaning is encompassed in a deictic directional system (D-AM). On the other hand, the AM meaning is the primary function of systems that also attest some deictic directional extensions (AM-D). Section 5 presents the means of expressing AM in the Atlantic languages and their geographical distribution. It also raises the question of the possible source(s) of the AM and DD systems in the Atlantic languages. Finally, section 6 concludes this chapter and summarizes the different systems of dynamic deixis found in Atlantic languages and their possible extensions.

2 Background on the Atlantic languages and the expression of spatial motion

The Atlantic language family consists of around 50 languages, which are listed in Figure 1. The Atlantic languages are mostly spoken in West Africa (Senegal, Gambia, Guinea and Guinea Bissau),⁴ in the vicinity of languages from Mande, Mel families and the Hassaniya language (Semitic), as shown in Map 2 in the Appendix. The family is divided into two distinct sub-branches, NORTH and BAK (Pozdniakov & Segerer to appear).

---

3 This configuration can probably extend to a large part of African languages (cf. for example the Cushitic languages described by Bourdin 2006). It should be noted, however, that Belkadi (2015a) indicates an extension towards an AM meaning of prior motion, at least for the Berber languages.
4 Except for FULA, whose dialectal continuum extends from the Atlantic coast to Chad, including some areas in Sudan.

ATLANTIC
NORTH
    WOLOF   Wolof, Lebu
    NYUNBUY
        NYUN   Gunyaamolo, Gubëeher, Gunyun, Nyun of Yacine, Gubelor, Gujaahar
        BUY   Kobiana, Kasanga
    TENDA-JAAD
        TENDA   Bedik, Bassari, Tenda, Konyagi
        JAAD   Jaad, Biafada
    FULA-SEREER
        FULA   Pulaar, Fulfulde of Nigeria, Fulfulde of Massina
        SEREER   Sereer-sine, Sereer of Mar Lodj
    CANGIN   Noon (Cangin-Noon, Pade-Noon), Laala, Saafi-saafi, Palor, Ndut
    NALU   Nalu, Baga
BAK
    BALANTE-JÓOLA-MANJAKU
        BALANTE   Balant-Ganja, Balant-Soofa, Balante Kentohe, Fraase
        JÓOLA-MANJAKU
            JÓOLA   Fóoñi, Banjal, Karon, Keeraak, Kwaatay, Bayot
            MANJAKU   Mankanya, Manjaku, Pepel
    BIJOGO   Kagbaaga,[5] Kamona, Kajoko

Figure 1: Internal classification of the Atlantic languages (adapted to Pozdniakov & Segerer to appear).

The documentation used in this chapter is based on the available grammatical descriptions, supplemented for some languages by personal communications with specialists. The languages surveyed are underlined in Figure 1. It should be noted that the Atlantic family includes a high proportion of under-described languages. Despite the recent attention that Atlantic languages have received, several linguistic domains are still under-documented. This gap of description concerns specifically verbal morphology, which is the main topic of this chapter. Languages with dashed underlining have reported data that need more exploration. In the current sample, special attention has been paid to taking into account most of the subgroups of the family. The only missing subgroup is NALU, since information on the dynamic deictic morphemes in these languages is completely lacking. The data available for the JAAD and TENDA groups need to be completed through a more detailed investigation in order for these languages to be better incorporated

---

5 Kagbaaga is a Bijogo variety spoken in Bubaque. It is the language documented in this chapter under the Bijogo name.

into the typology of the dynamic deixis systems of Atlantic languages. That is to say, except for the NALU group, for which no information is available, all subgroups of the family are attested with a system of dynamic deixis. The systems that are hard to characterize result more from lack of data than from the actual absence of specific morphemes with dynamic deictic meaning.

The morphemes examined in this chapter are regularly presented in the verbal morphology sections of descriptive studies and are commonly labeled as "centripetal /centrifugal", "ventive /itive" or simply "directional" morphemes without further precision. In contrast to better-known African language families, the separation between the branches of the Atlantic family is very ancient. Therefore, there is no uniformity in the morphological structure of verbs. TAM markers and verbal extensions occupy different positions with respect to the verbal root from one language to another. The constraints on subject indexation and the position occupied by subject indices also vary from one language to another.

Concerning the expression of translational motion in these languages, two features can be introduced, although they are not specific to the Atlantic family: the type of coding of motion events (verb-framed vs. satellite-framed) and the specificities of the most generic motion verbs. As pointed out by several analyses, such as those by Schaefer (1985), Schaefer & Gaines (1997) or Gaines (2014), African languages are generally verb-framed languages as defined in Talmy (2007), and Atlantic languages are not an exception. Only the second feature, the specificities of the 'go' and 'come' pair of verbs, will be discussed in this chapter. The differences which can be noticed between the 'come' and 'go' verbs in these languages shed some interesting light on the development of dynamic deictic systems in Atlantic languages. The behavior of these verbs is also a criterion taken into account in our survey, which traces the original system in the languages possessing a mixed system D-AM or AM-D.

3 AM functions expressed through dedicated suffixes

Dedicated associated motion systems, i.e. systems in which the morphemes encode exclusively AM functions (EAM), were first described for Pama-Nyungan languages spoken in Australia (Koch 1984; Wilkins 1991) and more recently for languages of South America (Guillaume 2000, 2006; Vuillermet 2013; Rose 2015). In some Atlantic languages, the verbal extensions labeled "directional" or "itive/ ventive" are considered as an EAM system. In this section, I show that the EAM systems are always simple in Atlantic languages, since these languages have from one to three AM markers (cf. Guillaume 2016 for more details on the degrees of the complexity of AM systems). The EAM systems for the languages presented in this section are summarized in Table 1 below. In this section, the main values of these EAM systems are described. The most commonly found meaning is a prior centrifugal movement involving the S/A argument (§ 3.1). But some other functions can be found. A distal meaning expressed by EAM morphemes, attested in at least two languages, is presented in section 3.2, an 'elsewhere' motion in section 3.3 and a 'hither' movement of the P argument in section 3.4. In Atlantic languages where the verbal derivations mainly express AM meanings (i.e. EAM), some semantic developments towards TAM functions can also be observed (§ 3.5).

Table 1: The dedicated AM system (EAM) in Atlantic languages.

		NORTH					
		WOLOF	FULA-SEREER	CANGIN			
		Wolof	FULA[6]	Saafi-saafi	Laala	Cangin-Noon	Pade-Noon
COME&DO	A	-si	-oy				
DISTAL							
GO&DO	A	-i		-a	-a	-naas/-nee	
MOVE&DO	A						-nee
OUT&DO	A	-aan			-itan		
DO.COMING	A / P						-doh

3.1 AM functions expressed through a dedicated AM system (EAM)

On the basis of the information at my disposal, my survey shows that the Atlantic languages exhibiting an EAM system are Wolof, Fulfulde, and several CANGIN languages: Saafi-saafi, Laala and two varieties of Noon. The EAM system in these languages is rather small as compared to those identified in some Australian or Amerindian languages. In all but one language (Wolof), the EAM system are asymmetrical, with a centrifugal marker (encoding prior motion involving the S/A argument) and no centripetal marker.

In the three following examples, the AM markers -i in Wolof (5), -a in Laala (6), -oy in Fulfulde (7) are suffixed to action verbs. These suffixes indicate that the subject of the sentence has moved or must move before realizing the action encoded by the verb.

---

[6] The suffix -oy is attested in several dialects of Fulfulde, with the same meanings. The analysis is proposed to the entire FULA group.

(5) B-u   xëy-ee   (moom   gaynde)   rëbb-**i**,
    CL-INDET leave_early-ANT   PRO3SG lioness   hunt-**GO&DO**
    'Every time, (she, lioness) she went hunting,'
    (Wolof: Kesteloot & Dieng 1989: 95)

(6) ka-faanok   ka-faanok-**a**   'go to sleep'
    INF-lay_down INF-lay_down-**CTF**
    ka-ñam   ka-ñam-**a**   'go to eat'
    INF-eat   INF-eat-**CTF**
    ka-ɓookok   ka-ɓookok-**a**   'go to wash'
    INF-wash   INF-wash-**CTF**
    (Laala: Dieye 2010: 218)

(7) dɔɔm-am   dɔɔ   faa   mi jɛɛ-ɔy-a   kaadɔ   mɛɛrɛɛjo   ʔɔɔ
    wait-IMP.SG-ME   here so_that   I   see-**GO&DO**-SUB   Bozo   worthless this
    'Wait here for me so that I **go** and look for this terrible Bozo and subsequently,
    dee,   min ⁿgar-t-id-a
    subsequently   we   come-PERF-COM-SUB
    we'll come back together.'
    (Fulfulde of Massina: Breedveld 1995: 252)

The AM systems of the Atlantic languages are unbalanced systems in the sense that the AM COME&DO is mainly expressed by periphrastic constructions (subordination, sequentiality) (8 and 10) or complex predicates in which the verb 'come' is an auxiliary (9).

(8) B-oo   dem-ee   nga   né   Buur   na   **ñów** rey   ma
    CL-TEMP.S.2SG leave-ANT   S.2SG say   king   OBL.S.3SG **come** kill O.1SG
    'When you leave, you will tell the king that he will come (and) kill me.'
    (Wolof: Kesteloot & Mbodj 1983: 123)

(9) Me   **hac**   na-raa   ka-andoh
    S.1SG   **come** with/and-O.2SG INF-accompany
    'I'm coming to accompany you.'
    (Laala: Dieye 2010: 177)

(10) mi-yahay   mi-suud'oo   bako   'o-**wara**   'o-naggga-yam
     1SG-go:TAM   1SG-hide   before 3SG-**come**   3SG-catch-O.1SG
     'I'll go (and) hide before he **comes** and catches me.'
     (Fulfulde of Nigeria: Arnott 1970: 40)

Wolof is the only language possessing two AM morphemes expressing prior movement with the opposite deictic meanings COME and GO. In the preceding example (5), the suffix -*i* involves a prior motion away from the deictic centre, while the suffix -*si* in (11) encodes a prior motion back to the deictic centre. Note that in Wolof, as illustrated by example (7), prior movement can also be expressed by the verb 'come' in a periphrastic construction.

(11) Dafa   jàq   moo   tax   mu   seet-**si**
      FOC.V.S.3SG be_worried   FOC.SUBJ.S.3SG   cause S.3SG visit-**COME&DO**
      la
      O.2SG
      'He's worried, that's why he **came** to see you.'
      (Wolof: Diouf 2003: 104)

The AM marker -*nee* of Pade-Noon (a Noon dialect belonging to the CANGIN cluster) adds a translational motion event without a specific path and is consequently labeled MOVE&DO. It has a default interpretation 'go and do' as in (12 and 13), but can also have a 'come and do' interpretation when it co-occurs[7] with the verb 'come' in the previous clause (14) (a construction that corresponds to what is named "echo construction" in Guillaume 2016), or in some specific contexts.

(12) ya   jom   ki-heel-**nee**   sookoo.
      s/he should   INF-get-**MOVE&DO**   firewood
      'She should **go** to get firewood.'
      (Pade-Noon: Soukka 2000: 172)

(13) ñam-id-is-**nee**!
      eat-CAUS-ITER-**MOVE&DO**
      '**Go** and feed again!'
      (Pade-Noon: Soukka 2000: 157)

(14) Hay-aa   dii,   fu   taas-**nee**   paam-fu!
      come-IMP   DEM.LOC   2SG   answer-**MOVE&DO**   father-2SG
      'Come here and answer your father! (lit. Come here and **come** answer your father!)'
      (Pade-Noon: Soukka 2000: 173)

---

7 It is important to note that in these constructions, the associated motion can be doubly marked, by the suffixation of the AM marker and by the independent motion verb (co-occurring verb).

Generally, the AM suffixes GO&DO and COME&DO can co-occur in "echo constructions" with the motion verbs 'go' / 'leave' and 'come', respectively, without any change in meaning, as in Wolof (15). In Pade-Noon, the presence of the motion verb confirms or disambiguates the 'go' vs. 'come' reading of the MOVE&DO suffix -*nee*.

(15) mu   dem   raxas-*i*   ko   géej-u   Ndaayaan.
     S.3SG   leave   wash-**GO&DO** O.3SG   sea-GEN   Ndayane
     'She goes to wash it at the sea of Ndayane.'
     (Wolof: Kesteloot & Mbodj 1983: 25)

Unlike Pade-Noon, in the other CANGIN languages, such as Laala, Saafi-saafi and Cangin-Noon, the presence of the motion verb 'go' in auxiliary position or in the previous clause is obligatory with the GO&DO AM marker (16), whereas the motion verb 'come' in auxiliary position or in the previous clause is in itself sufficient to express a COME&DO AM function.

(16) ɓete   c-aa   kaɗ-en   kaway-*a*
     woman   CL-DEM   go-PFT   look_for_wood-**GO&DO**
     'The women went to fetch wood'
     (Laala: Dieye 2010: 218)

This difference between the CANGIN varieties may explain the evolution of the -*nee* suffix in Pade-Noon. The systematic co-occurrence of a motion verb, such as 'go' or 'come', with the AM affixation has possibly led to the loss of some semantic substance of the AM suffix. The AM suffix retains the expression of prior motion but leaves the encoding of deixis to the independent motion co-occurring verb.

3.2 The altrilocative functions of AM affixes on motion verbs

In Fulfulde, the associated motion suffix -*oy* is more commonly used with another related function, often named "altrilocative". This function implies that the action of the derived verb "takes place in another place, different from where the subject is located" (Breedveld 1995: 178). This meaning occurs when -*oy* is associated with motion verbs, especially those that express a return motion. In this context, the AM suffix indicates that the event (often a motion encoded by the lexical verb) takes place away from the location of the speaker. The distal function conveyed by the GO&DO suffix is still present. This function can be related to the dissociative meaning of 'go' described in Bourdin (1992). It situates a (translational motion) event realized far away, from inception to completion, from the deictic centre. In this regard, the marker no longer means a movement before the realization of the state of affairs expressed by the verb. In (17), the translational motion *wart* 'come back' encodes a movement in which the path is directly expressed by the verbal lexeme. The suffix *-oy* indicates that the whole movement is realized far away from the deictic centre. The source and endpoint of the motion event are both distant from the deictic centre. Consequently, *-oy* locates the place where a motion occurs. In this function of localization, the AM morpheme loses its dynamic deictic value and acquires a non-dynamic/static location sense. This can explain the ability of derivation of locative state verbs, as in (18), where *-oy* means that the location is necessarily distant.

(17) Bello   wart-oy-ii
    Bello   come_back-**GO&DO**-PERF
    'Bello has come back there (from where he had gone).'
    (Fulfulde of Nigeria: Arnott 1970: 357)

(18) mi   'annd-aa   to   ɓe   'yiw-**oy**-i
    s.1SG   know-NEG   where   CL   be_native_of-**GO&DO**-TAM
    'I don't know where they came from (where they are originated from).'
    (*-oy-* implies a distant origin)'
    (Fulfulde of Nigeria: Arnott 1970: 357)

Another semantic extension which can be partly related to this altrilocative meaning is also attested in Wolof with the COME&DO suffix *-si*. When this suffix is affixed to motion verbs such as *àgg* 'to arrive', *dellu* 'to return' etc., it indicates that the S/A argument is situated away from the location of the speaker before performing the movement encoded by the derived verb. The motion event added by the AM suffix *-si* disappears and preserves only the centripetal value of the original AM morpheme (cf. 19 and 20b). In example (19), the motion event is directly encoded by the verb *àgg* 'arrive'. The suffix *-si* indicates that this movement is realized in the direction to the deictic centre situated in 'another village'.

(19) ñu=y   dem   di   dem   ba   ag-**si**   b-eneen
    s.3PL=IMPERF leave   IMPERF   leave   until   arrive-**COME&DO**   CL-another
    dëkk.
    village
    'They went away, went away till they arrived in another village.'
    (Wolof: Kesteloot & Mbodj 1983: 39)

In (20a) and (20b), the verb *dellu* 'return' is used. In (20a), the subject (S argument) goes back to a specific place. In (20b), the addition of *-si* implies that the movement has its endpoint located closer to or directed toward the deictic centre, whereas in (20a) the endpoint of the motion event can be viewed as far away from the deictic centre.

(20) a. *Sama   baay   dellu   na   Màkka.*
        POSS.1SG father return   PERFECT.S.3SG   Mecca
        'My father has gone back to Mecca.'
        (Wolof: Fal et al. 1990: 59)

   b. *Kañ   nga=y   dellu-**si**   Senegaal?*
      when   S.2SG-IMPERF   return-**COME&DO**   Senegal
      'When will you return to Senegal?'
      (Wolof: Diouf 2003: 52)

This meaning of the AM suffix can be explained by the loss of one of its semantic components. All AM suffixes combine indication of a translational motion and specification about the path taken during this movement, except the MOVE&DO suffix *-nee* in Pade-Noon. In both Fulfulde and Wolof, the AM suffixes lose the movement component while maintaining the path information when they are used with motion verbs. Due to the opposite meaning 'go' vs. 'come' of the involved AM markers in the two languages, the newly generated function is different in the end. The dissociative value of 'go' in Fulfulde provides an altrilocative marker, whereas, in Wolof, the value of 'come' leads to a centripetal Deictic Directional marker, but also implies that the source of the movement takes place in a distant location. Note that, curiously, the emergent functions have been predominantly found so far on verbs expressing a return movement.

3.3 OUT&DO, an atypical AM meaning

The AM suffixes glossed OUT&DO in Wolof and Laala imply the realizing of an action in a place other than that in which it is usually done. It is mostly illustrated with actions typically performed at home, such as sleeping, living, eating, etc., which limits the set of potential verbs (21 and 22).

The primary function of the AM suffixes OUT&DO is to highlight that the action is realized in different place from which it is usually done. I introduce this derivation into the AM markers, suggesting that the realization of an action in a place other than the usual place implies a movement out of this place. However, this associated motion remains as a background information in the translation. The appropriate situation and the small number of verbs concerned by this phenomenon can explain both the low frequency of its use and the fact that it is only described in two of the surveyed languages.

(21) b-i   jabar-am   demee   ba   tey
     CL-PROX   wife-POSS.3SG   leave-ANT   until   today
     dafa-y   añ-**aan**   rekk
     FOC.V.S.3SG-IMPERF   have_lunch-**OUT&DO**   only
     'Since his wife left, he's been having lunch here and there'
     (Wolof: Diouf 2003: 55)

(22) a. *ka-neh-**itan***   b. *ka-ñam-**itan***
         INF-sleep-**OUT&DO**   INF-eat-**OUT&DO**
         sleep out   eat elsewhere
         (Laala: Dieye 2010: 215)

In Wolof, a language for which a large documentation is available, the OUT&DO suffix can be found with verbs other than those denoting actions usually performed at home, as shown by 'flow' in (23). The example is extracted from a dictionary entry. Here, by using the OUT&DO suffix, the author underlines the multidirectionality taken by the water. The water flows abundantly, i.e. in several directions (not just in its natural course).

(23) ndox   m-a=a ngi   baaw-**aan**
     water   CL-DEF=PREST   flow-**OUT&DO**
     'The water flows abundantly.' *(couler à flot* in the original French translation)
     (Wolof: Fal, Santos & Doneux 1990: 42)

The distributive function of the OUT&DO suffix in Wolof is more obvious with other verbs. In example (24), with the verb *màng* 'to practice transhumance', the OUT&DO suffix is combined with the GO&DO suffix -*i*. The suffix -*i* indicates that the shepherds go away before the transhumance. The suffix -*aan* adds the information that, after this movement, they move their animals to places that are different from their traditional place of transhumance.

(24) B-u   ñax   am-at-ul   Jolof,
    TEMP-INDET   grass have-ITER-NEG Djolof
    dañu=y   màng-**aan-i**
    FOC.V.S.1SG=IMPERF transhumance-**OUT&DO-GO&DO**
    'When there is no more pasture in the Djolof, they go and practice transhumance in various places.'
    (Wolof: Diouf 2003: 148)

The co-occurrence of OUT&DO -*aan* and GO&DO -*i* seems to reinforce the distributive function (in several places) of the suffix -*aan*. In example (25), the sentence *dafa liggéeyaani* can be used as an answer to the question 'What is he doing for a living?', meaning 'he does odd jobs, he does not have steady jobs', literally 'he goes to work in different places'.

(25) Dafa   liggéey-**aan-i**
    FOC.V.3SG   work-**OUT&DO-GO&DO**
    'He works everywhere (here and there).'
    (Wolof[8])

The OUT&DO suffix attested in Wolof and Laala is an AM suffix whose precise status is unclear. The fact the OUT&DO suffix can co-occur with another AM suffix, as in (24) and (25), is unexpected in the typology of the AM system. It is possible that the associated motion co-event is only presupposed because the subject should have moved away from the normal place to carry out the activity "elsewhere", while the AM suffix involves a real motion of one of the arguments. Further investigation of Atlantic languages is in order. Exploration of the Wolof data shows that the set of verbs with which this suffix can probably occur goes beyond the usual activities most often mentioned in reference grammars. However, it also involves a more precise value than a strict AM suffix conveying an added motion event. The meaning of this suffix in Wolof is more related to a scattered action that can be interpreted either as an action not realized in the expected place, or an action done in various directions or in different places (24 and 25), displaying a distributive deictic meaning.

---

8 The Wolof and Kobiana data without any source indication have been collected by the author during fieldwork.

3.4 Simultaneous centripetal AM involving both S/A and P argument

Finally, in Pade-Noon, Soukka (2000) reports a valency-increasing morpheme -*doh*, which is labeled as an "apportative" and described as follows: "The suffix gives the verb a signification of movement when something is brought from one place to another" (Soukka 2000: 170). Example (26) is extracted from a narration of "Lion milk". This story is about a woman who seeks milk for her children. She went to the forest and saw a lioness that had given birth. "She came, took some of her goats, approached there and the lioness ate. The next morning, she brought a goat, she came a bit closer, the lioness ate (it). The next morning, she came even closer, the lioness ate (she did this) until the lioness got used to her".

(26) Ya   hay-ya,   ya   ɓeɓ-pa   ga   pe'-caa-gari,
     she   come-NARR   she   take-NARR   of   goats-DEF-POSS.3SG
     deey-**doh**-ha   da,
     be_close-**COMING.WITH**-narr   there
     'She (the woman) came (close to the lioness), she took some of her goats, approached there (lit. moved there together with the goats).'
     (Pade-Noon: Soukka 2000: 291)

In example (26), the suffix -*doh* adds a previous motion to the intransitive verb *deey* 'be close'. This suffix affects the S/A and introduces a P argument. The meaning conveyed by -*doh* gives the value of simultaneous centripetal motion for both arguments. This morpheme, like the centripetal described in Jóola Fóoñi by Creissels & Bassène (this volume), indicates that "the referent of the subject not only has taken or gotten something while coming, (s)he still has it upon arrival.".

The origin of this morpheme in Pade-Noon is probably a case of suffix stacking[9] incorporating an applicative morpheme -*oh*, which resulted in the meaning of doing something with someone or something (comitative / sociative participant). The suggested applicative origin is strengthened by the syntactic modification implied according to the verb involved. In examples (26), as also in (27), the involved verb is an intransitive motion verb. The derivation -*doh* increases the valence of the verb, as the applicative adds an applied argument. In (27), this applied argument *miismaa* 'milk' is also affected by the displacement. In other

---

9 Soukka (2000:170) makes the following assumption for the etymology of -*doh*: "It is possible that the spatial notion of the consonant *d*-, as a locative agreement marker in the nominal morphology, has an impact in this suffix as well". My interpretation is that the second component -*oh* is an applicative, not the durative marker, as Soukka suggests.

words, a presumably stacked applicative derivation develops an AM function with a comitative value. Note that this increase of the valence is not systematic with the AM suffix (28).

(27) *Kooh wiis-sa,   ya   hay-**doh**-ha   miis-maa,*
     God   make.day-NARR   she come-**COMING.WITH**-NARR   milk-DEF
     e'-ta   naah-aa.
     give-NARR   wise.man-DEF
     'The next morning, she brought the milk and gave it to the wise man.'
     (Pade-Noon: Soukka 2000: 336)

(28) *Ba   nak-ee   ki-ɓay-**doh**[10]   tesoh-taa   en*
     they use-PAST   INF-call-**COMING.WITH**   seeds-DEF   be
     'They used to bring seeds ...'
     (Pade-Noon: Soukka 2000: 283)

To summarize, morphemes dedicated to the expression of AM in Atlantic languages have the following properties:
- They mainly consist of one AM morpheme with a prior centrifugal function involving the S/A argument;
- The presence of a motion verb accompanying the derived verb in an echo construction is only obligatory in the CANGIN group of the family, except in Pade-Noon. Such constructions are allowed, but optional, in the other languages;
- Other values are attested in some languages with an AM system, without being widely shared:
    - Only Wolof has a centripetal COME&DO morpheme;
    - The GO&DO marker in the CANGIN Pade-Noon language is losing its centrifugal meaning, evolving into a deictically undetermined AM marker, labeled MOVE&DO;
    - In the same language, the emergence of a new AM morpheme has also been observed: the valency-increasing suffix *-doh*, which expresses a motion event involving the displacement of both the S/A and P arguments;
    - In Fulfulde, the GO&DO suffix *-oy* has developed an altrilocative function. With motion verbs, often 'go back' motion events, the suffix indicates that the event takes place in a different place from where the subject is

---

10 The meaning of 'bring', built through the derivation of the verb *ɓay* 'call' by the suffix *-doh*, is clearly noted in Soukka (2000:170). However, this kind of construction is not expected and is not frequent in Atlantic languages.

located. The translational event encoded by the verb is realized far away, from inception to completion, from the deictic centre.
- In Wolof, the COME&DO suffix -*si* has developed a distal meaning with a restricted set of motion verbs, indicating that the endpoint of motion encoded by the verb is located closer to or oriented toward the deictic centre.
- Finally, another suffix, glossed OUT&DO, is found expressing an elsewhere motion, at least in Wolof and Laala.

3.5 Expansion of the AM system towards TAM meanings with non-dynamic verbs

The evolution of the AM markers towards TAM meanings with non-dynamic verbs has been noted for some languages. This extension toward TAM meanings is reported in this section only for Wolof, but some indications of this semantic change can be found in Fula (Sow 1966) and it is probably present in other languages too, although investigation remains to be done.

Sow (1966: 19) notes that "when the realization of an action seems hypothetical, -*oy* tends to appear in the verbal element of that action."[11]

(29) a. mi   sikki   o   aray
       S.1SG believe:TAM S.3SG   come
       'I believe that he will came.'
       (Pulaar: Sow 1966: 19)

   b. mi   sikkaa   o   aray-**oy**
      S.1SG believe:NEG S.3SG   come-**HYP**
      'I don't believe that he will came.
      I don't believe that he's going to come'
      (Pulaar: Sow 1966: 19)

In African languages, and particularly in Atlantic languages, there is a simple test to distinguish non-dynamic verbs from dynamic ones.[12] The perfective receives two distinct interpretations depending on the semantics of the verb. With non-dynamic verbs, the perfective construction (in Wolof, no morpheme *vs. di* ~ =*y*

---
[11] Sow (1966: 19) "Lorsque la réalisation d'une action semble hypothétique, -*oy* a tendance à apparaître dans l'élément verbal de cette action."
[12] This verbal opposition is also labelled discrete *vs.* compact verbs, while it does not completely overlap with the stative *vs.* active verb distinction.

imperfective) conveys a present temporality (30). With dynamic verbs, the value of the perfective sentence is a retrospective present (past interpretation) (31).

(30) *Bëgg   na*
     love   PFT.S.3SG
     'He loves.'
     (Wolof)

(31) *Liggéey   na*
     work   PFT.S.3SG
     'He worked.'
     (Wolof)

According to this criterion, the inventory of non-dynamic and dynamic verbs can be different across the Atlantic languages, but this distribution is confirmed by other means, such as the AM derivations displaying TAM functions. The AM vs. TAM function of these markers is clearly identifiable, at least in some languages. In Wolof, for example, the morphemes *-si* COME&DO and *-i* GO&DO are used on non-dynamic verbs such as 'be good', 'be beautiful'. The clause has an inchoative interpretation with *-si* (32) and a prospective interpretation with *-i* (33).

(32) *Sa   liggéey=a ngi   baax-si   muñ-al   tuuti rekk*
     POSS.2SG   work=PREST   be_good-**INCHO**   wait-IMP   little just
     'Your work becomes good, be a little more patient.'
     (Wolof)

(33) *Xale   b-ii   dina   rafet-i*
     child   CL-DEM.PROX   FUT.S.3SG   be_beautiful-**PROSP**
     'This child will become beautiful.'
     (Wolof)

These suffixes are the same as those seen in the preceding section to encode AM on dynamic verbs such as 'work', 'eat', 'see', as the COME&DO suffix *-si* in (34) and the GO&DO suffix *-i* in (35). This shift from space to time is well documented and not surprising (cf. for instance Bybee et al. 1994 or Kuteva et al. 2019).

(34) *Dafa   ànd   ak   borom-bopp ;   du   liggéey-si*
     FOC.V.S.3SG   go_together   with   toothache   NEG.S.3SG   work-**COME&DO**
     'He has a toothache; he will not come to work.'
     (Wolof: Diouf 2003: 30)

(35) Bu   ko   fekk-*i*
     INJ.NEG   O.3SG   find-**GO&DO**
     'Do not go find him.'
     (Wolof: Diouf 2003: 72)

In some older grammars of Wolof, such as Boilat (1858), the AM affixation is integrated into the conjugation system. The suffixes are interpreted as FUTURE markers (36). In the present-day grammars, however, these suffixes are never included as TAM markers.

(36) *M'â-ngai-bakh'-i*
     Maa nga=y   baax-*i*
     PREST.S.1SG= IMPERF   be_good-**GO&DO**
     'I become good.'
     (Wolof: Boilat 1858: 111)

4 AM functions expressed through multifunctional suffixes

In this section, I introduce other markers encoding AM meanings in Atlantic languages. Contrary to the morphemes presented so far, the AM functions expressed by these markers are not incorporated into a dedicated AM system but are part of multifunctional systems in which the AM interpretation depends on specific contexts. Two distinct types of systems are distinguished, based on their primary meaning: D-AM when the expression of DD is primary (i.e. deictic direction with motion verbs) and the expression of AM secondary (section 4.1), and AM-D when the expression of AM is primary and the expression of DD secondary (section 4.2). In the last section 4.3, a number of additional systems are discussed in two groups of Atlantic languages, the JAAD and TENDA clusters, for which there is not sufficient information to classify them into any of the types discussed above. Moreover, these systems seem to have surprising particularities in contrast to the systems of other Atlantic languages, which make them an interesting subject for future investigation. The presentation here is only a preliminary account of the functions identifiable in the scarce documentation at my disposal.

4.1 AM functions expressed through a deictic directional system (D-AM)

Atlantic languages from this survey showing a D-AM system are listed in Table 2.[13] They belong either to the BAK branch or to the NYUN-BUY cluster of the NORTH branch.

Table 2: The D-AM system in Atlantic languages.

			CTP / DO&COME OR DO.COMING	CTF / DO&GO
NORTH	BUY	Kobiana	-Vtt (~ -Vh)	
	NUYN	Guñaamolo	-Vri	
		Gubëëher	-Vt	
		Gujaahar	-Vt	-an
BAK	BALANTE	Balant-Ganja	-tè /-ti	
	JÓOLA	Fóoñi	-úl(o)	
		Banjal	-úl(o)	
		Karon	-í(n)	
		Kwaatay	-in (~ -ina; -ino)	
	MANJAKU	Manjaku	-i	
		Mankanya	-ar	

For the expression of DD meanings, which is the primary function of these morphemes, one can see that all languages with a D-AM system have at least one morpheme with a centripetal (often named "ventive") function. With intransitive motion verbs, this morpheme encodes the fact that the motion performed by the subject is oriented toward the position occupied by the speaker or toward the deictic centre defined by the speaker, as illustrated in examples (37) to (39).

(37) *ngis-**eh**-a*
 III.go_down-CTP-S.2SG.IMP
 'Go down here!'
 (Kobiana: Doneux 1991: 78)

---

[13] Remember that in many descriptions these suffixes do not attract particular attention. More often, only a notification of their existence and some illustrative examples are given. In some languages, the absence of a precise description of their different functions and/or of the affected verbal classes makes it difficult to identify their possible extensions. This explains why, for instance, this extension cannot be proved in Bayot and this language is not included in the table.

(38) na-nogen-**ulo**-nogen   ni   y-aŋ   yayu
     s.3SG-enter-**CTP**-enter in   CL-house   CL-DEM
     'He entered in the house. (The speaker was inside)'
     (Jóola Banjal: Bassène 2006: 106)

(39) a. *tuk*   b. *tuk-**i***
        run   run-**CTP**
                    'run here'
     (Manjaku: Doneux 1993: 33)

With transitive motion verbs, the D-AM marker keeps the same centripetal value, but the centripetal direction applies to the object of the verb (40).

(40) *a   na-yel-**i**-in   b-yànk-ar-ul*
     and   s.3SG-sent-**CTP**-O.1SG   INF-take-APPL-O.3SG
     'and she sent me here to collect it.'
     (Manjaku: Karlik 1972: 151)

Gujaahar, of the NYUN group, is the sole language in my sample displaying both a centripetal morpheme and a centrifugal morpheme. In example (41), both morphemes are used. The centrifugal *-án* indicates that the subject *àm-* 'they' (S argument) arrives in a place distant from the speaker or the deictic centre (maybe a village indicated in the story), whereas the centripetal *-át* suffixed to *pííh* 'throw' interacts with a new deictic centre, i.e. the river, which is the place toward which the object *-ém* 'him' (P argument) is thrown. Note that in the other languages, which do not have a centrifugal marker, a default centrifugal interpretation applies to verbs without any directional marker.

(41) *biriŋ   ám-bár-án-**i**,*
     when   s.3PL-arrive-**CTF**-PAST.PUNC
     *ám-pííh-**át**-é-ém   a   ci-n-da*
     s.3PL-throw-**CTP**-PAST.PUNC-O.3SG in   CL-POST-river
     'When they arrived (**there**), they threw him into the river.'
     (Gujaahar: Goudiaby 2017: 229)

For the expression of AM meanings in the Atlantic languages with a D-AM system, a periphrastic construction can first be used, as in (42 to 44). In such constructions, AM is expressed by an independent motion verb root (with or without a directional) in combination with another verb.

(42) ti-yom-o   tí-dúk-ó   án-dék-**rí**-dék   án-lób   wol
CL-bee-DEF CL-other-DEF S.3PL-PERF.go-**CTP**-RED S.3PL-sting child
'The other bees came to sting a child.'
(Gunyaamolo: Bodian 2014: 103)

(43) a-kúuñ-a-kuuñ   e-kina   e-wun-e   a-**kaay**-ut   pa-haa.o.
S.3SG-be_sick~PERF   CL-DEM   CL-cause-FOC   S.3SG-**go**-NEG   CL-have_fun
'He's sick, which is why he didn't go to have fun.'
(Jóola Karon: Sambou 2014: 288)

(44) n-a-ragen   ka-ful-a-k   k-a-liir-i
PPF-CL-pick_up CL-cloth-D-CL CL-PTCP-WEAVE-PAS
k-a-jak-e   á-**já-ú**   a-sen   iñaay-ool   man
CL-PTCP-be_good-ACT   CL-**go-CTP**   CL-give   mother-CL   (CSC)_then
iñaay-ool   a-ŋar   a-**jaw**   a-nen
mother-CL   CL-take   CL-**go**   CL-put_away
'... then she picked up the beautiful woven cloth, came home and gave it to her mother in order for her mother to go and put it away.'
(Jóola Fóoñi: Creissels & Bassène this volume)

However, as in other languages with a D-AM system, AM meanings can also be expressed morphologically by way of the same deictic directional morphemes in Table 2. In Gujaahar, for instance, both centrifugal and centripetal suffixes show this extension; only the extension of the centrifugal marker through a DO&GO AM value is illustrated. In (45), this suffix adds a centrifugal motion co-event to the verb 'eat': the people ate and left. The added motion co-event is thus subsequent to the action.

(45) mi   yaah-**an**-i   bú-lúút   éém[14]
those   eat-**CTF**-PAST.PUNC   CL-meal   INTER
'Where are the people who ate the meal (and left)?'
(Gujaahar: Goudiaby 2017: 177)

In (46), the centripetal marker -*tè* of Balant Ganja expresses a DO.COMING AM function.

---

14 Note that the analysis and interpretation presented here is not the analysis proposed by the original author. Goudiaby identifies -*àn* as a causative marker, but nothing in the example supports this analysis. By contrast, the questioning of the location suggests a focus on spatial information.

(46) à-bɔ́ŋ-tɛ̀   à   b-sîn
    CL-get_hurt-**CTP** LOC CL-road
    'He got hurt on the road (while coming).'
    (Balant Ganja: Creissels & Biaye 2016: 175)

What is interesting to note with this semantic development of D-AM markers is the difference in the AM meanings. In the preceding section, the dedicated AM system displays mainly prior associated motion. By contrast, the D-AM markers add a subsequent (45, 47 and 48b) or sometimes a concurrent (46) associated motion co-event.

(47) *ñaaton-i!*
    put_on_pants-**CTP**
    'Put on your pants and come back!'
    (Jóola Karon: Sambou 2007: 178)

(48) a. *a-pên*
        s.3s-leave
        'He left'

   b. *a-pên-i*
        s.3s-leave-**CTP**
        'He left and is coming
        (Manjaku: Karlik 1972: 245)

The figure of motion is generally the S/A argument, but the P argument is also affected with transitive motion verbs, as illustrated in (49 and 50).

(49) 'á-yit-**in**   k-á-reŋ   kikina
    s.2SG-carry-**CTP** CLki-POST-kettle CLki.DEM6
    'Bring this kettle.'
    (Jóola Kwaatay: Coly 2010: 70)

(50) ki-ke   k-á-ji   ku-ruw-**ín**-o   diye
    CLki-some   CLki-POST-voice CLki-call-**CTP**-O.3SG here
    'A certain voice called him here.'
    (Jóola Kwaatay: Coly 2010: 84)

To conclude, in Atlantic languages, AM functions can be encoded through a D-AM system. However, the AM meanings displayed in D-AM differ from those encoded by a dedicated AM system with respect to several features. Firstly, the number of markers in the D-AM system is more often reduced to a single centripetal suffix. Secondly, the figure of the movement can be the P argument, generally when the D-AM marker is suffixed to transitive non-motion events. And finally, the relative order of the added motion event and the main event is in the D-AM system subsequent or concurrent motion, instead of the prior motion in the case of EAM systems (and also AM-D systems, see below).

4.2 DD functions expressed through an AM system (AM-D)

Two Atlantic languages, Bijogo and Sereer, possess an AM-D system. These languages have several morphemes whose distinct meanings are summarized in the following table.

Table 3: The AM-D systems in Atlantic languages.

				on non-motion verbs	on motion verbs
NORTH	FULA-SEREER	Sereer	-iid	COME&DO	CTP
			-ik	GO&DO	CTF
			-laan	OUT&DO	—
BAK	BIJOGO	Bijogo	-a	COME&DO	CTP
			-am	GO&DO	CTF

The morphemes of an AM-D mixed system, similarly to those of a D-AM system, are polyfunctional. They can have either DD or AM interpretations depending on whether they are used with motion or non-motion verbs. In Sereer, for instance, the centrifugal suffix -*ik* has a DD interpretation when suffixed to motion verbs, as in (51a), where it encodes the fact that the chasing of the antelope is done by moving away from the deictic centre, i.e. the island on which the hunters were located at the beginning of the hunt. And -*ik* has an AM interpretation when attached to dynamic non-motion verbs, as in (51b), where it encodes that a centrifugal motion is realized before the event encoded by the derived verb.

(51) a. bo i-mbeel-**ik** gi-mbaafal n-e
for S.1PL-PL.chase-**CTF** CL-antelope CL-PROX
'… so that we can pursue the antelope'
(Sereer: Renaudier 2012: 96)

b. *o-duuf-**ik***   *tiya*
S.2SG-sow-**GO&DO** peanut
'You are going to sow peanuts.'
(Sereer: Renaudier 2012: 97)

Similarly, in example (52a), the Sereer suffix *-iid* has a DD centripetal meaning with *yen* 'fall', implying that the person who fell was located away from the speaker, and that the fall of the person was directed towards the speaker's location. In (52b), the same suffix *-iid* is interpreted as a COME&DO AM suffix, indicating that the birds are moving and coming in the field to eat.

(52) a. *ten*   *yen-**iid**-u*   *ga-kall*   *al-e [...]*
3SG fall-**CTP**-FOC CL-arm_of_sea CL-PROX
'She fell into the inlet (towards the island where the speaker is located).'
(Sereer: Renaudier 2012: 41)

b. *tiit*   *k-e*   *a-ñaam-**iid**-aa*   *kaaf*   *k-e*
bird CL-PROX S.3-eat-**COME&DO**-IMPERF millet CL-PROX
'Birds come to eat millet.'
(Sereer: Renaudier 2012: 97)

However, unlike D-AM systems, which assume that a DD system can evolve to express some AM function (Bourdin 1992, 2005, 2006; Belkadi 2015a, 2015b), several features of AM-D systems lead us to consider a reverse path of extension, namely from a primary AM system towards DD function. A first reason is that AM-D systems, similarly to EAM systems (see §3.1), encode prior motion, as in (51b and 52b), whereas D-AM systems encode subsequent (or concurrent) motion.

This can be seen in the two Sereer examples above as well as those from Bijogo below. The suffix *-am*, in its AM function in (53a), expresses a prior GO&DO AM function, i.e. the toad moving from the place where it is located to see the pot. In (53b), the same suffix has a centrifugal DD meaning and indicates that the speaker will return to a place distant from his/her location at utterance time.

(53) a. *ɛ-pɔnɔ*   *ɛ-na*   *wa-ba-**jam***   *aŋ*   *ka-ṯuŋŋi*
CL-toad CL-tell.PERF S.LOG.SG-VIRT-see.**GO&DO** toward CL-pot
'The toad said he was going to look into the pot.'
(Bijogo: Segerer 2002: 54)

b. *ɲi-b(a)-eṭeb-**am*** ani Paris uraane
S.1SG-IMPERF-VIRT-step_back-**CTF** at Paris tomorrow
'I'll be back (there) in Paris tomorrow.'
(deictic centre is the place where the speaker was situated at the time of utterance)
(Bijogo: Segerer 2002: 55)

A second reason that points to the direction of an enlargement from a dedicated AM system relates to the size of the morpheme inventories across the various types of systems. AM-D systems, like EAM systems, have either two or three markers, while DD systems with two morphemes are exceptional in Atlantic languages (most of them have only one morpheme).

Finally, a third reason supporting the current analysis is the existence of OUT&DO morphemes in both AM-D systems (Sereer) and EAM systems but not in D-AM systems. Even though the integration of OUT&DO morphemes into the typology of AM system in Atlantic languages is not yet clear, this meaning is found only in languages with an AM system (EAM or AM-D).

The AM-D system of Bijogo seems to be older than that of Sereer. In Bijogo, the two dynamic deictic morphemes are sometimes obligatory. The stem of the verb is not attested. In the following examples; only the derived verbs with frozen CTP and CTF suffixes are found, as *dim-a* and *dim-am* in (54). The stem **dim* does not exist in Bijogo, or is no longer attested. In (55), the motion verb 'enter' is also only attested in centripetal or centrifugal derived forms.

(54) **dim*   *dim-**a***   *dim-**am***
     fall-**CTP**   fall-**CTF**
     fall (from a tree)   fall (into a well)   (the deictic centre is the ground)
(Bijogo: Segerer 2002: 208)

(55) **ɲuk*   *ɲuk-**a***   *ɲuk-**am***
     enter-**CTP**   enter-**CTF**
     enter (house)   enter (forest)   (the deictic centre is home)
(Bijogo: Segerer 2002: 208)

Other semantic extensions are also found in Bijogo. The dynamic deictic morphemes are regularly used with verbs involving a recipient (or beneficiary) argument. In the following examples, the distribution between centripetal or centrifugal meanings is always associated with the person of the recipient argument. Centripetal is correlated to the first person and centrifugal to the second and third persons. Segerer (2002) does not describe further the function of these derivations and the correlation between markers and person.

(56) ambe   mi-n-na   m-ba-ba-**da**   ɲu-mpɛs
     but   s.2SG.IMPERF-PAST-tell   s.2SG-VIRT-O.1SG-give.**CTP** CL-money
     'you said that you were going to give me money.'
     (Bijogo: Segerer 2002)

(57) mɔ-dɔ   na   n-na-rɛsɛk-an-**a**   ŋa-nde   ɛŋŋa   nko,
     s.2SG.PERF-go and   SEQ-O.1SG-sell-ASB-**CTP**   CL-skirt CL-DEM   there
     'go sell those skirts over there for me,'
     (Bijogo: Segerer 2002: 78)

(58) ma-na   ani   ɔ-g   ɔ-**dam**   ɔ-nkɔt-ɛɲ   ɛ-tɔnt
     s.2SG.PERF-tell to   CL-PRO   CL.PERF-give.**CTP**   CL-brother-1SG   CL-hen
     'tell him he's giving my brother a chicken'
     (Bijogo: Segerer 2002: 55)

(59) ɲi-b(a)-an-dit-**am**   ŋo-o   ŋ(ɔ)-an-de(ɲ)-ak-ɔ
     s.1SG.PERF-VIRT-O.2SG-tell-**CTF**   CL-thing   CL-O.2SG.PERF-eat-PERF-REL
     'I'll tell you what you ate.'
     (Bijogo: Segerer 2002)

Note that these extensions in Bijogo are different from the altrilocative extensions described for EAM systems in section 3.

To summarize, the AM-D systems of Bijogo and Sereer include at least two morphemes that encode centripetal and centrifugal DD meanings with motion verbs and prior motion co-events (AM) with non-motion verbs, in a similar manner to what is described for the dedicated AM (EAM) systems of other Atlantic languages. In the following section, I present cases of other spatial morphemes with both DD and AM meanings that cannot (yet) be straightforwardly classified as either AM-D or D-AM systems, due to lack of appropriate documentation.

4.3 Unclassified dynamic deictic morphemes

The spatial morphemes of the TENDA and JAAD language groups listed in Table 4 (and underlined with dashes lines in Figure 1) haven't yet attracted the attention of researchers.

Table 4: The supposed meanings of the dynamic deictic morphemes of four TENDA-JAAD languages.

					on non-motion verbs	on motion verbs
NORTH	TENDA-JAAD	TENDA	Bassari	-gu/-wu	DISTAL or DO&COME?	CTP
				-ə̀x	DO&GO	
			Bedik	-gú/-ú	ALTRILOCATIVE	CTP
				-e	COME&DO	CTF
				-ʌ̀ɗ	DO.COMING	CTP
			Konyagi	-ij (~-ĩ, -ə̀j)	DO&COME	CTP
				-ə̀rγì (ə́rγ)	DO&GO	CTF
				-ə̀x	DISTAL	
		JAAD	Jaad	-u	GO&DO&RETURN	CTF

With regard to the JAAD cluster, only data about Jaad (also called Badiaranke or Pajaade) can be found; no information is available for Biafada at this time. In Jaad, a sole suffix -*u* is described with a meaning related to a possible AM function. This suffix can be analyzed as a two-step reciprocating movement, GO&DO&RETURN. This suffix can be used with action and motion verbs and has AM readings with action verbs.

(60) a. *jaanaa-**u**-kõ-de*
 eat-**GO&DO&RETURN**-TAM-PERF
 'I had gone to lunch (and I came back)'
 (Jaad: Ducos 1971: 134)

 b. *be-ninaao-sę ka-bat-**u**-e k-bə̨*
 CL-cloud-DEF INF-approach-**CTF**-IMPERF COP-S.3PL
 'The clouds come and go.'
 (Jaad: Ducos 1971: 134)

In (60a), there are both 'go' and 'come' motion co-events associated with the main action of 'eating'. The first one is a centrifugal motion realized before the eating action and the second a centripetal motion back to the departure point, realized after the eating action. Similar meanings are described by Creissels & Bassène (this volume) for the -*úl(o)* suffix in Jóola Fóoñi, a language with a DD system (cf. § 4.1). The authors indicate that "this formulation emphasizes the return path, leaving implicit the first part of the path". There are not enough examples to be sure for Jaad, but it seems that in this language, the suffix -*u* only contributes a subsequent return motion which would be CTF, the first part of the motion being encoded by the verb root 'approach' (in 60b) or perhaps a return motion without a necessary deictic sense.

From these data, a D-AM system can be assumed for Jaad. However, some more investigation should be done before this can be confirmed, since no D-AM system with a single centrifugal marker has been described as yet for Atlantic languages.

The TENDA group consists of four languages spoken in eastern Senegal. Morphemes encoding spatial information have not received much attention in these languages. The data are not sufficient for a detailed survey. The inventories of morphemes in the individual languages are slightly different and their meanings are unclear in some respects. The following presentation is a preliminary analysis based on the limited data available. However, this limited information is still considered relevant for an overview of the dynamic deictic systems of the Atlantic languages.

As in all the other Atlantic languages, an AM co-event can first be expressed periphrastically by an independent motion verb. In Bedik (61), the verbal derivation with a deictic suffix is not necessary, whereas in Bassari and Konyagi all the examples of this kind show affixation on the main action verb, as we have seen in the cangin cluster, in which the AM suffixes are always associated with a motion verb (§ 3.1). In other words, in Bassari (62) and Konyagi (63), it seems that the derivation needs an "echo construction", i.e. the simultaneous use of a deictic suffix and a motion verb in a periphrastic proposition.

(61) ń-**ɗʸέ**   ń-yīty   sʸán   ā-yìɗ ...
      s.3PL-**go**   s.3PL-buy   at   genie
      'They were going to buy from the genie ...'
      (Bedik: Ferry 1967: 162)

(62) atáŋ   **yɛ-k'-mέ**   mέ-ɗeki-**ə́x**
      after   **go**-PERF-S.1SG   AOR:S.1SG-lie_down-**GO&DO**
      'Then I went to bed (over there).'
      (Bassari: Perrin 2019: 96)

(63) ... **njì-j**   cǽw̃ǽl-ì,
      ... III.3SG:**go-CTP**   urinate-**CTP**
      '... she's coming to urinate on (it)'
      (Konyagi: Santos 1996: 309)

Bassari has two suffixes, -ə̀x (illustrated in (62) above) and -gu (~ -wu) (64). They are affixed to motion verbs and indicate that the movement is towards the deictic centre (64a). Perrin (2019) also points out a distal value for the -gu (-wu) suffix, as in (64b). In this example, the action is realized in a place distant from the speaker's location. Further investigation would be necessary to rule out a possible AM interpretation, such as GO&DO ('what is he going to do there?') or DO&COME ('what is he doing over there before coming?'). The second interpretation seems to be the more probable. Otherwise, the use of a morpheme with a centripetal value in this context is difficult to explain. Note that if this reading is confirmed, this means that the AM function is a subsequent motion co-event.

(64) a. a-yɛ́ k'-mí-yamb-ra-d́ namána tamá
INF-be.good IMPF-S.1PL-eat-DUR-FUT before Tama
ɛ-xɔ́-ŋátu-**gu**.
AOR-S.3SG-arrive-**CTP**
'We will eat before Tama arrives (**here**).'
(Bassari: Perrin 2019: 96)

b. Cuní rɔ-dɔ́-ɛxɔ́. ínɛ k-ó-rí-**wu**-nd' ?
Tchouny here-irreal-AOR:S.3SG what IMPF-S.3SG-do-**DO&COME**-PROG
'Tchouny should be here. What's he doing (there)?'
(Bassari: Perrin 2019: 97)

In Bedik, Ferry (1991) identifies two kinds of spatial morphemes described respectively as distal (action realized far away)[15] and distanciative (action carried out by moving away). Examples are not sufficient to provide a fine description of the functions of each of these morphemes, nor a clear-cut distribution between function and morpheme. The few examples found of the *gú/-ú* suffix suggest that it has a DD centripetal value (named distanciative by Ferry) as in (65a &b), as well as probably a distal value (cf. 66 and 67). The reading of example (66) can be seen as a fictive motion. Thus the centripetal reading can be that the words come from over there toward the deictic centre. With the altrilocative reading, the suffix indicates that the action of talking is entirely realized far away from the deictic centre. In (67), a centripetal reading would mean that the departure of the action of falling is distant from the deictic centre, but that this action is carried out toward the deictic centre. In contrast, the altrilocative reading would mean that the entire action of falling is performed far away from the deictic centre.

---

15 This function is generally named altrilocative, as shown in section 3.2 for Fulfulde, for instance. In this chapter, the term *distal* is used for movement where the beginning of the motion is located away from the deictic centre, as in Wolof (see also 2.2).

(65) a. ɔ-dʸɛ́   u-dʸo-**gû**   b. u-sʸál   u-sʸól-**ú**
        INF-go   INF-go-**CTP**   INF-go_out   INF-go_out-**CTP**
        'go'   'come'   'go out'   'go out from there'
                 lit. 'go from there
                 and come here'
        (Bedik: Ferry 1991: 37)

(66) à-tʸōs-**ú**
     s.3SG-talk-**CTP/ALTRILOCATIVE**
     'He's talking from there.'
     (Bedik: Ferry 1967: 58)

(67) **a-màràsʸé**-gu
     s.3SG-make_fall_trees-CTP/ALTRILOCATIVE
     'It fell over there.'
     (Bedik: Ferry 1967: 58)

Still in Bedik, it appears necessary to carry on the examination of the other two suffixes, -*e* and -*ʌd*. These suffixes display distinct directions. In (68), the suffix -*e* added to the verb 'jump' gives the meaning of 'avoid', such as 'to jump', 'to go far away from something or someone'. This suffix can have a centrifugal DD interpretation or a subsequent or concurrent centrifugal AM interpretation, whereas the suffix -*ʌd* has a centripetal DD meaning (as with 'tell' in (69a)) or centripetal AM interpretations (as with 'run' in (69b)). If the AM meaning is confirmed in (69b), then the motion co-event is a concurrent AM.

(68) u-sʸíg   u-sʸíg-**e**
     INF-jump INF-jump-**CTF/COME&DO**
     'jump'   'avoid'
     (Bedik: Ferry 1991: 37)

(69) a. ma-sʸas-**ʌd**   b. u-ɓɤ̀r   mɤ-yɤr-**ʌd**
        INF-tell-**CTP**   INF-run   INF-run-**DO.COMING**
        'tell from there'   'run'   'come running'
        (Bedik: Ferry 1991: 37)

Finally, in Konyagi, the last TENDA language for which some information is available, Santos (1996) describes three morphemes carrying spatial information. She notes that the -*ǝx* suffix is a locative that does not involve motion, whereas the suffixes -*ij* (~ -*i*, -*ǝj*) and -*áryi* (~ -*áry*) involve a movement with respect to the deictic centre. The -*əx* suffix would have an altrilocative function, encoding the fact that an action is realized far away (70), as shown for the suffix -*oy* of Fulfulde in 2.2.

(70) gená   nkó-rún   bí   æ̀-fòf-ə́l-**əx**-ə̀nd-ú
     3SG:be:NEG   stay-2PL   INTER   S.2-braid-REC-**DISTAL**-IMPERF-S.PL
     'Is this not that you are braiding each other's hair over there?'
     (Konyagi: Santos 1996: 298)

Conversely, the -*ìj* (~ -*ì*, -*əj*) and -*ə́ryì* (~ -*ə́ry*) suffixes are explicitly described as adding a movement. Like AM suffixes, they are adjoined to an action verb and they add a motion co-event without any motion verb in the sentence (71, 72a, 72b). These suffixes encode subsequent or concurrent motion co-events, and maybe also prior motion co-events.[16]

(71) ỹắlĕ-fù-lǽ   mǽt-ǽl-**ì**-rún   kì
     LOC:AT-POSS.2PL-LOC   stand_up-LOC-**DO&COME**-S.2PL   MAN
     'From home, you left like this (to come here).'
     (Konyagi: Santos 1996: 299)

(72) a. ì-tòk   ì-tòk-**ì**   b. ì-tòk-**ə́ry**
         INF-eat   INF-eat-**DO&COME**   INF-eat-**DO&GO**
         'eat'   'eat before coming'   'eat before going/leaving'
         (Konyagi: Santos 1996: 299)

DD functions are not explicitly mentioned in the descriptions of these two morphemes and none of the few examples available lead us to associate this function with any of those.

Note that in Konyagi the suffix -*əx* develops an altrilocative function on non-motion verbs. This feature differs from those shown for Fulfulde (altrilocative) or Wolof (distal), where these meanings function only with some motion

---

[16] Further investigation is needed before confirming the temporal meaning of the AM markers of Konyagi, because of the contradictions between the available descriptions. In Santos (1996:298), two distinct constructions are described with AM values. The auxiliaries *fi* 'go' or *firy* 'come' can be used to convey prior AM. The AM suffixes -*i* and -*əry* are described as encoding the main action as concomitant with or preceding the movement: "-i approaching (come toward the speaker doing or after doing something) and -əry distant (go away from the speaker doing or after doing)". By contrast, in Jenkins et al. (2000), the same suffixes are described as encoding prior movement. However, in Jenkins et al. (2000) the illustrations are rare and always involve derivation of motion verbs, and in this combination the suffixes can have a deictic directional interpretation, as in *tenké-ry* 'enter-CTF' and *tenk-i* 'enter-CTP'.

verbs. As with other differences between TENDA and other Atlantic languages, Konyagi and Bedik display three spatial markers, but none of these markers has an OUT&DO function, as seen in Wolof, Laala and Sereer.

As summarized in Table 4 above, the information available on TENDA languages suggests that in Bassari the two suffixes -gú/-ú and -ə̀x can have a distal/altrilocative reading and an AM reading respectively: a DO&COME AM function (64b) and GO&DO AM function (60). Bedik and Konyagi have three spatial morphemes but seem to display opposite systems in the present state of their description. In both languages, AM, DD, altrilocative and distal functions are distributed among three morphemes. But once again, the data from this language cluster are partial and inadequate to consider this description as the final analysis.

A summary of the temporal relations expressed by the different types of AM systems in the Atlantic languages surveyed in this paper is provided in Table 5.

Table 5: The temporal relation in the major dynamic deictic system and in the system of TENDA languages.

				temporal relation
unidentified system	Bassari	-gu/-wu	DO&COME?	subsequent
		-ə̀x	DO&GO	subsequent
	Bedik	-e	COME&DO	prior
		-λd	DO.COMING	concurrent
	Konyagi	-ij (~-ì, -ə̀j)	DO&COME	subsequent (prior, Jenkins et al.)
		-ə̀ryì (ə́ry)	DO&GO	subsequent (prior, Jenkins et al.)
EAM	Wolof or CANGIN			prior
AM-D	Sereer or Bijogo			prior
D-AM	as in JOOLA cluster, for instance			subsequent or concurrent

We can see that, with the exception of TENDA languages, the temporal relations have a clear-cut distribution across system types. The prior temporal relation is attested in dedicated or mixed AM-D system, whereas subsequent and concurrent temporal relations are characteristic of D-AM systems.

5 Geographical distribution and possible source(s) of the dynamic deictic systems

In this section, I first discuss the geographical distribution of the three kinds of systems, EAM, AM-D and D-AM (section 5.1) and the historical origin of the verbal suffixes involved in these languages (section 5.2), while bearing in mind that the particularities of the verbal derivation in Atlantic languages prevent me from identifying lexical sources for these deictic suffixes.

5.1 Can a genetic distribution between original AM and original DD systems be drawn?

For the purpose of this section, the three specific types of systems described in the preceding sections (EAM, D-AM and AM-D) will be reduced to two major types: "original AM" systems and "original DD" systems. Original AM systems correspond to (i) dedicated AM (EAM) systems in which verbal morphemes add a prior translational motion co-event to the main verb event and (ii) AM-D systems in which I assume that, over time, a EAM system that only expressed prior AM developed some semantic extensions including a DD reading. Original DD systems, by contrast, correspond to D-AM systems in which I assume that over time a dedicated DD system (which originally did not express AM), has shown developments towards the expression of AM meanings when the centripetal morpheme is adjoined to non-motion verbs. These DD markers thus convey AM meanings of subsequent or concurrent motion. In this respect, they are opposed to the prior motion co-event value typical of the EAM and AM-D systems. This contrast plays a key role for the distinction between the two co-existing systems in the Atlantic family.

At first sight, it is difficult to find any genetic consistency in the distribution of original AM and original DD systems. The family has a first clear-cut division between the NORTH and BAK groups of languages. Nonetheless, the original AM and original DD systems are both attested in these two branches (cf. Table 6). The NYUN-BUY cluster belongs to the NORTH branch, and possesses a D-AM system (original DD), while other languages of the NORTH branch, such as the cangin group for instance, show an EAM (original AM) system. On the side of the BAK branch, Bijogo has been described as having an AM-D (original AM) system, whereas the other BAK groups possess a D-AM (original DD) system.

A closer inspection reveals that NYUN-BUY and Bijogo are in fact exceptions in their respective groups. The NYUN-BUY group is the sole sub-branch of the NORTH branch displaying a D-AM (original DD) system, and Bijogo is the sole language[17] exhibiting an AM-D (original AM) system in the BAK branch. The NORTH and

---

[17] This exception can probably be extended to the other languages of the BIJOGO cluster, but a survey of other Bijogo varieties should be done before.

Table 6: The different dynamic deictic systems of Atlantic.

				IDENTIFIED SYSTEM	OTHER SPATIAL EXTENSIONS	THIRD SUFFIX
NORTH	WOLOF		Wolof	EAM	distal	OUT&DO
	NYUN-BUY	NYUN	Gunyaamolo	D-AM		
			Gubëeher	D-AM		
			Gujaahar	D-AM		
		BUY	Kobiana	D-AM		
	TENDA-JAAD	TENDA	Bedik	*unidentified*		
			Bassari	*unidentified*		
			Konyagi	*unidentified*		
		JAAD	Jaad	*unidentified*		
	FULA-SEREER	FULA		EAM	altrilocative	
		SEREER		AM-D		OUT&DO
	CANGIN		Cangin-Noon	EAM		
			Pade-Noon	EAM		
			Laala	EAM		OUT&DO
			Saafi-saafi	EAM		
BAK	BALANTE-JÓOLA-MANJAKU	BALANTE	Balant-Ganja	D-AM		
	JÓOLA-MANJAKU	JÓOLA	Fóoñi	D-AM		
			Banjal	D-AM		
			Karon	D-AM		
			Kwaatay	D-AM		
			Bayot	D-AM?		
		MANJAKU	Mankanya	D-AM		
			Manjaku	D-AM		
	BIJOGO		Kagbaaga	AM-D		

BAK branches of the Atlantic family are themselves divided into several groups (cf. Figure 1 above). With the exception of Vehicular Wolof and Fula, which are spoken in large areas, the NORTH and BAK languages are spoken in well-localized smaller regions.[18]

---

18 JÓOLA has long been considered as a dialect cluster extending in a large part of the south western region of Senegal. Now, it is clear that within the JÓOLA group several languages must be distinguished (at least seven according to Segerer (2009), including Bayot). Only Jóola Fóoñi has a vehicular function in this region in competition with Creole, Mandinka, and more recently Wolof.

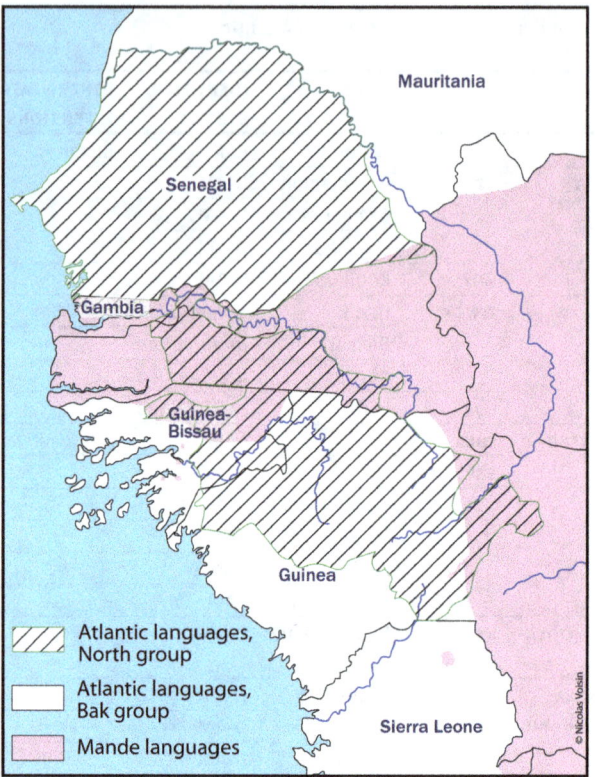

Map 1: The demarcation line made by Gambia and the area of Mande languages (Mandinka and Maninka two Senegalese dialects of the Manding language).[19]

The distribution of the original AM and original DD systems draws a boundary line between a northern and a southern geographical area separated from each other by Gambia and the Mandinka and Maninka dialects of Manding (Mande). As shown on Map 1, Gambia and the South of Senegal are recognizable by the presence of the Manding language (the zones in pink).[20] This differentiates this zone from the rest of Atlantic languages areas situated either to the North or to the South. All the languages of the northern area possess an original AM system. They all belong to the NORTH branch. The languages spoken in this boundary

---

19 This map is the enlargement of a map showing the extension of the Manding language and the localization of its different dialects, adapted from Vydrin et al. (2000).
20 Manding is a cover term for mostly mutually intelligible language varieties. Mandinka and Maninka are both varieties spoken in Senegal. The most known variety of Manding is Bambara (also called Bamana, Bamanankan). The Manding language belongs to the Mande family.

zone (together with Manding dialects) or to the South of this zone are languages with an original DD or an unidentified system. All the languages of the BAK branch are spoken in this area and possess an original DD system, except Bijogo. The languages affiliated with the NORTH branch located in this southern zone either have an original DD system, as the NYUN-BUY cluster, or belong at this time to the set of the languages with unclassified systems: the NALU cluster for lack of data, and the JAAD cluster because of the specific meaning of its AM morpheme (two-step reciprocating movement). The TENDA cluster has an intractable configuration, related to both i) the specific characteristics of the unexpected multiple morphemes attested in the different languages of this group and ii) the lack of data that would be necessary to establish a detailed and clear description of these suffixes and their respective meaning depending on verbal classes.

From a global perspective, the distribution of the original AM and original DD systems in the Atlantic family does not follow the genetic split between NORTH and BAK, but a geographical North vs. South distribution. Dedicated AM or AM-D (original AM) systems are only attested in languages affiliated with the NORTH branch and located within the northern area, whereas in the South, BAK and NORTH languages show a fuzzier distribution. No NORTH language has an AM or AM-D (original AM) system in this zone. As a result, a contact-induced change hypothesis can be formulated to explain the specific characteristics of the languages in this area.

Note that this hypothesis is not a plausible solution for a better understanding of the intricate data of TENDA and Jaad. These languages are in especially close contact with Fula, a widespread vehicular NORTH language. The 'go and do and return' meaning of the suffix -*u* in Jaad (cf. 60) may be explained by the deterioration of the previous system, and a linguistic transfer from the surrounding BAK languages. Future investigations of the TENDA group are necessary to clarify the configuration of the attested system(s). The unclassified systems expounded in section 4.3 can no longer be viewed as dedicated AM systems (EAM). The configuration of the TENDA languages can be considered as partially modified, keeping some features of the original AM system and adopting some others, which renders difficult the interpretation of both the morphemes and the current system. The specificities of their system can in no way be explained by a contact-induced change. The Fula and the Manding varieties spoken in this area could not transmit such complexity. Fula has a single suffix -*oy* and the Manding varieties of the zone have borrowed their spatial marker from the Atlantic languages, as it will be discussed later.

By contrast, the NYUN-BUY cluster is directly surrounded by BAK languages and this situation is ancient. The D-AM (original DD) system currently attested in NYUN-BUY languages of the NORTH spoken in the southern area may be plainly explained by a contact-induced change hypothesis. A linguistic change from an original AM system towards the original DD system induced by contact is a conceivable hypothesis explaining the unexpected configuration of this group of languages belonging to the NORTH branch. This hypothesis does not exclude that these languages originally had two AM markers (COME and GO), as suggested by the data of Gujaahar (cf. 42). But the transfer of the DD meaning from BAK languages has resulted in the persistence of a single AM marker in most of these languages, first reinterpreted as a centripetal marker (DD), and subsequently evolving towards the new meaning of a subsequent hither AM. This influence of the D-AM system of the BAK languages has already been suggested for Mandinka (Creissels 2014), a Mande language spoken in the demarcation zone (cf. Map 1). In the same way as the hypothesis put forward for the NYUN-BUY group, Mandinka has developed a D-AM system by contact-induced change based on its own morphology. Among Manding dialects, this function is only attested in varieties spoken in Western Senegal. Creissels (2014) suggests a contact-induced change due to the assimilation of speakers of Atlantic languages into Mandinka after the installation of Mandinka in the area. The centripetal marker *naŋ* of Mandinka is a verbal particle and therefore follows the typological profile of isolating languages of the Mande family. The *naŋ* morpheme in Mandinka has a centripetal DD meaning with motion verbs (73) and AM readings with non-motion verbs, as in (74), where the added motion co-event is centripetal and subsequent. In (75), the motion which is also subsequent refers to the motion of the P argument, also attested in the D-AM system of Atlantic languages (cf. for instance example 50).

(73) *Ali   kíní-tóo-lu   ji-ndí   naŋ*
2PL   food-residue.DEF-PL   go_down-CAUS   CTP
'Bring the leftover food here.'
(Mandinka: Creissels 2014: 3)

(74) *wŏ   le   yé   ñíŋ   sub-óo   fǎa   naŋ*
DEM   FOC   PERF   DEM   bushmeat.DEF   kill   **DO&COME**
'He killed that bushmeat and brought it back.'
(Mandinka: Creissels 2014: 5)

(75) *musu-kéebáa   ye   wul-ôo   kílí   naŋ*
woman-old.DEF   PERF   dog-DEF   call   **DO&COME**
'The old lady called the dog to come over.'
(Mandinka: Creissels 2014: 4)

The source of the centripetal marker in Mandinka suggested by Creissels (2014) is the contraction of *năa jaŋ*, literally 'come here'.

To summarize, the general hypothesis concerning the original dynamic deictic system of the Atlantic family can be sketched as follows. Considering that the surrounding families do not display a dedicated AM system (EAM), namely the Afroasiatic to the north (D-AM system according to Bourdin 2005, Belkadi 2015a) and the Mande family to the east (no dynamic deictic system at all) (cf. Creissels 2014), the dedicated AM system (EAM) of the NORTH Branch is most likely to have been inherited from Proto-Atlantic. Evidence supporting this hypothesis can be found in the existence of an AM-D system (original AM) in the single BAK branch language. Bijogo, belonging to the BAK branch and located below the demarcation line, should exhibit a D-AM system (original DD), as do other languages of this zone. The existence of an AM-D system (original AM) in this isolated language (spoken in several islands near the Coast of Guinea-Bissau) supports our hypothesis that dedicated AM system (EAM) is probably the first system developed in Atlantic languages. The development of the D-AM system (original DD) in the other BAK languages can be seen as an innovation.[21]

This hypothesis can also be reinforced by other convergence phenomena concerning deixis, and more precisely on the formation of the pair of 'go' and 'come' verbs. Cross-linguistically, 'come' and 'go' are commonly viewed as semantically distinct verbs. Nevertheless, 'go' is not always a deictic motion event,[22] whereas 'come' is always a deictic one. In contrast, all languages can encode a movement towards the speaker, although not always by means of a lexical verb, but using a compounded form. In some Atlantic languages, 'come' derives from 'go' by the adjunction of a centripetal deictic directional marker, as in (76) to (79).

(76) a-**dëët**-i a-ñoŋ ómlet a-han a gu-palat
 S3SG-**go:CTP**-PERF S3SG-take omelette S3SG-put PREP CL-plate
 'He came, took the omelette and put it on the plate.'
 (Gubëëher (Nyun): Cobbinah 2013: 160)

---

21 As shown in Map 2 (Appendix), the languages spoken to the south of the Atlantic languages area are also in contact with Mel languages, another Niger-Congo family. An influence of this family on the Atlantic languages of the southern area is a conceivable assumption, but it can not[?] be confirmed in the absence of data about these languages.
22 Wilkins and Hill (1995: 215) challenge two assumptions concerning the universality of the go/come opposition, and they note that there are some languages in which 'go' is not inherently deictic. Ricca (1993) demonstrates the existence of non-deictic languages in Europe. For example, in Russian, the centripetal and centrifugal movements are encoded by the same verb *idti* 'to go (on foot)', such as *On idët k nam*. "He's **going** towards us." [CTP movement] and *On idët k tomu domu*. "He's **going** towards this house." [CTF movement].

(77) a-wak βœ-**fa**-t
 S.2SG-HAB CL-**go**-CTP
 'He's used to coming.'
 (Kobiana)

(78) Ñénà **njí-jə̀**-dé túŋ
 Nyena III.**go**-CTP-IMPERF certainly
 'Nyena, she'll certainly come.'
 (Konyagi: Santos 1996: 513)

(79) au u-teg-e ni-**jo**-úl
 2SG S.2SG-cause-TAM S.1SG-**go**-CTP
 'It's for you that I came.'
 (Jóola Banjal: Bassène 2006: 150)

One would expect that languages resorting to derived 'come' verb have a D-AM system (original DD). Indeed, there is a restriction on the inflection of the motion verbs in the languages that attest an original AM system (EAM or AM-D). By definition, the AM affixes are applied to activity verbs, but cannot be attached to the set of intransitive motion verbs. As Wilkins (1991: 210) notes: "This co-occurrence restriction is not surprising given that 'associated motion' inflections convey much the same information as these verb roots".

As shown in Figure 2, all languages attesting an original AM system (EAM or AM-D) have a lexical 'go' and 'come' pair of verbs, and some languages displaying a D-AM system (original DD) also have a lexical verb 'come', such as languages of the manjaku cluster. By contrast, some jóola languages and some language groups of the NORTH branch spoken in the southern area share the same behavior. The languages of the NORTH branch that derive 'come' from 'go' either belong to the clusters whose system is clearly copied from jóola or are inadequately described. In any case, these languages do not fully maintain an original AM system. This distribution supports our assumption that the D-AM system (original DD) is an innovation in some languages of the family. The elaboration of a D-AM system (original DD) has led some languages to use another process to form the 'come' and 'go' opposition.

The JÓOLA group is not homogeneous. Some JÓOLA languages have underived pairs, such as Kwaatay (80) and Karon (81), or use morphological processes other than the D-AM suffix, such as reduplication in Bayot (cf. Table 7 in the Appendix for a complete list).

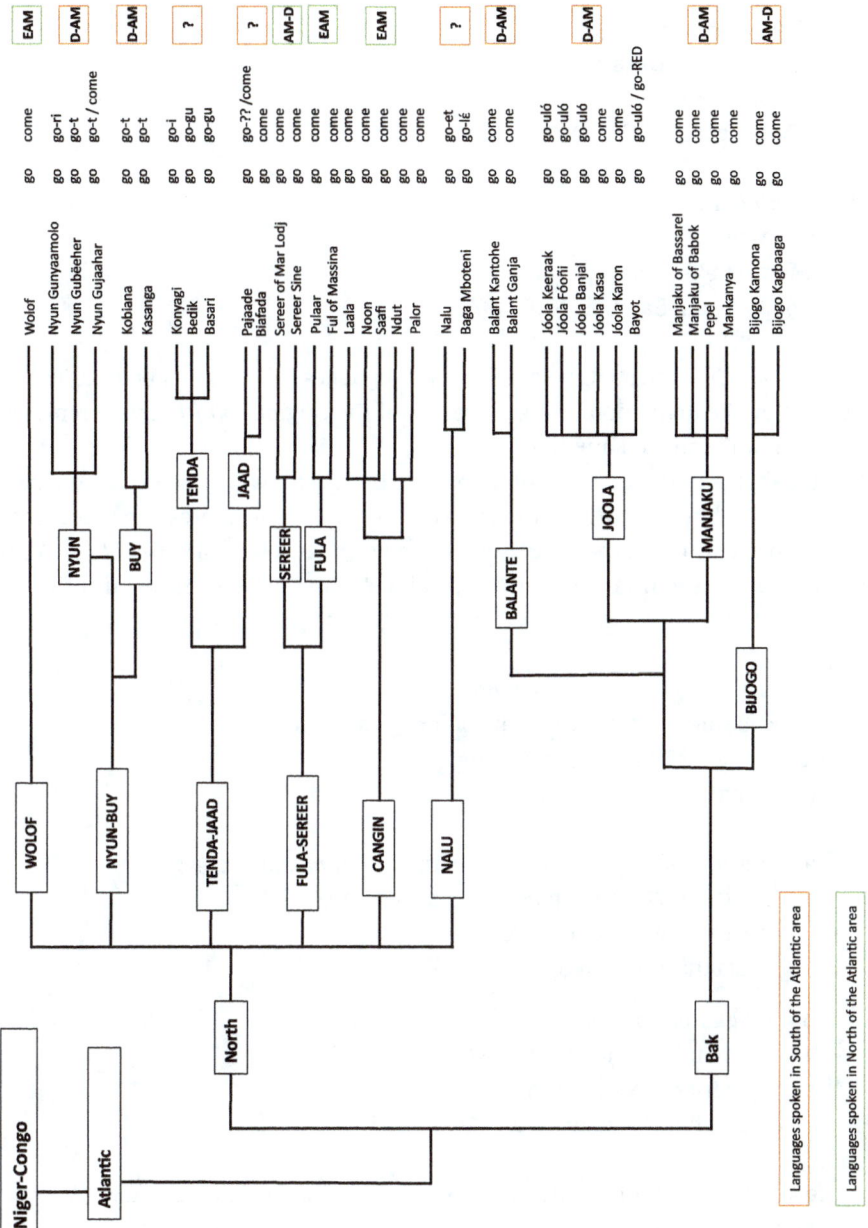

Figure 2: Distribution between AM and DD and absence/presence of derived directional verbs for *come*.

(80) *Fatu a-**bin**-a*
 Fatu s.3sg-**come**-TAM
 'Fatou came.'
 (Jóola Kwaatay: Coly 2010: 51)

(81) *mantàà-**kéy***
 PROB-**come**
 'Maybe he'll come'
 (Jóola Karon: Sambou 2007: 197)

The verb *bil / bin*, attested in some JÓOLA languages (cf. 80), has been replaced in others by the derivation of the *go* verb, but the original *bil / bin* verb remains attested as an aspectual auxiliary.

Gujaahar, a NYUN language of the NORTH branch for which a calque from BAK languages has been suggested, uses two possible means of expressing a centripetal motion event. The verb 'come' is expressed through a lexical verb *bát / bët* (82) or by a form derived from the verb *dák / dëk* 'go' with the DD centripetal suffix *-át* (cf. 83a and b).

(82) *á-**bát**-í*   *dohoon*
 s.3sg-**come**-PAST.PUNCT   day_before_yesterday
 'He came the day before yesterday.'
 (Gujaahar: Goudiaby 2017: 37)

(83) a. *á-**dák**-át-í*   *mati*   *u-muxubukoor*
     s.3sg-**go**-CTP-PAST.PUNCT   whitout   CL-chief
     'He came without the chief.'
     (Gujaahar: Goudiaby 2017: 164)

   b. *ba-gunda-aŋ **dák**-í*   *a*   *bú-nág*
     CL-friend-PL **go**-PAST.PUNCT to   CL-field
     'The friends went to the field.'
     (Gujaahar: Goudiaby 2017: 64)

As a result, we suggest that the original system of the Atlantic languages was an original AM system involving the existence of lexical verb pairs for the expression of the centripetal and centrifugal motion events 'come' and 'go'. The elaboration of a D-AM system (original DD) in some languages of the family allows the formation of *come* by DD suffixation to the 'go' verb. The continuation of the 'come' and 'go' verb pairs in some of these languages and the survival in other languages of the original 'come' verb through the path of grammaticalization support this assumption. The adoption of the complete system (D-AM system and 'come' by derivation) by languages that have changed their system by contact is not surprising.

5.2 Origin of the markers

In Atlantic languages, a verbal or prepositional origin cannot be reconstructed for most original AM and original DD markers, in contrast to many other languages in different parts of the world (Guillaume 2013). As illustrated in the various preceding sections and Tables 1–4 and 6, the dynamic deictic markers in Atlantic languages are all verbal suffixes and their forms are not related outside the different clusters. It is generally obvious that, within a given cluster, the morphemes are related to each other. However, in the present state of Atlantic comparative reconstruction, it is not possible to reconstruct the forms of proto-Atlantic. The verbs *come* or *go* in different languages are not good candidates for the lexical source of most dynamic deictic markers.[23] The provisional conclusion is that dynamic deictic markers were already verbal extensions in proto-Atlantic – or at least that different grammatical morphemes are at the origin of the dynamic deictic systems. The renewal of the verbal extensions system by further grammaticalization of already existing extensions can be observed in other semantic domains in this family (Voisin to appear).

One hypothesis relies on the frequently evoked possibility of a relationship between dynamic deictic markers and inversive/reversive morphemes[24] (Voisin to appear). The inversive is essentially used with contact verbs, i.e. verbs involving contact between two entities (such as 'close', 'cover'). The verb expresses a situation in which the entities are conjoined, and the inversive encodes their separation, as in (84a and b) with data of Wolof. In Wolof and several other Atlantic languages, the reversive and dynamic deictic morphemes are homophonous or phonologically similar affixes. Note that this inversive suffix can be described both as CTF/GO, since entities move away from one another,[25] and CTP/COME, since one

---

[23] The JÓOLA cluster could be an exception. The motion verb *bin* / *bil* 'come' still attested in some languages as a main verb or as an aspectual auxiliary could be a possible source for the dynamic deictic marker *-ul* / *-ʊl(ɔ)* and *-i(n)* / *-in(a/o)*.
[24] It is even quite common to find in the Atlantic languages at least two reversive suffixes, if not more. For instance, Wolof has four reversive morphemes *-i*, *-adi*, *-arñi* / *-arci*, *-ar*bi; and a reversive / anticausative *-ali* (Voisin to appear). Sereer is also described with two reversives *-it* and *-(a)tax* (Renaudier 2012: 93). In contrast, BALANT languages, at least Ganja and Kentohe, lack a reversive suffix (Creissels and Biaye 2016).
[25] Robert and Segerer (to appear) call it the separative, since it only occurs with contact verbs in Keerak (JÓOLA).

of the entities in its separating movement can be considered as moving towards the deictic centre or the speaker. The inversive and the dynamic deictic markers are not always similar in the Atlantic languages, but when they are, the inversive is similar to either CTF/GO or CTP/COME. In Wolof, the inversive -*i* has the same form as the AM GO&DO marker (compare (84) to (85)). In Jóola Fóoñi, the inversive and centripetal suffixes share the same -*úl* form (compare 86a vs. b and 87a *vs.* b).

(84) a. *ub*　　*ubb-i*　　　　　　b. *lem*　*lemm-i*
　　　close　close-**INV**　　　　　bend　bend-**INV**
　　　'close'　'open'　　　　　　　'bend'　'unfold'
　　　(Wolof)

(85) a. *ub*　　*ub-i*　　　　　　　b. *lem*　*lem-i*
　　　close　close-**GO&DO**　　　　bend　bend-**GO&DO**
　　　'close'　'go to close'　　　　'bend'　'go to bend'
　　　(Wolof)

(86) a. *e-kot*　　　　*ká-kót-úl*　　　b. *e-baj*　　*é-báj-úl*
　　　CL-be_sticky　CL-be_sticky-**INV**　　CL-have　CL-have-**CTP**
　　　'be sticky'　　'separate'　　　　　'have'　　'obtain'
　　　(Jóola Fóoñi : Hopkins 1995: 45)

(87) a. n-á-kamb-ul-kamb-**ul**
　　　PPF-S.3SG-close-**INV**-close-**INV**
　　　'He opened.'
　　　(Jóola Fóoñi: Creissels, p.c.)

　　b. *a-seek-a-w*　　　　*n-á-púr-**úló**-púr*　　　　*di*
　　　CL-woman-DEF-CL　　PPF-S.3SG-get_out-**CTP**-get_out　PREP
　　　e-luup-e-y
　　　CL-house-DEF-CL
　　　'The woman got out from the house. (I was outside)'
　　　(Jóola Fóoñi: Creissels, p.c.)

However, some important differences can be observed, which prevent us from considering that the inversive and the dynamic deictic suffixes are related to each other in a hierarchical path of grammaticalization. These differences concern morphology and morphophonology. In the preceding examples of Wolof, the gemination of the final consonant is the result of the affixation of the inversive (84), which is not attested with the AM morpheme (85). In Jóola Fóoñi, the suffixes also show different behaviors (for more details and a more recent analysis of these differences, see Creissels & Bassène, this volume).

As a result, the homophony of the inversive and the dynamic deictic morphemes is superficial and suggests parallel grammaticalization from a common source, rather than two steps in the same grammaticalization process. Note that in the reconstruction of verb extensions in proto-Niger-Congo, Voeltz (1977) proposes two reversive markers, a reversive-causative *TO and a reversive-stative *KO, but no dynamic deictic extensions. In the phylum of Niger-Congo, only three families or sub-groups have languages with dynamic deictic extensions. These correspond to Bantu, where the dynamic deictic markers are described as quite recent and sometimes reconstructible to verbal lexical sources (cf. Guérois et al. this volume). Some languages of the Kwa and Kordofanian families are also described with dynamic deictic markers (as in Koalib for example). In the other families of Niger-Congo (such as Ijoïd, Kru, Gur or Mande for instance), dynamic deictic extensions are lacking. The centripetal marker *naŋ* of Mandinka in Mande, discussed above, is clearly the result of a contact-induced change. Therefore, the dynamic deictic marking is not widespread across Niger-Congo, and is more likely to be an innovation in some of the families included in this phylum. Atlantic is a case in point, but unfortunately, the present state of comparative reconstruction of Atlantic does not make it possible to put forward firm hypotheses about the origin of Atlantic dynamic deictic markers.

6 Conclusion

This chapter focused on the verbal suffixes expressing AM functions in Atlantic languages, African languages which are generally underrepresented in typological and language-individual studies of space and even more in studies of motion -until this volume. In the descriptions of individual Atlantic languages, the spatial markers are frequently labeled as "directional", "centripetal" or "ventive". The Deictic Directional markers are clearly attested in Atlantic languages, and they are also used to encode AM meanings. This semantic expansion has been documented for other languages (see Belkadi or Ross, this volume) and has been confirmed in Atlantic languages (D-AM system) (§ 4.1).

The main contribution of this article is the identification and description of a dedicated AM system (EAM) in some Atlantic languages. In these systems, one to three suffixes are attested. The most common AM function is to indicate a prior centrifugal motion co-event. Frequent extensions of the EAM system have also been described, such as TAM functions or altrilocative meanings. This kind of extension of an AM system is also described for other languages, such as languages of the

Otomi family spoken in Central Mexico (Hernández-Green & Palancar this volume). A function expressing an 'elsewhere' motion has been added into EAM system as a specific marker, but this integration in not necessarily definitive. The dedicated AM system (EAM) seems to be the most ancient one in the family, whereas the D-AM system would be an innovation of some Atlantic languages spoken to the south of the Gambia River. This scenario is partially confirmed by the features of the AM-D system. Moreover, the prior motion added by these suffixes shows their relationship to a dedicated AM system (EAM). The extension of the original AM towards DD meanings also shows that it has the same semantic flexibility of the original DD system.

Abbreviations

1	first person	I	index (other than subject index, cf. si)
2	second person		
3	third person	III	third degree for consonant alternation
ANT	anterioriy		
AOR	aorist	IMP	imperative
APPL	applicative	IMPERF	imperfective
ASB	associative, benefactive	INCHO	inchoative
CAUS	causative	INDET	indeterminate
CL	noun class prefix or class agreement	INF	infinitive
		INJ	injunctive
COM	comitative	INTER	interrogative
DO.COMING	concurrent centripetal associated motion marker	INV	inversive
		ITER	iterative
COME&DO	prior centripetal associated motion marker	LOC	locative
		LOG	logophoric
CTP	centripetal directional deictic marker	MOVE&DO	prior associated motion marker
DEF	definite	NARR	narrative
LOC	locative	NEG	negation
DEM	demonstrative	O	object agreement
DET	determiner	OBL	obligative
DIST	distal	OUT&DO	prior associated motion marker
DUR	durative		
F	feminine	P.REL	relative pronoun
FIN	final vowel	PUNC	punctual
FOC	focalisation	PERF	perfective
FUT	future	PFT	perfect
GEN	genitive	PL	plural
GO&DO	prior centrifugal associated motion marker	POSS	possessive marker
		POST	post prefix
HAB	habitual	PREP	preposition

PREST	presentative	SG	singular
PROB	probability	SGF	singular feminine
PROSP	prospective	SUB	subordinate
PROX	proximate	SUBJ	subject
REC	reciprocal	TAM	tense-aspect-mood marker
RED	reduplication	TEMP	temporal
S	subject agreement	V	verb
SEQ	sequential	VIRT	virtual

Acknowledgments: I would like to thank Denis Creissels, Rozenn Guérois and Marc Tang for their comments on previous drafts. The editors of this volume, Antoine Guillaume and Harold Koch, also helped to further improve the manuscript. The collection of most of the data presented here was supported by the ANR in the "Senelangues project" (09-BLAN-0326), which made possible the description of Atlantic languages, without which the analysis could not have been carried out.

Appendix

Map 2: Atlantic languages and surrounding families.

Table 7: The verbs *go* and *come* in the Atlantic languages.

Languages	go	come	sources
Wolof	dem	ñow	Diouf 2003
Gubëëher	dëëk	dëë-t	Cobbinah 2013
Gunyaamolo	dék	dék-r	Bodian 2014
Gujaahar	dëk	dëk-t / bët	Goudiaby 2016
Kasanga	bet	bet-t	Bühnen 1988
Kobiana	fa(l) / pa(l)	fa-t / pa-t	Voisin
Konyagi	ì-fī	ì-fī-j	Santos 1996
Bedik	ɔ-fɛ́	u-foˊ-gú	Ferry 1991
Bassari	fè / ɲè	a-fò-wú	Ferry 1991
Pajaade	raa	ree	Ducos 1971
Biafada	raa	lee	Wilson 2008
Sereer	ret	gar	Crétois 1973/77
Fula	yaa	war	Sweetman 1981
Laala	kaɗ	hac	Dieye 2010
Noon	yah	hay	Soukka 2000
Saafi	fah	hay	Williams & Williams 1993
Ndut	pay	ʔac	Williams & Williams 1994
Palor	pay	ʔac / ʔaf	d'Alton 1987
Nalu	ŋɛy	ŋɛy-et	Seidel 2013
Baga Mboteni	cá	cá-lɛ́	Ferry sd
Balante	tɔ(ɔh)	bın	Creissels & Biaye 2015
Jóola Keeraak	ɲaŋ	ɲəŋ-ul	Barry 1987
Jóola Fóoñi	jaw	jaw-ul / jaw-ʊlɔ	Creissels, p.c.
Jóola Banjal	jow	jow-ul	Bassène 2006
Jóola Kasa	jaw	bıl	Barry 1987
Jóola Karon	kaay	kéy	Sambou 2014
Jóola Kwaatay	jaw	bin	Coly 2010
Jóola Bliss	jɔw	j-ul	Barry 1987
Bayot	lew	leelew	Diagne 2009
Bayot	ɬɛw	lew-ulo	Barry 1987
Manjaku of Calequisse	təp	biʔ	Wilson 2008
Manjaku of Bassarel	təp	bir	Buis 1990
Manjaku Cuur	həp	ya	Wilson 2008
Manjaku of Babok	təp	biʔ	Wilson 2008
Manjaku of Pecixe	ya	biʔ	Wilson 2008
Pepel	ya	biʔ	Wilson 2008
Mankanya	yaʔ	beʔ	Wilson 2007
Bijogo-kagbaaga	o	da	Segerer 2002
Bijago-Orango	ðɔ	ðɛna	Wilson 2008

References

Alamin, S, G Scheinder-Blum & Gerrit Jan Dimmendaal. 2012. Finding your way in Tima. In Angelika Mietzner & Ulrike Claudi (eds.), *Directionality in Grammar and Discourse: Case Studies from Africa*, 9–33. Köln: Rüdiger Köppe Verlag.

Arnott, David Whitehorn. 1970. *The nominal and verbal systems of Fula*. Oxford: Clarendon Press.

Bassène, Alain Christian. 2006. Description du Joola Banjal (Sénégal). Lyon 2 Thèse de 3e cycle, sous la direction de Denis Creissels.

Belkadi, Aicha. 2015a. Associated motion with deictic directionals: A comparative overview. SOAS *Working Papers in Linguistics* 17. 49–76.

Belkadi, Aicha. 2015b. Deictic directionals as markers of Associated Motion: examples from several African languages. http://eprints.soas.ac.uk/22027/1/Grammaticalization%20of%20directional s%20into%20Associated%20Motion.pdf

Belkadi, Aicha. This volume, chapter 5. Deictic directionality as associated motion: Motion, complex events and event integration in African languages.

Bodian, Lamine. 2014. Morphosyntaxe du guñaamolo, parler de baïnounk de Niamone. Dakar: Université Cheikh Anta Diop Thèse de doctorat unique, sous la direction de M. Ndiaye.

Boilat, P. D. 1858. *Grammaire de la langue Woloffe*: Ouvrage consonné par l'institut. Impr. imperiale.

Bourdin, Philippe. 1992. Constance et inconstances de la déicticité: la resémantisation des marques andatifs et ventifs. In Marie-Annick Morel & Laurent Danon-Boileau (eds.), *La deixis*, 287–296 & 303–307. Paris: Presses Universitaires de France.

Bourdin, Philippe. 2005. "Aller" et "venir" en somali : mise en perspective généalogique et typologique. *Faits de langues* 26. 247–258.

Bourdin, Philippe. 2006. The marking of directional deixis in Somali How typologically idiosyncratic is it? In Erhard F. Voeltz (ed.), *Studies in African Linguistic Typology*, 13–42. Amsterdam, Philadelphia: John Benjamins.

Breedveld, Johanna Odilia. 1995. *Form and meaning in Fulfulde: A morphophonological study of Maasinankoore*. Leiden: Reasearch School CNWS.

Bybee, Joan, Revere Perkins, & William Pagliuca. 1994. *The Evolution of Grammar: Tense, Aspect, and Modality in the Languages of the World*. University of Chicago Press.

Cobbinah, Alexander Yao. 2013. Nominal Classification and Verbal Nouns in Baïnounk Gubëeher. SOAS, University of London PhD.

Coly, Jules Jacques Georges. 2010. Morphosyntaxe du kuwaatay (Sénégal). Köln: Universität zu Köln PhD.

Creissels, Denis. 2014. Le développement d'un marqueur de déplacement centripète en mandinka. In Carole de Féral & Maarten Kossman (eds.) *In and Out of Africa, Languages in Question, In Honor of Robert Nicolaï*, vol2. Language Contact and Languge Change in Africa, 95–102. Louvain-la-Neuve / Walpole MA: Peeters.

Creissels, Denis. 2018. Dynamic deixis and associated motion in Jóola Fóoñi (Atlantic). Communication presented at the Events & Space: Associated Motion & Posture (ESAMP2) December, 5, Paris.

Denis Creissels & Bassène, Alain Christian. This volume, chapter 17. Ventive, associated motion and aspect in Joola Fooñi.

Creissels, Denis & Séckou Biaye. 2016. *Le balant ganja. Phonologie, morphosyntaxe, liste lexicale, textes.* Dakar: IFAN Cheikh Anta Diop.

Dieye, El Hadji. 2010. Description d'une langue cangin du Sénégal : le laalaa (léhar). Dakar – Paris, sous la direction de Stéphane Robert et Yéro Sylla: Université Cheikh Anta Diop et Institut National des langues et civilisations orientales Thèse de Doctorat de troisième cycle.

Diouf, Jean-Léopold. 2003. *Dictionnaire wolof-français et français-wolof.* Paris: KARTHALA Editions.

Doneux, Jean Léonce. 1991. La place du buy dans le groupe atlantique de la famille Kongo-Kordofan. Bruxelles: Université Libre de Bruxelles Thèse d'état, Faculté de Philosophie et de Lettres – Section Linguistique Africaine.

Doneux, Jean Léonce. 1993. Syllabus du cours de description du manjaku (Schéma proposé et commentaires). Manuscript. Aix-en-Provence, ms.

Ducos, Gisèle E. 1971. *La structure du badiaranké de Guinée et du Sénégal: phonologie et syntaxe.* Paris: Editions Klincksieck.

Fagard Benjamin, Jordan Zlatev, Anetta Kopecka, Massimo Cerruti & Johan Blomberg. 2013. The Expression of Motion Events: A Quantitative Study of Six Typologically Varied Languages. In *Berkeley Linguistics Society* 39, pp. 364–379.

Fal, Arame, Rosine Santos & Jean-Léonce Doneux. 1990. *Dictionnaire wolof-français suivi d'un index français-wolof.* Paris: Karthala.

Ferry, Marie-Paule. 1967. L'alternance consonantique et son utulisation dans la grammaire bedik. Paris: Ecole des Pratiques des Hautes Etudes Thèse de 3e cycle, sous la direction de André Martinet.

Ferry, Marie-Paule. 1991. *Thesaurus tenda. Dictionnaire ethnolinguistique de langues sénégalo-guinéennes (bassari-bedik-konyagi)* (Selaf 324). Editions Peeters. Vol. 1. 3 vols. Paris.

Gaines, Richard. 2014. On the Typology of Directional Verbs in Bantu. *IULC Working Papers* 1(01A).

Goudiaby, Arame. 2017. Eléments de grammaire du gújááhár, parler baïnounck de Niaguis (Casamance). Dakar Sénégal: Université Cheikh Anta Diop Thèse de doctorat unique.

Guérois, Rozenn, Hannah Gibson & Bastian Persohn. This volume, chapter 15. Associated motion in Bantu languages.

Guillaume, Antoine. 2000. Directionals versus associated motions in Cavineña. In Alan K. Melby & Arle L. Lommel (eds.), *LACUS Forum XXVI: The lexicon*, 395–401. Fullerton, CA: The Linguistic Association of Canada and the United States.

Guillaume, Antoine. 2006. La catégorie du "mouvement associé" en cavineña : apport à une typologie de l'encodage du mouvement et de la trajectoire. *Bulletin de la Société de Linguistique de Paris* 101(1). 415–436.

Guillaume, Antoine. 2013. Reconstructing the category of "associated motion" in Tacanan languages (Amazonian Bolivia and Peru). In Ritsuko Kikusawa & Lawrence A. Reid (eds.), *Historical Linguistics 2011. Selected papers from the 20th International Conference on Historical Linguistics, Osaka, 25–30 July 2011*, 129–151. Amsterdam & Philadelphia: John Benjamins Publishing Company.

Guillaume, Antoine. 2016. Associated motion in South America: typological and areal perspectives. *Linguistic Typology* 20:1.81–177.

Guillaume, Antoine & Harold Koch. This volume, chapter 1. Introduction: Associated Motion as a grammatical category in linguistic typology.

Hernández-Green, Néstor & Enrique L. Palancar. This volume, chapter 14. Associated motion in the Otomi family.
Hopkins, Bradley L. 1995. Contribution à une étude de la syntaxe diola-fogny. *Société Internationale de Linguistique*. (Cahiers de Recherche Linguistique) Vol. 4. Dakar, Sénégal.
Jenkins, Sue & Jay Jenkins. 2000. A Grammar of Weỹ. Archives Langues & Cultures Language and Culture Archives. http://creativecommons.org/licenses/by-nc-sa/3.0/deed.fr.
Karlik, Jan. 1972. A Manjako grammar whith special reference to the nominal group. Unpublished thesis, University of London.
Kesteloot, Lylian & Bassirou Dieng. 1989. *Du tieddo au Talibé, Contes et mythes wolof II*. Condé-sur-Noireau: Présence africaine.
Kesteloot, Lylian & Chérif Mbodj. 1983. *Contes et Mythes wolof*. Abbeville: Les Nouvelles Editions africaines. (Collection Traditions orales).
Koch, Harold. 1984. The category of 'Associated Motion' in Kaytej. *Language in Central Australia* 1.23–34.
Kuteva, Tania, Bernd Heine, Bo Hong, Haiping Long, Heiko Narrog, & Seongha Rhee. 2019. *World Lexicon of Grammaticalization*. Cambridge: Cambridge University Press.
Perrin, Loïc-Michel. 2019. *Description grammaticale du basari (oniyan). Langue atlantique du Sénégal Oriental*. Paris: Presses de l'INALCO. (Afrique(s)).
Pozdniakov, Konstantin & Guillaume Segerer. to appear. A Genealogical classification of Atlantic languages. In Friederike Lüpke (ed.), *The Oxford guide to the Atlantic languages of West Africa*. Oxford [England], New York: Oxford University Press.
Renaudier, Marie. 2012. Dérivation et valence en sereer. Lyon, sous la direction de Gérard Philippson: Université Lumière – Lyon2 Thèse de Doctorat de troisième cycle.
Ricca, Davide. 1993. *I Verbi Deittici di Movimento in Europa: Una Ricerca Interlinguistica*, Firenze, La Nuova Italia Editrice.
Robert, Stéphane & Guillaume Segerer. to appear. Joola Keeraak: A grammatical introduction. Friedrike Luepke. *The Oxford guide to the Atlantic languages of West Africa*. Oxford [England], New York: Oxford University Press.
Rose, Françoise. 2015. Associated motion in Mojeño Trinitario: some typological considerations. *Folia Linguistica* 49(1). 117–158
Ross, Daniel. This volume, chapter 2. A cross-linguistic survey of Associated Motion and Directionals.
Sambou, Pierre. 2007. Morphosyntaxe du Jóola karon. Dakar, Sénégal: Université Cheikh Anta Diop Thèse de Doctorat de troisième cycle.
Sambou, Pierre. 2014. Relations entre les rôles syntaxiques et les rôles sémantiques dans les langues jóola. Dakar, Sénégal: Université Cheikh Anta Diop Thèse d'état.
Santos, Rosine. 1996. Le Mey: langue ouest-atlantique de Guinée. Université de la Sorbonne nouvelle – Paris III Thèse d'état, sous la direction de Serge Sauvageot.
Schaefer, Ronald P. 1985. Motion in Tswana and its characteristic lexicalization. *Studies in African Linguistics* 16(1). 57–87.
Schaefer, Ronald P. & Richard Gaines. 1997. Toward a typology of directional motion for African languages. *Studies in African Linguistics* 26(2). 193–220.
Segerer, Guillaume. 2002. *La langue bijogo de Bubaque (Guinée Bissau)*. Louvain – Paris: Peeters. (Afrique et langage 3).
Segerer, Guillaume. 2009. Combien y a-t-il de langues joola ? 3ème journée d'étude sur les langues atlantiques. https://halshs.archives-ouvertes.fr/halshs-00728504.

Soukka, Maria. 2000. *A descriptive grammar of Noon: a Cangin language of Senegal.* Muenchen: LINCOM Europa.
Sow, Alfâ Ibrâhîm. 1966. Remarques sur les infixes de dérivation dans le fulfulde du Foûta-Djalon (Guinée). *The Journal of West African Languages*, III(1). 13–21. Cambridge University Press.
Talmy, Leonard. 2000. *Toward a cognitive semantics.* Cambridge, Mass: MIT Press.
Talmy, Leonard. 2007. Lexical typologies. In Timothy Shopen (ed.), *Language Typology and Syntactic Description*, 66–168. Cambridge: Cambridge University Press.
Voeltz, Erhard Friedrich Karl. 1977. Proto Niger-Congo extensions. Los Angeles: University of California Doctoral Dissertation.
Voisin, Sylvie. 2010. Les suffixes -i et -si en wolof. *Sciences et Techniques Du Langage 7.* 21–34. (CLAD)
Voisin, Sylvie. 2013. Expression de trajectoire dans quelques langues de la famille atlantique (Groupe Nord). (Ed.) Catherine Chauvin. *Faits de Langues* 42. 131–152.
Voisin, Sylvie. to appear. Verbal extensions of Atlantic languages. In Friederike Lüpke (ed.), *The Oxford guide to the Atlantic Languages of West Africa.* Oxford; New York: Oxford University Press.
Vuillermet, Marine. 2013. Dónde, cuándo, y con quién ocurren acciones: el movimiento asociado en ese ejja. In Ana María Ospina Bozzi (ed.), *Expresión de nociones espaciales en lenguas amazónicas*, 39–59. Bogota: Instituto Caro y Cuervo & Universidad Nacional de Colombia.
Vydrin, Valentin, T.G. Bergman, and Matthew Benjamin. 2000. "Mandé Language Family of West Africa: Location and Genetic Classification", SIL International 2000-003. SIL Electronic Survey Reports (April 1).
Wilkins, David P. 1991. The semantics, pragmatics and diachronic development of "associated motion" in Mparntwe Arrernte. *Buffalo papers in linguistics* 1. 207–257.
Wilkins, David P. & Deborah Hill. 1995. When GO means COME: Questioning the Basicness of Basic Motion Verbs. *Cognitive Linguistics* 6.2/3, 209–259.

Denis Creissels and Alain Christian Bassène
17 Ventive, associated motion and aspect in Jóola Fóoñi (Atlantic)

Abstract: Like the other Atlantic languages for which the relevant information is available, Jóola Fóoñi (aka Diola-Fogny) uses verb morphology to encode deictic orientation of motion events and associated motion. Jóola Fóoñi has a single marker fulfilling these two functions, a verbal suffix with two allomorphs -ʊlɔ and -ul. With motion verbs, this suffix indicates that the motion is oriented towards the deictic center, but in combination with verbs that do not encode movement, it acts as an associated movement marker, with a wide range of possible interpretations. Moreover, it is also used to encode aspectual meanings. This paper describes the uses of this suffix on the basis of a corpus of naturalistic texts.

Keywords: deictic directionals, ventive / centripetal, associated motion, Atlantic languages, Jóola / Diola.

1 Introduction

Jóola Fóoñi (aka Diola-Fogny), spoken in south western Senegal by approximately half a million speakers, belongs to the Bak group of languages included in the Atlantic family.[1]

The Atlantic languages for which the relevant information is available do not have non-deictic directionals of the type found among others in English (such as *back*, *up*, etc.), but use verb morphology to encode deictic directionality and/or associated motion (Voisin 2013, Forthcoming, this volume), and Jóola Fóoñi is no exception.

---

[1] Jóola languages can be divided into Central Jóola, a dialect continuum within the limits of which it is difficult (if not impossible) to decide what is a language and what is a dialect, and peripheral Jóola varieties whose status as separate languages is hardly disputable, in spite of their close relationship to Central Jóola, such as Karon, Kwaataay, Mulomp-North, or Bayot. Jóola Fóoñi is part of the Central Jóola dialect continuum.

Denis Creissels, Laboratoire Dynamique Du Langage (CNRS & Université Lumière Lyon 2), denis. creissels@univ-lyon2.fr
Alain Christian Bassène, Université Cheikh Anta Diop, Dakar, acbassene@hotmail.com

https://doi.org/10.1515/9783110692099-017

As discussed by Voisin (this volume), among Atlantic languages, systems similar to that described in this paper are found, not only in the other Jóola varieties, but also in their closest relatives within the Bak branch of Atlantic (Manjaku, Mankanya, Balant), and in the languages of the North branch that are in close contact with Bak languages (Nyun-Buy).

In Jóola Fóoñi, morphological encoding of deictic directionality is restricted to ventive (or centripetal) direction. In contrast to Australian or Amazonian languages having a variety of associated motion markers (see among others Koch 1984, this volume; Wilkins 1991; Guillaume 2016; Rose 2015), Jóola Fóoñi has a single associated motion marker coinciding with the marker encoding ventive (or centripetal) direction with movement verbs. This marker, henceforth designated as 'VEN marker', is widely used as an associated motion marker adding a motion component to verbs whose lexical meaning does not imply movement, with a very wide range of possible interpretations. In some cases, the movement implied by the presence of the VEN marker cannot be viewed as really 'associated' with the event encoded by the verbal lexeme, and the meaning is rather 'do something elsewhere than at deictic center' (sometimes called 'altrilocative' or 'distanciative'). Moreover, as in many other languages, the same VEN marker also has uses in which no movement is implied, and the semantic contribution of the VEN marker must be analyzed as purely aspectual.[2]

The importance of the uses of the VEN marker other than that of deictic directional with movement verbs follows from the observation that, in our corpus, about 60 % of the verbal lexemes occurring in combination with this marker are not movement verbs, and the second most frequent among the verbs attested in combination with the VEN marker (ŋar 'take') is not a movement verb.

Example (1) illustrates the use of the VEN marker to encode ventive direction with the movement verb pur 'get out'; example (2) illustrates its use as an associated motion marker with nɔɔm 'buy', example (3) illustrates its 'do away from here' use with the verb kʊr 'educate', and example (4) illustrates its use as an aspectual marker expressing the meaning 'development of a process in the direction of some outcome' in combination with jamɔ 'be famous'.[3]

---

[2] The choice of the label VEN marker does not imply that we analyze the polysemy of this marker as having necessarily developed from an original ventive meaning. This is a possibility, but a scenario of parallel developments from a common lexical source can also be imagined. As will be commented in the conclusion, we leave open the question of the historical scenario responsible for the polysemy pattern we observe in the present state of the language.

[3] Our transcription of Jóola Fóoñi differs from the official orthography in the notation of vowels, for which we use the IPA symbols, whereas the official orthography uses the acute accent to distinguish +ATR from −ATR vowels. As regards the consonants, we use the same letters as the

(1) a. *Aseekaw nepupur dɪ eluupey.*
A-seek-a-w   n-ɐ-pu-pur   dɪ   ɛ-luup-ɛ-y.
SG-woman-D-CLa PPF-sI:CLa-get.out-RDPL PREP SG-house-D-CLe
'The woman got out from the house.' (I was inside)

b. *Aseekaw nepurulopur dɪ eluupey.*
A-seek-a-w   n-ɐ-pur-**ulo**-pur   dɪ   ɛ-luup-ɛ-y.
SG-woman-D-CLa PPF-sI:CLa-get.out-**VEN**-RDPL PREP SG-house-D-CLe
'The woman got out from the house.' (I was outside)

(2) a. *Aseekaw nanɔnnɔɔm sɪwɔlas.*
A-seek-a-w   n-a-nɔn-nɔɔm   sɪ-wɔl-a-s.
SG-woman-D-CLa PPF-sI:CLa-buy-RDPL PL-fish-D-CLs
'The woman bought fish.'

b. *Aseekaw nanɔɔmʋlɔnɔɔm sɪwɔlas.*
A-seek-a-w   n-a-nɔɔm-**ʋlɔ**-nɔɔm   sɪ-wɔl-a-s.
SG-woman-D-CLa PPF-sI:CLa-buy-**VEN**-RDPL PL-fish-D-CLs
'The woman went to buy fish (and came back).'

(3) a. *Akʋrʋtɪ.*
A-kʋr-ʋt-ɪ.
sI:CLa-educate- NEG-PASS
'She has not been well-educated.'

b. A young bride has left her family to settle in her husband's house. In her new house, she doesn't behave properly. People say about her:
Akʋrʋlɔɔtɪ baaba sindeey.
A-kʋr-**ʋlɔ**-ʋt-ɪ   b-aa-b-a   sindo-ɐ-y.
sI:CLa-educate-**VEN**-NEG-PASS CLb-DEM-CLb-DIST home-D-CLe
'She has not been well-educated [when she was] there in her family.'

(4) a. *Najamɔjamɔ.*
N-a-jamɔ-jamɔ.
PPF-sI:cla-be.famous-RDPL
'He is famous.'

---

official orthography, since the phonetic values of the consonant letters in the official orthography do not depart from those usually found in West African orthographies.

b. *Najamɔʊlɔjamɔ waataay ʊyɛ.*
   N-a-jamɔ-**ʊlɔ**-jamɔ   waatɪ-a-y   ʊ-y-ɛ.
   PPF-sI:CLa-be.famous-**VEN**-RDPL   time-D-CLe   DEM-CLe-PROX
   'His reputation has been increasing lately.'

In previous descriptions of Jóola Fóoñi (Sapir 1965; Hopkins 1995), and more generally in descriptions of Jóola languages, this morpheme has been identified as a ventive marker, but its functions of associated motion marker and aspectual marker have not been clearly acknowledged so far, although descriptions of Jóola languages sometimes provide examples suggesting that the function of the VEN marker is not limited to the expression of orientation towards the deictic center with movement verbs. This is certainly due to the fact that, in elicitation sessions, deictic directionality is much easier to manipulate than associated motion or aspect.

The present paper analyzes the uses of this morpheme on the basis of a corpus of naturalistic texts.[4] All the examples we quote have been extracted from our corpus, with the only exceptions being (1) and (2) above, (5) in section 2.3, and (40) in section 7. As observed by a reviewer, the (almost) exclusive use of examples extracted from the corpus may make reading difficult, but this decision was motivated by a problem we had to face throughout this investigation. The point is that the use of the VEN marker as encoding ventive direction with movement verbs is the only one that speakers identify without hesitation, and about which they express clear judgments. As regards the uses of the VEN marker with non-movement verbs, most of the time, speakers show considerable hesitation about the possible semantic implications of the presence of the VEN marker as opposed to its absence. Moreover, the more we progressed in the study of the VEN marker, the more we became aware that there is considerable ambiguity in its possible meanings with non-movement verbs, and that even the context from which the examples are extracted is often insufficient to solve the ambiguity. In such conditions, it is more prudent to rely as far as possible on naturalistic data found in contexts that make it possible to reconstruct the intended meaning.

---

[4] The corpus on which the present study is based consists of about twelve hours of recorded naturalistic texts of various genres (narratives, discussions about Jóola tradition, discussions on themes relating to present-day society, procedural texts). Most of the recordings were kindly provided by two local radio stations that have programs in Jóola Fóoñi: Radio Awaña (Bignona) and Chaîne 4 (Ziguinchor). The corpus includes 1,689 occurrences of the VEN marker. The texts were transcribed by Boubacar Sambou (a graduate student in linguistics who is also a native speaker of the language), and then analyzed by Alain Christian Bassène and Denis Creissels with the assistance of Boubacar Sambou.

The paper is organized as follows. Section 2 describes the morphological identity and the morphological properties of the VEN marker of Jóola Fóoñi. Section 3 describes its use as a ventive marker with movement verbs. Section 4 describes its use as an associated motion marker. Section 5 describes the shift from associated motion proper to 'do elsewhere than at deictic center'. Section 6 discusses the use of the VEN marker as an aspectual marker. Section 7 analyzes the particular case of the verb *jʊk* 'see'. Section 8 summarizes the conclusions. An appendix provides the list of the 20 most frequent verbs occurring in combination with the VEN marker in our corpus.

2 Morphological properties of the VEN marker -*ul* / -*ʊlɔ*

2.1 Morphological structure of the verb forms of Jóola Fóoñi

With the exception of the imperative, in which the 2nd person prefix may optionally be deleted, the verb forms of Jóola Fóoñi consist minimally of a stem and a prefix. The stem may be a root (irreducible lexical element), or a root enlarged by one or more derivational suffixes. According to the nature of the prefix, verb forms can be characterized morphologically as finite or non-finite:

– in finite verb forms, the obligatory prefix preceding the root is a subject index[5] expressing the person (and in the third person, the gender and number)[6] of the subject argument;

---

[5] Like most of the languages of Subsaharan Africa, Jóola Fóoñi has a straightforward 'nominative-accusative' alignment system making it possible to define a grammatical relation 'subject' on the basis of a set of properties shared by A in the basic transitive construction and the sole argument of semantically monovalent verbs. The most obvious of the properties in question is obligatory indexation by means of the same set of verbal prefixes.

[6] In Jóola Fooñi, each noun form is associated with one of thirteen possible agreement patterns, and genders can be defined as sets of nominal lexemes that are associated with the same agreement pattern both in the singular and the plural. Agreement patterns and genders are designated here by labels that evoke the phonological form of the agreement markers. For example, 'dog' as a lexeme belongs to gender E/S, which means that the singular form *ɛ-yɛn* 'dog' is associated with the agreement pattern E (cf. *ɛ-yɛn ɛ-cɛɛn* 'some dog'), whereas the corresponding plural form *sɪ-yɛn* is associated with the agreement pattern S (cf *sɪ-yɛn sɪ-cɛɛn* 'some dogs'). The term 'class' refers to agreement patterns and their characteristic markers.

– non-finite verb forms do not include a subject index, and their obligatory prefix characterizes them as belonging to one of the following three types of non-finite forms: infinitive, participle, or converb.

Finite verb forms divide into independent verb forms, having the ability to act as the nucleus of independent clauses in which no noun phrase or adverb is focalized, and relative verb forms, whose use is restricted to relative clauses and clauses in which a noun phrase or adverb is focalized. Independent and relative verb forms have the same prefixes indexing the subject argument (with in particular a zero prefix expressing class D agreement), but differ in the details of their TAM and polarity inflection. In particular, independent verb forms may include TAM markers preceding the subject index, whereas the inflection of relative verb forms is purely suffixal. Moreover, the inflection of relative verb forms includes a special paradigm of three 'actualizers' (glossed ACT) that have no equivalent in the inflection of independent verb forms.[7]

There are, however, verbal suffixes that can be found in verb forms of any of the five sub-types (independent finite verb forms, relative finite verb forms, infinitive, participle, and converb), and that freely combine with all the suffixes involved in TAM-polarity inflection. The VEN marker belongs to this category, alongside with non-subject indexes.

2.2 The position of -ul / -ʊlɔ in relation to the other verbal suffixes

In the independent and relative verb forms of Jóola Fóoñi including one or more TAM-polarity markers and/or indexes suffixed to the stem, TAM-polarity markers and indexes are ordered according to the following template:[8]

---

[7] The actualizers characterize the event to which the relative verb form refers as irrealis (ACT_0), realis (ACT_1), or having a close relationship with the time of utterance (ACT_2). The ACT_2 marker -ñaa results from the grammaticalization of the adverb ñaa 'now'. In its presence, the incompletive aspect is interpreted as expressing present progressive, and the completive aspect is interpreted as expressing recent past.

[8] CPL = completive, hI = human index, ICPL = incompletive, INCL = inclusive, indep. = independent, neg. = negative, NEG = negative marker, nhI = non-human index, NONDUM = suffix found only in combination with the negative marker -ʊt with the meaning 'not yet', pos. = positive, PST = past, RDPL = reduplicative suffix. Note that: (a) NONDUM refers to a morpheme only found in negative verb forms, whose combination with the negative marker in slot 3 expresses 'not yet', (b) INCL 'inclusive' implies a 1st person plural subject, and (c) the reduplicative suffix

	1	2	3	4	5	6	7
indep. pos.	PST	INCL		ICPL	hI	RDPL / CPL	nhI	
indep. neg.	PST	NONDUM / ICPL	NEG	INCL	hI		nhI	
rel. pos.	PST	INCL		ICPL	hI	ACT$_0$	nhI	ACT$_{1/2}$
rel. neg.	PST	NONDUM / ICPL	NEG	INCL	hI		nhI	ACT$_{1/2}$

As regards the VEN marker -*ul* / -*ʊlɔ*, the general rule is that it immediately follows the stem, preceding the TAM-polarity suffixes and the non-subject indexes. There are however exceptions to this general rule:

- in the positive verb forms including the incompletive suffix -*ɛ*, the VEN suffix immediately follows the incompletive suffix occupying slot 3, as in *ɐ-tey-e-**uu**-ñaa* /(CLa)PTCP-run-ICPL-**VEN**-ACT$_2$/ 'running towards here';
- in the negative verb forms expressing the meaning 'not yet', the VEN suffix is inserted between the NONDUM marker -*ɔɔr*- (slot 2) and the negative marker -*ʊt* (slot 3), and the sequence -*ɔɔr*-**ʊlɔ**-*ʊt* surfaces as -*ɔɔrʊlɔɔt*, as in *ajawɔɔrʊlɔɔt*, segmentable as *a-jaw-ɔɔr-**ʊlɔ**-ʊt* /sI:CLa-go-NONDUM-**VEN**-NEG/ 'he has not come yet';
- in the relative verb forms including the 'irrealis' actualizer -*ɛ*, the VEN marker may optionally follow the actualizer occupying slot 7, as in *ɐjeeul*, segmentable as *ɐ-jɐw-e-ul* /(CLa)PTCP-go-ACT$_0$-VEN/ 'having come'.

2.3 The allomorphs of the VEN marker

The VEN marker of Jóola Fóoñi has two main allomorphs, -*ul* and -*ʊlɔ*. No other morpheme of Jóola Fooñi shows a similar allomorphy pattern, and consequently there would be no point in trying to posit a single underlying form and to describe the relationship between -*ul* and -*ʊlɔ* in terms of morphophonological processes.[9] By contrast, regular phonological processes explain the existence of several variants for each of the two main allomorphs of the VEN marker: depending on the phonological context, -*ul* may surface as -*ul*, -*uu*, or -*u*, and -*ʊlɔ* may surface as -*ulo*, -*ʊl*, -*ul*, -*lɔ*, -*lo*, or -*l*.

RDPL is an obligatory element of some finite verb forms, but cannot be analyzed as expressing a TAM value by itself.
9 We are aware of no comparative data that could suggest a historical explanation of this situation.

In conformity with the general rules governing ATR harmony, -*ul* is consistently +ATR, and may spread its +ATR feature to the neighboring formatives, whereas -*ʊlɔ* undergoes ATR harmony in combination with +ATR roots (as in example (1b) above, where -*ʊlɔ* surfaces as -*ulo*), or in the presence of a +ATR suffix.[10]

As regards the distribution of -*ul* and -*ʊlɔ*, the general rule is that the VEN marker occurs as -*ul* if it is not followed by any other verbal suffix, whereas the presence of another verbal suffix after the VEN marker triggers the choice of -*ʊlɔ*. There is no variation in this distribution that could be related to differences in the functions fulfilled by -*ul* / -*ʊlɔ*.

Interestingly, there is a tendency to use -*ul* rather than -*ʊlɔ* when the VEN marker is followed by morphemes whose status as suffixes or enclitics is unclear: the non-human indexes, the hypothetical marker -*jaa*, sometimes also (but more rarely) the actualizers -*mı* and -*ñaa*. However, the only true exception to the general rule accounting for the distribution of -*ul* and -*ʊlɔ* is that, when the VEN marker follows the incompletive marker -*ɛ*, it invariably occurs as -*ul*, even if it is followed by other suffixes.

There is also an apparent exception to the distribution of -*ul* and -*ʊlɔ*, which, however, can be explained by a rule according to which, as illustrated in (5), two suffixes (the completive marker -*ɛ* and the 'irrealis' actualizer -*ɛ*) have a zero allomorph in some contexts, in particular (but not only) when they immediately follow the VEN marker.[11] Comparison with (5a) shows that, in (5b), the VEN marker is underlyingly followed by the ACT_0 suffix. In this context, ACT_0 is realized as a zero-suffix, but its presence in the underlying string triggers the choice of the -*ʊlɔ* allomorph of the VEN marker (realized -*ulo* because of the +ATR feature of the root -*riiŋ*).

(5) a. *biriŋ nan kuriiŋe taata*
biriŋ n-an ku-riiŋ-e t-aa-t-a
since CLn-REL sI:CLbk-arrive-ACT_0 CLt-DEM-CLt-DIST
'since they arrived there'

---

10 In the vowel harmony system of Jóola Fóoñi, each morpheme (either root or affix) is lexically specified as +ATR or not. The morphemes underlyingly specified as +ATR (such as the allomorph -*ul* of the VEN marker) always surface as +ATR, and spread their +ATR feature to the neighboring formatives, whereas the realization of those that lack an underlying ATR specification (such as the allomorph -*ʊlɔ*) depends on the presence of a morpheme underlyingly specified as +ATR in their neighborhood. The spreading of the +ATR feature operates in both directions, but its precise scope cannot be specified in a straightforward way, since there is some variation depending on elocution speed.

11 The same markers also have a zero variant when they immediately follow a human index.

b. *biriŋ nan kuriiŋulo taatɛ*
   biriŋ   n-an   ku-riiŋ-**ulo**-Ø   t-aa-t-ɛ
   since   CLn-REL   sI:CLbk-arrive-**VEN**-ACT$_0$ CLt-DEM-CLt-PROX
   'since they arrived here'

2.4 The VEN marker -*ul* / -*ʊlɔ* and the separative suffix -*ul*

One of the two allomorphs of the VEN marker is homonymous with the separative suffix -*ul* (sometimes also called 'inversive' or 'reversive'). The separative suffix can be identified in verb pairs such as *kambɛn* 'close' / *kɛmbul* 'open', *kɔtɛn* 'glue' / *kɔtul* 'unglue', *lɔɔp* 'tie' / *loopul* 'untie'. The hypothesis of a historical link between the VEN marker and the separative suffix can be considered, but whatever the historical scenario responsible for this coincidence, synchronically, they must be analyzed as two distinct although partially homonymous morphemes, for several reasons:

- the separative suffix does not show the allomorphy pattern described above for the VEN marker;
- in the morphological structure of verb forms, the VEN marker follows some TAM-polarity suffixes, whereas the separative suffix consistently precedes all TAM-polarity suffixes, which can be viewed as evidence of its derivational status;
- in the forms involving reduplication of the verb stem,[12] the separative suffix is repeated, in the same way as the other derivational suffixes, cf. for example *n-ɐ-kɛmb-ul-kɛmb-u*l 'he opened'; by contrast, in the same tenses, the VEN marker is not repeated, which can be viewed as evidence of its inflectional status, cf. for example *n-ɐ-pur-**ulo**-pur* 'he came out';
- in the infinitive, with monosyllabic stems, the addition of the separative suffix triggers the replacement of the infinitive prefix *ɛ-* (the default infinitive suffix for monosyllabic stems)[13] by the infinitive prefix *ka-* (the default infinitive suffix for non-monosyllabic stems), cf. *e-lɔɔp* 'to tie' / *kɛ-loop-ul* 'untie' whereas the addition of the VEN suffix does not trigger any change in the infinitive prefix, cf. *ɛ-tɛy* 'run / *e-tey-**ul*** 'come running'; this provides addi-

---

12 As already mentioned above, the reduplicative suffix is an obligatory element of some finite verb forms, but cannot be analyzed as having a TAM value by itself, since it occurs in completive and incompletive forms as well. What marks the *completive* vs. *incompletive* distinction is the contrast between the incompletive marker -*ɛ* and its absence in a given morphological slot.

13 In Jóola Fóoñi, as in other Jóola varieties, several prefixes which are basically number prefixes of nouns can be used with verbal stems as infinitive prefixes, but statistically, the default choice is quite clearly *ɛ-* with monosyllabic stems, and *ka-* with non-monosyllabic stems.

tional evidence of the inflectional status of the VEN suffix, as opposed to the derivational status of the separative suffix.

Moreover, the separative suffix can only be found in a very limited set of verbs (ten or so), and is not productive anymore, whereas the VEN marker is productively used with all semantic kinds of verbs: in the corpus of naturalistic texts used for this study, 165 different verbs are attested in combination with the VEN marker.[14]

3 -ul / -ʊlɔ as a ventive marker

3.1 -ul / -ʊlɔ combined with movement verbs

With movement verbs, -ul / -ʊlɔ encodes that the movement of the figure is oriented towards the deictic center. As usual in deictic directional systems, in conversation, the deictic center consistently coincides with the location of the conversation, whereas in narration, the choice of the deictic center as evidenced by the use of the VEN marker is very flexible, producing 'camera effects' by suggesting the choice of one of the characters as the origin of perspective (Zubin & Hewitt 1995).

Depending on the verbs, the figure may be the referent of the subject (with intransitive verbs expressing spontaneous motion) or the object (with transitive verbs expressing caused motion). In example (6), both possibilities are illustrated by *jaw* 'go' and *bɔñ* 'send', respectively:

(6) The king's daughter has been captured by a dragon. A boy has been sent to liberate her. After finding the girl, he tells her:
Inje man ɩjaalɔñaa, paam ʊya abɔñʊlaam, naanɛ ijoo ɩŋarɩ.
Inje	m-an	ɩ-jaa-**lɔ**-ñaa,	paam	ʊya
1SG	CLm-REL	sI:1SG-go-**VEN**-ACT₂	father	(CLa)POSS.2SG

a-bɔñ-**ʊl**-aam,	n-aanɛ	i-je-**u**	ɩ-ŋar-ɩ.
sI:CLa-send-**VEN**-I:1SG	PPF-sI:CLa.tell	sI:1SG-go-**VEN**	sI:1SG-take-I:2SG

'I who am coming, it's your father who sent me, he told me to come and take you.'

---

14 The productivity of the VEN marker is confirmed by its ability to combine with verbs borrowed from French, as in (14) below.

In Jóola Fóoñi, morphological expression of the deictic orientation of motion verbs is restricted to ventive orientation. Nothing similar exists for itive orientation, which means that itive orientation constitutes the default interpretation of motion verbs not marked by the suffix -ul / -ʋlɔ in situations where deictic orientation cannot be inferred from the context.

Jóola Fóoñi does not have a verb root meaning 'come'.[15] As illustrated by example (6) above, the language encodes this meaning as *jaw* 'go' plus the VEN marker. In fact, this combination accounts for more than one third of the total number of occurrences of the VEN marker in the corpus (597 out of 1,689). Other movement verbs whose combination with the VEN marker is particularly frequent in the corpus include *laañ* 'return (intr.)', *riiŋ* 'arrive', *pur* 'go out', *tɛy* 'run', and their causative derivatives (*laañɛn* 'return (tr.)', etc.).

Examples (7) to (10) provide additional illustrations of the VEN marker encoding ventive direction with movement verbs.

(7) Hyena and Hare are in their field. They see Ground Squirrel running towards them. Hare says to Hyena:
Jɛmunuŋo, Jɛmɐɐp ɐteyeuuñaa naanɛ b'ɛɛtɛk bʋtʋmab bʋya barıɛm.
Jɛmunuŋo,   Jɛmɐɐp   ɐ-tey-e-**uu**-ñaa   n-aanɛ
Hyena   Ground Squirrel (CLa)PTCP-run-ICPL-**VEN**-ACT₂   PPF-sI:CLa.say
bɛɛ   ɛ-tɛk   bʋ-tʋm-a-b   b-ʋya   b-a-rı-ɛ-m.
DIR   INF-hit   SG-mouth-D-CLB   CLb-POSS.i:2SG CLb-PTCP-ache -ICPL-ACT₁
'Hyena, Ground Squirrel who is running towards us said he is going to hit your mouth which is aching.'

(8) Dog and Hyena are collecting honey. Dog has climbed a tree, he is filling the pot with honey, while Hyena has remained under the tree. Hyena says to Dog:
Kɐrumbɐɐk kʋmɛmmɛɛŋ, ñaa uwɐloul m'ʋʋjaal!
Kɐ-rumbɐ-ɐk   kʋ-mɛm-mɛɛŋ,   ñaa   u-wɐlo-**ul**
SG-pot-D-CLk   sI:CLk-be.full-RDPL   now   sI:2SG-go.down-**VEN**
man   ʋ-ja-al.
CSC   sI:1PL-go-INCL
'The pot is full, now come down and let's go!'

---

15 An entry *bıl* 'come' can be found in Sapir & al.'s (1993) dictionary of Jóola Fóoñi, without further details, but in our corpus, *bıl* is exclusively used in combination with other verbs as an aspectual auxiliary. In other Central Jóola varieties, for example, in the Kaasa variety described by P.M. Sambou (1979: 186), *bıl* occurs independently as a movement verb meaning 'come', but this is not the case in the Fóoñi variety described in the present article.

(9) A woman is pounding. A bird comes flying and drops something in her mortar. The woman says to her neighbor:
Jıcɛr ɛsʊaay man ɛfarʊlɔñaa saltaay bɛɛ dı ɛpɔrɛy yumbɐ!

Jıcɛr	ɛ-sʊa-a-y	m-an	ɛ-far-**ʊlɔ**-ñaa	saltɛ-a-y
look.at	SG-bird-D-CLe	CLm-REL	sI:CLe-throw-**VEN**-ACT	dirt-D-CLe

bɛɛ	dı	ɛ-pɔr-ɛ-y	y-umbɐ.	
DIR	PREP	SG-flour-D-CLe	CLe-POSS.I:1SG	

'Look at the bird, how it threw some dirty thing into my flour!'

(10) (from a text about malaria transmission and prophylaxis)
Mʊmɛlam mamɔcɛnaam muñɐkeuuñɐk bawɔlab.

Mʊ-mɛl-a-m	m-a-mɔcɛn-ɛ-a-m
PL-water-D-CLm	CLm-PTCP-be.dirty-ACT₀-D-CLm

mu-ñɐk-e-**uu**-ñɐk	ba-wɔl-a-b.
sI:CLm-draw-ICPL-**VEN**-RDPL	NN-mosquito-D-CLb

'Dirty water attracts mosquitos.'

3.2 *-ul / -ʊlɔ* and abstract motion

The etymology of light verb compounds such as French *jeter son regard sur* lit. 'throw one's gaze on' > 'have a look at' or English *give a ring to* constitutes a decisive proof that some events that do not involve physical movement or transfer of a concrete entity can be conceptualized as involving a kind of abstract (or fictive) motion or transfer, and the notion of abstract motion may also prove useful in the analysis of deictic directionals.[16]

In the Jóola Fóoñi corpus, the notion of abstract motion accounts in particular for the use of the VEN marker with *wɔnk* 'call' in the sense of 'do a phone call': in (11), there is no overt indication of first person, but *wonk-ul* is interpreted as 'give us a ring'.

---

[16] On fictive motion, see Vidal & Payne (this volume), Kawachi (this volume), Belkadi (this volume) and references therein.

(11) (announcement made by the host of a radio show)
Anɔɔsan amaŋʊm b'eewonkuley, nɛwonkuu dɪ nʊmɛrɔ ʊyɛ yalakɔm 339911048.
Anɔɔsan   a-maŋ-ʊ-m   bɛɛ   e-wonk-**ul**-e-y,
(CLa)DISTR sI:CLa-want-EP-ACT₁   DIR-   INF-call-**VEN**-D-CLe
n-e-wonk-**uu**   dɪ   nʊmɛrɔ   ʊ-y-ɛ
PPF-sI:CLa-call-**VEN**   PREP   number   DEM-CLe-PROX
y-a-lakɔ-m   339911048.
CLe-PTCP-be-ACT₁   339911048
'Any person who wants to call us, they may call the following number: 339911048.'

The notion of abstract motion can also be invoked to explain the use of *pur-ul*, ventive form of *pur* 'get out', in the sense of 'become'. As illustrated in example (1) at the beginning of the present paper, the VEN marker combined with *pur* 'get out' may carry its basic meaning of ventive orientation with reference to physical movement, but the same combination is also found with the meaning 'become', without any idea of physical movement, as in example (12).

(12) *Dɪ kʊñulak kɔɔla, babaj añul epurulo alʊñoora.*
Dɪ   kʊ-ñul-a-k   k-ɔɔl-a,   ba-baj   a-ñul
PREP   PL-child-D-CLbk   CLbk-POSS-I:CLa (sI:CLd)have-RDPL   SG-child
e-pur-**ulo**   a-lʊñɔɔra.
(CLa)PTCP-go.out-**VEN**(ACT₀)   SG-hunter
'Among his children, there is one who became a hunter.'

The co-lexification of 'get out' and 'become', cross-linguistically common, can be explained by viewing 'become' as a kind of abstract movement (i.e. a metaphorical extension of 'get out' to the expression of transition from a former state to a new one). In the case of Jóola Fóoñi, the use of the VEN marker in this metaphorical extension of 'get out' can be viewed as motivated by the fact that the present state of the world (as opposed to previous states) is construed as the deictic center.[17]

The same explanation can be considered for the use of the VEN marker with *cɛrɛ* 'create' (borrowed from French) in example (13), since 'create' can be paraphrased as 'make come into existence'.

---

[17] Note that this is also consistent with the etymology of English *be-come* or French *de-venir*.

(13) Pʊjaa, nakʊmaasɛ kacɛrɛʊlı sıprɔblɛm.
 Pʊ-jaa, n-a-kʊmaasɛ ka-cɛrɛ-**ʊl**-ı sı-prɔblɛm.
 (sI:CLd)continue-HYP PPF-sI:CLa-begin INF-create-**VEN**-I:2SG PL-problem
 'If things continue to be like this, she will begin to create problems for you.'

The notion of abstract motion also accounts for the possibility of using *jicer-ul* (from *jıcɛr* 'look') with the meaning 'look towards the deictic center'. This possibility is not attested in the corpus, but was confirmed in elicitation.

4 -ul / -ʊlɔ as an associated motion marker

4.1 Introductory remarks

As already illustrated by example (2), in addition to its use as a ventive directional marker with movement verbs, *-ul / -ʊlɔ* is productively used as an associated motion marker with verbs whose lexical meaning does not imply movement. In the use of the VEN marker as an associated motion marker, the movement it refers to is always performed by the referent of the subject, regardless of the transitive vs. intransitive distinction.

The temporal relationship between the event denoted by the verbal lexeme and the associated motion is very flexible.

4.2 'Do and come', 'do while coming', 'come and do'

In many occurrences of the VEN marker with non-motion verbs, it is clear from the context that the movement associated to the event encoded by the verbal lexeme is a one-way trip (i.e. a movement whose destination does not coincide with the point of departure) whose destination is the deictic center. The event may occur at any point of the path: it may coincide with the departure (subsequent motion), or with the arrival (prior motion), and it may also occur at some point in between (concurrent motion). (14) illustrates the possibility that the transitive verb event 'leave (something)' coincides with the departure.[18]

---

[18] *kat* is the equivalent of French 'laisser' or Spanish 'dejar', and corresponds only to the non-motion meaning of English 'leave'.

(14) An old woman is providing advice to a young bride who has just arrived at her husband's place:
Wan ʊkatʊlɔm deɐ paam ɩɩya, wɔɔ ʊkaawɔbɔ!
W-an   ʊ-kat-**ʊlɔ**-m   deɐ paam ɩɩya,   w-ɔɔ
CLu-REL   sI:2SG-leave-**VEN**-ACT₁ LOC father (CLa)POSS.I:2SG CLu-PRO
ʊ-kaa-wɔ-bɔ!
sI:2SG-leave-I:CLu-I:CLb
'What you left [behind you] when leaving your father's place, forget it!'
(lit. '... leave it there!')

In (15), the same verb *kat* 'leave' refers to an event occurring at some point during a journey whose destination is the deictic center.

(15) Samba and Maaria have fled their village. During the journey, under the effect of witchcraft, Samba forgets the existence of Maaria and leaves her. He arrives alone in another village where he settles. Later in the same village, a rooster is engaging sexual intercourse with a hen, and the hen says:
Tam ʊkaan nɛn Samba akatʊlɔm Maarɩa dɩ karambaak!
Tam   ʊ-kaan   nɛn   Samba   a-kat-**ʊlɔ**-m   Maarɩa
PROH   sI:2SG-do like Samba   (CLa)PTCP-leave-**VEN**-ACT₁ Maarɩa
dɩ   ka-ramba-a-k.
PREP   SG-bush-D-CLk
'Don't do like Samba who left Maaria in the bush!'

This configuration is particularly frequent in the narrative texts of our corpus. Examples (16) and (17) provide further illustrations.

(16) Two strangers arrive in a village. They look for a woman for whom they have a message. They say to her:
Babaj ɐniine an ʊyañɔɔrʊlɔ dɩ karambaak, naanɛ atɑɩ.
Ba-baj   ɐ-niine   an   ʊ-yañɔɔr-**ʊlɔ**   dɩ
(sI:CLd)have-RDPL   SG-man   (CLa)REL   sI:1PL-meet-**VEN**(ACT₀)   PREP
ka-ramba-a-k,   n-aanɛ   a-ta-ɩ.
SG-bush-D-CLk   PPF-sI:CLa.say   SG-husband-I:2SG
'There's a man we met in the bush, he said he was your husband.'

(17) Later in the same story, the woman becomes aware that her husband was killed by the two strangers. She says:
Ataɔm, jɩbʊjʊlɔɔbʊj dɩ bʊŋarab.
A-ta-ɔm, jɩ-bʊj-**ʊl**-ɔɔ-bʊj dɩ bʊ-ŋar-a-b.
SG-mari-I:1SG sI:2PL-kill-**VEN**-I:CLa-RDPL PREP SG-road-D-CLb
'My husband, you killed him on the way.'

In the corpus, coincidence between the event and the arrival at deictic center is mainly attested with *tɔɔk* 'find'. As illustrated by (18) and (19), depending on the context, *tookul* can be interpreted either as 'come in search of', 'come to visit' or as 'find upon arrival'.

(18) The mother of a boy complains that nowadays girls are not ashamed to chase after boys, and even to go to their parents' place to harass them:
Añʊlaw ʊya anaaraaw ɐtookuujaa añʊlaw umbɐ ɐniinɐɐw, nɩcɛsɔɔrɔɔ.
A-ñʊl-a-w ʊya a-naarɛ-a-w ɐ-took-**uu**-jaa
SG-child-D-CLa (CLa)POSS.I:2SG CLa-female-D-CLa sI:CLa-find-**VEN**-HYP
a-ñʊl-a-w umbɐ ɐ-niine-ɐ-w, n-ɩ-cɛsɔɔr-ɔɔ.
SG-child-D-CLa (CLa)POSS.I:1SG CLa-male-D-CLa PPF-sI:1SG-drive.out-I:CLa
'If your daughter comes to visit my son, I'll drive her out.'

(19) (When they marry, women leave their family's home and settle in the house of their husband's family)
kʊbɛtɩ kan ʊtɔɔkʊlɔdo dɩ ɛlʊʊpɛy mbaa katɔɔkʊlɩmdo
kʊ-bɛt-ɩ k-an ʊ-tɔɔk-**ʊlɔ**-do dɩ
PL-co.wife-I:2SG CLbk-REL sI:2SG-find-**VEN**-I:CLd´ PREP
ɛ-lʊʊp-ɛ-y mbaa k-a-tɔɔk-**ʊl**-ɩ-m-do,
SG-house-D-CLe or CLbk-PTCP-find-**VEN**-I:2SG-ACT₁-I:CLd´
'your co-wives whom you found when you arrived at your husband's place or who found you when they arrived'

With *ŋar* 'take' and *baj* 'get, have', the usual interpretation of the combination with the VEN marker is that the state resulting from an action performed by the referent of the subject while coming is still in place upon arrival at deictic center. As illustrated in (20) and (21), *ŋɐrul* (from *ŋar* 'take') and *bɐjul* (from *baj* 'get, have') are the usual equivalents of 'bring' in Jóola Fóoñi: the referent of the subject not only has taken or gotten something while coming, (s)he still has it upon arrival.

(20) A group of women are working in the rice field. Someone comes from the village with their breakfast. One of the women guesses that the food has been poisoned. She says to the others:
Daasɔɔmaay yan kɔmbɔm eŋeruley, tambɪ ʊrɪaayɔ!
Daasɔɔma-a-y   y-an   k-ɔm-bɔ-m   e-ŋer-**ul**-e-y,
breakfast-D-CLe CLe-REL CLbk-be-I:CLb-ACT₁ INF-take-**VEN**-D-CLe
tambɪ   ʊ-rɪ-aa-yɔ!
PROH.POT   sI:1PL-eat-INCL-I:CLe
'The breakfast they are bringing, let's not eat it!

(21) The hyenas have invited the goats to their place, and the goats are visiting them. In accordance with the traditional rules of hospitality, the goats are offered water.
Simunuŋees dɪ sibejuu mʊmɛlam sɪjaamɛɛnas sɪraan.
Si-munuŋo-e-s   dɪ   si-bej-**uu**   mʊ-mɛl-a-m   sɪ-jaamɛɛn-a-s
PL-hyena-D-CLs SEQ   sI:CLs-get-**VEN** PL-water-D-CLm   PL-goat-D-CLs
sɪ-raan.
sI:CLs-drink
'Then the hyenas brought some water and the goats drank.'

In the corpus, the combination of *ŋar* 'take' with the VEN marker, almost always with the meaning 'bring', accounts for 8.1 % of the total number of occurrences of the VEN marker, which makes *ŋar* 'take' the second most frequent verb among those attested in combination with the VEN marker (the first one being *jaw* 'go', whose combination with VEN is the translation equivalent of 'come').

4.3 'Go and do and come back'

The combination of the VEN marker with verbs whose lexical meaning includes no motion component is also widely attested in the corpus with reference to situations where the deictic center is at the same time the point of departure and the point of arrival of the associated motion. Example (2b), repeated here as (22), is a typical example, with *noomul* (ventive form of *nɔɔm* 'buy') interpreted as 'go to buy (and come back)'.

(22) *Asɛɛkaw nanɔɔmʊlɔnɔɔm sɪwɔlas.*
A-sɛɛk-a-w   n-a-nɔɔm-**ʊlɔ**-nɔɔm   sɪ-wɔl-a-s.
SG-woman-D-CLa   PPF-sI:CLa-buy-**VEN**-RDPL   PL-fish-D-CLs
'The woman went to buy fish (and came back).'

The way the event is encoded in Jóola Fóoñi sentences such as (22) leaves implicit the first part of the path and emphasizes the return path. In many other languages (including English), such events are commonly referred to by means of a verb 'go' in a construction 'motion verb + purposive complement' which highlights the first part of the path, the return path being usually left unexpressed. However, although commonly used with reference to the same situations, the formulation illustrated in (22) is not equivalent to a 'motion verb + purposive complement' construction, since in Jóola Fóoñi, a clause such as *Asɛɛkaw nanɔɔmʊlɔnɔɔm siwɔlas* implies that the woman came back after buying fish. This is evidenced by the impossibility of using it as the first part of a sentence whose second part would be something like '... but she didn't find any' or '... but she hasn't come back yet'.

Examples (23) to (25) provide further illustrations of this use of the VEN marker.

(23) A woman proposes to her husband's unmarried brother to do the washing for him:
Ñesuu seefuneey m'upɔsı.
Ñes-**uu** seefune-e-y man ι-pɔs-ι.
look.for-**VEN** soap-D-CLe CSC sI:1SG-wash-I:2SG
'Go fetch some soap and I'll do the washing for you.'

(24) The boys leave the village every morning to go herding cattle in the bush, and return to the village in the evening.
Kʊñulak, ban kumateuum, karambaak kʊcıla, kɔɔnɛkɔ Bagaya.
Kʊ-ñul-a-k, b-an ku-mat-e-**uu**-m,
PL-child-D-CLbk CLb-REL sI:CLbk-herd.cattle-ICPL-**VEN**-ACT₁
ka-ramba-a-k kʊ-cıla, k-ɔɔnɛ-kɔ Bagaya.
SG-bush-D-CLk CLk-ANA sI:CLbk-say-I:CLk Bagaya
'The children, the place where they go herding cattle, the bush in question, it is called (lit. they say to it) Bagaya.'

(25) A group of people have raised funds to send one of them in pilgrimage to Mecca. When the pilgrim comes back, they organize a meeting with him.
Bʊkanak dı kujoo kʊjam ehijinkeew ɔɔlu waa najamʊlɔm baa Maka.
Bʊk-an-a-k dı ku-je-**u** kʊ-jam e-hıijinke-e-w
SGuk-person-D-CLbk SEQ sI:CLbk-go-VEN sI:CLbk-hear SG-pilgrim-D-CLa
ɔɔl-u waa n-a-jam-**ʊlɔ**-m baa Maka.
(CLa)POSS-I:CLbk what PPF-sI:CLa-hear-**VEN**-ACT₁ LOC Mecca
'Then the people came to hear what their pilgrim had heard in Mecca.'

In example (26), the movement to which the VEN marker refers was intended as a round trip, but was interrupted precisely by the death of the boy, i.e. by the event encoded by the verbal lexeme to which the VEN marker is attached.

(26) A boy has come back from a trip with plenty of wealth. A woman orders her son to do the same trip in the hope that he will come back rich too. Later, learning that her son died during the trip, she says:
Nɛɛnɛ añulaw umbeem ajaw pɔɔp beebɔ, necetuubɔ.
N-ɛɛnɛ   a-ñul-a-w   umbeem   a-jaw   pɔɔp
PPF-sI:1SG.tell   SG-child-D-CLa   (CLa)POSS.I:1SG sI:CLa-go   also
bɛɛ-bɔ,   n-e-cet-**uu**-bɔ.
DIR-I:CLb   PPF-sI:CLa-die-**VEN**-I:CLb
'I told my son to go there too, and he died before returning.'

4.4 *Jaw* 'go' followed by another verb marked by the VEN suffιx

In the construction illustrated by examples (27) and (28), *jaw* 'go' is immediately followed by another verb in a form characterized by the lack of any overt TAM marker. This form is more generally the form taken by verbs in non-initial position in verb chains that constitute a functional equivalent of *and*-coordination of clauses in English.[19] Examples such as (27) and (28) suggest that the basic meaning of this construction is 'go and do and come back', and that the presence of *jaw* 'go' before the verb marked by the VEN suffix is motivated by some insistence on the first part of the path.

(27) A young boy doesn't know his paternal aunt, since she lives in another village and never comes to the boy's village. The boy says to his father:
Fɔk ιjaw ijukul asʊpaapɔm.
Fɔk   ι-jaw   i-juk-**ul**   a-sʊpaap-ɔm.
OBLG   sI:1SG-go   sI:1SG-see-**VEN**   SG-paternal.aunt-I:1SG
'I must go visit my aunt.'

---

[19] The same verb form, characterized by the lack of any overt TAM marker, is also found in independent clauses with a hortative, imperative or optative meaning, and in some types of subordinate clauses (i.e. in uses roughly comparable to those of European 'subjunctives').

(28) Two men are away from home. One of them becomes aware that the money he had with him has disappeared. His companion explains:
Sigoreɛs, inje ɩyabɛ dɩ aw, ɩjaw inenuu deɛ sindeɛy.

Si-gori-e-s,	inje	ɩ-yab-ɛ	dɩ	aw,	ɩ-jaw
PL-money-D-CLs	1SG	sI:1SG-take-CPL	PREP	2SG	sI:1SG-go

i-nen-**uu**	deɛ	sindo-e-y.
sI:1SG-put-**VEN**	LOC	hom-D-CLe

'The money, it is I who took it from you so that I go and put it at home (to keep it safe).'

However, at least in some cases, as in (29), there is clearly no idea of coming back, and the intended meaning is simply 'go and do'.

(29) (from a text about malaria transmission and prophylaxis)
Ɛwɔl ɛnaarɛ panɛjaw erumuu an ɐjuut m'eejool etipen dɩ an ɐjuwe.

Ɛ-wɔl	ɛ-naarɛ	pan	ɛ-jaw	e-rum-**uu**	an
SG-mosquito	CLe-female	FUT	sI:CLe-go	sI:CLe-bite-**VEN**	person

ɐ-ju-ut	man	e-je-**ul**	e-tipen
(CLa)PTCP-be.healthy-NEG	CSC	sI:CLe-go-**VEN**	sI:CLe-contaminate

dɩ	an	ɐ-ju-e.
PREP	person	(CLa)PTCP-be.healthy-ACT$_0$

'A female mosquito will go and bite an infected person, and then it will come and contaminate a healthy person.'

In fact, in elicitation, the judgment of the speakers is that, when 'go and do' is expressed by a construction in which *jaw* 'go' is followed by another verb, the VEN marker on the second verb is optional, and deleting it does not affect the meaning. There is in this respect a clear asymmetry between 'go' and 'come': when 'come and do' is expressed by a construction in which *jool* 'come' (decomposable as *jaw* 'go' + *ul* VEN) is followed by another verb, the second verb is never marked by the VEN marker in the corpus, and the judgment of the speakers is that it would not be correct to add it.

5 'Do something while being elsewhere than at deictic center'

The possibility that associated motion markers develop an 'altrilocative' or 'distanciative' meaning seems to have been first signaled for the Atlantic language Fulfulde (see in particular Breedveld 1995: 178). In Jóola Fóoñi, the possibility of a semantic shift from 'do before coming' to 'do something while being away from here', already illustrated by example (3) in section 1, is also illustrated by examples (30) to (33). In such cases, the referent of the subject is present at the deictic center at the time of utterance, and the use of the VEN marker was probably motivated originally by the fact that his/her involvement in an event that occurred elsewhere implies subsequent movement to deictic center. However, contrary to the situations we analyze in terms of associated motion, there is no immediate link (either in chronological terms or in terms of motivation) between the event and movement to or from the deictic center. In reference to such situations, a purely synchronic analysis in terms of 'associated motion' would imply understanding 'associated motion' in a very broad sense (and in most languages, the usual translation equivalent of such clauses only specifies the location of the event, without any reference to movement).

(30) Four brothers have left their village to learn vocational skills. When they come back, their father asks each of them:
Aw waa nʊlıtıcenʊlɔ?
Aw   waa   n-ʊ-lıtıcɛn-**ʊlɔ**?
2SG   what   PPF-sI:2SG-learn-**VEN**
'You, what did you learn there (while you were away)?'

(31) A boy spends the day in the bush herding cattle. In the evening he returns to the village. Upon arrival, he becomes aware that he doesn't have his knife anymore. He says:
Ɛlıbaay, nılɔŋʊlɔlɔŋyɔ dı karambaak.
Ɛ-lıba-a-y,   n-ı-lɔŋ-**ʊlɔ**-lɔŋ-yɔ   dı   ka-ramba-a-k.
SG-knife-D-CLe   PPF-sI:1SG-forget-**VEN**-RDPL-I:CLe   PREP   SG-bush-D-CLk
'The knife, I forgot it in the bush.'

(32) The following sentence is from a discussion about a kind of flute which is played at traditional ceremonies. The host asks the flute player about the origin of this instrument:
Jılıtaj ʊjɛ, jatı ɐjoolɐ, mantɛɛ bʊcɛɛ najʊkʊlɔjɔ?
Jı-lıt-a-j   ʊ-j-ɛ,   j-atı   ɐ-joolɐ,
SG-flute-D-CLj   DEM-CLj-PROX   CLj-GEN   SG-Jóola.person
mantɛɛ   bʊ-cɛɛ   n-a-jʊk-**ʊlɔ**-jɔ?
perhaps   CLb-some   PPF-sI:CLa-see-**VEN**-I:CLj
'This flute, does it belong to Jóola people, or perhaps they saw it somewhere else (before adopting it)?'

(33) A poor man's wife warns her daughter about the problems that may arise if she too marries a poor man.
Mbɩ inje ɩyɔk taatɛ, aw pɔɔ nuyokuu baaba, ay ajɛɛ b'ɛɛjʊkɩ?
Mbɩ inje ɩ-yɔk t-aat-ɛ aw pɔɔ
POT 1SG sI:1SG-suffer CLt-DEM-CLt-PROX 2SG also
n-u-yok-**uu** b-aa-b-a, ay a-ja-ɛ
PPF-sI:2SG-suffer-**VEN** CLb-DEM-CLb-DIST who sI:CLa-go-ACT$_0$
bɛɛ ɛ-jʊk-ɩ?
DIR INF-see-I:2SG
'If I suffer here, and you suffer there, who will pay attention to you?'

6 -ul / -ʊlɔ as an aspectual marker

In examples (34) to (36), the verb to which the VEN marker attaches is not a movement verb, and the VEN marker does not add a motion component to its meaning either. Its semantic contribution may rather be glossed as 'eventually' in English, or 'en venir à' in French. In other words, this use of the VEN marker can be described as 'development of a process in the direction of some outcome', which can be analyzed as a metaphorical extension of the original meaning 'movement of a concrete entity towards the deictic center'.

(34) (from a text about malaria transmission and prophylaxis)
Nanɔɔsan fɔɔcaay ɛtɔɔŋʊlɔ dɩ aw, fukɛɛf ɛfamb faŋ.
N-anɔɔsan fɔɔca-a-y ɛ-tɔɔŋ-**ʊlɔ** dɩ aw,
CLn-DISTR malaria-D-CLe sI:CLe-begin-**VEN**(ACT$_0$) PREP 2SG
fu-ko-ɐ-f ɛ-famb faŋ.
SG-head-D-CLf INF-ache INT
'Whenever malaria is in the stage where it is going to appear, your head hurts badly.'

(35) The following sentence is about holes made by mice in the walls of houses:
Naapɩ ɛmɩtey ɛlʊbʊlɔm, mʊmɛlam dɩ mʊnɔcɛn dɩ ʊsʊnaw ʊwʊ.
N-aapɩ ɛ-mɩt-ɛ-y ɛ-lʊb-**ʊlɔ**-m, mʊ-mɛl-a-m dɩ
CLn.REL.FUT SG-sky-D-CLe sI:CLe-rain-**VEN**-ACT$_1$ PL-water-D-CLm SEQ
mʊ-nɔcɛn dɩ ʊ-sʊn-a-w ʊ-wʊ.
sI:CLm-enter PREP PL-hole-D-CLu DEM-CLu
'When it will eventually rain, the water will enter through these holes.'

(36) A basic principle of traditional education: if an adult hits a child, there is certainly some good reason.
Añulaw, kʊnagʊlɔɔjaa, nʊmanj kaanak rajakʊt nakaanɛ.
A-ñul-a-w   kʊ-nag-**ʊl**-ɔɔ-jaa,   n-ʊ-manj
SG-child-D-CLa   sI:CLbk-hit-**VEN**-I:CLa-HYP   PPF-sI:2SG-know
ka-ɔn-a-k   r-a-jak-ʊt   n-a-kaan-ɛ.
INF-say-D-CLk   CLd-PTCP-be.good-NEG   sI:CLa-do-CPL
'A child, if someone eventually hits him/her, you know that it is because he/she has done something wrong.'

Example (37) includes two occurrences of the VEN marker. The second one is in deictic directional function, whereas the first one illustrates the aspectual function of the same marker.

(37) The following sentence is from a discussion about a kind of flute which is played in traditional ceremonies, and is supposed to have special powers. The host asks the flute player what happens if someone steals the flute, and the player answers:
Jɪlɪtaj ʊjɛ, suumi nʊsʊʊñ, aw bɛɛt ejukuu m'uuleeñenuu.
Jɪ-lɪt-a-j   ʊ-j-ɛ,   suum-i   n-ʊ-sʊʊñ,
SG-flute-D-CLj   DEM-CLj-PROX   (sI:CLd)please-I:2SG   PPF-sI:2SG-steal
aw   bɛɛt   e-juk-**uu**   man   u-leeñen-**uu**.
2SG   DIR   INF-see-**VEN**   CSC   sI:2SG-return.CAUS-**VEN**
'This flute, if you want you may steal it, you will eventually see (what happens to you), and you will return it.'

With verbs commonly interpreted as referring to states, as already noticed by Voisin (2013: 148–149) for other Atlantic languages, the VEN marker may trigger a dynamic reading. For example, in (38), *kajɔm keñouujaa* (with the VEN marker) is interpreted as 'if things eventually go wrong', 'if the situation evolves towards deterioration', whereas *kajɔm kañɔjaa* (without the VEN marker) would be interpreted simply as 'if later things are wrong'.

(38) In a debate about education, a participant evokes the attitude of men who don't take their responsibilities in the education of children and put the blame on their wife when problems arise with the children:
Kajɔm keñouujaa naanɛ asɛɛkaw amaŋʊt akʊr añulaw.
Kajɔm	keño-**uu**-jaa		n-aanɛ
tomorrow	(sI:CLd)-be(come).wrong-**VEN**-HYP		PPF-sI:CLa.say

a-sɛɛk-a-w	a-maŋ-ʊt	a-kʊr	a-ñul-a-w.
SG-woman-D-CLa	sI:CLa-want-NEG	sI:CLa-educate	SG-child-D-CLa

'Later if things eventually go wrong, he says that the woman doesn't want to educate the child.'

7 The particular case of *jʊk* 'see'

Among the verbs whose lexical meaning does not include a motion component, *jʊk* 'see' is attested several times in the corpus with reference to situations where the referent of the subject stays motionless, and sees the referent of the object coming towards him/her, as in example (39).

(39) A boy is waiting for his brother. He eventually sees him coming.
Nan ajʊkʊlɔm atıɔɔ, nakɔntaanı.
N-an	a-jʊk-**ʊlɔ**-m	a-tı-ɔɔ,	n-a-kɔntaanı.
CLn-REL	sI:CLa-see-**VEN**-ACT₁	SG-brother-I:CLa	PPF-sI:CLa-rejoice

'When he saw his brother coming, he rejoiced.'

Our first hypothesis was that, as suggested by the translation, this was an instance of associated motion. However, if this hypothesis were correct, this would be the only exception to the rule according to which, when the VEN marker encodes associated motion, the participant in movement is the referent of the subject. In fact, additional elicited examples showed us that, in this use of the ventive form of 'see', movement of the object is not essential, the general meaning being 'see at some distance'. For example, in (40), the nature of the object excludes any idea of movement.

(40) A man has got lost in the bush. He climbs a hill to orient himself. When he reaches the top of the hill, he sees his village on the horizon.
Nan ajʊkʊlɔm esukey yɔɔla, nakɔntaanı.
N-an   a-jʊk-**ʊlɔ**-m   e-suk-e-y   y-ɔɔl-a,
CLn-REL sI:CLa-see-**VEN**-ACT₁ SG-village-D-CLe CLe-POSS-I:CLa
n-a-kɔntaanı.
PPF-sI:CLa-rejoice
'When he saw his village in the distance, he rejoiced.'

This use of the VEN marker is therefore comparable to that described in section 5 ('do something elsewhere than at deictic center'), with, however, an important difference: with the verb 'see', it is not necessarily the whole event which is located at some distance from the deictic center, but only the referent of the object. Interestingly, Belkadi (2015: 63) mentions a similar use of the ventive form of 'see' in Huallaga Quechua.

Note that, in addition to this use, which has no equivalent with other verbs and can be viewed as conditioned by the particular lexical semantics of 'see', examples (28), (33) and (37) above show that the ventive form of *jʊk* 'see' can also express the meanings commonly attested with other verbs whose lexical meaning does not include a motion component.

8 Conclusion

In this article, we have shown that the *-ul / -ʊlɔ* marker of Jóola Fóoñi, used to encode ventive direction with movement verbs, is also widely used in combination with verbs whose lexical meaning does not imply movement. In the latter case, it may act as an associated motion marker with a wide variety of possible interpretations, but it may also encode that a person present at deictic center did or will do something while being somewhere else (which can be viewed as an extension of its use as an associated motion marker), and finally, it may act as an aspectual marker whose semantic contribution can be described as 'development of a process in the direction of some outcome'.

Belkadi (2015) rightly insists on the semantic flexibility of markers conflating the expression of deictic directionality and associated motion, in particular in systems with just a ventive marker without an itive counterpart. This is even more true of the ventive / associated motion marker of Jóola Fóoñi, which also has uses in which no movement is implied. However, further investigation would be necessary before putting forward precise hypotheses about the limits of this flexibility, and the interaction between the lexical semantics of verbs and the possible interpretations of the VEN marker in Jóola languages.

As regards the historical scenario responsible for the polysemy of *-ul* / *-ʊlɔ*, unfortunately, we are aware of no comparative data that could be used to reconstruct the history of this marker. Given the abundance of cross-linguistic data about multi-verb constructions (either of the serial type or of some other type) within the frame of which verbs of coming develop grammaticalized functions similar to those fulfilled by *-ul* / *-ʊlɔ* in Jóola Fóoñi (see in particular Lovestrand & Ross this volume), it is highly plausible that *-ul* / *ʊlɔ* originated from the grammaticalization of a verb of coming. However, we are not in a position to put forward anything precise about the details of the historical development of the various uses of *-ul* / *-ʊlɔ* attested in the present state of the language.

On the basis of comparative evidence, Voisin (this volume) argues that, in the type of system illustrated by Jóola Fóoñi, the expression of associated motion is a secondary development of systems whose primary function is the expression of deictic directionality. However, we do not think that, by themselves, the Jóola Fóoñi data we have analyzed can be viewed as suggesting a particular chronological order (either from associated motion to deictic directionality or the reverse). In fact, they leave open the possibility that the deictic directional and associated motion uses of the VEN marker are not ordered chronologically, and rather resulted from parallel developments in multiverbal constructions in which the same verb 'come' expressed associated motion in combination with non-movement verbs, and deictic directionality in combination with movement verbs, as widely attested in serializing languages.

As regards the lexical origin of *-ul* / *-ʊlɔ*, the only possible connection we are aware of, also evoked by Voisin (this volume), is with the Jóola verb *bɪl* (attested in Jóola Fóoñi as an aspectual auxiliary, but also attested with the lexical meaning 'come' in other Jóola varieties). However, the comparative data are not sufficient to exclude that the phonetic resemblance might simply be due to chance. Moreover, the fact that the allomorphy pattern of *-ul* / *-ʊlɔ* is unique in Jóola Fóoñi further complicates the analysis, since it suggests that the two allomorphs of the VEN suffix may have been originally distinct suffixes with distinct functions, one of them being possibly cognate with separative *-ul*. But here again, we are not aware of comparative data that could help us refine this hypothesis. In fact, the only conclusion that can be drawn from a precise description of the allomorphy pattern of *-ul* / *-ʊlɔ* is that it casts serious doubts on the very possibility of a straightforward etymological analysis of this marker, and rather supports the cautious stance adopted by Voisin (this volume) in her discussion of the possible origin of the associated motion and deictic directional markers found in Atlantic languages.

Abbreviations

ANA	anaphoric determiner	NEG	negation
CPL	completive	NN	number-neutral nominal prefix[21]
ACT	actualizer[20]	NONDUM	suffix whose addition to the negative suffix -ʊt expressses the meaning 'not yet'
CAUS	causative		
CL	class		
CSC	consecutive	OBLG	obligative
D	definite	PASS	passive
DEM	demonstrative	PL	plural
DIR	directive	POSS	possessive
DIST	distal	POT	potential
DISTR	distributive	PPF	pre-prefix[22]
EP	epenthetic vowel	PR	proximal
FUT	future	PREP	preposition
GEN	genitive	PRO	pronoun
HYP	hypothetical	PROH	prohibitive
I	index (other than subject index, cf. sI)	PTCP	participle
		RDPL	reduplicative affix
ICPL	incompletive	REL	relativizer
INCL	inclusive	SEQ	sequential
INDEF	indefinite	SG	singular
INF	infinitive	sI	subject index
INT	intensive	VEN	ventive
LOC	locative		

Acknowledgements: We are very grateful to Boubacar Sambou for his help in analyzing the examples, and to Françoise Rose, Tania Nikitina, Sylvie Voisin, and the editors of the volume, for their insightful comments and suggestions which helped improve the final version of our chapter.

---

[20] Actualizers are suffixes found in relative verb forms that characterize the event to which the relative verb form refers as irrealis, realis, or having a close relationship with the time of utterance.
[21] We use this gloss for nominal prefixes only found with nouns that do not have distinct singular and plural forms.
[22] The morpheme designated here as 'pre-prefix' precedes some subject indexes in some tenses. One of its functions is that fulfilled by the sequential marker *di* in combination with the other subject indexes, but it also occurs in contexts in which the verb forms including the other subject indexes show no particular marking.

Appendix

The 20 most frequent verbs attested in the corpus in combination with the VEN marker

The number in the left column indicates for each verb the total number of occurrences in combination with the VEN marker. Taken together, these 20 verbs represent 80% of the 1,689 occurrences of the VEN marker included in the corpus.

597	jaw 'go'
135	ŋar 'take'
95	laañ 'return'
91	riiŋ 'arrive'
90	pur 'go out'
44	wɔnk 'call'
35	tɔɔk 'find'
32	jʊk 'see'
32	puren 'bring out'
32	tɛy 'run'
29	baj 'have, get'
21	tɛb 'carry'
21	yitɔ 'stand up'
16	bɔñ 'send'
16	nɔcɛn 'enter'
15	kaan 'make'
15	lıtıcɛn 'learn'
15	walɔ 'go down'
14	ñɛs 'look for'
11	baal 'jump'

References

Belkadi, Aicha. 2015. Associated motion with deictic directionals: A comparative overview. *SOAS Working Papers in Linguistics* 17. 49–76.
Belkadi, Aicha. This volume, chapter 5. Deictic directionality as associated motion: Motion, complex events and event integration in African languages.
Breedveld, Johanna Odilia. 1995. *Form and meaning in Fulfulde: A morphophonological study of Maasinankoore*. Leiden: Research School CNWS.
Guillaume, Antoine. 2006. La catégorie du 'mouvement associé' en cavineña: apport à une typologie de l'encodage du mouvement et de la trajectoire. *Bulletin de la Société Linguistique de Paris* 101(2). 415–436.
Guillaume, Antoine. 2016. Associated motion in South America: Typological and areal perspectives. *Linguistic Typology* 20(1). 81–177.
Hopkins, Bradley L. 1995. *Contribution à une étude de la syntaxe diola-fogny*. Dakar: Société Internationale de Linguistique.
Kawachi, Kazuhiro. This volume, chapter 19. The 'along'-deictic-directional verb suffix complex in Kupsapiny.
Koch, Harold. 1984. The category of 'associated motion' in Kaytej. *Languages in Central Australia* 1. 23–34.
Lovestrand, Joseph & Daniel Ross. This volume, chapter 3. Serial verb constructions and motion semantics.
Rose, Françoise. 2015. Associated motion in Mojeño Trinitario: some typological considerations. *Folia Linguistica* 49(1). 117–158.
Sambou, Pierre-Marie. 1979. *Diola Kaasa Esuulaalur: phonologie, morphophonologie et morphologie*. University of Dakar dissertation.
Sapir, J. David. 1965. *A grammar of Diola-Fogny*. Cambridge: Cambridge University Press.
Sapir, J. David, Bara Goudjabi, Amang Badji, Kalilou Badji & Chérif Afo Coly. 1993. *Dictionnaire Jóola Kujamutay / A Dictionary of Jóola Kujamutay*. Charlottesville: University of Virginia.
Vidal, Alejandra & Doris L. Payne. This volume, chapter 12. Pilagá directionals and the typology of associated motion.
Voisin, Sylvie. 2013. Expression de trajectoire dans quelques langues de la famille atlantique (groupe nord). *Faits de langues* 42. 131–152.
Voisin, Sylvie. This volume, chapter 16. Associated motion and deictic directional in Atlantic languages.
Voisin, Sylvie. Forthcoming. Verbal extensions in Atlantic languages. In Friederike Lüpke (ed.), *The Oxford guide to the Atlantic languages of West Africa*. Oxford: Oxford University Press.
Wilkins, David P. 1991. The semantics, pragmatics and diachronic development of 'associated motion' in Mparntwe Arrernte. *Buffalo Papers in Linguistics* 1. 207–57.
Zubin, David A. & Lynne E. Hewitt. 1995. The deictic center: a theory of deixis in narrative. In J. F. Duchan, G. A. Bruder & L. E. Hewitt (eds.), *Deixis in narrative: A cognitive science perspective*. Hillsdale, NJ: Lawrence Erlbaum. 129–155.

Doris L. Payne
18 The extension of associated motion to direction, aspect and argument structure in Nilotic languages

Abstract: Itive and ventive directionals are common verbal categories in Nilotic (Nilo-Saharan phylum). The systems appear to be relatively old as they extend into the domain of aspect and are lexicalized in certain stems. In their directional use, itive and ventive forms are deictic, specifying orientation or direction relative to a point of reference. With certain lexical root types and contexts, they communicate (especially simultaneous) associated motion. They can manipulate argument structure, for instance creating <AGENT THEME> stems from <AGENT SOURCE> roots. This function is likely a consequence of their associated motion function, as translational movement necessarily entails a THEME that moves. However, a corpus study of Eastern Nilotic Maa (Maasai variety) shows that, modernly, associated motion is much less frequent than directional uses. If AM were the historically earlier function, the directionals have clearly diversified well beyond this.

Keywords: ambulative, applicative, aspect, deictic directional, itive, ventive

1 Introduction

Nilotic is a major but low-level family within the African Nilo-Saharan phylum (Greenberg 1966; Bender 1997; Ehret 2001). Directional verb morphology is common in Nilotic (cf. Mietzner 2009: 168-198). The commonly cited categories are 'ventive' and 'itive'.[1] The languages also have 'dative' ('goal reached, benefactive') and sometimes 'ambulative'[2] verb derivations that are closely involved, either paradigmatically or combinatorily, with the directionals. In this paper I

---

[1] These are variously referred to in the literature as 'centrifugal', 'away', 'thither', and 'andative' for itive; and 'centripetal', 'toward', and 'hither' for ventive (cf. Andersen 1999; Payne 2013; Kawachi, this volume; Rottland 1981). Here I consistently use 'ventive' and 'itive' and adapt the glossing of examples taken from other sources to this norm.
[2] The Southern Nilotic 'ambulative' (Zwarts 2004) is also called 'mobilative' (Mietzner 2016) and 'associated locomotion' (Kießling & Bruckhaus 2017).

Doris L. Payne, University of Oregon, dlpayne@uoregon.edu

https://doi.org/10.1515/9783110692099-018

focus on the ventive and itive categories. These appear to be old and are often phonologically eroded, sometimes surfacing in quite fused stem alternations. They are highly grammaticalized and also are lexicalized in certain stems. Not infrequently they are reported to have aspectual but more rarely temporal functions. In their directional use they are deictic, specifying orientation of a participant or situation in space, or direction or path of a (fictive or non-fictive motion) action relative to a point of reference. In certain pragmatic contexts, and in combination with certain roots, they communicate associated motion (AM). With some roots they may affect argument structure. In part, I will suggest that one of their argument-manipulating functions makes sense if associated motion was an earlier function; but even if so, the directionals have clearly diversified well beyond this. A corpus study shows that AM is not the dominant function in modern use in at least one Eastern Nilotic language (Maasai).

For purposes of this paper, I define a "directional" as a grammatical morpheme that, when added to a verb stem, indicates the orientation (without movement), direction (with or without movement) or path (Talmy 1985) in which a participant of the event or situation is headed, or in which the action of the verb itself is oriented or directed (e.g. 'upward', 'downward', 'inward', 'outward', 'toward/away from the deictic center', 'towards the listener', and other possible directional specifications). On a motion verb, a directional may indicate the orientation or direction of the movement of the AGENT, THEME, or other participant. On a non-motion verb, the interpretation of the (same) directional could be metaphorical and yield aspectual or phasal meanings. In Pingelapese, for instance, directional suffixes on non-motion verbs indicate phasal aspect including onset or competition of a situation (Hattori 2012: 31-33). Aspectual extensions of directionals are observed in several studies in this volume, especially phasal and various kinds of imperfective aspect (note especially the chapters by Otero; Creissels & Bassène; and Kawachi).

For this paper, I follow Koch (1984) and Guillaume (2016: 92-93) in defining an "associated motion" (AM) morpheme as a grammatical element associated with the verb and which, in and of itself, indicates a translational motion event (i.e., displacement in space), relative to the action or situation expressed by the lexical verb. Depending on the specific language, an AM may relate to the subject of the lexical event, or to the object of a lexical event or some other participant (cf. Wilkins 1989: 272). I this paper, I will use A for the most AGENT-like participant of a transitive event, S for the single argument of an intransitive event, and P for the most PATIENT-like participant of a transitive event. Based on a study of 66 South American languages, Guillaume (2016: 99) proposes that AM markers operate on a nominative-accusative basis; that is, the same markers will code AM of both A and S, but different markers will code AM of P. Guillaume (2016: 114) also proposes the implicational hierarchy that if a language has object AM, then it also has subject AM (i.e., **motion of subject > motion of object**). Though Guillaume (2016) does not mention this explicitly, the AM can assign an additional semantic role to a participant in the lexical event. In particular, insofar as a participant is understood to move, that participant must by definition be a semantic THEME of the movement (co-)event (Gruber 1965). Thus, a single participant could carry multiple semantic roles in the clause (e.g. AGENT of a transitive lexical event and also THEME of the movement co-event).

Prior works also discuss the fact that AM systems in at least some Australian and South American languages include information about whether the AM is prior, concurrent, or subsequent to the lexical event. Levinson & Wilkins (2006: 534) and Guillaume (2016: 120) propose the temporal implicational hierarchy (at least for subject AM forms) that if a language has AM morphemes which communicate that translational motion occurs subsequent to the lexical event, then it will likely also have morphemes that communicate concurrent motion; and if a language has AM morphemes which communicate concurrent motion, then it likely also has ones for prior motion (i.e. **prior motion > concurrent motion > subsequent motion**). In his South American sample, Guillaume also notes that some object AM markers communicate both "prior-or-concurrent" meanings (p. 122).

As defined above, a pure directional morpheme would not, in and of itself, communicate motion, and a pure AM morpheme might indicate just the fact of translational motion. However, actual morphemes are rarely so pure and relevant morphemes (or paradigms of morphemes) often conflate motion and direction, or motion and temporal/aspectual meaning, such as 'move away from the deictic center after another event finishes' or 'move toward the listener while performing another event'; or they may express translational motion with non-motion roots but only direction, path, or orientation with translational motion roots. Further, when combined with lexical roots not indicating translational motion, deictic directionals may contribute fictive motion, aspect, or other non-motion meanings (cf. Belkadi 2015 on directional functions in several African languages). What is conflated in any particular morpheme or paradigm is language specific, and the readings of the relevant morphemes may depend heavily on verb class and/or pragmatic context, as discussed on many chapters throughout this volume. Based on language-specific (e.g. Koch 1984; Wilkins 1991) and typological (e.g. Levinson and Wilkins 2006; Guillaume 2016) studies, including papers in this volume, I would venture that morphemes expressing pure associated motion are rare.

Across Nilotic, "(deictic) directional" has generally been used for the ventive and itive opposition, reflecting the fact that these morphemes often indicate some spatial notion involving a reference point (RP) (cf. Kawachi, this volume). At first glance, the term "directional" might be taken to imply that the itive and ventive morphemes, in themselves, lack any movement semantics. This might be inferred from the Maasai (Eastern Nilotic) examples in (1) and the Mabaan (Western Nilotic) examples in (2). The roots *sʊj* 'follow' and *lùul* 'take' themselves imply translational movement, while the itive and ventive morphemes add directionality to the movement relative to a primary or possibly displaced RP.

(1) Maasai (adapted from Tucker & Mpaayei 1955: 127 based on author's field data)
    a. *a-sʊ́j*   b. *a-sʊj-**aá***   c. *a-sʊj-**ʊ́***
       INF.SG-follow   INF.SG-follow-**ITV**   INF.SG-follow-**VEN**
       'to follow sth.'   'to follow sth. away from RP'   'to follow sth. toward rp'

(2) Mabaan (Andersen 1999: 108)
    a. *ʔékkèn bṹʌrŋ lùul-έ*
       3PL   cloth   take-PST.3PL.3
       'They took the cloth.'

    b. *ʔékkèn bṹʌrŋ lùul-ɟ-έ*
       3PL   cloth   take-**ITV**-PST.3PL.3
       'They took the cloth (somewhere).'

    c. *ʔékkèn bṹʌrŋ lùul-l-έ*
       3PL   cloth   take-**VEN**-PST.3PL.3
       'They brought the cloth.'

But since the roots themselves indicate motion, we cannot tell from (1) and (2) whether the ventive and itive do, or do not, have a [+MOTION] meaning component; even if present, it would be camouflaged or masked by the [+MOTION] meaning of the root. Thus, the directionals need to be evaluated against a variety of root or stem types in a variety of contexts.

Such evaluation across Nilotic is complicated by the nature of available studies. The morphological distinctions are attested in all three branches of the family (Southern, Eastern, Western), but they have rarely been systematically examined over a comprehensive range of root types or in corpora. Nevertheless, the state of studies allows us to confidently say that the directionals not only can indicate orientation of a lexically specified movement, but also can add the assertion of a movement event to an otherwise non-movement predicate. Further, there is evidence across branches that directionals have extended into aspect and argument structure domains. In Nilotic languages, their semantic interpretation appears to have high sensitivity to verb type as well as sometimes to pragmatic context.

The paper is structured as follows. Section 2 demonstrates the existence of deictic directionals in each branch of the family, based on representative languages. Section 3 discusses directional but non-motion (or less clearly motion) uses of the morphology. Section 4 documents their AM function. Section 5 considers argument-manipulating functions, and suggests that some of these uses may extend from the AM function. Section 6 addresses extension of the deictic directionals into the aspectual domain (though more detailed language-specific studies are merited). For completeness, Section 7 briefly observes lexicalization of directionals into certain stems. Section 8 presents a corpus-based case study of deictic directionals in Maasai (Eastern Nilotic), concluding that AM is not the dominant function at this point in time (the appendix tables show the meaning contribution of the directionals with specific lexical roots). Section 9 briefly concludes the paper.

2 Nilotic directional morphology

The Nilotic family has Western, Southern, and Eastern branches. Southern and Eastern Nilotic verbs are generally agglutinative with some fusional tendencies, including tone morphology. Southern Nilotic verbs generally have two morpheme slots relevant to the directional/associated motion domain, while Eastern Nilotic languages appear to have a single slot. Western Nilotic verbs are quite fusional and directional oppositions are indicated by stem-internal alternations and tone. I do not comprehensively address details of directional allomorphs–which are considerable– in the various languages; interested readers are referred to the cited sources.

2.1 Western Nilotic

Figure 1 presents a simplified Western Nilotic family tree, listing languages mentioned in this paper plus a few additional well-known ones. Subfamilies are indicated in capital letters.

Ventive and itive oppositions are found in both Dinka-Nuer and Luo-Burun branches; cf. Andersen (1992-1994) on Agar Dinka and Crazzolara (1933: 73-174) on Nuer; Reh (1996) on Anywa; Storch (2014: 128-129) on Luwo; Andersen (1988) on Päri; and Remijsen, Miller-Naudé & Gilley (2016) on Shilluk; Noonan (1992: 99-100) on Lango; and Andersen (1999) on Mabaan. Vowel and consonant variation, gemination, syllable length, and tonal alternations are involved in expression of Western Nilotic directional oppositions, depending on phonological shape of the lexical root and other interacting morphological categories (antipassive, benefactive, etc.).

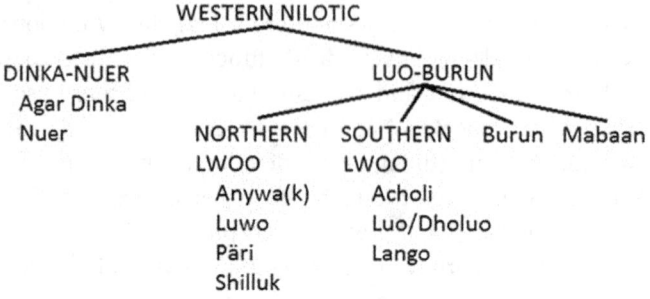

Figure 1: Western Nilotic (simplified).

In at least Northern Lwoo languages, directional forms may interact with stem transitivity. For Päri, Andersen (1988) states that transitive itive stems may have either +ATR or -ATR vowel quality depending on ATR value of the root, while intransitive itives are always +ATR. Ventive stems are always +ATR. Reh (1996) discusses similarities in Anywa. Remijsen, Miller-Naudé & Gilley (2016: 218-219) describe the Shilluk past tense ventive stems as involving a +ATR stem vowel along with possible increase in vowel height; while itive stems alternate between -ATR and +ATR depending on ATR of the root. In the Shilluk imperfective, just tone may mark the difference between a non-directional stem and its itive counterpart, depending on verb class. Northern Lwoo directional stems also display certain root-final consonant changes. Compare the Päri forms of 'dance' in (3), 'climb' in (4), and 'cut' in (5). Notice that the ventive in (4b) involves nasalization, while the same morphological category in (5b) involves voicing. Andersen claims that simple stems are inherently itive semantically, as in (4a); or–we might suggest–sometimes neutral based on data like (3a). In contrast, ventive stems are necessarily derived.

(3) Päri (Andersen 1988: 80)
    a. *dháagɔ̀ mìɛt̂*
       woman dance
       'The woman is dancing.'

    b. *dháagɔ̀ mìɛnd̂-ɔ̀*
       woman dance:**ITV**-INTR
       'The woman is going to dance.'

(4) Päri (Andersen 1988: 109)
    a. *á-ʔídȟ-ɔ̀*
       CPL-climb-INTR
       'He climbed (that way).'

b. á-ʔínnh̀-ò
CPL-climb:**VEN**-INTR
'He climbed (this way).'

(5) Päri (Andersen 1988: 87-88)
a. yàath á-ŋɔ̀t ùbúrr-ì
tree CPL-cut Ubur-ERG
'Ubur cut the tree.'

b. yàath á-ŋúɗ-ì ùbúrr-ì
tree CPL-cut:**VEN**-SUF Ubur-ERG
'Ubur cut the tree (this way).'

The Dinka-Nuer branch also displays complex stem-internal changes in vowel length, voice quality, and tone (Crazzolara 1933; Andersen 1992-1994) relative to directional forms. For Nuer, Crazzolara (1933: 173-174) shows some lexical motion stems with final nasals for direction toward the point of reference, versus non-nasals otherwise.

2.2 Southern Nilotic

Rottland (1981) distinguishes two branches within Southern Nilotic. Figure 2 shows the relationships of Southern Nilotic varieties mentioned in this paper plus a few additional ones. Rottland often refers to "common Datooga," but research shows that there are multiple Datooga varieties or languages (cf. Griscom 2019). There are also multiple Kalenjin varieties, some of which form dialect chains.

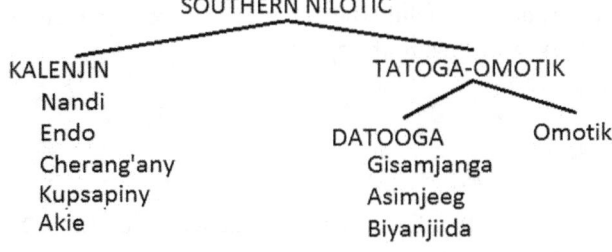

Figure 2: Southern Nilotic languages (simplified).

Examples in various sources demonstrate the existence of directionals across multiple Kalenjin varieties including Endo (Zwarts 2004), Kupsapiny (Kawachi

2011 and this volume), Cherang'any (Mietzner 2016), Nandi (Creider 2002), Akie (König, Heine and Legère 2015); Mietzner (2009) gives examples from several Kalenjin varieties. They also occur in Gisamjanga Datooga (Kießling and Bruckhaus 2017) and Asimjeeg Datooga (Griscom 2019).

Southern Nilotic languages have what is variously called an 'ambulative' (Zwarts 2004), 'mobilitive' (Mietzner 2016), 'along' (Kawachi, this volume), 'associated locomotion' (Kießling & Bruckhaus 2017), and 'associated motion' (Griscom 2019) morphological form, which is conceptually distinct from the directionals. Ventive and itive directionals can occur independently of the ambulative, but the ambulative cannot occur without a directional. For instance, Zwarts (2004) presents the Endo forms in (6).[3]

(6) Endo (Zwarts 2004: 122)
    Ventive   -u, -uun
    Itive   -ta, -taar
    Ambulative with ventive   -aanu
    Ambulative with itive   -aata

Nandi has a +ATR ventive -u and an itive -ta (Creider & Creider 1989: 86-88). The itive has various allomorphs, some of which are strictly tonal or strictly involve ATR variation. There are also the ambulative+ventive -aan and the ambulative+itive -aat (p. 89). The Cherang'any ventive is described as changing its ATR value if there is a contiguous morpheme with a +ATR vowel (Mietzner 2016: 59); this suggests the Cherang'any ventive may be underlyingly -ATR. Kupsapiny has forms clearly cognate to other Southern Nilotic ventive, itive, and ambulative combinations (Kawachi, this volume).

After considering both Datooga and Kalenjin varieties, Rottland (1981: 14) asserts that the simple Southern Nilotic directional morphemes indicate "direction away from and toward the speaker," while the ambulative+directional combinations involve "movement away or toward the speaker."

2.3 Eastern Nilotic

Figure 3 shows the genetic relationship of Eastern Nilotic language varieties discussed in this paper, plus some others. Dimmendaal (1983: 2) says that, with the

---

[3] Endo also has also innovative movement verb prefixes based on verbs for 'come' and 'go'.

exception of Teso, the Teso-Turkana varieties are mutually intelligible. Similarly, there are dialect-continua relationships among the Maa varieties.[4]

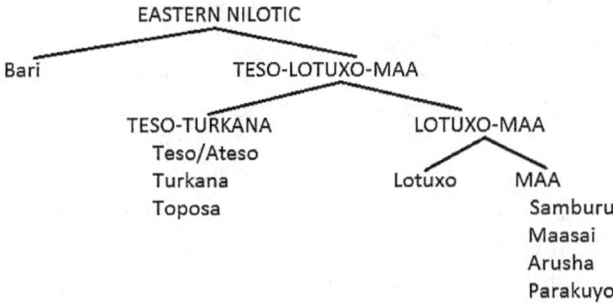

Figure 3: Eastern Nilotic languages (simplified).

Regarding directionals, Spangolo (1933: 143-144, 153-154) states that Bari *-un* indicates "linear movement out from some place toward the principal person concerned" (p. 143), and that *-VrV?* indicates "motion away from speaker or central point in no particular direction, scattering movement" (p. 146). Each has various allomorphs.

The Turkana ventive is *-ʊnị* and the itive is *-arị*, each with allomorphs (Dimmendaal 1983: 109-113). Dimmendaal suggests that the final vowel in each morpheme is historically a voice marker but that synchronically it is fused with the directionals. For Toposa, examples like (7) show an itive *-ar* (allomorph *-or*) and a ventive *-un* (or perhaps *-ʊn*) (Schroeder 1999).

(7) Toposa (Schroeder 1999; parsing and glossing mine)
    a. *nya-ar-**ar***
       GERUND-kill-**ITV**
       'kill(ing) and take(ing)'

    b. *nya-ar-**un***
       GERUND-kill-**VEN**
       'kill(ing) and bring(ing)'

Maasai directionals are illustrated in (1) above, but additional data show the ventive has allomorphs ending in /n/, and the itive has allomorphs with /ɾ/ (Payne 2012, 2013).

---

[4] Maa varieties form a dialect continuum. In this paper, I use the term "Maasai" to refer to the general variety spoken in southern Kenya and northern Tanzania but not including Arusha Maa.

2.4 Proto-Nilotic directionals

There is strong evidence that the Eastern Nilotic ventive was something like *-ʊn, and that the itive was something like *-ar or *-ara. For Southern Nilotic, Rottland (1981:13) reconstructs two itives (which he calls "andative") *-ta and *-a:ta, and two ventives *-u/*-nu and *-ɜ:nu; in each case, the longer forms contain the ambulative which he reconstructs as *-a:. Adding to Rottland's reconstructions, we note that the r-final allomorph of the itive in Endo (6) parallels Eastern Nilotic itive allomorphs. For Western Nilotic, both Andersen (1988: 105-106) and Reh (1996: 258) suggest that the directional stem alternations reflect historical suffix elements which can be reconstructed to Proto-Western Nilotic, if not to proto-Nilotic. The Western Nilotic details are complex and inter-twined with transitivity, but Reh (1996: 232, 248) suggests that the Proto-Western Nilotic benefactive, which may be related to one ventive form, had the form $*/\text{-}\hat{V}N/ \sim */N\hat{V}/$. Reh (1996: 252-244) suggests that one Western Nilotic bivalent itive morpheme reconstructs as $*/\text{-}\hat{V}_{[\text{-breathy}]}/$ while another form likely involved a consonant. In sum, allomorphs of ventive forms in all three branches involve a nasal (plus a high back rounded vowel in Eastern and Southern Nilotic), and (allomorphs of) itives in Southern and Eastern Nilotic involve oral coronal consonants, and various consonant, tone, and stem alternations in Western Nilotic. Table 1 summarizes the proposed reconstructions.

Table 1: Proposed reconstructions of Nilotic directionals.

	Eastern Nilotic	Southern Nilotic	Western Nilotic
VENTIVE	*-ʊn	*-u ~ *-nu	$*\text{-}\hat{V}N \sim *\text{-}N\hat{V}$
ITIVE	*-ar(a)	*-ta	$*\text{-}\hat{V}_{[\text{-breathy}]}$ / -C

Altogether, it seems clear that Proto-Nilotic had ventive and itive morphemes. The next sections consider the functional range of these morphemes in daughter languages. Wide attestation of both direction and AM functions, scattered across examples from various languages, suggests that directed AM was almost certainly a function in Proto-Nilotic, if not the dominant function of the ventive and itive. In Section 8, however, we will see that AM is not necessarily the dominant modern function in all daughter languages.

3 Directional non-motion function

We first demonstrate that Nilotic directional morphology can convey (deictic) orientation without motion. This surfaces when the directionals combine with lexical roots that in themselves convey translational motion; such instances do not meet Guillaume's (2016) definition of (a separate) "associated motion."[5] For instance, in (8a) from Päri (Western Nilotic), the root *bàac* means 'throw sth. (away from the reference point)', while the ventive derivation in (8b) specifies that the moving P is directed toward the reference point. The Mabaan root *lùul* 'take' in (2) above itself implies movement of A and P; the directional forms in (2b-c) give explicit information about direction of the movement.

(8) Päri (Andersen 1988: 90)
    a. *á-bàac*   *cícù̀-ê*
        CPL-throw   man-ERG
        'The man threw it (that way).'

    b. *á-bʌʌy*   *cícù̀-ê*
        CPL-throw:**VEN**   man-ERG
        'The man threw it (this way).'

Eastern Nilotic directionals likewise can add direction to lexical movement verbs. Observe (9) and (10) from Bari and Ateso.

(9) Bari (Spagnolo 1933: 144)
    a. *gʊm*
        'to throw'

    b. *gʊbara'*
        'to throw away' (**ITV**)

(10) Ateso (Barasa 2017: 125)
      à-dòl-ʊ̀n
      INF-arrive-**VEN**
      'to arrive (near the speaker)'

In Maasai (and Maa generally), *puon/pon* indicates 'go (plural)', while the ventive form in (11) specifies direction of the S participant (here, the colonial British) toward the reference point (East Africa).

---

[5] We noted earlier, however, that if the directionals in themselves include a [+MOTION] meaning, this could be masked when combined with lexical translational motion roots.

(11) Maasai
 peê   e-pon-**ú**   ɪl=áshʊmpá
 when   TEMP.3-go-**VEN**   M.PL=white.people.NOM
 'when the whites came ...' (aibartisho.033b)

For Southern Nilotic, Mietzner (2016) shows similar examples of directionals (without the 'ambulative') involving lexical roots like 'run', 'climb', 'go', etc. König et al. (2015: 52) state that in Akie the simple itive -*ta* is not productive, but is "commonly found as an obligatory or optional suffix" on verbs that lexically imply motion away, such as *lu-ta* 'push off accidentally', *tɔr-ta* 'push away', and *tii-ta* 'take along'. An Akie simple ventive -*ʊ(n)* is also no longer productive, but is parsable based on pairs like *kuur* 'call' versus *kurr-u* 'call here', and *amúti* 'I take sth. somewhere' versus *amútu* 'I bring sth. here' (p. 59).

We have just illustrated the directionals with translational motion roots. Even with non-translational motion and non-motion roots, they often do not add movement. Consider the following Southern Nilotic examples. While the root *tùk* in (12) does express a kind of rotational movement, the itive on *tùk* 'turn around' suggests orientation facing away from the first-person point of reference more than translational motion. In (13), if anything is "moving", it is the aroma of the ugali, not the ugali itself nor the person experiencing the smell. Sometimes one might argue there is fictive (metaphorical) motion, but bleaching of movement semantics has sometimes progressed so far that it is hard to make a case for even much fictive motion.

(12) Cherang'any (Mietzner (2016: 138))
 kí-ŋgù=cʌ́s-ɔ́   wàlákê   kú-tùk-tʌ́-c-eec   pátái
 PST3-COND=become.tired-CON   others   3-turn.round-**ITV**-APPL-DO1   back
 ák=kù-wék-**tà**-kéy   káà
 and=3-return-**ITV**-REFL home
 'When others got fatigued, they turned their back on us and went back home.'

(13) Cherang'any (Mietzner (2016: 137))
 í-ŋù-**tʌ**-i   iɲè   kímɲeet   ak   ŋwéék
 2SG-smell-**ITV**-IMPF 2sg   ugali   with   vegetable
 'Can you smell the ugali with vegetable?'

Spagnolo (1933) says the Eastern Nilotic Bari ventive indicates "linear movement out from some place toward the principal person concerned". The idea "out of" is often extended in various Nilotic languages to items metaphorically emerging from metaphorical spaces. This must be the basis for using the ventive to derive 'discover' from the root 'cover' in Turkana, and likely also 'remember' from the root 'think', as shown in (14).

(14) Turkana (Dimmendaal 1983: 110)
    a-rap-ʊ̀nɪ   'to discover'
    INF-cover-VEN
    a-tam-ʊ̀nɪ   'to remember'
    INF-think-VEN

On the other hand, use of the Turkana itive to derive 'think out loud' from 'think', as in (15), may be based on a distributive semantic extension of the itive (Section 6). How it comes to derive 'hear' from 'test' is more opaque, though a sound that is heard must be distributed out away from its source.

(15) Turkana (Dimmendaal 1983: 111)
    a-tam-àrɪ   'to think out loud'
    INF-think-ITV
    ak-ɪɪr-àrɪ   'to hear'
    INF-test-ITV

In Maasai, many instances of the directionals with non-motion roots (or senses thereof) contribute orientation without motion (or at best only fictive motion). A few examples follow.

(16) Maasai
    n-é-íbʊŋ-ɪ   *ɛnk=áíná*   *áa-yiat-**aa***
    CN1-3-hold-PASS   F.SG=arm   INF.PL-stretch-**ITV**
    'The hand is held to stretch them (fingers).' (speaking of treatment for a polio victim) (embul.015)

(17) Maasai
    *tá-wal-**ʊ́***   *ɛn=kʊ́tʊ́k*
    IMP.SG-exchange-**VEN**   F.SG=mouth
    'Translate (interpret) the language.'

(18) Maasai
    *k=é-íto-dól-ˈ**ú**-á*   *a-jó*   *il=ówúárâk*
    CN2-3-CAUS-see-**VEN**-PF   INF.SG-say   M.PL=beast.of.prey
    'It has shown that (they are) beasts.' (Iloikop.125)

Although sometimes one might argue there is a kind of metaphorical fictive motion, I have generally not considered these as AM. In the corpus study (Section 8) I count instances of the ventive as in (19) simply as directional, as it does not mean something like 'be fresh and come' or 'be fresh while coming' or even have a sense of freshness traveling over some distance.

(19) Maasai
 peê e-rropil-ú   ɛn=adúóó   âŋ   ényɛ
 so TEMP.3-be.fresh-VEN F.SG=previous home.NOM 3SG.PSR.NOM
 'so that his home is left with/emanates fragrance.' [from roasting meat, when a man dies] (enkeeya1.025)

Having demonstrated that the Nilotic deictic directionals can indicate direction, orientation, or perhaps in some cases figurative motion but without literal translational motion, we now turn to evidence that they can also express AM.

4 Associated motion function

There is evidence that, in all three branches of Nilotic, directionals can express AM. That is, the directionals are grammaticalized verb morphology (used alone, or in combination with the 'ambulative' in Southern Nilotic) which communicate a translational motion event co-associated with the event or situation expressed by the lexical verb root. This becomes evident when they occur with certain roots that do not normally imply translational motion.[6] For any given language, the available literature often does not allow comprehensive analysis of whether the AM can apply to S, A, P, or A+P arguments of lexical roots (and relative to what verb types), and whether the motion can be prior, simultaneous, and subsequent to the lexical event or situation. However, Table 2 summarizes what we find according to branches of the family. The blank cell for 'prior AM' for Southern Nilotic reflects the fact that such examples were not found in the literature (not that we know 'prior AM' interpretations cannot occur).[7]

---

[6] In this study I have counted roots with manner meanings like 'run', 'climb', 'migrate', etc., as translational motion, whether or not a point of departure or point of arrival is in view.
[7] Even Mietzner (2009), which includes examples showing 'prior motion' for Eastern and Western Nilotic languages, gives Southern Nilotic data demonstrating only simultaneous and subsequent or anticipated motion.

Table 2: Attested AM interpretations in branches of Nilotic.

		Eastern Nilotic	Southern Nilotic (with ambulative)	Western Nilotic
MOVING FIGURE	S	+	+	+
	A	+	+	+
	P	+	+	+
	A+P	+	+	+
TEMPORAL RELATION OF AM TO LEXICAL EVENT	prior	+		+
	simultaneous	+	+	+
	subsequent	+	+	+

Starting with Western Nilotic, Andersen (1999: 107) describes itive and ventive stems in Mabaan as having "directional meaning, indicating motion directed, respectively away from and towards the deictic center." The examples in (20) illustrate the directionals with a non-motion root; (20b) seems to show just directional orientation; while (20c) indicates 'prior' associated motion that applies to both the A and the P of 'tie'.[8]

(20) Mabaan (Andersen 1999: 109)
 a. ʔékkèn ḍiīēŋ wiiên-ɛ́
  3PL cow tie-PST.3PL.3
  'They tied the cow.'

 b. ʔékkèn ḍiīēŋ wiiên-ɟ-ɛ́
  3PL cow tie-ITV-PST.3PL.3
  'They tied the cow (onto something).'

 c. ʔékkèn ḍiīēŋ wiiên-n-ɛ́
  3PL cow tie-VEN-PST.3PL.3
  'They brought the cow and tied it.'

Similar facts hold in Päri. Andersen (1988) states that the ventive and itive stems indicate the action is performed in a direction toward or away from the deictic center, respectively. Comparison of (5a) and (5b) above shows the ventive with a

---

[8] Antoine Guillaume (p.c.) suggests that the pattern in (20c), of prior motion applying to A+P of the lexical event, may be previously unattested. Perhaps more commonly, subsequent motion may apply to both A and P of the lexical event in African languages, as in the Ateso example in (33b) 'buy and then bring', and examples in Belkadi (2015: 61).

directional function rather than a clearly AM one, but (21a) versus (21b) clarifies that at least the Päri itive can contribute prior AM attributed to the derived S (the semantic AGENT) of 'cut'.

(21) Päri (Andersen 1988: 87-88)
    a. *Ùbúr   á-ŋùd-ò*
       Ubur CPL-cut:ANTIP-INTR
       'Ubur cut.'

    b. *Ùbúr   á-ŋùt-o*
       Ubur CPL-cut:**ITV**:ANTIP-INTR
       'Ubur went to cut.'

Available Anywa examples show that on non-motion roots, the ventive and itive derivations can, but need not, express prior AM relevant to A and S arguments, as in (22a-e) (Reh 1996: 249-257; see also Reh 1991). Reh states that the ventive and itive may also be interpreted as just indicating that an action happens at the RP location without a necessary interpretation of associated motion, as seen in (22c-e). On motion roots, the directionals add deictic directionality.

(22) Anywa (Reh 1996: 43, 249, 257)
    a. *cìB-*   'give'   *cìmm-* (**VEN**) 'come and give hither'
    b. *láaJ-*   'urinate'   *láaɲɲ-* (**VEN**) 'come and urinate hither'
    c. *téeD-*   'do cooking'   *téenn-* (**VEN**) 'do cooking here'
    d. *càam-* 'feed sb.'   *cáamV-* (**ITV**) 'go and feed sb. there/feed sb. there'
    e. *bìɪJ-*   'squeeze sth.' *bíɪ-* (**ITV**) 'go and squeeze sth. there/squeeze sth. there'

For Shilluk, (23b) shows that a directional derivation can assert a prior motion event attributable to the A of a transitive lexical root.

(23) Shilluk (Remijsen, Miller-Naudé & Gilley 2016: 209)
    a. *gyèɛɛn-ɔ̀*   *ʊ̀-lôʊʊɲ-ɔ̀*
       chicken-SG IMPF-pluck-IMPF
       'Somebody is plucking the chicken.'

    b. *gyèɛɛn-ɔ̀*   *á-lôʊʊɲ*
       chicken-SG PST-pluck:**ITV**
       'Somebody went away to pluck a chicken.'

Shilluk directional forms can also indicate subsequent or prospective motion, as in (24b) where motion applies to the P argument of 'call'. Remijsen, Miller-Naudé & Gilley (2016: 216) state that reference to the P is characteristic for certain verbs including 'call', 'roll', and 'throw'.

(24) Shilluk (Remijsen, Miller-Naudé & Gilley 2016: 216)
    a. *jí*   *mʌ̂tɔ̀-à*   *ḍɔ́k*   *kàl*
        2SG greet:ANTIP.SG-FOC mouth compound
        'At the entrance to the compound you call out a greeting once,

    b. *ʊ̀*   *jí*   *cwôool*   *kàl*
        CONJ 2SG call:**VEN** compound
        and then they call you to come into the compound.'

For Nuer, Crazzolara (1933: 173) does not provide examples with non-translational-motion roots, yet he states: "The idea of motion, direction 'toward the speaker', or 'away from the speaker' is very often expressed by special forms in Nuer, even when the idea of motion or direction is not obviously included in the verb." His wording suggests that AM is found in at least certain derived stems.

Regarding Southern Nilotic, Kawachi (2011 and this volume) observes that Kupsapiny directionals in combination with the 'ambulative' can add a motion component to an otherwise non-motion event. Creider (2002) discusses two non-directional uses of the Nandi itive *-ta*, but suggests that it generally indicates 'motion away'. Zwarts (2004: 128) states that Endo 'ambulative+directional' combinations convey that the "action of the verb is performed while moving, away from or toward the speaker." In Cherang'any, the 'ambulative+directional' combinations "imply that a motion event takes place during another action" (Mietzner 2016: 139). Simultaneous motion on the part of a transitive A participant is seen in the following examples.

(25) Cherang'any (Mietzner 2016: 139)
    a. *kɔ-síŋíld-ʌ̀ʌ̀**ti***   *cùtɔ*
        PST2-spit-**AMB.ITV** person
        'While going away, the person spit saliva.'

    b. *kɔ-síŋíld-ʌ̀ʌ̀**nu***   *cùtɔ*
        PST2-spit-**AMB.VEN** person
        'While coming, the person spit saliva.'

(26) Cherang'any (Mietzner 2016: 139)
   a. *tíl-ʎʎtí*   *sùùswék*
      cut-**AMB.ITV**   grass
      'S/he cuts the grass while going.'

   b. *tíl-ʎʎnu*   *sùùswék*
      cut-**AMB.VEN**   grass
      'S/he cuts the grass while coming.'

Kießling & Bruckhaus (2017) discuss AM (their "associated locomotion") in Gisamjanga Datooga, based largely on a corpus compiled in the 1930's. They attribute AM to what corresponds to the Kalenjin 'ambulative' element, noting that—as in Kalenjin languages—this must co-occur with the ventive, itive, or a 'terminative' morpheme -*s*.[9] Their discussion and (27) show that the AM can apply to the A of an event, and that motion may be simultaneous to the event. It can also apply to an S, as in (28).

(27) Gisamjanga Datooga (Kießling & Bruckhaus 2017)
   a. *laj-aa-n*
      cut-**AMB-VEN**
      'cut (off) from a patient object while moving hither'

   b. *laj-aa-d*
      cut-**AMB-ITV**
      'cut (off) from a patient object while moving thither'

(28) Gisamjanga Datooga (Kießling & Bruckhaus 2017)
   a. *hiɲ*
      'bend, stoop'

   b. *hiɲ-aa-n*
      bend-**AMB-VEN**
      'move hither in bent position / stooping posture'

   c. *hiɲ-aa-d*
      bend-**AMB-ITV**
      'move thither in bent position / stooping posture'

---

9 This appears similar in function to the Eastern Nilotic 'dative' suffix, which (among other uses) can indicate 'goal reached', as well as 'benefactive/malefactive' senses. The term 'dative' is commonly used for these verb suffixes in Nilotic languages as there is a range of semantic uses.

In (29), AM applies only to the P, with a probably subsequent motion interpretation; but a subsequent temporal reading is infrequent in the available Southern Nilotic data. In (30), the AM applies to A and P together, per the authors.

(29) Gisamjanga Datooga (Kießling & Bruckhaus 2017)
 ákʰì-nùŋw-**àa-d**-í
 SEQ.2SG-allow-**AMB-ITV**-INFLECTION
 'So you may let them go away!'

(30) Gisamjanga Datooga (Kießling & Bruckhaus 2017)
 gàj-ée-ŋòɲ-**àa-d-a**
 FUT-3PL-catch-**AMB-ITV**-INFLECTION
 'They will catch them on the run.' (both A and P of 'catch' are moving)

For Eastern Nilotic, data on Bari directionals is sparse, but Spangolo (1933: 144, 153-154) gives translations of complex verb forms which suggest that AM is a reading of some directional stems, as in (31). In (32), addition of the ITV directional enforces the meaning that the spear moves (i.e. is thrown or somehow 'stabbing' occurs some distance away).

(31) Bari (Spagnolo 1933: 147; parsing and glossing mine)
 a. nan a-mɛt-**undya** Wani
  1SG 1SG-see-**VEN** Wani
  'I watched Wani coming.'

 b. nan a-mɛt-**ara'** Wani
  1SG 1SG-see-**ITV** Wani
  'I watched Wani go away.'

(32) Bari (Spagnolo 1933: 144)
 a. rem
  'to stab'

 b. rem-**orö**
  'to throw the spear' (**ITV**)
  (i.e. 'to stab by instrument moving away/to stab at a distance')

Some examples in Barasa (2017) suggest the Ateso ventive may communicate prior (33a) or subsequent (33b) AM. The translation of (33b) suggests the AM might apply to both the A and P of 'buy'.

(33) Ateso (Barasa 2017: 125)
    a. *à-kám-**ʊ̀n***
       INF-catch-**VEN**
       'to catch something thrown to the speaker' (i.e. THEME moves and then is caught)

    b. *à-gwêl-**ʊ̀n***
       INF-buy-**VEN**
       'to buy and bring to the speaker' (i.e. THEME is bought and then moves together with AGENT)

In (34) and (35) from Maasai, the roots *wal* 'exchange, change (e.g. colors)' and *ŋɪd* 'be proud' do not imply translational motion. Adding the itive creates translational movement events, in these instances simultaneous to changing colors and being proud. In (34) and (35), the motion applies to an intransitive S. In contrast, the discourse context of (36) suggests the motion may apply to just the P of 'beat', though in another context the same verb form could imply that both A and P are moving.[10] In (37) it applies to the A of 'attack', and the discourse context for (38) makes clear that the motion applies to both A and P of 'drive'.

(34) Maasai
    ɛ-gíra   ŋóto tankí   a-wal-***ar**-í*
    3-PROG   chameleon.NOM   INF.SG-exchange-**ITV**-MID
    'The chameleon is changing (colors) while moving away.'

(35) Maasai
    *ɛ-tɪ-ŋɪd-**á**-ítie*
    3-PF-be.proud-**ITV**-PF.PL
    'They were proud while going.'

(36) Maasai
    *n-ɛ́-ar-**áa**   ɛn=apá   tásat   ɛnyɛ́   bótór*
    CN1-3-beat-**ITV**   F.SG=prior   old   3SG.PSR   senior
    'He beat away/chased away his older senior wife.' (divorce 002)

---

10 In the story from which (36) comes, the senior wife departs while the man stays with the family and marries a younger woman. Thus, it is clear that the P moves, but less clear that the A (i.e. the man) also moves away.

(37) Maasai
pá⁺á   kán⁺ú   í-rás-ʊ́
then   when   2-attack-VEN
'Then when are you coming to attack (us)?' (ologol 058)

(38) Maasai
n-é-ósh-ú   aké
CN1-3-hit-VEN   just
'He drove them [animals].' (ilmurran.112a)

The pair in (39) from Arusha Maa involves the root *rriny* 'return something' which, in itself, implies translational motion of a P. Adding a directional can profile movement of an additional participant, thus effectively adding AM to an already (lexical) translational motion event. Note that in (39a) without a directional, only the P (the item returned) necessarily undergoes movement. In contrast, (39b) carries the itive and the speaker insisted that now both the A and the P would be moving. The data in (40) from Maasai, with the ditransitive root *pɪk* 'put', shows a similar difference.

(39) Arusha Maa
   a. á-rríny
      1SG-return.sth
      'I will return it back.' (I may or may not go with it.)

   b. á-rríny-óo
      1SG-return.sth-ITV
      'I will return it back (and I am going along with it).'

(40) Maasai
   a. á-pík   ɪl=ɔshɔ́   ɪl=álɛta
      1SG-put   M.PL=calves M.PL=pens
      'I will put the calves into pens.' (I may or may not move as I do so.)

   b. á-pík-áa   ɪl=ɔshɔ́   ɪl=álɛta
      1SG-put-ITV M.PL=calves M.PL=pens
      'I will move putting calves into pens.'

Section 8 below presents a corpus study on what roles are targeted by the Maasai directionals in AM functions, and on prior, simultaneous, and subsequent movement semantics. We will see that interpretations of simultaneous AM applying to the P of a transitive event are dominant in discourse.

5 Argument manipulation

Nilotic directionals can manipulate argument structure. There are two attested patterns: valence decreasing/increasing, and semantic role manipulation with no valence change.

5.1 Valence changing

In a (very) few reported instances, a directional appears to affect syntactic valence. This may be restricted to certain roots, and how robust it is across the family is unknown. In Gisamjanga Datooga, the ambulative+directionals can suppress a transitive P (Kießling & Bruckhaus 2017); compare the transitive forms in (41a, c) with the intransitives in (41b, e).

(41) Datooga (Kießling & Bruckhaus 2017)
    a. *duul-**un*** 'take hither several items grouped as a bundle' (ventive)

    b. *duul-**aa-n*** 'come in a single group, move hither in unification' (ambulative+ventive)

    c. *duul-**d*** 'take thither several items grouped as a bundle' (itive)

    d. *duul-**aa-d*** 'go there in a single group, move thither in unification' (ambulative+itive)

In Akie, the ventive without the ambulative can decrease valence. In (42a), the root *kas* 'hear' is transitive. The ventive is added in (42b). According to König et al. (2015: 59), if the item heard were to occur as an overt noun in (42b), it would be in the nominative case rather than the accusative, proving the intransitive nature of (42b).

(42) Akie (König et al. 2015: 59; my glossing)
    a. *a-kas-e*
       1SG-hear-IMPF
       'I hear it.'

    b. *a-kas-**ʊ***
       1SG-hear-VEN
       'I can be heard.'

In Maa, detransitivization via a directional is idiosyncratic to a very few roots. I illustrate just with the transitive root *man* 'surround'. First, in (43) *man* carries no directional and the scene involves static arrangement of dew around a kraal. 'Kraal' in (43) is the P of *man*. In (44) the relative clause 'that houses surround like a circle' is headed by *nk=anasâ* 'large village', which is the gapped P of the relative clause verb *man* (the relevant part of the sentence is bracketed and elements are labeled for clarity). The itive on *man* metaphorically signals the configuration of houses going (extending) around a central cattle pen but does not change transitivity: both with and without the directional, these examples use *man* with two arguments.

(43) Samburu Maa
n=kɛɛ́ya   pôs   n-á-mân   nk=áŋ   [sílíbít]
F.SG=disease blue   REL.F-F.SG.REL-surround F.SG=kraal   [dew]
'A blue sickness that surrounds the kraal' [Answer: 'dew'] (Samburu riddles.106)

(44) Maasai
                              [P
ém-i-yiolólo   iyíóók,   ɪl=mʊ́rran   l-ɛ́   nk=anasâ
NEG-2-know.2PL   us   MPL=warriors   M.PSD-FSG.PSR   FSG=large.village
V   A   ADJUNCT   ]
ɔ́ɔ́-man-**áa**   ɪnk=ajijík   ánaa   o=lekelél
M.PL.REL-surround-**ITV**   F.PL=houses.NOM   like   M.SG=circle
'You do not know us, the warriors of a big village that houses surround like a circle?' (enkijuka.002)

Transitive *man* can have a (non-)translational movement sense, as in (45) with the progressive.

(45) Kisonko Maa (author's field data)
á-mán-ɨ́ta   ol=órika
1SG-encircle-PROG   M.SG=chair
'I am going around/encircling the chair.'

In (46) and (47), a movement sense also occurs when the directionals are added. But as (47) shows, *man*+itive may mean 'rotation' in a single spot (i.e. there is no translational locomotion away from a deictic center), which is similar to the sense in (45) and possibly also in (48). Note that with the directionals in (46)–(48), the locations are in oblique phrases, unlike the locations in (44)–(45). In fact, (46)–(48) are ungrammatical with direct objects.

(46) Maasai
 óre   ɛ-man-ʊ́   tɛ   nde ...
 DSCN   TEMP.3-surround-VEN   OBL   there.NOM
 'as they come around at that place, ...' (Iloikop2.0039)

(47) Maasai
 á-mán-áa   to   l=óríkꜜá
 1SG-go.around-ITV   OBL   M.SG=chair.NOM
 'I am revolving on/above the chair.'

(48) Maasai
 n-ɛ́-man-áa,   n-ɛ́-man-áa,   tɔ   l=cháni
 CN1-3-surround-ITV   CN1-3-surround-ITV   OBL   M.SG=tree.NOM
 'They went round, they went round, under the tree.' (arinkoi.052)

Thus, while simultaneously allowing a transitive use, as in (44), it appears the directionals may optionally decrease the syntactic valence of *man*. Why should this be? If the deictic directionals are (historically) translational motion morphemes, by definition they would entail–and even give enhanced profiling to–a THEME undergoing movement. The enhanced profiling of one participant perhaps has the consequence of semantically deprofiling another to such an extent that the argument is also syntactically deprofiled; i.e. the stem has reduced valence. However, it is quite rare for directionals to decrease valence.

Shilluk is perhaps the only Nilotic language for which directionals are so-far claimed to sometimes increase valence. Remijsen, Miller-Naudé & Gilley (2016: 216-217) observe that when a Shilluk directional expresses spatial deixis, the destination of an AM can be overt, as in (49). The authors characterize the overt destination as an "internal argument" and hence argue that the derivation is valence-increasing. This would appear to be an applicative-like function.

(49) Shilluk (Remijsen, Miller-Naudé & Gilley 2016: 216)
 dɛ̄ɛŋ   mɔ̀ɔk   á-cǎaam-ɛ́   gɔ́l-ɛ̄
 Deng   kind.of.fish   PST-eat:ITV-3SG   compound-3SG
 'As for Deng, he went to eat the fish in his compound.'

5.2 Semantic role manipulation

Nilotic directionals can change the argument structure of transitive roots without manipulating valence. Two types of situations are found in the literature.

First, deictic directionals can operate on <AGENT SOURCE> roots, and in some languages also <AGENT GOAL> roots, to derive <AGENT THEME> stems. This argument manipulation makes sense if the directionals have (or historically had) their source in old translational motion roots or AM morphemes. Translational motion, by definition, implies there is a THEME that moves (Gruber 1965; Jackendoff 1972: 39). Though not valence increasing, effecting a change from <AGENT SOURCE>, or <AGENT GOAL>, to an <AGENT THEME> argument frame makes this function of directionals somewhat applicative-like. The Agar Dinka examples in (50) demonstrate with an <AGENT GOAL> root. In (50a) 'bird' is the GOAL object, but in (50b, c,) 'stone' is the moving THEME object.

(50) Agar Dinka (Andersen 1992-1994: 10)
    a.   d̪ɔ̂ɔk   à̰-bò̰k   d́ít
        boy   D-throw bird
        'The boy is throwing at the bird.'[11]

    b.   d̪ɔ̂ɔk   à̰-bò̰ok   doò̰ot
        boy   D-throw:ITV stone
        'The boy is throwing a stone thither.'

    c.   d̪ɔ̂ɔk   à̰-bò̰ok   doò̰ot
        boy   D-throw:VEN stone
        'The boy is throwing a stone hither.'

In (51a), one might initially suppose the argument structure of ɲìa̰c 'squeeze, wring' is <AGENT PATIENT> (or perhaps <AGENT THEME>), but it may be best analyzed as <AGENT SOURCE> as it is not clear there is a change of state (certainly not of location) for the cloth. By contrast, with the directional stems in (51b-c), the water moves from being in the cloth to being outside of it and hence is the THEME. 'Cloth' is no longer part of the syntactic structure.

(51) Agar Dinka (Andersen 1992-1994: 10)
    a.   tìik   à̰-ɲìa̰c   à̰lâ̰a̰t
        woman D-squeeze cloth
        'The woman is wringing the cloth.'

    b.   tìik   à̰-ɲìɛ̰ɛc   pîiw
        woman D-squeeze:ITV water
        'The woman is squeezing out water thither.'

---

[11] The English free translations here and in (54a) are intended to reflect the argument structure of the Dinka verb, even if they are somewhat unnatural-sounding English.

    c. *ṭik   à-ṇi̤ẹec   p̤îiw*
       woman D-squeeze:**VEN** water
       'The woman is squeezing water out hither.'

The Mabaan examples in (52) are similar.

(52) Mabaan (Andersen 1999: 109)
    a. *Ɂékkèn   Ɂʌ̃n   wiiêj-ɛ́*
       3PL   house sweep-PST.3PL.3
       'They swept the house.'

    b. *Ɂékkèn   jĩik-én   wiiêc-ɛ́*
       3PL   rubbish-PL sweep:**ITV**-PST.3PL.3
       'They swept the rubbish (into something).'

    c. *Ɂékkèn   jĩik-én   wêɛw-w-ɛ́*
       3PL   rubbish-PL sweep-**VEN**-PST.3PL.3
       'They swept the rubbish hither.'

In Eastern Nilotic Maasai, directionals also change <AGENT SOURCE> roots to become <AGENT THEME> stems, as in (53). Basic <AGENT GOAL> roots are not known to be affected.

(53) Maasai
    a. *á-púrr-íto   ol=dúka*
       1SG-rob-PROG M.SG=shop
       'I am stealing from the shop/robbing the shop.'

    b. *n-é-purr-**óo**   ɔl=áyíóní   il=mósorr*
       CN1-3-rob-**ITV** M.SG=boy.NOM M.PL=eggs
       'The boy stole eggs.' (He probably went away with them).

    c. *á-púrr-**ú**   ɛnk=alámu   tɔ   l=dúkâ*
       1SG-rob-**VEN** F.SG=pen OBL M.SG=shop.NOM
       'I will steal a pen from the market.'

In Southern Nilotic Nandi, the simple itive (without the ambulative) has a similar argument-manipulating function with some verbs (Creider 2002). In (54a), 'throw' has an <AGENT GOAL> frame, while the itive stem in (54b) has an <AGENT THEME> frame.

(54) Nandi (Creider 2002: 184)
 a. *ke:-wi:r   sè:sé:t*
    INF-throw.at   dog
    'to throw at the dog'

 b. *ke:-wi:r-tá   koytà*
    INF-throw.at-ITV stone
    'to throw the stone thither'

Creider (2002) also discusses what he analyzes as a second 'comitative' -*ta*. The comitative argument must be inanimate and, interestingly, can only be a CO-THEME, i.e. a participant 'associated with' a THEME (not CO-AGENT). In (55) and (56b) the 'comitative' -*ta* appears to increase valence and/or manipulate the semantic role of the object, like an applicative.[12] Creider suggests that conflation of formerly separate 'itive' and 'comitative' suffixes must have happened because (in his view) the uses are "unrelated" (p. 147). However, it is conceivable that the itive is added so that a second moving argument (i.e. CO-THEME) can occur; that is, the source for (56b) might have been 'grasp the pot while/by moving the cloth'.

(55) Nandi (Creider 2002: 147)
    ke:-ru-ta   ínkoráî:k
    INF-sleep-ITV   clothes
    'to sleep with clothes on'

(56) Nandi (Creider 2002: 147)
 a. *nám   la:kwé:t*
    grasp   child
    'Catch the child!'

 b. *nam-té: sapúryé:t ínkoryê:t si   ma-pé:l-în*
    grasp-ITV   pot   cloth   so   NEG-burn-2SG
    'Hold the pot together with a cloth so it doesn't burn you!'

A second, but less well established argument-related manipulation in Southern Nilotic is to use the ventive to indicate a benefactive role. For Endo, Zwarts (2004)

---

12 Creider (2002: 181-182) argues that any uses that might appear to be instrumental are due to ambiguity of Engish 'with'. In his view, the true instrumental applicative is -*e*; hence in contrast to (56b), *nam-é sapúryé:t ínkoryê:t* means 'Hold the pot with a cloth'.

observes that the ventive may indicate benefactive when combined with object suffixes; he does not elaborate on this relative to valence. A benefactive meaning may particularly arise in combination with first or second person participants, as something that arrives 'at me/you' may typically be for 'my/your benefit'. For Asimjeeg Datooga, Griscom (2019) states that the ventive is used to add 'benefactive' first and second person objects to the argument frame, as shown by the contrast between (57a-b), while the itive can sometimes add a third person 'instrument' object (57c).[13]

(57) Asimjeeg Datooga (Griscom 2019)
    a. *g-ì-dà-ʃà*   *dé:-d*
        AFF-FUT-1SG-buy   cow-SS.SG
        'I'll buy a cow.'

    b. *g-é:-ʃà-**n**-à:n*   *háŋ-d*
        AFF-IMPERS-buy-**VEN**-1SG   shawl-SS.SG
        'I was bought a shawl.'

    c. *m-ɛ́:-bár-**dà***
        NEG-IMPERS-hit-**ITV**
        'They (hoes) weren't used to farm.' (lit. hit away/with).

6 Aspectual extensions

Sources often comment on aspect or aspect-like uses of Nilotic directionals. In Southern Nilotic these are especially relevant to 'ambulative+directional' combinations, but in Western and Eastern branches they are reported for simple directional forms. Section 6.1 focuses on the ventive and Section 6.2 on the itive, though sometimes claims apply to both categories.[14]

---

[13] For Western Nilotic Anywa, Reh (1996: 229-233, 248) separately describes ventive, benefactive, and inchoative derivations, but observes that they can involve identical morphophonological changes; thus she explores possible semantic connections (p. 248). However, she also speculates on whether the Anywa benefactive might instead be related to a proto-Southern/Eastern Nilotic 'dative applicative' */-kIn/.

[14] Ateso directionals also figure in evidentiality, signalling that the speaker witnessed the event (Barasa 2017).

6.1 Aspectual and temporal extensions of the ventive

In Southern Nilotic, the 'ambulative+ventive' may express imperfective aspect notions. This may be due more to the ambulative than the ventive element. In Nandi and Kony, the combination has 'continuous' and in Kony also 'anticipative' uses (Mietzner 2009: 190-192). Consider (58), where Mietzner states that ambulative+ventive indicates the arrival of John is anticipated; there is no implication that the A or P of 'build' moves anywhere.[15]

(58) Kony (Mietzner 2009: 191; my re-parsing and glossing)
a-teech-ʌ:nʊ   ko:to   ku-mana:-cho   John
1SG-build-**AMB.VEN**   house   3SG-arrive-SUF   John
'I'll build a house anticipating John (will) arrive.'

The Kupsapiny 'ambulative+ventive' (as well as the 'ambulative+itive') may express 'continuative' (and in some circumsances 'iterative') throughout an associated motion event (Kawachi, this volume). Cherang'any 'ambulative+directionals' express 'continuity' on non-motion roots (Mietzner 2016: 139-140). The double ventive marking in (59) is very rare; in Mietzner's analysis the first ventive indicates that jumping occurred close to the deictic center, while the 'ambulative+ventive' indicates the jumping was continuous.

(59) Cherang'any (Mietzner 2016: 140)
*kú-rʌ̀   séséè-p   àsìkárì   ɲì   kì-síír-**un-ʌnu**   sùùs ...*
3-see   dog-POS   soldier   REL   PST3-jump-**VEN-AMB.VEN**   grass
'he saw a ranger's dog that was jumping continuously over the grass ...'

In various Eastern Nilotic languages, the ventive is reported to have inchoative (Maa), inceptive (Teso), prospective (Turkana), and perfective/perfect meanings. For the last, Spagnolo (1933: 143, 151) states that when the Bari ventive is used with the passive, it can communicate finishing off or completion. The Turkana ventive may be idiosyncratically extending into temporal and aspectual domains in combination with particular roots and other morphology. For instance, it can indicate 'prospective' meaning with some verbs, yielding 'shall look' from the

---

15 Mietzner (2009: 192) suggests that, in Eastern Nilotic, the Turkana itive and the Toposa ventive can indicate "temporal distance." However, her itive example for this claim involves a passive which has a past time implication, and her ventive example arguably suggests an inchoative sense. Citing examples from Otaala (1981), she claims the Teso ventive also has an 'attenuative' function, which may border on the aspectual domain.

root for 'look' (Dimmendaal 1983: 111). However the ventive of 'be somebody/something' indicates a "perfective situation in the past" (p. 466), except when combined with a distinct imperfective morpheme indicating "a state holding for the future" (p. 467).

In Maasai, 'ventive' and 'inchoative' have diverged phonologically and distributionally. The ventive occurs on lexically dynamic roots and is -ATR -ʊ(n), varying in ATR value depending on contiguous morphemes. The inchoative occurs on stative roots or stems, as in the derived middle in (60), and it is +ATR -u(n), causing a contiguous -ATR root to become +ATR. Assuming the inchoative and ventive came from the same historical source, these facts indicate a morphological split. Nevertheless, a few cases of -ATR -ʊ(n) do occur in text examples with seemingly inchoative meaning (Section 8).

(60) Maasai
o-m-e-tú-duŋ-oy-**ú**   ɔl=mʊ́rráni   ɛn=ámʊkɛ
until-SBJV-3-SBJV-cut-MID.NPF-**INCHO** M.SG=warrior F.SG=sandal.NOM
'until the shoe of a warrior became cut' (enamuke1.0002.c)

The Maasai ventive is common with ɪtɛr 'begin', seen in (61). With this root, an 'inceptive' meaning is understandably evident.

(61) Maasai
náa   té=íne   wúéjì   dúóó   é-ɪ́tér-**ʊ́**
FOC   OBL=that.place.NOM   stage.NOM   earlier   TEMP.3-begin-**VEN**
áa-tum   ɔ=sautí   l-oó   móruak
INF.PL-get M.SG=voice   M.PSD-PL.PSR   elders
'That is when they begin to get a voice of elders.' (bulunoto.063b)

6.2 Aspectual extensions of the itive

The itive is commonly reported to have imperfective semantics, but with some Western Nilotic transitive verbs it may convey telicity instead of spatial deixis. Remijsen, Miller-Naudé & Gilley (2016: 220) assert this for Shilluk, illustrating with the itive. Some free translations of their examples suggest 'inceptive' or 'inchoative' meaning, which is compatible with telicity in that 'entering' or 'starting' a new situation is, in itself, a type of finishable event. In (62a), for instance, the process of 'starting' is finished (even if the fire continues burning).

(62) Shilluk (Remijsen, Miller-Naudé & Gilley 2016: 220-221)
    a. *mâac á-kʊʊʊ̰́*
        fire   PST-blow.**ITV**
        'Somebody started the fire.'

    b. *mɔ́k-ɔ́*   *á-báaak*
        alcohol-SG PST-ferment.**ITV**
        'Somebody got the alcohol to ferment.'

Some Anywa itive verbs communicate successful completion of an event. Reh (1996: 255) reports that (63a) illustrates felicitous completion, while (63b) communicates both spatial movement and that the sent person successfully reached a destination.

(63) Anywa (Reh 1996: 255)
    a. *dhàanɔ́ Máyyá ā-cʌ̀DDó   k-ā-acàarā*
        person other PST-think:PD:**ITV** OBL-thought
        'Some other person got an idea.'

    b. *ācɔ́ɔ́G ā-jʌ́ʌGgó   kī   dhàanɔ́, ...*
        Acook PST-send:PD:**ITV** OBL person
        'Acook sent a person [and ...]'

In Eastern and Southern Nilotic, the itive may express pluractionality, distributivity, continuative, habitual and even plural participant number. Mietzner (2009: 190-191) discusses uses of the Kony (Southern Nilotic) itive that fit with distributive meaning.[16] König et al. (2015: 51-52) gloss the Akie form *-aat(ɛ)* as simply 'ambulative'; this is almost certainly cognate with the broader Southern Nilotic 'ambulative+itive'. The authors say it means 'to do habitually, carefully, and/or here and there', but in (64) I would say its sense is distributive and/or pluractional. Beyond adding the idea of 'do carefully' to (65), the free translation 'move on' may also suggest the itive adds a directional meaning, but it is not clear whether this is a motion event separate from that communicated by *went* 'go'.

(64) Akie (König, Heine & Legère 2015: 52)
    a. *a   táák-**aatéy**   kéétɪ*
        1SG see-**AMB.ITV** trees.A
        'I see many trees here and there.'

---

[16] Mietzer (2009: 190-191) refers to these itive uses as 'simultaneity'; but translations suggest action distributed over more than one object at a time, or pluractionality as in sowing seed.

b. *εεy-ááte*
drink-AMB.ITV
'He drinks little by little, or fairly regularly.'

(65) Akie (König, Heine & Legère 2015: 52)
went-ááte
go-AMB.ITV
'He goes carefully but moves on.'

In Cherang'any, the 'ambulative+itive' derivations of *pot* 'be lost' and *kás* 'listen' add motion as well as the idea of continuous or repeated action, as in *képòt-ʎʎt* 'walk and repeatedly get lost while trying to reach an unfamiliar destination' and *kàs-ààté* 'walk while keeping ears open so as to gather information' (Mietzner 2016: 141). In (66), by contrast, the 'ambulative+itive' indicates repeated or continuous action without any addition of motion.

(66) Cherang'any (Mietzner 2016: 139-140)
kì-kí-tyèm-aate   okoi kɔ́sɔlíɲ   kʊ-maa-kí-ŋɛɛt   kêy
PST3-1PL-try-AMB.ITV   until evening   SUBS-NEG-1PL-wake.up   anything
'We continuously tried until evening but didn't wake up anything.'

For Eastern Nilotic Bari, Spagnolo (1933: 146) states that an "emphatic"[17] form of the itive can indicate linear movement toward a far object and parallel movement, but also "action taking a long time," and sometimes a "scattering" sense. The last suggests pluractional or distributive meaning. The following examples are from Maasai, Ilchamus Maa, and North Samburu Maa. The itive communicates continuous aspect or distributed motion in (67) and (68), and in the southern Kenyan Maasai meaning of (69); the North Samburu meaning in (69) indicates distribution in space.

(67) Maasai
k-é-nár↓é   naá   k-é-ítʊ-bʊl-áa   ɪl=Maasáí
CN2-3-fit   FOC   CN2-3-caus-grow-ITV   M.PL=Maasai.PL.NOM
ɛn=apá   leŋón   enyê   apá-k↓é   n-a-át↓á.
F.SG=former   generosity 3PL.PSD before-just   REL.F-F.SG.REL-have
'It is fitting the Maasai keep making flourish their former generosity that they had.' (elengon.061)

---

17 It is difficult to know what Spagnolo means by "emphatic."

(68) Ilchamus Maa
n-έ-ˈákʊ́   k-é-niŋ-óo   aké nínchɛ   history te   idíê
CN1-3-become CN2-3-hear-ITV just they.NOM   OBL that.place.NOM
'so there they just hear history' (Camus4.401)

(69) Maa
á-bík-óo   t=ené
1SG-stay-ITV   OBL=here.NOM
i. 'I'll be staying around here' (e.g. for the holidays). (North Samburu Maa)
ii. 'I'll live forever.'(Southern Kenyan Maa)

The Maa itive is also used for pluractionality, including situations involving multiplicity of kinetic actions, multiple individuals (whether A and/or P), and non-kinetic situations distributed across each and every participant, as in (70a). The itive commonly occurs when there is a plural participant in the discourse context, to the point that, for some speakers of some dialects, it may possibly mark a 'plural' (Payne 2013), as in (71d, f) from Parakuyo Maa. Altogether, continuous, distributive, and other readings of the itive can depend on lexical aspect of the stem, discourse context, and may vary by dialect.

(70) Maasai
  a. k-é-adɔ́-ɔ   kʊlɔ́   popóŋ
     CN2-3-be.extended-ITV these.M.NOM euphorbia.NOM
     'Each and every one of these euporbia trees is tall.'

  Compare:
  b. k-é-adɔ́   kʊlɔ́   popóŋ
     CN2-3-be.extended these.M.NOM euphorbia.NOM
     'These euphorbia trees are tall.'

(71) Parakuyo Maa
  a. á-pír   'I am fat'   d. kí-pír-óo   'we are fat'
  b. í-pír   'you (sg.) are fat' e. í-píróró   'you (pl.) are fat'
  c. é-pír   'he/she is fat'   f. é-pír-óo   'they are fat'

The extension of Nilotic directionals into aspect is an area needing more research, with rigorous control of lexical and contextual factors that might affect aspectual interpretation. In the available literature, it is not always clear how much a given aspectual interpretation is grammaticalized versus inferred from context.

Information on potential aspectual and temporal extensions of directional forms is relatively sparser for Western Nilotic than in the other branches, and as the Southern Nilotic aspect readings typically involve a directional combined with the ambulative, it may be the latter which gives rise to 'continuative' and 'habitual' meanings across both ventive and itive contrasts. Nevertheless, as a basis for motivating further research, Table 3 summarizes aspectual and temporal claims about Nilotic directionals discussed here.

Table 3: Aspectual and temporal claims about uses of Nilotic directionals.

	Ventive	**Itive**
Southern Nilotic (with ambulative)	continuous, habitual, anticipative	continuous, habitual, pluractional, distributive, iterative, continuative
Eastern Nilotic	inchoative, inceptive, perfective/completive, attenuative, anticipative/prospective	continuative, pluractional, distributive
Western Nilotic		telicity, inchoative, inceptive, completive

7 Lexicalization

By now the reader may have asked whether directionals are not lexicalized with particular verb roots. This is almost certainly true in all Nilotic languages, as dictionary entries and scattered comments in the literature attest. Here I note just a few illustrative examples. Maasai *ŋamʊ* 'receive' has an allomorph *ŋamʊn*, which strongly suggests historical addition of the ventive; while *ŋamaa* has senses of 'receive, respond, answer' with allomorphs involving a stem-final /ɾ/, suggesting the historical itive. The directional stems are fully lexicalized, as **ŋam* does not occur with any related meaning (a root *ŋam* 'notch ears of an animal to indicate ownership, inoculate' does occur). The Turkana ventive derives 'remember' from 'think', 'discover' from 'cover', participates in idiomatic combinations as in (72a), and is synchronically frozen in (72b, c), as the simple roots no longer occur without a directional (Dimmendaal 1983: 109-111). The Turkana itive derives 'take down' from 'swallow', 'hear' from 'test', etc.

(72) Turkana (Dimmendaal 1983: 110)
    a. *a-cam-**ʊni**   asɛcɪ̀*
       to-like-**VEN**   sin
       'to admit guilt'

b. *a-limw-ùnɪ*
'tell' (no simple root form exists)

c. *a-ya-ʊnɪ*
'bring' (no simple root form exists)

8 Maasai (Eastern Nilotic) corpus study

Preceding sections have surveyed attested functions of the Nilotic directionals, ranging across orientation and direction on movement and non-movement roots, associated motion (on especially non-movement roots), argument role and valence manipulation, aspect-like and (marginal) temporal functions, and full lexicalization. However, simply giving such an inventory can be misleading about the modern usage profiles of the directionals. To provide a fuller picture of how these apparently old morphemes can develop, this section presents results of a corpus study from a particular language, Maasai. The study is based on 60 texts. Stems where roots no longer exist without a directional (e.g. Maasai *ŋamaa/ ŋamʊ(n)* discussed above) were excluded. The results suggest that the term "directional" is appropriate for modern Maasai relative to the dominant function. Of course, it should not be assumed that the Maasai profile is necessarily reflective of other Nilotic languages. To my knowledge, relevant corpus studies do not yet exist for other Nilotic languages.[18]

8.1 Distribution by root semantics and transitivity

A simple inventory of what root types directionals can occur with does not reveal whether collocations with particular roots types are dominant versus infrequent, and does not show the extent to which directionals may be specializing for particular uses. In this section we examine collocation of directionals according to root transitivity and translational motion semantics. Table 4 displays the distribution of Maasai directionals according to transitivity and translational motion semantics of the lexical root. Judgments about which of these categories a given lexeme or root should be assigned to is not always unambiguous and in a few instances I have categorized different senses of a root distinctly. For example, *rik*

---

[18] See Pakendorf & Stoynova (this volume) for a corpus-based study of AM constructions across Tungusic languages.

'lead' in the sense of 'administer, be the appointed leader of a group of people' is counted as a transitive non-movement root, while *rik* 'lead' in the sense of 'move at the head of a group of animals' or 'move to the husband's home in front of a new wife as part of the marriage event' is counted as a transitive movement root. (Hence, a given root form may register in more than one cell of Table 4.) In other cases translational movement seems incidental to the profiled meaning of a root. For instance, *bol* 'open' and *da* 'feed' could be argued to nearly always involve movement of something (the lid of a box or one's mouth for 'open', something nourishing entering a mouth for 'feed'), but translational motion is not profiled in their meaning. Such roots I have categorized as non-(translational) motion.[19] When a directional is added to some such verbs, a more clear assertion of a distinct (though potentially simultaneous) movement event may surface, like 'open while moving away' or 'open something while it moves away'.

Roots like *or* 'sweep', *purr* 'rob', *wuap* 'snatch from', possibly *sʊl* 'lop from, prune', etc. are <AGENT SOURCE> verbs in their simple form and disallow expression of a moved THEME. Adding a directional changes them to transitive <AGENT THEME> stems with the implication that the THEME moves (Section 5.2). Simple roots of this type are considered non-movement roots.

Table 4 shows that the ventive occurs with a greater variety of roots (or lexemes) than the itive (90 versus 65) in the corpus. Most roots with a directional in the corpus are transitive (104/131, 79%). Additionally, directionals occur with a greater variety of non-motion roots (101/131, 77%) than with translational motion ones. The strong skewing in favor of non-motion roots might suggest that the primary function of the directionals is to add a motion component, that is, to express AM; but we will see that this is not true.[20]

Table 5 shows the distribution of directionals across tokens, relative to type of root. The ventive is most frequent (594/767, 77%). When evaluated by token, 56% (429/767) of directionals occur with roots that do not lexically communicate translational motion (Figure 4), while 66% (510/767) of directionals occur with transitive roots (Figure 5).

---

[19] The appendix tables present decisions on root lexeme types. It should be kept in mind that the brief English glosses are not always full reflections of the senses in discourse context.

[20] In Table 4, the number of distinct roots (as just defined) at the top of each column is less than the sum of distinct roots with the ventive plus those with the itive. This is because some roots occur in the corpus with both directionals (though never simultaneously on the same token); see the appendix tables.

Table 4: Number of distinct root lexemes with directionals.

	Translational motion roots (N = 30; 23%)		Non-motion roots (N = 101; 77%)		Total
	Intransitive	Transitive	Intransitive	Transitive	
Total distinct roots with a directional	8	22	19	82	131
Distinct roots with ventive	6	16	12	56	90
Distinct roots with itive	3	10	9	43	65

Table 5: Distribution of directionals across verb tokens.

	Translational motion root lexeme tokens (N = 338)		Non-translational motion root lexeme tokens (N = 429)		Total Directional Instances
	Intransitive	Transitive	Intransitive	Transitive	
Ventive	183	106	54	251	594
Itive	7	42	13	111	173
Total	190	148	67	362	767

The Table 5 data show that the directionals favor transitive non-motion stems (362/767, 47%; Figure 6). Also, the hypothesis that there is no difference in distribution of the ventive versus itive relative to root lexeme type is rejected ($\chi2 = 55.6119$, $p < 0.00001$).

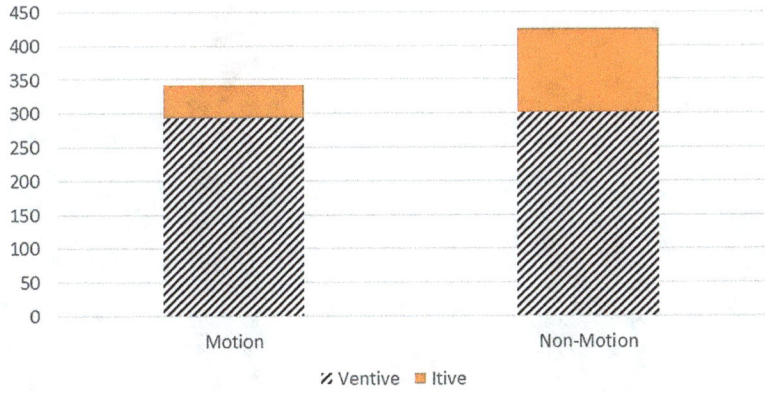

Figure 4: Directionals with motion vs. non-motion roots.

Table 4 shows that directionals occur with fewer distinct intransitive translational motion roots than any other type (less than 7%, whether calculated as

8/131 or 3+6/131). However, it is striking that of the 767 total directional tokens in Table 5, fully 22% (169) occur with one of the intransitive suppletive lexemes *lo(t)* 'go (singular)' or *puo(n)* 'go (plural)' (see the appendix tables). All but two of the 169 tokens are with ventive, which is the basic way to express 'come'. (The itive with these suppletive 'go' forms yields senses of 'roam, loiter', or imperfectivity.)

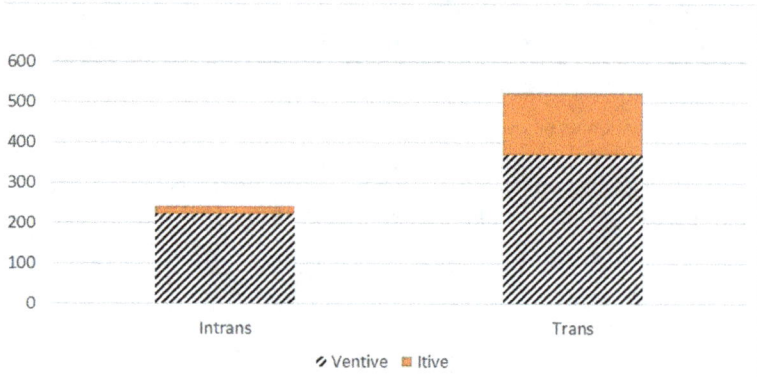

Figure 5: Directionals with intransitive vs. transitive roots.

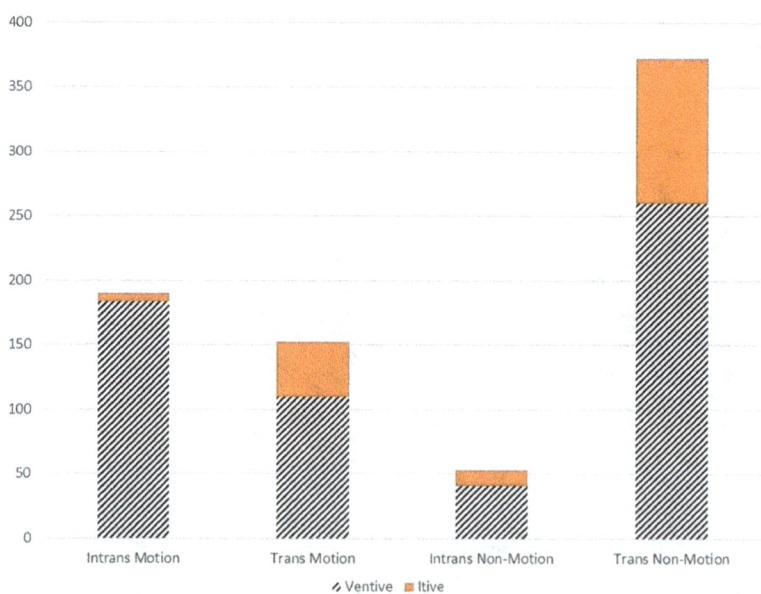

Figure 6: Combined distribution of directionals.

Against the backdrop of these co-occurrence distributions, Section 8.2 quantitatively examines functions of directionals in the Maasai corpus.

8.2 Functions in the corpus

Maasai directionals express: (1) direction (DIR) without clear AM, (2) translational motion relative to a point of reference, i.e. (directed) associated motion (AM), (3) ASPECT or aspect-like functions (continuous, pluractional, distributive with the itive; inchoative and possibly completive with the ventive), and (4) CHANGE argument structure of <AGENT SOURCE> roots; the last may or may not co-occur with AM. Table 6 tabulates the corpus distribution of these functions. The OTHER category in Table 6 reflects verbs with root lexemes that can occur without any directional, but where the contribution of the directional is synchronically idiosyncratic (highly lexicalized) and does not easily fit into any of the other four functions. For example, *nyɔrr* 'like' with the itive means 'agree', *duŋ* 'cut' with the ventive can mean 'decide, make a decision', etc. Lexicalization is a matter of degree, but where it seemed reasonable to assign use of a directional to one of the other four functions, it is not included under OTHER.

Table 6: Functions of directionals in the corpus.

	Dir (no AM)	AM (+/- Dir)	Aspect (no AM)	Argument Change (+/- AM)	Other
Ventive	458	68	58	2	1
Itive	92	51	26	10	3
Total	550	119	84	12	4

The aim of Table 6 is to evaluate how frequently directionals are used for a given function. Though I have endeavored to make decisions about whether a given use "is aspectual," "is directional," etc., tokens in the cells of Table 6 are not always fully independent. This is to be expected since morphology is always in the process of historical development. Note particularly that instances of directionals that manipulate argument structure are often simultaneously expressing AM. Nevertheless, Table 6 shows that a high number of ventive and itive tokens do not communicate AM. Strikingly, the appendix tables show that a large number of non-AM instances surface with lexical bases which, in themselves, do not express translational motion: the ventive with *bʊl* 'grow' yields 'mature/grow up'; *liki(n)* 'tell' with the itive yields 'tell about, report'; and so on.

Tables 7 and 8 break down the AM instances by whether the motion event targets S of an intransitive, or A or P of a transitive, and by whether the motion event is understood as prior, simultaneous, or subsequent to the lexical root event. For instance, Table 7 shows that out of the 68 instances in which the ventive expressed AM (column two of Table 6), 39 instances expressed simultaneous AM of the P. Here the analyses take into consideration valence derivations. For instance, if a directional occurred on a middle derivation of an otherwise transitive root, I count the argument as S since the middle derives an intransitive stem. If a directional occurs on a causative of an otherwise intransitive root, I count the argument as A or P.

Table 7: Ventive associated motion cases.

	S	A only	P only	A+P	Total
Prior AM		1			1
Simultaneous AM	9	6	39	10	64
Subsequent AM			3		3

Table 8: Itive associated motion cases.

	S	A only	P only	A+P	Total
Prior AM		1			1
Simultaneous AM	23	2	21	3	49
Subsequent AM	1				1

Tables 7 and 8 show that simultaneous AM readings predominate. Further, if the stem is transitive, AM most frequently applies to the P. There are a few arguable interpretations in the corpus of 'subsequent motion', though the examples are not clear assertions by themselves that subsequent movement necessarily occurred – only the hope of future motion, as in (73) and (74a).[21]

(73) Maasai
    n-é-ípot-**un**-í naá dúóó ɛnâ kúkuû
    CN1-3-call-**VEN**-PASS FOC relevant this.F wild.animal.NOM
    'and the animal is called [to come toward a dog]' (enkukuu.011b)

---

21 Several authors in this volume consider motion-with-purpose as instances of AM, as I have done here; but others do not so consider them.

(74) Maasai
  a. *N-é-pˈó-í   áa-ipot-u   in=tɔ́mɔ́nɔ́k*
     CN1-3-go.PL-PL INF.PL-call-VEN F.PL=women
     'They go to call women [to come],'

  b. *n-é-pˈón-ú   ɨ́nâ   dúóó   kítuaak   ɔ́   l=payíání*
     CN1-3-go.PL-VEN that.F.SG previous women.NOM M.SG.PSR M.PL=elders
     'and those wives of the men come'

  c. *é-étâ   ɪl=kɪlánˈí.*
     TEMP.3-have M.PL=clothes
     'wearing (traditional leather) clothes.' (ibaa.016)

The results in Tables 7 and 8 show that Maasai AM is almost always interpreted as simultaneous with the lexical event. This does not support Guillaume's (2016) proposal that that the existence of concurrent AM forms implies the existence of prior motion forms (i.e. **prior motion > concurrent motion**). Second, Tables 7 and 8 show that Maasai AM most frequently applies to transitive P's and least frequently to transitive A's. While these results do not absolutely contradict the proposed hierarchy that **motion of subject > motion of object**, the strong skewing in favor of P+S shows an absolutive preference, rather than a subject preference.

For transparency, I comment on coding decisions one might have treated differently. First, arguments of the non-promotional impersonal construction are counted as P, as they remain in the accusative case (5 instances).[22] Second, the moving argument of 'come, go' is counted as S, whether or not a specific goal is evident. Third, *ba* 'extend to' is considered a two-argument root when a clear locative occurs in a non-oblique form, as in (75) where the itive creates a motion event. (The A argument is a group of cattle, sheep and goats, mentioned lexically earlier in the paragraph.)

(75) Maasai
  n-é-ba-yá   ɛ=mówúó   ɔ́lˈɛ́ Katiany
  CN1-3-reach-ITV   F.SG=animal.horn of   Katiany
  'they [animals] reach "the horn of Ole-Katiany" [a place name].'
  (mapk01.010)

---

[22] Tucker & Mpaayei (1955) refer to the impersonal construction as a 'passive'. However, any understood agent is interpreted as "people" and cannot be overtly expressed; the understood P is not "promoted" to nominative/subject role (Payne 2011).

However, *ba* is counted as intransitive when 'time' is the nominative argument and there is no overt locative goal, as in (76a-b) (10 instances, all with the ventive).

(76) Maasai
    a. *n-ɛ́-ɛndɛléya mâ   ɔ=m-ɛ-tá-b↓á-ʊ́   ɛn=katá*
       CN1-3-go.on   that.NOM until=SBJV-3-SBJV-reach-VEN F.SG=time.NOM
       'That [staying with long ritual hair] goes on, until a time arrives.'

    b. *óre aké peê ɛ-bá-ʊ́   ɛn=katá*
       DSCN just when TEMP.3-reach-VEN F.SG=TIME.NOM
       n-á-ítayun-í   énâ dúóó kérái
       REL.F-F.SG.REL.NOM-remove-pass this.F previous child
       ɔl=masí ...
       M.SG=ritual.hair
       'When the time that the child's ritual hair is removed arrives ...'
       (eishoi.021-022)

Despite coding challenges with particular tokens, the corpus results unambiguously show that AM is not the dominant function of the Maasai directionals at this point in history, though it is clearly a well attested function.

9 Conclusions

Nilotic deictic directionals participate in communicating AM. In Southern Nilotic, this is dependent on the 'ambulative' element co-occurring with a directional, while Eastern and Western Nilotic directional forms alone can have this function. In at least Maasai, AM is almost always interpreted as simultaneous with the lexical event, and it most frequently applies to transitive P's and least frequently to transitive A's. Neither of these Maasai patterns particularly support Guillaume's (2016) proposed implicational hierarchies.

    The Nilotic directionals can derive <AGENT THEME> stems from <AGENT SOURCE/GOAL> roots. This would be consonant with the directionals having a translational movement semantic feature, as movement entails existence of a moving THEME, which may be so profiled as to displace what would otherwise be a SOURCE or GOAL grammatical object. But if AM were the historically earlier function, the directionals have clearly diversified well beyond this, and if the Maasai corpus study is indicative, the AM function of the directionals may be significantly less frequent than the directional function. At the same time, the meaning of this morphology is so grammaticalized and/or lexicalized that even 'direction relative to a reference point' is hard to discern in some instances.

The directionals also have aspectual functions. Across Nilotic, the itive commonly indicates some type of imperfectivity, whether continuous, iterative, pluractional, distributive, or some other shade of meaning. The ventive often indicates inchoativity and perfectiveness broadly understood. In Southern Nilotic, imperfectivity may be dependent on the ambulative element that requires a directional. Again assuming that AM functions are earlier, as translational motion necessarily takes place across some physical space, the aspectual extensions arise via space-to-time metaphorical extensions. Interaction of a directed motion with particular lexical elements and contextual factors may literally or figuratively entail coming to or crossing a boundary, thus giving rise to the inchoative or perfective meanings.

The wide attestation of the varied functions suggests these are old morphemes. The deictic and AM meanings cannot be neatly excised out as if one or the other was the "real" meaning and still be true to the modern polysemous nature of these morphemes. Nevertheless, the various modern uses find quite natural diachronic explanations if directed associated motion is taken as an earlier function.

Abbreviations

AFF	affirmative	FS	final suffix	PL	plural
AMB	ambulative	FUT	future	POS	possessive
AM	associated motion	IMP	imperative	PSD	possessed
ANTIP	antipassive	IMPF	imperfective	PSR	possessor
APPL	applicative	INCHO	inchoative	PST	past
CAUS	causative	INF	infinitive	REFL	reflexive
CN	connective	INTR	intransitive	REL	relative
CPL	completive	ITV	itive	SBJV	subjunctive
CON	contemporative	M	masculine	SEQ	sequential
COND	conditional	MID	middle	SG	singular
CONJ	conjunction	NEG	negative	SS	secondary number suffix
D	declarative	NOM	nominative		
DAT	dative	NPF	non-perfect(ive)	STH	something
DO	direct object	OBL	oblique	SUBS	subsecutive
DSCN	discontinuity	PASS	(impersonal) passive	SUF	suffix
ERG	ergative			TEMP	dependent temporal ('while, when')
F	feminine	PD	patient deleted		
FOC	focus	PF	perfect(ive)	VEN	ventive

Acknowledgements: I am grateful to Antoine Guillaume, Harold Koch, Kazuhiro Kawachi, and Jean-Christophe Verstraete, who have generously provided comments on this paper, and to the US Fulbright Foundation (1993-1994 and 2009-2010) and National Science Foundation (grants SBR-9616482 and SBR-9809387) for support related to the Maa work. Maa data in this paper come from elicitation or texts (the latter indicated by a code in parentheses after the free translation), gathered with assistance of multiple speakers. I am especially grateful to Maasai speakers Leonard Ole-Kotikash and A. Keswe Ole-Mapena for their generous collaboration. The work of other investigators who have published and made available data on Nilotic languages is also gratefully acknowledged.

Appendix

The Appendix reports results of a corpus study of Maasai texts, examining senses that result from adding the directionals to lexical roots. Tables A through D divide verbs according to transitivity and translational motion semantics. Numbers in the Ventive and Itive columns of each table give the number of instances in the corpus of the root with the relevant directional. Regarding Tables A and B, in accord with the definition of associated motion (AM) given in the introduction to this chapter, a directional was not counted as having an associated motion function if it occurred on a root that in itself already codes translational motion (unless the motion component contributed by the directional could clearly be argued to be a distinct motion event; this rarely if ever occurred in the data). The instances in Tables C and D marked with [AM] indicate uses in the corpus judged as associated motion. Aspectual, only directional, and other uses are not otherwise distinguished in the tables.

Table A: Meanings and number of instances of directionals with intransitive translational motion roots (no AM).

Root lexemes (N = 8)	Ventive	Itive
ıdʊrr 'migrate'	3 'migrate hither'	
ılany 'flee, outrun'		4 'run away'
ılɛp 'ascend, climb'	8 'climb up hither, increase, rise'	
ısarrısarr 'walk fast'	1 'come briskly'	
ıul 'stir, swerve, head toward'		1 'go near [distant place]'

Table A (continued)

Root lexemes (N = 8)	Ventive	Itive
kuɛt 'run'	4 'run hither'	
lot 'go (sg.)'	88 'come'	2 'go continuously'
puo 'go (pl.)'	79 'come'	
Total instances of directionals (N = 190)	183	7

Table B: Meanings and number of instances of directionals with (di)transitive translational motion bases (no AM).

Root lexemes (N = 22)	Ventive	Itive
ibuk 'pour back and forth'		2 'pour out'
ɪd 'jump over'		1 'jump over'
ɪkʊyʊkʊ 'drag'		1 'drag thither'
ɪm 'pass'	12 'pass'	3 'pass thither'
ɪŋat 'withdraw sth., outgrow'		4 'withdraw thither, flee from'
ɪpuŋ 'exit'	1 'exit'	
ɪrrɪ 'send'	3 'send'	
ɪshɔ(r) 'give'	7 'give, bring'	23 'give away, give out'
ɪt 'remove in installments'	1 'remove in installments'	
ɪtak 'send'	1 'distribute hither'	
ɪtau 'remove, give out'	1 'give out/cause'	
ɪturrurr 'gather'	1 'gather hither'	
jɪŋ 'enter'	4 'enter hither'	1 'enter (distributive)'
murut 'pass, overtake'		2 'precede'
naŋ 'throw'	1 'throw (toward self)'	
rɛʊ 'drive (e.g. cattle)'	16 'drive hither'	
rik 'lead s.o./sth.'	11 'lead hither, bring'	4 'lead thither'
rriny 'return sth.'	2 'come back, return'	
ruk 'flow thru, thread on'	18 'flow thru hither, flow out'	
shuk 'return sth.'	8 'return sth. hither'	
sʊj 'follow'		1 'follow thither'
ya 'take'	19 'bring hither'	
Total instances of directionals (N = 148)	106	42

Table C: Meanings and number of instances of directionals with intransitive non-motion roots.

Root lexemes (N = 19)	Ventive	Itive
ba 'extend (to)'	13 'arrive' [AM]; '(time) occur', 'reach (life stage)'	1 '(time) pass'
bʊl 'grow'	28 'mature, grow up'	1 'grow (pluractional)'
(ı)dɔrrɔp 'be short'	1 'become short'	
dʊp 'be effective'		5 'be very effective, be effective repeatedly'
ilab 'lap (liquid)'		1 'lap (pluractional)'
ıpus 'be blue'	1 'become blue'	
iriam 'do simultaneously'		1 'go simultaneously' [AM]
ishiu 'recover'	3 'completely recover'	
isho 'bear (children)'		1 'give birth'
isiadi 'be behind'	1 'logically result/be consequence'	
ıtʊmʊr 'be fed'	1 'get well fed'	
o 'ripen'		1 'ripen (imperfective)'
pırırıŋ '(be) narrow'		1 'run/roll away fast' [AM]
rany 'sing/dance'	2 'sing out, sing hither'	
rıny 'boast'		1 'disappear' [AM]
rropil 'be fresh'	1 'exude/emanate freshness'	
sıny '(be) holy'	1 'become wholesome'	
tɔn 'sit, stay'	1 'remain'	
wɔn 'sit, stay'	1 'repeatedly do coming hither' [AM]	
Total instances of directionals (N = 67)	54	13

Table D: Meanings and number of instances of directionals with transitive non-motion bases.

Root lexemes (N = 82)	Ventive	Itive
any 'await'	2 'wait while s.o. comes' [AM]	
ar 'beat, kill'	2 'bring by beating', 'beat so P moves to RP' [AM]	9 'kill while going', chase away by beating', send/take (forcefully) away' [AM]
ba 'be equal to, extend to, reach'	4 'come close to, move to reach RP', arrive at RP' [AM]; 'achieve (life stage); (time) "arrives"'	1 'extend to (time)'

Table D (continued)

Root lexemes (N = 82)	Ventive	Itive
baɾn 'shave'	2 'shave off (hairs)' [AM]; 'shave from'	
bɔr 'cut'	1 'carve out (create)'	
bol 'open'	6 'open while coming, roll (rock) over' [AM]; 'open (eyes)'	
da 'feed'		1 'graze while going' [AM]
dany 'burst sth.'	1 'burst sth. out' [AM]	
dɔl 'see'	14 'see while coming' [AM]; 'appear, reveal, indicate'	4 'go to see, see while being taken away' [AM]; 'see far off'
dot 'weed, disassemble' <AGENT SOURCE>	4 'uproot, pick up'	
duŋ 'cut'	3 'cut out, decide'	2 'cut off' [AM]; '(be) last born'
gɛl 'chose'	20 'collect while coming' [AM]; 'elect'	
gɪl 'break'	3 'break off (a leaf = die)'	
ibeleŋ 'overturn'	2 'roll hither' [AM]	
ibo(k) 'block'		2 'block (pluractional)'
ɪdɪp 'finish'	1 'end'	
ikilikuan 'ask'	3 'ask info. about/from'	
ɪkɔny 'seize, rape'		1 'snatch away by force' [AM]
ɪkʊ(n) 'do'	19 'do like (this)'	13 'do repeatedly'
ɪnɔs 'eat/tell'	1 'tell out, report'	2 'eat (pluractional), report'
ɪnyal 'damage'		2 'damage (pluractional)'
ɪnyaŋ 'trade with, barter from' <AGENT SOURCE>	3 'buy' [AM]; 'hire (people)'	
ɪŋat 'be insufficient'	1 'end up short'	
ɪŋɔr 'look'	33 'find out, investigate, look for'	3 'look around, look away, check on'
ɪpar 'inquire'	1 'inquire about/from'	
ɪpot 'call'	4 'call to come' [AM]; 'call hither'	
ɪrɪsh 'confront'		1 'confront (habitual/pluractional)'
ɪsh 'finish'	21 'end, come to an end'	2 'take all away, disappear by moving away' [AM]
ɪsham 'taste'	1 'try'	
ɪshɔ(r) 'allow'	1 'allow (us)'	
isud 'hide'		2 'hide by moving away' [AM]

Table D (continued)

Root lexemes (N = 82)	Ventive	Itive
ɪtɔbɪr 'prepare'	1 'prepare so it comes out' [AM]	
ɪtɛr 'begin'	28 'begin, start'	
ituku 'wash'		1 'wash'
juŋ 'inherit sth.; inherit from s.o.' ‹AGENT SOURCE›	7 'inherit sth.'	
kɔrd 'hook'	1 'save (us, from evil)'	
kurt 'stir, poke'	1 'gouge out (eye)' [AM]	
lak 'loose/pay'	10 'free, ask compensation for debt'	4 'pay (pluractional)'
lam 'avoid, be aloof from'		1 'avoid'
lep 'milk'		2 'milk going away' [AM]; 'milk (pluractional)'
liki(n) 'tell'		6 'report, say about s.o.'
man 'be surrounding'	1 'come around' [AM]	13 'go around' [AM]; 'surround (distributive)'
mɛn 'despise'		1 'despise (pluractional)'
mit 'defend (against)'	5 'defend (us)'	
naŋ 'die at/for'		2 'flow away' [AM]; 'be defeated (in election)'
niŋ 'hear'	4 'know, understand'	
nyɪk 'be close, be similar'	1 'move closer' [AM]	2 'go farther away' [AM]; 'approach life stage'
nʊk 'bury'		1 'bury'
nyɔrr 'agree/like'		4 'like (iterative), accept'
ŋad 'open up, dislodge'	1 'surround passing' [AM]	1 'drive (cattle) together' [AM]
ŋar 'share'		1 'share (distributive)'
ŋɛl 'disturb'		1 'fight'
ŋɛr 'destroy by tearing'	1 'uproot' [AM]	
ŋor 'stab'		1 'stab (pluractional)'
ŋɔb 'suck (illness)'	5 'remove by sucking' [AM]; 'suck outward'	
or 'divide'		1 'divide off'
or 'sweep (place)' ‹AGENT SOURCE›	1 'sweep sth.' [AM]	
osh 'hit'	3 'drive by hitting' [AM]	
paash 'differ'		5 'differ from each other'

18 The extension of associated motion to direction, aspect — 743

Table D (continued)

Root lexemes (N = 82)	Ventive	Itive
pɔn 'add, increase'		2 'increase (pluractional)'
poŋ 'miss'		1 'go astray' [AM]
purr 'rob' <AGENT SOURCE>		2 'rob (pluractional); steal' [AM]
raposh 'satiate'	1 'become satiated'	
ras 'attack, raid'	1 'come to attack' [AM]	
ret 'help'	1 'help'	
rresh 'ambush'	1 'ambush as it comes' [AM]	
rik 'lead administratively'		2 'administrate (pluractional)'
rrɪsh 'be tight on'	1 'hold firmly to'	
rʊj 'heap up'	1 'heap up'	
shɔr 'press'		1 'mix with' [AM]
shʊm 'store (above), hide'		1 'raise' [AM]
sɪr 'mark'	1 'choose'	
sot 'gather, contract'	6 'collect (cows)' [AM]; 'gather hither'	
sʊl 'lop from, prune' <AGENT SOURCE>	1 'bring down' [AM]	5 'throw down, fall down' [AM]
tur 'dig'	1 'cultivate'	1 'dig deep'
ʊt 'point'	1 'show the way'	1 'show the way'
wal 'answer'	1 'exchange' [AM]	
wuap 'snatch from <AGENT SOURCE>; attack'	2 'snatch sth. up hither' [AM]	1 'snatch sth. away' [AM]
yier 'cook'	1 'rend/extract (fat)' [AM]	
yiet 'stretch, tug on'	7 'pull hither' [AM]	1 'stretch out (fingers)'
yiolo 'know'	1 'get to know'	
yɔp 'cover'		1 'graze moving along' [AM]
Total instances of directionals (N = 362)	251	111

References

Andersen, Torben. 1988. Consonant alternation in the verbal morphology of Päri. *Afrika und Ubersee* 71. 63–113.
Andersen, Torben. 1992-1994. Morphological stratification in Dinka: On the alternations of voice quality, vowel length and tone in the morphology of transitive verbal roots in a monosyllabic language. *Studies in African Linguistics* 23 (1). 1–63.
Andersen, Torben. 1999. Vowel quality alternation in Mabaan and its Western Nilotic history. *Journal of African Languages and Linguistics* 20. 97–120.
Barasa, David. 2017. *Ateso Grammar: A Descriptive Account of an Eastern Nilotic Language.* Muenchen: LINCOM.
Belkadi, Aicha. 2015. Associated motion with deictic directionals: A comparative overview. *SOAS Working Papers in Linguistics* 17. 49–76.
Bender, Lionel M. 1997. *The Nilo-Saharan Languages: A Comparative Essay.* Muenchen: Lincom.
Crazzolara, Fr. J. P. 1933. Outlines of a Nuer grammar. *Anthropos* 13. v-xii, 1–218.
Creider, Chet. 2002. The semantics of participant types in derived verbs in Nandi. *Revue québécoise de linguistique* 31: 171–190.
Creider, Chet & Jane Tapsubei Creider. 1989. *A Grammar of Nandi.* Hamburg: Helmut Buske.
Creissels, Denis & Bassène, Alain Christian. This volume, chapter 17. Ventive, associated motion and aspect in Jóola Fóoñi (Atlantic).
Dimmendaal, Gerrit. 1983. *The Turkana Language.* Dordrecht: Foris.
Ehret, Christopher. 2001. *A Historical-Comparative Reconstruction of Nilo-Saharan.* Köln: Rüdiger Köppe.
Greenberg, Joseph. 1966. *The Languages of Africa* (2nd edn. with additions and corrections). Bloomington: Indiana University.
Griscom, Richard. 2019. *Topics in Asimjeeg Datooga Verbal Morphosyntax.* Eugene: University of Oregon PhD dissertation.
Gruber, Jeffrey. 1965. *Studies in Lexical Relations.* Cambridge, MA: MIT PhD Dissertation.
Guillaume, Antoine. 2016. Associated motion in South America: Typological and areal perspectives. *Linguistic Typology* 20. 81–177
Hattori, Ryoko. 2012. *Preverbal Particles in Pingelapese: A Language of Micronesia.* Manoa: University of Hawai'i at Manoa PhD dissertation.
Jackendoff, Ray. 1972. *Semantic Interpretation in Generative Grammar.* Cambridge, MA: MIT Press.
Kawachi, Kazuhiro. 2011. Meanings of the spatial deictic verb suffixes in Kupsapiny, the southern Nilotic language of the Sebei region of Uganda. In Osamu Hieda (ed.), *Descriptive studies of Nilotic Languages* (Studies in Nilotic Linguistics 3), 65–107. Tokyo: Research Institute for Languages and Cultures of Asia and Africa.
Kawachi, Kazuhiro. This volume, chapter 19. The 'along'–deictic-directional verb suffix complex in Kupsapiny.
Kießling, Roland & Stefan Bruckhaus. 2017. Associated locomotion in Datooga (Southern Nilotic). In Shigeki Kaji (ed.), *Proceedings of the 8th World Congress of African Linguistics (WOCAL), Kyoto 2015*, 243–258. Tokyo: Tokyo University of Foreign Studies.
Koch, Harold. 1984. The category of "associated motion" in Kaytej. *Language in Central Australia* 1. 23–34.

König, Christa, Bernd Heine & Karsten Legère. 2015. *The Akie language of Tanzania, a discourse grammar*. (Asian and African Lexicon Series 58.) Tokyo: Research Institute for Languages of Asia and Africa, Northisland Co.
Levinson, Stephen & David Wilkins. 2006. Patterns in the data: Toward a semantic typology of spatial description. In Stephen Levinson & David Wilkins (eds.), *Grammars of space: Explorations in cognitive diversity*, 512–552. Cambridge: Cambridge University Press.
Mietzner, Angelika. 2009. *Räumliche Orientierung in nilotischen Sprachen: Raumkonzepte – Direktionalität – Perspektiven*. [Spatial orientation in Nilotic languages: spatial concepts - directionality – perspectives.] Köln: Rüdiger Köppe.
Mietzner, Angelika. 2016. *Cherang'any, a Kalenjin language of Kenya*. Köln: Rüdiger Köppe.
Noonan, Michael. 1992. *A grammar of Lango*. Berlin: Mouton de Gruyter.
Otaala, Laura. 1981. Phonological and semantic aspects of Ateso derivational verbal morphology. Nairobi: University of Nairobi MA thesis.
Otero, Manuel A. This volume, chapter 20. At the intersection of associated motion, direction and exchoative aspect in the Koman languages.
Pakendorf, Brigitte & Natalja Stoynova. This volume, chapter 22. Associated motion in Tungusic languages: A case of mixed argument structure.
Payne, Doris L. 2011. The Maa (Eastern Nilotic) Impersonal Construction. In Anna Siewierska and Andrej Malchukov (eds.), *Impersonal constructions. A cross-linguistic perspective*, 257-284. Amsterdam: John Benjamins.
Payne, Doris L. 2012. Phonological variation in Maa varieties, with some implications for grammar. *Occasional Papers in Linguistics 4*, 35–65. Languages of Tanzania Project. University of Dar es Salaam.
Payne, Doris L. 2013. The challenge of Maa 'away'. In Tim Thornes, Erik Andvik, Gwendolyn Hyslop, & Joana Jansen (eds.), *Functional-historical approaches to explanation: In honor of Scott DeLancey*, 259–282. Amsterdam: John Benjamins.
Reh, Mechthild. 1991. Frequentative derivation in Anywa: Present-day reflexes of a Proto-Nilotic suffix. *Afrika und Übersee* 74. 223–246.
Reh, Mechthild. 1996. *Anywa language*. Köln: Rüdiger Köppe.
Remijsen, Bert, Cynthia Miller-Naudé & Leoma Gilley. 2016. The morphology of Shilluk transitive verbs. *Journal of African Languages and Linguistics* 37. 201–245.
Rottland, F. 1981. The segmental morphology of Proto-Southern Nilotic. *Nilo-Saharan; Proceedings of the First Nilo-Saharan Linguistics Colloquium, Leiden, September 8–10, 1980*, 5–17. Dordrecht: Cinnaminson.
Schroeder, M. 1999. *Dictionary Toposa-English, English-Toposa*. (Bilingual Dictionaries of Sudan 2) Nairobi: SIL International.
Spagnolo, L. M. 1933. *Bari Grammar*. Verona: Missioni Africane.
Storch, Anne. 2014. *A grammar of Luwo, An anthropological approach*. Amsterdam: John Benjamins.
Talmy, Leonard. 1985. Lexicalization patterns: Semantic structure in lexical forms. In Timothy Shopen (ed.), *Language typology and syntactic description, Vol. 3: Grammatical categories and the lexicon*, 57–149. Cambridge: Cambridge University Press.
Tucker, Archibald N. & John O. Mpaayei. 1955. *Maasai Grammar – with vocabulary*. London: Longman, Green.

Wilkins, David. 1989. *Mparntwe Arrernte (Aranda): Studies in the structure and semantics of grammar*. Canberra: Australian National University doctoral dissertation. http://hdl.handle.net/1885/9908.

Wilkins, David. 1991. The semantics, pragmatics, and diachronic development of 'associated motion' in Mparente Arrernte. *Buffalo Papers in Linguistics* 1. 207–57.

Zwarts, Joos. 2004. *The phonology of Endo*. (LINCOM Studies in African Linguistics 59) Muenchen: LINCOM.

Kazuhiro Kawachi
19 The 'along'–deictic-directional verb suffix complex in Kupsapiny

Abstract: The present study describes the use of a verb suffix complex consisting of the 'along' suffix and a deictic-directional suffix in Kupsapiny, a Southern Nilotic language of Uganda. In addition to specifying deictic direction of motion, this suffix complex can be used to emphasize the continuity or iteration of the translational motion expressed by a motion verb or to motionalize a non-motion verb to express associated motion (Koch 1984; Wilkins 1991; Guillaume 2013, 2016). It can also function as a pure aspectual marker, which involves no motion at all. Therefore, the use of this suffix complex always conveys the concept of continuation or iteration, and associated motion does not seem to be totally independent of the temporal category of aspect in Kupsapiny. Other typological implications of the findings are further discussed.

Keywords: aspect, continuative, iterative, motion typology, associated motion

1 Introduction

The present study[1] describes the use of a verb suffix complex in Kupsapiny, a Southern Nilotic language of Uganda, which is made up of a suffix that encodes continuous motion along some distance for a certain period of time ("'along' suffix", henceforth) plus a deictic-directional suffix ("DD suffix", henceforth). This suffix complex ("ALONG-DD complex" for short) has three functions. First, as illustrated in (1), it can be used with a motion verb to underscore the continuity or iteration of translational motion and provide information on deictic direction of motion.

---

[1] The present author examined data that he collected during his sixteen 3–5 week field trips in Kapchorwa, Sebei, in Uganda between 2009 and 2019. Data included conversations, folk tales, and true stories, as well as speakers' descriptions of video clips (specifically those for the Causality across Languages project designed by Jürgen Bohnemeyer and Erika Bellingham and those for the NINJAL motion projects designed by Yo Matsumoto) and memory-based descriptions of Wallace Chafe's Pear Film.

Kazuhiro Kawachi, National Defense Academy of Japan, kazuhirokawachi@gmail.com

https://doi.org/10.1515/9783110692099-019

(1) čèè-noomə̀n   čè-kkwa   čè-lapat-**óón**-u
    PTCP.1PL-leave PTCP.1PL-come.PL PTCP.1PL-run-**AL.H**-IPFV
    'We left, and came running along this way …'
    (Story 2018.3-2: M.E.)

Second, as in (2), it can be used with a non-motion verb to motionalize the verb to express associated motion (AM) (Koch 1984; Wilkins 1991; Guillaume 2013, 2016).

(2) à-kas-e   čoorwéé-ɲuu   ɲìmɲimèn-**òòn**-u
    PTCP.1SG-see-IPFV friend-1SG.POSS smile-**AL.H**-IPFV
    '… I saw my friend (continuously) smiling as s/he came along …'
    (NINJAL(-Kobe) Motion Project, Clip B8-04: Participant 5, C.P.)

Finally, as in (3), it can be used with any type of verb as a pure aspectual marker for continuation or iteration, without conveying the occurrence of any motion at all.

(3) kɨ-ššém   kàroomɨn   kù-pasèn-**aat**-ø
    D.PST.3-try   very.much   PTCP.3-ask.to.lend.money-**AL.TH**-3
    kàriik-í
    money.DEF.PL-EMPH
    'S/he tried very much to continuously ask people to lend him/her money …'
    (Story 2018.3-1: M.E.)

The ALONG-DD suffix complex is not dedicated to any specific type of function. Unlike in other languages that have been reported to have markers for AM (both those with affixes dedicated to AM and those with DDs that do not always, but can, express AM), in Kupsapiny, the use of the ALONG-DD complex always involves the concept of continuation or iteration, irrespective of whether it expresses deictic direction only, AM and deictic direction, or neither; hence, AM does not seem to be totally independent of the temporal category of aspect.

The present chapter is organized as follows. The rest of Section 1 provides a brief sketch of Kupsapiny. Section 2 reviews the literature on AM relevant to the present study, and raises pertinent issues. These issues include the (non-)independence of AM from tense and aspect, as well as what types of temporal relations AM markers preferably express, and how AM should be dealt with in the context of motion typology. Section 3 presents data on two Kupsapiny constructions that use DDs (DD and ALONG-DD). Section 4 discusses the findings. Section 5 concludes the chapter.

Kupsapiny is spoken by the Sebei people (also known as the Sapiny or Sabiny people) in the Sebei region in east Uganda, which is on the northern slopes of Mt.

Elgon, crossed by the Uganda-Kenya border, which runs northeast to southwest. According to the Uganda Bureau of Statistics 2014 national census, the population of the Sebei is 289,456, and almost all of them speak Kupsapiny. This language belongs to the Kalenjin branch of the Southern Nilotic language family. The dialect of Kupsapiny spoken on the Kenyan side of Mt. Elgon by about 280,000 people is called Sabaot. Most Sebei, especially those below the age of around 60, speak English as their second language. Many Sebei in the eastern Sebei region speak Swahili when they interact with Kenyan people for business purposes. Some Sebei people who live around the western border of the Sebei region neighboring the Gisu region speak Lumasaaba (called Masaaba in Simons & Fennig (eds.) 2018; Bantu, E.31) for business.

Kupsapiny is an agglutinating language with some fusion. It uses both prefixes and suffixes, and shows largely head-marking properties. Word order is relatively rigid VSO, though VOS is used depending on the properties of the subject and the object noun phrases, specifically, concreteness vs. abstractness, nounhood vs. pronounhood, and person (in the case of pronouns), as well as information structure. Kupsapiny has prepositions, but no postpositions. In this language, a noun precedes noun modifiers.

Kupsapiny distinguishes two cases, nominative and absolute (i.e. the case used for the grammatical object), by means of tone. It is difficult to determine which tone pattern is marked or unmarked, but because the absolute case has a wider range of uses than the nominative case, the case-marking system of this language can be regarded as marked nominative (Dixon 1994; König 2006, 2008).

In Kupsapiny, verbs and nouns have a series of prefix and suffix slots (Montgomery 1966; O'Brien and Cuyers 1975). The verb prefixes include tense and subject person-number elements (fused in some cases and analyzable into a tense prefix and a subject person-number prefix in other cases),[2] the participle prefix, and the negative prefix. There are verb suffixes for 'along', DDs, path/location 'via, at, from', intransitivization, instrumental, subject person, object person-number, imperfective aspect, reflexive, and anti-causative. The path/location suffix and the instrumental suffix each serve as applicatives, enabling a verb to take an applicative object as its direct object. The ordering relationship of suffixes relevant to the present study is: "V–along–DD–{APP>IPFV>SUBJ}(–REFL)", where various suffixes compete for the same slot { } and are selected in the indicated priority (i.e. a suffix to the left outranks ones to its right). For example, in (4),

---

[2] For example, in Table 1, tense and subject person-number prefix elements are fused in *kèè-* (T.PST.2SG-) and are analyzable into a tense prefix and a subject person-number prefix in *kà-čèè-/kà-čè-/kà-či-* (T.PST.1PL-).

which uses the applicative suffix for 'via, at, from', neither the imperfective suffix nor the first-person suffix occurs. In (5), which uses the imperfective suffix, the first-person suffix does not occur. In (6), where neither the applicative suffix nor the imperfective suffix occurs, the first-person suffix appears. (For the use of the hither suffix -n together with the thither suffix -t in (4), (5), and (6), see Section 3.2. These three sentences may express the deictic directions or may only express the continuation of non-deictic motion.)

(4) kà-à-miitè
 T.PST-1SG-exist
 à-muutù-**noon**-nw-éé-key/à-muutù-**noot**-éé-key   keetít.
 PTCP.1SG-move.around-**AL.H**-VAF-REFL/PTCP.1SG-move.around-   tree
 AL.TH-VAF-REFL
 'I was moving around the tree (this way/that way).'

(5) kà-à-miitè   à-muutù-**noon**-u-kéy/
 T.PST-1SG-exist   PTCP.1SG-move.around-**AL.H**-IPFV-REFL/
 à-muutù-**noot**-i-kéy   àm   keetít.
 PTCP.1SG-move.around-**AL.TH**-IPFV-REFL   LOC   tree
 'I was moving around the tree (this way/that way).'

(6) kà-à-muutù-**noon**-u-kéy/
 T.PST-1SG-move.around-**AL.H**-1-REFL/
 kà-à-muutù-**noot**-e-kéy   àm   keetít.
 T.PST-1SG-move.around-**AL.TH**-1-REFL   LOC   tree
 'I moved around the tree (this way/that way).'

Finite verb forms, which usually occur sentence-initially, contain the tense and subject person-number prefix. Non-finite verb forms carry what I call the participle prefix, which has a number of uses including a consecutive one. The citation form of a verb is the second-person singular participle form (with a zero prefix), one of whose uses is for a singular imperative.

Most verb stems can be classified into one of the three patterns shown in Table 1, depending on the form of the subject person suffix that they take. Verb stems ending in a vowel and many stems with monosyllabic verb roots ending in a consonant do not carry a subject person suffix (or take a zero subject person suffix) (e.g. siit- 'wash'). On the other hand, verb stems ending in some consonants take different forms of the subject person suffix for the first and second persons on the one hand and for the third person on the other, regardless of the finiteness and the tense of the verb. With some verb stems ending in /l/, /n/, /r/,

/w/, or /t/ (e.g. *lupul-* 'become frightened'), the first- and second-person suffix is *-u* and the third-person suffix is *-ø*, and with some verb stems ending in /t/ (e.g. *must-* 'imitate'), the first- and second-person suffix is *-e* and the third-person suffix is *-a*, *-o*, or *-ø*. There are also verb stems that do not take a subject person suffix, but change tone patterns depending on the person.

Table 1: Three patterns of person-number verb paradigms for today past.

verb root 'gloss'	*siit-* 'wash (sb/sth)'	*lupul-* 'become frightened'	*must-* 'imitate (sb/sth)'
1SG/2PL	*kà-à-siit*	*kà-à-lùpul-ú*	*kà-à-must-è*
1PL	*kà-čèè-siit*	*kà-čè-lùpul-ú*	*kà-čĭ-must-è*
2SG	*kèè-siit*	*kèè-lùpul-ú*	*kèè-must-è*
3	*kà-ø-siit*	*kà-ø-lùpul-ø*	*kèè-must-ò*

2 Literature review

In previous studies on AM, Wilkins (1991) and Guillaume (2016) state that the grammatical marking of AM is a phenomenon independent of tense and aspect. Wilkins (1991: 212) argues that in Mparntwe Arrernte, a Pama-Nyungan language of Australia, the grammatical category of AM expressed by AM suffixes is independent of tense and aspect for three reasons. First, the AM suffixes occur in a different slot from tense and aspect suffixes, and co-occur with them. Second, unlike the tense and aspect suffixes, the AM suffixes do not occur on basic motion verbs. Finally, the AM suffixes convey spatial notions, rather than the time of occurrence of an event or its internal temporal contour.

The claim about the distinctness of AM from tense and aspect has primarily been based on studies of AM marking systems in languages in Australia and South America. In some of these languages, a fine-grained distinction is made on the basis of such factors as deictic direction, a path type, and the temporal relation between the lexical event and the motion (and sometimes also what the moving entity is).

In contrast, Belkadi (2015) shows how DDs in some African languages, specifically, Päri (Western Nilotic), Somali (Cushitic), Pero (Chadic), Tima (Niger-Congo), and Berber languages, can be used not only to express the deictic direction of a lexical motion event, but also for AM as well as for non-spatial concepts, differently from affixes devoted to AM in languages in Australia and South America.[3]

---

[3] Belkadi (2015) calls AM-dedicated systems I-AM ('I' for 'inflectional') and AM expressed by DDs in AM-undedicated systems D-AM. However, the affixes in the former systems are not nec-

For example, the DDs in some of the languages that Belkadi looked at have grammaticalized uses as tense, aspect, or mood markers, as in (7), which she gives to show the use of the ventive particle in Somali as a recent past tense marker.[4]

(7) wuu   iga   **soo**   bax-ay
    FOC:3SG.M O:1SG.from   **hither**   go.out-PST.3SG.M
    'He has left my place not long ago.'
    (Somali (Cushitic): Bourdin 2006. 25; Some of the morpheme-by-morpheme glosses are modified by the present author)

However, the ALONG-DD complex in Kupsapiny belongs to neither type. In Kupsapiny, DD suffixes without the 'along' component are restricted to motion verbs, while the ALONG-DD complex is compatible with almost any verb. Moreover, the Kupsapiny DD suffixes alone cannot be used for AM, but need to be combined with the 'along' suffix to express AM. Furthermore, the ALONG-DD complex can be used not only for AM and its deictic direction (when attached to non-motion verbs), but also for pure deictic direction (when attached to motion verbs) as well as just for aspect. Therefore, the Kupsapiny system is of a different type from either what Belkadi (2015) describes for the African languages that she examined, or from what Wilkins (1991) and Guillaume (2016) describe for Mparntwe Arrernte and languages of South America.

Thus, the first research question that the present study addresses is: how does the Kupsapiny ALONG-DD complex, which is not devoted exclusively to AM, work? Is AM still independent of the temporal category of tense-aspect in Kupsapiny?

There are two other issues that the present study addresses. They also concern claims that have mainly been made based on the AM marking systems in Australian languages and South American languages.

First, Guillaume (2016) proposes two implicational hierarchies. (Levinson and Wilkins (2006) also proposed the second hierarchy, but their proposal is based on their observation of only two languages, Arrernte and Yélî Dnye.) One of them is (8), according to which AM markers in a particular language are more

---

essarily inflectional (Antoine Guillaume, p.c.) (see also Reed & Lindsey (this volume) for their criticism of Belkadi's terminology).

4 See also other chapters in this volume, especially those by Creissels and Bassène, Guérois et al., Jacques et al., Osgarby, Otero, Payne, Ross, and Tallman, for the grammaticalization of AM markers or directionals into tense/aspect markers or their use as pure tense/aspect markers in various languages.

likely to express the motion of subject than that of object, and if they can express the motion of object, then they can also express that of subject.

(8) Subject > Object

The other implicational hierarchy is in (9) (adapted from Levinson and Wilkins 2006: 534), which concerns the temporal relations between the action or state (-change) encoded by the verb root and the motion expressed by the grammatical morpheme for AM – if an AM marker expresses a relation on the hierarchy, then it can also express any other relation to the left.

(9) Prior motion (e.g. 'go then/to VERB') > Concurrent motion (e.g. 'do VERB while going') > Subsequent motion (e.g. 'VERB then go')

In fact, the temporal relation that an AM marker can express is one of the semantic criteria for the formal distinction that can be made between different affixes in a complex AM-dedicated system (Wilkins 1991). It will be interesting to see how this hierarchy is applicable to the Kupsapiny system, which seems to be different from the AM-marking systems described so far.

Second, according to Levinson and Wilkins (2006) and Guillaume (2016), AM constructions are unusual in that they do not follow any of the patterns in the framework of Talmy's (1985, 1991, 2000) motion typology – the fact of motion shows up not in the verb root, but in a grammatical morpheme (specifically, in a verb affix), unlike in constructions of any typological type proposed by Talmy, where the fact of motion is expressed by the verb root at least. This peculiarity may appear to apply to constructions devoted to AM. However, it does not apply to the Kupsapiny ALONG-DD complex. The ALONG-DD complex is used not only for AM, but also for motion events in Talmy's sense, namely complex motion events made up of a main event (framing event) component consisting of the fact of motion as well as the path of motion and a secondary event (co-event) component such as a manner or cause of motion, where the co-event has a support relation to the framing event. When the ALONG-DD complex is used for AM, the verb root does not express the fact of motion, but when it is used for complex motion events, the verb root does express the fact of motion. Furthermore, there are questions of whether AM is a type of motion event to be dealt with in Talmy's typology (what he calls a macro-event) first of all, as well as which is the main event component of AM, the action or state change expressed in the verb root or the motion.

In this paper, I will explore all of these issues in Kupsapiny.

There are descriptions of the ALONG-DD complex in Southern Nilotic languages, but previous studies have either only touched on the use of this complex (e.g. Toweett 1979: 138–139; Creider and Creider 1989: 89; Zwarts 2004: 122, 128; Mietzner 2016: 139–141), or have focused on its spatial use without looking at other uses (e.g. Kawachi 2011, 2014; Kießling and Bruckhaus 2017).[5] Eastern and Western Nilotic languages have also been reported to have DD verb suffixes (see Tucker and Mpaayei 1955: 123–129 and Payne 2013 for Maa (Maasai) (Eastern); Noonan 1992: 98–100, 134–136 for Lango (Eastern); Dimmendaal 1983: 109–113 for Turkana (Eastern); Reh 1996: 249–259 for Anywa (Western); Barasa 2017: 160–164 for Ateso (Eastern)).[6] However, unlike in Southern Nilotic languages, the DD suffixes by themselves (without any other affix) in these languages seem to directly attach not only to motion verbs but also to non-motion verbs to indicate the deictic direction of the action denoted by the verb (or AM: described as a minor pattern of the use of the Maa 'thither' suffix by Payne 2013; also, e.g. Reh 1996: 257–258 judging from the glosses for a limited number of examples of the Anywa suffixes).[7] Moreover, unlike Southern Nilotic languages, no Eastern or Western Nilotic languages have been described as having a suffix for continuous motion or any other morpheme that is combined with the DD suffixes on a non-motion verb to express AM.

3 Kupsapiny deictic-directional system

This section describes two Kupsapiny DD constructions. Section 3.1 briefly describes the use of the DD suffixes, and Section 3.2 discusses the use of these suffixes combined with the 'along' suffix for continuous motion.

3.1 Deictic-directional suffixes

As in other languages, it is difficult to draw a clear line between motion verbs and non-motion verbs in Kupsapiny. However, for this study, the category of "motion verbs" is defined to include (A) translational motion verbs (path of motion verbs,

---

5 The 'along' suffix is called by different names in the literature: the 'ambulative' (Zwarts 2004), 'mobilitive' (Mietzner 2016), or 'associated locomotion' (Kießling & Bruckhaus 2017) suffix.
6 See Payne (this volume) for a detailed comparison of the AM and other functions of DDs across the branches of the Nilotic language family.
7 However, according to Noonan (1992: 135), the use of the ventive suffix in Lango is restricted to a small number of motion verbs.

manner of motion verbs, cause of motion verbs, etc.) and (B) object-maneuvering verbs, which express the figure entity's local motion along a relatively short path in relation to the ground entity (e.g. 'put', 'lift').

Most translational motion verbs and some object-maneuvering verbs in Kupsapiny can take different DD suffixes, depending on the combination of the person of the subject and that of the entity at the goal of or in the direction of motion. A majority of them show a deictic contrast with -ø 'H (third-person subject and first- or second-person goal/direction)', -u 'H (either first-person subject and second-person goal/direction or second-person subject and first-person goal/direction)', and -t 'TH', as illustrated in (11)–(13), and many additionally have unsuffixed forms, as in (10).[8]

(10) kà-wiir   ku-kkwà   ɲuɲ-í.
     T.PST.3-throw PTCP.3-come.PL ground.INDEF.SG-EMPH
     '… s/he threw them (fruits) down this way (toward the speaker or toward the addressee).' (Pear story 11: S. H.)

(11) kà-wììr-ø   màtùntaanɨk   ɲuɲ-í.
     T.PST.3-throw-H fruit.DEF.PL   ground.INDEF.SG-EMPH
     'S/he threw the fruits this way (toward the speaker or toward the addressee).'

(12) kà-à-wiir-ù màtùntaanɨk ku-kkwà   ɲuɲ-í.
     T.PST-1SG-throw-H fruit.DEF.PL PTCP.3-come.PL ground.INDEF.SG-EMPH
     'I threw the fruits down that way (toward the addressee).'

---

8 This does not apply to the progressive construction, which uses the verb of existence mììte and the participle form of a verb in the imperfective. In this construction, the imperfective suffix shows a two-way contrast: -ú 'hither' and -é 'thither'.

(i) kà-à-mììtè   à-wiir-ú   màtùntaanik ɲuɲ-í.
     T.PST-1SG-exist PTCP.1-throw-IPFV.H fruit.DEF.PL ground.INDEF.SG-EMPH
     'I am throwing the fruits down this way.'

(ii) kà-à-mììtè   à-wiir-é   màtùntaanik ɲuɲ-í.
     T.PST-1SG-exist PTCP.1-throw-IPFV.TH fruit.DEF.PL ground.INDEF.SG-EMPH
     'I am throwing the fruits down that way.'

(13) kà-à-wiir-t-é   màtùntaanik kù-pa   ŋuɲ-í.
     T.PST-1SG-throw-TH-1/2 fruit.DEF.PL PTCP.3-go.PL ground.INDEF.SG-EMPH
     'I threw the fruits down that way (neither toward the speaker nor toward the addressee).'

The use of the DD suffixes (without being accompanied by the 'along' suffix) is restricted to motion verbs, and to verbs for looking, where they express fictive motion (*kas* 'look', *kà-kos-ø* (T.PST.3, first- or second-person goal/direction), *kà-à-kas-ú* (T.PST-1SG, second-person goal/direction), *kà-à-kas-t-e* (T.PST-1SG, third-person goal/direction); *čil* 'look carefully from a distance', *kà-čil-ø* (T.PST.3, first- or second-person goal), *ka-a-číl-ú* (T.PST-1SG, second-person goal/direction), *kà-à-čil-t-e* (T.PST-1SG, third-person goal/direction)).

Table 2 shows examples of today past forms of verbs with the DD suffixes as well as unsuffixed forms of the verbs in the today past. The 'hither' suffix for a motion event involving a third-person subject and a first- or second-person goal/direction is *-ø*, the 'hither' suffix for a motion event involving a combination of the first person and the second person used for subject and goal/direction is *-u*, and the 'thither' suffix is *-t*.[9] (The first- and second-person subject suffix for the 'thither' form of a verb is *-e*, and the third-person suffix for it is *-a* or *-o*.) Many motion verbs also have unsuffixed forms, which differ from forms with the DD suffix *-ø* segmentally, suprasegmentally, or both (compare the third-person subject forms in Table 2). There are different types of verbs with respect to the deictic distinction that they make. Some verbs exhibit a three-way distinction between their two 'hither' forms and their 'thither' form (verbs in (a) of Table 2). There are also verbs that show the three-way distinction and additionally have unsuffixed forms, which can be used regardless of deictic direction (verbs in (b) of Table 2, *wiir-* 'throw' in (10)–(13)), and those that show the three-way contrast, where the unsuffixed forms express 'thither', and lack 'thither' forms (verbs in (c) of Table 2). In the first pattern, the basic form (i.e. the minimum citation form, which carries no prefix) of a verb is the 'thither' form (e.g. *sap-t-è* 'tiptoe, move slowly'), whereas in the second and third patterns, the basic form is the unsuffixed form (e.g. *yèèl* 'move aside').

---

[9] The DD suffix *-u* is different from the first- and second-person suffix *-u* in Table 1, which is exemplified with *lupul-* 'become frightened'. It cannot be used for 'thither' motion. Moreover, many motion verbs have unsuffixed forms, which do not take a subject person suffix.

Table 2: Verbs with the deictic directional suffixes (today past forms).

	verb root 'gloss'	unsuffixed (T.PST.3)	-ø (T.PST.3) (goal/ direction: 1 or 2)	-u (T.PST.1SG) (goal/ direction: 2)	-t (T.PST.1SG) (goal/ direction: 3)
(a)	sap- 'tiptoe, move slowly'	—	kèè-sop-ø	kàà-sap-ù	kàà-sap-t-è
	teereer- 'fly'	—	kà-tèèreer-ø	kàà-tèèreer-ù	kàà-tèèreer-t-è
	siriir- 'throw (a long distance)'	—	kèè-sìriir-ø	kàà-sìriir-ù	kàà-sìriir-t-è
(b)	siir- 'move over'	kèè-siir	kèè-sììr-ø	kà-siir-ù	kà-siir-t-è
	mukurkuur- 'roll'	kèè-mùkurkúúr	kèè-mùkurkùùr-ø	kàà-mùkùrkuur-ù	kàà-mùkùrkuur-t-è
	taar- 'kick'	kee-táár	kèè-toor-ø	kàà-toor-ù	kàà-taar-t-è
(c)	yeel- 'move aside'	kà-yèèl	kà-yeel-ø	kàà-yeel-ù	—
	lapat- 'run'	kà-lapát	kà-llopot-ø	kàà-làpot-ú	—
	tooč- 'ascend'	kee-tóóč	kèè-took-ø	kàà-took-ù	—

A small number of translational motion verbs in their simple stem form (i.e. when the stem contains just a root) do not allow any deictic contrast, and are always deictically neutral by themselves (e.g. lèèkité 'approach', nòòmən 'leave').

Applicative derived stems of some translational motion verbs allow a three-way directional contrast between their 'deictically neutral', 'hither', and 'thither' forms or a two-way 'deictically neutral'–'hither' or a two-way 'hither'–'thither' distinction, using (two or all of) the suffix complexes in (14), which consist of the DD suffix (deictically neutral: -ø, 'hither': -u, 'thither': -t) and the applicative suffix -ee 'via, at, from'.

(14) (i) -ø-ee 'deictically neutrally via/at/from'
    (ii) -un-ee (-nw-ee in the case of a stem ending in n) 'hither via/at/from' (u of -un-ee and w of -nw-ee could be analyzed as epenthetic.)
    (iii) -t-ee 'thither via/at/from'

Examples are given in Table 3. (Applicative derived stems take the same form, irrespective of the person, because the suffix slot already occupied by the applicative suffix cannot be used for a subject person suffix.)

Table 3: Verbs with the applicative suffix for 'via, at, from' (citation forms).

	verb root 'gloss'	deictically neutral via/at/from	'hither via/at/from'	'thither via/at/from'
(a)	tampuliil- 'float'	tampuliil-ø-éé	tampuliil-un-éé	tampuliil-t-éé
(b)	sareet- 'scatter'	sareet-ø-éé	sәreet-un-éé	—
(c)	tɨl- 'cross, pass by, move through'	—	tɨl-un-éé	tɨl-t-éé

There is (at least) one verb that always contains the applicative suffix for 'via, at, from' (e.g. *pun-nw-éé* (hither), *pun-t-éé* (thither; basic form) 'cross, pass through'), presumably because it intrinsically has the notion of 'via'.

3.2 'Along'–deictic-directional suffix complex

As stated earlier, the Kupsapiny ALONG-DD complex[10] consists of the 'along' suffix *-aa/-oo* and one of the DD suffixes, *-n* 'hither' or *-t* 'thither'.[11] (The 'hither' suffix is *-ø* or *-u* in the absence of the 'along' suffix and *-un* (or *-n*) in the DD-applicative complex, but in the ALONG-DD complex, it is *-n*.[12])

Table 4 shows forms of the ALONG-DD complex, and Table 5 gives examples of citation forms of verbs with the ALONG-DD complex. Between the verb root and the 'along' suffix *-aa/-oo*, there can usually be *-n* (preceded by an epenthetic

---

10 The 'along' suffix requires one of the DD suffixes, and cannot occur without it. Most motion verbs can take one of the DD suffixes alone, without carrying the 'along' suffix. On the other hand, non-motion verbs cannot take one of the DD suffixes alone directly, but can only be accompanied by the ALONG-DD complex as a whole.
11 The choice between *-aa* and *-oo* is often lexically determined. With certain lexemes, however, these forms may be in free variation or may be dialectal variants (e.g. *kù-pasèn-aat-ø* (PTCP.3-ask.to.lend.money-AL.TH-3) in (3) used in the Western dialect; *kù-pasèn-oot-ø* used in other dialects).
12 This is also reported for other Southern Nilotic languages. The following table compares the Kupsapiny DD suffixes and ALONG-DD complexes with those in Cherang'any (Mietzner 2016), Endo (Zwarts 2004), and Nandi (Creider 1989, 2002) (see also Payne this volume).

	DD suffix		ALONG-DD complex	
	'hither'	'thither'	'hither along'	'thither along'
Kupsapiny	-ø, -u; -un	-t	-áán, -óón, etc.	-áát, -óót, etc.
Cherang'any	-u	-ta	-aan	-aati
Endo	-u, -uun	-ta, -taar	-aanu	-aata
Nandi	-u	-ta	-aan	-aat

u) in the case of 'hither', as in *siir-unóón-u* (move.over-AL.H-1/2), or *-t* in the case of 'thither', as in *siir-tóót-e* (move.over-AL.TH-1/2). There are also cases where *-n* (preceded by an epenthetic *u*) occurs immediately before the ALONG-DD complex for 'thither' *-aat/-oot* to express 'hither along' (rather than 'thither along') as in *siir-unáát-e/siir-unóót-e* (move.over-AL.H-1/2). On the other hand, the sequence of *-n* and the ALONG-DD complex *-aat/-oot* for 'thither' (without any epenthetic vowel) expresses 'thither along' (rather than 'hither along') (e.g. *kà-à-muutù-noot-e-kéy* (T.PST-1SG-move.around-AL.TH-1/2-REFL) in (6), and *ɲèèru-nóót-e* (become.angry-AL.TH-1/2)).

Table 4: Forms of the 'along'–deictic-directional suffix complex (citation forms).

'hither along' (V-AL.H-1/2)	'thither along' (V-AL.TH-1/2)
V-*aan-u*	V-*aat-e*
V-*oon-u*	V-*oot-e*
V-*unoon-u*	V-*toot-e*
V-*toon-u*	V-*taat-e*
V-*unaat-e*	V-*naat-e*
V-*unoot-e*	V-*noot-e*

Table 5: Verbs with the 'along'–deictic-directional suffix complex (citation forms).

verb root 'gloss'	'hither along' (V-AL.H-1/2)	'thither along' (V-AL.TH-1/2)
siir- 'move over'	*siir-óón-u/* *siir-unóón-u/* *siir-tóón-u/* *siir-unáát-e/* *siir-unóót-e*	*siir-áát-e/* *siir-óót-e/* *siir-tóót-e/* *siir-táát-e*
mukurkuur- 'roll'	*mùkurkuur-óón-u/* *mùkurkuur-unóón-u/* *mùkurkuur-tóón-u/* *mùkurkuur-unóót-e*	*mùkurkuur-óót-e/* *mùkurkuur-tóót-e*
taar- 'kick'	*toor-óón-u/* *toor-unóón-u/* *toor-tóón-u/* *toor-unáát-e/* *toor-unóót-e*	*taar-áát-e/* *taar-táát-e*
yeel- 'move aside'	*yeel-óón-u/* *yeel-unóón-u/* *yeel-unóót-e*	*yeel-áát-e/* *yeel-táát-e*

Table 5 (continued)

verb root 'gloss'	'hither along' (V-AL.H-1/2)	'thither along' (V-AL.TH-1/2)
lapat- 'run'	*lapat-óón-u/* *lapat-unóón-u/* *lapat-unáát-e/* *lapat-unóót-e*	*lapat-áát-e*
tooč- 'ascend'	*took-óón-u/* *took-unóón-u/* *took-unáát-e/* *took-unóót-e*	*took-áát-e/* *took-táát-e*
sap- 'tiptoe, move slowly'	*sap-óón-u/* *sap-unóón-u/* *sap-tóón-u/* *sap-unáát-e/* *sap-unóót-e*	*sap-áát-e/* *sap-táát-e*
teereer- 'fly'	*tèèreer-óón-u/* *tèèreer-unóón-u/* *tèèreer-tóón-u/* *tèèreer-unáát-e/* *tèèreer-unóót-e*	*tèèreer-áát-e/* *tèèreer-táát-e*
siriir- 'throw (a long distance)'	*sìriir-óón-u/* *sìriir-unóón-u/* *sìriir-tóón-u/* *sìriir-unáát-e/* *sìriir-unóót-e*	*sìriir-áát-e/* *sìriir-táát-e*

As shown in Tables 4 and 5, when the subject is first or second person, the ALONG-DD complex is immediately followed by the subject person suffix (*-u* for 'hither' and *-e* for 'thither') to form *-aan-u/-oon-u* 'hither along' and *-aat-e/-oot-e* 'thither along'. Because the suffix for the third person right after the ALONG-DD complex is zero, such third-person verbs take the forms in Tables 4 and 5 minus *-u* ('hither') or minus *-e* ('thither') (e.g. 'move over' *siir-óón* with 'hither along'/ *siir-táát* with 'thither along') when one of the tense and subject person-number prefixes attaches to them.

The ALONG-DD complex is often followed by the applicative suffix *-ee* 'via, at, from' to form *-oon-nw-ee* '-AL.H-VAF' or *-aat-ee/-oot-ee* '-AL.TH-VAF', as in (4). It is also often followed by an imperfective aspect suffix, which has different forms depending on the directional, either *-u* 'hither' or *-i* 'thither', to form *-oon-u* '-AL.H-IPFV' or *-aat-i/-oot-i* '-AL.TH-IPFV', as in (5).[13]

---

[13] There are also cases where *-u* (for 'hither') or *-i* (for 'thither') is used emphatically, e.g. (31).

The use of the ALONG-DD complex is normally optional, though the verb for 'walk' in central and western dialects requires the 'along'–'thither' complex, yielding *wost-óót-e*; however, when not accompanied by the applicative or the imperfective suffix, this form is used regardless of deictic direction (whether the direction is 'hither', 'thither', or 'deictic neutral'), and the 'hither along' counterpart *wost-óón-u* is not commonly used.

Unlike the simple DD suffixes, whose use is mostly limited to motion verbs, the ALONG-DD complex can attach both to motion verbs (including deictic motion verbs) and to non-motion verbs (e.g. *miite-* 'exist', *roopən-* 'rain'), including verbs borrowed from English (e.g. *koolinken-* 'call', *respoontinken-* 'respond'). There are only two verbs in the present author's data that cannot carry this suffix complex: *čara-* 'injure, hurt' (and its anti-causative form *čara-kay* 'become injured, become hurt') and *pun-* 'arrive'.

The ALONG-DD complex often expresses translational motion with a deictic direction in space, but there are cases where its meaning is not at all spatial but purely temporal. The next two subsections discuss these two uses.

3.2.1 Spatial notions conveyed by the 'along'–deictic-directional suffix complex

Belkadi (2015) states that DDs that are used for AM can express different types of situations relative to time relations, path shapes, or the grammatical relation of the noun phrase referring to a moving entity (subject vs. object), depending on the semantics of the verb and the pragmatic context.

In Kupsapiny, the temporal relation between the lexically-designated event and the deictic motion imparted by the ALONG-DD complex allows different interpretations depending on the lexical aspectual property expressed by the verb. When the lexical event is durative or iterative, the lexical and the deictic motion events are interpreted as occurring concurrently ('V continuously/iteratively this/that way'). When the lexical event is understood to be punctual, the motion event is subsequent to the lexical event ('V and [then] come/go continuously').

When the lexical event is understood to be durative or iterative, the ALONG-DD complex construction bears different semantic functions, depending on the type of the lexical verb.

On a motion verb expressing a durative event, the complex adds one of the two DD notions ('hither' or 'thither') as well as a sense of continuity of the translational motion. The deictic specification expressed by the complex and the translational motion expressed by the verb root occur concurrently and continuously (e.g. (15): path of motion verb, (16A): manner of motion verb, (16B) and (17): cause of motion verbs).

(15) ku-čáč   yéč   m̀po   paapà   kù-nòòk-**ùnoon**-ø
     PTCP.3-start again also father.DEF.SG.NOM PTCP.3-approach-**AL.H**-3
     yootò
     that.time
     '... the father again started to continuously come close (to the home) at that time ...'
     (Conversation 2016.8-6: C. F. and C. E.)

(16) (A)ø-tĭk-**oot**-ì   ŋúɲ
     PTCP.2SG-step.on-**AL.TH**-IPFV ground.INDEF.SG
     (B)ø-čuut-**oot**-éé   keréénkok   ŋúɲ.
     PTCP.2SG-pull-**AL.TH**-VAF   leg.DEF.PL   ground.INDEF.SG
     '... one (*lit.* the generic second-person singular)(A)walked along that way barefoot (*lit.* stepped along that way on the ground)'), while(B)dragging his/her legs along that way on the surface of the ground.'
     (Conversation 2016.8-8: C. F. and C. E.)

(17) kà-toor-**taat**-ø   pasukùlît   kù-wo   ká
     T.PST.3-push-**AL.TH**-3 bicycle.DEF.SG PTCP.3-go.sg   home.INDEF.SG
     '... he pushed a bicycle along that way, and went home ...'
     (Pear story 11: S. H.)

When the ALONG-DD complex attaches to a non-motion verb lexeme denoting a durative or iterative event, it can convey AM of the subject in a direction toward or not toward the deictic center, concomitantly with the continuous or iterative action or state change (or the continuous state) encoded by the verb root. Thus, it motionalizes non-motion verbs, and the temporal relation between the lexical event and the deictic motion is concurrent.

With an action verb, the action continues concurrently with the motion expressed by the suffix complex (e.g. (18), (19)).

(18) kii-yè   čá=tilé   kààriimanîk   čo,
     D.PST.3-when   come.3SG=pass.by   young.man.DEF.PL.NOM   those
     kà-mii   kwòòm-**oot**-i   mùyèmpèènik.
     T.PST.3-exist PTCP.3-eat-**AL.TH**-IPFV   mango.DEF.PL
     '... when those young men came and passed by, they were eating mangoes as they went along.'
     (Pear story 20: C. E.)

(19) ku-ĩm   neetó   làttyet   kù-ŋolool-**oon**-ú
      PTCP.3-hear   3SG.NOM   neighbor.DEF.SG   PTCP.3-talk-**AL.H**-IPFV
      ak   čìt=aake.
      other   person.DEF.SG=certain
      '... she heard a neighbor talking with some other person as she
      (= the neighbor) came along.'
      (Story 2015.7/8-5: C. F.)

When the verb is stative, as in (20), the subject referent moves while maintaining the state.

(20) a-čil   čìt=aakè   ɲèè   ø-póónt-**oot**-i
      PTCP.1SG-see person.DEF.SG=certain   REL.SG   PRS.3-have-**AL.TH**-IPFV
      wààrwet
      goat.DEF.SG
      '... I saw someone who was taking a goat along that way (*lit.* has a goat as he is going) ...'
      (Pear story 8: C. E.)

When the lexical event expresses a gradual change of state, and the ALONG-DD construction conveys an incremental, continual change of state during the motion (e.g. (21), (22)).[14]

(21) kà-čaas-**ààt**-ø   neetó.
      T.PST.3-become.tired-**AL.TH**-3   3SG.NOM
      'S/he became increasingly tired as s/he went along.'

(22) kà-ŋàràk-**oon**-ø   neetó.
      T.PST.3-become.happy-**AL.H**-3   3SG.NOM
      'S/he became increasingly happy as s/he came along.'

---

14 In Kupsapiny, physical sensations and emotions are often expressed with an idiomatic expression with the noun for the feeling as subject and the main verb predicate being a verb for eating, killing, or finishing. For example, 'X becomes hungry' is expressed as 'Hunger eats/kills/finishes X'. In the ALONG-DD complex construction, the verb is an action verb, but the construction conveys a gradual intensification of a physical sensation or an emotion.

(i)   kà-kkaam-**aat**-ø   nééto   rupèt.
      T.PST.3-eat-**AL.TH**-3 3SG   hunger.DEF.SG.NOM
      'S/he became increasingly hungry as s/he went along (*lit.* Hunger ate him/her (continuously) as s/he went along).'

When the suffix complex accompanies a verb denoting a change of state that is potentially punctual and iterative (a "one-way resettable change" in Talmy 2000: 68; e.g. 'fall', 'drop'), the construction conveys an iterable full-cycle state change (e.g. 'fall and get up', 'drop something and pick it up'), as in (23). Other verbs used this way include *pùrtekey* 'fall down' and *mìstè* 'faint'.

(23) kà-ru-w-**oon**-ø   neetó.
     T.PST.3-fall.asleep-EP-**AL.H**-3   3SG.NOM
     'S/he fell asleep and woke up repeatedly as s/he came along.'[15]

When the event expressed by the verb of the ALONG-DD complex construction is punctual but non-iterative (i.e. unlikely to occur multiple times), the meaning of the construction is usually interpreted as 'V and come/go continuously' (subsequent motion). Motion verbs that typically express this type of event have the path vector FROM or VIA, when they take a singular noun phrase for the ground entity. Examples include *noomàn* 'leave', *pukáákte* 'leave', *mwèy* 'escape', *tur* 'escape', *yay* 'cross' (when the ground is regarded as a linear or ribbonal (long thin strip-like) object, rather than a planar object bounded both at a pair of axes parallel to and at another perpendicular to the figure entity's path; e.g. a line, a road, a border), *wùt* 'enter', and *mùŋte* 'cross a boundary (enter/exit)'. Motion events expressed with such verbs usually involve no or little temporal duration, and the figure entity goes through an immediate change of location, normally one time, before the deictic translational motion starts, as in (24) and (25). For example, in (24), one of the verbs for leaving involves the vector FROM. The event of his/her leaving a market precedes his/her going along from there.

(24) kà-noomən-**òòt**-ee   neetó   màkit.
     T.PST.3-leave-**AL.TH**-VAF 3SG.NOM market.INDEF.SG
     'S/he left a market, and went along.'

---

15 Because the verb *ru* also has the stative sense of 'be asleep', (23) could also mean 'S/he kept asleep as s/he came along' (as well as 'S/he has been asleep' when the ALONG-DD complex is in its purely temporal sense).

(25) kìì-taŋáɲ piikò kàpusa kot
 D.PST.3-suffer person.DEF.PL.NOM very.much until
 kù-mwèy-**oot**-ø yáát piikò, ku-mwîy
 PTCP.3-escape-**AL.TH**-3 DM person.DEF.PL.NOM PTCP.3-escape
 alák akóy wook ...
 other up.to forest.DEF.PL
 'People suffered very much, and as a result, they escaped and went along, and others escaped up to the forest ...'
 (Conversation 2016-8: C. F. and C. E.)

Object-maneuvering verbs including clothing verbs usually express punctual but non-iterative events. When they are accompanied by the suffix complex, the construction preferably means 'V and [then] come/go continuously' (subsequent motion), as in (26) and (27).[16] Such verbs include *kàlaŋ* 'lift up', *kànap* 'lift up (something heavy)', *kasán* 'put on the back', *nùmu* 'remove', *čwìy* 'separate, divide into pieces', *sòru* 'grab forcefully', *nam* 'hold, grab', *lač* 'put on (a clothing item)', *rèèku* 'take off (a clothing item)', *rat* 'tie', *tyač* 'untie'.

(26) à-wo kéélly-a wòòk wùlin
 PTCP.1SG-go.SG way-POSS forest.DEF.PL there
 à-toor-**óót**-i kiššéérok,
 PTCP.1SG-put.on.head-**AL.TH**-IPFV skin.DEF.PL
 à-pùn-t-ee wòòk lìn ...
 PTCP.1SG-pass.through-TH-VAF forest.DEF.PL there
 '... I went through the forest there (*lit.* the way of the forest there), put animal skins on the head, and went along, and passed that way through the forest there ...'
 (Conversation 2016.8-8: C. F. and C. E.)

(27) yòòto kyàà-kasan-**óót**-i àni lèèkok.
 at.that.time D.PST.1SG-put.on.back-**AL.TH**-IPFV 1SG.NOM child.DEF.PL
 'At that time, I put the children on my back, and went along.'
 (Story 2012.7-1: M. M. K.)

---

16 However, this does not apply to *ywee* 'put'. When accompanied by the suffix complex, this verb expresses concurrent motion, 'keep on putting iteratively', rather than subsequent motion (*'put and [then] come/go continuously'), perhaps because of its polysemy with 'give', or possibly because its basic sense is 'give'.

Nevertheless, events expressed by these verbs with the ALONG-DD complex could be interpreted as durative or iterative, and when such an interpretation occurs, the lexical and the deictic motion events are taken as concurrent (e.g. kà-rat-aat-í 'tie, fasten' in (31) could mean, 'he tied (a certain person) continuously as he went along').

Some non-motion verbs can express either punctual or iterative events (e.g. láál 'cough', pur 'knock', tol 'explode'). When such a verb is used with the ALONG-DD complex, the interpretation may be either subsequent motion or concurrent motion, as in (28).

(28) ka-láál-**oon**-ø   neetó.
T.PST.3-cough-**AL.H**-3   3SG.NOM
'S/he coughed once, and [then] came along.' or 'S/he coughed repetitively as s/he came along.'

Lexemes used as posture or posture-change verbs (e.g. yoɲ 'stand (up)', puur 'sit (down)') can express different types of events with the ALONG-DD complex, as in (29). These cannot be classified into any single aspectual type, either.

(29) kèè-yoŋ-**oot**-ø   neetó   àm   rapét.
T.PST.3-stand-**AL.TH**-3   3SG.NOM LOC   boat.DEF.SG
 (a) 'S/he went along standing on the boat.' (lexical event: stative)
 (b) 'S/he stood up and sat down repeatedly as s/he went along on the boat.' (lexical event: iterable full-cycle posture change)
 (c) 'S/he stood up, and [then] went along on the boat.' (lexical event: punctual and non-iterative)

Unlike those AM-dedicated systems, which can make several fine-grained distinctions in which each affix has a fixed temporal interpretation, the Kupsapiny ALONG-DD complex can express different temporal relations, depending on the aspectual interpretation of the lexical event. Belkadi (2015) attributes the difference between AM affixes in AM-dedicated systems and DDs in AM-undedicated systems to the difference in the degree of grammaticalization – AM affixes in AM-dedicated systems are more grammaticalized and more resistant to semantic and pragmatic factors than AM-expressible DDs. However, this claim does not seem reasonable if polysemy is "a natural outcome of grammaticalization" (Heine et al. 1991: 261), motivated by "paradigmatic economy" (Haiman 1985: 159), which "economizes on the inventory of signs within a system". In fact, the Kupsapiny suffix complex is highly grammaticalized, and is not invariant in meaning. The simplicity of the ALONG-DD complex seems to make its meaning further context-dependent or ambiguous in some cases, as discussed in Section 3.2.2.

3.2.2 Aspectual notions conveyed by the 'along'–deictic-directional suffix complex

As shown in Section 3.2.1, the ALONG-DD complex appears to consistently convey spatial motion in a particular deictic direction. However, the temporal relation between the lexical event and the deictic motion event depends on the aspectual property of the expressed event – it is that of concurrent motion when the event is durative or iterative, and it is that of subsequent motion when the event is punctual and non-iterative. Thus, the use of the ALONG-DD complex is not independent of aspect. Furthermore, there are four other phenomena that suggest that the use of this suffix complex is not purely spatial, but aspectual.

First, regardless of whether the temporal relation between the lexical event and the deictic motion event expressed by the ALONG-DD complex construction is concurrent or subsequent, the deictic motion always continues for some time, in the course of which the figure entity travels a certain distance, rather than instantaneously changing its location. That is, a certain duration of time is required for the deictic motion.

Second, when the ALONG-DD complex construction expresses concurrent motion, the action or state (change) encoded by the verb root has to be continuative (or iterative in the case of an action and a state change) throughout the motion. For example, in (18), the young men's eating activity has to persist during their motion away from the speaker. It would be inappropriate for an event where their activity stops intermittently during the motion.

Third, when no ground entity (e.g. source or goal of motion) is mentioned, the ALONG-DD complex construction with a non-motion verb can normally have both an AM interpretation, and also the aspectual interpretation of either the continuation or iteration of the action or state change or the continuation of the state encoded by the verb root (e.g. (30–35)). When the verb is in one of the past tenses, the continuation or iteration lasts up to a certain reference point in time (typically, the time of speaking), additionally yielding a perfect aspect meaning (e.g. (30), (31)). In the purely aspectual interpretation, which seems to have developed from the spatial interpretation, no motion is involved, and it does not matter which of the deictic suffixes is used. For example, in (30) and (31), *kii-póónt-**oot**-í* and *kà-rat-**aat**-í* could be replaced by *kii-póónt-**oon**-ú* (D.PST.3-have-**AL.H**-IPFV) and *kà-rat-**oon**-u* (T.PST.3-tie-**AL.H**-EMPH), respectively, without any difference in meaning.

(30) *kii-póónt-**oot**-í*   *tùkuk*   *álak*
D.PST.3-have-**AL.TH**-IPFV thing.DEF.PL other
'… he had had other things (for some time) …'
(Conversation 2016.8-1: C. F. and C. F.)

(31) kà-nam mèrèèt=akè čìt=aakè ɲèè
T.PST.3-catch man.DEF.SG.NOM=certain person.DEF.SG=certain REL.SG
kà-rat-**aat**-í
T.PST.3-tie-**AL.TH**-EMPH
'A certain man caught a certain person who had been tied (*lit*, he had tied) (for some time) …'
("Causality across Languages" Discourse Subproject Experiment, ID07: #42 HM2_strongman)

(32) a. ø-mìite ànu waarwèt?
PRS.3-exist where goat.DEF.SG

b. ø-riip-**òòn**-u/ø-riip-**òòt**-i čeeròp waarwèt.
PRS.3-have-**AL.H**-IPFV/PRS.3-have-**AL.TH**-IPFV Cheerop.NOM goat.DEF.SG

a. 'Where is the goat?'

b. 'Cheerop has been keeping the goat.'

(33) CFR: ø-wèè=ø-soot-**áát**-e ɲi ŋàlee-ča.
PTCP.2SG-go.2SG=PTCP.2SG-think-**AL.TH**-1/2 2SG.NOM word.DEF.PL-those

CFA: ma-a-soot-**áát**-e àni.
FUT-PTCP.1SG-think-**AL.TH**-1/2 1SG.NOM

CFR: 'Keep thinking about those things wherever you are. (*lit*. Go and keep thinking about those words.)'

CFA: 'I will keep thinking about them.'
(Conversation 2016.8-1: C. F. and C. F.)

(34) ø-mìite ŋalèèk čèè ø-tòòku-**nòòn**-u àm àrañ.
PRS.3-exist word.DEF.PL REL.PL PRS.3-happen-**AL.H**-IPFV LOC road.INDEF.SG
'There are situations (*lit*. words) that keep happening on the road.'
(Conversation 2018.1-4: C. F. and C. P.)

(35) (A)kù-miŋiš-**oot** yáát piikò
PTCP.3-live-**AL.TH** DM person.DEF.PL.NOM
(B)kù-taŋàŋ-**áát**-ø kùčakee yootò páka paantáɲ.
PTCP.3-suffer-**AL.TH**-3 since that.time until now
'… the people (A)have been living there and (B)have been suffering since that time until now.'
(Conversation 2016-8: C. F. and C. E.; continued from (25))

The meaning of the ALONG-DD complex can also be purely temporal when it attaches to certain motion verbs with no specific goal or source, or with verbs expressing self-contained motion (or those used for self-contained motion) (e.g. (36b)) rather than translational motion (e.g. (36a)) (see also (4), (5), and (6)). In such a case, no deictic direction is specified.

(36) kà-toor-**taat**-ø   neetó   pásukulìt.
 T.PST.3-push-**AL.TH**-3   3SG.NOM   bicycle.DEF.SG
 (a) 'S/he pushed a bicycle along that way.'
 (b) 'S/he repeatedly pushed the bicycle in one place.'

This purely temporal use of the ALONG-DD complex is very frequent in my conversation data. Out of 42 instances of the use of the ALONG-DD complex in the conversation data that I collected, 11 were examples of its purely temporal use as an aspectual marker.[17]

Fourth, the ALONG-DD complex construction is ambiguous between a one-time occurrence of the lexical event and repeated occurrences. For example, in (37), the complex event of a combination of getting out of the car or getting off the motorcycle and walking is interpreted as happening repeatedly in this context. Another example is provided in (38), whose free translation reflects the repeated occurrence of the event, which the speaker had in mind.

(37) či-péé-t-i   čèè-rok-**unòòt**-i   mpo
 PTCP.1PL-go.PL-TH-IPFV   PTCP.1PL-descend-**AL.H**-IPFV   even
 '... we traveled (*lit*. go) (on the very bad road), and even came out (of the car or off the motorcycle) (*lit*. get down) (and walked) repeatedly ...'
 (Conversation 2018.1-3: C. F. and S. H.)

(38) ku-kkwáy   yáát   čoo   tukúk,
 PTCP.3-pick   DM   those   thing.DEF.PL
 ku-kéttyi-**nóón**-ø   kèrèpoon-tèŋo
 PTCP.3-return-**AL.H**-3   basket.DEF.SG-that
 '... now they (the children) picked those things, and returned them to that basket repetitively ...'
 (Pear story 11: S. H.)

---

17 I collected the data in August 2016 and January 2018 (total number of conversations: 14, total amount of time: 58 minutes and 31 seconds).

The repeated interpretation is always possible, and seems to be likely especially in the following three types of cases, judging from the ways that my consultants interpret meanings of examples of the ALONG-DD complex construction: (i) when a source of motion is mentioned, (ii) when the vector of the motion verb is intrinsically FROM, and (iii) when the expressed event involves the vector FROM.

According to Belkadi (2015), DDs commonly grammaticalize into tense, aspect, or modality markers because of associations of spatial concepts with the domain of time (e.g. Lakoff and Johnson 1980). In the case of Kupsapiny, the DDs without the 'along' suffix do not have any non-spatial use. When they are combined with the 'along' suffix, which expresses continuous motion in space over a certain duration of time, the suffix complex as a whole can yield the aspectual notion of continuation or iteration, and can even be used as a pure aspectual marker.[18]

4 Discussion

This section discusses some of the findings of the present study. Section 4.1 speculates on how the Kupsapiny ALONG-DD complex came to be used as an aspectual marker. Section 4.2 shows how the Kupsapiny ALONG-DD complex is a counterexample to one of the implicational hierarchies (the temporal implicational hierarchy in (9)) proposed for AM by Guillaume (2016). Section 4.3 discusses the treatment of AM in the context of motion typology, in particular Talmy's (1991, 2000) typology of event integration.

4.1 Development of the 'along'–deictic-directional suffix complex into an aspectual marker

As shown in Section 3, the ALONG-DD complex construction in Kupsapiny is not devoted to any specific type of motion, but may be used to describe DD, AM, or neither, partially depending on the verb root that it combines with. The meaning of the Kupsapiny ALONG-DD complex is largely spatio-temporal and sometimes exclusively temporal.

---

[18] Crazzolara (1978: 103) states that the suffix complex in another Kalenjin language, Pokot, expresses the non-spatial notion of "intensity, exertion, applied to some action". This seems to differ from the aspectual notion that the Kupsapiny ALONG-DD complex can express, but it still needs to be investigated exactly how it differs from it.

There seem to be several possible motivations for this. First, as Belkadi (2015) points out about DDs in other languages, the Kupsapiny ALONG-DD complex may have grammaticalized into an aspectual marker, because of a general cognitive tendency to conceptualize time in terms of spatial concepts (e.g. Clark 1973; Lakoff and Johnson 1980: 41–45, 1999: 139–161). Second, unlike AM affixes in AM-devoted systems and DDs that can be used to describe AM, in the Kupsapiny ALONG-DD complex, the 'along' element seems to have the function of an aspect marker, independently of the DD suffixes, even though it requires the presence of one of them. The meaning of the 'along' suffix may be seemingly purely spatial. However, motion is a spatio-temporal phenomenon, and when the 'along' suffix motionalizes a non-motion verb in expressing AM, the concept of continuation or iteration, which is inherent in the meaning of the suffix, necessarily involves this process.

4.2 Implicational hierarchy for the temporal relation of associated motion

As mentioned in Section 2, two implicational hierarchies have been proposed regarding crosslinguistic patterns of AM by Guillaume (2016) (also Levinson and Wilkins 2006). However, they were primarily based on data on AM-dedicated systems in Australian and South American languages, where AM systems may be sensitive to the grammatical relation of the moving entity, and to the temporal relation between the lexical event and the deictic motion event. The Kupsapiny data supports the implicational hierarchy in (8) (Subject > Object: an AM marker is more likely to express the motion of subject than that of object, and if it can express the motion of object, then it can also express that of subject).[19] In transitive AM examples, (16B), (17), (18), (20), (26), and (27), the moving entity has to be the subject. However, the second proposed implicational hierarchy in (9) (Prior motion > Concurrent motion > Subsequent motion: if an AM marker expresses a

---

19 There are two exceptions. First, when the subject is a possessed body-part noun, the moving entity is the possessor, as in (i).

(i)   *kèè-wutùt-**oot**-ø*   *ryoonté-mmwaaní.*
      T.PST.3-become.itchy-**AL.TH**-3 skin.DEF.SG-1SG.POSS
      'My skin became more and more itchy as I went along.' (Also, 'My skin has been itchy.')

Second, when the verb for 'eat', 'kill', or 'finish' with the ALONG-DD complex is used in an idiomatic expression for a physical sensation or emotion (Footnote 14), the moving entity is the referent of the object noun phrase rather than the subject noun phrase.

relation on the hierarchy, then it can also express any other relation to the left) does not hold for the Kupsapiny ALONG-DD complex – when used for AM, this suffix complex can express concurrent motion or subsequent motion, but not prior motion, which is the highest in the proposed hierarchy.

As discussed in Section 3.2, the interpretation of the motion event as being subsequent versus concurrent depends on the aspectual property of the lexical event. In subsequent motion, the path of deictic motion is always bounded at its starting point, when the lexical event finishes, and is neutral as to boundedness at its endpoint (it may be bounded or unbounded at its endpoint depending on the context). On the other hand, in concurrent motion, the path is neutral with respect to boundedness at both ends. Therefore, both in subsequent motion and concurrent motion, the path is neutral in boundedness at its final point. The neutrality of boundedness at the end of the path is the temporal property of the Kupsapiny ALONG-DD complex as used for AM.

The hierarchy in (9) can accommodate polysemous cases, and the two types of relations on the left (prior motion and concurrent motion) and those on the right (concurrent motion and subsequent motion) each have a property in common and form a continuum. Because prior motion is a mirror image of and has characteristics opposite to subsequent motion, the path is neutral with respect to boundedness at its starting point, and is always bounded at its end, where the verb event starts. Thus, prior motion shares the neutrality of the boundedness of the path at its starting point with concurrent motion. This is unlike subsequent motion, which shares the neutrality of the boundedness of the path at its end point with concurrent motion.

The hierarchy in (9) predicts that there is no language where (at least) a single construction expresses prior motion and subsequent motion, excluding concurrent motion, because the two end-situations have no path boundedness property in common. One may wonder why the relations sharing unboundedness at the starting point of the path (prior motion and concurrent motion), rather than those sharing unboundedness at the end point of the path (subsequent motion and concurrent motion), is placed higher on the hierarchy. A possible reason for this arrangement may be the goal-source asymmetry (e.g. Ikegami 1987), whereby goal is more salient and more frequently mentioned than and more likely to be grammaticalized and easily specifiable than source across languages. The Kupsapiny ALONG-DD suffix might be a counterexample to this tendency.

The Kupsapiny ALONG-DD complex cannot be used for prior motion. Nevertheless, prior motion can be expressed by another construction in this language: 'come=V'/'go=V'. It takes the form of čee=V/wee=V in the case of the second-person singular subject and different forms depending on the person and number of the subject. In this construction, the proclitic for 'come' or 'go' is followed by a verb in its unprefixed form or its participle form, usually to express 'come/go and V' (e.g. čá=tílé in (18), ø-wèè=ø-soot-áát-e in (33)). Thus, it is not the case that Kupsapiny as a whole does not have a way to express the uppermost part of the hierarchy in (9) at all. However, it does not seem to be reasonable to place formally different types of constructions on the same hierarchy to talk about an implicational relationship between them.

4.3 Associated motion in the context of motion typology

As mentioned in Section 2, according to Levinson and Wilkins (2006) and Guillaume (2016), in AM, the fact of motion appears, not in the verb root, but in a grammatical morpheme, and such a system is not included in any typological pattern proposed in Talmy (1985, 1991, 2000, 2007). However, a fundamental question is whether or not AM is a type of complex event that is dealt with in Talmy's typology of event integration (a motion event as a macro-event). According to Talmy, a macro-event in general is a complex event consisting of two event components, a main event component (a framing event) and a secondary or subordinate event component (a co-event), which supports the framing event. The framing event has a framing function relative to the macro-event. Talmy (2000: 219) states that the framing event "provides for the whole macro-event the overarching conceptual framework or reference frame within which the other included activities are conceived of as taking place". It represents "the upshot – relative to the whole macro-event" in the sense that "it is the framing event that is asserted in a positive declarative sentence, that is denied under negation, that is demanded in an imperative, and that is asked about in an interrogative". It also determines the overall temporal and spatial frameworks, the argument structure, and the syntactic complement structure. Thus, a framing event component assumes the function of framing the core schema of a macro-event.

Motion is one of the five domains to which Talmy claims his typology of event integration applies. (The other domains are state change, realization, temporal contouring (aspect), and action correlating.) In the case of motion, the framing event is the figure entity's motion along a path relative to a ground entity – it is made up of a figure entity, a ground entity, a path of motion, and the fact of motion (or locatedness); the co-event may be a manner of motion, a cause of motion, a concomitance of motion, and so on. The most schematic component of a motion macro-event is a path of motion, and languages are classified into typological types depending on what type of morpheme frames the core schema of a macro-event, specifically, whether a path of motion is expressed in the main verb root (verb-framed languages: e.g. Spanish, *La botella **entró** a la cueva* *flotando.* 'The bottle **entered** the cave, floating') or the satellite (including affixes and particles; "the grammatical category of any constituent other than a noun-phrase or prepositional-phrase complement that is in a sister relation to the verb" (Talmy 2000: 102)) (satellite-framed languages: e.g. English, *The bottle floated **into** the cave.*). Formally, AM markers seem to satisfy the definition of a satellite.[20]

If AM were assumed to be a type of macro-event that Talmy's typology deals with, the question is whether its framing event is the figure entity's motion along a path (as in other types of complex motion events) or the lexical event or situation. If one employs Talmy's above-cited definition of the framing event in terms of what event component is associated with each speech act (e.g. command) and determines important facets of grammatical structure (e.g, the argument structure), AM seems to be different from motion as a macro-event as far as the Kupsapiny ALONG-DD complex is concerned, judging from my Sebei consultants' comments – when the ALONG-DD complex is used for AM, it is the verb event that satisfies the definition, and the deictic motion is secondary. This also turns out to be most likely the case if one examines contexts where the ALONG-DD complex is used for AM. For example, the important event components in the clauses of examples (18) and (19) in which the verb marked with the ALONG-DD complex appears are the young men's eating mangoes and a neighbor's talking, respectively, rather than the deictic motion event components, which could go unmentioned in these contexts.

This seems to accord with Belkadi's (2015) characterization of the motion component of AM as a "motion co-event". If the framing event is the verb event, another remaining question is whether or not AM is a different semantic domain from motion.

5 Conclusion

As discussed, the Kupsapiny ALONG-DD complex construction differs both from AM markers in AM-dedicated systems and from DDs in AM-undedicated systems – it involves the addition of the 'along' suffix to the DD suffixes. Its use is not limited only to emphasizing the continuity or iteration of motion and describing AM by motionalizing non-motion verbs. Its meaning is not purely spatial, but always spatio-temporal or only temporal. Therefore, in such a system, AM does not seem to be independent of aspect.

---

20 In one of my previous papers (Kawachi 2016: 62–63), I analyzed the ALONG-DD complex as a satellite-framed construction wherein the fact of motion and a concomitance are conflated.

Abbreviations

AL	along	INDEF	indefinite	REL	relative clause marker
AM	associated motion	IPFV	imperfective		
APP	applicative	LOC	locative	sb	somebody
D.PST	distant past	NEUT	deictically neutral	SG	singular
DD	deictic directional	NOM	nominative	sth	something
DEF	definite	O	object	T.PST	today past
DM	discourse marker	PL	plural	TH	thither
EMPH	emphasis	POSS	possessive	VAF	via/at/from
EP	epenthesis	PRS	present	1	first person
FOC	focus	PTCP	participle	2	second person
FUT	future	REFL	reflexive	3	third person
H	hither				

Acknowledgments: I would like to express my deepest gratitude to my consultants, especially, Chebet Francis (Sipi and Kapchorwa), Mwanga Elvis (Kasseren), and Chebet Mercy (Kapchorwa), for providing me Kupsapiny data. My sincere thanks also go to Doris Payne, Antoine Guillaume, Harold Koch, and Jean-Christophe Verstraete for their highly insightful comments, as well as the audience at the 8th Association for Linguistic Typology Conference and at the 156th meeting of the Linguistic Society of Japan for their questions and comments. Any errors or inaccuracies are, of course, my responsibility alone. The present study has been supported by grants from the Japan Society for the Promotion of Science (KAKENHI Project IDs: 15H05157 and 19K00565, PI: Kazuhiro Kawachi, KAKENHI Project IDs: 15H03206 and 19H01264, PI: Yo Matsumoto) and from the National Institute for Japanese Language and Linguistics. It also used data that I collected for studies supported by the National Science Foundation (Project ID: BCS-1535846, PI: Jürgen Bohnemeyer). I owe a video file for Wallace Chafe's Pear Film to Mary Erbaugh.

References

Barasa, David. 2017. *Ateso grammar: A descriptive account of an Eastern Nilotic language*. Cape Town: University of Cape Town, dissertation.
Belkadi, Aicha. 2015. Associated motion with deictic directionals: A comparative overview. *SOAS Working Papers in Linguistics* 17. 49–76.
Bourdin, Philippe. 2006. The marking of directional deixis in Somali: How typologically idiosyncratic is it? In Voeltz, F. K. Erhard (ed.), *Studies in African linguistic typology*, 13–41. Amsterdam: John Benjamins.
Clark, Herbert H. 1973. Space, time, semantics and the child. In Timothy E. Moore (ed.), *Cognitive development and the acquisition of language*, 27–63. New York: Academic Press.

Crazzolara, Pasquale. 1978. *A Study of the Pokot (Suk) language: Grammar and vocabulary*. Bologna: Editrice Missionaria Italiana.
Creider, Chet A. & Jane Tapsubei Creider. 1989. *A grammar of Nandi*. Hamburg: Helmut Buske Verlag.
Creider, Chet. 2002. The semantics of participant types in derived verbs in Nandi. *Revue Québécoise de Linguistique* 31 (2). 171–190.
Creissels, Denis & Alain Christian Bassène. This volume, chapter 17. Ventive, associated motion and aspect in Jóola Fóoñi (Atlantic).
Dimmendaal, Gerrit J. 1983. *The Turkana language*. Dordrecht: Foris.
Dixon, R. M. W. 1994. *Ergativity*. Cambridge: Cambridge University Press.
Guérois, Rozenn, Hannah Gibson & Bastian Persohn. This volume, chapter 15. Associated motion in Bantu languages.
Guillaume, Antoine. 2013. Reconstructing the category of "associated motion" in Tacanan languages (Amazonian Bolivia and Peru). In Ritsuko Kikusawa & Lawrence A. Reid (eds.), *Historical linguistics 2011: Selected papers from the 20th international conference on historical linguistics, Osaka, 25–30 July 2011*, 129–151. Amsterdam: John Benjamins.
Guillaume, Antoine. 2016. Associated motion in South America: Typological and areal perspectives. *Linguistic Typology* 20 (1). 81–177.
Haiman, John. 1985. *Natural syntax: Iconicity and erosion*. Cambridge: Cambridge University Press.
Heine, Bernd, Ulrike Claudi & Friederike Hünnemeyer. 1991. *Grammaticalization: A conceptual framework*. Chicago: University of Chicago Press.
Ikegami, Yoshihiko. 1987. 'Source' vs. 'goal': A case of linguistic dissymmetry. In René Dirven & Günter Radden (eds.), *Concepts of case*, 122–146. Tübingen: Gunter Narr Verlag.
Jacques, Guillaume, Aimée Lahaussois & Shuya Zhang. This volume, chapter 21. Associated motion in Trans-Himalayan, with a focus on Gyalrongic and Kiranti.
Kawachi, Kazuhiro. 2011. Meanings of the spatial deictic verb suffixes in Kupsapiny. In Osamu Hieda (ed.), *Descriptive studies of Nilotic languages (Studies in Nilotic linguistics vol. 3)*, 65–107. Tokyo: Research Institute for Languages and Cultures of Asia and Africa, Tokyo University of Foreign Studies.
Kawachi, Kazuhiro. 2014. Patterns of expressing motion events in Kupsapiny. In Osamu Hieda (ed.), *Recent advances in Nilotic linguistics (Studies in Nilotic linguistics vol. 8)*, 103–136. Tokyo: Research Institute for Languages and Cultures of Asia and Africa, Tokyo University of Foreign Studies.
Kawachi, Kazuhiro. 2016. Event integration patterns in Kupsapiny. *Asian and African Languages and Linguistics* 10. 37–91.
Kießling, Roland & Stefan Bruckhaus. 2017. Associated locomotion in Datooga (Southern Nilotic). In Shigeki Kaji (ed.), *Proceedings of the 8th World Congress of African Linguistics, Kyoto 2015*, 243–258. Tokyo: Research Institute for Languages and Cultures of Asia and Africa, Tokyo University of Foreign Studies.
Koch, Harold. 1984. The category of 'associated motion' in Kaytej. *Language in Central Australia* 1 (1). 23–34.
König, Christa. 2006. Marked nominative in Africa. *Studies in Language* 30 (4). 655–732.
König, Christa. 2008. *Case in Africa*. Oxford: Oxford University Press.
Lakoff, George & Mark Johnson. 1980. *Metaphors we live by*. Chicago: The University of Chicago Press.

Lakoff, George & Mark Johnson. 1999. *Philosophy in the flesh: The embodied mind and its challenge to western thought*. Chicago: University of Chicago Press.
Levinson, Stephen C. & David P. Wilkins. 2006. Patterns in the data: Toward a semantic typology of spatial description. In Stephen C. Levinson & David P. Wilkins (eds.), *Grammars of space: Explorations in cognitive diversity*, 512–552. Cambridge: Cambridge University Press.
Mietzner, Angelika. 2016. *Cherang'any: A Kalenjin language of Kenya*. Köln: Köppe.
Montgomery, Christine Anne. 1966. *The morphology of Sebei*. Los Angeles, CA: University of California, Los Angeles, dissertation.
Noonan, Michael. 1992. *A grammar of Lango*. Berlin & New York: Mouton de Gruyter.
O'Brien, Richard J. & Wim A. M. Cuyers. 1975. A descriptive sketch of the grammar of Sebei. *Georgetown University Working Papers on Languages and Linguistics* 9. 1–108. Washington, D.C.: Georgetown University Press.
Osgarby, David. This volume, chapter 8. Mudburra associated motion in an areal perspective.
Otero, Manuel. This volume, chapter 20. At the intersection of associated motion, direction and exchoative aspect in the Koman languages.
Payne, Doris L. 2013. The challenge of Maa 'Away'. In Tim Thornes, Erik Andvik, Gwendolyn Hyslop & Joana Jansen (eds.), *Functional-historical approaches to explanation: In honor of Scott DeLancey*, 259–282. Amsterdam: John Benjamins.
Payne, Doris L. This volume, chapter 18. The extension of associated motion to direction, aspect and argument structure in Nilotic languages.
Reed, Lauren W. & Kate L. Lindsey. This volume, chapter 9. "Now the story's turning around": Associated motion and directionality in Ende, a language of Papua New Guinea.
Reh, Mechthild. 1996. *Anywa language*. Köln: Rüdiger Köppe.
Ross, Daniel. This volume, chapter 2. A cross-linguistic survey of associated motion and directionals.
Simons, Gary F. & Charles D. Fennig. (eds.). 2018. *Ethnologue: Languages of the world, twenty-first edition*. Dallas, Texas: SIL International. (Online version: http://www.ethnologue.com).
Tallman, Adam J. R. This volume, chapter 11. Associated motion in Chácobo (Pano) in typological perspective.
Talmy, Leonard. 1985. Lexicalization patterns. In Timothy Shopen (ed.), *Language typology and syntactic description, volume 3: Grammatical categories and the lexicon*, 57–149. Cambridge: Cambridge University Press.
Talmy, Leonard. 1991. Path to realization: A typology of event conflation. *Proceedings of the 17th annual meeting of the Berkeley linguistics society*, 480–519. Berkeley, CA: Berkeley Linguistics Society.
Talmy, Leonard. 2000. *Toward a cognitive semantics, volume II: Typology and process in concept structuring*. Cambridge, MA: MIT Press.
Talmy, Leonard. 2007. Lexical typologies. In Timothy Shopen (ed.), *Language typology and syntactic description, second edition, volume 3: Grammatical categories and the lexicon*, 66–168. Cambridge: Cambridge University Press.
Toweett, Taitta. 1979. *Kalenjin linguistics*. Nirobi: Kenya Literature Bureau.
Tucker, Archibald N. & J. Tompo Ole Mpaayei. 1955. *A Maasai grammar with vocabulary*. London, New York & Toronto: Longmans, Green & Co.
Wilkins, David P. 1991. The semantics, pragmatics and diachronic development of 'associated motion' in Mparntwe Arrernte. *Buffalo Working Papers in Linguistics* 91. 207–257.
Zwarts, Joos. 2004. *The phonology of Endo, a Sothern Nilotic language of Kenya*. München: LINCOM.

Manuel A. Otero
20 At the intersection of associated motion, direction and exchoative aspect in the Koman languages

Abstract: The living Koman languages of the Ethiopia-Sudan borderlands all display Deictic Directional (DD) verb morphology which, when occurring on verbs of distinct semantic classes, can express three main conceptual categories. Associated motion is expressed on dynamic verbs that do not contain motion in their inherent semantics, (deictic) direction is expressed on translational motion verbs, and exchoative aspect, or the "exiting from a state", a heretofore cross-linguistically unattested category, entails that the state expressed by the verb no longer holds. This paper examines the Koman DD system in light of current associated motion typologies and through the lens of a motion event. While the function of a particular DD morpheme can generally be predicted by the semantic class of verb on which it occurs, an examination of lower-lever semantic verb classes reveals that alternate construals of events and states can lead to the expression of more than one conceptual category.

Keywords: Koman, direction, associated motion, path, exchoative

1 Introduction

The conceptual category of Associated Motion (AM), commonly coded by verbal grammatical markers that add a translational motion event to a (generally) non-motion event, has been well-documented in the languages of Australia and South America (e.g. Koch 1984, this volume; Tunbridge 1988; Wilkins 1991; Guillaume 2000, 2013, 2016, 2017; Vuillermet 2013; Rose 2015; Tallman, this volume). In Africa by contrast, the term "Associated Motion" as such doesn't surface until the 2010s (e.g. Renaudier 2012; Voisin 2010, 2013, this volume; Belkadi 2013, 2015, 2016, this volume). Yet prior to this, descriptions of what appears to be associated motion are found nestled within descriptions of directional systems (e.g. Serzisko 1988; Reh 1996; Heath 2005; Bourdin 2006; Andersen 2012; Storch 2014; Dimmendaal 2015). Further, recent descriptions of (deictic) directional morphology in African

---
Manuel A. Otero, Eastern Connecticut State University, oterom@easternct.edu

https://doi.org/10.1515/9783110692099-020

languages discuss their relationship to AM and/or aspectual-temporal concepts (Bourdin 2002; Payne 2013, this volume; Creissels 2014; Kramer 2017; Kawachi this volume; Guérois, Gibson and Persohn this volume). Based on original data, this paper examines the highly polyfunctional Deictic Directional (DD) verbal morphology in the living Koman languages of the Ethiopia/Sudan borderlands in light of current AM typologies and through the lens of a motion event (Talmy 1985, 2000).

This paper aims to contribute to the discussion of Associated Motion in several ways. First, it explores the range of heterogeneity across conceptual categories that a DD morpheme can express. When occurring on verbs of distinct semantic classes, the Koman DD morphemes code three distinct categories: associated motion (1a, 1c, 2a), (deictic) direction towards a 1st person (1b) or a 2nd person goal (2b) and exchoative aspect (2c).[1]

(1) Gwama (Lowland)
   a. *ʊ̃hāj*   *ʃɛ̃-í-ná*   *njã*
       3SG.M   slaughter-**DD1**-3SG.M   goat
       'He slaughtered a goat (then came here).'

   b. *ʊ̄sīt*   *zɛ̀*   *kĭs'-í-ná*   *í=swī*
       man   PROG   enter-**DD1**-3SG.M   LOC=house
       '(The) man is entering the house (towards me).'

   c. *zɛ̀*   *tĭnd-í-ná~tĭndĭ*
       PROG   be.fat-**DD1**-3SG.M~REDUP
       'He was getting fat (then came here)'.

(2) Komo (Ethiopia)
   a. *ĭp-**kʊ́**-p'*   *ʃwĭ*   b. *pà-**kʊ́**-p'*   c. *yís'-**kʊ́**-p'*
       drink.SG-**DD2**-3SG.F   beer   run.SG-**DD2**-3SG.F   be.old.SG-**DD2**-3SG.F
       'She drank beer   'She runs (to you   'She was old (She is
       (then left).'   or where you   no longer old).'
                                                   have been).'

Typically, deictic Direction is expressed on (intransitive) verbs of motion while AM is most often realized on dynamic verbs that do not inherently contain motion

---

[1] All of the Gwama, Komo, Opo and Dana data were collected in the Benishangul-Gumuz and Gambella regions of Ethiopia from a variety of native speakers over several fieldtrips from 2011–2017. Uduk data were collected from native speakers residing in Salt Lake City over several trips in 2016–2017.

in their semantics. Grammatical aspect, namely the exchoative ("exiting from a state"), a rare if unattested aspectual category, is expressed on stative verbs. While these general patterns largely conform to Belkadi's (2016) typology of polysemous associated motion/direction systems in African languages, a deeper investigation reveals that certain semantic subclasses of verbs can have alternate construals, which can result in the expression of more than one category.

Second, this paper presents counterevidence to Guillaume's (2016) implicational hierarchy regarding the temporal relationship between the lexical event and the motion co-event. Guillaume's typology proposes that if a language displays *subsequent* AM, it will also display *concurrent* and *prior* AM. The Koman DDs only code subsequent associated motion (1a, 1c, 2a) and do not code concurrent nor prior associated motion on such verbs, contrary to what is predicted by Guillaume's typology.

Third, in light of the second point, this paper addresses what constitutes *bona fide* AM coding material. Following Guillaume's (2016) proposal, an AM morpheme can only be a verbal affix, clitic, particle, or auxiliary. The Koman DD system is the only grammaticalized morphology that expresses subsequent AM, but prior and concurrent AM can be realized through serial verb constructions involving non-grammaticalized lexical motion verbs.

The paper proceeds as follows: §1.1 provides a background on the Koman family, §1.2 briefly discusses Koman grammar and §1.3 provides some theoretical preliminaries. §2 explores the three functions expressed by the Koman DD systems. To describe the general patterns, the subsections are organized by semantic macro-classes– §2.1 describes the directional function on intransitive verbs of motion, §2.2 examines subsequent AM on dynamic (non-motion) verbs and §2.3 looks at AM and exchoativity on stative verbs. Lastly, §2.4 examines alternate construals of lower-level verb subclasses. The role of the Koman DD systems in light of current AM typologies is explored in §3, and §4 offers a brief conclusion.

1.1 Koman background

Koman is a small family of five living languages spoken along the rugged mountains and verdant lowlands of the Ethiopia/(South)Sudan borderlands– Gwama, Komo, Uduk, Opo and Dana.[2] Figure 1 contains a map of the living Koman languages

---

[2] Dana is spoken in Dajo (Daga Post) of what is currently South Sudan. Otero (2019) reconstructs Dana as an initial split from Proto-Dana-Opo (cf. Figure 2). Prior to this classification, Dana was not mentioned in the literature as such but Schuver's 1881 wordlist of Gambiel (James et al.

adapted from Killian (2015: 6).[3] Note that in Figure 1, "Tw'ampa" corresponds to Uduk, "Kwama" to Gwama and "Opoo" to Opo. Koman groups have historically been the subject of slave-raiding from both sides of the border which resulted in the scattering of groups and fracturing of communities which continues to the present day (e.g. James 1979; Meckelburg 2016). Koman groups range in population from 1,000 to 25,000 and with regard to vitality, Komo and Opo are considered seriously endangered (Moseley 2010).

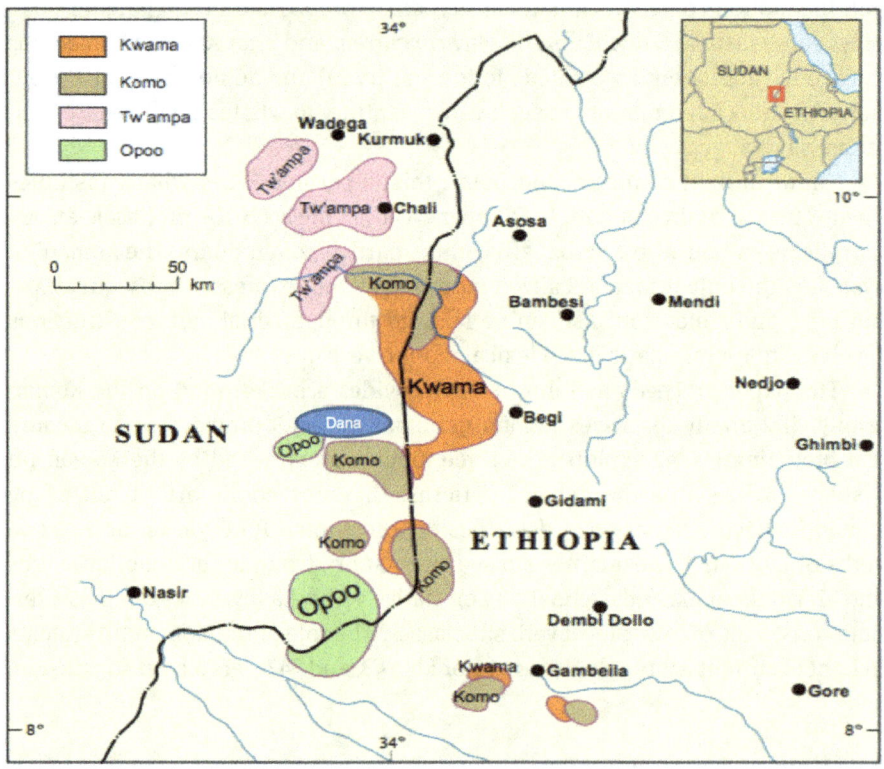

Figure 1: The living Koman languages (adapted from Killian 2015:6).

1996: 335–340) and Corfield's (1938: 158–164) wordlist of *Buldiit* correspond to modern-day Dana (see Otero 2019 for details). The now extinct language Gule is also possibly of Koman origin.

3 The map in Figure 1, which Killian (2015) attributes to an unpublished manuscript by Roger Blench, appears to have been adapted from the map in James (1975: 80). I have added an approximation of where Dana is spoken to this map.

Koman was first classified as Nilo-Saharan by Greenberg (1963). Bender (1997) situates Koman within what he calls the 'core' of Nilo-Saharan, coordinate with Gumuz, Kadu and the East Sudanic branch while Ehret (2001) reconstructs Koman as one branch of an initial binary split from Proto Nilo-Saharan. However, the inclusion of Koman within Nilo-Saharan is still under debate. Dimmendaal (2011) and Güldemann (2018) classify Koman as an independent family for lack of substantial comparative data and Dimmendaal (2018) argues that Koman does not exhibit a sufficient number of "stable" Nilo-Saharan grammatical features to warrant genetic affiliation. The internal structure of Koman, with the exception of Dana, is less controversial than its purported Nilo-Saharan affiliation. The Koman internal classification is seen in Figure.[4]

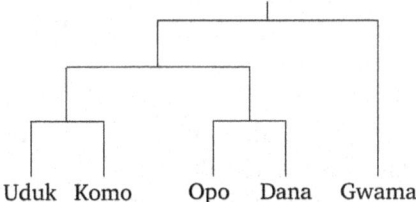

Figure 2: Koman internal subgrouping (Otero 2019).

1.2 Koman structural preliminaries

Koman languages are somewhat synthetic, largely head-marking and predominantly display verb second word order. Alignment patterns are generally Nominative-Accusative, though Killian (2015: 79–84) analyzes residual ergativity in Chali Uduk. All of the languages display a seven-vowel /i, ɪ, ɛ, a, ɔ, ʊ, u/ system with ATR contrast in the high vowels with the exception of Uduk, which has lost the ATR distinction and exhibits a five-vowel /i, ɛ, a, ɔ, u/ system. Nominal morphology occurs in varying degrees across the family, but verbal morphology is more common. Many Koman languages display derivational strategies generally through (partial) reduplication of the verb to create distinctions in participant number and/or pluractionality (cf. Otero 2015, Hellenthal 2017, Smolders forthcoming).[5] One core feature of the Koman verb systems is the existence of

---
[4] All dialects are indicated in the data. Komo has Ethiopian and Sudanese varieties, Gwama has Lowland and Highland varieties, Uduk has the Chali, Yabus and Bonya varieties and Opo has the Bilugu, Modin, Pame, Kigile and Pilakoy dialects.
[5] Verb roots that are suppletive in number are also common in the family.

paradigms of Deictic Directional (DD) suffixes, which generally occur immediately after the verb root or derived stem. Depending on the language, a DD can be followed by bound pronominal person marking suffixes and/or other inflectional/derivational morphology.[6] Figure 3 contains a schematized version of a "maximal" Koman verb. Note that morphemes in parentheses are not obligatory.

ROOT(~PLU)-(DRV)-**DD**-BP$_1$-(APPL)-(BP$_2$)-(BP$_3$)

Figure 3: Schematized Koman "maximal" verb template.

The Koman Deictic Directional suffixes are seen in Table 1. Given the dialectal variation within the language groups, some clarifications are in order. Yabus Uduk is the only language that lacks DD2 or any derivational strategy to encode similar functions expressed by DD2 in the other Koman varieties, while the Chali and Bonya Uduk varieties exhibit a DD2 morpheme. In the Opo cluster, the DD1 morpheme is realized as /-(w)ʊ́/ in the Bilugu, Kigile and Modin varieties, and it is realized as /-(j)ɪ/ in the Pame variety. Komo is the only language with DD$\emptyset$ morphemes. The Komo DD$\emptyset$ morphemes only appear in restricted contexts[7] and are virtually devoid of any semantic content though in these contexts they stand in paradigmatic opposition to the DD1/2 morphemes. As such, I consider the Komo DD$\emptyset$ morphemes akin to the unmarked form of the verb seen in the other Koman languages.

Table 1: Koman Deictic Directional (dd) verb suffixes.

	Uduk	Komo	Opo	Dana	Gwama
DD1	-í	-ʊ́	-(w)ʊ́ -(j)ɪ	-í	-í
DD2	-kú / -kí	-úk	-(j)á -(h)á	-á	-gí
DD$\emptyset$	–	-í / -á	–	–	–

---

[6] One exception is Gwama -gí DD2 (seen in Table 1), which occurs after subject (BP1) bound pronominal person marking suffixes.

[7] Komo DD$\emptyset$ morphemes only occur in particular morphophonological environments: /-í/ occurs before a non-nasal bound pronominal suffix on a finite verb and /-á/ occurs on an initial (non-finite) verb in a serial verb construction. In all other contexts, they don't appear, as in (4c).

While all of the Koman DD morphemes are not necessarily similar in form across the languages, they are to a large extent similar in expressing direction/AM/aspect with respect to the semantic class of verb on which they occur. Prior studies have identified the polyfunctionality of Koman DD morphology, though in some instances, the term "associated motion" is not explicitly stated. For instance, in Chali Uduk, Killian (2015: 187) describes one function of the "Aspect-Directional" morpheme /-í/ (which is currently analyzed as DD1) as "actor doing an action and then coming to the current location" (i.e. subsequent AM). Otero (2018) provides a preliminary analysis of the Ethiopian Komo deictic directional system, which includes associated motion, though it is not explicitly labeled as such. Hellenthal (2018), Otero (2020) and Smolders (forthcoming) describe associated motion within an analysis of DD morphology in Lowland Gwama, Ethiopian Komo and Bilugu Opo, respectively. Otero (2019) describes associated motion in all of the living Koman languages and provides a preliminary reconstruction of DD morphology to Proto-Koman. The data for this study were collected firsthand in the field from native speakers of all of the living Koman languages. The data is from elicitation unless stated otherwise.

1.3 Theoretical and typological preliminaries

Of all of the conceptual categories expressed by the Koman DD systems, associated motion contains the richest semantic content– a complete motion event. Talmy's (1985, 2000) motion event schema comprises four semantic primitives– figure, ground, motion and path. The figure, a conceptual "entity" can undergo motion (spatial displacement) relative to a ground.[8] Path is defined as the route followed or site occupied by the figure with respect to the ground (Talmy 2000: 24–25).

The notion of path is important here as it can be employed synonymously with direction. In order to keep the two notions distinct, I consider path a semantic notion and direction a formal notion, the latter of which specifically refers to the encoding on verbs by morphological or derivational means. This distinction has partly to do with the fact that in Koman languages, DD morphemes can encode deictic goals of motion on verbs that lexicalize path (see §2.1).[9]

---
[8] Note that Talmy's motion event subsumes both translational (or translocational) motion and stasis ('be located').
[9] Talmy (1985, 2000) includes deixis as a subcomponent of path, though which categories are universal and/or primitive to a motion event and what constitutes path is still under debate (e.g. Jackendoff 1983; Langacker 1987; Zlatev 2003, 2007).

In a typological study of 20 African languages, Belkadi (2016) examines the expression of AM and direction across several semantic classes of verbs. She proposes a ranking of verb classes based on the likelihood of a directional or AM expression. Belkadi's (2016: 64) proposal is reproduced in Figure 4. Note that verb classes towards the left, the motion verbs, are more likely to trigger directional readings while those towards the right, such as "activities not involving motion", are more likely to express AM. According to this ranking, stative verbs are the most likely verb class to trigger AM, though Belkadi only provides one example of a purported stative verb 'stay' expressing AM (Belkadi 2016: 62).

Expression: Direction	←	→	Associated Motion
Verb Class	Path Motion	Perception	States
	Motion	Natural phenomena and bodily secretions	
		Causative Motion	Activities not involving motion

Figure 4: Belkadi's (2016: 64) ranking of semantic verb class and direction or AM expression.

Belkadi (2016) also observes that the distinction between motion and non-motion verbs according to their behavior with DD morphemes (i.e. triggering deictic direction or AM readings) is not categorical but gradient, depending on the semantic verb class. In light of this observation, the semantic properties of the Koman DD system are examined across and within three semantic macro-classes of verbs: Motion, Dynamic (non-motion) and Stative (Table 2). These verb classes are derived from two basic semantic features– whether or not the verb denotes change over time [± DYNAMIC], and whether or not the verb contains translational motion in its semantics [± MOTION]. In the last column, the general expressions of the Koman DD morphology is listed for each verb class. In §2, I show that the Koman data largely conforms to Belkadi's (2016) typology particularly with respect to dynamic motion vs. non-motion verbs. The stative verbs, by contrast, exhibit a semantic extension into the aspectual realm.

Table 2: Koman verb semantic macro-classes.

± DYNAMIC	± MOTION	Macro-class	Expression of DD1/2
+ DYNAMIC	+ MOTION	Motion	Direction
	– MOTION	Dynamic (non-motion)	Associated Motion
– DYNAMIC		Stative	Associated Motion / Exchoative Aspect

2 The Koman deictic directional system

The following sections examine the Koman DD1/2 morphemes across three semantic verb macro-classes – Motion, Dynamic (non-motion) and Stative. Transitive and intransitive constructions are discussed as well as the role of external aspectual marking, negation and imperative constructions.

2.1 DD morphemes with motion verbs

The Koman DD systems express deictic direction of motion on motion verbs, regardless of whether the root lexicalizes manner or path, and whether it is intransitive or transitive. Consider the data in (3), which contain a full contrast for the Gwama manner of intransitive motion verb *tìndí* 'roll'. In (3a), the DD1 morpheme orients the trajectory of the subject's motion towards the speaker while in (3b), the DD2 morpheme directs the motion towards the addressee.[10] Compare these to the unmarked form in (3c), in which the direction of motion is unspecified. Also note that in (3c) the unmarked form cannot mean that the direction of motion is oriented towards the speaker or addressee.

(3) Gwama (Lowland)
    a. *mā=pīdìn tìndì-í-bá~tìndì*   b. *mā=pīdìn tìndì-bí-gí~tìndì*
       PL=stone roll-**DD1**-3PL~REDUP   PL=stone roll-3PL-**DD2**~REDUP
       'The stones roll (towards me).'   'The stones roll (towards you).'

    c. *mā=pīdìn tìndì-bí~tìndì*
       PL=stone roll-3PL~ REDUP
       'The stones roll.' (not towards me or towards you)
       *'The stones roll to me/you.'

In the Komo examples in (4), with the intransitive path verb *pŭk* 'cross', we can see identical directional encoding of the subject's motion with speaker and addressee goals of motion. In (4a), the goal of motion is directed towards the speaker with DD1 while in (4b) it is directed towards the addressee with DD2. Note that in these cases, the DDs impart deictic goals to the lexical path. In (4c) by contrast, the lexical path is expressed but deictic direction is unspecified as the verb does not take a DD.

---

[10] The DD1/2 morpheme labels are partially mnemonic as DD1 can express motion towards the 1st person and DD2 towards the 2nd person.

(4) Komo (Ethiopia)
   a. ʊ́-r   pʊ́k-**ʊ́**   s'ʊ́   b. ʊ́-r   pʊ́k-**kʊ́**   s'ʊ́
      INT-3SG.M cross-**DD1** river   INT-3SG.M cross-**DD2** river
      'He will cross the river   'He will cross the river
      (towards me).'   (towards you).'

   c. ʊ́-r   pʊ́k   s'ʊ́
      INT-3SG.M cross   river
      'He will cross the river.' (not towards me or towards you)

The Opo data in (5) illustrate two additional features of the DD morphemes on motion verbs: (i) on transitive motion verbs, an object can be profiled if it undergoes motion and (ii), when a goal of motion is lexically specified, the speaker or addressee's location must coincide with this goal. Observe that in (5) hàm 'brother' undergoes motion as the object of tʃàŋ 'send someone' to the village of Wanke. In (5a), DD1 orients the direction of motion towards the speaker, and she must be in Wanke for the utterance to be felicitous. Similarly, in (5b), DD2 orients the direction of motion towards the addressee, who must be in Wanke for the utterance to be felicitous. Lastly, in (5c), if the unmarked form of the verb is employed, the direction of motion is unspecified and neither the speaker nor the addressee can be in Wanke at the time of utterance.

(5) Opo (Bilugu)
   a. āb=tʃàŋ-**ʊ́**   hàm   wánkɛ̀   b. āb=tʃàŋ-**á**   hàm   wánkɛ̀
      3SG.F=send-**DD1** brother   W.   3SG.F=send-**DD2** brother   W.
      'She sent her brother to Wanke.'   'She sent her brother to Wanke.'
      (speaker is in Wanke)   (addressee is in Wanke)

   c. āb=tʃàŋi   hàm   wánkɛ̀
      3SG.F=send   brother   W.
      'She sent her brother to Wanke.' (neither speaker nor addressee is in Wanke)

There is a very interesting outcome for the DD morphemes in imperative constructions with intransitive motion verbs. In these constructions, the direction of motion of the addressee (the recipient of the command) is profiled with DD1, but with DD2, there are also implications for the (associated) motion of the speaker. In (6a), the DD1 morpheme only expresses the direction of motion towards the speaker after the command is given. But in (6b), the DD2 morpheme, which expresses motion towards the addressee in declarative clauses, has a double function. First, DD2 signals to the addressee that she should move *away* from the speaker. Second, it also indicates that the speaker will *follow* the addressee after she has moved. Thus, both the direction of the addressee (departing from the deictic center) as well as the subsequent associated motion of the speaker (following the addressee) are expressed by DD2 in this construction. Compare this to the unmarked form in (6c), which indicates that the addressee move (in any direction other than towards the speaker) and also that the speaker will *not follow* the addressee subsequent to her moving.

(6) Dana
    a. $k^h\grave{a}j$-$\hat{\imath}$ $\underaccent{.}{t}\hat{\imath}n$ b. $k^h\hat{\jmath}j$-$\acute{a}$ $j\bar{\imath}s$ c. $k^h\grave{a}c^h$ $j\bar{\imath}s$
       climb-**DD1**   ground   climb-**DD2**   sky   climb   sky
       'Climb downwards   'Climb up!' (then I   'Climb up! (I will
       toward me (I am below)!'   will follow you)   not follow you)

Similar behavior is seen in negative imperative constructions. It is important to note that negation only has scope over the lexical verb, i.e., over the motion of the addressee given in the command, not the direction of motion or the associated motion of the speaker. Consider the Komo data in (7), which contain negative imperative constructions with the path verb *gìz* 'enter'. In (7a), the addressee is instructed to not enter (towards the speaker) with the DD1 morpheme. To be clear, (7a) *cannot* mean, 'Don't enter towards me (but you may enter in any other direction)'. In (7b), negation has scope over the verb in the command but not over the subsequent AM co-event expressed by DD2. Compare this to the unmarked form in (7c), which does not express AM of the speaker.

(7) Komo (Ethiopia)
    a. *lāk-í*   *gìz-ʊ́*   b. *lāk-í*   *gìz-úk*
       NEG.IMP-2SG   enter.SG-**DD1**   NEG.IMP-2SG   enter.SG-**DD2**
       'Don't enter!'   'Don't enter!'
       (towards me)   (then I will enter)

    c. *lāk-í*   *gìz*
       NEG.IMP-2SG   enter.SG
       'Don't enter!'
       (I will not enter)

The deictic direction expressed by the Koman DD morphemes on motion verbs in declarative clauses is peculiar given that they do not exhibit a prototypical binary opposition of directional encoding (i.e. *away* from a source and *towards* a goal), but rather, encode direction towards two goals– speaker and addressee. This said, in imperative clauses with motion verbs, there does appear to be a binary (towards/away) directional opposition profiling the addressee but there is also a subsequent AM co-event that profiles the speaker moving towards the addressee's location. The deictic speaker and addressee goals of motion are also profiled in the AM function described in the following section.

2.2 DD morphemes with dynamic non-motion verbs

The Koman DD systems robustly express subsequent AM of the subject on dynamic verbs that do not contain motion in their inherent semantics. This is seen in (8–9), which contain transitive dynamic verbs with DD1/2 in Gwama and Komo respectively. In (8a) and (9a), DD1 codes subsequent AM of the subject with a 1st person/speaker goal. The encoding of the motion co-event goal is identical to the directional encoding on motion verbs with DD1. In (8b) and (9b), DD2 expresses subsequent AM of the subject directed *away* from the source. This is distinct from the directional function motion verbs in which DD2 expresses direction of motion towards the 2nd person/addressee. Note also that in Gwama and Komo, the subsequent AM expressed by DD1/2 also add temporal telicity to the lexical event by virtue of the fact that the subject has come to the deictic center (with DD1) or left the deictic center (with DD2).

(8) Gwama (Lowland)
    a. ʃɛ̂-**ɨ**-ná   njã   b. ʃɛ̂-ní-**gɨ́**   njã
        slaughter-**DD1**-3SG.M   goat   slaughter-3SG.M-**DD2**   goat
        'He slaughtered a goat   'He slaughtered a goat
        (then came here).'   (then left).'

(9) Komo (Ethiopia)
    a. k'ɛ̄r-**ú**-p'   kāmā   b. k'ɛ̄r-**kú**-p'   kāmā
        break-**DD1**-3SG.F   corn   break-**DD2**-3SG.F   corn
        'She broke (the) corn   'She broke (the) corn (then left).'
        (then came here).'

The Koman languages all exhibit a default speaker goal of the subsequent AM co-event with DD1 as seen above in (8a, 9a) and below in (10a, 11a), but the semantics of the DD2 AM co-event are not uniform across the family. In Gwama and Komo, the source of motion is profiled, and the subject of the AM co-event expressed by DD2 departs from the point of reference subsequent to the lexical event denoted by the verb (8b, 9b). By contrast, in Dana and Opo, the goal of

20 At the intersection of associated motion, direction and exchoative aspect — 791

motion is profiled, and the subject of the AM co-event moves towards an addressee goal as seen in (10b, 11b).

(10) Dana
    a. ɓāpʰā nìŋ-**í** mā
       woman cook-**DD1** food
       'The woman cooked food.'
       (then came here)

    b. ɓāpʰā nìŋ-**á** mā
       woman cook-**DD2** food
       'The woman cooked food.'
       (then left towards you)

(11) Opo (Bilugu)
    a. ʊ̀kàdʒ ɔ̄l-**ʊ́** mɛ̀
       man bump.into-**DD1** goat
       'The man bumped into a goat.'
       (then came here)

    b. ʊ̀kàdʒ ɔ̄l-**á** mɛ̀
       man bump.into-**DD2** goat
       'The man bumped into a goat.'
       (then left towards you)

The Chali and Bonya Uduk varieties express subsequent AM with DD1 (12a, 13a). In (13a), it is likely that the prior AM in the translation (i.e. 'going somewhere else to fish') is implied rather than explicitly expressed by DD1. (As discussed in §3.1, Koman languages have a distinct construction for expressing prior AM, involving a lexical verb). The DD2 morpheme, by contrast, has lost its subsequent AM meaning and has become semantically extended into the temporal/aspectual realm. For Chali and Bonya Uduk speakers, DD2 on dynamic (non-motion) verbs expresses perfective aspect/(remote) past time as seen in (12b, 13b).

(12) Uduk (Bonya)
    a. jè k'ɔ́ʃɔ́-**j**-ɔ́d=ā k'á
       elephant kill-**DD1**-3SG=CL dog
       '(The) elephant killed a/the dog.'
       (then came here)

    b. jè k'ɔ́ʃ-**k**-ɔ́d=ā k'á
       elephant kill-**DD2**-3SG=CL dog
       '(The) elephant killed a/the dog.'
       (in the past, somewhere)

(13) Uduk (Chali)
    a. ádĩ k'ɔ́ʃ-**í** wàc' mɔ̀
       3SG hit-**DD1** fish MO
       'S/he has gone somewhere else to fish (lit. hit fish) and has now come back here.' (Killian 2015: 190)

    b. áhā ʃwá-**kí**-ná mà mɔ̀
       1SG eat.PFV-**DD2**-1SG food MO
       'I have already eaten the food.'
       (Killian 2015: 185)

The examples thus far in this section show that subjects of dynamic transitive verbs undergo subsequent AM. The following data in (14) show subsequent AM of an intransitive subject, *tījā* 'pot', which cannot undergo motion in the real world unless acted upon by an outside force. Nonetheless, it can still undergo subsequent AM by being transported. In (14a), DD1 expresses that the pot broke at another location and was then brought to the deictic center, while in (14b), DD2 indicates that the pot was taken away from the deictic center towards the location of the addressee after having broken.

(14) Dana
    a. tījā́ tā́j-**ɪ́**
       pot break-**DD1**
       'The pot broke.' (then it was brought here)

    b. tījā́ tów-**ā́**
       pot break-**DD2**
       'The pot broke.' (it is on the way to you)

The degree of event integration between the lexical event and the AM co-event can be investigated through the use of external operators.[11] Interestingly, external aspectual marking only has scope over the lexical event, not the AM co-event. The Bilugu Opo data in (15) show full contrast for subsequent AM with DD1/2 in two aspectual constructions– the perfective and the progressive. The unmarked forms in (15a-b) are of perfective aspect by default and express subsequent AM. In (15c-d), progressive marking only has scope over the lexical event with both DD1/2. This is evidenced by the fact that progressive marking does not target the AM co-event and concurrent AM is not expressed (i.e. examples (15c-d) cannot mean 'He plastered the hut *while coming/going*.').

(15) Opo (Bilugu)
    a. ār=tʰáp-**ʊ́** kù
       3SG.M=plaster-**DD1** hut
       'He plastered the hut.' (then came here)

    b. ār=tʰáp-**á** kù
       3SG.M=plaster-**DD2** hut
       'He plastered the hut.' (then left towards you)

    c. àr-à=tʰáp-**ʊ́** kù
       3SG.M-PROG=plaster-**DD1** hut
       'He was plastering the hut.' (then came here)

    d. àr-à=tʰáp-**á** kù
       3SG.M-PROG=plaster-**DD2** hut
       'He was plastering the hut.' (then left towards you)

---

[11] See Jacques, Lahaussois and Zhang (this volume) for a discussion of event integration in Sino-Tibetan.

Similarly, negation also only has scope over the lexical event, not the AM co-event. Negation is generally expressed by an auxiliary verb that precedes the lexical verb, which takes a DD. In the Komo data in (16a), the lexical slaughtering event is negated but the AM component is still expressed with DD1– the subject has come to the deictic center. In (16b), the lexical event is again negated, but subsequent AM with DD2 is expressed– the subject has departed from the deictic center.

(16) Komo (Ethiopia)
    a. *bāʃ-í-n*   *t'ɔr-ú*   *mɛ́*
       NEG-DDØ-3PL slaughter-**DD1** goat
       'They didn't slaughter a goat.'
       (at other location, then came here)

    b. *bāʃ-í-n*   *t'ɔr-úk*   *mɛ́*
       NEG-DDØ-3PL slaughter-**DD2** goat
       'They didn't slaughter a goat.'
       (then they left)

Recall that in motion verb imperative constructions, DD1 expresses the (intended) direction of the addressee towards the speaker and DD2 expresses subsequent AM in which the speaker will follow the addressee after she has moved, as seen in (6a,b). In imperative constructions with dynamic (non-motion) verbs, subsequent AM of the addressee is expressed with DD1 and subsequent AM of the speaker is expressed with DD2. Full contrast in affirmative and negative imperatives is given in (17).[12] In (17a), DD1 on the verb instructs the addressee to return to the deictic center after having realized the event denoted by the lexical verb, while in (17b), DD2 expresses the fact that the speaker will subsequently follow the addressee after the lexical event has been realized. The translation of 'go (and X)' in these examples appears to be a pragmatic inference rather than a strict grammatical encoding. In (17d-e), negation only has scope over the lexical event, but the AM co-events expressed by DD1/2 remain expressed. Thus, on dynamic verbs in the imperative, DD1 expresses subsequent AM of the addressee (17a, d), while DD2 expresses subsequent AM of the speaker (as is also the case when used with motion verb; see (6–7) above).

---

[12] I am grateful to Joshua Smolders for remotely eliciting the Bilugu Opo imperative data in Ethiopia seen in (17).

(17) Opo (Bilugu)
    a. *k'ám-ʊ́*   *wàc'à*   b. *k'ám-há*   *wàc'à*   c. *k'ámá*   *wàc'à*
       eat.SG-**DD1**   fish   eat.SG-**DD2**   fish   eat.SG   fish
       '(Go) Eat fish!'   '(Go) Eat fish!'   'Eat fish!'
       (then come here)   (I will follow you)

    d. *nāná*   *wàc'à*   *k'ám-ʊ́*   e. *nāná*   *wàc'à*   *k'ám-há*
       NEG.INT   fish   eat.SG-**DD1**   NEG.INT   fish   eat.SG-**DD2**
       '(Go) Don't eat fish!'   '(Go) Don't eat fish!'
       (then come here)   (I will follow you)

    f. *nāná*   *wàc'à*   *k'ámá*
       NEG.INT   fish   eat.SG
       'Don't eat fish!'

Subsequent AM is by default expressed on transitive and intransitive dynamic (non-motion) verbs. The DD1 morpheme robustly encodes subsequent AM of the subject toward the speaker in all of the languages. By contrast, the DD2 morpheme expresses subsequent AM of the subject toward the addressee in Dana and Opo. In the remaining languages (Gwama, Komo and Uduk), DD2 can express either subsequent AM of the subject departing away from the deictic center, or it can also be extended into past/perfective aspect. In terms of semantic event integration, external aspectual marking as well as negation generally has scope over the lexical event denoted by the verb, not the motion co-event expressed by a given DD morpheme. This suggests a strong degree of integration between the AM co-event and the semantics of the lexical verb as the AM component does not fall under the scope of external operators.

2.3 DD morphemes with stative verbs

Koman languages lack a robust class of adjectives and instead employ stative verbs to fulfill adjectival functions. Koman stative verbs are not morphologically distinct from other lexical verbs such as the motion or dynamic (non-motion) verbs seen thus far. The outcomes of DD morphology with stative verbs are discussed in this section.

    Belkadi's (2016: 64) ranking, reproduced in Figure 4, proposes that out of all verb classes, stative verbs are most likely to display AM. In Koman, this is the case for the DD1 morpheme, which strongly expresses deictic subsequent AM of the subject moving to the speaker's location by default. Subsequent AM in a stative verb entails that the subject either enters the state or is in the state and then undergoes the AM co-event. To illustrate, consider the Dana data in (18), which contain stative verbs with DD1 and express subsequent AM of an animate subject. Note that the motion co-event expresses the arrival of the moving figure at the speaker's location by default.

(18) Dana
    a. hār-â būd-**í**
       3SG-INT be.tall.SG-**DD1**
       'He will get tall.'
       (then come here)

    b. hŏn k'ɔ́-**jī** á=dájʊ̀
       3PL live.PL-**DD1** LOC=D.
       'They lived in Dajo.'
       (then came here)

In Komo and Gwama, DD1 also expresses subsequent AM of the subject as seen in (19). Note that the subject of the verb can be inanimate and still undergo subsequent AM. In (19a), DD1 expresses subsequent AM of an inanimate subject– the mangos were in the state of being red and then were brought to the deictic center, while in (20b), DD1 expresses subsequent AM of an animate subject– the girl became tall at another location and has since come to the deictic center.[13]

(19) Komo (Ethiopia)
    a. máŋgà p'ɛ̀l-**ʊ́**-n   (ɨ̄=ĵángú)
       mango be.red-**DD1**-3PL LOC=J.
       '(The) mangos were red (in Yangu).'
       (then were brought here)

    Gwama (Lowland)
    b. wār-tɔ̀ tù-**ʊ́**-bá~tŭ
       child-DIST.F be.tall-**DD1**-3SG.F~REDUP
       'That girl became tall (while she was away).'
       (she has come back here) (Hellenthal 2018)

While the DD1 morpheme uniformly expresses subsequent AM, DD2 on stative verbs behaves differently across the languages. The Dana data in (20) show that in this language the DD2 morpheme on stative verbs expresses subsequent AM towards the addressee, as it does on dynamic (non-motion) verbs. In (20a), DD2 expresses subsequent AM of the subject to the addressee after having entered the state of being tall and in (20b), DD2 indicates that the subject has left Dajo and is either

---

[13] In (19a), the use of the verb 'be red' here is akin to 'be ripe' for mangos. Note also that (19a) can occur with an optional oblique constituent ĵángú 'in Yangu', which is indicated in parentheses.

going towards the addressee or is with the addressee at the time of utterance. Note that the AM co-event expressed with DD2 does not necessarily entail arrival at the goal of motion as opposed to DD1, which does entail arrival (cf. (18)).

(20) Dana
    a. hār-â   būd-**á**   b. hūn k'ɔ́-**wā**   á=dájò
        3SG-INT be.tall.SG-**DD2**   3PL live.PL-**DD2** LOC=D.
        'He will get tall.'   'They lived in Dajo.'
        (then go to you)   (then left towards you or they are with you now)

In Komo and Gwama, by contrast, DD2 on stative verbs does not normally express subsequent AM but rather expresses *exchoativity*, or the 'exiting from a state', meaning that the state described by the verb no longer holds. To illustrate, consider the data in (21). In (21a), the mangos were red at one point, but are no longer red, or, have 'left the state of being red'.[14] Example (21b) also expresses exchoativity of the subject as having left the state of being tall. The translation of (21b) also shows that a subsequent AM reading is ungrammatical; only the exchoative interpretation is possible.

(21) Komo (Ethiopia)
    a. máŋgà   p'èl-**kû**-n   (í=jángú)
        mango   be.red-**DD2**-3PL LOC=J.
        '(The) mangos were red (in Yangu).'
        (no longer red)

    Gwama (Lowland)
    b. wār-tɔ̀   tǔ-á-**gá**~tǔ
        child-DIST.F be.tall-3SG.F-**DD2**~REDUP
        'That girl was tall (but not anymore).'
        *'That girl became tall (and left).' (Hellenthal 2018)

However, there are contexts in which DD2 on stative verbs expresses subsequent AM and not exchoativity. For instance, Komo has a morpheme =*kɛ́* PRF which expresses the inchoative on stative verbs (i.e. 'entering into a state').[15] This is seen

---

[14] Note that (21a) holds true in a mythical world in which mangos can somehow "unripen".
[15] This morpheme expresses perfect aspect on non-stative verbs (see Otero (2020) for more details).

in (22a), together with DD1, in which the mangos have entered the state of being red and have subsequently been brought to the deictic center. Example (22b), where =ké is used with DD2, is notable due to the fact that the DD2 morpheme is expected to express exchoativity. This semantic predicament has an elegant solution in that in this context, DD2 does not express exchoativity, but rather subsequent AM of the subject physically moving away from the deictic center. Thus (22b) behaves more like a dynamic verb in which DD2 expresses subsequent AM as seen in §2.2.

(22) Komo (Ethiopia)
    a. *máŋgà p'ɛ̀l-ʉ́-n=ké*   (*ı̃=ĵángú*)
       mango be.red-**DD1**-3PL=PRF LOC=J.
       '(The) mangos became red (in Yangu).'
       (then were brought here)

    b. *máŋgà p'ɛ̀l-kʉ́-n=ké*   (*ı̃=ĵángú*)
       mango be.red-**DD2**-3PL=PRF LOC=J.
       '(The) mangos became red (in Yangu).'
       (then were taken away; they are still red)

In Gwama, external progressive marking on a stative verb is marked by the preverbal particle *zè* which indicates an ongoing process of inchoativity into the state. In (23a), DD1 expresses subsequent AM of the subject, who, before coming to the deictic center, enters in the state denoted by the verb. Contrary to Komo, even though ongoing inchoativity is expressed via progressive marking, DD2 retains exchoative encoding in Gwama. In (23b), DD2 expresses that the subject exited the state of being fat after having entered it.

(23) Gwama (Lowland)
    a. *zè*   *tı̆nd-ı̆-ná~tı̆ndı̆*   b. *zè*   *tı̆n-nı́-gı̆~tı̆ndı̆*
       PROG be.fat-**DD1**-3SG.M~REDUP   PROG be.fat-3SG.M-**DD2**~REDUP
       'He was becoming fat.'   'He was becoming fat.'
       (then came here, still fat)   (no longer fat)

Thus far we have examined DD morphology on intransitive stative verbs. The Gwama data in (24) show DD1/2 on a transitive stative verb *jı́s* 'resemble'. In (24a), DD1 expresses that the subject resembled her mother at another location and has since travelled to the deictic center where she still resembles her mother. By contrast in (24b), the DD2 expresses the exchoative– the subject no longer resembles her mother.

(24) Gwama (Lowland)
    a. *dwā   jís-í-ná*   *nă=dáp'*
        girl   resemble-**DD1**-3SG.F   mother=3SG.F.POSS
        'The girl resembled her mother.' (then came here, resembles her mother)

    b. *dwā   jís-á-**gí***   *nă=dáp'*
        girl   resemble-3SG.F-**DD2**   mother=3SG.F.POSS
        'The girl resembled her mother.' (no longer resembles her mother)

Stative verbs (with optional DD morphology) can also be employed in imperative constructions. Consider the Opo affirmative and negative imperatives in (25).[16] The DD1 forms in (25a, d) instruct the addressee to (go), (not) become strong, and subsequently return to the deictic center. In (25b, e) by contrast, the DD2 forms signal to the addressee that the speaker will subsequently follow.[17] Compare these to the unmarked forms in (25c, f) which lack AM or specification about the speaker or addressee's whereabouts.

(25) Opo (Bilugu)
    a. *k'āw-**ʊ́***   b. *k'āw-**há***   c. *k'āw*
        be.strong.SG-**DD1**   be.strong.SG-**DD2**   be.strong.SG
        '(Go) Be strong!'   '(Go) Be strong!'   'Be strong!'
        (then return)   (then I will follow you)

    d. *nāná   k'āw-**ʊ́***   e. *nāná   k'ám-**há***
        NEG.INT be.strong.SG-**DD1**   NEG.INT eat.SG-**DD2**
        '(Go) Don't be strong!'   '(Go) Don't be strong!'
        (then return)   (then I will follow you)

    f. *nāná   k'āw*
        NEG.INT be.strong.SG
        'Don't be strong!

2.4 Alternate construals

While the conceptual categories expressed by the Koman DD systems (direction, AM, exchoativity) can largely be predicted from the semantic macro-class of verb

---

[16] I am grateful to Josh Smolders for remotely eliciting the imperative forms in Ethiopia seen in (25).
[17] The DD1/2 forms are all translated with '(Go) X', which does appear to describe prior AM, though this appears to be a pragmatic inference rather than strict grammatical encoding. More research is needed.

on which they occur, this is not always the case. States and events can have alternate construals and the conceptual categories expressed by a given DD are not always predictable. Nevertheless, there are some general tendencies. This section examines alternate construals on more fine-grained, low-level semantic classes of verbs. Where there are alternate construals for a given utterance, I employ the symbols (i) and (ii) to indicate the distinct interpretations.

One major pattern in determining the expression of the DD morphology within a subclass of verbs is whether or not motion can be profiled in the meaning of a verb that does not *necessarily* profile motion. To illustrate, consider the Opo data in (26) with the transitive verb *p'ɔ́t'* 'pick', in which either a directional or an AM reading can be construed. In its semantics, 'pick' denotes an event of taking something from something else to which it is attached. If the 'picking motion' is profiled, then the DD morphology expresses the direction of the picking, as seen in the (i) interpretations in (26a-b). By contrast, if the motion of the picking is not profiled, then the subject of the picking event can undergo subsequent AM, as seen in the (ii) interpretations in (26a-b).

(26) Opo (Bilugu)
a. āb=p'ɔ́t'-**ʊ́**   máŋgà   b. āb=p'ɔ́t'-**á**   máŋgà
   3SG.F=pick-**DD1** mango   3SG.F=pick-**DD2** mango
   (i) 'She picked a mango   (i) 'She picked a mango (towards you).'
   (towards me).'   (ii) 'She picked a mango
   (ii) 'She picked a mango   (then went to you).'
   (then came here).'

A similar pattern of alternate construals can occur with more canonical motion verbs, such as the path verb *kǐs* 'enter' in (27). If the trajectory of motion is profiled, the DDs encode the direction of motion, but if the event is conceptually packaged as a whole, the DDs can express subsequent AM as seen above in (26). In (27a-b), the (i) interpretations reflect the directional expression of DD1/2, which results from the profiling of the trajectory of motion– in (27a), DD1 expresses motion toward the speaker and in (27b), DD2 directs the motion towards the addressee.[18] By contrast, if the trajectory of motion is not profiled, an alternate construal can have interesting results with respect to AM. In interpretation (ii) in (27a), the *speaker* undergoes subsequent AM with DD1– she witnessed the man

---

18 Note that the speaker must be situated within the enclosure for interpretation (i) of (27a) to be felicitous and the addressee must be inside the enclosure for interpretation (i) of (27b) to be felicitous. Note also that *-gí* DD2 is realized as *-gá* after a suffix that contains /ɪ/ in (27b).

entering a house at a distinct location from that of the utterance location (the deictic center) to which she has since travelled. In this case, AM does not target the subject but rather the experiencer, which in this case is instantiated by the speaker. By contrast, in (ii) of (27b), DD2 expresses subsequent associated motion of the subject as having left the location after having entered. The fact that a verb that lexicalizes path can also have an AM interpretation must be highlighted here as it challenges Belkadi's (2016) ranking of verb classes and the expression of AM or direction (cf. Figure 4).

(27) Gwama (Lowland)
    a. ōsīt   zè   kĭs'-ɨ́-ná   ɨ̂=swī
       man   PROG enter-**DD1**-3SG.M LOC=house
       (i) '(The) man is entering the house (towards me).'
       (ii) '(The) man was entering a house at another location.'
       (Speaker is now here.)

    b. ōsīt   zè   kĭs'-nɨ́-**gá**   ɨ̂=swī
       man   PROG enter-3SG.M-**DD2** LOC=house
       (i) '(The) man is entering the house (towards you).'
       (ii) '(The) man was entering the house (and left).'

Before proceeding, some clarification must be made on aspectual/temporal interpretations in these alternate construals. In Gwama (and Komo), unmarked dynamic verbs have a default imperfective aspectual profile, which is translated into English present tense when the event denoted by the verb occurs at the time of utterance. Thus, interpretations (i) in (27a-b) have been translated into English present tense– these events are construed as occurring at the time of utterance. Nevertheless, subsequent AM imparts temporal/aspectual telicity to the lexical verb event and these events, such as interpretation (ii) in (27a-b), have been translated into English past tense. Unmarked Dana and Opo dynamic verbs are by default perfective and do not exhibit this distinction in tense/aspect (cf. (26)).

Verbs that express bodily emissions can also result in alternate construals with DD1/2. The lexical event denoted by the verb can be construed as expressing motion, to which a directional specification can be imparted. Alternatively, the event can be conceived in its entirety and the subject can undergo subsequent AM. The examples in (28), with the verb bǔʃ 'fart', illustrate this alternate construal, with a directional reading in interpretation (i) and subsequent AM in interpretation (ii).

(28) Gwama (Lowland)
    a. kānā zè bǔʃ-**í**-ná tūʃ
        dog PROG fart-**DD1**-3SG.M feces
        (i) 'The dog is farting (towards me).'
        (ii) 'The dog was farting (then came here).'

    b. kānā zè bǔʃ-ní-**gí** tūʃ
        dog PROG fart-3SG.M-**DD2** feces
        (i) 'The dog is farting (towards you).'
        (ii) 'The dog was farting (then left).'

Recall that with DD2, Dana and Opo express a subsequent AM co-event oriented towards the addressee while the remaining languages express subsequent AM of the subject departing away from the deictic center (cf. §2.2). This distinction also holds in the AM interpretation of an alternate construal. Interpretation (i) in (29a-b) show a directional construal of the body emission verb *k'ɛ̄rɛ̄m* 'burp' while a subsequent AM construal is seen in interpretation (ii). The AM co-event is directed towards the addressee in (29b) in Opo, while in (28b) the AM co-event profiles the subject as departing the event location in Gwama. Identical alternate construals for DD1 are seen in Yabus Uduk in (30).

(29) Opo (Bilugu)
    a. àb=à k'ɛ̄rɛ̄m-**ʊ́**   b. àb=à k'ɛ̄rɛ̄m-**á**
        3SG.F=PROG burp-**DD1**   3SG.F=PROG burp-**DD2**
        (i) 'She is burping (towards me).'   (i) 'She is burping (towards you).'
        (ii) 'She was burping   (ii) 'She was burping (then left
        (then came here).'   towards you).'

(30) Uduk (Yabus)
    wàzí gàr:-**í**-d
    man burp-**DD1**-3SG
    (i) 'She is burping (towards me).'
    (ii) 'She was burping (then came here).'

Verbs that express the static location of a referent can also have directional or AM construals. In interpretation (i) in (31), DD1 on the verb *sɔk* 'sit.SG' can express the direction (i.e. the 'facing') of the sitting as oriented towards the speaker.[19]

---

19 Recall that Talmy (2001) subsumes both motion and stasis ('be located') within a motion event, as similar coding can be employed to express either category. Talmy's claim is supported

Alternatively in interpretation (ii), subsequent AM is expressed– the sitting event is construed as having occurred at a distinct location from the deictic center to which the subject has come.

(31) Komo (Ethiopia)
 bāɓɔ́nk'ɔ́ sɔ̀k-**ʉ́**-p'   î=míʃ=ī=ɔ̀ʃ
 frog   sit.SG-**DD1**-3SG.F LOC=sky=ASS=rock
 (i) 'The frog sat on a rock (facing me).'
 (ii) 'The frog sat on a rock (then came here).'

Profiling the direction of motion on stative verbs that denote natural events such as weather or temperature verbs is also common. For instance, the DD1/2 morphemes can express the direction of the temperature of an area as moving towards or away from a reference point. This is seen in (32a), in which DD1 expresses that the heat will move towards the speaker's location and in (32b), where DD2 expresses motion of the heat away from the speaker. Compare this to the data in (33), where the aspectual profile of the predicate also contributes to the construal of the situation. In (33a), DD1 on the unmarked form of the verb expresses subsequent AM of the speaker, who experienced the temperature at another location and has since travelled to the utterance location. By contrast in (33b), progressive marking construes a directional interpretation of the cold as coming towards the speaker.

(32) Gwama (Lowland)
 a. jàs   á-ní   tàwàn-**í**~tàwàn
   ground INT-3SG.M be.hot-**DD1**~REDUP
   'It will get hot (towards here).'

 b. jàs   á-ní   tàwàn-**gí**~tàwàn
   ground INT-3SG.M be.hot-**DD2**~REDUP
   'It will get hot (from here away).'

---

by certain languages, especially those lacking adpositions, which employ "directionals" to encode the static location of a figure (cf. Craig 1993, Grinevald 2006).

(33) Opo (Bilugu)
    a. *tʃém sá-wʊ́*
       cold eat.SG-**DD1**
       'It was cold (at other location).'
       (Lit. 'Cold ate (at other location).')

    b. *tʃém-à sá-wʊ́*
       cold-PROG eat.SG-**DD1**
       'It's getting cold (from elsewhere towards here).'
       (Lit. 'Cold was eating (towards here).')

Some verbs that describe natural events, such as rain, have motion implicit in their meaning, and this readily allows for a directional interpretation of the event, although AM interpretations are also possible. In Gwama, the DD1 morpheme can allow for two construals of an event of rain. With external perfect aspect marking, a directional construal of the rain coming towards the speaker is expressed with DD1 as in interpretation (i) in (34a), although subsequent AM of the speaker as having experienced the rain at another location is also possible as in interpretation (ii). Interestingly, in (34b), with DD2 and perfect marking, an exchoative interpretation is only possible, while in (34c) progressive marking can coerce a directional interpretation of the rain as moving away from the deictic center.

(34) Gwama (Lowland)
    a. *ʃʊ́ mǎ-n ʃāp'-**ɨ**~ʃāp'*
       rain PRF-3SG.M hit-**DD1**~REDUP
       (i) 'It has (just) started raining (towards here).'
       (ii) 'It is/was raining (at other location).'

    b. *ʃʊ́ mǎ-n ʃāp'-**gɨ**~ʃāp'*
       rain PRF-3SG.M hit-**DD2**~REDUP
       'It has rained.' (It is no longer raining)

    c. *ʃʊ́ á-ní ʃāp'-**gɨ**~ʃāp'*
       rain INT-3SG.M hit-**DD2**~REDUP
       'It will rain (from here away).'

While Belkadi's (2016) typology generally holds for semantic macro-classes of verbs in Koman languages, alternate construals are frequent when examining low-level verb classes. Further, external aspectual marking can also influence the category that is expressed (direction versus AM). One general pattern across the alternate construals is that direction can be expressed if motion is somehow construed in the event. By contrast, if direction of motion (or stasis) is not profiled, the event is cognitively packaged as a whole and subsequent AM of the subject or the speaker is expressed.

3 Koman and AM typologies

Guillaume's (2016) landmark typology of South American AM systems puts forth an implicational hierarchy regarding the temporal relationship between the lexical event and the motion co-event: if a language displays *subsequent* AM, it will also display *concurrent* and *prior* AM. The Koman languages present counter-evidence to this claim as only subsequent AM is robustly expressed by the grammaticalized DD morphology (cf. §2.2). This section explores other means by which prior and concurrent AM interpretations arise. §3.1 examines the role of lexical deictic 'go' and 'come' verbs in serial verb constructions that express what translates to prior AM of the subject, as well their interaction with the DD system. §3.2 discusses how concurrent AM interpretations can be inferred through a combination of DD1/2 and specific external aspectual marking. Lastly, §3.3 provides a brief discussion of AM profiling the Object in light of Guillaume's (2016) observations.

3.1 Prior (and subsequent) AM: serial verb constructions with lexical 'go' and 'come'

Koman languages employ serial verb constructions (SVC) consisting of a bare lexical deictic path verb ('go' or 'come') followed by a finite lexical verb to express what translates to "prior" AM of the subject. In these SVCs, the deictic path verb imparts a "prior" AM meaning, which can be combined with DD1/2 on the lexical verb to also express subsequent AM.

Consider the Komo data in (35), which contain serial verb constructions with 'go' followed by a dynamic (non-motion) finite verb. In (35a), *jà* 'go' expresses spatial displacement directed away from a reference point to where the lexical eating event will take place. Further, DD1 on the lexical verb *ʃá* 'eat.SG' expresses subsequent AM– the subject will return to the deictic reference point of the initial departure, resulting in what Bourdin (2006: 17) describes as "roundtrip motion". In (35b), DD2 also adds a subsequent AM event. But in this case, the subject will leave the eating location after the eating is realized and will crucially *not* come to the original point of departure (the utterance location). The data in (35a-b) provide examples of two instances of AM via the interaction between the SVC and the DD morphology– the 'go' verb in the SVC expresses prior AM and the DD expresses subsequent AM. Compare these to (35c), in which the lexical verb in the SVC does not take a DD. In this example only "prior" AM is expressed through the lexical 'go' verb.

(35) Komo (Ethiopia)
   a. ʊ́-ná **jà** ʃá-**ʊ́** mèī   b. ʊ́-ná **jà** ʃá-**ûk** mèī
      INT-1SG **go.SG** eat.SG-**DD1** food   INT-1SG **go.SG** eat.SG-**DD2** food
      'I will go eat food (then come   'I will go eat food (then leave).'
      back here).'

   c. ʊ́-ná **jà** ʃá mèī
      INT-1SG **go.SG** eat.SG food
      'I will go eat food.'

Similar encoding of "prior" AM through a serial verb construction is seen in the Opo example in (36). In all cases, the lexical 'go' verb indicates spatial displacement prior to the lexical event. The only difference from the Komo data in (35) is that in (36b), DD2 expresses subsequent AM towards the addressee, whereas in (35b), subsequent AM is directed away from the point of reference.

(36) Opo (Bilugu)
   a. ʊ̀kàdʒ **dʒà** táp-**ʊ́** kù   b. ʊ̀kàdʒ **dʒà** táp-**á** kù
      man **go.SG** plaster-**DD1** hut   man **go.SG** plaster-**DD2** hut
      'The man went and plastered   'The man went and plastered
      the hut.' (then came back here)   the hut.' (then left towards you)

   c. ʊ̀kàdʒ **dʒà** táp kù
      man **go.SG** plaster hut
      'The man went and plastered the hut.'

A serial verb construction involving a lexical 'come' verb can also be employed to express "prior" AM to the deictic center. Further, if the following finite lexical verb occurs with DD2, subsequent AM away from the deictic center is also expressed. In (37), the subject came to the deictic center (expressed by the lexical verb 'come'), realized the event denoted by the verb, and then departed the deictic center (via DD2 on k'ɔ́ʃ 'kill').

(37) Komo (Ethiopia)
   hà-ʊ́   k'ɔ́ʃ-**kú**-r   gwà
   come.SG-DD1 kill-**DD2**-3SG.M elephant
   'He came (and) killed an elephant (and left).'

In Komo, negation of the serial verb construction appears to have scope over the entire series of events, but this appears to be a pragmatic implicature. In (38), negation targets the 'go' verb, which, by negating the 'prior' AM, entails that the subject does not travel to the location where the lexical verb event is to be realized.

(38) Komo (Ethiopia)
    a. *bāʃ-í-n*   *ì*   *k'ɔ́ʃ-ʊ́*   *gwà*
       NEG-DDØ-3PL   **go.PL**   kill-**DD1**   elephant
       'They didn't go kill an elephant (and come back here).'

    b. *bāʃ-í-n*   *ì*   *k'ɔ́ʃ-úk*   *gwà*
       NEG-DDØ-3PL   **go.PL**   kill-**DD2**   elephant
       'They didn't go kill an elephant (and leave).'

By contrast, in Dana, negation only has scope over the motion event expressed by the 'go' verb, not the lexical verb or the subsequent AM co-event expressed by a DD. Consider (39), in which the motion expressed by *ḍâ* 'go.SG' is subject to negation but the lexical verb event and subsequent AM are not.[20]

(39) Dana
    a. *hār-â*   *ḍâ*   *k'à*   *mē*   *tɔ́r-ī*
       3SG.M-INT   **go.SG**   NEG   goat   hit-**DD1**
       'He will not go (but will) hit a goat (then come back here).'

    b. *hār-â*   *ḍâ*   *k'à*   *mē*   *tɔ́r-á*
       3SG.M-INT   **go.SG**   NEG   goat   hit-**DD2**
       'He will not go (but will) hit a goat (then go to you).'

Serial verb constructions with 'go' can also occur with stative verbs, though there appear to be more restrictions with the DD that can occur on the following lexical verb. In (40a), the lexical 'go' verb expresses translational motion to where the state denoted by the verb is realized. Further, subsequent AM to the deictic center is expressed by DD1 on the lexical stative verb *tùr* 'be tall'. Compare this to (40b), in which only departure is expressed by the 'go' verb as the lexical stative verb does not take a DD.

---

[20] Note that the clause structure in Dana in this negative construction is distinct from that of Komo. The Dana negative morpheme *k'à* occurs after the 'go' verb whereas in (38), the Komo negative auxiliary occurs before the 'go' verb.

20 At the intersection of associated motion, direction and exchoative aspect — 807

(40) Uduk (Yabus)
 a. hádī mɔ̀r-íd **jà** tùr-**í**   b. hádī mɔ̀r-íd **jà** tùr
   3SG INT-3SG **go.SG** be.tall-**DD1**   3SG INT-3SG **go.SG** be.tall
   'S/he will go get tall (then come   'S/he will go get tall.'
   back here).'

Many languages exhibit 'go' serial verb constructions with DD1 but not DD2 on the lexical stative verb. Compare (41a), which is perfectly felicitous with DD1, to (41b), which is ungrammatical with DD2. Recall that in Gwama, DD2 on stative verbs express the exchoative aspect ('no longer be X'). As such, departure from a source via the 'go' verb, followed by the exchoative, seems odd to express (e.g. 'She went and was no longer X').

(41) Gwama (Lowland)
 a. á-ní hɔ̃ tĭnd-ĭ~tĭndĭ   b. *á-ní hɔ̃ tĭnd-gí~tĭndĭ
   INT-3SG.M **go** be.fat-**DD1**~REDUP   INT-3SG.M **go** be.fat-**DD2**~REDUP
   'He will go get fat (then come   (Intended: 'He will go get fat
   back here).'   (and leave).')

Similar restrictions with DD2 on the lexical stative verb in a 'go' serial verb construction are seen in Opo in (42). In (42a), the 'go' serial verb construction is possible with DD1 and in the unmarked form in (42b), but not with DD2 in (42c).

(42) Opo (Bilugu)
 a. ār-á **dʒà** k'áj-**ú**   b. ār-á **dʒà** k'áj
   3SG.M-INT **go.SG** be.good-**DD1**   3SG.M-INT **go.SG** be.good
   'He will go become good (then   'He will go become good.'
   come back here).'

 c. *ār-á **dʒà** k'áj-á
   3SG.M-INT **go.SG** be.good-**DD2**
   (Intended: 'He will go become good (and go to you).')

'Come' serial verb constructions with lexical stative verbs are also possible. These constructions have undergone further semantic extensions which, in some cases, can be correlated with external aspectual marking in the clause. Consider the Opo example (43a), in which the 'come' verb does not express translational motion to the deictic center. When combined with the unmarked form of the stative verb sĭk' 'be tall', this construction expresses the speaker's surprise at the subject's entering into the state (of being tall).²¹ By contrast, in (43b), when future marking is expressed in the clause, motion to the deictic center via the 'come' verb is expressed. The construction in (43b) does not convey the speaker's surprise as compared to (43a). Lastly, example (43c) shows that the use of DD1 on the lexical stative verb in a serial verb construction with 'come' is ungrammatical.

(43) Opo (Bilugu)
    a. *ār*   **dʒū**   *sík'*   b. *ār-á*   **dʒū**   *sík'*
        3SG.M **come.SG** be.tall   3SG.M-INT **come.SG** be.tall
        'He has become tall!'   'He will come and get tall.'
        (Speaker surprised)

    c. **ār-á*   **dʒū**   *sík'-ʊ́*
        3SG.M-INT **come.SG** be.tall-**DD1**

In Dana, this apparent mirative interpretation can also be expressed through either a 'go' or 'come' serial verb construction, as seen in (44).

(44) Dana
    a. *mángà* **jʊ́**   *kʰāpʰā*   b. *mángà* **ʔjâ**   *kʰápʰá*
        mango   **come.SG** be.red.SG   mango   **go.PL** be.red.PL
        'The mango has become red!'   'The mangos have become red!'
        (Speaker surprised)   (Speaker surprised)

To summarize, serial verb constructions involving a lexical 'go' or 'come' verb followed by a finite lexical verb express "prior" AM meanings. If the finite verb in the construction takes a DD, then both prior and subsequent AM meanings are expressed. Particular 'go/come' serial verb constructions involving stative verbs have become semantically extended to express the speaker's surprise at the subject's entering into a state.

3.2 Concurrent associated motion?

As Guillaume's (2016) typology predicts, languages that exhibit subsequent AM should also display concurrent (and prior) AM. Concurrent AM in Koman is not

---

21 This resembles *mirativity*, or the grammatical expression of the speaker's surprise at unexpected information (DeLancey 1997). Further research is needed to determine whether this is a productive construction in Koman.

robustly attested by any dedicated morphological means, though concurrent AM *meanings* can arise via a combination of DD and external aspectual marking and/ or by pragmatic inference. The first example, in the progressive aspect, comes from Opo. In elicitation, some Opo speakers volunteered either a subsequent or concurrent AM reading as seen in (45).[22]

(45) Opo (Bilugu)
 ùn-à k'ám-**ʊ́** kʰɔ̀bà
 3PL-PROG eat.PL-**DD1** corn
 (i) 'They were eating corn (then came here).'
 (ii) 'They are eating corn (coming towards here).'

The examples from Dana in (46) show concurrent AM meanings in transitive and intransitive clauses. In (46a), concurrent AM can be construed as a pragmatic inference and DD2 indicates that the speaker was hungry on the way to the hearer.[23] In (46b), progressive marking and DD2 can imply concurrent AM directed towards the addressee.[24]

(46) Dana
 a. tʰá̠d̠ ʃʊ́w-āgā á=jàrābúth b. tījā-í tʊ́wā
  hunger **eat.SG.DD2**-1SG.O LOC=road pot-PROG **break.DD2**
  'I was hungry on the road.' 'The pot is breaking.'
  (on the way to you) (on the way to you)

The Komo example in (47) contains a serial verb construction that is distinct from the 'go/come' serial verb constructions seen in §3.1. The construction in (47) contains a non-finite lexical dynamic (non-motion) verb followed by a finite translational motion verb. The meaning given (or inferred) is concurrent AM of the subject directed towards the deictic center. Whether or not this is a productive concurrent AM strategy remains to be investigated. Eliciting similar concurrent AM with this construction and distinct lexical verbs did not yield any results. More research is needed to test concurrent AM in Koman, but preliminary investigations reveal that it is marginal at best.

---

22 This is the only example I have of concurrent AM in this language. Note also that concurrent AM was not possible for the DD2 form of this construction.
23 In the Koman languages, the state of 'being hungry' is not expressed by a lexical verb but a construction that translates to 'hunger eats X', where X is the semantic experiencer of hunger and the syntactic object.
24 Interestingly, DD1 on this verb only expresses subsequent AM.

(47) Komo (Ethiopia)
 k'à-ā   ì-ū-n   gì=mángà
 eat.PL-DD∅ go.PL-DD1-3PL OBL=mango
 'They came eating mangos.'

3.3 AM profiling the object

Guillaume's (2016: 114) typology observed that AM of the object was rare overall. It also predicts that if a language expresses AM of the object, it will also express AM of the subject. AM in Koman robustly profiles the subject (or the speaker). Attempts at direct elicitation of AM of the object have proved futile thus far,[25] but an excerpt from a text shows what may well be AM of the object. Example (48) was uttered by a Komo speaker describing a scene in the Pear Story video (Chafe 1980). In this scene, a boy on a bicycle drops his hat while riding past a group of children. The group of children then whistle to the boy in order for him to return and pick up his hat. The Komo speaker in (48) employs DD1 on the verb úl 'call' to indicate the intended AM of the object to move towards the deictic center, which in this case is the location of the group of children. Whether or not this example constitutes bona fide AM of the object and/or whether it may be restricted to a certain class of verbs remains to be investigated.

(48) Komo (Ethiopia)
 ʃít-á   úl-ú-ār
 whistle-DD∅   call-**DD1**-3SG.M.O
 'They whistled (and) called him (towards them).' [SP_PS_2014:21]

4 Conclusion

This paper has examined three conceptual categories expressed by the Koman Deictic Directional (DD) morphological systems: associated motion (AM), direction and (exchoative) aspect. Subsequent AM profiling the subject is expressed on dynamic verbs that do not contain translational motion in their inherent semantics. The semantic properties of the path within the AM co-event can vary. Some of the languages express subsequent AM towards speaker and addressee goals

---

25 In attempting to elicit AM of the object, Koman speakers often employ full relative clauses such as "I see the man *who is coming/going.*" etc.

while others express subsequent AM towards the speaker and away from a source. This *depart source* encoding is also semantically extending into a perfective/past temporal/aspectual domain on dynamic (non-motion) verbs. The exchoative ("exiting from a state"), a heretofore unattested comparative category expressed on stative verbs, can be interpreted as the metaphorical mapping of a motion event to a state (i.e. 'move away from state' has extended into 'state no longer holds'). Deictic direction is expressed on motion verbs, regardless of whether path or manner is lexicalized in the root. While the semantic behavior of the Koman DD morphemes largely conforms to Belkadi's (2016) typology for African languages with polysemous DD/AM systems, examining low-level verb classes reveals that alternate construals of events and states can lead to the expression of more than one conceptual category on a given verb.

The Koman DD system is the only grammaticalized morphology that expresses subsequent AM. This presents counterevidence to Guillaume's (2016) AM typology regarding the temporal relationship between the lexical event and the AM co-event– depending on what constitutes *bona fide* AM coding material. Guillaume proposes that an AM morpheme can only be a verbal affix, clitic, particle, or auxiliary. In Koman, prior AM *meanings* can be expressed via serial verb constructions involving lexical deictic motion verbs. Concurrent AM, if at all expressed, is realized through serial verb constructions or through pragmatic inference. Whether or not these serial verb constructions are in fact markers of AM remains to be determined. Nevertheless, the DD system, a core feature of Koman grammar, is a window into the grammaticalization of space into the aspectual/temporal realm and AM appears to be one step along this diachronic pathway.

Abbreviations

APPL	applicative	PFV	perfective
ASS	associative	PL	plural
BP	bound pronominal	PLU	pluractional
CL	class	POSS	possessive
DD	deictic directional	PRF	perfect
DIST	distal	PROG	progressive
DRV	derivational	REDUP	reduplication
IMP	imperative	SG	singular
INT	intentative	Tone: v̂	(H)igh
LOC	locative	v̄	(M)id
M	masculine	v̀	(L)ow
NEG	negative	v̌	(R)ise
O	object	v̂	(F)all

Acknowledgements: My heartfelt gratitude is extended to all of the Koman speakers with whom I have worked over the last decade. I am grateful to Antoine Guillaume and Harold Koch for organizing the Workshop on Associated Motion held during the 12th Conference of the Association for Linguistic Typology at the Australian National University, Canberra on 15 December 2017 and for serving as editors of this volume. I am also grateful to them and to Aïcha Belkadi for serving as external reviewers of this manuscript. Many thanks go to Doris Payne, the University of Oregon department of Linguistics, the Benishangul-Gumuz Ministry of Education, and to fellow Koman scholars Anne-Christie Hellenthal, Don Killian, Joshua Smolders and Justin Goldberg. This research was partially funded by the U.S. National Science Foundation Doctoral Dissertation Research Grant (BCS 1628750).

References

Andersen, Torben. 2012. Verbal directionality and argument alternation in Dinka. In Angelika Mietzner & Ulrike Claudi (eds.), *Directionality in grammar and discourse: Case studies from Africa*, 35–53. Köln: Rüdiger Köppe Verlag.

Belkadi, Aïcha. 2013. Verb meaning and deictic path in Taqbaylit Berber. In Aicha Belkadi, Kakia Chatsiou, & Kirsty Rowan (eds.), *Proceedings of Conference on Language Documentation and Linguistic Theory 4*, London: SOAS.

Belkadi, Aïcha. 2015. Associated motion with deictic directionals: A comparative overview. *SOAS Working Papers in Linguistics* 17. 49–76.

Belkadi, Aïcha. 2016. Associated motion constructions in African languages. *Africana Linguistica* 22. 43–70.

Belkadi, Aïcha. This volume, chapter 5. Deictic directionality as associated motion: Motion, complex events and event integration in African languages.

Bender, M. Lionel. 1997. *The Nilo-Saharan languages: A comparative essay*. München: Lincom Europa.

Bourdin, Philippe. 2002. The grammaticalization of deictic directionals into modulators of temporal distance. In Ilse Wischer & Gabriele Diewald (eds.), *New reflections on grammaticalization*, 181–199. Amsterdam: John Benjamins.

Bourdin, Philippe. 2006. The marking of directional deixis in Somali: How typologically idiosyncratic is it? In Erhard Voeltz (ed.), *Studies in African linguistic typology*, 13–41. Amsterdam: John Benjamins.

Chafe, Wallace L. 1980. *The pear stories: Cognitive, cultural, and linguistic aspects of narrative production*. Norwood, N.J.: Ablex Publishing.

Corfield, Frank D. 1938. The Koma. *Sudan Notes and Records* 21(1). 123–165.

Craig, Collette. 1993. Jakaltek directionals: Their meaning and discourse function. *Languages of the world* 7(2). 23–36.

Creissels, Denis. 2014. Le développement d'un marqueur de déplacement centripète en mandinka. In Carolede Féral, Maarten Kossmann, & Mauro Tosco (eds.), *In and out of Africa: Languages in question, vol II*. 95–102. Leuven, Belgium: Peeters.

Delancey, Scott. 1997. Mirativity: The grammatical marking of unexpected information. *Linguistic Typology* 1. 33–52.
Dimmendaal, Gerrit J. 2011. *Historical linguistics and the comparative study of African languages*. Amsterdam: John Benjamins.
Dimmendaal, Gerrit J. 2015. Alloying as an economy principle in morphology. *SKASE Journal of Theoretical Linguistics* 13(2). 2–14.
Dimmendaal, Gerrit J. 2018. On stable and unstable features in Nilo-Saharan. In Helga Schröder & Prisca Jerono (eds.), *Nilo-Saharan issues and perspectives*, 9–24. Köln: Rüdiger Köppe Verlag.
Ehret, Christopher. 2001. *A historical-comparative reconstruction of Nilo-Saharan*. Köln: Rüdiger Köppe Verlag.
Greenberg, Joseph H. 1963. *The languages of Africa*. Bloomington: Indiana University.
Grinevald, Colette. 2006. The expression of static location in a typological perspective. In Maya Hickmann & Stephane Robert (eds.), *Space in languages: Linguistic systems and cognitive categories*, 29–58. Amsterdam: John Benjamins.
Guérois, Rozenn, Hannah Gibson & Bastian Persohn. This volume, chapter 15. Associated motion in Bantu languages.
Guillaume, Antoine. 2000. Directionals versus associated motions in Cavineña. In Alan Melby & Arle Lommel (eds.), *LACUS Forum XXVI: The lexicon*, 395–401. Fullerton, CA: Linguistic Association of Canada and the United States.
Guillaume, Antoine. 2013. Reconstructing the category of "associated motion" in Tacanan languages (Amazonian Bolivia and Peru). In Ritsuko Kilkusawa & Lawrence A. Reid (eds.), *Historical Linguistics 2011*, 129–151. Amsterdam: John Benjamins.
Guillaume, Antoine. 2016. Associated motion in South America: Typological and areal perspectives. *Linguistic Typology* 20(1). 81–177.
Guillaume, Antoine. 2017. Sistemas complejos de movimiento asociado en las lenguas Takana y Pano: perspectivas descriptiva, tipológica e histórico-comparativa. *Amerindia* 39(1). 211–261.
Güldemann, Tom. 2018. Historical linguistics and genealogical language classification in Africa. In Tom Güldemann (ed.), *The languages and linguistics of Africa*, 58–444. Berlin: De Gruyter Mouton.
Hellenthal, Anne-Christie. 2017. Reduplication in Gwama. Paper presented at the 13th Nilo-Saharan Linguistics Colloquium, Addis Ababa, Ethiopia.
Hellenthal, Anne-Christie. 2018. Semantics of directional verb morphology in Gwama. In Helga Schröder & Prisca Jerono (eds.), *Nilo-Saharan issues and perspectives*, 179–192. Köln: Rüdiger Köppe Verlag.
Jackendoff, Ray. 1983. *Semantics and cognition*. Cambridge: MIT press.
James, Wendy. 1975. Sister-exchange marriage. *Scientific American* 233(6). 84–94.
James, Wendy. 1979. *'Kwanim Pa: The making of the Uduk people: An ethnographic study of survival in the Sudan-Ethiopian borderlands*. Oxford: Clarendon Press.
James, Wendy, Gerd Baumann, & Douglas Hamilton Johnson (eds.). 1996. *Juan Maria Schuver's travels in North-East Africa: 1880–1883*. London: The Hakluyt Society.
Jacques, Guillaume, Aimée Lahaussois & Shuya Zhang. This volume, chapter 21. Associated motion in Sino-Tibetan, with a focus on Gyalrongic and Kiranti.
Heath, Jeffrey. 2005. *A grammar of Tamashek (Tuareg of Mali)*. Berlin: Mouton de Gruyter.
Kawachi, Kazuhiro. This volume, chapter 19. The 'along'-deictic-directional verb suffix complex in Kupsapiny.

Killian, Don. 2015. *Topics in Uduk phonology and morphosyntax*. Helsinki: University of Helsinki PhD dissertation.
Koch, Harold. 1984. The category of 'associated motion' in Kaytej. *Language in central Australia* 1. 23–34.
Koch, Harold. This volume, chapter 7. Associated motion in the Pama-Nyungan languages of Australia.
Kramer, Raija L. 2017. On locomotion, spatial orientation and lexical aspect: The functional diversity of deictic directional suffixes in Fali ("Adamawa", North Cameroon). In Raija L. Kramer & Roland Kiessling (eds.), *Mechthildian approaches to Afrikanistik: Advances in language based research on Africa: Festschrift für Mechthild Reh*, 225–242. Köln: Rüdiger Köppe Verlag.
Langacker, Ronald W. 1987. *Foundations of cognitive grammar, vol. I: Theoretical prerequisites*. Stanford: Stanford University Press.
Meckelburg, Alexander. 2016. *From "subject to citizen"? History, identity and minority citizenship: The case of the Mao and Komo of Western Ethiopia*. Hamburg: Universität Hamburg PhD dissertation.
Mietzner, Angelika, & Claudi Ulrike (eds.). 2012. *Directionality in grammar and discourse: Case studies from Africa*. Köln: Köppe.
Moseley, Christopher (ed.). 2010. Atlas of the world's languages in danger, 3rd edn. Paris: UNESCO Publishing. Online: http://www.unesco.org/culture/en/endangeredlanguages/atlas
Otero, Manuel A. 2015. Dual number in Ethiopian Komo. In Angelika Mietzner & Anne Storch (eds.), *Nilo-Saharan: Models and descriptions*, 123–134. Köln: Rüdiger Köppe Verlag.
Otero, Manuel A. 2018. Directional verb morphology in Ethiopian Komo. In Helga Schröder & Prisca Jerono (eds.), *Nilo-Saharan issues and perspectives*, 165–177. Köln: Rüdiger Köppe Verlag.
Otero, Manuel, A. 2019. *A historical reconstruction of the Koman language family*. Eugene: University of Oregon PhD Dissertation.
Otero, Manuel A. 2020. Associated motion, direction and (exchoative) aspect in Ethiopian Komo. *Studies in Language* 44(4). 737–787.
Payne, Doris L. 2013. The challenge of Maa 'Away'. In Tim Thornes, Gwendolyn Hyslop & Joana Jansen (eds.), *Functional-historical approaches to explanation: In honor of Scott DeLancey*, 259–282. Amsterdam: John Benjamins.
Payne, Doris L. This volume, chapter 18. The extension of 'Associated Motion' to aspect and argument structure in Nilotic languages.
Reh, Mechthild. 1996. *Anywa language: Description and internal reconstructions*. Köln: Rüdiger Köppe Verlag.
Renaudier, Marie. 2012. *Dérivation et valence en sereer: Variété de Mar Lodj (Sénégal)*. Lyon: Université Lumière Lyon 2 PhD dissertation.
Rose, Françoise. 2015. Associated motion in Mojeño Trinitario: Some typological considerations. *Folia Linguistica* 49(1). 117–158.
Serzisko, Fritz. 1988. On bounding in Ik. In Brygida Rudzka-Ostyn (ed.), *Topics in cognitive linguistics*, 429–445. Amsterdam: John Benjamins.
Schaefer, Ronald P., & Richard Gaines. 1997. Toward a typology of directional motion for African languages. *Studies in African Linguistics* 26(2). 193–220.

Smolders, Joshua A. G. forthcoming. Aspects of spatial grams in Bilugu Opo. In Anbessa Teferra, Azeb Amha, & Binyam S. Mendisu (eds.), *Spatial expressions in Ethiopian languages*.
Storch, Anne. 2014. *A Grammar of Luwo: An anthropological approach*. Philadelphia: John Benjamins.
Tallman, Adam J. R. This volume, chapter 11. Associated motion in Chácobo (Pano) in typological perspective.
Talmy, Leonard. 1985. Lexicalization patterns: Semantic structure in lexical forms. In Timothy Shopen (ed.), *Language typology and syntactic description, vol. III: Grammatical categories and the lexicon*, 57–149. Cambridge, UK: Cambridge University Press.
Talmy, Leonard. 2000. *Toward a cognitive semantics, vol. II: Typology and process in concept structuring*. Cambridge, MA: MIT Press.
Tunbridge, Dorothy. 1988. Affixes of motion and direction in Adnyamathanha. In Peter Austin (ed.), *Complex sentence constructions in Australian languages*, 267–284. Amsterdam: John Benjamins.
Vuillermet, Marine. 2013. Dónde, cuándo, y con quién ocurren acciones: El movimiento asociado en ese ejja. In Ana María Ospina Bozzi (ed.), *Expresión de nociones espaciales en lenguas amazónicas*, 39–59. Bogota: Universidad Nacional de Colombia.
Voisin, Sylvie. 2010. Les morphèmes *-i* et *-si* en wolof. *Sciences et Techniques du Langage 7*. 25–34.
Voisin, Sylvie. 2013. Expressions de trajectoire dans quelques langues atlantiques (groupe Nord). *Faits de langues* 42(2). 131–152.
Voisin, Sylvie. This volume, chapter 16. Associated motion and deictic directionals in Atlantic languages.
Wilkins, David P. 1991. The semantics, pragmatics and diachronic development of 'associated motion' in Mparntwe Arrernte. *Buffalo Papers in Linguistics* 1. 207–257.
Zlatev, Jordan. 2003. Holistic spatial semantics of Thai. In Gary B. Palmer & Eugene H. Casad (eds.), *Cognitive linguistics and non-Indo-European languages*, 305–336. Berlin: Mouton de Gruyter.
Zlatev, Jordan. 2007. Spatial semantics. In Dirk Geeraerts & Hubert Cuyckens (eds.), *The Oxford handbook of cognitive linguistics*, 318–350. Oxford: Oxford University Press.

—
Part V: **Asia**

Guillaume Jacques, Aimée Lahaussois and Shuya Zhang
21 Associated motion in Sino-Tibetan, with a focus on Gyalrongic and Kiranti

Abstract: This chapter presents the category of associated motion in the Sino-Tibetan family, with a special focus on the two groups with the most developed systems of associated motion, namely Gyalrongic and Kiranti. While the Gyalrongic languages have simple two-way systems, the Kiranti languages are more diverse, ranging from zero to seven sssociated motion markers.

Our survey of languages from these two groups reveals the importance of accounting for additional parameters in the description of associated motion, namely vertical dimension, circumambulative deixis, and degree of event integration. Another contribution of our chapter is to highlight differences between associated motion and purposive motion verb constructions, on the one hand, and orientation markers, on the other. This appears particularly important in light of the sometimes ambiguous examples provided in language descriptions, making it impossible to establish whether the formative in question codes associated motion or another category.

Keywords: associated motion, purposive, motion verbs, orientation event integration, elevational deixis, Gyalrongic, Kiranti, Japhug, Situ, Khaling, Dhimal

1 Introduction

This article aims to examine associated motion (henceforth AM) in a few language groups of the Sino- Tibetan family. We seek to determine the contribution that the study of the phenomenon in Sino-Tibetan languages can bring to a wider typological discussion of this linguistic category, through the consideration of additional parameters and questions that have not yet been taken up in the existing literature.

Guillaume Jacques, Centre de recherches linguistiques sur l'Asie orientale (CNRS, EHESS & INALCO), rgyalrongskad@gmail.com
Aimée Lahaussois, Laboratoire d'histoire des théories linguistiques (CNRS, Université Paris Diderot & Université de la Sorbonne Nouvelle), aimee.lahaussois@linguist.univ-paris-diderot.fr
Shuya Zhang, Centre de recherches linguistiques sur l'Asie orientale (INALCO & CRLAO), bragbarskad@gmail.com

The language groups considered in this study are Gyalrongic and Kiranti, the two groups in which AM appears to form a system, but we also take into account some data from Sinitic and a few additional languages where AM has been found. For both Gyalrongic and Kiranti, we examine the main characteristics of AM marking, highlighting the ways in which the configurations of AM are quite different across the two groups. The comparison grid that we apply is based on previously identified parameters of AM which have been described in the literature for different linguistic areas (in particular Koch 1984, Wilkins 1991 and Guillaume 2016), namely temporal relation, deixis and argument of motion, in addition to a few extra parameters which are particularly relevant for the Sino-Tibetan languages (vertical dimension and degree of event integration).

In this survey, we follow Guillaume (2016) in considering only affixal markers for AM, such as we find in Gyalrongic and Kiranti languages,[1] even though we mention cases of non-affixal AM in some languages (section 5). We take into account any affixal marker of AM, even if the primary function of the marker is to express some other feature, most commonly aspect or orientation. We do not, however, take into account markers which do not encode any AM – even though these may in many cases come from source verbs which indicate motion –, or those for which the examples are questionable as to the interpretation that should be given to the marker in question.

This paper first situates our work within the framework of Guillaume & Koch (This volume), and highlights the importance of distinguishing AM from purposive motion verb constructions (MVC) on the one hand, and orientation markers on the other. Second, we present a detailed description of the two-way AM systems in Gyalrongic languages, in particular the interaction of the AM prefixes with orientation prefixes, echo phenomena and degree of event integration. Third, we discuss the much more diverse AM systems found in Kiranti languages, ranging from zero to seven markers. This section focuses on the parameters that are usually used to describe these systems, to which we add a discussion of the vertical dimension. Finally, we briefly present data from other Sino-Tibetan languages whose descriptions either suggest or claim the existence of AM.

---

[1] Gyalrongic languages are spoken in Western Sichuan (China), and Kiranti languages in Eastern Nepal and Sikkim (Michailovsky 2017). On their phylogenetic position within Sino-Tibetan/Trans-Himalayan, see Sagart et al. (2019).

2 Definition of associated motion

The term 'Associated Motion' was originally proposed to describe a morphological category in Arandic languages (Koch 1984 and Wilkins 1991) and was more recently extended to the description of various languages of South America, in particular Tacanan and Arawakan (Guillaume 2009, Rose 2015, Guillaume 2016) as well as to some Sino-Tibetan languages (Jacques 2013, Konnerth 2015). The present work adopts Guillaume's (2016: 13) definition of associated motion in (1).

(1) An AM marker is a grammatical morpheme that is associated with the verb and that has among its possible functions the coding of translational motion.

A clear example of an AM marker in a Sino-Tibetan language is provided for instance by the cislocative *yɯ-* prefix in Japhug (in bold), as in (2) and (3).

(2) Japhug (Gyalrongic)
qajɯ ra tu-ndze   ma tɤ-rɤku
bugs PL IPFV-eat[III]   LNK INDEF.POSS-crops
yɯ-tu-ndze   mɤ-ŋgrɤl
COME&DO-IPFV-eat[III] NEG-be.usually.the.case:FACT
'It eats bugs, and does not **come and** eat the crops.' (24-ZmbrWpGa, 129)

(3) Japhug (Gyalrongic)
nɯ   ma   azo   a-mɤ-**yɯ**-kɯ-sɯzdɯɣ-a   ra
DEM apart.from 1SG   IRR-NEG-**COME&DO**-2→1-bother-1SG have.to:FACT
'Don't **come and** bother me again!' (150901 changfamei, 166)

This prefix expresses a motion event linked to the action of the main verb, but nevertheless distinct from it, that involves not only the motion of a body part of the referent (unlike orientation markers, see below), but the translational motion of its whole body from one place to the other. It is distinct from orientation markers (which occupy a different slot, see 3.2) and from a motion verb in a purposive construction.

While the definition in (1) does not specifically exclude motion auxiliaries and clitics, the present work, like Guillaume (2016: 19–20), focuses on AM markers that are verbal affixes. Potential examples of AM clitics and auxiliaries are briefly treated in section 5.

In existing grammars of Sino-Tibetan languages, AM markers are almost never described as a distinct class, but treated in chapters discussing morphemes expressing orientation or even aspect (see however King 2009, §5, Table 9).

The terms 'directionals' or 'directives' (see for instance DeLancey 1985) encompass the domain of AM, but do not distinguish it from other notions such as orientation.

In order to clarify the sampling method used in this chapter, and also to provide a terminology that may be useful for field linguists, we provide here a list of criteria to consider in determining how AM functions in a particular language. It is important to distinguish AM from other markers and constructions that involve motion, in particular from purposive motion verb constructions (see 2.1) and orientation markers (2.2).

2.1 Purposive motion verb constructions

Most, if not all, languages of the Sino-Tibetan family have at least one supine/purposive motion verb constructions (henceforth MVC), with the main verb in non-finite form, and the motion verb acting as the syntactic head of the clause. As an example, in the case of Japhug, compare the AM forms in (2) and (3) above with the MVC in (4).

(4) Japhug (Gyalrongic)
 tɕe mbarkʰom kɯ-rɣ-βzjoz tʰɯ-ye-a
 LNK Mbarkham NMIZ:S/A-ANTIP-learn PFV:DOWNSTREAM-come[II]-1SG
 'I came to Mbarkham to study.' (140501 tshering skyid, 49) (Japhug)

In (4), the verb expressing the main action is a distinct word in non-finite form (in this particular case, a subject participle). The motion verb is the main verb of the sentence and takes full TAME and person inflection, in this case the first singular suffix -a. In (3), by contrast, person inflection markers (1SG suffix and 2→1 portmanteau prefix) are affixed to the verb stem (in addition, in Gyalrongic the AM marker has no verbal properties, in particular no indexation affixes).

In some languages, the motion verb and the main verb of the purposive clause, when adjacent, may become a single phonological constituent and undergo sandhi phenomena. This is not however a sufficient criterion in itself to analyze the motion verb as an AM marker, so long as that motion verb displays full verbal morphology and the verb in the purposive clause is non-finite.

While the distinction between AM, on the one hand, and a motion verb phonologically fused with an adjacent non-finite verb, on the other, is quite trivial in the case of languages with inflectional morphology, it can be less clear with more isolating languages. Borderline cases are presented in section 5.

2.2 Orientation

The terms 'directional' has been used in the literature to refer to quite distinct phenomena such as AM, but also static orientation (see for instance Lin 2002) and even person configuration (Zúñiga 2006: 20).

In some languages, in particular Gyalrongic and neighbouring languages, directional prefixes mark orientation and TAME, but cannot express motion by themselves. In Japhug, for instance, all finite verb forms require a directional prefix specifying one of six distinct orientations (up, down, upstream, downstream, east, west; in addition, there is a series of unspecified orientation prefixes used with some verbs, see Jacques 2017). Motion verbs and verbs of manipulation are compatible with all directional prefixes, but other verbs generally have one or two fixed possible lexicalized orientations. For instance, the verb *tsʰi* 'drink' is generally used with the 'towards east; centripetal' prefixes, though it does occur with the 'downstream' prefixes with the meaning 'drink from a straw' and with the 'down' prefixes to express the meaning 'drink from below (as an animal)' as in (5).

(5) Japhug (Gyalrongic)
tɕe   ɯ-tɤ-lu   pjɯ -wɣ-rku   tɕe nɯnɯ
LNK   3SG.POSS-INDEX.POSS-milk   IPFV:DOWN-INV-put.in   LNK DEM
pjɯ-tsʰi   qʰe, tɯ-sɲi   tɕe tɯ-kʰɯtsa jamar tɯ-rdoʁ kɯ
IPFV:DOWN-drink LNK one-day   LNK one-bowl about one-CL ERG
pjɯ-tsʰi   ɲɯ-cʰa.
IPFV:DOWN-drink   SENS-can
'People pour drink for it (the cat) to drink, and it drinks it, one cat can drink about a bowl of milk per day.' (21-lWLU, 45)

The fact that the form *pjɯ-tsʰi* absolutely cannot be interpreted as meaning 'it goes down and drinks it' shows that the directional prefixes in Japhug exclusively express orientation and not AM. To test the difference between the two, it is important not to use motion verbs or verb of manipulation that have an intrinsic motion, like *ɣɯt* 'bring', which means 'bring down' when used with the prefix *pjɯ*, as in (6).

(6) Japhug (Gyalrongic)
sci   tɕe **pjɯ**-ɣɯt-a   ŋu
be.born:FACT   LNK **IPFV:DOWN**-bring-1SG   be:FACT
'When he is born, I will bring him down (from heaven).' (150828 donglang)

3 Gyalrongic

3.1 General overview

Associated motion prefixes are reported in Japhug (Jacques 2013), Zbu (Gong 2018), Tshobdun (Sun 2014) and Situ (Zhang 2016: 200–204, Prins 2016: 497–500, Lin 2017), but not found in other Gyalrongic languages (for example in Khroskyabs, cf Lai 2017).

3.1.1 Temporal relation

AM prefixes in Japhug and other Gyalrongic languages refer to a motion event occurring before the action of the main verb, resulting in a prior temporal relation with respect to the main verb, as in (7) and (8).

(7) Japhug (Gyalrongic)
 tɕe tɯ-ci ɣɯ-pjɯ-nɯ-tsʰi-nɯ
 LNK INDEF POSS-water **COME&DO**-IPFV-AUTO-drink-PL
 '(The wild yaks) come and drink water there.' (20-RmbroN, 46)

(8) Japhug (Gyalrongic)
 tɕe tɯ-ci ɕ-pjɤ-nɯ-tsʰi.
 LNK INDEF.POSS-water **GO&DO**-IFR-AUTO-drink
 'She went and drank water.' (140428 mu e guniang, 72)

3.1.2 Deixis

All four Gyalrongic languages distinguish cislocative (see examples 7 and 9) and translocative AM (see example 8). They mark the category through two prefixes each (see Table 1 from Zhang 2016: 201, Tshobdun data from Sun 2012, Zbu from Gong 2018), grammaticalized from the motion verbs 'go' and 'come' (except in the case of the translocative in the Cogtse dialect of Situ). The fact that motion verbs were grammaticalized as prefixes rather than suffixes in strict verb-final languages like Japhug and Situ can be accounted for by assuming that they come from the first member of a former serial verb construction (Jacques 2013). AM markers in Gyalrongic do not have redundant person and TAM markers, as they do in Kiranti languages.

(9) Zbu (Gyalrongic)
ɐ-kóm?   və-tə-twí?
1SG-door   COME&DO-IMP-open
'Come and open the door for me!' (Gong 2018)

Table 1: Associated motion prefixes in Gyalrongic languages.

	come	CISLOC	go	TRANSLOC
Japhug	γi	γɯ-	ɕe	ɕɯ-, ɕ-, ʑ-, z-
Kyom-kyo (Situ)	vi	və-	tʃʰi	ʃi-
Bragbar (Situ)	βʑê, və	ɟɐ-	tɕʰê	ɕɐ-
Tshobdun	wî	o-	ʃê	ʃə-
Zbu	vâ	və-	xwé?	ɕə-

Note that in Situ, the cislocative can be used with a prospective aspectual value (Lin 2003, Zhang 2016: 203), whereas in the other Gyalrongic languages, it only marks associated motion.

3.1.3 Argument of motion

The argument undergoing the motion event is always the subject (S/A), except in the case of causative constructions, where it can be either causer (A) or causee (P). For instance, Japhug *γɯ-cʰɯ-sɯ-χtɯ- nɯ* could either mean 'they send (cause to come) X here to buy Y' or 'they come and make X buy Y'; illustrates the first interpretation.

(10) Japhug (Gyalrongic)
tɕe   kupa   cʰu   nɯra   atʰi   pɕoʁ   nɯra,
LNK   Chinese   LOC   DEM:PL   DOWNSTREAM   direction   DEM:PL
ɯ-pɕi   nɯra   kɯ   kɯreri
3SG-outside   DEM:PL   ERG   here
γɯ-cʰɯ-sɯ-χtɯ-nɯ   ŋu.
COME&DO-IPFV:DOWNSTREAM-CAUS-buy-PL   be:FACT
'People from the Chinese areas, people from outside send people here to buy (matsutake).' (20 grWBgrWB 58)

3.1.4 Motion verbs and AM prefixes

In Gyalrongic, there is no constraint on AM prefixes occurring redundantly on motion verbs with the same deixis. Examples (11) and (12) respectively illustrate the cislocative on the verb *yi* 'come' and the translocative on the verb *ɕe* 'go'. Such examples are not common enough to allow a clear analysis of the semantic value of the redundant AM.

(11) Japhug (Gyalrongic)
<jiazhang> ra ju-yi-nɯ   tɕe   <laoshi> ɯ-ɕki,
parents   PL IPFV-come-PL   LNK   teacher   3SG.POSS-DAT
ɯ-ɕki   zo   **yɯ**-ju-yi-nɯ   ɕti
GENRPOSS-DAT   EMPH   **COME&DO**-IPFV-come-PL be.AFFIRM:FACT
netɕi?
SFP
'The parents come to (see) the teachers (us).' (conversation140501 01, 60)

(12) Japhug (Gyalrongic)
li   nɤki iɕqʰa   nɯ   tɤjlu   kɤ-rku
again   DEM the.aforementioned   DEM   flour   NMLZ:P-put.in
ɯ-ŋgɯ   zɯ   **ɕ**-pjɤ-ɕe
3SG.POSS-inside   LOC   **GO&DO**-IFR:DOWN-go
'He went into a bag of flour.' (140519 chou xiaoya-zh, 145)

The opposite combinations, namely cislocative with *ɕe* 'go' and translocative with *yi* 'come', are not grammatical.

3.2 Orientation and AM

The first characteristic of note is that Gyalrongic languages have devoted AM markers. These markers are only used for AM, and occur in a distinct slot within the verbal template. Orientation markers can thus be reliably distinguished from AM markers, clarifying the function of the two markers when they co-occur.

Non-orientable verbs (verbs expressing actions other than motion, manipulation, sight or actions with a single direction) select one or two lexicalized orientation prefixes. For instance, in Japhug the verb *mɯrkɯ* 'steal' occurs with the orientation 'up'.

When non-orientable verbs occur with AM, they normally keep the lexicalized orientation prefix, as in (13), where *mɯrkɯ* 'steal' is used with the *tu-* 'up' prefix (here the orientation is not indicated in the gloss since it is lexicalized); the orientation prefix is thus irrelevant to the motion event.

(13) Japhug (Gyalrongic)
kɯ-nɲo nɯ qʰe ci ci ɕ-tu-mɯrki
NMLZ:S/A-be.defeated DEM LNK one one GO&DO-IPFV-steal[III]
kɯ-fse ma nɯ ma tɯ-ɲɯ-ɣʁe.
NMLZ:S/A-be.like apart.from DEM apart.from NEG-SENS-have.to.eat
'The (lion) which is defeated goes and steals a little out from (the preys), but apart from that has nothing to eat.' (20-sWNgi, 65)

However, some verbs with an AM marker select the orientational prefix not on the basis of the lexicalized orientation, but of the motion expressed by that AM marker,[2] as in (14), where the 'down' orientation (instead of expected 'west, centrifugal' orientation selected by the verb *ntsye* 'sell') represents the motion from Gyalrong areas to Chinese areas.

(14) Japhug (Gyalrongic)
pot ɣɯ ɯ-laχtɕʰa pjɯ-ɣɯt-a tɕe, ŋa zɯ
Tibet GEN 3SG.POSS-thing IPFV:DOWN-BRING-1SG LNK China LOC
ɕ-pjɯ-ntsye-a.
GO&DO-IPFV:DOWN-sell-1SG
'I bring things (down) from central Tibet, and I go (down) and sell them to China.' (28- qAjdoskAt)

3.3 Echo phenomena

Previous literature on AM has reported the existence of 'echo phenomena' in the use of AM markers (Wilkins 1991: 251, Vuillermet 2012: 681–683, Rose 2015: 128–130, Guillaume 2016: 91, fn. 11), namely that the same motion event can be expressed by more than one AM marker or by one AM marker and one motion verb. This phenomenon is common in Japhug narratives. Two subtypes of AM echo can be distinguished.

First, in examples such as (15) and (16), a motion verb (ɕe 'go' and ɣi 'come' respectively) is followed by a verb with an AM prefix with the same deixis, though there is a single motion event.

---

[2] This phenomenon is even more frequent in Situ, where AM prefixes can modify the orientation prefixes of the main verb so long as the motion co-event is prominent (For details see Zhang 2020).

(15) Japhug (Gyalrongic)
tɕʰi ɯ-taʁ to-ɕe tɕe ɕ-tɤ-ru
stairs 3SG.POSS-on IFR:UP-GO LNK GO&DO-PFV:UP-look
'He went up the stairs and looked up.' (08-kWqhi, 18)

(16) Japhug (Gyalrongic)
kʰa mɯ-pɯ-rɤzi tɕe tɕe, ftɕar nɯ wuma zo
house NEG-PST.IPFV-stay LNK LNK summer DEM really EMPH
βɣɯz pjɤ-rɯɲɯŋɤn tɕe maka, kɯmtʰoʁ ra
badger IFR.IPFV-cause.damage LNK completely threshold PL
kɯnɤ ju-ɣi ɣɯ-ɲɯ-sloʁ pjɤ-ŋu.
also IPFV-come COME&DO-IPFV-dig.UP IFR.IPFV-be
'He was not home, and badgers were causing a lot of damage that summer, they came and even dug up the threshold of the house.' (27-spjaNkW, 107)

Second, we also find cases, such as (17), without a motion verb, but with two verbs redundantly prefixed with the same AM marker (here *ɣɯ-*).

(17) Japhug (Gyalrongic)
tɕe a-kʰa ra ɣɯ-ta-rɤroʁrɯz, a-mgo
LNK 1SG.POSS-house PL COME&DO-PFV:3→3'-tidy 1SG.POSS-food
ra ɣɯ-ta-βzu ŋu ɕi
PL COME&DO-PFV:3→3'-make be:FACT QU
'Did she (the neighbour's wife who took pity on me) come and tidy my house and make food for me?' (150827 tianluo, 76)

Echo AM is required in serial verb constructions (Jacques 2016a: 253–255), as shown in (18), where the verbs *stu* 'do like' and the *nɯrtɕa* 'tease' share the same person (3→3'), TAME (imperfective) and AM (translocative) markers.

(18) Japhug (Gyalrongic)
kɯra ɕ-tu-ste tɕe ɕ-ku-nɯrtɕe
DEM:PROX:PL GO&DO-IPFV-do.like[III] LNK GO&DO-IPFV-tease[III]
ra pjɤ-ŋu.
PL IFR.IPFV-be
'(The mouse) went and teased (the cat) like that.' (150902 dashu, 31)

3.4 Degree of event integration

Another topic of interest in Gyalrongic is the issue of the separability of the motion event and the verbal action. Unlike other languages with AM such as Kiranti, Tungusic or Koman (Stoynova 2016, Alonso de la Fuente & Jacques 2018, Pakendorf & Stoynova This volume, Otero This volume) in Japhug the scope of negation, interrogation, conditionals and complement-taking verbs applies to the entire verbal event (motion+main action). In cases where the verbal action is outside their scope, an alternative purposive construction with a motion verb is used. This is however not common to all Gyalrongic languages: in the closely related Situ language, the semantic distinction between AM and the corresponding purposive construction is less clear (§ 3.4.5).

To express the meaning of motion prior to an action, associated motion prefixes are nearly two times as common as corresponding MVCs in the Japhug corpus. There is however a clear semantic difference between the two constructions, which was briefly described in Jacques (2013), but is presented here in more detail.

AM and MVC differ from each other in that in the former, the completion of both motion event and verbal action is presupposed (AM is completely integrated into the event), whereas in the case of the latter, the two can be separated (in other words, have a low degree of event integration). This contrast in event integration is most conspicuous in past perfective forms, and can be observed in four types of constructions: concessives (with negation of the verbal action), interrogatives, conditionals and complement clauses.

MVCs are built by combining a deictic motion verb (ɕe 'go' or ɣi 'come') with a purposive clause whose main verb is in kɯ- subject participle form. Deictic motion verbs, and in the case of Situ, orientation verbs (Zhang 2020), are compatible with this type of purposive clause.

3.4.1 Concessive

A MVC with the motion verb in perfective form can be followed by a clause negating the purposive action, as in (19). In this example, only the motion is realized, while the action expressed by the verb rtoʁ 'look' could not be accomplished.

(19) Japhug (Gyalrongic)
nɤ-kɯ-rtoʁ   jɤ-ɣe-a   ri,   mɯ-nɯ-atɯɣ-tɕi,
1SG.POSS-NMLZ:S/A-see PFV-come[II]-1SG LNK NEG-PFV-meet-1DU
mɯ-pɯ-ta-mto.
NEG-PFV-1→2-see
'I came to see you but I did not see you.'

With the corresponding AM verb form *ɣɯ-jɤ-ta-rtoʁ* 'I came and saw you', negating the action of the verb is self-contradictory and nonsensical, and a sentence such as (20) is incorrect.

(20) Japhug (Gyalrongic)
†ɣɯ-jɤ-ta-rtoʁ ri mɯ-pɯ-ta-mto
COME&DO-PFV-1→2-look LNK NEG-PFV-1→2-see
Intended meaning: 'I came and saw you but I did not see you.'

Additional minimal pairs of the same type are presented in Jacques (2013: 202–203).

3.4.2 Interrogative

In interrogative clauses, MVCs are required to express meanings such as 'What/ who have you come/ gone to X', as in example (21), an example which occurs nine times in the corpus on Pangloss.

(21) Japhug (Gyalrongic)
tɕʰi ɯ-kɯ-pa jɤ-tɯ-ye?
what 3SG.POSS-do PFV-2-come[II]
'What did you come to do?'

The difference between a MVC and AM in interrogatives can be illustrated by comparing the minimal pair (21) and (22). Example (21), implies that the addressee has not done anything yet, while (22) with AM can only be used if the action is already done, requiring a different translation.

(22) Japhug (Gyalrongic)
tɕʰi **ɣɯ-tɤ-tɯ-pa-t**
what COME&DO-PFV-2-do-PST:TR
'What did you do upon coming here?' (elicited)

3.4.3 Conditional

The presuppositional difference between a MVC and AM is also perceptible in the protasis of conditional clauses.

With a MVC in the protasis as in (23), there is no presupposition that the verbal action took place, and the motion event alone constitutes a condition to the state of affair described in the apodosis.

(23) Japhug (Gyalrongic)
nɤ-wa   ɯ-kɯ-rtoʁ   mɯ~mɤ-jɤ-tɯ-ye
2SG.POSS-father 3SG.POSS-NMLZ:S/A-look COND~NEG-PFV-2-come[II]
nɤ azo mɯ-pɯ-kɯ-mto-a.
LNK 1SG NEG-PFV-2→1-1SG
'If you had not come to see your father, you would not have seen me.' (you saw me, but your father was not here)

By contrast, with AM, the verbal action necessarily took place, as in example (24).

(24) Japhug (Gyalrongic)
nɤ-wa   mɯ~mɤ-**yɯ**-jɤ-tɯ-rtoʁ   nɤ
2SG.POSS-father COND~NEG-**COME&DO**-PFV-2-look   LNK
pɯ-sɤzdɯxpa
PST.IPFV-be.pitiful
'If you had not come and seen your father, he would have felt sorry.' (but you did see him, so he does not feel sorry)

3.4.4 Complement clauses

In complement clauses, verbs with AM prefixes are attested, and complement-taking verbs always have scope over both the action of the verb and the motion event.

In (25), the modal verb cʰa 'can' and the double negations (with the specific meaning 'cannot help') have scope over both the motion event and the verbal action – this example is taken from a passage in a story where the king reproaches a small child, who has just returned from a mission the king sent him on, for not having first come to greet him upon his return home; the child says these words to justify why he first went to see his mother before greeting the king.

(25) Japhug (Gyalrongic)
tɯ-nɯ   ɯ-kɯ-tsʰi   ɲɯ-ɕti-a
INDEF.POSS-breast 3SG.POSS-NMLZ:S/A-drink SENS-be.AFFIRM-1SG
tɕe, jɤ-azɣɯt-a   tɕe, tɯ-nɯ   ci
LNK PFV-arrive-1SG LNK INDEF.POSS-breast INDEF

mɤ-ɕɯ-kɤ-tsʰi   nɯ   mú j-cʰa-a
NEG-GO&DO-INF-drink   DEM   NEG:SENS-can-1SG
'I am (a toddler) who (still) drinks (his mother's) milk, when I arrived, I could not help but go and drink milk.' (Norbzang, 262)

The context makes it clear that both the motion event (going to his mother's house, the reason for the child's failure to go to see the king) and the action 'drink milk' (the reason for that motion event) are equally important to the plot and inseparable. In (26), the negated modal verb applies to both the main verb and the motion event – the guards prevent the main character not only from stealing, but also from going to the location of the potential theft.

(26) Japhug (Gyalrongic)
ʁmaʁ   χsɯ-tɤkʰar   kɯ   ɲɯ-ɤz-nɤkʰar-nɯ   ɕti
soldier three-rounds   ERG   SENS-PROG-surround-PL be.AFFIRM:FACT
tɕe,   ɕɯ-kɤ-mɯrkɯ   mɤ-tɯ-cʰa
LNK   GO&DO-INF-steal   NEG-2-can:FACT
'Three rounds of soldiers will be surrounding it, you will not be able to go (there) and steal it.' (2003qachga, 55)

The same observation also applies to verbs with AM in complement clauses selected by a verb in the protasis, as in (27): the realization of the verbal action (in addition to that of the motion event) belongs to the condition.

(27) Japhug (Gyalrongic)
nɤzo   ɕɯ-kɤ-mɯrkɯ   a-pɯ-tɯ-cʰa   nɤ   azo
2SG   GO&DO-INF-steal   IRR-IPFV-2-can   LNK   1SG
cʰɯ-sɯ-jɣat-a   jɤɣ
IPFV-CAUS-go.back-1SG   be.agreed:FACT
'If you succeed in going and stealing it, I can make him to go back there.' (02-montagnes- kamnyu, 46)

By contrast, in (28), in the case of the infinitival complement kɯ-rɤma kɤ-ɕe 'go to work' with a purposive clause (kɯ-rɤma), the main verb mda 'be time to' only has scope over the motion event expressed by the verb ɕe 'go' – the time that is indicated by the stars refers to the beginning of the journey to work, not the start of the work itself.

(28) Japhug (Gyalrongic)
tɕe kɯɕɯŋgɯ tɕe tutsʰot pɯ-me tɕe nɯnɯ
LNK long.ago LNK clock PST.IPFV-not.exist LNK DEM
cʰɯ-ɬoʁ lu-ɕqʰlɤt nɯra
IPFV:DOWNSTREAM-come.out IPFV:UPSTREAM-disappear DEM:PL
ɕ-tu-kɯ-rɯ tɕe, nɯnɯ kɤ-rɤru
GO&DO-IPFV:up-GENR:S/P-look LNK DEM INF-get.up
mda mɤ-mda cʰondɤre kɯ-rɤma kɤ-ɕe
be.time:FACT NEG-be.time:FACT COMIT NMLZ:S/A-work INF-go
mda mɤ-mda nɯtɕu
be.time:FACT NEG-be.time:FACT DEM:LOC
ɕ-tu-kɯ-rɯ pɯ-ŋgrɤl.
GO&DO-IPFV:up-GENR:S/P-look PST.IPFV-be.usually.the.case
'In former times, there was no clock, and people used to go and watch when (these stars) came out or disappeared (to know) whether it was time to get up or go to work.' (29-LAntshAm, 66)

3.4.5 Degree of event integration in situ

Minimal pairs similar to those presented above in Japhug have been elicited in Situ. However, it appears that in this language, the use of verbs in perfective form with AM markers does not presuppose that both the verbal action and the motion event have been accomplished. The degree of event integration is thus lower than in Japhug.

In (29), the action of the verb nə-ɟe-ta-natsô-n 'I came to see you' with the AM prefix ɟe- is negated by the following clauses, while the motion event clearly took place; the corresponding Japhug example (20 in § 3.4.1) is considered to be not only agrammatical, but also non-sensical. Example (29) has little discernible semantic difference with the corresponding MVC in (30).

(29) Situ (Gyalrongic)
nə-ɟe-ta-natsô-n rɐ, nəɟɔ̂ nə-'tə-mɐ-n,
PFV:DOWN-COME&DO-2→1-look$_{II}$-2 CONJ 2SG SENS-2-do.not.exist$_I$-2SG
majnə ma-na-tə-mətê-n.
CONJ NEG-PFV-2→1-see$_{II}$-2SG
'I came to see you, but you were not here, so I didn't see you.'

(30) Situ (Gyalrongic)
nə-kə-natsō   nə-və̄-ŋ   rɐnə,   nəɟə̂
POSS.2SG-NMLZ-see   PFV:DOWN-come_II-1SG   CONJ   2SG
nə-ˈtə-mɐ-n,   majnə ma-na-tə-mətê-n.
SENS-2-do.not.exist_I-2SG   CONJ NEG-PFV-2→1-see_II-
'I came to see you, but you were not here, so I didn't see you.'

Similarly, in (31), the verb form nə-ɟɐ-ˈtə-va-n 'What did you come to do?' with the AM prefix ɟɐ- does not imply that the action of the verb has already taken place, unlike the corresponding construction in Japhug in § 3.4.2. The interpretation of (31) is the same as for example (32), the latter featuring a MVC.

(31) Situ (Gyalrongic)
nəɟə̂   tɕē   thə̂   nə-**ɟɐ**-ˈtə-va-n?
2SG   here   what PFV:DOWN-**COME&DO**-2-do_II-2SG
'What did you come to do?'

(32) Situ (Gyalrongic)
nəɟə̂   tɕē   thə̂   kə-viê   nə-ˈtə-va-n   gɐ?
2SG   here   what   INF-do   PFV:DOWN-2-come_II-2SG   Q
'What did you come to do?'

This difference between Japhug and Situ, two otherwise relatively closely related languages, suggests that features such as degree of integration between the motion event and the verbal action may not be diachronically stable.

3.4.6 Lack of volitionality and control

An additional difference between AM and MVC has to do with volitionality and/or controllability. In the case of an MVC, the verb in the purposive clause, whose action follows the motion event, is always necessarily volitional and controllable. By contrast, in the case of AM, it is possible to find examples where the verbal action expresses a non-controllable event, such as the action of finding a lost object in example (33) with echo phenomenon (cf § 3.3). Note that there are no examples of the non-volitional verb *mto* 'see' with the MVC in the corpus (the volitional *rtoʁ* 'see, look' or *ru* 'look' occur instead).

(33) Japhug (Gyalrongic)
nɯɕɯmɯma zo tɯ-ci ɯ-ŋgɯ pjɤ-ɕe
immediately EMPH INDEF.POSS-water 3SG.POSS-inside IFR:DOWN-go
qʰe icqʰa   tɤɕime   kɯ   ɯ-sɤcɯ
LNK the.aforementioned lady ERG 3SG.POSS-key
pɯ-kɤ-nɯ-ɕluɣ   nɯ   ɕ-pjɤ-mto.
PFV:DOWN-NMLZ:P-AUTO-drop DEM   **GO&DO**-IFR-see
'He immediately went into the water and saw there the key that the lady had dropped by mistake.' (140510 fengwang, 118)

3.5 Relativizability of objects

MVC and AM present another contrast, which cannot be ascribed to the question of event integration: the relativizability of objects. In the MVC, the common subject of the motion verb and the verb of the purposive clause (which can be a transitive or an intransitive subject) can be relativized, and if overt, the head can be internal, between the purposive clause and the nominalized motion verb, as *tɤ-tɕɯ* 'son, boy' in (34), or occur after the whole clause.

(34) [[tɤ-mu   ɯ-kɯ-rtoʁ]   tɤ-tɕɯ
     INDEF.POSS-mother   3SG.POSS-NMLZ:S/A-see INDEF.POSS-son
     jɤ-kɯ-ɤri]   nɯ   a-ʁi   ŋu
     PFV-NMLZ:S/A-go[II] DEM   1SG.POSS-younger.sibling be:FACT
'The boy who went to see the old lady is my brother.' (elicited)

On the other hand, when the verb of the purposive clause is transitive, it is not possible to relativize its object. Example (35), with an overt transitive subject *a-ʁi kɯ*, is thus non-grammatical, and the phrase *ɯ-kɯ-rtoʁ jɤ-kɯ-ɤri tɤ-mu* can only be interpreted as a subject relative 'the old lady who went to see him'.

(35) †a-ʁi   kɯ   ɯ-kɯ-rtoʁ
     1SG.POSS-younger.sibling ERG   3SG.POSS-SUBJ:PCP-see
     jɤ-kɯ-ɤri   tɤ-mu
     PFV-NMLZ:S/A-go[II] INDEF.POSS-mother
     nɯ   a-ɬaʁ   ŋu
     DEM   1SG.POSS-aunt   be:FACT
Intended meaning: 'The old lady that my younger brother went to see is my aunt.'

The only way to build a relative clause with this meaning is to use AM prefixes. In (36) for instance, the finite relative[3] *a-ʁi kɯ z-ja-rtoʁ* does not contain any additional embedded clause, and is a simple case of object relativization.

(36) [*a-ʁi   kɯ   z-ja-rtoʁ*]
     1SG.POSS-younger.sibling ERG   TRANSLOC-PFV:3→3'-see
     tɤ-mu   nɯ   a-ɬaʁ   ŋu
     INDEF.POSS-mother DEM   1SG.POSS-aunt be:FACT
     'The old lady that my younger brother went to see is my aunt.' (elicited)

Using AM in object relativization is a thus strategy to circumvent the syntactic constraint against relativization outside of purposive clauses.

4 Kiranti

The most complex AM systems of the Sino-Tibetan family are found in Kiranti, with systems with up to seven distinct markers (Khaling; Yamphu, Rutgers 1998: 137–194). The main characteristics of AM marking in Kiranti are the following:
1. AM systems are of greatly differing complexity across the subgroup.
2. AM systems can encode vertical dimension.
3. AM markers are labile: they can be either intransitive or transitive (usually matching the main verb, but not always); when transitive, the argument of motion is not only the A but also includes the P.
4. AM markers often have multiple uses, with the same marker variously also marking aspect, as well as orientation, and, in one description, even voice.
5. Verbs with AM marking have a low degree of event integration (true of Khaling; unclear of other languages)

In Kiranti, AM markers are erstwhile auxiliaries (variously called 'aspectivizers', 'bound roots', 'motionalizers', 'general motion auxiliaries', 'V₂s', 'vector verbs', 'oriented motion verbs' and 'modal verbs' in different descriptions of Kiranti languages) which often come from motion verbs, though in many cases the source verb does not exist anymore.

---

[3] In Japhug relative clause with a finite verb can only be used to relativize objects and goals, are not used for subject relativization (Jacques 2016b).

There is evidence that such complex verb forms originate from serial verb constructions (Loves-trand & Ross This volume), in which a motion verb (as well as other auxiliaries) occupied the second position, but became progressively integrated into a single word (though with differences across Kiranti; see Bickel et al. 2007, Schiering et al. 2010). For some languages, the second verb has grammaticalized into an aspectual marker (see Bickel 1996), but some of these languages still show, within the examples given in grammars, some situations where the marker clearly indicates AM and not aspect. In other cases, it is not aspect but orientation which is the main function of the markers. However, some languages have AM markers which are devoted to motion. These different degrees of grammaticalization of auxiliary motion verbs explain one of the interesting features of AM in Kiranti: even with cognate morphemes, the languages range from zero to seven AM markers (including markers that do not exclusively encode AM).

Example (37) illustrates a typical AM-marked verb in Khaling, with the circumambulative **-le-** 'go around doing'. Note the multiple exponence of the 2PL: the reduced form *-n-* between the stem of the verb *-ŋô-* and the AM marker *-le-* and the full form *-ni* at the end of the verb complex. This suggests that at an earlier stage both the main verb and the AM marker had the full array of person indexation and TAM markers.[4]

(37) Khaling (Kiranti)
      *ʔi-ŋô-n-**le**-ni*
      2/INV-cry-2PL:N.PST-**GO.AROUND.DOING**-2PL:N.PST
      'You$_{pl}$ went around crying.'

4.1 Morphosyntactic parameters of AM in Kiranti

The Khaling AM system, which ranks among the most complex in the Kiranti branch, can be used to illustrate the general typological characteristics of AM systems in this group. Table 2 summarizes the data concerning four parameters (temporal relation, deixis, vertical dimension and argument of motion) relating to the AM markers of Khaling. The following sections will illustrate each of these parameters using data from various Kiranti languages.

---

[4] This reduced inflectional material is also found with infinitives as in example (50) below.

Table 2: The Khaling AM system.

Source	AM marker	Temp.	Deixis	Vertical	Argument
?	|-le(t)-| 'go around doing X'	C	CIRCUM	∅	S/A
|kʰot| 'go'	|-kʰo(t)-| 'do X and go'	S	TRANS	∅	S/A(+P)
?	|-pɛ(t)-| 'go and do X'	P	TRANS	∅	S/A
|ɦo| 'come'	|-ɦo(t)-| 'do X and come'	S	CIS	∅	S/A(+P)
|kʰoŋ| 'come up'	|-kʰoŋ-| 'do X and come up'	S	CIS	up	S/A
|pi| 'come (same level)'	|-pi(t)-| 'do X and come (same level)'	S	CIS	same level	S/A(+P)
|tɛn| 'fall'	|-tɛ(nt)-| 'do X and come/bring down'	S/P	CIS	down	S/A(+P)

4.1.1 Temporal relation

As seen in Table 2, AM markers in Kiranti languages can indicate prior, concurrent or subsequent motion (abbreviated as P, C and S respectively) with respect to the main verb. This is exemplified (38) in from Khaling and (39) from Belhare, where the AM markers |-kʰot-| 'do and go' and |-thaŋ-| 'go up and do' respectively express subsequent and prior motion.

(38) Khaling (Kiranti)
 tûŋ-**kʰʌ**-tɛ
 drink-AWAY/**DO&GO**-2/3:PST
 'He drank it up' or 'He drank it and left.'

(39) Belhare (Kiranti)
 cia thuŋ-**dhaŋŋ**-itt-u!
 tea set.up.to.cook-**go.UPWARDS**-ACCELERATIVE-3U
 'Go up and cook up some tea!' (Bickel 1999: 73)

In some cases, pragmatics will trump the usual temporal relation for a given AM marker. This is seen in the set of examples below, where |-tɛ(nt)-| 'do X and come/ bring down', which generally implies subsequent motion (as in 40), can instead be used to express prior motion if the scenario triggers that interpretation.

(40) Khaling (Kiranti)
 sirise?-ɛ   bʰrêm   rɛp-**tɛnd**-ʉ
 p.n.-ERG   buckwheat beat-**COME.DOWN**-3SG→3.N.PST
 'Sirise beats the buckwheat and comes down.'

(41) Khaling (Kiranti)
 dzirise-?ɛ rê: rɛp-**tɛnd**-ʉ
 p.n.-ERG   rice beat-**COME.DOWN**-3SG→3.N.PST
 'Jirise comes down, beats the rice (and returns).'

In (40), there is no obstacle to a default subsequent motion interpretation (buckwheat is cultivated at the same altitude as the villages, and the grain can be beaten without Sirise needing to ascend or descend first), but in (41), the fact that the rice is cultivated lower in altitude than the household means that only an interpretation whereby Jirise first descends to the level of the rice field before beating the rice makes sense to Khaling speakers.

4.1.2 Deixis and vertical dimension

Most AM systems in Kiranti languages have a circumambulative 'go around doing' (see (42 from Yakkha), although its form is cognate only in very closely related languages, such as Khaling and Dumi.

(42) Yakkha (Kiranti)
 ŋkha i=ya   het-u-**ghond**-wa-ga?
 that what=NMLZ.SG   cut-3P-**V₂ROAM**-NPST-2
 'What are you cutting (at various places)?' (Schackow 2015: 326)

The circumambulative marker is not necessarily always interpreted as AM in all languages; for instance in Belhare, Bickel (1996: 164) shows that the marker which he glosses as 'spatially distributed temporary' (SDT) has both AM and non-AM uses (compare 43 and 44).

(43) Belhare (Kiranti)
 rot-de   i-baŋ-ŋa   chap-**kon**-u
 road-LOC   one-HUM-OBL   write-**SDT**-3U
 'Somebody is walking around taking notes on the road.'

(44) Belhare (Kiranti)
thali khore wat chi-gon
plat cup clean clean-SDT
'He is cleaning plates and cups.'

The traditional deictic categories of cis- and translocative are clearly present in Kiranti languages, and always identifiable through the glosses. With the addition of circumambulative deixis, this results in a three-way deictic system for the languages in the subgroup.

Kiranti languages also mark the vertical dimension with cislocative (or more rarely, translocative) deixis (motion down, up, and on the same level), as shown by (45) and (46) from Yamphu.

(45) Yamphu (Kiranti)
mo.ba ka sem.so semlu-ʔug-iŋ
that:ELA I sing.too sing-**COME.DOWN**-EXPS
'I came down a-singing' (Rutgers 1998: 143)

(46) Yamphu (Kiranti)
i.doʔ ik-kætt-u
this.like grind-**BRING.UP**-3P
'He ground and brought up [the chutney]' (Rutgers 1998: 144)

Since the AM markers are transparently grammaticalized from motion verbs (and their applicative/causative counterparts), some of which encode the vertical dimension (§4.2), it is hardly surprising that this contrast is also found in the AM system. Note that a distinction is often made in Kiranti languages between verbs and AM markers for 'same level' and 'unspecified for level'.

4.1.3 Argument of motion

With all AM markers for Kiranti languages, the argument undergoing the motion event always includes the subject (S/A). The AM markers tend to present distinct allomorphs depending on the transitivity of the main verb. When the AM is marked on a transitive verb, in many cases the motion is to be interpreted transitively, resulting in a 'manipulative' meaning whereby translocatives are interpreted as 'take away' and cislocatives as 'bring', the latter exemplified in (47). The result of this is that the P is an argument of motion, along with the A. We have indicated this with the formula 'S/A(+P)' in tables presenting Kiranti data.

(47) Yakkha (Kiranti)
*eko   phuŋ   chikt-u-**ra**=na*
one   flower   pluck:PST-3.P-**V₂.BRING**=NMLZ.SG
'She plucked a flower and brought it' (Schackow 2015: 312)

While it is never possible for an intransitive main verb to be accompanied by a transitive version of the AM marker, it must be noted that the AM marker is not always interpreted transitively with a transitive main verb as in (48). Considering that the interpretation for the transitivity of the AM marker is contextual, this is another instance (as with the temporal relation being affected by context) of default[5] interpretations being trumped by pragmatics.

(48) Khaling (Kiranti)
ʔin   kʰɵs-tʰer-e   uŋʌ   ʔʌ-dʌrʌm
2sg   go-HABIT-IMP:2SG   1SG.ERG   1SG.POSS-friend
*ɦûŋ-**kʰond**-u*
wait-**DO&COME.UP**-1SG.A.N.PST
'You keep going, I will wait for my friends and come up then.' [NOT 'bring them up'] (Khaling)

4.1.4 Non-AM meanings

As mentioned earlier, what accounts for the diversity of AM systems in Kiranti languages is the fact that different languages have undergone different degrees of grammaticalization of motion verbs in the second position of what were presumably originally serial verb constructions. In some languages, the motion verbs have all grammaticalized to the point that none can be used to encode AM (this is the case with Bantawa, for example); in other languages, most markers have undergone considerable grammaticalization, but occasionally some uses will encode AM (see examples 43 and 44 from Belhare). In yet other cases, most markers derived from motion verbs are used for AM (this is the case of Khaling, where one AM marker – -*kʰot*- – is also used to mark completive aspect/telicity, as shown by the first translation given for (38) above, while the others are used exclusively for AM). The primary non-AM meaning found is aspect.

---

5 The reason for considering the transitive interpretation here as default is because the AM markers in these forms morphologically match the transitivity of the V₁, and therefore contain traces of transitive morphology. For instance, in the AM marker *kʰond-* contains a *d-* suffix which originates from an earlier applicative suffix (Michailovsky 1985, Jacques 2015).

In yet other situations, AM markers can also be used to encode orientation without motion. One of the great difficulties in decoding the examples found in grammars is that AM markers are often given with verbs of motion or of transfer, resulting in a situation where it is not clear whether the marker in question merely encodes orientation or whether it also carries motion. For instance, since the verb |yok| 'seek' implies an intrinsic motion, an example such as (49) is not sufficient to prove that the V_2 -tus- can be analyzed as AM rather than orientation.

(49) Yamphu (Kiranti)
 mo-ba pa:tro yok-tus-iŋ
 that-ELA patro seek-AROUND-EXPS
 'So then I went around looking for a calendar' (Rutgers 1998: 153)

4.1.5 Degree of event integration

As with Gyalrongic languages, it is interesting to consider the degree of event integration of the verb+AM unit in Kiranti. Again, one of the difficulties in broadening this discussion to Kiranti as a whole results from the fact that it is rarely possible to determine the degree of event integration from the examples found in many grammars. Nonetheless the first-hand data we have collected on Khaling suggests that AM markers form verbal events with low event integration: when examples are negated, the scope of the negation is limited to the main event and does not cover the AM. This can be seen in example (50) (compare with 48 above).

(50) Khaling (Kiranti)
 ʔuŋʌ ʔʌ̃m mʌ-ĥû-n-**kʰō:**-nɛ-ʔɛ ʔu-nû:
 1SG.ERG 3SG NEG-wait-INF-**DO&COME.UP**-INF-ERG 3SG.POSS-mind
 ŋes-tɛ
 hurt-2/3:PST
 'Because I did not wait for him before going up, he was sad. (I had already gone up by the time he arrived at the waiting place).'

The low degree of event integration for the verb+AM in Khaling has only been tested with negation, but presumably the tests described for Gyalrongic languages would work equally well with Kiranti languages.

4.2 Survey of AM systems in Kiranti

A large number of grammars of Kiranti languages have been consulted for the present survey, but not all languages have been included, as shorter grammars (Ebert 1997b, Ebert 1997a, Opgenort 2005, Tolsma 2006) do not always include data on potential AM constructions.

Not all Kiranti languages have AM. Although Bantawa (Doornenbal 2009) is among the better described languages, no example of constructions with clearly analyzable AM could be found in the available publications.

The simplest AM system is that of Thulung (Lahaussois 2002 and additional fieldwork) with only one AM marker, the circumambulative -*bal* (Table 3).

Table 3: The Thulung AM system.

Source	AM marker	Temp.	Deix.	Vert.	Arg.
|*bal*| 'wind around'	-*bal*- 'go around doing'	C	CIRCUM	Ø	S/A+P

Dumi, the closest relative of Khaling, has at least the four markers indicated in Table 4, and possibly more (van Driem 1993: 199–214). Note that all the markers in this Table have Khaling cognates, with similar functions (Table 2), and that the AM systems in these two languages may go back to their common ancestor.

Table 4: The Dumi AM system (van Driem 1993: 199–214).

AM marker	Gloss	Temp.	Deix.	Vert.	Arg.
-*pad*- 'to go off to do something'	Allative	P	TRANS	Ø	S/A
-*li(lit)*- 'to be up and about while doing'	Frolicsome	C	CIRCUM	Ø	S/A
-*hu:d*- 'do and bring back here'	fetch	S	CIS	Ø	S/A+P
-*pid*- 'do and bring it over here'	bring	S	CIS	Ø	S/A+P

Wambule (Opgenort 2004) has five AM markers, all of which can have a manipulative 'bring/ take' meaning (Table 5). The verb form (51) with -*lwa*- 'go/take and do' provides a clear example of the AM value of the marker.

(51) Wambule (Kiranti)
sei-**lwa**-*s*-*ta*
kill.self-**go/take**-DETR-IMP:sAS
'go and kill yourself' (Opgenort 2004: 439)

Table 5: The Wambule AM system (Opgenort 2004).

Source	AM marker	Gloss	Temp.	Deix.	Vert.	Arg.
|pi| 'come (horizontal)', |phit| 'bring (horizontal)'	-phi- 'come/bring and do'	come/bring:HRZ	P	CISL	same level	S/A+P
|ga| 'come up', |khat| 'bring up'	-kha- 'come/bring up'	?	P	CISL	up	S/A+P
|ywa| 'come down', |hywat| 'bring down'	-ywa, hywa- 'come/bring down'	come/bring:DOWN	P	CISL	down	S/A+P
|di| 'go and come back'	-di, du- 'go/take (and come back)'	go/take/come	P	TRANSL	∅	S/A+P
|lwa| 'go', |lyat| 'take away'	-lwa- 'go/take and do'	go/take	P	CISL	same level	S/A+P

Yamphu has a particularly rich AM system, with at least seven markers (Rutgers 1998: 137–194). Among the AM markers in Table 6, note that *-phæt(t)-* essentially has non-AM functions, but does occur with the meaning 'do and leave' as in example (52), hence its analysis as a subsequent translocative AM marker.

Table 6: The Yamphu AM system (Rutgers 1998: 137–194).

Source	AM marker	Gloss	Temp.	Deix.	Vert.	Arg.
	-ca/cæt- 'come and do'	come/bring	P	CISL	∅	S/A+P
|ap| 'come (horizontal)'	-ap(t)- 'come and do'	come/bring	P	CISL	same level	S/A+P
|uks| 'come down'	-uk(t)- 'come down and do'	come/bring down	P/C	CISL	same level	S/A+P
|kæt| 'come up'	-kæt(t)- 'do and come/bring up'	come/bring up	S	CISL	same level	S/A+P
	-phæt(t)- 'do and leave'	away	S	TRANSLOC	∅	S/A
|las| 'go and come back'	-las- 'go, do and come back'	go come	S+P	CISL	∅	S/A+P
	-tus/tit- 'go around doing'	around	C	CIRCUM	∅	S/A

Table 7: The Yakkha AM system (Schackow 2015: 283–328).

Source	AM marker	Gloss	Temp.	Deix.	Vert.	Arg.
	-khe?/t- 'do and go/carry'	V$_2$.GO/CARRY.OFF	S	TRANS	Ø	S/A, A+P
	-uks/t- 'do and come/bring down'	V$_2$.COME.DOWN/ BRING.DOWN	S	CIS	down	S/A+P
	-ap(t)- 'do and come/bring'	V$_2$.COME/BRING	S	CIS	same level	S/A+P
	-ghond- 'go around doing'	V$_2$.ROAM	C	CIRCUM	Ø	S/A

Table 8: The Belhare AM system (Bickel 1996, 1997, 2017).

Source	AM marker	Gloss	Temp.	Deix.	Vert.	Arg.
	-itt- 'go up and do'	go.upwards	S	CIS	down	S/A+P
	-ap(t)- 'do and come/bring'	bring.across	P	TRANS	up	S/A+P
	-kon- 'go around doing'	spatially distributed temporary	C	CIRCUM	Ø	S/A

(52) Yamphu (Kiranti)
uŋ-**bhæ:tt**-o   uŋ-**bhæ:tt**-o   sapphi
drink-**away**-ARQ drink-**away**-ARQ abundantly
'Drink before you leave, drink before you leave, [drink] as much as you can.'
(Rutgers 1998: 150).

The Yamphu marker -las- 'go, do and come back' (Table 6) implies two motion events, and may be similar to the 'interrupted motion' category proposed by Rose (2015: 123) to describe a "situation where the realization of the lexical event occurs between two stretches of motion and where the motion is encoded by a marker distinct from that of 'concurrent motion'".

Tables 7 and 8 present the AM systems of Yakkha and Belhare respectively, both featuring an ambulative-type marker.

5 Other languages

The term 'AM' has rarely been used to describe the grammar of Sino-Tibetan languages other than Gyalrongic and Kiranti, although the phenomenon is clearly present in other branches of the family. To our knowledge, only the grammars of

Karbi (Konnerth 2014, 2015) and Hakhun Tangsa (Boro 2017), some recent works on Sinitic (such as Lamarre 2020, Lamarre et al. To appear) and Burmese (Vittrant 2015) make use of this term. Potential additional examples of associated motion markers in Sino-Tibetan are discussed in Genetti et al.'s (in press) survey. Their paper partially overlaps with the present chapter (it includes the Kyomkyo dialect of Situ) but has a different scope, since it includes discussion of orientation markers without associated motion functions, with only a limited treatment of affixal AM markers, which are the focus of the present work.

Outside of Gyalrongic and Kiranti, affixal AM markers are uncommon in Sino-Tibetan; most AM markers observed in other branches are clitics, and have many non-AM functions.

For instance, in Karbi, the cislocative proclitic *nang=*, in addition to marking AM as in (53), also occurs as a person indexation marker, used for first or second person non-subject (including local scenarios 1→2 and 2→1) as in (54) and as a marker of cislocative orientation with (55) or without motion (56) (Konnerth 2015).

(53) Karbi
*alàng-lì=ke   là-tūm   a-hēm=si   **nang**=vùr-si   sá*
3-HON=TOP   this-PL   POSS-house=FOC   **CIS**=drop.in-NF:RL   tea
*aját   **nang**=jùn-lò*
GENEX   **CIS**=drink-RL
'…it was him, at their house we stopped by and had tea [come and drink tea] and everything.'

(54) Karbi
nang-phān=ke   nang=kV-pòn-pò
you-NSUBJ=top   1/2:NSUBJ=IPFV-take.away-IRR1
'[…] (I) will carry you away'

(55) Karbi
lasō   a-hūt   amāt   [e-nūt   a-kV-prék
this   POSS-during and.then   one-CLF:HUM.SG   POSS-NMLZ-be.different
a-monít   abàng=ke]   saikél   nang=ardòn-si   vàng-lò…
POSS-man NPDL=TOP   bicycle(<Eng)   CIS=ride-NF:RL   come-RL
'in this moment, another person riding on a bicycle came'

(56) Karbi
angsóng=pen=si   phén   nang=jāng-lìng
up.high=from=FOC   fan(<Eng)   CIS=hang-small:S
'the fan is hanging down from up high (from the ceiling)'

In the case of Tangsa, although Boro (2017: 311–312) uses the term AM to refer to the construction in (57), it remains unclear from the description whether an alternative analysis as a MVC is possible.

(57) Hakhun Tangsa (Sal, Northern Naga)
 inɣ́   ʒuk   kà   l-o?
 there drink **go** IMP-2SG
 'Go and drink (tea) there.' (Hakhun Tangsa)

Branches of Sino-Tibetan other than Gyalrongic and Kiranti that have affixal AM include Kuki-Chin (Chelliah & Utt 2017) and Dhimal (King 2009: 173–188). In Dhimal, King (2009) identifies five 'deictic motion' markers and provides an extremely detailed description of their uses; three of these markers (all except the 'indeterminate motion' *-gil* suffix and the 'relinquitive *-dhi*) are clearly AM markers. Table (9) summarizes the data.

Note that unlike most of the sources of AM in Sino-Tibetan languages, King explicitly provides a clear account of the degree of event integration for each AM marker. For instance, concerning the intentive *-lha*, King (2009: 177) writes 'while the motion encoded by <-lha> is viewed as preceding the action of the main verb, the completeness of the movement does not necessarily entail completeness of the action, as is the case with the distal, only that the subject went with the intention.'

Table 9: The Dhimal AM system (King 2009: 173–188).

Source	Label	Form	Temp.	Deix.	Arg.	Volitionality
puli 'go out'	Distal	*-pu* 'go and do'	P	TRANS	S/A	✓
?	Intentive	*-lha* 'go to do'	P	TRANS	S/A	✗
?	Venitive	*-pa* 'come and do'	P	CIS	S/A	✓

6 Conclusion

AM systems have been grammaticalized from motion verbs independently several times in the Sino-Tibetan family and present considerable typological diversity. Table 10 summarizes the main findings of this paper regarding affixal AM systems in the family.

Table 10: Affixal AM systems in Sino-Tibetan languages.

Subgroup	Language	Number	Temp. relation	Deixis	Vertical dimension	Other functions	Event integration	Arg.
Gyalrong	Japhug	2	P	CIS/TRANS	∅	∅	✓	S/A
	Tshobdun	2	P	CIS/TRANS	∅	∅	?	S/A
	Zbu	2	P	CIS/TRANS	∅	∅	?	S/A
	Situ	2	P	CIS/TRANS	∅	Aspect	✗	S/A
Kiranti	Khaling	7	P, C, S	CIS/TRANS/CIRCUM	✓	Aspect, Orientation	✗	S/A, S/A+P
	Dumi	4?	P, C, S	CIS/TRANS/CIRCUM	∅	Aspect, Orientation	?	S/A, S/A+P
	Thulung	1	C	CIRCUM	∅	∅	?	S/A
	Wambule	5	P	CIS/TRANS/CIRCUM	✓	Aspect, Orientation	?	S/A, S/A+P
	Yamphu	7	P, C, S	CIS/TRANS/CIRCUM	✓	Aspect, Orientation	?	S/A, S/A+P
	Yakkha	4?	P, C, S	CIS/TRANS/CIRCUM	✓	Aspect, Orientation	?	S/A, S/A+P
	Belhare	3?	P, C, S	CIS/TRANS/CIRCUM	✓	Aspect, Orientation	?	S/A, S/A+P
Dhimalish	Dhimal	3	P	CIS/TRANS/CIRCUM	∅	Aspect	✓	S/A

Gyalrongic and Kiranti, the two subgroups surveyed in detail in this work, contribute to the typology of AM in different ways.

Gyalrongic languages have simple AM systems with only two members, but the high frequency of the markers in texts makes it possible to describe in greater detail the semantic properties of AM in these languages. A corpus study on Japhug shows in particular that AM markers differ in many ways from the corresponding purposive construction with motion verbs (MVC): several syntactic tests show that the motion event cannot be separated from the action of the main verbs in the case of AM, showing a high degree of event integration. Moreover, AM can be used with non-volitional verbs, unlike MVCs.

Kiranti languages have richer AM systems, but AM markers are less common in texts, do not show echo phenomena (unlike Gyalrong, §3.3) and possibly have a low degree of event integration. They do however encode more parameters, in particular in terms of temporal relations (AM markers for prior, concurrent and subsequent motion are found), of the necessity to take into consideration the vertical dimension and an additional deictic component (adding circumlocative to cis- and translocative), and of the presence of manipulative AM markers ('bring/take and X') which add the P as an argument of motion. The languages with the highest number of AM markers in the Sino-Tibetan family (Khaling and Yamphu) are found in this branch.

Outside of Gyalrongic and Kiranti, affixal AM systems are found at least in Dhimal and probably in Kuki-Chin; non-affixal AM systems may be more widespread.

The present work contributes to the typology of AM by presenting in more detail a range of tests and criteria that can be used to refine the study of the semantic contrast between AM and other constructions. Previous descriptive work on AM in Sino-Tibetan, even in detailed grammars, rarely provides explicit examples making it possible to determine the degree of event integration of the motion event + action. Additionally, examples provided to illustrate the function of AM markers are often difficult to interpret, as they often feature verbs of manipulation, the intrinsic motion component of which makes it impossible to tell whether the marker contributes AM or orientation. It is our hope that this contribution will be a stepping stone in the production of future descriptions of the phenomenon of AM in various Sino-Tibetan languages, so that we are some day able to determine the true extent of the phenomenon in the family, and to discover other criteria that may be helpful to the cross-linguistic study of this linguistic category.

Abbreviations

This paper follows the Leipzig Glossing Rules. Other abbreviations used are as follow:

I	Stem I	FACT	factual
II	Stem II	GENEX	general extender
III	Stem III	GENR	generic
AFFIRM	affirmative	HABIT	habitual
AUTO	autobenefactive-spontaneous	HON	honorific
		HUM	human
ANTIP	antipassive	IFR	Inferential
ARQ	attention requestive suffix	INV	inverse
CIS(L)	cislocative	LNK	linker
CIRCUM	circumambulative	NF	non-final
CL	classifier	NPDF	noun phrase delimiter
COMIT	comitative	NSUB	non-subject
CONJ	conjunction	p.n.	person name
DOWN	downward orientation	QU	question particle
DOWNSTREAM	downstream orientation	RL	realis
DETR	detransitivizing marker	SENS	sensory
ELA	elative	TRANS(LOC)	translocative
EMPH	emphatic	UP	upward orientation
EXPS	first person exclusive patient subject marker		

Acknowledgements: The Japhug, Situ, Khaling and Thulung data are from the authors' fieldwork. The Japhug and Khaling examples are taken from corpora that are progressively being made available on the Pangloss archive (Michailovsky et al. 2014, http://lacito.vjf.cnrs.fr/pangloss/corpus/list_rsc.php? lg=Japhug and http://lacito.vjf.cnrs.fr/pangloss/corpus/list_rsc.php?lg=Khaling). This contribution is based on an earlier presentation which discussed a much larger language sample, including a number of Sinitic languages. Because of the near impossibility of using Guillaume's (2016) definition of AM when working with second-hand data on isolating languages, we ultimately decided to exclusively refocus the morphologically richest languages in the family, with clearly affixally-marked AM. The author wish to thank the editors, as well as Jean-Christophe Verstraete and one anonymous reviewer, for useful comments on this work.

References

Alonso de la Fuente, José Andrés & Guillaume Jacques. 2018. Associated motion in Manchu in typological perspective. *Language and Linguistics* 19(4). 501–524.
Bickel, Balthasar. 1996. *Aspect, mood, and time in Belhare: studies in the semantics-pragmatics interface of a Himalayan language*: Universität Zürich dissertation.
Bickel, Balthasar. 1997. Spatial operations in deixis, cognition, and culture: where to orient oneself in Belhare. In Jan Nuyts & Eric Pederson (eds.), *Language and conceptualization*, 46–83. Cambridge: Cambridge University Press.
Bickel, Balthasar. 1999. Cultural formalism and spatial language in Belhara. In Balthasar Bickel & Martin Gaenszle (eds.), *Himalayan space: cultural horizons and practices*, 73–101. Zürich: Museum of Ethnography.
Bickel, Balthasar. 2017. Belhare. In Graham Thurgood & Randy LaPolla (eds.), *The Sino-Tibetan Languages*, 696–721. London: Routledge.
Bickel, Balthasar, Goma Banjade, Martin Gaenszle, Elena Lieven, Netra Paudyal, Ichchha Purna Rai, Manoj Rai, Novel Kishore Rai & Sabine Stoll. 2007. Free prefix ordering in Chintang. *Language* 83(1). 43–73.
Boro, Krishna. 2017. *A Grammar of Hakhun Tangsa*: University of Oregon dissertation.
Chelliah, Shobhana & Tyler Utt. 2017. The Syntax and Semantics of Spatial Reference in Lamkang Verb. *Himalayan Linguistics* 16(1). 28–40.
DeLancey, Scott. 1985. The analysis-synthesis-lexis cycle in Tibeto-Burman: a case study in motivated change. In John Haiman (ed.), *Iconicity in Syntax*, 367–390. Amsterdam: Benjamins.
Doornenbal, Marius. 2009. *A Grammar of Bantawa: Grammar, paradigm tables, glossary and texts of a Rai language of Eastern Nepal*. Leiden: Leiden University dissertation.
van Driem, George. 1993. *A Grammar of Dumi*. Berlin and New York: Mouton De Gruyter.
Ebert, Karen H. 1997a. *Camling*. München: Lincom Europa.
Ebert, Karen H. 1997b. *Grammar of Athpare*. München: Lincom Europa.
Genetti, Carol, Kristine A. Hildebrandt, Alexia Fawcett & Nathaniel Sims. In press. Direction and Associated Motion in Tibeto-Burman. *Linguistic Typology*.
Gong, Xun. 2018. *Le rgyalrong zbu, une langue tibéto-birmane de Chine du Sud-ouest: une étude descriptive, typologique et comparative*. Paris: Institut national des langues et civilisations orientales dissertation.
Guillaume, Antoine. 2009. Les suffixes verbaux de mouvement associé en cavineña. *Faits de Langues: Les Cahiers* 1. 181–204.
Guillaume, Antoine. 2016. Associated motion in South America: Typological and areal perspectives. *Linguistic Typology* 20(1).
Guillaume, Antoine & Harold Koch. This volume. Introduction: Associated motion as a grammatical category in linguistic typology, chap. 1.
Jacques, Guillaume. 2013. Harmonization and disharmonization of affix ordering and basic word order. *Linguistic Typology* 17(2). 187–217.
Jacques, Guillaume. 2015. Derivational morphology in Khaling. *Bulletin of Chinese Linguistics* 8(1). 78–85.
Jacques, Guillaume. 2016a. Complementation in Japhug. *Linguistics of the Tibeto Burman Area* 39(2). 222–281.

Jacques, Guillaume. 2016b. Subjects, objects and relativization in Japhug. *Journal of Chinese Linguistics* 44(1). 1–28.
Jacques, Guillaume. 2017. Japhug. In Graham Thurgood & Randy LaPolla (eds.), *The Sino-Tibetan Languages*, 614–634. London: Routledge.
King, John T. 2009. *Grammar of Dhimal*. Leiden: Brill.
Koch, Harold. 1984. The category of 'Associated Motion' in Kaytej. *Language in Central Australia* 1. 23–34.
Konnerth, Linda. 2014. *A grammar of Karbi*: University of Oregon dissertation.
Konnerth, Linda. 2015. A new type of convergence at the deictic center: Second person and cislocative in Karbi (Tibeto-Burman). *Studies in Language* 39(1). 24–45.
Lahaussois, Aimée. 2002. *Aspects of the grammar of Thulung Rai: an endangered Himalayan language*: University of California, Berkeley dissertation.
Lai, Yunfan. 2017. *Grammaire du khroskyabs de Wobzi*. Paris: Université Paris III dissertation.
Lamarre, Christine. 2020. An Associated Motion approach to northern Mandarin MOTION-CUM-PURPOSE patterns. In Janet Xing (ed.), *A typological approach to grammaticalization and lexicaliza-tion: East meets west*, 131–163. Berlin: De Gruyter Mouton.
Lamarre, Christine, Alice Vittrant, Anetta Kopecka, Sylvie Voisin, Noëllie Bon, Benjamin Fagard, Colette Grinevald, Claire Moyse-Faurie, Annie Risler, Jinke Song, Adeline Tan & Clément Voirin. To appear. Deictic directionals revisited in the light of advances in typology. In Laure Sarda & Benjamin Fagard (eds.), *Neglected aspects of motion-event description*. (Human Cognitive Processing). Amsterdam: John Benjamins.
Lin, You-Jing. 2017. How Grammar Encodes Space in Cogtse Rgyalrong. *Himalayan Linguistics* 16(1). 59–83.
Lin, Youjing. 2002. A Dimension Missed: East and West in Situ rGyalrong Orientation Marking. *Language and Linguistics* 3(1). 27–42.
Lin, Youjing. 2003. Tense and aspect morphology in the Zhuokeji rGyalrong verb. *Cahiers de linguistique – Asie orientale* 32(2). 245–286.
Lovestrand, Joseph & Daniel Ross. This volume. Serial verb constructions and motion semantics, chap. 3.
Michailovsky, Boyd. 1985. Tibeto-Burman dental suffixes: Evidence from Limbu (Nepal). In Graham Thurgood, James A. Matisoff & David Bradley (eds.), *Linguistics of the Sino-Tibetan Area, the state of the art*, 363–375. Canberra: Pacific Linguistics.
Michailovsky, Boyd. 2017. Kiranti languages. In Graham Thurgood & Randy LaPolla (eds.), *The Sino-Tibetan Languages*, 646–679. London: Routledge.
Michailovsky, Boyd, Martine Mazaudon, Alexis Michaud, Séverine Guillaume, Alexandre François & Evangelia Adamou. 2014. Documenting and researching endangered languages: the Pangloss Collection. *Language Documentation and Conservation* 8. 119–135.
Opgenort, Jean-Robert. 2004. *A Grammar of Wambule*. Leiden: Brill.
Opgenort, Jean-Robert. 2005. *A grammar of Jero, with a historical comparative study of the Kiranti languages*. Leiden: Brill.
Otero, Manuel A. This volume. At the intersection of associated motion, direction and exchoative aspect in the koman languages, chap. 20.
Pakendorf, Brigitte & Natalia M. Stoynova. This volume. Associated motion in Tungusic languages: a case of mixed argument structure, chap. 22.
Prins, Marielle. 2016. *A grammar of rGyalrong Jiaomuzu (Kyom-kyo) dialects, A web of relations*. Leiden: Brill.

Rose, Françoise. 2015. Associated motion in Mojeño Trinitario: Some typological considerations. *Folia Linguistica* 49(1). 117–158.
Rutgers, Roland. 1998. *Yamphu, Grammar, Texts and Lexicon*. Leiden: Research School CNWS.
Sagart, Laurent, Guillaume Jacques, Yunfan Lai, Robin J. Ryder, Valentin Thouzeau, Simon J. Greenhill & Johann-Mattis List. 2019. Dated language phylogenies shed light on the ancestry of Sino-Tibetan. *Proceedings of the National Academy of Sciences* 116(21). 10317–10322. doi: 10.1073/pnas.1817972116. https://www.pnas.org/content/116/21/10317.
Schackow, Diana. 2015. *A grammar of Yakkha*. Berlin: Language Science Press. http:// langsci-press.org/catalog/book/66.
Schiering, René, Balthasar Bickel & Kristine A. Hildebrandt. 2010. The prosodic word is not universal (but emergent). *Journal of Linguistics* 46. 657–709.
Stoynova, Natalia M. 2016. Pokazateli "dvizhenija s cel'ju" i sobytijnaja struktura: suffiks -nda v nanajskom jazyke. *Voprosy Jazykoznanija* (4). 86–111.
Sun, Jackson T.-S. 2012. Complementation in Caodeng rGyalrong. *Language and Linguistics* 13(3). 471–498.
Sun, Jackson T.-S. 2014. Sino-Tibetan: Rgyalrong. In Rochelle Lieber & Pavol Štekauer (eds.), *The Oxford Handbook of Derivational Morphology*, 630–650. Oxford: Oxford University Press.
Tolsma, Gerard Jacobus. 2006. *A Grammar of Kulung*. Leiden: Brill.
Vittrant, Alice. 2015. Expressing motion. the contribution of Southeast Asian languages with reference to East Asian languages. In Nick J. Enfield & Bernard Comrie (eds.), *Languages of Mainland Southeast Asia: the state of the art*, 586–632. Berlin: De Gruyter Mouton.
Vuillermet, Marine. 2012. *A grammar of Ese Ejja, a Takanan language of the Bolivian Amazon*: Université Lyon II dissertation.
Wilkins, David P. 1991. The Semantics, Pragmatics and Diachronic Development of 'Associated Motion' in Mparntwe Arrernte. *Buffalo Papers in Linguistics* 1. 207–57.
Zhang, Shuya. 2016. *La phonologie et la morphologie du dialecte de Brag-bar du rgyalrong situ*. Université Paris III MA thesis.
Zhang, Shuya. 2020. *Le rgyalrong situ de Brag-bar et sa contribution à la typologie de l'expression des relations spatiales : L'orientation et le mouvement associé*. Paris: Institut National des Langues et Civilisations Orientales doctoral dissertation.
Zúñiga, Fernando. 2006. *Deixis and Alignment – Inverse systems in indigenous languages of the Americas*. Amsterdam: Benjamins.

Brigitte Pakendorf and Natalia Stoynova
22 Associated motion in Tungusic languages: a case of mixed argument structure

Abstract: The languages of South America and Australia are known for their morphologically and semantically elaborate systems of Associated Motion (AM). In contrast, the five Tungusic languages discussed here, which belong to the Northern and the Southern branch of the family, have only a single suffix pertaining to this category. This morpheme expresses a motion event that precedes the verb event. It is deictically neutral, i.e. can refer to both translocative and cislocative motion, although translocative readings predominate.

The cross-linguistically most striking feature of AM in the Tungusic languages is the fact that not only base verb arguments can be expressed, but so can arguments typical of motion verbs, called 'spatial arguments' in the paper. We explore the argument structure of verbs marked with the AM-suffix in detail and find that both formal considerations (a preference for only one overt argument) and pragmatic considerations (the choice to foreground the spatial argument over the verb argument) play a role in which argument(s) get expressed.

Keywords: Siberia, Russian Far East, corpus data, independent construction, echo construction, converbial construction, foregrounding, base verb argument, spatial argument

1 Introduction

The grammatical category of Associated Motion (AM) has been described in some detail for the languages of Australia and South America (e.g. Koch 1984; Wilkins 1991; Rose 2015; Guillaume 2016), while the related category of Motion-cum-Purpose has been described mainly in Mesoamerican languages (e.g. Haviland 1993; Zavala Maldonado 2000). These domains of verbal morphology have only recently been investigated in the languages of Northern Asia in general (Volkov

---

Brigitte Pakendorf, Laboratoire Dynamique du Langage (CNRS & Université Lumière Lyon 2), brigitte.pakendorf@cnrs.fr
Natalia Stoynova, Russian Language Institute RAS & National Research University Higher School of Economics, stoynova@yandex.ru

https://doi.org/10.1515/9783110692099-022

and Stenin 2019) and the Tungusic family in particular (Stoynova 2016, 2017; Alonso de la Fuente and Jacques 2018). This paucity of previous descriptions of Associated Motion (including Motion-cum-Purpose) in the languages of Northern Asia can probably be partly explained by the fact that this is a rare morphological category in the languages of Eurasia overall, as can be seen from the survey conducted by Ross (this volume).

All the Tungusic languages, including the now-extinct Classical Manchu, have a productive suffix with the meaning of 'to go and V' or 'to go in order to V' (1). We will here refer to it as the *ndA*-suffix, following the reconstruction proposed in Benzing (1955: 120). In this article, we focus on the argument structure of verbs with the *ndA*-suffix in several Tungusic languages, based on frequency counts of various constructions in narrative corpora (for other studies that make use of frequency counts in narrative corpora see Payne, this volume, and Tallman, this volume). The languages we discuss, namely Nanai, Ulch, Udihe, Even, and Negidal, belong to two major branches of the Tungusic family, Southern and Northern Tungusic (see Figure 1 for an attempt at a consensus tree of the Tungusic languages; for more information, see Section 2).

(1) Udihe (Nikolaeva et al. 2002: 144, txt 17, 3)
 emende ise-**ne**-je ni em'e
 witch see-**AM**-IMP who come
 'Witch, go and see who's come.'

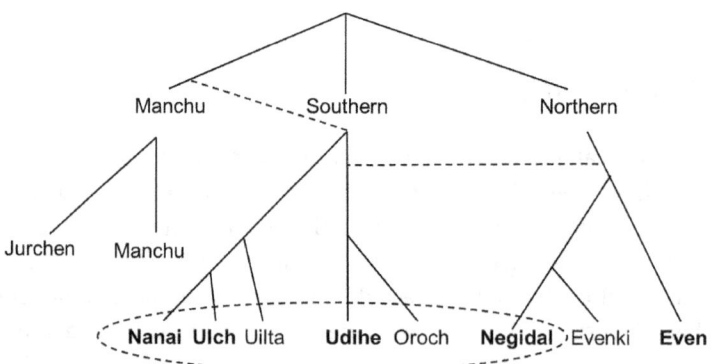

Figure 1: Attempt at a consensus tree of Tungusic genealogical relationships. The tree shown with solid branches is based on Atknine (1997: 111), while the dotted branches indicate the proposals of Comrie (1981: 58 – the Manchu branch together with the Southern branch – and Janhunen (2012: 16): Udihe/Oroch together with the Northern Tungusic languages, and the Manchu branch together with Nanai/Ulch/Uilta. The languages that the article is based on are indicated in bold font, and the dotted circle unites the languages spoken in the Lower Amur region.

A notable feature of verbs carrying the *ndA*-suffix is their mixed argument structure. They can both inherit the arguments of the base verb and take arguments that are typical of motion verbs (Goal, Source, Trajectory). For instance, in (2) the accusative argument 'girl' is inherited from the base verb 'take', while the allative argument 'to her father' is licensed by the *ndA*-suffix. Note that there is no overt motion verb in the sentence that could license the Goal argument.

(2) Bystraja Even (NIG_legend_Alngej_062)[1]
 nan ga-sči-**na**-ri-n akan-**taki**-n asatkam
 and take-CONAT-**AM**-PST-3SG father-**ALL**-POSS.3SG girl.ACC
 'And he went to her father to ask for (lit. take) the girl (in marriage).'

Few studies of AM-markers in languages of the world have explicitly addressed the argument structure of AM-verbs, but where it is mentioned it is nearly always the base verb argument that is expressed, not the argument of the motion verb. Thus, Wilkins (1991: 211) writes that in Mparntwe Arrernte "… a verb form inflected for AM takes exactly the same case frame(s) and adjunct possibilities as the verb stem without any AM inflection. Moreover, the use of associated motion inflections does not appear to license, nor increase the likelihood of, the occurrence of those spatial adjuncts that typically cooccur with motion verbs (such as ablative and allative phrases)" (see also Zavala Maldonado [2000: 143] on Olutec and O'Connor [2007: 111–112] on Lowland Chontal). Indeed, Rose (2015: 122) argues that in languages where the associated motion marker is identical to a motion verb, a grammatical category of AM can be posited only when the argument structure of the clause is provided solely by the base verb. The Pama-Nyungan languages Warlpiri and Kaytetye constitute a marked exception, since here the element expressing the motion event can add a Goal or Source argument (Simpson 2001: 180; Koch, this volume). However, while in Kaytetye a bound AM-marker appears to occasionally license a Goal or Source argument (Koch, this volume: examples [40b] and [41]), in Warlpiri a Goal argument can only be added if in participle-verb compounds it is the finite element of the compound that expresses the motion. This is quite different from what we find in the Tungusic languages studied here, where it is a bound morpheme that can add a spatial argument. The Tungusic AM

---

[1] Examples from our own text collections are provided with short source labels following the conventions used in the respective corpora (usually the speaker code, the title of the text, and the number of the sentence). For examples taken from published sources, we indicate the page, text and sentence number. See Section 2 and the Appendix for information on the text collections used in the study. Elicited examples are marked as such, with the speaker code added.

constructions discussed here thus appear to be cross-linguistically quite rare and will add to our understanding of AM as a grammatical category.

The following terms are used in the paper. The suffix *-ndA* is here called the associated motion suffix (abbreviated as AM-suffix or *ndA*-suffix), following Guillaume's (2016: 92) definition: "An AM marker is a grammatical morpheme that is associated with the verb and that has among its possible functions the coding of translational motion". See Section 3.2 for some remarks on its semantics in the Tungusic languages. Verbs marked with this suffix are referred to as *ndA*-verbs. The two events that are introduced by a *ndA*-verb are called in the paper the "motion event" and the "base verb event" or simply the "verb event". The arguments of the *ndA*-verb are divided into "base verb arguments" or simply "verb arguments" (i.e. arguments that are inherited from the base verb, often direct objects) and "spatial arguments"[2] (i.e. arguments or adjuncts that are typical of motion verbs, most notably Goal arguments).

The *ndA*-suffix is attested in the languages under consideration in three types of constructions with one and the same meaning. Firstly, it can mark the single independent verb (i.e. a finite verb in main clauses or a non-finite verb in subordinate clauses), as illustrated in (1) and (2) above and (5) below, a construction that we label "independent" here. Secondly, it can mark the converb in biverbal constructions consisting of a simultaneous converb plus finite motion verb (3a); these are called "converbial constructions/uses" here. Lastly, as shown in (3b), it can mark a finite base verb that follows (or very rarely precedes) a finite verb of motion, a type of use that we here label "echo construction" following Guillaume (2006: 424). Since both the converbial and the echo constructions contain a seemingly redundant verb of motion in addition to the *ndA*-verb, we subsume them under the cover term "pleonastic constructions/uses".

(3) a. Lamunkhin Even (AXK_svatovstvo_006)
    ta-la   *orin-či-d-deke-tne*   *honte*
    DIST-LOC   set.up.camp-RES-PROG-COND.CVB-POSS.3PL other
    ebe-hel   *gori-nuk*   *em-nidʒur*   *ukčem-met-**ne**-mi*
    Even-PL far-ADVB.ABL come-ANT.CVB.PL tell-RECP-**AM**-COND.CVB

---

[2] Note that we choose this term over the more iconic term "motion argument" in order to avoid confusion with the notion of 'argument of motion' or 'moving argument', which is used with reference to the argument of the base verb (S, A or O) that is moving when the AM-marker is attached; cf. Guillaume (2016: 113–116). From the point of view of the moving argument parameter, the *ndA*-suffix belongs to subject AM-markers: it expresses consistently the movement of the A or S argument, but not the movement of the O-argument.

em-gere-če-l
come-HAB-PST.PTCP-PL
'While they were living in their camp like this, other Evens, having come from afar, came to talk with them.'

b. Udihe (Nikolaeva et al. 2002: 50, txt 10, 19)
zeu-ŋi-na-mie   zawa-mie   ŋene-li-e-ni
food-ALN-DEST-PREFL take-COND.CVB   go-INCEP-PST-3SG
ge:-**ne**-gi-li-e-ni
bring-**AM**-REP-INCEP-PST-3SG
'(She) took some food with her and set out to bring her granddaughter back.'

As we show in this paper, both spatial arguments and verb arguments can be expressed with *ndA*-verbs (Section 4.1). However, there are differences in the occurrence of spatial arguments across syntactic constructions: they are expressed more frequently with intransitive *ndA*-verbs and in pleonastic constructions than in independent constructions with transitive *ndA*-verbs. Furthermore, from a cursory analysis it would appear that in pleonastic constructions with an overtly expressed spatial argument this is more often governed by the motion verb than the AM-marked lexical verb (Section 4.2). In those cases where both the verb event and the motion event share an argument (e.g. when the Goal of the motion event is the Location where the verb event takes place) it is the Goal that is more frequently expressed overtly. Nevertheless, some interesting variation occurs, indicating that pragmatic considerations about which event to foreground might play a role in argument expression (Section 4.3).

The paper has the following structure. In Section 2, we give some background information on the languages under discussion as well as on the methodology and the data used in the study. Section 3 contains an overview of formal (3.1) and semantic (3.2) features of AM-constructions in Tungusic languages, while Section 4 deals with the main topic of the paper, namely the argument structure of *ndA*-verbs. In Section 5, we discuss some differences in AM-constructions attested across the Tungusic languages included in the study. Finally, in Section 6 we discuss the empirical data on AM-constructions in the Tungusic languages in a wider cross-linguistic perspective.

2 Languages included in the study and data used

Tungusic languages are spoken in Siberia, the Russian Far East, and Northern China (Figure 2). The family includes Evenki, Solon, Even, Negidal, Nanai, Kilen,

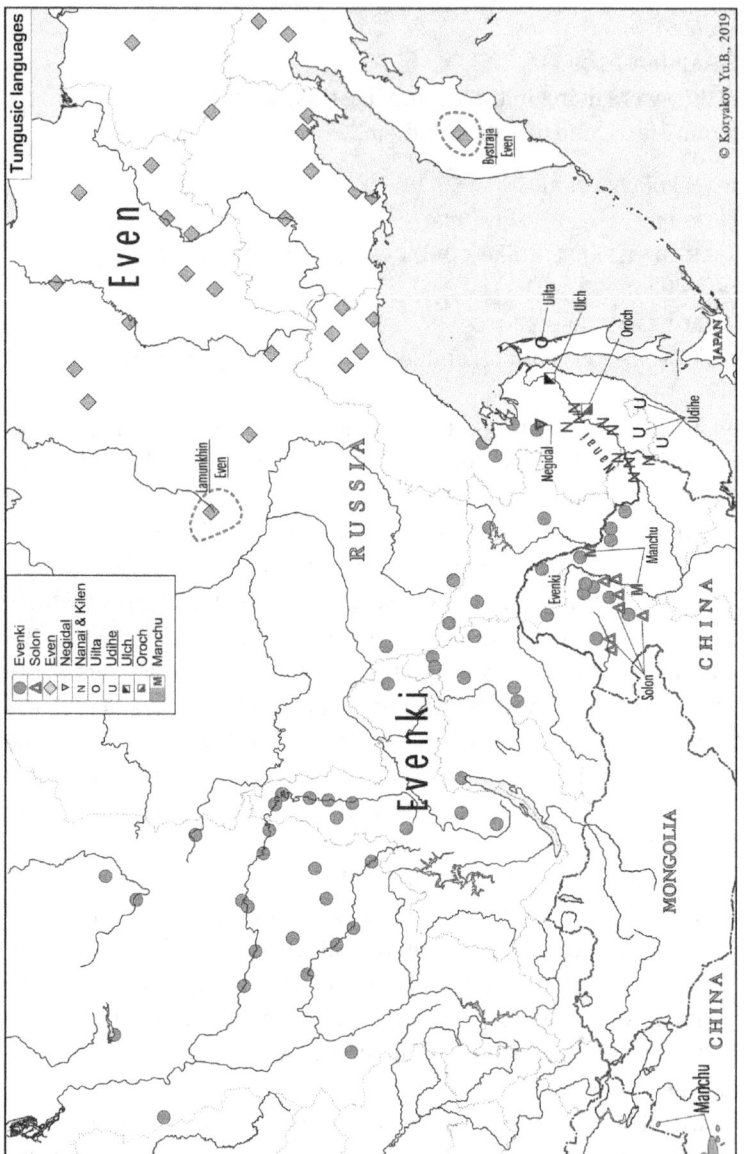

Figure 2: Map of northeastern Asia showing the areas where Tungusic languages are spoken. The underlined names in the legend refer to the five languages which we discuss in detail in the paper.

Uilta (aka Orok), Udihe, Ulch, Oroch, and Manchu. For some of these lects it is questionable whether they are languages (each with several dialects) or rather small language groups. While the classification of the Tungusic languages into one family is uncontroversial, no consensus has yet been achieved on its internal branching. Whereas all classifications agree about the close relationship of Nanai, Ulch, and Uilta on the one hand and Even, Evenki, and Negidal on the other (e.g. Sunik 1968; Atknine 1997; Janhunen 2012; cf. Figure 1), it is uncertain whether Udihe and Oroch cluster with Nanai and Ulch as part of the Southern Tungusic languages (as envisioned by Sunik 1968 and Atknine 1997, among others) or whether they are more closely related to Even, Evenki, and Negidal and thus form part of the Northern Tungusic languages (as suggested by Janhunen 2012). A further branch of the Tungusic family is represented by the extinct language Jurchen as well as Manchu and the closely related Sibe.

In this paper, we discuss data from five Tungusic languages of different genealogical subgroups. These are Nanai, Ulch, Udihe, Even, and Negidal, all of which are spoken in the Far East of Russia and in northeastern Siberia.

1) Nanai is spoken in Khabarovsk Krai (and to a lesser extent in Primorsky Krai and on Sakhalin). The language is endangered, with at most 1347 speakers (Census 2010), 11% of the ethnic group. See Kalinina and Oskolskaya (2016) on the current sociolinguistic situation. It is quite well described (Avrorin 1959, 1961, 1981). There are different dialects of Nanai. The data used in the paper come from the Middle Amur dialect (mostly from the village of Naikhin).
2) Ulch (Ulcha) is spoken in the Ulchsky district of Khabarovsk Krai. It is severely endangered, with only 154 speakers recorded in the 2010 census (Census 2010), 6% of the ethnic group (cf. Gerasimova 2002; Sumbatova and Gusev 2016). It is underdescribed: only two short grammatical sketches exist to date (Petrova 1936; Sunik 1985).
3) Udihe is spoken in Primorsky Krai by at most 103 individuals (Census 2010), 5.5% of the ethnic group. The language is severely endangered. It is quite well described (Nikolaeva and Tolskaya 2001).
4) Even is spoken by small and widely dispersed speech communities in northeastern Siberia, from the Lena river in the west to Chukotka, Kamchatka, and the coast of the Okhotsk Sea in the east. It is dialectally highly fragmented (Burykin 2004), and at most 4,900 Evens (22% of the total ethnic group) still speak the language (Census 2010). These largely belong to the older generation, and the language overall is severely endangered. However, there are big differences in language maintenance among different dialect communities (Pakendorf and Kuz'mina 2016: 587). The data in this study come from two of the geographically and linguistically most differentiated dialects (indicated

by dotted circles in Figure 2): the Lamunkhin dialect spoken in central Yakutia and the Bystraja dialect spoken in central Kamchatka. Neither of these dialects has been described in any detail.

5) Negidal used to comprise two dialects, Upper Negidal (Verxovskoj) and Lower Negidal (Nizovskoj). However, the Lower dialect is by now extinct, and Upper Negidal is spoken with varying degrees of proficiency by only five[3] elderly women in the village Vladimirovka and the nearby district centre Polina Osipenko in Khabarovsk Krai (Pakendorf and Aralova 2018). Only very brief grammar sketches exist (Cincius 1982; Kolesnikova and Konstantinova 1968; Khasanova and Pevnov 2003).

The current article is based mostly on textual data (see the Appendix for detailed information on the text collections):

1) The sample of *ndA*-uses in Nanai was extracted from Avrorin (1986), Bel'dy and Bulgakova (2012), and from our own collection of field recordings. Since some variation is attested across different dialects of Nanai, only Middle Amur texts (mostly of the Naikhin variety) were included in the sample.
2) The sample of *ndA*-uses in Ulch was extracted from the archive of L. I. Sem and from our own collection of field recordings (c. 47,500 words in total). When data from these separate sources were combined, we refer simply to "Ulch".
3) The sample of *ndA*-uses in Udihe was extracted from Nikolaeva et al. (2002, 2003), which are based on the Bikin dialect.
4) The data on Even come from corpora of transcribed, translated and glossed field recordings totalling c. 52,000 words for the Lamunkhin dialect and c. 34,000 words for the Bystraja dialect. The data from the two Even dialects were kept separate given their extreme linguistic differentiation.
5) The Negidal data were taken from a corpus of transcribed, translated, and glossed audio recordings of the Upper dialect comprising c. 47,000 words at time of writing (Pakendorf and Aralova 2017).

There is no unified analysis of the *ndA*-suffix in the literature on Tungusic languages, with some authors including it among the aspectual markers (e.g. Cincius 1982 on Negidal), others among the modal markers (e.g. Malchukov 1995 on Even), and yet others describing them among general verbal derivational suffixes (e.g. Avrorin 1961 on Nanai or Novikova 1980 on Even).[4] In the text collections

---

[3] Pakendorf & Aralova (2018) list seven speakers, but speaker 1 and speaker 5 (in their Table 1) have since passed away.
[4] Some terms occurring in different grammatical descriptions of the languages included in this paper are: "purposive derivation" ("poroda celi"; Nanai, Avrorin 1961: 59); "complex verb

we used for the study, the marker is glossed in the following way: PURP (purposive) for Nanai, MPURP (motion-cum-purpose) for Ulch, DIR (directive) for Udihe, INTENT (intentional) for Even, and AM (associated motion) for Negidal. Note that we adapted the glosses for all languages to provide consistency throughout the paper, and that we do not mark epenthetic vowels separately.

3 The *ndA*-suffix: formal aspects and semantics

3.1 Form, frequency, and syntax of the *ndA*-suffix

In this section, we briefly describe the main morphosyntactic features of the associated motion suffix and discuss its frequency in different Tungusic languages and in different types of constructions. The argument structure of *ndA*-verbs and especially the encoding of spatial arguments will be discussed in detail in Section 4.

With the exception of Classical Manchu, the Tungusic languages have only one associated motion suffix.[5] This has the following form in the languages under discussion: *-ndA* (with the allomorph *-ni* [Naikhin] ~ *-nindA* [Gorin]) or *-nA* in different dialects of Nanai (cf. Avrorin 1961: 61–62), *-ŋdA* in Ulch (cf. Sunik 1985: 50), *-nA* in Udihe (Nikolaeva and Tolskaya 2001: 232–233), *-nA* in Even and *-nA:* in Negidal. In these languages the suffix expresses prior motion by the subject/agent. It is deictically neutral, i.e. depending on the context it has an itive ('go')

---

base with such general meanings as 'depart to perform the action expressed by the primary base'" ("složnye glagol'nye osnovy s takimi, naprimer, obščimi značenijami, kak 'otpravit'sja soveršit' dejstvie oboznačennoe pervoobraznoj osnovoj'" (Ulch, Sunik 1985: 50); "directive" (Udihe, Nikolaeva, Tolskaya 2001: 232–233); "directional-intentional" (Even, Malchukov 1995: 15); "secondary verb base expressing motion or departure of the agent with the goal of performing an action" ("vtoroobraznye glagol'nye osnovy, oboznačajuščie dviženie, otpravlenie dejstvujuščego lica s cel'ju soveršit' to ili inoe dejstvie"; Even, Novikova 1980: 37); and "aspect of departure to perform an action" ("vid otpravlenija dlja soveršenija dejstvija"; Negidal, Cincius 1982: 23).

5 Note, however, that a second suffix with the meaning of 'go and V and return' is grammaticalizing out of the combination of the associated motion suffix and an erstwhile imperfective suffix, as we discuss in Section 3.2. In Bystraja Even and Negidal, this grammaticalization process appears to be completed, so that one could speak of two associated motion suffixes in these lects from a synchronic perspective.

or ventive ('come') reading (see Section 3.2 for more detail). Classical Manchu, in contrast, has both an itive suffix -nA and a distinct ventive suffix -ndʒi (Alonso de la Fuente and Jacques 2018: 505). While the ndA-suffix in the Tungusic languages (including the Classical Manchu itive) is most probably at least partially cognate and can thus be assumed to go back to Proto-Tungusic, the precise etymology of the variants in the different languages remains opaque (see Alonso de la Fuente & Jacques 2018: 519–520 for discussion).

The ndA-suffix belongs to the derivational suffixes in Tungusic. The verb stem marked by this suffix is compatible with the whole set of mood, tense, and person-number inflections. Within the stem, the ndA-suffix can be followed by some other derivational suffixes, e.g. the causative and desiderative (see Stoynova [2016: 25–31] for more detail on possible combinations attested in Nanai).

Table 1 contains comparative data on the frequency of -ndA in the languages under discussion. Note that we excluded clearly lexicalized cases, such as tu:ndə- 'to fall down, crash down' in Nanai, which can be analysed as tu:-ndə- 'fall-AM', as well as incomplete utterances (that consisted of only a converb carrying the ndA-suffix) and examples in which the suffix didn't add any motion event to the verb, but appeared rather to have aspectual readings. The latter are relatively frequent in the Udihe texts and appear to express perfective meanings, with the specific reading depending on the aspectual features of the verb stem, e.g. inceptive in (4a) and completive in (4b). Such aspectual extensions of AM markers are also reported for Kiranti languages (Jacques et al., this volume), the Pano language Chácobo, where subsequent motion AM markers indicate completive semantics of the main event (Tallman, this volume), and Nilotic directionals, where the itive indicates imperfectivity and the ventive tends to indicate inchoativity and perfectiveness (Payne, this volume).

(4) a. Udihe (Nikolaeva et al. 2003: 17; txt 1, 7)
    tukca awa-ʐa muda-tigi-ni tukä-**ŋi**-si:-ni nautu bi:-ni
    hare this-SIDE end-LAT-SG run-**AM**-ANT-3SG raccoon be-3SG
    'The hare began to run to the other end, (but) the raccoon dog was already there (as well).'

  b. Udihe (Nikolaeva et al. 2002: 180; txt 24, 13)
    diga-mi mute:-si činda gabzi-**ne**-gi-e-ni ...
    eat-SIM.CVB finish-ANT.CVB bird cheer-**AM**-REP-PST-3SG
    'Having finished eating, the bird cheered up ...'

Table 1: The frequency of -ndA.

Language	N of uses	N of sentences	N uses / 1000 sentences
Nanai	138	6356	22
Ulch	98	7477	13
Udihe	188	3313	57
Lamunkhin Even	100	8641	12
Bystraja Even	166	7140	23
Negidal	156	8554	18

There are notable differences in frequency of use of the *ndA*-suffix: Udihe exhibits a nearly three- to fivefold higher frequency of use of the AM-suffix than its sisters, and there are big differences even between the closely related languages Nanai and Ulch or the two Even dialects. Given that the Even dialectal corpora are quite similar in genre composition, as are the different sources for the Southern Tungusic languages (see Appendix), these discrepancies are likely to reflect actual linguistic divergence rather than merely being due to differences in the make-up of the corpora. However, it should be kept in mind that the corpora are rather small, so that the observed differences might simply be due to chance.

Overall, the frequency of the AM-suffix in the Tungusic languages is quite low: all except Udihe have a lower frequency than that observed by Rose (2015: 148) in Mojeño Trinitario – a language which she qualifies as making "infrequent" use of associated motion in comparison with other languages, especially with Arrernte, where in some texts more than 30% of the verbs carry an AM-marker.[6] Similarly, for the Pama-Nyungan language Kaytetye Koch (this volume) counts "some 240 AM forms" in 2870 sentences, i.e. 84 uses/1000 sentences. The AM-suffix is also infrequent in comparison to other derivational suffixes attested in the same languages. For instance, the token frequency of the most frequent verbal derivational suffix in Nanai, the repetitive -*gO*, is 260/1000 sentences, ten times higher than that of -*ndA*.

As mentioned in the introduction, the suffix is used in three types of syntactic constructions: independent, pleonastic converbial, and pleonastic echo. Examples (1) and (2) above and (5) below illustrate the independent use of the suffix, in which it is attached to the single finite verb, e.g. 'search' in (5). Examples (3a and 6a) illustrate its pleonastic converbial use, which consists of a finite motion verb and a lexical verb marked with -*ndA* in a non-finite converbial form (the

---

[6] Rose mentions 62 occurrences of the two most frequent AM-markers in nearly 2000 sentences, i.e. a frequency of use of c. 31/1000 sentences.

simultaneous converb -*mi*). The same meaning can be expressed by a combination of the finite motion verb and the plain simultaneous converb, without the AM-marker, cf. (6b). Such examples are, however, quite rare in Nanai and Ulch, and practically absent in Even and Negidal. In the Bystraja dialect of Even only two examples of the converbial construction are found; these carry the purposive converb instead of the simultaneous converb -*mi* (6c). Nanai speakers also accept such constructions with the purposive converb; however, no examples occur in the narrative corpus. The echo construction, which consists of a finite verb of motion and a finite *ndA*-verb, is exemplified in (3b) above and (7). In Udihe, one example was found in which the *ndA*-verb is finite and the motion verb carries the converb suffix (8).

(5) Ulch (Sunik 1985: 74, txt 3, 155)
    *ịlan-ʒị   bəgdi-ču   gịvụ   galə-**ndə**-xə-n*
    three-INS   leg-COM   roe   search-**AM**-PST-3SG
    'He went to search for a roe with three legs.'

(6) a. Nanai (fna_110820_so_Skazka.023)
       *sogdata-wa   waː-**nda**-mị̣   ənə-xə-či*
       fish-ACC   kill-**AM**-SIM.CVB.SG   go-PST-3PL
       'They went to fish (lit. they went while going to kill fish).'

    b. Ulch (lpd_20180720_nst_SluchajMuzhUpalVProrubj)
       umbuču-m   ŋənə-xə-ni
       fish-SIM.CVB.SG   go-PST-3SG
       'He went fishing.'

    c. Bystraja Even (SPA_ life_006)
       *ńan   ta-duk   noka   tor-teki-n   **or**-ri-wu*
       and   DIST-ABL   Sakha   earth-ALL-POSS.3SG   **go**-PST-1SG
       *upkuči-d-**ne-de**-ji   korowa   doktor-du-n*
       learn-PROG-**AM-PURP**-PREFL.SG   cow.R   doctor.R-DAT-POSS.3SG
       'And from there I went to Yakutia to study veterinary medicine (lit. cow doctor).'

(7) Negidal (Pakendorf and Aralova 2017, DIN_savkan: 77)
    *saβkan   əmə-kəl   ɉep-**na**-kal*
    pers.name   **come**-IMP.SG   eat-**AM**-IMP.SG
    'Savkan, come to eat/come and eat.'

(8) Udihe (Nikolaeva et al. 2002: 81, txt 13, 143)
    uta-digi   eme-gi-m(i)   (g)une:-n(i)
    DIST-ABL   come-REP-SIM.CVB   say.PST-3SG
    sine-we   mamasa-na-mi   **eme**-mi   ge:-**ne**-zeŋe-i
    you-ACC   wife-DEST-PREFL   **come**-SIM.CVB   bring-**AM**-FUT-1SG
    'After returning from there, he said: "I will come and marry you".'

The independent use is more frequent than the pleonastic ones in all the lects examined, with the exception of the Lamunkhin dialect of Even (Table 2): here, the pleonastic constructions are as frequent as the independent ones. Furthermore, the frequency of the converbial vs. echo subtype of the pleonastic construction differs among the languages. In Nanai, Ulch, and Lamunkhin Even, the main subtype is converbial, and echo constructions are very rare. In contrast, in Bystraja Even the main subtype is the echo construction, with hardly any converbial constructions occurring. In Udihe and Negidal the converbial and echo constructions occur with comparable frequency. These patterns of frequency do not correlate with genealogical or areal groupings (cf. Figures 1 and 2).

Table 2: Frequency of the different types of constructions.

Language	Independent	Pleonastic		Proportion of pleonastic uses (over all constructions)	Proportion of echo uses (over pleonastic constructions)
		converbial	echo		
Nanai	96	40	2	30%	5%
Ulch	68	27	3	31%	10%
Udihe	135	25	28	28%	53%
Lamunkhin Even	50	47	3	50%	6%
Bystraja Even	138	2	26	17%	93%
Negidal	114	18	24	27%	57%

3.2 The semantics of -ndA

The AM-suffix can take different directional interpretations in the independent construction.[7] In particular, both the 'go'-reading (as in [1], [2], and [5] above) and the 'come'-reading (9a) are available, although the first one is more typical: only

---

[7] However, as mentioned in the introduction, two separate markers with different spatial meanings are attested in Manchu (cf. Avrorin 2000: 173–175; Alonso de la Fuente and Jacques 2018): -nA (the cognate of the suffix under discussion) for 'go to V' and -nǯi for 'come to V'.

9% of Udihe and 27% of Nanai examples carry a come-reading (Stoynova 2018); in the Northern Tungusic lects only c. 16% of the examples are ventive. Thus, the AM-suffix appears to be deictically neutral, with the specific interpretation furnished either by the context or by additional deictic elements in the sentence. For instance, (9a) is part of a conversation between two sisters that takes place in the older sister's house, and the context makes it clear that the older sister, who is speaking and thus represents the deictic centre, assumes that her younger sister, who lives far away, will come and visit her frequently. In contrast, if the implicit goal of motion of this utterance were a third person, then the reading would be one of translocative motion ('you will probably go to see him/her frequently'). In (9b), the allative-marked proximal demonstrative *eweski* clearly signals the cislocative motion (see the similar example [19b] below), while in (9c) it is the 1SG pronoun that signals that the motion carried by the AM-suffix on 'help' is cislocative (see also [17a] with an overt 2SG addressee).

(9) a. Negidal (Pakendorf and Aralova 2017, APN_two_sisters: 55)
    *itɕe-**naː**-si-ktə-na-sun=jəkə*
    see-**AM**-IPFV-MULT-POT-2PL=PRES
    'You will probably **come** to see (me) frequently.'

   b. Bystraja Even (RME_Uindja_041)
    *Uindʒa   ia-sči-d-**na**-ri-s   **ewe-ski***
    pers.name   do.what-CONAT-PROG-**AM**-PST-2SG   **PROX-ADV.ALL**
    'Uindja, what did you **come here** to do?'

   c. Negidal (Pakendorf and Aralova 2017, DIN_Emeksikan: 35)
    *oj   **min-du**=da   osa   oː-da-ki-n*
    PROX   **1SG-DAT**=PTL   bad   become-NFUT-COND-3SG
    *ni=da   o-ta-tin   bələ-**naː**-ja*
    who=PTL   NEG-FUT-3PL   help-**AM**-NEG.CVB
    'And when it will be bad for **me**, no-one will **come** help (me).'

Within both subtypes of pleonastic constructions, the *ndA*-verb can be combined with different motion verbs: not only 'to go' (3b, 6a) and 'to come' (3a, 7), but also verbs which describe a specific manner or trajectory of motion, such as 'run', 'ascend' (10a), 'exit', as well as derived causatives such as *emu-* 'bring' (< *em-* 'come') and *horu-* 'take along' (< *hor-* 'go' [10b]). This picture differs radically from that of the rich associated motion systems frequently found in languages of Australia and South America. In such systems cumulative expression of AM-meanings and differentiated spatial meanings is attested (i.e. different markers for 'go and V' and 'come and V', etc.); cf. the overviews in Guillaume (2016) and Koch (this volume).

(10) a. Bystraja Even (PMB_pear_story21)
 nan=da uge-ski **ojči**-*ri-n uŋ-na-ji*
 again=PTL top-ADV.ALL **go.up**-PST-3SG HESIT-LOC-PREFL.SG
 gruša-n mo:-ŋa-n-dula-ji
 pear.R-POSS.3SG tree-ALN-POSS.3SG-LOC-PREFL.SG
 *čaka-d-**na**-ri-n nan=da gruša-ŋ-i*
 gather-PROG-**AM**-PST-3SG again=PTL pear.R-ALN-PREFL.SG
 '... and then climbed up the tree again and picked pears again.'

 b. Lamunkhin Even (IVK_memories_122)
 *kosči-**ne**-mi igin* **hor-u**-*wre-n,*
 herd.reindeer(day)-**AM**-SIM.CVB etc.Y **go-CAUS**-HAB[NFUT]-3SG
 *iawči-**na**-mi=da*
 herd.reindeer(night)-**AM**-SIM.CVB=PTL
 '... (he) took us along to the day reindeer herding and to the night reindeer herding.'

The combination of the suffixes *-ndA* and *-sV* (probably derived from an imperfective marker) has the meaning 'go and V and then return' (11a-b). This is also found in the example (9a) above, where the speaker implies that her sister will come repeatedly to see her, returning to her own home in between every visit. In the text data from the Naikhin dialect of Nanai and Ulch this combination is attested only in habitual contexts (11c, and see also 18d below), even though in elicitation readings with a single event are obtained. This construction is lacking in the Lamunkhin Even and Udihe data and is infrequent in Nanai.

(11) a. Bystraja Even (TEB_childhood_043)
 *a bi uže upkut-**ne-sči**-ǯi*
 but.R 1SG already.R learn-**AM-IPFV**-ANT.CVB
 gurge:wči-l-li-wu e-du
 work-INCEP-PST-1SG PROX-DAT
 'But I worked here, having gone to study (i.e. having gone to study and returned).'

b. Negidal (Pakendorf & Aralova 2017, GIK_2tatarskoe: 54)
   səktəβ-βə-βun   aː-sin-da-βaj   ɲeko-jaːn
   make.bed-NFUT-1PL.EXCL sleep-TAM1-PURP-PREFL.PL do-ANT.CVB
   itɕe-**naː-si**-ja-βun   ŋənu-tɕa-l(=gu)   ə-tɕa-l=gu
   see-**AM-IPFV**-NFUT-1PL.EXCL leave-PST-PL(=Q) NEG-PST-PL=Q
   taj   ɟaː-l-βun
   DIST relative-PL-1PL.EXCL
   'We made up our beds; before going to sleep, we went to look whether our relatives had left.'

c. Ulch (spk_170802_so_roditeli)
   mənə su̧gdata waː-**ŋda-su̧**-j
   self fish   kill-**AM-IPFV**-PRS
   'She herself goes fishing.'

The combination -ndA-sV is on its way to being grammaticalized into a dedicated 'go and V and return' marker, with different stages of this process attested in the languages discussed here. In Negidal and Bystraja Even it is more grammaticalized than in Nanai and Ulch, as can be seen from the fact that in Nanai and Ulch the suffix -sV occurs on its own (with a multiplicative/distributive/habitual meaning), whereas in Negidal and Bystraja Even the suffix -si is attested only in combination with -ndA. Thus for these two languages -ndAsi can be analyzed synchronically as an additional AM-marker distinct from -ndA. However, we here gloss -ndA and -sV as two separate suffixes for all four languages where the combination is attested, in order to retain a uniform analysis.

The grammaticalization process presumably started from habitual contexts such as that illustrated in (11c), which are appropriate for the initial meaning of -sV on its own. The next step is a reinterpretation of -ndA-sV as 'go and return' (since going somewhere repeatedly to perform an action implies a return in between each going event). From this follows the extension to uses with reference to a single event, as illustrated in (11a) and (11b). Note that in (9a) above from Negidal the erstwhile imperfective suffix co-occurs with a multiplicative suffix that expresses iterativity of the action. This shows clearly that the habitual meaning still inherent in the imperfective suffix in Nanai and Ulch has been completely bleached in Negidal (and possibly in Even as well).

The meaning 'go and V and return' (called 'roundtrip' by Ross [this volume] and Dryer [this volume]) belongs to the cross-linguistic inventory of AM-meanings. Although it is not very widespread (Guillaume 2016: 117–118; Ross, this volume), it is attested in 7.5% of the North American languages included in Dryer's sample (this volume), in the Pama-Nyungan language Kaytetye (Koch, this volume), and the Kiranti language Yamphu (Jacques et al., this volume). In the Pano language Chácobo the marker called 'counterdirectional' by Tallman (this volume) can have a 'go and V and return' meaning, but can also be used to express circular motion and is thus not dedicated to the expression of returning after performing the verb event. A semantic feature of the 'go and V and return' affix combination is that it describes a motion event with two Goals: one of them is an interim point, while the other (the endpoint) coincides with the Source. This is relevant for the argument structure, since in theory either of the two Goal arguments could be expressed. However, in our data, if an overt Goal argument is present, this refers to the interim point and not to the endpoint of the motion event – probably because the latter is implied in the 'return' meaning provided by the suffix combination.

The *ndA*-suffix can be categorized as a "prior motion" marker in the classification of AM-markers of Levinson and Wilkins (2006), since the motion event precedes the verb event. The Tungusic languages thus fit the hierarchy proposed in Levinson and Wilkins (2006) and Guillaume (2016): if there is only one AM-marker in a language, this marker expresses prior motion and not concurrent or subsequent motion (12). Thus, prior motion is the most widespread type of AM cross-linguistically, confirmed by the cross-linguistic study of Ross (this volume), who finds it in 73.5% of the languages of his sample that have a morphological category of AM.

(12) **prior motion** > concurrent motion > subsequent motion

A closely related category is Motion-cum-Purpose, where the motion event is "specifically aimed at the realization of the non-motion event" (Rose 2015: 121). This category has been primarily identified in languages of Mesoamerica that have distinct Associated Motion and Motion-cum-Purpose constructions (e.g. Haviland 1993; Zavala Maldonado 2000). In practice the distinction between Associated Motion expressing prior motion and Motion-cum-Purpose is quite subtle (cf. Guillaume 2006: 426; Ross, this volume), since in both cases the motion event precedes the verb event. In particular, in irrealis contexts such as imperatives or hortatives (which in the Tungusic languages very frequently carry the *ndA*-suffix) the two meanings are totally indistinguishable:

(13) a. Udihe (Nikolaeva et al. 2003: 68, txt 10, 165)
 *ute ge-**ne**-gi-e*
 DIST take-**AM**-REP-IMP.2SG
 'Go and take it / go to take it (meat)!'

b. Ulch (spk_170725_nst_SkazkaDochka)
   muru-č-i-n   əs   bi   žustə   ga-**ŋd**-i̦
   think-DUR-PRS-3SG   now   1SG   blueberry gather-**AM**-PRS.1SG
   '(She) thinks: Now, I'll go to gather blueberries / go and gather blueberries!'

There are numerous examples in the Tungusic corpora analysed here where the *ndA*-suffix has a clear sequential reading without a purposive nuance, e.g. (14a, b). In (14a) the sitting event is achieved after the scuffling movement across the floor, while in (14b) the next sentence makes it clear that the people did indeed search (and didn't only intend to do so), since they found the bear they were looking for.

(14) a. Nanai (Bel'dy and Bulgakova 2012: 178, txt 16, 60)
       palan-dola   sisox   sisox   sisox
       floor-LOC   sisox   sisox   sisox
       *golžon   žuliə-či-ə-ni   tə:-**ndə**-gu-xə-ni*
       stove   in.front.of-ALL-OBL-POSS.3SG sit-**AM**-REP-PST-3SG
       'She was scuffling on the floor: sisoh, sisoh, sisoh and then she sat at the fire.'

   b. Lamunkhin Even (RDA_shatun_035)
      o̦ka:t   ča:w-da-li-n   emie   iak
      river   far-SIDE-PROL-POSS.3SG   also.Y   what
      *bi-h-ni   ta-li   mende-**nə**-če-l*
      be-NFUT-3SG   DIST-PROL   search-**AM**-PST.PTCP-PL
      '... behind the river there is also something, there they went and searched. {There he found it.}'

Such unambiguous sequential readings show that -*ndA* cannot be defined as a dedicated motion-cum-purpose marker. However, there are also many examples in the Tungusic corpora which have a purposive reading rather than a specifically sequential reading. This can be clearly seen in those cases where the motion event is completed while the verb event is not (see [15a] for the independent use, [15b] for the pleonastic construction), as also discussed in detail by Jacques et al. (this volume).

(15) a. Nanai (nmch_110815_ns_MatjJagody.069)
       *simbi-ə   xaj   bəlači-**ndə**-xəm-bi-ə   un-ǯi*
       you-ACC   what   help-**AM**-PST-1SG-EMPH   say-PRS
       '{Why have you come here?} – I've come to help you – she says.'

b. Udihe (Nikolaeva et. al. 2003: 80, txt 12, 48)
   xuku   zawa:-k   me-mi   käusala-**na:**-mi   ŋene:-ni
   string take.PST-EXPR self-ACC   strangle-**AM**-SIM.CVB   go.PST-3SG
   'She took a string and went to strangle herself. {She found one place she wanted to hang herself, but it was a bad place.}'

In (15a) the motion event ('come') has already been realized at the time of the speech act, while the verb event ('help') has clearly not been realized yet. In (15b) the motion event ('go') is being realized, while the verb event ('strangle herself') has not been started by the reference time (the next sentence shows that she failed to strangle herself). In both of these examples the *ndA*-suffix thus conveys a motion-cum-purpose ('go to V') meaning, and not an associated motion ('go and V') meaning. Interestingly, according to Alonso de la Fuente and Jacques (2018) the cognate marker in Classical Manchu differs in its function from what we find in the languages of our sample: it appears to lack the motion-cum-purpose reading, having solely a sequential meaning, and can thus be regarded as a dedicated AM-marker.[8]

4 The argument structure of *ndA*-verbs

The arguments and adjuncts of motion verbs are expressed in Tungusic languages by a rich system of dedicated spatial case forms and by postpositional phrases (see Table 3 for an overview of the most important ones). Note that in this section (and in the paper overall), we ignore the core S and A arguments, which are irrelevant for our discussion.

1) In Nanai, there are four spatial cases. Location is expressed by the dative/essive case *-dO*, Source is expressed by the ablative case *-ʒiA(ʒi)* (Gorin *-dOki*), and Goal is expressed by the allative case *-či*. It shares this function with the postposition *ba:roani*. The "locative" case *-(dO)lA* expresses Trajectory ('via, through, across') and also competes in some uses with all the other spatial cases. See Avrorin (1959: 177–183) for more detail.
2) The spatial case system of Ulch is similar to that of Nanai. In addition to the Nanai inventory, it has a dedicated prolative case (*-ki*) to express Trajectory. Unlike Nanai, it has no dedicated form to express Source: this is marked by

---

[8] It is notable that related Gyalrongic languages of the Trans-Himalayan family also differ with respect to the degree of event integration, suggesting diachronic instability of this feature (Jacques et al., this volume).

Table 3: The spatial case system in Tungusic.

	Location	Goal	Source	Trajectory
Nanai	-dO	-či, ba:roani	-ǯiAǯi	-(dO)lA
Ulch	-du	=bA:n, -ti	-ǯi	-ki, (-lA)
Udihe	-du, (-lA)	-tigi, (-lA)	-digi	-li
Even	-(du)lA, (-du)	Bystr.: -t(A)ki, (-klA) Lam.: -(du)lA, (-t(A)ki)	-duk, (-gič/-git)	-(du)li
Negidal	-du	-(du)lA, -t(i)ki	-duk	-(du)li

the instrumental case -ǯi. The clitic =bA:n (the cognate of the Nanai postposition ba:roani) competes with the allative case -ti in the Goal function; cf. Petrova (1936: 27–29, 43).

3) In Udihe, Location is expressed by the essive/dative -du (as in Nanai and Ulch). Source is expressed by the ablative -digi, Goal is expressed by the allative -tigi, Trajectory is expressed by the prolative -li. The locative -lA competes with the essive/dative case and with the allative case. See Nikolaeva and Tolskaya (2001: 118–127) for more detail.

4) The complement of spatial cases in Even differs from dialect to dialect. Static Location is mostly marked by the locative case -(du)lA, although the dative case -du can also fulfil this function. Source is marked by the ablative case -duk and infrequently by the elative case -gič/-git, and Trajectory is marked by the prolative case -(du)li. The two dialects included here differ in the marking of Goal: in the Bystraja dialect, this is achieved mostly by the allative case -t(A)ki or much more infrequently the allative-locative -klA and occasionally by the locative case. In the Lamunkhin dialect, in contrast, Goal is mostly marked by the locative case, with the allative being used much less frequently, and some rare examples of the dative occurring in this function as well.

5) In Negidal, static Location is marked by the dative case -du, while Goal is marked by both the locative -(du)lA and the allative -t(i)ki. As in Even, Source is marked by the ablative case -duk, and Trajectory by the prolative -(du)li. The elative and allative-locative cases do not exist.

4.1 Verb arguments vs. spatial arguments

The argument structure of ndA-verbs is mixed. On the one hand, they can take the same arguments (highlighted in bold in the following examples) as the base verb, i.e. the verb without -ndA. Thus, in (16a) the verb gələ-ndə-gu- 'to go to search' takes the direct object *ag-bi* 'brother', as would the base verb *gələ-(gu)-* 'to search', and in (16b) the reciprocal-marked verb *tore-met-ne-* 'to go to speak with someone' takes a comitative argument, as would the reciprocal-marked verb *tore-met-*.

(16) a. Nanai (Bel'dy and Bulgakova 2012: 106, txt 11, 141)
   *mi   ag-**bi**   gələ-**ndə**-gu-əm-bi*
   1SG elder.brother-**PREFL.SG** search-**AM**-REP-ASSERT-1SG
   'I'll go to search for **my brother**.'

   b. Bystraja Even (AEI_ASA_muzej2_001)
   *Manja-**gli**   tore-met-**ne**-ger*
   pers.name-**COM**   speak-RECP-**AM**-IMP.1PL.INCL
   'Let's go to speak **with Manja**!'

On the other hand, they can also take arguments which are typical of motion verbs (indicated by both bold and underlined font in the following examples): in (17a) the verb *xupi-ndə-* 'to come to play' takes the same allative-marked Goal argument *sin-či* 'to you' as would the motion verb 'come', while in (17b) *taŋ-na-* 'to go and study' takes both an allative- and an ablative-marked argument, as would the motion verb 'go'. Neither *xupi-* 'to play', nor *taŋ-* 'to study' can take such arguments without the *ndA*-suffix, as can be seen in (19b) below, where the base form 'I studied' occurs with a dative-marked static Location. A similar case of the AM marker licensing the overt expression of a Goal argument is mentioned for the Nilotic language Shilluk (Payne, this volume).

(17) a. Nanai (Avrorin 1986: 65, txt 13, 3)
   *sin-**či**   xupi-**ndə**-xəm-bi*
   2SG-**ALL**   play-**AM**-PST-1SG
   'I've come **to you** to play.'

   b. Bystraja Even (RMS_childhood.083)
   ńan   boloni   o:-kla-n
   and   late.autumn   become-ALL.LOC-POSS.3SG
   *bi   ńan   škole-**tki**   tar   rybelke-**duk***
   1SG and   school.R-**ALL**   DIST fishing.camp.R-**ABL**
   *taŋ-**na**-wa:t[-te-m]*
   study-**AM**-GNR[-NFUT-1SG]
   'And until it became autumn I went **to school** to study **from that fishing camp**.'

Interestingly, both the arguments typical of motion verbs (spatial arguments) and the arguments inherited from the initial verb stem (base verb arguments) can be expressed in one and the same clause; see (2) above and the examples in (18):

(18) a. Negidal (Pakendorf and Aralova 2017, AET_grandmother: 73)
  oɲin-mi   amin-mi   amin-ŋasa-β
  mother-POSS.1SG   father-POSS.1SG father-DECES-POSS.1SG
  *tatkat-**na**:-βkan-tɕa-tin   naːn-**ma**-n*
  study-**AM**-CAUS-PST-3PL   3SG-**ACC**-3SG
  *nikolaevski-**teki**   učitel-**du***
  geo.name-**ALL**   teacher.R-**DAT**
  'My mother and father sent **her** **to Nikolaevsk** to study **for teacher** (i.e. to become a teacher).'

b. Lamunkhin Even (ZAS_naled_096)
  dʒapk-is   stada-l   ọran-tan   tar-tiki,
  eight-ORD.Y   herd.R-PL   reindeer-POSS.3PL DIST-ALL
  *tara-w   nọŋartan   tar-**tiki**   it-**ne**-wre-r*
  DIST-ACC   3PL   DIST-**ALL**   see-**AM**-HAB[NFUT]-3PL
  'The reindeer of the eighth herd (went) there, and they (my father and brother) went **there** to watch **them** …'

c. Udihe (Nikolaeva et al. 2002: 45; txt 9, 24)
  *zugdi-**tigi**   geː-**ne**-gie   suese-we   moː-wo*
  house-**ALL**   take-**AM**-REP.IMP   axe-**ACC** tree-ACC
  xua-ŋni-laga-mi
  cut-AM-PURP-PREFL
  'Go **home** to get **an axe** to cut down the tree.'

d. Ulch (BD_legend1)
  *ụgda-ʒị   əj   qalta-**tị**   əj   duəntə   qalta-**tị**-n*
  boat-INS   PROX   part-**ALL**   PROX   forest   part-**ALL**-POSS.3SG
  *talụ-**wa**   uku-**ŋdə**-su-mi   bi-či-ti*
  birch.bark-**ACC**   peel-**AM**-IPFV-SIM.CVB.SG   be-PST-3Pl
  '(They) used to go by boat **to this forest side** to peel **the birch-bark**.'

There are no evident restrictions on spatial arguments, as can be seen from the elicited example from Nanai (19a). Here, all the possible types of spatial roles (Source, Goal, and Trajectory) are expressed within one and the same clause. Similarly, in the text examples in (17b) above and (19b) both Source and Goal are expressed.

(19) a. Nanai (elicited, NCHB)
　　　əktə-səl　　　exon-ʒia　　　xoton-či　goj　　pokto-la
　　　woman-PL　　village-ABL　　town-ALL　other　road-LOC
　　　amtaka-wa　xodasi-**na**-xa-či
　　　berry-ACC　sell-**AM**-PST-3PL
　　　'The women went to sell berries **from the village** (Source) **to the town** (Goal) **by another road** (Trajectory).'

　　b. Bystraja Even (EIA_leaving_Twajan_117)
　　　Ketačan-**gič**=kal　　　　　nan　ewe-**ski**　　　taŋ-**na**-ri-wu
　　　geo.name-ELAT=COORD　and　PROX-ADV.ALL　read-**AM**-PST-1SG
　　　Essoː-**tki**,　　　Essoː-du　　nan
　　　geo.name-ALL　geo.name-DAT　and
　　　taŋa-ʤaːn-ni-wu　　mudaka-kla-n
　　　read-DUR-PST-1SG　finish-ALL.LOC-POSS.3SG
　　　'And **from Ketachan** I came **here to Esso** to attend school, and in Esso I studied until the end.'

To a certain extent the AM-suffix in the Tungusic languages thus resembles an applicative, since it allows the addition of an argument that isn't licensed by the lexical verb on its own; cf. Mithun (2002: 73): "Prototypical applicatives are derivational processes within the verbal morphology that add a participant to the set of core arguments. The added argument usually represents a semantic recipient, beneficiary, instrument, associate, direction, or location …". However, in contrast to true applicatives, there is no promotion of an oblique argument to a core argument in the AM construction, since the case-marking of all the arguments remains the same as in non-AM constructions: Goals are marked with allative or locative case, and the base verb arguments carry the case-marking licensed by the lexical verb.

Spatial arguments are overtly expressed in c. 15–20% of the independent *ndA*-constructions (for pleonastic constructions see Section 4.2), as shown in Table 4. Ulch expresses spatial arguments more frequently than do the other languages; however, this difference is not statistically significant.

Interestingly, non-spatial arguments typical of motion verbs can also be expressed with *ndA*-verbs. Even though in a judgement task speakers of Ulch were doubtful of examples in which the role "Transport" (marked with the instrumental case [20a]) was expressed (20b), similar examples are found in the Ulch narrative corpus, e.g. (18d) above and (21a) below. Such examples are also found in the Bystraja Even (21b) corpus:

Table 4: Spatial arguments with *ndA*-verbs (independent constructions).

Language	With spatial arguments	All independent	% with spatial arguments
Nanai	14	96	15%
Ulch	15	68	22%
Udihe	18	135	13%
Lamunkhin Even	8	50	16%
Bystraja Even	24	138	17%
Negidal	17	114	15%

(20) a. Ulch (elicited, IPR)
    xusə pikta pojez-ǯi ŋən-i-n
    male child train.R-**INS** go-PRS-3SG
    'The boy goes **by train**.'

  b. Ulch (elicited, IPR)
    ???*xusə pikta pojez-ǯi tatųčị-**nda**-xa-nị*
    male child train.R-**INS** learn-**AM**-PST-3SG
    'The boy went to study **by train**.'

(21) a. Ulch (spk_171112_Biografia)
    *Kiǯi=bən murin-ǯi gələ-**ndə**-su-xə*
    geo.name=ALL horse-**INS** search-**AM**-IPFV-PST
    'They used to go for it (lit. go to search for it) to the lake Kizi **by horse**.'

  b. Bystraja Even (GIK_life_Anavgaj_183)
    *motocikli-č eŋe-**ne**-dʒi-ru mura-l-ba*
    motorcycle.R-**INS** look-**AM**-FUT-1PL.EXCL horse-PL-ACC
    'We will go to look at the horses **by motorbike**.'

4.2 Argument structure in different syntactic constructions

Although it is possible to express spatial arguments overtly in AM-constructions, it is nevertheless the verb argument that is expressed more commonly. In Table 5, we summarize the occurrences of different kinds of overt arguments found in independent *ndA*-constructions with transitive base verbs. These constructions have at least two possible argument slots (along with that of the subject), one for the spatial argument and one for the verb argument (i.e. the direct object in this case), and in theory both could be filled equally. However, in the corpora the verb argument is overtly expressed three to nine times more frequently than the spatial argument.[9] The greatest difference is attested in Udihe and Nanai, the smallest is found in Ulch. Importantly, the co-expression of spatial arguments and verb arguments is very rare in all the languages, i.e. usually only one slot is filled, a point we come back to below.

Table 5: The argument structure of *ndA*-verbs (independent constructions with transitive verbs).

Language	Only spatial argument	Only verb argument (O)	Spatial argument and verb argument	No argument	Ratio verb/ spatial argument
Nanai	5	46	1	13	7.8
Ulch	6	28	3	15	3.4
Udihe	3	58	4	43	8.9
Lamunkhin Even	3	24	3	12	4.5
Bystraja Even	3	31	2	36	6.6
Negidal	4	35	6	39	4.1

Interestingly, *ndA*-constructions with intransitive base verbs occur more frequently with overt spatial arguments than do *ndA*-constructions with transitive base verbs (Table 6), suggesting a potential preference for overtly expressing only one of the two possible arguments per verb; this effect is significant for Nanai, Udihe and Bystraja Even (2-tailed Fisher's exact test, $p<0.05$). This might be an indication that the availability of the transitive verb argument 'blocks' expression of the spatial argument unless the speaker chooses to give the motion event equal or more discourse prominence by overtly expressing its argument. We return to the choice of foregrounding the motion event over the verb event in the discussion below (Section 6).

In pleonastic constructions the motion event is expressed twice: once via the motion verb and once via the AM-suffix on the base verb, be this coded as a finite verb (in the echo construction) or as a converb. It is thus possible that the pleonastic constructions contain more overt spatial arguments than independent AM-constructions, which have only one verb that expresses both the verb event and the motion event. As can be seen in Table 7, this is indeed the case at least for some of the languages under consideration (for examples of the converbial construction with overt spatial argument see 22a and 23a below; for examples

---

[9] Quite frequently neither argument is expressed, since argument-dropping is common in Tungusic languages.

Table 6: Spatial arguments with transitive vs. intransitive verbs (independent constructions).

Language	Transitive verbs			Intransitive verbs		
	Spat arg*	No spat arg	% with spat arg	Spat arg	No spat arg	% with spat arg
Nanai	6	59	9%	6	14	30%
Ulch	9	43	17%	5	9	36%
Udihe	7	101	6%	11	8	58%
Lamunkhin Even	6	36	14%	0	5	0%
Bystraja Even	5	67	7%	14	31	31%
Negidal	10	74	12%	5	15	25%

*spat arg = spatial argument.

of the echo construction with overt spatial argument see 22b and 24a): in all languages except Ulch and Negidal pleonastic constructions code spatial arguments significantly more frequently than do independent constructions (2-tailed Fisher's exact test, p<0.05).

(22) a. Lamunkhin Even (AEK_reindeer_herd_011)
 ejmu no:-n kuŋa-l-čal
 mother.POSS.1SG younger.sib-POSS.3SG child-PL-COM
 mut-**tule** ńo:-wre-ri-n deremket-**ne**-mi
 1PL-**LOC** exit-HAB-PST-3SG rest-**AM**-SIM.CVB
 '… my mother's younger sister […] also **went to us** […] with her children to rest.'

 b. Udihe (Nikolaeva et al. 2002: 70, txt 12, 77)
 ti: emne-gde **ŋene:**-n(i)
 DIST once-FOC **go**.PST-3SG
 ba-**ixi** uli gaŋ-**na**-gi-e-n(i)
 place-**ALL** water fetch-**AM**-REP-PST-3SG
 'One day (the mother) **went outdoors** to fetch some water.'

The data on overtly expressed verb arguments, in contrast, are rather less clear: although both pleonastic and independent constructions express the verb event via the single *ndA*-verb, so that one wouldn't expect any difference in argument expression, there is variation between the languages. Only in Nanai, Bystraja Even, and Negidal do we find roughly equal amounts of overtly expressed verb arguments in pleonastic and independent constructions, as expected. In Ulch and Lamunkhin Even, in contrast, the verb event is expressed significantly more often in independent constructions than in pleonastic ones (2-tailed Fisher's exact test, p<0.05), whereas in Udihe it is expressed significantly less frequently in independent constructions (2-tailed Fisher's exact test, p<0.05). These patterns do not correlate with the proportion of converbial vs. echo pleonastic constructions, as a comparison with Table 2 shows. What factors determine the overt expression of verb arguments is thus still unclear.

Table 7: Spatial arguments in independent and pleonastic constructions.

Language	Pleonastic with ...		Independent with ...	
	Spatial arguments	Verb arguments	Spatial arguments	Verb arguments
Nanai	21 (50%)	23 (55%)	14 (15%)	50 (52%)
Ulch	8 (27%)	8 (26%)	14 (21%)	34 (50%)
Udihe	18 (35%)	34 (64%)	18 (16%)	63 (47%)
Lamunkhin Even	20 (40%)	10 (20%)	8 (16%)	28 (56%)
Bystraja Even	16 (57%)	7 (25%)	24 (17%)	35 (25%)
Negidal	11 (26%)	16 (38%)	17 (15%)	45 (40%)

In pleonastic constructions with an overt spatial argument, this might be governed by the motion verb or the *ndA*-verb. Without in-depth syntactic analysis it is not easy to distinguish between these options, and it might even be the case that the spatial argument is governed by both verbs. Based simply on word order and distance between the spatial argument and the motion verb vs. *ndA*-verb, it would appear that both options are indeed available (23a, b).

(23) a. Nanai (znb_110821_so_SkazkaZheleznajaPtitsa.046)
  gə: əm modan=tani xaj piktə-n'=təni
  DP one time=COORD what child-POSS.3SG=COORD
  du**si** to:-ri-ni xaj-wa=də xəm
  to.forest **go.from.bank**-PRS-3SG what-ACC=PTL all
  icə-**ndə**-m
  see-**AM**-SIM.CVB.SG
  'Once, the son **goes to the forest** to see lots of things.'

b. Bystraja Even (NIG_shkola_remesel_1_293)
  ŋen-de-ku gu:n-e-m čas
  go-PURP-1SG say-NFUT-1SG PTL
  bi čepuki-w aŋani-ldewu ...
  1SG boots.R-ACC sew-NMLZ

> *unta-l-ba aŋani-ldewun-**teki** upkut-**ne**-de-ku*
> fur.boots-PL-ACC sew-NMLZ-**ALL** learn-**AM**-PURP-1SG
> 'And I said "well, let me go, let me **go** to study **where they sew boots**, where they sew fur boots".'

In (23a) the Goal argument *dujsi* 'to the forest' precedes the motion verb *to:-* 'go from the riverbank' and is separated from the *ndA*-verb by the verb argument 'a lot of things' and by the motion verb. It is thus arguably the motion verb that triggers the overt Goal marking here. In contrast, in (23b) the Goal argument is adjacent to the *ndA*-verb and is separated from the motion verb by the self-corrected speech error; arguably, in this case it is the *ndA*-verb that governs the Goal argument. Judging purely from such very superficial considerations (by simply counting constructions where the spatial argument is closer to the motion verb than the *ndA*-verb and vice versa), it would appear that in pleonastic constructions the spatial argument is more frequently governed by the motion verb than by the *ndA*-verb (this can also be seen in [22a-b], where it is more likely that the spatial argument is governed by the motion verb). However, this conclusion needs to be ascertained with more detailed investigations.

In pleonastic constructions, the motion verb and the *ndA*-verb can be syntactically independent, as shown by (24a-c). In the echo construction in (24a) the spatial argument is repeated in near-identical form: since in Negidal both the allative and the locative can mark Goal arguments, as outlined in Section 4 above, *okin-tiki-j* and *okin-dula-j* both mean 'to my older sister'. Thus here the clause 'go to my older sister' is repeated using two different verbs. Such independence of the two verbs is possible not only with echo constructions, but also with converbial pleonastic constructions, as shown in (24b) and (24c).

(24) a. Negidal (Pakendorf & Aralova 2017, APN_two_sisters: 82)
> *okin-**tiki**-j ŋənə-mtɕə-lti gun-ə-n*
> older.sister-**ALL**-PREFL.SG **go**-SBJV-1PL.INCL say-NFUT-3SG
> *okin-**dula**-j itɕe-**na**-mtɕa-lti*
> older.sister-**LOC**-PREFL.SG see-**AM**-SBJV-1PL.INCL
> '... we should **go to my sister**, we should **go** see **my sister**.'

b. Lamunkhin Even (SPK_oxota_047)
> *iril-du ... amm-u ia-**la** hor-ger-e-n*
> summer-DAT ... father-POSS.1SG HESIT-**LOC** go-HAB-NFUT-3SG
> *stada-**du** orolčimŋa-l-du kömölöh-**ne**-mi*
> herd.R-**DAT** reindeer.herder-PL-DAT help.Y-**AM**-SIM.CVB
> 'In summer my father **goes to whatchamallit**, he **goes to the herd** to help the reindeer herders.'

c. Nanai (Avrorin 1986: 83, txt 18)
ńoači   žog-**či**-a-či   tuə-ri-**ndə**-gu-məri
they   house-**ALL**-OBL-POSS.3PL   winter-VBLZ-**AM**-REP-SIM.CVB.PL
palan-**či**   i:-xə-či
floor-**ALL** enter-PST-3PL
'(The rats) **came** to spend winter **to their house, into the cellar**.'

In (24b) the Goal argument of the motion verb is first introduced via the hesitative *iak* (literally 'what'), marked with the locative case. It is repeated in the subordinate clause with the dative-marked noun *stada-du* 'to the reindeer herd', where it is governed by the converb *kömölöh-ne-mi* 'going to help'. (Note that the dative case-marking on *ọrọlčimŋa-l* 'reindeer herders' is governed by the base verb *kömölöh-* 'to help', and not by the motion event.) As described above, in Lamunkhin Even the dative case is occasionally used to mark Goal arguments in addition to the more frequent locative case, accounting for the variation in case marking on the hesitative and lexical noun. Example (24c) from Nanai illustrates the converbial construction with two different spatial arguments – one governed by the converb ('to the house') and the other governed by the finite verb ('to the cellar'). The linear position seems to reflect semantic differences: 'the house' is a more general location (the rats came to the house to spend the winter there), 'the cellar' is a more specific one (they entered into this particular part of the house). Such examples provide evidence for the high degree of autonomy of the components of the pleonastic construction.

4.3 Competition between spatial argument and verb argument

The motion event and the verb event sometimes share an argument (other than the subject, which is always shared). The most prominent case is when the Goal of the motion event coincides with the Location of the verb event. It is an open question which coding strategy is chosen in this case: that of the motion event (Goal) or that of the verb event (Location).

As seen in examples (25a) and (25b) from Ulch, both options are available. In example (25a) the pronoun 'that' is marked with the essive/dative case as the Location of the verb event ('to set a net in that place'). In (25b), the noun 'hill' is marked with the allative case as the Goal of the motion event ('to go to the hill'). Coding of both Goal and Location is not attested and is rejected by speakers (25c).

(25) a. Ulch (lpd_170626_SluchajNaRybalke)
tara tį-wa tį-**dų** tulə-**ŋdə**-xə-t=gun
then DIST-ACC DIST-**DAT** set.net-**AM**-PST-3PL=PTL
'Then they went to set **there** a net for this (fish).' – Location (the verb event argument)

b. Ulch (elicited, GIP)
xurəm=**bən** boqto-wa ga-**ŋda**-xa-n
hill=**ALL** pine.nut-ACC gather-**AM**-PST-3SG
'(He) went **to the hill** to gather pine nuts.' – Goal (the spatial argument)

c. Ulch (elicited, GIP)
*xurəm=**bən** boqto-wa tį-**dų** ga-**ŋda**-xa-n
hill=**ALL** pine.nut-ACC DIST-**DAT** gather-**AM**-PST-3SG
expected: '(He) went **to the hill** to gather pine nuts **there**.'

Nevertheless, in general it is the Goal argument that tends to be expressed, not the Location. For example, an elicitation task conducted with Nanai and Ulch speakers shows that with the verb 'study' only the encoding of the Goal argument was accepted (27a), and examples with Location-encoding were rejected or judged as dubious (27b) (cf. [26], which illustrates Location-encoding in the absence of the ndA-suffix). Although overt expression of Location was judged acceptable with the verb 'be, live' (27c), in the Nanai text corpus only an example with overtly expressed Goal was found.

(26) Nanai (elicited, NCHB)
xoton-**do** tačeo-če-xa-ni / balʒe-xa-ni
town-**DAT** learn-DUR-PST-3SG / live-PST-3SG
'(He) studied / lived in the town.' =Location

(27) a. Nanai (elicited, NCHB)
ᴼᴷxoton-**či** tačeo-če-**nda**-xa-ni
town-**ALL** learn-DUR-**AM**-PST-3SG
'(He) went **to the town** to study.' =Goal

b. Nanai (elicited, NCHB)
???xoton-**do** tačeo-če-**nda**-xa-ni
town-**DAT** learn-DUR-**AM**-PST-3SG
expected: '(He) went (away) to study **in the town**.' =Location

c. Nanai (elicited, NCHB)
   goj   boa-**du**   balže-**nda**-xa-ni
   other place-DAT   live-AM-PST-3SG
   'He went away to live **in some other place**.' =Location

The compatibility of the *ndA*-marked verb *bi*- 'to be, live' with Location arguments is also demonstrated by data from Bystraja Even: in the corpus there are two examples where the *ndA*-verb *bi(d)ne-* takes an overtly expressed Goal, e.g. (28a), and one example where it takes an overtly expressed Location (28b). It is possible that the Location argument in (28b) is triggered by the progressive suffix on the verb, which emphasizes the duration of the event and is thus more compatible with static location.

(28) a. Bystraja Even (JIP_RME_razgovor_454)
       e-te-m   gu:n-ni   bi   kuren=de   Maksim-**teki**
       NEG-FUT-1SG   say[NFUT]-3SG   1SG   on.purpose=PTL   pers.name-**ALL**
       bi-**ne**-dʒi-m
       be-**AM**-FUT-1SG
       'No, she said, I will go on purpose **to Maksim** to live.' =Goal

   b. Bystraja Even (TEB_childhood_042)
       potom   ewe-ski   em-ni-ten,
       then.R   PROX-ADV.ALL   come-PST-3PL
       nan   e-**du**   bi-d-**ne**-ri-ten
       and   PROX-DAT   be-PROG-AM-PST-3PL
       'Then they came here to live **here**.' =Location

Text examples with Location arguments are much less common than those with overt Goal arguments, as summarized in Table 8 (only independent constructions were taken into account). Since in Udihe and especially Lamunkhin Even one and the same case form (the locative) can encode both Goal and Location arguments, as outlined above (see Table 3), it is not clear in all cases which of these is encoded.

In some cases, the direct object of the base verb can be perceived as the Goal of the motion event, opening up a choice of which of these roles to encode, Theme/Patient or Goal. As shown in (29) taken from the Negidal corpus, it is indeed possible for speakers to encode the Goal argument rather than the Theme. However, there are only two examples of this kind in the corpora used for this study, both produced by the same speaker (see [24a] above for the other example).

Table 8: Goal-encoding vs. Location-encoding in independent constructions.

Language	Goal	Location	Unclear	% of Location among clear examples
Nanai	14	0	0	0%
Ulch	14	1	3	7%
Udihe	17	2	7	11%
Lamunkhin Even	4	2	0	33%
Bystraja Even	24	4	4	14%
Negidal	16	0	1	0%

(29) Negidal (Pakendorf & Aralova 2017, APN_zabludilisj: 13)
 gə taj uj bəjə-l ŋənə-tɕa:-**tki**-tin
 DP DIST recently person-PL go-PST.PTCP-**ALL**-3PL
 itɕe-**na:**-gaj gun-ə-n
 see-**AM**-IMP.1PL.INCL say-NFUT-3SG
 '"Let's go see that **place** where those people recently went to", she says.'

In example (29) the place recently visited by 'those people' is marked with the allative case expected for a Goal argument instead of the accusative case expected for the Theme of 'see'. The choice of encoding the Goal rather than the Theme might here be due to the importance of the motion event in this case,[10] since the principal participants in the narrative spent a lot of time walking to the place referred to here and ultimately got lost. We discuss a similar example of choice of encoding triggered by the weight accorded to the motion event, taken from Negidal's close sister Evenki, in the discussion in Section 6.

Some arguments are semantically compatible both with the motion event and with the verb event, for example when both events have a valency for the Goal argument. In this case, there is competition between the interpretation of the Goal as argument of the motion event and the Goal as argument of the verb event. These uses are quite marginal, since -ndA is compatible with only very few motion verbs;[11] however, examples such as (30) are possible. Elicitation tasks

---

[10] It should be noted that there is a possibility that the allative case is simply a non-standard means of marking the Theme: although this speaker produced many more accusative-marked Theme arguments, she did produce two examples where the Theme of the simple verb itɕe- 'to see' was marked with the allative case (in addition to the two examples mentioned in the text where the allative-marked Theme was the argument of AM-marked 'go and see').

[11] We find motion verbs occurring with the AM-suffix only in the corpora of the Southern Tungusic languages Nanai, Ulch, and Udihe; these are verbs of manner of motion (e.g. 'to run', 'to

conducted with Nanai speakers show that in (30) – where it is the AM-suffix that provides the meaning of 'arrived' – only the interpretation of 'Naikhin' being the argument of the motion event is possible. No such examples are found in the texts analysed here.

(30) Nanai (elicited, SSB)
    *Najxin-**či***   *solo-**nda**-xa-či*
    geo.name-**ALL**   go.upriver-**AM**-PST-3PL
    '(They arrived) **at Naikhin** to go (from there) upriver.'
    *'(They arrived) to go upriver **to Naikhin**.'

5 Differences in AM constructions between Tungusic languages

As shown by the data from the six more or less closely related lects included in this study, there are small but notable differences in AM constructions between the individual lects. We summarize these differences in Table 9; details were provided in the preceding sections. No obvious clustering of the lects by their genealogical or areal groupings can be discerned (cf. Figures 1 and 2).

Table 9: Summary of differences in AM constructions in six Tungusic lects.

Parameter	Language hierarchy
Frequency of use	Udihe ≫ Nanai, Bystraja Ev., Negidal > Ulch, Lamunkhin Ev.
% pleonastic constructions	Lamunkhin Ev. > Ulch, Nanai, Udihe, Negidal > Bystraja Ev.
% echo (over all pleonastic)	Bystraja Ev. ≫ Negidal, Udihe ≫ Ulch, Lamunkhin Ev., Nanai
Ratio verb arg/spat arg*	Udihe > Nanai > Bystraja Ev. > Lamunkhin Ev., Negidal > Ulch
% intr with spat arg/ % trns with spat arg	Udihe ≫ Bystraja Ev. > Nanai > Ulch, Negidal ≫ Lamunkhin Ev.
% spat arg pleonastic/ % spat arg independent	Bystraja Ev., Nanai > Lamunkhin Ev., Udihe > Negidal > Ulch

*arg = argument; spat = spatial; % = proportion of uses; Ev. = Even.

---

float', 'to jump') and verbs expressing the trajectory of motion (e.g. 'to pass', 'to enter', 'to reach'). In the spontaneous text examples, the *ndA*-suffix doesn't add any further motion event or any specification of trajectory, in contrast to the elicited example (30), where the motion event that precedes the 'going upriver' is expressed by the AM-marker.

Udihe stands out in making extensive use of the *ndA*-suffix overall, with nearly three times as many examples counted in the published text collections than what we found in Nanai and Bystraja Even, and nearly five times as many examples as those found for Ulch and Lamunkhin Even. The frequency of the individual constructions differs, too, with independent constructions predominating heavily in Bystraja Even, and pleonastic constructions making up half of all examples in Lamunkhin Even. In the other languages, pleonastic uses comprise about one quarter to one third of all examples. There are also differences in the preferred subtype of pleonastic construction, with Nanai, Ulch, and Lamunkhin Even demonstrating a strong preference for converbial constructions and Bystraja Even having a marked preference for echo constructions. The frequency of pleonastic converbial constructions in Lamunkhin Even might have increased through contact influence from the neighbouring Turkic language Sakha (Yakut), since in this language finite motion verbs with simultaneous converbs of the lexical verb express 'go to V/go and V', as in (31):

(31) Sakha (Pakendorf field data, XatR_274)
 ʤaχtal-lar barï ot-**tu:** **bar**-bït-tar
 woman-PL all hay-VBLZ.**CVB** **go**-PST.PTCP-PL
 '... the women had all gone to make hay.'

There are also fine-grained differences in the argument structure between the lects. While all the lects overtly express the verb argument more frequently than the spatial argument in independent transitive constructions, this preference is more pronounced in Udihe and Nanai than in Lamunkhin Even, Negidal, and especially Ulch. Furthermore, in all lects the proportion of overtly expressed spatial arguments with intransitive AM-verbs is higher than with transitive AM-verbs – with the exception of Lamunkhin Even, where no intransitive *ndA*-verbs occur with an overtly expressed spatial argument. (It should be noted, however, that the frequency of intransitive verbs is overall rather low.) Finally, whereas the proportion of overtly expressed spatial arguments is higher in pleonastic constructions than in independent ones in all lects, the difference is far more pronounced for Bystraja Even and Nanai than it is for Negidal or Ulch – in accordance with the fact that in these languages spatial arguments tend to be less frequently expressed than verb arguments.

6 Discussion and conclusions

To summarize, in the six Tungusic lects investigated for this study, the single AM-marker is used with various meanings, not only 'go and V' and 'go in order to V', but also 'come and V', 'come in order to V', and – in conjunction with the suffix -*sV* – 'go and V and return' (a combination that appears to have grammaticalized into a distinct AM-marker in Bystraja Even and Negidal, as discussed in Section 4.2). The *ndA*-verb occurs in three different constructions in the Tungusic languages: 1) as the sole verb in independent constructions, or accompanying a verb of motion in pleonastic constructions, where the *ndA*-verb can 2) either be finite ('echo' constructions) or 3) a converb. There are pronounced differences in frequency of these different constructions between the languages examined here, although independent constructions tend to be preferred by most. The languages also differ in their overall frequency of use of the *ndA*-suffix, but it is infrequent everywhere in comparison to other derivational affixes attested in the same languages. It is hard to evaluate the frequency of use of the AM-suffix in the Tungusic languages in a cross-linguistic perspective, since most studies to date do not mention frequency of use, rather focusing on the form and function of the markers found in a particular language. Among the few exceptions are Koch (this volume), who counts 240 AM forms in Kaytetye in 2870 sentences and Rose (2015), whose count of the two most frequent AM markers in Mojeño Trinitario is higher than what we find in the languages investigated here with the exception of Udihe (cf. footnote 10 above). For Mparntwe Arrernte Wilkins (1991: 215) counts between 0–36% of AM-verbs (i.e. in some texts a full third of all verbs carry an AM-marker), while O'Connor (2004) counts 234 examples of the two morphemes with a translocative meaning in 22 texts of Lowland Chontal (without giving a precise count for the two morphemes with a cislocative meaning). While it is of course difficult to compare counts based simply on the number of texts (which can vary enormously in length), in Udihe, the language in our sample showing the highest frequency of the *ndA*-suffix, we find 188 examples in 42 texts. Thus, based on the scanty information available to us it would seem that the AM-suffix in the Tungusic languages investigated here is not only infrequent in comparison to other derivational morphemes within the languages, but also in comparison to other languages.[12]

Intriguingly from a cross-linguistic point of view, in all the languages studied here *ndA*-verbs can express not only the argument of the base verb, but also the

---

[12] However, it is of course possible that there is a bias in the studies up to date, with the category being described mainly in languages that use it frequently.

spatial argument, and occasionally both. While overall overtly expressed verb arguments occur more commonly than overtly expressed spatial arguments, in most languages intransitive verbs and pleonastic constructions occur with spatial arguments more frequently than do independent transitive constructions. This might be an indication that there is a constraint towards expressing only one argument per verb, so that the spatial argument is 'blocked' by the verb argument in independent constructions with transitive base verbs. In contrast, constructions with intransitive base verbs – where there is no verb argument that could block expression of the spatial argument – and pleonastic constructions, where the spatial argument can be governed not only by the *ndA*-verb, but also by the semantically redundant motion verb, would offer more free slots for overt spatial arguments.

However, while formal considerations indeed seem to play a role in the choice of argument encoding, this is clearly not the whole story. Rather, as we argue here, this choice seems to be guided partly by which event is being foregrounded, as shown in examples (28a), (28b), and (29). In (28a), with the location of living being marked as the Goal (carrying allative case), the entire event is still in the future, and emphasis is on the move from the current living space to the new one. In (28b), in contrast, where the location of living is marked as the Location (with the dative case), the entire event is in the past and the focus is on the verb event, the duration of which is expressed by the progressive aspect. Similarly, as mentioned above, in the Negidal example (29) the focus of the narrative is on motion, on walking towards the place that other people had gone to, but never reaching it and getting hopelessly lost. The motion event is thus foregrounded here, which might account for the choice of encoding the direct object of the verb event not as Theme (which is the most common encoding chosen for objects of AM-marked 'see' in the languages included here), but as Goal.

The importance of discourse prominence of the motion event vs. the verb event in the choice of argument encoding in Tungusic languages is shown particularly clearly in (32) below by a 'minimal pair' taken from a narrative in Evenki, a close sister of Negidal and Even. As can be seen from the sequence provided here, the narrative is about going to hunt a bear (referred to by the euphemism 'bandit'). In (32a), in which the hunters take the decision to hunt and kill the bear, this is encoded as the direct object of the verb event 'hunt', as expressed by the accusative case. In (32c), in contrast, it is encoded as the Goal argument of the motion event, taking the locative-allative suffix *-tula:*. This choice is arguably due to the shift of discourse prominence onto the motion event, as shown by the sequence of utterances referring to the motion (32b, d, e).

(32) a. Stony Tunguska Evenki (Kazakevich et al. 2007)
čaŋit tar čaŋit-pa tarə aŋi-wa:t
bandit DIST bandit-ACC DIST.ACC HESIT-IMP.1PL.INCL
čok-na:-ya:t
kill-AM-IMP.1PL.INCL
'Let's do this, let's go and kill **that bear** (lit. 'bandit').'

b. Stony Tunguska Evenki (Kazakevich et al. 2007)
nu bu suru-rə-w ta:-la
well.R 1PL.EXCL go-NFUT-1PL.EXCL DIST-LOC
'Well, we went there.'

c. Stony Tunguska Evenki (Kazakevich et al. 2007)
čok-na:-s-tə-w čaŋit-tula:
kill-AM-INCEP-NFUT-1PL.EXCL bandit-LOC
'We went **to the bear** to kill.'

d. Stony Tunguska Evenki (Kazakevich et al. 2007)
oro-r-d'i suru-rə-w
reindeer-PL-INS go-NFUT-1PL.EXCL
'We went by reindeer.'

e. Stony Tunguska Evenki (Kazakevich et al. 2007)
əmə-rə-w
come-NFUT-1PL.EXCL
'We arrived.'

Nevertheless, although examples such as (32a-e) clearly show that the discourse prominence of the motion event vs. the verb event plays a role in the choice of argument structure, this cannot be the only factor. This is shown by examples such as (21b): here the presence of the noun phrase 'by motorbike', which is licensed by the motion event, indicates that the motion event is quite prominent, yet it is not the Goal of the motion event that is coded, but the direct object of the verb event. It is thus likely that the choice of argument structure in AM-constructions in the Tungusic languages depends on a complex interplay of formal preferences with respect to the number of overt arguments to be expressed and pragmatic needs of foregrounding specific events.

In this context it is possible that the vagueness between prior motion and motion-cum-purpose readings of the *ndA*-verbs described in Section 3.2 plays a role in their mixed argument structure. In motion-cum-purpose readings the motion event can be considered more central than the verb event (as shown by the fact that the motion event can be completed while the verb event has not yet begun), and this might facilitate overt expression of spatial arguments. Whether overt spatial arguments occur more frequently in constructions with motion-cum-purpose readings than in those with clear sequential readings needs further investigation. However, it should be noted that constructions with a clear motion-cum-purpose reading in which it is the verb argument, and not the spatial argument, that is expressed, are also cross-linguistically attested; cf. Aissen (1994) for Tzotzil and Zavala Maldonado (2000: 142–144) for Olutec.

In summary, the Tungusic languages investigated here show flexibility of argument encoding in AM-constructions. From the extant literature this kind of flexibility and the possibility of overtly expressing the spatial argument appear to be cross-linguistically rare. However, more typological studies of AM-constructions that explicitly address argument encoding strategies are needed before this claim can be considered conclusive.

Abbreviations

1, 2, 3	1, 2, 3 person	ELAT	elative	PRES	presumptive
ABL	ablative	EMPH	emphatic	PROG	progressive
ACC	accusative	EXCL	exclusive	PROL	prolative
ADV	adverbial	EXPR	expressive	PROX	proximal demonstrative
ALL	allative	FOC	focus		
ALN	alienable	FUT	future	PRS	present
AM	associated motion	GNR	generic	PST	past
		HAB	habitual	PTCP	participle
ANT	anterior	HESIT	hesitative	PTL	particle
ASSERT	assertive	IMP	imperative	PURP	purposive
CAUS	causative	IPFV	imperfective	Q	question particle
COM	comitative	INCEP	inceptive	QUOT	quotative
CONAT	conative	INCL	inclusive	R	Russian copy
COND	conditional	INS	instrumental	RECP	reciprocal
COORD	coordinative	LOC	locative	REP	repeated action
CVB	converb	MULT	multiplicative	RES	resultative
DAT	dative	NEG	negative	RSTR	restrictive
DECES	decessive	NFUT	non-future	SBJV	subjunctive
DEST	destinative	NMLZ	nominalizer	SG	singular
DIM	diminutive	OBL	oblique	SIDE	side (nominal derivation)
DIST	distal demonstrative	ORD	ordinal		
		PL	plural	SIM	simultaneous
DISTR	distributive	POSS	possessive	TAM1	tense-aspect-modality 1
DP	discourse particle	POT	potential		
		PREFL	possessive reflexive	VBLZ	verbalizer
DUR	durative			Y	Yakut copy

Acknowledgements: Brigitte Pakendorf thanks the Volkswagen Foundation, the Max Planck Society, the CNRS, and the Endangered Languages Documentation Programme (ELDP, www.eldp.net) for funding the field trips to collect the Even and Negidal data, and also acknowledges the LABEX ASLAN (ANR-10-LABX-0081) of Université de Lyon for its financial support within the program "Investissements d'Avenir" (ANR-11-IDEX-0007) of the French government operated by the National Research Agency (ANR). Furthermore, we thank our colleagues from Dynamique du Langage for helpful discussion of our data during a seminar, Antoine Guillaume, Harold Koch, Guillaume Jacques, and Jean-Christophe Verstraete for feedback on our manuscript, and Yuriy Koryakov for providing the map in Figure 2. For help with transcriptions, translations and clarification of the narrative data we thank: Ekaterina Shadrina, Ija Krivoshapkina, and Rimma Egorova (Even), Daria Nadeina, Galina Kandakova, and Antonina Kazarova (Negidal), Raisa Bel'dy and Nikolay Bel'dy (Naikhin Nanai), and Natalia Kuchekta, Natalia Kujsali, Alla Kujsali and Nadezhda Dechuli (Ulch). We are grateful to Natalia Aralova for access to the Even narratives which she recorded and glossed and to Sofia Oskolskaya, who was the organizer of the field trips to the Nanai and who collected, transcribed and glossed the Nanai and Ulch text collections used in the study together with Natalia Stoynova. Last, but definitely not least, we thank all the speakers who contributed to the corpora and participated in the elicitation tasks.

Appendix

Text collections used in this study

Language	Genres	Source	Comments
Nanai	folklore	Avrorin 1986	Middle Amur (Naikhin) Nanai texts (№ 13–24)
Nanai	folklore	Bel'dy, Bulgakova 2012	Middle Amur Nanai texts (all except № 4, № 22)
Nanai	folklore, biographic texts, ethnographic descriptions	unpublished collection of S. Oskolskaya and N. Stoynova	The texts were collected by S. Oskolskaya, N. Stoynova and K. Shagal in Khabarovsk Kray between 2008–2017 (only Middle Amur Nanai texts were used in the study).
Ulch	folklore, biographic texts, ethnographic descriptions	unpublished collection of S. Oskolskaya and N. Stoynova	The texts were collected in 2017–2018 by NS and S. Oskolskaya in Bulava and Bogorodskoje (Ulchsky district).

(continued)

Language	Genres	Source	Comments
Ulch	folklore, biographic texts	unpublished collection of L.I. Sem	The texts were recorded in 1971 and 1979 by L. I. Sem and Yu. A. Sem in Bulava (Ulchsky district), digitalized by S. Oskolskaya and transcribed by NS.
Udihe	folklore	Nikolaeva et al. 2003	Texts № 1–15
Udihe	folklore	Nikolaeva et al. 2002	
Lamunkhin Even	biographical and historical narratives, folklore, procedural text, conversation	Pakendorf corpus (partly available at: http://dobes.mpi.nl/projects/even/)	The corpus was collected by BP in Sebjan-Küöl between 2008–2012, with assistance by N. Aralova in 2010.
Bystraja Even	biographical and historical narratives, folklore, procedural text, conversation	Pakendorf corpus (partly available at: http://dobes.mpi.nl/projects/even/)	The corpus was collected by BP in Kamchatka between 2007–2016, with assistance by N. Aralova in 2009; some of the audio recordings were done by A. Lavrillier in 2010.
Negidal	biographical and historical narratives, folklore, procedural text, conversation	Pakendorf and Aralova 2017 (https://elar.soas.ac.uk/Collection/MPI1041287)	

References

Aissen, Judith L. 1994. Tzotzil auxiliaries. *Linguistics* 32 (4–5). 657–690.

Alonso de la Fuente, José Andrés & Guillaume Jacques. 2018. Associated motion in Manchu in typological perspective. *Language and Linguistics* 19 (4). 501–524.

Atknine, Victor. 1997. The Evenki Language from the Yenisei to Sakhalin. In Hiroshi Shoji & Juha Janhunen (eds.), *Northern Minority Languages. Problems of Survival. Papers Presented at the Eighteenth Taniguchi International Symposium: Division of Ethnology*, 109–121. Osaka: National Museum of Ethnology.

Avrorin, Valentin A. 1959. *Grammatika nanajskogo jazyka. Tom pervyj* [A grammar of Nanai. vol. 1]. Moscow, Leningrad: Izdatel'stvo Akademii Nauk SSSR.

Avrorin, Valentin A. 1961. *Grammatika nanajskogo jazyka. Tom vtoroj* [A grammar of Nanai. vol. 2]. Moscow, Leningrad: Izdatel'stvo Akademii Nauk SSSR.

Avrorin, Valentin A. 1981. *Sintaksičeskije issledovanija po nanajskomu jazyku* [Studies of Nanai syntax]. Leningrad: 'Nauka.'

Avrorin, Valentin A. 1986. *Materialy po nanajskomu jazyku i fol'kloru* [Materials on the Nanai language and folklore]. Leningrad: Nauka.
Avrorin, Valentin A. 2000. *Grammatika man'čžurskogo pis'mennogo jazyka* [A grammar of written Manchu]. Saint Petersburg: Nauka.
Bel'dy, Raisa A. & Tatiana D. Bulgakova. 2012. *Nanajskie skazki* [Nanai fairy tales] (Languages and Cultures of the Russian Far East). Fürstenberg: Verlag der Kulturstiftung Sibirien / SEC Publications.
Benzing, Johannes. 1955. *Die tungusischen Sprachen. Versuch einer vergleichenden Grammatik* (Akademie der Wissenschaften und Der Literatur. Abhandlungen der Geistes- Und Sozialwissenschaftlichen Klasse). Vol. 11. Wiesbaden: Verlag der Akademie der Wissenschaften und der Literatur in Mainz in Kommission bei Franz Steiner Verlag.
Burykin, Aleksej A. 2004. *Jazyk maločislennogo naroda v ego pis'mennoj forme. Sociolingvističeskie i sobstvenno lingvističeskie aspekty* [The language of a minority people in its written form. Sociolinguistic and linguistic aspects]. St Petersburg: Peterburgskoe Vostokovedenie.
Census 2010. http://www.gks.ru/free_doc/new_site/perepis2010/croc/Documents/Vol4/pub-04-20.pdf. (Accessed on 01.09.2018).
Cincius, Vera I. 1982. *Negidal'skij jazyk. Issledovanija i materialy* [Negidal. Analysis and materials]. Leningrad: Nauka.
Comrie, Bernard. 1981. *The Languages of the Soviet Union*. Cambridge: Cambridge University Press.
Dryer, Matthew S. This volume, chapter 13. Associated Motion in North America (including Mexico and Central America).
Gerasimova, Anna N. 2002. Nanajskij i ul'čskij jazyki v Rossii: sravnitel'naja xarakteristika sociolingvističeskoj situacii [Nanai and Ulch in Russia: comparative characteristics of the sociolinguistic situation]. *Jazyki korennyx narodov Sibiri* 12. 246–257.
Guillaume, Antoine. 2006. La catégorie du "mouvement associé" en cavineña: Apport à une typologie de l'encodage du mouvement et de la trajectoire. *Bulletin de la Société de Linguistique de Paris* 101 (1). 415–436.
Guillaume, Antoine. 2016. Associated motion in South America: Typological and areal perspectives. *Linguistic Typology* 20 (1). 81–177.
Haviland, John B. 1993. The syntax of Tzotzil auxiliaries and directionals: the grammaticalization of motion. *Berkeley Linguistics Society* 19 (2). 35–49.
Jacques, Guillaume, Aimée Lahaussois, and Shuya Zhang. This volume, chapter 21. Associated motion in Sino-Tibetan, with a focus on Gyalrongic and Kiranti.
Janhunen, Juha. 2012. The expansion of Tungusic as an ethnic and linguistic process. In Andrei L. Malchukov & Lindsay J. Whaley (eds.), *Recent Advances in Tungusic Linguistics* (Turcologica 89), 5–16. Wiesbaden: Harrassowitz.
Kalinina, Elena Ju & Sofia A. Oskolskaya. 2016. Nanajskij jazyk. [Nanai]. In Vida Ju. Mixal'čenko (ed.), *Jazyk i obščestvo. Ènciklopedija* [Language and Society. An Encyclopaedia], 293–296. Moscow: Azbukovnik.
Kazakevich, Ol'ga A., Evgenija A. Renkovskaja, Darija Vaxoneva and Nadežda Mamontova. 2007. Èkspedicija k èvenkam Podkamennoj Tunguski [Expedition to the Evenks of the Stony Tunguska]. Na Severnoj Tajmure [On the Northern Tajmur], told by S.M. Andreeva. http://siberian-lang.srcc.msu.ru/ru/text/na-severnoy-taymure-s-m-andreeva. (Accessed on 29.01.2018).

Khasanova, Marina M. & Aleksandr M. Pevnov. 2003. *Mify i skazki negidal'cev* [Myths and tales of the Negidals.] (Endangered Languages of the Pacific Rim A2-024). Kyoto: Nakanishi.
Koch, Harold. 1984. The category of 'associated motion' in Kaytej. *Language in central Australia* 1 (1). 23–34.
Koch, Harold. This volume, chapter 7. Associated Motion in the Pama-Nyungan languages of Australia.
Kolesnikova, Vera D. & Ol'ga A. Konstantinova. 1968. Negidal'skij jazyk [Negidal]. In Pëtr Ja. Skorik, Valentin A. Avrorin, Trofim A. Bertagaev, Georgij A. Menovščikov, Orest P. Sunik & Ol'ga A. Konstantinova (eds.), *Mongol'skie, tunguso-man'čžurskie i paleoaziatskie jazyki.* [Mongolian, Tungusic, and Paleoasiatic languages] (Jazyki Narodov SSSR [Languages of the Peoples of the USSR.] 5), 109–128. Leningrad: Nauka, Leningradskoe otdelenie.
Levinson, Stephen C. & David P. Wilkins. 2006. Patterns in the data: Toward a semantic typology of spatial description. In Stephen C. Levinson & David P. Wilkins (eds.), *Grammars of Space: Explorations in Cognitive Diversity*, 512–552. Cambridge: Cambridge University Press.
Malchukov, Andrey L. 1995. *Even*. München, Newcastle: LINCOM Europa.
Mithun, Marianne. 2002. Understanding and explaining applicatives. In Mary Andronis, Christopher Ball, Heidi Elston & Sylvain Neuvel (eds.), *Proceedings of the Thirty-seventh Meeting of the Chicago Linguistic Society: Functionalism and formalism in linguistic theory*, 37 (2), 73–98. Chicago.
Nikolaeva, Irina, Elena Perekhvalskaya & Maria Tolskaya. 2002. *Udeghe (Udihe) Folk Tales* (Tunguso-Sibirica). Vol. 10. Wiesbaden: Harrassowitz Verlag.
Nikolaeva, Irina, Elena Perekhvalskaya & Maria Tolskaya. 2003. *Udeghe Texts* (Endangered Languages of the Pacific Rim). Vol. A2-025. Kyoto: ELPR.
Nikolaeva, Irina & Maria Tolskaya. 2001. *A grammar of Udihe*. Berlin, New York: Mouton de Gruyter.
Novikova, Klavdija A. 1980. *Očerki dialektov èvenskogo jazyka. Glagol, služebnye slova, teksty, glossarij*. [Sketches of Even dialects. Verb, auxiliary words, texts, glossary]. Leningrad: Nauka.
O'Connor, Loretta. 2004. Going getting tired: Associated motion through space and time in Lowland Chontal. In Michel Achard & Suzanne Kemmer (eds.), *Language, culture and mind*, 181–199. Stanford: Centre for the Study of Language and Information.
O'Connor, Loretta. 2007. *Motion, transfer and transformation: The grammar of change in lowland Chontal*. Amsterdam, Philadelphia: John Benjamins.
Pakendorf, Brigitte & Natalia Aralova. 2017. *Documentation of Negidal, a nearly extinct Northern Tungusic language of the Lower Amur*. London: SOAS, Endangered Languages Archive. https://elar.soas.ac.uk/Collection/MPI1041287.
Pakendorf, Brigitte & Natalia Aralova. 2018. The endangered state of Negidal: A field report. *Language Documentation and Conservation*. http://scholarspace.manoa.hawaii.edu/handle/10125/24760.
Pakendorf, Brigitte & Raisa P. Kuz'mina. 2016. Èvenskij jazyk [Even]. In Vida Ju. Mixal'čenko (ed.), *Jazyk i obščestvo. Ènciklopedija* [Language and Society. An Encyclopaedia], 583–587. Moscow: Azbukovnik.
Payne, Doris L. This volume, chapter 18. The extension of Associated Motion to Direction, Aspect and Argument Structure in Nilotic languages.
Petrova, Taisija I. 1936. *Ul'čskij dialect nanajskogo jazyka* [The Ulch dialect of Nanai]. Moscow, Leningrad: Učpedgiz.

Rose, Françoise. 2015. Associated motion in Mojeño Trinitario: Some typological considerations. *Folia Linguistica* 49 (1). 117–158.
Ross, Daniel. This volume, chapter 2. A cross-linguistic survey of Associated Motion and Directionals.
Simpson, Jane. 2001. Preferred word order and the grammaticalization of Associated Path. In Miriam Butt & Tracy Holloway King (eds.), *Time over matter: diachronic perspectives on morphosyntax*, 173–208. Stanford: Centre for the Study of Language and Information.
Stoynova, Natal'ja M. 2016. Pokazateli "dviženija s cel'ju" i sobytijnaja struktura: suffiks -nda v nanajskom jazyke [Markers of "motion-cum-purpose" and event structure: *-nda* suffix in Nanai]. *Voprosy Jazykoznanija* 4. 86–111.
Stoynova, Natal'ja M. 2017. Pokazateli dviženija s cel'ju v južnotungusskix jazykax i kategorija associated motion [Motion-cum-purpose markers in the Southern Tungusic languages and the typology of associated motion]. *Problemy jazyka. Sbornik naučnyx statej po materialam Pjatej konferencii-školy "Problemy jazyka: vzgljad molodyx učenyx"* [Problems of Language: Collection of Scientific Papers from the Materials of the Third Conference-School "Problems of Language: A View of Young Scholars"], 321–339. Moscow: Institut jazykoznanija RAN, Izdatel'stvo "Kancler."
Sumbatova, Nina R. & Valentin Ju. Gusev. 2016. Ul'čskij jazyk [Ulch]. In Vida Ju. Mixal'čenko (ed.), *Jazyk i obščestvo. Ènciklopedija* [Language and Society. An Encyclopaedia], 513–515. Moscow: Azbukovnik.
Sunik, Orest P. 1968. Tunguso-man'čžurskie jazyki (vvedenie) [Tungus-Manchu languages (introduction)]. In Pëtr Ja. Skorik, Valentin A. Avrorin, Trofim A. Bertagaev, Georgij A. Menovščikov, Orest P. Sunik & Ol'ga A. Konstantinova (eds.), *Jazyki narodov SSSR: Mongol'skie, tunguso-man'čžurskie i paleoaziatskie jazyki* [Languages of the peoples of the USSR: Mongolic, Tungusic and Paleoasiatic languages], 53–67. Leningrad: Izdatel'stvo 'Nauka' Lenigradskoe otdelenie.
Sunik, Orest P. 1985. *Ul'čskij jazyk. Issledovanija i materialy* [Ulča. Study and materials]. Leningrad: Nauka.
Tallman Adam J.R. This volume, chapter 11. Associated motion in Chácobo (Pano) in typological perspective.
Volkov, Oleg S. & Ivan A. Stenin. 2019. Andativ i ventiv v jazykax Sibiri: k tipologii glagol'noj orientacii [Andative and ventive in the languages of Siberia: towards a typology of verb orientation]. *Acta Linguistica Petropolitana* 15 (1) [Special issue for A.P. Volodin's 80th birthday]. 289–319.
Wilkins, David P. 1991. The semantics, pragmatics and diachronic development of "associated motion" in Mparntwe Arrernte. *Buffalo Papers in Linguistics* 1. 207–257.
Zavala Maldonado, Roberto. 2000. Olutec motion verbs: Grammaticalization under Mayan contact. *Berkeley Linguistics Society* 26 (2). 139–151.

Subject Index

Absolute Frame of Reference 213–214, 224, 390, 407
Absolutive 451, 454, 467, 476, 481, 735
Abstract motion / movement 113, 336, 676–678
Adlocative 10, 21, 528, 539–540, 581, 584, 590
Adverbial infection 529, 548
Affixal AM 846–847, 849
Agglutinative 699
Aimless (motion) 10, 55–56, 143
ALONG-DD complex 747, 752–753, 758, 760–762, 764, 766–767, 769–772, 774
ALONG-DD construction 763
'Along'–deictic-directional suffix complex 748, 759
Alternate construals 781, 799–801, 803
Altrilocal / Altrilocative 13, 16, 22–23, 593–594, 620–622, 640, 642, 666, 684
Ambulative 10, 21, 23, 221, 301, 403, 491, 497, 527–528, 538–539, 695, 702, 704, 708, 754, 845
AM-D (AM system with deictic directional extensions) 12, 23, 613–614, 616, 629, 634–637, 643–644, 647, 649–650, 656
Analogies 314
Analysability 252
Andative 4, 10, 20–21, 32, 131–132, 134–139, 141–142, 145–146, 148–149, 152, 154, 156, 291, 308, 346, 362, 425, 427, 490, 537–538
Andative prefixes varying for distance traveled 517
Anticipated ventive 374
Anticipatory 15
Applicatives 21, 451, 456, 458, 463, 466, 469, 471, 477, 480–481, 625–626, 696, 718–719, 721, 749–750, 757–758, 840–841, 877
Areal convergence 352
Argument expression 25
Argument manipulation 719–720
Argument of motion 820
Argument role of the moving figure 6

Arguments 402, 404, 406, 408, 410–413
Argument structure 13, 253, 302, 314, 716, 718–719, 733
Around 10, 21, 24, 43, 143, 179, 232, 251, 837, 839
Arriving AM / direction 10, 21, 202, 237, 247–248, 258, 494, 515–516, 539, 581
Aspect 3, 12–13, 16, 20, 32, 60, 69, 233, 242, 256, 260, 271, 273, 279, 305, 315–316, 330, 665–666, 668–669, 675, 686–687, 689, 728, 733, 737, 747–748, 751, 767, 771, 774, 820
Aspect-like distinctions 269, 315
Aspectual 22–24, 237, 256, 295, 309, 433, 436, 770, 811
Aspectual contrasts 257, 261, 270, 287, 312
Aspectual distinctions 263, 286, 288, 316
Aspectual readings 864
Aspectual realisation 6, 233, 242, 316
Aspectual usage 277
Aspectual values 237
Associated motion of transitive objects alone 370
Associated motion of intransitive subjects 370
Associated motion typological tendencies 369
Associated movement 665
Associated Posture 69, 265, 306, 394
Assumption or intention of motion 374, 379
Atelic 435
Atelic-durative 435–436
Attenuative 244, 266
Auxiliaries 360, 573, 576
Auxiliary constructions 14
Auxiliary motion verb 266
Auxiliary phrases 15, 266
Auxiliary verbs 252–253, 301, 305
Away 330

Backgrounded 422
Base verb arguments 855, 857–858, 876–877
Bayesian phylogenetic methods 234

Benefactive 704, 721–722
Bi-clausal constructions 222
Bi-clausal strategies 224
Bidirectional 10
Binary systems 310–312
Borrowed 289, 311
Borrowing 270, 315

Calquing 315
Canonical AM 12, 361
Causative 675
Caused motion 11, 674
Centrifugal 4, 10, 32, 276
Centripetal 4, 10, 32, 276, 666
Cessative 13
Chained subordinate clauses 223
Circular motion 10, 20, 247, 428, 871
Circumambulative deixis 819, 827, 839–840
Circumlocative 10, 24, 849
Cislocative 10, 32, 855, 868
Class size 431
Clause chaining 224
Clitics 16, 266, 360
Co-event 232
Coextensive 188–192, 312
Co-indexation 15
Co-lexification 677
Collocation 729
Combination of affixes 55
Come 649
'Come'-reading 867
Coming-into-view 430
Comitative 63, 721
Comparison across languages 224
Completive 443, 864
Complex 9
Complex AM systems 19, 20, 24, 312, 316
Complex inventory 9
Complexity 8, 14, 21–22, 231, 233, 235, 306, 310–311, 571, 578–579, 586, 599
Complexity of exponence 22
Complex predicate 350
Compositionality 66, 266
Compounding 278–279, 285, 314
Compounds 66, 276
Concurrent 6, 11, 17, 19–21, 24, 46–47, 55–56, 61, 66, 255, 372, 441, 762, 871

Concurrent associated motion 132, 137, 140–144, 148–150, 152–156, 294, 298, 373, 486, 493, 804, 809
Concurrent motion 8–9, 22, 232, 242, 244, 256–257, 260–261, 264, 266, 270–273, 275, 286–288, 299–300, 302, 311–312, 314–316, 339, 343, 378, 678, 753, 765–767, 771–772
Concurrent or Prior motion 295–296
Concurrently 761
Concurrent-subsequent 425
Conjugation classes 550–551
Conjugation class of the verb 22
Conjunctive 284, 295
Consonant mutations 22, 554
Contact influence 41, 313, 315, 351, 888
Continuation 747–748, 750, 767, 770
Continuative 441, 546
Continuative aspect 441
Continuing 288
Continuing action 295
Continuity 761, 774
Continuous 6, 257, 260, 265, 286, 288, 312
Continuous Aspect 263–264, 297
Converb 88
Converbial 858, 867, 881
Converbial constructions 866–867, 879, 883, 888
Converbial constructions/uses 858
Converbial pleonastic constructions 882
Convergence area 352
Coordinated 221
Coordinator 222
Core-layer SVCs 408
Corpus 729
Counterdirectional 10, 20, 423, 428–430, 871
Coverb 328
Cross-linguistically 214
Cross-linguistic comparison 205
Crosslinguistic proposals 373
Cultural conceptualization 57
Customary 22

D-AM (AM marked by deictic directionals) 7, 9, 11–12, 18–20, 22–23, 233, 290, 292, 338, 344, 350, 358, 360–361, 377, 379,

612, 614, 616, 629–637, 639, 643–644, 647–650, 652–653, 655–656
Dative 695, 712
DD (deictic directional) 754, 756, 758, 761, 770–771
Dedicated affixes 357–358, 373
Dedicated AM 12
Dedicated associated motion 357, 360, 373, 378
Dedicated associated motion systems 616–617
Dedicated marker 234
Dedicated motion 379
Definitions of AM 35, 52, 54, 65, 99, 129, 133, 165–166, 388, 419–420, 434, 436–437, 577, 593, 650, 821, 858
Degree of complexity 19
Deictic 39, 42, 275, 388–392, 394–395, 398–401, 404, 407, 411, 413, 443, 697
Deictic associated motion (D-AM) 338, 341, 357–361, 377–379
Deictic center 9–10, 329, 363–364, 366, 379, 665–666, 668, 674, 677–681, 685–686, 689
Deictic direction 19, 23, 291, 747–748, 751–752, 761, 787, 789
Deictic Directional 4, 23, 611, 666, 674, 687, 690, 698, 757, 780, 784
Deictic directionality 18, 665–666, 668, 689–690
Deictic directionals 7, 23, 233, 676
Deictic directions 276, 755–777
Deictic distinctions 755–757
Deictic enclitic 293
Deictic markers 292
Deictic motion 280, 847
Deictic orientation 665, 675
Deictic postposition 376
Deictically neutral 10, 20–21, 148, 155–156, 251, 490–492, 757, 772, 855, 863, 868
Deictically orientated non-motion verb 377
Deixis 256, 283, 571, 597, 599–600, 820
Derivational 5
Derivational affixes 360
Derivational morphology 69
Derivations 378
Derived lexemes 251

Descriptive grammars 32
Diachronic 52
Diachronic developments 16, 46, 266
Diachronic pathway 811
Diachronic sources 19, 111, 236, 263, 281
Diachronic typology 232
Direction of motion 18, 315
Directional adverb 376
Directional affix 357, 359
Directional Associated Motion 341
Directional clitics 314
Directional contrasts 68
Directional enclitic 335
Directional function 343, 346
Directionality 163–171, 178, 181–186, 188, 190–192, 357, 376, 452–454, 459–462
Directional markers 18, 311
Directional marking 284
Directional morpheme 370, 379
Directionals 16–17, 21, 24, 31, 87, 129–157, 163, 165, 184, 274, 290, 344, 363, 374, 376, 379, 385, 388–408, 410–413, 451, 453–467, 469–477, 480–481, 487–489, 696–697, 732, 737, 822–823
Directional SVCs 17
Directional systems 20, 358, 779
Directions 3, 9, 12, 16–17, 19, 21, 23, 233, 237, 240, 268, 292, 307, 335, 358, 488–489, 705, 708, 733
Directives 4, 822
Discourse prominence 879, 890–891
Discourse use 15, 18, 204–205
Displaced directionality 378
Dissociative 620, 622
Distal 13, 54, 58, 168, 397, 534, 570, 594–595, 640, 645
Distanciative 640, 666, 684
Distributed exponence 362–363
Distribution 36
Distributional 430
Distributive construction 314
Distributives 10, 20, 43, 55, 302, 423, 426, 429, 431, 623–624, 707, 725–728
Doing while carrying 517
Downward 6, 144, 203, 207, 261–262
Durative 435
Dynamic verbs 790

EAM (Exclusive Associated Motion) 613–614, 616–617, 634–637, 643–644, 647, 649–650, 655–656
Echo constructions 396, 591, 619, 639, 858, 866–867, 879–880, 882, 888–889
Echo phenomena 15, 68–69, 204, 232, 238, 272, 275, 279–280, 282, 427, 431, 577, 820, 827, 834, 849
Elevational(s) 59, 820
Entailment 374
Ergative-absolutive 64
Etymological sources 15
Etymology 348
Event integration 18, 163, 187, 770, 773, 792, 794, 819–820, 829, 833, 836, 842, 847, 849, 873
Events 163–171, 173–176, 178–180, 182–192
Evolution of AM markers to non-AM values 16
Exchoative (aspect) 13, 24, 780–781, 796–797, 803, 811
Exclusive Associated Motion system (EAM) 613
Exlocative 13, 22, 397, 534–537, 594

Fact-of-motion 4, 10, 33, 35, 44, 65, 68, 278, 753, 773–774
Fictive motion 60, 176, 180–181, 249, 336, 372, 474–475, 640, 676, 696, 706–708, 756
Fieldwork 35, 211–212, 224
Fieldworkers 224
Figures 166–168, 170–171, 174–179, 182, 187, 189–190, 389, 408, 410, 412, 785
Flexibility 267
Foregrounding 859, 879, 890–891
Frequency 864–865, 888–889
Frequency of use 15
Fusional 699
Future 12, 22
Fuzzy category membership 437

Genetic classification 328
Genetic distribution 644
Geographical distribution 236, 614
Glosses (standardization of) 36, 53
Go 649
Go and V and return 869–871
Go back and do 516

Go out to do something 517
'Go'-reading 867
GOAL 719–720, 736
Goals 857–859, 871, 873–877, 882–886, 890
Grammatical category 3, 12, 17–18, 87, 89, 116–117, 315
Grammaticalization 15, 39–40, 50–52, 289, 305, 314, 348, 350, 395, 413, 486, 573, 576, 583, 591–592, 600, 766, 811, 870
Grammaticalized 274, 349, 403, 581, 585, 591, 771, 870
Grammatical marking 232
Grammatical relation 771
Grammatical role 232
Grammatical role of the moving entity 9, 247

Habitual 547, 557, 725, 870
HENCE 10
Hierarchies 17, 24, 311, 772–773
Hierarchy of semantic classes of verbs 13
Historical development 23
Historical origin 643
Historical scenario 690
Hither deixis 10, 257
Hortatives 871

I-AM (AM expressed by inflectional affixes) 360–361, 378–379
Iconic 108, 412
Iconicity 50, 52, 111, 413
Imperative AM 511
Imperative constructions 788–789, 793, 798
Imperatives 12, 22, 66, 871
Imperfective 6, 25, 290, 724
Imperfective aspect 265, 340, 723
Imperfectivity 737
Implicational hierarchy of semantic classes of verbs 18
Implicational scales / hierarchies 5, 8–9, 46, 63–64, 204, 311, 697, 736, 752–753, 771, 781, 804
Implicature 428
Inceptive 13, 289, 723–724, 864
Inchoative 723–724, 737, 797
Independent 858, 865, 867, 877–879, 881–882, 888, 890

Subject Index — 903

Independent constructions 859, 867, 880–881, 885, 888–890
Indirect motion 10, 427–428
Inferential associated motion (I-AM) 12, 20, 357, 361, 369, 377–379, 403
Inflectional 5, 22
Inflectional affixes 360
Inflectional category 251
Inflectional formatives 529
Inflectional morphology 69
Instrument 722
Integration 163, 166, 182, 186–188, 190, 192
Intentional 4
Interrupted motion / interruptive 11, 56–57, 66, 93, 142, 179, 247, 496–497, 845
Intransitive 732
Irrealis 12
Iterable 764
Iteration 747–748, 767, 770, 774
Itive 4, 9–10, 17–18, 21–23, 32–33, 42–43, 168, 172, 174, 177, 183, 185, 290, 308, 675, 689, 695, 704, 730, 737, 836

Joint movement of subject and object 24

Language contact 16
Leaving AM / direction 10, 103, 202, 213, 269, 509, 516, 844
Lexicalization 733
Lexicalized 219
Lexicalized orientations 823, 826–827
Lexical means 224
Lexical motion-manner 441
Lexical motion verbs 423, 443
Ligatives 265–266
Locational(s) 22–23, 39, 52, 57, 534, 537, 578, 580, 593–594, 596, 600
Locations 10, 12–13, 21–22, 859, 873–875, 883–885, 890

Macro-event 773–774
Mande 646
Manding language 646
Manipulative AM markers 849
Manner+motion verbs 441, 443
Metaphorical extension 677, 686
Metaphorical uses 249, 297, 344, 368

Methodological tool for eliciting AM 18
Mirative 808
Mirativity 808
Mobilative 10, 696
Moderately complex 271, 310–311
Momentary 260, 287–288
Mood 3, 12, 330
Morphological complexity 66
Morphological structure 237
Morphology 31
Motion auxiliary 314
Motion complex 378
Motion-cum-purpose 561, 855–856, 871–873, 891–892
Motion events 665
Motion event typology 4
Motion+manner verb 443
Motion of the object 9, 372
Motion of the subject 9
Motion-path verbs 441
Motion phrases 268
Motion semantics 372
Motion subevent 335, 346
Motion typology 753
Motion verbs 43, 665, 675, 868
Motion-with-purpose 4, 12, 24, 130, 233, 265, 278, 282, 284, 316, 375, 503, 734
Motive marker 283
Movement 666
Movement of a non-subject 11
Movement of the object 11
Movement of the subject 11
Movement verbs 666, 668–669, 674–675, 678, 686, 689–690
Moving 297
Moving argument / entity / figure 9, 11, 17, 237, 250, 256, 311, 315, 571, 586, 599
Moving suffix 297
Multi-functional 36, 40, 60
Multi-verb constructions 17, 52, 67, 88, 117, 221, 690

Neutral 148, 155–156, 330
Neutral direction 491
Non-affixal AM 820, 849
Non-dedicated systems 361
Non-deictic directionals 665

Non-motion 730–731
Non-motion roots 710
Non-motional functions 433–434, 436, 443
Non-motional lexical verbs 441
Non-motion/movement verbs 668, 678, 690
Non-orientable verbs 826
Non-spatial arguments 877
Non-subject AM 60, 258
Non-translational motion roots 711
Nuclear-layer SVCs 394, 408
Number of markers 44

Object 674, 688
Object-only motion 372
Oceanic 388
Orientation 9, 20, 23–24, 89, 113, 182, 233, 275, 363, 369, 378, 388, 424, 426–427, 443, 528, 696–697, 708, 819–820, 822–823, 836–837, 842
Orientational 59
Origin 295
Origin of the markers 653
Overlap of categories 40, 66

Paradigm 65
Paradigm gaps 22, 559
Paradigmatic relations 424
Parameters 232–233, 237, 256, 307, 310–311
Particles 14, 16, 35, 360, 378, 388–389, 392–395, 408
Passing-by 11, 21, 142, 147, 496–499
Path/Direction 273, 311
Path of motion 337
Path-oriented intentionality 375
Paths 6–7, 9, 163–164, 166–170, 172, 174, 176, 178, 180–181, 183–184, 187–188, 190–192, 256, 682–683, 785
Patient 885
Patient agreement 363
Perception verbs 61
Perfective 6, 290
Perfective aspect 791
Perfective meanings 864
Perfectiveness 737
Perfective/perfect 723
Phrasal structure 252

Pleonastic constructions 858–859, 867–868, 872, 877, 879–883, 888–890
Pleonastic converbial constructions 865, 888
Pleonastic echo 865
Pleonastic uses 15, 25, 858, 888
Pluractionals 55, 546, 725–727
Plural 725, 727
Polyfunctional 23, 758
Polysemous DD/AM systems 9, 11, 811
Polysemous markers 311, 425
Portmanteau morphemes 333, 347, 551, 559–560
Pragmatic backgrounding 431
Pragmatic context 8, 358
Pragmatically 377
Pragmatics 361, 373, 379
Precursor constructions 231, 236, 302, 317
Prefixing 39, 50
Preverbal and postverbal directionals 373
Prior 6, 11–13, 17, 19–22, 24, 46–47, 54, 61, 255, 372, 425, 715
Prior Arrival of a non-subject 262, 264, 308
Prior associated motion 130–132, 137–139, 142, 144, 146, 148–156, 373, 486, 492, 708, 804
Prior motion 8–9, 18, 22, 24, 232, 238–239, 264, 266, 268, 270, 272, 275, 277, 282, 286, 289–290, 296, 302, 314, 316, 339, 360, 369, 375, 396, 398, 402, 412–413, 678, 753, 771–772, 863, 871, 891
Prior motion SVCs 17
Prior plus subsequent AM 8, 20–21, 24, 137, 146–147, 233, 245, 258, 262, 311, 486, 493
Profiling 718
Progressive 22, 546
Prolative 288
Prospective 94, 576, 587, 628, 711, 723, 825
Prototypical associated motion 358
Proximal 13, 54, 58
Pseudocoordination 35, 52–53, 88
Punctual 6, 11, 257, 286, 312
Punctual Aspect 263
Pure AM 12
Pure direction(al) 18, 21
Purposive 4, 53, 402, 872
Purposive motion 47

Purposive motion SVCs 17
Purposive motion verb constructions 819–820, 822
Purposive reading 872

Quasi-inflections 254
Quick succession 443, 447

Random direction / motion 10, 21, 137, 143, 154, 157, 490–492
Ranking of verb classes 800
Reconstruction 15, 267–268
Redundant use 15, 280, 284
Reduplication 242–244, 261, 272–273, 303, 330
Reference points 204, 211
Relative temporality / time of the motion event 20–21, 233, 237, 247, 256, 262, 273, 283, 290, 310–311, 315, 339–340
Repeated 6
Repurposing 351
Respect Language 250
Resultative 94, 111
Return path 681–682
Returnative 10, 137, 140, 142, 150, 578, 638
Reversive 10, 43, 48, 55, 57, 203, 247
Round-trip motion 10, 11, 21, 48–49, 54–57, 64, 66, 93, 103, 147, 233, 411, 497–499, 561, 683, 804, 870

Same Subject subordinate 265
Sample 34
Satellite frame 4, 774
Scale 9
Selection 431
Semantic classes of verbs 799, 803
Semantic contrasts 237
Semantic extensions 807
Semantic shifts 245, 265–266, 315
Semantic variation 39
Semantic verb class 786
Semantics of the host verb 368
Semantics of the verb 8
Separative 64, 673–674, 690
Sequential meaning 872–873, 892
Serial verb 388, 404

Serial verb constructions (SVC) 14–17, 20, 24, 39, 50–52, 87, 222, 360, 378, 781, 804–809, 811, 824, 828, 837, 841
Shift in the deictic centre 367
Simultaneous 708, 715, 735–736
Simultaneous AM (Concurrent AM) 734
Source 719, 736, 857, 871, 873–874, 876
Source constructions 15, 313
Spatial arguments 13, 25, 855, 858–859, 876–883, 888, 890, 892
Spatial distribution 294, 302–304
Spatial extension 303
Speed of motion 12–13, 233, 237, 239–240, 256–257, 263, 268, 270, 309, 312, 316
Spontaneous motion 674
Stative verbs 365, 794
Stem alternations 550
Stimulus 201
Storybook 201
Stylistic 376
Subcategories 236
Subgrouping 783
Subgroups 234–235
Subject 674, 678, 680, 685, 688
Subject-Marking 14
Subordinated/coordinated clauses 224
Subsequent 6, 11, 17, 20–21, 24, 46, 48, 54, 61, 255, 372, 425, 443, 708, 761
Subsequent associated motion (AM) 133, 137, 145–147, 151–152, 154, 373, 486, 493, 790, 795, 800, 805
Subsequent motion with purpose 375
Subsequent movement 715
Subsequent (S) Motion 8–9, 144, 232, 240–241, 264–265, 268, 271, 292, 314, 678, 753, 764–767, 771–772, 871
Suffixing 39, 50
Suppletive allomorphy 429
Survey 31, 34
SVC 224, 392, 395, 398, 403–404, 406, 408, 411–413
Syncretism 559–560
Syntactic valence 716, 718
System complexity 19

TAM settings 8
Telicity 724

Temporal relation hierarchy 11, 311
Temporal relations 6, 8–9, 11, 17, 18, 21, 46, 280, 753, 761, 767, 771, 804, 811, 820, 824, 838, 849
Tense 3, 12, 14, 60, 69, 233, 315, 330, 751
Tense-mood 19
Terminology 32, 36
Theme 697, 719–721, 736, 885–886, 890
THITHER 10
Time referentials 378
Tonal alternation 555–556
Tone changes 22
Towards 330
Towards/ventive-orientation 441
Trajectory 799, 857, 873–874, 876
Transitive 94, 730
Transitive motion 94, 112
Transitive subjects and objects together 370
Transitive subjects without their object 370
Transitive verbs 362
Transitivity 14, 20, 25, 240, 242, 253, 700, 729
Transitivity harmony 14, 422, 424
TRANSITORY 271, 273
Translational motion 232, 329, 705, 714, 729–730, 733, 737
Translocative 10, 32, 855, 868, 889
Typologically unusual 372
Typology 31, 35, 39, 44, 87, 781
Typology of event encoding 18
Typology of event integration 773

Unitary systems 310–311
Univerbation 266, 277

Unspecified orientation / direction 10, 20, 24, 43, 238, 241–242, 269, 349, 528, 787–788, 823
Upward 6, 137, 144, 203, 261–262

Valence change 14, 23
Ven(i)tive 4
VEN(TIVE) 308
Ventive Orientation 441
Ventive prefix 361
Ventives 9–10, 17–18, 20–23, 25, 32–33, 42–43, 131–142, 144–149, 151–156, 164–165, 168, 170–181, 183, 185, 188–190, 290, 362, 441, 490, 532–533, 666, 668–669, 674–675, 677–678, 688–689, 695, 704, 730, 737, 864, 868
Verbal inflections 378
Verbal paradigm 332
Verb arguments 858–859, 878–882, 888, 890, 892
Verb frame 4
Verb-framed languages 773
Verb serialisation 306
Verb-verb compounds 67, 88, 91–92, 95–97
Vertical 42, 65
Vertical cline 403
Vertical dimension 9, 24, 257, 263, 819–820, 836, 840
Vertical motion 261
Very complex systems 310–312
Viewpoint aspect 340
Visual stimuli 18
Vowel harmony 362

Language Index

Abipón 452
Abkhaz 62, 71
Abun 113, 118
Acazulco Otomi 527–528, 530, 533, 535, 537–539, 541, 543–544, 547, 549–552, 554–557, 559–560
Acehnese 118, 122
Achumawi 517, 521
Acoma 71, 521
Adnyamathanha 231, 235, 240, 246, 257, 264–265, 268–270, 301, 305, 307–308, 310–314, 350, 358, 372–373, 378
African languages 6–7, 9, 12–13, 22, 752, 779, 786
Afro-Asiatic 7, 96–97
Agar Dinka 699, 719
Ainu 122
Akan 92
Akie 702, 706, 716, 725–726
Alamblak 59, 71, 122
Algic 21, 511, 522
Algonquian 143, 155, 160, 487, 491, 495, 511, 868
Alyawarr/Alyawarra 42, 49, 62, 71, 249, 254, 257–258, 260–262, 264, 267, 307, 312
Amazonian languages 3, 6, 18, 666
Ambae (Lolovoli Northeast) 93
Andoke 594
Anmatyerr 249, 254, 257, 260, 262, 267, 289, 310, 312
Anywa 172–173, 699–700, 710, 722, 725, 754
Apurinã 56, 71, 122, 143, 159, 491
Arabana 150, 160, 271, 273, 308, 310, 312
Arabana-Wangkangurru 236, 271, 274, 305, 309, 312–313
Arabic (Egyptian) 118
Aranda 254, 263–265, 312
Arandic 5–6, 15, 19, 137, 141, 145, 231, 235, 240, 244, 246–248, 254, 259, 262–263, 266–268, 271, 285, 289, 305, 307, 310–314, 325, 329, 821
Araona 48–49, 71, 122
Arapaho 522
Arapesh 64, 89
Arapesh (Mountain) 71, 118
Arawak 6, 37, 48, 71, 203, 360
Arawakan 135, 139, 143, 147, 159, 489, 493, 519, 821
Arop-Lokep 108–109, 111, 112, 118, 122
Arrernte 42, 49, 52, 60, 62, 66, 203–204, 314–315, 358
Arusha Maa 703, 715
Asheninca 62
Asian languages 5
Asimjeeg Datooga 702, 722
Asmat 67, 72, 122
Ateso 705, 713–714, 722, 754
Athapaskan 489
Atlantic languages 6, 12, 17, 22–23, 611, 665–666, 687
Atsugewi 521
Australian languages 19, 666, 751, 752, 771
Austronesian 88, 90, 95–97, 109–110, 220, 358

Babungo 118
Bagirmi 118
Bak 665–666
Balant 666
Balant Ganja 632–633
Banoni 72, 118, 122
Bantawa 841, 843
Bantoid 96
Bantu 12, 15, 22, 569
Barasano 44, 72, 122
Barbareño Chumash 511, 521
Bari 703, 705–706, 713, 726
Bassari 639–640, 643
Batak (Karo) 118
Baure 139, 159, 360
Bayot 645, 650, 665
Bedik 639–641, 643
Belhare 838–839
Berber 7, 60, 134, 149, 152, 159, 165, 169, 171, 751
Berber (Middle Atlas) 118
Biafada 638
Bidyara 293–294, 296, 309, 314

Bijogo 181, 634–637, 644, 647, 649
Bikin 862
Bilinarra 326, 336
Bininj Gun-Wok 45, 49, 72, 118
Blackfoot 522
Bole 133, 145, 159
Bora 63–64
Border 132, 160, 359
Boro 109
Bozo (Tigemaxo) 118
Brahui 118
Brokskat 122
Buduma 118
Bularnu 285, 308
Buma 118
Burmese 118, 122, 846
Buwal 138, 145, 159
Bystraja 862, 866, 874, 880
Bystraja Even 863, 867, 870, 877, 879, 885, 888–889

Caddo 521
Caddoan 521
Cahuilla 53, 72, 118, 122
Camus 145–146, 159
Cantonese 105, 118, 122
Cavineña 3–4, 61, 65, 170, 189, 203, 358, 360, 378, 476, 558, 560
Cayuga 72, 522
Central Arrernte 254
Central Jóola 665
Central Karnic (CKarnic) 278, 308
Central New South Wales (Central NSW/ CNSW) 235, 290, 298, 309, 313
Central Sudanic 159
Central Tarahumara 500
Chácobo 13, 17, 20, 419–428, 431, 434–436, 445–447, 543, 864, 871
Chadic 7, 89, 96, 133, 138, 159, 751
Changana 573–574, 590, 597
Chemehuevi 72, 122
Cherang'any 163–164, 184, 702, 706, 711–712, 723, 726, 758
Cherokee 522
Chewa 590–591, 595–596
Cheyenne 522
Chibchan 88, 159, 503, 519

Chichewa 72
Chichimec 561
Chimariko 140, 142, 150, 160, 516, 521
Chinantec 159, 486, 519, 527, 562
Chinantecan 136, 491, 494–495, 515, 561
Chinook 509
Chinookan 521
Choapan Zapotec 220
Choctaw 521
Chontal 490
Chuj 519
Chukchi 72, 122
Chumash 138, 160, 503
Chumashan 521
Classical Manchu 24, 25, 856, 863–864, 873
Cogtse 824
Colonial Otomi 547–548
Comaltepec Chinantec 511, 515, 520
Coos (Hanis) 72
Coptic 118
Cora 131, 160, 520
Cree 138, 155, 160, 491, 522
Cree (Plains) 72
Creek 138, 160, 517, 521
Cupeño 144, 160, 492, 500, 502, 504–506, 511, 513, 520
Cushitic 7, 8, 751–752
Cuwabo 577, 579, 586–587, 591

Dagbani 73, 118
Dana 780–781, 789, 791–792, 795–796, 806, 808–809
Dani (Lower Grand Valley) 73, 122
Dargwa 73
Datooga 135, 701
Dâw 220, 222
Degema 118
Dhanggati 302, 317
Dhimal 847, 849
Dhirari 289
Digo 573–575, 577, 582–583, 587–588, 590, 595
Dinka 40, 172
Dinka-Nuer 699, 701
Diola-Fogny 23
Diyari 278, 288–289, 305, 308, 312
Djabugay (Jabugay) 52, 67

Djambarrpuyngu 305
Djapu 305
Djinang 305–306, 317
Djinpa 305
Doyayo 73
Drehu 122
Dumi 839, 843

Eastern and Central (EC) Arrernte 246,
  254–258, 260, 262, 266–267, 307, 312
Eastern Anmatyerr 261
Eastern Arrernte 254
Eastern Highlands Otomi 536
Eastern Nilotic 698, 702, 704–706, 713, 720,
  723, 725–726, 728, 736, 754
East Karnic (EKarnic) 278, 308
Egyptian Arabic 97
Ende 19–20, 365
Endo 701–702, 711, 721, 758
English 33, 35, 53, 57, 60, 64, 99, 104, 118,
  168–169, 180, 186, 422, 532, 665,
  677–678, 682–683, 686, 749, 761, 774
Erromangan 73, 119
Ese Ejja 18, 62, 170, 189, 201–205, 212–214,
  218, 221
Eskimo-Aleut 522
Eudeve 520
Even 856, 860–863, 865–867, 870, 874,
  880, 890
Evenki 73, 860–861, 886, 890
Ewe 99
Ewondo 119

Fijian 119
Filomena Mata Totonac 497, 499
Finnish 119
Fon 105–106, 113
Fongbe 119
Fóoñi 666, 671, 675, 690
Formosan 88
French 168, 192, 674, 677–678, 686
Fula 627, 645, 647
Fulfulde 617, 620–622, 626, 640, 642, 684
Fuliiru 22, 576, 582–585, 588, 590, 597–599

Gamilaraay 297
Gapapaiwa 119, 122

Garifuna 141, 159, 493, 500, 505, 519
Garo 73, 122
Georgian 73
German 73
Ghadamsi 169
Gisamjanga Datooga 702, 712–713, 716
Gola 119
Gorin 863, 873
Greek (Modern) 73
Greenlandic (West) 73
Guaraní 119
Guatusa 138, 159, 503, 519
Guaycuruan 17, 21, 451–452
Gubëëher 649
Gude 145, 159
Gujaahar 631–632, 648, 652
Gule 782
Gunbalang 73, 119
Gundungurra 298–299, 309
Gunya 295, 309, 313
Gunyaamolo 632
Gurindji 326
Gurr-goni 111, 114, 119
Gwama 780–781, 784, 787, 790, 795,
  797–798, 800–803, 807
Gyalrong 849
Gyalrongic 15, 17, 24, 819–820, 822–826,
  829, 842, 845–849, 873

Haida 48, 73, 107, 119, 122
Hakhun Tangsa 109, 846
Hatam 119
Hausa 40, 60, 62, 74, 172, 177, 180
Hindi 119
Hixkaryana 37, 66, 74
Hmong Njua 119, 122
Hoava 119
Huallaga Quechua 147, 689
Huasteca Nahuatl 501, 511, 516
Huehuetla Tepehua 144, 159, 506, 510, 520
Hungarian 74, 119

Ika 37, 51, 74
Ilchamus Maa 726–727
Imonda 122, 132, 160, 359
Indo-Aryan 103
Indo-European 96, 108

Indonesian 119
Ineseño Chumash 160, 521
Iraqw 66, 74
Iroquoian 522
Italian 37
Itzaj 119
Ixil 519
Ixtenco Otomi 536
Iyaa 579

Jaad 638–639, 647
Jabêm 74, 119
Jabugay (Djabugay) 278, 280–281, 308, 313
Jakaltek 60, 74
Japanese 5, 168, 187
Japhug 6, 821–827, 829, 833–834, 849
Japonic 24
Jingulu 327, 349–351
Jóola 665–666, 668, 673, 690
Jóola Banjal 172, 631, 650
Jóola Fóoñi 13, 17, 23, 534, 537, 549, 594, 612–613, 625, 632, 638, 654, 665–666, 668–673, 675–677, 680, 682, 685, 689–690
Jóola Karon 632–633, 652
Jóola Kwaatay 633, 652
Ju|'hoan 119

Kaasa 675
Kadiwéu 451–452
Kairiru 119, 122
Kalenjin 701, 749, 770
Kalkatungic 235, 290–291, 309, 313
Kalkatungu 66, 74, 119, 291–292, 313
Kamaiurá 119, 122
Kambera 122
Kana 74, 119
Kanamari 139, 159
Kaonde 579, 589, 595
Kara 389
Karbi 131, 160, 846
Karen (Pwo) 119, 122
Karnic 150, 235, 268, 271, 278, 290, 304–306, 312, 314
Karok 74, 508, 521
Karon 650, 665
Kashaya 500, 521

Kashibo-Kakataibo 142, 153, 159, 427
Kashinawa 143, 159, 427
Kâte 122
Kathlamet 521
Katukinan 159
Kayardild 89, 94, 102–103, 107, 108, 110–112, 114–115, 119, 378
Kaytej (Kaytetye) 487, 528
Kaytetye 19–20, 48, 62, 137, 141, 145, 160, 183, 185, 203, 231, 235–237, 240, 242–243, 246–247, 252–254, 256, 258, 260–267, 269, 274, 289, 307, 311–312, 314–315, 329, 357, 360, 378–379, 498, 857, 865, 870, 889
Kekchí 138, 159, 496, 497, 514, 519
Kenga 172
Kera 74
Keresan 521
Ket 74, 122
Khaling 836–839, 841–843, 849
Kham 75, 97
Khasi 122
Khmu' 119
Khoekhoe 56, 75, 122
Khoisan 94, 96
Khroskyabs 824
Khwe 94, 169
Kickapoo 522
Kinga 598–599
Kiowa 75, 122, 521
Kiowa-Tanoan 521
Kiranti 17, 24, 220, 819–820, 824, 829, 836–843, 845–849, 864, 871
Kiribati 33, 35, 39, 43, 75
Kisonko Maa 717
Klamath 521
Koasati 75, 135, 521
Kobiana 630, 650
Kobon 119
Koman 12–13, 17, 23–24, 373, 480, 780–783, 785–787, 804, 810–811, 829
Kombai 122
Komo 780–781, 784, 788–790, 793, 795–797, 802, 805–806, 810
Kony 723, 725
Konyagi 639, 641–643
Kordofanian 145, 159

Language Index

Korean 122
Korku 75, 122
Koro 389
Koromfe 119
Korowai 122
Koyraboro (Koroboro) Senni 75, 119, 145, 159
Koyra Chiini 145, 159
Krongo 75
Ktunaxa 495
Kui 37
Kukata 301
Kuki-Chin 847, 849
Kukú 75
Kuna 519
Kuot 119
Kupsapiny 17, 23, 48, 701, 711, 723, 747–749, 751–755, 757–759, 761, 763, 765–767, 769–777
Kuuk Thaayorre 240, 276–277, 281, 308, 312–314
Kuyani 235, 268, 270, 301, 305, 307, 310, 312–313
Kwa 138
Kwaataay 665
Kwaatay 650
Kwaio 119
Kwak'wala 141, 160, 522
Kwarandzyey 145, 159
Kyomkyo 846

Laala 617, 620, 622–624, 627, 643
Lai 42, 59, 64, 75
Lakhota 119, 122
Lamang 40, 42, 75, 119
Lamunkhin 862, 867, 874
Lamunkhin Even 867, 869, 880, 883, 885, 888
Lango 75, 119, 699, 754
Latin 266
Latvian 75
Lavukaleve 109, 119
Laz 75
Lealao Chinantec 520
Lega 593
Lele 119, 145, 159, 173
Lepcha 122
Lillooet 119

Longgu 122
Loniu 392
Lower (L) Arrernte 254, 257, 260–264, 307, 310, 312
Lower Chinook 521
Lower Negidal 862
Lowland Chontal 159, 490, 499, 520, 857, 889
Lucazi 577
Lugbara 75, 119
Luiseño 511, 520
Lumasaaba 749
Luo-Burun 699
Luvale 75
Luwo 699

Maa 703, 705, 716, 723, 727, 754
Maasai 23, 41, 61–62, 177, 181, 698, 703, 705, 707–708, 714–715, 717–718, 720, 724, 726–728, 733–736, 738, 754
Mabaan 698–699, 705, 709, 720
Macro-Ge 159
Ma'di 76, 145, 159
Madurese 119
Máíhɨ̃ki 220, 223
Maithili 103, 120
Makah 66, 76, 120, 511, 522
Malecite-Passamaquoddy 149, 160, 487, 491, 495, 504, 522
Mam 76, 492, 511, 519
Manchu 861
Mandarin 5, 120, 122
Mande 646
Manding 646–647
Mandinka 173, 175–176, 648
Mangarla 301
Mangghuer 120
Manjaku 631, 633, 666
Mankanya 666
Mapudungun 37, 57, 76, 122
Margany 294–296, 309, 313
Maric 235, 290, 293, 309–310, 313
Maricopa 76
Marquesan 120
Marrngu 235, 290, 309, 313
Masaaba 749
Mataguayan 374, 480

Matlatzinca 561
Matsés 42, 56–57, 65–66, 76, 122, 499
Matukar Panau 358
Maung 76, 120
Mayan 159, 492–493, 496, 514, 519
Maybrat 112, 120
Mayo 510, 520
Mayrinax Atayal 88
Mazahua 536, 561
Mbay 110, 112, 120
Mbugwe 579
Mbuun 579
Meithei 49, 58, 76
Menomini 21, 160, 497, 511, 522
Meskwaki 511, 522
Mesoamerican 527, 561, 563
Mezquital Otomi 527, 536
Middle Amur 861–862
Midob 76, 123
Mirndi 19, 109, 290, 326–327, 349
Misantla Totonac 510, 520
Miwok 521
Mocoví 76, 120, 451–452
Mohawk 76, 522, 537
Mojeño Trinitario 203, 247, 358, 865, 889
Mongo 575–576, 579
Mono-Alu 389
Montagnais 522
Monumbo 120, 123
Mosetén 6, 57, 76, 139, 159
Mparntwe (Central) Arrernte 6, 71, 141–142, 150, 160, 205, 231, 247, 252, 254, 257, 258, 260, 264, 267, 436, 751–752, 857
Mpoto 570
Mudburra 17, 19, 235, 278, 290, 308, 314, 315, 325–332, 334–335, 337–338, 351–352, 543, 551, 557
Mulomp-North 665
Mundari 123
Mupun 120
Muskogean 135, 160, 517, 521
Mussau 120
Mutsun 511, 521

Nabak 120, 123
Nadahup 220
Nagatman 76
Nahuatl 45, 51, 55, 66, 148, 159, 501, 516, 520, 527, 561
Nahuatl (Mecayapan Isthmus) 77
Nahuatl (Tetelcingo) 77, 120
Naikhin 863, 869
Nalu 22
Nambikuára (Southern) 123
Nanai 856, 860–870, 873–874, 876, 879–880, 884, 886–888
Nandi 702, 711, 720–721, 723, 758
Nanti 147, 154, 159
Nara 88
Natchez 521
Navajo 77
Ndali 590, 597
Ndjébbana 77, 120
Negidal 856, 860–863, 866–867, 870, 874, 880, 882, 885–886, 888–890
Nelemwa 120
Nez Perce 48–49, 61–62, 77, 120, 123, 486, 496, 500, 511, 521
Ngalakan 40, 77, 123
Ngamini 278, 288, 305, 308, 312
Ngarna 235, 278, 290, 308–309
Ngarnka 327, 349–350
Ngiyambaa 77, 120, 123, 296, 309
Ngizim 145, 159
Ngumpin 278
Ngumpin-Yapa 235, 271, 276, 278, 290, 308, 326, 351
Ngunawal 298, 309
Nhanda 77, 301
Niger-Congo 6, 22, 96, 99, 105–106, 113, 159, 751
Nilo-Saharan 7, 22–23, 88, 96, 110, 695, 783
Nilotic 7, 15, 17, 23, 135, 146, 151, 159, 695, 754, 864, 875
Nisgha 39–40, 59, 77
Niuean 113–114, 120
Nivacle 62–63, 374, 480
Nivkh 123
Nkore-Kiga 120
Nomatsigenga 139, 159
Nomatsiguenga 61–62
Non-Pama-Nyungan 305, 327
Noon 183, 617
Northern (N) Karnic 308–309

Northern Lwoo 700
Northern Otomi 528
Northern Paiute 139, 490, 500, 504, 510, 521
Northern Sahaptin 501, 511, 521
Northern Tungusic 856, 861, 868
North Samburu Maa 726
Nsenga 77
Nuaulu 88, 120
Nuer 184, 699, 701, 711
Nuuchahnulth 511, 522
Nxa'amxcin 489
Nyakyusa 572, 576–577, 580–581, 587–590, 595, 597, 599
Nyamwezi 573, 579
Nyangumarta 301, 309, 313–314
Nyun-Buy 666
Nzebi 593

Oceanic 17, 19–20, 93, 96, 109, 114, 220, 373, 385, 388–390, 392, 396–397, 404, 413
Ocuilteco 519
Ojibwa 143, 160, 504, 506, 522
Ojibwa (Eastern) 77
Olutec 857, 892
Oneida 59, 77, 522, 534, 537
O'odham 77
Opo 533, 780–781, 783–784, 788, 791–792, 794, 798–799, 801, 803, 805, 807–809
Oromo (Harar) 77
Oto-Manguean/Otomanguean 159, 220, 511, 519–520, 527, 561
Otomi 15, 17, 21–22, 527, 594
Otomi-Mazahua 537, 548
Oto-Pamean 527, 537, 561
Otoro 172–173

Paamese 120
Pade-Noon 619–620, 625–626
Páez 77
Pahoturi River language family 17, 20, 359
Paiute 160, 506
Paiute (Northern) 77, 123
Palaihnihan 521
Palantla Chinantec 520
Palauan 120
Paluai 15, 20, 112, 373

Paman 235, 271, 278, 308, 313
Pama-Nyungan 15, 17, 19, 96, 137, 141, 145, 150, 160, 203, 231–232, 234–236, 289–290, 305–312, 316–318, 326, 357, 372, 528, 751, 857, 865, 870
Panamint 21, 144, 150, 160, 486, 504, 506, 509, 511, 520
Pano 20, 419, 421–423, 430, 864, 871
Panoan 6, 17, 142, 144, 159, 247, 425, 427
Pano-Takanan 203, 220
Papitalai 222
Papitalai (Koro dialect) 220
Papuan 89, 96, 109, 112–113, 358–359
Parakuyo Maa 727
Päri 145, 151, 159, 174, 699–701, 705, 709–710, 751
Passamaquoddy-Maliseet 51, 78
Pech 55, 123
Penutian 521
Pero 62–63, 78, 89, 120, 174, 178–179, 751
Persian 78, 120
Pilagá 11, 17, 21, 41, 64, 451–455, 458–460, 465, 467, 469, 471, 473, 476–481, 544
Pilaga-Toba 452
Pintupi 300, 303, 309
Pirahã 123
Pitjantjatjara 78, 300, 304, 309
Pitta-Pitta 260, 278, 290, 292–293, 304, 309
Plateau Penutian 511
Pokot 770
Polynesian 33, 35
Pomoan 500, 521
Popoloca 66
Popoloca (Metzontla) 78
Proto-Arandic 257, 260, 264, 267
Proto-Atlantic 23
Proto-Koman 785
Proto-Ngumpin-Yapa 348
Proto-Oto-Pamean 561
Proto Pama-Nyungan 313
Pulaar 627
Puluwat 62–63, 78
Purépecha 78, 220
Pwo Karen 103–104, 109–111

Qiang 78, 123
Qom 452

Quechua 37, 41–43, 54, 58, 146, 159, 358, 535, 594
Quechua (Huallaga) 78
Quechua (Imbabura) 78, 120
Querétaro Otomi 21, 527–528, 530, 533, 535, 537, 539, 544, 551, 554, 557, 559–560
Quiché 519

Rama 78, 88, 123
Rangi 591
Retuarã 42, 62, 78, 123
Rgyalongic 6
Rikbaktsa 138, 159
Ritharrngu 305
Romance 266
Ronga 591
Rotuman 78, 120
Russian 78, 108, 111, 120, 168, 180–181

Saafi-saafi 617, 620
Saami (Northern) 120
Sabaot 749
Sahaptian/Sahaptin 134, 156, 486, 496, 501
Sakha 888
Salishan 96, 489
Salt-Yui 120
Samburu Maa 717
Sangu 78
San Juan Guelavía Zapotec 519
Sanuma 78, 123
Seneca 522
Sentani 78, 120
Sereer 178–179, 613, 634–636, 643
Shasta 521
Shawnee 522
Shilluk 699–700, 710–711, 718, 724–725, 875
Shipibo 425
Shipibo-Konibo 144, 153, 159
Shona 573–575, 581–582, 590–591
Shoshone 78, 123, 139, 160, 520
Siar 120
Siberian Yupik 522
Sierra Miwok 521
Sinitic 820, 846
Sino-Tibetan 6, 17, 24, 96, 104–105, 109–110, 131, 160, 220, 792, 819–822, 836, 845–847, 849

Sipakapense 493, 499–500, 515–516, 519
Situ 824–825, 829, 833–834
Slave 78
So 78
Sochiapan Chinantec 136, 139, 144, 491, 500, 504, 506–507, 509, 511, 519
Somali 8, 175, 177, 751–752
Songhai 159
South American languages 3, 6, 8, 20, 21, 240, 247, 751, 752, 771, 804
Southeast Ambrym 120
Southeastern Tepehuan 102, 110–112, 508–510
Southern Arrernte 259
Southern Ndebele 592
Southern Nilotic 23, 701, 702, 704, 706, 708, 711, 713, 720, 723, 725, 728, 736, 747, 749, 753–754, 758
Southern Sotho 580, 592
Southern Tungusic 856, 861, 865, 886
Southwest Paman 276
Spanish 53, 422, 427, 452, 540, 773
Squamish 79, 120
Sranan 99
Sudest 79, 123
Sundanese 120
Swahili 79, 749

Taba 90, 103, 120
Tacana 61–62, 220, 560
Tacanan 242, 360, 821
Tafi 138, 159
Tai-Kadai 93
Taiof 120
Takanan 5–6, 18, 476, 558
Tamabo 123
Tamashek/Tamasheq 134, 145, 149, 152, 159, 174, 177–178
Tangkic 378
Tangsa 847
Taqbaylit 7, 165, 171, 174, 176–179, 188
Taqbaylit Berber 358–361, 377
Tarahumara 141, 160, 500, 505, 520
Tarao 79
Tarascan 220
Tariana 594
Tauya 120, 123

Tepehuan 520
Tepehuan (Southeastern) 79, 120
Tepetotutla Chinantec 494–495, 499
Tequistlatecan 159, 490, 520
Tequixistlan Chontal 520
Teribe 121
Teso 703, 723
Teso-Turkana 703
Tetelcingo Nahuatl 148, 504–505, 520
Tetun 121
Thai 93, 121
Thompson 79
Thulung 220–221, 843
Thura-Yura 235, 268, 270–271, 290, 301, 307, 309–313
Tibetan 66
Tibetan (Shigatse) 79, 121
Tibeto-Burman 49
Tidore 79, 103, 121
Tikar 79, 121
Tilapa Otomi 519, 527–530, 533, 537–540, 543–544, 547–554, 559–560
Tima 145, 159, 189–190, 751
Tinrin 79, 121
Tiwi 66, 79, 121
Tlachichilco Tepehua 510, 520
Toba 451–452, 460
Tobelo 79
Tolowa 489
Tonkawa 141, 160, 510, 521
Toposa 703, 723
Torricelli 96
Totela 595
Totonac 51
Totonac (Xicotepec de Juárez) 79, 121
Totonacan 159, 494, 496–497
Trans-Himalayan 873
Trans-New Guinea 96
Trinitario 6
Trumai 67
Tsat 121
Tshobdun 824
Tugun 121, 123
Tukang Besi 109–110, 121, 123
Tukanoan 220
Tumbuka 590
Tumpisa Shoshone 149

Tungusic 15, 17, 24–25, 729, 829, 855, 861–862, 879, 889–890, 892
Tupian 96
Turkana 703, 707, 723, 728, 754
Turkic 888
Turkish 121
Tuvaluan 121
Tzotzil 892
Tzutujil 33, 80, 519

Udihe 48, 55, 80, 856, 861–869, 874, 879, 881, 885–886, 888–889
Udmurt 121
Uduk 780–781, 783–784, 791, 801, 807
Ulch 856, 861–863, 865–867, 869–870, 873–874, 877, 879–880, 883–884, 886, 888
Umbundu 589
Upper Aranda 254
Upper Kuskokwim 80
Upper Necaxa Totonac 494, 496–497, 520
Upper Negidal 862
Uralic 96
Urubú-Kaapor 108, 121
Usan 121
Utian 521
Uto-Aztecan 21, 96, 102, 131, 141, 148, 150, 159–160, 486, 490, 492, 511, 513, 516, 520–521, 561

Vafsi 80
Vietnamese 121, 123

Wakashan 160, 511, 522
Wakaya 278, 290–291, 309, 326, 346–347, 352
Walman 121
Wambaya 19, 109, 290, 325–327, 330, 336, 341–342, 349, 352
Wambule 843
Wangkangurru 271, 273, 308, 310, 312
Wangka-Yutyuru 278, 285–286, 293, 304, 308, 310, 312
Wangkumara 278, 286, 305, 308
Wappo 510, 517, 521
Wari' 80, 123
Warlmanpa 236, 271, 276, 308, 313, 326, 346, 352

Warlpiri 253, 276, 278, 289–290, 302–303, 308, 311, 314, 326, 335, 345, 348, 352, 857
Warluwarra 283, 285, 292, 308, 310, 314
Warluwarric 235, 278
Warnman 299
Warumungu 235–236, 264, 271, 274–276, 285, 308, 310, 313–314, 326, 343–345, 350–352, 551
Washo 494, 510, 521
Wati 235, 290, 299, 309
Western Amazonian 233, 311
Western (W) Arrernte 254, 258, 260, 262, 264, 267, 289, 310, 312
Western Desert 235, 270, 290, 299, 301–304, 309, 314
Western Nilotic 698–699, 704–705, 709, 722, 724, 728, 736, 751, 754
West Greenlandic 491, 522
West (W) Karnic 271, 308
West Papuan 96
Wichí 80, 121
Wichita 123
Wiradjuri 298, 309
Wirangu 141, 160, 270, 290, 301, 309, 313, 315
Wiyot 522
Wolof 6, 80, 612–613, 617, 619–624, 626–629, 640, 642–643, 645, 653–654
Wyandot 522

Yagua 46, 49, 57, 80, 123, 204, 560
Yakima 134, 156, 521
Yakkha 839
Yalarnnga 234, 290–292, 309, 311, 313–314
Yaminahua 142, 159, 220, 221
Yamphu 836, 840, 844–845, 849, 871
Yana 521
Yandruwandha 278, 287, 305, 308, 312
Yankunytjatjara 299, 309
Yanomami 138, 141, 152, 159
Yanyuwa 278
Yapa 276, 278, 308
Yaqui 80, 123, 520
Yarluyandi 305
Yélî Dnye 20, 359, 752
Yeyi 594
Yidiny 80, 111, 121, 278–281, 299, 308, 313
Yimas 80, 123
Yine 135, 139, 159, 489
Yir-Yoront 236, 271, 276–278, 308, 310, 313
Yolngu 305–306
Yoruba 121
Yosondúa Mixtec 519
Yuin 235, 290, 298–299, 309–310, 313
Yukaghir (Kolyma) 80
Yupik 522
Yurok 491, 522
Yuwaalaraay 297, 309
Yuwaaliyaay 297–298

Zapotec 519
Zapotec (Quiegolani) 121, 123
Zbu 824
Zoque (Chimalapa) 80, 123
Zulu 80, 576–577, 592
Zuni 80, 123

Name Index

Abbott, C. 59
Accattoli, M. 37
Agnew, B. 301
Aikhenvald, A. Y. 88–89, 92–93, 437
Aissen, J. L. 892
Alamin, S. 165, 171, 189–190
Alonso de la Fuente, J. A. 5, 856, 864, 867, 873
Alpher, B. 276–277
Ameka, F. K. 168
Andersen, T. 40, 172, 174, 695, 698–701, 704–705, 709–710, 719–720
Anderson, G. D. S. 358, 389
Anderson, S. R. 560
Andrews, H. 530
Ansre, G. 92
Antonov, A. 60
Aoki, H. 61
Aralova, N. 862
Aronoff, M. 529, 550, 559
Aske, J. 180
Atkinson, Q. D. 234
Atknine, V. 861
Austin, P. K. 15–16, 67, 111, 170, 182, 271, 286, 288, 304–305, 313–315, 406
Avrorin, V. A. 861–862, 867, 873

Baerman, M. 559
Baird, L. 298
Barasa, D. 705, 713–714, 722, 754
Barth, D. 358, 389
Bartholomew, D. A. 536
Bassène, A. C. 11, 13, 16–17, 23, 42, 165, 172, 413, 534, 537, 549, 594, 611–612, 625, 638, 655, 696, 752
Beavers, J. 107, 168, 181, 186
Beck, D. 497
Belkadi, A. 4, 7, 9, 11–14, 16, 18, 22, 24, 32, 42, 45, 48, 60, 62–63, 103, 112, 130, 156, 164–166, 169–172, 178, 181–184, 190–191, 233, 249, 292, 338, 341, 344, 357–361, 368, 372, 377, 379, 388, 395, 411, 413, 436, 453, 461, 480, 490, 506, 570, 611–612, 614, 635, 649, 655, 676, 689, 697, 709, 751–752, 761, 766, 770–771, 774, 779, 781, 786, 794, 800, 803, 811
Bellingham, E. 747
Bender, M. L. 695, 783
Benedicto, E. 539
Benzing, J. 856
Bergmann, T. 60
Berry, C. 113
Berry, K. 113
Besold, J. 299
Biaye, S. 653
Bibiko, H.-J. 95
Bickel, B. 837–839, 845
Bills, G. D. 42
Black, P. 276, 328
Blake, B. J. 285, 291–293
Blevins, J. 301
Blevins, J. P. 445
Blomberg, J. 166–168, 179
Bloomfield, L. 252
Bohnemeyer, J. 166–167, 186–188, 192, 747, 775
Boilat, P. D. 629
Bolton, R. A. 88
Bond, O. 170, 172, 184
Boro, K. 5, 109
Botne, R. 60
Bouckaert, R. R. 234
Bourdin, P. 7–8, 32, 103, 165, 171, 175, 177, 185–186, 358, 611, 614, 620, 635, 649, 752, 780, 804
Bowden, J. 90
Bowern, C. 234
Breedveld, J. O. 620, 685
Breen, G. 285, 287, 291–292, 347
Breen, J. G. 283, 285–288, 291, 293–296
Brousseau, A.-M. 113
Browne, M. 276, 346
Bruce, L. 59
Bruckhaus, S. 4, 695, 702, 712–713, 716, 754
Bryan, M. A. 88
Bubenik, V. 39
Bybee, J. 628

Cáceres, N. 209
Campbell, L. 563
Carceres, F. P. de 528
Cardinaletti, A. 116
Carlson, R. 92
Carrió, C. 451
Caudal, P. 87
Chadwick, N. 330
Chafe, W. L. 747, 775
Chelliah, S. L. 58, 847
Choi-Jonin, I. 169
Cincius, V. I. 862–863
Clark, H. H. 771
Claudi, U. 165, 171, 177
Cleary-Kemp, J. 5, 87, 389
Comrie, B. 237
Conrad, R. J. 64, 89
Córdoba, L. 421
Craig, C. G. 60, 88, 414
Crazzolara, Fr. J. P. 699, 701, 711, 770
Creider, C. A. 702, 711, 720–721, 754, 758
Creider, J. T. 702, 754
Creissels, D. 11, 13, 16–17, 23, 42, 165, 172–173, 175–176, 413, 534, 537, 549, 594, 611–612, 625, 638, 648–649, 653, 655, 696, 752, 780
Croft, W. 178
Crowley, T. 92, 113, 394, 396, 404
Cuyers, W. A. M. 749

Danielson, S. 360
David, C. 166–168
Davidson, D. 186
Dayley, J. P. 33
Déchaine, R.-M. 92
Deering, N. 537
DeLancey, S. 808, 822
Dench, A. 348
Desnoyers, A. 201
Di Caro, V. 37
Dimmendaal, G. J. 165, 171, 188, 702–703, 707, 724, 728, 754, 783
Dixon, R. M. W. 16, 32, 187, 234, 279–281, 291–292, 313, 315, 749
D'Jernes, L. 109
Dobson, V. 254, 258, 267

Dol, P. H. 112
Donaldson, T. 296–297
Donohue, M. 110
Dooley, R. A. 187
Doornenbal, M. 843
Doxtator, M. 59
Drabbe, P. 67
Dras, M. 66
Dryer, M. S. 4–5, 10–12, 14, 16, 18, 21, 34, 37, 39, 41–42, 44, 55, 57, 95, 112–113, 130, 147, 153, 165, 171, 185, 192, 204, 215, 234, 249, 359–360, 368, 370, 377, 389, 413, 436, 453, 461, 480, 503, 528, 532, 535, 561, 563, 868, 870
Durie, M. 88–89, 92, 111, 385, 389, 404

Ebert, K. H. 843
Ebneter, T. 590
Echegoyen, A. 536
Eckert, P. 300, 304
Ehret, C. 695, 783
Elbert, S. H. 62
Enfield, N. J. 69, 394
Epps, P. 317
Erbaugh, M. 775
Essegbey, J. 99, 168
Evans, N. D. 45, 89, 102–103, 108, 110, 114–115, 291, 313, 359, 378

Fabre, A. 374, 453, 480
Facundes, S. S. 56
Fagard, B. 166, 168, 367, 612
Fennig, C. D. 749
Ferry, M.-P. 640
Fillmore, C. J. 180
Finkel, R. 558
Fleck, D. W. 56–57, 65, 423
Fleisch, A. 169
Fleischman, S. 43
Foley, W. A. 88–89, 92, 394
Foris, D. P. 561–562
Forker, D. 59
Fortis, J.-M. 367
Frajzyngier, Z. 32, 63, 89, 171, 173–174, 179
Francis, C. 775
Frawley, W. 363

Gaby, A. R. 281–283
Gaines, R. 616
García Salido, G. 102, 110
Gast, V. 362
Gehrke, B. 166, 178, 192
Genetti, C. 5, 165, 846
Gerasimova, A. N. 861
Giacon, J. 297–298
Gibson, H. 22, 57, 780
Gilley, L. 699–700, 710–711, 718, 724–725
Giusti, G. 116
Givón, T. 40, 91, 187, 435
Goddard, C. 299
Gong, X. 824–825
Good, J. 111
Goudiaby, A. 633
Grant, S. 298
Greenberg, J. H. 172, 695, 783
Green, J. 258
Green, R. 114
Grinevald, C. 455
Griscom, R. 701–702, 722
Groves, T. R. 33
Gruber, J. 697
Gualdieri, B. 451
Guérois, R. 12–15, 17, 22, 57, 549, 655, 752, 780
Guillaume, A. 4–6, 8, 11, 14–17, 21, 32, 34–35, 37–38, 45–46, 48, 52, 54–57, 60–65, 69, 87, 89, 94, 106, 112, 116–117, 129–130, 142, 163–164, 169–171, 182, 189, 201, 203–204, 220, 232–233, 242, 247, 311, 314, 316–317, 329, 358, 362–363, 368, 372–373, 375, 388–389, 396–397, 402–403, 419–420, 423, 425, 427, 434, 436–437, 443, 447–448, 451–454, 461, 475–476, 478–479, 481, 486–487, 489, 494, 496, 506, 528–529, 532, 541, 558, 560, 563, 569, 577–579, 586, 588, 594, 611, 613, 616, 619, 653, 666, 696–697, 705, 709, 735–736, 738, 747–748, 751–753, 770–771, 773, 775, 781, 804, 808, 810–811, 820–821, 827, 850, 855, 858, 869–871
Guirardello-Damian, R. 67
Güldemann, T. 172, 783
Gurzdeva, E. 191
Gusev, V. J. 861

Hagman, R. S. 56
Haiman, J. 766
Hale, K. 186, 254, 278–279
Hamel, P. J. 92, 389, 392
Hansen, K. C. 300, 303–304
Hansen, L. E. 300, 303–304
Harries-Delisle, H. 537
Harvey, M. 252
Haspelmath, M. 34, 91, 95, 404
Hattori, R. 696
Haviland, J. B. 358, 361, 377–378, 855, 871
Heath, J. 171, 174, 178
Heine, B. 182, 702, 725–726, 766
Heine, S. J. 209
Hellenthal, A.-C. 785
Henderson, J. 66, 254, 258, 267
Henrich, J. 209
Hercus, L. A. 268, 270–273, 301
Hernández-Green, N. 13–15, 17, 21, 57, 436, 529–530, 537, 541, 544, 547, 551–552, 594, 656
Hewitt, L. E. 674
Hewson, J. 39
Hill, D. 389, 428, 588, 597, 649
Hilpert, M. 590
Himmelmann, N. P. 209
Holt, D. 55
Hooper, R. 35, 377
Hopkins, B. L. 668
Hopper, P. J. 182
Hudson, J. 300, 304
Humphris, K. C. 257, 260, 262, 264
Hyman, L. M. 92
Hyslop, C. 93

Jackendoff, R. 186, 364, 454
Jacobs, R. 33
Jacques, G. 4–6, 10–12, 15, 17, 24, 32, 39, 52–53, 60, 68, 98, 116, 403, 752, 792, 821, 824, 830, 841, 856, 864, 867, 871–873
Jaggar, P. 171, 177, 180
Janhunen, J. 861
Jenkins, S. 642
Johnson-Laird, P. N. 186
Johnson, M. 60, 180, 770–771
Jones, P. 44

Jones, W. 44
Joseph, B. D. 88

Kakumasu, J. 108
Kalinina, E. J. 861
Kato, A. 104, 110
Kawachi, K. 4, 11, 13, 17, 23, 44, 48, 165, 676, 695–697, 701–702, 711, 738, 747, 774–775, 780
Keegan, J. M. 110
Kempe, H. 258, 267
Keyser, S. J. 186
Khasanova, M. M. 862
Kießling, R. 4, 172, 695, 702, 712–713, 716, 754
Kilian-Hatz, C. 94, 169, 172
Killian, D. 782–783, 785
King, J. T. 821, 847
Klamer, M. 359
Klein, H. M. 451, 460
Klein, W. 436
Koch, H. 4–5, 9–16, 19, 32, 34–35, 37, 42, 45, 47–48, 52, 54–57, 62–63, 65, 67, 87, 89, 117–118, 129, 163–164, 166, 169–170, 183, 185, 191, 201, 203–204, 231, 234, 236, 247, 252, 254, 266–267, 314–315, 329–330, 338, 348, 351–352, 357–358, 362–363, 368, 388, 396–397, 402, 436–437, 461, 475, 487, 496, 528, 551, 569, 578, 588, 611, 616, 666, 696–697, 738, 747–748, 775, 779, 820–821, 855, 857, 865, 869–870, 889
Kolesnikova, V. D. 862
König, C. 702, 706, 716, 725–726, 749
Konnerth, L. 4, 821, 846
Konstantinova, O. A. 862
Kopecka, A. 167, 178, 201
Kossmann, M. 169, 171
Kramer, R. L. 780
Krifka, M. 166, 186–187
Kuteva, T. 182, 628
Kuz'mina, R. P. 861

Lahaussois, A. 24, 53, 68, 98, 116, 203, 792, 843
Lai, Y. 824
Lakoff, G. 60, 180, 770–771
Lamarre, C. 5, 42, 169, 846
Langacker, R. 166, 597
Lastra, Y. 536
Lee, T. 106
Lefebvre, C. 88, 105–106, 113
Legère, K. 702, 725–726
Lehmann, C. 182
Levin, B. 107, 111, 166, 168, 178, 180, 186–189
Levinson, S. C. 4, 9, 19, 46, 164, 168–170, 192, 201, 233, 359, 373, 390, 411, 494, 597, 697, 752–753, 771, 773, 871
Lichtenberk, F. 358, 378, 397
Lindsey, K. L. 11–12, 14, 17, 19, 42, 62, 68, 165, 361, 403, 752
Link, G. 186
Lin, Y.-J. 823–825
Lissarrague, A. 302
Li, Y. 111
Lord, C. 92
Lovestrand, J. 12, 14, 16–17, 35, 39, 46, 50, 52–53, 65, 67, 69, 88, 91, 95, 98, 130, 170, 360, 402, 413, 503, 837
Lüpke, F. 208
Lynch, J. 396

Majid, A. 204, 208
Malchukov, A. L. 862–863
Margetts, A. 104, 406
Mathews, R. H. 298–299
Matlock, T. 60
Matsumoto, Y. 113, 747, 775
Matthews, S. 105
Mattiola, S. 55
Maurer, P. 94
McConvell, B. 317
McConvell, P. 328
McFarland, T. A. 60
Meakins, F. 328, 336
Meier, S. C. 389
Messerschmidt, M. 37, 60
Messineo, C. 451
Mettouchi, A. 178
Miceli, L. 234
Michael, L. D. 437
Michaelis, S. M. 94
Michailovsky, B. 820, 841

Michelson, K. 59
Mietzner, A. 164, 171, 184, 695, 702, 706, 708, 711, 723, 725–726, 754, 758
Miller, G. A. 186
Miller, R. J. 209
Miller-Naudé, C. 699–700, 710–711, 718, 724–725
Mithun, M. 32, 38–39, 59, 877
Montgomery, C. A. 749
Moore, D. 257, 260–262, 264, 267, 317
Morita, T. 169
Mpaayei, J. T. O. 41, 177, 181, 698, 735, 754
Muansuwan, N. 93
Munro, P. 53
Muysken, P. 42, 58

Næss, Å. 389
Nakazawa, T. 168
Narasimhan, B. 105, 201
Nash, D. 289, 302–303
Neukom, L. 172
Newman, J. 394
Newman, P. 60, 171
Nielsen, M. 37, 60
Nikitina, T. 178, 192
Nikolaeva, I. 55, 861, 863, 874
Nishiyama, K. 92
Noonan, M. 699, 754
Nordhoff, S. 43
Nordlinger, R. 19, 87, 109, 325, 330, 336, 341–342, 349
Norenzayan, A. 209
Novikova, K. A. 862–863

O'Brien, R. J. 749
O'Connor, L. 4, 32, 170, 857, 889
Ole-Kotikash, L. 738
Ole-Mapena, A. K. 738
Olson, M. 88–89, 92, 394
Opgenort, J.-R. 843–844
Osgarby, D. 16–17, 19, 52, 231, 235, 290, 314–315, 334, 349, 360, 543, 551, 557, 752
Oskolskaya, S. A. 861
Otaala, L. 723
Otero, M. A. 9, 11–13, 17, 23–24, 35, 48, 61, 116–117, 165, 171, 373, 436, 447, 453, 455–456, 480, 533, 696, 752, 781, 785, 796

Pakendorf, B. 11–13, 15, 17, 24, 53, 55, 68, 98, 116, 232, 729, 861–862
Palancar, E. L. 13–15, 17, 21, 57, 436, 528–529, 541, 548, 557, 594, 656
Panther, F. 252
Parsons, T. 186
Patz, E. 67, 278–279
Pawley, A. 187, 385, 389, 393
Payne, D. L. 11–12, 14–17, 21, 23, 40–42, 44, 46, 57, 60, 64, 165, 171–172, 360, 399, 453, 455–456, 467, 480, 544, 549, 676, 695, 703, 727, 735, 752, 754, 758, 775, 780, 856, 864, 875
Payne, J. 358, 378
Payne, T. 204
Pensalfini, R. 328, 330, 349
Perrin, L.-M. 639
Persohn, B. 4, 22, 57, 172, 780
Peterson, D. A. 64
Petrova, T. I. 861, 874
Pevnov, A. 862
Ponsonnet, M. 209
Pourcel, S. 167
Pozdniakov, K. 614
Prins, M. 824
Prost, G. 420
Pustejovsky, J. 166, 186

Ramchand, G. 166, 186, 192
Rappaport Hovav, M. 107, 111, 166, 180–181, 186–189
Reed, L. W. 11–12, 14, 17, 19, 42, 62, 68, 165, 403, 752
Reesink, G. 94–95, 105
Reh, M. 172–173, 699–700, 704, 710, 754
Reichenbach, H. 186
Reid, T. 170, 172, 184
Remijsen, B. 699–700, 710–711, 724–725
Renaudier, M. 4, 653, 779
Ricca, D. 649
Riis, H. N. 92
Robert, S. 653
Rose, F. 6, 32, 55, 57, 93, 170, 184, 203, 233, 240, 247, 315, 358, 434, 436–437, 446–447, 453, 616, 666, 779, 821, 827, 845, 855, 857, 865, 871
Ross, A. 236, 241, 244, 246, 249–250

Ross, D. 11–14, 16–17, 32, 34–36, 39, 41, 46, 50, 52–53, 60, 65, 67–69, 71, 87–88, 90–91, 93, 95, 97–99, 104, 106, 111–113, 116, 118, 130, 153, 165, 170, 234, 249, 311, 360, 372–373, 402, 413, 453, 503, 506, 534, 537, 542, 578, 594–595, 612, 655, 752, 837, 856, 868, 870–871
Ross, M. 389, 396
Rottland, F. 695, 701, 704
Round, E. R. 108
Rudder, J. 298
Rutgers, R. 836, 840, 842, 844–845

Sagart, L. 820
Sagot, B. 558
Sakel, J. 4, 6, 57
Salomón, E. 539
Sambou, P.-M. 675
Sandalo, F. 451
San Roque, L. 209
Santos, R. 641–642
Sapir, J. D. 668, 675
Sarda, L. 169
Sauvel, K. S. 53
Schackow, D. 845
Schaefer, R. P. 616
Schalley, A. C. 93
Schebeck, B. 268
Schiering, R. 837
Schokkin, D. 10–12, 14–15, 17, 20, 35, 112, 360, 373, 389
Schroeder, M. 703
Schultze-Berndt, E. 4
Sebba, M. 88, 93, 99
Segerer, G. 614, 637, 653
Seiter, W. J. 114
Senft, G. 389
Sharp, J. C. 301
Shibatani, M. 88, 92
Shluinsky, A. 106
Simons, G. F. 749
Simpson, J. 253, 268, 274–275, 289, 302, 314, 344–345, 857
Slobin, D. I. 4, 168, 176, 180–181
Smith, C. 435
Smolders, J. A. G. 785, 793, 798
Soukka, M. 625–626

Sow, A. I. 627
Spagnolo, L. M. 703, 705–706, 713, 723, 726
Stenin, I. A. 856
Stevenson, R. C. 173
Stewart, D. 536
Storch, A. 699
Stoynova, N. 5, 11–13, 15, 17, 24, 53, 55, 68, 98, 116, 232, 729, 856, 864, 868
Strehlow, C. 258–259, 261, 267
Strehlow, T. G. H. 258–260
Stump, G. 558
Sumbatova, N. R. 861
Sunik, O. P. 861, 863
Sun, J. T.-S. 824

Tai, J. H.-Y. 111
Tallman, A. J. R. 10–11, 13–17, 20, 55, 92, 420–423, 425–426, 430–431, 437, 543, 752, 779, 856, 864, 871
Talmy, L. 4, 32, 60, 107, 166–169, 176, 180, 186–188, 364, 369, 436, 454–455, 588, 616, 696, 753, 764, 770, 773–774, 780, 785, 801
Tarpent, M.-L. 39
Tenny, C. 166, 186
Tham, S. W. 107, 168
Thiesen, W. 63
Tluangneh, T. 59
Todaro, G. 37
Tolskaya, M. 55, 861, 863, 874
Tolsma, G. J. 843
Toweett, T. 754
Traugott, E. C. 60, 182, 590
Tucker, A. N. 41, 88, 177, 181, 698, 735, 754
Tunbridge, D. 4, 32, 231, 235, 268, 270, 313, 315, 350, 358, 372, 779
Turpin, M. 236, 241, 244, 246, 249–250, 317

Unterladstetter, V. 95, 97
Utt, T. 847

Valenzuela, P. M. 421–423, 425
Valle, D. 423
VanBik, K. 59
van de Kerke, S. 42, 58
van Driem, G. 843
van Staden, M. 94–95, 105

Van Valin, R. D. 394
Veerman-Leichsenring, A. 66
Versteegh, K. 97
Verstraete, J.-C. 118, 317, 775
Vidal, A. 11–12, 16–17, 21, 41–42, 60, 64, 165, 360, 399, 451, 453–456, 459–460, 463, 473, 544, 676
Viegas Barros, J. P. 452
Villar, D. 421
Vittrant, A. 5, 846
Voeltz, E. F. K. 655
Voigtlander, K. 536
Voisin, S. 4, 6, 11–13, 16–17, 22, 42, 57, 112, 164–165, 170–172, 179, 181, 183–184, 215, 413, 436, 612–613, 653, 665, 687, 779
Volkov, O. S. 855
Vuillermet, M. 5, 13, 15, 18, 20, 35, 117, 164, 169–170, 184, 189, 201, 204, 212–213, 215, 233, 426, 453, 616, 779, 827

Waldie, R. 447
Walther, G. 558
Waters, B. E. 306
Watters, D. E. 97
Weber, D. J. 42, 54, 58, 63, 165
Weiss, D. 108
Westermann, D. 92

Wilkins, D. P. 4–5, 9, 15–16, 19, 32, 42–43, 46, 52, 54, 60, 62, 66–68, 87, 112, 163–164, 166, 168–170, 182, 191–192, 201, 203–205, 209, 231, 233, 247, 252, 254, 256–257, 260, 263–264, 267, 313–317, 358, 373, 389–390, 428, 434, 436–437, 461, 494, 569, 577–578, 586, 588, 597, 616, 649–650, 666, 696–697, 747–748, 751–753, 771, 773, 779, 820–821, 827, 855, 857, 871, 889
Williams, A. 111
Williams, C. 298
Winfield, W. W. 38
Wogiga, K. 64, 89
Woidich, M. 97
Wolgemuth, C. 55, 561

Yadav, R. 103
Yangklang, P. 168

Zariquiey, R. 423
Zavala Maldonado, R. 4, 855, 857, 871, 892
Zhang, S. 24, 53, 68, 98, 116, 792, 824–825
Zingg, P. 420
Zlatev, J. 166–168, 179
Zubin, D. A. 674
Zúñiga, F. 823
Zwarts, J. 695, 701–702, 711, 721, 754, 758
Zwicky, A. M. 88

www.ingramcontent.com/pod-product-compliance
Lightning Source LLC
Chambersburg PA
CBHW050521300426
44113CB00012B/1912